Less managing. More teaching. Greater learning.

 INSTRUCTORS...

Would you like your **students** to show up for class more **prepared**? *(Let's face it, class is much more fun if everyone is engaged and prepared...)*

Want ready-made application-level **interactive assignments,** student progress reporting, and auto-assignment grading? *(Less time grading means more time teaching...)*

Want an **instant view of student or class performance** relative to learning objectives? *(No more wondering if students understand...)*

Need to **collect data and generate reports** required for administration or accreditation? *(Say goodbye to manually tracking student learning outcomes...)*

Want to **record and post your lectures** for students to view online?

 With McGraw-Hill's *Connect*® Management,

INSTRUCTORS GET:

- Interactive Applications – **book-specific interactive assignments** that require students to APPLY what they've learned.

- Simple **assignment management,** allowing you to spend more time teaching.

- **Auto-graded** assignments, quizzes, and tests.

- **Detailed Visual Reporting** where student and section results can be viewed and analyzed.

- Sophisticated **online testing** capability.

- A **filtering and reporting** function that allows you to easily assign and report on materials that are correlated to accreditation standards, learning outcomes, and Bloom's taxonomy.

- An easy-to-use **lecture capture** tool.

STUDENTS...

Want an online, **searchable version** of your textbook?

Wish your textbook could be **available online** while you're doing your assignments?

Connect® Plus Management eBook

If you choose to use *Connect® Plus Management*, you have an affordable and searchable online version of your book integrated with your other online tools.

Connect® Plus Management eBook offers features like:

- Topic search
- Direct links from assignments
- Adjustable text size
- Jump to page number
- Print by section

STUDENTS...

Want to get more **value** from your textbook purchase?

Think learning management should be a bit more **interesting**?

Check out the STUDENT RESOURCES section under the *Connect®* Library tab.

Here you'll find a wealth of resources designed to help you achieve your goals in the course. You'll find things like **quizzes, PowerPoints, and Internet activities** to help you study. Every student has different needs, so explore the STUDENT RESOURCES to find the materials best suited to you.

MANAGEMENT

Leading & Collaborating in a Competitive World

TENTH EDITION

THOMAS S. BATEMAN
McIntire School of Commerce
University of Virginia

SCOTT A. SNELL
Darden Graduate School of Business
University of Virginia

McGraw-Hill
Irwin

McGraw-Hill
Irwin

MANAGEMENT: LEADING & COLLABORATING IN A COMPETITIVE WORLD
Published by McGraw-Hill/Irwin, a business unit of The McGraw-Hill Companies, Inc., 1221 Avenue of
the Americas, New York, NY, 10020. Copyright © 2013, 2011, 2009, 2007, 2004, 2002, 1999, 1996, 1993,
1990 by The McGraw-Hill Companies, Inc. All rights reserved. Printed in the United States of America.
No part of this publication may be reproduced or distributed in any form or by any means, or stored in
a database or retrieval system, without the prior written consent of The McGraw-Hill Companies, Inc.,
including, but not limited to, in any network or other electronic storage or transmission, or broadcast for
distance learning.

Some ancillaries, including electronic and print components, may not be available to customers outside
the United States.

This book is printed on acid-free paper.

1 2 3 4 5 6 7 8 9 0 RJE/RJE 1 0 9 8 7 6 5 4 3 2

ISBN 978-0-07-802933-2
MHID 0-07-802933-3

Vice president and editor-in-chief: *Brent Gordon*
Editorial director: *Paul Ducham*
Executive editor: *Michael Ablassmeir*
Executive director of development: *Ann Torbert*
Development editor II: *Laura Griffin*
Editorial coordinator: *Andrea Heirendt*
Vice president and director of marketing: *Robin J. Zwettler*
Marketing director: *Amee Mosley*
Senior marketing manager: *Michelle Heaster*
Vice president of editing, design, and production: *Sesha Bolisetty*
Senior project manager: *Dana M. Pauley*
Senior buyer: *Michael R. McCormick*
Senior designer: *Matt Diamond*
Senior photo research coordinator: *Jeremy Cheshareck*
Photo researcher: *Allison Grimes*
Senior media project manager: *Bruce Gin*
Media project manager: *Rachel Townsend*
Media project manager: *Ron Nelms*
Cover and interior design: *Maureen McCutcheon*
Typeface: *10/12 Jenson*
Compositor: *Laserwords Private Limited*
Printer: *R. R. Donnelley*

Library of Congress Cataloging-in-Publication Data

Bateman, Thomas S.
    Management : leading & collaborating in a competitive world / Thomas S. Bateman,
Scott A. Snell. — 10th ed.
        p. cm.
    Includes index.
    ISBN-13: 978-0-07-802933-2 (alk. paper)
    ISBN-10: 0-07-802933-3 (alk. paper)
    1. Management. I. Snell, Scott, 1958- II. Title.
HD31.B369485 2013
658—dc23
                                                        2011045057

www.mhhe.com

For my parents, Tom and Jeanine Bateman,
and Mary Jo, Lauren, T.J., and James

AND

My parents, John and Clara Snell,
and Marybeth, Sara, Jack, and Emily

About the Authors

THOMAS S. BATEMAN

Thomas S. Bateman is Bank of America Professor and management area coordinator in the McIntire School of Commerce at the University of Virginia. He teaches leadership courses and is director of a new leadership minor open to undergraduate students of all majors. Prior to joining the University of Virginia, he taught organizational behavior at the Kenan-Flager Business School of the University of North Carolina to undergraduates, MBA students, PhD students, and practicing managers. He also taught for two years in Europe as a visiting professor at the Institute for Management Development (IMD), one of the world's leaders in the design and delivery of executive education. Professor Bateman completed his doctoral program in business administration in 1980 at Indiana University. Prior to receiving his doctorate, Dr. Bateman received his BA from Miami University. In addition to Virginia, UNC–Chapel Hill, and IMD, Dr. Bateman has taught at Texas A&M, Tulane, and Indiana universities.

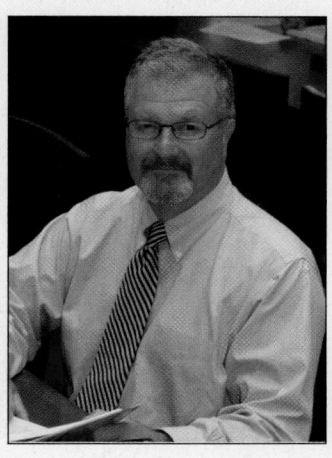

Professor Bateman is an active management researcher, writer, and consultant. He serves on the editorial boards of the *Academy of Management Review*, the *Academy of Management Journal*, and the *Asia Pacific Journal of Business and Management*. His articles have appeared in professional journals such as the *Academy of Management Journal*, *Academy of Management Review*, *Journal of Applied Psychology*, *Organizational Behavior and Human Decision Processes*, *Journal of Management*, *Business Horizons*, *Journal of Organizational Behavior*, and *Decision Sciences*.

Tom's current consulting and research center on practical wisdom in business executives, leadership in the form of problem solving at all organizational levels, various types of proactive behavior by employees at all levels, and the successful pursuit of long-term work goals. He works with organizations including Singapore Airlines, the Brookings Institution, the U.S. Chamber of Commerce, the Nature Conservancy, and LexisNexis.

SCOTT A. SNELL

Scott Snell is the E. Thayer Bigelow Professor of Business Administration at the University of Virginia's Darden Business School, where he teaches courses in leadership and strategic management. His research focuses on strategic human resource management, and he was recently listed among the top 150 most cited authors in the field of management. He is coauthor of four books: *Management: Leading and Collaborating in a Competitive World*, *M: Management*, *Managing Human Resources*, and *Managing People and Knowledge in Professional Service Firms*. His research has been published in a number of journals such as the *Academy of Management Journal*, *Academy of Management Review*, *Strategic Management Journal*, *Journal of Management*, *Journal of Management Studies*, and *Human Resource Management*, and he has served on the boards of the Society for Human Resource Management Foundation, the Academy of Management's Human Resource Division, the *Human Resource Management Journal*, the *Academy of Management Journal*, and the *Academy of Management Review*. Scott has worked with companies such as AstraZeneca, Deutsche Telekom, Shell, and United Technologies to align investments in talent and strategic capability. Prior to joining the Darden faculty in 2007, Scott was professor and director of executive education at Cornell University's Center for Advanced Human Resource Studies and a professor of management in the Smeal College of Business at Pennsylvania State University. He received a BA in psychology from Miami University, as well as MBA and PhD degrees in business administration from Michigan State University.

Preface

Welcome to our 10th edition! Thank you to everyone who has used and learned from previous editions and helped make this book such a success. We are proud to present the newest edition.

With the many challenges that we all face, this is truly an exciting time in business. Technology, innovation, and global commerce are transforming industries. Companies like Facebook, Whole Foods, NetFlix, and others are revolutionizing not only their industries but also the way we live our lives. The fact that they are unseating their more traditional rivals shows that entrepreneurs and courageous leaders can have a significant impact on business and on the world. Whether it's driving creativity and innovation (Google), continuously improving quality (Mayo Clinic), or relentlessly pursuing productivity and cost (Southwest), managers are uniquely positioned to work with their people to achieve competitive advantage in business and to make a difference in the world.

But succeeding in a challenging work world is not just about competing; collaborating with others is more essential than ever, too. Joint ventures and strategic alliances such as Apple's partnership with Rovio (maker of Angry Birds) show just how important it is that people within and between different organizations—even rivals—work together effectively. This collaboration is more global than ever. Countries like India and China are center stage not just because of the rapid growth and sheer size of their economies and consumer markets, but because of the productive power of their people and the growing capability of their companies.

As things change in business and in the world more broadly, the metaphorical glass sometimes seems half-empty. Unfortunate world events, disconcerting trends, and ineffective and unethical management practices will continue. But good people will continue to step up and take on important leadership roles, managing well and making things better, as they always have. In this book you will read about many managers, some doing things brilliantly, others making mistakes (with some learning from their mistakes, and some not). Some organizations rise from the ashes, or come from seemingly nowhere, to become the next hot investment. Some organizations are high-flyers one day and come crashing down the next. Some achieve greatness, and have occasional downturns, but continue being great.

These performance shifts occur in large part due to the ways in which they are managed, and partly from how circumstances change. Business environments, like pendulums, swing from one extreme to another. These changes will contribute to the fall of some currently successful companies and managers and the rise of others who currently struggle or are now just dreaming of new business ideas.

For you, as a businessperson as in life, uncertainty will be a constant state of affairs. That is, no one knows for certain what will happen, or what to do in pursuit of a successful future. Luck and the right circumstances can help companies (and people) succeed in the short run. But in the long run good management is essential.

Fortunately, you have access to current knowledge about how to manage. We have learned a lot from the companies that have succeeded and failed. The continuing experiment created by the vast array of management practices that exist in the business world, combined with sound research that helps tease out what works from what doesn't, helps us learn from mistakes and identify the most important lessons and useful practices that managers can employ. We hope that you will not only learn as much as you can about this vital activity but also commit to applying it—by reading and learning, and by using it in the best possible ways.

This book and the course you are taking will help you face the managerial challenges of a changing world. In doing so, they will help you identify what's important and what's not, make good decisions, and take effective action on behalf of yourself, your colleagues, and the organizations for which you work.

Our Goals

Our mission with this text hasn't changed from that of our previous editions: to inform, instruct, and inspire. We hope to *inform* by providing descriptions of the important concepts and practices of modern management. We hope to *instruct* by describing how you can take action on the ideas discussed. We hope to *inspire* not only by writing in a positive, interesting, and optimistic way but also by providing a real sense of the opportunities ahead of you. Whether your goal is starting your own company, leading a team to greatness, building a strong organization, delighting your customers, or generally forging a positive future, we want to inspire you to take positive actions.

We hope to inspire you to be both a thinker and a doer. We want you to think about the issues, think about the impact of your actions, think before you act. But being a good thinker is not enough; you also must be a doer. Management is a world of action. It is a world that requires timely and appropriate action. It is a world not for the passive but for those who commit to positive accomplishments.

Keep applying the ideas you learn in this course, read about management in sources outside of this course, and keep learning about management after you leave school and continue your career. Make no mistake about it: learning about management is a personal voyage that will last years, an entire career, your entire lifetime.

Competitive Advantage

Today's world is competitive. Never before has the world of work been so challenging. Never before has it been so imperative to your career that you learn the skills of management. Never before have people had so many opportunities and challenges with so many potential risks and rewards.

You will compete with other people for jobs, resources, and promotions. Your organization will compete with other firms for contracts, clients, and customers. To survive the competition, and to thrive, you must perform in ways that give you an edge over your competitors, that make the other party want to hire you, buy from you, and do repeat business with you. You will want them to choose you, not your competitor.

To survive and thrive, today's managers have to think and act strategically. Today's customers are well educated, aware of their options, and demanding of excellence. For this reason, managers today must think constantly about how to build a capable workforce and manage in a way that delivers the goods and services that provide the best possible value to the customer.

By this standard, managers and organizations must perform. Six essential types of performance, on which the organization beats, equals, or loses to the competition, are *cost*, *quality*, *speed*, *innovation*, *service* and *sustainability*. These six performance dimensions, when managed well, deliver value to the customer and competitive advantage to you and your organization. We will elaborate on all of these topics throughout the book.

The idea is to keep you focused on a type of "bottom line," to make sure you think continually about "delivering the goods" that make both you and your organization a competitive success. This results-oriented approach is unique among management textbooks.

Leading & Collaborating

Yes, business is competitive. But it's not that simple. In fact, to think strictly in terms of competition is overly cynical, and such cynicism can sabotage your performance. The other fundamental elements in the success equation are collaboration and leadership. People working with, rather than against, one another are essential to competitive advantage. Put another way, you can't do it alone—the world is too complex, and business is too challenging.

You need to work with your teammates. Leaders and followers need to work as collaborators more than as adversaries. Work groups throughout your organization need to cooperate with one another. Business and government, often viewed as antagonists, can work productively together. And today more than ever, companies that traditionally were competitors engage in joint ventures and find other ways to collaborate on some things even as they compete in others. Leadership is needed to make these collaborations happen.

How does an organization create competitive advantage through collaboration? It's all about the people, and it derives from good leadership. Three stereotypes of leadership are that it comes from the top of the company, that it comes from one's immediate boss, and that it means being decisive and issuing commands. These stereotypes may contain grains of truth, but the reality is much more complex. First, the person at the top may or may not provide effective leadership—in fact, many observers believe that good leadership is far too rare. Second, organizations need leaders at all levels, in every team and work unit. This includes you, beginning early in your career, and this is why leadership is an important theme in this book. Third, leaders should be capable of decisiveness and of giving commands, but relying too much on this traditional approach isn't enough. Great leadership is far more inspirational than this, and helps people both to think differently and also to work differently—including working collaboratively with a focus on results.

Leadership—from your boss as well as from you—generates collaboration, which in turn creates results that are good for the company and good for the people involved.

As Always, Currency and Variety in the 10th Edition

It goes without saying that this textbook, in its 10th edition, remains on the cutting edge of topical coverage, as updated via both current business examples and recent management research. Chapters have been thoroughly updated, and students are exposed to a broad array of important current topics.

We have done our very best to draw from a wide variety of subject matter, sources, and personal experiences. We continue to emphasize throughout the book themes such as real results, ethics, cultural considerations, and leadership and collaboration. Here is just a small sampling of new highlights in the 10th edition—enough to convey the wide variety of people, organizations, issues, and contexts represented throughout the text.

Chapter 1

- A new title for this chapter, "Managing and Performing."
- The Management Connection discusses how Tesla Motors managers keep the company productive.
- New examples include ReCellular, Dunkin' Brands Culinary Innovation Team, Singapore Airlines, Aetna, and basic practices of good management at textile factories in India.
- A new section on sustainability has been added to the chapter.

Chapter 2

- A new title for this chapter, "The External and Internal Environments."
- The Management Connection examines how Apple concentrates on being a winner in a fast-changing environment.
- Information on the Affordable Care Act of 2010 discusses the legal provisions aimed at health care.
- A new section on the natural environment.
- New examples include Tata Motors and breaks in supplier chains caused by the external environment.
- New Table 2.1.

Chapter 3

- A new Management Connection on Pandora Media, one of the world's most innovative companies according to *Fast Company* magazine.
- New examples include Capterra, Chargify, and Integrated Medical Solutions.
- Updated graphics on organizations' strategy decisions.
- BP's Deepwater Horizon disaster is used as an example to discuss management decision making.

Chapter 4

- A new Management Connection on General Electric.
- New examples include General Motors, Price Chopper Supermarkets, an Iraqi commercial sign store, AXA Canada, and Cisco Systems.
- A discussion of the trends shaping how companies grow.

Chapter 5

- The Management Connection looks at corporate social responsibility at Patagonia.
- New examples include overbooked hotel practices, Hilton Worldwide call centers, Countrywide Financial, and 3M.
- Updated graphics on ethics.

Chapter 6

- The Management Connection discusses IKEA's global presence and sustainability.
- The need for employees and sales from other countries outside the United States to meet their objectives.
- New Table 6.1.
- India's growing role in the global marketplace.
- New examples include Stanbic IBTC Bank in Nigeria, Master Lock, and Ignighter.com.
- A new Figure 6.3 on the top 10 global firms.

Chapter 7

- A new Management Connection about Chipotle's founder, Steve Ells.
- New examples include inDinero, research on entrepreneurs, Toepener, CopyShark.net, and the Unreasonable Institute.
- A new section on social entrepreneurship.
- Updated graphics on money management.

Chapter 8

- The Management Connection discusses the organization chart at Cisco Systems.
- New examples include Harmonix Music Systems, Valve Software, Walt Disney Studios, and LoveMachine.
- Updated graphics on delegating leadership responsibilities.
- New Tables 8.1 and 8.2.

Chapter 9

- A new Management Connection on how Pixar thrives in a changing industry.
- A discussion of ambidextrous organizations.
- New examples include Pfizer, Salesforce.com, and Miles Chemical.
- A new key term definition of six sigma quality.

Chapter 10

- The Management Connection looks at Google's ability to hire great employees.
- New examples include GM's Chevy Volt, Walmart, and Sprint.
- Updated section on drug testing.
- New Figure 10.4.

Chapter 11

- A new Management Connection on PepsiCo.
- New examples include CH2M Hill, Procter & Gamble, and Ernst & Young.
- New Tables 11.1, 11.2, 11.4, and 11.5.
- Updated graphics on employee resource groups.
- A discussion of leveraging difference.

Chapter 12

- The Management Connection looks at Howard Schultz and Starbucks.
- New examples include George Buckley of 3M, Linda Parker Hudson of General Dynamics, and Kathy Savitt of Lockerz.

Chapter 13

- A new Management Connection about Intuit being a great place to work.
- Updated graphics on employee engagement.
- New examples include Quick Lane Tire & Auto Center, Rable Machine, and K Hotels Sales & Marketing.

Chapter 14

- The Management Connection discusses teamwork at Toyota.
- New examples include Wells's Dairy and IBM.
- Updated graphics on how senior managers spend their time.

Chapter 15

- A new Management Connection on Zingerman's Delicatessen.
- Updated graphics on the variety of communication methods.
- New examples include SlideShare, Hilcorp Energy Company, Applied Materials, and Royal Caribbean Cruises.

Chapter 16

- The Management Connection examines controls at Southwest Airlines.
- New examples include Hertz, Family Practice Association, and Netflix.
- Updated graphics on quality control.

Chapter 17

- A new Management Connection on BP's alternative energy future.
- Discussion of innovation and its three fundamental types.
- New examples include Pratt & Whitney, Facebook, and the military's use of solar technology.
- The limits organizations have put on information technology at work.
- New Figure 17.5.

Chapter 18

- The Management Connection discusses Dr. Peter Pronovost.
- New examples include Goodrich Aerostructures and Jacqueline Woods.
- Updated graphics on the length of time people spend with the same employer.

A Team Effort

This book is the product of a fantastic McGraw-Hill/Irwin team. Moreover, we wrote this book believing that we are part of a team with the course instructor and with students. The entire team is responsible for the learning process.

Our goal, and that of your instructor, is to create a positive learning environment in which you can excel. But in the end, the raw material of this course is just words. It is up to you to use them as a basis for further thinking, deep learning, and constructive action.

What you do with the things you learn from this course, and with the opportunities the future holds, *counts*. As a manager, you can make a dramatic difference for yourself and for other people. What managers do matters, *tremendously*.

Acknowledgments

This book could not have been written and published without the valuable contributions of many individuals.

Ingrid Benson and her colleagues at Integra-Chicago were instrumental in creating a strong 10th edition.

Many thanks for their meticulous attention to detail, ideas, and contributions. Ingrid has become a valued friend throughout the process; we couldn't have done it, or had as much fun, without Ingrid.

Special thanks to Lily Bowles for contributing her knowledge, insights, and research to Appendix B: Managing in Our Natural Environment.

Our reviewers over the last eight editions contributed time, expertise, and terrific ideas that significantly enhanced the quality of the text. The reviewers of the 10th edition are

David P. Arseneau
Eastern Illinois University

Carol Bormann Young
Metropolitan State University, MN

Tom Deckelman
Owens Community College

Ann Gilley
Ferris State University

John Guess
Delgado Community College

Samuel E. Hazen
Tarleton State University

Dan Hallock
University of North Alabama

Nathan Himelstein
Essex County College

Anne Kelly Hoel
University of Wisconsin–Stout

Coy A. Jones
The University of Memphis

Lori Merlak
Kirkwood Community College

Stephanie B. Narvell
Wilmington University

Thomas J. Norman
California State University–Dominguez Hills

Eren Ozgen
Troy University

Marc Siegall
California State University–Chico

R. Scott Taylor
Moberly Area Community College

Wynn Teasley
University of West Florida

Neal F. Thomson
Columbus State University

Many individuals contributed directly to our development as textbook authors. Dennis Organ provided one of the authors with an initial opportunity and guidance in textbook writing. Executive Editor John Weimeister has been a friend and adviser from the very beginning. The entire McGraw-Hill/Irwin team, starting with Executive Editor Mike Ablassmeir (who spontaneously and impressively knew *Rolling Stone*'s top three drummers of all time) provided great support and expertise to this new edition. Many thanks to Managing Development Editor Christine Scheid for so much good work on previous editions and for continued friendship. And to our superb Development Editor II Laura Griffin, and to Michelle Heaster, senior marketing manager, thank you for your skills, professionalism, collegiality, good fun, and for making the new edition *rock!* What a team!

Finally, we thank our families. Our parents, Jeanine and Tom Bateman and Clara and John Snell, provided us with the foundation on which we have built our careers. They continue to be a source of great support. Our wives, Mary Jo and Marybeth, demonstrated great encouragement, insight, and understanding throughout the process. Our children, Lauren, T. J., and James Bateman and Sara, Jack, and Emily Snell, inspire us in every way.

Thomas S. Bateman
Charlottesville, VA

Scott A. Snell
Charlottesville, VA

BOTTOM LINE

from page 324

Bottom Line

Large size often leads to scale economics.

How has General Motor's large size affected its ability to compete?

from page 420

Bottom Line

Retaining qualified employees increases workforce quality.

What makes you feel that your employer values who you are and what you contribute?

from page 294

Bottom Line

Decentralization often speeds decision making.

What makes centralized decision making slower?

from page 246

Bottom Line

Entrepreneurship is inherently about innovation—creating a new venture where one didn't exist before.

How is entrepreneurship different from inventing a new product?

from page 62

Bottom Line

In all businesses—services as well as manufacturing—strategies that emphasize good customer service provide a critical competitive advantage.

Name a company that has delivered good customer service to you.

from page 76

Bottom Line

A culture aligned with its environment helps the organization succeed.

To be aligned with its environment, what values should an oil company have?

In this ever more competitive environment there are six essential types of performance, on which the organization beats, equals, or loses to the competition: cost, quality, speed, innovation, service and sustainability. These six performance dimensions, when done well, deliver value to the customer and competitive advantage to you and your organization.

Throughout the text, Bateman and Snell remind students of these six dimensions and their impact on the bottom line with marginal icons. This results-oriented approach is a unique hallmark of this textbook.

Questions have also now been added to this edition to further emphasize the bottom line. Answers to these questions can be found in the Instructor's Manual.

In CASE You Haven't Noticed . . .

Bateman and Snell have once again put together an outstanding selection of case studies of various lengths that highlight companies' ups and downs, stimulate learning and understanding, and challenge students to respond.

Instructors will find a wealth of relevant and updated cases in every chapter, using companies—big and small—that students will enjoy learning about.

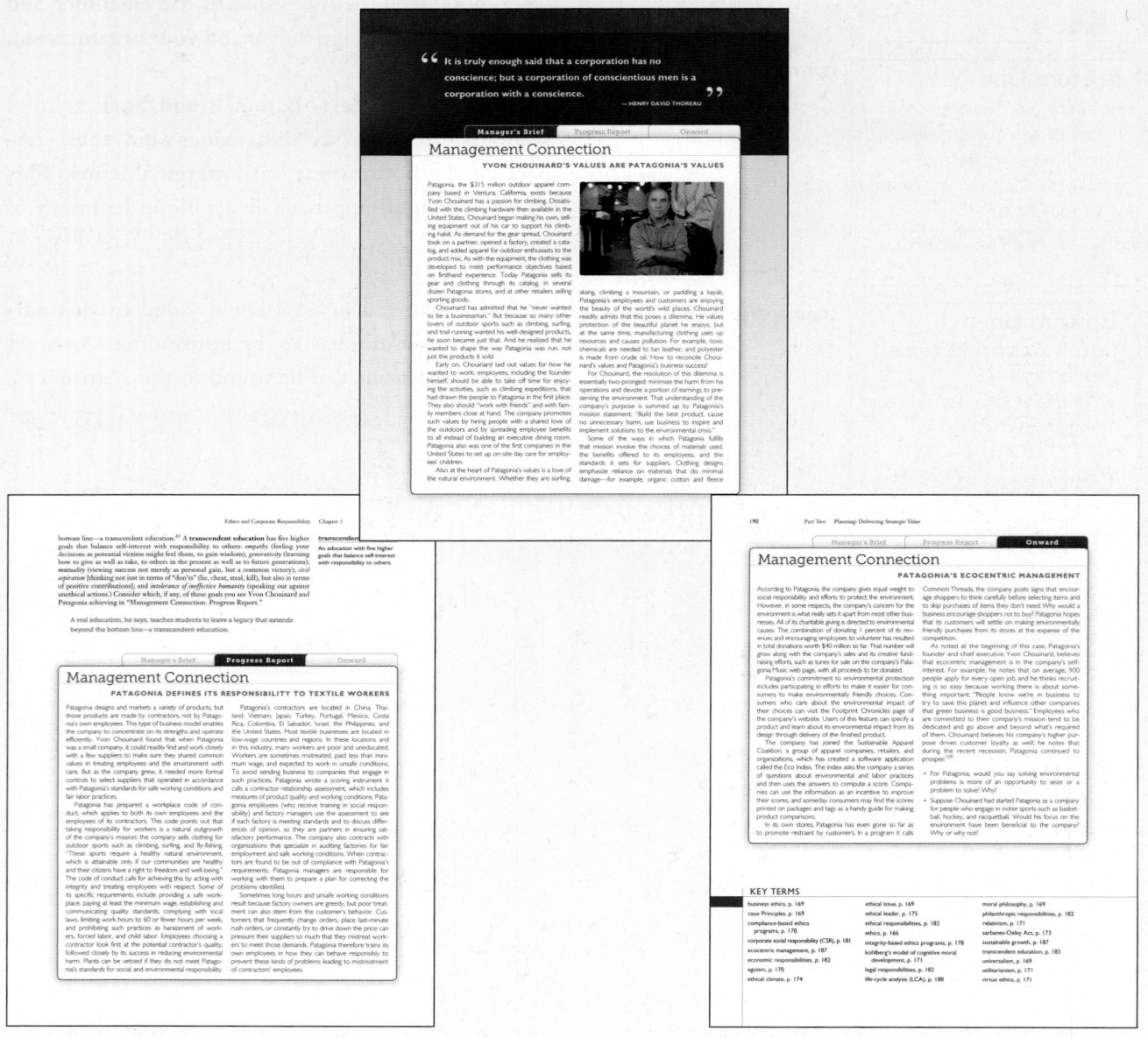

CHAPTER UNFOLDING CASES

Each chapter begins with a "Management Connection: Manager's Brief" section that describes an actual organizational situation, leader, or company. The Manager's Brief is referred to again within the chapter in the "Progress Report" section, showing the student how the chapter material relates back to the company, situation, or leader highlighted in the chapter opener. At the end of the chapter, the "Onward" section ties up loose ends and brings the material full circle for the student. Answers to Management Connection section questions can be found in the Instructor's Manual.

IN PRACTICE
In Practice boxes have been added to this edition to reinforce concepts learned in the chapter. Answers to In Practice box questions are also included in the Instructor's Manual.

CONCLUDING CASES
Each chapter ends with a case based on disguised but real companies and people that reinforces key chapter elements and themes.

SUPPLEMENTARY CASES
At the end of each part, an additional case is provided for professors who want students to delve further into part topics.

Assurance of Learning

① This 10th edition contains revised learning objectives for each chapter, and ② learning objectives are called out within the chapter where the content begins. ③ The summary for each chapter ties the learning objectives back together as well. ④ Our test bank provides tagging for the learning objective that the question covers, so instructors will be able to test material covering all learning objectives, thus ensuring that students have mastered the important topics.

ASSURANCE OF LEARNING READY

Many educational institutions today are focused on the notion of *assurance of learning*, an important element of some accreditation standards. The edition of *Management: Leading & Collaborating in a Competitive World* is designed specifically to support your assurance of learning initiatives with a simple yet powerful solution.

Each test bank question for *Management: Leading & Collaborating in a Competitive World*, 10e, maps to a specific chapter learning outcome/objective listed in the text. You can use our test bank software, EZ Test and EZ Test Online, or *Connect Management* to easily query for learning outcomes/objectives that directly relate to the learning objectives for your course. You can then use the reporting features of EZ Test to aggregate student results in similar fashion, making the collection and presentation of assurance of learning data simple and easy.

AACSB STATEMENT

The McGraw-Hill Companies are a proud corporate member of AACSB International. Understanding the importance and value of AACSB accreditation, *Management: Leading & Collaborating in a Competitive World*, 10e, recognizes the curricula guidelines detailed in the AACSB standards for business accreditation by connecting selected questions in the text and/or the test bank to the six general knowledge and skill guidelines in the AACSB standards.

The statements contained in *Management: Leading & Collaborating in a Competitive World*, 10e, are provided only as a guide for the users of this textbook. The AACSB leaves content coverage and assessment within the purview of individual schools, the mission of the school, and the faculty. While this book and the teaching package make no claim of any specific AACSB qualification or evaluation, we have within *Management: Leading & Collaborating in a Competitive World*, 10e, labeled selected questions according to the six general knowledge and skills areas.

Outstanding Pedagogy

Management: Leading & Collaborating in a Competitive World is pedagogically stimulating and is intended to maximize student learning. With this in mind, we used a wide array of pedagogical features—some tried and true, others new and novel:

RANDOM POP-UPS
Throughout the chapter, these marginal boxes highlight interesting factoids, statistics, and quotes relating to chapter content.

A recent survey by a human resource consulting firm found that over half of employees were engaged, defined as knowing what to do (vision) and wanting to do it (commitment). This was 5 percentage point improvement from three years earlier, when more employees were lacking in commitment.[5]

- Engaged employees (commitment, vision)
- Enthusiasts (commitment, no vision)
- Renegades (vision, no commitment)
- Disengaged employees (no commitment, no vision)

END-OF-CHAPTER ELEMENTS

- **Key terms** are page-referenced to the text and are part of the vocabulary-building emphasis. These terms are defined again in the glossary at the end of the book.

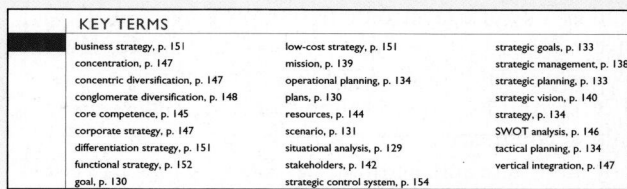

KEY TERMS

business strategy, p. 151	low-cost strategy, p. 151	strategic goals, p. 133
concentration, p. 147	mission, p. 139	strategic management, p. 138
concentric diversification, p. 147	operational planning, p. 134	strategic planning, p. 133
conglomerate diversification, p. 148	plans, p. 130	strategic vision, p. 140
core competence, p. 145	resources, p. 144	strategy, p. 134
corporate strategy, p. 147	scenario, p. 131	SWOT analysis, p. 146
differentiation strategy, p. 151	situational analysis, p. 129	tactical planning, p. 134
functional strategy, p. 152	stakeholders, p. 142	vertical integration, p. 147
goal, p. 130	strategic control system, p. 154	

- A **Summary of Learning Objectives** provides clear, concise responses to the learning objectives, giving students a quick reference for reviewing the important concepts in the chapter.

SUMMARY OF LEARNING OBJECTIVES

Now that you have studied Chapter 4, you should be able to:

LO 1 Summarize the basic steps in any planning process.

The planning process begins with a situation analysis of the external and internal forces affecting the organization. This examination helps identify and diagnose issues and problems and may bring to the surface alternative goals and plans for the firm. Next, the advantages and disadvantages of these goals and

LO 2 Describe how strategic planning should be integrated with tactical and operational planning.

Strategic planning is different from operational planning in that it involves making long-term decisions about the entire organization. Tactical planning translates broad goals and strategies into specific actions to be taken within parts of the organization. Operational planning identifies the specific short-term procedures and processes required at lower levels of the organization.

- **Discussion Questions,** which follow the Summary of Learning Objectives, are thought-provoking questions on concepts covered in the chapter and ask for opinions on controversial issues.

DISCUSSION QUESTIONS

1. This chapter opened with a quote from former CEO of GE Jack Welch: "Manage your destiny, or someone else will." What does this mean for strategic management? What does it mean when Welch adds, "or someone else will"?

2. List the six steps in the formal planning process. Suppose you are a top executive of a home improvement chain and you want to launch a new company website. Provide examples of activities you would carry out during each step to create the site.

5. How might an organization such as Urban Outfitters use a strategy map? With your classmates and using Figure 4.3 as a guide, develop a possible strategy map for the company.

6. What accounts for the shift from strategic planning to strategic management? In which industries would you be most likely to observe these trends? Why?

7. Review Table 4.1, which lists the components of an environmental analysis. Why would this analysis be important to a company's strategic planning process?

- Each chapter ends with a **Concluding Case,** based on disguised but real companies and people, that reinforces key chapter elements and themes.

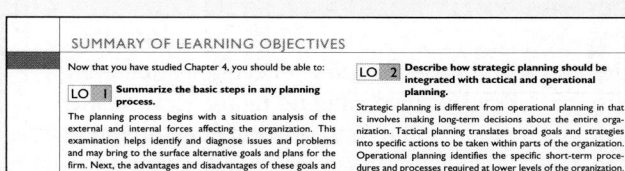

162   Part Two   Planning: Delivering Strategic Value

CONCLUDING CASE

CUSTOM COFFEE & CHOCOLATE

Bonnie Brewer and Stacy Kim were college roommates. While at school, they shared dreams of opening their own business. To prepare themselves, they took business and marketing courses, along with courses in management. When they graduated, they each found jobs in Seattle, near where they'd gone to school.

Several years later, after working at other companies to gain

their attention toward longer-term planning. They had exhausted their savings and their initial small business loan, and their six-month lease was up. They needed to decide whether they were in this for the long haul.

The two women met to consider their options. Right away, they decided they wanted to extend their hours and hire two

Comprehensive Supplements

INSTRUCTOR'S MANUAL

Authored by Kerry S. Webb, Texas Woman's University, the Instructor's Manual was revised and updated to include thorough coverage of each chapter as well as time-saving features such as an outline, key student questions, class prep work assignments, guidance for using the "unfolding" cases, video supplements, and finally, PowerPoint ® slides.

TEST BANK

Prepared by Tia Quinlan-Wilder, University of Denver, the Test Bank includes more than 100 questions per chapter in a variety of formats. It has been revised for accuracy and expanded to include a greater variety of comprehension and application (scenario-based) questions as well as tagged with Bloom's Taxonomy levels and AACSB requirements. **EZ Test** is a flexible and easy-to-use electronic testing program that allows instructors to create tests from book-specific items. A downloadable desktop version can be found on the IRCD. And **EZ Test Online** (*www.eztestonline.com*) allows you to access the test bank from the OLC virtually anywhere and anytime. EZ Test–created exams and quizzes can be administered online, providing instant feedback for students.

POWERPOINT PRESENTATION SLIDES

Prepared by Brad Cox, Midlands Technical College, the PowerPoint presentation collection contains an easy-to-follow outline including figures downloaded from the text. In addition to providing lecture notes, the slides also include questions for class discussion as well as company examples not found in the textbook. This versatility allows you to create a custom presentation suitable for your own classroom experience.

Note: All of the above can be found on the Instructor's Resource CD-ROM. It allows instructors to easily create their own custom presentations using the following resources: Instructor's Manual, Test Bank, EZ Test, and PowerPoint Presentations.

MCGRAW-HILL *CONNECT MANAGEMENT*

LESS MANAGING. MORE TEACHING. GREATER LEARNING

McGraw-Hill *Connect Management* is an online assignment and assessment solution that connects students with the tools and resources they'll need to achieve success.

McGraw-Hill *Connect Management* helps prepare students for their future by enabling faster learning, more efficient studying, and higher retention of knowledge.

MCGRAW-HILL *CONNECT MANAGEMENT* FEATURES

Connect Management offers a number of powerful tools and features to make managing assignments easier, so faculty can spend more time teaching. With *Connect Management*, students can engage with their coursework anytime and anywhere, making the learning process more accessible and efficient. *Connect Management* offers you the features described next.

Diagnostic and Adaptive Learning of Concepts: LearnSmart Students want to make the best use of their study time. The LearnSmart adaptive self-study technology within *Connect Management* provides students with a seamless combination of practice, assessment, and remediation for every concept in the textbook. LearnSmart's intelligent software adapts to every student response and automatically delivers concepts that advance the student's understanding while reducing time devoted to the concepts already mastered. The result for every student is the fastest path to mastery of the chapter concepts.

- Applies an intelligent concept engine to identify the relationships between concepts and to serve new concepts to each student only when he or she is ready.

- Adapts automatically to each student, so students spend less time on the topics they understand and practice more those they have yet to master.

- Provides continual reinforcement and remediation, but gives only as much guidance as students need.

- Integrates diagnostics as part of the learning experience.

- Enables you to assess which concepts students have efficiently learned on their own, thus freeing class time for more applications and discussion.

Online Interactives   Online Interactives are engaging tools that teach students to apply key concepts in practice. These interactives provide them with immersive, experiential learning opportunities. Students will engage in a variety of interactive scenarios to deepen critical knowledge of key course topics. They receive immediate feedback at intermediate steps throughout each exercise, as well as comprehensive feedback at the end of the assignment. All interactives are automatically scored and entered into the instructor grade book.

Lecture Capture via Tegrity Campus   *Increase the attention* paid to lecture discussion by decreasing the attention paid to note taking. For an additional charge, Lecture Capture offers new ways for students to focus on the in-class discussion, knowing they can revisit important topics later.

McGraw-Hill *Connect Plus Management*   McGraw-Hill reinvents the textbook learning experience for the modern student with *Connect Plus Management*. A seamless integration of an eBook and *Management*, *Connect Plus Management* provides all of the *Connect Management* features plus the following:

- An integrated eBook, allowing for anytime, anywhere access to the textbook.
- Dynamic links between the problems or questions you assign to your students and the location in the eBook where that problem or question is covered.
- A powerful search function to pinpoint and connect key concepts in a snap.

In short, *Connect Management* offers you and your students powerful tools and features that optimize your time and energies, enabling you to focus on course content, teaching, and student learning. *Connect Management* also offers a wealth of content resources for both instructors and students. This state-of-the-art, thoroughly tested system supports you in preparing students for the world that awaits.

For more information about *Connect*, go to **www.mcgrawhillconnect.com,** or contact your local McGraw-Hill sales representative.

TEGRITY CAMPUS

Lectures 24/7:   Tegrity Campus is a service that makes class time available 24/7 by automatically capturing every lecture in a searchable format for students to review when they study and complete assignments. With a simple one-click start-and-stop process, you capture all computer screens and corresponding audio. Students can replay any part of any class with easy-to-use browser-based viewing on a PC or Mac.

Educators know that the more students can see, hear, and experience class resources, the better they learn. In fact, studies prove it. With Tegrity Campus, students quickly recall key moments by using Tegrity Campus's unique search feature. This search helps students efficiently find what they need, when they need it, across an entire semester of class recordings. Help turn all your students' study time into learning moments immediately supported by your lecture. Lecture Capture enables you to

- Record and distribute your lecture with a click of button.
- Record and index PowerPoint presentations and anything shown on your computer so it is easily searchable, frame by frame.
- Offer access to lectures anytime and anywhere by computer, iPod, or mobile device.
- Increase intent listening and class participation by easing students' concerns about note taking. Lecture Capture will make it more likely you will see students' faces, not the tops of their heads.

To learn more about Tegrity, watch a two-minute Flash demo at **http://tegritycampus.mhhe.com.**

Student Progress Tracking   *Connect Management* keeps instructors informed about how each student, section, and class is performing, allowing for more productive use of lecture and office hours. The progress-tracking function enables you to

- View scored work immediately and track individual or group performance with assignment and grade reports.
- Access an instant view of student or class performance relative to learning objectives.
- Collect data and generate reports required by many accreditation organizations, such as AACSB.

Smart Grading   When it comes to studying, time is precious. *Connect Management* helps students learn more efficiently by providing feedback and practice material when they need it, where they need it. When it comes to teaching, your time also is precious. The grading function enables you to

- Have assignments scored automatically, giving students immediate feedback on their work and side-by-side comparisons with correct answers.
- Access and review each response; manually change grades or leave comments for students to review.
- Reinforce classroom concepts with practice tests and instant quizzes.

Simple Assignment Management   With *Connect Management*, creating assignments is easier than ever, so you can spend more time teaching and less time managing. The assignment management function enables you to

- Create and deliver assignments easily with selectable end-of-chapter questions and test bank items.
- Streamline lesson planning, student progress reporting, and assignment grading to make classroom management more efficient than ever.
- Go paperless with the eBook and online submission and grading of student assignments.

Instructor Library   The *Connect Management* Instructor Library is your repository for additional resources to improve student engagement in and out of class. You can select and use any asset that enhances your lecture. The *Connect Management* Instructor Library includes

- Instructor Manual.
- PowerPoint files.
- Test Bank.
- Management Asset Gallery.
- eBook.

Student Study Center   The *Connect Management* Student Study Center is the place for students to access additional resources. The Student Study Center

- Offers students quick access to lectures, practice materials, eBooks, and more.
- Provides instant practice material and study questions, easily accessible on the go.

- Gives students access to self-assessments, video materials, Manager's Hot Seat, and more.

E-BOOK OPTIONS

e-books are an innovative way for students to save money and to "go green." McGraw-Hill's e-books are typically 40 percent of bookstore price. Students have the choice between an online and a downloadable CourseSmart e-book.

Through *CourseSmart*, students have the flexibility to access an exact replica of their textbook from any computer that has Internet service without plug-ins or special software via the version, or create a library of books on their hard drive via the downloadable version. Access to the CourseSmart e-books lasts for one year.

Features   *CourseSmart* e-books allow students to highlight, take notes, organize notes, and share the notes with other *CourseSmart* users. Students can also search terms across all e-books in their purchased *CourseSmart* library. *CourseSmart* e-books can be printed (five pages at a time).

More Info and Purchase   Please visit www. coursesmart.com for more information and to purchase access to our e-books. *CourseSmart* allows students to try one chapter of the e-book, free of charge, before purchase.

Create

 Craft your teaching resources to match the way you teach! With McGraw-Hill *Create*, *www.mcgrawhillcreate.com*, you can easily rearrange chapters, combine material from other content sources, and quickly upload content you have written, like your course syllabus or teaching notes. Find the content you need in *Create* by searching through thousands of leading McGraw-Hill textbooks. Arrange your book to fit your teaching style. *Create* even allows you to personalize your book's appearance by selecting the cover and adding your name, school, and course information. Order a *Create* book and you'll receive a complimentary print review copy in three to five business days or a complimentary electronic review copy (eComp) via e-mail in about one hour. Go to *www.mcgrawhillcreate.com* today and register. Experience how McGraw-Hill *Create* empowers you to teach *your* students *your* way.

McGraw-Hill Higher Education and Blackboard

McGraw-Hill Higher Education and Blackboard have teamed up. What does this mean for you?

1. **Your life, simplified.** Now you and your students can access McGraw-Hill's *Connect* and *Create* right from within your Blackboard course—all with one single sign-on. Say goodbye to the days of logging into multiple applications.
2. **Deep integration of content and tools.** Not only do you get single sign-on with *Connect* and *Create*, you also get deep integration of McGraw-Hill content and content engines right in Blackboard. Whether you're choosing a book for your course or building Connect assignments, all the tools you need are right where you want them—inside of Blackboard.
3. **Seamless gradebooks.** Are you tired of keeping multiple gradebooks and manually synchronizing grades into Blackboard? We thought so. When a student completes an integrated Connect assignment, the grade for that assignment automatically (and instantly) feeds your Blackboard grade center.
4. **A solution for everyone.** Whether your institution is already using Blackboard or you just want to try Blackboard on your own, we have a solution for you. McGraw-Hill and Blackboard can now offer you easy access to industry-leading technology and content, whether your campus hosts it or we do. Be sure to ask your local McGraw-Hill representative for details.

McGraw-Hill Customer Experience

At McGraw-Hill, we understand that getting the most from new technology can be challenging. That's why our services don't stop after you purchase our products. You can e-mail our product specialists 24 hours a day to get product training online. Or you can search our knowledge bank of frequently asked questions on our support website. For customer support, call **800-331-5094**, submit a support request using our contact us form, **http://mpss.mhhe.com/contact.php**, or visit **www.mhhe.com/support**. One of our technical support analysts will be able to assist you in a timely fashion.

Instructor & Student Asset Gallery!

McGraw-Hill/Irwin Management still provides a one-stop shop for our wealth of assets, making it quick and easy for instructors to locate specific materials to enhance their courses.

The Instructor & Student Asset Gallery is intuitively organized and designed, allowing instructors ease of use in previewing our wealth of resources. These resources correlate with specific asset categories and more than 40 topics in management.

The Asset Gallery includes all of our non-text-specific management resources (Self-Assessments, Test Your Knowledge exercises, videos and information, additional group and individual exercises) along with supporting PowerPoint® and Instructor Manual materials. Additionally, to help incorporate the assets in the classroom, a guide is provided specific to McGraw-Hill/Irwin texts. Instructors can reach the Asset Gallery through a link from the Instructor area of the Online Learning Center.

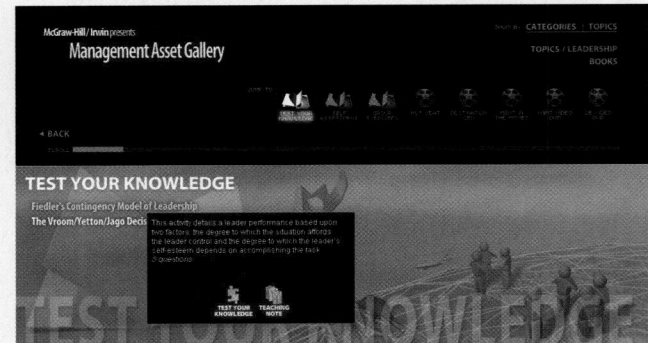

All of the following can be accessed within the Management Asset Gallery:

MANAGER'S HOT SEAT

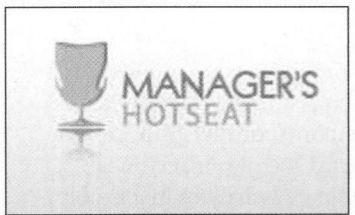

This interactive, video-based application puts students in the manager's hot seat, building critical thinking and decision-making skills and allowing students to apply concepts to real managerial challenges. Students watch as 21 real managers apply their years of experience when confronting unscripted issues such as bullying in the workplace, cyber loafing, globalization, intergenerational work conflicts, workplace violence, and leadership versus management.

SELF-ASSESSMENT GALLERY

Unique among publisher-provided self-assessments, our 23 self-assessments provide students with background information to ensure that students understand the purpose of the assessment. Students test their values, beliefs, skills, and interests in a wide variety of areas allowing them to apply chapter content to their own lives and careers.

Every self-assessment is supported with Power-Points and an instructor's manual in the Instructor & Student Asset Gallery, making it easy for the instructor to create an engaging classroom discussion surrounding the assessments.

TEST YOUR KNOWLEDGE

To help reinforce students' understanding of key management concepts, Test Your Knowledge activities give students a review of the conceptual materials followed by application-based questions to work through. Students can choose practice mode, which provides them with detailed feedback after each question, or test mode, which provides feedback after the entire test has been completed. Every Test Your Knowledge activity is supported by instructor notes in the Instructor & Student Asset Gallery to make it easy for the instructor to create engaging classroom discussions surrounding the materials students have completed.

MANAGEMENT HISTORY TIMELINE

This web application allows instructors to present and students to learn the history of management in an engaging and interactive way. Management history is presented along an intuitive timeline that can be traveled through sequentially or by selected decade. With the click of a mouse students learn the important dates, see the people who influenced the field, and understand the general management theories that have molded and shaped management as we know it today.

PRINCIPLES OF MANAGEMENT VIDEO DVD VOLUMES 1 AND 2 & NEW! VOLUME 3

More than 95 video clips from sources such as *BusinessWeek* Online, BBC, CBS, FiftyLessons, NBC, PBS, and McGraw-Hill are provided on three DVD sets. These company videos are organized by the four functions of management and feature companies such as AFLAC, Goldman Sachs, Google, IDEO, Zappos, PlayStation, Panera Bread, Patagonia, Mini Cooper, the Greater Chicago Food Depository, Employer-Subsidized Commuting, Grounded: Are U.S. Airlines Safe?, Using Facebook at Work, Adult Bullies, and Encore Careers in 2½- to 15-minute clips. Corresponding video cases and a guide that ties the videos closely to the chapter can be found in the Instructor's Manual and online.

Online Learning Center

WWW.MHHE.COM/BATEMAN10E
More and more students are studying online and on the go.

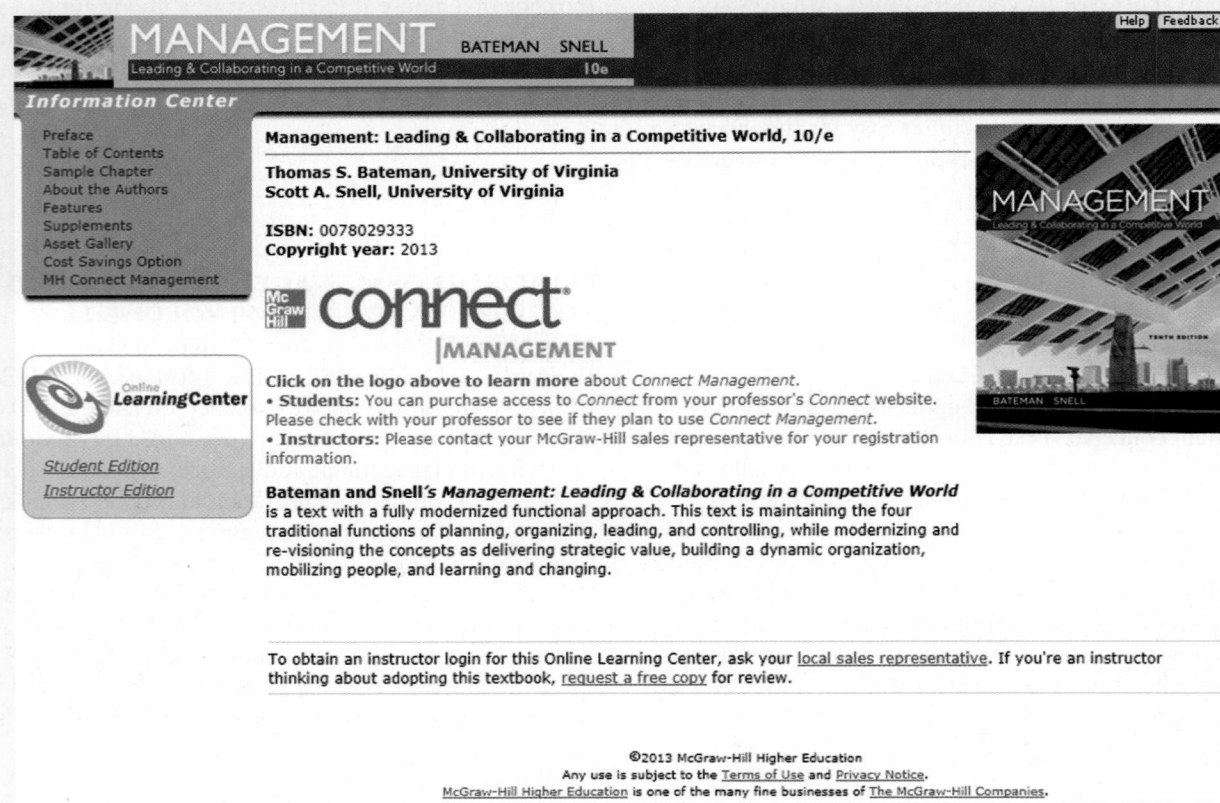

To obtain an instructor login for this Online Learning Center, ask your local sales representative. If you're an instructor thinking about adopting this textbook, request a free copy for review.

Brief Contents

Contents

Preface   vi

Part One

Foundations of Management

Chapter 3

Managerial Decision Making   84

Part Two
Planning: Delivering Strategic Value

Chapter 4
Planning and Strategic Management   126

Part Three
Organizing: Building a Dynamic Organization

Chapter 11
Managing the Diverse Workforce   392

Part Four
Leading: Mobilizing People

Chapter 12
Leadership   430

Chapter 13
Motivating for Performance   468

Part Five

Controlling: Learning and Changing

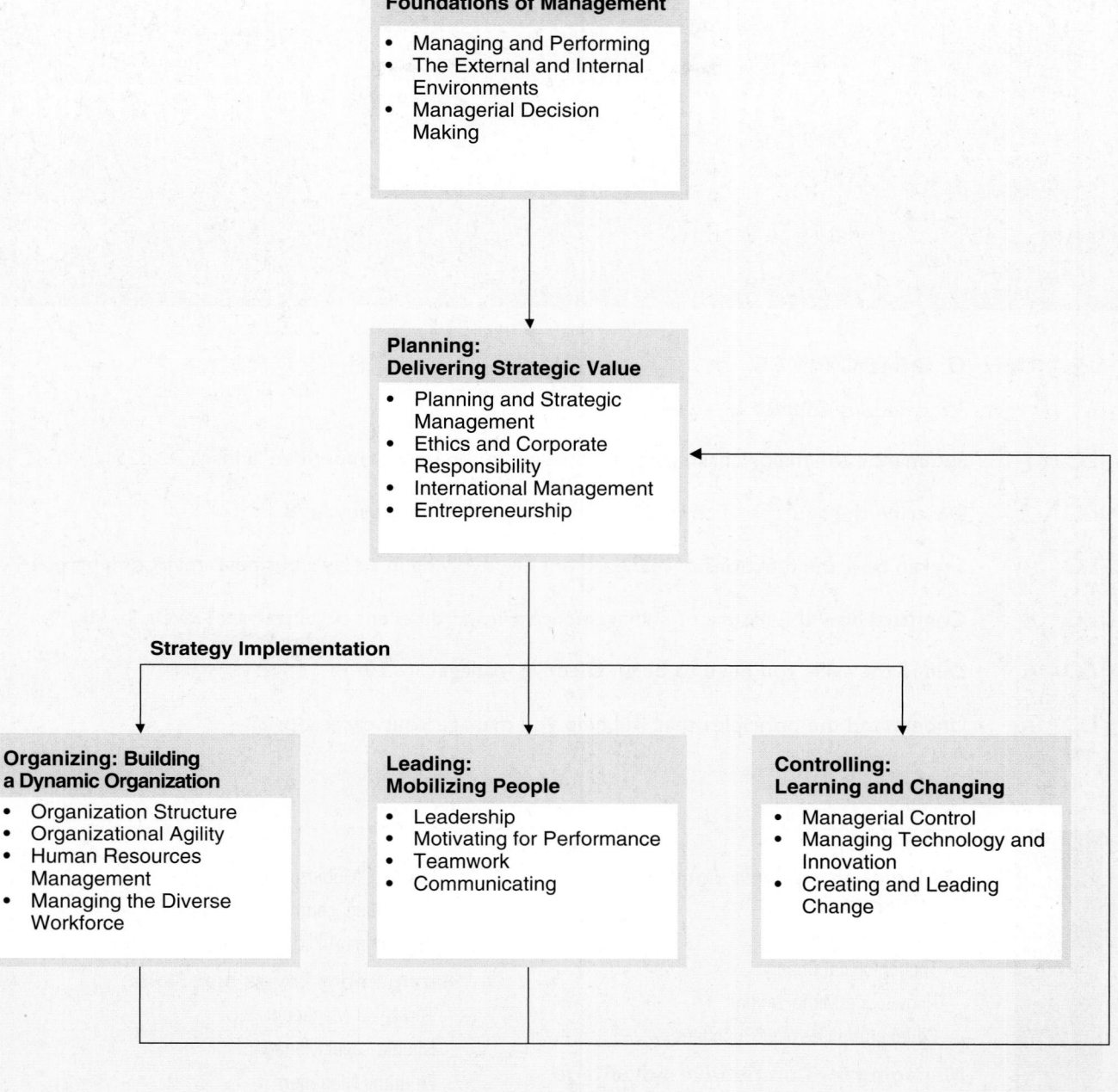

Foundations of Management

- Managing and Performing
- The External and Internal Environments
- Managerial Decision Making

Planning:
Delivering Strategic Value

- Planning and Strategic Management
- Ethics and Corporate Responsibility
- International Management
- Entrepreneurship

Strategy Implementation

Organizing: Building a Dynamic Organization

- Organization Structure
- Organizational Agility
- Human Resources Management
- Managing the Diverse Workforce

Leading:
Mobilizing People

- Leadership
- Motivating for Performance
- Teamwork
- Communicating

Controlling:
Learning and Changing

- Managerial Control
- Managing Technology and Innovation
- Creating and Leading Change

Managing and Performing

LEARNING OBJECTIVES

After studying Chapter 1, you will be able to:

LO 1 Summarize the major challenges of managing in the new competitive landscape. p. 5

LO 2 Describe the sources of competitive advantage for a company. p. 8

LO 3 Explain how the functions of management are evolving in today's business environment. p. 14

LO 4 Compare how the nature of management varies at different organizational levels. p. 18

LO 5 Define the skills you need to be an effective manager. p. 20

LO 6 Understand the principles that will help you manage your career. p. 22

CHAPTER OUTLINE

Managing in the New Competitive Landscape
Globalization
Technological Change
Knowledge Management
Collaboration across "Boundaries"

Managing for Competitive Advantage
Innovation
Quality
Service
Speed
Cost Competitiveness
Sustainability
Delivering All Types of Performance

The Functions of Management
Planning: Delivering Strategic Value
Organizing: Building a Dynamic Organization

Leading: Mobilizing People
Controlling: Learning and Changing
Performing All Four Management Functions

Management Levels and Skills
Top-Level Managers
Middle-Level Managers
Frontline Managers
Working Leaders with Broad Responsibilities
Management Skills

You and Your Career
Be Both a Specialist and a Generalist
Be Self-Reliant
Be Connected
Actively Manage Your Relationship with Your Organization
Survive and Thrive

| Manager's Brief | Progress Report | Onward |

Management Connection

HOW MANAGERS KEEP TESLA MOTORING

What does it take to turn a vision into an ongoing, productive reality? If your vision is to lead an automotive revolution by selling all-electric cars that deliver a comfortable, convenient ride while cutting dependence on fossil fuels, it takes engineering genius, quality-driven workers, marketing know-how, and cash. And then it takes people who can harness all these resources, figure out the best way to direct them, and get the whole organization to outperform the competition. In other words, achieving the vision requires talented managers.

For a picture of what this means, think about how the managers of Tesla Motors have pulled together a host of resources aimed at achieving an ambitious goal: selling the world's first marketable all-electric car. As envisioned, Tesla's car would be priced competitively with midsize sedans and would run on a battery with enough power to carry the car 300 miles on a single charge. So far, the company has begun selling its $109,000 battery-powered Roadster, which is a high-performance vehicle but doesn't fulfill the affordability part of the Tesla equation. The company planned to begin making a sedan, the Model S, targeted to sell for $54,700, beginning in 2012.

A project like that requires sizable fund-raising—millions of dollars, in fact—and Tesla's chief executive, Elon Musk, has come up with some creative financing ideas and persuaded investors with deep pockets to buy in. Musk also negotiated with Toyota's president, Akio Toyoda, to set up a joint venture in which Tesla helped Toyota develop an electric version of Toyota's RAV4 sport utility vehicle. The deal called for Toyota to invest $50 million for an ownership share of Tesla. It might seem strange to share technology with a potential competitor, but the deal gives Tesla much-needed

cash and makes it more attractive to other potential investors. For example, Panasonic, which has been a leader in developing powerful lithium ion batteries and hopes to supply electric vehicles, invested $30 million in Tesla in exchange for an ownership share. The deal gives Tesla not only cash but also access to expertise in designing one of the trickiest parts of an electric car.

Building an innovative automobile also requires a great design and a factory located near the right kind of talent to bring a new design to market. The responsibility for designing a battery that is safe yet delivers enough power and costs less than $10,000 to make falls to Wes Hermann, manager of Tesla's battery safety and technology lab. Hermann studied engineering in college and then worked for a foundation that studies the environmental impact of energy use. Working for Tesla was a chance to put theory into practice. Of course Hermann can't achieve those goals on his own; he has to hire and direct a team of engineers.

The hit to the auto industry from the recent financial crisis brought Tesla an opportunity in the form of an empty factory. General Motors closed a plant it had jointly operated with Toyota in Fremont, California, not far from Tesla's Palo Alto headquarters in the heart of Silicon Valley. Tesla bought the plant and set up a temporary office in the parking lot. Preparing the plant to make the Model S is the responsibility of Gilbert Passin, Tesla's vice president of manufacturing. Passin is aiming to meet the ambitious goal of assembling Model S cars within two years. The people who report to him are busy preparing diagrams and schedules to set up workstations for building high-tech automobiles. Meanwhile, Tesla's vice president of human resources, Arnnon Geshuri, is overseeing the task of hiring hundreds of new workers. Geshuri has the background for a challenge; before working at Tesla, he managed human resources at Google when that company's head count was rising exponentially.[1]

As you read this chapter, notice the wide variety of skills required of the managers at Tesla Motors. Also think about how managing people, money, and other resources enables Tesla and other organizations to accomplish far more than individuals acting independently could ever achieve.

Tesla Motors' CEO, Elon Musk, is arguably one of the most interesting leaders in business today. He combines strong creative skills with a keen ability to see the big picture—and he's been remarkably successful at building organizations. Of course not every manager or organization succeeds. A story of failure that shocked many Americans involved the care provided to wounded soldiers at the Walter Reed Army Medical Center in Washington, DC. Reporters investigating outpatient facilities of Walter Reed—which ranks among the nation's top military hospitals—discovered that in some facilities, outpatients were coping with mold, roaches, rodents, and damaged walls and doors. Many outpatients, some with serious injuries and mental impairments, complained of paperwork problems that kept them from receiving services. Testifying before Congress, the Army's vice chief of staff admitted fundamental management problems:

> Our counselors and case managers are overworked, and they do not receive enough training. We do not adequately communicate necessary information. Our administrative processes are needlessly cumbersome and . . . take too long. Our medical holding units are not manned to the proper level, and we do not assign leaders who can ensure a proper accountability, proper discipline and well-being, . . . and our facilities are not maintained to the standards that we know is [sic] right.[2]

Major General George W. Weightman, who lost his job as Walter Reed's commander as a result of the scandal, acknowledged that the organization had experienced a "failure of leadership."[3]

On brighter notes, capable managers have made improvements at Walter Reed. And *Harvard Business Review* ranks and spotlights the best CEOs in the world not on position or fame or charisma or short-term flash, but on the consistently high performance they deliver over many years in office.[4] For 2011, number one was no surprise: Steve Jobs, who took over Apple in 1997 when the company was in bad shape and delivered sterling returns and market value year after year. The list ranked Yun Jong-Yong of South Korea's Samsung Electronics in the number two spot.

Companies, like individuals, succeed or fail for a variety of reasons. Some of these reasons are circumstantial. Most are personal and human and include the decisions managers make and the actions they take.

In business, there is no replacement for effective management. Companies may fly high for a while, but they cannot do well for very long without good management. It's the same for individuals: *Bloomberg Businessweek*'s managers succeed by focusing on fundamentals, knowing what's important, and managing well. The aim of this book is to help you succeed in those pursuits.

Managing in the New Competitive Landscape

When the economy is soaring, business seems easy. Starting an Internet company looked easy in the 1990s, and ventures related to the real estate boom looked like a sure thing just a few years ago. But investors grew wary of dot-com start-ups, and the demand for new homes dropped off the table when the economy crashed in late 2008. At such times, it becomes evident that management is a challenge requiring constant adaptation to new circumstances.

What defines the competitive landscape of today's business? You will be reading about many relevant issues in the coming chapters, but we begin here by highlighting four key elements that make the current business landscape different from the past: globalization, technological change, the importance of knowledge and ideas, and collaboration across organizational "boundaries."

LO 1

> Management is a challenge requiring constant adaptation to new circumstances.

Globalization

Far more than in the past, today's enterprises are global, with offices and production facilities in countries all over the world. Corporations operate worldwide, transcending national borders. Companies that want to grow often need to tap international markets, where incomes are rising and demand is increasing. The change from a local to a global marketplace is gaining momentum and is irreversible.[5]

Fortune magazine annually publishes a list of the world's most admired companies. Whereas U.S. companies used to dominate, Madrid-based Telefonica was the most admired telecom in 2011. South Korea's POSCO was the most admired metals company, and Norway's Statoil was number one in petroleum refining, with Brazil's Petrobras coming on strong. McDonald's was number one in the category for effectiveness in conducting its business globally.[6] Who are other or more recent leaders?

Globalization also means that a company's talent can come from anywhere. As with its sales, more than half of GE's employees work outside the United States.[7] Cisco, a leader in equipment for computer networking, considers maintaining operations in India to be an essential tactic for staying competitive. Cisco serves the fast-growing Indian Internet market at a crucial time: the growth in demand is attracting low-cost competition from Chinese businesses.[8]

PepsiCo's chief executive, Indra Nooyi, brings a much-needed global viewpoint to a company whose international business has been growing three times faster than sales in the United States. Nooyi, who was raised in India and educated there and in the United States, has steered the company toward more "better for you" and "good for you" snacks with acquisitions including a nut packager in Bulgaria and a hummus producer in Israel.[9]

Meanwhile Coca-Cola has higher sales in Mexico than in any other country at 665 servings per year per

Globalization has changed the face of the workforce. Management in this new competitive landscape will need to attract and effectively manage a talent pool from all over the globe.

capita. In Kenya the rate is 39 servings per year per capita. Coca-Cola is already Africa's largest employer, and the continent is a key to Coke's future growth. Coke's CEO Muhtar Kent says, "Africa is the untold story, and could be the big story, of the next decade, like India and China were this past decade."[10]

Globalization affects small companies as well as large. Many small companies export their goods. Many domestic firms assemble their products in other countries. And companies are under pressure to improve their products in the face of intense competition from foreign manufacturers. Firms today must ask themselves, "How can we be the best in the world?"

Firms today must ask themselves, "How can we be the best in the world?"

For students, it's not too early to think about the personal ramifications. In the words of CEO Jim Goodnight of SAS, the largest privately held software company in the world, "The best thing business schools can do to prepare their students is to encourage them to look beyond their own backyards. Globalization has opened the world for many opportunities, and schools should encourage their students to take advantage of them."[11]

Technological Change

The Internet's impact on globalization is only one of the ways that technology is vitally important in the business world. Technology both complicates things and creates new opportunities. The challenges come from the rapid rate at which communication, transportation, information, and other technologies change.[12] For example, after just a couple of decades of widespread desktop use, customers switched to laptop models, which require different accessories.[13] Any company that serves desktop users had to rethink its customers' wants and needs, not to mention the possibility that these customers are now working at the airport or a local Starbucks outlet, rather than in an office.

Google search sites span the Internet in more than 50 languages.

Later chapters will discuss technology further, but here we highlight the rise of the Internet and its effects. Why is the Internet so important to business?[14] It is a marketplace, a means for manufacturing goods and services, a distribution channel, an information service, and more. It drives down costs and speeds up globalization. It improves efficiency of decision making. It facilitates design of new products, from pharmaceuticals to financial services. Managers can watch and learn what other companies are doing— on the other side of the world. While these advantages create business opportunities, they also create threats as competitors sometimes capitalize on new developments more than you do.

It may be hard to imagine that just a few years ago, going online to order plane tickets, read the news, or share photos was a novelty. Some online success stories, such as Amazon, Monster, and Google, were founded as purely Internet businesses. Other companies, including Barnes & Noble, Best Buy, and Office Depot, incorporated online channels into an established business strategy.

Among people who work long hours in high-stress jobs, 59% said technology lengthens rather than shortens their workday.[16]

And things continue to change at breakneck speed. In 2003 tech guru Tim O'Reilly coined the term "Web 2.0" to describe the exciting new wave of social networking start-ups that allow users to publish and share information. But most failed or are stalled; many fired their chief executives and laid off employees. Very few, other than Facebook, make a profit.[15]

Knowledge Management

Companies and managers need good new ideas. Because companies in advanced economies have become so efficient at producing physical goods, most workers have been freed up to provide services or "abstract goods" such as software, entertainment, data, and advertising. Efficient factories with fewer workers produce the cereals and cell phones the market demands; meanwhile, more and more workers create software and invent new goods and services. These workers, whose primary contributions are ideas and problem-solving expertise, are often referred to as *knowledge workers*. Managing these workers poses some particular challenges, which we will examine throughout this book. For example, determining whether they are doing a good job can be difficult because the manager cannot simply count or measure a knowledge worker's output. Also, these workers often are most motivated to do their best when the work is interesting, not because of a carrot or stick dangled by the manager.[17]

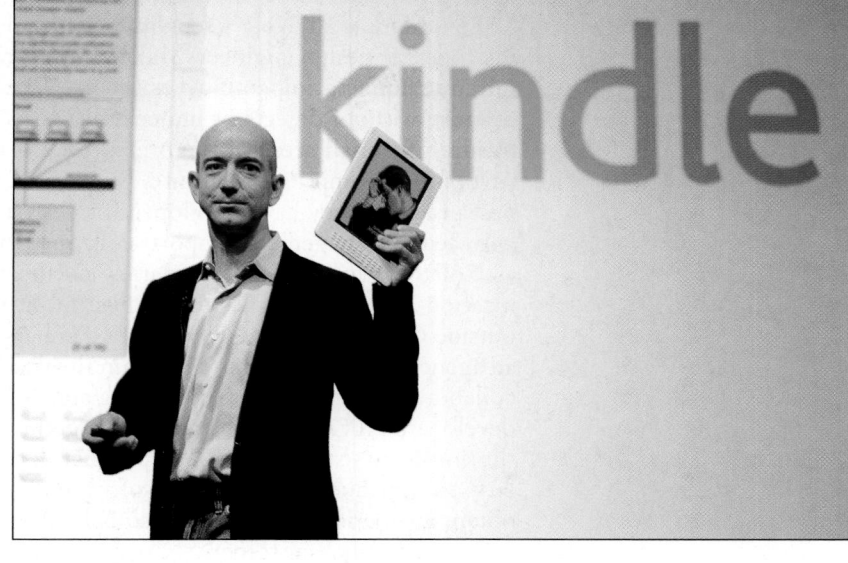

Jeff Bezos, founder and CEO of Amazon.com, holds the Kindle DX, a large-screen version of the standard Kindle eBook reader. Via a 3G wireless connection, users have access to Amazon's library containing about 2 million free, public domain e-books and can subscribe to several online newspapers, magazines, and blogs.

Because the success of modern businesses so often depends on the knowledge used for innovation and the delivery of services, organizations need to manage that knowledge. **Knowledge management** is the set of practices aimed at discovering and harnessing an organization's intellectual resources—fully utilizing the intellects of the organization's people.

> Knowledge management is about finding, unlocking, sharing, and altogether capitalizing on the most precious resources of an organization: people's expertise, skills, wisdom, and relationships.

Knowledge managers find these human assets, help people collaborate and learn, help people generate new ideas, and harness those ideas into successful innovations.

In hospitals, important knowledge includes patients' histories, doctors' orders, billing information, dietary requirements, prescriptions administered, and much more. With lives at stake, many hospitals have embraced knowledge management. For example, at Virginia Commonwealth University (VCU) Health System, a single information system lets doctors write prescriptions, look up patient information and lab results, and consult with one another. Billing also is automated as part of VCU's knowledge management system, making the process more efficient and connecting with patient data so that it can remind the physician of all the conditions being treated—and billed for.[18] Hospitals can also give patients access to the knowledge management system so that they can schedule appointments, request prescription refills, and send questions to their doctors.

knowledge management

Practices aimed at discovering and harnessing an organization's intellectual resources.

Collaboration across "Boundaries"

One of the most important processes of knowledge management is to ensure that people in different parts of the organization collaborate effectively with one another. This requires productive communications among different departments, divisions, or other subunits of the organization. For example, "T-shaped" managers break out of the traditional corporate hierarchy to share knowledge freely across the organization (the horizontal part of the T) while remaining fiercely committed to the bottom-line performance of their individual business units (the vertical part). This emphasis on dual responsibilities for performance and knowledge sharing occurs at pharmaceutical giant GlaxoSmithKline, large German industrial company Siemens, and London-based steelmaker Ispat International.[19]

For example, Toyota keeps its product development process efficient by bringing together design engineers and manufacturing employees from the very beginning. Often manufacturing employees can see ways to simplify a design so that it is easier to make without defects or unnecessary costs. Toyota expects its employees to listen to input from all areas of the organization, so this type of collaboration is a natural part of the organization's culture. Employees use software to share their knowledge—best practices they have developed for design and manufacturing.[20] Thus, at Toyota, knowledge management supports collaboration, and vice versa.

Collaboration across "boundaries" occurs even beyond the boundaries of the organization itself. Companies today must motivate and capitalize on the ideas of people outside the organization. How can a company best use the services of its consultants, ad agencies, and suppliers? To obtain the product development software that supports collaboration between manufacturing and design, Toyota collaborated with a software developer, PTC. Toyota and PTC together identified how software could support the company's strategy of "lean product development," and they kept meeting regularly to continue improving the software. This collaboration not only helped Toyota obtain a superior product but also helped PTC improve the value of the software it offers to its other customers.[21]

Customers, too, can be collaborators. Companies must realize that the need to serve the customer drives everything else. Best serving the customer can start with involving the customer more in company decisions. For example, companies like Procter & Gamble are getting customers to think creatively and talk with one another online to come up with new product and service ideas.[22] Tapping into the popularity of social networking websites like Facebook, P&G has set up websites aimed at bringing its customers together. One site is a discussion group for women, where they can discuss health and other concerns. Although such sites offer advertising opportunities, P&G uses them primarily as a way to learn more about consumers' attitudes.[23]

Managing for Competitive Advantage

 LO 2

Bottom Line

Because it's easy for managers to get so caught up in being busy, get distracted, and lose sight of what really drives performance, you will periodically see icons as "bottom-line" reminders of the need for innovation, quality, service, speed, cost competitiveness, and sustainability.

Which of these advantages do you think it would be hard to deliver at the same time?

The rise of the Internet turned careers (and lives) upside down. Students dropped out of school to join Internet start-ups or start their own. Managers in big corporations quit their jobs to do the same. Investors salivated, and invested heavily. The risks were often ignored or downplayed—sometimes tragically as the boom went bust. Or consider an earlier industry with similar transforming power: automobiles. There have been at least 2,000 car makers, but now only three U.S. car companies are left in the United States, with the rest either long gone or in serious trouble.

What is the lesson to be learned from the failures in these important transformational industries? A key to understanding the success of a company—whether traditional, Internet-based, or a combination of both—is not how much the industry in which it operates will affect society or how much it will grow. The key is the competitive advantage held by a particular company and how well it can sustain that advantage. Good managers know that they are in a competitive struggle to survive and win.

To survive and win, you have to gain advantage over your competitors and earn a profit. You gain competitive advantage by being better than your competitors at doing valuable things for your customers. But what does this mean, specifically? To succeed, managers must **deliver performance.** The fundamental success drivers of performance are innovation, quality, service, speed, cost competitiveness, and sustainability.

Innovation

While some cell phone users are always on the lookout for the latest in wireless technology and the most elegant design, many others simply want a phone they can afford. For the latter group, creative businesses are figuring out how to unite unwanted old cell phones with cost-conscious buyers. One of the most successful is ReCellular, which acquires used phones from charity collections and retailers looking for a place to dispose of returned products. It refurbishes the phones and then sells them at a modest price. ReCellular has seen its sales more than double in five years, but competitors are entering the market. However, companies like ReCellular have to be ready with an answer to what may be the next big trend: low-priced phones made in China.[24]

As ReCellular's experience illustrates, companies must continually innovate. **Innovation** is the introduction of new goods and services. Your firm must adapt to changes in consumer demands and to new competitors. Products don't sell forever; in fact, they don't sell for nearly as long as they used to because so many competitors are introducing so many new products all the time. Your firm must innovate, or it will die. Likewise, you have to be ready with new ways to communicate with customers and deliver the products to them. When the net allowed merchants to bypass traditional distribution channels and reach buyers directly, traditional marketers had to learn how to innovate to remain competitive.

Innovation isn't all about high tech. Dunkin' Brands Culinary Innovation Team is a group of 18 chefs led by executive chef Stan Frankenthaler. They send out about 20 new product launches to market each year for Dunkin' Donuts and Baskin-Robbins in a constant effort to boost revenues and profits. Bagel twists are a recent success; whole wheat donuts are not. The team is working long-term to create a zero-grams trans-fat menu.[25]

The need for innovation is driven in part by globalization. One obvious reason is that when facilities in other countries can manufacture appliances or write software code at a lower cost than facilities in the United States, U.S. facilities are operating at a disadvantage. They have to deliver something that their foreign competitors don't offer—and often that means something new. Philips, which started out making light bulbs in the Netherlands in the 1890s, has set up research as well as manufacturing operations in China because that country is becoming a key source of technical know-how, not just cheap labor.[26] Developing countries are becoming hotbeds of business innovation, providing new goods and services far more cheaply than their Western counterparts.[27] They are also reinventing production and distribution systems and experimenting with entirely new business models. Companies in developed countries need to learn from their new rivals in those developing countries.

Innovation is today's holy grail (2011's number one most admired company in *Fortune*'s innovativeness category was Apple).[28] Like the other sources of competitive advantage, innovation comes from people, it must be a strategic goal, and it must be managed properly. Later chapters will show you how great companies innovate.

Quality

When Spectrum Health, a hospital chain based in Grand Rapids, Michigan, asked patients how well they were served, patients rated staff low on helpfulness and their attitude toward visitors and said they didn't get good information about procedures or how to take care of themselves after being released to go home. Spectrum set

Good managers know that they are in a competitive struggle to survive and win.

innovation

The introduction of new goods and services.

People entering the Dans le Noir (In the Black) restaurant in Paris where they will enjoy a dining experience in complete darkness as if they were blind. Blind waiters serve as guides. The concept is an innovative approach to fine dining, and restaurants such as this are spreading around the globe.

up an advisory council of patients and family members, making visiting hours more flexible, getting patient input into who was allowed to hear medical information and make decisions about treatment, and calling discharged patients at home to make sure they understood the directions they had received. Satisfaction scores of Spectrum patients improved dramatically.[29]

quality

The excellence of your product (goods or services).

Spectrum Health's efforts reflect a commitment to quality. In general, **quality** is the excellence of your product. The importance of quality and the standards for acceptable quality have increased dramatically in recent years. Customers now demand high-quality goods and services, and often they will accept nothing less. In the hospital industry, the government is contributing to that trend. To receive full reimbursement from Medicare, hospitals must participate in a national program of patient satisfaction surveys. Results of these surveys are posted on the Department of Health and Human Service's Medicare information website, hospitalcompare.hhs.gov, so that patients can compare the rankings of hospitals in their area when choosing services.[30]

Historically, quality pertained primarily to the physical goods that customers bought, and it referred to attractiveness, lack of defects, reliability, and long-term dependability. The traditional approach to quality was to check work after it was completed and then eliminate defects, using inspection and statistical data to determine whether products were up to standards. But then W. Edwards Deming, J. M. Juran, and other quality gurus convinced managers to take a more complete approach to achieving *total* quality. This includes *preventing* defects before they occur, *achieving zero defects* in manufacturing, and *designing* products for quality. The goal is to solve and eradicate from the beginning all quality-related problems and to live a philosophy of *continuous improvement* in the way the company operates.[31]

Quality is further provided when companies customize goods and services to the wishes of the individual consumer. Choices at Starbucks give consumers thousands of variations on the drinks they can order, whether it's half-caff or all caffeine, skim milk or soy milk, or shots of espresso and any of a variety of flavored syrups. Car buyers can go online to "build their own" Mini Cooper, down to the color of the light for the speedometer. And for a premium price, candy lovers can select M&M's candies bearing the message of their own creation.[32] Similarly, Jones Soda Company lets visitors to its website order a 12-pack of soda with their photo on the bottles. They upload the photo to the myJones website (www.myjones.com) and choose a soda flavor.[33]

Providing world-class quality requires a thorough understanding of what quality really is.

Providing world-class quality requires a thorough understanding of what quality really is.[34] Quality can be measured in terms of product performance, customer service, reliability (avoidance of failure or breakdowns), conformance to standards, durability, and aesthetics. At the beginning of this section, we mentioned how hospitals are using patient surveys to measure quality and meet Medicare requirements. However, a recent study conducted by the University of Pennsylvania School of Medicine determined that a patient's risk of dying was not significantly less at hospitals that scored well on Medicare's quality measures.[35] But quality care is more than staying alive. Only when you move beyond broad, generic concepts such as "quality" and identify specific quality requirements can you identify problems, target needs, set performance standards more precisely, and deliver world-class value.

By the way, *Fortune* magazine's 2011 number one company for quality of products and services was Amazon.com. Who has it been since?

Service

As noted, important quality measures often pertain to the level of service received by customers. This dimension of quality is particularly important because the service sector has come to dominate the U.S. economy. According to the federal government, the value of services produced in the United States is more than three times the value of tangible goods produced.[36] In recent years, the fastest-growing job categories have been almost entirely services and retailing jobs, and the jobs with the greatest declines are almost all in manufacturing.[37] Services include intangible products such as insurance, hotel accommodations, medical care, and haircuts.

In a competitive context, **service** means giving customers what they want or need, when they want it. So service is focused on continually meeting the needs of customers to establish mutually beneficial long-term relationships. Thus software companies, in addition to providing the actual programs, may help their customers identify requirements, set up computer systems, and perform maintenance.

An important dimension of service quality is making it easy and enjoyable for customers to experience a service or to buy and use products. The Detroit Institute of Arts recently hired a manager formerly with the Ritz-Carlton hotel chain, noted for its exceptional level of service, to be vice president of museum operations. As the art museum prepared for a grand reopening following a major renovation, the manager analyzed the types of customer interactions that occur in a museum, identifying ways to make the experience more pleasant. He also worked with his staff to identify ways to customize services, such as offering tours tailored to the interests of particular groups.[38]

Every time you get a haircut at a salon, you are contributing to the employment of someone in one of the fastest-growing job categories, the service sector.

Speed

Google constantly improves its search product at a rapid rate. In fact, its entire culture is based on rapid innovation. Sheryl Sandberg, a Google vice president, once made a mistake because she was moving too fast to plan carefully. Although the mistake cost the company a few million dollars, Google cofounder Larry Page responded to her explanation and apology by saying he was actually glad she had made the mistake. It showed that she appreciated the company's values. Page told Sandberg, "I want to run a company where we are moving too quickly and doing too much, not being too cautious and doing too little. If we don't have any of these mistakes, we're just not taking enough risks."[39]

While it's unlikely that Google actually favors mistakes over moneymaking ideas, Page's statement expressed an appreciation that in the modern business environment, **speed**—rapid execution, response, and delivery of results—often separates the winners from the losers. How fast can you develop and get a new product to market? How quickly can you respond to customer requests? You are far better off if you are faster than the competition—and if you can respond quickly to your competitors' actions.

Speed isn't everything—you can't get sloppy in your quest to be first. But other things being equal, faster companies are more likely to be the winners, slow ones the losers. Even pre-Internet, companies were getting products to market and in the hands of customers faster than ever. Now the speed requirement has increased exponentially. Everything, it seems, is on fast-forward.

Speed is no longer just a goal of some companies; it is a strategic imperative. In the auto industry, getting faster is essential just for keeping up with the competition. A recent study found that the top assembly plant in the United States was Ford's Atlanta facility, where employees needed just 15.4 hours to assemble a vehicle. Compare that with the 1980s, when GM employees needed 40 hours to assemble a vehicle.[40] Another important measure of speed in the auto industry is the time the company takes to go from product concept to availability of the vehicle in the showroom. During the 1980s, that time was about 30 or 40 months. Today Toyota has cut the process to an average of 24 months; it needed just 22 months to launch its Tundra pickup.[41]

service

The speed and dependability with which an organization delivers what customers want.

speed

Fast and timely execution, response, and delivery of results.

Speed is no longer just a goal of some companies; it is a strategic imperative.

Walmart's goal is to provide products at low costs in order to retain its large customer base. To remain successful and cost competitive, it has devised and followed through with several plans to lower its operational costs.

cost competitiveness

Keeping costs low to achieve profits and be able to offer prices that are attractive to consumers.

Cost Competitiveness

Walmart keeps driving hard to find new ways to cut billions of dollars from its already very low distribution costs. It leads the industry in efficient distribution, but competitors are copying Walmart's methods, so the efficiency no longer gives it as much of an advantage.[42] Walmart has sought to keep costs down by scheduling store employees more efficiently. It introduced a computerized system that schedules employees based on each store's sales, transactions, units sold, and customer traffic. The system is intended to schedule just enough workers, with full staffing only at the busiest times of day and days of the week, so it requires more flexibility from Walmart's employees.[43]

Walmart's efforts are aimed at **cost competitiveness,** which means keeping costs low enough so that the company can realize profits and price its products (goods or services) at levels that are attractive to consumers. Needless to say, if you can offer a desirable product at a lower price, it is more likely to sell.

Singapore Airlines, one of the world's most admired companies, kept profiting during the economic recession while the global airline industry lost money. It did so by cutting costs more strategically than the competition. While competitors cut prices and still didn't fill their planes (and risked a backlash to later price hikes), SA slashed flights, parked planes, and reduced salaries, including the CEO's.[44]

In contrast to the high-quality, even luxurious flying experience offered by Singapore Airlines, Ryanair is a European low-cost airline. *Bloomberg BusinessWeek* reports that CEO Michael O'Leary is "remaking commercial air travel in his image: shabby, crabby, and cheap, cheap, cheap." O'Leary thinks that short flights need only one toilet, and every flight needs only one pilot because the computer or a trained member of the cabin crew can fly if necessary. Less frighteningly, he believes that commercial air passengers do not need free pillows, blankets, and snacks; they just want to arrive at their destination cheaply and with their luggage. His vision is for profits to come from inflight sales, high luggage fees, low-cost secondary airports, and commissions on travel products sold through the airline's website.[45]

Managing your costs and keeping them down requires being efficient: accomplishing your goals by using your resources wisely and minimizing waste. Many top executives fly on private jets, which of course is more expensive than buying a ticket on a commercial airline. If the company can arrange to participate in a service such as NetJets, where the company buys only shares in a jet with the rights to use it, this can trim the price and make the arrangement more worthwhile.[46]

One reason every company must worry about cost is that consumers can easily compare prices on the Internet from thousands of competitors. Consumers looking to buy popular items, such as cameras, printers, and plane fares, can go online to research the best models and the best deals. If you can't cut costs and offer attractive prices, you can't compete.

Sustainability

Avoiding wasteful use of energy can bolster a company's financial performance while being kind to the environment. For example, a company called Performance Fibers cut its costs by more than $200,000 by fixing steam leaks.[47] Efforts to cut energy waste are just one way to achieve a popular form of competitive advantage: **sustainability,** which is the effort to minimize the use of resources, especially those that are polluting and nonrenewable.

Sustainability can have other meanings, but in this text we will focus on environmental sustainability. In the United States, corporate efforts aimed at sustainability have fluctuated somewhat as environmental controls are strengthened or loosened; overall, the worldwide trend has been in the direction of greater concern for sustainability. The clashes among the rising demand for resources, limited supplies, and changing social attitudes toward environmental protection mean that the coming decade is likely to have greater focus on resource productivity, the emergence of clean-tech industries, and regulation.[48]

As many companies have discovered, addressing that concern often produces bottom-line benefits. Sustainability is more than a cost-cutting effort. Besides reductions in the use of resources consumed for operations, it includes the sale of sustainable products, such as Tesla Motors' goal to sell vehicles that run on electricity rather than burning gasoline.

Patagonia Sur is a for-profit company that has created the first private land trust in Patagonia to permanently protect the company's land; it plans to create up to 10 profitable environmentally sustained businesses on that land.[49] The goals are to apply free-market forces to develop the land for profit, do no harm, and spread this radically different land management model to developing nations around the world.

Sustainability is about protecting our options.[50] Done properly, sustainability allows people to live and work in ways that can be maintained over the long term (generations) without depleting or harming our environmental, social, and economic resources. In 2011 the number one company for responsibility to the community and environment was Norway's Statoil. What companies can you think of that are great, and not so great, in their sustainability practices?

Delivering All Types of Performance

Don't assume that you can settle for delivering just one of the six competitive advantages: low cost alone, or quality alone, for example. The best managers and companies perform on all of these criteria.

Virginia Mason Medical Center, like many hospitals, felt challenged in delivering low costs along with high quality and superior services. Virginia Mason has a reputation for high-quality care, but it was losing money treating certain patients. So Virginia Mason collaborated with Aetna, an insurer that pays for 10 percent of the medical center's business, and found ways to treat some of the most expensive conditions so that they became more economical to insure but were paid for at higher rates that would be profitable for Virginia Mason. The medical center has also improved quality through measures that enhance speed—in this case, cutting waiting times for patients, such as a reduction in the four-hour wait for chemotherapy to 90 minutes.[51]

Trade-offs may occur among the six sources of competitive advantage, but this doesn't need to be a zero-sum game where one has to suffer at the expense of another.

> This doesn't need to be a zero-sum game where one has to suffer at the expense of another.

Avon focused on cost savings when it contracted with IBM Global Services to handle human resources tasks such as payroll and benefits management. Turning over those responsibilities to a company that specializes in performing them efficiently also frees Avon to concentrate on innovating in areas it knows best: direct selling of cosmetics to new customers. Avon's CEO, Andrea Jung, launched an effort to sell cosmetics to Chinese consumers through hundreds of thousands of representatives who are licensed with the government.[52] Avon also has tapped into the trend toward customization by introducing the Hook Up Connector, a packaging product that allows consumers to snap together items of their choice, such as a lipstick and mascara.[53]

The Functions of Management

management

The process of working with people and resources to accomplish organizational goals.

Management is the process of working with people and resources to accomplish organizational goals. Good managers do those things both effectively and efficiently. To be *effective* is to achieve organizational goals. To be *efficient* is to achieve goals with minimal waste of resources—that is, to make the best possible use of money, time, materials, and people. Some managers fail on both criteria, or focus on one at the expense of another. The best managers achieve high performance by focusing on both effectiveness *and* efficiency. These definitions have been around for a long time. But as you know, business is changing radically. The real issue is how to *do* these things.[54]

Although the context of business and the specifics of doing business are changing, there are still plenty of timeless principles that make great managers, and great companies, great. While fresh thinking and new approaches are required now more than ever, much of what has already been learned about successful management practices remains relevant, useful, and adaptable, with fresh thinking, to the 21st century business environment.

In the business world today,

> great executives not only adapt to changing conditions but also apply—fanatically, rigorously, consistently, and with discipline—the fundamental management principles.

These fundamentals include the four traditional functions of management: *planning*, *organizing*, *leading*, and *controlling*. They remain as relevant as ever, and they still provide the fundamentals that are needed in start-ups as much as in established corporations. But their form has evolved.

Planning: Delivering Strategic Value

planning

The management function of systematically making decisions about the goals and activities that an individual, a group, a work unit, or the overall organization will pursue.

value

The monetary amount associated with how well a job, task, good, or service meets users' needs.

Planning is specifying the goals to be achieved and deciding in advance the appropriate actions needed to achieve those goals. Planning activities include analyzing current situations, anticipating the future, determining objectives, deciding in what types of activities the company will engage, choosing corporate and business strategies, and determining the resources needed to achieve the organization's goals. Plans set the stage for action and for major achievements.

The planning function for the new business environment, discussed in Part 2 of this book, is more dynamically described as *delivering strategic value*. **Value** is a complex concept.[55] Fundamentally, it describes the monetary amount associated with how well a job, task, good, or service meets users' needs. Those users might be business owners, customers, employees, society, and even nations. The better you meet those needs (in terms of quality, speed, efficiency, and so on), the more value you deliver. That value is "strategic" when it contributes to meeting the organization's goals. On a personal level, you will do well when you periodically ask yourself and your boss, "How can I add value?" Answering that question will enhance your contributions, your job performance, and your career.

> You will do well when you periodically ask yourself and your boss, "How can I add value?"

Historically, planning described a top-down approach in which top executives establish business plans and tell others to implement them. Now and in the future, delivering strategic value is a continual process in which people throughout the organization use their brains and the brains of customers, suppliers, and other stakeholders to identify opportunities to create, seize, strengthen, and sustain competitive advantage. This dynamic process swirls around the objective of creating more and more value for the customer. Effectively creating value requires fully considering a new and changing set of stakeholders and issues, including the government, the natural environment, globalization, and the dynamic economy in which ideas are king and entrepreneurs are both formidable competitors and potential collaborators. You will learn about these and related topics in Chapter 4 (planning and strategic management), Chapter 5 (ethics and corporate responsibility), Chapter 6 (international management), and Chapter 7 (entrepreneurship).

Organizing: Building a Dynamic Organization

Organizing is assembling and coordinating the human, financial, physical, informational, and other resources needed to achieve goals. Organizing activities include attracting people to the organization, specifying job responsibilities, grouping jobs into work units, marshaling and allocating resources, and creating conditions so that people and things work together to achieve maximum success.

Part 3 of the book describes the organizing function as *building a dynamic organization*. Historically, organizing involved creating an organization chart by identifying business functions, establishing reporting relationships, and having a personnel department that administered plans, programs, and paperwork. Now and in the future,

> effective managers will be using new forms of organizing and viewing their people as perhaps their most valuable resources.

They will build organizations that are flexible and adaptive, particularly in response to competitive threats and customer needs. Progressive human resource practices that attract and retain the very best of a highly diverse population will be essential aspects of the successful company. You will learn about these topics in Chapter 8 (organization structure), Chapter 9 (organizational agility), Chapter 10 (human resources management), and Chapter 11 (managing the diverse workforce).

Leading: Mobilizing People

Leading is stimulating people to be high performers. It includes motivating and communicating with employees, individually and in groups. Leading involves close day-to-day contact with people, helping to guide and inspire them toward achieving team and organizational goals. Leading takes place in teams, departments, and divisions, as well as at the tops of large organizations.

In earlier textbooks, the leading function described how managers motivate workers to come to work and execute top management's plans by doing their jobs. Today and in the

organizing

The management function of assembling and coordinating human, financial, physical, informational, and other resources needed to achieve goals.

leading

The management function that involves the manager's efforts to stimulate high performance by employees.

Shona Brown of Google makes decisions about organizing. She says, "The company's goal is to determine precisely the amount of management it needs—and then use a little bit less."

managers must be good at mobilizing people to contribute their ideas—
to use their brains in ways never needed or dreamed of in the past.

future, managers must be good at *mobilizing people* to contribute their ideas—to use their brains in ways never needed or dreamed of in the past.

As described in Part 4, managers must rely on a very different kind of leadership (Chapter 12) that empowers and motivates people (Chapter 13). Far more than in the past, great work must be done via great teamwork (Chapter 14), both within work groups and across group boundaries. Ideally, underlying these processes will be effective interpersonal and organizational communication (Chapter 15).

In a recent nationwide survey of frontline managers (the first rung of management), the managers overwhelmingly had a high opinion of their leadership skills.[56] However, when the researchers looked at the skills of a group of managers in a leader assessment program, they found that the managers frequently overrated their skills in areas such as gaining commitment and coaching employees.

Controlling: Learning and Changing

controlling

The management function of monitoring performance and making needed changes.

Planning, organizing, and leading do not guarantee success. The fourth function, **controlling,** monitors performance and implements necessary changes. By controlling, managers make sure the organization's resources are being used as planned and that the organization is meeting its goals such as quality and safety.

When managers implement their plans, they often find that things are not working out as planned. The controlling function makes sure that goals are met. It asks and answers the question, "Are our actual outcomes consistent with our goals?" It then makes adjustments as needed.

Successful organizations, large and small, pay close attention to the controlling function. But Part 5 of the book makes it clear that today and for the future, the key managerial challenges are far more dynamic than in the past; they involve continually *learning and changing.* Controls must still be in place, as described in Chapter 16. But new technologies and other innovations (Chapter 17) make it possible to achieve controls in more effective ways and to help all the people throughout the company, and across company boundaries (including customers and suppliers), to use their brains, learn, make a variety of new contributions, and help the organization change in ways that forge a successful future (Chapter 18).

The four management functions apply to you personally, as well. You must find ways to create value, organize for your own personal effectiveness, mobilize your own talents and skills as well as those of others, monitor performance, and constantly learn, develop, and change for the future. As you proceed through this book and this course, we encourage you to not merely do your "textbook learning" of an impersonal course subject but to think about these issues from a personal perspective as well, using the ideas for your own personal development.

The four management functions apply to you personally, as well.
Think about these issues from a personal perspective as well, using the
ideas for your own personal development.

Performing All Four Management Functions

As a manager, your typical day will not be neatly divided into the four functions. You will be doing many things more or less simultaneously.[57] Your days will be busy and fractionated, spent dealing with interruptions, meetings, and firefighting. There will be plenty to do that you wish you could be doing but can't seem to get to. These activities will include all four management functions.

Some managers are particularly interested in, devoted to, or skilled in one or two of the four functions but not in the others. But you should devote adequate attention and resources to *all four* functions. You can be a skilled planner and controller, but if you organize your people improperly or fail to inspire them to perform at high levels, you will not be realizing your potential as a manager. Likewise, it does no good to be the kind of manager who loves to organize and lead, but who doesn't really understand where to go or how to determine whether you are on the right track. Good managers don't neglect any of the four management functions. Knowing what they are, you can periodically ask yourself if you are devoting adequate attention to *all* of them.

Manager's Brief | **Progress Report** | Onward

Management Connection

SPEED BUMPS FOR TESLA MANAGEMENT

Tesla Motors needs excellence in all the management functions to face the very real challenges of being an innovator in an intensely competitive industry.

A primary challenge facing Wes Hermann, the manager of battery safety and technology, is the fundamental difficulty of his team's goal: battery technology has all along been the design problem that has interfered with development of an affordable electric car that can travel far enough to be useful to potential buyers. So far, Hermann's lab has figured out how to make batteries that are much safer, smaller, and lighter. However, just two years before Tesla was planning to begin selling the Model S, making the batteries was still far too expensive, so Hermann's team needed to begin excelling in cost competitiveness.

Gilbert Passin, the vice president of manufacturing, must simultaneously meet demands for speed, quality, and cost competitiveness as his team prepares to open a new factory in Fremont, California. The purchase of the facility included 210 acres occupied by several buildings covering about 5.5 million square feet. Passin's team has been planning to start out by using about 20 percent of the floor space and then gradually expand along with demand for the Model S. Passin has experience in his favor. Before taking a job with Tesla, he was vice president of manufacturing at Toyota's Lexus facility in Ontario, Canada, and was a general manager at the same Toyota–GM facility Tesla purchased. Toyota is known for establishing exacting processes aimed at maximum efficiency and quality.

Another challenge facing management is to hire enough qualified people for a variety of positions as the company moves from product development to production. By a recent count, Tesla had 800 employees and expected to reach 2,000 employees if it met its goals to start producing the Model S by 2012. As thousands of résumés flood the company, Amnon Geshuri, the vice president for human resources, directs his employees to find ambitious people who excel at teamwork, collaboration, and juggling multiple tasks. Geshuri says Tesla doesn't limit its hiring to people with automotive experience; rather, the human resource department has concluded that a variety of electrical and electromechanical engineers who have "tackled challenging problems" are well suited to help Tesla meet its own challenges. Finding these people has required a variety of efforts from posting jobs on the company's website to partnering with universities.

And of course the Tesla management challenges include selling cars. A start-up company, it has the disadvantage of an unfamiliar brand and even an unfamiliar product. Many consumers simply are unaware of the benefits of driving an electric car—not just low pollution, but also an extremely quiet ride and fast acceleration. So far, Tesla has sold about 1,500 of its Roadsters at over $100,000 each, and its goal is to sell about 20,000 Model S sedans each year. Management needs to figure out how to meet sales goals so the company can become profitable. Although Tesla has raised enough capital to keep development moving forward and cover its rapidly rising research and development costs, it has not yet earned a profit.[58]

- Of the four management functions described in the text (planning, organizing, leading, and controlling), which do you think would be most important for Wes Hermann to use in achieving cost competitiveness? Why?
- As Tesla managers Gilbert Passin and Amnon Geshuri prepare for opening a new production facility in Fresno, how might they deliver high performance via achieving competitive advantage?

Management Levels and Skills

  Organizations—particularly large organizations—have many levels. In this section, you will learn about the types of managers found at three different organizational levels: top level, middle level, and frontline.

Top-Level Managers

top-level managers

Senior executives responsible for the overall management and effectiveness of the organization.

Top-level managers are the senior executives of an organization and are responsible for its overall management. Top-level managers, often referred to as *strategic managers*, are supposed to focus on long-term issues and emphasize the survival, growth, and overall effectiveness of the organization.

Top managers are concerned not only with the organization as a whole but also with the interaction between the organization and its external environment. This interaction often requires managers to work extensively with outside individuals and organizations.

The chief executive officer (CEO) is one type of top-level manager found in large corporations. This individual is the primary strategic manager of the firm and has authority over everyone else. Others include the chief operating officer (COO), company presidents, vice presidents, and members of the top management team. As companies are appreciating the potential of modern technology and knowledge management to help them achieve and maintain a competitive advantage, more are creating the position of chief information officer (CIO). At defense contractor Northrop Grumman, CIO Tom Shelman used to focus on managing the company's computer systems. But in the last few years, he has become directly involved with strategy; Shelman's job includes meeting with customers to help identify ways the company can use its technology to serve them better and help the company grow.[59]

In a recent poll of chief information officers, half said their responsibilities extend beyond information technology to include top-level concerns such as developing the company's strategy.[60]

Traditionally, the role of top-level managers has been to set overall direction by formulating strategy and controlling resources. But now top managers are more commonly called on to be not only strategic architects but also true organizational leaders. As leaders, they must create and articulate a broader corporate purpose with which people can identify—and one to which people will enthusiastically commit.

> Top managers are more commonly called on to be not only strategic architects but also true organizational leaders.

Middle-Level Managers

middle-level managers

Managers located in the middle layers of the organizational hierarchy, reporting to top-level executives.

As the name implies, **middle-level managers** are located in the organization's hierarchy below top-level management and above the frontline managers. Sometimes called *tactical managers*, they are responsible for translating the general goals and plans developed by strategic managers into more specific objectives and activities.

Traditionally, the role of the middle manager is to be an administrative controller who bridges the gap between higher and lower levels. Middle-level managers take corporate objectives and break them down into business unit targets; put together separate business unit plans from the units below them for higher-level corporate review; and serve as linchpins of internal communication, interpreting and broadcasting top management's priorities downward and channeling and translating information from the front lines upward.

As a stereotype, the term *middle manager* connotes mediocrity: unimaginative people behaving like bureaucrats and defending the status quo. But middle managers are closer than top managers to day-to-day operations, customers, frontline managers, and employees—so they know the problems and opportunities. They also have many creative ideas—often better than their bosses'. Good middle managers provide the operating skills and practical problem solving that keep the company working.[61]

Frontline Managers

Frontline managers, or *operational managers*, are lower-level managers who supervise the operations of the organization. These managers often have titles such as *supervisor* or *sales manager*. They are directly involved with nonmanagement employees, implementing the specific plans developed with middle managers. This role is critical in the organization because operational managers are the link between management and nonmanagement personnel. Your first management position probably will fit into this category.

Traditionally, frontline managers have been directed and controlled from above to make sure that they successfully implement operations in support of company strategy. But in leading companies, the role has expanded. Whereas the operational execution aspect of the role remains vital, in leading companies frontline managers are increasingly called on to be innovative and entrepreneurial, managing for growth and new business development.

Managers on the front line are crucial to creating and sustaining quality, innovation, and other drivers of financial performance.[62] In outstanding organizations, talented frontline managers are not only *allowed* to initiate new activities but are *expected* to by their top- and middle-level managers. And they are given freedom, incentives, and support to find ways to do so.[63]

Table 1.1 elaborates on the changing aspects of different management levels. You will learn about each of these aspects of management throughout this course.

frontline managers

Lower-level managers who supervise the operational activities of the organization.

Your first management position probably will fit into this category.

	Frontline Managers	Middle-Level Managers	Top-Level Managers
Changing Roles	• From operational implementers to aggressive entrepreneurs.	• From administrative controllers to supportive coaches.	• From resource allocators to institutional leaders.
Key Activities	• Creating and pursuing new growth opportunities for the business.	• Developing individuals and supporting their activities.	• Establishing high performance standards.
	• Attracting and developing resources.	• Linking dispersed knowledge and skills across units.	• Institutionalizing a set of norms and values to support cooperation and trust.
	• Managing continuous improvement within the unit.	• Managing the tension between short-term purpose and long-term ambition.	• Creating an overarching corporate purpose and ambition.

TABLE 1.1

Transformation of Management Roles and Activities

SOURCE: Adapted from C. Bartlett and S. Goshal, "The Myth of the Generic Manager: New Personal Competencies for New Management Roles," *California Management Review* 40, no. 1, Fall 1977, pp. 92–116.

IN PRACTICE

A dramatic look at the benefits contributed by capable middle-level managers comes from a study of factories that weren't implementing any of the basic practices the managers should, such as recording quality defects, specifying job requirements, and tracking inventory. A group of Stanford researchers visited randomly selected textile factories in India to evaluate their use of basic practices of good management. At many of the facilities, managers were simply unfamiliar with controls that are widely used in developed economies. Consequently, the factories were in disarray, and waste was the norm. Unsorted yarn rotted in storerooms, dirty machinery blocked hallways, and tools were strewn about.

The researchers then dispatched a locally based team of management consultants to spend several months teaching management basics to managers at most of the factories they visited (leaving the rest as a control group, which received just one month of consulting services). The newly trained managers began requiring employees to sort and stack yarn, clean workspaces, and post schedules of workflows. Defect rates tumbled, as did the amount of raw materials and finished goods taking up space in inventory. Information flow increased, so the factories set up computers, enabling managers to keep better track of what was happening day by day, and freeing them to delegate more work. According to the researchers' estimates, the improvements added more than $200,000 to profits at each factory they assisted—an average increase of about 11 percent.[64]

- Managers at the textile factories initially doubted that the changes would have practical benefits. Why might this be so? How common or unusual do you think this attitude is?

Working Leaders with Broad Responsibilities

In small firms—and in those large companies that have adapted to the times—managers have strategic, tactical, *and* operational responsibilities. They are *complete* businesspeople; they have knowledge of all business functions, are accountable for results, and focus on serving customers both inside and outside their firms. All of this requires the ability to think strategically, translate strategies into specific objectives, coordinate resources, and do real work with lower-level people.

They get dirty, do hard work themselves, solve problems, and produce value.

In short, today's best managers can do it all; they are "working leaders."[65] They focus on relationships with other people and on achieving results. They don't just make decisions, give orders, wait for others to produce, and then evaluate results. They get dirty, do hard work themselves, solve problems, and produce value.

What does all of this mean in practice? How do managers spend their time—what do they actually do? A classic study of top executives found that they spend their time engaging in 10 key activities or roles, falling into three categories: interpersonal, informational, and decisional.[66] Table 1.2 summarizes these roles. Even though the study was done decades ago, it remains highly relevant as a description of what executives do. And even though the study focused on top executives, managers at all levels engage in all these activities. As you study the table, you might ask yourself, "Which of these activities do I enjoy most (and least)? Where do I excel (and not excel)? Which would I like to improve?" Whatever your answers, you will be learning more about these activities throughout this course.

Management Skills

 LO 5

Performing management functions and roles, and achieving competitive advantage, are the cornerstones of a manager's job. However, understanding this fact does not ensure success. Managers need a variety of skills to *do* these things *well*. Skills are

Interpersonal Roles	*Leader:* Staffing, training, and motivating people.
	Liaison: Maintaining a network of outside contacts who provide information and favors.
	Figurehead: Performing symbolic duties (ceremonies and serving other social and legal demands).
Informational Roles	*Monitor:* Seeking and receiving information to develop a thorough understanding of the organization and its environment; serving as the "nerve center" of communication.
	Disseminator: Transmitting information from source to source, sometimes interpreting and integrating diverse perspectives.
	Spokesperson: Speaking on behalf of the organization about plans, policies, actions, and results.
Decisional Roles	*Entrepreneur:* Searching for new business opportunities and initiating new projects to create change.
	Disturbance handler: Taking corrective action during crises or other conflicts.
	Resource allocator: Providing funding and other resources to units or people; includes making or approving significant organizational decisions.
	Negotiator: Engaging in negotiations with parties outside the organization as well as inside (e.g., resource exchanges).

TABLE 1.2
Managerial Roles: What Managers Do

SOURCE: Adapted from H. Mintzberg, *The Nature of Managerial Work* (New York: Harper & Row, 1973), pp. 92–93.

specific abilities that result from knowledge, information, practice, and aptitude. Although managers need many individual skills, which you will learn about throughout this textbook, there are three essential categories: technical skills, interpersonal and communication skills, and conceptual and decision skills.[67]

First-timers can underestimate the challenges of the many technical, human, and conceptual competencies required.[68] But when the key management functions are performed by managers who have these critical management skills, the result is high performance.

A **technical skill** is the ability to perform a specialized task that involves a certain method or process. Most people develop a set of technical skills to complete the activities that are part of their daily work lives. The technical skills you learn in school will provide you with the opportunity to get an entry-level position; they will also help you as a manager. For example, your accounting and finance courses will develop the technical skills you need to understand and manage the financial resources of an organization.

Conceptual and decision skills involve the ability to identify and resolve problems for the benefit of the organization and everyone concerned. Managers use these skills when they consider the overall objectives and strategy of the firm, the interactions among different parts of the organization, and the role of the business in its external environment. As you acquire greater responsibility, you must exercise your conceptual and decision skills with increasing frequency. You will confront issues that involve all aspects of the organization and must consider a larger and more interrelated set of decision factors. Much of this book is devoted to enhancing your conceptual and decision skills, but experience also plays an important part in their development.

Interpersonal and communication skills influence the manager's ability to work well with people. These skills are often called *people skills.* Managers spend the great

technical skill

The ability to perform a specialized task involving a particular method or process.

conceptual and decision skills

Skills pertaining to the ability to identify and resolve problems for the benefit of the organization and its members.

interpersonal and communication skills

People skills; the ability to lead, motivate, and communicate effectively with others.

majority of their time interacting with people,[69] and they must develop their abilities to lead, motivate, and communicate effectively with those around them. Your people skills often make the difference in how high you go. Management professor Michael Morris emphasizes that it is vital for future managers to realize the importance of these skills in getting a job, keeping it, and performing well in it, especially in the 21st century, where managers tend to be supervisors of independent-minded knowledge workers. He explains, "You have to get high performance out of people in your organization whom you don't have any authority over. You need to read other people, know their motivators, know how you affect them."[70]

The importance of these skills varies by managerial level. Technical skills are most important early in your career. Conceptual and decision skills become more important than technical skills as you rise higher in the company. But interpersonal skills are important throughout your career, at every level of management. Several biomedical companies in California's Orange County collaborated to provide training because they observed that managers originally hired for their technical expertise needed to develop their people skills so that they could handle higher-level assignments successfully.[71]

An example of a manager with these skills is Mark Bertolini, chief executive of Aetna, which provides health insurance and related services. As a young man doing assembly work for Ford Motor Company, Bertolini acquired an interest in union management, so he decided to study business and earned a degree in accounting and then a master's degree in finance. Those two specialties involve valuable technical skills, but Bertolini rose through the management ranks at a series of insurance companies because he also has a passion for people. He recently told an interviewer that he is constantly engaged in learning about people and forging networks with them. He sees tapping into those networks and figuring out how to lead people as the kinds of skills that allow managers to get results. At Aetna, Bertolini is not only an expert at insurance matters, but also a promoter of employee diversity. Furthermore, challenges in his personal life—he survives a spinal cord injury and donated a kidney to his son—have placed him in a position to empathize with others, including clients who use his company's services.[72]

You and Your Career

LO 6

At the beginning of your career, your contribution to your employer depends on your own performance; that's all you're responsible for. But on becoming a manager, you are responsible for a whole group. To use an orchestra analogy, instead of playing an instrument, you're a conductor, coordinating others' efforts.[73] The challenge is much greater than most first-time managers expect it to be.

Throughout your career you'll need to lead teams effectively, as well as influence people over whom you have no authority; thus the human skills are especially important. Businesspeople often talk about **emotional intelligence**,[74] or "EQ"—the skills of understanding yourself (including strengths and limitations), managing yourself (dealing with emotions, making good decisions, seeking and using feedback, exercising self-control), and dealing effectively with others (listening, showing empathy, motivating, leading, and so on).

emotional intelligence

The skills of understanding yourself, managing yourself, and dealing effectively with others.

A common complaint about leaders, especially newly promoted ones who had been outstanding individual performers, is that they lack what is perhaps the most fundamental of EQ skills: empathy. The issue is not lack of ability to change (you can), but the lack of motivation to change.[75] William George, former chair and CEO of Medtronic, says some people can go a long way in their careers based on sheer determination and aggressiveness, but personal development—including EQ—ultimately

Managing and Performing   Chapter 1   23

becomes essential.[76] Executives who score low on EQ are less likely to be rated as excellent on their performance reviews, and their divisions tend not to perform as well.[77] A vice president at an aerospace company underwent a program to improve her EQ after colleagues kept complaining that she was overly demanding and inclined to put people down. An assessment found that she lacked social awareness. The vice president eventually learned to respond after calming herself, as well as to explore colleagues' ideas rather than demeaning them. Before long, her colleagues began to appreciate the change, and her career took a more successful path.[78]

What should you do to forge a successful, gratifying career? You are well advised to be both a specialist and a generalist, to be self-reliant and connected, to actively manage your relationship with your organization, and to know what is required not only to survive but also to thrive in today's world.

Be Both a Specialist and a Generalist

If you think your career will be as a specialist, think again. Chances are, you will not want to stay forever in strictly technical jobs with no managerial responsibilities. Accountants are promoted to accounting department heads and team leaders, sales representatives become sales managers, writers become editors, and nurses become nursing directors. As your responsibilities increase, you must deal with more people, understand more about other aspects of the organization, and make bigger and more complex decisions. Beginning to learn now about these managerial challenges may yield benefits sooner than you think.

If you think your career will be as a specialist, think again.

So it will help if you can become both a specialist and a generalist.[79] Seek to become a *specialist:* you should be an expert in something. This will give you specific skills that help you provide concrete, identifiable value to your firm and to customers. And over time, you should learn to be a *generalist*, knowing enough about a variety of business disciplines so that you can think strategically and work with different perspectives.

IN PRACTICE

Patricia Calkins broadened her focus gradually and ambitiously from specialties in the sciences, expanding first to engineering and then to management. She started her career with AT&T's Western Electric subsidiary as a chemist; when she was considering a master's degree in chemistry, she heeded advice to develop her career opportunities by studying engineering. Once Calkins had her master's in civil and environmental engineering, the company saw her management talent and wanted to promote her, so she returned to school for another master's degree, this time in business administration. She developed her generalist skills by consulting, and from that work moved to her current—and favorite—position as vice president of environment, health, and safety at Xerox.[80]

Patricia Calkins, VP of Environment, Health, and Safety at Xerox, became successful by being both a specialist and a generalist. She developed her specialty skills in the sciences and in business administration, and then acquired her generalist skills as a business consultant. What steps do you need to take to become a specialist and a generalist?

- When Calkins started her career at Western Electric, what was her specialty? To become a consultant and then a manager, what else did she have to learn about?

Be Self-Reliant

To be self-reliant means to take full responsibility for yourself, your actions, and your career, as Patricia Calkins did when she furthered her education and tackled consulting assignments that applied her technical knowledge to the business world. You cannot count on your boss or your company to take care of you. A useful metaphor is to think of yourself as a business, with you as president and sole employee.

> Don't just do your work and wait for orders; look for opportunities to contribute in new ways.

To be self-reliant, find new ways to make your overall performance better. Take responsibility for change; be an innovator.[81] Don't just do your work and wait for orders; look for opportunities to contribute in new ways, to develop new products and processes, and to generate constructive change that strengthens the company and benefits customers and colleagues. Success requires more than talent; you also have to be willing to work hard. The elite, world-class performers in many fields reach the top tier only after 10 years or more of hard work.[82] The key is to engage in consistent practice, looking at the results and identifying where to improve.

It's easy to see how this works for violinists or basketball players, but what about business managers? The answer is to focus on getting better results each time you try any business task, whether it's writing a report, chairing a meeting, or interpreting a financial statement. To know whether you're getting better, make a point of asking for feedback from customers, colleagues, and bosses.

To develop your full potential, assess yourself, including your interests, aptitudes, and personal character strengths. Think about it, ask others who know you well, conduct a formal exercise in which you learn what others consider to be your "best self,"[83] and use the resources of recent advances in psychology to identify your signature strengths.[84] Consider the professional image and reputation you would like to develop,[85] and continue building your capabilities. Consider the suggestions found throughout this book, and your courses, as you pursue these objectives.

IN PRACTICE

Atour Eyvazian epitomizes self-reliance. He worked his way up from janitor at a Jack in the Box restaurant through management positions at the fast-food restaurant chain's headquarters to owning 59 Jack in the Box franchises. Eyvazian's career with Jack in the Box started when, as a 19-year-old, he left Iran for Los Angeles, where he initially lived with his uncle. Taking a night class in English as a second language, he spent the days cleaning his neighborhood's Jack in the Box and offering to fill in with other responsibilities, first as fry cook and eventually, as his English improved, taking customer orders. As his supervisors saw how hard he worked, they promoted him to team leader, then assistant manager, then manager of the restaurant.

His commitment to his work and the company paid off further when Eyvazian was offered a job with headquarters. In his first position, he audited restaurants to ensure they were meeting standards for quality, cleanliness, and food safety. Then he was promoted to manager of guest service systems, responsible for 677 Jack in the Box restaurants. Taking advantage of the company's tuition reimbursement benefit, he went to school at night, earning bachelor's and master's degrees. As if a job and college courses weren't enough, he also set aside money and used it to invest in real estate, generating cash he later combined with a partner's to buy 10 Jack in the Box franchises in Sacramento and 49 more around Houston.[86]

- Thinking about your schoolwork, a job, and your career goals, what are some areas in which you would like to improve your performance? What are some steps you could take to start improving?

Be Connected

Being *connected* means having many good working relationships and interpersonal contacts and being a team player with strong interpersonal skills. For example, those who want to become partners in professional service organizations like accounting, advertising, and consulting firms strive constantly to build a network of contacts. Their "connectedness" goal is to work not only with lots of clients but also with a half dozen or more senior partners, including several from outside their home offices and some from outside their country. A study of new auditors showed that social relationships improved newcomers' knowledge of the organization and their jobs, their social integration into the firm, and their commitment to the organization.[87]

Social capital is the goodwill stemming from your social relationships, and it can be mobilized on your behalf. It aids career success, compensation, employment, team effectiveness, successful entrepreneurship, and relationships with suppliers and other outsiders.[88] Today much of that social capital can be tapped online at social networking websites. Besides the purely social sites like MySpace and Facebook, some of these sites are aimed at helping people tap business networks. For example, LinkedIn has more than 100 million registered users, with membership growing rapidly.

States *Fortune*, "Facebook is for fun . . . If you're serious about managing your career, the only social site that really matters is LinkedIn."[89]

Look at this another way: all business is a function of human relationships.[90] Building competitive advantage depends not only on you but on other people. Management is personal. Commercial dealings are personal. Purchase decisions, repurchase decisions, and contracts all hinge on relationships. Even the biggest business deals—takeovers—are intensely personal and emotional. Without good work relationships, you are an outsider, not an effective manager and leader.

Actively Manage Your Relationship with Your Organization

Many of the previous comments suggest the importance of taking responsibility for your own actions and your own career. Unless you are self-employed and your own boss, one way to do this is to think about the nature of the relationship between you and your employer. Figure 1.1 shows two possible relationships—and you have some control over which relationship you will be in.

Relationship #1 is one in which you view yourself as an employee and passively expect your employer to tell you what to do and give you pay and benefits. Your employer is in charge, and you are a passive recipient of its actions. Your contributions are likely to be adequate but minimal—you won't make the added contributions that strengthen your organization, and if all organizational members take this perspective, the organization is not likely to be strong for the long run. Personally, you may lose your job, or keep your job in a declining organization, or receive few positive benefits from working there and either quit or become cynical and unhappy in your work.

In contrast, relationship #2 is a two-way relationship in which you and your organization both benefit from one another. The mind-set is different: instead of doing what

Bottom Line

If you want people who see your Facebook profile to think of you as a future manager, what should *not* be on the profile?

social capital

Goodwill stemming from your social relationships.

#1	#2
You as a passive employee	**You as an active contributor in a productive relationship**

FIGURE 1.1

Two Relationships: Which Will You Choose?

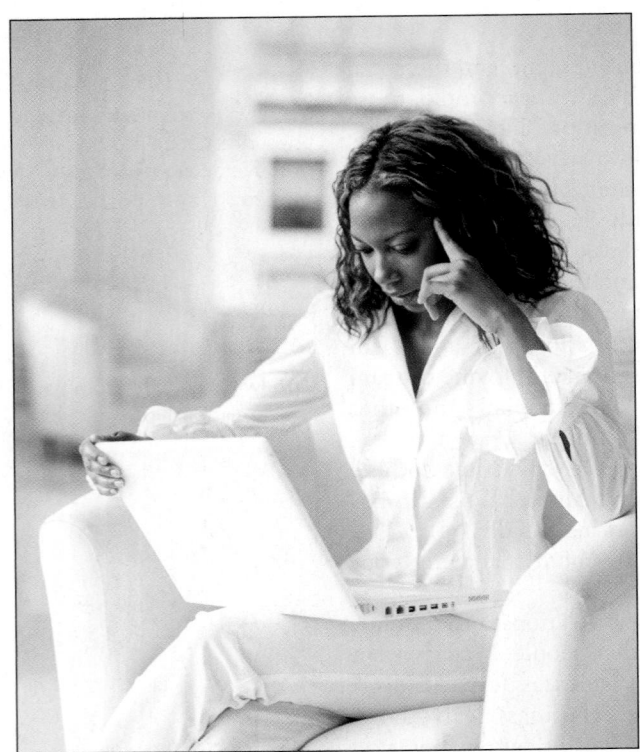

Social networking via websites such as Facebook and LinkedIn is an important way to stay "connected" and build social relationships within and outside of the workplace.

you are told, you think about how you can contribute—and you act accordingly. To the extent that your organization values your contributions, you are likely to benefit in return by receiving full and fair rewards, support for further personal development, and a more gratifying work environment. If you think in broad terms about how you can help your company, and if others think like this as well, there is likely to be continuous improvement in the company's ability to innovate, cut costs, and deliver quality products quickly to an expanding customer base. As the company's bottom line strengthens, benefits accrue to shareholders as well as to you and other employees.

What contributions can you make? You can do your basic work. But you can, and should, go further. You can also figure out new ways to add value—by thinking of and implementing new ideas that improve processes and results. You can do this by using your technical knowledge and skills, as in developing a better information system, accounting technique, or sales strategy.

You also can contribute with your conceptual and human skills and your managerial actions (see Figure 1.2). You can execute the essential management functions and deliver competitive advantage. You can deliver strategic value (Part 2 of this book). You can take actions that help build a more dynamic organization (Part 3). You can mobilize people to contribute to their fullest potential (Part 4). And you can learn and change—and help your colleagues and company learn and change—to adapt to changing realities and forge a successful future (Part 5).

Survive and Thrive

Now—far more than ever—you will be accountable for your actions and for results. In the past, people at many companies could show up, do an OK job, get a decent evaluation, and get a raise equal to the cost of living and maybe higher. Today managers

FIGURE 1.2
Managerial Action Is Your Opportunity to Contribute

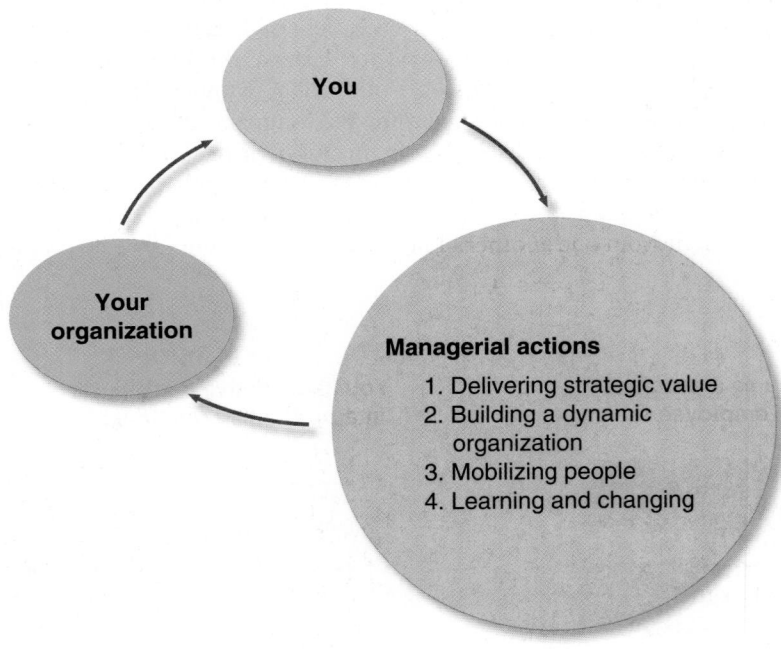

must do more, better. Eminent management scholar Peter Drucker, in considering what makes managers effective, noted that some are charismatic while some are not, and some are visionary while others are more numbers-oriented.[91] But successful executives do share some common practices:

> Successful executives do share some common practices

- They ask "What needs to be done?" rather than "What do I want to do?"
- They write an action plan. They don't just think, they do, based on a sound, ethical plan.
- They take responsibility for decisions. This requires checking up, revisiting, and changing if necessary.
- They focus on opportunities rather than problems. Problems have to be solved, and problem solving prevents more damage. But exploiting opportunities is what creates great results.

This creative approach can make each employee a standout in some unique way. Career adviser Rachelle Canter advises identifying where you deliver superior results and thinking of that as your "brand." For instance, an executive might develop a track record of consistently improving productivity in various organizations, and an entry-level customer service worker might become the company's go-to employee for handling the toughest customers.[92]

Career success is most likely if you are flexible, creative, and ambitious. You will need to learn how to think strategically, discern and convey your business vision, make decisions, and work in teams. You will need to deliver competitive advantage and thrive on change, just as the managers of Tesla Motors do, as discussed in the "Management Connection: Onward" feature. These and other topics, essential to your successful career, provide the focus for the following chapters.

| Manager's Brief | Progress Report | **Onward** |

Management Connection

MANAGING FOR TESLA'S FUTURE

The managers of Tesla Motors will be accountable for their results following an industry shakeup in a fast-changing environment. Not only are they aiming to offer consumers an alternative that is friendly to the environment, but they must do so with a product that delivers on its quality promise at a price consumers are willing to pay. And even more basic is this question: Will consumers want to buy what Tesla is selling? That question is especially challenging for managers when a product is as innovative as the electric car.

As Tesla's managers, from chief executive Elon Musk on down, plan for the production and rollout of the Model S, they have to keep an eye on developments that can shape consumers' demand for electric vehicles. One plus is that the U.S. government has recently offered buyers a $7,500 tax credit, and some states also are offering incentives for the purchase of these environmentally friendly vehicles. On the down side is the high sticker prices on electric vehicles. Industry analysts predict growth in demand for electric vehicles, but mainly as a niche product. For example, industry experts have seen potential for this type of car in large cities where drivers often go short distances and are especially troubled by air pollution.

Management decisions also shape Tesla's actions relative to competitors. For example, a key decision was whether to approach the design of the electric car as a completely new product or as a modification of gasoline-powered or hybrid vehicles. Ford chose to develop an electric version of its popular Ford Focus. General Motors started with the front-wheel-drive Chevrolet Cruze as the base for its Chevy Volt. Tesla's management, in contrast, sees the Model S as a chance to design a superior product from scratch. (Its earlier Roadster was designed to be built on the chassis of the Lotus, a British sports car.) The rationale for the completely original design of the Model S is that modifying a gas-powered car won't be innovative enough to achieve the promise of a well-designed electric vehicle. For example, in the Model S, the battery pack will be in a relative flat arrangement across the bottom of the car, versus squeezing a big battery somewhere into an existing car design. According to Peter Rawlinson, Tesla's vice president and chief engineer, this design offers "significant ride and handling advantages" because of how the weight is distributed.

At the time of this writing, it's still too early to say whether Elon Musk and the other managers of Tesla Motors will be acclaimed as heroes of innovation or written off as overly optimistic dreamers. Tesla's corporate reply is that its sale of over 1,500 Roadsters to customers in more than 30 countries shows that "Tesla is raising the bar for [electric vehicles]." And while some doubters wonder if the 2012 release of the Model S is a fantasy, too fast to be true, the company has begun road tests ahead of schedule. Looking at how far managers have brought Tesla to date,

a writer at *Automotive News* referred to the company as an "upstart" that has made "credible progress"—an encouraging assessment of a company that promises it will be profitable when it's several more years down the road. With careful handling, Tesla could yet speed ahead of the pack.[93]

- Give examples of conceptual and technical skills Tesla managers will need to prepare for the future. How might strong interpersonal and communication skills help a manager get the best results from using those skills?
- The chapter says that managers who thrive tend to focus on opportunities rather than problems. In one to three sentences, summarize the future facing Tesla Motors in terms of opportunities rather than problems. Is this a realistic view? Why or why not?

KEY TERMS

conceptual and decision skills, p. 21	knowledge management, p. 7	service, p. 11
controlling, p. 16	leading, p. 15	social capital, p. 25
cost competitiveness, p. 12	management, p. 14	speed, p. 11
emotional intelligence, p. 22	middle-level managers, p. 18	sustainability, p. 13
frontline managers, p. 19	organizing, p. 15	technical skill, p. 21
innovation, p. 9	planning, p. 14	top-level managers, p. 18
interpersonal and communication skills, p. 21	quality, p. 10	value, p. 14

SUMMARY OF LEARNING OBJECTIVES

Now that you have studied Chapter 1, you should be able to:

LO 1 **Summarize the major challenges of managing in the new competitive landscape.**

Managers today must deal with dynamic forces that create greater change than ever before. Among many forces that are creating a need for managers to rethink their approaches, there have recently been four major waves of change: globalization, technological change including the development and applications of the Internet, knowledge management, and collaboration across organizational boundaries.

LO 2 **Describe the sources of competitive advantage for a company.**

Because business is a competitive arena, you need to deliver value to customers in ways that are superior to what your competitors do. Competitive advantages result from innovation, quality, service, speed, cost, and sustainability.

LO 3 **Explain how the functions of management are evolving in today's business environment.**

Despite massive change, management retains certain foundations that will not disappear. The primary functions of management are planning, organizing, leading, and controlling. Planning is analyzing a situation, determining the goals that will be pursued, and deciding in advance the actions needed to pursue these goals. Organizing is assembling the resources needed to complete the job and coordinating employees and tasks for maximum success. Leading is motivating people and stimulating high performance. Controlling is monitoring the progress of the organization or the work unit toward goals and then taking corrective action, as necessary. In today's business environment, these functions more broadly require creating strategic value, building a dynamic organization, mobilizing people, and learning and changing.

LO 4 Compare how the nature of management varies at different organizational levels.

Top-level, strategic managers are the senior executives responsible for the organization's overall management. Middle-level, tactical managers translate general goals and plans into more specific objectives and activities. Frontline, operational managers are lower-level managers who supervise operations. Today managers at all levels must perform a variety of interpersonal, informational, and decisional roles. Even at the operational level, the best managers think strategically and operate like complete businesspeople.

LO 5 Define the skills you need to be an effective manager.

To execute management functions successfully, managers need technical skills, conceptual and decision skills, and interpersonal and communication skills. A technical skill is the ability to perform a specialized task involving certain methods or processes.

Conceptual and decision skills help the manager recognize complex and dynamic issues, analyze the factors that influence those issues or problems, and make appropriate decisions. Interpersonal and communication skills enable the manager to interact and work well with people. As you rise to higher organizational levels, technical skills tend to become less important and conceptual skills become more important, while interpersonal and communication skills remain extremely important at every level.

LO 6 Understand the principles that will help you manage your career.

You are more likely to succeed in your career if you become both a specialist and a generalist. You should be self-reliant but also connected. You should actively manage your relationship with your organization and continuously improve your skills so you can perform in the ways demanded in the changing work environment.

DISCUSSION QUESTIONS

1. Identify and describe a great manager. What makes him or her stand out from the crowd?

2. Have you ever seen or worked for an ineffective manager? Describe the causes and the consequences of the ineffectiveness.

3. Describe in as much detail as possible how the Internet and globalization affect your daily life.

4. Identify some examples of how different organizations collaborate "across boundaries."

5. Name a great organization. How do you think management contributes to making it great?

6. Name an ineffective organization. What can management do to improve it?

7. Give examples you have seen of firms that are outstanding and weak on each of the six pillars of competitive advantage. Why do you choose the firms you do?

8. Describe your use of the four management functions in the management of your daily life.

9. Discuss the importance of technical, conceptual, and interpersonal skills at school and in jobs you have held.

10. What are your strengths and weaknesses as you contemplate your career? How do they correlate with the skills and behaviors identified in the chapter?

11. Devise a plan for developing yourself and making yourself attractive to potential employers. How would you go about improving your managerial skills?

12. Consider the managers and companies discussed in the chapter. Have they been in the news lately, and what is the latest? If their image, performance, or fortunes have gone up or down, what has changed to affect how they have fared?

13. Who are *Bloomberg Businessweek*'s most recent "best and worst managers," and why were they selected?

EXPERIENTIAL EXERCISES

1.1   PERSONAL ASSESSMENT OF MANAGEMENT SKILLS (PAMS)

To get an overall profile of your level of skill competence, respond to the following statements using the following rating scale. Please rate your behavior as it is, not as you would like it to be. If you have not engaged in a specific activity, answer according to how you think you would behave based on your experience in similar activities. Be honest; this instrument is designed to help you tailor your learning to your specific needs.

RATING SCALE

1 Strongly disagree
2 Disagree
3 Slightly disagree

4 Slightly agree
5 Agree
6 Strongly agree

In regard to my level of self-knowledge:

_____ 1. I seek information about my strengths and weaknesses from others as a basis for self-improvement.

_____ 2. To improve, I am willing to be self-disclosing to others (i.e., to share my beliefs and feelings).

_____ 3. I am aware of my preferred style in gathering information and making decisions.

_____ 4. I understand how I cope with situations that are ambiguous and uncertain.

_____ 5. I have a well-developed set of personal standards and principles that guide my behavior.

When faced with stressful or time-pressured situations:

_____ 6. I use effective time management methods such as keeping track of my time, making to-do lists, and prioritizing tasks.

_____ 7. I reaffirm my priorities so that less important things don't drive out more important things.

_____ 8. I maintain a program of regular exercise for fitness.

_____ 9. I maintain an open, trusting relationship with someone with whom I can share my frustrations.

_____ 10. I know and practice several temporary relaxation techniques such as deep breathing and muscle relaxation.

_____ 11. I maintain balance in my life by pursuing a variety of interests outside work.

When I approach a typical, routine problem:

_____ 12. I state clearly and explicitly what the problem is. I avoid trying to solve it until I have defined it.

_____ 13. I generate more than one alternative solution to the problem instead of identifying only one obvious solution.

_____ 14. I keep steps in the problem-solving process distinct; that is, I define the problem before proposing alternative solutions, and I generate alternatives before selecting a single solution.

When faced with a complex or difficult problem that does not have an easy solution:

_____ 15. I define a problem in multiple ways. I don't limit myself to just one problem definition.

_____ 16. I unfreeze my thinking by asking lots of questions about the nature of the problem before considering ways to solve it.

_____ 17. I think about the problem from both the left (logical) side of my brain and the right (intuitive) side of my brain.

_____ 18. I avoid selecting a solution until I have developed many possible alternatives.

_____ 19. I have specific techniques that I use to help develop creative and innovative solutions to problems.

When trying to foster more creativity and innovation among those with whom I work:

_____ 20. I make sure there are divergent points of view represented or expressed in every complex problem-solving situation.

_____ 21. I try to acquire information from individuals outside the problem-solving group who will be affected by the decision, mainly to determine their preferences and expectations.

_____ 22. I provide recognition not only for those who come up with creative ideas (the idea champions) but also for those who support others' ideas (supporters) and who provide resources to implement them (orchestrators).

_____ 23. I encourage informed rule breaking in pursuit of creative solutions.

In situations where I have to provide negative feedback or offer corrective advice:

_____ 24. I help others recognize and define their own problems when I counsel them.

_____ 25. I am clear about when I should coach someone and when I should provide counseling instead.

_____ 26. When I give feedback to others, I avoid referring to personal characteristics and focus on problems or solutions instead.

_____ 27. When I try to correct someone's behavior, our relationship is strengthened.

_____ 28. I am descriptive in giving negative feedback to others. That is, I objectively describe events, their consequences, and my feelings about them.

_____ 29. I take responsibility for my statements and point of view—for example, "I have decided" instead of "They have decided."

_____ 30. I identify some area of agreement in a discussion with someone who has a different point of view.

_____ 31. I don't talk down to those who have less power or less information than I do.

_____ 32. When discussing someone's problem, I respond with a reply that indicates understanding rather than advice.

In a situation where it is important to obtain more power:

_____ 33. I put forth more effort and take more initiative than expected in my work.

_____ 34. I am continually upgrading my skills and knowledge.

_____ 35. I support organizational ceremonial events and activities.

_____ 36. I form a broad network of relationships with people throughout the organization at all levels.

_____ 37. In my work I strive to generate new ideas, initiate new activities, and minimize routine tasks.

_____ 38. I send personal notes to others when they accomplish something significant or when I pass along important information to them.

_____ 39. I refuse to bargain with individuals who use high-pressure negotiation tactics.

_____ 40. I avoid using threats or demands to impose my will on others.

When another person needs to be motivated:

_____ 41. I determine if the person has the necessary resources and support to succeed in a task.

_____ 42. I use a variety of rewards to reinforce exceptional performances.

_____ 43. I design task assignments to make them interesting and challenging.

_____ 44. I make sure the person gets timely feedback from those affected by task performance.

_____ 45. I help the person establish performance goals that are challenging, specific, and time bound.

_____ 46. Only as a last resort do I attempt to reassign or release a poorly performing individual.

_____ 47. I discipline when effort is below expectations and capabilities.

_____ 48. I make sure that people feel fairly and equitably treated.

_____ 49. I provide immediate compliments and other forms of recognition for meaningful accomplishments.

When I see someone doing something that needs correcting:

_____ 50. I avoid making personal accusations and attributing self-serving motives to the other person.

_____ 51. I encourage two-way interaction by inviting the respondent to express his or her perspective and to ask questions.

_____ 52. I make a specific request, detailing a more acceptable option.

When someone complains about something I've done:

_____ 53. I show genuine concern and interest, even when I disagree.

_____ 54. I seek additional information by asking questions that provide specific and descriptive information.

_____ 55. I ask the other person to suggest more acceptable behaviors.

When two people are in conflict and I am the mediator:

_____ 56. I do not take sides but remain neutral.

_____ 57. I help the parties generate multiple alternatives.

_____ 58. I help the parties find areas on which they agree.

In situations where I have an opportunity to empower others:

_____ 59. I help people feel competent in their work by recognizing and celebrating their small successes.

_____ 60. I provide regular feedback and needed support.

_____ 61. I provide all the information that people need to accomplish their tasks.

_____ 62. I highlight the important impact that a person's work will have.

When delegating work to others:

_____ 63. I specify clearly the results I desire.

_____ 64. I specify clearly the level of initiative I want others to take (e.g., wait for directions, do part of the task and then report, do the whole task and then report).

_____ 65. I allow participation by those accepting assignments regarding when and how work will be done.

_____ 66. I avoid upward delegation by asking people to recommend solutions, rather than merely asking for advice or answers, when a problem is encountered.

_____ 67. I follow up and maintain accountability for delegated tasks on a regular basis.

When I am in the role of leader in a team:

_____ 68. I know how to establish credibility and influence among team members.

_____ 69. I am clear and consistent about what I want to achieve.

_____ 70. I build a common base of agreement in the team before moving forward with task accomplishment.

_____ 71. I articulate a clear, motivating vision of what the team can achieve along with specific short-term goals.

When I am in the role of team member:

_____ 72. I know a variety of ways to facilitate task accomplishment in the team.

_____ 73. I know a variety of ways to help build strong relationships and cohesion among team members.

When I desire to make my team perform well, regardless of whether I am a leader or member:

_____ 74. I am knowledgeable about the different stages of team development experienced by most teams.

_____ 75. I help the team avoid groupthink by making sure that sufficient diversity of opinions is expressed in the team.

_____ 76. I diagnose and capitalize on my team's core competencies or unique strengths.

_____ 77. I encourage exceptionally high standards of performance and outcomes that far exceed expectations.

When I am leading change:

_____ 78. I usually emphasize a higher purpose or meaning associated with the work I do.

_____ 79. I keep track of things that go right, not just things that go wrong.

_____ 80. I frequently give other people positive feedback.

_____ 81. I work to close performance gaps—the difference between good performance and great performance.

_____ 82. I express gratitude frequently and conspicuously, even for small acts.

_____ 83. I know how to get people to commit to my vision of positive change.

_____ 84. I know how to unlock the positive energy in other people.

_____ 85. I express compassion toward people who are facing pain or difficulty.

SOURCE: David A. Whetten and Kim S. Cameron, _Developing Management Skills_, 6th ed. pp. 23–27. Copyright 2005. Reproduced by permission of Pearson Education, Inc., Upper Saddle River, New Jersey.

1.2   YOUR PERSONAL NETWORK

1. See the figure on page 33. Working on your own, write down all of your primary contacts—individuals you know personally who can support you in attaining your professional goals. Then begin to explore their secondary connections. Make assumptions about possible secondary connections that can be made for you by contacting your primary connections. For example, through one of your teachers (primary), you might be able to obtain some names of potential employers (secondary). (10–15 min.)

2. Then meet with your partner or small group to exchange information about your primary and secondary networks and to exchange advice and information on how to best use these connections, as well as how you could be helpful to them. (about 5 min. per person; 10–30 min. total, depending on group size)

3. Add names or types of names to your list based on ideas you get by talking with others in your group. (2–5 min.)

4. Discuss with your large group or class, using the following discussion questions. (10 min.)

QUESTIONS

1. What were some of the best primary sources identified by your group?

2. What were some of the best sources for secondary contacts identified by your group?

3. What are some suggestions for approaching primary contacts?

4. What are some suggestions for approaching secondary contacts, and how is contacting secondary sources different from contacting primary contacts?

5. What did you learn about yourself and others from this exercise?

SOURCE: Suzanne C. de Janasz, Karen O'. Dowd, and Beth Z. Schneider, _Interpersonal Skills in Organizations_ (New York: McGraw-Hill, 2002), p. 211. © 2002 The McGraw-Hill Companies, Inc. Reprinted with permission.

1.3   EFFECTIVE MANAGERS

OBJECTIVES

1. To better understand what behaviors contribute to effective management.

2. To conceive a ranking of critical behaviors that you personally believe reflects their importance to your success as a manager.

INSTRUCTIONS

1. Following is a partial list of behaviors in which managers may engage. Rank these items in terms of their importance for effective performance as a manager. Put a 1 next to the item that you think is most important, 2 for the next most important, down to 10 for the least important.

2. Bring your rankings to class. Be prepared to justify your results and rationale. If you can add any behaviors to this list that might lead to success or greater management effectiveness, write them in.

Effective Managers Worksheet

_____ Communicates and interprets policy so that it is understood by the members of the organization.

_____ Makes prompt and clear decisions.

_____ Assigns subordinates to the jobs for which they are best suited.

_____ Encourages associates to submit ideas and plans.

_____ Stimulates subordinates by means of competition among employees.

_____ Seeks means of improving management capabilities and competence.

_____ Fully supports and carries out company policies.

Primary and Secondary
Connections

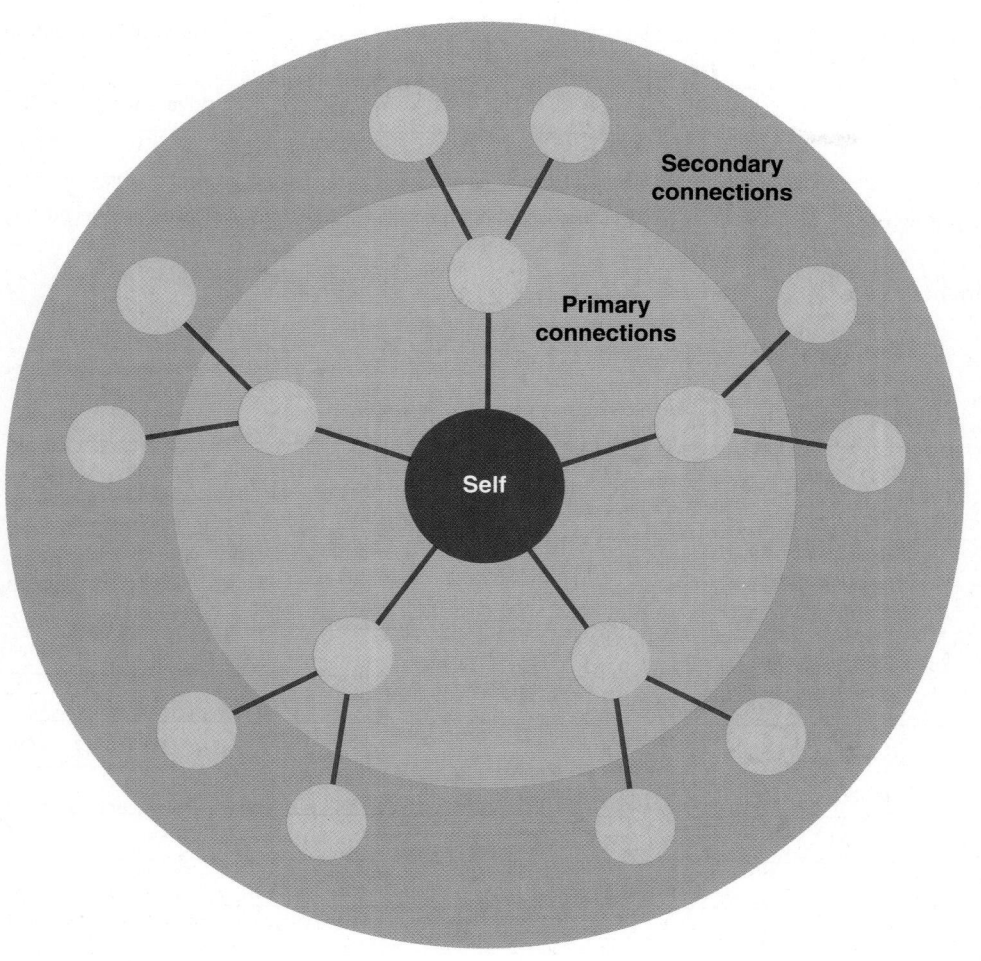

_____   Participates in community activities as opportunities arise.

_____   Is neat in appearance.

_____   Is honest in all matters pertaining to company property
          or funds.

SOURCE: Excerpted from Lawrence R. Jauch, Arthur G. Bedeian, Sally A. Coltrin, and William F. Glueck, *The Managerial Experience: Cases, Exercises, and Readings,* 5th ed. Copyright © 1989 South-Western, a part of Cengage Learning, Inc. Reproduced with permission. www.cengage.com/permissions.

1.4   CAREER PLANNING

OBJECTIVES

1. To explore your career thinking.

2. To visualize your ideal job in terms as concrete as possible.

3. To summarize the state of your career planning, and to become conscious of the main questions you have about it at this point.

INSTRUCTIONS

Read the instructions for each activity, reflect on them, and then write your response. Be as brief or extensive as you like.

Career Planning Worksheet

1. Describe your ideal occupation in terms of responsibilities, skills, and how you would know if you were successful.

    _____

    _____

    _____

    _____

_____
_____
_____
_____

2. Identify 10 statements you can make today about your current career planning. Identify 10 questions you need answered for career planning.

10 statements

1. _____
_____

2. _____
_____

3. _____
_____

4. _____
_____

5. _____
_____

6. _____
_____

7. _____
_____

8. _____
_____

9. _____
_____

10. _____
_____

10 questions

1. _____
_____

2. _____
_____

3. _____
_____

4. _____
_____

5. _____
_____

6. _____
_____

7. _____
_____

8. _____
_____

9. _____
_____

10. _____
_____

CONCLUDING CASE

A NEW MANAGER AT USA HOSPITAL SUPPLY

As Charlie Greer drove to work, he smiled, recalling the meeting at the end of the previous day. Inez Rodriguez, the owner of the company where he worked, USA Hospital Supply, had summoned him to her office, where she warmly shook his hand and exclaimed, "Congratulations!" As they settled into chairs, Inez reviewed the conversation she'd had with the company's board of directors that morning: USA Hospital had been growing steadily for the past 10 years despite the economy's ups and downs. As the company's founder, Inez had always been an insightful and enthusiastic leader of the five-person sales team, but the level of activity was becoming too much of a distraction. Inez needed to think about the long-range vision of the company, so she needed a leader who could focus on sales. She had interviewed several candidates outside the firm, as well as Charlie and two of the other sales representatives. In the end, Inez told Charlie, the choice was obvious: Charlie was far and away the best sales rep on the team, he had extensive knowledge of the company's product mix, and if anyone could help the sales team achieve its goals, it was Charlie. She offered him the job as the company's first sales manager. He eagerly accepted. When he left work that evening, his head was full of ideas, and his heart was full of confidence.

Now Charlie pulled into the office park where USA Hospital Supply was located and easily found a parking space in the lot outside the one-story office and warehouse facility. As usual, he was one of the first employees to arrive. By habit, he strode toward his cubicle, but after a second, he recalled that Inez had arranged for the small firm's accountant and computer systems manager to share an office so he could have an office of his own. Charlie entered his new domain and settled into the swivel chair behind his desk.

At that instant, the eagerness to enjoy his new status and responsibility began to give way to nervousness. Charlie realized that although he knew a lot about selling supplies to hospitals and doctor's offices, he had never given much thought to managing. Obviously, he mused, his job was to see that his department met or exceeded its sales targets. But how?

Charlie booted up his computer and then opened his e-mail and his word-processing software, intending to get some ideas into writing. He typed out a list of the four other sales reps: Cindy, Paula, John, and Doreen. Cindy handled the large corporate accounts, Paula covered the East Coast, John called on accounts in the South, and Doreen handled the Midwest. Until today, Charlie had been building a fast-growing territory west of the Mississippi. Now who was going to do that? Charlie was tempted to keep that work for himself; he knew he could build a base of loyal clients better than anyone else. Still, he wondered if he could excel as a manager and as a sales rep at the same time.

While he was pondering that challenge, Cindy walked past the office door and, without stopping, politely called, "Congratulations!" through the doorway. Charlie's heart sank as he realized that Cindy had also wanted this job. They had always enjoyed a friendly rivalry as talented salespeople; now what would happen to the fun of being team members? It was easier to think about the other representatives at the moment. Charlie scanned his e-mail inbox and saw status reports from John and Doreen, both of them out of the office to call on clients. What about Paula? Charlie wasn't quite sure he remembered her plans for this week. Obviously he needed to catch up on what everyone was doing, and that gave him a new idea. He could build on his strengths by traveling with each of the sales reps and coaching them. That way, he could show them all his proven methods for closing a sale, and they could learn to sell as well as he did. Charlie thought, "That's what a good manager does: shows employees how to do the job right." He was starting to feel less nervous as he began to compose an e-mail to Paula.

QUESTIONS

1. How will Charlie's approach to quality and service affect his company's performance?

2. Which of the basic functions of management has Charlie considered? How well is he preparing to carry out these functions?

3. Which management skills does Charlie have? In what areas do you think he has the greatest need to develop skills? How can he actively manage his development as a manager?

The Evolution of Management

For thousands of years, managers have wrestled with the same issues and problems confronting executives today. Around 1100 BC the Chinese practiced the four management functions—planning, organizing, leading, and controlling—discussed in Chapter 1. Between 400 BC and 350 BC the Greeks recognized management as a separate art and advocated a scientific approach to work. The Romans decentralized the management of their vast empire before the birth of Christ. During medieval times, the Venetians standardized production through the use of an assembly line, building warehouses and using an inventory system to monitor the contents.[1]

But throughout history most managers operated strictly on a trial-and-error basis. The challenges of the Industrial Revolution changed that. Management emerged as a formal discipline at the turn of the century. The first university programs to offer management and business education, the Wharton School at the University of Pennsylvania and the Amos Tuck School at Dartmouth, were founded in the late 19th century. By 1914, 25 business schools existed.[2]

Thus the management profession as we know it today is relatively new. This appendix explores the roots of modern management theory. Understanding the origins of management thought will help you grasp the underlying contexts of the ideas and concepts presented in the chapters ahead.

Although this appendix is titled "The Evolution of Management," it might be more appropriately called "The Revolutions of Management" because it documents the wide swings in management approaches over the last 100 years. Out of the great variety of ideas about how to improve management, parts of each approach have survived and been incorporated into modern perspectives on management. Thus the legacy of past efforts, triumphs, and failures has become our guide to future management practice.

EARLY MANAGEMENT CONCEPTS AND INFLUENCES

Communication and transportation constraints hindered the growth of earlier businesses. Therefore, improvements in management techniques did not substantially improve performance. However, the Industrial Revolution changed that. As companies grew and became more complex, minor improvements in management tactics produced impressive increases in production quantity and quality.[3]

The emergence of **economies of scale**—reductions in the average cost of a unit of production as the total volume produced increases—drove managers to strive for further growth. The opportunities for mass production created by the Industrial Revolution spawned intense and systematic thought about management problems and issues—particularly efficiency, production processes, and cost savings.[4]

Figure A.1 provides a time line depicting the evolution of management thought through the decades. This historical perspective is divided into two major sections: classical approaches and contemporary approaches. Many of these approaches overlapped as they developed, and they often had a significant impact on one another. Some approaches were a direct reaction to the perceived deficiencies of previous approaches. Others developed as the needs and issues confronting managers changed over the years. All the approaches attempted to explain the real issues facing managers and provide them with tools to solve future problems.

Figure A.1 will reinforce your understanding of the key relationships among the approaches and place each perspective in its historical context.

FIGURE A.1
The Evolution of Management Thought

The oldest company on the *Fortune* 500 list is the Bank of New York, founded in 1784 by Alexander Hamilton. The oldest industrial company is DuPont, begun in 1802 after E. I. du Pont fled persecution during the French Revolution.[5]

CLASSICAL APPROACHES

The classical period extended from the mid-19th century through the early 1950s. The major approaches that emerged during this period were systematic management, scientific management, administrative management, human relations, and bureaucracy.

Systematic Management During the 19th century, growth in U.S. business centered on manufacturing.[6] Early writers such as Adam Smith believed the management of these firms was chaotic, and their ideas helped to systematize it. Most organizational tasks were subdivided and performed by specialized labor. However, poor coordination caused frequent problems and breakdowns of the manufacturing process.

The **systematic management** approach attempted to build specific procedures and processes into operations to ensure coordination of effort. Systematic management emphasized economical operations, adequate staffing, maintenance of inventories to meet consumer demand, and organizational control. These goals were achieved through

- Careful definition of duties and responsibilities.
- Standardized techniques for performing these duties.
- Specific means of gathering, handling, transmitting, and analyzing information.
- Cost accounting, wage, and production control systems to facilitate internal coordination and communications.

Systematic management emphasized internal operations because managers were concerned primarily with meeting the explosive

Production costs dropped as mass manufacturing lowered unit costs. Thus economies of scale were born—a concept that persists in the modern manufacturing era.

growth in demand brought about by the Industrial Revolution. In addition, managers were free to focus on internal issues of efficiency, in part because the government did not constrain business practices significantly. Finally, labor was poorly organized. As a result, many managers were oriented more toward things than toward people.

Systematic management did not address all the issues 19th-century managers faced, but it tried to raise managers' awareness about the most pressing concerns of their job.

An Early Labor Contract

The following rules, taken from the records of Cocheco Company, were typical of labor contract provisions in the 1850s.

1. The hours of work shall be from sunrise to sunset, from the 21st of March to the 20th of September inclusively; and from sunrise until eight o'clock, p.m., during the remainder of the year. One hour shall be allowed for dinner, and half an hour for breakfast during the first mentioned six months; and one hour for dinner during the other half of the year; on Saturdays, the mill shall be stopped one hour before sunset, for the purpose of cleaning the machinery.

2. Every hand coming to work a quarter of an hour after the mill has been started shall be docked a quarter of a day; and every hand absenting him or herself, without absolute necessity, shall be docked in a sum double the amount of the wages such hand shall have earned during the time of such absence. No more than one hand is allowed to leave any one of the rooms at the same time—a quarter of a day shall be deducted for every breach of this rule.

3. No smoking or spiritous liquors shall be allowed in the factory under any pretense whatsoever. It is also forbidden to carry into the factory, nuts, fruits, etc. books, or papers during the hours of work.

SOURCE: W. Sullivan, "The Industrial Revolution and the Factory Operative in Pennsylvania," *The Pennsylvania Magazine of History and Biography* 78 (1954), pp. 478–79.

Scientific Management Systematic management failed to lead to widespread production efficiency. This shortcoming became apparent to a young engineer named Frederick Taylor, who was hired by Midvale Steel Company in 1878. Taylor discovered that production and pay were poor, inefficiency and waste were prevalent, and most companies had tremendous unused potential. He concluded that management decisions were unsystematic and that no research to determine the best means of production existed.

In response, Taylor introduced a second approach to management, known as **scientific management.**[7] This approach advocated the application of scientific methods to analyze work and to determine how to complete production tasks efficiently.

For example, U.S. Steel's contract with the United Steel Workers of America specified that sand shovelers should move 12.5 shovelfuls per minute; shovelfuls should average 15 pounds of river sand composed of 5.5 percent moisture.[8]

Taylor identified four principles of scientific management:

1. Management should develop a precise, scientific approach for each element of one's work to replace general guidelines.
2. Management should scientifically select, train, teach, and develop each worker so that the right person has the right job.
3. Management should cooperate with workers to ensure that jobs match plans and principles.
4. Management should ensure an appropriate division of work and responsibility between managers and workers.

To implement this approach, Taylor used techniques such as time-and-motion studies. With this technique, a task was divided into its basic movements, and different motions were timed to determine the most efficient way to complete the task.

After the "one best way" to perform the job was identified, Taylor stressed the importance of hiring and training the proper worker to do that job. Taylor advocated the standardization of tools, the use of instruction cards to help workers, and breaks to eliminate fatigue.

Another key element of Taylor's approach was the use of the differential piecerate system. Taylor assumed workers were motivated by receiving money. Therefore, he implemented a pay system in which workers were paid additional wages when they exceeded a standard level of output for each job. Taylor concluded that both workers and management would benefit from such an approach.

Scientific management principles were widely embraced. Other proponents, including Henry Gantt and Frank and Lillian Gilbreth, introduced many refinements and techniques for applying scientific management on the factory floor. One of the most famous examples of the application of scientific management is the factory Henry Ford built to produce the Model T.[9]

The legacy of Taylor's scientific management approach is broad and pervasive. Most important, productivity and efficiency in manufacturing improved dramatically. The concepts of scientific methods and research were introduced to manufacturing. The piecerate system gained wide acceptance because it more closely aligned effort and reward. Taylor also emphasized the need for cooperation between management and workers. And the concept of a management specialist gained prominence.

Scientific Management and the Model T

> At the turn of the century, automobiles were a luxury that only the wealthy could afford. They were assembled by craftspeople who put an entire car together at one spot on the factory floor. These workers were not specialized, and Henry Ford believed they wasted time and energy bringing the needed parts to the car. Ford took a revolutionary approach to automobile manufacturing by using scientific management principles.
>
> After much study, machines and workers in Ford's new factory were placed in sequence so that an automobile could be assembled without interruption along a moving production line. Mechanical energy and a conveyor belt were used to take the work to the workers.
>
> The manufacture of parts likewise was revolutionized. For example, formerly it had taken one worker 20 minutes to assemble a flywheel magneto. By splitting the job into 29 different operations, putting the product on a mechanical conveyor, and changing the height of the conveyor, Ford cut production time to 5 minutes.
>
> By 1914 chassis assembly time had been trimmed from almost 13 hours to 1½ hours. The new methods of production required complete standardization, new machines, and an adaptable labor force. Costs dropped significantly, the Model T became the first car accessible to the majority of Americans, and Ford dominated the industry for many years.

SOURCE: H. Kroos and C. Gilbert, *The Principles of Scientific Management* (New York: Harper & Row, 1911).

Frederick Taylor (left) and Dr. Lillian Gilbreth (right) were early experts in management efficiency.

The first female executive to head a company on the *Fortune* 500 list was Katharine Graham of *The Washington Post* (first listed in 1972).[10]

Despite these gains, not everyone was convinced that scientific management was the best solution to all business problems. First, critics claimed that Taylor ignored many job-related social and psychological factors by emphasizing only money as a worker incentive. Second, production tasks were reduced to a set of routine, machinelike procedures that led to boredom, apathy, and quality control problems. Third, unions strongly opposed scientific management techniques because they believed management might abuse its power to set the standards and the piecerates, thus exploiting workers and diminishing their importance. Finally, although scientific management resulted in intense scrutiny of the internal efficiency of organizations, it did not help managers deal with broader external issues such as competitors and government regulations, especially at the senior management level.

Administrative Management The **administrative management** approach emphasized the perspective of senior managers within the organization, and argued that management was a profession and could be taught.

An explicit and broad framework for administrative management emerged in 1916, when Henri Fayol, a French mining engineer and executive, published a book summarizing his management experiences. Fayol identified five functions and 14 principles of management. The five functions, which are very similar to the four functions discussed in Chapter 1, are planning, organizing, commanding, coordinating, and controlling. Table A.1 lists and defines the 14 principles. Although some critics claim Fayol treated the principles as universal truths for management, he actually wanted them applied flexibly.[11]

A host of other executives contributed to the administrative management literature. These writers discussed a broad spectrum of management topics, including the social responsibilities of management, the philosophy of management, clarification of business terms and concepts, and organizational principles. Chester Barnard's and Mary Parker Follet's contributions have become classic works in this area.[12]

Barnard, former president of New Jersey Bell Telephone Company, published his landmark book *The Functions of the Executive* in 1938. He outlined the role of the senior executive: formulating the purpose of the organization, hiring key individuals, and maintaining organizational communications.[13] Mary Parker Follet's 1942 book *Dynamic Organization* extended Barnard's work by emphasizing the continually changing situations that managers face.[14] Two of her key contributions—the notion that managers desire flexibility and the differences between motivating groups and individuals—laid the groundwork for the modern contingency approach discussed later in the chapter.

All the writings in the administrative management area emphasize management as a profession along with fields such as law and medicine. In addition, these authors offered many recommendations based on their personal experiences, which often included managing large corporations. Although these perspectives and recommendations were considered sound, critics

TABLE A.1
Fayol's 14 Principles of Management

1. *Division of work*—divide work into specialized tasks and assign responsibilities to specific individuals.
2. *Authority*—delegate authority along with responsibility.
3. *Discipline*—make expectations clear and punish violations.
4. *Unity of command*—each employee should be assigned to only one supervisor.
5. *Unity of direction*—employees' efforts should be focused on achieving organizational objectives.
6. *Subordination of individual interest to the general interest*—the general interest must predominate.
7. *Remuneration*—systematically reward efforts that support the organization's direction.
8. *Centralization*—determine the relative importance of superior and subordinate roles.
9. *Scalar chain*—keep communications within the chain of command.
10. *Order*—order jobs and material so they support the organization's direction.
11. *Equity*—fair discipline and order enhance employee commitment.
12. *Stability and tenure of personnel*—promote employee loyalty and longevity.
13. *Initiative*—encourage employees to act on their own in support of the organization's direction.
14. *Esprit de corps*—promote a unity of interests between employees and management.

noted that they might not work in all settings. Different types of personnel, industry conditions, and technologies may affect the appropriateness of these principles.

1955 Ray Kroc's first McDonald's opens. Bill Gates and Steve Jobs are born.[15]

Human Relations A fourth approach to management, **human relations,** developed during the 1930s. This approach aimed at understanding how psychological and social processes interact with the work situation to influence performance. Human relations was the first major approach to emphasize informal work relationships and worker satisfaction.

This approach owes much to other major schools of thought. For example, many of the ideas of the Gilbreths (scientific management) and Barnard and Follet (administrative management) influenced the development of human relations from 1930 to 1955. In fact, human relations emerged from a research project that began as a scientific management study.

Western Electric Company, a manufacturer of communications equipment, hired a team of Harvard researchers led by Elton Mayo and Fritz Roethlisberger. They were to investigate the influence of physical working conditions on workers' productivity and efficiency in one of the company's factories outside Chicago. This research project, known as the *Hawthorne Studies,* provided some of the most interesting and controversial results in the history of management.[16]

The Hawthorne Studies were a series of experiments conducted from 1924 to 1932. During the first stage of the project (the illumination experiments), various working conditions, particularly the lighting in the factory, were altered to determine the effects of those changes on productivity. The researchers found no systematic relationship between the factory lighting and production levels. In some cases, productivity continued to increase even when the illumination was reduced to the level of moonlight. The researchers concluded that the workers performed and reacted differently because the researchers were observing them. This reaction is known as the **Hawthorne Effect.**

This conclusion led the researchers to believe productivity may be affected more by psychological and social factors than by physical or objective influences. With this thought in mind, they initiated the other four stages of the project. During these stages, the researchers performed various work group experiments and had extensive interviews with employees. Mayo and his team eventually concluded that productivity and employee behavior were influenced by the informal work group.

Human relations proponents argued that managers should stress primarily employee welfare, motivation, and communication. They believed social needs had precedence over economic needs. Therefore, management must gain the cooperation of the group and promote job satisfaction and group norms consistent with the goals of the organization.

Another noted contributor to the field of human relations was Abraham Maslow.[17] In 1943 Maslow suggested that humans have five levels of needs. The most basic needs are the physical needs for food, water, and shelter; the most advanced need is for self-actualization, or personal fulfillment. Maslow argued that people try to satisfy their lower-level needs and then progress upward to the higher-level needs. Managers can facilitate this process and achieve organizational goals by removing obstacles and encouraging behaviors that satisfy people's needs and organizational goals simultaneously.

Although the human relations approach generated research into leadership, job attitudes, and group dynamics, it drew heavy criticism.[18] Critics believed that one result of human relations—a belief that a happy worker was a productive worker—was too simplistic. While scientific management overemphasized the economic and formal aspects of the workplace, human relations ignored the more rational side of the worker and the important characteristics of the formal organization. However, human relations was a significant step in the development of management thought because it prompted managers and researchers to consider the psychological and social factors that influence performance.

Bureaucracy Max Weber, a German sociologist, lawyer, and social historian, showed how management itself could be more efficient and consistent in his book *The Theory of Social and Economic Organizations.*[19] The ideal model for management, according to Weber, is the **bureaucracy** approach.

Weber believed bureaucratic structures can eliminate the variability that results when managers in the same organization

A Human Relations Pioneer

In 1837 William Procter, a ruined English retailer, and James Gamble, son of a Methodist minister, formed a partnership in Cincinnati to make soap and candles. Both were known for their integrity, and soon their business was thriving.

By 1883 the business had grown substantially. When William Cooper Procter, grandson of the founder, left Princeton University to work for the firm, he wanted to learn the business from the ground up. He started working on the factory floor. "He did every menial job from shoveling rosin and soap to pouring fatty mixtures into crutchers. He brought his lunch in a paper bag . . . and sat on the floor [with the other workers] and ate with them, learning their feelings about work."

By 1884 Cooper Procter believed, from his own experience, that increasing workers' psychological commitment to the company would lead to higher productivity. His passion to increase employee commitment to the firm led him to propose a scandalous plan: share profits with workers to increase their sense of responsibility and job satisfaction. The surprise was audible on the first "dividend day," when workers held checks equivalent to seven weeks' pay.

Still, the plan was not complete. Workers saw the profit sharing as extra pay rather than as an incentive to improve. In addition, Cooper Procter recognized that a fundamental issue for the workers, some of whom continued to be his good friends, was the insecurity of old age. Public incorporation in 1890 gave Procter a new idea. After trying several versions, by 1903 he had discovered a way to meet all his goals for labor: a stock purchase plan. For every dollar a worker invested in P&G stock, the company would contribute four dollars' worth of stock.

Finally, Cooper Procter had resolved some key issues for labor that paid off in worker loyalty, improved productivity, and an increasing corporate reputation for caring and integrity. He went on to become CEO of the firm, and P&G today remains one of the most admired corporations in the United States.

SOURCES: O. Schisgall, *Eyes on Tomorrow* (Chicago: J. G. Ferguson, 1981); T. Welsh, "Best and Worst Corporate Reputations," *Fortune,* February 7, 1994, pp. 58–66.

have different skills, experiences, and goals. Weber advocated that the jobs themselves be standardized so that personnel changes would not disrupt the organization. He emphasized a structured, formal network of relationships among specialized positions in an organization. Rules and regulations standardize behavior, and authority resides in positions rather than in individuals. As a result, the organization need not rely on a particular individual, but will realize efficiency and success by following the rules in a routine and unbiased manner.

1962 The first Walmart store opens in Rogers, Arkansas.
1964 Blue Ribbon Sports ships its first shoes. It's now called Nike.
1969 Don and Doris Fisher open the first Gap store in San Francisco.

According to Weber, bureaucracies are especially important because they allow large organizations to perform the many routine activities necessary for their survival. Also, bureaucratic positions foster specialized skills, eliminating many subjective judgments by managers. In addition, if the rules and controls are established properly, bureaucracies should be unbiased in their treatment of people—both customers and employees.

Many organizations today are bureaucratic. Bureaucracy can be efficient and productive. However, bureaucracy is not the appropriate model for every organization. Organizations or departments that need rapid decision making and flexibility may suffer under a bureaucratic approach. Some people may not perform their best with excessive bureaucratic rules and procedures.

Other shortcomings stem from a faulty execution of bureaucratic principles rather than from the approach itself. Too much authority may be vested in too few people; the procedures may become the ends rather than the means; or managers may ignore appropriate rules and regulations. Finally, one advantage of a bureaucracy—its permanence—can also be a problem. Once a bureaucracy is established, dismantling it is difficult.

CONTEMPORARY APPROACHES

The contemporary approaches to management include quantitative management, organizational behavior, systems theory, and the contingency perspective. The contemporary approaches have developed at various times since World War II, and they continue to represent the cornerstones of modern management thought.

Quantitative Management Although Taylor introduced the use of science as a management tool early in the 20th century, most organizations did not adopt the use of quantitative techniques for management problems until the 1940s and 1950s.[20] During World War II, military planners began to apply mathematical techniques to defense and logistics problems. After the war, private corporations began assembling teams of quantitative experts to tackle many of the complex issues confronting large organizations. This approach, referred to as **quantitative management,** emphasizes the application of quantitative analysis to management decisions and problems.

Quantitative management helps a manager make a decision by developing formal mathematical models of the problem. Computers facilitated the development of specific quantitative methods. These include such techniques as statistical decision theory, linear programming, queuing theory, simulation, forecasting, inventory modeling, network modeling, and break-even analysis. Organizations apply these techniques in many areas, including production, quality control, marketing, human resources, finance, distribution, planning, and research and development.

Despite the promise quantitative management holds, managers do not rely on these methods as the primary approach to decision making. Typically they use these techniques as a supplement or tool in the decision process. Many managers will use results that are consistent with their experience, intuition, and judgment, but they often reject results that contradict their beliefs. Also, managers may use the process to compare alternatives and eliminate weaker options.

Several explanations account for the limited use of quantitative management. Many managers have not been trained in using these techniques. Also, many aspects of a management decision cannot be expressed through mathematical symbols and formulas. Finally, many of the decisions managers face are nonroutine and unpredictable.

1971 Intel introduces the first microprocessor, and IBM introduces the floppy disk.
1976 Steve Jobs and Steve Wozniak start Apple Computer in their garage.

Organizational Behavior During the 1950s, a transition took place in the human relations approach. Scholars began to recognize that worker productivity and organizational success are based on more than the satisfaction of economic or social needs. The revised perspective, known as **organizational behavior,** studies and identifies management activities that promote employee effectiveness through an understanding of the complex nature of individual, group, and organizational processes. Organizational behavior draws from a variety of disciplines, including psychology and sociology, to explain the behavior of people on the job.

During the 1960s, organizational behaviorists heavily influenced the field of management. Douglas McGregor's Theory X and Theory Y marked the transition from human relations.[21] According to McGregor, Theory X managers assume workers are lazy and irresponsible and require constant supervision and external motivation to achieve organizational goals. Theory Y managers assume employees *want* to work and can direct and control themselves. McGregor advocated a Theory Y perspective, suggesting that managers who encourage participation and allow opportunities for individual challenge and initiative would achieve superior performance.

Other major organizational behaviorists include Chris Argyris, who recommended greater autonomy and better jobs for workers,[22] and Rensis Likert, who stressed the value of participative management.[23] Through the years, organizational behavior has consistently emphasized development of the organization's human resources to achieve individual and organizational goals. Like other approaches, it has been criticized for its limited perspective, although more recent contributions have a broader and more situational viewpoint. In the past few years, many of the primary issues addressed by organizational behavior have experienced a rebirth with a greater interest in leadership, employee involvement, and self-management.

1980 Microsoft licenses its operating system to IBM.
1981 MTV launches on cable.
1995 Netscape goes public and kicks off the dot-com boom.

Systems Theory The classical approaches as a whole were criticized because they (1) ignored the relationship between the organization and its external environment, and (2) usually stressed one aspect of the organization or its employees at the expense of other considerations. In response to these criticisms, management scholars during the 1950s stepped back from the details of the organization to attempt to understand it as a whole system. These efforts were based on a general scientific approach called **systems theory**.[24] Organizations are open systems, dependent on inputs from the outside world, such as raw materials, human resources, and capital. They transform these inputs into outputs that (ideally) meet the market's needs for goods and services. The environment reacts to the outputs through a feedback loop; this feedback provides input for the next cycle of the system. The process repeats itself for the life of the system, and is illustrated in Figure A.2.

Systems theory also emphasizes that an organization is one system in a series of subsystems. For instance, Southwest Airlines is a subsystem of the airline industry, and the flight crews are a subsystem of Southwest. Systems theory points out that each subsystem is a component of the whole and is interdependent with other subsystems.

Contingency Perspective Building on systems theory ideas, the **contingency perspective** refutes universal principles of management by stating that a variety of factors, both internal and external to the firm, may affect the organization's performance.[25] Therefore, there is no "one best way" to manage and organize because circumstances vary.

Situational characteristics are called **contingencies**. Understanding contingencies helps a manager know which sets of circumstances dictate which management actions. You will learn recommendations for the major contingencies throughout this text. The contingencies include

1. Circumstances in the organization's external environment.
2. The internal strengths and weaknesses of the organization.
3. The values, goals, skills, and attitudes of managers and workers in the organization.
4. The types of tasks, resources, and technologies the organization uses.

With an eye to these contingencies, a manager may categorize the situation and then choose the proper competitive strategy, organization structure, or management process for the circumstances.

Researchers continue to identify key contingency variables and their effects on management issues. As you read the topics covered in each chapter, you will notice similarities and differences among management situations and the appropriate responses. This perspective should represent a cornerstone of your own approach to management. Many of the things you will learn about throughout this course apply a contingency perspective.

1998 Google registers google.com domain.
2000 AOL becomes the first pure Internet company to make the *Fortune* 500 list and merges with Time Warner the same year.
2001 Enron files for bankruptcy.
2003 AOL Time Warner posts a record $98.7 billion loss.[26]
2007 Housing bubble bursts.
2008 Market meltdown.
2008 Wall Street gets bailout.
2008–2009 Auto industry collapses.

AN EYE ON THE FUTURE

All of these historical perspectives have left legacies that affect contemporary management thought and practice. Their undercurrents continue to flow, even as the context and the specifics change.

Times pass, and things change. This may sound obvious, but it isn't to those managers who sit by idly while their firms fail to adapt to changing times. Business becomes global. New technologies change how we work, produce goods, and deliver services. Change continually creates both new opportunities and new demands for lowering costs and for achieving greater innovation, quality, and speed. Management knowledge and practices evolve accordingly.

The essential facts about change are these. First, change is happening more rapidly and dramatically than at any other time in history. Second, if you don't anticipate change and adapt to it, you and your firm will not thrive in a competitive business world. The theme of change—what is happening now, what lies ahead, how it affects management, and how you can deal with it—permeates this entire book.

What are the implications of these changes for you and your career? How can you best be ready to meet the challenges? You

FIGURE A.2
Open-System Perspective of an Organization

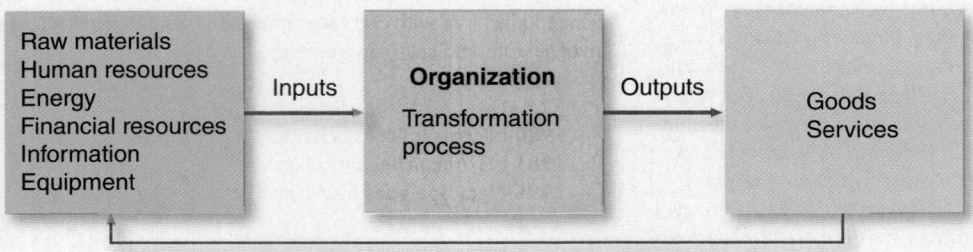

EXTERNAL ENVIRONMENT

Raw materials / Human resources / Energy / Financial resources / Information / Equipment → Inputs → **Organization** Transformation process → Outputs → Goods / Services must ask questions about the future, anticipate changes, know your responsibilities, and be prepared to meet them head-on. We hope you study the remaining chapters with these goals in mind.

KEY TERMS

administrative management   A classical management approach that attempted to identify major principles and functions that managers could use to achieve superior organizational performance, p. 39.

bureaucracy   A classical management approach emphasizing a structured, formal network of relationships among specialized positions in the organization, p. 40.

contingencies   Factors that determine the appropriateness of managerial actions, p. 42.

contingency perspective   An approach to the study of management proposing that the managerial strategies, structures, and processes that result in high performance depend on the characteristics, or important contingencies, of the situation in which they are applied, p. 42.

economies of scale   Reductions in the average cost of a unit of production as the total volume produced increases, p. 36.

Hawthorne Effect   People's reactions to being observed or studied resulting in superficial rather than meaningful changes in behavior, p. 40.

human relations   A classical management approach that attempted to understand and explain how human psychological and social processes interact with the formal aspects of the work situation to influence performance, p. 39.

organizational behavior   A contemporary management approach that studies and identifies management activities that promote employee effectiveness by examining the complex and dynamic nature of individual, group, and organizational processes, p. 41.

quantitative management   A contemporary management approach that emphasizes the application of quantitative analysis to managerial decisions and problems, p. 41.

scientific management   A classical management approach that applied scientific methods to analyze and determine the "one best way" to complete production tasks, p. 37.

systematic management   A classical management approach that attempted to build into operations the specific procedures and processes that would ensure coordination of effort to achieve established goals and plans, p. 37.

systems theory   A theory stating that an organization is a managed system that changes inputs into outputs, p. 42.

DISCUSSION QUESTIONS

1. How does today's business world compare with the one of 40 years ago? What is different about today, and what is not so different?

2. What is scientific management? How might today's organizations use it?

3. Table A.1 lists Fayol's 14 principles of management, first published in 1916. Are they as useful today as they were then? Why or why not? *When* are they most, and least, useful?

4. What are the advantages and disadvantages of a bureaucratic organization?

5. In what situations are quantitative management concepts and tools applicable?

6. Choose any organization and describe its system of inputs and outputs.

7. Why did the contingency perspective become such an important approach to management? Generate a list of contingencies that might affect the decisions you make in your life or as a manager.

8. For each of the management approaches discussed in the appendix, give examples you have seen. How effective or ineffective were they?

9. The appendix highlighted a few landmark events in recent business history. What additional landmarks during those decades would you include?

10. The final landmark was from 2008 to 2009. What are the most important landmarks since then, and why?

Experiential Exercises

A.1 APPROACHES TO MANAGEMENT

OBJECTIVES
1. To help you conceive a wide variety of management approaches.
2. To clarify the appropriateness of different management approaches in different situations.

INSTRUCTIONS
Your instructor will divide your class randomly into groups of four to six people. Acting as a team, with everyone offering ideas and one person serving as official recorder, each group will be responsible for writing a one-page memo to your present class. The subject matter of your group's memo will be "My advice for managing people today is . . ." The fun part of this exercise (and its creative element) involves writing the memo from the viewpoint of the person assigned to your group by your instructor.

Among the memo viewpoints your instructor may assign are

- An ancient Egyptian slave master (building the great pyramids).
- Henri Fayol.
- Frederick Taylor.
- Mary Parker Follet.
- Douglas McGregor.
- A contingency management theorist.
- A Japanese auto company executive.

- The chief executive officer of IBM in the year 2030.
- Commander of the Starship Enterprise II in the year 3001.
- Others as assigned by your instructor.

Use your imagination, make sure everyone participates, and try to be true to any historical facts you've encountered. Attempt to be as specific and realistic as possible. Remember, the idea is to provide advice about managing people from another point in time (or from a particular point of view at the present time).

Make sure you manage your 20-minute time limit carefully. A recommended approach is to spend 2 to 3 minutes

putting the exercise into proper perspective. Next, take about 10 to 12 minutes brainstorming ideas for your memo, with your recorder jotting down key ideas and phrases. Have your recorder use the remaining time to write your group's one-page memo, with constructive comments and help from the others. Pick a spokesperson to read your group's memo to the class.

SOURCE: R. Krietner and A. Kinicki, *Organization Behavior*, 3rd ed. (New York: Richard D. Irwin, 1994), pp. 30–31.

A.2 THE UNIVERSITY GRADING SYSTEM ANALYSIS

OBJECTIVES

1. To learn to identify the components of a complex system.
2. To better understand organizations as systems.
3. To visualize how a change in policy affects the functioning of an organization system.

INSTRUCTIONS

1. Assume that your university has decided to institute a pass–fail system of grading instead of the letter-grade

system it presently has. Apply the systems perspective learned from this chapter to understanding this decision.

2. Answer the questions on the Grading System Analysis Worksheet individually, or in small groups, as directed by your instructor.

DISCUSSION QUESTIONS

Share your own or your group's responses with the entire class. Then answer the following questions:

1. Did you diagram the system in the same way?
2. Did you identify the same system components?
3. Which subsystems will be affected by the change?
4. How do you explain differences in your responses?

Grading System Analysis Worksheet

DESCRIPTION

1. What subsystems compose the system (the university)? Diagram the system.

    _____

    _____

    _____

2. Identify the following in this system: inputs, outputs, transformations.

    _____

    _____

    _____

DIAGNOSIS

3. Which of the subsystems will be affected by the change; that is, what changes are likely to occur throughout the system as a result of the policy change?

    _____

    _____

    _____

SOURCE: J. Gordon, *A Diagnostic Approach to Organizational Behavior* (Englewood Cliffs, NJ: Prentice Hall, 1983), p. 38. Reprinted with permission of Prentice Hall, Inc., Englewood Cliffs, NJ.

2

The External and Internal Environments

LEARNING OBJECTIVES

After studying Chapter 2, you will be able to:

LO 1   Describe how environmental forces influence organizations and how organizations can influence their environments. p. 48

LO 2   Distinguish between the macroenvironment and the competitive environment. p. 49

LO 3   Explain why managers and organizations should attend to economic and social developments. p. 49

LO 4   Identify elements of the competitive environment. p. 55

LO 5   Summarize how organizations respond to environmental uncertainty. p. 64

LO 6   Define elements of an organization's culture. p. 72

LO 7   Discuss how an organization's culture and climate affect its response to its external environment. p. 72

> ❝ **The essence of a business is outside itself.**
> — PETER DRUCKER ❞

Management Connection

WHAT MAKES APPLE A WINNER IN A FAST-CHANGING ENVIRONMENT?

In the 1970s consumers loved the spreadsheet and desktop publishing software they could run on their Apple II personal computers. But over the next two decades, Apple Computer watched its market share drop as more and more businesses and consumers chose from the wide variety of PCs and software using a Microsoft operating system. After Microsoft launched Windows 95 in 1995, it seemed that Apple's computers were destined to be a niche product for a small but intensely loyal band of customers.

Today, however, Apple—which dropped "Computer" from the company name—is widely admired. Investors have driven up the stock price of Apple to the point that the company is valued at roughly 50 percent more than Microsoft.

One explanation for Apple's dramatic comeback is that it became far more than a personal computer company as computing came to mean far more than using a machine to crunch numbers and create documents. As technological advances have redefined computers, shifting the emphasis from machines to the Internet, Apple has readied a host of ways to tap into and enjoy that potential. The iPod music player (and its offspring, the iTouch), iTunes music store, iPhone cell phone with its App Store, and iPad tablet computer have generated excitement and long lines of eager customers.

In some cases, Apple's management seems to anticipate the new directions taken by technology and society. The company developed the iPod in tandem with the creation of iTunes. Many companies already were selling MP3 players offering a variety of features. But creating its music player in conjunction with an easy—and legal—way to buy and download music helped make the iPod the runaway hit in a still-young product category.

In other cases, Apple seems to have been surprised but responsive. At the launch of the iPhone

in 2007, chief executive Steve Jobs described how this device would serve as a phone, iPod, and mobile device for browsing the Internet. That combination of features made it a handsome smartphone, but smartphones such as the BlackBerry were already available. What would make the iPhone amazing was something new for Apple. Whereas in the past the company had maintained tight control over every aspect of its technology, it made a software development kit available a year after the iPhone's launch. With the development kit, any programmer could write code for additional applications and sell them online at Apple's App Store.

This bow to the power of Web 2.0 with its emphasis on information sharing and online collaboration opened the door to an explosion of creativity. Apps made the iPhone fun to use, and more than 100 million apps were downloaded in the first two months. Within a few years, the App Store had sold over $1.8 billion in apps. Many of them are games, something Jobs and his development team hadn't seen as a significant use for the iPhone. In fact, Apple developed only one game for the iPhone; the real creative work in this area came from outsiders such as Stanford's Ge Wang, who wrote a program to make the iPhone play music that sounds like an ocarina, and FireMint, a company that wrote the popular game "Flight Control." This approach not only added "game device" to the list of the iPhone's uses—it also helped to make the iPhone the world's top-selling handset in terms of revenue.

Apple's approach has been to focus on the ways consumers can use the Internet, rather than on the capabilities of particular machines—even the machines that made it famous, such as the iMac computer. So, for example, the company has shifted its research and development spending away from the operating system for its personal computers and into mobile computing. This strategy has made Apple a tremendous success.

The question is whether Apple's management will continue to anticipate where society and technology are headed. One challenge is how to participate responsibly in an online, interconnected society where the standards of conduct for sharing information are still evolving. For example, mobile devices such as the iPhone can track the user's location. That information has some valuable applications, such as quickly generating directions to the nearest coffee shop. However, people have raised privacy concerns that the company might build databases of unencrypted information about phone users' locations. Tests showed company databases being updated even if the user turned off a phone's location feature. Apple initially offered assurances that data would remain anonymous, but as complaints persisted, it promised to release a software update that would limit the collection and storage of information. The company also promised to upgrade its operating system to encrypt location information. That response seemed to quell concerns as revenues poured in from still-accelerating iPhone and iPad sales.[1]

> Technology and society are just two of the forces shaping the environment in which Apple operates. As you study this chapter, consider what other forces Apple's managers should be monitoring and engaging with.

open systems

Organizations that are affected by, and that affect, their environment.

 LO 1

inputs

Goods and services organizations take in and use to create products or services.

outputs

The products and services organizations create.

external environment

All relevant forces outside a firm's boundaries, such as competitors, customers, the government, and the economy.

As a technology leader, Apple is affecting how people work, play, shop, and communicate today, as well as preparing for how they might want to do so in the future. Its management must therefore keep a sharp watch on a broad spectrum of influences and events that can affect its operations. In this chapter, we discuss in detail how pressures from outside the organization help create the context in which managers and their companies must operate.

As we suggested in the first chapter, organizations are **open systems**—that is, they are affected by and in turn affect their external environments. For example, they take in **inputs** such as goods or services from their environment and use them to create products and services that are **outputs** to their environment, as shown in Figure 2.1. But when we use the term **external environment** here, we mean more than an organization's clients or customers; the external environment includes *all* relevant forces outside the organization's boundaries.

> Managers must stay abreast of external developments and react effectively.

Many of these factors are uncontrollable. Companies large and small are buffeted or battered by recession, government regulations, competitors' actions, and other factors. But their lack of control does not mean that managers can ignore such forces, use them as excuses for poor performance, and try to just get by. Managers must stay abreast of external developments and react effectively. Moreover, as we will discuss later in this chapter, sometimes managers can influence components of the external environment. We will examine ways in which organizations can do just that.

FIGURE 2.1

Organization Inputs and Outputs

Environments

FIGURE 2.2
The External Environment

Figure 2.2 shows the external environment of a business organization. The organization exists in its **competitive environment**, which is composed of the firm and its rivals, suppliers, customers (buyers), new entrants, and substitute or complementary products. At the more general level is the **macroenvironment**, which includes legal, political, economic, technological, demographic, and social and natural factors that generally affect all organizations.

A Look Ahead

This chapter discusses the basic characteristics of an organization's environment and the importance of that environment for strategic management. We also examine the *internal environment*, or *culture*, of the organization and the way that culture may influence the organization's response to its environment. Later chapters elaborate on many of the basic environmental forces introduced here. For example, technology will be discussed again in Chapter 17. The global environment gets a thorough treatment in Chapter 6, which is devoted to international management. Other chapters focus on ethics, social responsibility, and the natural environment. Chapter 18 reiterates the theme that recurs throughout this text: organizations must change continually because environments change continually.

competitive environment

The immediate environment surrounding a firm; includes suppliers, customers, rivals, and the like.

macroenvironment

The general environment; includes governments, economic conditions, and other fundamental factors that generally affect all organizations.

The Macroenvironment

All organizations operate in a macroenvironment, which is defined by the most general elements in the external environment that potentially can influence strategic decisions. Although a top executive team may have unique internal strengths and ideas about its goals, it must consider external factors before taking action.

The Economy

Although most Americans think in terms of the U.S. economy, the economic environment for organizations is much larger—created by complex interconnections among the economies of different countries. Wall Street investment analysts begin their workday thinking not just about what the New York Stock Exchange did yesterday but also about how the London and Tokyo exchanges did overnight. Growth and recessions occur worldwide as well as domestically.

The economic environment dramatically affects managers' ability to function effectively and influences their strategic choices. Interest and inflation rates affect the availability and cost of capital, growth opportunities, prices, costs, and consumer demand for products. Unemployment rates affect labor availability and the wages the firm must pay, as well as product demand. Steeply rising energy and health care costs have had a great effect on companies' ability to hire and their cost of doing business. Changes in the value of the dollar on world exchanges may make American products cheaper or more expensive than their foreign competitors.

An important economic influence is the stock market. When investors bid up stock prices, they are paying more to own shares in companies, which means the companies have more capital to fuel their strategies. Observers of the stock market watch trends in major indexes such as the Dow Jones Industrial Average, Standard and Poor's 500, and Nasdaq Composite, which combine many companies' performance into a single

Bottom Line

With increased competition from foreign and domestic companies, managers must pay particular attention to cost. *Does low-cost mean low-quality? Why or why not?*

IN PRACTICE

Economic forces have caused the fortunes of corn-based ethanol producers to swing wildly. For a time, soaring gasoline prices intensified the demand for alternative fuel sources for automobiles. That fact, coupled with a belief that ethanol fuel would reduce emissions of greenhouse gases, inspired the U.S. government to mandate the use of ethanol. Farmers responded by planting more corn, and energy companies built ethanol refineries.

But soon other forces pummeled the ethanol producers. First flooding in the Midwest led to forecasts of high corn prices, and many ethanol producers tried to protect themselves by signing contracts for a generous $7 and more per bushel. Then fields dried and prospects for a good harvest improved, so corn prices started falling, leaving ethanol producers with contracts for overpriced corn.

More recently, the economy swung downward. A "bubble" of inflated real estate prices burst, contributing to problems for mortgage lenders that quickly spread to the entire financial industry. As credit dried up, the overall pace of business slowed dramatically, and oil prices fell, erasing some of ethanol's competitive advantage in the marketplace for fuel. But prices for corn also fell, keeping production costs down. Ethanol producers are hopeful that in the long run, drivers will need to rely more and more on alternative fuels. Meanwhile, ethanol companies need steady and farsighted management to guide them through the ups and downs of commodity prices and demand.[2] Besides corn, what are some other products for which prices have swung dramatically?

measurement. Figure 2.3 shows how two of these indexes performed over a year's worth of trading. They are measured against their price level at the beginning of the period, set at an index value of 100. Both indexes had risen to great heights at the beginning of the period, and then they dropped rapidly during the autumn months. The falling prices reflected an economy in which demand for homes and cars had shriveled, credit was difficult to obtain, exports tumbled, and unemployment rates soared.[3] Lower stock values coupled with tight credit made it hard for most businesses to find capital for expansion and innovation. Governments launched a variety of stimulus efforts to help companies get financing and to encourage consumers to start spending again. Stock markets have always rebounded eventually, even after a steep decline such as this one, as investors see hope for renewed business growth.

The stock market may also have a profound effect on the behavior of individual managers. In publicly held companies, managers throughout the organization may feel required to meet Wall Street's earnings expectations. It is quite likely that you, too,

SOURCE: www.nasdaq.com.

FIGURE 2.3
Twelve-Month Comparison
of Stock Markets

at some point in your career, will be asked to improve a budget or estimate because your company does not want to disappoint "the Street." Such external pressures usually have a positive effect—they help make many firms more efficient and profitable. But failure to meet those expectations can cause a company's stock price to drop, making it more difficult for the firm to raise additional capital for investment. The compensation of managers may also be affected, particularly if they have been issued stock options. The net effect of these pressures may sometimes be that managers focus on short-term results at the expense of the long-term success of their organizations. Even worse, a few managers may be tempted to engage in unethical or unlawful behavior that misleads investors.[4] We will discuss managerial ethics in Chapter 5 and stock options in Chapter 10.

Economic conditions change over time and are difficult to predict. Bull and bear markets come and go. Periods of dramatic growth may be followed by a recession. Every trend undoubtedly will end—but when? Even when times seem good, budget deficits or other considerations create concern about the future.

> Economic conditions change over time and are difficult to predict.

Technology

Today a company cannot succeed without incorporating into its strategy the astonishing technologies that exist and continue to evolve. Technological advances create new products, advanced production techniques, and better ways of managing and communicating. In addition, as technology evolves, new industries, markets, and competitive niches develop. For example, early entrants in biotechnology are trying to establish dominant positions, while later entrants work on technological advances that will give them a competitive niche. Advances in technology also permit companies to enter markets that would otherwise be unavailable to them, such as when cable TV companies adapted their technology to enter the market for Internet services.

New technologies also provide new production techniques. In manufacturing, sophisticated robots perform jobs without suffering fatigue, requiring vacations or weekends off, or demanding wage increases. New methods, such as injecting steam into oil fields at high pressure, are enabling Shell, ExxonMobil, and other oil companies to extract that valuable resource from locations that had once been considered depleted. In this case, technological and economic forces overlap: the rising price of oil has made it worthwhile for companies to develop and try the new technology.[5]

In addition, new technologies provide new ways to manage and communicate. Computerized management information systems (MISs) make information available when needed, and networking via the Internet makes that information available where it is needed. Computers monitor productivity and note performance deficiencies. Telecommunications allow conferences to take place without requiring people to travel to the same location. Such technological advances create innovations in business. Strategies developed around the cutting edge of technological advances create a

Bottom Line
Managers with ready access to information gain a significant competitive edge.
What are some technologies that have given managers fast access to information?

competitive advantage; strategies that ignore or lag behind competitors' technology lead to obsolescence and extinction. This issue is so important that we devote an entire chapter (Chapter 17) to the topic.

Laws and Regulations

U.S. government policies impose strategic constraints on organizations but may also provide opportunities. In the United States, for example, the Affordable Care Act of 2010 includes a host of legal provisions aimed at making health care more widely available. Many of these affect businesses; some apply differently depending on whether a company is large or small. Thus companies that have up to 25 employees and provide health insurance coverage to their employees may receive a tax credit to offset part of that expense. By 2014 the states are supposed to set up insurance exchanges to make coverage available to individuals and small businesses; companies with fewer than 100 employees will be eligible to shop in these exchanges, which are intended to offer better deals than are currently available. The law's major impact on larger companies will depend on whether they offer their employees insurance that the government considers adequate. If companies with at least 50 employees do not, their employees may be eligible for tax credits to offset their cost of insurance, and these companies will have to pay the government an assessment of $2,000 for each eligible employee. The law also includes a variety of provisions imposing requirements on insurers, establishing incentives for cost containment and expansion of primary care, and requiring reporting of more data on insurance costs and patient outcomes.[6] In sum, whether this law introduces primarily constraints (say, higher cost of employee benefits) or opportunities (greater ability to attract talent by being able to afford insurance) will depend on the situation of a particular company.

> Strategies that ignore or lag behind competitors' technology lead to obsolescence and extinction.

The government can affect business opportunities through tax laws, economic policies, and international trade rulings. An example of restraint on business action is the U.S. government's standards regarding bribery. In some countries, bribes and kickbacks are common and expected ways of doing business, but for U.S. firms they are illegal practices. Some U.S. businesses have, in fact, been fined for using bribery when competing internationally. But laws can also assist organizations. Because U.S. federal and state governments protect property rights, including copyrights, trademarks, and patents, it is economically more attractive to start businesses in the United States than in countries where laws and law enforcement offer less protection.

Regulators are specific government organizations in a firm's more immediate task environment. Regulatory agencies such as the Occupational Safety and Health Administration (OSHA), the Interstate Commerce Commission (ICC), the Federal Aviation Administration (FAA), the Equal Employment Opportunity Commission (EEOC), the National Labor Relations Board (NLRB), the Office of Federal Contract Compliance Programs (OFCCP), and the Environmental Protection Agency (EPA) have the power to investigate company practices and take legal action to ensure compliance with laws.

The Securities and Exchange Commission (SEC) regulates U.S. financial markets. Its regulations are intended to protect investors. For instance, the SEC has proposed regulations requiring companies to disclose more details about the total compensation paid to executives, including deferred compensation (pensions, severance pay) and perks (such as free housing and personal use of a corporate jet). The objective of the regulations is to help investors in a company evaluate whether executives are being compensated at an appropriate level.[7]

Another example of a regulatory body is the Food and Drug Administration (FDA), which can prevent a company from selling an unsafe or ineffective product to the public. Following recent highly publicized incidents of illness from people who ate tainted peanuts, lettuce, spinach, and green onions, the FDA came under pressure to tighten its regulations for food safety.

Often the corporate community sees government as an adversary. However, many organizations realize that government can be a source of competitive advantages for an individual company or an entire industry. Public policy may prevent or limit new foreign or domestic competitors from entering an industry. Government may subsidize failing companies or provide tax breaks to some. Federal patents protect innovative products or production process technologies. Legislation may be passed to support industry prices, thereby guaranteeing profits or survival. The government may even intervene to ensure the survival of certain key industries or companies, as it has done to help auto companies, airlines, and agricultural businesses.

> The U.S. Department of Commerce's Trade Advocacy Center, at www.export.gov/advocacy/, was established to help U.S. businesses overcome hurdles that make it difficult for them to export goods or compete against foreign firms.

Demographics

Demographics are measures of various characteristics of the people who make up groups or other social units. Work groups, organizations, countries, markets, and societies can be described statistically by referring to demographic measures such as their members' age, gender, family size, income, education, occupation, and so forth.

demographics

Measures of various characteristics of the people who make up groups or other social units.

Managers must consider workforce demographics in formulating their human resources strategies. Population growth influences the size and composition of the labor force. In the decade from 2008 to 2018, the U.S. civilian labor force is expected to grow at a rate of 8.2 percent, reaching 166.9 million.[8] This growth is slower than during the previous decade, partly because young workers—those between the ages of 16 and 24— are declining in numbers. The fastest-growing age group will

> Will the next generation of workers change the way we work? Researchers found that teens studying at their computers are also doing something else 65 percent of the time, and 26 percent of teens use several media at once. A study of multitasking and brain activity found that we use different parts of the brain when we multitask while learning. Multitaskers used the part of the brain involved in repetitive skills, while those engaged only in learning used the area associated with memory.[9] Will this influence future managers' ability to think deeply about problems?

be workers who are 55 and older, who are expected to represent close to one-fourth of the labor force in 2018. What does this mean for employers? They will need to find ways to retain and fully use the talents of their experienced workers while competing for relatively scarce entry-level workers. They may find that many of their older employees are willing to work past the traditional retirement age of 65; one reason is that research suggests that a lack of pensions and adequate savings will make retirement unaffordable for many of today's baby boomers.[10] Eventually, however, declining participation in work by older persons will require managers to find replacements for these highly experienced workers.

The education and skill levels of the workforce are another demographic factor managers must consider. The share of the U.S. labor force with at least some college education has been increasing steadily over the past several decades, from less than one-fourth of the workforce in 1970 to more than three-fourths today.[11] Even so, many companies find that they must invest heavily in training their entry-level workers, who may not have been adequately prepared for some of the more complex tasks the modern workplace requires. (We discuss training in greater detail in Chapter 10.) Also, as college has become a more popular option, employers are finding it difficult to recruit employees for jobs that require knowledge of a skilled trade, such as machinists and toolmakers, especially in areas where the cost of living is so high that most residents are professionals.[12] However, as education levels improve around the globe, more managers find they are able to send even technical tasks to lower-priced but highly trained workers overseas, which we discuss further in Chapter 6.

As the number of people in the workforce with a college education increases, managers must consider how this impacts their work.

Another factor that significantly influences the U.S. population and labor force is immigration. Immigrants represent over 15 percent of the U.S. workforce, although they are a stronger presence in the West (almost 24 percent of the workforce) than in the Midwest (less than 8 percent).[13] Immigrants are frequently of working age but have different educational and occupational backgrounds from the rest of the labor force. Immigration is one reason the labor force in the future will be more ethnically diverse than it is today. The biggest percentage employment increases will be by Hispanics and Asian Americans, followed by African Americans. The demographic importance of immigration intersects with legal issues governing who is permitted to work in the United States. For example, the federal government has recently cracked down not only on undocumented workers but also on the managers who hired them. Other companies have asked the government to admit more foreign workers with technical expertise that may be hard to find in the United States.

> Immigration is one reason the labor force in the future will be more ethnically diverse than it is today.

Since the last quarter of the 20th century, women have joined the U.S. labor force in record numbers. Throughout the 1970s and 1980s, they became much more likely to take paying jobs. In the 1970s only about one-third of women were in the labor force, but 60 percent had jobs in 1999. Since then, women's labor force participation rate has stayed near that level, declining only slightly. Women's participation contrasts with a participation rate of 72 percent for men, also declining gradually as the workforce ages and more adults retire.[14]

A more diverse workforce has many advantages, but managers have to make certain they provide equality for women and minorities with respect to employment, advancement opportunities, and compensation. They must make strategic plans to recruit, retain, train, motivate, and effectively utilize people of diverse demographic backgrounds who have the skills to achieve the company's mission. We discuss the issue of managing the diverse workforce in detail in Chapter 11.

Social Issues

Societal trends regarding how people think and behave have major implications for management of the labor force, corporate social actions, and strategic decisions about products and markets. For example, during the 1980s and 1990s women in the workforce often chose to delay having children as they focused on their careers, but today more women are having children and then returning to the workforce. As a result, companies have introduced more supportive policies, including family leave, flexible working hours, and child care assistance. Many firms also extend these benefits to all employees or allow them to design their own benefits packages, where they can choose from a menu of available benefits that suit their individual situations. Domestic partners, whether they are in a marital relationship or not, also are covered by many employee benefit programs. Firms provide these benefits as a way of increasing a source of competitive advantage: an experienced workforce.

How companies respond to these and other social issues may also affect their reputation in the marketplace, which in turn may help or hinder their competitiveness. The public health issue of childhood obesity has given video games a bad name among those who advocate for children to get off the couch and get more exercise. But two games have generated favorable publicity: Konami's Dance Dance Revolution (DDR), where players compete with dance moves, and Nintendo's Wii Sports, where players swing a remote control containing motion sensors to move a virtual tennis racket, bowling ball, baseball bat, or boxing gloves. The games have also been praised as an alternative to the violent themes of many games. Dean Bender, the public relations agent for DDR, said of his client, "With all the bad PR about violence, we became the white knights."[15] And Wii Sports players have reported breaking into a sweat and even straining muscles.[16] However, one side effect of that vigorous play with the Wii system was a safety hazard. The company's first wrist straps for the remote controls occasionally broke. But within weeks, the company began replacing the straps with a stronger

> How companies respond to these and other social issues may also affect their reputation in the marketplace.

version at no charge, a rapid response that cemented customer satisfaction more than the defect harmed Nintendo's reputation.[17]

The Natural Environment

Directly or indirectly, organizations depend on the natural environment to provide them with resources. Depending on their processes, they may need trees for paper, steel for manufacturing goods, petroleum to fuel transportation or make plastics, and adequate air and water quality to maintain a healthy workforce. In addition, the ways in which organizations operate will have some impact on the quantity and quality of natural resources available. When the quantity is depleted or the quality is damaged, costs for resources skyrocket. Furthermore, the impact on natural resources—whether negatively by poisoning wells or positively by restoring forests—affects the quality of life for citizens in the areas where companies operate. Decisions that affect the natural environment therefore shape the climate of social issues and the political and legal environment in which organizations operate.

A dramatic example was the explosion of BP's Deepwater Horizon drilling rig in the Gulf of Mexico, which killed 11 workers and caused millions of barrels of oil to gush into the gulf and spread toward the coastlands of Mississippi and Louisiana. During the weeks that followed, fisheries closed, and tourists vacationed elsewhere. BP was forced to set aside tens of billions of dollars to cover all costs of the spill and its cleanup. In addition, the U.S. government was expected to assess severe fines against the company; and to prevent similar accidents in the future, it imposed additional regulations on any oil companies that want to drill in the Gulf.[18]

Protecting the natural environment has become so important to managerial decisions that we devote Appendix B following Chapter 5 to that subject.

The Competitive Environment

All managers are affected by the components of the macroenvironment we just discussed. But each organization also functions in a closer, more immediate competitive environment. The competitive environment includes the organizations with which the organization directly interacts. As shown in Figure 2.4, the competitive environment includes rivalry among current competitors and the impact of new entrants, substitute and complementary products, suppliers, and customers. This model was originally developed by Michael Porter, a Harvard professor and a noted authority on strategic management.

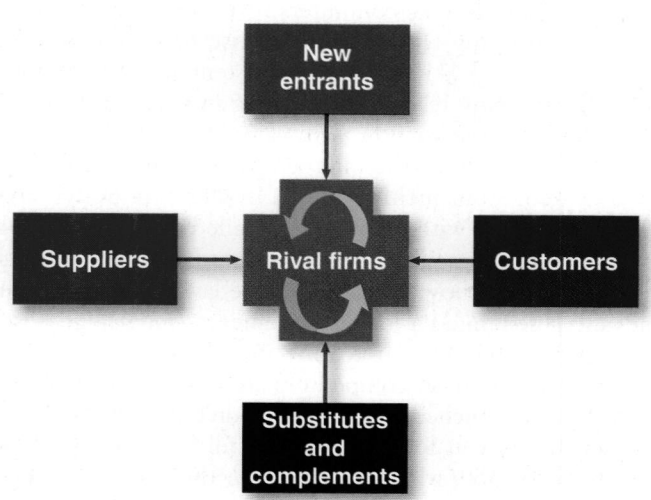

FIGURE 2.4
The Competitive Environment

According to Porter, successful managers do more than simply react to the environment; they act in ways that actually shape or change the organization's environment. In strategic decision making, Porter's model is an excellent method to help managers analyze the competitive environment and adapt to or influence the nature of their competition.

Competitors

Bottom Line

Companies often compete through innovation, quality, service, and cost. We will discuss the issue of competitors and strategy in further detail in Chapter 4.

In which of these areas would you say Nintendo tried to create a competitive advantage for the Wii console? (If you aren't sure, come back to this question after you've studied this section.)

Among the various components of the competitive environment, competitors within the industry must first deal with one another. When organizations compete for the same customers and try to win market share at the others' expense, all must react to and anticipate their competitors' actions.

The first question to consider is this: Who is the competition? Sometimes the answer is obvious. The major competitors in the market for video game consoles are Sony (whose brand is the PlayStation), Microsoft (Xbox 360), and Nintendo (maker of the Wii). However, if organizations focus exclusively on traditional rivalries, they miss the emerging ones. Video games today are played on cell phones and tablet computers, not just on consoles. Likewise, Coca-Cola and PepsiCo are obvious competitors, but consumer tastes have shifted away from soda to bottled water and other beverages. The two companies have had to compete in introducing new products, not just in winning consumers over to their brand of cola.

Thus, as a first step in understanding their competitive environment, organizations must identify their competitors. Competitors may include (1) small domestic firms, especially their entry into tiny, premium markets; (2) strong regional competitors; (3) big new domestic companies exploring new markets; (4) overseas firms, especially those that either try to solidify their position in small niches (a traditional Japanese tactic) or are able to draw on an inexpensive labor force on a large scale (as in China); and (5) newer entries, such as firms offering their products on the web. The growth in competition from other countries has been especially significant in recent years with the worldwide reduction in international trade barriers. For example, the North American Free Trade Agreement (NAFTA) sharply reduced tariffs on trade between the United States, Canada, and Mexico. Managers today confront a particular challenge from low-cost producers abroad (see Chapter 6).

Once competitors have been identified, the next step is to analyze how they compete. Competitors use tactics such as price reductions, new product introductions, and advertising campaigns to gain advantage over their rivals. In the market for video game consoles, Sony had been a leader and was expected to maintain its dominance when it launched its powerful PS3 model, choosing a technology-based strategy. The PS3 is a technological marvel, which by one account combines "the [processing] speed of a low-end supercomputer with the [component] cooling techniques of a network server" (a high-end computer used to handle the needs of a network of personal computers).[19] Rather than using an existing processor, Sony tapped the expertise of suppliers to develop a new processor and interface. The system generates so much power that engineering teams had to bring in a special team of designers to simulate the air flow with various cooling designs and figure out how to arrange the microchips within the box to keep the whole system from melting down. In addition, Sony's engineers developed a high-definition display, with graphics so detailed that software engineers had to calculate the motions of the game's activities precisely. If something in a game bounces or breaks, the software must show it moving as the laws of physics would in the real world. These advances generated a lot of excitement—and a high cost. By one estimate, making a top-of-the-line PS3 costs Sony about $840.

It's essential to understand what competitors are doing when you are honing your own strategy.

It's essential to understand what competitors are doing when you are honing your own strategy. When Sony launched its PS3, it couldn't charge a high enough price to cover its costs. It set the price at $599, which was still far above the prices charged by its competitors. The Xbox 360, which had been on the market for a year, was a less

Video game enthusiasts welcomed the invention of Microsoft's Kinect for Xbox 360 in late 2010. Kinect allows users to play Xbox games without holding a controller, making it a major competitor of Nintendo's Wii.

advanced but comparable product selling for $399. But Nintendo became a surprise winner in the initial competition with PS3 by choosing an entirely different strategy for its Wii. Rather than competing on the basis of advanced graphics and powerful processing, the company chose to offer something new and easy to use—its remote-control motion sensors—and set the price at just $249. While the PS3 and Wii both flew off store shelves in the early weeks of the products' launch, PS3 sales over the next few years continually fell below expectations, while Wii became the top-selling game console in the United States. It would be years before Nintendo's competitors unveiled their own motion-sensing technology: Sony's Move controller and Microsoft's Kinect camera.[20]

Competition is most intense when there are many direct competitors (including foreign contenders), when industry growth is slow, and when the product or service cannot be differentiated in some way. New, high-growth industries offer enormous opportunities for profits. When an industry matures and growth slows, profits drop. Then intense competition causes an industry shakeout: weaker companies are eliminated, and the strong companies survive.[21] We will discuss the issue of competitors and strategy in further detail in Chapter 4.

New Entrants

New entrants into an industry compete with established companies. New entrants in the market for entertainment have come from unexpected quarters as increasing broadband speeds and more powerful microprocessors have enabled a whole host of ways to enjoy videos and games online. Cable and satellite television saw viewers flock to Hulu, Blockbuster lost movie sales to Netflix, and the makers of game consoles have watched sales dry up as consumers switched to playing Farmville via Facebook and downloading the Angry Birds app for their smart phones.

If many factors prevent new companies from entering an industry, the threat to established firms is less serious. If there are few such **barriers to entry,** the threat of new entrants is more serious. Some major barriers to entry are government policy, capital requirements, brand identification, cost disadvantages, and distribution channels. The government can limit or prevent entry, as occurs when the FDA forbids a new drug entrant. Some industries, such as liquor retailing, are regulated; more subtle government controls operate in fields such as mining and ski area development. Patents are also entry barriers. When a patent expires, other companies can then enter

barriers to entry

Conditions that prevent new companies from entering an industry.

the market. For example, the patents have recently expired on several drugs made by Pfizer, including antidepressant Zoloft, allergy medicine Zyrtec, and blood pressure medicine Norvasc. At the same time, several research projects to introduce new, patented medicines have failed, so Pfizer was forced to lay off employees and close some facilities to cut costs.[22]

Other barriers are less formal but can have the same effect. Capital requirements may be so high that companies won't risk or try to raise such large amounts of money. Brand identification forces new entrants to spend heavily to overcome customer loyalty. Imagine, for example, the costs involved in trying to launch a new cola against Coke or Pepsi. The cost advantages established companies hold—due to large size, favorable locations, existing assets, and so forth—can also be formidable entry barriers.

Finally, existing competitors may have such tight distribution channels that new entrants have difficulty getting their goods or services to customers. For example, established food products already have supermarket shelf space. New entrants must displace existing products with promotions, price breaks, intensive selling, and other tactics.

IN PRACTICE

The barriers to entry are so high in the automotive industry that it's rare to see a new entrant. A notable exception has been India's Tata Motors, the country's largest maker of commercial vehicles, which a few years ago promised to become a leading car maker in the fast-growing economies of the developing world. Tata announced it was developing a "people's car." Priced at $2,000 to $2,500 (or 1 lakh in Indian currency), the Nano would become the standard transportation for Indian families working their way up to the middle class.

However, it is not yet clear whether Tata will overcome the industry's barriers to success. The promised launch was so ambitious that Tata could not realistically meet expectations. Production was postponed for about a year and a half, and then the company determined it couldn't afford to sell the Nano profitably at the promised price. The first Nanos to roll off assembly lines were priced just $800 below Suzuki's competing Alto, which offers more storage space and a bigger engine. The Nano's safety performance also ran into embarrassing problems; some reportedly caught fire.

Tata has responded with price adjustments, maintenance contracts, test drives, and safety improvements. It has revenues from its commercial vehicles and its Jaguar Land Rover operations to stay afloat. Perhaps the Nano will still become the people's car. Start-ups often make mistakes, and some of them recover brilliantly. What made Tata's stumble remarkable was its grand scale.[23]

- What barriers to entry would you expect for entering the auto market at the low end, as Tata did with the Nano?

Substitutes and Complements

Besides products that directly compete, other products can affect a company's performance by being substitutes for or complements of the company's offerings. A *substitute* is a potential threat; customers use it as an alternative, buying less of one kind of product but more of another. A *complement* is a potential opportunity because customers buy more of a given product if they also demand more of the complementary product. Table 2.1 lists a dozen products and their potential substitutes and complements.

Technological advances and economic efficiencies are among the ways that firms can develop substitutes for existing products. The introduction of video game systems created a substitute for television viewing that has drawn a large share of young men away from TV audiences. More recently, the makers of video games have said that Internet offerings such as YouTube and MySpace have attracted video game players away from their TV sets to interact with one another online. This example shows that

If the Product Is . . .	The Substitute Might Be . . .
Starbucks coffee	Red Bull energy drink
Blockbuster DVD rental	Netflix streaming video
Nissan Sentra (purchased)	Nissan Sentra and Honda CR-V (shared via Zipcar)
SanDisk USB flash drive	CrashPlan online backup service
If the Product Is . . .	**The Complement Might Be . . .**
Starbucks coffee	Starbucks Cake Pops
Netflix streaming video	Orville Redenbacher's popcorn
iTouch media player	iTunes music store
Apartment rental	IKEA furniture

TABLE 2.1
Potential Substitutes
for and Complements
of Products

substitute products or services can limit another industry's revenue potential. Companies in those industries are likely to suffer growth and earnings problems unless they improve quality or launch aggressive marketing campaigns. Nintendo's success with the Wii game console partly resulted from its offering games such as Wii Sports that enticed people who want to interact with the game, as well as by allowing them to create avatars to represent themselves in the various games, a feature that computer users enjoy in many online games and worlds. More recently, Microsoft's introduction of the Kinect camera gave users a gaming experience they can't get from other kinds of entertainment by allowing them to control games via body movements without holding a controller. Within months, the Kinect had become the fastest-selling consumer electronic device, making substitutes for the Xbox 360 less attractive. Meantime, as Nintendo worked on the next-generation console to replace its Wii, it acknowledged the threat from substitutes and hinted that the next product would be aimed at offering an experience consumers could get only in their homes—not in a coffee shop on a handheld device.[24]

Bottom Line
Cost is often a major barrier to entry.
Would cost be a bigger barrier for a game console maker or a developer of video games? Why?

IN PRACTICE

In addition to current substitutes, companies need to think about potential substitutes that may be viable in the near future. For example, as alternatives to fossil fuels, experts suggest that nuclear fusion, solar power, and wind energy may prove useful one day. The advantages promised by each of these technologies are many: inexhaustible fuel supplies, electricity "too cheap to meter," zero emissions, universal public acceptance, and so on. Yet while they may look good on paper—and make us feel good about our choice—they often come up short in economic feasibility or technical viability.

Besides identifying and planning for substitutes, companies must consider complements for their products. When people are buying new homes, they are also buying appliances and landscaping products. When they buy a car, they buy insurance for it. And as we have noted, game consoles and video games are complementary products. For this reason, console makers work closely with developers, giving them the information they need to create products to lure customers to their gaming systems. The complexity of the PS3 created another hurdle for Sony in this area. Because the system is so sophisticated, programming a game for PS3 costs roughly 30 percent more than creating a similar title for Microsoft's Xbox. That has made game developers cautious about launching PS3 titles, which in turn has made game players think twice about buying the new console. In the January following release of the PS3, only 2 of the top 20 games sold ("Resistance: Fall of Man" and "Madden NFL 07") were PS3 games.[25] To collaborate better with the game industry, Sony released programming tools for game developers.[26] The effort was especially important because developers such as Electronic Arts were quick to adjust their own product plans when sales of PS3 titles were lower than expected while sales of Wii titles were better than expected.[27]

As with substitutes, a company needs to watch for new complements that can change the competitive landscape. When Microsoft launched its Kinect device, intended for playing games on the Xbox 360, hackers quickly figured out how to write code that would enable the Kinect to control applications on their personal computers. At first Microsoft saw this as a problem: hackers misusing proprietary information and perhaps not paying the royalties Microsoft would traditionally get from a game developer. However, within months, Microsoft showed that it understood these applications as potentially valuable complementary products for the Kinect. The company announced that it would release a software toolkit so that programmers could write applications legitimately.[28]

> Organizations are at a disadvantage if they become overly dependent on any powerful supplier.

Suppliers

Recall from our earlier mention of open systems that organizations must acquire resources (inputs) from their environment and convert those resources into products or services (outputs) to sell. Suppliers provide the resources needed for production, and those resources may come in the form of people (supplied by trade schools and universities), raw materials (from producers, wholesalers, and distributors), information (supplied by researchers and consulting firms), and financial capital (from banks and other sources). But suppliers are important to an organization for reasons that go beyond the resources they provide. Suppliers can raise their prices or provide poor-quality goods and services. Labor unions can go on strike or demand higher wages. Workers may produce defective work. Powerful suppliers, then, can reduce an organization's profits, particularly if the organization cannot pass on price increases to its customers.

Organizations are at a disadvantage if they become overly dependent on any powerful supplier. A supplier is powerful if the buyer has few other sources of supply or if the supplier has many other buyers. One of the problems plaguing the launch of the PS3 was a shortage of parts, and during the weeks leading up to the console's first Christmas, it was often out of stock in U.S. stores. Sony depended on Panasonic to provide disk drives and on IBM and ATI Technologies to deliver core processors and graphics chips.[29] For such a sophisticated product, the company couldn't go elsewhere for these components. Dependence also results from high **switching costs**—the fixed costs buyers face if they change suppliers. For example, once a buyer learns how to operate a supplier's equipment, such as computer software, the buyer faces both economic and psychological costs in changing to a new supplier.

In recent years, supply chain management has become an increasingly important contributor to a company's competitiveness and profitability. By **supply chain management,** we mean the managing of the entire network of facilities and people that obtain raw materials from outside the organization, transform them into products, and distribute them to customers.[30] In the past, managers did not have to pay as much attention to supply chain management as they do today. Products tended to be standardized, overseas competition was still years in the future, and the pace of change was slower. But increased competition has required managers to pay very close attention to their costs. For example, they can no longer afford to hold large and costly inventories, waiting for orders to come in. Also, once orders do come in, some products still sitting in inventory might well be out of date.

With the emergence of the Internet, customers look for products built to their specific needs and preferences—and they want them delivered quickly at the lowest available price. This requires the supply chain to be not only efficient but also *flexible,* so that the organization's output can quickly respond to changes in demand.

---

switching costs

Fixed costs buyers face when they change suppliers.

supply chain management

The managing of the network of facilities and people that obtain materials from outside the organization, transform them into products, and distribute them to customers.

Bottom Line

The ability to manufacture even customized products quickly has become a competitive requirement.

To meet this requirement, what qualities would a company need in its employees?

Today the goal of effective supply chain management is to have *the right product in the right quantity available at the right place at the right cost.* Boeing, the aircraft and defense systems company, provides a good example of effective supply chain management. Boeing forges partnerships with its suppliers to share knowledge that will help them learn how to operate more efficiently. For example, at Boeing Integrated Defense Systems (IDS), Rick Behrens is senior manager of supplier development, charged with building close supplier relationships and helping them understand Boeing's commitment to "lean" operations, aimed at eliminating waste. Behrens tailors the supplier relationships to each supplier's familiarity with lean processes. He educates some suppliers in the basics of how to run lean operations; for others, he sends a supplier development team to the organization to help them streamline certain activities. He also identifies Boeing specialists who can help suppliers with particularly challenging problems. Along the way, Behrens helps suppliers develop their abilities so that they can move from simply selling parts to providing complete subassemblies. In Behrens's words, "We need suppliers that can grow with us."[31]

In sum, choosing the right supplier is an important strategic decision. Suppliers can affect manufacturing time, product quality, and inventory levels. The relationship between suppliers and the organization is changing in many companies. The close supplier relationship has become a new model for many organizations that are using a just-in-time manufacturing approach (discussed further in Chapters 16 and 17). And in some companies, innovative managers are forming strategic partnerships with their key suppliers in developing new products or new production techniques. We describe this kind of strategic partnership in more detail in Chapter 9.

A Keurig single-serving coffee maker is shown at the Green Mountain Coffee Roasters outlet store in Waterbury, Vermont. Green Mountain Coffee Roasters was granted approval by the Federal Trade Commission to buy single-cup brewing systems maker Keurig Incorporated. Green Mountain already owned 35 percent of Keurig and announced that it would acquire the company outright. Do you think this collaboration will benefit the company or the customers?

IN PRACTICE

Highly efficient supply chains depend on reliable suppliers, and recent events have shown that the external environment can break those chains. The 2011 earthquake and tsunami that devastated Japan created supply chain headaches for automakers in the United States, which depend on Japanese suppliers for a variety of components, including microchips, LCD panels, and optical sensors.

One response was to cut production processes that depend on parts from Japan. For example, in a facility north of Tokyo, Hitachi Automotive Systems makes an electronic part used in mass airflow sensors. Hitachi's share of the market for airflow sensors is about 60 percent, so when its facility was damaged, automakers feared they wouldn't have enough of these sensors to meet production goals. General Motors stopped production at factories in Louisiana, Germany, and Spain, and Peugeot-Citroën reduced production of several models. Ford initially announced no production cuts but said it was monitoring its supply of sensors on an hourly basis.

Other companies have spotted opportunities to solve supply chain problems. Gage Products Company, located near Detroit, cleans and maintains painting systems for automakers. When the earthquake shut down a paint-manufacturing plant in Japan, auto companies were limited in the paints they could use. Before switching from a paint from Japan to an available alternative, they had to clean out their equipment. Gage quickly filled up its schedule with jobs to clean out paint machines.[32]

• Given these problems, why would auto companies want close relationships with a few suppliers?

Customers

final consumer

A customer who purchases products in their finished form.

intermediate consumer

A customer who purchases raw materials or wholesale products before selling them to final customers.

Customers purchase the goods or services an organization offers. Without customers, a company won't survive. Customers can be intermediate (wholesalers and retailers) or final (end users), depending on where they are in the value chain. You are a **final consumer** when you buy a McDonald's hamburger or a pair of jeans from Aéropostale. **Intermediate consumers** buy raw materials or wholesale products and then sell to final consumers, as when Sony buys components from IBM and ATI Technologies and uses them to make PS3 consoles. Intermediate customers actually make more purchases than individual final consumers do. Types of intermediate customers include retailers, who buy clothes from wholesalers and manufacturers' representatives before selling them to their customers, and industrial buyers, who buy raw materials (such as chemicals) before converting them into final products. Selling to intermediate customers is often called *business-to-business* (B2B) selling. Notice in these B2B examples that the intermediate customer eventually goes on to become a seller.

Consumers using the Internet have an easier time comparing products and prices. This saves them money and time.

Like suppliers, customers are important to organizations for reasons other than the money they provide for goods and services. Customers can demand lower prices, higher quality, unique product specifications, or better service. They also can play competitors against one another, as occurs when a car buyer (or a purchasing agent) collects different offers and negotiates for the best price. Many companies are finding that today's customers want to be actively involved with their products, as when Wii users create a Mii avatar so that the person playing the game looks like a cartoon version of themselves. Dell Inc. has taken customer input a step further by asking customers what they want the company to develop next. At Dell's IdeaStorm website (www.dellideastorm.com), visitors can post ideas for the next generation of computers and vote on the ideas they like best.[33]

The Internet has further empowered customers. It provides an easy source of information—both about product features and about pricing. In addition, today's Internet users informally create and share messages about a product, which provides flattering free "advertising" at best or embarrassing and even erroneous bad publicity at worst. For example, enthusiastic gamers who favor one device or another have posted their homemade "commercials" pairing scenes from games with musical backgrounds on YouTube, as well as blunt point-by-point product comparisons about competing brands. Fans of the Wii mocked Sony's claims that its PS3 was popular by visiting stores and filming inventory sitting on shelves. Among the hackers who developed computer applications for Microsoft's Kinect, half the fun was posting videos on YouTube, showing how they used the Kinect to do something fun, whether displaying a stick as a light saber à la *Star Wars* or gesturing with a hand puppet to control an animal's movements on the screen.[34] Today's companies may find it difficult to identify, much less respond to, these unofficial messages.

As we discussed in Chapter 1, customer service means giving customers what they want or need, the way they want it, the first time. This usually depends on the speed and dependability with which an organization can deliver its products. Actions and attitudes that provide excellent customer service include the following:

Speed of filling and delivering normal orders.
Willingness to meet emergency needs.
Merchandise delivered in good condition.
Readiness to take back defective goods and resupply quickly.

Bottom Line

In all businesses—services as well as manufacturing—strategies that emphasize good customer service provide a critical competitive advantage.

Name a company that has delivered good customer service to you.

Management Connection

APPLE'S ROCKY RELATIONSHIPS

As Apple has innovated, it has found itself a party to ever-fluctuating relationships with the members of its competitive environment. Managing these relationships has been as complex as maintaining its position at the forefront of technology.

Apple's move from personal computers to devices such as iPods and iPads that get content from the Internet has introduced a new kind of "supplier" into its competitive environment: content creators. Instead of merely ordering parts for its devices, Apple needs to forge ties with the creators of the content customers want to buy online.

When Apple launched the iTunes music store, it needed contracts with recording companies. Apple persuaded the companies to accept a deal in which Apple would sell songs for 99 cents apiece, rather than requiring consumers to shop for entire albums. The iPod caught on so fast that Apple soon transformed the way music is sold. Sales of CDs plummeted as consumers flocked to downloaded music. Overall, recording companies saw revenues fall—but perhaps by less than they would have experienced without the ability to distribute music through legal sales on iTunes.

When Apple began selling iPads, it predicted that a major use for this device would be downloading content from publishers. Based on the popularity of its brand, Apple has been bold to insist on favorable terms from publishers. As it does with iPhone and iPad apps, Apple keeps 30 percent of the revenue from in-app subscriptions. Thus if a reader spends $2.99 per month to subscribe to *Bloomberg Businessweek*, the publisher keeps $2.09 of that revenue stream. Much as the music industry did, magazine and newspaper publishers are trying to find their way through a period of transformation. Revenues are dropping as consumers prefer to find free information online. Many publishers complain that the terms Apple is offering are unfavorable, but they are nervous to miss out on what may be the primary method for delivering stories in the future. Consumers may not be willing to pay much for an iPad app, but at least they pay something. And other makers of e-readers, such as Amazon's Kindle, have made deals that leave even smaller amounts on the table for publishers.

Initially publishers balked at the low prices of Apple's App Store, a requirement that subscriptions be sold only in the App Store, and Apple's unwillingness to share subscriber data (something magazine publishers have long collected for themselves). Recently, however, some have been coming around. Besides *Bloomberg Businessweek*, some publishers offering app subscriptions include *Popular Science* and *Elle*. Time Inc., which publishes the *Time* newsweekly plus *Fortune* and *Sports Illustrated*, recently agreed to make its iPad editions free to print subscribers but continued to resist selling online subscriptions because of Apple's lock on the subscriber data.

Apple also has inked deals with companies providing complementary products. Apple produces cell phones, for instance, but other companies have the infrastructure to offer wireless service. Apple first worked solely with AT&T in an arrangement that gave Apple control over the specifications for the iPhone. More recently, it began offering iPhones with service from Verizon Communications. Adding Verizon resulted in a near-doubling of iPhone sales in the first quarter of the deal with Verizon. Even AT&T managed to maintain its customer numbers by cutting prices on its earlier-generation iPhones.

The realm of Apple's competitors is large and complex. When Apple was a personal computer company, the competition was basically Windows-based computers. Now Apple has competitors in music players, e-readers, tablet computers, gaming systems, and any other way people obtain information and content. It also competes with other companies offering apps and online services, notably Google's Android platform. Sometimes the competition is unexpected even to the competitors. Software developers, acting independently, recently published software that enables the Barnes & Noble Nook Color e-reader to use Google's Android platform to run a variety of online applications. Downloading that program essentially turns an e-reader into a tablet computer for half the price of an iPad. Barnes & Noble had not intended this use and announced that the software would void the Nook's warranty. However, if Barnes & Noble decided to add these features to the Nook in the future, the company could instantly put downward pressure on the price of tablets, including the iPad.

Furthermore, companies that compete with Apple in some markets sell components or complementary products in others. These complex relationships sometimes get stormy. For example, Apple buys computer chips, screens, and other components of its devices from Samsung. But Samsung and Apple also make competing mobile phones and tablet computers. The two companies have sued each other over allegations of infringing their patents. As a result, they have to try to maintain cordial working relationships even as they battle in court.[35]

- What substitutes and complements can you identify for the iPhone and iPad?
- Which company do you think has the most power in Apple's supply chain? Why?

Availability of installation and repair services and parts.

Service charges (that is, whether services are "free" or priced separately).[36]

An organization is at a disadvantage if it depends too heavily on powerful customers. Customers are powerful if they make large purchases or if they can easily find alternative places to buy. If you are the largest customer of a firm and you can buy

> "Your most unhappy customers are your greatest source of learning."
> Bill Gates

from others, you have power over that firm, and you most likely can negotiate with it successfully. Your firm's biggest customers—especially if they can buy from other sources—will have the greatest negotiating power over you. Customer relationship management is discussed more fully in Chapter 9. As you read "Management Connection: Progress Report," consider how Apple distinguishes itself with customers by seeking advantages in its relationships with other parties in the competitive environment.

Environmental Analysis

LO 5

environmental uncertainty

Lack of information needed to understand or predict the future.

If managers do not understand how the environment affects their organizations or cannot identify opportunities and threats that are likely to be important, their ability to make decisions and execute plans will be severely limited. For example, if little is known about customer likes and dislikes, organizations will have a difficult time designing new products, scheduling production, or developing marketing plans. In short, timely and accurate environmental information is critical for running a business.

But information about the environment is not always readily available. For example, even economists have difficulty predicting whether an upturn or a downturn in the economy is likely. Moreover, managers find it difficult to forecast how well their own products will sell, let alone how a competitor might respond. In other words, managers often operate under conditions of uncertainty. **Environmental uncertainty** means that managers do not have enough information about the environment to understand or predict the future. Uncertainty arises from two related factors: complexity and dynamism. Environmental *complexity* refers to the number of issues to which a manager must attend as well as their interconnectedness. For example, industries that have many different firms that compete in vastly different ways tend to be more complex—and uncertain—than industries with only a few key competitors. Similarly, environmental *dynamism* refers to the degree of discontinuous change that occurs within the industry. High-growth industries with products and technologies that change rapidly tend to be more uncertain than stable industries where change is less dramatic and more predictable.[37]

> If managers do not understand how the environment affects their organizations, their ability to make decisions and execute plans will be severely limited.

As environmental uncertainty increases, managers must develop techniques and methods for collecting, sorting through, and interpreting information about the environment. We discuss some of these approaches in this section of the chapter. (In the next chapter, we will also discuss how managers make decisions under conditions of uncertainty.) By analyzing environmental forces—in both the macroenvironment and the competitive environment—managers can identify opportunities and threats that might affect the organization.

Environmental Scanning

Perhaps the first step in coping with uncertainty in the environment is pinning down what might be important. Frequently, organizations and individuals act out of ignorance, only to regret those actions in the future. IBM, for example, had the opportunity to purchase the technology behind xerography but turned it down. Xerox saw the potential, and the rest is history. However, Xerox researchers later developed the technology for the original computer mouse, but not seeing the potential, the company missed an important market opportunity.

To understand and predict changes, opportunities, and threats, organizations such as Monsanto, Weyerhaeuser, and Union Carbide spend a good deal of time and money monitoring events in the environment. **Environmental scanning** means both searching out information that is unavailable to most people and sorting through that information to interpret what is important and what is not. Managers can ask questions such as these:

Who are our current competitors?
Are there few or many entry barriers to our industry?
What substitutes exist for our product or service?
Is the company too dependent on powerful suppliers?
Is the company too dependent on powerful customers?[38]

Answers to these questions help managers develop **competitive intelligence,** the information necessary to decide how best to manage in the competitive environment they have identified. Porter's competitive analysis, discussed earlier, can guide environmental scanning and help managers evaluate the competitive potential of different environments. Table 2.2 describes two extreme environments: an attractive environment, which gives a firm a competitive advantage, and an unattractive environment, which puts a firm at a competitive disadvantage.[39]

Scenario Development

As managers attempt to determine the effect of environmental forces on their organizations, they frequently develop **scenarios** of the future. Scenarios create alternative combinations of different factors into a total picture of the environment and the firm. For example, when Congress and the president must forecast the size of the federal budget deficit, they develop several different scenarios about what the economy is likely to do over the next decade or so. Frequently, organizations develop a *best-case scenario* (the occurrence of events that are favorable to the firm), a *worst-case scenario* (the occurrence of unfavorable events), and some middle-ground alternatives. The value of scenario development is that it helps managers develop contingency plans for what they might do given different outcomes.[40] For example, as a manager, you will quite likely be involved in budgeting for your area. You will almost certainly be asked to list initiatives that you would eliminate in case of an economic downturn and new investments you would make if your firm does better than expected.

environmental scanning

Searching for and sorting through information about the environment.

competitive intelligence

Information that helps managers determine how to compete better.

scenario

A narrative that describes a particular set of future conditions.

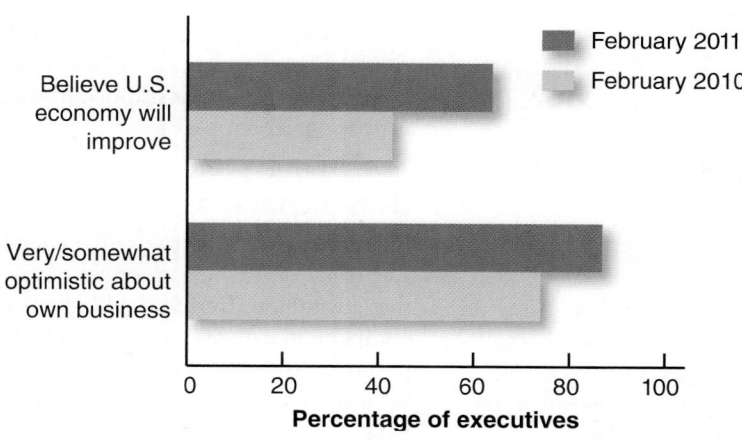

Environmental Factor	Unattractive	Attractive
Competitors	Many; low industry growth; equal size; commodity	Few; high industry growth; unequal size; differentiated
Threat of entry	High threat; few entry barriers	Low threat; many entry barriers
Substitutes	Many	Few
Suppliers	Few; high bargaining power	Many; low bargaining power
Customers	Few; high bargaining power	Many; low bargaining power

TABLE 2.2

Attractive and Unattractive Environments

When the economy was on an upswing, U.S. executives became more optimistic about the scenarios they expected to be true for the nation's economy and their own companies in the six months ahead. Notice that these business leaders tend to be more positive about their own companies than about the overall economy.[41]

Effective managers regard the scenarios they develop as living documents, not merely prepared once and put aside. Instead they constantly update the scenarios to take into account relevant new factors that emerge, such as significant changes in the economy or actions by competitors.

Forecasting

forecasting

Method for predicting how variables will change the future.

Whereas environmental scanning is used to identify important factors and scenario development is used to develop alternative pictures of the future, **forecasting** is used to predict exactly how some variable or variables will change in the future. For example, in making capital investments, firms may try to forecast how interest rates will change. In deciding to expand or downsize a business, firms may try to forecast the demand for goods and services or forecast the supply and demand of labor they probably would use. Publications such as *Bloomberg Businessweek*'s *Business Outlook* provide forecasts to businesses both large and small.

Although forecasts are designed to help executives make predictions about the future, their accuracy varies from application to application. Because they extrapolate from the past to project the future, forecasts tend to be most accurate when the future ends up looking a lot like the past. Of course, we don't need sophisticated forecasts in those instances. Forecasts are most useful when the future will look radically different from the past. Unfortunately, that is when forecasts tend to be less accurate. The more things change, the less confidence we tend to have in our forecasts. The best advice for using forecasts might include the following ideas:

Use multiple forecasts, and perhaps average their predictions.
Remember that accuracy decreases the further into the future you are trying to predict.
Forecasts are no better than the data used to construct them.
Use simple forecasts (rather than complicated ones) where possible.
Keep in mind that important events often are surprises and represent a departure from predictions.[42]

Benchmarking

benchmarking

The process of comparing an organization's practices and technologies with those of other companies.

In addition to trying to predict changes in the environment, firms can undertake intensive study of the best practices of various firms to understand their sources of competitive advantage. **Benchmarking** means identifying the best-in-class performance by a company in a given area, say, product development or customer service, and then comparing your processes to theirs. To accomplish this, a benchmarking team would collect information on its own company's operations and those of the other firm to determine gaps. These gaps serve as a point of entry to learn the underlying causes of performance differences. Ultimately the team would map out a set of best practices that lead to world-class performance. We will discuss benchmarking further in Chapter 4.

Responding to the Environment

For managers and organizations, responding effectively to their environments is almost always essential. Clothing retailers who pay no attention to changes in the public's style preferences, or manufacturers who don't make sure they have steady sources of supply, are soon out of business. To respond to their environment, managers and companies have a number of options, which can be grouped into three categories: (1) selecting a new environment, (2) influencing the environment, and (3) adapting to the environment.

Changing the Environment You Are In

Organizations need not be stuck within some given environment; they have options for defining where they operate. We refer to this category of responses as **strategic maneuvering.** By making a conscious effort to change the boundaries of its competitive environment, a firm can maneuver around potential threats and capitalize on arising opportunities.[43] Managers can use several strategic maneuvers, including domain selection, diversification, merger and acquisition, and divestiture.[44]

Domain selection is the entrance by a company into another suitable market or industry. For example, the market may have limited competition or regulation, ample suppliers and customers, or high growth. An example is Nintendo's decision to create products such as the Wii that appeal to customer segments that have not been enthusiastic to purchase video games—for instance, people intimidated by complicated game controllers and parents concerned about the violent content and sedentary play involved in video games. By avoiding head-on competition to be the product with the best graphics or most advanced play, Nintendo was able to enjoy immediate profits from its new console. This approach built on the company's earlier success with its DS, which lured not only young game players but also women and older-than-average players with its touch screens and games like "Brain Age" and "Nintendogs."[45] Thus Nintendo used an existing expertise to broaden the goods and services it offers.

Diversification occurs when a firm invests in different types of businesses or products or when it expands geographically to reduce its dependence on a single market or technology. Apple successfully diversified its product line when it added the iPod, iTouch, iPad, and iPhone to its offerings of personal computers. As the popularity of the devices has spread, Apple has identified an opportunity to diversify its customer base as well. Apple recently partnered with Unisys to provide tech support so that Apple can better serve organizational customers. Besides maintaining systems, Unisys will write business- and government-related apps. For example, Unisys provides border patrol agents with an iPhone app that lets them easily look up border-crossing data.[46]

A **merger** or **acquisition** takes place when two or more firms combine, or one firm buys another, to form a single company. Mergers and acquisitions can offer greater efficiency from combined operations or can give companies relatively quick access to new markets or industries. After Bayer acquired Schering, it announced plans to cut more than 6,000 jobs to "create an internationally successful pharmaceutical company with competitive cost structures," in the words of Werner Wenning, Bayer Schering Pharma's board chairman.[47] Electronic Arts, publisher of video games, acquired Headgate Studios, a smaller game publisher whose titles include "Tiger Woods PGA Tour" and "Madden NFL." The acquisition helped Electronic Arts add quickly to its list of games for the Wii when sales of the console and its games exceeded expectations.[48]

Divestiture occurs when a company sells one or more businesses. At Ford Motor Company, recent operating losses and the costs of restructuring its workforce have brought about a cash shortage. To raise cash, Ford sold its Aston Martin sports car brand and its Hertz rental car unit.[49]

Organizations engage in strategic maneuvering when they move into different environments. Some companies, called **prospectors,** are more likely than others to engage in strategic maneuvering.[50] Aggressive companies continuously change the boundaries of their competitive environments by seeking new products and markets, diversifying, and merging or acquiring new enterprises. In these and other ways, corporations put their competitors on the defensive and force them to react. **Defenders,** in contrast, stay within a more limited, stable product domain.

> Organizations need not be stuck within some given environment; they have options for defining where they operate.

strategic maneuvering

An organization's conscious efforts to change the boundaries of its task environment.

domain selection

Entering a new market or industry with an existing expertise.

diversification

A firm's investment in a different product, business, or geographic area.

merger

One or more companies combining with another.

acquisition

One firm buying another.

divestiture

A firm selling one or more businesses.

prospectors

Companies that continually change the boundaries for their task environments by seeking new products and markets, diversifying and merging, or acquiring new enterprises.

defenders

Companies that stay within a stable product domain as a strategic maneuver.

Influencing Your Environment

In addition to redefining the boundaries of their environment, managers and organizations can develop proactive responses aimed at changing the environment. Two general types of proactive responses are independent action and cooperative action.

independent strategies

Strategies that an organization acting on its own uses to change some aspect of its current environment.

cooperative strategies

Strategies used by two or more organizations working together to manage the external environment.

empowerment

The process of sharing power with employees, thereby enhancing their confidence in their ability to perform their jobs and their belief that they are influential contributors to the organization.

Independent Action   A company uses **independent strategies** when it acts on its own to change some aspect of its current environment.[51] Table 2.3 shows the definitions and uses of these strategies. For example, Southwest Airlines demonstrates competitive aggression by cutting fares when it enters a new market, and Sony used competitive aggression when it aimed to position itself as the gaming industry's technological leader with the launch of the PS3. In contrast, when Kellogg Company promotes the cereal industry as a whole, it demonstrates competitive pacification. Weyerhaeuser Company advertises its reforestation efforts (public relations). The Gap, Motorola, Nike, American Express, Converse, and other companies have signed on to Product Red, a program in which they market special Red-themed products and donate a percentage of the profits to the Global Fund, a project to help end AIDS in Africa (voluntary action). Viacom sued Google for allowing users to post copyrighted video clips on the Google-owned YouTube website (legal action). In a recent year, pharmaceutical companies spent $1.1 billion to lobby members of Congress (political action); insurers, the second biggest spenders on lobbying, paid out almost $900 million.[52] Each of these examples shows how organizations—on their own—can have an impact on the environment.

Cooperative Action   In some situations, two or more organizations work together using **cooperative strategies** to influence the environment.[53] Table 2.4 shows several examples of cooperative strategies. An example of contracting occurs when suppliers and customers, or managers and labor unions, sign formal agreements about the terms and conditions of their future relationships. These contracts are explicit attempts to make their future relationship predictable. An example of cooptation might occur when universities invite wealthy alumni to join their boards of directors.

TABLE 2.3   Independent Action

Strategy	Definition	Examples
Competitive aggression	Exploiting a distinctive competence or improving internal efficiency for competitive advantage	Aggressive pricing, comparative advertising (e.g., Walmart)
Competitive pacification	Independent action to improve relations with competitors	Helping competitors find raw materials
Public relations	Establishing and maintaining favorable images in the minds of those making up the environment	Sponsoring sporting events
Voluntary action	Voluntary commitment to various interest groups, causes, and social problems	Johnson & Johnson donating supplies to tsunami victims
Legal action	Engaging company in private legal battle	Warner Music lawsuits against illegal music copying
Political action	Efforts to influence elected representatives to create a more favorable business environment or limit competition	Issue advertising; lobbying at state and national levels

SOURCE: Adapted from *Journal of Marketing*, published by the American Marketing Association. C. Zeithaml and V. Zeithaml, "Environmental Management: Revising the Marketing Perspective," Spring 1984.

Strategy	Definition	Examples
Contraction	Negotiation of an agreement between the organization and another group to exchange goods, services, information, patents, and so on	Contractual marketing systems
Cooptation	Absorbing new elements into the organization's leadership structure to avert threats to its stability or existence	Consumer and labor representatives and bankers on boards of directors
Coalition	Two or more groups that coalesce and act jointly with respect to some set of issues for some period of time	Industry associations; political initiatives of the Business Roundtable and the U.S. Chamber of Commerce

TABLE 2.4
Cooperative Action

SOURCE: Reprinted from *Journal of Marketing*, published by the American Marketing Association. C. Zeithaml and V. Zeithaml, "Environmental Management: Revising the Marketing Perspective," Spring 1984.

Finally, an example of coalition formation might be when local businesses band together to curb the rise of employee health care costs and when organizations in the same industry form industry associations and special interest groups. You may have seen cooperative advertising strategies, such as when dairy producers, beef producers, orange growers, and the like jointly pay for television commercials. Life Is Good, a New England–based T-shirt company, used the latest economic downturn as an opportunity to strengthen cooperative action with the retailers that stock its products. According to cofounder Bert Jacobs, employees at Life Is Good began calling retailers to ask how they could help them through the slow times. Based on the feedback, Jacobs identified a need to establish online networks that retailers—his company's customers—could use for sharing ideas.[54]

At the organizational level, firms establish strategic alliances, partnerships, joint ventures, and mergers with competitors to deal with environmental uncertainties. Cooperative strategies such as these make most sense when (1) taking joint action will reduce the organizations' costs and risks and (2) cooperation will increase their power—that is, their ability to successfully accomplish the changes they desire.

Adapting to the Environment: Changing Yourself

To cope with environmental uncertainty, organizations frequently make adjustments in their structures and work processes. When uncertainty arises from environmental complexity, organizations tend to adapt by *decentralizing* decision making. For example, if a company faces a growing number of competitors in various markets, if different customers want different things, if the dissimilar characteristics of different products keep increasing, and if production facilities are being built in different regions of the world, it may be impossible for the chief executive (or a small group of top executives) to keep abreast of all activities and understand all the operational details of a business. In these cases, the top management team is likely to give authority to lower-level managers to make decisions that benefit the firm. The term **empowerment** is used frequently today to talk about this type of decentralized authority. We will address empowerment and decision making in more detail in Chapters 3 and 9.

Celebrities Bono and Oprah have supported organizations participating in the Product Red Program to help end AIDS in Africa through the Global Fund. What other opportunities do companies have to participate in voluntary actions to change their environment?

IN PRACTICE

Organizations can compete more effectively in volatile environments if they have knowledgeable and skilled workers. One way to obtain these workers is to sponsor training programs. Alliances among employers, community colleges, universities, and nonprofit training programs are producing workers with much-needed skills in many industries, and those workers now can earn higher wages. One program in New York, Per Scholas, trains computer repair technicians in one of the country's poorest areas—the Bronx. Funded by grants from private foundations and the New York City Council, the program gained momentum through its collaboration with companies such as Time Warner Cable that were looking for skilled employees.

Per Scholas boasts a job placement rate of 80 percent of its graduates, who earn about $12 per hour in the first year and $15 per hour in two years—often double what they would have earned without the training. One such graduate, Cristina Rodriguez, now works at Time Warner Cable as a broadband specialist for a similar wage plus health insurance coverage. Her new skills have empowered her to become a high-performing employee. "What feels great is when I resolve someone's issue," she says. Rodriguez, fluent in both English and Spanish, is able to solve customers' problems in both languages.

Training programs such as Per Scholas have grown more sophisticated in the last few years because of their close association with the companies that hire their graduates. These relationships foster "the deep understanding these programs develop of the workings of industries where they place people," explains MIT Professor Paul Osterman. Connie Ciliberti, vice president of human resources for Time Warner Cable, confirms the importance of this collaboration. "Per Scholas has spent time learning our business, understanding our measures of success," she says.[55]

* In what ways might a business benefit from helping to sponsor a training program in the community?

In response to uncertainty caused by change (dynamism) in the environment, organizations tend to establish more flexible structures. In today's business world, the term *bureaucracy* generally has a bad connotation. Most of us recognize that bureaucratic organizations tend to be formal and very stable; frequently they are unable to adjust to change or exceptional circumstances that "don't fit the rules." And while bureaucratic organizations may be efficient and controlled if the environment is stable, they tend to be slow-moving and plodding when products, technologies, customers, or competitors are changing over time. In these cases, more *organic* structures give organizations the flexibility to adjust to change. We will discuss organic structures in more detail in Chapter 9, but we can simply say here that they are less formal than bureaucratic organizations—making decisions through interaction and mutual adjustment among individuals rather than from a set of predefined rules. Table 2.5 shows four different approaches that organizations can take in adapting to environmental uncertainty.

TABLE 2.5

Four Approaches for Managing Uncertainty

		Stable	Dynamic
Complex		Decentralized	Decentralized
		Bureaucratic (standardized skills)	Organic (mutual adjustment)
Simple		Centralized	Centralized
		Bureaucratic (standardized work processes)	Organic (direct supervision)

Adapting at the Boundaries   Because they are open systems, organizations are exposed to uncertainties from both their inputs and outputs. To help them compete, they can create buffers on both the input and output boundaries with the environment. **Buffering** creates supplies of excess resources to meet unpredictable needs. On the input side, organizations establish relationships with employment agencies to hire part-time and temporary help during rush periods when labor demand is difficult to predict. In the U.S. labor force, these workers, known as *contingent workers*, include 2.5 million on-call workers, 1.2 million temporary help agency workers, and more than 800,000 workers provided by contract firms, suggesting widespread use of this approach to buffering labor input uncertainties.[56] On the output side of the system, most organizations use some type of ending inventories that allow them to keep merchandise on hand in case a rush of customers decide to buy their products. Auto dealers are a common example of this use of buffers, but we can see similar use of buffer inventories in fast-food restaurants, bookstores, clothing stores, and even real estate agencies.[57]

In addition to buffering, organizations may try **smoothing,** or leveling normal fluctuations at the boundaries of the environment. For example, during winter months in the north, when automobile sales drop off, it is not uncommon for dealers to cut the price of their in-stock vehicles to increase demand. At the end of each clothing season, retailers discount their merchandise to clear it out to make room for incoming inventories. These are examples of smoothing environmental cycles to level off fluctuations in demand.

Adapting at the Core   While buffering and smoothing manage uncertainties at the boundaries of the organization, firms also can establish **flexible processes** that allow for adaptation in their technical core. For example, firms increasingly try to customize their goods and services to meet the varied and changing demands of customers. Even in manufacturing, where it is difficult to change basic core processes, firms are adopting techniques of mass customization that help them create flexible factories. Instead of mass-producing large quantities of a "one-size-fits-all" product, organizations can use mass customization to produce individually customized products at an equally low cost. Whereas Henry Ford used to claim that "you could have a Model T in any color you wanted, as long as it was black," auto companies now offer a wide array of colors and trim lines, with different options and accessories. The process of mass customization involves the use of a network of independent operating units in which each performs a specific process or task such as making a dashboard assembly on an automobile. When an order comes in, different modules join forces to deliver the product or service as specified by the customer.[58] We will discuss mass customization and flexible factories in more depth in Chapter 9.

Choosing a Response Approach

Three general considerations help guide management's response to the environment. First, organizations should attempt to *change appropriate elements of the environment.* Environmental responses are most useful when aimed at elements of the environment that (1) cause the company problems, (2) provide it with opportunities, and (3) allow the company to change successfully. Thus Nintendo recognized that its Wii game console would have difficulty competing on superior graphics, so it addressed underserved segments of the market, where customers and favorable publicity made the Wii a successful entrant.

Second, organizations should *choose responses that focus on pertinent elements of the environment.* If a company wants to better manage its competitive environment, competitive aggression and pacification are viable options. Political action influences the legal environment, and contracting helps manage customers and suppliers.

Third, companies should *choose responses that offer the most benefit at the lowest cost.* Return-on-investment calculations should incorporate short-term financial considerations as well as long-term impact. Strategic managers who consider these factors carefully will guide their organizations to competitive advantage more effectively.

---

buffering

Creating supplies of excess resources in case of unpredictable needs.

smoothing

Leveling normal fluctuations at the boundaries of the environment.

flexible processes

Methods for adapting the technical core to changes in the environment.

Bottom Line

The Internet lets customers quickly find products with the cost and quality features they want.
What might "flexible processes" mean for a fast-food restaurant? For an auto company?

The Internal Environment of Organizations: Culture and Climate

One of the most important factors that influence an organization's response to its external environment is its culture.

Of course an organization is more than a collection of responses to the external environment. The ways people in an organization behave, including the goals they set and the manner in which they treat their customers, are also shaped by forces within the organization. These forces, which include an organization's culture and its climate, are sets of conditions that influence the decisions and behavior of employees at all levels of the organization. On a day-to-day basis, an employee's experience of an organization's culture and climate may feel hard to sort out, much as your experience of a hot summer day may result from a combination of your region's climate and the day's weather, or your experience of happiness from a combination of your general personality and your mood in response to recent events.

Organization Culture

organization culture

The set of important assumptions about the organization and its goals and practices that members of the company share.

One of the most important factors that influence an organization's response to its external environment is its culture. **Organization culture** is the set of important assumptions about the organization and its goals and practices that members of the company share. It is a system of shared values about what is important and beliefs about how the world works. In this way, a company's culture provides a framework that organizes and directs people's behavior on the job.[59] The culture of an organization may be difficult for an observer to define easily, yet like an individual's personality, it can often

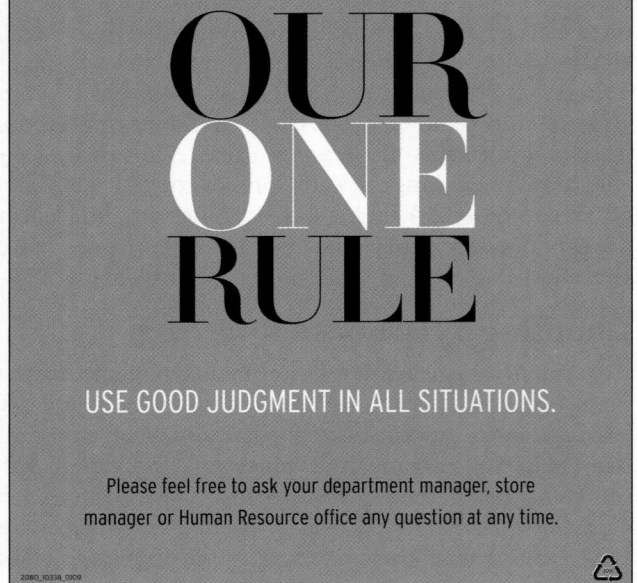

At Nordstrom, the fashion retailer, new employees are given a five-by-eight-inch card with one rule on it, along with a full handbook containing policies and legal regulations.

be sensed almost immediately. For example, the way people dress and behave, the way they interact with each other and with customers, and the qualities that are likely to be valued by their managers are usually quite different at a bank than they are at a rock music company, and different again at a law firm or an advertising agency.

Cultures can be strong or weak; strong cultures can have great influence on how people think and behave. A strong culture is one in which everyone understands and believes in the firm's goals, priorities, and practices. A strong culture can be a real advantage to the organization if the behaviors it encourages and facilitates are

In its relatively short life as a company, Google quickly has become a role model for its brainy culture of innovation. Software writers and engineers were attracted to Google not just for its famous perks such as free meals and laundry facilities but also for a climate in which they were encouraged to let their imaginations roam free, dreaming up ideas that could be crazy but just might be the next big thing on the Internet.

During a long-running business boom, that culture served Google well. The best engineers were thrilled to work for a company that let them spend one-fifth of their time on new projects of their own choosing. But when the economy slowed and the stock market nosedived, Google's managers had to cope with a new reality in which money was tight. Google could no longer afford its free-spending culture. Managers had to figure out how to maintain the best of the culture while innovating at a more prudent pace.

Google's modified culture now values setting priorities. New ideas are still welcome if they are focused on core businesses of search, advertising, and web-based software applications. Managers are reassigning employees away from teams working on unrelated projects and using them to staff teams working on profitable ideas in the core areas. Employees who have an idea that can improve the computer user's experience are asked to consider also what impact that idea might have on Google's bottom line. Similarly, hiring has slowed because managers must not only justify the talent of a candidate but also target hiring to particular business needs. The challenge will be to keep employees as excited about targeted innovation as they have been about freewheeling innovation.[60]

• What do you think could make employees feel excited about targeted innovation?

appropriate ones. For example, the Walt Disney Company's culture encourages extraordinary devotion to customer service; the culture at Apple Inc. encourages innovation. Employees in these companies don't need rule books to dictate how they act because these behaviors are conveyed as "the way we do things around here"; they are rooted in their companies' cultures.

In contrast, a strong culture that encourages inappropriate behaviors can severely hinder an organization's ability to deal effectively with its external environment—particularly if the environment is undergoing change, as is almost always the case today. A culture that was suitable and even advantageous in a prior era may become counterproductive in a new environment. For instance, a small start-up may have an informal culture that becomes less suitable when the company grows, faces more competition, and requires decision making by a wide range of specialized employees spread out over many locations.

Similarly, when a merger or acquisition brings together organizations with strong cultures, cultural differences can encourage behaviors that are harmful to the combined organization. After Sprint acquired Nextel, conflicts arose because the two wireless carriers had different cultures. Sprint moved cautiously, whereas Nextel's culture was more entrepreneurial. Such differences in style can be unsettling to employees on both sides and may help to explain why research has found much higher turnover rates among managers at companies that have been acquired.[61]

In contrast to strong cultures, weak cultures have the following characteristics: different people hold different values, there is confusion about corporate goals, and it is not clear from one day to the next what principles should guide decisions. Some managers may pay lip service to some aspects of the culture ("we would never cheat a customer") but behave very differently ("don't tell him about the flaw"). As you can guess, such a culture fosters confusion, conflict, and poor performance. Most managers would agree that they want to create a strong culture that encourages and supports goals and useful behaviors that will make the company more effective. In other words, they want to create a culture that is appropriately aligned with the organization's competitive environment.[62]

Diagnosing Culture   Let's say you want to understand a company's culture. Perhaps you are thinking about working there and you want a good "fit," or perhaps you are working there right now and want to deepen your understanding of the organization and determine whether its culture matches the challenges it faces. How would you go about making the diagnosis? A variety of things will give you useful clues about culture:

Corporate mission statements and official goals are a starting point because they will tell you the firm's desired public image. Most companies have a mission statement— even the CIA, as shown in Figure 2.5. Your school has one, and you can probably find it online. But are these statements a true expression of culture? A study of hospital employees and their managers found that managers rated their mission statement more positively than nonmanagers (even though employees had participated in developing it), and 3 out of 10 employees were not even aware that the hospital had a mission statement (even though the hospital had processes for communicating about it).[63] So, even after reading statements of mission and goals, you still need to figure out whether the statements truly reflect how the firm conducts business.

Business practices can be observed. How a company responds to problems, makes strategic decisions, and treats employees and customers tells a lot about what top management really values. The Tribune Company's repeated efforts to cut costs at the *Los Angeles Times* and consolidate its Washington bureau with that of the chain's other newspapers told the acquired company's employees about the parent company's priorities.

Symbols, rites, and ceremonies give further clues about culture. For instance, status symbols can give you a feel for how rigid the hierarchy is and for the nature of relationships between lower and higher levels. Who is hired and fired—and why—and the activities that are rewarded indicate the firm's real values.

The stories people tell carry a lot of information about the company's culture. Every company has its myths, legends, and true stories about important past decisions and actions that convey the company's main values. The stories often feature the

FIGURE 2.5
CIA Vision, Mission, and Values

Vision	We will provide knowledge and take action to ensure the national security of the United States and the preservation of American life and ideals.
Mission	We are the eyes and ears of the nation and at times its hidden hand. We accomplish this mission by:
	• Collecting intelligence that matters.
	• Providing relevant, timely, and objective all-source analysis.
	• Conducting covert action at the direction of the president to preempt threats or achieve United States policy objectives.
Values	In pursuit of our country's interests, we put Nation before Agency, Agency before unit, and all before self. What we do matters.
	• Our success depends on our ability to act with total discretion and an ability to protect sources and methods.
	• We provide objective, unbiased information and analysis.
	• Our mission requires complete personal integrity and personal courage, physical and intellectual.
	• We accomplish things others cannot, often at great risk. When the stakes are highest and the dangers greatest, we are there and there first.
	• We stand by one another and behind one another. Service, sacrifice, flexibility, teamwork, and quiet patriotism are our hallmarks.

SOURCE: CIA website at www.cia.gov/information/mission.html.

company's heroes: people once or still active who possessed the qualities and characteristics that the culture especially values and who act as models for others about how to behave.

A strong culture combines these measures in a consistent way. The Ritz-Carlton hotel chain gives each employee a laminated card listing its 12 service values. Each day it carries out a type of ceremony: a 15-minute meeting during which employees from every department resolve problems and discuss areas of potential improvement. At these meetings, the focus is on the day's "wow story," which details an extraordinary way that a Ritz-Carlton employee lived up to one of the service values. For example, a family arrived at the Bali Ritz-Carlton with special eggs and milk because of their son's allergies, but the food had spoiled. The manager and dining staff couldn't find replacements in town, so the executive chef called his mother-in-law in Singapore and asked her to buy the necessary products and fly with them to Bali.[64]

In general, cultures can be categorized according to whether they emphasize flexibility or control and whether their focus is internal or external to the organization. By juxtaposing these two dimensions, we can describe four types of organizational cultures, depicted in Figure 2.6:

> *Group culture.* A group culture is internally oriented and flexible. It tends to be based on the values and norms associated with affiliation. An organizational member's compliance with organizational directives flows from trust, tradition, and long-term commitment. It tends to emphasize member development and values

FIGURE 2.6
Competing Values Model of Culture

Flexible

Type: Group
Dominant attribute:
  Cohesiveness, participation, teamwork, sense of family
Leadership style: Mentor, facilitator, parent figure
Bonding: Loyalty, tradition, interpersonal cohesion
Strategic emphasis: Toward developing human resources, commitment, and morale

Type: Adhocracy
Dominant attribute:
  Entrepreneurship, creativity, adaptability, dynamism
Leadership style: Innovator, entrepreneur, risk taker
Bonding: Flexibility, risk, entrepreneur
Strategic emphasis: Toward innovation, growth, new resources

Internal maintenance   **External positioning**

Type: Hierarchy
Dominant attribute: Order, rules and regulations, uniformity, efficiency
Leadership style: Coordinator, organizer, administrator
Bonding: Rules, policies and procedures, clear expectations
Strategic emphasis: Toward stability, predictability, smooth

Type: Rational
Dominant attribute: Goal achievement, environment exchange, competitiveness
Leadership style: Production- and achievement-oriented, decisive
Bonding: Goal orientation, production, competition
Strategic emphasis: Toward competitive advantage and market superiority

Control–oriented

SOURCE: Kim S. Cameron and Robert E. Quinn, *Diagnosing and Changing Organizational Culture* 3rd Edition (San Francisco: Jossey Bass, 2011). Used by permission of the authors.

participation in decision making. The strategic orientation associated with this cultural type is one of implementation through consensus building. Leaders tend to act as mentors and facilitators.

Hierarchical culture. The hierarchical culture is internally oriented by more focus on control and stability. It has the values and norms associated with a bureaucracy. It values stability and assumes that individuals will comply with organizational mandates when roles are stated formally and enforced through rules and procedures.

Rational culture. The rational culture is externally oriented and focused on control. Its primary objectives are productivity, planning, and efficiency. Organizational members are motivated by the belief that performance that leads to the desired organizational objectives will be rewarded.

Adhocracy. The adhocracy is externally oriented and flexible. This culture type emphasizes change in which growth, resource acquisition, and innovation are stressed. Organizational members are motivated by the importance or ideological appeal of the task. Leaders tend to be entrepreneurial and risk takers. Other members tend to have these characteristics as well.[65]

This type of diagnosis is important when two companies are considering combining operations, as in a merger, acquisition, or joint venture, because as we noted, cultural differences can sink these arrangements. In some cases, organizations investigating this type of change can benefit from setting up a "clean team" of third-party experts who investigate the details of each company's culture. For example, they might conduct employee focus groups to learn about leadership styles, the way policies are established, and the kinds of behavior that are rewarded. They can look for systems that indicate employees are empowered to make independent decisions or that directions are handed down from above. They can note how management talks about the company's founder, customers, and employees. In this way, the clean team can identify for the organizations' leaders the types of issues they will have to resolve and the values they must choose among as they try to establish a combined culture.[66]

Managing Culture We mentioned earlier in this chapter that one important way organizations have of responding to the environment is to *adapt* to it by changing the organization itself. One of the most important tools managers have for implementing such a change lies in their management of their organization's culture. A culture that is inwardly instead of customer focused, for example, when the new competitive environment requires excellence in customer service, can delay or even defeat a manager's efforts to effect change. Simple directives alone are often ineffective; the underlying values of the organization also have to be shifted in the desired direction. Most companies today know that adopting a customer orientation, improving quality, and making other moves necessary to remain competitive are so essential that they require deep-rooted cultural changes. When that kind of change occurs, organization members may then begin to internalize the new values and display the appropriate behaviors on their own.

Top managers can take several approaches to managing culture. First, they should espouse lofty ideals and visions for the company that will inspire organization members. (We will discuss vision more fully in Chapter 4, on strategy, and in Chapter 12, on leadership.) That vision—whether it concerns quality, integrity, innovation, or whatever—should be articulated over and over until it becomes a tangible presence throughout the organization.

Second, executives must give constant attention to the mundane details of daily affairs such as communicating regularly, being visible and active throughout the company, and setting examples. Not only should the CEO talk about the vision, but he or she should also embody it day in and day out. This makes the CEO's pronouncements credible, creates a personal example others can emulate, and builds trust that the organization's progress toward the vision will continue over the long run.

Bottom Line

A culture aligned with its environment helps the organization succeed.

To be aligned with its environment, what values should an oil company have?

Important here are the moments of truth when hard choices must be made. Imagine top management trumpeting a culture that emphasizes quality and then discovering that a part used in a batch of assembled products is defective. Whether to replace the part at great expense in the interest of quality or to ship the defective part just to save time and money is a decision that will go a long way toward reinforcing or destroying a quality-oriented culture.

To reinforce the organization's culture, the CEO and other executives should routinely celebrate and reward those who exemplify the new values. Another key to managing culture involves hiring, socializing newcomers, and promoting employees on the basis of the new corporate values. In this way, the new culture will begin to permeate the organization. While this may seem a time-consuming approach to building a new culture, effective managers recognize that replacing a long-term culture of traditional values with one that embodies the competitive values needed in the future can take years. But as suggested by Apple's example in "Management Connection: Onward," the rewards of that effort will be an organization much more effective and responsive to its environmental challenges and opportunities.

Organizational Climate

In contrast to a culture's deeply held beliefs, values, and so on, an organization's climate can be measured more readily. **Organizational climate** consists of the patterns of attitudes and behavior that shape people's experience of an organization.[67] For example, an organization's climate might include clear performance standards, frequent conflict, great trust in leaders, and open communication between supervisors and their employees. Researchers have developed and tested surveys for measuring organizational climate in terms of factors such as morale, employees' relationships with managers and coworkers, handling of conflicts, openness and effectiveness of communication, methods for measuring and rewarding performance, and the clarity of one's role in the organization.

An organization's climate and its culture both shape the experience of working there and the organization's effectiveness. However, because organizational climate is easier to measure, managers often find that dimensions of organizational climate are more manageable. Later chapters explore a variety of management responsibilities that shape organizational climate, including ethical conduct (Chapter 5), creating a structure for the organization (Chapter 8), appraising and rewarding performance (Chapter 10), valuing diversity (Chapter 11), leading (Chapter 12), motivating employees (Chapter 13), fostering teamwork (Chapter 14), communicating (Chapter 15), and leading change (Chapter 18). An organization is most effective when it has a climate that motivates and enables workers to achieve the organization's strategy.

organizational climate

The patterns of attitudes and behavior that shape people's experience of an organization.

| Manager's Brief | Progress Report | **Onward** |

Management Connection

THE POWER OF APPLE'S CULTURE

As it prepares for the future, Apple's environment will surely continue to be fast-moving and turbulent. Many credit Apple's culture for the company's ability to prosper in that kind of situation.

Apple's former CEO, Steve Jobs, had described Apple's culture as "that of a start-up." A new company typically is run by the founder, who has a passion for some new idea or a desire to create something new (the organization) to

deliver a product or service better than others do. New companies tend to move fast, and successful new companies grow fast. So Jobs likely saw his company as one where people value speed, innovation, and passion for what Apple does—connecting ideas, people, and technology using elegantly designed products.

As noted at the beginning of this chapter, Apple ended the previous century with a doubtful future. The customers for its computers were a loyal but small sliver of the personal computer market. Investors were so doubtful about Apple's prospects that the company's stock was trading for a few dollars per share. At that point Steve Jobs had left the company to run Pixar, and the managers who remained seemed to be floundering.

Jobs returned to Apple and made some changes that refocused the company on its start-up culture. He discontinued projects that were unrelated to his vision, encouraged active debate about new ideas, and forced people in different functions to work together on strategy—for example, seeing the retail activities as related to product design activities. Together, these efforts enabled the company to drive innovation as it had when it was a start-up. Jobs was able to lead this effort because he was respected as the founder and as someone with visionary ideas plus the ability to sell them.

This history gives rise to an important question for the future: To what extent can Apple's management keep that culture strong without the presence of Apple's dynamic founding partner Steve Jobs? This is a poignant question because Jobs had been seriously ill, and recently passed away, a stark reminder that no executive can remain at the helm forever. In early 2011 he took a medical leave of absence. The reason was unspecified, but past medical problems for Jobs have been serious: pancreatic cancer and a liver transplant.

As he did during two previous leaves of absence, Jobs appointed Apple's chief operating officer, Tim Cook, to lead the company. Cook is widely respected, but not because he is a clone of Jobs. Quite the contrary— he is known for being calm, quiet, and serious-minded, managing processes more than pitching new products. Cook is, however, respected for his track record. While Jobs was often given credit for meeting previously unrealized consumer needs with product and design innovation, Cook is known for streamlining the way work gets done at Apple. Under Cook, Apple's production activities and supply chain reached new heights of efficiency. In addition, Cook shares Jobs's vision of Apple as a company that can make the world better.

Can Cook keep the magic of Apple alive? Some are worried: in the past, design decisions and product ideas have often sprung from Jobs's intuition, rather than some process, such as consumer research, that can be copied by others. Few companies as large as Apple have a chief executive so involved in detailed product decisions. Still, the question might be whether Cook really has to do it alone. Along with his expertise in operations, Apple has other strong leaders, including Paul Schiller in marketing and Jonathan Ive in product design—both of them respected in their own right. Some employees have even hinted to the press that they have implemented some of their own great ideas by working around Jobs rather than blindly following him.[68]

- Using the model of cultural types in Figure 2.6, which type of culture do you think Apple has? Why?
- How can Apple's managers reinforce Apple's culture since the death of Steve Jobs?

KEY TERMS

SUMMARY OF LEARNING OBJECTIVES

Now that you have studied Chapter 2, you should be able to:

LO 1 Describe how environmental forces influence organizations and how organizations can influence their environments.

Organizations are open systems that are affected by, and in turn affect, their external environments. Organizations receive financial, human, material, and information resources from the environment; transform those resources into finished goods and services; and then send those outputs back into the environment.

LO 2 Distinguish between the macroenvironment and the competitive environment.

The macroenvironment is composed of economic, legal and political, technological, demographic, social, and natural environment forces that influence strategic decisions. The competitive environment is composed of forces closer to the organization, such as current competitors, new entrants, substitute and complementary products, suppliers, and customers. Perhaps the simplest distinction between the macroenvironment and the competitive environment is in the amount of control a firm can exert on external forces. Macroenvironmental forces such as the economy and social trends are much less controllable than are forces in the competitive environment such as suppliers and customers.

LO 3 Explain why managers and organizations should attend to economic and social developments.

Developments outside the organization can have a profound effect on the way managers and their companies operate. For example, higher energy costs or increased spending on security may make it harder for managers to keep their prices low. The growing diversity of the labor force gives managers access to a much broader range of talent but also requires them to make sure different types of employees are treated equally. Effective managers stay aware of trends like these and respond to them effectively.

LO 4 Identify elements of the competitive environment.

Elements in the environment can range from favorable to unfavorable. To determine how favorable a competitive environment is, managers should consider the nature of the competitors, potential new entrants, threat of substitutes, opportunities from complements, and relationships with suppliers and customers. Analyzing how these forces influence the organization provides an indication of potential threats and opportunities. Effective management of the firm's supply chain is one way to achieve a competitive advantage. Attractive environments tend to be those with high industry growth, few competitors, products that

can be differentiated, few potential entrants, many barriers to entry, few substitutes, many suppliers (none with much power), and many customers. After identifying and analyzing competitive forces, managers must formulate a strategy that minimizes the power external forces have over the organization.

LO 5 Summarize how organizations respond to environmental uncertainty.

Responding effectively to the environment often requires devising proactive strategies to change the environment. Strategic maneuvering involves changing the boundaries of the competitive environment through domain selection, diversification, mergers, and the like. Independent strategies require not moving into a new environment but rather changing some aspect of the current environment through competitive aggression, public relations, legal action, and so on. Cooperative strategies, such as contracting, cooptation, and coalition building, involve the working together of two or more organizations. Organizations also may make themselves better able to handle environmental change by decentralizing authority, buffering or smoothing, and establishing flexible processes.

LO 6 Define elements of an organization's culture.

An organization's culture is its set of shared values and practices related to what is important and how the world works. The culture provides a framework that organizes and directs people's behavior at work. Elements of the culture may be expressed in corporate mission statements and official goals, assuming these reflect how the organization actually operates. Business practices are a basic measure of culture. Symbols, rites, ceremonies, and the stories people tell express and reinforce their cultural values.

LO 7 Discuss how an organization's culture and climate affect its response to its external environment.

A culture may be strong or weak and may be one of four types: group, hierarchical, rational, or adhocracy. These cultures shape whether they are flexible and whether the focus is on the external or internal environment. Managing and changing the culture to align it with the organization's environment will require strong, long-term commitment by the CEO and other managers. Managers should espouse high ideals and pay constant attention to conveying values by communicating and modeling them, making decisions that are consistent with cultural values, and rewarding those who demonstrate the organization's values. In addition, an organization's climate shapes the attitudes and behaviors of its people. When the climate is positive, employees want to and are able to carry out its strategy for responding to the external environment.

DISCUSSION QUESTIONS

1. This chapter's opening quote by Peter Drucker said, "The essence of a business is outside itself." What do you think this means? Do you agree?

2. What are the most important forces in the macroenvironment facing companies today?

3. What are the main differences between the macroenvironment and the competitive environment?

4. What kinds of changes do companies make in response to environmental uncertainty?

5. We outlined several proactive responses that organizations can make to the environment. What examples have you seen recently of an organization's responding effectively to its environment? Did the effectiveness of the response depend on whether the organization was facing a threat or an opportunity?

6. Select two organizations that you are interested in. Research information about the firms or talk with an employee, if possible. What types of cultures do they have? Write a paragraph that describes each culture.

7. When you visited colleges to select one to attend, were there cultural differences in the campuses that made a difference in your choice? Did these differences help you decide which college to attend?

EXPERIENTIAL EXERCISES

2.1   EXTERNAL ENVIRONMENT ANALYSIS

OBJECTIVE
To give you the experience of performing an analysis of a company's external environment

INSTRUCTIONS
Select a company you like in the music industry. Using online and/or library resources, including websites on the music industry and your company's website and annual report, fill out the following External Environment Worksheet for that company:

External Environment Worksheet

Laws and regulations
What are some key laws and regulations under which this company and the music industry must operate?

_____

_____

The economy
How does the state of the economy influence the sales of this company's products?

_____

_____

Technology
What new technologies strongly affect the company you have selected?

_____

_____

Demographics
What changes in the population might affect the company's customer base?

_____

_____

Social issues
What changes in society affect the market for your company's music products?

_____

_____

Suppliers
How does your company's relationship with suppliers affect its profitability?

_____

_____

Competitors

What companies compete with the firm you have selected? Do they compete on price, on quality, or on other factors?

_____

_____

New entrants

Are new competitors to the company likely? Possible?

_____

_____

Substitutes and complements

Is there a threat of substitutes for the music industry's existing products? Are there complementary products that suggest an opportunity for collaboration?

_____

_____

Customers

What characteristics of the company's customer base influence the company's competitiveness?

_____

_____

DISCUSSION QUESTIONS

1. What has the company done to adapt to its environment?

2. How does the company attempt to influence its environment?

2.2 CORPORATE CULTURE PREFERENCE SCALE

OBJECTIVE

This self-assessment is designed to help you to identify a corporate culture that fits most closely with your personal values and assumptions.

INSTRUCTIONS

Read each pair of the statements in the Corporate Culture Preference Scale and circle the statement that describes the organization you would prefer to work in. This exercise is completed alone so students assess themselves honestly without concerns of social comparison. However, class discussion will focus on the importance of matching job applicants to the organization's dominant values.

Corporate Culture Preference Scale

I would prefer to work in an organization:

1a.	Where employees work well together in teams.	**OR**	1b.	That produces highly respected products or services.
2a.	Where top management maintains a sense of order in the workplace.	**OR**	2b.	Where the organization listens to customers and responds quickly to their needs.
3a.	Where employees are treated fairly.	**OR**	3b.	Where employees continuously search for ways to work more efficiently.
4a.	Where employees adapt quickly to new work requirements.	**OR**	4b.	Where corporate leaders work hard to keep employees happy.
5a.	Where senior executives receive special benefits not available to other employees.	**OR**	5b.	Where employees are proud when the organization achieves its performance goals.
6a.	Where employees who perform the best get paid the most.	**OR**	6b.	Where senior executives are respected.
7a.	Where everyone gets his or her job done like clockwork.	**OR**	7b.	That is on top of new innovations in the industry.

8a. Where employees receive assistance to overcome any personal problems.	**OR**	8b. Where employees abide by company rules.
9a. That is always experimenting with new ideas in the marketplace.	**OR**	9b. That expects everyone to put in 110 percent for peak performance.
10a. That quickly benefits from market opportunities.	**OR**	10b. Where employees are always kept informed of what's happening in the organization.
11a. That can quickly respond to competitive threats.	**OR**	11b. Where most decisions are made by the top executives.
12a. Where management keeps everything under control.	**OR**	12b. Where employees care for each other.

SOURCE: Steven L. McShane and Mary Ann Von Glinow, *Organizational Behavior,* 3rd Ed., McGraw-Hill, 2005, p. 499. Copyright. © 2005 The McGraw-Hill Companies, Inc. Reprinted with permission..

Scoring Key for the Corporate Culture Preference Scale

Scoring instructions: In each space, write in a "1" if you circled the statement and "0" if you did not. Then add up the scores for each subscale.

Control culture   ___(2a)___ + ___(5a)___ + ___(6b)___ + ___(8b)___ + ___(11b)___ + ___(12a)___ = _____

Performance culture   ___(1b)___ + ___(3b)___ + ___(5b)___ + ___(6a)___ + ___(7a)___ + ___(9a)___ = _____

Relationship culture   ___(1a)___ + ___(3a)___ + ___(4b)___ + ___(8a)___ + ___(10b)___ + ___(12b)___ = _____

Responsive culture   ___(2b)___ + ___(4a)___ + ___(7b)___ + ___(9a)___ + ___(10a)___ + ___(11a)___ = _____

Interpreting your score: These corporate cultures may be found in many organizations, but they represent only four of many possible organizational cultures. Also, keep in mind none of these subscales is inherently good or bad. Each is effective in different situations. The four corporate cultures are defined here, along with the range of scores for high, medium, and low levels of each dimension based on a sample of MBA students:

Corporate Culture Dimension and Definition	Score Interpretation
Control culture: This culture values the role of senior executives to lead the organization. Its goal is to keep everyone aligned and under control.	High: 3 to 6 Medium: 1 to 2 Low: 0
Performance culture: This culture values individual and organizational performance and strives for effectiveness and efficiency.	High: 5 to 6 Medium: 3 to 4 Low: 0 to 2
Relationship culture: This culture values nurturing and well-being. It considers open communication, fairness, teamwork, and sharing a vital part of organizational life.	High: 6 Medium: 4 to 5 Low: 0 to 3
Responsive culture: This culture values its ability to keep in tune with the external environment, including being competitive and realizing new opportunities.	High: 6 Medium: 4 to 5 Low: 0 to 3

CONCLUDING CASE

WILD WATER GETS SOAKED

Jason and Marie Salerno, brother and sister, have been running their family business, a water park called Wild Water, since they both graduated from college. The Salernos operate the park, which is located near the New Jersey shore, with help from their parents. Marie's husband and Jason's wife are also involved in the business. Wild Water has now been in business for more than 40 years—it is a landmark to both locals and summer tourists. The water park features such attractions as a wave pool, several water slides, a flume ride, a kiddie pool, and a tube ride. A picnic park, shaded petting zoo, aquarium, snack bar, and restaurant called the Seafood Shack round out the park's offerings.

The park opens on Memorial Day and cuts back to weekends only after Labor Day, typically closing in the fall. With just a few months to accumulate revenue, the family and employees of the park work extremely hard. Marie oversees the financial aspects of the business, while Jason manages the staff. The staff—ride operators, ticket takers, lifeguards, and the like—are very loyal. Some have parents who once worked at the water park, and many have siblings who also work there. By its very nature, the organization culture of Wild Water is hierarchical—but most who work there, including Jason and Marie, would refer to their employees as part of the family. Jason holds weekly staff meetings, where employees are encouraged to voice their ideas about any aspect of the park's operations. Photos of workers and customers line the walls of Jason and Marie's tiny office, and stories about the park and its people abound, including sightings of celebrity visitors and near-disasters such as a close call with a hurricane.

While the organization culture has remained largely unchanged for the past four decades, the environment in which the park operates is changing. A new state safety law requires some expensive updating to meet the code. The Salernos recently learned that some of the smaller beach cottages in the area are going to be torn down to make way for a development of expensive condominiums. Vacationers who rent the condos are more likely to be looking for entertainment in the form of golf, deep-sea fishing trips, and exclusive restaurants. One of the major amusement park chains has been looking at a piece of real estate nearby. This chain is well known for its high-end rides, shows, and eating establishments. The Salernos point out that an entire family could enter Wild Water for the cost of one ticket at one of the chain's parks.

While the Salernos acknowledge that they have serious challenges ahead, they remain upbeat. Wild Water has been a favorite of families for more than two generations, and they expect it to continue to be a destination for local residents as well as vacationers. But they need to make some changes to keep those visitors—and the new condo owners—coming through the turnstile.

QUESTIONS

1. Imagine that you are a management consultant hired by the Salernos to help them navigate the choppy waters ahead. First describe the elements of the macroenvironment and competitive environment that affect Wild Water now. Then describe elements that you anticipate will affect the water park in the next few years.

2. Next describe the organization's culture. Discuss how the current culture affects the way it responds to the organization's external environment.

3. Now create a plan for Wild Water. In your plan, describe what changes the organization needs to make in its culture to meet upcoming challenges in the external environment. Then describe steps that Wild Water can take to compete successfully against the new amusement park. How can the Salernos keep their loyal customers happy while attracting new ones?

3 Managerial Decision Making

LEARNING OBJECTIVES

After studying Chapter 3, you will be able to:

LO 1 Describe the kinds of decisions you will face as a manager. p. 86

LO 2 Summarize the steps in making "rational" decisions. p. 89

LO 3 Recognize the pitfalls you should avoid when making decisions. p. 96

LO 4 Evaluate the pros and cons of using a group to make decisions. p. 100

LO 5 Identify procedures to use in leading a decision-making group. p. 102

LO 6 Explain how to encourage creative decisions. p. 103

LO 7 Discuss the processes by which decisions are made in organizations. p. 105

LO 8 Describe how to make decisions in a crisis. p. 107

| Manager's Brief | Progress Report | Onward |

Management Connection

PANDORA'S WESTERGREN DECIDES HOW TO MAKE MUSIC PERSONAL

Some 80 million music lovers use their smartphones, computers, or other connected devices to stream music from Pandora's Internet radio service. What is today a popular Internet company—Pandora Media, based in Oakland, California—began as a series of decisions by a musician, Tim Westergren.

Back in 2000, Westergren wondered how he could introduce more people to his band. He could see that a lot of people were creating good music but struggling to find an audience, and he identified an opportunity: a software tool that would recommend music based on what listeners already like. Westergren developed a system he branded the Music Genome Project, which categorizes any piece of music according to hundreds of possible attributes. He decided that the project would be based on human input from skilled musicians and musicologists who listen to every piece of music they enter into the system and identify its characteristics. Users of the application enter the name of a song or piece they already enjoy, and the software looks up that music's features and recommends other music with the same features. The application makes recommendations based on the music itself, rather than the popularity of a band or song, so an unknown artist's music can be recommended alongside Lady Gaga or Kanye West.

Building this software took several years. Then, under the name Savage Beast Technologies, Westergren's company tried to convince music sellers such as Amazon to use the software, but they weren't interested. However, Westergren's company did set up music recommendation kiosks in music stores and music sections of bookstores. Use of the kiosks gave Westergren a customer base to identify when he went looking for investors' dollars. That helped to keep the company going as Westergren maxed out a dozen credit cards and failed to earn a profit.

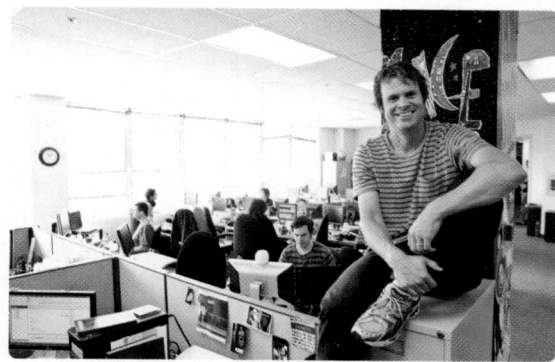

(In fact, for nearly two years of the company's early life, he asked his employees to work for free, in hopes of a better future.)

In 2004 Westergren made another major decision: Pandora would switch from being primarily a software company to becoming an online radio-type service using the software. The service launched the following year. Pandora's users can enjoy music they love by registering and then setting up stations by entering a "seed"—the name of a song, musician, or genre they want to hear on that station. The Music Genome Project software then plays that music plus other tunes with similar qualities, occasionally crossing strict genre categories or introducing little-known artists, thanks to the intuitive decisions by the company's music experts. Users provide feedback by giving particular songs thumbs-up or thumbs-down votes, and the additional data enable the software to further tailor its future offerings to each listener's tastes.

The switch from selling software to selling a way of listening to music opened up a need for some other decisions—most critically, decisions related to generating money. The company needed to cover the costs of buying music (CDs as well as downloads), hiring skilled musicologists to analyze it, and paying royalties for streaming it online. Westergren settled on an advertising model, where listeners could stream music for free, and advertisers would pay to post ads on the website. He believed the site would be a desirable advertising vehicle because companies could target their ads to people based not only on listening habits, but also on demographic information provided when Pandora users registered for the service. And in fact Nike, Procter & Gamble, and other companies signed on, providing ad revenue to keep the service going.

Pandora started out as an innovative idea of one person, Tim Westergren, now founder and chief strategy officer of Pandora Media. As you will see in later parts of this case, the company's growth and popularity introduced new challenges requiring a continuing series of difficult and creative decisions by its managers.[1]

Starting Pandora Media was possible for Tim Westergren because he interprets challenges as opportunities and devises innovative ways to meet those challenges. As you read this chapter, consider what makes managers' decisions difficult and what skills and resources can help managers overcome those difficulties to make the right choices.

The best managers make decisions constantly. Some are big, difficult, and strategic, like those Tim Westergren faced when starting up his new company. But managers also make countless smaller decisions that affect day-to-day operations and procedures. Karen Lancaster, chief information officer at Western Marine Insurance, makes many decisions about her firm's computer systems. For example, she had to decide on a plan to back up and store the company's data. If Western Marine's computers ever lost power or failed, the company needed to store data off-site. So Lancaster compared offers from three vendors and chose Courtesy Computers, which uses an Internet connection to back up the company's data automatically at the end of each day.

Backing up data is hardly glamorous, but a crisis can bring home the importance of these decisions, as Lancaster well knows. One day the phone company was digging outside Western Marine's building in Stockton, California, and cut a line, causing the company's Internet firewall to go down, which in turn allowed a hacker access to the company's server, clogging it with spam so that it crashed. Another time a power surge caused a loss of data in the computers. In both situations, the online backup solved the problem. Lancaster says, "When you're creating your disaster plan, you need to think about every scenario."[2]

The typical organization has the potential to more than double its decision effectiveness in terms of impact on financial results.[3] If you can't make decisions, you won't be an effective manager. This chapter discusses what kinds of decisions managers face, how they are made, and how they *should* be made.

Bottom Line

You'll be making decisions constantly. It may seem obvious, but it's worth stating: If you know how to make good decisions, you'll deliver good results.

What qualities or results of a management decision make it a "good" decision?

Characteristics of Managerial Decisions

 LO 1

Managers face problems and opportunities constantly. Some situations that require a decision are relatively simple; others seem overwhelming. Some demand immediate action, while others take months or even years to unfold.

Actually, managers often ignore challenges.[4] For several reasons, they avoid taking action.[5] First, managers can't be sure how much time, energy, or trouble lies ahead once they start working on a challenge. Second, getting involved is risky; tackling a problem but failing to solve it successfully can hurt a manager's track record. Third, because problems can be so perplexing, it is easier to procrastinate or to get busy with less demanding activities. For these reasons, managers may lack the insight, courage, or will to decide.

FIGURE 3.1

Characteristics of
Managerial Decisions

It is important to understand why decision making can be so challenging. Figure 3.1 illustrates several characteristics of managerial decisions that contribute to their difficulty and pressure. Most managerial decisions lack structure and entail risk, uncertainty, and conflict.

Lack of Structure

Lack of structure is the usual state of affairs in managerial decision making.[6] Although some decisions

> A moderate ego demonstrates wisdom.
> Lao-tzu

are routine and clear-cut, for most there is no automatic procedure to follow. Problems are novel and unstructured, leaving the decision maker uncertain about how to proceed.

An important distinction illustrating this point is between programmed and nonprogrammed decisions. **Programmed decisions** have been encountered and made before. They have objectively correct answers and can be solved by using simple rules, policies, or numerical computations. If you face a programmed decision, a clear procedure or structure exists for arriving at the right decision. For example, if you are a small business owner and must decide the amounts for your employees' paychecks, you can use a formula—and if the amounts are wrong, your employees will prove it to you. Table 3.1 gives some other examples.

If most important decisions were programmed, managerial life would be much easier. But managers typically face **nonprogrammed decisions:** new, novel, complex decisions having no certain outcomes. They have a variety of possible solutions, all of which have merits and drawbacks. The decision maker must create or impose a method for making the decision; there is no predetermined structure on which to rely. As Table 3.1 suggests, important, difficult decisions tend to be nonprogrammed, and they demand creative approaches.

Uncertainty and Risk

If you have all the information you need, and can predict precisely the consequences of your actions, you are operating under a condition of **certainty**.[7] Managers are expressing their preference for certainty when they are not satisfied hearing about what *might have* happened or *may* happen, and insist on hearing what *did* or *will* happen.[8] But perfect certainty is rare. For important, nonprogrammed managerial decisions, uncertainty is the rule.

Uncertainty means the manager has insufficient information to know the consequences of different actions. Decision makers may have strong opinions—they may

programmed decisions

Decisions encountered and made before, having objectively correct answers, and solvable by using simple rules, policies, or numerical computations.

nonprogrammed decisions

New, novel, complex decisions having no proven answers.

certainty

The state that exists when decision makers have accurate and comprehensive information.

uncertainty

The state that exists when decision makers have insufficient information.

TABLE 3.1
Comparison of Types
of Decisions

	Programmed Decisions	Nonprogrammed Decisions
Problem	Frequent, repetitive, routine. Much certainty regarding cause-and-effect relationships.	Novel, unstructured. Much uncertainty regarding cause-and-effect relationships.
Procedure	Dependence on policies, rules, and definite procedures.	Necessity for creativity, intuition, tolerance for ambiguity, creative problem solving.
Examples		
Business firm	Periodic reorders of inventory.	Diversification into new products and markets.
University	Necessary grade point average for good academic standing.	Construction of new classroom facilities.
Health care	Procedure for admitting patients.	Purchase of experimental equipment.
Government	Merit system for promotion of state employees.	Reorganization of state government agencies.

SOURCE: J. Gibson, J. Ivancevich, and J. Donnelly Jr., *Organizations: Behavior, Structure, Processes*, 10th ed. 2000. Copyright © 2000 by The McGraw-Hill Companies, Inc. Reprinted with permission.

feel sure of themselves—but they are still operating under conditions of uncertainty if they lack pertinent information and cannot estimate accurately the likelihood of different results of their actions. Businesspeople do not like uncertainty: it can hold them back from taking action. For example, uncertainty about the strength and timing of the economic recovery in 2010 and 2011 made businesses slow to start hiring.[9] But economies don't strengthen until consumer demand picks up, which doesn't happen until employment rises.

When you can estimate the likelihood of various consequences but still do not know with certainty what will happen, you are facing **risk**. Risk exists when the probability of an action being successful is less than 100 percent and losses may occur. If the decision is the wrong one, you may lose money, time, reputation, or other important assets.

Risk, like uncertainty, is a fact of life in managerial decision making. But this is not the same as *taking* a risk. Although it sometimes seems as though risk takers are admired and entrepreneurs and investors thrive on taking risks, the reality is that good decision makers prefer to *manage* risk. They accept the fact that decisions have consequences entailing risk, but they do everything they can to anticipate the risk, minimize it, and control it.

Consider the choices involved in preparing a restaurant menu. The Center for Science in the Public Interest recently criticized restaurant chains for selling entrées, appetizers, and desserts containing 1,400 calories or more (a typical American might eat 2,000 calories in an entire day). Making no changes could give those restaurants a reputation for contributing to obesity, but if a restaurant offers more healthful alternatives, will diners bite? The riskiest approach would be to change the entire menu. Instead restaurateurs including T.G.I. Friday's are more likely to lower uncertainty by retaining popular choices and adding some new selections. Some entrées are smaller versions of items already being offered, and others are new but similar to popular dishes.[10]

A T-shirt company called Threadless reduces uncertainty and manages risk by basing its whole marketing model on collaboration with customers. Professional and amateur graphic designers submit their ideas for T-shirt designs at the Threadless

risk

The state that exists when the probability of success is less than 100 percent and losses may occur.

website, where customers vote on the designs they like. From hundreds of submissions, the company selects four to six of the top vote getters each week and pays their designers $1,000. But it makes and sells them only after a minimum number of customers have already ordered the shirt design.[11]

Conflict

Important decisions are even more difficult because of the conflict managers face. **Conflict,** which exists when a manager must consider opposing pressures from different sources, occurs at two levels.

First, individual decision makers experience psychological conflict when several options are attractive, or when none of the options is attractive. For instance, a manager may have to decide whom to lay off when she doesn't want to lay off anyone. Or she may have three promising job applicants for one position—but choosing one means she has to reject the other two.

Second, conflict arises between people. A chief financial officer argues in favor of increasing long-term debt to finance an acquisition. The chief executive officer, however, prefers to minimize such debt and find the funds elsewhere. A marketing department wants more product lines to sell, and the engineers want higher-quality products. But the production people want to lower costs by having longer production runs of fewer products with no changes. Few decisions are without conflict.

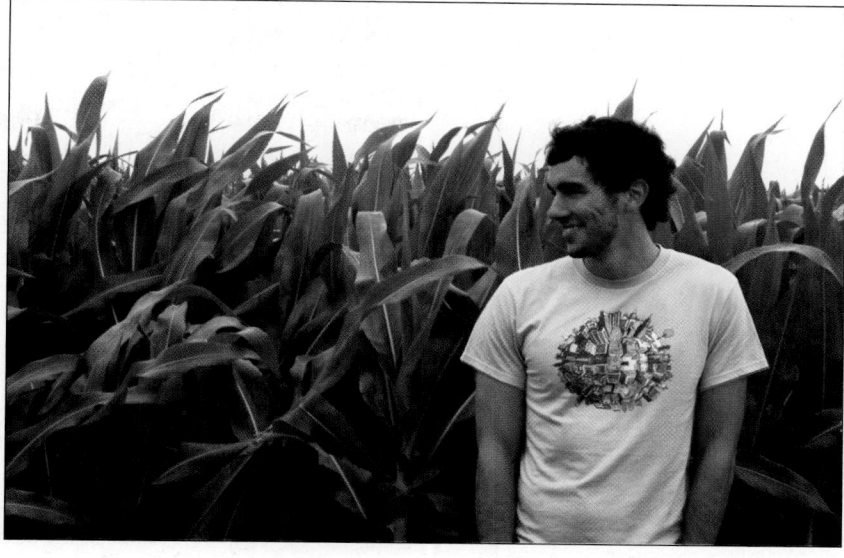

T-shirt designers have a chance to get their designs printed through the Threadless website, but only after enough customers have given them high ratings and ordered a shirt.

conflict

Opposing pressures from different sources, occurring on the level of psychological conflict or of conflict between individuals or groups.

The Stages of Decision Making

Faced with these challenges, how can you make good decisions? The ideal decision-making process includes six stages. As Figure 3.2 illustrates, decision makers should (1) identify and diagnose the problem, (2) generate alternative solutions, (3) evaluate alternatives, (4) make the choice, (5) implement the decision, and (6) evaluate the decision.

LO 2

Identifying and Diagnosing the Problem

The first stage in the decision-making process is to recognize that a problem exists and must be solved. Typically, a manager realizes some discrepancy between the current state (the way things are) and a desired state (the way things ought to be). Such discrepancies—say, in organizational or unit performance—may be detected by comparing current performance against (1) *past* performance, (2) the *current* performance of other organizations or units, or (3) *future* expected performance as determined by plans and forecasts.[12] Michael Ortner and Rakesh Chilakapati cofounded a company called Capterra, which created an online directory of companies that sell business software. Their problem was that they wanted to bring more traffic to their website; more listings would make the site more valuable to buyers, and more buyers would make the site more attractive to vendors.[13] We will refer to this example throughout this section.

FIGURE 3.2
The Stages of Decision Making

The "problem" may be an opportunity that needs to be exploited: a gap between what the organization is doing now and what it can do to create a more positive future. In that case, decisions involve choosing how to seize the opportunity. To recognize important opportunities as a manager, you will need to understand your company's macro- and competitive environments (described in Chapter 2).

Recognizing that a problem or opportunity exists is only the beginning of this stage. The decision maker must dig in deeper and attempt to *diagnose* the situation. For example, a sales manager knows that sales have dropped drastically. If he is leaving the company soon or believes the decreased sales volume is due to the economy (which he can't do anything about), he won't take action. But if he does try to solve the problem, he should not automatically reprimand his sales staff, add new people, or increase the advertising budget. He must analyze *why* sales are down and then develop a solution appropriate to his analysis. Asking why, of yourself and others, is essential to understanding the real problem. In the case of Capterra, the company had asked *why* traffic was low by conducting surveys of the directory's users. The results showed that buyers wanted to find reviews of the vendors—a feature that the directory was not offering. To Capterra's founders, it seemed plausible that the underlying problem was that their website lacked a key feature that would make it helpful.[14]

The following questions are useful to ask and answer in this stage:[15]

Is there a difference between what is actually happening and what should be happening?
How can you describe the deviation, as specifically as possible?
What is/are the cause(s) of the deviation?
What specific goals should be met?
Which of these goals are absolutely critical to the success of the decision?

Generating Alternative Solutions

The second stage of decision making links problem diagnosis to the development of alternative courses of action aimed at solving the problem. Managers generate at least some alternative solutions based on past experiences.[16]

Solutions range from ready made to custom made.[17] Decision makers who search for **ready-made solutions** use ideas they have tried before or follow the advice of others who have faced similar problems. **Custom-made solutions,** by contrast, must be designed for specific problems. This technique often combines ideas into new, creative solutions. For example, Yamaha Corporation drew on ideas from its customer community, which said that hobby guitarists were interested in an instrument they could play without a lot of practice. Designers at Yamaha created an idea for a guitar that could read electronically entered songs and display lights on the fingerboard showing users where to put their fingers. Customers provided ideas for modifications, and the back and forth eventually generated more than the minimum number of orders for the company to produce the innovative product.[18] Potentially, custom-made solutions can be devised for any challenge. Later in the chapter, we will discuss how to generate creative ideas.

ready-made solutions

Ideas that have been seen or tried before.

custom-made solutions

New, creative solutions designed specifically for the problem.

Often, many more alternatives are available than managers may realize. For example, what would you do if one of your competitors reduced prices? Managers sometimes assume that cutting prices in response to a competitor's price cuts is their only option, but it is not. Alternatives include emphasizing consumer risks to low-priced products, building awareness of your products' features and overall quality, and communicating your cost advantage to your competitors so they realize that they can't win a price war. If you do decide to cut your price as a last resort, do it fast—if you do it slowly, your competitors will gain sales in the meantime, which may embolden them to employ the same tactic again in the future.[19]

Returning to the example of Capterra, Michael Ortner, whose background was in sales, was eager to launch the product reviews, but his colleague Rakesh Chilakapati, the company's technology manager, wanted to proceed cautiously because of the time and expense required to add the feature, along with fear that some vendors would get bad reviews and leave the directory. So to generate alternatives, the two partners studied existing websites with product reviews (for example, Amazon, eBay, and Edmunds.com). They identified a variety of ways to offer some kind of reviewing feature. They could simply post testimonials from satisfied customers. They could allow or forbid anonymous comments. They could require reviewers to list both positive and negative points. The big question that remained was whether the features attractive to buyers would repel sellers.[20]

> Often, many more alternatives are available than managers may realize.

IN PRACTICE

Generating more alternatives could have prevented some problems for the managers of Chargify, an online service for small businesses to use in managing their billing activities. To stand out from its competition, Chargify distinguished itself based on price: businesses with up to 50 customers could use the service for free; larger customers could choose from packages priced at $49 to $2,500 per month. Chargify's founders, Siamak Taghaddos and David Hauser, assumed that after about three to six months with the service, the small, nonpaying customers would build their businesses and migrate to the fee-based service. Unfortunately, they were wrong; the pricing model actually attracted people who were content to run their businesses on a small scale, and fewer than 1 percent of Chargify's customers ever paid. The problem was how to bring in more paying customers.

Chargify's executives met and quickly agreed that the solution was to change the pricing structure. The free service seemed to be an obvious mistake, so they announced to customers that it would end in 45 days. Clients who had up to 500 customers would have to select a service priced at $49 to $99 per month, and the paid service would come with additional features to make it worthwhile. But clients howled at the unexpected change. Only when bad publicity sped around the Internet and Hauser began fielding complaints from angry customers did the executive team start coming up with alternatives: a low rate for existing customers, a reduced rate for the smallest customers, and a 12-month guaranteed rate for all customers. In the end, Chargify lost 35 customers, gained 225, and learned a valuable lesson about thinking carefully and generating more alternatives before making important decisions.[21]

- What was the problem with the executives' initial solution? What alternative solutions were available besides a choice between offering a free service and ending it?

Evaluating Alternatives

The third stage of decision making involves determining the value or adequacy of the alternatives that were generated. In other words, which solution will be the best?

Especially when decisions are important, alternatives should be evaluated with careful thought and logic. Fundamental to this process is to predict the consequences that will occur if the various options are put into effect. Managers should consider several types of consequences, including quantifiable measures of success, such as lower costs, higher sales, lower employee turnover, and higher profits. The evaluation of alternatives at Capterra weighed the expected impact of reviews on buyers against the expected impact on vendors. Posting testimonials instead of inviting reviews seemed likely to protect the goodwill of vendors, but this one-sided approach seemed unlikely to satisfy buyers, so the founders doubted it would have much impact on traffic to the website. Anonymous reviews seemed risky because vendors' competitors could abuse the system, so that alternative was easily abandoned. Requiring both pros and cons in the reviews would encourage balanced information about vendors, an apparent plus. One issue that remained was that any review feature opened the possibility that vendors would be upset by negative comments. Ortner investigated further by sending a survey to the site's vendors, and he learned that many, in fact, did worry about that risk.[22]

Environmental changes require companies to think through new alternatives and their consequences. When the recent downturn in the U.S. economy required cutbacks, organizations as diverse as the State of California, Gulfstream Aerospace, and Gannett evaluated the alternatives of layoffs (permanent job cuts) versus furloughs (requiring employees to take some unpaid time off until demand picks up again). While layoffs save more money per employee because the company doesn't have to continue paying for benefits, furloughs attempt to maintain relationships with talented employees, who are more likely than laid-off workers to return when the company needs them again. Furloughs may seem kinder to employees, who can hope to return to work eventually, but workers may not be eligible for unemployment compensation during the furlough period.[23]

To evaluate alternatives, refer to your original goals.

To evaluate alternatives, refer to your original goals, defined in the first stage. Which goals does each alternative meet and fail to meet? Which alternatives are most acceptable to you and to other important stakeholders? If several alternatives may solve the problem, which can be implemented at the lowest cost or greatest profit? If no alternative achieves all your goals, perhaps you can combine two or more of the best ones. Several additional questions help:[24]

Is our information about alternatives complete and current? If not, can we get more and better information?
Does the alternative meet our primary objectives?
What problems could we have if we implement the alternative?

As you read the "Management Connection: Progress Report" feature, consider how well Pandora's managers seem to have evaluated the alternatives facing them.

Of course results cannot be forecast with perfect accuracy. But sometimes decision makers can build in safeguards against an uncertain future by considering the potential consequences of several different scenarios. Then they generate **contingency plans**—alternative courses of action that can be implemented depending on how the future unfolds.

contingency plans
Alternative courses of action that can be implemented based on how the future unfolds.

For example, during an economic crisis when it is unclear when a recovery might begin and how strong it will be or what shape it will take, the range of potential outcomes is very large, and many companies will not survive. Firms could consider at least four scenarios:[25]

A scenario may use numbers that sound reasonable, but you should look at the data in different ways to check your assumptions. As Dean Kamen's company developed the Segway scooter, Kamen decided that each year Segway could capture 0.1 percent of the world's population. That percentage might sound conservative, but consider that 0.1 percent of 6 billion people is 6 million Segways a year! Kamen decided to build a factory that could produce 40,000 units a month; five years later, sales had reached fewer than 25,000.[26]

Manager's Brief   **Progress Report**   Onward

Management Connection

FINDING INCOME STREAMS FOR PANDORA

As Pandora's music service has grown to 80 million registered users and a database of over 800,000 pieces of music, a constant challenge has been how to generate sufficient revenue to turn a profit. Because the service launched when the whole concept of Internet radio was new, the company's management had no clear models to imitate. Therefore, decisions about revenue generation were unprogrammed decisions with tremendous uncertainty and risk.

Pandora's managers have by and large stuck to Tim Westergren's original model of a free, advertising-supported medium. Most of their revenue-generating decisions have focused on identifying and pursuing advertisers and sponsors for various promotions.

Early on, the obvious alternative was to sell ads on computer screens. Pandora partnered with Google's DoubleClick and offered advertisers the opportunity to target messages based on users' age, sex, zip code, and music preferences. John Trimble, the company's chief revenue officer with a background in media ad sales, developed a program that matches potential advertisers' brands with artists who appeal to the brands' target markets. Because ads on Pandora are so well targeted, the company can charge a premium.

But the promotional game suddenly changed when smartphones, especially the iPhone, became popular around 2008. A smartphone user not only can launch Pandora's service from the phone, but also can plug it into a home or car stereo as an input device. As membership numbers soared and Pandora's app became one of the most popular for the iPhone, Pandora transformed from a computer application into a new, personalized version of a radio, available on the go. Managers quickly realized they were facing a completely new situation, with its own set of opportunities for a larger audience and new kinds of sponsorship. They just had to figure out what those opportunities were.

Pandora's managers began ramping up their efforts to partner with anyone who could provide an easy, enjoyable way to listen to music. Pandora signed deals with car and car stereo makers to put Pandora-enabled stereos in their cars so users can operate Pandora with dashboard controls, rather than fiddling with their phones while driving. Westergren notes that half of all radio listening occurs while people are in their cars so he sees these capabilities as enabling Pandora to earn money as traditional stations do: by selling targeted advertising. But because Pandora is also available over more kinds of media, including computers and Blu-Ray players on television, the company can sell video as well as audio ads. Trimble, the chief revenue officer, is researching solutions to a new challenge from this expansion: figuring out how to target ads played in cars or on TV rather than on computers.

Pandora also built on its origins as a musician-friendly service. Matt Ostrower, senior manager of artist development, works with artists to craft deals in which they provide exclusive, sponsored content to build their relationships with (and sell music to) their fan base. For example, in the week before the Dave Matthews Band released its album *Big Whiskey and the Groogrux King,* Pandora set up a special page to stream the album (sponsored by an advertiser), and it alerted all users who had seeded or given a thumbs-up to one of the band's songs that the music was available. This kind of win–win deal generates ad revenue for Pandora as well as sales and publicity for the band. In addition, musicians themselves can run advertisements with Pandora, targeting only people who have already indicated that they enjoy the band's music. Aimee Mann filled a Los Angeles venue just by having Pandora send an e-mail to people who had liked one of her songs.

Finally, Pandora has even modified its original commitment to the free radio model, offering users an alternative. Listeners who would prefer to skip the advertising have an option to pay $36 per year for ad-free streaming of their music. So far, however, most are opting for the free version.[25]

- What problem did Pandora's managers identify? How well did they diagnose it?
- What alternatives did they identify? Do you think they missed any alternatives?

1. A most optimistic scenario in which trade and capital flows resume, further recession is averted, globalization stays on course, and developed and emerging economies continue to integrate as confidence rebounds quickly.
2. A battered-but-resilient scenario in which the recession continues for a long period, recovery is slow, confidence is shaken but does rebound, and globalization slowly gets back on course.

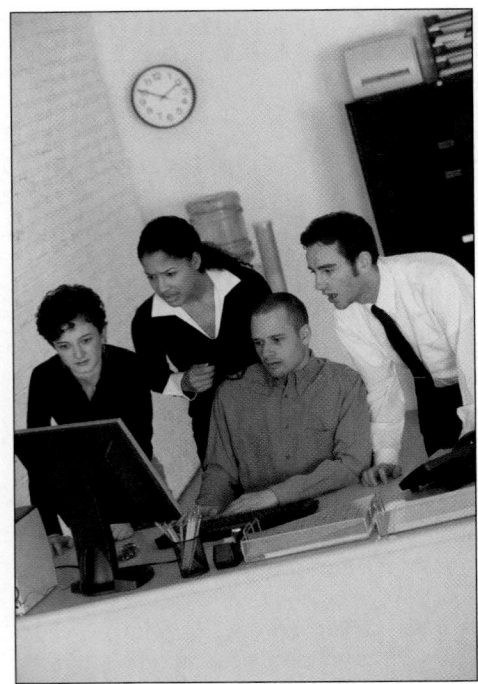

Some decisions do not work out. Although it can be surprising and frustrating, you will need to create alternative courses of action, or contingency plans, that will allow you to achieve your desired goals.

3. Stalled globalization, in which the global recession is significant, the intensity varies greatly from nation to nation (for example, with China and the United States proving resilient), but the integration of the world's economies stalls and growth is slow.
4. A long freeze, in which the recession lasts more than five years, economies everywhere stagnate, and globalization goes into reverse.

Some scenarios will seem more likely than others, and some may seem highly improbable. Ultimately one of the scenarios will prove to be more accurate than the others.

The process of considering multiple scenarios raises important "what if?" questions for decision makers and highlights the need for preparedness and contingency plans.

As you read this, what economic scenario is unfolding? What are the important current events and trends? What scenarios could evolve six or eight years from now? How will *you* prepare?

Making the Choice

Once you have considered the possible consequences of your options, it is time to make your decision. Some managers are more comfortable with the analysis stage. Especially with all the advanced technology that is available, quantitatively inclined people can easily tweak the assumptions behind every scenario in countless ways. But the temptation can lead to "paralysis by analysis"—that is, indecisiveness caused by too much analysis rather than the assertive decision making that can help an organization seize new opportunities or thwart challenges. This kind of indecisiveness became a risk at Capterra because Ortner and Chilakapati had conflicting worries. Ortner continued to see the lack of reviews as a missed opportunity, while Chilakapati remained focused on the risks of adding this feature. Ortner further researched the situation by calling vendors who had expressed concerns about reviews; he became convinced that they, too, were simply failing to see the opportunities of this additional feature and would come around when experience showed them the value of reviews. Finally, after three months of debate, Ortner was enjoying his regular five-mile run when he concluded that the analysis had to end, and a decision must be made. As president, he made the final call, respecting Chilakapati's concerns but announcing that it was time to try the reviews.[27]

As you make your decision, important concepts include maximizing, satisficing, and optimizing.[28]

maximizing

A decision realizing the best possible outcome.

Maximizing is achieving the best possible outcome. The maximizing decision realizes the greatest positive consequences and the fewest negative consequences. In other words, maximizing results in the greatest benefit at the lowest cost, with the largest expected total return. Maximizing requires searching thoroughly for a complete range of alternatives, carefully assessing each alternative, comparing one to another, and then choosing or creating the very best.

satisficing

Choosing an option that is acceptable, although not necessarily the best or perfect.

Satisficing is choosing the first option that is minimally acceptable or adequate. When you satisfice, you compare your choice against your goal, not against other options. Satisficing means that a search for alternatives stops after you find one that is okay. Commonly, people do not expend the time or energy to gather more information. Instead they make the expedient decision based on readily available information.

Let's say you are purchasing new equipment, and your goal is to avoid spending too much money. You would be maximizing if you checked out all your options and their prices, and then bought the cheapest one that met your performance requirements.

But you would be satisficing if you bought the first adequate option that was within your budget and failed to look for less expensive options.

Satisficing is sometimes a result of laziness; other times, there is no other known option because time is short, information is unavailable, or other constraints make maximizing impossible. When the consequences are not huge, satisficing can even be the ideal approach. But in other situations, when managers satisfice, they fail to consider important options.

Optimizing means that you achieve the best possible balance among several goals. Perhaps, in purchasing equipment, you are interested in quality and durability as well as price. So instead of buying the cheapest piece of equipment that works, you buy the one with the best combination of attributes, even though there may be options that are better on the price criterion and others that are better on the quality and durability criteria. The same idea applies to achieving business goals: one marketing strategy could maximize sales, while a different strategy might maximize profit. An optimizing strategy is the one that achieves the best balance among multiple goals.

optimizing

Achieving the best possible balance among several goals.

Implementing the Decision

The decision-making process does not end once a choice is made. The chosen alternative must be implemented. Sometimes the people involved in making the choice must put it into effect. At other times, they delegate the responsibility for implementation to others, such as when a top management team changes a policy or operating procedure and has operational managers carry out the change. At Capterra, implementation of the decision to add customer reviews included 10 months of software development, followed by invitations to vendors to encourage their customers to submit reviews. Notice that the implementation took into account the concerns about negative reviews by giving the vendors some control over who submitted the initial reviews.[29]

Unfortunately, sometimes people make decisions but don't take action. Implementing may fail to occur when talking a lot is mistaken for doing a lot; if people just assume that a decision will "happen"; when people forget that merely making a decision changes nothing; when meetings, plans, and reports are seen as "actions," even if they have no effect on what people actually do; and if managers don't check to ensure that what was decided was actually done.[30]

Managers should plan implementation carefully. Adequate planning requires several steps:[31]

1. Determine how things will look when the decision is fully operational.
2. Chronologically order, perhaps with a flow diagram, the steps necessary to achieve a fully operational decision.
3. List the resources and activities required to implement each step.
4. Estimate the time needed for each step.
5. Assign responsibility for each step to specific individuals.

Decision makers should assume that things will *not* go smoothly during implementation. It is useful to take a little extra time to *identify potential problems* and *identify potential opportunities* associated with implementation. Then you can take actions to prevent problems and also be ready to seize on unexpected opportunities. The following questions are useful:

What problems could this action cause?
What can we do to prevent the problems?
What unintended benefits or opportunities could arise?
How can we make sure they happen?
How can we be ready to act when the opportunities come?

Bottom Line
It's easy to become so focused on maximizing one goal that you lose sight of other important goals. You're optimizing if you make sure that no important result suffers too much unnecessarily.
What could be the negative consequences of making decisions that maximize only innovation?

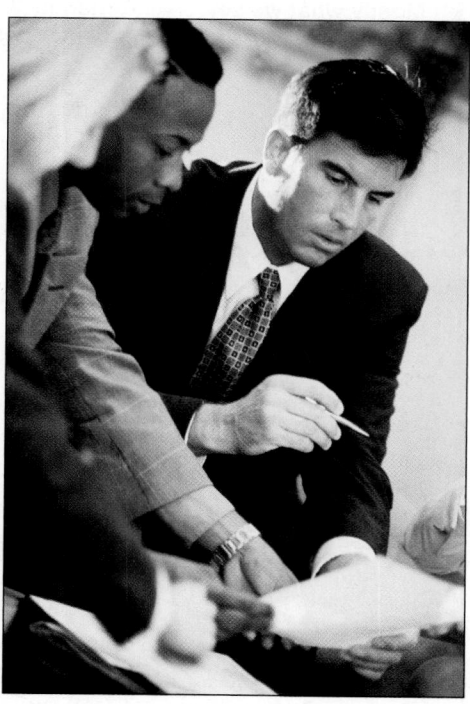

Evaluating decisions after they have been implemented is an important final step to determine if they were successful, need to be altered, or have failed.

Decision makers should assume that things will *not* go smoothly during implementation.

Many of the chapters in this book are concerned with implementation issues: how to implement strategy, allocate resources, organize for results, lead and motivate people, manage change, and so on. View the chapters from that perspective, and learn as much as you can about how to implement properly.

Evaluating the Decision

The final stage in the decision-making process is evaluating the decision. It involves collecting information on how well the decision is working. Quantifiable goals—a 20 percent increase in sales, a 95 percent reduction in accidents, 100 percent on-time deliveries—can be set before the solution to the problem is implemented. Then objective data can be gathered to accurately determine its success or failure.

In a global survey of executives, a majority said the results of their organizations' decisions about strategy were inconsistent at best. Many of them blamed the decision-making process, saying assumptions too often went unchallenged, decisions got bogged down in company politics, too little time was devoted to the decision, and the investigation of alternatives was too narrowly focused.[32]

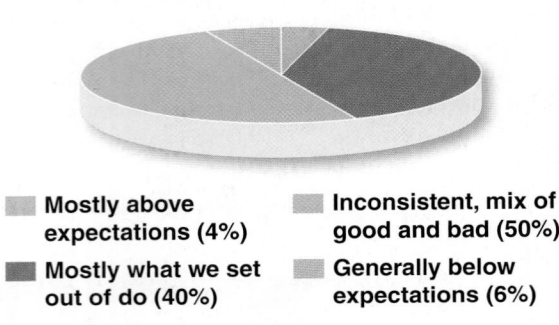

Results of managers' strategic decisions

■ **Mostly above expectations (4%)**
■ **Mostly what we set out of do (40%)**
■ **Inconsistent, mix of good and bad (50%)**
■ **Generally below expectations (6%)**

Decision evaluation is useful whether the conclusion is positive or negative. Feedback that suggests the decision is working implies that the decision should be continued and perhaps applied elsewhere in the organization. Negative feedback means that either (1) implementation will require more time, resources, effort, or thought or (2) the decision was a bad one. The feedback for Capterra was positive. In the first year of offering customer reviews, the site gathered about 500 reviews. Another year after that, the site had 2,000 reviews, with about 40 percent of them unsolicited. Most of the reviews are positive. Even though some are less than glowing, traffic to the site has grown so much that vendors see the review feature as a benefit because they are getting more business. Revenues to Capterra have jumped almost 30 percent, and Ortner and Chilakapati are finally in agreement: customer reviews were a great idea.[33]

If the decision appears inappropriate, it's back to the drawing board. Then the process cycles back to the first stage: (re)defining the problem. The decision-making process begins anew, preferably with more information, new suggestions, and an approach that attempts to eliminate the mistakes made the first time around.

The Best Decision

LO 3

How can managers tell whether they have made the best decision? While nothing can guarantee a "best" decision, managers should at least be confident that they followed proper *procedures* that will yield the best possible decision under the circumstances. This means that the decision makers were appropriately vigilant in making the decision. **Vigilance** occurs when the decision makers carefully and conscientiously execute all six stages of decision making, including making provisions for implementation and evaluation.[34]

Author and CEO Luda Kopeikina says managers can learn to make better decisions by improving the processes they use. First, your decisions will get better if you learn to manage stress, get enough rest, and put distractions aside when you need to

vigilance

A process in which a decision maker carefully executes all stages of decision making.

make important decisions. Next, you should define the consequences you are trying to achieve and make sure the data you gather match the goals for your decision. Along with this comes the vision of how your decision can play out when you implement it. Finally, you need to develop the strength of character to take responsibility for the consequences of your decision. Encourage debate so you can see all the alternatives; but if you are the decision maker, you must eventually end the debate, exercise courage, and act on your responsibility as decision maker.[35]

Even if managers reflect on their decision-making activities and conclude that they executed each step conscientiously, they still will not know whether the decision will work; after all, nothing guarantees a good outcome. But they *will* know that they did their best to make the best possible decision.

Barriers to Effective Decision Making

Vigilance and full execution of the six-stage decision-making process are the exception rather than the rule. But when managers use such rational processes, better decisions result.[36] Managers who make sure they engage in these processes are more effective.

Why don't people automatically invoke such rational processes? It is easy to neglect or improperly execute these processes. The problem may be improperly defined, or goals misidentified. Not enough solutions may be generated, or they may be evaluated incompletely. A satisficing rather than maximizing choice may be made. Implementation may be poorly planned or executed, or monitoring may be inadequate or nonexistent. And decisions are influenced by subjective psychological biases, time pressures, and social realities.

> It is easy to neglect or improperly execute these processes.

Psychological Biases

Decision makers are far from objective in the way they gather, evaluate, and apply information in making their choices. People have biases that interfere with objective rationality. The examples that follow represent only a few of the many documented subjective biases.[37]

The **illusion of control** is a belief that one can influence events even when one has no control over what will happen. Gambling is one example: some people believe they

illusion of control

People's belief that they can influence events even when they have no control over what will happen.

> Some people believe they have the skill to beat the odds, even though most of the time they cannot.

have the skill to beat the odds, even though most of the time they cannot. In business, such overconfidence can lead to failure because decision makers ignore risks and fail to objectively evaluate the odds of success.

In addition, managers may believe they can do no wrong, or hold a general optimism about the future that can lead them to believe they are immune to risk and failure.[38] In addition, managers may overrate the value of their experience. They may believe that a previous project met its goals because of their decisions, so they can succeed by doing everything the same way on the next project. Rohit Girdhar admits that he held this type of bias until he tried a computer simulation that he assumed would confirm his skills as an experienced manager of software programmers. In the simulation, the workload increased and he hired more workers, as he had in his prior jobs. But the added workers weren't as productive as his experience told him they would be, and his project fell behind. Girdhar learned to question his assumptions before making decisions.[39]

framing effects

A decision bias influenced by the way in which a problem or decision alternative is phrased or presented.

discounting the future

A bias weighting short-term costs and benefits more heavily than longer-term costs and benefits.

Bottom Line

As in this example, when you want to pursue sustainability, think in terms of the *long-term consequences* of your decisions.

Framing effects refer to how problems or decision alternatives are phrased or presented and how these subjective influences can override objective facts. In one example, managers indicated a desire to invest more money in a course of action that was reported to have a 70 percent chance of profit than in one said to have a 30 percent chance of loss.[40] The choices were equivalent in their chances of success; it was the way the options were framed that determined the managers' choices.

Managers may be quick to frame a problem as being similar to problems they have already handled, so they don't search for new alternatives. For example, when CEO Richard Fuld tackled financial problems at Lehman Brothers as the mortgage market tumbled, he assumed that the situation was much the same as when he had handled a previous financial crisis in the late 1990s. Unfortunately for Lehman Brothers, the recent crisis was far worse. In late 2008 the firm declared bankruptcy—the largest in U.S. history—helping to send global financial markets into a tailspin. Similarly, when the head of the operations center of the Department of Homeland Security prepared for Hurricane Katrina as it headed for New Orleans, he assumed the storm would be like Florida hurricanes he had prepared for in the past. As information came in, he focused on the data that fit his expectations, but Katrina turned out to be far more devastating.[41]

Often decision makers **discount the future.** That is, in their evaluation of alternatives, they weigh short-term costs and benefits more heavily than longer-term costs and benefits. Consider your own decision about whether to go for a dental checkup. The choice to go poses short-term financial costs, anxiety, and perhaps physical pain. The choice not to go will inflict even greater costs and more severe pain if dental problems worsen. How do you choose? Many people decide to avoid the short-term costs by not going for regular checkups, but end up facing greater pain in the long run.

The same bias applies to students who don't study, weight watchers who sneak dessert or skip an exercise routine, and people who take the afternoon off to play golf when they really need to work. It can also affect managers who hesitate to invest funds in research and development programs that may not pay off until far into the future. In all these cases, the avoidance of short-term costs or the seeking of short-term rewards results in negative long-term consequences.

Asian managers tend to think with a longer-term outlook than do American managers, and many believe that this provides competitive advantage for long-term success.[42] Western myopia is driven in part by Wall Street's focus on quarterly earnings, causing managers to make decisions based primarily on short-run considerations and to neglect long-term problems and opportunities.

In contrast, when U.S. companies sacrifice present value to invest for the future—such as when Weyerhaeuser incurs enormous costs for its reforestation efforts that won't lead to harvest until 60 years in the future—it seems the exception rather than the rule. Discounting the future partly explains governmental budget deficits, environmental destruction, and decaying urban infrastructure.[43]

Time Pressures

In today's rapidly changing business environment, the premium is on acting quickly and keeping pace. The most conscientiously made business decisions can become irrelevant and even disastrous if managers take too long to make them.

How can managers make decisions quickly? Some natural tendencies, at least for North Americans, might be to skimp on analysis (not be too vigilant), suppress conflict, and make decisions on one's own without consulting other managers.[44] These strategies may speed up decision making, but they reduce decision *quality*.

Delaying dental checkups can have a negative impact on the future. It may save money today but may lead to larger costs later.

Carl Camden, CEO of Kelly Services, believed that rapid-fire decisions were the sign of a dynamic executive until he saw how this approach could hurt decision quality. In light of some early mistakes, Camden now believes the habit of fast decisions is related to the "trap of being all-knowing."[45]

In fact, the "speed trap" can be as dangerous as moving too slowly.[46] In an Internet start-up that went bankrupt, fast decisions initially helped the firm achieve its growth objectives. Early on, the founders did everything they could to create a sense of urgency: they planned a meeting to "light a fire under the company," calling it a "state-of-emergency address" with the purpose of creating "the idea of panic with an emerging deadline." Speed became more important than content. They failed to consider multiple alternatives, used little information, didn't fully acknowledge competing views, and didn't consult outside advisers. They never considered slowing down to be an option. This speed trap syndrome is a potential pathology for organizations under pressure to make fast decisions.

Timing is essential, and firms must be able to identify critical issues at the earliest possible opportunity.[47] Can managers under time pressure make decisions that are timely and of high quality? A study of effective decision-making processes in microcomputer firms—a high-tech, fast-paced industry—revealed the tactics that such companies use.[48] First, instead of relying on old data, long-range planning, and futuristic forecasts, they focus on *real-time information:* current information obtained with little or no time delay. For example, they constantly monitor daily operating measures like work in process rather than checking periodically the traditional accounting-based indicators such as profitability.

Second, they *involve people more effectively and efficiently* in the decision-making process. They rely heavily on trusted experts, and this yields both good advice and the

> The "speed trap" can be as dangerous as moving too slowly.

Bottom Line

You'll feel pressure to make quick decisions, but then it becomes easier to make mistakes. Fortunately, you can be vigilant while moving quickly, and you can avoid the "speed trap."

When you are under time pressure, what can you do to avoid mistakes?

IN PRACTICE

In April 2010 the explosion of leaking gas at BP's Deepwater Horizon oil rig caused 11 deaths and the worst-ever oil spill off the shores of the United States. Even before the oil leak was contained, questions were emerging about what kinds of decisions and actions led to this catastrophe. The answers have been complex and not always consistent. However, they illustrate significant barriers to effective decision making.

Initial investigations and a later report by BP suggest that the disaster arose from a unique series of poor decisions. On the final day of the rig's operation, employees were feeling intense time and cost pressure. The well had posed a series of problems that were driving the drilling project behind schedule and over budget. However, the well was finally drilled and lined with cement to prevent gas from escaping and causing an explosion, so it was ready for testing. On the day of the test, BP engineers decided to modify the typical testing procedures. Crew members who were to implement the procedure weren't clear about the rationale, but they went ahead. The test results were mixed, so workers consulted managers on the rig. Those managers divided their time between trying to make sense of the results and giving a tour to a delegation of managers from the rig's owner, Transocean. They decided the well was OK. Transocean workers who were monitoring the well then missed further indications of trouble. Gas escaped from the well, and attempts to trigger a blowout preventer failed.

A report by the presidential commission charged with investigating the spill found that all the companies involved in the project failed to evaluate risks and communicate problems adequately. The commission's report implied that the disaster was the result of a flawed system, not just a unique set of decisions. In fact, the trend toward more deepwater drilling has been making drilling operations more complex, and the rate of drilling spills has been rising in recent years.[49]

- What barriers to effective decision making can you identify in this situation?

confidence to act quickly despite uncertainty. They also take a *realistic view of conflict:* they value differing opinions, but they know that if disagreements are not resolved, the top executive must make the final choice in the end. Slow-moving firms, in contrast, are stymied by conflict. Like the fast-moving firms, they seek consensus; but when disagreements persist, they fail to come to a decision.

Social Realities

Many decisions are made by a group rather than by an individual manager. In slow-moving firms, interpersonal factors decrease decision-making effectiveness. Even the manager acting alone is accountable to the boss and to others and must consider the preferences and reactions of many people. Important managerial decisions are marked by conflict among interested parties. Therefore, many decisions are the result of intensive social interactions, bargaining, and politicking.

> Many decisions are the result of intensive social interactions, bargaining, and politicking.

The remainder of this chapter focuses on the social context of decisions, including decision making in groups and the realities of decision making in organizations.

Decision Making in Groups

Sometimes a manager finds it necessary to convene a group of people for the purpose of making an important decision. Some advise that in today's complex business environment, significant problems should *always* be tackled by groups.[50] As a result, managers must understand how groups operate and how to use them to improve decision making. You will learn much more about how groups work later in the book.

The basic philosophy behind using a group to make decisions is captured by the adage "two heads are better than one." But is this statement really valid? Yes, it is—potentially.

If enough time is available, groups usually make higher-quality decisions than most individuals acting alone. However, groups often are inferior to the *best* individual.[51]

How well the group performs depends on how effectively it capitalizes on the potential advantages and minimizes the potential problems of using a group. Table 3.2 summarizes these issues.

Potential Advantages of Using a Group

If other people have something to contribute, using groups to make a decision offers at least five potential advantages:[52]

1. More *information* is available when several people are making the decision. If one member doesn't have all the facts or the pertinent expertise, another member might.

TABLE 3.2
Pros and Cons of Using a Group to Make Decisions

Potential Advantages	Potential Disadvantages
1. Larger pool of information.	1. One person dominates.
2. More perspectives and approaches.	2. Satisficing.
3. Intellectual stimulation.	3. Groupthink.
4. People understand the decision.	4. Goal displacement.
5. People are committed to the decision.	

2. A greater number of *perspectives* on the issues, or different *approaches* to solving the problem, are available. The problem may be new to one group member but familiar to another. Or the group may need to consider other viewpoints—financial, legal, marketing, human resources, and so on—to achieve an optimal solution.
3. Group discussion provides an opportunity for *intellectual stimulation*. It can get people thinking and unleash their creativity to a far greater extent than would be possible with individual decision making.

These three potential advantages of using a group improve the odds that a more fully informed, higher-quality decision will result. Thus managers should involve people with different backgrounds, perspectives, and access to information. They should not involve only their cronies who think the same way they do.

4. People who participate in a group discussion are more likely to *understand* why the decision was made. They will have heard the relevant arguments both for the chosen alternative and against the rejected alternatives.
5. Group discussion typically leads to a higher level of *commitment* to the decision. Buying into the proposed solution translates into high motivation to ensure that it is executed well.

The last two advantages improve the chances that the decision will be implemented successfully. Therefore, managers should involve the people who will be responsible for implementing the decision as early in the deliberations as possible.

Potential Problems of Using a Group

Things *can* go wrong when groups make decisions. Most of the potential problems concern the process through which group members interact with one another:[53]

1. Sometimes one group member *dominates* the discussion. When this occurs—such as when a strong leader makes his or her preferences clear—the result is the same as it would be if the dominant individual made the decision alone. Individual dominance has two disadvantages. First, the dominant person does not necessarily have the most valid opinions—and may even have the most unsound ideas. Second, even if that person's preference leads to a good decision, convening as a group will have been a waste of everyone else's time.
2. *Satisficing* is more likely with groups. Most people don't like meetings and will do what they can to end them. This may include criticizing members who want to continue exploring new and better alternatives. The result is a satisficing rather than an optimizing or maximizing decision.
3. *Pressure to avoid disagreement* can lead to a phenomenon called *groupthink*. **Groupthink** occurs when people choose not to disagree or raise objections because they don't want to break up a positive team spirit. Some groups want to think as one, tolerate no dissension, and strive to remain cordial. Such groups are overconfident, complacent, and perhaps too willing to take risks. Pressure to go along with the group's preferred solution stifles creativity and the other behaviors characteristic of vigilant decision making.

groupthink

A phenomenon that occurs in decision making when group members avoid disagreement as they strive for consensus.

Heated arguments can arise when team members have differing opinions and are more concerned with winning the dispute than resolving the initial problem.

goal displacement

A condition that occurs when a decision-making group loses sight of its original goal and a new, less important goal emerges.

4. *Goal displacement* often occurs in groups. The goal of group members should be to come up with the best possible solution to the problem. But when **goal displacement** occurs, new goals emerge to replace the original ones. It is common for two or more group members to have different opinions and present their conflicting cases. Attempts at rational persuasion become heated disagreement. Winning the argument becomes the new goal.

Saving face and defeating the other person's idea become more important than solving the problem.

Effective managers pay close attention to the group process; they manage it carefully. You have just read about the pros and cons of using a group to make decisions, and you are about to read *how* to manage the group's decision-making process. Chapter 12, on leadership, helps you decide *when* to use groups to make decisions.

Managing Group Decision Making

 LO 5   As Figure 3.3 illustrates, effectively managing group decision making has three requirements: (1) an appropriate leadership style, (2) the constructive use of disagreement and conflict, and (3) the enhancement of creativity.

Leadership Style

The leader of a decision-making body must attempt to minimize process-related problems. The leader should avoid dominating the discussion or allowing another individual to dominate. Less vocal group members should be encouraged to air their opinions and suggestions, and all members should be asked for dissenting viewpoints.

FIGURE 3.3
Managing Group Decision Making

At the same time, the leader should not allow the group to pressure people into conforming. The leader should be alert to the dangers of groupthink and satisficing. Also, she should be attuned to indications that group members are losing sight of the primary objective: to come up with the best possible solution to the problem.

These suggestions have two implications. First, don't lose sight of the problem and your goals. Second, make a decision! Slow-moving organizations whose group members can't come to an agreement will be standing still while their competitors move ahead.

> First, don't lose sight of the problem and your goals. Second, make a decision!

Constructive Conflict

Total and consistent agreement among group members can be destructive. It can lead to groupthink, uncreative solutions, and a waste of the knowledge and diverse viewpoints that individuals bring to the group. Therefore, a certain amount of *constructive* conflict should exist.[54] Some companies, including United Parcel Service, take steps to ensure that conflict and debate are generated within their management teams.[55]

The most constructive type of conflict is **cognitive conflict,** or differences in perspectives or judgments about issues. In contrast, **affective conflict** is emotional and directed at other people. Affective conflict is likely to be destructive to the group because it can lead to anger, bitterness, goal displacement, and lower-quality decisions. Cognitive conflict, in contrast, can air legitimate differences of opinion and develop better ideas and problem solutions. Conflict, then, should be task related rather than personal.[56] But even task-related conflict can hurt performance;[57] disagreement is good only when managed properly.

Conflict can be generated formally through structured processes.[58] Two techniques that purposely program cognitive conflict into the decision-making process are devil's advocacy and the dialectic method.

A **devil's advocate** has the job of criticizing ideas. The group leader can formally assign people to play this role. Requiring people to point out problems can lessen inhibitions about disagreeing and make the conflict less personal and emotional.

An alternative to devil's advocacy is the dialectic. The **dialectic** goes a step beyond devil's advocacy by requiring a structured debate about two conflicting courses of action.[59] The philosophy of the dialectic stems from Plato and Aristotle, who advocated synthesizing the conflicting views of a thesis and an antithesis. Structured debates between plans and counterplans can be useful prior to making a strategic decision. For example, one team might present the case for acquiring a firm while another team advocates not making the acquisition.

Constructive conflict does not need to be generated on such a formal basis and is not solely the leader's responsibility. Any team member can introduce cognitive conflict by being honest with opinions, by being unafraid to disagree with others, by pushing the group to action if it is taking too long or making the group slow down if necessary, and by advocating long-term considerations if the group is too focused on short-term results. Introducing constructive conflict is a legitimate and necessary responsibility of all group members interested in improving the group's decision-making effectiveness.

cognitive conflict

Issue-based differences in perspectives or judgments.

affective conflict

Emotional disagreement directed toward other people.

devil's advocate

A person who has the job of criticizing ideas to ensure that their downsides are fully explored.

dialectic

A structured debate comparing two conflicting courses of action.

Encouraging Creativity

As you've already learned, ready-made solutions to a problem can be inadequate or unavailable. In such cases, custom-made solutions are necessary, so the group must be creative in generating ideas.

Some have said we are in the midst of the next great business revolution: the "creative revolution."[60] Said to transcend the agricultural, industrial, and information revolutions, the most fundamental unit of value in the creativity revolution is ideas. Creativity is more than just an option; it is essential to survival. Allowing people to

The most fundamental unit of value in the creativity revolution is ideas.

be creative may be one of the manager's most important and challenging responsibilities.

You might be saying to yourself, "I'm not creative." But even if you are not an artist or a musician, you do have potential to be creative in countless other ways. You are being creative if you (1) bring a new thing into being (*creation*); (2) join two previously unrelated things (*synthesis*); or (3) improve something or give it a new application (*modification*). You don't need to be a genius in school either—Thomas Edison and Albert Einstein were not particularly good students. Nor does something need to change the world to be creative; the "little things" can always be done in new, creative ways that add value to the product and the customer.

> "I invented nothing new. I simply assembled into a car the discoveries of other men behind whom were centuries of work."
>
> Henry Ford

How do you "get" creative?[61] Recognize the almost infinite "little" opportunities to be creative. Assume you can be creative if you give it a try. Escape from work once in a while. Read widely, and try new experiences. Take a course or find a good book about creative thought processes; plenty are available. And be aware that creativity is social; your creativity will be affected by your social relationships at work, including your connections with other people outside your immediate close network.[62] Talk to people, often, about the issues and ideas with which you are wrestling.

How do you "get" creativity out of other people?[63] Give creative efforts the credit they are due, and don't punish creative failures. Avoid extreme time pressure, if possible.[64] Stimulate and challenge people intellectually. Listen to employees' ideas, and allow enough time to explore different ideas. Put together groups of people with different styles of thinking and behaving. Get your people in touch with customers, and let them bounce ideas around. Protect your people from managers who demand immediate payoffs, who don't understand the importance of creative contributions, or who try to take credit for others' successes. And strive to be creative yourself—you'll set a good example.

People are likely to be more creative if they believe they are capable, if they know that their coworkers expect creativity, and if they believe that their employer values creativity.[65] As a manager, you can do much to help employees develop these beliefs by how you listen, what you allow, and what you reward and punish. At a large consumer products company, management signals that it values creativity by inviting managers to post stories on the company's intranet about ideas their employees have suggested and the results of implementation. The company also awards "innovation bonuses" linked to how these innovations have benefited the organization.[66]

Bottom Line

Most creative ideas come not from the lone genius in the basement laboratory, but from people talking and working together.

Why is listening a part of stimulating creativity?

brainstorming

A process in which group members generate as many ideas about a problem as they can; criticism is withheld until all ideas have been proposed.

IN PRACTICE

At Miron Construction Company, Theresa Lehman fosters creative thinking about sustainability. In addition to helping clients plan more sustainable buildings, Lehman, the director of sustainable services at the Neenah, Wisconsin, building contractor, helps Miron itself operate more sustainably.

Lehman defines the problem—or opportunity—of running a sustainable construction company as one that extends beyond a building's features. Rather, all efforts to reduce waste contribute to sustainability. Says Lehman, "Everyone needs to focus on doing things more effectively and efficiently by reducing resources and eliminating waste." She seeks ideas from all employees and ensures that every idea receives careful consideration. For example, an employee suggested switching from paper paychecks to direct deposit for all employees. Besides saving paper, that change cuts printing and postage expenses. By taking ideas seriously and then communicating the practical benefits, Lehman reinforces the value of sustainability.

Lehman is ready with plenty of examples about the financial soundness of sustainability. For example, as Miron added to and renovated its own headquarters, it installed geothermal heating and cooling, which will pay for itself in five years, and it replaced interior lights with LED bulbs that are expected to save about $12,000 in energy costs over the life of the bulbs. With benefits like these, it's no wonder that Lehman has been able to make sustainability a widely shared value at Miron.[67]

- What other ideas for getting creativity out of employees might Lehman use to promote sustainability at Miron?

Brainstorming

A common technique used to elicit creative ideas is brainstorming. In **brainstorming,** group members generate as many ideas about a problem as they can. As the ideas are presented, they are posted so that everyone can read them, and people can use the ideas as building blocks. The group is encouraged to say anything that comes to mind, with one exception: no criticism of other people or their ideas is allowed.

In the proper brainstorming environment—free of criticism—people are less inhibited and more likely to voice their unusual, creative, or even wild ideas. By the time people have exhausted their ideas, a long list of alternatives has been generated. Only then does the group turn to the evaluation stage. At that point, many different ideas can be considered, modified, or combined into a creative, custom-made solution to the problem.

Brainstorming isn't necessarily as effective as some people think. Sometimes in a brainstorming session people are inhibited and anxious, they conform to others' ideas, they set low standards, and they engage in noncreative behaviors including cocktail party–type conversations—complimenting one another, repeating ideas, telling stories—that are nice but don't promote creativity. Fortunately, there are techniques that help, including brainwriting (taking time to silently write down ideas), using trained facilitators, setting high performance goals, brainstorming electronically so that people aren't competing for air time, and even building a playground with fun elements that can foster creativity.[68]

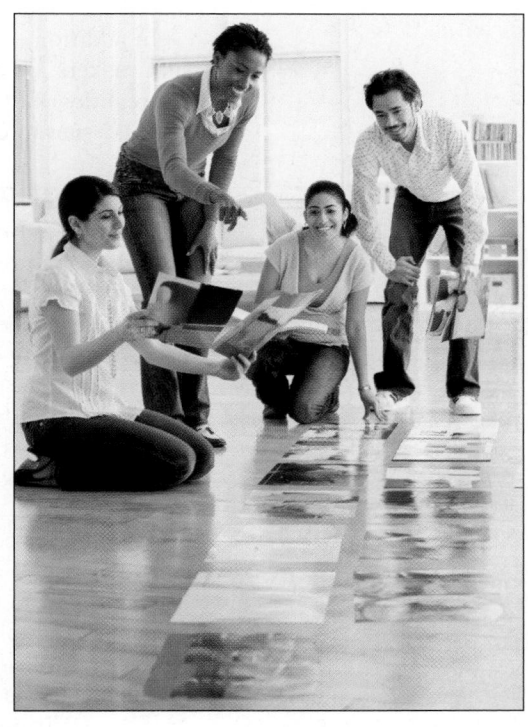

Brainstorming is a technique used to generate as many ideas as possible to solve a problem. You have probably engaged in brainstorming sessions for various class or work projects.

Organizational Decision Making

Individuals and groups make decisions constantly throughout every organization. To understand decision making in organizations, a manager must consider (1) the constraints decision makers face, (2) organizational decision processes, and (3) decision making during a crisis.

Constraints on Decision Makers

Organizations—or, more accurately, the people who make important decisions—cannot do whatever they wish. They face various constraints—financial, legal, market,

Bottom Line

You may be an innovator if you come up with a creative idea. But you're not yet, until you implement it.

Say you're a manager who dreamed up a great process for cutting costs. Whose buy-in might you need to implement this innovation?

human, and organizational—that inhibit certain actions. Capital or product markets may make an expensive new venture impossible. Legal restrictions may constrain the kinds of international business activities in which a firm can participate. Labor unions may defeat a contract proposed by management, and managers and investors may block a takeover attempt. Even brilliant ideas must take into account the practical matters of implementation.[69]

Suppose you have a great idea that will provide a revolutionary service for your bank's customers. You won't be able to put your idea into action immediately. You will have to sell it to the people who can give you the go-ahead and also to those whose help you will need to carry out the project. You might start by convincing your boss of your idea's merit. Next, the two of you may have to hash it out with a vice president. Then maybe the president has to be sold. At each stage, you must listen to these individuals' opinions and suggestions and often incorporate them into your original concept. Ultimately, you will have to derive a proposal acceptable to others.

In addition, ethical and legal considerations must be thought out carefully. Decision makers must consider ethics and the preferences of many constituent groups—the realities of life in organizations. You will have plenty of opportunity to think about ethical issues in Chapter 5.

Organizational Decision Processes

Just as with individuals and groups, organizational decision making historically was described with rational models like the one depicted earlier in Figure 3.2. But Nobel laureate Herbert Simon challenged the rational model and proposed an important alternative called *bounded rationality*. According to Simon's **bounded rationality,** decision makers cannot be truly rational because (1) they have imperfect, incomplete information about alternatives and consequences; (2) the problems they face are so complex; (3) human beings simply cannot process all the information to which they are exposed; (4) there is not enough time to process all relevant information fully; and (5) people, including managers within the same firm, have conflicting goals.

When these conditions hold—and they do for most consequential managerial decisions—perfect rationality will give way to more biased, subjective, messier decision processes. For example, the **incremental model** of decision making occurs when decision makers make small decisions, take little steps, move cautiously, and move in piecemeal fashion toward a bigger solution. The classic example is the budget process, which traditionally begins with the budget from the previous period and makes incremental decisions from that starting point.

The **coalitional model** of decision making arises when people disagree on goals or compete with one another for resources. The decision process becomes political as groups of individuals band together and try collectively to influence the decision. Two or more coalitions form, each representing a different preference, and each tries to use power and negotiations to sway the decision.

Organizational politics, in which people try to influence organizational decisions so that their own interests will be served, can reduce decision-making effectiveness.[70] One of the best ways to reduce such politics, and to make sure that constructive cognitive conflict does not degenerate into affective conflict, is to *create common goals* for members of the team—that is, make the decision-making process a collaborative, rather than a competitive, exercise by establishing a goal around which the group can rally. In one study, top management teams with stated goals like "build the biggest financial war chest" for an upcoming competitive battle, or "create *the* computer firm of the decade," or "build the best damn machine on the market" were less likely to have dysfunctional conflict and politics between members.[71] On a personal level, if you find yourself in a conflict, you and your adversary may be focused on the wrong goals. Work to find common ground in the form of an important goal that you both want to achieve.

The **garbage can model** of decision making occurs when people aren't sure of their goals, or disagree about the goals, and likewise are unsure of or in disagreement

---

bounded rationality

A less-than-perfect form of rationality in which decision makers cannot be perfectly rational because decisions are complex and complete information is unavailable or cannot be fully processed.

incremental model

Model of organizational decision making in which major solutions arise through a series of smaller decisions.

coalitional model

Model of organizational decision making in which groups with differing preferences use power and negotiation to influence decisions.

garbage can model

Model of organizational decision making depicting a chaotic process and seemingly random decisions.

about what to do. This situation occurs because some problems are so complex that they are not well understood and also because decision makers move in and out of the decision process because they have so many other things to attend to as well. This model implies that some decisions are chaotic and almost random. You can see that this is a dramatic departure from rationality in decision making.

Decision Making in a Crisis

In crises, managers must make decisions under a great deal of pressure.[72] You may know some of the most famous recent crises: the explosion of BP's oil rig in the Gulf of Mexico, the devastation of hurricanes along the Gulf Coast, the financial crisis that brought turmoil to the housing industry, and the political crises that have shaken many governments in the Middle East.

LO 8

In two famous cases from the past, Union Carbide's gas leak in Bhopal, India, killed thousands of people, and several people were killed in the cyanide poisonings using Johnson & Johnson's Tylenol. As outlined in Table 3.3, Union Carbide and J&J handled their crises in very different ways. Today J&J is still known for its effective handling of the crisis, as outlined in the table.

Information technology is a new arena for a crisis. Businesses, homes, government agencies, hospitals, and other organizations send critical information through the Internet and private networks around the clock, and any technical failure—sometimes accidental, sometimes maliciously intentional—could be magnified by the speed and

Information technology is a new arena for a crisis.

TABLE 3.3
Two Disasters

Union Carbide	Johnson & Johnson
Failed to identify as a crisis the public perception that the company was a negligent, uncaring killer.	Identified the crisis of public perception that Tylenol was unsafe and J&J was not in control.

No planning before reacting:
 	
   CEO immediately went to India to inspect damage.
 	
   All executives involved.
	Planned before reacting:
	
	   CEO picked one executive to head crisis team.
	
	   Rest of company involved only on a need-to-know basis.

Set no goals	Set goals:
	
	   Stop the killings.
	
	   Find reasons for the killings.
	
	   Provide assistance to the victims.
	
	   Restore Tylenol's credibility.

Action: Damage control/stonewalling.
 	
   Distanced itself.
 	
   Misrepresented safety conditions.
 	
   Did not inform spokespeople
 	
   Adopted bunker mentality
	Action: Gave complete information.
	
	   Worked with authorities.
	
	   Pulled Tylenol from shelves (first-year cost: $150 million).
	
	   Used strong marketing program.
	
	   Reissued Tylenol with tamper-proof packaging.

Chronic problems continued:
 	
   Public confidence low.
 	
   Costly litigation.
 	
   No formal crisis plan resulted.
	Crisis resolved:
	
	   Public confidence high.
	
	   Sales high again.
	
	   Well-documented crisis management plan.

widespread use of information technology. One vulnerable area is the electrical grid, which links utilities and carries power to each user. Information technology systems allow utility employees to control the grid remotely. Recently, information came to light that hackers have gained access to the U.S. electrical grid, leaving behind computer programs that theoretically would permit them to interfere with the grid's operations.[73] Such programs can be purged, but the biggest challenge is preventing or catching each attempt to gain unauthorized access to the system.

The response to IT-related crises must involve senior executives in online communication, both to protect the firm's reputation and to communicate with outside experts, news sources, and key external and internal stakeholders. Managers can use IT to monitor and respond immediately to problems including scandals, boycotts, rumors, cyberattacks, and other crises.[74]

Although many companies don't concern themselves with crisis management, it is imperative that it be on management's agenda. An effective plan for crisis management (CM) should include the following elements:[75]

1. *Strategic actions* such as integrating CM into strategic planning and official policies.
2. *Technical and structural actions* such as creating a CM team and dedicating a budget to CM.
3. *Evaluation and diagnostic actions* such as conducting audits of threats and liabilities, and establishing tracking systems for early warning signals.
4. *Communication actions* such as providing training for dealing with the media, local communities, and police and government officials.
5. *Psychological and cultural actions* such as showing a strong top management commitment to CM and providing training and psychological support services regarding the human and emotional impacts of crises.

Ultimately, management should be able to answer the following questions:[76]

What kinds of crises could your company face?
Can your company detect a crisis in its early stages?
How will it manage a crisis if one occurs?
How can it benefit from a crisis after it has passed?

The last question makes an important point: a crisis, managed effectively, can have *benefits*. For example, a prison riot helped Jerry Heftler create a firm bond with one of his company's first clients. Heftler set up Integrated Medical Solutions (IMS) to manage medical care for prison inmates who need to visit doctors, hospitals, and rehabilitation centers outside prison walls. The company contacts providers located near prisons to identify who will be willing to serve inmates, and then it makes appointments and handles insurance paperwork for prisons that sign contracts with his company. A few days after IMS had signed a contract with its second customer but a week before the contract was to go into effect, Heftler learned that prisoners at his new client's facility were rioting. Heftler called the prison's health services director and offered to be of assistance immediately. Drawing on earlier experience in hostage negotiation, Heftler kept cool as he worked overtime to locate injured prisoners who had been loaded onto medevac helicopters without identification and sent to any hospital that would take them. He set up a system to track them by their tattoos until they could be properly identified, and he stayed in constant touch with the health services director. In the years since then, that prison's management has had unfailing confidence in IMS's abilities.[77]

And if someone steps in and manages the crisis well, a hero is born.

With effective crisis management, old as well as new problems can be resolved, new strategies and competitive advantages may appear, and positive change can emerge. And if someone steps in and manages the crisis well, a hero is born. The ability of Pandora's managers to steer the company through the nearly devastating period during which it was being required to pay royalty fees that might consume all its revenues gave many observers hope that the company will continue thriving and transforming the music business. You will read about and evaluate those decisions in "Management Connection: Onward."

As a leader during a crisis, don't pretend that nothing happened (as did managers at one firm after a visitor died in the hallway despite employees' efforts to save him).[78] Communicate and reinforce the organization's values. Try to find ways for people to support one another, and remember that people will take cues from your behavior. You should be optimistic but brutally honest. Show emotion, but not fear. "You have to be cooler than cool," says Gene Krantz of *Apollo 13* ground control fame. But don't ignore the problems or downplay them and reassure too much; don't create false hopes. Give people the bad news straight—you'll gain credibility, and when the good news comes, it will really mean something.

Manager's Brief	Progress Report	**Onward**

Management Connection

POSITIONING PANDORA FOR THE FUTURE

Despite all the efforts of Tim Westergren and Pandora Media's other managers to expand the subscriber base and sign up advertisers, the company endured a financial crisis that almost destroyed Pandora. The problem came not from a competitor but from the Copyright Royalty Board, the music industry nonprofit group that sets royalty rates for performances of sound recordings. Several years ago, the board announced an increase in royalty fees that would be required from Internet radio providers. Unlike AM/FM radio broadcasters, Internet radio providers would be expected to pay a performance royalty to musicians as well as a publishing royalty to recording companies for each song they stream.

Founder Westergren, chief executive officer Joe Kennedy, and other Pandora managers considered their options. Eventually, Westergren recalls, the only option that seemed realistic was to "pull the plug" on Pandora. But they decided to try one more desperate idea: beg their most loyal users to put pressure on their representatives in Congress, asking them to step in. Here the company had some resources—specifically its database of user registrations. Pandora sent out an e-mail that provided information about contacting representatives based on the users' zip codes. The desperate idea worked: more than a million and a half users contacted Congress, which then pressed for easing the rate schedule. According to Kennedy, the new rate schedule was one that would allow Pandora to survive. That struggle for survival took two years from the announced rate increase until the negotiation of the lower increase.

Even at the lower royalty rates, profitability would be difficult, but managers stepped up to the challenge. In a recent year, performance royalties equaled 60 percent of Pandora's revenue (compared with 15 percent for satellite radio and zero for AM/FM radio). More recently, the company has been bringing down many of its costs, including licensing fees for music. Managers also decided that Pandora would have to adjust its pricing by asking its heaviest users to help share the burden.

Having weathered that storm, Pandora's managers felt they were ready to begin enjoying a profitable future. The company, which had invested heavily in building its Music Genome Project, has been narrowing its losses and marked its first operating profits. Management prepared a plan to take the company public, offering stock for sale in an initial public offering.

Risk and uncertainty continue, of course. Apple's App Store is currently an important source of revenue—iPhone and iPad users go there if they want a paid subscription to Pandora for their devices. Apple recently announced that it would begin taking a 30 percent cut of the payments for those subscriptions. So far, most of Pandora's revenues come from advertising, but subscription revenues have been growing. In addition, assuming Pandora becomes consistently profitable, other companies will see opportunities in offering similar kinds of services. For example, if Apple were to offer music streaming, it has a contractual right to stop offering a similar, competing service such as Pandora. In that case, Pandora would lose a chunk of its subscriber base—unless creative managers could decide on a plan to make Pandora more attractive to music lovers than an iPhone. Given the company's track record of innovation (*Fast Company* recently named it one of the world's 50 most innovative companies), that could be the next big surprise.[79]

- Did the announcement of higher royalties for Internet radio companies amount to a crisis for Pandora? Why or why not? Could Pandora's managers have planned for it?
- What are some other constraints on decision making at Pandora?

KEY TERMS

affective conflict, p. 103

bounded rationality, p. 106

brainstorming, p. 104

certainty, p. 87

coalitional model, p. 106

cognitive conflict, p. 103

conflict, p. 89

contingency plans, p. 92

custom-made solutions, p. 90

devil's advocate, p. 103

dialectic, p. 103

discounting the future, p. 98

framing effects, p. 98

garbage can model, p. 106

goal displacement, p. 102

groupthink, p. 101

illusion of control, p. 97

incremental model, p. 106

maximizing, p. 94

nonprogrammed decisions, p. 87

optimizing, p. 95

programmed decisions, p. 87

ready-made solutions, p. 90

risk, p. 88

satisficing, p. 94

uncertainty, p. 87

vigilance, p. 96

SUMMARY OF LEARNING OBJECTIVES

Now that you have studied Chapter 3, you should be able to:

LO 1   Describe the kinds of decisions you will face as a manager.

Most important managerial decisions are ill structured and characterized by uncertainty, risk, and conflict. Yet managers are expected to make rational decisions in the face of these challenges.

LO 2   Summarize the steps in making "rational" decisions.

The ideal decision-making process involves six stages. The first, identifying and diagnosing the problem (or opportunity), requires recognizing a discrepancy between the current state and a desired state and then delving below surface symptoms to uncover the underlying causes of the problem. The second stage, generating alternative solutions, requires adopting ready-made or designing custom-made solutions. The third, evaluating alternatives, means predicting the consequences of different alternatives, sometimes through building scenarios of the future. Fourth, a solution is chosen; the solution might maximize, satisfice, or optimize. Fifth, people implement the decision; this stage requires more careful planning than it often receives. Finally, managers should evaluate how well the decision is working. This means gathering objective, valid information about the impact the decision is having. If the evidence suggests the problem is not getting solved, either a better decision or a better implementation plan must be developed.

LO 3   Recognize the pitfalls you should avoid when making decisions.

Situational and human limitations lead most decision makers to satisfice rather than maximize. Psychological biases, time pressures, and the social realities of organizational life may prevent rational execution of the six decision-making stages. But vigilance and an understanding of how to manage decision-making groups and organizational constraints will improve the process and result in better decisions.

LO 4   Evaluate the pros and cons of using a group to make decisions.

Advantages of using groups include more information, perspectives, and approaches brought to bear on problem solving; intellectual stimulation; greater understanding by all of the final decision;

and higher commitment to the decision once it is made. Potential dangers or disadvantages of using groups include individual domination of discussions, satisficing, groupthink, and goal displacement.

LO 5   Identify procedures to use in leading a decision-making group.

Effective leaders in decision-making teams avoid dominating the discussion; encourage people's input; avoid groupthink and satisficing; and stay focused on the group's goals. They encourage constructive conflict via devil's advocacy and the dialectic, posing opposite sides of an issue or solutions to a problem. They also encourage creativity through a variety of techniques.

LO 6   Explain how to encourage creative decisions.

When creative ideas are needed, leaders should set a good example by being creative themselves. They should recognize the almost infinite "little" opportunities for creativity and have confidence in their own creative abilities. They can inspire creativity in others by pushing for creative freedom, rewarding creativity, and not punishing creative failures. They should encourage interaction with customers, stimulate discussion, and protect people from managers who might squelch the creative process. Brainstorming is one of the most popular techniques for generating creative ideas.

LO 7   Discuss the processes by which decisions are made in organizations.

Decision making in organizations is often a highly complex process. Individuals and groups are constrained by a variety of factors and constituencies. In practice, decision makers are boundedly rational rather than purely rational. Some decisions are made on an incremental basis. Coalitions form to represent different preferences. The process is often chaotic, as depicted in the garbage can model. Politics can also enter the process, decisions are negotiated, and crises come and go.

LO 8   Describe how to make decisions in a crisis.

Crisis conditions make sound, effective decision making more difficult. However, it is possible for crises to be managed well. A strategy for crisis management can be developed beforehand, and the mechanisms readied, so that if crises do arise, decision makers are prepared.

DISCUSSION QUESTIONS

1. Discuss Pandora Media in terms of risk, uncertainty, and how its managers handled the company's challenges. What is the current news on this company?

2. Identify some risky decisions you have made. Why did you take the risks? How did they work out? Looking back, what did you learn?

3. Identify a decision you made that had important unexpected consequences. Were the consequences good, bad, or both? Should you, and could you, have done anything differently in making the decision?

4. What effects does time pressure have on your decision making? In what ways do you handle it well and not so well?

5. Recall a recent decision that you had difficulty making. Describe it in terms of the characteristics of managerial decisions.

6. What do you think are some advantages and disadvantages to using computer technology in decision making?

7. Do you think that when managers make decisions they follow the decision-making steps as presented in this chapter? Which steps are apt to be overlooked or given inadequate attention? What can people do to make sure they do a more thorough job?

8. Discuss the potential advantages and disadvantages of using a group to make decisions. Give examples from your experience.

9. Suppose you are the CEO of a major corporation and one of your company's oil tanks has ruptured, spilling thousands of gallons of oil into a river that empties into the ocean. What do you need to do to handle the crisis?

10. Identify some problems you want to solve. Brainstorm with others a variety of creative solutions.

EXPERIENTIAL EXERCISES

3.1   COMPETITIVE ESCALATION: THE DOLLAR AUCTION

OBJECTIVE
To explore the effects of competition on decision making.

INSTRUCTIONS

Step 1: *5 minutes.* The instructor will play the role of auctioneer. In this auction, the instructor will auction off $1 bills (the instructor will inform you whether this money is real or imaginary). All members of the class may participate in the auction at the same time.

The rules for this auction are slightly different from those of a normal auction. In this version, *both the highest bidder and the next highest bidder will play their last bids* even though the dollar is awarded only to the highest bidder. For example, if Bidder A bids 15 cents for the dollar and Bidder B bids 10 cents, and there is no further bidding, then A pays 15 cents for the dollar and receives the dollar, while B pays 10 cents and receives nothing. The auctioneer will lose 75 cents on the dollar just sold.

Bids must be made in multiples of 5 cents. The dollar will be sold when there is no further bidding. If two individuals bid the same amount at the same time, ties are resolved in favor of the bidder located physically closest to the auctioneer. *During each round, there is to be no talking except for making bids.*

Step 2: *15 minutes.* The instructor (auctioneer) will auction off five individual dollars to the class. Any student may bid in an effort to win the dollar. A record sheet of the bidding and winners can be kept in the worksheet that follows.

DISCUSSION QUESTIONS

1. Who made the most money in this exercise—one of the bidders or the auctioneer? Why?

2. As the auction proceeded, did bidders become more competitive or more cooperative? Why?

3. Did two bidders ever pay more for the money being auctioned than the value of the money itself? Explain how and why this happened.

4. Did you become involved in the bidding? Why?
   a. If you became involved, what were your motivations? Did you accomplish your objectives?
   b. If not, why didn't you become involved? What did you think were the goals and objectives of those who did become involved?

5. Did people say things to one another during the bidding to influence their actions? What was said, and how was it influential?

Dollar Auction Worksheet

	Amount Paid by Winning Bidder	Amount Paid by Second Bidder	Total Paid for This Dollar
First dollar			
Second dollar			
Third dollar			
Fourth dollar			
Fifth dollar			

SOURCE: Excerpted from R. Lewicki, *Experiences in Management and Organizational Behavior*, 3rd ed. 1991. Reprinted with permission of John Wiley and Sons, Inc.

3.2 GROUP PROBLEM-SOLVING MEETING AT THE COMMUNITY AGENCY

OBJECTIVE

To understand the interactions in group decision making through role playing a meeting between a chairman and his subordinates.

INSTRUCTIONS

1. Gather role sheets for each character and instructions for observers.

2. Set up a table in front of the room with five chairs around it arranged in such a way that participants can talk comfortably and have their faces visible to observers.

3. Read the introduction and cast of characters.

4. Five members from the class are selected to role-play the five characters. All other members act as observers. The participants study the roles. All should play their roles without referring to the role sheets.

5. The observers read the instructions for observers.

6. When everyone is ready, John Cabot enters his office, joins the others at the table, and the scene begins. Allow 20 minutes to complete the meeting. The meeting is carried to the point of completion unless an argument develops and no progress is evident after 10 or 15 minutes of conflict.

DISCUSSION QUESTIONS

1. Describe the group's behavior. What did each member say? Do?

2. Evaluate the effectiveness of the group's decision making.

3. Did any problems exist in leadership, power, motivation, communication, or perception?

4. How could the group's effectiveness be increased?

INTRODUCTION

The Community Agency is a role-play exercise of a meeting between the chairman of the board of a social service agency and four of his subordinates. Each character's role is designed to re-create the reality of a business meeting. Each character comes to the meeting with a unique perspective on a major problem facing the agency as well as some personal impressions of the other characters developed over several years of business and social associations.

CAST OF CHARACTERS

John Cabot, the chairman, was the principal force behind the formation of the Community Agency, a multiservice agency. The agency employs 50 people, and during its 19 years of operations has enjoyed better client relations, a better service record, and a better reputation than other local agencies because of a reputation for high-quality service at a moderate cost to funding agencies. Recently, however, competitors have begun to overtake the Community Agency, resulting in declining contracts. John Cabot is expending every possible effort to keep his agency comfortably at the top.

Ron Smith, director of the agency, reports directly to Cabot. He has held this position since he helped Cabot establish the agency 19 years ago.

Joan Sweet, head of client services, reports to Smith. She has been with the agency 12 years, having worked before that for the government as a contracting officer.

Tom Lynch, head community liaison, reports to Joan Sweet. He came to the Community Agency at Sweet's request, having worked with Sweet previously.

Jane Cox, head case worker, also works for Joan Sweet. Cox was promoted to this position two years ago. Prior to that time, Jane had gone through a year's training program after receiving an MSW from a large urban university.

TODAY'S MEETING

John Cabot has called the meeting with these four managers to solve some problems that have developed in meeting service schedules and contract requirements. Cabot must catch a plane to Washington in half an hour; he has an appointment to negotiate a key contract that means a great deal to the future of the Community Agency. He has only 20 minutes to meet with his managers and still catch the plane. Cabot feels that getting the Washington contract is absolutely crucial to the future of the agency.

CONCLUDING CASE

THE WALLINGFORD BOWLING CENTER

A group of 12 lifelong friends put together $1,200,000 of their own funds and built a $6,000,000, 48-lane bowling alley near Norfolk, Virginia. Two of the investors became employees of the corporation. Ned Flanders works full-time as general manager, and James Ahmad, a licensed CPA, serves as controller on a part-time basis.

The beautiful, modern-day facility features a multilevel spacious interior with three rows of 16 lanes on two separate levels of the building, a full-service bar, a small restaurant, a game room (pool, videogames, pinball), and two locker rooms. The facility sits on a spacious lot with plenty of parking and room to grow.

The bowling center is located in the small blue-collar town of Wallingford. There is no direct competition within the town. The surrounding communities include a wide-ranging mix of ethnic groups, professionals, middle- to upper-middle-class private homes, and apartment and condominium complexes ranging from singles to young married couples to senior citizen retirement units. Nearly 200,000 people live within 15 miles of Wallingford.

The bowling center is open 24 hours per day and has a staff of 27 part- and full-time employees. After four years of operation, the partners find themselves frustrated with the low profit performance of the business. While sales are covering expenses, the partners are not happy with the end-of-year profit-sharing pool. The most recent income statement follows:

Sales	$1,844,000
CGS	315,000
GM	1,529,000
Operating expenses	1,466,000
Mortgage	460,000
Depreciation	95,000
Utilities	188,000
Maintenance	70,000
Payroll	490,000
Supplies	27,000
Insurance	136,000
Taxable income	63,000
Taxes	19,000
Net income	$ 44,000

The bowling center operates at 100 percent capacity on Sunday through Thursday nights from 6:00 p.m. until midnight. Two sets of men's leagues come and go on each of those nights, occupying each lane with mostly five-person teams. Bowlers from each league consistently spend money at both the bar and restaurant. In fact, the men's leagues combine to generate about 60 percent of total current sales.

The bowling center operates at about 50 percent capacity on Friday and Saturday nights and on Saturday morning. The Friday and Saturday "open bowling" nights include mostly teenagers, young couples, and league members who come to practice in groups of two or three. The Saturday morning group is a kids' league, ages 10 through 14.

There are four women's leagues that bowl on Monday and Wednesday afternoons.

Business is extremely slow at the bowling center on Monday through Friday and Sunday mornings, and on the afternoons of Tuesday, Thursday, Friday, Saturday, and Sunday. It is not uncommon to have just three or four lanes in operation during those time periods.

The owners have taken a close look at the cost side of their business as a way to improve profitability. They concluded that while the total operating expense of $1,466,000 might appear to be high, there was in fact little room for expense cutting.

At a recent meeting of the partners, James Ahmad reported on the results of his three-month-long investigation into the operating cost side of other bowling alleys and discovered that the Wallingford Bowling Center was very much in keeping with their industry. James went on to report that bowling alleys were considered to be "heavy fixed cost operations" and that the key to success and profitability lies in maximizing capacity and sales dollars.

QUESTIONS

1. Apply the decision-making process described in the chapter to this case. What is the major problem facing Wallingford? List five specific alternative solutions that could be implemented to solve that major problem.

2. As general manager of this company, how could you utilize and manage the group decision-making process and technique to improve company profits? Which employees would you include in the group?

PART ONE   SUPPORTING CASE

SSS Software In-Basket Exercise

One way to assess your own strengths and weaknesses in management skills is to engage in an actual managerial work experience. The following exercise gives you a realistic glimpse of the tasks faced regularly by practicing managers. Complete the exercise, and then compare your own decisions and actions with those of classmates.

SSS Software designs and develops customized software for businesses. It also integrates this software with the customer's existing systems and provides system maintenance. SSS Software has customers in the following industries: airlines, automotive, finance/banking, health/hospital, consumer products, electronics, and government. The company has also begun to attract important international clients. These include the European Airbus consortium and a consortium of banks and financial firms based in Kenya.

SSS Software has grown rapidly since its inception just over a decade ago. Its revenue, net income, and earnings per share have all been above the industry average for the past several years. However, competition in this technologically sophisticated field has grown very rapidly. Recently, it has become more difficult to compete for major contracts. Moreover, although SSS Software's revenue and net income continue to grow, the rate of growth declined during the last fiscal year.

SSS Software's 250 employees are divided into several operating divisions with employees at four levels: nonmanagement, technical/professional, managerial, and executive. Nonmanagement employees take care of the clerical and facilities support functions. The technical/professional staff perform the core technical work for the firm. Most managerial employees are group managers who supervise a team of technical/professional employees working on a project for a particular customer. Staff who work in specialized areas such as finance, accounting, human resources, nursing, and law are also considered

FIGURE A

Partial Organization Chart of the Health and Financial Services Division managerial employees. The executive level includes the 12 highest-ranking employees at SSS Software. An organization chart in Figure A illustrates SSS Software's structure. There is also an employee classification report that lists the number of employees at each level of the organization.

In this exercise, you will play the role of Chris Perillo, vice president of operations for health and financial services. You learned last Wednesday, October 13, that your predecessor, Michael Grant, has resigned and gone to Universal Business Solutions, Inc. You were offered his former job, and you accepted it. Previously, you were the group manager for a team of 15 software developers assigned to work on the Airbus consortium project in the Airline Services Division. You spent all of Thursday and Friday and most of the weekend finishing up parts of the project, briefing your successor, and preparing for an interim report you will deliver in Paris on October 21.

It is now 7 a.m. Monday, and you are in your new office. You have arrived at work early so you can spend the next two hours reviewing material in your in-basket (including some memos and messages to Michael Grant), as well as your voice mail and e-mail. Your daily planning book indicates that you have no appointments today or tomorrow but will have to catch a plane for Paris early Wednesday morning. You have a full schedule for the remainder of the week and all of next week.

ASSIGNMENT

During the next two hours, review all the material in your in-basket, as well as your voice mail and e-mail. Take only two hours. Using the following response form as a model, indicate how you want to respond to each item (that is, via letter/memo, e-mail, phone/voice mail, or personal meeting). If you decide not to respond to an item, check "no response" on the response form. All of your responses must be written on the response forms. Write your precise, detailed response (do not merely jot down a few notes). For example, you might draft a memo or write out a message that you will deliver via phone/voice mail. You may also decide to meet with an individual (or individuals) during the limited time available on your calendar today or tomorrow. If so, prepare an agenda for a personal meeting and list your goals for the meeting. As you read through the items, you may occasionally observe some information that you think is relevant and want to remember (or attend to in the future) but that you decide not to include in any of your responses to employees. Write down such information on a sheet of paper titled "note to self."

SOURCE: D. Whetten and K. Cameron, *Developing Management Skills,* 6th ed. Copyright 2005. Reproduced by permission of Pearson Education, Inc., Upper Saddle River, New Jersey.

SAMPLE RESPONSE FORM

Relates to:

Memo # _____   E-mail # _____   Voice mail # _____

Response form:

_____ Letter/memo   _____ Meet with person (when, where)

_____ E-mail   _____ Note to self

_____ Phone call/voice mail _____ No response

ITEM 1 MEMO

TO: All employees

FROM: Roger Steiner, chief executive officer

DATE: October 15

I am pleased to announce that Chris Perillo has been appointed as vice president of operations for health and financial services. Chris will immediately assume responsibility for all operations previously managed by Michael Grant. Chris will have end-to-end responsibility for the design, development, integration, and maintenance of custom software for the health and finance/banking industries. This responsibility includes all technical, financial, and staffing issues. Chris will also manage our program of software support and integration for the recently announced merger of three large health maintenance organizations (HMOs). Chris will be responsible for our recently announced project with a consortium of banks and financial firms operating in Kenya. This project represents an exciting opportunity for us, and Chris's background seems ideally suited to the task.

Chris comes to this position with an undergraduate degree in computer science from the California Institute of Technology and an MBA from the University of Virginia. Chris began as a member of our technical/professional staff six years ago and has most recently served for three years as a group manager supporting domestic and international projects for our airlines industry group, including our recent work for the European Airbus consortium.

I am sure you all join me in offering congratulations to Chris for this promotion.

ITEM 2 MEMO

TO: All managers

FROM: Hal Harris, vice president, community and public relations

DATE: October 15

For your information, the following article appeared on the front page of the business section of Thursday's *Los Angeles Times*.

In a move that may create problems for SSS Software, Michael Grant and Janice Ramos have left SSS Software and moved to Universal Business Solutions Inc. Industry analysts see the move as another victory for Universal Business Solutions Inc. in their battle with SSS Software for share of the growing software development and integration business. Both Grant and Ramos had been with SSS Software for over seven years. Grant was most recently vice president of operations for all SSS Software's work in two industries: health and hospitals, and finance and banking. Ramos brings to Universal Business Solutions Inc. her special expertise in the growing area of international software development and integration.

Hillary Collins, an industry analyst with Merrill Lynch, said "The loss of key staff to a competitor can often create serious problems for a firm such as SSS Software. Grant and Ramos have an insider's understanding of SSS Software's strategic and technical limitations. It will be interesting to see if they can exploit this knowledge to the advantage of Universal Business Solutions Inc."

ITEM 3 MEMO

TO: Chris Perillo

FROM: Paula Sprague, executive assistant to Roger Steiner

DATE: October 15

Chris, I know that in your former position as a group manager in the Airline Services Division, you probably have met most of the group managers in the Health and Financial Services Division, but I thought you might like some more personal information about them. These people will be your direct reports on the management team.

Group #1: Bob Miller, 55-year-old white male, married (Anne) with two children and three grandchildren. Active in local Republican politics. Well regarded as a "hands-off" manager heading a high-performing team. Plays golf regularly with Mark McIntyre, John Small, and a couple of V.P.s from other divisions.

Group #2: Wanda Manners, 38-year-old white female, single with one school-age child. A fitness "nut," has run in several marathons. Some experience in Germany and Japan. Considered a hard-driving manager with a constant focus on the task at hand. Will be the first person to show up every morning.

Group #3: William Chen, 31-year-old male of Chinese descent, married (Harriet), two young children from his first marriage. Enjoys tennis and is quite good at it. A rising star in the company, he is highly respected by his peers as a "man of action" and a good friend.

Group #4: Leo Jones, 36-year-old white male, married (Janet) with an infant daughter. Recently returned from paternity leave. Has traveled extensively on projects because he speaks three languages. Has liked hockey ever since the time he spent in Montreal. Considered a strong manager who gets the most out of his people.

Group #5: Mark McIntyre, 45-year-old white male, married (Mary Theresa) to an executive in the banking industry. No children. A lot of experience in Germany and Eastern Europe. Has been writing a mystery novel. Has always been a good "team player," but several members of his technical staff are not well respected, and he hasn't addressed the problem.

Group #6: John Small, 38-year-old white male, recently divorced. Three children living with his wife. A gregarious individual who likes sports. He spent a lot of time in Mexico and Central America before he came to SSS Software. Recently has been doing mostly contract work with the federal government. An average manager, has had some trouble keeping his people on schedule.

Group #7: This position has been vacant since Janice Ramos left. Roger thinks we ought to fill this position quickly. Get in touch with me if you want information on any in-house candidates for any position.

Group #8: Marcus Harper, 42-year-old black male, married (Tamara) with two teenage children. Recently won an award in a local photography contest. Considered a strong manager who gets along with peers and works long hours.

Customer Services: Armand Marke, 38-year-old Armenian male, divorced. A basketball fan. Originally from Armenia. Previously a group manager. Worked hard to establish the technical services phone line, but now has pretty much left it alone.

Office administrator: Michelle Harrison, 41-year-old white female, single. Grew up on a ranch and still rides horses whenever she can. A strict administrator.

There are a number of good folks here, but they don't function well as a management team. I think Michael played favorites, especially with Janice and Leo. There are a few cliques in this group, and I'm not sure how effectively Michael dealt with them. I expect you will find it a challenge to build a cohesive team.

ITEM 4 MEMO

TO: Chris Perillo

FROM: Wanda Manners, Group 2 manager

DATE: October 15

CONFIDENTIAL AND RESTRICTED

Although I know you are new to your job, I feel it is important that I let you know about some information I just obtained concerning the development work we recently completed for First National Investment. Our project involved the development of asset management software for managing their international funds. This was a very complex project due to the volatile exchange rates and the forecasting tools we needed to develop.

As part of this project, we had to integrate the software and reports with all their existing systems and reporting mechanisms. To do this we were given access to all of their existing software (much of which was developed by Universal Business Solutions Inc.). Of course, we signed an agreement acknowledging that the software to which we were given access was proprietary and that our access was solely for the purpose of our system integration work associated with the project.

Unfortunately, I have learned that some parts of the software we developed actually "borrow" heavily from complex application programs developed for First National Investment by Universal Business Solutions Inc. It seems obvious to me that one or more of the software developers from Group 5 (that is, Mark McIntyre's group) inappropriately "borrowed" algorithms developed by Universal Business Solutions Inc. I am sure that doing so saved us significant development time on some aspects of the project. It seems very unlikely that First National Investment or Universal Business Solutions Inc. will ever become aware of this issue.

Finally, First National Investment is successfully using the software we developed and is thrilled with the work we did. We brought the project in on time and under budget. You probably know that they have invited us to bid on several other substantial projects.

I'm sorry to bring this delicate matter to your attention, but I thought you should know about it.

ITEM 5A MEMO

TO: Chris Perillo

FROM: Paula Sprague, executive assistant to Roger Steiner

DATE: October 15

RE: Letter from C.A.R.E. Services (copies attached)

Roger asked me to work on this C.A.R.E. project and obviously wants some fast action. A lot of the staff are already booked solid for the next couple of weeks. I knew that Elise Soto and Chu Hung Woo have the expertise to do this system, and when I checked with them, they were relatively free. I had them pencil in the next two weeks and wanted to let you know. Hopefully, it will take a "hot potato" out of your hands.

ITEM 5B COPY OF FAX

C.A.R.E.
Child and Adolescent Rehabilitative and Educational Services
A United Way Member Agency
200 Main Street
Los Angeles, California 90230

DATE: October 11

Mr. Roger Steiner, CEO
SSS Software
13 Miller Way
Los Angeles, California 90224

Dear Roger,

This letter is a follow-up to our conversation after last night's board meeting. I appreciated your comments during the board meeting about the need for sophisticated computer systems in nonprofit organizations, and I especially appreciate your generous offer of assistance to have SSS Software provide assistance to deal with the immediate problem with our accounting system. Since the board voted to fire the computer consultant, I am very worried about getting our reports done in time to meet the state funding cycle.

Thanks again for your offer of help during this crisis.

Sincerely yours,

Janice Polocizwic

Janice Polocizwic
Executive Director

ITEM 5C COPY OF LETTER

SSS SOFTWARE
13 Miller Way
Los Angeles, CA 90224
213-635-2000

DATE: October 12

Janice Polocizwic
Executive Director, C.A.R.E. Services
200 Main Street
Los Angeles, California 90230

Dear Janice,

I received your fax of October 11. I have asked Paula Sprague, my executive assistant, to line up people to work on your accounting system as soon as possible. You can expect to hear from her shortly.

Sincerely,

Roger Steiner

Roger Steiner

cc: Paula Sprague, Executive Assistant

ITEM 6 MEMO

TO: Michael Grant

FROM: Harry Withers, Group 6 technical staff

DATE: October 12

PERSONAL AND CONFIDENTIAL

Our team is having difficulty meeting the submission deadline of November 5 for the Halstrom project. Kim, Fred, Peter, Kyoto, Susan, Mala, and I have been working on the project for several weeks, but are experiencing some problems and may need additional time. I hesitate to write this letter, but the main problem is that our group manager, John Small, is involved in a relationship with Mala. Mala gets John's support for her ideas and brings them to the team as required components of the project. Needless to say, this has posed some problems for the group. Mala's background is especially valuable for this project, but Kim and Fred, who have both worked very hard on the project, do not want to work with her. In addition, one member of the team has been unavailable recently because of child care needs. Commitment to the project and team morale have plummeted. However, we'll do our best to get the project finished as soon as possible. Mala will be on vacation the next two weeks, so I'm expecting that some of us can complete it in her absence.

ITEM 7 VOICE MAIL

Hello, Michael. This is Jim Bishop of United Hospitals. I wanted to talk with you about the quality assurance project that you are working on for us. When José Martinez first started talking with us, I was impressed with his friendliness and expertise. But recently he doesn't seem to be getting much accomplished and has seemed distant and on-edge in conversations. Today I asked him about the schedule, and he seemed very defensive and not entirely in control of his emotions. I am quite concerned about our project. Please give me a call at 213-951-1234.

ITEM 8 VOICE MAIL

Hi, Michael. This is Armand. I wanted to talk with you about some issues with the technical services phone line. I've recently received some complaint letters from phone line customers whose complaints have included long delays while waiting for a technician to answer the phone; technicians who are not knowledgeable enough to solve problems; and, on occasion, rude service. Needless to say, I'm quite concerned about these complaints.

I believe that the overall quality of the phone line staff is very good, but we continue to be understaffed, even with the recent hires. The new technicians look strong but are working on the help line before being fully trained. Antolina, our best tech, often brings her child to work, which is adding to the craziness around here.

I think you should know that we're feeling a lot of stress here. I'll talk to you soon.

ITEM 9 VOICE MAIL

Hi Chris, it's Pat. Congratulations on your promotion. They definitely picked the right person. It's great news—for me, too. You've been a terrific mentor so far, so I'm expecting to learn a lot from you in your new position. How about lunch next week?

ITEM 10 VOICE MAIL

Chris, this is Bob Miller. Just thought you'd like to know that John's joke during our planning meeting has disturbed a few of the women in my group. Frankly, I think the thing's being blown out of proportion, especially since we all know this is a good place for both men and women to work. Give me a call if you want to chat about this.

ITEM 11 VOICE MAIL

Hello. This is Lorraine Adams from Westside Hospital. I read in today's Los Angeles Times that you will be taking over from Michael Grant. We haven't met yet, but your division has recently finished two large million-dollar projects for Westside. Michael Grant and I had some discussion about a small conversion of a piece of existing software to be compatible with the new systems. The original vendor had said that they would do the work but has been stalling, and I need to move quickly. Can you see if Harris Wilson, Chu Hung Woo, and Elise Soto are available to do this work as soon as possible? They were on the original project and work well with our people. You can call me at 213-555-3456.

Um . . . (long pause) I guess I should tell you that I got a call from Michael offering to do this work. But I think I should stick with SSS Software. Give me a call.

ITEM 12 VOICE MAIL

Hi, Chris. This is Roosevelt Moore calling. I'm a member of your technical/professional staff. I used to report to Janice Ramos, but since she left the firm, I thought I'd bring my concerns directly to you. I'd like to arrange some time to talk with you about my experience since returning from six weeks of paternity leave. Some of my major responsibilities have been turned over to others. I seem to be out of the loop and wonder if my career is at risk. Also, I am afraid that I won't be supported or seriously considered for the opening created by Janice's departure. Frankly, I feel I'm being screwed for taking my leave. I'd like to talk with you this week.

ITEM 13 E-MAIL

TO: Michael Grant

FROM: José Martinez, Group 1 technical staff

DATE: October 12

I would like to set up a meeting with you as soon as possible. I suspect that you will get a call from Jim Bishop of United Hospitals and want to be sure that you hear my side of the story first. I have been working on a customized system design for quality assurance for them using a variation of the J-3 product we developed several years ago. They had a number of special requirements and some quirks in their accounting systems, so I have had to put in especially long hours. I've worked hard to meet their demands, but they keep changing the ground rules. I keep thinking, this is just another J-3 I'm working on, but they have been interfering with an elegant design I have developed. It seems I'm not getting anywhere on this project. Then Mr. Bishop asked me if the system was running yet. I was worn out from dealing with the controller, and I made a sarcastic comment to Mr. Bishop. He gave me a funny look and just walked out of the room.

I would like to talk with you about this situation at your earliest convenience.

ITEM 14 E-MAIL

TO: Chris Perillo
FROM: John Small, Group 6 manager
DATE: October 15

Welcome aboard, Chris. I look forward to meeting with you. I just wanted to put a bug in your ear about finding a replacement for Janice Ramos. One of my technical staff, Mala Abendano, has the ability and drive to make an excellent group manager. I have encouraged her to apply for the position. I'd be happy to talk with you further about this at your convenience.

ITEM 15 E-MAIL

TO: Chris Perillo
FROM: Paula Sprague, executive assistant to Roger Steiner
DATE: October 15

Roger asked me to let you know about the large contract we have gotten in Kenya. It means that a team of four managers will be making a short trip to determine current needs. They will assign their technical staff the task of developing a system and software here over the next six months, and then the managers and possibly some team members will be spending about 10 months on site in Kenya to handle the implementation. Roger would appreciate an e-mail of your thoughts about the issues to be discussed at this meeting, additional considerations about sending people to Kenya, and about how you will put together an effective team to work on this project. The October 15 memo I sent to you will provide you with some information you'll need to start making these decisions.

ITEM 16 E-MAIL

TO: Chris Perillo
FROM: Sharon Shapiro, V.P. of Human Resources
DATE: October 15
RE: Upcoming meeting

I want to update you on the rippling effect of John Small's sexual joke at last week's planning meeting. Quite a few women have been very upset and have met informally to talk about it. They have decided to call a meeting of all the people concerned about this kind of behavior throughout the firm. I plan to attend, so I'll keep you posted.

ITEM 17 E-MAIL

TO: All SSS Software managers

FROM: Sharon Shapiro, Vice President, Human Resources

DATE: October 14

RE: Promotions and External Hires

Year-to-date (January through September) promotions and external hires

Level	Race					Sex		Total
	White	Black	Asian	Hispanic	Native American	M	F	
Hires into executive level	0 (0%)	0 (0%)	0 (0%)	0 (0%)	0 (0%)	0 (0%)	0 (0%)	0
Promotions to executive level	0 (0%)	0 (0%)	0 (0%)	0 (0%)	0 (0%)	0 (0%)	0 (0%)	0
Hires into management level	2 (67%)	1 (33%)	0 (0%)	0 (0%)	0 (0%)	2 (67%)	1 (33%)	3
Promotions to management level	7 (88%)	0 (0%)	1 (12%)	0 (0%)	0 (0%)	7 (88%)	1 (12%)	8
Hires into technical/ professional level	10 (36%)	6 (21%)	10 (36%)	2 (7%)	0 (0%)	14 (50%)	14 (50%)	28
Promotions to technical/ professional level	0 (0%)	0 (0%)	0 (0%)	0 (0%)	0 (0%)	0 (0%)	0 (0%)	0
Hires into nonmanagement	4 (20%)	10 (50%)	2 (10%)	4 (20%)	0 (0%)	6 (30%)	14 (70%)	20
Promotions to nonmanagement level	NA	NA	NA	NA	NA	NA	NA	NA

SSS Software employee (EEO) classification report as of June 30

Level	Race					Sex		Total
	White	Black	Asian	Hispanic	Native American	M	F	
Executive level	11 (92%)	0 (0%)	1 (8%)	0 (0%)	0 (0%)	11 (92%)	1 (8%)	12
Management level	43 (90%)	2 (4%)	2 (4%)	1 (2%)	0 (0%)	38 (79%)	10 (21%)	48
Technical/ professional level	58 (45%)	20 (15%)	37 (28%)	14 (11%)	1 (1%)	80 (62%)	50 (38%)	130
Nonmanagement level	29 (48%)	22 (37%)	4 (7%)	4 (7%)	1 (2%)	12 (20%)	48 (80%)	60
Total	141 (56%)	44 (18%)	44 (18%)	19 (8%)	2 (1%)	141 (56%)	109 (44%)	250

Employee Raiding

Litson Cotton Yarn Manufacturing Company, located in Murray, New Jersey, decided as a result of increasing labor costs to relocate its plant in Fairlee, a southern community of 4,200. Plant construction was started, and a human resources office was opened in the state employment office, located in Fairlee.

Because of ineffective HR practices in the other three textile mills located within a 50-mile radius of Fairlee, Litson was receiving applications from some of the most highly skilled and trained textile operators in the state. After receiving applications from approximately 500 people, employment was offered to 260 male and female applicants. These employees would be placed immediately on the payroll with instructions to await final installation of machinery, which was expected within the following six weeks.

The managers of the three other textile companies, faced with resignations from their most efficient and best-trained employees, approached the Litson managers with the complaint that their labor force was being "raided." They registered a strong protest to cease such practices and demanded an immediate cancellation of the employment of the 260 people hired by Litson.

Litson managers discussed the ethical and moral considerations involved in offering employment to the 260 people. Litson clearly faced a tight labor market in Fairlee, and management thought that if the 260 employees were discharged, the company would face cancellation of its plans and large construction losses. Litson management also felt obligated to the 260 employees who had resigned from their previous employment in favor of Litson.

The dilemma was compounded when the manager of one community plant reminded Litson that his plant was part of a nationwide chain supplied with cotton yarn from Litson. He implied that Litson's attempts to continue operations in Fairlee could result in cancellation of orders and the possible loss of approximately 18 percent market share. It was also suggested to Litson managers that actions taken by the nationwide textile chain could result in cancellation of orders from other textile companies. Litson's president held an urgent meeting of his top subordinates to (1) decide what to do about the situation in Fairlee, (2) formulate a written policy statement indicating Litson's position regarding employee raiding, and (3) develop a plan for implementing the policy.

How would you prepare for the meeting, and what would you say at the meeting?

Effective Management

Dr. Sam Perkins, a graduate of the Harvard University College of Medicine, had a private practice in internal medicine for 12 years. Fourteen months ago, he was persuaded by the Massachusetts governor to give up private practice to be director of the State Division of Human Services.

After one year as director, Perkins recognized he had made little progress in reducing the considerable inefficiency in the division. Employee morale and effectiveness seemed even lower than when he had assumed the position. He realized his past training and experiences were of a clinical nature with little exposure to effective management techniques. Perkins decided to research literature on the subject of management available to him at a local university.

Perkins soon realized that management scholars are divided on the question of what constitutes effective management. Some believe people are born with certain identifiable personality traits that make them effective managers. Others believe a manager can learn to be effective by treating subordinates with a personal and considerate approach and by giving particular attention to their need for favorable working conditions. Still others emphasize the importance of developing a management style characterized by an authoritarian, democratic, or laissez-faire approach. Perkins was further confused when he learned that a growing number of scholars advocate that effective management is contingent on the situation.

Because a state university was located nearby, Perkins contacted the dean of its college of business administration. The dean referred him to the director of the college's management center, Professor Joel McCann. Discussions between Perkins and McCann resulted in a tentative agreement that the management center would organize a series of management training sessions for the State Division of Human Services. Before agreeing on the price tag for the management conference, Perkins asked McCann to prepare a proposal reflecting his thoughts on the following questions:

1. How will the question of what constitutes effective management be answered during the conference?
2. What will be the specific subject content of the conference?
3. Who will the instructors be?
4. What will be the conference's duration?
5. How can the conference's effectiveness be evaluated?
6. What policies should the State Division of Human Services adopt regarding who the conference participants should be and how they should be selected? How can these policies be best implemented?

4 Planning and Strategic Management

LEARNING OBJECTIVES

After studying Chapter 4, you will be able to:

LO 1   Summarize the basic steps in any planning process. p. 128

LO 2   Describe how strategic planning should be integrated with tactical and operational planning. p. 133

LO 3   Identify elements of the external environment and internal resources of the firm to analyze before formulating a strategy. p. 141

LO 4   Define core competencies and explain how they provide the foundation for business strategy. p. 144

LO 5   Summarize the types of choices available for corporate strategy. p. 147

LO 6   Discuss how companies can achieve competitive advantage through business strategy. p. 151

LO 7   Describe the keys to effective strategy implementation. p. 153

> **" Manage your destiny, or someone else will. "**
>
> — JACK WELCH, FORMER CEO, GENERAL ELECTRIC

| Manager's Brief | Progress Report | Onward |

Management Connection

EVEN MUCH-ADMIRED GE NEEDS TO RETHINK ITS PLANS SOMETIMES

General Electric is a huge company with a stellar reputation for good management. In one measure of its importance to the economy, for example, GE's stock has been included in the Dow Jones Industrial Average longer than any other corporation's. The company's 300,000 employees in 160 countries help it bring in revenues of $150 billion a year from selling a diverse range of products including jet engines, medical scanning devices, power generation equipment, commercial loans, home appliances, and more. But in the years after Jeffrey Immelt was appointed to the top job at GE, the situation facing the company could hardly have been much worse.

Immelt started his tenure as CEO on September 7, 2001, just days before terrorist attacks rattled the world, including the business markets. Then in 2008 came the near-collapse of the banking system, an event that hit GE hard. Throughout the decade, financial institutions were generating tremendous profits, so under Immelt's predecessor, Jack Welch, GE aggressively built up its GE Capital group. A key advantage of expansion in the financial arena was that new products could be introduced without long-range investment in research and development or construction of factories to make industrial equipment. Under Immelt, GE continued its expansion into commercial real estate and other types of loans, and GE Capital eventually grew to become the largest nonbank financial company in the United States. The profitability of GE Capital (before the credit crisis, it was earning half of GE's profits) made investors happy. But then came the financial crisis, and the group's profits suddenly turned to losses as borrowers defaulted on their loans. Adding to GE's woes, the credit crisis contributed to the worst economic downturn since the Great Depression, and orders for the company's equipment tumbled.

Shocked investors sold off their GE stock, driving its price down from $29 per share before the financial crisis to less than $6. It would be many months before the share price crept back up near $20 per share.

Immelt, a widely respected and experienced manager, set goals and led the development of plans for GE to return to its past track record of success. Instead of relying on the financial industry to drive profits, Immelt refocused the company on making innovative physical products, the strategy that was the company's heritage from the days when Thomas Edison developed the incandescent lightbulb.

Immelt insists that GE is well on the road to recovery and future success. And one advantage of the company's massive size is that it earns money on a massive scale. GE recently posted profits of $10 billion. Still, a few years earlier, the company was earning double those profits.

The challenge facing Immelt is how to devise plans for returning to the kind of reliable success that investors have come to count on. Immelt's approach to meeting that challenge is to focus on GE's strength as an innovator and to apply innovation in business areas with growth potential while selling or scaling back business units with less potential for future success. Whereas a smaller, more focused company might struggle with finding enough resources to expand in a few directions, the trick for GE's planners is to figure out which of the many possible activities are most important to pursue. Under Immelt, the company is looking for opportunities where innovation can give GE an edge in infrastructure (for example, transportation, water treatment, and power generation), finance, and media (the company owns NBC Universal). Although these criteria impose some priorities, they are still very broad. Succeeding in such a complicated environment calls for expert planning—and implementation of those plans—at all levels of the organization.[1]

As you read this chapter, think about the challenge of crafting goals and strategies that provide useful direction to a massive enterprise involved in multiple industries. What planning methods could help managers zero in on the best opportunities? Which of these methods would be equally useful for a small enterprise?

To imagine the global conglomerate General Electric—or any organization—dealing with the significant challenges it faces without developing a plan beforehand is almost impossible. Planning is a formal expression of managerial intent. It describes what managers decide to do and how they will do it. It provides the framework, focus, and direction required for a meaningful effort. Without planning, any improvements in an organization's innovation, speed, quality, service, and cost will be accidental, if they occur at all. This chapter examines the most important concepts and processes involved in planning and strategic management. By learning these concepts and reviewing the steps outlined, you will be on your way to understanding the current approaches to the strategic management of today's organizations.

An Overview of Planning Fundamentals

The importance of formal planning in organizations has grown dramatically. Until the mid-1900s, most planning was unstructured and fragmented, and formal planning was restricted to a few large corporations. Although management pioneers such as Alfred Sloan of General Motors instituted formal planning processes, planning became a widespread management function only during the last few decades. Initially, larger organizations adopted formal planning, but today even small firms operated by aggressive, opportunistic entrepreneurs engage in formal planning.[2]

Planning provides individuals and work units with a clear map to follow their future activities.

Planning is the conscious, systematic process of making decisions about goals and activities that an individual, group, work unit, or organization will pursue in the future. Planning is not an informal or haphazard response to a crisis; it is a purposeful effort that is directed and controlled by managers and often draws on the knowledge and experience of employees throughout the organization. Planning provides individuals and work units with a clear map to follow in their future activities; at the same time this map may be flexible enough to allow for individual circumstances and changing conditions.

The Basic Planning Process

LO 1

Because planning is a decision process—you're deciding what to do and how to go about doing it—the important steps followed during formal planning are similar to the basic decision-making steps we discussed in Chapter 3. Figure 4.1 summarizes the similarities between decision making and planning—including the fact that both move not just in one direction but in a *cycle*. The outcomes of decisions and plans are evaluated, and if necessary, they are revised.

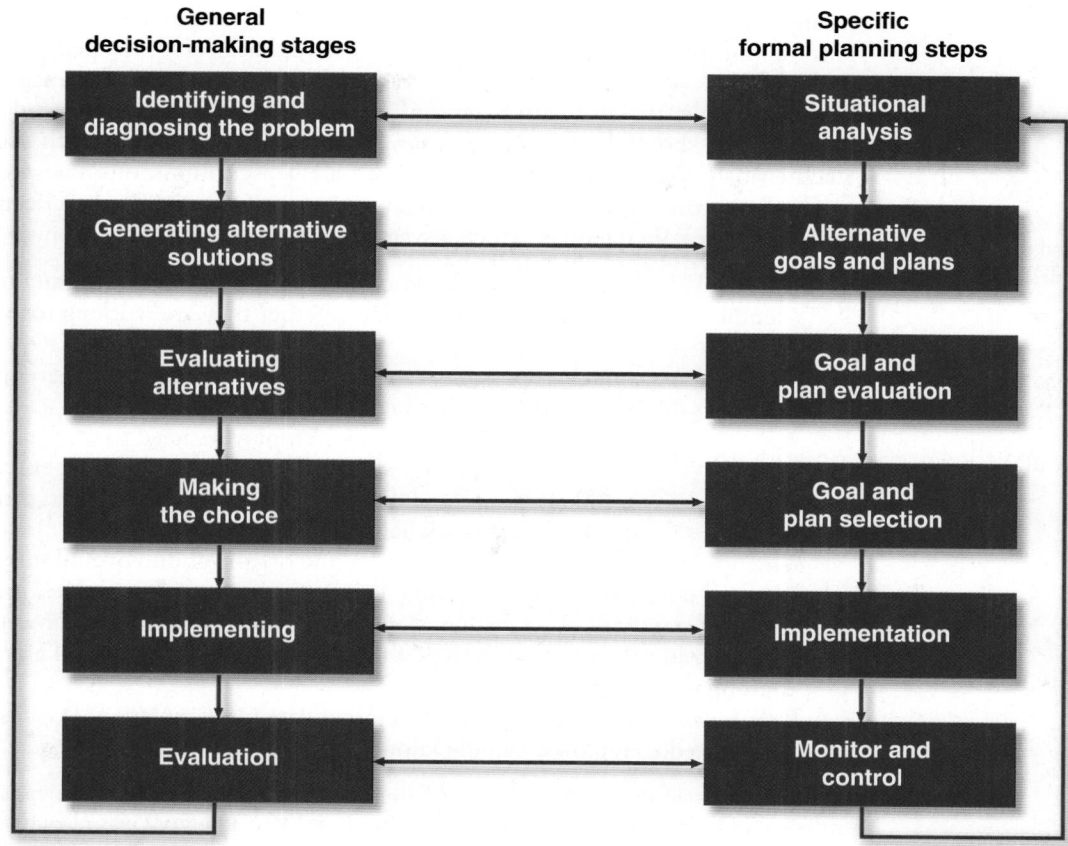

**General
decision-making stages**

- Identifying and diagnosing the problem
- Generating alternative solutions
- Evaluating alternatives
- Making the choice
- Implementing
- Evaluation

**Specific
formal planning steps**

- Situational analysis
- Alternative goals and plans
- Goal and plan evaluation
- Goal and plan selection
- Implementation
- Monitor and control

FIGURE 4.1

Decision-Making Stages
(Chapter 3) and Formal
Planning Steps (Chapter 4)

We now describe the basic planning process in more detail. Later in this chapter, we will discuss how managerial decisions and plans fit into the larger purposes of the organization—its ultimate strategy, mission, vision, and goals.

Step 1: Situational Analysis   As the contingency approach advocates, planning begins with a **situational analysis.** Within their time and resource constraints, planners should gather, interpret, and summarize all information relevant to the planning issue in question. A thorough situational analysis studies past events, examines current conditions, and attempts to forecast future trends. It focuses on the internal forces at work in the organization or work unit and, consistent with the open-systems approach (see Chapter 2), examines influences from the external environment. The outcome of this step is the identification and diagnosis of planning assumptions, issues, and problems.

A thorough situational analysis will provide information about the planning decisions you need to make. For example, if you are a manager in a magazine company considering the launch of a sports publication for the teen market, your analysis will include such factors as the number of teens who subscribe to magazines, the appeal of the teen market to advertisers, your firm's ability to serve this market effectively, current economic conditions, the level of teen interest in sports, and any sports magazines already serving this market and their current sales. Such a detailed analysis will help you decide whether to proceed with the next step in your magazine launch.

Step 2: Alternative Goals and Plans   Based on the situational analysis, the planning process should generate alternative goals that may be pursued in the future and the alternative plans that may be used to achieve those goals. This step in the process

situational analysis

A process planners use, within time and resource constraints, to gather, interpret, and summarize all information relevant to the planning issue under consideration.

should stress creativity and encourage managers and employees to think in broad terms about their jobs. Once a range of alternatives has been developed, the merits of these different plans and goals will be evaluated. Continuing with our magazine publishing example, the alternatives you might want to consider could include whether the magazine should be targeted at young men, young women, or both groups, and whether it should be sold mainly online, through subscriptions, or on newsstands.

goal

A target or end that management desires to reach.

Goals are the targets or ends the manager wants to reach. To be effective, goals should have certain qualities, which are easy to remember with the acronym SMART:

> Goals are the targets or ends the manager wants to reach.

Specific—When goals are precise, describing particular behaviors and outcomes, employees can more easily determine whether they are working toward the goals.

Measurable—As much as possible, each goal should quantify the desired results so there is no doubt whether it has been achieved.

Attainable (but challenging)—Employees need to recognize that they can attain the goals they are responsible for, or else they are likely to become discouraged. However, they also should feel challenged to work hard and be creative.

Relevant—Each goal should contribute to the organization's overall mission (discussed later in this chapter), while being consistent with its values, including ethical standards (see Chapter 5). Goals are most likely to be relevant to the organization's overall objectives if they are consistent within and among work groups.

Time-bound—Effective goals specify a target date for completion. Besides knowing what to do, employees should know when they need to deliver results.

General Electric met at least some of these criteria with its goal to increase sales in India to $8 billion by 2010 from $1.9 billion in 2006.[3] The goal was clearly *measurable* and *time-bound*. It also was *relevant* because the fast-growing Indian economy is a logical source of sales, not only because of its size, but also because a developing economy needs many of the kinds of products GE sells. While the sales number was *specific*, GE's people would need to settle on many details of how to achieve it: $8 billion from selling which products to whom? And the goal to quadruple sales was challenging to the point that some would question whether it was *achievable*. In fact, GE did not meet this target, but perhaps it could have done so with a clearer vision of how to achieve it. Ideally, SMART goals not only point individual employees in the direction they should be going but also tend to be accepted by the managers and employees who are charged with achieving them. Thus they both direct employees and motivate them (for more on the importance of motivation, see Chapter 13).

plans

The actions or means managers intend to use to achieve organizational goals.

Plans are the actions or means the manager intends to use to achieve goals. At a minimum, planning should outline alternative actions that may lead to the attainment of each goal, the resources required to reach the goal through those means, and the obstacles that may develop. After General Motors declared bankruptcy and borrowed millions from the U.S. government in 2009, management made plans for a return to profitability. The plans included reducing costs by producing fewer trucks, eliminating several brands, introducing smaller vehicles, keeping fewer vehicles in inventory, and closing hundreds of dealerships. GM had relied on trucks to generate comfortable profits, but those plans were no longer effective as a poor economy and high gas prices shifted demand toward fuel-efficient models. So besides cutting costs, GM introduced cars it hoped would be more popular, including the Cruze compact and the Sonic subcompact. Despite obstacles such as difficulty meeting demand with a reduced workforce and the lower profitability of smaller vehicles, the company moved back into the black a year after the bankruptcy, and in two years it reported its strongest financial performance in over a decade.[4]

In this chapter we will talk about various types of plans. Some plans, called *contingency plans*, might be referred to as "what if" plans. They include sets of actions to be taken when a company's initial plans have not worked well or if events in the external environment require a sudden change. Disasters of recent years, including the 2001 terrorist attacks and Hurricanes Katrina and Rita, have reminded many businesses how important contingency planning can be.

Most major corporations now have contingency plans in place to respond to a major disaster—to make sure vital data are backed up and can be recovered in an emergency, for instance, or that employees know what to do when a crisis occurs. But contingency plans are important for more common situations as well. For example, many businesses are affected by snowstorms, increases in gasoline prices, computer breakdowns, or changes in consumer tastes. JetBlue initially achieved success as an airline that would "bring humanity back to air travel" by caring about its customers and employees. But the airline was humiliated by its inability to cope with a February snowstorm during which at least one plane notoriously sat on a runway for 10 hours; the company took days to recover, canceling a thousand flights.[5]

Step 3: Goal and Plan Evaluation   Next managers will evaluate the advantages, disadvantages, and potential effects of each alternative goal and plan. They must prioritize those goals and even eliminate some of them. Also, managers will consider carefully the implications of alternative plans for meeting high-priority goals. In particular, they will pay a great deal of attention to the cost of any initiative and the investment return that is likely to result. In our magazine publishing example, your evaluation might determine that newsstand sales alone wouldn't be profitable enough to justify the launch. Perhaps you could improve profits with an online edition supplemented by podcasts. To decide, you would estimate the costs and expected returns of such alternatives, trying to follow the decision steps advised in Chapter 3.

Step 4: Goal and Plan Selection   Once managers have assessed the various goals and plans, they will select the one that is most appropriate and feasible. The evaluation process will identify the priorities and trade-offs among the goals and plans. For example, if your plan is to launch a number of new publications, and you're trying to choose among them,

> "Most discussions of decision making assume that only senior executives make decisions or that only senior executives' decisions matter. This is a dangerous mistake."
>
> Peter Drucker

you might weigh the different up-front investment each requires, the size of each market, which one fits best with your existing product line or company image, and so on. Experienced judgment always plays an important role in this process. However, as you will discover later in the chapter, relying on judgment alone may not be the best way to proceed.

Typically, a formal planning process leads to a written set of goals and plans that are appropriate and feasible for a particular set of circumstances. In some organizations, the alternative generation, evaluation, and selection steps generate planning **scenarios,** as discussed in Chapter 2. A different contingency plan is attached to each scenario. The manager pursues the goals and implements the plans associated with the most likely scenario. However, the manager will also be prepared to switch to another set of plans if the situation changes and

Bottom Line
Contingency plans that keep service levels high during a crisis can seal a company's reputation for caring about customers. But this commitment requires highly dedicated and creative employees, and access to the necessary resources can be expensive. Managers must decide how crucial service is to their strategy—and how willing customers will be to forgive them for service lapses under pressure.
During a major storm, what services do you expect to be able to receive without interruption? Would you pay more to make these services more reliable?

scenario

A narrative that describes a particular set of future conditions.

The Hard Rock Café carries its strategy—to be identified with rock 'n' roll—through to its hotel signs.

another scenario becomes relevant. This approach helps the firm anticipate and manage crises and allows greater flexibility and responsiveness.

IN PRACTICE

If a company hasn't already considered relevant scenarios, managers have to be prepared to restart the planning process when an unexpected change brings disappointing results. This flexible approach to planning can help a company survive and even thrive in a turbulent environment. For example, when the economy recently took a downturn, major clients stopped calling on Cor Business, a management coaching firm, for help in developing their managers. Jeffrey Hull and the other partners of Cor Business realized their firm's survival required a new plan for bringing in business.

The partners brainstormed ideas for a new business plan. Looking over the prior year's results, they noticed that most of Cor Business's growth that year had come from small businesses, even though the partners had been directing most of their energy toward large companies like MasterCard and AT&T. As a matter of fact, as the economy had slowed, more and more nervous small business owners had been looking for help from their firm.

Hull and the other partners drew up a new plan in which they would focus on serving small clients, helping them do what Cor Business's managers were doing—move beyond their fear of change to find new opportunities in challenging times. Hull counseled the owner of a real estate investment company to set aside his fears about the real estate downturn, reevaluate his data on the prospects for converting a warehouse into a restaurant, and go ahead with plans for what was in fact a well-researched, practical idea.[6]

- Now that Cor Business's managers have a plan for surviving difficult times, do they still need to consider different scenarios? Why or why not?

Step 5: Implementation   Once managers have selected the goals and plans, they must implement the plans designed to achieve the goals. Even the best plans are use-

> Even the best plans are useless if they are not implemented properly.

less if they are not implemented properly. Managers and employees must understand the plan, have the resources to implement it, and be motivated to do so. Including employees in the previous steps of the planning process paves the way for the implementation phase. As we mentioned earlier, employees usually are better informed, more committed, and more highly motivated when a goal or plan is one they helped develop.

Finally, successful implementation requires a plan to be linked to other systems in the organization, particularly the budget and reward systems. If the manager does not have a budget with financial resources to execute the plan, the plan is probably doomed. Similarly, goal achievement must be linked to the organization's reward system. Many organizations use incentive programs to encourage employees to achieve goals and to implement plans properly. Commissions, salaries, promotions, bonuses, and other rewards are based on successful performance.

At Wells Fargo, chairman of the board Dick Kovacevich saw that the bank—one of the nation's largest—could stay competitive by excelling at "cross-selling," the practice of encouraging the bank's existing customers to use more of its financial services. Bank customers typically go to different institutions for different services, but Wells Fargo beat the odds by getting employees at all levels to focus on customer needs rather than product lines. Tellers and branch managers receive training aimed at this goal, and pay systems reward employees for cross-selling. As a result, Wells Fargo customers use an average of 5.2 of the bank's products, roughly double the average for the industry. Selling to existing customers is much more profitable than winning new ones, so this strategy might seem obvious. Perhaps it is, but Wells Fargo board member Robert Joss says, "It's simple in concept but very hard in execution," adding that this successful implementation reflects Kovacevich's "great capacity to motivate people."[7]

Bottom Line

Tying plans to a firm's financials is a key element of success. *How might a plan to improve employees' job satisfaction be tied to a company's financial measures?*

Step 6: Monitor and Control   Although it is sometimes ignored, the sixth step in the formal planning process—monitoring and controlling—is essential. Without it, you will never know whether your plan is succeeding. As we mentioned earlier, planning works in a cycle; it is an ongoing, repetitive process. Managers must continually monitor the actual performance of their work units against the units' goals and plans. They also need to develop control systems to measure that performance and allow them to take corrective action when the plans are implemented improperly or when the situation changes. In our magazine publishing example, newsstand and subscription sales reports are essential for letting you know how well your new magazine launch is going. If subscription sales aren't doing as well as expected, you may need to revise your marketing plan. We will discuss the important issue of control systems in greater detail later in this chapter and in Chapter 16.

strategic planning

A set of procedures for making decisions about the organization's long-term goals and strategies.

strategic goals

Major targets or end results relating to the organization's long-term survival, value, and growth.

A strategy is a pattern of actions and resource allocations designed to achieve the goals of the organization.

Levels of Planning

In Chapter 1 you learned about the three major types of managers: top-level (*strategic* managers), middle-level (*tactical* managers), and frontline (*operational* managers). Because planning is an important management function, managers at all three levels use it. However, the scope and activities of the planning process at each level of the organization often differ.

Strategic Planning

Strategic planning involves making decisions about the organization's long-term goals and strategies. Strategic plans have a strong external orientation and cover major portions of the organization. Senior executives are responsible for the development and execution of the strategic plan, although they usually do not formulate or implement the entire plan personally.

LO 2

The Chicago Sun-Times and the Chicago Tribune are the only two major daily newspapers that remain in Chicago, a city of 3 million. Both papers are in serious trouble from declining circulation and poor advertising revenues. What kind of new strategy do you think would help to ensure the survival of these two organizations?

Strategic goals are major targets or end results that relate to the long-term survival, value, and growth of the organization. Strategic managers—top-level managers— usually establish goals that reflect both effectiveness (providing appropriate outputs) and efficiency (a high ratio of outputs to inputs). Typical strategic goals include growth, increasing market share, improving profitability, boosting return on investment, fostering both quantity and quality of outputs, increasing productivity, improving customer service, and contributing to society.

Organizations usually have a number of mutually reinforcing strategic goals. For example, a computer manufacturer may have as its strategic goals the launch of a specified number of new products in a particular time frame, of higher quality, with a targeted increase in market share. Each of these goals supports and contributes to the others.

A strategy is a pattern of actions and resource allocations designed to achieve the goals of the organization. An effective strategy provides a basis for answering five broad questions about how the organization will meet its objectives: (1) Where will we be active? (2) How will we get there (e.g., by increasing sales or acquiring another company)? (3) How will we win in the marketplace (e.g.,

strategy

A pattern of actions and resource allocations designed to achieve the organization's goals.

by keeping prices low or offering the best service)? (4) How fast will we move and in what sequence will we make changes? (5) How will we obtain financial returns (low costs or premium prices)?[8] In setting a strategy, managers try to match the organization's skills and resources to the opportunities found in the external environment. Every organization has certain strengths and weaknesses, so the actions, or strategies, the organization implements should help build on strengths in areas that satisfy the wants and needs of consumers and other key factors in the organization's external environment. Also, some organizations may implement strategies that change or influence the external environment, as discussed in Chapter 2.

Tactical and Operational Planning

Once the organization's strategic goals and plans are identified, they serve as the foundation for planning done by middle-level and frontline managers. As you can see in Figure 4.2, goals and plans become more specific and involve shorter periods of time as they move from the strategic level to the tactical level and then to the operational level. A strategic plan will typically have a time horizon of from three to seven years—but sometimes even decades, as with the successful plan to land a probe on Titan, Saturn's moon. Tactical plans may have a time horizon of a year or two, and operational plans may cover a period of months.

> In setting a strategy, managers try to match the organization's skills and resources to the opportunities found in the external environment.

Tactical planning translates broad strategic goals and plans into specific goals and plans that are relevant to a definite portion of the organization, often a functional area like marketing or human resources, as discussed in Chapter 10. Tactical plans focus on the major actions a unit must take to fulfill its part of the strategic plan. For example, if the strategy calls for the rollout of a new product line, the tactical plan for the manufacturing unit might involve the design, testing, and installation of the equipment needed to produce the new line.

tactical planning

A set of procedures for translating broad strategic goals and plans into specific goals and plans that are relevant to a distinct portion of the organization, such as a functional area like marketing.

operational planning

The process of identifying the specific procedures and processes required at lower levels of the organization.

Operational planning identifies the specific procedures and processes required at lower levels of the organization. Frontline managers usually focus on routine tasks such as production runs, delivery schedules, and human resource requirements, as we discuss in Chapters 16 and 17.

The planning model we have been describing is a hierarchical one, with top-level strategies flowing down through the levels of the organization into more specific goals and plans and an ever-more-limited timetable. But in today's complex organizations, the planning sequence is often not as rigid as this traditional view. As we will see later in this chapter, managers throughout an organization may be involved in developing the strategic plan and contributing critical elements to it. Also, in practice, lower-level managers may be making decisions that shape strategy, whether or not top executives realize it. When Intel senior adviser Andy Grove suggested that the company exit the computer memory business, Intel was directing about one-third of its research dollars to memory-related projects. However, on a practical level, the company had already been exiting the business; only 4 percent of its total sales were for computer memory

FIGURE 4.2

Hierarchy of Goals and Plans

Managerial Level	Level of Detail	Time Horizon
Top	Low	Long (3–7 years)
Middle	Medium	Medium (1–2 years)
Frontline	High	Short (<1 year)

products. Why was this occurring if it wasn't yet a defined strategy? Manufacturing managers had been directed by finance executives to set up factories in a way that would generate the biggest margins (revenues minus costs) per square inch of microchips produced. As computer memory became a money-losing commodity, manufacturing made fewer of those products. So when Intel announced it would get out of the memory business, its strategy was catching up with its operational planning, which had been driven by tactical plans.[9] The lesson for top managers is to make sure they are communicating strategy to all levels of the organization *and* paying attention to what is happening at all levels in the organization. In the "Management Connection: Progress Report," consider whether GE's top management applied that principle.

| Manager's Brief | **Progress Report** | Onward |

Management Connection

ALIGNING GE'S STRATEGY AND PLANS

As we saw at the beginning of this chapter, GE is looking for opportunities where innovation can give the company an edge in infrastructure, finance, and media. This is a very broad strategy. How do managers translate it into activities they can control?

For GE's human resources management, supporting GE's strategies includes development of the kind of management talent that can meet the demands of running a massive global corporation. Intensive training and development activities are one feature of GE that has distinguished the corporation for years. The company's tremendous size and resources enable it to establish its own intensive training programs; GE spends $1 billion a year on training. As the company positions itself for a future in which past practices are no longer guarantees of success, it is expanding the management development activities to bring in more outside ideas. Under CEO Jeffrey Immelt, 30 top managers have begun studying and visiting other companies to learn from their strengths—innovation at Google, for example, and resilience amid uncertainty at the U.S. Military Academy. The goal is to identify ways the company can better prepare all of its leaders and evaluate their performance. Immelt also brought in personal coaches to try out their effectiveness in working with some of the company's high-potential managers.

Immelt assigned his chief learning officer, Susan Peters, to evaluate which traits are most needed in leaders of the 21st century, to be sure these are the qualities the company is selecting for and developing. The company measures managers in terms of their external focus, clear thinking, imagination, inclusiveness, and expertise—broad qualities that can be adjusted for particular situations and need to be redefined periodically to ensure they are up-to-date. For example, under Welch, the previous CEO, there was more emphasis on efficiency, and recently

under Immelt, there has been more of a drive for customer focus and innovation. To achieve this, the company is pushing more responsibility for making decisions further down to levels of the organization where managers interact with customers. GE increased the funding for its global research center in Niskayuna, New York. Immelt had a guesthouse built near the facility and encourages business leaders and customers to stay there so they can interact directly with GE's researchers. One sign that this has created a fertile environment for new ideas is the growth in GE's patent awards, which rose from 1,991 in 2001 to 2,945 in 2010.

The company's recommitment to its background as a technological innovator is evident in GE's production facilities. For example, in Batesville, Mississippi, GE is expanding a factory that makes parts for fuel-efficient jet engines. The products use lightweight but strong composite materials, and production processes include computer-controlled machine tools for cutting the materials precisely. The people who carry out this work have been organized into teams of 6 to 12 workers each, and each team is charged with continually identifying and implementing ways to improve efficiency. So far, the teams have slashed the time it takes to go from cutting fabric to shipping parts by 80 percent. At plants like these, GE has committed itself to expand by hiring 6,300 more manufacturing workers in the United States.

As in the case of using high-tech materials to make fuel-efficient jet engines, many of GE's innovation projects are targeting ways customers can reduce their impact on the environment. Starting in 2005, GE launched a project it calls "ecomagination," which addresses what Immelt sees as two growth markets: energy efficiency and alternative energy sources. Immelt himself spends much of his time talking with customers, analysts, government officials, and others about the opportunities for pursuing sustainability. He is supported in this effort by Beth Comstock, a senior vice president and GE's chief marketing officer. Initially Immelt and Comstock found there was little enthusiasm for ecomagination inside GE; but as customers have been impressed by the energy savings GE can help them realize, acceptance of the program quickly spread through the company. Besides the jet engines, other products that fit under the ecomagination umbrella include batteries for hybrid vehicles, a hybrid train locomotive, equipment for solar and wind power, parts for nuclear power plants, and recharging stations for electric vehicles. The ecomagination campaign also covers efforts to run GE itself more efficiently. The company recently announced plans to buy 25,000 electric vehicles for its corporate fleet and its fleet management business by 2015. Not only does that save money on gas, but it helps to stimulate the market for electric cars—and, indirectly, for the charging stations that GE sells.[10]

- Identify a goal that a GE manager might set to achieve the strategy described here. Write that example as a SMART goal, inventing the details if information is not given.
- Based on the examples given, how well do you think GE's tactical and operational plans are aligned with its overall strategy? Why?

Aligning Tactical, Operational, and Strategic Planning

To be fully effective, the organization's strategic, tactical, and operational goals and plans must be *aligned*—that is, they must be consistent, mutually supportive, and focused on achieving the common purpose and direction. Whole Foods Market, for example, links its tactical and operational planning directly to its strategic planning. The firm describes itself on its website as a mission-driven company that aims to set the standards for excellence for food retailers. The firm measures its success in fulfilling its vision by "customer satisfaction, team member excellence and happiness, return on capital investment, improvement in the state of the environment, and local and larger community support."

Whole Foods's strategic goal is "to sell the highest-quality products that also offer high value for our customers." Its operational goals focus on ingredients, freshness, taste, nutritional value, safety, and appearance that meet or exceed its customers' expectations, including guaranteeing product satisfaction. Tactical goals include store environments that are "inviting, fun, unique, informal, comfortable, attractive, nurturing, and educational" and safe and inviting work environments for its employees.

One method for aligning the organization's strategic and operational goals is a *strategy map*. A strategy map provides a tool managers can use to communicate their strategic goals and enable members of the organization at every level to understand the parts they will play in helping to achieve them. The map illustrates the four key drivers (or "balanced scorecard") of a firm's long-term success: the skills of its people and their ability to grow and learn; the effectiveness of its internal processes; its ability to deliver value to customers; and ultimately its ability to grow its financial assets. The map shows how specific plans and goals in each area link to the others and can generate real improvements in an organization's performance.

Figure 4.3 shows how a strategy map might be built and how the various goals of the organization relate to each other to create long-term value for the firm. As an example, let us assume that a company's primary *financial goal* is "to increase revenues by enhancing the value we offer to existing customers by making our prices the lowest available." (Target and Walmart might be good examples of companies with this kind of strategy.) The company will then have corresponding goals and plans in the other sections of the map to support that strategy. Its *learning and growth goals* might include bringing in the most efficient production technologies or work processes and training the staff to use them. These in turn will lead to the *internal goals* of improved production speed and lower cost, which in turn lead to the *customer goal* of competitive pricing, making the original financial goal feasible. On the other hand, a financial strategy of revenue growth through new products might lead to people and technology goals that speed up product design, to internal processes that lead to innovation,

Bottom Line

Ideally, strategic plans integrate all the bottom-line practices of the firm.

What could be the consequences if a company's innovation practices were not aligned with its strategy?

Bottom Line

The strategy map shows the relationship between a firm's practices and its long-term success.

Where do a company's quality practices show up in the strategy map (Figure 4.3)?

SOURCE: Adapted from R. Kaplan and D. Norton, "Plotting Success with Strategy Maps," *Optimize,* February 2004, online; and R. Kaplan and D. Norton, "Having Trouble with Your Strategy? Then Map It," *Harvard Business Review,* September–October 2000.

FIGURE 4.3
The Strategy Map: Creating Value by Aligning Goals

and to a customer goal of perceived product leadership. Whatever the strategy, the strategy map can be used to develop the appropriate measures and standards in each operational area for that strategy and to show how they are all linked.[11]

IN PRACTICE

Many supermarkets address consumers' concerns about getting and staying healthy by using tactics such as selling organic produce and placing informational brochures next to the pharmacy. But Price Chopper Supermarkets has taken this to a new level: its commitment to wellness is an overarching strategy. Efforts throughout the business contribute to promoting the wellness of Price Chopper's customers and community.

The 128 Price Chopper stores, all in the northeastern United States, and the company's website employ a communications program called Healthy U. Under the slogan "Eat Smart, Get Moving, Live Well," the Healthy U program educates shoppers about topics such as heart health and diabetes and offers shopping tips, such as a list of gluten-free products. In addition, the company uses the NuVal nutrition rating system to inform consumers about the products on its shelves. With a rating scale of 1 to 100, NuVal gives shoppers a handy way to identify which products deliver the most nutritional value. The ratings include Price Chopper's store brand, and when those products get low scores, Price Chopper has its suppliers reformulate them.

The commitment to wellness extends beyond customers. Employees from all departments send representatives to a Wellness Committee, which looks for ways to encourage healthy behaviors through information and events. Prizes are awarded for participating in programs such as weight loss challenges. And to care for the well-being of the environment, the company is reducing energy use in its stores, cutting waste, and researching other ways to make the business more ecofriendly and sustainable.[12]

- How might Price Chopper's financial goals support this strategy?

Strategic Planning

Strategic decision making is one of the most exciting and controversial topics in management today. In fact, many organizations currently are changing the ways they develop and execute their strategic plans.

Traditionally, strategic planning emphasized a top-down approach—senior executives and specialized planning units developed goals and plans for the entire organization. Tactical and operational managers received those goals and plans, and their own planning activities were limited to specific procedures and budgets for the units.

Over the years, managers and consulting firms innovated with a variety of analytical techniques and planning approaches, many of which have been critical for analyzing complex business situations and competitive issues. In many instances, however, senior executives spent too much time with their planning specialists to the exclusion of line managers in the rest of the organization. As a result, a gap often developed between strategic managers and tactical and operational managers, and managers and employees throughout the organization became alienated and uncommitted to the organization's success.[13]

Today, however, senior executives increasingly are involving managers throughout the organization in the strategy formation process.[14] The problems just described and the rapidly changing environment of the past 25 years have forced executives to look to all levels of the organization for ideas and innovations to make their firms more competitive. Although the CEO and other top managers continue to furnish the strategic direction, or "vision," of the organization, tactical and even operational managers often provide valuable inputs to the organization's strategic plan. In some cases, these managers also have substantial autonomy to formulate or change their own plans. This authority increases flexibility and responsiveness, critical requirements for success in today's organizations.

Because of this trend, a new term for the strategic planning process has emerged: *strategic management*. **Strategic management** involves managers from all parts of the organization in the formulation and implementation of strategic goals and strategies. It integrates strategic planning and management into a single process. Strategic planning becomes an ongoing activity in which all managers are encouraged to think strategically and focus on long-term, externally oriented issues as well as short-term tactical and operational issues.

Bottom Line

New ideas from managers throughout the organization can contribute to a plan's effectiveness.

What experiences might give frontline managers ideas that top-level executives haven't thought of?

strategic management

A process that involves managers from all parts of the organization in the formulation and implementation of strategic goals and strategies.

FIGURE 4.4
The Strategic Management Process

As shown in Figure 4.4, the strategic management process has six major components:

1. Establishment of mission, vision, and goals.
2. Analysis of external opportunities and threats.
3. Analysis of internal strengths and weaknesses.
4. SWOT (strengths, weaknesses, opportunities, and threats) analysis and strategy formulation.
5. Strategy implementation.
6. Strategic control.

The mission is a clear and concise expression of the basic purpose of the organization.

Because this process is a planning and decision process, it is similar to the planning framework discussed earlier. Although organizations may use different terms or emphasize different parts of the process, the components and concepts described in this section are found either explicitly or implicitly in every organization. Even a small entrepreneurial firm can benefit from the kind of planning framework we describe here.

mission

An organization's basic purpose and scope of operations.

Step 1: Establishment of Mission, Vision, and Goals

The first step in strategic planning is establishing a mission, a vision, and goals for the organization. The **mission** is a clear and concise expression of the basic purpose of the organization. It describes what the organization does, whom it does it for, its basic good or service, and its values. Here are some mission statements from firms you will recognize:[15]

The mission statemant at McDonald's is "to be our customers' favorite place and way to eat." How do you see that translated into the atmosphere at your local McDonald's?

McDonald's: "To be our customers' favorite place and way to eat."

Microsoft: "We work to help people and businesses throughout the world to realize their full potential."

Allstate: "To be the best . . . serving our customers by providing peace of mind and enriching their quality of life through our partnership in the management of the risks they face."

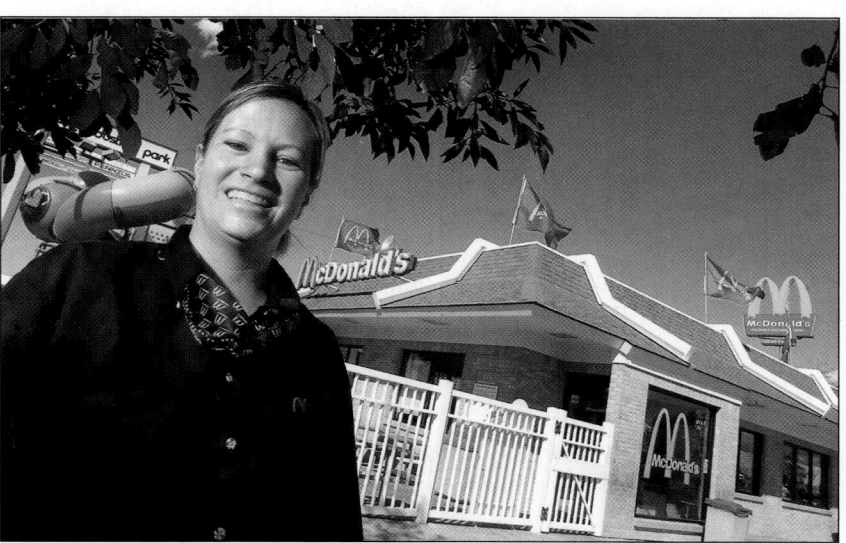

strategic vision

The long-term direction and strategic intent of a company.

Smaller organizations, of course, may have missions that aren't as broad as these. For example, the local bar found next to most campuses has this implicit mission: "to sell large quantities of inexpensive beer to college students in a noisily enjoyable environment."

The mission describes the organization as it currently operates. The **strategic vision** points to the future—it provides a perspective on where the organization is headed and what it can become. Ideally the vision statement clarifies the long-term direction of the company and its *strategic intent*. Here are some actual vision statements:[16]

> *DuPont:* "To be the world's most dynamic science company, creating sustainable solutions essential to a better, safer, and healthier life for people everywhere."
> *City of Redmond, Washington:* "Together we create a community of good neighbors."
> *Great Lakes Naval Museum:* "To enhance and become an integral part of the training mission of the Naval Service Training Command, Great Lakes, by instilling in our newest sailors a strong sense of tradition and heritage of naval service in the United States."

The strategic vision points to the future—where the organization is headed and what it can become.

The most effective vision statements inspire organization members. They offer a worthwhile target for the entire organization to work together to achieve. Often these statements are not strictly financial because financial targets alone may not motivate all organization members. For example, DuPont's vision refers to being a "dynamic science company" that works toward a "better, safer, and healthier life" for people. This vision inspires innovation aimed at making the world better—the type of work that is likely to motivate the scientists and other knowledge workers who can give the company an edge, ultimately improving DuPont's competitive position. Likewise, "instilling . . . a strong sense of tradition and heritage" provides an inspirational basis for operating the Great Lakes Naval Museum, in contrast to planning based only on budgets and historical artifacts.

Strategic goals evolve from the mission and vision of the organization. The chief executive officer of the organization, with the input and approval of the board of directors, establishes the mission, vision, and major strategic goals. The concepts and information within the mission statement, vision statement, and strategic goals statement may not be identified as such, but they should be communicated to everyone who has contact with the organization. Large firms generally provide public formal statements of their missions, visions, goals, and even values. For example, in support of its vision that "creating a community of good neighbors" is best done "together" with all sectors of the community, the City of Redmond has established goals such as these:

> Enhance citizen engagement in city issues.
> Sustain the natural systems and beauty of the community.
> Sustain a safe community with a coherent, comprehensive, cohesive approach to safety.
> Maintain economic vitality.

Different city departments would contribute to various aspects of this vision in the way they carry out their operational plans with an emphasis on collaborating with local businesses and residents.

Lofty words in a vision and mission statement cannot be meaningful without strong leadership support. At McDonald's, the commitment of past and present CEOs has played a large role in the success of the company's strategy implementation. Several years ago, the company was floundering as it lost sight of its commitment to quality, value, speed, and convenience. Under the leadership of James Cantalupo, the company created the mission statement quoted earlier, which placed the emphasis on the customer's experience. In a "Plan to Win," strategic goals such as revamping restaurants for a better

"There is no more powerful engine driving an organization toward excellence and long-term success than an attractive, worthwhile, and achievable vision of the future."
Burt Nanus

SOURCE: *Visionary Leadership* (San Francisco: Jossey-Bass, 1992).

drive-through experience and improving the quality of the menu supported the mission. When Jim Skinner took the job of chief executive, he enthusiastically backed the mission statement and its supporting Plan to Win, not hesitating to share credit for the company's continued success.[17]

Where leadership is strong, statements of visions and goals clarify the organization's purpose to key constituencies outside the organization. They also help employees focus their talent, energy, and commitment in pursuit of the organization's goals. When the time comes for you to seek employment with a firm, reviewing the firm's statements of mission, vision, and goals is a good first step in determining whether the firm's purposes and values will be compatible with your own.

Step 2: Analysis of External Opportunities and Threats

The mission and vision drive the second component of the strategic management process: analysis of the external environment. Successful strategic management depends on an accurate and thorough evaluation of the competitive environment and macroenvironment. The various components of these environments were introduced in Chapter 2.

The important activities in an environmental analysis include the ones listed in Table 4.1. The analysis begins with an examination of the industry. Next,

TABLE 4.1
Environmental Analysis

Industry and Market Analysis

- *Industry profile:* major product lines and significant market segments in the industry.
- *Industry growth:* growth rates for the entire industry, growth rates for key market segments, projected changes in patterns of growth, and the determinants of growth.
- *Industry forces:* threat of new industry entrants, threat of substitutes, economic power of buyers, economic power of suppliers, and internal industry rivalry (recall Chapter 2).

Competitor Analysis

- *Competitor profile:* major competitors and their market shares.
- *Competitor analysis:* goals, strategies, strengths, and weaknesses of each major competitor.
- *Competitor advantages:* the degree to which industry competitors have differentiated their products or services or achieved cost leadership.

Political and Regulatory Analysis

- *Legislation and regulatory activities* and their effects on the industry.
- *Political activity:* the level of political activity that organizations and associations within the industry undertake (see Chapter 5).

Social Analysis

- *Social issues:* current and potential social issues and their effects on the industry.
- *Social interest groups:* consumer, environmental, and similar activist groups that attempt to influence the industry (see Chapters 5 and 6).

Human Resources Analysis

- *Labor issues:* key labor needs, shortages, opportunities, and problems confronting the industry (see Chapters 10 and 11).

Macroeconomic Analysis

- *Macroeconomic conditions:* economic factors that affect supply, demand, growth, competition, and profitability within the industry.

Technological Analysis

- *Technological factors:* scientific or technical methods that affect the industry, particularly recent and potential innovations (see Chapter 17).

stakeholders

Groups and individuals who affect and are affected by the achievement of the organization's mission, goals, and strategies.

organizational stakeholders are examined. **Stakeholders** are groups and individuals who affect and are affected by the achievement of the organization's mission, goals, and strategies. They include buyers, suppliers, competitors, government and regulatory agencies, unions and employee groups, the financial community, owners and shareholders, and trade associations. The environmental analysis provides a map of these stakeholders and the ways they influence the organization.[18]

IN PRACTICE

Stakeholders are groups and individuals who affect and are affected by the organization.

Frequently the difference between an opportunity and a threat depends on how a company positions itself.

Collaborating with key stakeholders can help organizations successfully develop and implement their strategic plan. At software company Intuit, CEO Brad Smith launched strategy development by learning what was on the minds of some key stakeholders. He visited with his board of directors and investors and set up meetings with groups of employees who work directly with Intuit's customers.

Smith asked each group of stakeholders some key questions related to strategic analysis: "What is Intuit's biggest untapped opportunity? What is the biggest risk facing Intuit that keeps you up at night? What is the biggest mistake I can make as a CEO in my first year?" From the answers, Smith gained insights that helped him establish priorities for Intuit's strategy.

Smith learned that a sizable number of Intuit's business customers have international activities, so he determined that Intuit would have to become a more global company. Its QuickBooks financial software now handles multiple currencies for international transactions. In response to the competitive threat of a new release of financial software from Microsoft, Smith assembled managers to craft a marketing strategy that would convince customers to wait two more months for the next version of QuickBooks. That campaign caused QuickBooks sales to jump despite Microsoft's efforts.[19]

- Now that Smith has launched his strategy development process, what can he do to continue learning from environmental analysis?

Since some states require the use of renewable sources to generate power, it is up to these companies to turn the negative aspect of higher costs into an overall positive outcome.

The environmental analysis also should examine other forces in the environment, such as economic conditions and technological factors. One critical task in environmental analysis is forecasting future trends. As noted in Chapter 2, forecasting techniques range from simple judgment to complex mathematical models that examine systematic relationships among many variables. Even simple quantitative techniques outperform the intuitive assessments of experts. Judgment is susceptible to bias, and managers have a limited ability to process information. Managers should use subjective judgments as inputs to quantitative models or when they confront new situations.

Frequently the difference between an opportunity and a threat depends on how a company positions itself strategically. For example, some states have required that electric utilities get a certain share of their power from renewable sources such as wind and solar energy, rather than from fossil fuels, including coal, oil, and natural gas. This requirement poses an obvious threat to utilities because the costs of fossil fuel energy are less, and customers demand low prices.

However, some companies see strategic opportunities in renewable power. For example, the German conglomerate Schott has developed a solar thermal technology in which sunlight heats oil in metal tubes enclosed in coated glass; the heated oil makes steam, which powers a turbine and generates electricity. Solar thermal energy, although it now costs more than fossil fuels, is more efficient than the solar panels installed on buildings, and it can store extra power to be used on cloudy days.[20] Similarly, overflowing landfills are an expensive challenge for many municipalities, but a growing number are seeing an opportunity in the form of energy generation. As garbage decomposes, it produces methane gas, which is used as a fuel to power generators. In East Brunswick, New Jersey, for example, the Edgeboro landfill generates electricity that powers the county's wastewater treatment plant.[21]

Some changes in the environment can bring one company a combination of threats and opportunities. One example is when the United States and European Union deregulated air travel between their respective countries, allowing any European air carrier to fly to any city in the United States, while U.S. carriers were granted access to all airports in EU countries. Before this agreement, airlines had to negotiate permission with each country whose airport they wanted to use. The deregulation allows American Airlines, for example, to broaden the variety of flights it offers in its one-world alliance with British Airways—an opportunity. But it also means threats, such as new competition to serve London's Heathrow Airport, where Continental and Delta previously could not land.[22]

> "We wanted Nike to be the world's best sports and fitness company. Once you say that, you have a focus. You don't end up making wing tips or sponsoring the next Rolling Stone world tour."
>
> Philip Knight, Nike Founder

In some environments, it takes an especially creative mind to see opportunities among severe threats. For Farif Ali Abood, who opened a shop to make commercial signs in his hometown of Najaf, Iraq, the difficulties have included sporadic electrical service, lack of funds to borrow, and even occasional sniper fire in the area. Despite these challenges, Abood has managed to keep the business running by using a generator when the power goes out. As conditions in the city have stabilized, business has grown enough for Abood to hire several full-time employees and earn a modest profit.

Halfway across the world in Haiti, the potentially devastating threat to businesses was the massive earthquake of 2010. Mathias Pierre had launched an information technology company to serve schools and the government. When his client base was effectively wiped out or at least disabled by the quake, Pierre managed to locate his key managers, and together they worked tirelessly to ensure communications for all the organizations at work on the relief effort. Eventually these agencies became the new clients for Pierre's business.[23] The brave few who, like Pierre and Abood, can fill needs amidst such difficult threats are well positioned to benefit from the business relationships they create with loyal customers.

Step 3: Analysis of Internal Strengths and Weaknesses

As managers conduct an external analysis, they will also assess the strengths and weaknesses of major functional areas inside their organization. Table 4.2 lists some of the major components of this internal resource analysis. For example, is your firm strong enough financially to handle the lengthy and costly investment new projects often require? Can your existing staff carry out its part of the plan, or will additional training or hiring be needed? Is your firm's image compatible with the strategy, or will it have to persuade key stakeholders that a change in direction makes sense? This kind of internal analysis gives strategic decision makers an inventory of the organization's existing functions, skills, and resources as well as its overall performance level. Many of your other business courses will prepare you to conduct an internal analysis.

TABLE 4.2
Internal Resource Analysis

Financial Analysis
Examines financial strengths and weaknesses through financial statements such as a balance sheet and an income statement and compares trends to historical and industry figures (see Chapter 18).
Marketing Audit
Examines strengths and weaknesses of major marketing activities and identifies markets, key market segments, and the competitive position (market share) of the organization within key markets.
Operations Analysis
Examines the strengths and weaknesses of the manufacturing, production, or service delivery activities of the organization (see Chapters 9, 16, and 17).
Other Internal Resource Analyses
Examine, as necessary and appropriate, the strengths and weaknesses of other organizational activities, such as research and development (product and process), management information systems, engineering, and purchasing.
Human Resources Assessment
Examines strengths and weaknesses of all levels of management and employees and focuses on key human resources activities, including recruitment, selection, placement, training, labor (union) relationships, compensation, promotion, appraisal, quality of work life, and human resources planning (see Chapters 10 and 11).

LO 4

resources

Inputs to a system that can enhance performance.

Bottom Line

Amazon's key customer benefits are speed and excellence of service.

What are some resources Amazon needs in order to deliver these benefits?

Resources are a source of competitive advantage only under certain circumstances.

Resources and Core Competencies   Without question, strategic planning has been strongly influenced in recent years by a focus on internal resources. **Resources** are inputs to production (recall systems theory) that can be accumulated over time to enhance the performance of a firm. Resources can take many forms, but they tend to fall into two broad categories: (1) *tangible assets* such as real estate, production facilities, raw materials, and so on, and (2) *intangible assets* such as company reputation, culture, technical knowledge, and patents, as well as accumulated learning and experience. The Walt Disney Company, for example, has developed its strategic plan on combinations of tangible assets (e.g., hotels and theme parks) as well as intangible assets (brand recognition, talented craftspeople, culture focused on customer service).[24]

Effective internal analysis provides a clearer understanding of how a company can compete through its resources. Resources are a source of competitive advantage only under certain circumstances. First, if the resource is instrumental for creating customer *value*—that is, if it increases the benefits customers derive from a good or service relative to the costs they incur—the resource can lead to a competitive advantage.[25] For example, Amazon's powerful search technology and its ability to track customer preferences and offer personalized recommendations each time its site is accessed, as well as its quick product delivery system, are clearly valuable resources that enhance Amazon's competitiveness.

Second, resources are a source of advantage if they are *rare* and not equally available to all competitors. Even for extremely valuable resources, if all competitors have equal access, the resource cannot provide a source of competitive advantage. For companies such as Merck, DuPont, Dow Chemical, and others, patented formulas represent important resources that are both rare and valuable. Amazon, too, sought a patent for its one-click shopping technique.

Third, if resources are *difficult to imitate*, they provide a source of competitive advantage. Earlier in this chapter, we saw that Wells Fargo has managed to compete with larger banks by developing expertise in cross-selling. Unlike, say, free checking accounts, this intangible resource is difficult to imitate because it requires training and motivating employees at all levels to adopt customer-oriented thinking and collaborate across divisions. Under the strong leadership of Dick Kovacevich, Wells Fargo was able to inspire its employees to learn and use the necessary skills. Industry analyst Richard Bove says the strategy succeeded because of a hard-to-imitate resource, "the force of [Kovacevich's] personality, which is so strong and so positive that it infects other people."[26] As in this example, where success relies on leadership and collaboration practices, resources tend to be harder to imitate if they are complex, with many interdependent variables and no obvious links between easily explained behaviors and desired outcomes.[27]

Imagine how skilled Coca-Cola's global network of bottlers is to be able to deliver their product worldwide and more efficiently than any of their competitors. Shown here is a small market in Indonesia.

Finally, resources can enhance a firm's competitive advantage when they are well *organized*. For example, Coca-Cola's well-organized and global network of bottlers allows the company to quickly introduce a new soft drink worldwide and to distribute it more efficiently than any competitor. IBM, known primarily for computer hardware until it became more of a commodity than a source of competitive advantage, has organized its staff and systems to efficiently produce a consolidated technology product for its corporate clients—hardware, software, and service in one package. This spares its clients the cost of managing technology on their own.

As shown in Figure 4.5, when resources are valuable, rare, inimitable, and organized, they can be viewed as a company's core competencies. Simply stated, a **core competence** is something a company does especially well relative to its competitors.

core competence

A unique skill and/or knowledge an organization possesses that gives it an edge over competitors.

FIGURE 4.5
Resources and Core Competence

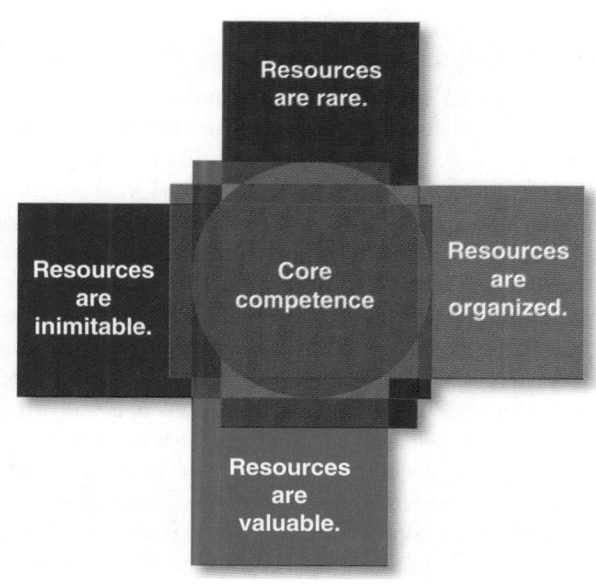

Honda, for example, has a core competence in small engine design and manufacturing; Sony has a core competence in miniaturization; Federal Express has a core competence in logistics and customer service. As in these examples, a core competence typically refers to a set of skills or expertise in some activity rather than physical or financial assets.

Benchmarking   To assess and improve performance, some companies use benchmarking, the process of assessing how well one company's basic functions and skills compare with those of another company or set of companies. The goal of benchmarking is to thoroughly understand the "best practices" of other firms and to undertake actions to achieve both better performance and lower costs. Benchmarking programs have helped a myriad of companies, such as Ford, Corning, Hewlett-Packard, Xerox, and Anheuser-Busch, make great strides in eliminating inefficiencies and improving competitiveness.

Depending on how it is applied, benchmarking may be of limited help in that it only helps a company perform as well as its competitors; strategic management ultimately is about surpassing those companies. Besides benchmarking against leading organizations in other industries, companies may address this problem by engaging in internal benchmarking. That approach involves benchmarking their different internal operations and departments against one another to disseminate the company's best practices throughout the organization and thereby gain a competitive advantage.

One company that has experienced the pros and cons of benchmarking is AXA Canada, an insurance company. The company turned to benchmarking as a way to identify how it could improve its processes and lower its costs. AXA Canada used internal benchmarking to compare results among its regions. However, employees objected that in a country as vast as Canada, the differences among regions were so great that performance couldn't really be compared. More energy went to arguing about the numbers than looking for ways to close performance gaps. The company made similar efforts to compare Canadian performance with insurers in other countries, and it ran into even greater difficulty making comparisons. The most success came from an arrangement with the Ward Group to gather performance data from several insurance companies, analyze it, and report on areas of strength and weakness. Using this benchmarking information, AXA Canada has found areas where it can operate more efficiently by applying other companies' practices. The company uses the benchmarking data primarily for cutting costs and identifying potential new markets.[28]

Step 4: SWOT Analysis and Strategy Formulation

Once managers have analyzed the external environment and the internal resources of the organization, they will have the information they need to assess the organization's strengths, weaknesses, opportunities, and threats. Such an assessment normally is referred to as a **SWOT analysis.** Strengths and weaknesses refer to internal resources. For example, an organization's *strengths* might include skilled management, positive cash flow, and well-known and highly regarded brands. *Weaknesses* might be lack of spare production capacity and the absence of reliable suppliers. Opportunities and threats arise in the macroenvironment and competitive environment. Examples of *opportunities* are a new technology that could make the supply chain more efficient and a market niche that is currently underserved. *Threats* might include the possibility that competitors will enter the underserved niche once it has been shown to be profitable.

SWOT analysis helps managers summarize the relevant, important facts from their external and internal analyses. Based on this summary, they can identify the primary and secondary strategic issues their organization faces. The managers then formulate a strategy that will build on the SWOT analysis to take advantage of available opportunities by capitalizing on the organization's strengths, neutralizing its weakness, and countering potential threats.

Bottom Line

Aligning a firm's bottom-line practices with best practices can improve its competitiveness. *In some famous benchmarking examples, businesses have learned from pit crews for race car teams. What kinds of bottom-line practices could such an organization demonstrate?*

SWOT analysis

A comparison of strengths, weaknesses, opportunities, and threats that helps executives formulate strategy.

To take an example, consider how SWOT analysis might be carried out at Microsoft. The company's size and earnings from its dominant operating system and Office suite of software are an obvious strength. The company has weaknesses as well. One of the fastest-growing areas of the computer business is Internet applications, especially profits from the sale of online advertising. Microsoft has struggled in this area, with its Internet search engine losing market share year after year, and online ad sales growing but only as a tiny segment of the market. The dominant threat to Microsoft in this area is widely considered to be Google, which not only dominates the search business—and its related advertising—but even has challenged Microsoft with free business applications. This analysis would explain Microsoft's recent efforts to buy DoubleClick, which arranges deals between advertisers and online publishers. DoubleClick is a big player in the online advertising business and has expertise that Microsoft lacks.[29] By purchasing DoubleClick, Microsoft would use one of its strengths (its capital) to neutralize a weakness (inexperience and small market share in online advertising) and counter a threat (Google). Ironically, before the deal could close, Google emerged as another bidder for DoubleClick.[30] In the real world, as a company is formulating strategy, so are its competitors. As a result, the process must be continually evolving through contingency planning. The more uncertainty that exists in the external environment, the more the strategy needs to focus on building internal capabilities through practices such as knowledge sharing and continuous process improvement.[31] Yet at a basic level, strategy formulation moves from analysis to devising a coherent course of action, such as Microsoft's plan to purchase (and eventually operate) DoubleClick. In this way, the organization's corporate, business, and functional strategies will begin to take shape.

Before we continue our strategy discussion, we note that many individuals seeking a job or a career change can find a "self-SWOT analysis" helpful. What are you particularly good at? What weaknesses might you need to overcome to improve your employment chances? What firms offer the best opportunity to market your skills to full advantage? Will you have a lot of competition from other job seekers? As with companies, this kind of analysis can be the beginning of a plan of action and can improve the plan's effectiveness.

Corporate Strategy   A **corporate strategy** identifies the set of businesses, markets, or industries in which the organization competes and the distribution of resources among those businesses. Figure 4.6 shows four basic alternatives for a corporate strategy, ranging from very specialized to highly diverse. A **concentration** strategy focuses on a single business competing in a single industry. In the food retailing industry, Kroger, Safeway, and A&P all pursue concentration strategies. Frequently companies pursue concentration strategies to gain entry into an industry when industry growth is good, or when the company has a narrow range of competencies. An example is C. F. Martin & Company, which pursues a concentration strategy by focusing on making the best possible guitars and guitar strings, a strategy that has enabled the family-owned business to operate successfully for more than 150 years.

A **vertical integration** strategy involves expanding the domain of the organization into supply channels or to distributors. At one time, Henry Ford had fully integrated his company from the ore mines needed to make steel all the way to the showrooms where his cars were sold. Vertical integration generally is used to eliminate uncertainties and reduce costs associated with suppliers or distributors.

A strategy of **concentric diversification** involves moving into new businesses that are related to the company's original core business. William Marriott expanded his original restaurant business outside Washington, DC, by moving into airline catering, hotels, and fast food. Each of these businesses within the hospitality industry is related in terms of the services it provides, the skills necessary for success, and the customers it attracts. Often companies such as Marriott pursue a strategy of concentric diversification to take advantage of their strengths in one business to gain advantage

corporate strategy

The set of businesses, markets, or industries in which an organization competes and the distribution of resources among those entities.

concentration

A strategy employed for an organization that operates a single business and competes in a single industry.

vertical integration

The acquisition or development of new businesses that produce parts or components of the organization's product.

concentric diversification

A strategy used to add new businesses that produce related products or are involved in related markets and activities.

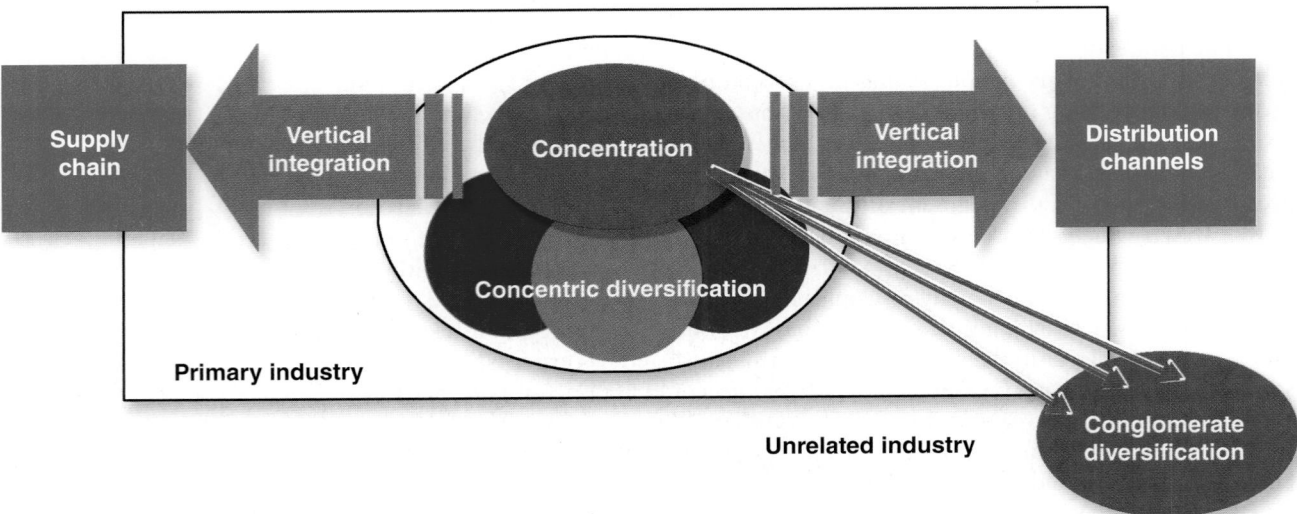

FIGURE 4.6
Summary of Corporate Strategies

in another. Because the businesses are related, the products, markets, technologies, or capabilities used in one business can be transferred to another. Success in a concentric diversification strategy requires adequate management and other resources for operating more than one business. Guitar maker C. F. Martin once tried expanding through purchases of other instrument companies, but management was stretched too thin to run them all well, so the company eventually divested the acquisitions and returned to its concentration strategy.[32]

IN PRACTICE

Concentric diversification can melt national boundaries. Internet search giant Google recently acquired a portion of the rapidly growing Chinese website Xunlei.com, which allows users to download music and video clips from the Internet. Google's investment in—and partnership with—Xunlei.com will allow the Chinese site to use Google's search capabilities while giving Google direct access to China's 130 million Internet users. Google has also formed an alliance with China Mobile, the country's largest mobile phone carrier, to offer mobile Internet search service to Chinese consumers.

Despite its ranking as the world's largest search engine, in China Google is dwarfed by the Chinese search engine Baidu.com, which claims about 63 percent of China's market share. (Google claims only about 19 percent.) In addition, China is filled with tiny start-ups that have, thus far, shut out U.S. Internet firms. So Google's strategy is to diversify within that country to capture more of the market. Because of government and cultural restraints in China, Google would have a much more difficult time entering the market there alone. By creating alliances with Chinese firms, Google will have a better chance of gaining the attention of Chinese consumers who are in the market for downloads of videos, music, games, software, and cell phone ringtones.[33]

conglomerate diversification

A strategy used to add new businesses that produce unrelated products or are involved in unrelated markets and activities.

In contrast to concentric diversification, **conglomerate diversification** is a corporate strategy that involves expansion into unrelated businesses. For example, General Electric Corporation has diversified from its original base in electrical and home appliance products to such wide-ranging industries as health, finance, insurance, truck and air transportation, and even media with its ownership of NBC (now owned with Comcast). Typically companies pursue a conglomerate diversification strategy to minimize risks due to market fluctuations in one industry.

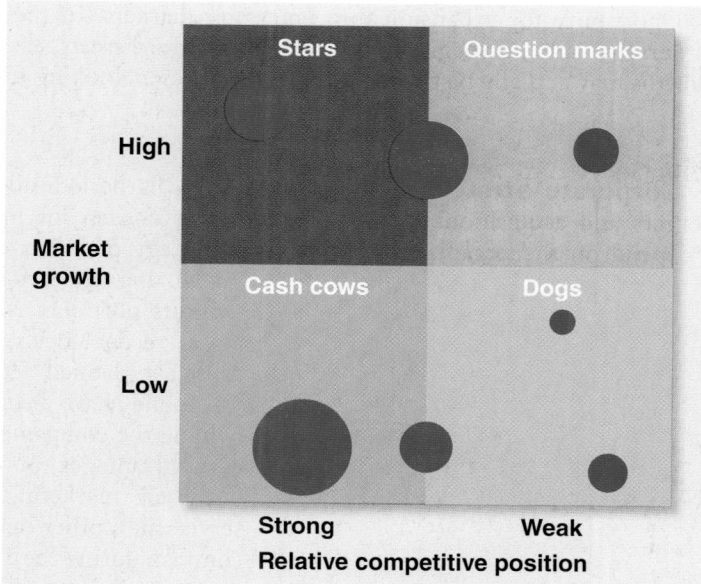

FIGURE 4.7
The BCG Matrix

The diversified businesses of an organization are sometimes called its business *portfolio*. One of the most popular techniques for analyzing a corporation's strategy for managing its portfolio is the BCG matrix, developed by the Boston Consulting Group. The BCG matrix is shown in Figure 4.7. Each business in the corporation is plotted on the matrix on the basis of the growth rate of its market and the relative strength of its competitive position in that market (market share). The business is represented by a circle whose size depends on the business's contribution to corporate revenues.

High-growth, weak-competitive-position businesses are called *question marks*. They require substantial investment to improve their position; otherwise divestiture is recommended. High-growth, strong-competitive-position businesses are called *stars*. These businesses require heavy investment, but their strong position allows them to generate the needed revenues. Low-growth, strong-competitive-position businesses are called *cash cows*. These businesses generate revenues in excess of their investment needs and therefore fund other businesses. Finally, low-growth, weak-competitive-position businesses are called *dogs*. The remaining revenues from these businesses are realized, and then the businesses are divested.

The BCG matrix is not intended as a substitute for management judgment, creativity, insight, or leadership. But it is a tool that can, along with other techniques, help managers of the firm as a whole and of its individual businesses evaluate their strategy alternatives.[34] This approach can help a company such as PepsiCo that needs to weigh the relative merits of many current and possible product lines. While the company sells only snacks and beverages, it has many choices about the products offered around the world within those two broad categories. As the public has raised concerns about overconsumption of soft drinks and snacks, the company has treated its flagship brand as a cash cow and has actively pursued opportunities in products that can claim superior nutrition, such as oatmeal and orange juice. Growth in sales of noncarbonated beverages has propelled the recent success of Pepsi's beverages, and the company has set a goal to triple its sales of "good-for-you" products that feature whole grains, fruits, vegetables, nuts, and seeds. Another way to look at Pepsi's portfolio of businesses is by region served. Pepsi's presence in North America shows little evidence of growth potential, but management sees

Bottom Line
Companies that integrate vertically often do so to reduce their costs.
Why might buying from a division of your company be less costly than buying on the open market?

tremendous opportunity for expansion into emerging markets. In these markets, where consumers are only just beginning to be able to afford treats, cash cows like Pepsi and Doritos may actually be the stars among consumers looking for "fun-for-you" products.[35]

Trends in Corporate Strategy   Corporate America is periodically swept by waves of mergers and acquisitions (M&As). The targets chosen for mergers and acquisitions depend on the organization's corporate strategy of either concentrating in one industry or diversifying its portfolio. Many of the most recent deals, including AT&T's planned acquisition of T-Mobile, have been aimed at helping the companies enjoy the cost advantages of consolidating their marketing, customer service, and other operations. In contrast, during the 1990s, many deals—including the merger of America Online and Time Warner—were made to help traditional businesses enter the hot Internet market.

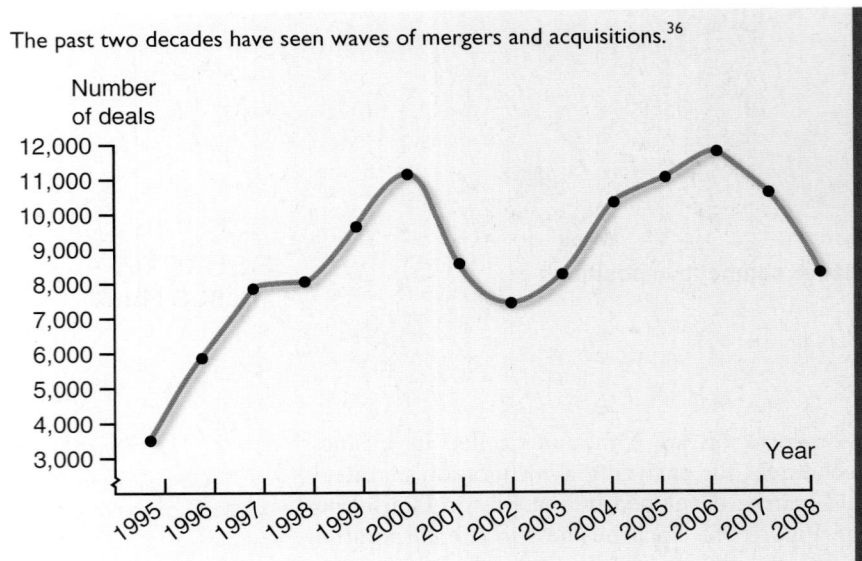

The past two decades have seen waves of mergers and acquisitions.[36]

The value of implementing a diversified corporate strategy depends on individual circumstances. Many critics have argued that unrelated diversification hurts a company more often than it helps it. In recent years, many diversified companies have sold their peripheral businesses so they could concentrate on a more focused portfolio. In contrast, the diversification efforts of an organization competing in a slow-growth, mature, or threatened industry often are applauded. Although the merits of diversification are an issue for continued study, most observers agree that organizations usually perform better if they implement a more concentric diversification strategy, in which businesses are related somehow or similar to one another.

Within the various types of corporate strategies, other trends are shaping the ways that today's companies are seeking growth. One huge trend affecting almost every company's strategy is the degree to which business today takes place across national boundaries. Today there is hardly any organization that does not buy at least some of its supplies and equipment from, or sell at least some of its products to, individuals and organizations in other countries. In terms of strategy, companies are often finding the best opportunities for growth where economies are expanding the fastest, as in Brazil, India, and China. Chapter 6 explores this trend, known as *globalization*.

Other trends are related to the business arrangements used to carry out the strategy. Rather than expanding through organic growth—that is, adding employees, equipment, offices, and so on—an organization can find a partner that already has the expertise it needs in a particular market, technology, or product. Choosing such partners in support of a strategy and entering a business arrangement with them can be called a *joint venture, strategic partnership*, or *strategic alliance*, depending on the details of the arrangement. Chapter 9 describes how some organizations use strategic alliances to become more agile, and Chapter 17 tells how joint ventures can give companies quick access to new technology.

Cisco Systems has struggled with decisions about how to expand. Cisco is primarily known as the world's largest producer of computer networking equipment. That expertise has won the company respect and a sizable income as customers pay a premium for it when they set up computer networks. However, as more customers shift to wireless modes of connecting, Cisco's management has seen less demand for its hardware in the future and has had to make tough choices about where the company will find success.

Cisco tried to get involved in video technology. It acquired Pure Digital, which makes the Flip camera, and it tried developing the idea of using separate networks for video and other kinds of information traffic in computer networks. Also in the video arena, Cisco began offering a technology called TelePresence, which delivers high-quality video messages to others on a network; for example, colleagues in different cities can participate in a meeting by viewing each other on screens. However, the Flip camera flopped when consumers found that it was handier to record videos on their smartphones, and the expense of setting up Cisco's TelePresence system in special locations was less attractive to businesses than using a service such as Skype on their laptop computers.

In light of these missteps, Cisco has refocused on five priorities related to the company's deep knowledge of computer networks and business customers: routing and switching, user collaboration, cloud computing, network architectures, and video. The company also decided to move out of less profitable areas of businesses aimed at serving consumers, such as set-top boxes and digital cameras.[37]

• What type of corporate strategy is Cisco following in this example?

Business Strategy   After the top management team and board make the corporate strategic decisions, executives must determine how they will compete in each business area. **Business strategy** defines the major actions by which an organization builds and strengthens its competitive position in the marketplace. A competitive advantage typically results from one of two generic business strategies introduced here and elaborated in Chapter 7.[38]

First, organizations such as Walmart and Southwest Airlines pursue competitive advantage through **low-cost strategies.** Businesses using a low-cost strategy attempt to be efficient and offer a standard, no-frills product. Walmart Stores expresses its low-price strategy with the slogan "save money, live better." The company uses the power of its giant size to negotiate favorable prices from suppliers, enabling it to sell at prices below those of most competing retailers. Recently, when gasoline prices soared, the company promoted its stores as a place where consumers can save on transportation costs by purchasing everything they need at low prices in one trip.[39] Companies that succeed with a low-cost strategy often are large and try to take advantage of economies of scale in production or distribution. In many cases, their scale allows them to buy and sell their goods and services at a lower price, which leads to higher market share, volume, and ultimately profits. To succeed, an organization using this strategy generally must be the cost leader in its industry or market segment. However, even a cost leader must offer a product that is acceptable to customers compared with competitors' products.

Second, an organization may pursue a **differentiation strategy.** With a differentiation strategy, a company attempts to be unique in its industry or market segment along some dimensions that customers value. This unique or differentiated position within the industry often is based on high product quality, excellent marketing and distribution, or superior service.

Nordstrom's commitment to quality and customer service in the retail apparel industry is an excellent example of a differentiation strategy. For example, Nordstrom's

LO 6

business strategy
The major actions by which a business competes in a particular industry or market.

low-cost strategy
A strategy an organization uses to build competitive advantage by being efficient and offering a standard, no-frills product.

Bottom Line
Low-price strategies usually require low production costs.
How do you think Walmart keeps costs low?

differentiation strategy
A strategy an organization uses to build competitive advantage by being unique in its industry or market segment along one or more dimensions.

Nordstrom differentiates itself from its competitors with superior customer service and broad product selection.

Bottom Line

A high-quality strategy is often more difficult for competitors to imitate.

What would be hard about imitating Nordstrom's strategy for top-quality service?

functional strategies

Strategies implemented by each functional area of the organization to support the organization's business strategy.

personal shoppers are available online, by phone, or in stores to select items for shoppers' consideration at no charge. Innovation, too, is an important ingredient of a differentiation strategy. In the market for toilet paper, Scott Paper Company once determined that it could not afford to compete for institutional sales based on price. Instead the company began offering institutions a free dispenser that would hold larger rolls of paper, saving its customers the labor cost of replacing empty rolls more frequently. Scott initially was the only company selling the larger rolls, so it gained market share while competitors scrambled to catch up.[40]

Whatever strategy managers adopt, *the most effective strategy is one that competitors are unwilling or unable to imitate.* If the organization's strategic plan is one that could easily be adopted by industry competitors, it may not be sufficiently distinctive or, in the long run, contribute significantly to the organization's competitiveness. For example, a strategy to gain market share and profits by being the "first mover" to offer an innovative product may or may not succeed, depending in part on competitive responses. In some industries, such as computers, technology advances so fast that the first company to provide a new product is quickly challenged by later entrants offering superior products.[41]

Functional Strategy   The final step in strategy formulation is to establish the major functional strategies. **Functional strategies** are implemented by each functional area of the organization to support the business strategy. The typical functional areas include production, human resources, marketing, research and development, finance, and distribution. For example, IBM's plan to grow through acquisitions of software companies requires functional strategies for training its sales force to understand the new products and for training the acquired company's employees to understand IBM's culture and procedures. Part of the functional strategy includes assigning each new employee to an experienced IBM mentor. At Wells Fargo, the strategy to grow through cross-selling requires functional strategies for advertising, training employees to cross-sell, and developing systems for sharing information across department boundaries. And at Boeing, the strategy to grow at a steady pace, rather than ramping up production until high costs force cutbacks, requires functional strategies related to hiring and training employees, scheduling production, and negotiating sales.[42]

Functional strategies typically are developed by functional area executives with input of and approval from the executives responsible for business strategy. Senior strategic decision makers review the functional strategies to ensure that each major department is operating consistently with the business strategies of the organization. For example, automated production techniques—even if they saved money—would not be appropriate for a piano company like Steinway, whose products are strategically positioned (and priced) as high-quality and handcrafted. At companies that compete based on product innovation, strategies for research and development are especially critical. But in the recession that occurred at the beginning of this decade, General Electric cut back on research in lighting technology just as other companies were making advances in LED lighting. When the economy recovered, customers were looking for innovative lighting, but GE had fallen behind. Based on that experience, GE committed itself to an R&D strategy of maintaining budgets even when sales slow down. In the latest economic downturn, the company continued to fund a project in which it is developing new aircraft engines with Honda Motor Company.[43]

Step 5: Strategy Implementation

As with any plan, simply formulating a good strategy is not enough. Strategic managers also must ensure that the new strategies are implemented effectively and efficiently. Recently corporations and strategy consultants have been paying more attention to implementation. They realize that clever techniques and a good plan do not guarantee success. This greater appreciation is reflected in two major trends.

First, organizations are adopting a more comprehensive view of implementation. The organization structure, technology, human resources, employee reward systems, information systems, organization culture, and leadership style must all support the strategy. Just as an organization's strategy must be matched to the external environment, so must it also fit the multiple factors through which it is implemented. The remainder of this section discusses these factors and the ways they can be used to implement strategy.

A recent survey found that when it comes to strategy implementation, companies have plenty of room for improving and outperforming the competition.[44]

Executives describing their company as very good at given activity

Second, many organizations are extending the more participative strategic management process to implementation. Managers at all levels are involved with formulating strategy and identifying and executing ways to implement it. Senior executives still may oversee the implementation process, but they are placing much greater responsibility and authority in the hands of others. In general, strategy implementation involves four related steps:

Step 1: *Define strategic tasks.* Articulate in simple language what a particular business must do to create or sustain a competitive advantage. Define strategic tasks to help employees understand how they contribute to the organization, including redefining relationships among the parts of the organization.

Step 2: *Assess organization capabilities.* Evaluate the organization's ability to implement the strategic tasks. A task force typically interviews employees and managers to identify specific issues that help or hinder effective implementation. Then the results are summarized for top management. In the course of your career, you will likely be asked to participate in a task force. We discuss working effectively in teams in Chapter 14.

Step 3: *Develop an implementation agenda.* Management decides how it will change its own activities and procedures; how critical interdependencies will be managed; what skills and individuals are needed in key roles; and what structures, measures, information, and rewards might ultimately support the needed behavior. A philosophy statement, communicated in terms of value, is the outcome of this process.

Step 4: *Create an implementation plan.* The top management team, the employee task force, and others develop the implementation plan. The top management team then monitors progress. The employee task force continues its work by providing feedback about how others in the organization are responding to the changes.

TABLE 4.3

Attacking the Six Barriers
to Strategy Implementation

Change starts with the leader	
The Silent Killers	**Principles for Engaging and Changing the Silent Killers**
Top-down or laissez-faire senior management style	With the top team and lower levels, the CEO/general manager creates a partnership built around the development of a compelling business direction, the creation of an enabling organizational context, and the delegation of authority to clearly accountable individuals and teams.
Unclear strategy and conflicting priorities	The top team, as a group, develops a statement of strategy, and priorities that members are willing to stand behind are developed.
An ineffective senior management team	The top team, as a group, is involved in all steps in the change process so that its effectiveness is tested and developed.
Poor vertical communication	An honest, fact-based dialogue is established with lower levels about the new strategy and the barriers to implementing it.
Poor coordination across functions, businesses, or borders	A set of businesswide initiatives and new organizational roles and responsibilities are defined that require "the right people to work together on the right things in the right way" to implement the strategy.
Inadequate down-the-line leadership skills and development	Lower-level managers develop skills through newly created opportunities to lead change and drive key business initiatives. They are supported with just-in-time coaching, training, and targeted recruitment. Those who still are not able to make the grade must be replaced.

SOURCE: From M. Beer and R. A Eisenstat, "The Silent Killers of Strategy Implementation and Learning," *MIT Sloan Management Review*, Summer 2000. Copyright © 2000 by Massachusetts Institute of Technology. All rights reserved. Distributed by Tribune Media Services.

This process, though straightforward, does not always go smoothly. Table 4.3 shows six different barriers to strategy implementation and provides a description of some key principles for overcoming these "silent killers." By paying closer attention to the processes by which strategies are implemented, executives, managers, and employees can make sure that strategic plans are actually carried out.[45]

Step 6: Strategic Control

strategic control system

A system designed to support managers in evaluating the organization's progress regarding its strategy and, when discrepancies exist, taking corrective action.

The final component of the strategic management process is strategic control. A **strategic control system** is designed to support managers in evaluating the organization's progress with its strategy and, when discrepancies exist, taking corrective action. The system must encourage efficient operations that are consistent with the plan while allowing flexibility to adapt to changing conditions. As with all control systems, the organization must develop performance indicators, an information system, and specific mechanisms to monitor progress. At Boeing, one obvious measure of its strategy to partner with suppliers is whether suppliers are keeping up with Boeing's need for components that meet its quality standards. In fact, as orders flowed in for the 787 Dreamliner, several suppliers began missing deadlines. Boeing dispatched teams of experts from various functions to visit the suppliers, diagnose the reasons for their difficulties, and help them catch up. It also has modified its strategy by having its own employees do more of the final assembly work to avoid falling further behind.[46]

Most strategic control systems include a budget to monitor and control major financial expenditures. In fact, as a first-time manager, you will most likely confront your work unit's budget—a key aspect of your organization's strategic plan. Your executive team may give you budget assumptions and targets for your area, reflecting your part in the overall plan, and you may be asked to revise your budget once all the budgets in your organization have been consolidated and reviewed.

The dual responsibilities of a control system—efficiency and flexibility—often seem contradictory with respect to budgets. The budget usually establishes spending limits, but changing conditions or the need for innovation may require different financial commitments during the period. To solve this dilemma, some companies have created two budgets: strategic and operational. For example, managers at Texas Instruments control two budgets under the OST (objectives–strategies–tactics) system. The strategic budget is used to create and maintain long-term effectiveness, and the operational budget is tightly monitored to achieve short-term efficiency. In "Management Connection: Onward," consider how GE's top managers are trying to balance efficiency and flexibility as they position GE for the future. The topic of control in general—and budgets in particular—is discussed in more detail in Chapter 16.

| Manager's Brief | Progress Report | **Onward** |

Management Connection

GE POLISHES ITS PORTFOLIO FOR THE FUTURE

After the shock of watching GE Capital pull down the entire corporation's fortunes in 2008, CEO Jeffrey Immelt and his executive team quickly got to work on revamping GE's portfolio of businesses. Some businesses and operations would be spun off; others would be positioned to seize growth opportunities.

GE Capital was ripe for change. Within the new strategy's focus on engineering innovation, the financial unit would not be abandoned; it still generates strong profits in some areas but has a lesser, more targeted role. Whereas the past growth in GE Capital occurred wherever its managers spotted potential for big returns, GE Capital now chooses investments based on their fit with the company's knowledge of its markets. Thus GE would pursue lending capital in the power generation or aviation industry, or to a midsize industrial company. In contrast, the company has discontinued its subprime lending, and it is reducing its exposure to or getting out of other risky financial activities.

GE sees low potential in other businesses. The company sold off its plastics and insurance units. It sold Comcast a majority share of NBC Universal. The NBC sale could bring in significant cash for investing in areas where GE sees itself as having superior strength. GE considered selling its home and business division, which includes appliances, but lacking a buyer, decided to reinvest in it. Although sales have been slow since the housing market fell, the products enjoy solid profit margins, and appliances are an area where the company can apply innovation in energy efficiency.

GE also has been making acquisitions aimed at its strategy of innovating in what it expects will be high-growth manufacturing industries, including health care and power generation. The company spent $11 billion over six months to increase its participation in the market for energy equipment, and it spent $7 billion to expand its oil services division. The commitment to making huge, complex products for infrastructure and transportation seizes on one of GE's obvious strengths: its size. Few companies have GE's ability to set up factories for making jet engines, power turbines, and locomotives. Even a facility for making solar panels can cost tens of millions of dollars to start. And products such as nuclear power plants are so specialized and complex that few companies could assemble all the talent and expertise needed to compete with GE.

On the down side, the size of these investments means the industries are hard to exit quickly if the growth potential isn't there. Nuclear power is one obvious example; the recent earthquake and tsunami in Japan, with the subsequent breakdowns of some nuclear reactors, led to questions about that industry's future. In situations such as this, GE relies on its diversification strategy: if nuclear power (less than $2 billion of GE's revenue) should fall further out of favor, perhaps more countries will turn to other energy sources, and GE also sells gas and wind turbines (already $31 billion of revenue).

In developing this strategy, GE's leadership is thinking globally. Under Immelt, GE expanded its sales outside the United States from $51 billion in 2001 to $81 billion in 2009. In 2010 one-fourth of GE's revenues came from developing countries such as China and India; sales from all countries outside the United States account for more than half of GE's revenues. GE has a goal to increase those sales to 60 percent of revenues. Sales in China alone have tripled over the past 10 years, and sales in Africa and the Middle East have grown by four times. The international growth, while impressive, has fallen short of the company's targets. To focus more on growth in other countries, Immelt made GE's international business the responsibility of one executive, John G. Rice.

GE plans for international growth according to the opportunities in particular markets. In China, for example, the company looks not only at its business rivals, but also at the threats and opportunities from the government. Thus when China makes increasing use of solar and wind power part of its five-year economic plan, GE explores whether commercial businesses will be allowed to compete for that work (an opportunity for GE) or whether the government will run that area of the energy sector. Investments by the Chinese government in research and development for alternative energy could place GE at a competitive disadvantage relative to up-and-coming Chinese competitors.

With its efforts to address these challenges, GE seems to have left the bad times behind. Profits are on the rise again, and Immelt assures investors that even better performance lies ahead. This vision is reinforced by GE's slogan "imagination at work," which Immelt calls the company's "reason for being." It is symbolized at GE's global research center with a desk used by the company's founder, Thomas Edison. Immelt is committed to seeing the spirit of that great inventor live on at GE.[47]

- For the various GE businesses described, where would you place them in the BCG matrix?
- How well does GE's strategy of conglomerate diversification enable the company to seize opportunities and address threats? Why?

KEY TERMS

business strategy, p. 151

concentration, p. 147

concentric diversification, p. 147

conglomerate diversification, p. 148

core competence, p. 145

corporate strategy, p. 147

differentiation strategy, p. 151

functional strategy, p. 152

goal, p. 130

low-cost strategy, p. 151

mission, p. 139

operational planning, p. 134

plans, p. 130

resources, p. 144

scenario, p. 131

situational analysis, p. 129

stakeholders, p. 142

strategic control system, p. 154

strategic goals, p. 133

strategic management, p. 138

strategic planning, p. 133

strategic vision, p. 140

strategy, p. 134

SWOT analysis, p. 146

tactical planning, p. 134

vertical integration, p. 147

SUMMARY OF LEARNING OBJECTIVES

Now that you have studied Chapter 4, you should be able to:

LO 1 Summarize the basic steps in any planning process.

The planning process begins with a situation analysis of the external and internal forces affecting the organization. This examination helps identify and diagnose issues and problems and may bring to the surface alternative goals and plans for the firm. Next, the advantages and disadvantages of these goals and plans should be evaluated against one another. Once a set of goals and a plan have been selected, implementation involves communicating the plan to employees, allocating resources, and making certain that other systems such as rewards and budgets support the plan. Finally, planning requires instituting control systems to monitor progress toward the goals.

LO 2 Describe how strategic planning should be integrated with tactical and operational planning.

Strategic planning is different from operational planning in that it involves making long-term decisions about the entire organization. Tactical planning translates broad goals and strategies into specific actions to be taken within parts of the organization. Operational planning identifies the specific short-term procedures and processes required at lower levels of the organization.

LO 3 Identify elements of the external environment and internal resources of the firm to analyze before formulating a strategy.

Strategic planning is designed to leverage the strengths of a firm while minimizing the effects of its weaknesses. It is difficult to know the potential advantage a firm may have unless external analysis is done well. For example, a company may have a talented marketing department or an efficient production system. However, the organization cannot determine whether these internal characteristics are sources of competitive advantage until it knows something about how well the competitors stack up in these areas.

LO 4 Define core competencies and explain how they provide the foundation for business strategy.

A core competence is something a company does especially well relative to its competitors. When this competence, say, in engineering or marketing, is in some area important to market success, it becomes the foundation for developing a competitive advantage. It can provide a sustainable advantage if it is valuable, rare, difficult to imitate, and well organized.

LO 5 Summarize the types of choices available for corporate strategy.

Corporate strategy identifies the breadth of a firm's competitive domain. Corporate strategy can be kept narrow, as in a concentration strategy, or can move to suppliers and buyers via vertical integration. Corporate strategy also can broaden a firm's domain via concentric (related) diversification or conglomerate (unrelated) diversification.

LO 6 Discuss how companies can achieve competitive advantage through business strategy.

Companies gain competitive advantage in two primary ways. They can attempt to be unique in some way by pursuing a differentiation strategy, or they can focus on efficiency and price by pursuing a low-cost strategy.

LO 7 Describe the keys to effective strategy implementation.

Many good plans are doomed to failure because they are not implemented correctly. Strategy must be supported by structure, technology, human resources, rewards, information systems, culture, leadership, and so on. Ultimately, the success of a plan depends on how well employees at low levels are able and willing to implement it. Participative management is one of the more popular approaches executives use to gain employees' input and ensure their commitment to strategy implementation.

DISCUSSION QUESTIONS

1. This chapter opened with a quote from former CEO of GE Jack Welch: "Manage your destiny, or someone else will." What does this mean for strategic management? What does it mean when Welch adds, "or someone else will"?

2. List the six steps in the formal planning process. Suppose you are a top executive of a home improvement chain and you want to launch a new company website. Provide examples of activities you would carry out during each step to create the site.

3. Your friend is frustrated because he's having trouble selecting a career. He says, "I can't plan because the future is too complicated. Anything can happen, and there are too many choices." What would you say to him to change his mind?

4. How do strategic, operational, and tactical planning differ? How might the three levels complement one another in an organization?

5. How might an organization such as Urban Outfitters use a strategy map? With your classmates and using Figure 4.3 as a guide, develop a possible strategy map for the company.

6. What accounts for the shift from strategic planning to strategic management? In which industries would you be most likely to observe these trends? Why?

7. Review Table 4.1, which lists the components of an environmental analysis. Why would this analysis be important to a company's strategic planning process?

8. In your opinion, what are the core competencies of Harley-Davidson Motor Company motorcycles? How do these competencies help Harley-Davidson compete against foreign competitors such as Yamaha and Suzuki?

9. How could SWOT analysis help newspaper companies remain competitive in the new media environment?

10. What are the key challenges in strategy implementation? What barriers might prevent strategy implementation?

EXPERIENTIAL EXERCISES

4.1   STRATEGIC PLANNING

OBJECTIVE

To study the strategic planning of a corporation recently in the news.

INSTRUCTIONS

Bloomberg Businessweek magazine frequently has articles on the strategies of various corporations. Find a recent article on a corporation in an industry of interest to you. Read the article and answer the following questions.

Strategic Planning Worksheet

1. Has the firm clearly identified what business it is in and how it is different from its competitors? Explain.

_____
_____
_____
_____
_____
_____

2. What key assumptions about the future have shaped the firm's new strategy?

_____
_____
_____
_____
_____
_____

3. What key strengths and weaknesses of the firm influenced the selection of the new strategy?

_____
_____
_____
_____
_____
_____

4. What specific objectives has the firm set in conjunction with the new strategy?

_____
_____
_____
_____
_____
_____

SOURCE: R. R. McGrath Jr., *Exercises in Management Fundamentals,* 1st, p. 15. Copyright © 1985. Reprinted by permission of Pearson Education, Inc., Upper Saddle River, New Jersy.

4.2 FORMULATING BUSINESS STRATEGY

OBJECTIVES

1. To illustrate the complex interrelationships central to the formulation of business strategy.
2. To demonstrate the use of SWOT (strengths, weaknesses, opportunities, and threats) analysis in a business situation.

INSTRUCTIONS

1. Your instructor will divide the class into small groups and assign each group a well-known organization for analysis.
2. Each group will
   a. Study the SWOT Introduction and the SWOT Worksheet to understand the work needed to complete the assignment.
   b. Obtain the needed information about the organization under study through library research, interviews, and so on.
   c. Complete the SWOT Worksheet.
   d. Prepare group responses to the discussion questions.
3. After the class reconvenes, group spokespersons will present group findings.

DISCUSSION QUESTIONS

1. Why would most organizations not develop strategies for matches between opportunities and strengths?
2. Why would most organizations not develop strategies for matches between opportunities and weaknesses?
3. Why do most organizations want to deal from strength?

SWOT INTRODUCTION

One of the more commonly used strategy tools is SWOT (strengths, weaknesses, opportunities, and threats) analysis, which is accomplished in four steps:

Step 1: Analyze the organization's internal environment, identifying its strengths and weaknesses.

Step 2: Analyze the organization's external environment, identifying its opportunities and threats.

Step 3: Match (a) strengths with opportunities, (b) weaknesses with threats, (c) strengths with threats, and (d) weaknesses with opportunities.

Step 4: Develop strategies for those matches that appear to be of greatest importance to the organization. Most organizations give top priority to strategies that involve the matching of strengths with opportunities and second priority to strategies that involve the matching of weaknesses with threats. The key is to exploit opportunities in areas where the organization has a strength and to defend against threats in areas where the organization has a weakness.

SWOT Worksheet
Organization being analyzed: _____

Internal Analysis   **External Analysis**

Strengths   Opportunities

_____   _____
_____   _____
_____   _____
_____   _____
_____   _____
_____   _____
_____   _____
_____   _____
_____   _____
_____   _____

Weaknesses   Threats

_____   _____
_____   _____
_____   _____
_____   _____
_____   _____
_____   _____
_____   _____
_____   _____

Strategies That Match Strengths with Opportunities

_____
_____
_____
_____
_____
_____
_____
_____
_____
_____
_____
_____
_____

Strategies That Match Weaknesses with Threats

_____
_____
_____
_____
_____
_____
_____
_____
_____
_____
_____
_____
_____

Strategies That Match Strengths with Threats

_____
_____
_____
_____
_____
_____
_____
_____
_____
_____
_____
_____

Strategies That Match Weaknesses with Opportunities

_____
_____
_____
_____
_____
_____
_____
_____
_____
_____
_____
_____

CONCLUDING CASE
CUSTOM COFFEE & CHOCOLATE

Bonnie Brewer and Stacy Kim were college roommates. While at school, they shared dreams of opening their own business. To prepare themselves, they took business and marketing courses, along with courses in management. When they graduated, they each found jobs in Seattle, near where they'd gone to school.

Several years later, after working at other companies to gain experience, the two women decided to take the plunge together and made a plan to open a small café where they and their customers could indulge their love of good coffee and fine chocolate. They looked at two locations for their café: one near Pike Place Market, which gets a lot of foot traffic from shoppers and businesspeople, and one near the university, where shops and restaurants are patronized by students, faculty, staff, and local residents. They chose the university location because they thought they knew and understood those customers well. The doors to Custom Coffee & Chocolate opened several months later, with both Brewer and Kim working hard to serve unique coffee blends and specialty chocolates, maintain the shop, and handle the finances.

Custom Coffee & Chocolate's business plan included purchasing only fair trade coffee (priced to provide living wages to coffee growers) and chocolates made by a few local suppliers. Their café was small, but it had several comfortable chairs, couches, and coffee tables to encourage customers to stay and chat or read the newspaper between classes. However, the majority of their business was takeout.

At the beginning, business was slow. Brewer and Kim had struggled to find the right price points for their coffee and chocolates, and they worried they might be set too high. But everyone who came in to the café loved what they bought and came back—and began to bring friends. Business increased over a period of about five months, when Brewer and Kim had to turn their attention toward longer-term planning. They had exhausted their savings and their initial small business loan, and their six-month lease was up. They needed to decide whether they were in this for the long haul.

The two women met to consider their options. Right away, they decided they wanted to extend their hours and hire two part-time employees. They would investigate a wireless connection that customers could use. Kim would take over more of the finances, while Brewer would handle marketing—which they both agreed they needed for the café to grow. They evaluated whether to expand the menu to include baked chocolate desserts, tea, and other beverages. They considered delivery service to locations on campus, such as dorms and lounges where students were studying. They discussed holding events at the café such as poetry readings or discussion groups. And they talked about establishing a website with a menu and phone number, updates on current coffees and chocolate flavors, and a blog written by Brewer with opportunities for customers to respond. They agreed they were not yet ready to accept online orders, but eventually they might.

As Kim and Brewer finalized their planning, they agreed that managing their own business was a challenge, but one they would never regret.

QUESTIONS

1. What do you think Custom Coffee & Chocolate's mission is?
2. Create a SWOT analysis for Custom Coffee & Chocolate.
3. Using the owners' ideas for the future of their café, as well as your own ideas, outline a tactical plan for Custom Coffee & Chocolate.

5

Ethics and Corporate Responsibility

LEARNING OBJECTIVES

After studying Chapter 5, you will be able to:

LO 1 Describe how different ethical perspectives guide decision making. p. 169

LO 2 Explain how companies influence their ethics environment. p. 172

LO 3 Outline a process for making ethical decisions. p. 178

LO 4 Summarize the important issues surrounding corporate social responsibility. p. 181

LO 5 Discuss reasons for businesses' growing interest in the natural environment. p. 186

LO 6 Identify actions managers can take to manage with the environment in mind and Appendix B. p. 187

Management Connection

YVON CHOUINARD'S VALUES ARE PATAGONIA'S VALUES

Patagonia, the $315 million outdoor apparel company based in Ventura, California, exists because Yvon Chouinard has a passion for climbing. Dissatisfied with the climbing hardware then available in the United States, Chouinard began making his own, selling equipment out of his car to support his climbing habit. As demand for the gear spread, Chouinard took on a partner, opened a factory, created a catalog, and added apparel for outdoor enthusiasts to the product mix. As with the equipment, the clothing was developed to meet performance objectives based on firsthand experience. Today Patagonia sells its gear and clothing through its catalog, in several dozen Patagonia stores, and at other retailers selling sporting goods.

Chouinard has admitted that he "never wanted to be a businessman." But because so many other lovers of outdoor sports such as climbing, surfing, and trail running wanted his well-designed products, he soon became just that. And he realized that he wanted to shape the way Patagonia was run, not just the products it sold.

Early on, Chouinard laid out values for how he wanted to work: employees, including the founder himself, should be able to take off time for enjoying the activities, such as climbing expeditions, that had drawn the people to Patagonia in the first place. They also should "work with friends" and with family members close at hand. The company promotes such values by hiring people with a shared love of the outdoors and by spreading employee benefits to all instead of building an executive dining room. Patagonia also was one of the first companies in the United States to set up on-site day care for employees' children.

Also at the heart of Patagonia's values is a love of the natural environment. Whether they are surfing,

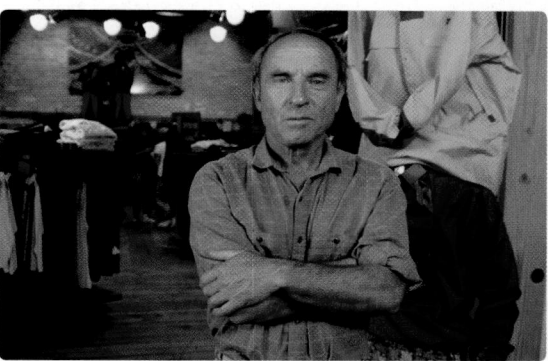

skiing, climbing a mountain, or paddling a kayak, Patagonia's employees and customers are enjoying the beauty of the world's wild places. Chouinard readily admits that this poses a dilemma. He values protection of the beautiful planet he enjoys, but at the same time, manufacturing clothing uses up resources and causes pollution. For example, toxic chemicals are needed to tan leather, and polyester is made from crude oil. How to reconcile Chouinard's values and Patagonia's business success?

For Chouinard, the resolution of this dilemma is essentially two-pronged: minimize the harm from his operations and devote a portion of earnings to preserving the environment. That understanding of the company's purpose is summed up by Patagonia's mission statement: "Build the best product, cause no unnecessary harm, use business to inspire and implement solutions to the environmental crisis."

Some of the ways in which Patagonia fulfills that mission involve the choices of materials used, the benefits offered to its employees, and the standards it sets for suppliers. Clothing designs emphasize reliance on materials that do minimal damage—for example, organic cotton and fleece made from recycled soda bottles. Employee benefits at Patagonia—recently named one of *Inc.* magazine's top small company workplaces—include two weeks of paid time off to work on the environmental cause of their choice. The company has established standards for measuring the environmental performance of the manufacturers it buys from, and it uses those criteria in selecting contractors. Furthermore, since 1985 the company has donated 1 percent of its revenues (not just profits) to organizations working to protect the environment. In the end, Chouinard insists, this concern for the environment makes perfect sense for a business: "We make outdoor products, so it's to our benefit that there be some nature left" for Patagonia's customers to enjoy—while wearing Patagonia gear, of course.[1]

How does a manager who believes we should protect the environment justify running a company that manufactures goods, engaging in processes that almost by definition use resources and create pollution? For Patagonia's Yvon Chouinard, the answer involves identifying important values and figuring out how the company can live up to them. As you read this chapter, think about how Chouinard's values-driven approach positions his company to be both ethical and successful.

Most companies are not started by someone who "never wanted to be" in business, and it might seem doubtful that someone who values outdoor adventure more than selling and managing could run a successful company. Still, under the continued leadership of Yvon Chouinard, Patagonia is prospering and widely respected. This example might, however, raise some questions, including whether managers can usually afford to put personal values first and what values are consistent with a company's long-term success.

This chapter addresses the values and manner of doing business adopted by managers as they carry out their corporate and business strategies. In particular, we will explore ways of applying **ethics,** the system of rules that governs the ordering of values. We do so based on the premise that

ethics

The system of rules that governs the ordering of values.

managers, their organizations, and their communities thrive over the long term when the managers apply ethical standards that direct them to act with integrity.

In addition, we consider the idea that organizations may have a responsibility to meet social obligations beyond earning profits within legal and ethical constraints. As you study this chapter, consider what kind of manager you want to be. What reputation do you hope to have? How would you like others to describe your behavior as a manager?

It's a Big Issue

Recent scandals have engulfed company executives, independent auditors, politicians and regulators, and shareholders and employees.[2] In some, executives at public companies have made misleading statements to inflate stock prices, undermining the public's trust in the integrity of the financial markets. Often the scandals are perpetrated by a number of people cooperating with one another, and many of the guilty parties had been otherwise upstanding individuals. Lobbyists have been accused—and some convicted—of buying influence with lavish gifts to politicians. Executives have admitted they received huge bonuses or stock options that were backdated to guarantee they would make money from investing in their company, regardless of whether their performance caused the stock's value to rise or fall. What other news disturbs you about managers' behavior? Tainted products in the food supply . . . actions that harm the environment . . . Internet scams . . . employees pressured to meet sales or production targets by any means? The list goes on, and the public becomes cynical. According to a

Temptations exist in every organization.

survey by the public relations firm Edelman, people are often suspicious of their own company's management; only 31 percent said they trust their own CEO.[3] Try to imagine the challenge of leading employees who don't trust you.

Sadly, when corporations behave badly, it's often not the top executives but the rank-and-file employees who suffer most. When companies such as energy trader Enron and insurance brokerage firm Marsh & McLennan saw their stocks tumble following scandals, executives had millions invested from generous pay and bonus packages. In contrast, employees, who had been encouraged to invest their retirement packages heavily in their company's stock, saw their savings disappear along with their company's reputation.

Still, simply talking about Enron and other famous cases as examples of lax company ethics doesn't get at the heart of the problem. Clearly these cases involve "bad guys," and the ethical lapses are obvious. But saying, "I would never do things like that," becomes too easy. The fact is that temptations exist in every organization. Many of the decisions you will face as a manager will pose ethical dilemmas, and the right thing to do is not always evident.

Bernard Madoff was convicted for running a multibillion-dollar ponzi scheme. He was sentenced to 150 years in prison for fraud that totaled an estimated $65 billion. The incident has been referred to as the largest white-collar fraud in history.

It's a Personal Issue

"Answer true or false: 'I am an ethical manager.' If you answered 'true,' here's an uncomfortable fact: You're probably not."[4] These sentences are the first in a *Harvard Business Review* article called "How (Un)Ethical Are You?" The point is that most of us think we are good decision makers, ethical, and unbiased. But the fact is, most people have unconscious biases that favor themselves and their own group. For example, managers often hire people who are like them, think they are immune to conflicts of interest, take more credit than they deserve, and blame others when they deserve some blame themselves.

Knowing that you have biases may help you try to overcome them, but usually that's not enough. Consider the basic ethical issue of telling a lie. Many people lie—some more than others, and in part depending on the situation, usually presuming that they will benefit from the lie. At a basic level, we all can make ethical arguments against lying and in favor of honesty. Yet it is useful to think thoroughly about the real consequences of lying.[5] Table 5.1 summarizes the possible outcomes of telling the truth or lying in different situations. People often lie or commit other ethical transgressions somewhat mindlessly, without realizing the full array of negative personal consequences.

> Knowing that you have biases may help you try to overcome them, but usually that's not enough.

Ethics issues are not easy, and they are not just for newsworthy corporate CEOs. For example, people at work use computers with Internet access. If the employer pays for the computer and the time you spend sitting in front of it, is it ethical for you to use the computer to do tasks unrelated to your work?

Maybe you think it's OK to do a little online shopping during your lunch hour or to check scores during the World Series or March Madness.

But what if you stream video of the games for your own and your coworkers' enjoyment or take a two-hour lunch to locate the best deal on a flat-panel TV?

TABLE 5.1   Telling the Truth and Lying: Possible Outcomes

Reason and Context of the Lie	Results of Lying	Results of Truth Telling
Conflicting expectations	• Easier to lie than to address the underlying conflict. • Offers quick relief of the issue. • Leaves the underlying problem unresolved. • May have no meaningful consequences, good or bad. • Liar must rationalize the action to preserve positive self-concept.	• Emotionally more difficult than lying. • May correct underlying problem. • May provoke further conflict. • Sometimes difficult to have an impact on an impermeable structure. • Develops one's reputation as an "honest" person.
Negotiation	• Short-term gain. • Economically positive. • Harms long-term relationship. • Must rationalize to oneself.	• Supports high-quality long-term relationship. • Develops reputation of integrity. • Models behavior to others.
Keeping a confidence (that may require at least a lie of omission)	• Protects whatever good reason there is for the confidence. • Maintains a long-term relationship with the party for whom confidence is kept. • May project deceitfulness to the deceived party.	• Violates a trust to the confiding party. • Makes one appear deceitful to all parties in the long run. • Creates the impression of honesty beyond utility.
Reporting your own performance within an organization	• Might advance oneself or one's cause. • Develops dishonest reputation over time. • Must continue the sequence of lies to appear consistent.	• Creates reputation of integrity. • May not always be positive.

SOURCE: From *Academy of Management Executive: The Thinking Manager's Source* by S.L. Gover, "The Truth, the Whole Truth, and Nothing but the Truth: The Causes and Management of Workplace Lying." Copyright © 2005. Reproduced with permission of Academy of Management via Copyright Clearance Center.

Besides lost productivity, employers are most concerned about computer users introducing viruses, leaking confidential information, and creating a hostile work environment by downloading inappropriate web content.

Sometimes employees write blogs or post comments online about their company and its products. Obviously companies do not want their employees to say bad things about them, but some companies are concerned about employees who are overly enthusiastic. When employees plug their companies and products on comments pages, this practice is considered spamming at best and deceptive if the employees don't disclose their relationship with their company. Another practice considered deceptive is when companies create fictional blogs as a marketing tactic without disclosing their sponsorship. And in a practice known as Astroturfing—because the "grassroots" interest it builds is fake—businesses pay bloggers to write positive comments about them. A Florida company known as PayPerPost will match advertisers with bloggers but now requires bloggers to disclose the relationship. Companies such as Coca-Cola, UPS, and IBM have established guidelines directing

Here's a small but potentially powerful suggestion.[6] Change your vocabulary: the word "ethics" is too loaded, even trite. Substitute "responsibility" or "decency." And act accordingly.

employees to identify themselves accurately in online communications so that they can participate in online conversations about their companies without being accused of deception.[7]

Are these examples too small to worry about? This chapter will help you think through decisions with ethical ramifications.

Are women more ethical than men?

Ethics

The aim of ethics is to identify both the rules that should govern people's behavior and the "goods" that are worth seeking. Ethical decisions are guided by the underlying values of the individual. Values are principles of conduct such as caring, being honest, keeping promises, pursuing excellence, showing loyalty, being fair, acting with integrity, respecting others, and being a responsible citizen.[8]

Most people would agree that all of these values are admirable guidelines for behavior. However, ethics becomes a more complicated issue when a situation dictates that one value overrules others. An **ethical issue** is a situation, problem, or opportunity in which an individual must choose among several actions that must be evaluated as morally right or wrong.[10]

> Are women more ethical than men? Studies have implied they are, at least by some measures. Surveys of business students found an increase in their interest in studying ethics, with a greater increase among women. Compared with their female counterparts, undergraduate male students in business and psychology showed stronger unethical attitudes and a tendency to behave unethically. When business students took an ethics curriculum, women made greater strides than men in improving their moral awareness and decision-making processes.[9]

> Ethics becomes a more complicated issue when a situation dictates that one value overrules others.

Ethical issues arise in every facet of life; we concern ourselves here with business ethics in particular. **Business ethics** comprises the moral principles and standards that guide behavior in the world of business.[11]

Ethical Systems

Moral philosophy refers to the principles, rules, and values people use in deciding what is right or wrong. This is a simple definition in the abstract but often terribly complex and difficult when facing real choices. How do you decide what is right and wrong? Do you know what criteria you apply and how you apply them?

Ethics scholars point to various major ethical systems as guides.[12] The first ethical system, **universalism**, states that all people should uphold certain values, such as honesty, that society needs to function. Universal values are principles so fundamental to human existence that they are important in all societies—for example, rules against murder, deceit, torture, and oppression.

Some efforts have been made to establish global, universal ethical principles for business. The Caux Roundtable, a group of international executives based in Caux, Switzerland, worked with business leaders from Japan, Europe, and the United States to create the **Caux Principles.** Two basic ethical ideals underpin the Caux Principles: *kyosei* and human dignity. *Kyosei* means living and working together for the common good, allowing cooperation and mutual prosperity to coexist with healthy and fair competition. Human dignity concerns the value of each person as an end, not a means to the fulfillment of others' purposes.

ethical issue

Situation, problem, or opportunity in which an individual must choose among several actions that must be evaluated as morally right or wrong.

business ethics

The moral principles and standards that guide behavior in the world of business.

moral philosophy

Principles, rules, and values people use in deciding what is right or wrong.

universalism

The ethical system stating that all people should uphold certain values that society needs to function.

Caux Principles

Ethical principles established by international executives based in Caux, Switzerland, in collaboration with business leaders from Japan, Europe, and the United States.

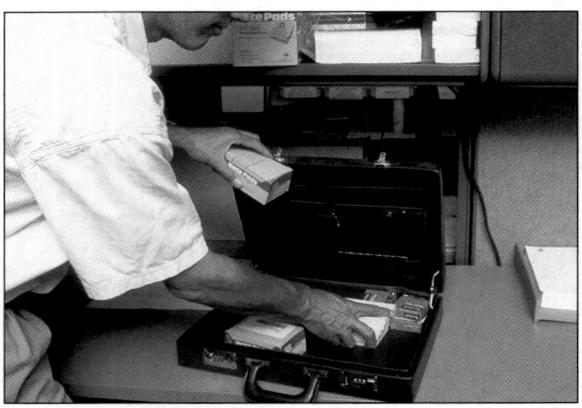

Employees sometimes feel that "borrowing" a few office supplies from their company helps compensate for any perceived inequities in pay or other benefits.

Universal principles can be powerful and useful, but what people say, hope, or think they would do is often different from what they *really* do, faced with conflicting demands in real situations. Before we describe other ethical systems, consider the following "In Practice" example, and think about how you or others would resolve it.

Not everyone would behave the same in this scenario. Different individuals would apply different moral philosophies. Consider each of the following moral philosophies and the actions to which they might lead in the bridge example.[13]

Egoism and Utilitarianism   According to **egoism,** acceptable behavior is that which maximizes benefits for the individual. "Doing the right thing," the focus of moral philosophy, is defined by egoism as "do the act that promotes the greatest good for oneself." If everyone follows this system, according to its proponents, the well-being of society as a whole should increase.

IN PRACTICE

Suppose that Sam Colt, a sales representative, is preparing a sales presentation on behalf of his firm, Midwest Hardware, which manufactures nuts and bolts. Colt hopes to obtain a large sale from a construction firm that is building a bridge across the Missouri River near St. Louis. The bolts manufactured by Midwest Hardware have a 3 percent defect rate, which, although acceptable in the industry, makes them unsuitable for use in certain types of projects, such as those that might be subject to sudden, severe stress. The new bridge will be located near the New Madrid fault line, the source of a major earthquake in 1811. The epicenter of that earthquake, which caused extensive damage and altered the flow of the Missouri, is about 190 miles from the new bridge site.

Bridge construction in the area is not regulated by earthquake codes. If Colt wins the sale, he will earn a commission of $25,000 on top of his regular salary. But if he tells the contractors about the defect rate, Midwest may lose the sale to a competitor whose bolts are slightly more reliable. Thus Colt's ethical issue is whether to point out to the bridge contractor that in the event of an earthquake, some Midwest bolts could fail.

• What should Colt do? Is that what you believe you would do in this situation?

SOURCE: O. C. Ferrell and J. Fraedrich, *Business Ethics: Ethical Decision Making and Cases,* 3rd ed. p. 53. Copyright 1997 South-Western, a part of Cengage Learning, Inc. Reproduced with permission. www.cengage.com/permission.

This notion is similar to Adam Smith's concept of the invisible hand in business. Smith argued that if every organization follows its own economic self-interest, the total wealth of society will be maximized.

Not everyone would behave the same in this scenario.

egoism

An ethical system defining acceptable behavior as that which maximizes consequences for the individual.

Unlike egoism, **utilitarianism** directly seeks the greatest good for the greatest number of people. Consider whether utilitarianism would help guide ethical decision making with regard to student loan programs. New York's attorney general investigated 100 colleges and half a dozen lenders for arrangements in which the lenders allegedly offered payments, stock grants, and perks to schools, and the schools listed the companies as "preferred lenders" in information given to students who wanted to borrow tuition money from private sources. The attorney general called the arrangements "kickbacks"; some schools replied that they were not being corrupted but used the money to add to the financial aid they could award to students.[14]

Whereas ethics based on egoism would accept actions that allow the lenders to maximize their earnings and the financial aid officers to pursue whatever arrangements benefit themselves and their schools, utilitarianism requires a broader view. Most obviously, there is the question of what these arrangements cost students who make borrowing decisions on the assumption that "preferred" lenders will give students the best deals. But other students benefited if payments from lenders were used to augment the financial aid given to other students. The utilitarian approach might consider how many students benefited—and by how much—and how many students paid extra for loans and how much more they paid. One company responded to the allegations by agreeing to a code of conduct that forbids gifts in exchange for "preferred" status.[15]

Relativism   Perhaps it seems that an individual makes ethical choices on a personal basis, applying personal perspectives. But this is not necessarily the case. **Relativism** defines ethical behavior based on the opinions and behaviors of relevant other people. In the previous example of student loans, U.S. business, government, and society largely agree that bribes, kickbacks, and conflicts of interest would not be acceptable behaviors for people in the lending industry—perhaps even less so for those charged with serving students. Those standards help to explain the rapid actions taken by the organizations when they found out about the situation.

Relativism acknowledges the existence of different ethical viewpoints. For example, *norms*, or standards of expected and acceptable behavior, vary from one culture to another. A study of Russian versus U.S. managers found that all followed norms of informed consent about chemical hazards in work situations and paying wages on time. But in Russia more than in the United States, businesspeople were likely to consider the interests of a broader set of stakeholders (in this study, keeping factories open for the sake of local employment), to keep double books to hide information from tax inspectors and criminal organizations, and to make personal payments to government officials in charge of awarding contracts.[17] Relativism defines ethical behavior according to how others behave.

> In a recent survey ranking 180 nations from most to least honest, the United States came in 18th (tied with Japan and Belgium). The U.S. rating of 7.3 on a 10-point scale placed it among only 22 countries that scored at least a 7.0. The top ratings went to Denmark, Sweden, and New Zealand, each with 9.3. The bottom-ranked nations, including Somalia, Myanmar, and Iraq, tend to be among the poorest. Sadly, the combination of corruption and poverty in these nations can literally amount to a death sentence for many of their citizens.[16]

Virtue ethics   The moral philosophies just described apply different types of rules and reasoning. **Virtue ethics** is a perspective that goes beyond the conventional rules of society by suggesting that what is moral must also come from what a mature person with good "moral character" would deem right. Society's rules provide a moral minimum, and then moral individuals can transcend rules by applying their personal virtues such as faith, honesty, and integrity.

Individuals differ in this regard. **Kohlberg's model of cognitive moral development** classifies people into categories based on their level of moral judgment.[18] People in the *preconventional* stage make decisions based on concrete rewards and punishments and immediate self-interest. People in the *conventional* stage conform to the expectations of ethical behavior held by groups or institutions such as society, family, or peers. People in the *principled* stage see beyond authority, laws, and norms and follow their self-chosen ethical principles.[19] Some people forever reside in the preconventional stage, some move into the conventional stage, and some develop further yet into the principled stage. Over time, and through education and experience, people may change their values and ethical behavior.

Returning to the bolts-in-the-bridge example, *egoism* would result in keeping quiet about the bolts' defect rate. *Utilitarianism* would dictate a more thorough cost–benefit

---

utilitarianism

An ethical system stating that the greatest good for the greatest number should be the overriding concern of decision makers.

relativism

Philosophy that bases ethical behavior on the opinions and behaviors of relevant other people.

virtue ethics

Classification of people based on their level of moral judgment.

Kohlberg's model of cognitive moral development

Perspective that what is moral comes from what a mature person with "good" moral character would deem right.

analysis and possibly the conclusion that the probability of a bridge collapse is so low compared to the utility of jobs, economic growth, and company growth that the defect rate is not worth mentioning. The *relativist* perspective might prompt the salesperson to look at company policy and general industry practice, and to seek opinions from colleagues and perhaps trade journals and ethics codes. Whatever is then perceived to be a consensus or normal practice would dictate action. Finally, *virtue ethics*, applied by people in the principled stage of moral development, would likely lead to full disclosure about the product and risks, and perhaps suggestions for alternatives that would reduce the risk.[20]

These major ethical systems underlie personal moral choices and ethical decisions in business.

IN PRACTICE

The Waldorf-Astoria Hotel is an icon of luxurious accommodations in New York City, so Linda and Michael Morgan were understandably excited about their family's plans to celebrate the Thanksgiving holiday there. The summer before, they reserved four rooms, including three suites. But shortly before Thanksgiving, Linda Morgan's mother decided not to travel, so Michael called to cancel one of the rooms. That's when he learned that the rooms previously reserved would not be available. The Waldorf offered alternative accommodations at the Hilton New York, including one night for free. The Morgans went ahead with their trip, but they were unhappy; compared with what they'd expected, the Hilton was a letdown.

Trial lawyer Allen Stewart can tell many such stories. He recalls at least a dozen situations in which he was turned away from full hotels where he had reservations. Wondering if it was a common practice, he investigated and learned that hotels routinely overbook because their experience is that some percentage of people with reservations will cancel at the last minute. A desirable hotel such as the Waldorf can run into especially sticky situations. At the time the Morgans were trying to stay there, Saudi Arabia's King Abdullah made last-minute plans to visit with an entourage because he had surgery scheduled for late November. In such a situation, hotel management would have to choose between housing VIPs who would pay a premium and honoring reservations from holiday travelers, who tend to take advantage of discounts.[21]

- Imagine you are a Waldorf-Astoria manager who must decide which guests to accommodate when you are overbooked. Would you honor the Morgan's reservations? What ethical issues come into play in your decision?

Business Ethics

Insider trading, illegal campaign contributions, bribery and kickbacks, famous court cases, and other scandals have created a perception that business leaders use illegal means to gain competitive advantage, increase profits, or improve their personal positions. Neither young managers nor consumers believe top executives are doing a good job of establishing high ethical standards.[22] Some even joke that *business ethics* has become a contradiction in terms.

Most business leaders believe they uphold ethical standards in business practices.[23] But many managers and their organizations must deal frequently with ethical dilemmas, and the issues are becoming increasingly complex. For example,

> many people seek spiritual renewal in the workplace, in part reflecting a broader religious awakening in America, while others argue that this trend violates religious freedom and the separation of church and boardroom.[24]

Table 5.2 shows some other important examples of ethical dilemmas in business.

Artistic control	Rock musicians, independent filmmakers, and other artists are rebelling against control by big media and retail companies.
Brands	In-your-face marketing campaigns have sparked antibrand attitudes among students.
CEO pay	Nearly three-fourths of Americans see executive pay packages as excessive.
Commercialism in schools	Parent groups have mounted battles in hundreds of communities against advertising in the public schools.
Consumerism	Anger and frustration are mounting over high gasoline and drug prices, poor airline service, and HMOs that override doctors' decisions.
Frankenfoods	Europeans' skepticism about genetically modified food is taking hold in the United States, making targets of companies such as Monsanto.
Globalization	Environmentalists, students, and unionists charge that global trade and economic bodies operate in the interests of multinational companies.
Politics	Public revulsion over the corporate bankrolling of politicians has energized campaign finance reform activists.
Sweatshops	Anti-sweatshop groups have sprung up on college campuses; they routinely picket clothing manufacturers, toymakers, and retailers.
Urban sprawl	Groups in more than 100 cities have blocked big-box superstores by Walmart and other chains.
Wages	Some 56 percent of workers feel they are underpaid, especially as wages since 1992 have topped inflation by 7.6 percent, while productivity is up 17.9 percent.

TABLE 5.2
Some Ethical Issues in Business. What Is Happening Today with These Issues?

The Ethics Environment

Responding to a series of corporate scandals—particularly the high-profile cases of Enron and WorldCom—Congress passed the **Sarbanes-Oxley Act** in 2002 to improve and maintain investor confidence. The law requires companies to have more independent board directors (not just company insiders), to adhere strictly to accounting rules, and to have senior managers personally sign off on financial results. Violations could result in heavy fines and criminal prosecution. One of the biggest impacts of the law is the requirement for companies and their auditors to provide reports to financial statement users about the effectiveness of internal controls over the financial reporting process.

Companies that make the effort to meet or exceed these requirements can reduce their risks by lowering the likelihood of misdeeds and the consequences if an employee does break the law.[25] But some executives say Sarbanes-Oxley distracts from their real work and makes them more risk-averse. Some complain about the time and money needed to comply with the internal control reporting—millions of dollars at big businesses. But as companies have implemented tighter controls, many have discovered

Sarbanes-Oxley Act

An act passed into law by Congress in 2002 to establish strict accounting and reporting rules in order to make senior managers more accountable and to improve and maintain investor confidence.

that the effort is helping them avoid mistakes and improve efficiency. Regardless of managers' attitudes toward Sarbanes-Oxley, it creates legal requirements intended to improve ethical behavior.

According to a global survey of almost 500,000 employees, efforts to promote ethics are associated with better business performance. In high-integrity company cultures, employees were far less likely to see significant business misconduct. And at companies where employees were encouraged to speak up about wrongdoing, financial returns to shareholders were higher.[26]

Ethics are not shaped only by laws and by individual virtue. They also may be influenced by the company's work environment.

Unethical corporate behavior may be the responsibility of an unethical individual, but it often also reveals a company culture that is ethically lax.[27]

Maintaining a positive ethical climate is always challenging, but it is especially complex for organizations with international activities. Different cultures and countries may have different standards of behavior, and managers have to decide when relativism is appropriate, rather than adherence to firm standards. Table 5.3 gives examples of real situations where ethics-related decisions have arisen in an international context.

ethical climate

In an organization, the processes by which decisions are evaluated and made on the basis of right and wrong.

The **ethical climate** of an organization refers to the processes by which decisions are evaluated and made on the basis of right and wrong.[28] For example, General Electric's top executives have demonstrated a commitment to promoting high levels of integrity without sacrificing the company's well-known commitment to business results. The measures taken by GE to maintain a positive ethical climate include establishing global standards for behavior to prevent ethical problems such as conflicts of interest and money laundering. As managers monitor the external environment, they are expected to consider legal and ethical developments, along with other concerns,

TABLE 5.3
Ethical Decision Making in the International Context

What would you do in each of these true-life situations, and why?

- You are a sales representative for a construction company in the Middle East. Your company wants very much to land a particular project. The cousin of the minister who will award the contract informs you that the minister wants $20,000 in addition to the standard fees. If you do not make this payment, your competition certainly will—and will get the contract.

- You are the international vice president of a multinational chemical corporation. Your company is the sole producer of an insecticide that will effectively combat a recent infestation of West African crops. The minister of agriculture in a small, developing African country has put in a large order for your product. Your insecticide is highly toxic and is banned in the United States. You inform the minister of the risks of using your product, but he insists on using it and claims it will be used "intelligently." The president of your company believes you should fill the order, but the decision ultimately is yours.

- You are a new marketing manager for a large automobile tire manufacturer. Your company's advertising agency has just presented plans for introducing a new tire into the Southeast Asia market. Your tire is a truly good product, but the proposed advertising is deceptive. For example, the "reduced price" was reduced from a hypothetical amount that was established only so it could be "reduced," and claims that the tire was tested under the "most adverse" conditions ignore the fact that it was not tested in prolonged tropical heat and humidity. Your superiors are not concerned about deceptive advertising, and they are counting on you to see that the tire does extremely well in the new market. Will you approve the ad plan?

SOURCE: N. Adler, *International Dimensions of Organizational Behavior*, 2nd ed. (Boston: Kent, 1997).

so that the company can be prepared for new issues as they arise. Managers at all levels are rewarded for their performance in meeting both integrity and business standards, and when violations occur, even managers who were otherwise successful are disciplined, sending a powerful message that ethical behavior is truly valued at GE.[29]

Danger Signs   Maintaining consistent ethical behavior by all employees is an ongoing challenge. What are some danger signs that an organization may be allowing or even encouraging unethical behavior? Many factors create a climate conducive to unethical behavior:

1. Excessive emphasis on short-term revenues over longer-term considerations.
2. Failure to establish a written code of ethics.
3. A desire for simple, "quick fix" solutions to ethical problems.
4. An unwillingness to take an ethical stand that may impose financial costs.
5. Consideration of ethics solely as a legal issue or a public relations tool.
6. Lack of clear procedures for handling ethical problems.
7. Responding to the demands of shareholders at the expense of other constituencies.[30]

Do you see danger signs for AutoAdmit? The small company operates a message board website targeting college and law school students. Some students have complained that participants on the site's law school message board have posted false and insulting messages about them that have humiliated them and may have interfered with their ability to find summer internships. Many employers use Internet searches as part of their background checks, and sites such as AutoAdmit might surface in search results. AutoAdmit founder Jarret Cohen told the *Washington Post* that he is reluctant to interfere with postings: "I want [the message board] to be a place where people can express themselves freely." He and his partner, Anthony Ciolli, define the matter in terms of free speech, insisting that "one finds overall a much deeper and much more mature level of insight in a community where the ugliest depths of human opinion are confronted, rather than ignored." Ciolli claims that only Cohen has the authority to remove offensive postings, and Cohen refuses to "selectively remove" comments. The site also does not keep information that would identify participants, using only screen names, because "people would not have as much fun" if employers could identify them. Ciolli and Cohen have so far avoided any accusation that their message boards are violating the law; AutoAdmit isn't liable for the content of messages written by visitors to the site.[31]

AutoAdmit claims to be the most prestigious law school discussion in the world. What do you think about the organization's ethical climate? Should it uphold values other than freedom of expression?

It's been said that your reputation is your most precious asset. Here's a suggestion: Set a goal for yourself to be seen by others as both a "moral person" and also as a "moral manager," someone who influences others to behave ethically. When you are both personally moral and a moral manager, you will truly be an **ethical leader**.[32] You can have strong personal character, but if you pay more attention to other things, and ethics is "managed" by "benign neglect," you won't have a reputation as an ethical leader.

Corporate Ethical Standards   To create a culture that encourages ethical behavior, managers must be more than ethical people. They also should lead others to behave ethically.[33] At General Electric, chief executive Jeffrey Immelt demonstrates

Ethical climate is heating up! Former Enron treasurer Ben Glisan, Jr. pleaded guilty to conspiracy and became the first ex-Enron executive to go to prison. Former Enron executives Jeff Skilling and Ken Lay were later arrested for their participation in the high-profile scandal case that led to the passage of the Sarbanes-Oxley Act in 2002. This case is considered to be one of the biggest business scandals in U.S. history.

ethical leader

One who is both a moral person and a moral manager influencing others to behave ethically.

you won't have a reputation as an ethical leader.

his concern for ethical leadership by beginning and ending each annual meeting with a statement of the company's integrity principles, emphasizing that "GE's business success is built on our reputation with all stakeholders for lawful and ethical behavior." These words are backed up with a reward system in which managers are evaluated for how well they meet ethics-related standards such as the use of audits, minimal customer complaints and lawsuits, avoidance of compliance actions by government regulators, and high ratings on employee surveys.[34]

IBM uses a guideline for business conduct that asks employees to determine whether under the full glare of examination by associates, friends, and family, they would remain comfortable with their decisions. One suggestion is to imagine how you would feel if you saw your decision and its consequences on the front page of the newspaper.[36] This "light of day" or "sunshine" ethical framework can be powerful.

Trust and ethics matter to employees. Among executives concerned that employee turnover will grow as the economy improves, 65 percent say loss of trust in the company will contribute to the problem. Almost half of employees who plan to look for a new job blame their decision to leave on loss of trust.[35]

Employees' reasons for planning to look for a new job

Such fear of exposure compels people more strongly in some cultures than in others. In Asia, anxiety about losing face often makes executives resign immediately if they are caught in ethical transgressions or if their companies are embarrassed by revelations in the press. By contrast, in the United States, exposed executives might respond with indignation, intransigence, pleading the Fifth Amendment, stonewalling, and an everyone-else-does-it self-defense, or by not admitting wrongdoing and giving no sign that resignation ever crossed their minds. Partly because of legal tradition, the attitude often is never explain, never apologize, don't admit the mistake, and do not resign, even if the entire world knows exactly what happened.[37]

Fear of exposure compels people more strongly in some cultures than in others.

Ethics Codes   The Sarbanes-Oxley Act requires that public companies periodically disclose whether they have adopted a code of ethics for senior financial officers—and if not, why not. Often the statements are just for show, but when implemented well they can change a company's ethical climate for the better and truly encourage ethical behavior. Executives say they pay most attention to their company's code of ethics when they feel that stakeholders (customers, investors, lenders, and suppliers) try to influence them to do so, and their reasons for paying attention to the code are that doing so will help create a strong ethical culture and promote a positive image.[38]

Ethics codes must be carefully written and tailored to individual companies' philosophies. Aetna Life & Casualty believes that tending to the broader needs of society is essential to fulfilling its economic role. Johnson & Johnson has one of the most famous ethics codes; it is featured in Table 5.4. J&J consistently receives high rankings for community and social responsibility in *Fortune*'s annual survey of corporate reputations.

Most ethics codes address subjects such as employee conduct, community and environment, shareholders, customers, suppliers and contractors, political activity, and technology. Often the codes are drawn up by the organizations' legal departments and begin with research into other companies' codes. The nonprofit Ethics Resource Center assists companies interested in establishing a corporate code of ethics.[39]

TABLE 5.4
Johnson & Johnson's
Ethics Code

We believe our first responsibility is to the doctors, nurses, and patients, to mothers and all others who use our products and services. In meeting their needs everything we do must be of high quality. We must constantly strive to reduce our costs in order to maintain reasonable prices. Customers' orders must be serviced promptly and accurately. Our suppliers and distributors must have an opportunity to make a fair profit.

We are responsible to our employees: the men and women who work with us throughout the world. Everyone must be considered as an individual. We must respect their dignity and recognize their merit. They must have a sense of security in their jobs. Compensation must be fair and adequate, and working conditions clean, orderly, and safe. Employees must feel free to make suggestions and complaints. There must be equal opportunity for employment, development, and advancement for those qualified. We must provide competent management, and their actions must be just and ethical.

We are responsible to the communities in which we live and work and to the world community as well.

We must be good citizens — support good works and charities and bear our fair share of taxes. We must encourage civic improvements and better health and education.

We must maintain in good order the property we are privileged to use, protecting the environment and natural resources.

Our final responsibility is to our stockholders. Business must make a sound profit. We must experiment with new ideas. Research must be carried on, innovative programs developed, and mistakes paid for. New equipment must be purchased, new facilities provided, and new products launched. Reserves must be created to provide for adverse times.

When we operate according to these principles, the stockholders should realize a fair return.

SOURCE: Reprinted with permission of Johnson & Johnson.

To make an ethics code effective, do the following: (1) involve those who have to live with it in writing the statement; (2) focus on real-life situations that employees can relate to; (3) keep it short and simple, so it is easy to understand and remember; (4) write about values and shared beliefs that are important and that people can really believe in; and (5) set the tone at the top, having executives talk about and live up to the statement.[40] When reality differs from the statement—as when a motto says people are our most precious asset or a product is the finest in the world, but in fact people are treated poorly or product quality is weak—the statement becomes a joke to employees rather than a guiding light.

The "sunshine" principle encourages employees to consider first if they would like to see their actions displayed on the front page of the newspaper. If yes, then it is likely an appropriate course of action.

> When reality differs from the statement
> the statement becomes a joke to employees rather than a
> guiding light.

Ethics Programs   Corporate ethics programs commonly include formal ethics codes that articulate the company's expectations regarding ethics; ethics committees that develop policies, evaluate actions, and investigate violations; ethics communication systems that give employees a means of reporting problems or getting guidance; ethics officers or ombudspersons who investigate allegations and provide education; ethics training programs; and disciplinary processes for addressing unethical behavior.[41]

Ethics programs can range from compliance-based to integrity-based.[42] **Compliance-based ethics programs** are designed by corporate counsel to prevent, detect, and punish legal violations. Compliance-based programs increase surveillance and controls on people and impose

**compliance-based
ethics programs**

Company mechanisms typically
designed by corporate counsel
to prevent, detect, and punish
legal violations.

**integrity-based ethics
programs**

Company mechanisms
designed to instill in people
a personal responsibility for
ethical behavior.

punishments on wrongdoers. Program elements include establishing and communicating legal standards and procedures, assigning high-level managers to oversee compliance, auditing and monitoring compliance, reporting criminal misconduct, punishing wrongdoers, and taking steps to prevent offenses in the future.

Such programs should reduce illegal behavior and help a company stay out of court. But they do not create a moral commitment to ethical conduct; they merely ensure moral mediocrity. As Richard Breeden, former chairman of the Securities and Exchange Commission, said, "It is not an adequate ethical standard to aspire to get through the day without being indicted."

Integrity-based ethics programs go beyond the mere avoidance of illegality; they are concerned with the law but also with instilling in people a personal responsibility for ethical behavior. With such a program, companies and people govern themselves through a set of guiding principles that they embrace.

For example, the Americans with Disabilities Act (ADA) required companies to change the physical work environment so it will allow people with disabilities to function on the job. Mere compliance would involve making the changes necessary to avoid legal problems. Integrity-based programs would go further by training people to understand and perhaps change attitudes toward people with disabilities and sending clear signals that people with disabilities also have valued abilities. This effort goes far beyond taking action to stay out of trouble with the law.[43]

When top management has a personal commitment to responsible ethical behavior, programs tend to be better integrated into operations, thinking, and behavior. For example, at a meeting of about 25 middle managers at a major financial services firm, every one of them told the company's general counsel that they had never seen or heard of the company's ethics policy document.[44] The policies existed but were not a part of the everyday thinking of managers. In contrast, a health care products company bases one-third of managers' annual pay raises on how well they carry out the company's ethical ideals. Their ethical behavior is assessed by superiors, peers, and subordinates—making ethics a thoroughly integrated aspect of the way the company and its people do business.

Ethical Decision Making

We've said it's not easy to make ethical decisions. Such decisions are complex. For starters, you may face pressures that are difficult to resist. Furthermore,

> it's not always clear that a problem has ethical dimensions; they don't hold up signs that say "Hey, I'm an ethical issue, so think about me in moral terms!"[45]

Making ethical decisions takes *moral awareness* (realizing the issue has ethical implications), *moral judgment* (knowing what actions are morally defensible), and *moral character* (the strength and persistence to act in accordance with your ethics despite the challenges).[46]

Moral awareness begins with considering whether a decision has ramifications that disadvantage employees, the environment, or other stakeholders. Then the challenge is to apply moral judgment.

The philosopher John Rawls created a thought experiment based on the "veil of ignorance."[47] Imagine that you are making a decision about a policy that will benefit or disadvantage some groups more than others. For example, a policy might provide extra vacation time for all employees but eliminate flextime, which allows parents of young children to balance their work and family responsibilities. Or you're a university president considering raising tuition or cutting financial support for study abroad.

Now pretend that you belong to one of the affected groups, but you don't know which one—for instance, those who can afford to study abroad or those who can't, or a young parent or a young single person. You won't find out until after the decision is made. How would you decide? Would you be willing to risk being in the

SOURCE: L. T. Hosmer, *The Ethics of Management*, 4th ed. McGraw-Hill/Irwin, 2003, p. 32. Fig. 5.1A. © 2003 The McGraw-Hill Companies, Inc. Reprinted with permission.

FIGURE 5.1

A Process for Ethical Decision Making

disadvantaged group? Would your decision be different if you were in a group other than your own? Rawls maintained that only a person ignorant of his own identity can make a truly ethical decision. A decision maker can apply the veil of ignorance to help minimize personal bias.

To resolve ethical problems, you can use the process illustrated in Figure 5.1. Understand the various moral standards (universalism, relativism, etc.), as described on pp. 169–171. Go through the problem-solving model from Chapter 3, and recognize the impacts of your alternatives: which people do they benefit and harm, which are able to exercise their rights, and whose rights are denied? You now know the full scope of the moral problem.

Finding excuses and rationalizations for unethical behavior is easy. Only days after the U.S. government had posted $85 billion to keep insurance giant American International Group from collapsing, AIG sent executives on a luxurious retreat. When questioned about this, executives initially replied with excuses: the $440,000 spent was far, far less than the amount of the government bailout, and the executives who participated in the retreat did not work in the AIG division where the company's financial problems had originated. Eventually they had to concede that these responses did not really address the question of whether the retreat was an ethical use of company money at a time when the company—along with many of the taxpayers whose money was bailing out AIG—was undergoing an economic crisis.[48]

Excuses are often bogus.[49] "I was told to do it" implies a person has no thought and blindly obeys. "Everybody's doing it" often really means that someone is doing it, but it's rarely everybody; regardless, following convention doesn't mean correctness. "Might equals right" is just a rationalization. "It's not my problem" is sometimes a wise perspective, if it's a battle you can't win, but sometimes it's a cop-out. "I didn't mean for that to happen, it just felt right at the time" can be prevented with more forethought and analysis.

You must also consider legal requirements to ensure full compliance, and the economic outcomes of your options, including costs and potential profits. Figure 5.2 shows some of the costs associated with unethical behavior.[50] Some are obvious: fines and penalties. Others, like administrative costs and corrective actions, are less obvious. Ultimately the effects on customers, employees, and government reactions can be huge. Being fully aware of the potential costs can help prevent people from straying into unethical terrain.

Courage

Behaving ethically requires not just moral awareness and moral judgment but also moral character, including the courage to take actions consistent with your ethical

Excuses are often bogus.

Bottom Line

"Costs" aren't exactly synonymous with "ethics." But by considering all costs to all parties, you can make high-quality ethical decisions that you can more convincingly "sell" to others who might otherwise balk.

What are some costs of treating employees unethically?

Level 3 Costs

Customer defections
Loss of reputation
Employee cynicism
Lost employee morale
Employee turnover
Government cynicism
Government regulation

Level 2 Costs

Administrative and audit
Legal and investigative
Remedial education
Corrective actions
Government oversight

Level 1 Costs

Government fines
and penalties

Less damaging
costs, get
more executive
attention.

More damaging
costs, get
less executive
attention.

FIGURE 5.2
The Business Costs of
Ethical Failures

SOURCE: From *Academy of Management Executive: The Thinking Manager's Source* by T. Thomas, et al., "Strategic Leadership of Ethical Behavior in Business." Copyright © 2004. Reproduced with permission of Academy of Management via Copyright Clearance Center.

decisions. Think about how hard it can be to do the right thing.[51] On the job, how hard would it be to walk away from lots of money in order to "stick to your ethics"? To tell colleagues or your boss that you believe they've crossed an ethical line? To disobey a boss's order? To go over your boss's head to someone in senior management with your suspicions about accounting practices? To go outside the company to alert others if someone is being hurt and management refuses to correct the problem?

Courage plays a role in the moral awareness involved in identifying an act as unethical, the moral judgment to fully consider the repercussions, and the moral character to take the ethical action. Consider, for example, how difficult it is to deliver unpleasant news, even if you agree that honesty is required for justice and is the way you would want to be treated. This was a hurdle for some Hilton Worldwide managers as they made staffing decisions for their call centers. Hilton, which operates call centers in five countries and contracts with call centers in the Philippines, reportedly sent employees from its Hemet, California, center to a new call center in Manila to train employees in handling reservation changes and other customer service activities. Only afterward were the California employees told that the company would be closing the Hemet facility, located southeast of Los Angeles, and laying off the workers there unless they chose to relocate to jobs in Texas or Florida. Perhaps the managers feared that telling employees they were training their replacements would have hurt performance; honesty takes courage when it is risky, and the risks of complete honesty are real.[52]

The road for whistleblowers is rocky.

Behaving ethically in an ethical climate is complicated enough, but even more courage is necessary when you decide that the only ethical course of action is *whistleblowing*—telling others, inside or outside the organization, of wrongdoing. The road for whistleblowers is rocky. When whistleblowers go public, they are often seen as acting against the company's interests. Many, perhaps most, whistleblowers suffer consequences such as being ostracized, treated rudely, or given undesirable assignments. Not even high-level executives are immune from the risks, as Michael G. Winston discovered after uncovering reckless lending practices at Countrywide Financial Corporation. Countrywide had hired Winston to develop the company's management team, and before long he began hearing stories about the mortgage lender's strategy to grant loans to just about anyone, regardless of ability to pay. Winston urged the company's leaders to redefine their strategy, but instead of seeing improvements, Winston began to suspect he was the target of harassment: a frozen budget, shrinking staff, no more invitations to meetings, frequent requests that he relocate his office, and even an unexplained release of a toxic substance in his office. Then, months after Winston refused a request that he fabricate a report to investors, Countrywide's CEO requested that Winston be terminated for his negative attitude. That decision was carried out a year later, after Countrywide collapsed along with the housing market and was taken over by Bank of America. Winston sued for wrongful termination. It was a battle he won, but only after three more years.[53]

For this reason, and in response to the revised sentencing guidelines under the Sarbanes-Oxley Act, organizations set up channels for employees to report ethics problems so the organization can respond without the matter becoming a scandal. Ideally the reporting method should keep the whistleblower's identity secret, management should investigate and respond quickly, and there should be no retaliation against whistleblowers who use proper channels. Besides online reporting systems, such as e-mail and web-based tools, companies can use drop boxes and telephone hotlines.[55]

> According to a study by the Association of Certified Fraud Examiners, companies that uncovered fraud most often learned about it from a coworker's tip, rather than from a formal audit.[54]

Corporate Social Responsibility

- Ford Motor Company fights HIV/AIDs in South Africa.
- Levi Strauss fights racism.
- Green Mountain Coffee promotes fair trade coffee around the world.
- Bank Boston fosters economic development in communities of moderate income and in the inner city.
- United Parcel Service works to help people on welfare find employment.
- McDonald's and Bank of America support sustainable development in a variety of strategic ways.[56]

LO 4

Should business be responsible for social concerns beyond its own economic well-being? Do social concerns affect a corporation's financial performance? The extent of business's responsibility for noneconomic concerns has been hotly debated for years. In the 1960s and 1970s, the political and social environment became more important to U.S. corporations as society turned its attention to issues like equal opportunity, pollution control, energy and natural resource conservation, and consumer and worker protection.[57] Public debate addressed these issues and the ways business should respond to them. This controversy focused on the concept of corporate social responsibility (CSR).

The extent to which companies practice CSR has varied over time and differs across companies and countries.[58] For example, Transparency International is an anticorruption watchdog that flags Greece as a particular problem area for Europe, and more broadly the Middle East, sub-Saharan Africa, and the old Soviet bloc.[59]

Corporate social responsibility is the obligation toward society assumed by business.[60] Corporate social responsibility reflects the social imperatives and the social consequences of business success, and consists broadly of policies and practices that reflect business responsibility for some of the wider societal good. The precise policies and practices underlying this responsibility lie at the discretion of the corporation.[61]

corporate social responsibility (CSR)

Obligation toward society assumed by business.

Be a good
global
corporate
citizen.

Do what is *desired*
by global stakeholders.

**Philanthropic
responsibility**

Be
ethical.

Do what is *expected*
by global stakeholders.

**Ethical
responsibility**

Obey
the
law.

Do what is
required by global
stakeholders.

**Legal
responsibility**

Be
profitable.

Do what is
required by
global
capitalism.

**Economic
responsibility**

FIGURE 5.3
Pyramid of Global
Corporate Social
Responsibility and
Performance

SOURCE: From *Academy of Management Executive: The Thinking Manager's Source* by A. Carroll, "Management Ethically with Global Stakeholders: A Present and Future Challenge." Copyright © 2004. Reproduced with permission of Academy of Management via Copyright Clearance Center.

**economic
responsibilities**

To produce goods and
services that society wants
at a price that perpetuates
the business and satisfies its
obligations to investors.

legal responsibilities

To obey local, state, federal,
and relevant international laws.

ethical responsibilities

Meeting other social expectations,
not written as law.

**philanthropic
responsibilities**

Additional behaviors and
activities that society finds
desirable and that the values of
the business support.

Social responsibilities can be categorized[62] as shown in Figure 5.3. The **economic responsibilities** of business are to produce goods and services that society wants at a price that perpetuates the business and satisfies its obligations to investors. For Smithfield Foods, the largest pork producer in the United States, this means selling bacon, ham, and other products to customers at prices that maximize Smithfield's profits and keep the company growing over the long term. Economic responsibility may also extend to offering certain products to needy consumers at a reduced price.

Legal responsibilities are to obey local, state, federal, and relevant international laws. Laws affecting Smithfield cover a wide range of requirements, from filing tax returns to meeting worker safety standards. **Ethical responsibilities** include meeting other societal expectations, not written as law. Smithfield took on this level of responsibility when it responded to requests by major customers, including McDonald's and Walmart, that it discontinue the practice of using gestation crates to house its sows. The customers were reacting to pressure from animal rights advocates who consider it cruel for sows to live in the two-foot by seven-foot crates during their entire gestation period, which means they cannot walk, turn around, or stretch their legs for months at a time.[63] Smithfield was not legally required to make the change (except in two states), and the arrangement was costly, but the company's decision helped its public image— that is, until it backed out of the plan, citing economic woes.

Finally, **philanthropic responsibilities** are additional behaviors and activities that society finds desirable and that the values of the business support. Examples include supporting community projects and making charitable contributions. Philanthropic activities can be more than mere altruism; managed properly, "strategic philanthropy" can become not an oxymoron but a way to build goodwill in a variety of stakeholders and even add to shareholder wealth.[64]

Robert Giacalone, who teaches business ethics at Temple University, believes that a 21st century education must help students think beyond self-interest and profitability. A real education, he says, teaches students to leave a legacy that extends beyond the bottom line—a transcendent education.[65] A **transcendent education** has five higher goals that balance self-interest with responsibility to others: *empathy* (feeling your decisions as potential victims might feel them, to gain wisdom); *generativity* (learning how to give as well as take, to others in the present as well as to future generations); *mutuality* (viewing success not merely as personal gain, but a common victory); *civil aspiration* (thinking not just in terms of "don'ts" [lie, cheat, steal, kill], but also in terms of positive contributions); and *intolerance of ineffective humanity* (speaking out against unethical actions). Consider which, if any, of these goals you see Yvon Chouinard and Patagonia achieving in "Management Connection: Progress Report."

transcendent education

An education with five higher goals that balance self-interest with responsibility to others.

A real education, he says, teaches students to leave a legacy that extends beyond the bottom line—a transcendent education.

| Manager's Brief | **Progress Report** | Onward |

Management Connection

PATAGONIA DEFINES ITS RESPONSIBILITY TO TEXTILE WORKERS

Patagonia designs and markets a variety of products, but those products are made by contractors, not by Patagonia's own employees. This type of business model enables the company to concentrate on its strengths and operate efficiently. Yvon Chouinard found that when Patagonia was a small company, it could readily find and work closely with a few suppliers to make sure they shared common values in treating employees and the environment with care. But as the company grew, it needed more formal controls to select suppliers that operated in accordance with Patagonia's standards for safe working conditions and fair labor practices.

Patagonia has prepared a workplace code of conduct, which applies to both its own employees and the employees of its contractors. This code points out that taking responsibility for workers is a natural outgrowth of the company's mission: the company sells clothing for outdoor sports such as climbing, surfing, and fly-fishing. "These sports require a healthy natural environment, which is attainable only if our communities are healthy and their citizens have a right to freedom and well-being." The code of conduct calls for achieving this by acting with integrity and treating employees with respect. Some of its specific requirements include providing a safe workplace, paying at least the minimum wage, establishing and communicating quality standards, complying with local laws, limiting work hours to 60 or fewer hours per week, and prohibiting such practices as harassment of workers, forced labor, and child labor. Employees choosing a contractor look first at the potential contractor's quality, followed closely by its success in reducing environmental harm. Plants can be vetoed if they do not meet Patagonia's standards for social and environmental responsibility.

Patagonia's contractors are located in China, Thailand, Vietnam, Japan, Turkey, Portugal, Mexico, Costa Rica, Colombia, El Salvador, Israel, the Philippines, and the United States. Most textile businesses are located in low-wage countries and regions. In these locations and in this industry, many workers are poor and uneducated. Workers are sometimes mistreated, paid less than minimum wage, and expected to work in unsafe conditions. To avoid sending business to companies that engage in such practices, Patagonia wrote a scoring instrument it calls a contractor relationship assessment, which includes measures of product quality and working conditions. Patagonia employees (who receive training in social responsibility) and factory managers use the assessment to see if each factory is meeting standards and to discuss differences of opinion, so they are partners in ensuring satisfactory performance. The company also contracts with organizations that specialize in auditing factories for fair employment and safe working conditions. When contractors are found to be out of compliance with Patagonia's requirements, Patagonia managers are responsible for working with them to prepare a plan for correcting the problems identified.

Sometimes long hours and unsafe working conditions result because factory owners are greedy, but poor treatment can also stem from the customer's behavior. Customers that frequently change orders, place last-minute rush orders, or constantly try to drive down the price can pressure their suppliers so much that they mistreat workers to meet those demands. Patagonia therefore trains its own employees in how they can behave responsibly to prevent these kinds of problems leading to mistreatment of contractors' employees.

One area in which Patagonia hopes to make further improvement has to do with payment of a "living wage"—that is, paying workers enough that they can provide for the basic needs of themselves and their families. While the company requires that all suppliers pay workers at least the local minimum wage and prefers that they pay a living wage, it acknowledges that sewing jobs tend to be low-paid in a highly competitive industry. Because factories sell to more than one customer, they generally can't afford to pay a higher wage if only Patagonia will pay a higher price for their products. The company also notes that even at its Ventura, California, headquarters, meeting this standard is difficult. There a living wage for a single parent supporting one child is $22.49 per hour, which in the United States is high for many kinds of work. The company's response to this apparent disconnect between values and practices is to participate in the Fair Labor Association, whose goals include promoting the requirement of a living wage.[66]

- According to this description of Patagonia's efforts at corporate social responsibility, how does the company address the four categories of social responsibility? (See Figure 5.3 to review the categories.)
- How would you expect Patagonia's commitment to social responsibility to affect its profits?

Contrasting Views

Two basic and contrasting views describe principles that should guide managerial responsibility. The first holds that managers act as agents for shareholders and, as such, are obligated to maximize the present value of the firm. This tenet of capitalism is widely associated with the early writings of Adam Smith in *The Wealth of Nations*, and more recently with Milton Friedman, the Nobel Prize–winning economist of the University of Chicago. With his now-famous dictum "The social responsibility of business is to increase profits," Friedman contended that organizations may help improve the quality of life as long as such actions are directed at increasing profits.

Some considered Friedman to be "the enemy of business ethics," but his position was ethical: he believed that it was unethical for unelected business leaders to decide what was best for society and unethical for them to spend shareholders' money on projects unconnected to key business interests.[67] Furthermore, the context of Friedman's famous statement includes the qualifier that business should increase its profits while conforming to society's laws and ethical customs.

The second perspective, different from the profit maximization perspective, is that managers should be motivated by principled moral reasoning. Adam Smith wrote about a world different from the one we are in now, driven in the 18th century by the self-interest of small owner-operated farms and craft shops trying to generate a living income for themselves and their families. This self-interest was quite different from that of top executives of modern corporations.[68] It is noteworthy that Adam Smith also wrote *A Theory of Moral Sentiments*, in which he argued that "sympathy," defined as a proper regard for others, is the basis of a civilized society.[69] Smith argued further that "the wise and virtuous man is at all times willing that this own private interest should be sacrificed to public interest" if circumstance require it.[70]

Advocates of corporate social responsibility argue that organizations have a wider range of responsibilities that extend beyond the production of

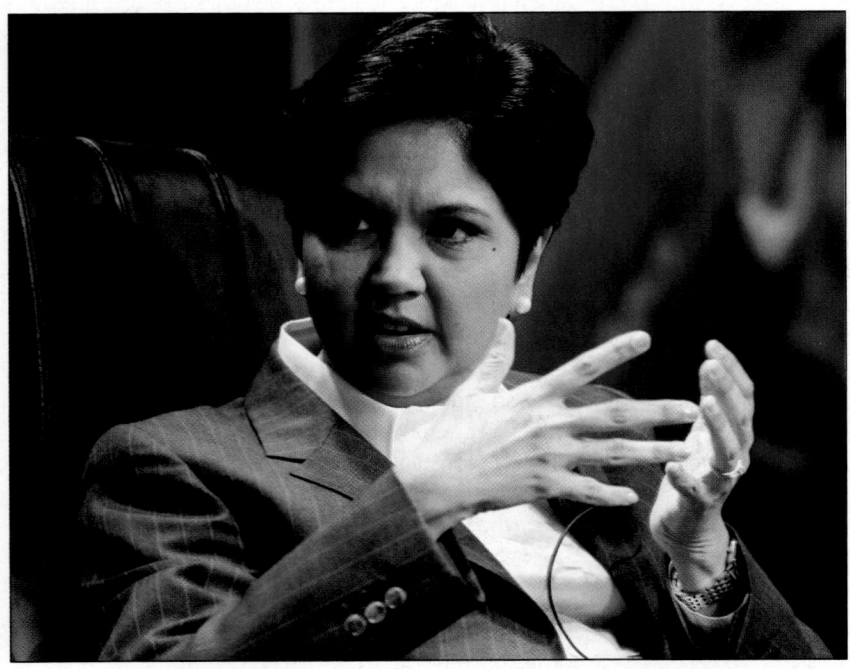

Indra Nooyi, PepsiCo chair and CEO, discussed the recent development of the first plastic bottle made completely from agricultural waste. The company plans to utilize the discarded materials from its own food businesses, which would keep costs down. With the invention of this new "green" bottle, not only does PepsiCo show corporate social responsibility toward the environment, but it also takes into account the economic responsibility of keeping the price of its products unchanged for consumers.

goods and services at a profit. As members of society, organizations should actively and responsibly participate in the community and in the larger environment. From this perspective, many people criticized insurance companies after Hurricanes Katrina and Rita devastated homes and businesses along the Gulf Coast. From a social responsibility perspective, it was wrong for companies to watch out for their bottom line and avoid paying claims where they could make a case that the damage wasn't covered; the insurers should have been more concerned about their devastated customers.

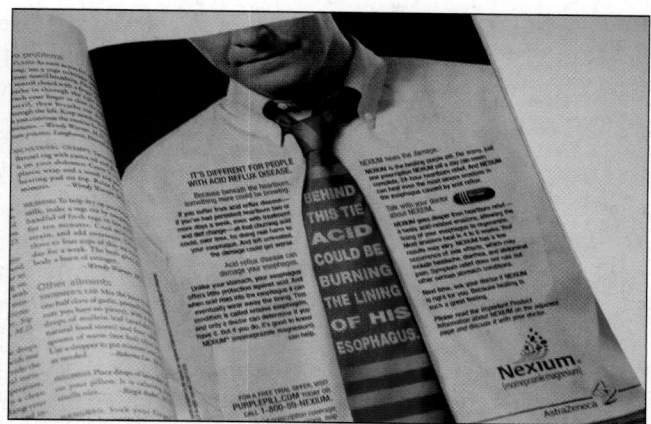

Should pharmaceutical companies be allowed to advertise directly to the consumer if the medicine can be obtained only with a prescription from a doctor? When patients request a particular product, doctors are more likely to prescribe it—even if the patients haven't reported the corresponding symptoms.

Reconciliation

Profit maximization and corporate social responsibility used to be regarded as antagonistic, leading to opposing policies. But the two views can converge.[71] The Coca-Cola Company has set up about 70 charitable projects to provide clean water in 40 countries. These projects are helping some of the 1.2 billion people without access to safe drinking water. The company is constructing structures to "harvest" rainwater in India, building extensions of the municipal water supply in Mali, and delivering water purification systems and storage urns to Kenya. These projects are aimed at burnishing the company's image and targeting complaints that the company is using up too much of the world's water supply to manufacture its beverages. From a practical perspective, Coca-Cola's strategic planners have identified water shortages as a strategic risk; from a values perspective, water is, in the words of executive Neville Isdell, "at the very core of our ethos," so "responsible use of that resource is very important to us."[72]

Earlier attention to corporate social responsibility focused on alleged wrongdoing and how to control it. More recently, attention has also been centered on the possible competitive advantage of socially responsible actions. DuPont has been incorporating care for the environment into its business in two ways it hopes will put it ahead of the competition. First, the company has been reducing its pollution. It hopes these efforts will give it an advantage in a future where the government more heavily regulates emissions, requiring competitors to play catch-up. In addition, reducing emissions goes hand in hand with reducing waste and unnecessary use of energy, saving the company money and directly benefiting the bottom line. Second, DuPont has been developing products that are sustainable, meaning they don't use up the earth's resources. Examples include corn-based fabrics and new applications of its Tyvek material to make buildings more energy-efficient. DuPont expects these innovations to give the company profitable access to the growing market for environmentally friendly products.[73]

> Recently, attention has also been centered on the possible competitive advantage of socially responsible actions.

The real relationship between corporate social performance and corporate financial performance is highly complex; socially responsible organizations are not necessarily more or less successful in financial terms.[74] But on net, the accumulated evidence indicates that social responsibility is associated with better financial performance.[75] Some advantages are clear. For example, socially responsible actions can have long-term benefits. Companies can avoid unnecessary and costly regulation if they are socially responsible. Honesty and fairness may pay great dividends to the conscience, to the personal reputation, and to the public

Managers can treat corporate social responsibility as they would treat all investment decisions.

image of the company as well as in the market response.[76] In addition, society's problems can offer business opportunities, and profits can be made from systematic and vigorous efforts to solve these problems. Firms can perform a cost–benefit analysis to identify actions that will maximize profits while satisfying the demand for corporate social responsibility from multiple stakeholders.[77] In other words, managers can treat corporate social responsibility as they would treat all investment decisions. This has been the case as firms attempt to reconcile their business practices with their effect on the natural environment.

In this way, organizations can identify social issues as part of environmental scanning and SWOT analysis and then choose issues that make the most strategic sense. This approach to social responsibility requires not only careful choice of the initiatives to pursue but also monitoring of results as the company would do for other initiatives. For example, Microsoft has partnered with the American Association of Community Colleges (AACC), whose institutions educate 45 percent of U.S. undergraduates. Microsoft contributes money, equipment, and volunteers to the colleges in the AACC, helping to develop IT curricula and train faculty. In this way, Microsoft is using its own strengths (its volunteers are serving in their areas of expertise) to address an environmental threat (the shortage of IT workers). These accomplishments are all measurable in terms of the number of training programs that meet Microsoft's standards and the number of new IT workers who have completed the programs. Thus the company is benefiting the community and enhancing its reputation while expanding the market for its products.[79]

> "The essential test that should guide corporate social responsibility is not whether a cause is worthy but whether it presents an opportunity to create shared value—that is, a meaningful benefit for society that is also valuable to the business."
> Michael E. Porter and Mark R. Kramer[78]

The Natural Environment and Sustainability

Sustainability is a central factor in long-term competitiveness, not just a "nice-to-have." Ecofriendly product launches went up by more than 500 percent in a recent two-year span.[80] Many companies are placing strategic bets on innovations in energy efficiency, pollution control, and renewable control. Some maintain that sustainability is now *the* key driver of innovation.[81]

Most large corporations developed in an era of abundant raw materials, cheap energy, and unconstrained waste disposal.[82] But many of the technologies developed during this era are contributing to the destruction of ecosystems. Industrial-age systems follow a linear flow of extract, produce, sell, use, and discard—what some call a "take–make–waste" approach.[83] But perhaps no time in history has offered greater possibilities for a change in business thinking than the 21st century.

Business used to look at environmental issues as a no-win situation: you either help the environment and hurt your business, or help your business at a cost to the environment. But now a paradigm shift is taking place in corporate environmental management: the deliberate incorporation of environmental values into competitive strategies and into the design and manufacturing of products.[84] Why? In addition to philosophical reasons, companies "go green" to satisfy consumer demand, to react to a competitor's actions, to meet requests from customers or suppliers, to comply with guidelines, and to create competitive advantage.

Business used to look at environmental issues as a no-win situation:
But now a paradigm shift is taking place

General Electric CEO Jeff Immelt used to view environmental rules as a burden and a cost. Now he sees environmentally friendly technologies as one of the global economy's most significant business opportunities. Under a business initiative called Ecomagination, GE is looking for business opportunities from solving environmental problems. Ecomagination solutions include wind turbines, materials for solar energy cells, and energy-efficient home appliances. Ecomagination delivered $25 billion in revenues by 2011. It also has built a green image for the GE brand and positioned the company as a leader in many rapidly growing markets, including high-efficiency jet engines and locomotives.[85]

A Risk Society

We live in a risk society. That is, the creation and distribution of wealth generate by-products that can cause injury, loss, or danger to people and the environment. The fundamental sources of risk in modern society are the excessive production of hazards and ecologically unsustainable consumption of natural resources.[86] Risk has proliferated through population explosion, industrial pollution, and environmental degradation.[87]

Industrial pollution risks include air pollution, smog, global warming, ozone depletion, acid rain, toxic waste sites, nuclear hazards, obsolete weapons arsenals, industrial accidents, and hazardous products. Well over 30,000 uncontrolled toxic waste sites have been documented in the United States alone. The situation is far worse in other parts of the world. The pattern, for toxic waste and many other risks, is one of accumulating risks and inadequate remedies.

The institutions that create environmental and technological risk (corporations and government agencies) are responsible for controlling and managing the risks.[88] For example, as a manufacturer, 3M acknowledges that its activities result in pollution, so the company has committed itself to reducing its impact on the environment. Since 1990, a combination of reduced energy use, improvements in manufacturing processes, redesign of products, and the use of pollution control equipment have enabled the company to cut its global emissions of greenhouse gases by 77 percent. And building on its culture of innovation, 3M recently installed charging stations for electric vehicles at its headquarters in St. Paul, Minnesota.[89]

> Despite the 2010 explosion of its Deepwater Horizon rig that sent oil leaking into the Gulf of Mexico and killed 11 people working on the rig, Transocean executives got two-thirds of their target safety bonus. The company called it their best safety year ever. What is your reaction, and why?

Some of the world's worst environmental problems are in China because of its rapid industrialization and its huge population and size. About one-third of China's rural population—hundreds of millions of people—drink unhealthful, unclean water. At least the problem is recognized: local authorities are beginning to experience pressure from the central government to clean up or shut down dirty factories.[90] Still, most cleanup efforts focus on big cities while rural areas get worse.

Ecocentric Management

Ecocentric management has as its goal the creation of sustainable economic development and improvement of quality of life worldwide for all organizational stakeholders.[91] **Sustainable growth** is economic growth and development that meet the organization's present needs without harming the ability of future generations to meet their needs.[92] Sustainability is fully compatible with the natural ecosystems that generate and preserve life.[93]

The concept of sustainable growth offers (1) a framework for organizations to use in communicating to all stakeholders, (2) a planning and strategy guide, and (3) a tool for evaluating and improving the ability to compete.[94] The principle can begin at the highest organizational levels and be made explicit in performance appraisals and reward systems.

ecocentric management

Its goal is the creation of sustainable economic development and improvement of quality of life worldwide for all organizational stakeholders.

LO 6

sustainable growth

Economic growth and development that meet present needs without harming the needs of future generations.

life-cycle analysis (LCA)

A process of analyzing all inputs and outputs, through the entire "cradle-to-grave" life of a product, to determine total environmental impact.

Increasingly, firms are paying attention to the total environmental impact throughout the life cycle of their products.[95] **Life-cycle analysis (LCA)** is a process of analyzing all inputs and outputs, through the entire "cradle-to-grave" life of a product, to determine the total environmental impact of the production and use of a product. LCA quantifies the total use of resources and the releases into the air, water, and land. Apple used LCA in 2009 to calculate and then report its entire carbon footprint worldwide—a big step in environmental reporting in that industry.

LCA considers the extraction of raw materials, product packaging, transportation, and disposal. Consider packaging alone. Goods make the journey from manufacturer to wholesaler to retailer to customer; then they are recycled back to the manufacturer. They may be packaged and repackaged several times, from bulk transport, to large crates, to cardboard boxes, to individual consumer sizes. Repackaging not only creates waste but also costs time. The design of initial packaging in sizes and formats adaptable to the final customer can minimize the need for repackaging, cut waste, and realize financial benefits.

Rather than the linear "take–make–waste" production model described earlier, a fully sustainable model applies a circular "borrow–use–return" approach.[96] Whereas the former model engages in harmful extraction, generates huge quantities of waste and pollution, and depletes natural resources (a process in which resources move from "cradle to grave"), the "cradle-to-cradle" approach is ecologically benign and restorative. In its ideal form, this sustainable approach extracts energy and raw materials without harm, phases out the use of nonrenewable resources, designs processes and products (goods and services) that recirculate so they don't cause environmental or socioeconomic harm, keeps toxic substances in closed-loop industrial cycles, and recirculates biological materials back into nature without harm.[97]

Profitability need not suffer and may be positively affected by ecocentric philosophies and practices. Some, but not all, research has shown a positive relationship between corporate environmental performance and profitability.[98] Of course, whether the relationship is positive, negative, or neutral depends on the strategies chosen and the effectiveness of implementation.

Companies can integrate green practices with strategy in a variety of ways. Certainly they develop and market green products; Toyota's bold move to develop the Prius paid off handsomely with market dominance.[99] Companies also can emphasize green attributes in their marketing, but need to avoid misleading claims ("greenwashing") and public backlash. For instance, Arm & Hammer positioned its baking soda brand as "the number one environmentally sensible alternative for cleaning and deodorizing" and "committed to the environment since 1846." On the other hand, the company ignored a major problem: it used animal testing. The blogosphere began touting equally green but cruelty-free Bob's Red Mill baking soda.[100]

Companies also can acquire other companies with sustainability (and image) in mind. L'Oreal bought The Body Shop, Colgate-Palmolive bought Tom's of Maine, Unilever bought Ben & Jerry's, and Group Danone bought Stonyfield's.[101] When Clorox bought Burt's Bees, which had decades of leadership and experience with sustainability, it did so for growth and to convince environmental stakeholders that the company's strategic change was genuine, but also to acquire knowledge about the green product space.[102]

For those interested in reading more about this subject, Appendix B of this chapter discusses in greater detail the reasons for managing with the environment in mind, some history of the environmental movement, economic issues, and a wide array of "green" examples pertaining to strategy, public affairs, legal issues, operations, marketing, accounting, and finance.

You also can check out the Global Reporting Initiatives list of more than 70 sustainability performance indicators. This useful resource, at www.gri.com, aims to help companies improve their sustainability practices, including transparent reporting.

Environmental Agendas for the Future

In the past, most companies were oblivious to their negative environmental impact. More recently, many began striving for low impact. Now some strive for positive impact, eager to sell solutions to the world's problems. IBM has three decades of experience in lowering its environmental impact through efforts such as reducing packaging waste and measuring carbon emissions. It has begun to use that experience as a strength—a basis for expertise it can sell to other organizations, along with its computing power and other consulting services. Thus one application might be to help clients measure and forecast the carbon emissions of their entire supply chain. By running calculations on its supercomputers, IBM consultants could help clients find ways to lower their energy use.[103]

Or consider climate change and the world's shortage of clean water. When Dow Chemical's Freeport, Texas, site had trouble getting enough water to run its processes during droughts, it installed technology to monitor the water system 24/7 and reduced water consumption by a billion gallons a year.[104] Coca-Cola pursues its water neutrality pledge, aiming to replenish watersheds to the full extent of the water it extracts. And for Nestlé, a major strategic challenge is water security for farmers who supply factories (and people) the world over.[105] Nestlé saves up to 1,375 cubic meters of water per year since improving how it collects and transports milk from farmers.

You don't have to be a manufacturer or a utility to jump on the green bandwagon. Web search giant Google is applying a three-pronged strategy aimed at reducing its "carbon footprint"—that is, its output of carbon dioxide and other greenhouse gases. At Google, most greenhouse gas emissions are related to electricity consumption by its buildings and computers. So Google is seeking ways to make buildings and computers more energy-efficient, such as by using high-efficiency lighting and installing power management software in its computers. Also, the company is developing ways to get more of its power from renewable sources, such as the solar power system at its facility in Mountain View, California. Finally, recognizing that its other efforts cannot yet eliminate Google's release of greenhouse gases, the company is purchasing "offsets"—funding projects that reduce greenhouse gas emissions elsewhere.[106]

Webs of companies with a common ecological vision can combine their efforts into high-leverage, impactful action.[107] In cities like San Antonio, Texas, and Columbus, Ohio, federal partner agencies work closely with city governments, utilities, and multiple manufacturers to reduce pollutants and energy consumption and to increase energy savings. In Kalundborg, Denmark, such a collaborative alliance exists among an electric power generating plant, an oil refiner, a biotech production plant, a plaster-board factory, cement producers, heating utilities, a sulfuric acid producer, and local agriculture and horticulture. Chemicals, energy (for both heating and cooling), water, and organic materials flow among companies. Resources are conserved, "waste" materials generate revenues, and water, air, and ground pollution all are reduced.

Companies not only have the *ability* to solve environmental problems; they are coming to see and acquire the *motivation* as well, as Patagonia has had since its beginning (see "Management Connection: Onward"). In addition to the benefits to the world of sustainable practices, many now believe that solving environmental problems is one of the biggest opportunities in the history of commerce.[108]

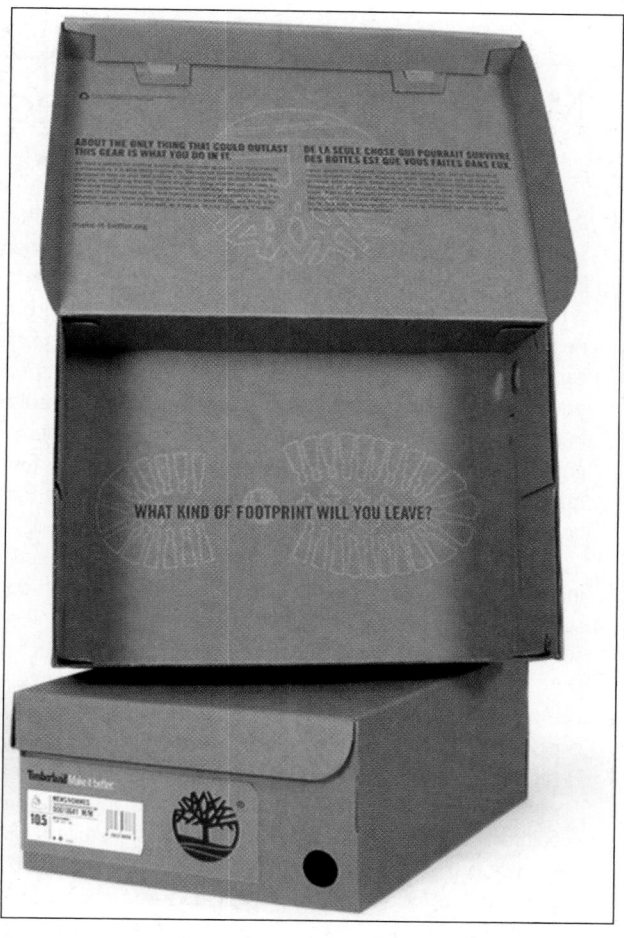

Timberland has paid particular attention to life cycle analysis, as implied by what is printed on their recycled material shoe boxes.

Bottom Line

Packaging isn't the most glamorous of business topics, but it holds great potential for reducing costs and increasing speed while helping the environment. You can always find opportunities to improve results in unexpected places, where others haven't tried.

Think of a product you recently purchased. How could its packaging have been more environmentally friendly?

Manager's Brief   Progress Report   **Onward**

Management Connection

PATAGONIA'S ECOCENTRIC MANAGEMENT

According to Patagonia, the company gives equal weight to social responsibility and efforts to protect the environment. However, in some respects, the company's concern for the environment is what really sets it apart from most other businesses. All of its charitable giving is directed to environmental causes. The combination of donating 1 percent of its revenues and encouraging employees to volunteer has resulted in total donations worth $40 million so far. That number will grow along with the company's sales and its creative fundraising efforts, such as tunes for sale on the company's Patagonia Music web page, with all proceeds to be donated.

Patagonia's commitment to environmental protection includes participating in efforts to make it easier for consumers to make environmentally friendly choices. Consumers who care about the environmental impact of their choices can visit the Footprint Chronicles page of the company's website. Users of this feature can specify a product and learn about its environmental impact from its design through delivery of the finished product.

The company has joined the Sustainable Apparel Coalition, a group of apparel companies, retailers, and organizations, which has created a software application called the Eco Index. The index asks the company a series of questions about environmental and labor practices and then uses the answers to compute a score. Companies can use the information as an incentive to improve their scores, and someday consumers may find the scores printed on packages and tags as a handy guide for making product comparisons.

In its own stores, Patagonia has even gone so far as to promote restraint by customers. In a program it calls

Common Threads, the company posts signs that encourage shoppers to think carefully before selecting items and to skip purchases of items they don't need. Why would a business encourage shoppers *not* to buy? Patagonia hopes that its customers will settle on making environmentally friendly purchases from its stores at the expense of the competition.

As noted at the beginning of this case, Patagonia's founder and chief executive, Yvon Chouinard, believes that ecocentric management is in the company's self-interest. For example, he notes that on average, 900 people apply for every open job, and he thinks recruiting is so easy because working there is about something important: "People know we're in business to try to save this planet and influence other companies that green business is good business." Employees who are committed to their company's mission tend to be dedicated and go above and beyond what's required of them. Chouinard believes his company's higher purpose drives customer loyalty as well; he notes that during the recent recession, Patagonia continued to prosper.[109]

- For Patagonia, would you say solving environmental problems is more of an opportunity to seize or a problem to solve? Why?

- Suppose Chouinard had started Patagonia as a company for people who engage in *indoor* sports such as basketball, hockey, and racquetball. Would his focus on the environment have been beneficial to the company? Why or why not?

KEY TERMS

business ethics, p. 169

Caux Principles, p. 169

compliance-based ethics
  programs, p. 178

corporate social responsibility (CSR), p. 181

ecocentric management, p. 187

economic responsibilities, p. 182

egoism, p. 170

ethical climate, p. 174

ethical issue, p. 169

ethical leader, p. 175

ethical responsibilities, p. 182

ethics, p. 166

integrity-based ethics programs, p. 178

Kohlberg's model of cognitive moral
  development, p. 171

legal responsibilities, p. 182

life-cycle analysis (LCA), p. 188

moral philosophy, p. 169

philanthropic responsibilities, p. 182

relativism, p. 171

Sarbanes-Oxley Act, p. 173

sustainable growth, p. 187

transcendent education, p. 183

universalism, p. 169

utilitarianism, p. 171

virtue ethics, p. 171

SUMMARY OF LEARNING OBJECTIVES

Now that you have studied Chapter 5, you should be able to:

LO 1 Describe how different ethical perspectives guide decision making.

The purpose of ethics is to identify the rules that govern human behavior and the "goods" that are worth seeking. Ethical decisions are guided by the individual's values or principles of conduct such as honesty, fairness, integrity, respect for others, and responsible citizenship. Different ethical systems include universalism, egoism and utilitarianism, relativism, and virtue ethics. These philosophical systems, as practiced by different individuals according to their level of cognitive moral development and other factors, underlie the ethical stances of individuals and organizations.

LO 2 Explain how companies influence their ethics environment.

Different organizations apply different ethical perspectives and standards. Ethics codes sometimes are helpful, although they must be implemented properly. Ethics programs can range from compliance-based to integrity-based. An increasing number of organizations are adopting ethics codes. Such codes address employee conduct, community and environment, shareholders, customers, suppliers and contractors, political activity, and technology.

LO 3 Outline a process for making ethical decisions.

Making ethical decisions requires moral awareness, moral judgment, and moral character. When faced with ethical dilemmas, the veil of ignorance is a useful metaphor. More precisely, you can know various moral standards (universalism, relativism, and so on), use the problem-solving model described in Chapter 3, identify the positive and negative effects of your alternatives on different parties, consider legal requirements and the costs of unethical actions, and then evaluate your ethical duties using criteria specified in the chapter.

LO 4 Summarize the important issues surrounding corporate social responsibility.

Corporate social responsibility is the extension of the corporate role beyond economic pursuits. It includes not only economic but also legal, ethical, and philanthropic responsibilities. Advocates believe managers should consider societal and human needs in their business decisions because corporations are members of society and carry a wide range of responsibilities. Critics of corporate responsibility believe managers' first responsibility is to increase profits for the shareholders who own the corporation. The two perspectives are potentially reconcilable, especially if managers choose to address areas of social responsibility that contribute to the organization's strategy.

LO 5 Discuss reasons for businesses' growing interest in the natural environment.

In the past, most companies viewed the natural environment as a resource to be used for raw materials and profit. But consumer, regulatory, and other pressures arose. Executives often viewed these pressures as burdens, constraints, and costs to be borne. Now more companies view the interface between business and the natural environment as a potential win–win opportunity. Some are adopting a "greener" agenda for philosophical reasons and personal commitment to sustainable development. Many also are recognizing the potential financial benefits of managing with the environment in mind, and are integrating environmental issues into corporate and business strategy. Some see entering businesses that help rather than harm the natural environment as one of the great commercial opportunities in history.

LO 6 Identify actions managers can take to manage with the environment in mind.

Organizations have contributed risk to society and have some responsibility for reducing risk to the environment. They also have the capability to help solve environmental problems. Ecocentric management attempts to minimize negative environment impact, create sustainable economic development, and improve the quality of life worldwide. Relevant actions are described in the chapter, including strategic initiatives, life-cycle analysis, and interorganizational alliances. A chapter appendix provides a wide variety of specific examples of strategic, operations, finance, legal and public affairs, marketing, and accounting practices that are environmentally friendly.

DISCUSSION QUESTIONS

1. Consider the various ethical systems described early in the chapter. Identify concrete examples from your own past decisions or the decisions of others you have seen or read about.

2. Choose one or more topics from Table 5.2 and discuss their current status and the ethical issues surrounding them.

3. What would you do in each of the scenarios described in Table 5.3?

4. Identify and discuss illegal, unethical, and socially responsible business actions in the current news.

5. Does your school have a code of ethics? If so, what does it say? Is it effective? Why or why not?

6. You have a job you like at which you work 40 to 45 hours per week. How much off-the-job volunteer work would you do? What kinds of volunteer work? How will you react if your boss makes it clear he or she wants you to cut back on the outside activities and devote more hours to your job?

7. What are the arguments for and against the concept of corporate social responsibility? Where do you stand, and why? Give your opinions, specifically, with respect to the text examples.

8. What do you think of the concept of a transcendent education, as described in the chapter? What can be done to implement such a vision for education?

9. What is the current status of the Sarbanes-Oxley Act? Have there been any changes? What do executives think of it now? What impact has it had?

10. A company in England slaughtered 70,000 baby ostrich chicks each year for their meat. It told a teen magazine that it would stop if it received enough complaints. Analyze this policy, practice, and public statement using the concepts discussed in the chapter.

11. A Nike ad in the U.S. magazine *Seventeen* showed a picture of a girl, aged perhaps 8 or 9. The ad read,

    If you let me play . . .

    I will like myself more.

    I will have more self-confidence.

    I will suffer less depression.

    I will be 60 percent less likely to get breast cancer.

    I will be more likely to leave a man who beats me.

    I will be less likely to get pregnant before I want to.

    I will learn what it means to be strong.

    If you let me play sports.

    Assess this ad in terms of chapter concepts surrounding ethics and social responsibility. What questions would you ask in doing this analysis?

12. Should companies like GE and Monsanto be held accountable for actions of decades past, then legal but since made illegal, as their harmful effects became known? Why or why not?

13. Discuss courage as a requirement for ethical behavior. What personal examples can you offer, either as an actor or as an observer? What examples are in the news?

EXPERIENTIAL EXERCISES

5.1   MEASURING YOUR ETHICAL WORK BEHAVIOR

OBJECTIVES

1. To explore a range of ethically perplexing situations.
2. To understand your own ethical attitudes.

INSTRUCTIONS

Make decisions in the situations described in the Ethical Behavior Worksheet. You will not have all the background information on each situation; instead you should make whatever assumptions you feel you would make if you were actually confronted with the decision choices described. Select the decision choice that most closely represents the decision you feel you would make personally. You should choose decision options even though you can envision other creative solutions that were not included in the exercise.

Ethical Behavior Worksheet

Situation I. You are taking a very difficult chemistry course, which you must pass to maintain your scholarship and to avoid damaging your application for graduate school. Chemistry is not your strong suit, and, because of a just-below-failing average in the course, you will have to receive a grade of 90 or better on the final exam, which is two days away. A janitor, who is aware of your plight, informs you that he found the master for the chemistry final in a trash barrel and has saved it. He will make it available to you for a price, which is high but which you could afford. What would you do?

_____ (a) I would tell the janitor thanks, but no thanks.

_____ (b) I would report the janitor to the proper officials.

_____ (c) I would buy the exam and keep it to myself.

_____ (d) I would not buy the exam myself, but I would let some of my friends, who are also flunking the course, know that it is available.

Situation 2. You have been working on some financial projections manually for two days now. It seems that each time you think you have them completed your boss shows up with a new assumption or another "what if" question. If you only had a copy of a spreadsheet software program for your personal computer, you could plug in the new assumptions and revise the estimates with ease. Then a colleague offers to let you make a copy of some software that is copyrighted. What would you do?

_____ (a) I would accept my friend's generous offer and make a copy of the software.

_____ (b) I would decline to copy it and plug away manually on the numbers.

_____ (c) I would decide to go buy a copy of the software myself, for $300, and hope I would be reimbursed by the company in a month or two.

_____ (d) I would request another extension on an already overdue project date.

Situation 3. Your small manufacturing company is in serious financial difficulty. A large order of your products is ready to be delivered to a key customer when you discover that the product is simply not right. It will not meet all performance specifications, will cause problems for your customer, and will require rework in the field; however, this, you know, will not become evident until after the customer has received and paid for the order. If you do not ship the order and receive the payment as expected, your business may be forced into bankruptcy. And if you delay the shipment or inform the customer of these problems, you may lose the order and also go bankrupt. What would you do?

_____ (a) I would not ship the order and place my firm in voluntary bankruptcy.

_____ (b) I would inform the customer and declare voluntary bankruptcy.

_____ (c) I would ship the order and inform the customer after I received payment.

_____ (d) I would ship the order and not inform the customer.

Situation 4. You are the cofounder and president of a new venture, manufacturing products for the recreational market. Five months after launching the business, one of your suppliers informs you it can no longer supply you with a critical raw material because you are not a large-quantity user. Without the raw material, the business cannot continue. What would you do?

_____ (a) I would grossly overstate my requirements to another supplier to make the supplier think I am a much larger potential customer to secure the raw material from that supplier, even though this would mean the supplier will no longer be able to supply another, noncompeting small manufacturer who may thus be forced out of business.

_____ (b) I would steal raw material from another firm (noncompeting) where I am aware of a sizable stockpile.

_____ (c) I would pay off the supplier because I have reason to believe that the supplier could be "persuaded" to meet my needs with a sizable "under the table" payoff that my company could afford.

_____ (d) I would declare voluntary bankruptcy.

Situation 5. You are on a marketing trip for your new venture for the purpose of calling on the purchasing agent of a major prospective client. Your company is manufacturing an electronic system that you hope the purchasing agent will buy. During your conversation, you notice on the cluttered desk of the purchasing agent several copies of a cost proposal for a system from one of your direct competitors. This purchasing agent has previously reported mislaying several of your own company's proposals and has asked for additional copies. The purchasing agent leaves the room momentarily to get you a cup of coffee, leaving you alone with your competitor's proposals less than an arm's length away. What would you do?

_____ (a) I would do nothing but await the man's return.

_____ (b) I would sneak a quick peek at the proposal, looking for bottom-line numbers.

_____ (c) I would put the copy of the proposal in my briefcase.

_____ (d) I would wait until the man returns and ask his permission to see the copy.

SOURCE: Jeffry A. Timmons, *New Venture Creation*, 3rd ed. 1994, pp. 160–161. Copyright 1994 The McGraw-Hill Companies, Inc. Reprinted with permission.

5.2   ETHICAL STANCE

Are the following actions ethical or unethical in your opinion? Why? Consider the actions individually, and discuss them in small groups.

- Calling in sick when you really are not.
- Taking office supplies home for personal use.
- Cheating on a test.
- Turning someone in for cheating on a test or paper.
- Overcharging on your company expense report.
- Trying to flirt your way out of a speeding ticket.
- Splicing cable from your neighbor.
- Surfing the net on company time.

- Cheating on income tax.
- Lying (exaggerating) about yourself to influence someone of the opposite sex.
- Looking at pornographic sites on the web through the company network.
- Lying about your education on a job application.
- Lying about experience in a job interview.
- Making a copy of a rental DVD before returning it to the store.

SOURCE: Suzanne C. de Janasz, Karen O'. Dowd, and Beth Z. Schneider, *Interpersonal Skills in Organizations*, McGraw-Hill, 2002, p. 211. Copyright 2002 The McGraw-Hill Companies, Inc. Reprinted with permission.

CONCLUDING CASE

MA EARTH SKIN CARE TRIES TO STAY NATURAL

Heather Franklin is a marketing manager for Ma Earth Skin Care. Four years ago, when she was hired to help with the paperwork for promotional campaigns, she was thrilled to become a part of this company because she loved Ma Earth's lotions, soaps, and cosmetics. Besides smelling heavenly and offering exquisite colors for eye shadow and lipstick, the products spoke to Heather's values: Ma Earth promised to use all natural ingredients, sustainably grown or mined, and to operate with minimal adverse impact on

the planet. So for Heather, going to work was almost like carrying out a mission, promoting both beauty and concern for the planet's well-being. No doubt, her commitment and enthusiasm helped to pave the way when the position of marketing manager opened up.

Currently Heather and her team are preparing a promotional campaign for a new product line, Oré Essentials, which includes lipsticks, foundation, and eye shadows tinted with a plant extract called orellana. The exciting feature of Oré Essentials is that orellana is harvested deep in the Amazon rain forest, and because of its sustainable practices, Ma Earth will obtain this special ingredient in a socially responsible manner. The company set up a contract with a tribe living in a remote village. The people of the tribe are supposed to grow and harvest the orellana, which is naturally part of the area's ecosystem, and Ma Earth has promised to pay a fair price to the whole tribe so the people can use the money to maintain their village and their way of life. Consumers will get a beautiful product and the pleasure of knowing that they are helping to preserve an endangered ecology—and an endangered way of life for the rain forest people.

But when Heather sat down for a meeting with the photography crew that traveled to the village, some concerns began to surface. She was looking at stunning photos of tribe members arrayed in grass skirts as they stood behind a pile of fruit from the orellana tree. As she was selecting her favorite shots, one of the photographers commented that the translator had made some surprising remarks on the return trip from the village. Apparently the pile of orellana fruit had been gathered just for the photo shoot. The tribe doesn't really bother with growing and harvesting orellana; the people of this area aren't primarily farmers, and there aren't actually many orellana trees within a day's walk of the village. The first year they had tried selling orellana to Ma Earth, they grew only enough to earn a few hundred dollars, not really worth the effort. Heather felt confused by these statements and planned to take a closer look at spending on her product later that day.

Hours later, when the other employees had gone home, Heather finally had a chance to spend some time researching her product on the company's employee website. She found purchasing transactions for "orellana/annatto," and after a little research learned that under either name, the product is just an inexpensive dye. Under the latter name, it is used as a common food coloring. It turns out that Ma Earth made most of its purchases from a mainstream supplier, which is cheaper than persuading remote villagers to provide orellana.

That evening Heather went home feeling betrayed and upset. The next day she asked her boss, the divisional vice president, why the company pretended to care about a remote village if it was just a front for a brand. Heather's boss, Megan McDonough, said, "But we *do* care! We send them tens of thousands of dollars every year. Sure, they don't actually grow that stuff for us, but they could, and we'll buy it if they do. Anyway, our aid has provided a school and a health clinic, not to mention food and clothing. We've helped the tribe members stay healthy and preserve their language and culture."

Heather considered what Megan said. "So," she asked, "does this mean we're using their culture to build an image for our brand, and in exchange, they get money from us to keep that culture alive?" She thought about the traditional designs the marketing department had copied from the tribe as decorations for the Oré Essentials packaging.

Megan nodded encouragingly. "That's exactly what I'm saying. It's a win–win situation." Heather felt relieved but not quite sure that her original idealism would withstand her deeper knowledge of how Ma Earth defined its mission.

QUESTIONS

1. What ethical issues is Heather facing in this situation? What possible marketing claims about the company's relationship with the Amazonian tribe would cross a line into unethical territory? What claims could it make ethically?

2. How could Ma Earth create an ethical climate that would help managers such as Heather ensure that they are behaving ethically?

3. How effectively do you think Ma Earth is practicing corporate social responsibility in this situation? Explain the reasoning behind your evaluation.

Managing in Our Natural Environment

BUSINESS AND THE ENVIRONMENT: CONFLICTING VIEWS

Some people believe everyone wins when business tackles environmental issues.[1] Others disagree.

The Win–Win Mentality Business used to look at environmental issues as a no-win situation: you either help the environment and hurt your business, or help your business only at a cost to the environment. Fortunately things have changed. "When Americans first demanded a cleanup of the environment during the early 1970s, corporations threw a tantrum. Their response ran the psychological gamut from denial to hostility, defiance, obstinacy, and fear. But today, when it comes to green issues, many U.S. companies have turned from rebellious underachievers to active problem solvers."[2] This appendix gives just a few examples of things U.S. corporations are doing to help solve environmental problems.

The Earth Summit in Rio in 1992 helped increase awareness of environmental issues. This led to the Kyoto Protocol, an international effort to control global warming that included subsequent meetings in The Hague in 2000 and Copenhagen in 2009.[3] "There has been an evolution of most groups—whether industry, governments, or nongovernmental organizations—toward a recognition that everyone plays a part in reaching a solution."[4]

Being "green" is potentially a catalyst for innovation, new market opportunities, and wealth creation. Advocates believe that this is truly a win–win situation; actions can be taken that benefit both business and the environment. For example, Procter & Gamble in a span of five years reduced disposable wastes by over 50 percent while increasing sales by 25 percent.[5] Win–win companies will come out ahead of those companies that have an us-versus-them, we-can't-afford-to-protect-the-environment mentality.

Is the easy part over?[6] Companies have found a lot of easy-to-harvest, "low-hanging fruit"—that is, overly costly practices that were made environmentally friendlier and that saved money at the same time. Many big companies have made these easy changes and reaped benefits from them. Many small companies still have such low-hanging fruit to harvest,[7] and plenty remains to be done.

The Dissenting View The critics of environmentalism in business are vocal. Some economists maintain that not a single empirical analysis supports the "free lunch view" that spending money on environmental problems provides full payback to the firm.[8] Skepticism should continue, they say; the belief that everyone will come out a winner is naive.

What really upsets many businesspeople is the financial cost of complying with environmental regulations.[9] Consider a few examples:

- GM spent $1.3 billion to comply with California requirements that 10 percent of the cars sold there be emission-free. European automakers spent $7 billion to install pollution control equipment in all new cars during a five-year period.

- At Bayer, 20 percent of manufacturing costs were for the environment. This is approximately the same amount spent for labor.
- The Clean Air Act alone was expected to cost U.S. petroleum refiners $37 billion, more than the book value of the entire industry.
- California's tough laws are a major reason why manufacturers moved to Arkansas or Nevada.

In industries like chemicals and petroleum, environmental regulations were once considered a threat to their very survival.[10]

Balance A more balanced view is that business must weigh the environmental benefits of an action against value destruction. The advice here is this: don't obstruct progress, but pick your environmental initiatives carefully. Compliance and remediation efforts will protect, but not increase, shareholder value.[11] And it is shareholder value, rather than compliance, emissions, or costs, that should be the focus of objective cost–benefit analyses. Such an approach is environmentally sound but also hardheaded in a business sense, and is the one approach that is truly sustainable over the long term.

Johan Piet said, "Only win–win companies will survive, but that does not mean that all win–win ideas will be successful."[12] In other words, rigorous analysis is essential. Thus some companies maintain continuous improvement in environmental performance, but fund only projects that meet financial objectives.

Most people understand that business has the resources and the competence to bring about constructive change, and that this creates great opportunity—if well managed—for both business and the environment.

WHY MANAGE WITH THE ENVIRONMENT IN MIND?

Business is turning its full attention to environmental issues for many reasons, including legal compliance, cost effectiveness, competitive advantage, public opinion, and long-term thinking.

Legal Compliance Table B.1 shows just some of the most important U.S. environmental laws. Government regulations and liability for damages provide strong economic incentives to comply with environmental guidelines. Most industries already have made environmental protection regulation and liability an integral part of their business planning.[13] The U.S. Justice Department has handed out tough prison sentences to executives whose companies violate hazardous waste requirements.

Some businesspeople consider the regulations to be too rigid, inflexible, and unfair. In response to this concern, regulatory reform may become more creative. The Aspen Institute Series on the Environment in the Twenty-First Century has tried to increase the cost-effectiveness of compliance measures through more flexibility in meeting standards and relying on market-based incentives. Such mechanisms, including tradable permits, pollution charges, and deposit refund systems, provide positive financial incentives for good environmental performance.[14]

Cost Effectiveness Environmentally conscious strategies can be cost-effective.[15] In the short run, company after company is realizing cost savings from repackaging, recycling, and other

TABLE B.1
Some U.S Environmental Laws

Superfund [Comprehensive Environmental Response, Compensation, and Liability Act (CERCLA)]: Establishes potential liability for any person or organization responsible for creating an environmental health hazard. Individuals may be prosecuted, fined, or taxed to fund cleanup.

Clean Water Act [Federal Water Pollution Control Act]: Regulates all discharges into surface waters, and affects the construction and performance of sewer systems. The Safe Drinking Water Act similarly protects groundwaters.

Clean Air Act: Regulates the emission into the air of any substance that affects air quality, including nitrous oxides, sulfur dioxide, and carbon dioxide.

Community Response and Right-to-Know Act: Mandates that all facilities producing, transporting, storing, using, or releasing hazardous substances provide full information to local and state authorities and maintain emergency action plans.

Federal Hazardous Substances Act: Regulates hazards to health and safety associated with consumer products. The Consumer Product Safety Commission has the right to recall hazardous products.

Hazardous Materials Transportation Act: Regulates the packaging, marketing, and labeling of shipments of flammable, toxic, and radioactive materials.

Resource Conservation and Recovery Act: Extends to small-quantity generators the laws regulating generation, treatment, and disposal of solid and hazardous wastes.

Surface Mining Control and Reclamation Act: Establishes environmental standards for all surface mining operations.

Toxic Substances Control Act: Addresses the manufacture, processing, distribution, use, and disposal of dangerous chemical substances and mixtures.

SOURCE: Dennis C. Kinlaw, *Competitive and Green: Sustainable Performance in the Environmental Age* (Amsterdam: Pfeiffer & Co., 1993). Reprinted by permission of the author.

approaches. Union Carbide faced costs of $30 a ton for disposal of solid wastes and $2,000 a ton for disposal of hazardous wastes. By recycling, reclaiming, or selling its waste, it avoided $8.5 million in costs *and* generated $3.5 million in income during a six-month period. Dow Chemical launched a 10-year program to improve its environmental, health, and safety performance worldwide. Dow projected savings of $1.8 billion over the 10-year period.[16]

Environmentally conscious strategies offer long-run cost advantages as well. Companies that are functioning barely within legal limits today may incur big costs—being forced to pay damages or upgrade technologies and practices—when laws change down the road.

A few of the other cost savings include fines, cleanups, and litigation; lower raw materials costs; reduced energy use; less expensive waste handling and disposal; lower insurance rates; and possibly higher interest rates.

Competitive Advantage Corporations gain a competitive advantage by channeling their environmental concerns into entrepreneurial opportunities and by producing higher-quality products that meet consumer demand. Business opportunities abound in pollution protection equipment and processes, waste cleanup, low-water-use plumbing, new lightbulb technology, and marketing of environmentally safe products like biodegradable plastics. With new pools of venture capital, government funding, and specialized investment funds available, environmental technology has become a major sector of the venture capital industry.[17]

In addition, companies that fail to innovate in this area will be at a competitive *disadvantage*. Environmental protection is not only a universal need; it is also a major export industry. U.S. trade suffered as other countries—notably Germany—took the lead in patenting and exporting anti–air pollution and other environmental technologies. If the United States does not produce innovative, competitive new technologies, it will forsake a growth industry and see most of its domestic spending for environmental protection go to imports.[18]

In short, competitive advantage can be gained by maintaining market share with old customers, and by creating new products for new market opportunities. And if you are an environmental leader, you may set the standards for future regulations—regulations that you are prepared to meet while your competitors are not.

Public Opinion The majority of the U.S. population believes business must clean up; few people think it is doing its job well. Gallup surveys have shown that more than 80 percent of U.S. consumers consider environmentalism in making purchases. An international survey of 22 countries found that majorities in 20 countries gave priority to environmental protection even at the risk of slowing economic growth. Consumers seem to have reached the point of routinely expecting companies to come up with environmentally friendly alternatives to current products and practices.[19]

Companies also receive pressure from local communities and from their own employees. Sometimes the pressure is informal and low-key, but much pressure is exerted by environmental organizations, aroused citizen groups, societies and associations, international codes of conduct, and environmentally conscious investors.[20]

Another important reason for paying attention to environmental impact is TRI, the Toxic Release Inventory.[21] Starting in 1986, the EPA required all the plants of approximately 10,000 U.S. manufacturers to report annual releases of 317 toxic chemicals into the air, ground, and water. The substances include freon, PCBs, asbestos, and lead compounds. Hundreds of others have been added to the list. The releases are not necessarily illegal, but they provide the public with an annual environmental benchmark. TRI provides a powerful incentive to reduce emissions.

Finally, it is useful to remember that companies recover very slowly in public opinion from the impact of an environmental disaster. Adverse public opinion may affect sales as well as the firm's ability to attract and retain talented people. You can see why companies like P&G consider concern for the environment a consumer need, making it a basic and critical business issue.

Long-Term Thinking
Long-term thinking about resources helps business leaders understand the nature of their responsibilities with regard to environmental concerns. For example, you read about sustainable growth in the chapter.[22] Economic arguments and the tragedy of the commons also highlight the need for long-term thinking.

Economic arguments In Chapter 3, we discussed long-term versus short-term decision making. We stated that it is common for managers to succumb to short-term pressure for profits and to avoid spending now when the potential payoff is years down the road. In addition, some economists maintain that it is the responsibility of management to maximize returns for shareholders, implying the preeminence of the short-term profit goal.

But other economists argue that such a strategy caters to immediate profit maximization for stock speculators and neglects serious investors who are with the company for the long haul. Attention to environmental issues enhances the organization's long-term viability because the goal is the long-term creation of wealth for the patient, serious investors in the company[23]—not to mention the future state of our planet and the new generations of humans and other species who will inhabit it.

The tragedy of the commons In a classic article in *Science,* Garrett Hardin described a situation that applies to all business decisions and social concerns regarding scarce resources like clean water, air, and land.[24] Throughout human history, a commons was a tract of community land on which people grazed their animals. A commons has limited **carrying capacity,** or the ability to sustain a population, because it is a finite resource. For individual herders, short-term interest lies in adding as many animals to the commons as they can. But problems develop as more herders add more animals to graze the commons. This leads to tragedy: as each herder acts in his short-term interest, the long-run impact is the destruction of the commons. The solution is to make choices according to long-run rather than short-run consequences.

In many ways, we are witnessing this **tragedy of the commons.** Carrying capacities are shrinking as precious resources, water chief among them, become scarcer. Inevitably conflict arises—and solutions are urgently needed.

The Environmental Movement
The 1990s were labeled the "earth decade" when a "new environmentalism" with new features emerged.[25] For example, proponents of the new environmentalism asked companies to reduce their wastes, use resources prudently, market safe products, and take responsibility for past damages. These requests are updated and formalized in the CERES Roadmap of the 21st Century.

The new environmentalism combined many diverse viewpoints, but initially it did not blend easily with traditional business values. Some of the key aspects of this philosophy are noted in the following discussion of the history of the movement.[26]

Conservation and Environmentalism A strand of environmental philosophy that is not at odds with business management is **conservation.** The conservation movement is anthropocentric (human centered), technologically optimistic, and concerned chiefly with the efficient use of resources. The movement seeks to avoid waste, promote the rational and efficient use of natural resources, and maximize long-term yields, especially of renewable resources.

The **environmental movement,** in contrast, historically has posed dilemmas for business management. Following the lead of early thinkers like George Perkins Marsh (1801–1882), it has shown that the unintended negative effects of human economic activities on the environment often are greater than the benefits. For example, there are links between forest cutting and soil erosion and between the draining of marshes and lakes and the decline of animal life.

Other early environmentalists, such as John Muir (1838–1914) and Aldo Leopold (1886–1948), argued that humans are not above nature but a part of it. Nature is not for humans to subdue but is sacred and should be preserved not simply for economic use but for its own sake—and for what people can learn from it.

Science and the Environment Rachel Carson's 1962 bestselling book, *The Silent Spring,* helped ignite the modern environmental movement by alerting the public to the dangers of unrestricted pesticide use.[27] Carson brought together the findings of toxicology, ecology, and epidemiology in a form accessible to the public. Blending scientific, moral, and political arguments, she connected environmental politics and values with scientific knowledge.

Barry Commoner's *Science and Survival* (1963) continued in this vein. Commoner expanded the scope of ecology to include everything in the physical, chemical, biological, social, political, economic, and philosophical worlds.[28] He argued that all of these elements fit together and have to be understood as a whole. According to Commoner, the symptoms of environmental problems are in the biological world, but their source lies in economic and political organizations.

Economics and the Environment Economists promote growth for many reasons: to restore the balance of payments, to make nations more competitive, to create jobs, to reduce the deficit, to provide for the elderly and the sick, and to reduce poverty. Environmentalists criticize economics for its notions of efficiency and its emphasis on economic growth.[29] For example, environmentalists argue that economists do not adequately consider the unintended side effects of efficiency. Environmentalists hold that economists need to supplement estimates of the economic costs and benefits of growth with estimates of other factors that historically were not measured in economic terms.[30]

Economists and public policy analysts argue that the benefits of eliminating risk to the environment and to people must be balanced against the costs. Reducing risk involves determining how effective the proposed methods of reduction are likely to be and how much they will cost. There are many ways to consider cost factors. Analysts can perform cost-effectiveness analyses, in which they attempt to figure out how to achieve a given goal with limited resources, or they can conduct more formal risk–benefit and cost–benefit analyses, in which they quantify both the benefits and the costs of risk reduction.[31]

Qualitative Judgments in Cost–Benefit Analysis Formal, quantitative approaches to balancing costs and benefits do not eliminate the need for qualitative judgments. For example, how does one assess the value of a magnificent vista obscured by air pollution? What is the loss to society if a particular genetic strain of grass or animal species becomes extinct? How does one assess the lost opportunity costs of spending vast amounts of money on air pollution that could have been spent on productivity enhancement and global competitiveness?

Fairness cannot be ignored when doing cost–benefit analysis.[32] For example, the costs of air pollution reduction may have to be borne disproportionately by the poor in the form of higher gasoline and automobile prices. Intergenerational fairness also plays a role.[33] Future generations have no representatives in the current market and political processes. To what extent should the current generation hold back on its own consumption for the sake of posterity? This question is particularly poignant because few people in the world today are well off. To ask the poor to reduce their life's chances for the sake of a generation yet to come is asking for a great sacrifice.

International Perspectives Environmental problems present a different face in various countries and regions of the world. The United States and Great Britain lagged behind Germany and Japan in mandated emissions standards.[34] In Europe, the Dutch, the Germans, and the Danes are among the most environmentally conscious. Italy, Ireland, Spain, Portugal, and Greece are in earlier stages of developing environmental policies. Poland, Hungary, the Czech Republic, and former East Germany are among the most polluted of the world's industrialized nations.[35]

U.S. companies need to realize that there is a large market in western Europe for environmentally "friendly" products. U.S. managers also need to be fully aware of the environmental movement in western Europe. Environmentalists in Europe have been successful in halting many projects, and consumers generally have been much more resistance to genetically modified foods than in the United States.[36] China has been paying a high ecological price for its rapid economic growth. But the government has begun recognizing the problem and is creating some antipollution laws.[37]

Industries that pollute or make polluting products will have to adjust to the new reality, and companies selling products in certain parts of the world must take into account a growing consumer consciousness about environmental protection. Manufacturers may even be legally required to take products and packaging back from customers after use, to recycle or dispose of. To meet these requirements in Germany, and to be prepared for similar demands in other countries, Hewlett-Packard redesigned its office machine packaging worldwide.

WHAT MANAGERS CAN DO

To be truly "green"—that is, a cutting-edge company with respect to environmental concerns—legal compliance is not enough. Progressive companies stay abreast *and ahead* of the laws by going beyond marginal compliance and anticipating future requirements and needs.[38] But companies can go further still by experimenting continually with innovations that protect the environment. McDonald's, for example, conducted tests and pilot projects in composting food scraps and in offering refillable coffee mugs and starch-based (biodegradable) cutlery.[39]

Systems Thinking The first thing managers can do to better understand environmental issues in their companies is to engage in systems thinking. Environmental considerations relate to the organization's inputs, processes, and outputs.[40] *Inputs* include raw materials and energy. Environmental pressures are causing prices of some raw materials, such as metals, to rise. This greatly increases the costs of production. Higher energy costs are causing firms to switch to more efficient sources.

Firms are considering new *processes* or methods of production that will reduce water pollution, air pollution, noise and vibration, and waste. They are incorporating technologies that sample and monitor (control) these by-products of business processes. Chemical plants have computerized systems that flash warnings when a maximum allowable pollution level is soon to be reached. Many companies keep only minimal stocks of hazardous materials, making serious accidents less likely.

Outputs have environmental impact, whether the products themselves or the waste or by-products of processes. To reduce the impact of its outputs, Herman Miller recycles or reuses nearly all waste from the manufacturing process. It sells fabric scraps to the auto industry, leather trim to luggage makers, and vinyl to stereo and auto manufacturers. It buys back its old furniture, refurbishes it, and resells it. Its corporatewide goal is to send zero waste to landfills. Environmental manager Paul Murray says, "There is never an acceptable level of waste at Miller. There are always new things we can learn."[41]

Strategic Integration Systems thinking reveals that environmental issues permeate the firm, and therefore should be addressed in a comprehensive, integrative fashion. Perhaps the first step is to create the proper mind-set. Does your firm see environmental concerns merely in terms of a business versus environment trade-off, or does it see a potential source of competitive advantage and an important part of a strategy for long-term survival and effectiveness? The latter attitude, of course, is more likely to set the stage for the following strategic actions.

These ideas help to strategically integrate environmental considerations into the firm's ongoing activities:[42]

1. *Develop a mission statement and strong values supporting environmental advocacy.* See P&G, Genworth, Bayer, or other examples online.
2. *Establish a framework for managing environmental initiatives.* Some industries have created voluntary codes of environmental practice, such as the chemical industry's Responsible Care Initiative. Not all standard practices are adopted by all companies, however.[43] At J&J, Environmental Regulatory Affairs uses external audit teams to conduct environmental audits.[44] The Community Environmental Responsibility Program includes strategy and planning, and the development of products and processes with neutral environmental impact.
3. *Engage in "green" process and product design.* The German furniture maker Wilkhahn uses an integrated strategic approach that minimizes the use of virgin resources and uses recycled materials in an environmentally designed plant.[45]
4. *Establish environmentally focused stakeholder relationships.* The E3 Initiative is a coordinated federal and local technical assistance initiative that helps manufacturer adapt and thrive in a new era that focuses on sustainability. It became official

in September 2010. To defray costs as well as develop new ideas, small companies like WHYCO Chromium Company establish environmental management partnerships with firms like IBM and GM.[46]

5. *Provide internal and external education.* Engage employees in environmental actions. Dow's WRAP program has cut millions of pounds of hazardous and solid waste and emissions, and achieved annual cost savings of over $10 million, all through employee suggestions.[47] At the same time, inform the public of your firm's environmental initiatives. For example, ecolabeling can urge consumers to recycle and communicate the environmental friendliness of your product. But don't "greenwash"— that is, engage in deceptive communication practices that do not accurately reflect the company's behavior.[48]

Implementation How can companies implement "greening" strategies? One tactic you read about in the chapter is life-cycle analysis.[49] That and other approaches begin with a commitment by top management. Specific actions could include commissioning an environmental audit in which an outside company checks for environmental hazards, drafting (or reviewing) the organization's environmental policy, communicating the policy and making it highly visible throughout the organization, having environmental professionals within the company report directly to the president or CEO, allocating sufficient resources to support the environmental effort, and building bridges between the organization and other companies, governments, environmentalists, and local communities.

Ultimately it is essential to make employees accountable for any of their actions that have environmental impact.[50] Texaco, Du Pont, and other companies evaluate managers on their ideas for minimizing pollution and for new, environment-friendly products. Kodak ties some managers' compensation to the prevention of chemical spills; the company attributes to this policy a dramatic reduction in accidents.[51]

Companies can employ all areas of the organization to meet the challenges posed by pollution and environmental challenges. A variety of companies have responded creatively to these challenges[52] and may serve as models for other organizations. The following sections describe specific actions companies can take to address environmental issues.

Strategy Actions companies can take in the area of strategy include the following:

1. *Cut back on environmentally unsafe businesses.* Du Pont, the leading producer of CFCs, voluntarily pulled out of this $750 million business.[53]

2. *Carry out R&D on environmentally safe activities.* GM is spending millions to develop hydrogen-powered cars that don't emit carbon dioxide. GE is doing research on earth-friendly hydrogen and lower-emission locomotives and jet engines.[54]

3. *Develop and expand environmental cleanup services.* Building on the expertise gained in cleaning up its own plants, Du Pont formed a safety and environmental resources division to help industrial customers clean up their toxic wastes.[55] Global Research Technologies LLC is trying to use solvents to grab carbon dioxide out of the air to isolate it for disposal.[56]

4. *Compensate for environmentally risky projects.* AES has a long-standing policy of planting trees to offset its power plants' carbon emission.[57]

5. *Make your company accountable to others.* Royal Dutch Shell and Bristol-Myers Squibb are trendsetters in green reporting.[58] Danish health care and enzymes company Novo Nordisk purposely asked for feedback from environmentalists, regulators, and other interested bodies from around Europe. Its reputation has been enhanced, its people have learned a lot, and new market opportunities have been identified.[59]

6. *Make every new product environmentally better than the last.* Intel is developing ultra-energy-efficient chips.[60] IBM uses recyclable materials, reduces hazardous materials, reduces emissions, and uses natural energy and resources in packaging.[61]

7. *Invest in green businesses.* American Electric Power Co. invested in renewable energy in Chile and retrofitted Bulgarian schools for greater efficiency.[62]

Public affairs In the area of public affairs, companies can take a variety of actions:

1. *Attempt to gain environmental legitimacy and credibility.* The cosponsors of Earth Day included Apple Computer, Hewlett-Packard, and the Chemical Manufacturers Association. McDonald's has tried to become a corporate environmental "educator." Ethel M. Chocolates, in public tours of its Las Vegas factory, showcases effective handling of its industrial wastes. 1% for the Planet has inspired members of the business community to contribute 1 percent of sales to environmental groups around the world.[63]

2. *Try to avoid losses caused by insensitivity to environmental issues.* As a result of Exxon's apparent lack of concern after the *Valdez* oil spill, 41 percent of Americans polled said they would consider boycotting the company.[64] MacMillan Bloedel lost a big chunk of sales almost overnight when it was targeted publicly as a clear-cutter and chlorine user.[65] The BP Gulf oil spill in 2010 was a disaster on many levels, including the company's inadequate and insensitive communications with the public.

3. *Collaborate with environmentalists.* Executives at Pacific Gas & Electric seek discussions and joint projects with any willing environmental group.

The legal area Actions companies can take in the legal area include the following:

1. *Try to avoid confrontation with state or federal pollution control agencies.* W. R. Grace faced expensive and time-consuming lawsuits as a result of its toxic dumps. Browning-Ferris, Waste Management Inc., and Louisiana-Pacific were charged with pollution control violations, damaging their reputations.

2. *Comply early.* Because compliance costs only increase over time, the first companies to act will have lower costs. This will enable them to increase their market share and profits and win competitive advantage. 3M's goal was to meet government requirements to replace or improve underground storage tanks five years ahead of the legally mandated year.

3. *Take advantage of innovative compliance programs.* The EU started a carbon-cutting and trading system in 2005.[66] Instead of source-by-source reduction, the EPA's bubble policy allows

factories to reduce pollution at different sources by different amounts, provided the overall result is equivalent. Therefore, 3M installed equipment on only certain production lines at its tape-manufacturing facility in Pennsylvania, thereby lowering its compliance costs.[67] Today there is greater use of economic instruments like tradable pollution permits, charges, and taxes to encourage improvements.[68] *Joint implementation* involves companies in industrialized nations working with businesses in developing countries to help them reduce greenhouse gas emissions. The company lending a hand then receives credit toward fulfilling its environmental obligations at home. The developing country receives investment, technology, and jobs; the company giving a lending hand receives environmental credits; and the world gets cleaner air.[69]

4. *Don't deal with fly-by-night subcontractors for waste disposal.* They are more likely to cut corners, break laws, and do a poor job. Moreover, the result for you could be bad publicity and legal problems.[70]

Operations   The actions companies can take in the area of operations include the following:

1. *Promote new manufacturing technologies.* Louisville Gas and Electric took the lead in installing smokestack scrubbers, Consolidated Natural Gas pioneered the use of clean-burning technologies, and Nucor developed state-of-the-art steel mills.
2. *Practice reverse logistics.* Firms move packaging and other used goods from the consumer back up the distribution channel to the firm. Make them not just costs, but a source of revenue—inputs to production. Fuji Australia believes that remanufacturing has generated returns in the tens of millions of dollars.[71]
3. *Encourage technological advances that reduce pollution from products and manufacturing processes.* Cinergy and AEP are working on technologies that capture carbon as coal is burned and pump it deep into the ground to be stored for thousands of years.[72] 3M's Pollution Prevention Pays has saved the company more than $1 billion.[73] Pollution prevention, more than pollution control, is related to both better environmental performance and better manufacturing performance, including cost and speed.[74]
4. *Develop new product formulations.* The Chicago Transit Authority and Union Pacific Corporation replaced traditional wood railroad ties with plastic ties. Other companies experimented with making recycled cross-ties of old tires, grocery bags, milk jugs, and Styrofoam cups.[75] Weyerhaeuser, recognizing the decreasing supply of timber and growing demand, is working to produce high-quality wood on fewer, continuously regenerated acres.[76] Electrolux has developed a sun-powered lawn mower and a chainsaw that runs on vegetable oil.[77] Many companies are developing green pesticides.
5. *Eliminate manufacturing wastes.* 3M replaced volatile solvents with water-based ones, thereby eliminating the need for costly air pollution control equipment. DuPont, consistent with its "zero waste" commitment, shed its carpet and nylon businesses, in part because of their big eco-footprints.[78] Walmart, establishing tough targets for reducing suppliers' packaging waste, expects to save $12 billion.[79] More

comprehensively, its Sustainability 360 established goals to purchase 100 percent renewable energy, create zero waste, and slash greenhouse gas emissions.[80]

6. *Find alternative uses for wastes.* When DuPont halted ocean dumping of acid iron salts, it discovered that the salts could be sold to water treatment plants at a profit. A Queensland sugarcane facility powers production via sugarcane waste.[81]
7. *Insist that your suppliers have strong environmental performance.* Environmental Defense asked McDonald's to influence the practices of chicken suppliers; Tyson Foods then slashed its use of antibiotics. Scott Paper discovered that many of its environmental problems were "imported" through the supply chain. Initially focusing on pulp suppliers, the company sent questionnaires asking for figures on air, water, and land releases, energy consumption, and energy sources. Scott was astonished at the variance. For example, carbon dioxide emissions varied by a factor of 17 among different suppliers. Scott dropped the worst performers and announced that the best performers would in the future receive preference in its purchasing decisions.[82]
8. *Assemble products with the environment in mind.* Make them easy to snap apart, sort, and recycle, and avoid glues and screws.

Marketing   Companies can also take action in the marketing area:

1. *Cast products in an environment-friendly light.* Most Americans believe a company's environmental reputation influences what they buy.[83] Seventh Generation Products are not tested on animals, are kosher-certified, and use hydrogen peroxide rather than chlorine bleach and plant-derived cleaning agents rather than petroleum-based cleaners. Walmart has made efforts to provide customers with recycled or recyclable products. A Chinese entrepreneur is making underwear out of soybean by-products.[84] Other eco-friendly fibers are made from hemp and bamboo, which require little pesticide.
2. *Avoid attacks by environmentalists for unsubstantiated or inappropriate claims.* When Hefty marketed "biodegradable" garbage bags, that claim was technically true, but it turned out that landfill conditions didn't allow decomposition to occur.[85] The extensive public backlash affected not only Hefty bags but also other Hefty products. Hefty didn't lie, but it did exaggerate. Its tactics overshadowed well-intentioned greening actions.
3. *Differentiate your product via environmental services.* Apple gives discounts for turning in old iPods. Teach customers how to use and dispose of products; for instance, farmers inadvertently abuse pesticides. Make education a part of a firm's after-sales service.
4. *Take advantage of the net.* The EcoMall (www.ecomall.com/biz/) promotes a number of environmentally oriented firms in 68 product categories. Firms using the net target green consumers globally, effectively, and efficiently.[86]

Accounting   Actions companies can take in the accounting area include the following:

1. *Collect useful data.* The best reporters of environmental information include Dow Europe, Danish Steel, BSO/Origin, 3M, and Monsanto.[87]

2. *Make polluters pay.* CIBA-GEIGY has a "polluter pays" principle throughout the firm, so managers have the incentive to combat pollution at the sources they can influence.[88]

3. *Demonstrate that antipollution programs pay off.* 3M's Pollution Prevention Pays program is based on the premise that only if the program pays will there be the motivation to carry it out. Every company needs to be cost-effective in its pollution reduction efforts.

4. *Use an advanced waste accounting system.* Do this in addition to standard management accounting, which can hinder investment in new technologies. Waste accounting makes sure all costs are identified and better decisions can be made.

5. *Adopt full-cost accounting.* This approach ensures that the price of a product reflects its full environmental cost.[89]

6. *Show the overall impact of the pollution reduction program.* Companies have an obligation to account for the costs and benefits of their pollution reduction programs. 3M claims a *billion* dollars in savings from pollution prevention efforts.

Finance In the area of finance, companies can do the following:

1. *Gain the respect of the socially responsible investment community.* Deutsche Asset Management, CalPERS, and Nikko Asset management are integrating sustainability into investment decision making in all asset classes.[90] Many investment funds in the United States and Europe take environmental criteria into account. A study concluded that environmental improvements could lead to significant reduction in the perceived risk of a firm, with a possible 5 percent increase in the stock price.[91] Socially responsible rating services and investment funds try to help people invest with a "clean conscience."[92]

2. *Recognize true liability.* Investment houses often employ environmental analysts who search for companies' true environmental liability in evaluating their potential performance. Bankers look at environmental risks and environmental market opportunities when evaluating a company's credit rating.[93] The Securities and Exchange Commission in New York requires some companies to report certain environmental costs.

3. *Fund and then assist green companies.* Ann Winblad of Hummer Winblad Venture Partners was one of the first venture capitalists to coach green entrepreneurs to increase their business skills and chances of success.[94]

4. *Recognize financial opportunities.* Worldwide, one of these great opportunities is water. Water must be purified and delivered reliably to everyone worldwide. Billions of people lack sanitary sewage facilities and have poor access to drinking water. Infrastructures in big cities, including those in the United States, are seriously deteriorating. Supplying clean water to people and companies is a $400 billion-a-year industry. Companies are aggressively pursuing this market. They are betting that water in the 21st century will be like oil in the 20th century.

KEY TERMS

carrying capacity The ability of a finite resource to sustain a population. p. 197

conservation An environmental philosophy that seeks to avoid waste, promote the rational and efficient use of natural resources, and maximize long-term yields, especially of renewable resources. p. 197

environmental movement An environmental philosophy postulating that the unintended negative effects of human economic activities on the environment are often greater than the benefits, and that nature should be preserved. p. 197

tragedy of the commons The environmental destruction that results as individuals and businesses consume finite resources (the "commons") to serve their short-term interests without regard for the long-term consequences. p. 197

DISCUSSION QUESTIONS

1. To what extent can and should we rely on government to solve environmental problems? What are some of government's limitations? Take a stand on the role and usefulness of government regulations on business activities.

2. To what extent should managers today be responsible for cleaning up mistakes from years past that have hurt the environment?

3. How would you characterize the environmental movement in western Europe? How does it differ from the U.S. movement? What difference will this make to a multinational company that wants to produce and market goods in many countries?

4. What business opportunities can you see in meeting environmental challenges? Be specific.

5. You are appointed environmental manager of XYZ Company. Describe some actions you will take to address environmental challenges. Discuss obstacles you are likely to encounter in the company and how you will manage them.

6. Interview a businessperson about environmental regulations and report your findings to the class. How would you characterize his or her attitude? How constructive is his or her attitude?

7. Interview a businessperson about actions he or she has taken that have helped the environment. Report your findings to the class and discuss.

8. Identify and discuss some examples of the tragedy of the commons. How can the tragedies be avoided?

9. Discuss the status of recycling efforts in your community or school, your perspectives on it as a consumer, and what business opportunities could be available.

10. What companies currently come to mind as having the best and worst reputations with respect to the environment? Why do they have these reputations?

11. Choose one product and discuss its environmental impact through its entire life cycle.

12. What are you, your college or university, and your community doing about the environment? What would you recommend doing?

6

International Management

LEARNING OBJECTIVES

After studying Chapter 6, you will be able to:

CHAPTER OUTLINE

Managing in a (Sometimes) Flat World
Implications of a Flat World
The Role of Outsourcing

The Global Environment
European Unification
Asia: China and India's Ascent
The Americas
The Rest of the World

Global Strategy
Pressures for Global Integration
Pressures for Local Responsiveness

Choosing a Global Strategy

Entry Mode
Exporting
Licensing
Franchising
Joint Ventures
Wholly Owned Subsidiaries

Managing across Borders
Skills of the Global Manager
Understanding Cultural Issues
Ethical Issues in International Management

Manager's Brief	Progress Report	Onward

Management Connection

HOW IKEA IS MAKING SWEDISH DESIGN A GLOBAL PHENOMENON

Throughout the United States, dorm rooms and apartments feature stylish bookshelves, chairs, desks, and other furniture assembled by the owners from kits purchased at IKEA stores or at the retailer's website. The company, which started as one Swedish teenager's dream in the 1940s, is today an international enterprise with hundreds of stores in 38 countries generating revenues of more than $32 billion a year by selling its own distinctive line of furniture and housewares. Even when most other retailers saw customers disappear during the last recession, IKEA recorded growing sales.

What management ideas and methods made IKEA so popular around the world? One primary consideration has to be the practicality of the company's founder, Ingvar Kamprad. From the start, when Kamprad was just 17, he was committed to finding useful products he could sell at a low price to the residents of his village of Agunnaryd, Sweden, where people were used to making do with limited resources. Kamprad named his company IKEA, using his initials, the first letter of his family's farm (Elmtaryd), and the first letter of the village's name. IKEA initially sold small items such as pens, wallets, and stockings. As advertising increased sales to a wider area, Kamprad began the rudiments of a mail-order business, using the village's milk truck to carry products to the closest train station. As the business grew, IKEA added a line of locally made furniture and published its first catalog.

Practical solutions continued to drive the innovations that make IKEA distinctive today. In the 1950s competitors began applying price pressure, threatening to drive down quality as suppliers looked for ways to reduce costs. So IKEA opened its first showroom as a way to demonstrate the quality of its furniture. Then competitors pressured furniture

makers to discontinue business with IKEA, so the company began to design its own furniture. And one day, when workers were trying to fit a table into the back of a car, they removed the legs to avoid damage. That experience provided the germ of an idea to pack furniture into flat boxes and let the buyers assemble it at home. Today the flat packaging remains a way to minimize costs without compromising quality.

These roots helped shape the company's vision as it is described today. IKEA's stated vision is "to create a better everyday life for the many people." Keeping costs low means more people can afford to furnish their homes with IKEA's products. Control over design helps the company make daily life better by enabling people to enjoy beautiful design and functionality, even if they aren't wealthy. Attractive, affordable products at reasonable prices for use at home: this strategy resonates in Sweden and far beyond.

Innovative thinking helps IKEA carry out its low-cost strategy. The company is out front when it comes to applying efficiency and renewable energy sources to reduce its stores' energy usage. For example, outside Denver, IKEA partnered with the

National Renewable Energy Laboratory to build a store with a geothermal heating system. Pipes installed below the store's parking garage carry warmer air in the winter or cooler air in the summer to the surface, where it is used to keep the store at a comfortable temperature. (In the summer, a backup ice storage system will deliver additional cooling.) In California IKEA installed solar panels on seven stores plus its distribution center. The 20,000 panels in its plan were expected to generate about 6.7 million kilowatt-hours of electricity for the facilities each year.

Sustainability is not just about costs, however. IKEA communicates a message of commitment to the environment. For example, a drive to continually improve the efficiency of packaging enables the company to both drive down prices and reduce the energy consumption required to transport the goods to warehouses. IKEA is also trying to make its products themselves more environmentally friendly. The company set up a venture capital fund, called the GreenTech Fund, to invest in start-ups such as a maker of high-tech batteries that may someday contribute to ecofriendly IKEA products. IKEA creatively communicates the value of sustainability to its employees as well. In a recent year, IKEA's 12,400 employees in the United States received a thank-you gift: a mountain bike painted in the blue and yellow of IKEA's logo (and Sweden's flag)—packaged in a box with assembly instructions. The choice of this gift was both an expression of gratitude for hard work and a message in support of living a lifestyle that is both healthy and sustainable.

Sustainability is a value near and dear to the hearts of many consumers in IKEA's original markets in Sweden and nearby European countries. That counts for a lot, given that 80 percent of IKEA's sales still come from Europe. As IKEA continues its expansion in fast-growing markets of Eastern Europe and Asia, time will tell whether that message continues to resonate around the world.[1]

How well can IKEA's commitment to affordability and sustainability appeal to consumers around the world? As you read this chapter, consider what qualities of the international business environment present threats and opportunities for this company.

The direction of IKEA's growth resembles that of many successful businesses in recent decades. The company started out by satisfying customers in a local market. As sales increased, the company hired employees and began serving a larger region. Eventually it began selling goods to and running operations in other countries. Now it boasts sales and develops managers around the globe.

Today's corporate giants—and many ambitious, creative small businesses—need employees and sales in other countries to meet their objectives. U.S. multinational corporations now employ almost one-third of their workers outside the United States, and the overseas share is growing. Sales of some product categories also are growing faster outside the United States. That's why GE, for example, earns 60 percent of its revenues outside the United States (versus 30 percent in 2000) and has over half its workforce outside the United States (54 percent, up from 46 percent in 2000).[2] Or consider Walt Disney Company. After years of negotiations, the iconic U.S. company began construction of a theme park and resort in Shanghai. The deal is complex because the Chinese government insisted on Chinese ownership, but for Disney it was worthwhile because it wants to bring its brand of entertainment to China's vast population and rapidly developing economy.[3]

Because of such trends, today's managers need to be able to plan how their company will enter markets around the world. That planning begins with understanding the importance of the global economy and the opportunities and threats of the fast-changing global environment.

Managing in a (Sometimes) Flat World

The global economy matters precisely because it *is* global—because your customers, employees, and suppliers could be located anywhere in the world. Several years ago, *New York Times* columnist Thomas Friedman wrote a best seller about this phenomenon. His book, *The World Is Flat*, described how such trends as the Internet and trade agreements between more and more nations have made international business the norm today. Whether you are a large or small company looking for financing, supplies, employees, machinery, natural resources, or transportation services, you can readily go online and find the mix of price and quality that is right for you. In that way, according to Friedman, the business environment has become a level playing field—in a word, "flat."

But if "flat" is taken to mean everyone has the same advantages or buys the same products, it hardly describes the real world. Internet connectivity doesn't necessarily make us more aware of every idea or interested in every global trend. Sometimes individuals go online to connect with people they already know and to buy products that are tailored to their own particular tastes. And sometimes a local government still makes it hard for a business to grow, or a community lacks the resources to encourage development. In that sense, the world is not always flat; it is often bumpy.[4] For managers, that makes the business environment more complex and exciting than ever: a global economy with threats and opportunities around the world, accompanied by a requirement to know their customers' specific needs and values, which may vary considerably from place to place.

Later in this chapter, we will describe how managers can select strategies for the world's "bumpiness." But first, let's see how the ever-greater interconnection, or integration, of the world economy is shaping the way business is done today.

The world is not always flat; it is often bumpy.

Implications of a Flat World

As you will see later in the chapter, increasing prosperity and the lowering of trade barriers have increased the extent to which the economies of different nations are integrated into one global economy. The increasing integration of the global economy has had many consequences. First, even as the output of the world's economies surged during the middle of the past decade, international trade expanded even faster. When trouble in the financial industry sparked an economic downturn, European and North American imports declined, and other world trade growth slowed. But those trends are expected to be temporary, eventually reversing as economic conditions improve.[5] Years of emphasis on international commerce by major industrial countries, recent liberalized trading brought about by free trade agreements, and market reforms in China have resulted in lowering the barriers to the free flow of goods, services, and capital among nation–states. The impact of these trends is staggering. The dollar value of international trade (merchandise exports and commercial services) is over $16 trillion—up from just a few hundred billion dollars in the 1960s and 1970s. For example, Figure 6.1 shows how the international trade of the United States (particularly for goods) increased relative to the country's output since 1990. The dollar value of trade in goods grew from 12 percent to almost 18 percent of the country's total output of goods, even as total U.S. output also grew. Most experts expect competition to increase as trade is liberalized, and as is often the case, the more efficient players will survive. To succeed in this industrial climate, managers need to study opportunities in existing markets, as well as work to enhance the competitiveness of their firms.

A second consequence of increased global integration is that *foreign direct investment (FDI)* is playing an ever-increasing role in the global economy as companies of all sizes invest overseas. In particular, the foreign direct investment flows to less developed countries from firms in developed countries investment flows have risen substantially.[6] Investment by foreign companies and individuals in U.S. firms is also huge: $2.3 trillion, close to double the 2000 level, with the majority coming from European investors. In recent years, the United States has received more foreign direct investment than any other country.[7] To give two examples, Deutsche Boerse, a German provider of securities trading, arranged to buy the parent company of the New York Stock Exchange, and a Chinese company called Geely bought the Volvo business unit

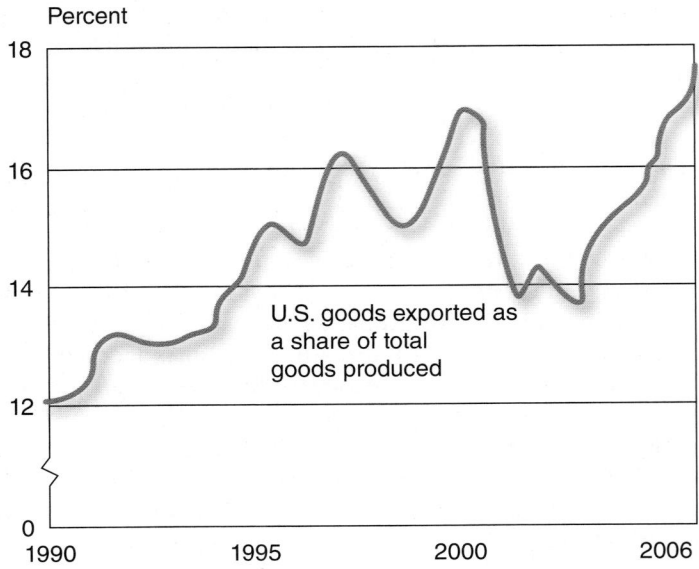

Percent

FIGURE 6.1
Growing Proportion of
Goods Being Exported

SOURCE: Data from U.S. Bureau of Economic Analysis, as cited in James C. Cooper, "Exports Are Giving the Economy a Surprise Lift," *Bloomberg Businessweek*, November 27, 2006.

from Ford Motor Company.[8] In recent years, China's role as an export powerhouse has allowed the Chinese government to amass about $1 trillion in foreign exchange reserves, of which it is expected to invest hundreds of billions of dollars.[9]

A third consequence of an increasingly integrated global economy is that imports are penetrating deeper into the world's largest economies. For example, high percentages of the clothing and textile products, paper, cut diamonds, and electronics consumed in the United States are imported. Until recently, most of the canned peaches sold in the United States were cling peaches grown in California, but China's share of this market has been skyrocketing and now represents more than 1 out of every 10 cans sold. And in the automobile industry, over half of the new cars sold in the United States in 2010 were from automakers based in other countries, primarily in Asia.[10] Figure 6.2 shows how the world trade of manufactured merchandise has grown relative to other product groups. The growth of imports is a natural by-product of the growth of world trade and the trend toward the manufacture of component parts, or even entire products, overseas before shipping them back home for final sale.

Finally, the growth of world trade, FDI, and imports implies that companies around the globe are finding their home markets under attack from foreign competitors. This is true in the United States, where Japanese automakers have captured market share from General Motors, Ford, and Chrysler; and in western Europe, where the once-dominant Dutch company Philips N. V. has lost market share in the consumer electronics industry to Japan's JVC, Matsushita, and Sony.

What does all this mean for today's managers? Compared with only a few years ago, *opportunities are greater* because the movement toward free trade has opened up many formerly protected national markets. The potential for export and for making direct investments overseas is greater today than ever before. *The environment is more complex* because today's manager often has to deal with the challenges of doing business in countries with radically different cultures and coordinating globally dispersed operations. *The environment is more competitive* because in addition to domestic competitors, the manager must deal with cost-efficient overseas competitors.

Companies both large and small now view the world, rather than a single country, as their marketplace. As Figure 6.3 shows, the United States

Companies both large and small now view the world as their marketplace.

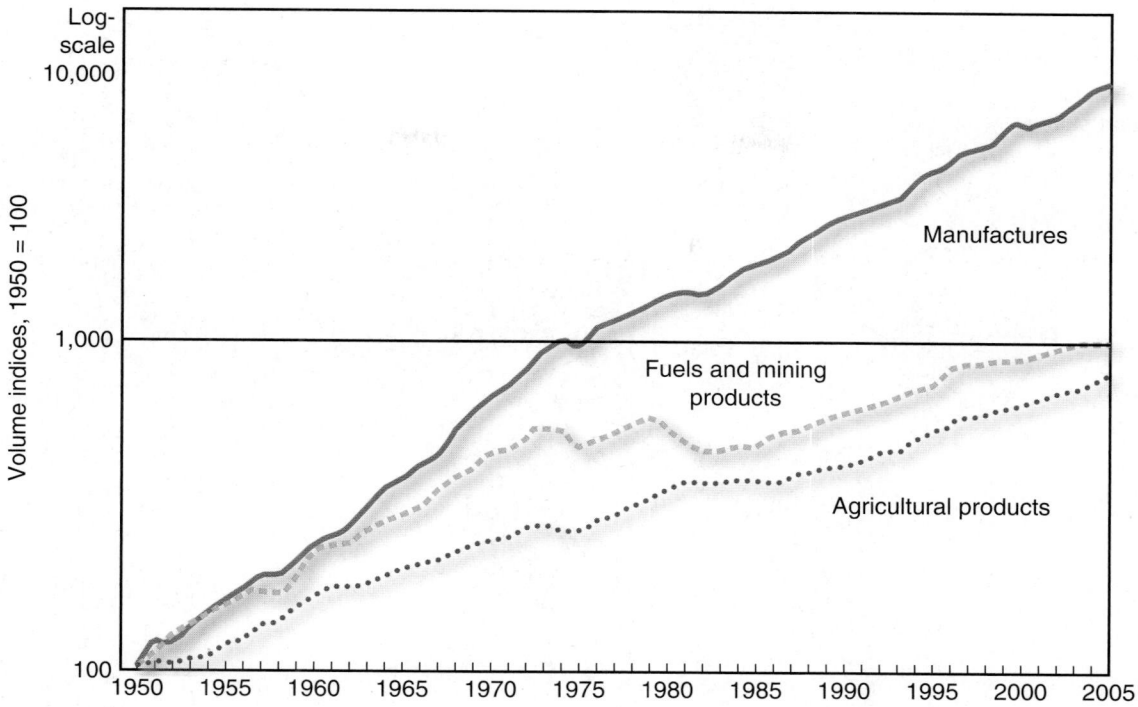

SOURCE: World Trade Organization, "Selected Long-Term Trends," *International Trade Statistics 2006*, pp. 25–32, http://www.wto.org.

FIGURE 6.2

Relative Growth in World Merchandise Trade by Major Product Group, 1950–2005

has no monopoly on international business. Of the top 25 corporations in the world, 16 are based in countries outside the United States. Also, companies have dispersed their manufacturing, marketing, and research facilities to those locations around the globe where cost and skill conditions are most favorable. This trend is now so pervasive in industries such as automobiles, aerospace, and electronics that it is becoming increasingly irrelevant to talk about "American products" or "Japanese products" or "German products."

For example, the headquarters of an automaker no longer says much about where a particular car is made. According to the National Highway Traffic Safety Administration, despite the Jeep Patriot's red-white-and-blue name, only 66 percent of its components are made in the United States. In contrast, although Toyota is a Japanese-headquartered company, 80 percent of the parts in a Toyota Sequoia are produced in the United States. A U.S. headquarters doesn't limit a U.S. car company either. General Motors reports that it employs more people, sells more cars, and sees its best growth prospects outside the United States.[11]

Such internationalization is not limited to the largest corporations. An increasing number of medium-size and small firms also engage in international trade. Some companies have limited their involvement to exporting, while others set up production facilities overseas. Jade Corporation, which started out as a tool and die maker, operates three facilities with a few hundred employees. The company found it difficult to compete as U.S. manufacturing operations moved overseas, but creative management continued to find opportunities. As the company moved into making more specialized products, it developed its engineering capabilities and its experience in working with a Singapore manufacturer. Eventually Jade began working with clients to set up manufacturing facilities in Asia. Jade employees first learn about the customer's product and the way to make it, and then they use their overseas connections to get the customer's foreign plant running.[12] Responding to the dominance of English on the Internet, an Israeli software start-up developed a program called WhiteSmoke, which uses artificial intelligence to analyze written English, not only checking for spelling

FIGURE 6.3
Top 10 Global Firms

and grammar errors but also suggesting ways to make the writing clearer and more natural. The company originally found a customer base among Israeli lawyers and tech workers. Since then, the ease of downloading a program online has expanded the market to computer users in the United States. The company next began negotiating with distributors to sell WhiteSmoke in China and India. The global nature of the Internet has provided both the need and a major means of distributing WhiteSmoke.[13]

> Some of the reasons managers collaborate with their overseas counterparts on trade are obvious.

Some of the reasons managers collaborate with their overseas counterparts on trade are obvious. Other countries offer expanded markets for one's own products. In turn, they might have natural resources, products, or cost structures that managers need but that aren't available in the home country. But there are other, perhaps less obvious, benefits to collaborating with other countries on trade. Because trade allows each country to obtain more efficiently what it cannot as easily produce on its own, it lowers prices overall and makes more goods more widely available. This in turn raises living standards—and may broaden the market for a manager's own products, both locally and abroad. Trade also makes new technologies and methods more widely available, again raising the standard of living and improving efficiency. Finally, collaborating with others on trade creates links between people and cultures that, particularly over the long run, can lead to cooperation in other areas.

The Role of Outsourcing

outsourcing

Contracting with an outside provider to produce one or more of an organization's goods or services.

offshoring

Moving work to other countries.

In recent years, the issues of offshoring and outsourcing have become sources of controversy. **Outsourcing** occurs when an organization contracts with an outside provider to produce one or more of its goods or services. **Offshoring** occurs when companies move jobs to another country, typically where wages are lower. This practice does not necessarily require using an outside provider. Companies with large workforces can resource globally. However, most of the concerns expressed about offshoring refer to outsourcing because people conclude that high-paying U.S. jobs are being lost to low-cost countries overseas. The concern is prompted by widespread reports of major corporations relocating assembly lines, computer programming, help centers, and other parts of their operations to India or China. One study has estimated that by 2015 more than 3 million U.S. jobs will be sent abroad.[14] Economist Alan Blinder raised the possibility that communication technology will lead to the offshoring of at least 30 million jobs over the longer term. For example, the work of bookkeepers, accounting clerks, computer programmers, data entry keyers, and financial analysts can be performed anywhere and submitted to the customer or employer electronically.[15]

Even as manufacturing employment has declined, manufacturing output in the United States has grown.

The decline in manufacturing employment in the United States is evident. During the previous decade, the United States lost 2 million manufacturing jobs, as well as 1.6 million office and administrative support jobs. During the recession in 2009, more workers in the United States were laid off than abroad. Some economists blame certain conditions in the United States for making the business climate relatively unfavorable: taxes, declining infrastructure, inadequate education, and barriers to hiring skilled immigrant workers.[17] However, considerable evidence suggests that the cause of this job decline is not offshoring, but innovation. Because of new technology and processes, managers simply need fewer workers to produce the same quantity of goods. Even as manufacturing

At many big U.S. corporations, employees outside the United States represent a significant and growing part of the workforce.[16]

employment has declined, manufacturing output in the United States has grown. In addition, technology and trade enable the creation of new jobs. Even as manufacturing jobs have been lost, the United States has gained millions of new jobs, including 3.2 million service jobs, 2.5 million professional jobs, and 1.3 million managerial jobs. Thus the important question may not be how to prevent offshoring from "taking" jobs but how to prepare the workforce for the types of jobs that will be needed in the United States of the future—jobs requiring personal interaction (such as the work of doctors or counselors), hands-on activity (plumbers, janitors), and tailoring to particular situations (identifying clients' needs rather than following a routine).[18]

The statistics on offshoring often overlook that the job transfers from offshoring represent a small fraction of the 135 million jobs in the United States. Most jobs require workers to be close to their markets—people still shop at their local supermarkets and appliance dealers, visit their doctors, and attend a community school. Perhaps most important, as offshoring increases efficiency, it frees funds for expansion and additional employment. The challenge is primarily one in which individual workers are deeply affected when their jobs are lost. Some

An increasing number of American companies are outsourcing and offshoring divisions and departments of their organizations to save money. Many call centers are now located in India, where wages are still much lower than in the United States. Here is a photo of a typical call center in Hyderabad, India.

organizations determine that they have a social responsibility to participate in retraining programs to help these displaced workers identify and prepare for jobs that are less likely to move overseas. The controversy over offshoring also overlooks the extent to which foreign companies hire workers in the United States—for example, when Germany's BMW runs a South Carolina assembly plant for its X5 sport utility vehicle.

One less positive effect of offshoring has been wage stagnation in industries where offshoring is common, as workers in those areas compete with their lower-wage counterparts abroad. On the other hand, wages, energy costs, and other expenses in some of those other countries have started to rise, reducing the benefits of offshoring.[19] Some firms have looked for lower costs outside India and China by heading for Bangladesh, Vietnam, and Indonesia, while others are testing the potential of operations in African countries.

In recent years automation has reduced the percentage of product costs that can be attributed to labor, making it less necessary to consider moving jobs overseas. Also, managers who offshore to achieve wage savings alone often incur unexpected additional costs in travel, training, quality control, language barriers, and the resistance of some customers who

> "Competitiveness is not a zero-sum game and the success of other economies is not a failure of U.S. competitiveness. As all nations improve their productivity, wages rise and markets expand, creating the potential for rising prosperity for all."
> Michael Porter[20]

prefer to deal with local personnel. However, offshoring is a continuing trend because in some cases it delivers advantages other than cost. For some types of work, companies use offshoring as a way to find talent that is in short supply at home. A survey of software firms found that the main reasons for offshoring were to enable the company to grow and to get products to market faster. The companies either have difficulty finding enough programmers in the United States or determine that they can keep a project moving ahead around the clock as U.S. and overseas teams hand the project back and forth. Similarly, by outsourcing a project to a specialist firm, a company can quickly have hundreds of people devoted to it, dramatically shortening the turnaround time.[21]

In short, in deciding whether to offshore, managers should not start out with the assumption that it will be cheaper for them to do so. Instead, here are some of the factors they might take into account:

What is the competitive advantage of the products they offer? If, say, rapid delivery, reliability, and customer contact are paramount, then offshoring is a less attractive option. But if the product is widely available and standardized, like a calculator, and the only competitive advantage is price, the lowest possible production cost becomes essential and offshoring becomes something managers will consider.

Is the business in its early stages? If so, offshoring may well be inappropriate because managers need to stay close to the business and its customers to solve problems and make sure everything is going according to plan. When the business is more mature, managers can afford to consider moving some operations overseas.

Can production savings be achieved locally? Automation can often achieve significant labor cost savings and eliminate the advantage of moving production abroad. Where automation savings are not feasible, as with computer call centers, then offshoring becomes a more attractive option.

Can the entire supply chain be improved? As we discussed in Chapter 2, enormous productivity savings are possible when managers develop an efficient supply chain, from suppliers to manufacturing to customers. These improvements permit both lower cost and high customer responsiveness. If the supply chain is not a major consideration, or is already highly efficient or routine, and more savings are needed, then offshoring may be one way for managers to achieve additional efficiencies.[22]

These considerations lead to a variety of decisions about where to operate. The high costs of transporting heavy appliances are one reason why GE decided to move some of its appliance manufacturing back to the United States. Master Lock, based in Milwaukee, Wisconsin, also found that returning production to the United States from China had become more cost-effective. Fortunately for the company, it still had some production facilities and employees in the United States; companies that previously outsourced all production have found that their options for bringing manufacturing home are now more limited.[23]

The Global Environment

As we saw in Chapter 2, an organization's external environment includes its economic, technological, legal/regulatory, demographic, social, and natural environments. When today's managers think about, for example, the economic potential of a market, the laws that both protect their property and restrain their conduct, and the resources they need for making products, they should be thinking about these in terms of where the best opportunities lie anywhere in the world. The simple fact is that technology and an integrated economy are making international business inescapable. Table 6.1 provides examples of current issues we will consider in each area of this international environment.

LO 2

The global economy is becoming more integrated than ever before.

The global economy is becoming more integrated than ever before. For example, the World Trade Organization (WTO), formed in 1995, now has 153 member countries involved in more than 95 percent of the world's trade. The newest members are Cambodia, Nepal, Russia, Saudi Arabia, Tonga, Ukraine, and Vietnam. (The International Monetary Fund, set up by the United Nations in 1945, serves a similar purpose and includes 187 countries.) The WTO provides a forum for nations to negotiate trade agreements and procedures for administering the agreements and resolving disputes. Issues that are currently under negotiation because they have been difficult for the parties to resolve include objections to environmental regulations and subsidies to farmers in developed countries, on the grounds that they conflict with free trade. To follow how these issues are playing out, you can explore the "Trade Topics" section of the WTO website, http://www.wto.org.

The global economy is dominated by countries in three regions: North America, western Europe, and Asia. However, other developing countries and regions represent important areas for economic growth as well. Figure 6.4 shows the major international trade areas and countries of the world.

Economic environment	Foreign investment; growth of developing nations; rising wages in developing nations
Technological environment	Internet and wireless technology
Legal/regulatory environment	Free trade agreements; anticorruption laws
Demographics	Aging population in developed nations; growing population worldwide, especially in the developing world
Social issues	Cultural differences; bribery concerns
Natural environment	Intensifying demand for resources, including oil, water, and food; growing desire for sustainable products and operations; increasingly endangered species; climate change

TABLE 6.1

Key Issues of the Global Environment

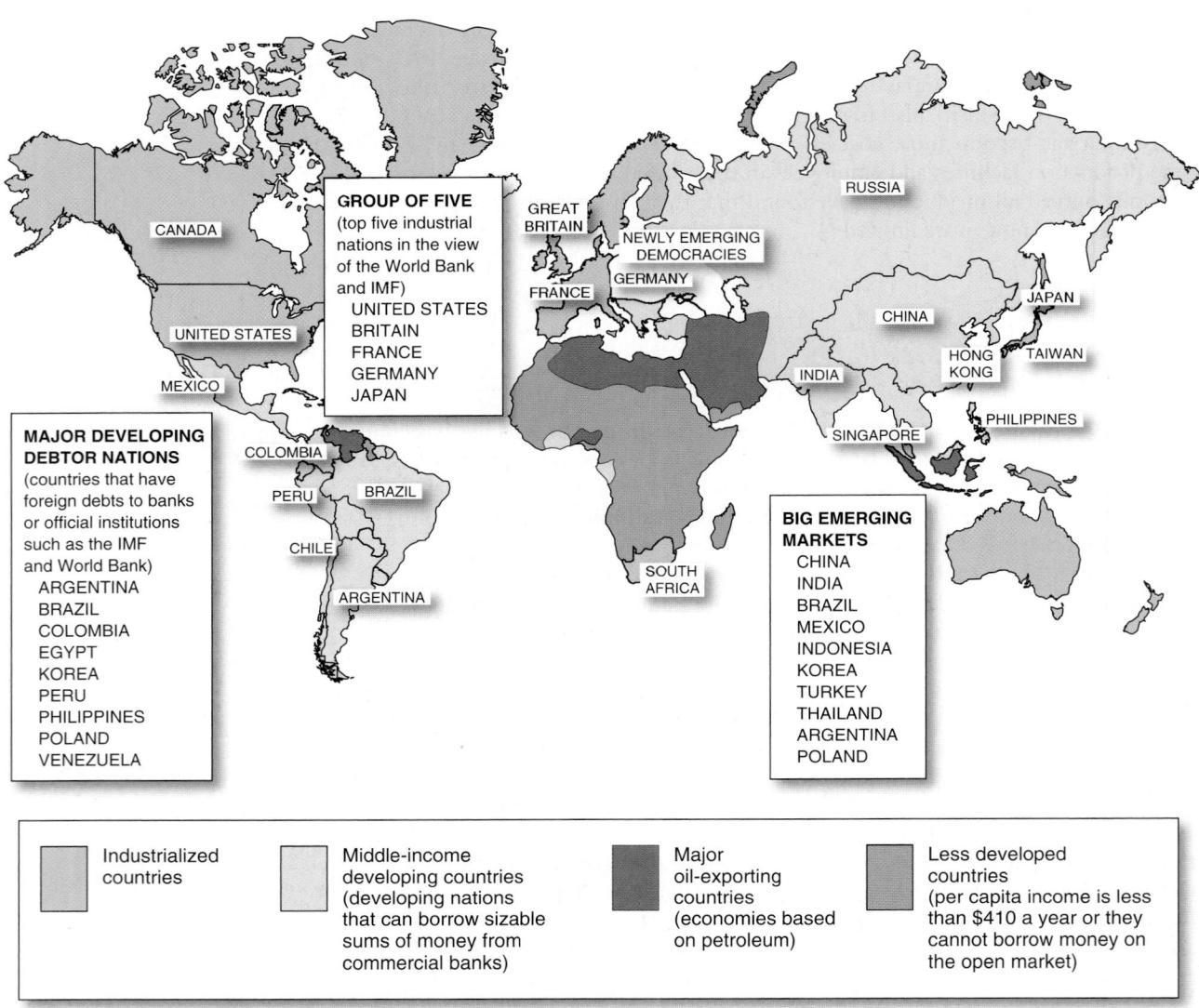

FIGURE 6.4
The Global Economy

European Unification

Europe is integrating economically to form the biggest market in the world. Under the Maastricht Treaty, which formally established the European Union (EU), the euro was adopted as a common currency among 13 member countries. Currencies with a long history like the franc and the mark are now relics of the past. The EU allows most goods, services, capital, and human resources to flow freely across its national borders. The EU was originally formed after World War II to foster cooperation through trade in place of military conflict, but the efforts have also created an economic superpower. Its 27 members now boast a population of more than 492 million and a GDP (gross domestic product) exceeding that of the United States.[24]

The pace of European unification accelerated in 2004 with the addition of former Eastern-bloc countries including Poland and Hungary, and in 2007 Bulgaria and Romania joined. Many of these new members offer a particular challenge to full integration because as former communist countries they do not have extensive experience as modern market economies. Other even less wealthy countries—Croatia, Macedonia, and Turkey—have also applied to join the EU.

In addition to the difficulty of integrating widely divergent economies, certain structural issues within Europe need to be corrected for the EU to function effectively. In particular, western Europeans on average work fewer hours, earn more pay, take longer vacations, and enjoy far more social entitlements than do their counterparts in North America and Asia. To be competitive in a global economy, Europeans must increase their level of productivity. Other problems will present even greater challenges, such as Europe's aging population, low birthrates, and low immigration, all of which are threatening to cause Europe's population to drop, even as America's is increasing. Recently EU relationships were tested by the global financial crisis and recession, which hit some member nations harder than others. For example, Ireland, which had been enjoying impressive growth in the banking and insurance sectors, suffered the near-collapse of those industries. With tax revenues falling even as citizens needed more help, the governments of Portugal, Ireland, and Greece found themselves begging other EU nations for financial assistance. The economically stronger nations were reluctant to ask their own citizens to support a bailout of other countries but eventually agreed to provide loans through the EU and International Monetary Fund. That assistance is accompanied by requirements that the less stable governments bring more discipline to their spending habits. That, in the end, may make the EU even more potent than it was before.[25]

Still, unification is creating a more competitive Europe, one that U.S. managers will increasingly have to take into account. One reason is that although growth in the developed economies of western Europe has been modest, it is strong in the eastern part of the continent. Companies are investing in Poland, the Czech Republic, Romania, and nearby countries because of their relatively low wages, trained workers, and access to markets. Nokia, the Finland-based maker of telecommunications equipment, is building a factory in Romania, where it can provide products not only to European customers but also to Africa and the Middle East. Moving from the other direction, Chinese and Taiwanese companies have seen central Europe as a convenient and affordable location for building facilities to develop their positions in Europe. For example, Sichuan Changhong, a Chinese electronics company, is building a factory in Numburk, Czech Republic, and Foxconn, a Taiwanese maker of components for name-brand computers, operates a factory in the Czech city of Pardubice.[26]

The EU also presents a regulatory challenge to the United States and other countries. For example, the EU has supported excluding genetically engineered food products from American firms, over objections from the WTO. It has fined Microsoft for what it says are unreasonable prices Microsoft charges rival software firms to give them the information and documentation they need to develop products compatible with the Windows operating system. The EU required the documentation as a remedy to remove its antitrust charges.[27]

The EU's more competitive and regulatory environment clearly presents new challenges to managers and their employees. Managers in U.S. companies that wish to export to that market must become more knowledgeable about the new business environment the EU is creating. Management and labor will have to work cooperatively to achieve high levels of quality to make U.S. goods and services attractive to consumers in Europe and other markets around the world. The United States needs managers who will stay on top of worldwide developments and manage high-quality, efficient organizations as well as a well-educated, well-trained, and continually *retrained* labor force to remain competitive with the Europeans and other formidable competitors.

Asia: China and India's Ascent

Among the Pacific Rim countries, and particularly in the United States, Japan dominated world attention toward the end of the last century. Today Japan is America's fourth-largest export market, after Canada, China, and Mexico, as you can see in Figure 6.5. And Japan is in fourth place as a source of U.S. imports. Japanese

Bottom Line

Globalization requires improvements in all bottom-line practices.

Why might innovation be important for a U.S. company in a global market?

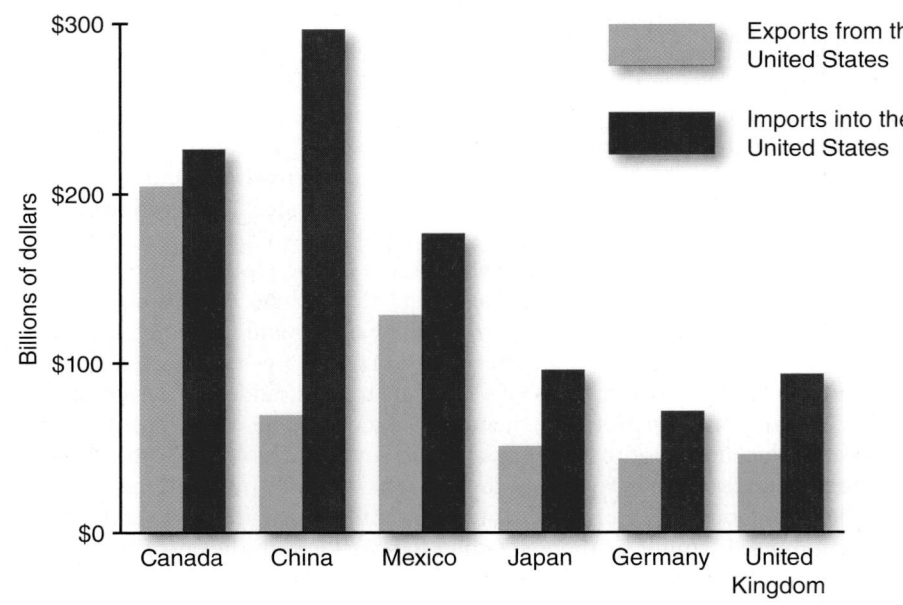

FIGURE 6.5
Top U.S. Trading Partners,
Based on Total Imports and
Exports

SOURCE: U.S. Census Bureau, *Statistical Abstract of the United States: 2011*, Table 1306, http://www.census.gov.

companies like Toyota are both a major source of goods and, as competitors, a growing influence in the ways U.S. managers seek quality and efficiency.

> China is on its way to becoming the largest producer and consumer of many of the world's goods.

As successful as Japan is, a bigger force is rising in Asia: China. With the world's largest population and increasing industrialization, China is on its way to becoming the largest producer and consumer of many of the world's goods. Its large and growing demand for oil is a cost factor that managers everywhere must consider in their long-range planning. The country has also become the world's largest consumer of basic raw materials like steel and cement, as well as the world's largest cell phone market. Not only is China the largest source of imports to the United States (see Figure 6.5), but it is on track to surpass the United States as the world's second-largest exporter overall, after Germany.[28]

As a consuming nation, China's appeal to managers lies in its large population of 1.3 billion people and its extremely rapid economic growth. Even as global economic growth stalled during the recent financial crisis, China's economy continued expanding. During the past decade, it has tripled its imports and quadrupled its exports. The nation was recently ranked as the world's second-largest exporter and third-largest importer, primarily trading manufactured goods but also importing huge quantities of materials used in manufacturing and construction.[29] Several American companies have invested heavily in the Chinese market, with some success. Intel recently announced plans to build a silicon wafer fabrication factory in Dalian, China. Building the facility is an element of Intel's strategy to operate closer to China's information technology market, which the company predicts may become the world's largest. The company already operates laboratories and testing and packaging facilities in China.[30] Microsoft and Chinese computer maker Lenovo have entered into a partnership in an effort to expand in the Chinese market, as well.

Even with its growing consumption, China has had an even greater global impact in its role as an exporting nation. The enormous size of its labor force, combined with its extremely low labor costs, has given it a huge competitive advantage in manufacturing. Estimates suggest that labor costs in China are less than $1 an hour, compared with $2.92 for manufacturing workers in Mexico and $24.59 for manufacturing

Several U.S. and European companies have sensed opportunity in the estimated 300 million Chinese people learning English—and presumably many millions more who want to learn, given the chance. British publisher Pearson PLC and Sweden-based school operator English First SV have emphasized adult education, but Walt Disney Company sees a profitable niche market in teaching children.

Disney has opened a chain of Disney English schools in Shanghai and has drawn up plans to operate in Beijing. Managers insist that the mission of the schools is simply to teach English to Chinese children, but that mission requires books and worksheets, and they just happen to be populated with Buzz Lightyear, Ariel the Mermaid, and other characters from Disney's movies. Young students can earn rewards such as stickers and CDs featuring Disney characters and productions. Rather than being repelled by the marketing angle, Chinese parents see a chance for their children to learn from a company that is familiar and truly international.

For Disney, the schools offer an opportunity to connect with families in an environment that is otherwise politically tricky. While the Chinese government limits movie and television distribution of Disney productions, Disney English can offer students all the Disney-themed worksheets, backpacks, and toys they need to develop a lasting love for Mickey Mouse.[31]

• What threats and opportunities did Disney identify in China?

workers in the United States.[32] These low wage rates have led many managers to relocate operations to China or to import an increasing number and variety of Chinese products instead of continuing to do business with local manufacturers. This trend is one reason that the value of U.S. imports from China is more than five times the value of U.S exports to China.

This type of trade imbalance may well have contributed to the loss of manufacturing jobs in the United States and Europe. But it has also led to the continuing availability of comparatively low-priced goods, helping consumers everywhere and leading to overall economic and job growth at home. Yet jobs in certain industries, such as textiles, may have been transferred abroad permanently to lower-cost producers like China and India. Those affected workers and communities experience real hardships. We will be discussing the effects of *outsourcing* or *offshoring* in more detail later in this chapter.

Threats to China's growing dominance include political instability as the growing prosperity of its cities and industrial enclaves leaves millions of poor rural residents further behind. Also, countries that have experienced job loss may face growing pressure to restrict Chinese imports, particularly in the EU, with its strong labor unions. But for the foreseeable future, China's growing presence in the world economy, as an importer *and* exporter, is one that you as a manager will increasingly have to take into account.

Besides China, India has become an important player in the global marketplace. The nation is still developing, and its poverty is often severe, but its 1.2 billion people (the world's second-largest population), many of them entering the working and professional classes, make India

While still growing, India has become one of the most rapidly developed economies in the world. Many citizens within this populous country have entered or are entering the workforce. Like China, India's labor costs are low, making it a desirable location for outsourced jobs.

an essential market for more and more companies. For many U.S. companies, India is seen as a provider of online support for computer software, software development, and other services. In fact, so many companies have set up shop there that the demand for Indian workers with strong technical and English language skills is exceeding the supply. Companies such as Wipro and Tata Group are responding with expanded training programs.[33] Thanks to India's fast-growing economy and huge population, more U.S. businesses are beginning to see the country as a source of customers as well as workers. Citigroup, for example, has made plans to open more branches in India and expand service such as microfinance (small loans), as well as to add thousands more staff members there.[34]

Other rapidly growing countries in the region that have strong trade relationships with the United States include South Korea, Taiwan, and Singapore. These countries are important trading partners not merely because of their wage rates but because many of their companies have developed competitive advantages in areas such as engineering and technological know-how. South Korea's Samsung has the largest share of the world's markets for flat-screen televisions and flash memory cards, and Taiwan's Hon Hai is the leader in contract manufacturing of electronics. The reason you may not have heard of Hon Hai is that it specializes in making components for brand-name products of other companies, including Sony (PlayStations), Apple (iPods), and Dell (computers).[35]

These Asian countries and others have joined with the United States, Australia, and Russia to form the 21-member Asia-Pacific Economic Cooperation (APEC) trade group. Combined, APEC members' economies account for more than half of world output (GDP) and almost half of world trade.[36] In recent years the APEC countries have been working to establish policies that encourage international commerce and reduce trade barriers. APEC members address these objectives through dialogue and nonbinding commitments rather than treaties.

Another international organization, the Association of Southeast Asian Nations (ASEAN), brings together 10 developing nations, including Indonesia, Malaysia, and the Philippines. Along with economic development, ASEAN is aimed at promoting cultural development and political security.

The Americas

North and South America constitute a mix of industrialized countries, such as Canada and the United States, as well as countries with growing economies, such as Argentina, Brazil, Chile, and Mexico. The winter fruit you eat may come from Chile, the coffee you drink from Jamaica, and the shirt you wear from Honduras. Increasingly, businesses are looking to establish freer trade among countries in the Western Hemisphere—and with other parts of the world.

North American Free Trade Agreement (NAFTA)

An economic pact that combined the economies of the United States, Canada, and Mexico into one of the world's largest trading blocs.

The **North American Free Trade Agreement (NAFTA)** combined the economies of the United States, Canada, and Mexico into the world's largest trading bloc with nearly 450 million U.S., Canadian, and Mexican consumers and a total output of $17 trillion. By 2008 virtually all U.S. industrial exports into Mexico and Canada were duty-free. Although the United States has had a longer-standing agreement with Canada, Mexico has quickly emerged as the United States's third largest trading partner as a result of NAFTA. U.S. industries that have benefited in the short run include capital goods suppliers, manufacturers of consumer durables, grain producers and distributors, construction equipment manufacturers, the auto industry, and the financial industry, which now has privileged access into a previously protected market. Besides importing and exporting, companies in the NAFTA countries have invested in facilities across national borders. Mexico-based CEMEX, the world's third-largest cement company, is actually the largest cement supplier in the United States. Twenty-two percent of CEMEX's employees and 27 percent of its sales are in the United States, and it conducts management meetings in English because the majority of its employees do not speak Spanish.[37]

Even as most of the world was struggling to leave behind a severe recession in 2010, Brazil announced a stunning 9 percent growth rate for the first quarter of that year and almost kept up the pace for the following two quarters. Much of Brazil's economic activity is in the agricultural sector, including exports of soybeans and coffee. Other growth is coming from the energy sector, including the production of ethanol and potential leadership in wind power from harnessing its steady trade winds at wind farms built on land being auctioned by the government.[38] As in Asia, more South American companies are relying on innovation and technology rather than simply cost to compete in the global marketplace. For example, one reason that Argentina's Tenaris is the global leader in the market for oil pipes is that management of a predecessor company, Siderca, decided to focus on building a global network of facilities that could research customer needs, develop products, and deliver pipes just as needed by their customers. This focus gave Siderca, now part of Tenaris, a competitive advantage.[39]

Among the list of the greatest places to work in Mexico are several U.S.-based companies, including McDonald's, which ranked as the third best company in 2011.

Other agreements have been proposed to promote trade with Central and South America. In 2005 President George W. Bush signed into law U.S. participation in a Central America–Dominican Republic–United States Free Trade Agreement (CAFTA-DR). Other nations that have agreed to participate include Costa Rica, the Dominican Republic, El Salvador, Guatemala, Honduras, and Nicaragua. CAFTA-DR creates the second-largest free trade zone with the United States (NAFTA being the largest). As part of the negotiations for CAFTA-DR, Central American nations promised to protect workers' rights in their countries. Complaints that some countries have not delivered on this promise have led the U.S. government to request consultations with Guatemala on "apparent violations of its obligations."[40] Other trade agreements have been negotiated on a country-by-country basis with Chile and Peru, and President Obama's administration is trying to resolve labor issues so Congress will ratify agreements with Colombia and Panama. In addition, the countries of South America formed their own trading bloc, called Mercosur, to promote trade among nations of that continent.

The Rest of the World

We can't begin to fully discuss all the important developments, markets, and competitors shaping the global environment. These trends leave huge and promising areas of the world—the Middle East, parts of South America, and much of Africa—that have not yet participated as much in globalization. These regions account for a major share of the world's natural resources, and managers are watching the global environment, looking for areas with potential.

The economy of the Middle East is, of course, best known for its export of oil. While oil exploration and drilling take place in many parts of the world, the oil-rich countries of the Middle East supply by far the most oil to the world's buyers, most of it going to buyers in Asia. The Middle East is not, however, the largest supplier of oil to the United States, which imports oil primarily from closer sources: Canada, Mexico, and Venezuela. The main Middle Eastern supplier of U.S. oil imports is Saudi Arabia.[41] Nevertheless, U.S. businesses are concerned about the Middle East because activities there can shape the price of oil, which is important not only for transportation but also for the manufacture of many products, including fertilizer and plastic. Recently, for example, many Middle Eastern and North African governments have been shaken by public protests over corruption and limited economic and political opportunity; that instability has been blamed as one cause of a spike in oil prices.

Africa has long been seen only as a place of dire poverty. Indeed, the continent is still plagued by an epidemic of AIDS and many unstable political situations, including outright wars. The continent has, however, been enjoying overall economic growth at a pace exceeding that of Latin America or Central and Eastern Europe. That growth is led by strength in the economies of Algeria, Botswana, Egypt, Libya (until the recent civil war), Mauritius, Morocco, South Africa, and Tunisia. While part of the growth comes from the rising value of commodities, other evidence points to entrepreneurship as a primary factor.[42]

IN PRACTICE

Managers thinking about doing business in Nigeria will find an intense entrepreneurial spirit that persists despite governmental red tape. That combination of forces can sometimes create a perverse incentive to find ways around the rules. Managers have to establish specific and reasonable guidelines for behavior.

One manager who has found the challenge worthwhile is Chris Newsom, who left his home in South Africa to work in Lagos, Nigeria, where he is chief executive of Stanbic IBTC Bank Nigeria. The bank has 2,100 employees, with a team of managers who include Nigerians, South Africans, Zimbabweans, and Congolese with the right mix of functional skills and relationship skills. The Nigerian managers help the others learn the day-to-day realities of doing business in their country. Their insights helped the bank craft operating guidelines that are practical and appropriate to the culture.

Newsom's way of tapping into the Nigerian passion for entrepreneurship is to encourage innovation among managers and their employees. The bank rewards new ideas and takes a forgiving attitude toward the inevitable failures. At the same time, Newsom expects managers to monitor each person's conduct closely to ensure that no one puts the organization's reputation or assets at risk by straying from ethical norms.[43]

Global Strategy

One of the critical tasks an international manager faces is to identify the best strategy for competing in a global marketplace. To approach this issue, managers can plot a company's position on an integration–responsiveness grid, such as that shown in Figure 6.6. The vertical axis measures pressures for *global integration*, and the horizontal axis measures pressures for *local responsiveness*. Borrowing language from early in this chapter, we might say that much of the pressure for global integration comes from today's business world being flat, while the pressure for local responsiveness reflects the world's bumpiness.

Pressures for Global Integration

Managers may have several reasons to want or need a common global strategy, rather than one tailored to individual markets. These factors include the existence of universal needs, pressures to reduce costs, or the presence of competitors with a global strategy.

Universal needs create strong pressure for a global strategy. Universal needs exist when the tastes and preferences of consumers in different countries with regard to a product are similar. Products that serve universal needs require little adaptation across national markets; thus global integration is facilitated. This is the case in many industrial markets. For example, electronic products such as semiconductor chips meet universal needs. Certain basic foodstuffs (like

Universal needs create strong pressure for a global strategy.

GLOBAL

Views the world as a single market. Operations are controlled centrally from the corporate office.

TRANSNATIONAL

Specialized facilities permit local responsiveness. Complex coordination mechanisms provide global integration.

INTERNATIONAL

Uses existing capabilities to expand into foreign markets.

MULTINATIONAL

Several subsidiaries operating as stand-alone business units in multiple countries.

Pressures for global integration — High / Low
Low   High
Pressures for local responsiveness

SOURCES: C. A. Bartlett and S. Ghoshal, *Managing across Borders: The Transnational Solution* (Boston: Harvard Business School Press, 1991); and A. W. Harzing, "An Empirical Analysis and Extension of the Bartlett and Ghoshal Typology of Multinational Companies," *Journal of International Business Studies* 31, no. 1 (2000), pp. 101–20.

FIGURE 6.6
Organizational Models

colas) and appliances (like can openers) are also increasingly available and regarded in similar ways globally.

Competitive *pressures to reduce costs* may cause managers to seek to integrate manufacturing globally. Cost can be particularly important in industries in which price is the main competitive weapon and competition is intense (e.g., as with smartphones). It is also important if key international competitors are based in countries where labor and other operating costs are low. In these cases, products are more likely to be standardized and perhaps produced in a few locations to capture economies of scale.

The presence of competitors engaged in *global strategic coordination* is another factor that creates pressures for global integration. For example, a competitor that centrally coordinates the purchase of raw materials worldwide may achieve significant price reductions compared with firms that allow subsidiaries to handle purchases locally. Global competition can often create pressures to centralize in corporate headquarters certain decisions being made by different national subsidiaries. And once one multinational company adopts global strategic coordination, its competitors may be forced to do the same.

Pressures for Local Responsiveness

In some circumstances, managers need to make sure their companies can adapt to different needs in different locations. Strong pressures for local responsiveness emerge when *consumer tastes and preferences differ significantly* among countries. In such cases, products and/or marketing messages have to be customized. In the automobile industry, for example, U.S. consumers' demand for pickup trucks is strong in the South and West, where many families have a pickup truck as a second or third vehicle. In contrast, in Europe pickup trucks are viewed as utility vehicles and are purchased primarily by companies rather than by individuals. As a result, automakers must tailor their marketing messages to these differences in consumer demand.

Pressures for local responsiveness also emerge when there are *differences in traditional practices* among countries. For example, in Great Britain people drive on the left side of the road, creating a demand for right-hand-drive cars, whereas in neighboring France people drive on the right side of the road. Obviously automobiles must be customized to accommodate this difference in traditional practices.

Bottom Line
The need to lower costs is a key globalization driver.
What is one way in which a global strategy can help reduce costs?

"When you travel, remember that a foreign country is not designed to make you comfortable. It is designed to make its own people comfortable."

—Clifton Fadiman

Ignighter.com is an Internet start-up that surprised its founders by appealing to traditional practices far from its home base in New York City. Dan Osit, Kevin Owocki, and Adam Sachs created Ignighter.com as a dating site that would make dating "safer, less awkward, and more fun." Its distinction was the founders' assumption that dating would be more comfortable if the individuals met up with others in a group. Thus one customer coordinates a date by inviting a group of people to join him or her for an outing.

After a year, 50,000 people in the United States had registered for the service—not an embarrassing start, but also not enough for a viable business. It turned out that many people in the target group—singles in their twenties—were confused by the concept. But Osit studied user data and picked up on an unexpected trend: the site was generating a lot of traffic from Singapore, Malaysia, India, and South Korea. At first the founders brushed off that information as just a quirk.

The trend persisted, however, especially in India, where hundreds of users were signing up for Ignighter every day. After another year, the founders acknowledged that they had accidentally created a website for dating Indian-style. In many parts of India, young people are not supposed to be out with someone from the opposite sex; but from their exposure to Western media, the idea of dating appeals to them. Group outings meet their desire in a socially acceptable way. With that realization, Ignighter's founders laid plans to hire employees in India and let the U.S. website coast.[44]

- How might Ignighter's founders have better prepared for local responsiveness?

To re-create the delicate dynamic of its popular U.S. ads, Apple used local TV actors in England, shown here in the U.K. advertisement. They did the same with Japanese actors. Apple faced a difficult issue in bringing its series of ads to different countries since what is funny in one culture can seem ill-mannered in another.

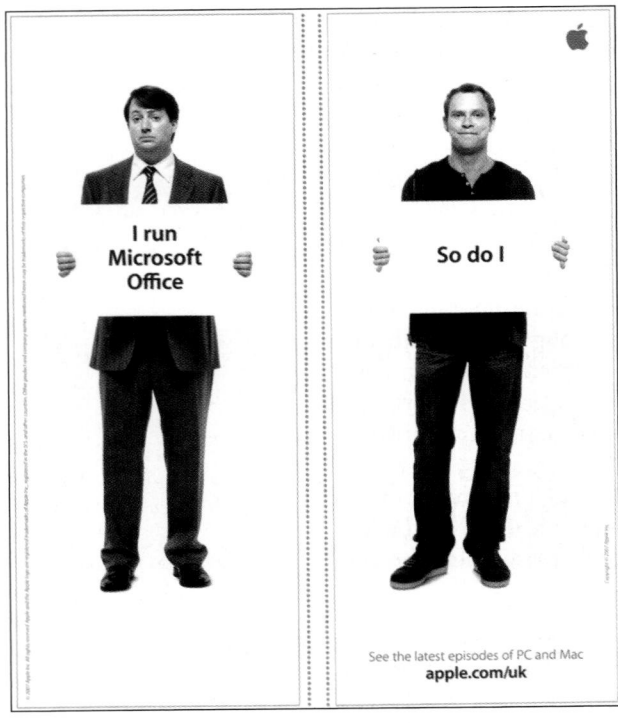

See the latest episodes of PC and Mac
apple.com/uk

Differences in distribution channels and sales practices among countries also may create pressures for local responsiveness. In India people are used to buying their groceries at small, local shops, creating challenges for Walmart as it develops plans to open supermarkets and larger stores in that country.[45] And cultural differences in selling have led Apple to adjust its "Mac vs. PC" advertising campaign in some countries. In Japan people think it's rude to make direct comparisons, so the comedians hired for the Japanese ads deemphasize differences in product features, instead distinguishing them more in terms of the work-oriented PC versus the Mac's appeal for leisure activities. In the United Kingdom, Apple's ad agency hired two British actors to portray the products in terms of the characters the actors play in a sitcom; the more sensible character represents PC, and the more fun-loving character represents Apple. Even with these adjustments, the ads generated some criticism. A poll found that respect for Apple actually declined after the ads started running in Britain, and in Japan the Mac character's casual attire generated some confusion. Instead of seeing the casually dressed character as a hip entrepreneur, some saw him as merely cheap or unsuccessful, wearing low-cost clothing.[46]

Finally, *economic and political demands* that host-country governments impose may necessitate a degree of local responsiveness. Most important, threats of protectionism, economic nationalism, and local content rules (rules requiring that a certain percentage of a product be manufactured locally) dictate that international companies manufacture locally. For example, countries may impose tariffs (taxes on imports) or quotas (restrictions on the number of imports allowed into a country) to protect domestic industries from foreign competition perceived to be unfair or not in the nation's interests. Recently the United States began imposing tariffs on paper imported from China. The U.S. government justi-fied the tariffs as a response to complaints that the Chinese companies were selling the paper below the cost of the raw materials, presumably because the Chinese gov-ernment was subsidizing the industry. Others interpret this and other protectionist actions as being motivated primarily by political objectives.[47] Whatever the reasons for them, tariffs and quotas influence managers' decisions about whether it is eco-nomically advantageous, or even possible, to operate locally or rely on exporting.

Choosing a Global Strategy

As Figure 6.6 shows, managers can use four approaches to international competition, depending on their company's position on the integration–responsiveness grid: the international model, the multinational model, the global model, and the transnational model. Organizations in each model compete globally, but they differ in the strategy they use and in the structure and systems that drive their operations.

The International Model   In the **international model,** managers use their organization's existing core capabilities to expand into foreign markets. As the grid suggests, it is most appropriate when there are few pressures for economies of scale *or* local responsiveness. Pfizer is an example of a company operating in the international model. It is in an industry that doesn't compete on cost, and its drugs obvi-ously don't need to be tailored for local tastes. The international model uses subsidiaries in each country in which the company does business, with ultimate control exercised by the parent company. In particular, while subsidiaries may have some latitude to adapt products to local conditions, core functions such as research and development tend to be centralized in the parent company. Consequently, the dependence of subsidiaries on the parent company for new products, processes, and ideas requires a great deal of coordination and control by the parent company.

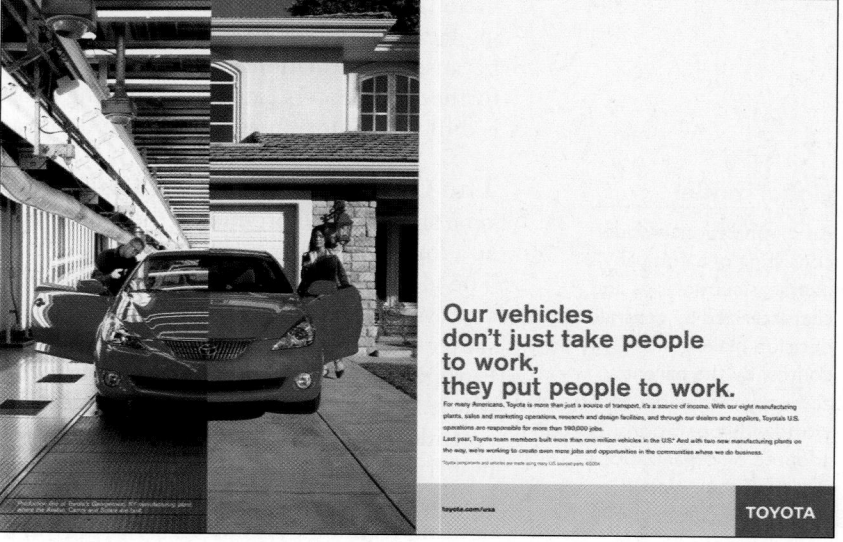

The advantage of this model is that it facilitates the transfer of skills and know-how from the parent company to subsidiar-ies around the globe. For example, IBM and Xerox profited from the transfer of their core skills in technology and research and development (R&D) overseas. The over-seas successes of Kellogg, Coca-Cola, Heinz, and Procter & Gamble are based more on marketing know-how than on technological expertise. Toyota and Honda suc-cessfully penetrated U.S. markets from their base in Japan with their core competen-cies in manufacturing relative to local competitors. Still other companies have based their competitive advantage on general management skills. These factors explain the growth of international hotel chains such as Hilton International, Intercontinental, and Sheraton.

One disadvantage of the international model is that it does not provide maximum latitude for responding to local conditions. In addition, it frequently does not provide the opportunity to achieve a low-cost position via scale economies.

The Multinational Model   Where global efficiency is not required but adapt-ing to local conditions offers advantages, the multinational model is appropriate. The

---

international model

An organizational model that is composed of a company's overseas subsidiaries and characterized by greater control by the parent company over the research function and local product and marketing strategies than is the case in the multinational model.

In this ad, Toyota counters the perception that foreign auto companies take jobs from Americans. The production line above is actually its Georgetown, KY, manufacturing plant. According to the organizational model in Figure 6.6, what type of company is Toyota?

Bottom Line

The international model helps spread quality and service standards globally. *Give an example of a product for which quality standards would apply globally.*

multinational model

An organizational model that consists of the subsidiaries in each country in which a company does business, and provides a great deal of discretion to those subsidiaries to respond to local conditions.

Bottom Line

The multinational model helps speed up local response.
What kind of product might experience rapid changes in local demand?

multinational model, sometimes referred to as *multidomestic,* uses subsidiaries in each country in which the company does business and provides a great deal of discretion to those subsidiaries to respond to local conditions. Each local subsidiary is a self-contained unit with all the functions required for operating in the host market. Thus each subsidiary has its own manufacturing, marketing, research, and human resources functions. Because of this autonomy, each multinational subsidiary can customize its products and strategies according to the tastes and preferences of local consumers; the competitive conditions; and political, legal, and social structures.

A good example of a multinational firm is Heineken, a Netherlands-based brewing company. Heineken has three major global brands—Heineken, Amstel, and Murphy's Stout—but it also offers regional and local brands. The company understands that every country is unique, with its own culture and business practices. So it attempts to adapt its products to local attitudes and tastes while maintaining its high quality. As a result, the company produces more than 170 different brands around the world, from its international brands to local and specialty brews. The localized portfolio includes such brands as Primus and Star in Africa, Vitamalt and Piton in the Caribbean, and Tiger in Asia. Individual countries have considerable autonomy in the beer that is brewed locally.[48]

A major disadvantage of the multinational form is higher manufacturing costs and duplication of effort. Although a multinational can transfer core skills among its international operations, it cannot realize scale economies from centralizing manufacturing facilities and offering a standardized product to the global marketplace. Moreover, because a multinational approach tends to decentralize strategy decisions (discussed further in Chapters 8 and 9), launching coordinated global attacks against competitors is difficult. This can be a significant disadvantage when competitors have this ability.

global model

An organizational model consisting of a company's overseas subsidiaries and characterized by centralized decision making and tight control by the parent company over most aspects of worldwide operations; typically adopted by organizations that base their global competitive strategy on cost considerations.

Bottom Line

The global model of standardization lowers cost.
Could this model apply to a jewelry company? If so, how? If not, why not?

The Global Model   The **global model** is designed to enable a company to market a standardized product in the global marketplace and to manufacture that product in a limited number of locations where the mix of costs and skills is most favorable. The global model has been adopted by companies that view the world as one market and assume that no tangible differences exist among countries with regard to consumer tastes and preferences. Procter & Gamble, for example, has been successful in Europe against Unilever because it has approached the entire continent as a unified whole. As part of its effort to improve efficiency while broadening its appeal, Ford recently launched a line of compact cars under the Ford Focus brand as the company's first truly global product. The Focus models include hybrid, plug-in hybrid, and electric cars, and promotional plans are built around a unified advertising campaign highlighting technology features.[49]

Companies that adopt the global model tend to construct global-scale manufacturing facilities in a few selected locations so they can realize scale economies. These scale economies come from spreading the fixed costs of investments in new product development, plants and equipment, and the like over worldwide sales. By using centralized manufacturing facilities and global marketing strategies, Sony was able to push down its unit costs to the point where it became the low-cost player in the global television market. This advantage enabled Sony to take market share away from Philips, RCA, and Zenith, all of which used traditionally based manufacturing operations in each major national market (a characteristic of the multinational approach). Because operations are centralized, subsidiaries usually are limited to marketing and service functions.

On the downside, because a company pursuing a purely global approach tries to standardize its goods and services, it may be less responsive to consumer tastes and demands in different countries. Attempts to lower costs through global product standardization may result in a product that fails to satisfy anyone. For example, while Procter & Gamble has been quite successful using a global approach, the company experienced problems when it tried to market Cheer laundry detergent in Japan.

Unfortunately for P&G, the product did not "suds up" as promoted in Japan because the Japanese use a great deal of fabric softener, which suppresses suds. Moreover, the claim that Cheer worked in all water temperatures was irrelevant in Japan, where most washing is done in cold water. The global model also requires a great deal of coordination, with significant additional management and paperwork costs.

> The transnational model enables managers to think globally but act locally.

The Transnational Model   In today's global economy, achieving a competitive advantage often requires managers to simultaneously pursue local responsiveness, transfer of know-how, and cost economies.[50] The transnational model is designed to help them do just that. It is an approach that enables managers to "think globally but act locally."

In companies that adopt the **transnational model,** functions are centralized where it makes sense to do so, but a great deal of decision making also takes place at the local level. In addition, the experiences of local subsidiaries are shared worldwide to improve the firm's overall knowledge and capabilities. For example, research, training, and the overall development of the organization's strategy and global brand image tend to be centralized at home. Other functions may be centralized as well, but not necessarily in the home country.

To achieve cost economies, companies may base global-scale production plants for labor-intensive products in low-wage countries such as Mexico, Poland, and China and locate production plants that require a skilled workforce in high-skill countries such as Germany and Japan. Increasingly, companies are able to find locations where the workforce includes the optimal balance of needed skills and relatively low costs. Thus, although wages have begun rising in India, the level of technical skill of its workforce has made that country an attractive place to locate many kinds of knowledge-based operations, such as loan approvals, legal research, and biotech R&D. These types of skilled occupations are growing faster in India than jobs in call centers, the work that once brought India to prominence as an offshoring location.[51]

Marketing, service, and final assembly functions tend to be based in the national subsidiaries to facilitate greater local responsiveness. Thus major components may be manufactured in centralized production plants to realize scale economies and then shipped to local plants, where the final product is assembled and customized to fit local needs.

Caterpillar, which manufactures construction and mining equipment, is a transnational company.[52] The need to compete with low-cost competitors such as Komatsu has forced Caterpillar to look for greater cost economies by centralizing global production at locations where the mix of costs and skills is most favorable. At the same time, variations in construction practices and government regulations across countries mean that Caterpillar must be responsive to local needs. On the integration–responsiveness grid in Figure 6.6, therefore, Caterpillar is situated toward the top right corner.

To deal with these simultaneous demands, Caterpillar has designed its products to use many identical components and has invested in a few large-scale component-manufacturing facilities to fill global demand and realize scale economies. But while the company manufactures components centrally, it has assembly plants in each of its major markets. At these plants Caterpillar adds local product features, tailoring the finished product to local needs. In addition, most of its dealerships, located in more than 200 countries, are locally owned. Thus Caterpillar can realize many of the benefits of global manufacturing while managing pressure for local responsiveness by differentiating its product among national markets.

Perhaps the most important distinguishing characteristic of the transnational organization is the fostering of communications among subsidiaries and the ability to integrate the efforts of subsidiaries when doing so makes sense. For example, when Caterpillar was developing certain medium-size engines, it enlisted the efforts of Caterpillar facilities in the United Kingdom, Mexico, Belgium, and several U.S. locations.

transnational model

An organizational model characterized by centralizing certain functions in locations that best achieve cost economies; basing other functions in the company's national subsidiaries to facilitate greater local responsiveness; and fostering communication among subsidiaries to permit transfer of technological expertise and skills.

Bottom Line

The transnational model tries to deliver on all bottom-line practices.
Does that mean the transnational model is always best? Why or why not?

Achieving such communications across subsidiaries requires elaborate formal mechanisms, such as transnational committees staffed by people from the various subsidiaries who are responsible for monitoring coordination among subsidiaries. Equally important is to transfer managers among subsidiaries on a regular basis. This enables international managers to establish a global network of personal contacts in different subsidiaries with whom they can share information as the need arises. Finally, achieving coordination among subsidiaries requires that the head office play a proactive role in coordinating their activities.

Now that you have seen examples of the need to balance global integration and local responsiveness, consider how those pressures apply to IKEA's situation as described in "Management Connection: Progress Report."

Manager's Brief   **Progress Report**   Onward

Management Connection

IKEA'S FAVORABLE ENVIRONMENT

IKEA's vision to "create a better everyday life for the many people" has been well received in 38 countries, with more planned for the future. Not every company is so well received in foreign markets, but IKEA meets widely shared needs and stands for widely shared values.

Some of these advantages arise from IKEA's origins in a small town in Sweden. IKEA's founder, Ingvar Kamprad, lived in southern Sweden, where poor soil contributed to a culture in which farmers expected to work hard and make do with less. Thriftiness and creative use of limited resources became prized qualities shared by Kamprad and his business. Along with this frugality came the application of Swedish style, building on influences such as cheery folk designs, functionalism, and the fresh look of natural textiles and light woods. The blend of styles is easily enjoyable and appealing to many. Furthermore, the Sweden of Kamprad's time was developing an egalitarian society—a quality that plays out in IKEA's commitment to affordability and its "partnership" with customers, who play a role in making the furniture by assembling the parts themselves. The Swedish influence of IKEA's heritage continues today, not only in the store's logo (using the colors of Sweden's flag), but in its leadership: all six members of its board of directors are Swedish.

The drive for continual cost reduction shapes decisions about the products offered, the prices charged, the materials and packaging used, and the transportation of merchandise to warehouses, stores, and customers' homes. Design is as important for packaging as for the products themselves. For example, in the case of a sofa model, IKEA designers figured out how to pack the parts more tightly into a smaller box. The savings on transportation and packaging materials enabled the company to cut the sofa's price by $135. While prices for food and energy have been on the rise, IKEA has been able to reduce prices 2 to 3 percent every year of the past decade.

The low-price strategy has been a key for weathering a global economic downturn in recent years. Even in the hardest-hit countries of Europe, IKEA has enjoyed sales growth during the past few years. Chief executive Mikael Ohlsson observes, "People still need furniture in the homes and our offer to consumers always wins in an economically tough climate." But cost-conscious shoppers are everywhere: Germany, which suffered less during the recession, provides the biggest share of IKEA customers (15 percent of sales). In the United States, the economic downturn brought more consumers to IKEA as families joined college students and recent graduates in looking for low-cost but appealing furniture.

The United States has become IKEA's second-largest market (after Germany). In response, the company has begun making furniture in the United States to save on transportation costs. The company opened its first U.S. factory in Danville, Virginia, in 2008. Part of the attraction of opening factories in the U.S. South is that compared with Sweden or Germany, this region offers less restrictive labor laws and lower wages.

Developing nations such as China and India present further opportunities. In fact, a decade ago, IKEA's management expected these to be the key areas of growth. They were surprised when economically stressed consumers in Europe brought an equal pace of sales growth in countries such as France and Spain. But the developing country market potential remains important, and IKEA's managers seem to be careful students of customers' needs in new markets. The company is waiting for legal restrictions on foreign retailers to ease so it can open stores in India. In China IKEA has strived even as Home

Depot initially stumbled. Because home ownership in China is a widespread but new phenomenon, Chinese home owners tend to have little experience in furnishing and maintaining a home. They didn't care for Home Depot's do-it-yourself ideas because it was relatively inexpensive to hire someone to do repairs or remodeling. At the same time, Chinese consumers are eager to learn ideas for furnishing a home, so they flocked to IKEA's stores, which feature model rooms showing ways to make homes functional and stylish. In fact, some Chinese consumers treat a visit to IKEA as a form of entertainment where they can get a firsthand look at how Westerners live.[53]

- Where in this example do you see pressures for global integration? Where do you see pressures for local responsiveness?
- Which global strategy (international, multinational, global, or transnational) do you think is most appropriate for IKEA? Why?

Entry Mode

When considering global expansion, international managers must decide on the best means of entering an overseas market. The five basic ways to expand overseas are exporting, licensing, franchising, entering into a joint venture with a host-country company, and setting up a wholly owned subsidiary in the host country.[54] Table 6.2 compares the entry modes.

LO 4

Exporting

Most manufacturing companies begin global expansion as exporters and later switch to one of the other modes for serving an overseas market. The advantages of exporting are that it (1) provides scale economies by avoiding the costs of manufacturing in other countries and (2) is consistent with a pure global strategy. By manufacturing the product in a centralized location and then exporting it to other national markets, the company may be able to realize substantial scale economies from its global sales volume.

TABLE 6.2   Comparison of Entry Modes

Exporting	Licensing	Franchising	Joint Venture	Wholly Owned Subsidiary
Advantages				
Scale economies	Lower development costs	Lower development costs	Local knowledge	Maintains control over technology
Consistent with pure global strategy	Lower political risk	Lower political risk	Shared costs and risk	Maintains control over operations
			May be the only option	
Disadvantages				
No low-cost sites	Loss of control over technology	Loss of control over quality	Loss of control over technology	High cost
High transportation costs			Conflict between partners	High risk
Tariff barriers				

IN PRACTICE

Television networks have long exported popular U.S. television programs such as *Dallas* and *Friends* to Europe, where they have become hits again. In the old days, Europeans had to wait many months for episodes of their favorite programs. But today studios such as Buena Vista International (the sales division of Disney's ABC network) and British Sky Broadcasting Group have teamed up to get the hits across the ocean within a matter of days. This speed of delivery is an important step as networks scramble to nab their share of the $110 billion overseas television market, which is fast falling prey to online pirating. The movie industry meets a similar challenge by opening new releases worldwide. For example, Disney's fourth movie in the *Pirates of the Caribbean* series opened in 70 countries. Although it disappointed expectations in the United States, its $346.4 million global take on opening weekend placed it among the top five worldwide.

Still, exporting is not a simple task. Although foreign TV companies have already paid more than $500 million for reruns of NBC's *Law & Order* (with subtitles), the network is closing in on the preference of foreign audiences for shows that reflect their own culture. So instead of just translating scripts, writers are now adapting certain scenes to reflect France's Napoleonic legal code and changing the set to look like a Paris police station with the Eiffel Tower in the background. The series will even have a new name: *Paris Enquêtes Criminelles*. This kind of adapting and exporting flows in the other direction too as U.S. TV networks have aired U.S. versions of *The Office* and *American Idol*, concepts imported from Britain (where the latter show originated as *Pop Idol*).[55]

- What primary advantage of exporting was lost when NBC adapted *Law & Order* for a French audience?

However, exporting has a number of drawbacks. First, exporting from the company's home base may be inappropriate if other countries offer lower-cost locations for manufacturing the product. An alternative is to manufacture in a location where the mix of factor costs and skills is most favorable and then export from that location to other markets to achieve scale economies. Several U.S. electronics companies have moved some manufacturing operations to parts of Asia where low-cost, high-skill labor is available, and export from that location to other countries, including the United States.

A second drawback of exporting is that high transportation costs can make it uneconomical, particularly in the case of bulk products. Chemical companies get around this by manufacturing their products on a regional basis, serving several countries in a region from one facility.

A third drawback is that host countries can impose (or threaten to impose) tariff barriers. Trade arrangements described earlier, including the World Trade Organization, NAFTA, and APEC, work to minimize this risk. However, tariffs continue to affect trade between particular countries in various industries. Examples include U.S.-imposed tariffs on sugar imported from Mexico and, as mentioned earlier, paper imported from China. Dell has lobbied the Indian government to reduce tariffs on computers exported to that country, where they can increase a computer's price by one-third. In the meantime, the company has decided to manufacture in India rather than relying on exports.[56]

Licensing

International licensing is an arrangement by which a licensee in another country buys the rights to manufacture a company's product in its own country for a negotiated fee (typically royalty payments on the number of units sold). The licensee then puts up most of the capital necessary to get the overseas operation going. The advantage of licensing is that the company need not bear the costs and risks of opening up an overseas market.

However, a problem arises when a company licenses its technological expertise to overseas companies. Technological know-how is the basis of the competitive advantage of many multinational companies. But RCA Corporation lost control over its color TV technology by licensing it to a number of Japanese companies. The Japanese companies quickly assimilated RCA's technology and then used it to enter the U.S. market, eventually gaining a bigger share of the U.S. market than RCA held.

Franchising

In many respects, franchising is similar to licensing. However, whereas licensing is a strategy pursued primarily by manufacturing companies, franchising is used primarily by service companies. McDonald's, Hilton International, and many other companies have expanded overseas by franchising. Pretzel maker Auntie Anne's has expanded through franchising in the Asia-Pacific region, where its sales are growing at 30 percent a year, far more quickly than in the United States.[57]

In six years Cold Stone Creamery has expanded its franchises into 17 countries outside of the United States, including South Korea, shown here.

In franchising, the company sells limited rights to use its brand name to franchisees in return for a lump-sum payment and a share of the franchisee's profits. However, unlike most licensing agreements, the franchisee has to agree to abide by strict rules regarding how it does business. Thus, when McDonald's enters into a franchising agreement with an overseas company, it expects the franchisee to run its restaurants in a manner identical to that used under the McDonald's name elsewhere in the world.

The advantages of franchising as an entry mode are similar to those of licensing. The franchisees put up capital and assume most of the business risk. However, local laws can limit this advantage. Until recently, China required that franchisors had to operate at least two company-owned outlets in that country profitably for at least a year before they would be allowed to offer franchises to Chinese entrepreneurs. Relaxation of that requirement made franchising in China's high-growth market far more attractive to businesses like Ruby Tuesday, all of whose restaurants are operated by franchisees with knowledge of their local markets.[58]

The most significant disadvantage of franchising concerns quality control. The company's brand name guarantees consistency in the company's product. Thus a business traveler booking into a Hilton International hotel in Hong Kong can reasonably expect the same quality of room, food, and service that he or she would receive in New York. But if overseas franchisees are less concerned about quality than they should be, the impact can go beyond lost sales in the local market to a decline in the company's reputation worldwide. If a business traveler has an unpleasant experience at the Hilton in Hong Kong, she or he may decide never to go to another Hilton hotel—and urge colleagues to do likewise. To make matters worse, the geographic distance between the franchisor and its overseas franchisees makes poor quality difficult to detect.

Joint Ventures

Establishing a joint venture (a formal business agreement discussed in more detail in Chapter 17) with a company in another country has long been a popular means of entering a new market. Joint ventures benefit a company through (1) the local partner's

> **Bottom Line**
> Franchising is one way to maintain standards globally.
> *Why does quality control pose a risk in franchising?*

knowledge of the host country's competitive conditions, culture, language, political systems, and business systems and (2) the sharing of development costs and/or risks with the local partner. Hershey recently announced a joint venture with India's Godrej Beverages and Foods as a way to achieve growth in an industry that has matured in the United States. Hershey will own a 51 percent share of the joint business, which combines Hershey's brands and recipes with Godrej's manufacturing facilities and distribution network. The venture will start by selling Hershey's Syrup in India and later add other products.[59] In addition, many countries' political considerations make joint ventures the only feasible entry mode. Before China opened its borders to trade, many U.S. companies, including Eastman Kodak, AT&T, Ford, and GM, did business in the country via joint ventures.

But as attractive as they sound, joint ventures have their problems. First, as in the case of licensing, a company runs the risk of losing control over its technology to its venture partner. For example, Japan's Kawasaki Heavy Industries and Germany's Siemens entered into joint ventures with Chinese partners to build China's high-speed rail network, but now those Chinese companies are using some of the technology they learned from the venture to compete with Kawasaki and Siemens for contracts elsewhere.[60] Second, companies may find themselves at odds with one another. For example, one joint venture partner may want to move production to a country where demand is growing, while the other would prefer to keep its factories at home running at full capacity. Conflict over who controls what within a joint venture is a primary reason why many fail.[61] In fact, many of the early joint ventures American and European companies entered into with companies in China lost money or failed precisely because of conflicts over control. To offset these disadvantages, experienced managers strive to iron out technology, control, and other potential conflicts up front, when they first negotiate the joint venture agreement.

Wholly Owned Subsidiaries

Establishing a wholly owned subsidiary—that is, an independent company owned by the parent corporation—is the most costly method of serving an overseas market. Companies that use this approach must bear the full costs and risks associated with setting up overseas operations (as opposed to joint ventures, in which the costs and risks are shared, or licensing, in which the licensee bears most of the costs and risks).

Nevertheless, setting up a wholly owned subsidiary offers two clear advantages. First, when a company's competitive advantage is based on technology, a wholly owned subsidiary normally is the preferred entry mode because it reduces the risk of losing control over the technology. Wholly owned subsidiaries are thus the preferred mode of entry in the semiconductor, electronics, and pharmaceutical industries. However, this advantage is limited by the extent to which the Chinese government will protect intellectual property such as patents and trademarks. Seven years after SI Group, a U.S. chemical company, began making rubber-bonding resins in China for the local tire industry, a competitor hired away SI Group's plant manager and began making a product that was virtually identical. Both sides aggressively defended their actions in the ensuing court battle. In the past, U.S. companies tended to lose such battles, but U.S. Commerce Secretary Gary Locke recently said the situation has been improving.[62]

Second, a wholly owned subsidiary gives a company tight control over operations in other countries, which is necessary if the company chooses to pursue a global strategy. Establishing a global manufacturing system requires world headquarters to have a high degree of control over the operations of national affiliates. Unlike licensees or joint venture partners, wholly owned subsidiaries usually accept centrally determined decisions about how to produce, how much to produce, and how to price output for transfer among operations.

Managing across Borders

When establishing operations overseas, headquarters executives have a choice among sending **expatriates** (individuals from the parent country), using **host-country nationals** (natives of the host country), and deploying **third-country nationals** (natives of a country other than the home country or the host country). While most corporations use some combination of all three types of employees, there are advantages and disadvantages for each. Colgate-Palmolive and Procter & Gamble, for example, use expatriates to get their products to market abroad more quickly. AT&T and Toyota have used expatriates to transfer their corporate cultures and best practices to other countries—in Toyota's case, to its U.S. plants.

Because sending employees abroad can cost three to four times as much as employing host-country nationals, other companies, including Texas Instruments, have made more limited use of expatriates. Moreover, in many countries—particularly developing countries in which firms are trying to get an economic foothold—the personal security of expatriates is an issue. As a result, more firms may send their expatriates on shorter assignments and engage in telecommuting, teleconferencing, and other electronic means to facilitate communications between their international divisions. In fact, working internationally can be very stressful, even for experienced "globalites." Table 6.3 shows some of the primary stressors for expatriates at different stages of their assignments. It also shows ways for executives to cope with the stress, as well as some of the things companies can do to help with the adjustment.

Although developing a valuable pool of expatriates is important, local employees are more available, tend to be familiar with the culture and language, and usually cost less because they do not have to be relocated. In addition, local governments often provide incentives to companies that create good jobs for their citizens, or they may place restrictions on the use of expatriates. Such advantages, coupled with the often-inadequate educational systems of developing nations, combine to create stiff competition for local management talent. The result is that China, India, and Latin America do not have enough qualified talent to fill the demand for local executives.

> Most of the growth in IBM's workforce is occurring in India, where employees handle software development, services, and customer support. IBM has more employees in India than in any other country outside the United States.[63]

For example, in China, recruiting firm Russell Reynolds finds that local managers offer technical skills but often lack conceptual skills and a strategic perspective. Motorola Mobility meets the challenge in mainland China with a mix of executives—about one-third from mainland China, one-third from other Asian countries, and one-third from the West.[64]

Skills of the Global Manager

It is estimated that nearly 15 percent of all employee transfers are to an international location. However, the **failure rate** among expatriates (defined as those who come home early) ranges from an estimated 20 percent to 70 percent, depending on the country of assignment. The cost of each of these failed assignments ranges from tens of thousands to hundreds of thousands of dollars.[65] Typically the causes for failure overseas extend beyond technical capability and include personal and social issues. In a recent survey of human resource managers around the globe, two-thirds said the main reason for the failures is family issues, especially dissatisfaction of the employee's spouse or partner.[66] The problem may be compounded in this era of dual-career couples, in which one spouse may have to give up his or her job to accompany the expatriate manager to the new location. To ensure that an overseas posting will succeed, managers can encourage an employee to talk to her or his spouse about what he or she

LO 5

expatriates

Parent-company nationals who are sent to work at a foreign subsidiary.

host-country nationals

Natives of the country where an overseas subsidiary is located.

third-country nationals

Natives of a country other than the home country or the host country of an overseas subsidiary.

Bottom Line

Expatriate hiring increases cost; training raises quality.

How might training an expatriate manager differ from training a local manager?

It is estimated that nearly 15 percent of all employee transfers are to an international location.

LO 6

failure rate

The number of expatriate managers of an overseas operation who come home early.

TABLE 6.3   Stressors and Coping Responses in the Developmental Stages of Expatriate Executives

Stage	Primary Stressors	Executive Coping Response	Employer Coping Response
Expatriate selection	Cross-cultural unreadiness.	Engage in self-evaluation.	Encourage expatriate's self- and family evaluation. Perform an assessment of potential and interests.
Assignment acceptance	Unrealistic evaluation of stressors to come. Hurried time frame.	Think of assignment as a growth opportunity rather than an instrument to vertical promotion.	Do not make hard-to-keep promises. Clarify expectations.
Pre- and postarrival	Ignorance of cultural differences.	Do not make unwarranted assumptions of cultural competence and cultural rules.	Provide pre-, during-, and postassignment training. Encourage support-seeking behavior.
Arrival	Cultural shock. Stressor reevaluation. Feelings of lack of fit and differential treatment.	Do not construe identification with the host and parent cultures as mutually exclusive. Seek social support.	Provide postarrival training. Facilitate integration in expatriate network.
Novice	Cultural blunders or inadequacy of coping responses. Ambiguity owing to inability to decipher meaning of situations.	Observe and study functional value of coping responses among locals. Do not simply replicate responses that worked at home.	Provide follow-up training. Seek advice from locals and expatriate network.
Transitional	Rejection of host or parent culture.	Form and maintain attachments with both cultures.	Promote culturally sensitive policies in host country. Provide Internet access to family and friends at home. Maintain constant communication and periodic visits to parent organization.
Mastery	Frustration with inability to perform boundary-spanning role. Bothered by living with a cultural paradox.	Internalize and enjoy identification with both cultures and walking between two cultures.	Reinforce rather than punish dual identification by defining common goals.
Repatriation	Disappointment with unfulfilled expectations. Sense of isolation. Loss of autonomy.	Realistically reevaluate assignment as a personal and professional growth opportunity.	Arrange prerepatriation briefings and interviews. Schedule postrepatriation support meetings.

SOURCE: From *Academy of Management Executive,* J. Sanchez, P. Spector, and C. Cooper, May 2000, pp. 96–106. Copyright © 2000. Reproduced with permission of Academy of Management via Copyright Clearance Center.

will do in the foreign country. For both the expatriate and the spouse, adjustment requires flexibility, emotional stability, empathy for the culture, communication skills, resourcefulness, initiative, and diplomatic skills.[67] When Kent Millington took the position of vice president of Asia operations for an Internet hosting company, his wife Linda quit her job to move with him to Japan. Especially for Linda Millington, the first three months were difficult because she didn't speak Japanese, found the transit system confusing, and even struggled to buy food because she couldn't translate the labels. But she persevered and participated in classes and volunteer activities. Eventually she and her husband learned to enjoy the experience and appreciated the chance to see just how well they could tackle a challenge.[68]

Companies such as Levi Strauss, Bechtel, Monsanto, Whirlpool, and Dow Chemical have worked to identify the characteristics of individuals that will predict their success abroad. Table 6.4 shows skills that can be used to identify candidates who are likely to succeed in a global environment. Interestingly, in addition to such characteristics as cultural sensitivity, technical expertise, and business knowledge, an individual's success abroad may depend greatly on his or her ability to learn from experience.[69]

> "If there is any great secret of success in life, it lies in the ability to put yourself in the other person's place and to see things from his point of view as well as your own."
>
> —Henry Ford

Companies such as BPAmocos, Global Hyatt, and others with large international staffs have extensive training programs to prepare employees for international assignments. Table 6.5 suggests ways to improve their likelihood of success. Other organizations, such as Coca-Cola, Motorola, Chevron, and Mattel, have extended this training to include employees who may be located in the United States but who also deal in international markets. These programs focus on areas such as language, culture, and career development.

Managers who are sent on an overseas assignment usually wonder about the effect such an assignment will have on their careers. Certainly their selection for a post overseas is usually an indication that they are being groomed to become more effective managers in an era of globalization. In addition, they will often have more responsibility, challenge, and operating leeway than they might have at home. Yet they may be concerned that they will soon be "out of the loop" on key developments back home. Good companies and managers address that issue with effective communication between subsidiaries and headquarters and by a program of visitations to and from the home office. Communication technology now makes it easy for expatriates to keep in

TABLE 6.4   **Identifying International Executives**

End-State Dimensions	Sample Items
1. Sensitivity to cultural differences	When working with people from other cultures, works hard to understand their perspective.
2. Business knowledge.	Has a solid understanding of the company's products and services.
3. Courage to take a stand.	Is willing to take a stand on issues.
4. Brings out the best in people.	Has a special talent for dealing with people.
5. Acts with integrity.	Can be depended on to tell the truth regardless of circumstances.
6. Is insightful.	Is good at identifying the most important part of a complex problem.
7. Is committed to success.	Clearly demonstrates commitment to seeing the organization succeed.
8. Takes risks.	Takes personal as well as business risks.
Learning-Oriented Dimensions	**Sample Items**
1. Uses feedback.	Has changed as a result of feedback.
2. Is culturally adventurous.	Enjoys the challenge of working in countries other than his or her own.
3. Seeks opportunities to learn.	Takes advantage of opportunities to do new things.
4. Is open to criticism.	Does not appear brittle—as if criticism might cause him or her to break.
5. Seeks feedback.	Pursues feedback even when others are reluctant to give it.
6. Is flexible.	Doesn't get so invested in things that he or she cannot change when something doesn't work.

SOURCE: Copyright © 1997 by the American Psychological Association. G. M. Spreitzer, M. W. McCall, and J. D. Mahoney, "Early Identification of International Executive Potential," *Journal of Applied Psychology* 82, no. 1 (1997), pp. 6–29.

TABLE 6.5   How to Prevent Failed Global Assignments

- Structure assignments clearly: develop clear reporting relationships and job responsibilities.
- Create clear job objectives.
- Develop performance measurements based on objectives.
- Use effective, validated selection and screening criteria (both personal and technical attributes).
- Prepare expatriates and families for assignments (briefings, training, support).
- Create a vehicle for ongoing communication with expatriates.
- Anticipate repatriation to facilitate reentry when they come back home.
- Consider developing a mentor program that will help monitor and intervene in case of trouble.

touch with colleagues in their home country on a daily or even more frequent basis, through e-mail and phone calls. Alan Paul, an American journalist working in China, says Internet phone service, a webcam, and podcasts of favorite radio programs also enable him to stay in touch with family and friends back home, even to the extent that he has to work hard to have "a fully engaged existence in China."[70]

Understanding Cultural Issues

LO 7

ethnocentrism

The tendency to judge others by the standards of one's group or culture, which are seen as superior.

In this era where people from all over the globe are collaborating on business issues, it is important to continue learning about and respecting different cultures in order to succeed.

In many ways, cultural issues represent the most elusive aspect of international business. In an era when modern transportation and communication technologies have created a "global village," it is easy to forget how deep and enduring the differences among nations can be. The fact that people everywhere drink Coke, wear blue jeans, and drive Toyotas doesn't mean we are all becoming alike. Each country is unique for reasons rooted in history, culture, language, geography, social conditions, race, and religion. These differences complicate any international activity and represent the fundamental issues that inform and guide how a company should conduct business across borders. For example, while working in Hong Kong, Geoffrey Fowler discovered that his coworkers there choose topics for small talk—people's weight, salary, and the size of their apartment—that would horrify Americans. At the same time, Chinese workers are put off by the American custom of combining lunch with a business meeting, meaning junior employees are chewing away while a superior in the company is talking.[71]

Ironically, while most of us would guess that the trick to working abroad is learning about a foreign culture, in reality our problems often stem from our being oblivious to our own cultural conditioning. Most of us pay no attention to how culture influences our everyday behavior, and because of this, we tend to adapt poorly to situations that are unique or foreign to us. Without realizing it, some managers may even act out of **ethnocentrism**— a tendency to judge foreign people or groups by the standards of one's own culture or group, and to see one's own standards as superior. Such tendencies may be totally unconscious— for example, the assumption that "in England they drive on the *wrong* side of the road," rather than merely on the left. Or they may reflect a lack of awareness of the values underlying a local culture—for example, an assumption that the culture is backward because it does not air American or European television programming, when it is actually focused on maintaining its traditional values and norms.

Assumptions such as these are one reason why people traveling abroad frequently experience **culture shock**—the disorientation and stress associated with being in a foreign environment. Managers are better able to navigate this transition if they are sensitive to their surroundings, including social norms and customs, and readily able to adjust their behavior to such circumstances.[72] Employers can help by identifying some of the cultural norms to expect and by establishing performance measures for behaviors that contribute to success in the host country (for example, the types of communication and direction employees will expect from their manager).

A wealth of cross-cultural research has been conducted on the differences and similarities among various countries. Geert Hofstede, for example, has identified four dimensions along which managers in multinational corporations tend to view cultural differences:

> *Power distance:* the extent to which a society accepts the fact that power in organizations is distributed unequally.
> *Individualism/collectivism:* the extent to which people act on their own or as a part of a group.
> *Uncertainty avoidance:* the extent to which people in a society feel threatened by uncertain and ambiguous situations.
> *Masculinity/femininity:* the extent to which a society values quantity of life (e.g., accomplishment, money) over quality of life (e.g., compassion, beauty).

Figure 6.7 offers a graphic depiction of how 40 different nations differ on the dimensions of individualism/collectivism and power distance. Of course this depiction exaggerates the differences between national traits to some extent. Many Americans prefer to act as part of a group, just as many Taiwanese prefer to act individualistically. And globalization may have already begun to blur some of these distinctions. Still, to suggest no cultural differences exist is equally simplistic. Clearly, cultures such as the United States, which emphasize "rugged individualism," differ significantly from collectivistic cultures such as those of Pakistan, Taiwan, and Colombia. To be effective in cultures that exhibit a greater power distance, managers often must behave more autocratically, perhaps being less participative in decision making. Conversely, in Scandinavian cultures such as Sweden's, for instance, where power distance is low, the very idea that management would make decisions on its own may be questioned. Here managers tend to work more toward creating processes that reflect an "industrial democracy."

culture shock

The disorientation and stress associated with being in a foreign environment.

IN PRACTICE

In starting an insurance company in the United Arab Emirates, Texas native Michael Weinberg has learned a lot about that country's business culture. One surprise was the Arabs' far looser sense of time. On an early visit, Weinberg was doubtful when his partners—both Lebanese American and more familiar with the culture—assured him that showing up a few hours late for an appointment would be fine. As it turned out, their hosts were unruffled by their late arrival.

Traditionally, in Arabic culture, people's activities fit around the appointed times for prayer (related to the sun's position) and the climate's cycles of heating and cooling. In addition, participants in a meeting are focused more on the relationships being built than on the next event on their calendar, so appointments often run longer than scheduled. These cultural norms result in a fluid understanding of time.

Still, visitors must be conscientious. They have to take into account the status of their host; a higher-status person expects visitors to be available, even if that means a wait. Weinberg has learned to use waiting time as a chance to catch up on his e-mail. He also calls ahead to confirm meeting times and to notify his host if he'll be late. Also, the office of a company headquartered elsewhere typically follows the customs of its headquarters. Thus a German company in the UAE will be run with the precision of a German company anywhere else.

Acknowledging the challenges of learning a culture, Weinberg has also experienced the joys, noting the "hospitality, warmth, love, education, and charity" valued by the Arab people he has met.[73]

- How would Weinberg's experience have differed if he had expected his Arab clients to adapt to U.S. business culture instead?

FIGURE 6.7
Positions of 40 Countries on the Power Distance and Individualism Scales

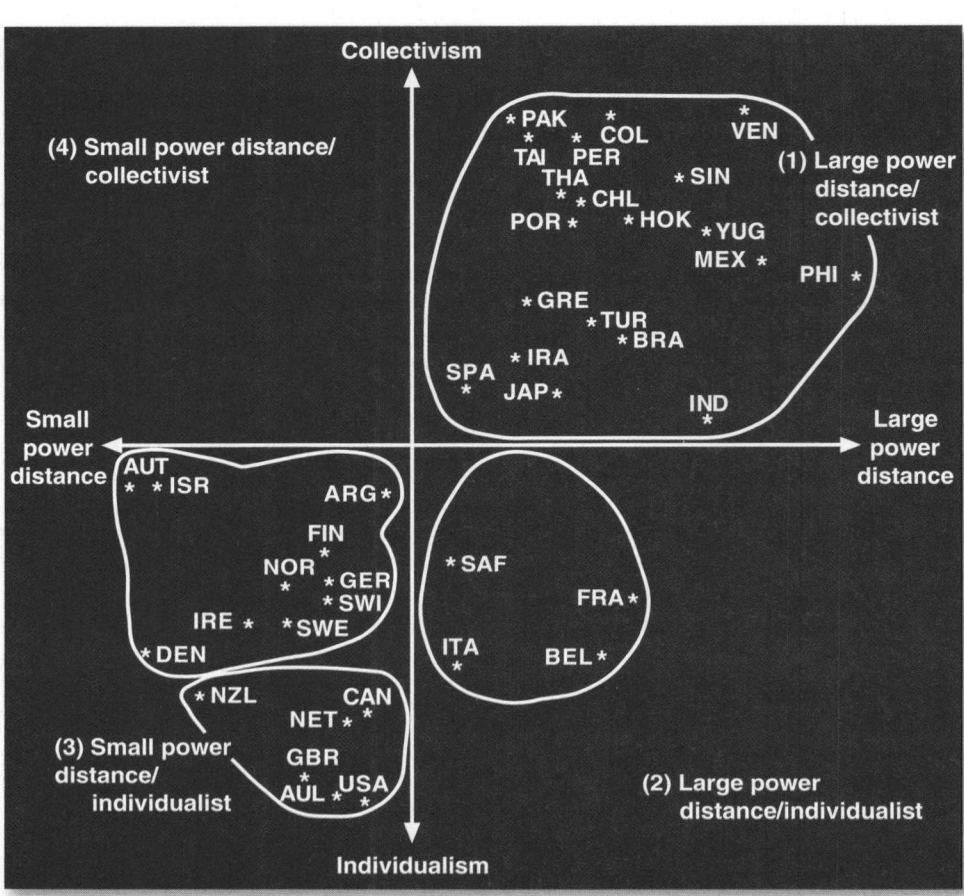

The 40 Countries
(showing abbreviations used above)

ARG Argentina	FRA France	JAP Japan	SIN Singapore
AUL Australia	GBR Great Britain	MEX Mexico	SPA Spain
AUT Austria	GER Germany (West)	NET Netherlands	SWE Sweden
BEL Belgium	GRE Greece	NOR Norway	SWI Switzerland
BRA Brazil	HOK Hong Kong	NZL New Zealand	TAI Taiwan
CAN Canada	IND India	PAK Pakistan	THA Thailand
CHL Chile	IRA Iran	PER Peru	TUR Turkey
COL Colombia	IRE Ireland	PHI Philippines	USA United States
DEN Denmark	ISR Israel	POR Portugal	VEN Venezuela
FIN Finland	ITA Italy	SAF SouthAfrica	YUG Yugoslavia

SOURCE: G. Hofstede, "Motivation, Leadership, and Organization: Do American Theories Apply Abroad?" *Organizational Dynamics* 9, no. 1 (Summer 1980), pp. 42–63. Reprinted by permission.

Cross-cultural management extends beyond U.S. employees going abroad. It also includes effective management of **inpatriates**—foreign nationals who are brought in to work at the parent company. These employees provide a valuable service to global companies because they bring extensive knowledge about how to operate effectively in their home countries. They will also be better prepared to communicate their organization's products and values when they return. But they often have the same types of problems as expatriates and may be even more neglected because parent–company managers either are more focused on their expatriate program or unconsciously see the home country as normal—requiring no period of adjustment. Yet the language, customs, expense, and lack of local community support in the United States are at least as daunting to inpatriates as the experience of American nationals abroad. Culture shock works both ways.

inpatriate

A foreign national brought in to work at the parent company.

Effective managers are sensitive to these issues and take them into account in dealing with foreign-national employees. In contrast to American-born employees, coworkers or customers from other countries might tend to communicate less directly, place more emphasis on hierarchy and authority, or make decisions more slowly. For example, an American manager working in Japan sent an e-mail to her American supervisor and Japanese colleagues in which she pointed out flaws in the process they were working on. The supervisor appreciated the alert, but her colleagues were embarrassed by behavior they considered rude; she should have inquired indirectly—say, by wondering what might happen if such a problem did exist. In another situation, a manager from Mexico showed respect for authority by phrasing ideas as questions when he was in a meeting with superiors. Instead of seeing him as appropriately humble, his American colleagues concluded that he was indecisive. In general, managers of international groups can manage these types of misunderstandings by acknowledging cultural differences frankly and finding ways to work around them by modifying the group (e.g., assigning tasks to subgroups), by setting rules to correct problems that are upsetting group members, or by removing group members who demonstrate they cannot work effectively within a particular situation.[74]

In addition, when working in the United States, foreign nationals will encounter a number of work-related differences. Alert managers help their employees adjust. A few basic categories include the following:

Meetings: Americans tend to have specific views about the purpose of meetings and how much time can be spent. International workers may have different preconceptions about the nature and length of meetings, and managers should make sure foreign nationals are comfortable with the American approach.

Work(aholic) schedules: Workers from other countries can work long hours but, in countries with strong labor organizations, often get many more weeks of vacation than American workers. And Europeans in particular may balk at working on weekends. Obviously matters such as these are most helpfully raised and addressed at the beginning of the work assignment.

E-mail: Parts of the world have not yet embraced e-mail and voice mail the way U.S. workers have. Often others prefer to communicate face to face. Particularly when potential language difficulties exist, at the outset managers will probably want to avoid using e-mail for important matters.

Fast-trackers: Although U.S. companies may take a young MBA graduate and put him or her on the fast track to management, most other cultures still see no substitute for the wisdom gained through experience. (This is something U.S. managers working abroad will also want to keep in mind.) More experienced managers are often a better choice for mentoring inpatriates.

Feedback: Everyone likes praise, but the use of excessive positive feedback tends to be less prevalent in other cultures than in the United States—a useful fact for managers when they give foreign nationals their performance reviews.[75]

Ethical Issues in International Management

If managers are to function effectively in a foreign setting, they must understand how culture influences both how they are perceived and how others behave. One of the most sensitive issues in this regard is how culture plays out in terms of ethical behavior.[76] Issues of right and wrong get blurred as we move from one culture to another, and actions that may be normal and customary in one setting may be unethical—even illegal—in another. The use of bribes, for example, is perceived to be an accepted part of commercial transactions in many Asian, African, Latin American, and Middle Eastern cultures; and even in cultures that view bribery as a form of corruption, some companies offer bribes when they think that it is part of the culture.[77]

In the United States, of course, such behavior is illegal, but what should a U.S. businessperson do when working abroad? Failure to "sweeten" the deal with bribes can result in lost business. Although the Foreign Corrupt Practices Act of 1977 prohibits U.S. employees from bribing foreign officials, one study published in the United States found that fewer than half of U.S. managers said bribes were unacceptable, and 20 percent actually said they were always acceptable. (Small business gifts or "grease payments" to lower-level officials are permissible under the act if the dollar amount of the payments would not influence the outcome of the negotiations.) Internationally, countries of the Organization for Economic Cooperation and Development, including the United States, have also prohibited bribes since 1977.[78] Companies that conduct business in Britain are also subject to that country's Bribery Act, which prohibits not only bribes of foreign officials but also bribes between businesspeople.[79] That sweeping law took effect in 2011; as of this writing, it is not yet clear how aggressive the British government will be in pursuing cases involving small bribes and companies based outside Britain.

Britain's law comes at a time when other governments are getting tough on bribery and other forms of corruption. Other European countries have recently strengthened their laws against bribery, and China has begun to prosecute corporations for bribery. In the United States, the Justice Department has been charging more firms with violating the Foreign Corrupt Practices Act (FCPA). In one case, for example, IBM paid $10 million to settle charges by the Securities and Exchange Commission that its people had been engaging in bribery to win contracts. (That settlement was actually small; fines in FCPA cases can exceed $100 million.) In this case, IBM neither admitted wrongdoing nor denied it, and the company said it was taking remedial action to ensure that violations didn't occur in the future.[80]

Without an understanding of local customs, ethical standards, and applicable laws, an expatriate may be woefully unprepared to work internationally. To safeguard against the problems and mitigate the punishment if an organization should be found guilty of bribery, the U.S. Sentencing Commission has deemed it essential for firms to establish effective ethics programs and see that they are enforced. Companies such as Caterpillar, General Dynamics, and United Technologies established official codes of conduct for their employees years ago. In addition, many other companies have hired official ethics officers and increased their efforts to ensure ethical conduct. UPS couples an international code of conduct (available in 12 languages) with tools to ensure compliance: a corporate compliance department headed by a senior vice president, ethics training for all managers and employees, a toll-free line for requesting guidance or reporting problems, and regular audits of compliance with the code. In developing the international code of ethics, the compliance department sought input from employees in many positions and countries to ensure that the policies would be relevant throughout the company. Employees are invited to submit any ideas they have for improving the code's current language.[81]

To put teeth into the corporate ethics initiative, companies with global operations should be at least as engaged in establishing and enforcing standards for ethical behavior as domestic corporations. In Chapter 5 we identified a number of steps organizations should take. They include establishing and communicating the company's values, measuring performance in meeting ethical standards, rewarding employees at all levels for meeting those standards, and taking swift but fair action when violations occur. The primary difference in the international context is that these activities must be carried out with foreign business partners and employees in any subsidiary, franchise, or other company operation.

Interestingly, despite some obvious differences across cultures, research suggests that regardless of nationality or religion, most people embrace a set of five core values: *compassion, fairness, honesty, responsibility,* and *respect for others.* These values lie at the heart of human rights issues and seem to transcend more superficial differences among Americans, Europeans, and Asians. Finding shared values such as these allows companies to build more effective partnerships and alliances, especially across cultures. Perhaps as long as people understand that there is a set of core values, they can permit all kinds of differences in strategy and tactics.[82]

To a large extent, the challenge of managing across borders comes down to the philosophies and systems used to manage people. In moving from domestic to international management, managers need to develop a wide portfolio of behaviors along with the capacity to adjust their behavior for a particular situation. This adjustment, however, should not compromise the values, integrity, and strengths of their home country. When managers can transcend national borders and move among different cultures, they can leverage the strategic capabilities of their organization and take advantage of the opportunities that our global economy has to offer. This is certainly what IKEA's managers have tried to do, as described in "Management Connection: Onward."

Taking these management principles beyond national borders is an exciting challenge that should be irresistible to today's and tomorrow's leaders. As we saw in the early sections of this chapter, the business environment is spreading wider. People around the world are seizing the chance to get an education, launch a business, and enjoy a higher standard of living. The opportunities to serve their needs are enormous. Thanks to modern technology, the ability to learn about needs and meet them globally is available even to small, local businesses. Whether you are addressing unique desires in a "bumpy" world or delivering your product to all continents in a "flat" one, you must pay attention to what is happening far beyond your neighborhood.

> Perhaps as long as people understand that there is a set of core values, they can permit all kinds of differences in strategy and tactics.

Management Connection

Manager's Brief   Progress Report   **Onward**

MANAGING IKEA FOR FUTURE GROWTH

As IKEA's leaders position the company for future growth, two internal factors are especially relevant. The entry mode used by IKEA has given the privately held company strong control over maintaining its values. And efforts to develop future managers have hit some bumps but show concern for keeping a large pool of talent focused on the company's mission.

By the standards of a U.S. company traded on the stock exchanges, IKEA's ownership structure is complex and opaque. At the top is the Stichting Ingka Foundation, a tax-exempt nonprofit organization registered in Holland. Stichting Ingka is controlled by a five-member executive committee, chaired by founder Ingvar Kamprad, now in his 80s. This organization owns Ingka Holding, a privately

owned business also registered in Holland. And Ingka Holding owns the subsidiary IKEA Group, which controls 284 of IKEA's stores. This arrangement limits the amount of information the company must disclose to the public, as well as the taxes it must pay. The 284 stores owned by IKEA Group and the 35 owned by others (mostly in the Middle East and Asia) all operate under franchise agreements in which they pay 3 percent of sales as royalties.

IKEA's concern for privacy does not please some members of the public. The idea that management might keep details of its performance private, as well as its structure that minimizes taxation, seems to some observers inconsistent with a commitment to social responsibility. IKEA has responded to the concerns by beginning to report performance data such as annual sales and expansion plans.

Others would like more information about IKEA's sustainability claims. They note that inexpensive furniture tends to have a short life span and is not necessarily made from wood grown in the most ecofriendly ways. IKEA has responded with an effort to buy used IKEA products and resell them at a discount; the trial of this program has been running in Sweden with hopes to expand it internationally. IKEA also developed a Sustainability Product Scorecard as an internal measure of how sustainably its products are made, with the aim of improving the scores on 90 percent of its products.

As we saw in earlier parts of this case, the company draws strength from the values of the company's Swedish founder and his culture. These traditions are carried on by company practices such as the drive to continuously shave costs without compromising quality. The traditions are also maintained by the all-Swedish board of directors. However, diversity also plays a role. Among IKEA's 200 top managers, 40 percent are women. In addition, local operations tend to have local managers.

At IKEA's first U.S. factory, in Danville, Virginia, most of the managers are American, although a few are Swedish expatriates. This gives control to individuals who know the rules for operating in the United States, but it means values or practices can stray from what the company is used to at its home base in Europe. Workers at the Danville plant have been signing cards expressing interest in forming a union. Their dissatisfaction with management includes complaints that the company cut some pay packages, skipped scheduled pay increases, and frequently scheduled them to work overtime at the last minute. They also complained that management was resisting their efforts to form a union. Per-Olaf Sjoo, the head of the Swedish union

in Swedwood, where workers make similar furniture, expressed surprise when he learned about the complaints. According to Sjoo, IKEA has a code of conduct that makes overtime voluntary and guarantees workers the right to organize a union. In addition, in Sweden, workers are paid $19 an hour and have five weeks of vacation, as required by law. In Danville, starting pay is $8 an hour with 12 vacation days, and up to one-third of workers come from temp agencies with lower pay and benefits. These differences are consistent with company policy because they relate to differences in laws and standards of living between the two countries.

Retailing is highly competitive, and most retailers cope by minimizing labor costs. Often management development is seen as a luxury. At IKEA, however, development of future leaders is treated as an important activity. Building its strength as a global brand, for example, the company has a development program called Backpacker, aimed at given its people exposure to other cultures. Aimed at high-potential workers near the beginning of their careers, the Backpacker program sends them to operations in other countries so they can experience retailing there firsthand. For example, a department manager from Belfast recently went to Shanghai. From there, he told a reporter that the program was "a fabulous opportunity . . . to experience different cultures and working patterns whilst developing . . . leadership skills." Surely those are skills the company will be relying on as it continues to spread its promise of "a better everyday life."[83]

- How does IKEA's use of subsidiaries and franchises support its mission?
- What cross-cultural issues faced by IKEA's managers are described here? How is the company handling these?

KEY TERMS

culture shock, p. 233

ethnocentrism, p. 232

expatriates, p. 229

failure rate, p. 229

global model, p. 222

host-country nationals, p. 229

inpatriate, p. 235

international model, p. 221

multinational model, p. 222

North American Free Trade Agreement (NAFTA), p. 216

offshoring, p. 208

outsourcing, p. 208

third-country nationals, p. 229

transnational model, p. 223

SUMMARY OF LEARNING OBJECTIVES

Now that you have studied Chapter 6, you should be able to:

 Discuss what integration of the global economy means for individual companies and their managers.

In recent years, rapid growth has occurred in world trade, foreign direct investment, and imports. One consequence is that

companies around the globe are now finding their home markets under attack from international competitors. The global competitive environment is becoming a much tougher place in which to do business. However, companies now have access to markets that previously were denied to them.

LO 2 Describe how the world economy is becoming more integrated than ever before.

The gradual lowering of barriers to free trade is making the world economy more integrated. This means that the modern manager operates in an environment that offers more opportunities but is also more complex and competitive than that faced by the manager of a generation ago.

LO 3 Define the strategies organizations use to compete in the global marketplace.

The international corporation builds on its existing core capabilities in R&D, marketing, manufacturing, and so on to penetrate overseas markets. A multinational is a more complex form that usually has fully autonomous units operating in multiple countries. Subsidiaries are given latitude to address local issues such as consumer preferences, political pressures, and economic trends in different regions of the world. The global organization pulls control of overseas operations back into the headquarters and tends to approach the world market as a "unified whole" by combining activities in each country to maximize efficiency on a global scale. A transnational attempts to achieve both local responsiveness and global integration by utilizing a network structure that coordinates specialized facilities positioned around the world.

LO 4 Compare the various entry modes organizations use to enter overseas markets.

There are five ways to enter an overseas market: exporting, licensing, franchising, entering into a joint venture, and setting up a wholly owned subsidiary. Each mode has advantages and disadvantages.

LO 5 Explain how companies can approach the task of staffing overseas operations.

Most executives use a combination of expatriates, host-country nationals, and third-country nationals. Expatriates sometimes are used to quickly establish new country operations, transfer the company's culture, and bring in a specific technical skill. Host-country nationals have the advantages that they are familiar with local customs and culture, may cost less, and are viewed more favorably by local governments. Third-country nationals often are used as a compromise in politically touchy situations or when home-country expatriates are not available.

LO 6 Summarize the skills and knowledge managers need to manage globally.

The causes for failure overseas extend beyond technical capability and include personal and social issues as well. Success depends on a manager's core skills, such as having a multidimensional perspective; having proficiency in line management and decision making; and having resourcefulness, cultural adaptability, sensitivity, team-building skills, and mental maturity. In addition, helpful augmented skills include computer literacy, negotiating skills, strategic vision, and the ability to delegate.

LO 7 Identify ways in which cultural differences across countries influence management.

Culture influences our actions and perceptions as well as the actions and perceptions of others. Unfortunately we are often unaware of how culture influences us, and this can cause problems. Today managers must be able to change their behavior to match the needs and customs of local cultures. For example, in various cultures, employees expect a manager to be either more or less autocratic or participative. By recognizing their cultural differences, people can find it easier to work together collaboratively and benefit from the exchange.

DISCUSSION QUESTIONS

1. Why is the world economy becoming more integrated? What are the implications of this integration for international managers?

2. Imagine you were the CEO of a major company. What approach to global competition would you choose for your firm: international, multinational, global, or transnational? Why?

3. Why have franchises been so popular as a method of international expansion in the fast-food industry? Contrast this with high-tech manufacturing, where joint ventures and partnerships have been more popular. What accounts for the differences across industries?

4. What are the pros and cons of using expatriates, host-country nationals, and third-country nationals to run overseas operations? If you were expanding your business, what approach would you use?

5. If you had entered into a joint venture with a foreign company but knew that women were not treated fairly in that culture, would you consider sending a female expatriate to handle the start-up? Why or why not?

6. What are the biggest cultural obstacles that we must overcome if we are to work effectively in Mexico? Are there different obstacles in France? Japan? China?

EXPERIENTIAL EXERCISES

6.1   UNDERSTANDING MULTINATIONAL CORPORATIONS

OBJECTIVE

To gain a more thorough picture of how a multinational corporation operates.

INSTRUCTIONS

Perhaps the best way to gain an understanding of multinational corporations is to study a specific organization and how it operates throughout the world. Select a multinational corporation, find several articles on that company, and answer the questions on the Multinational Worksheet.

Multinational Worksheet

1. What is the primary business of this organization?

_____

_____

_____

_____

2. To what extent does the company engage in multinational operations? For example, does it market its products and/or services only in other countries, or does it also have overseas manufacturing facilities? What portion of the firm's operating income comes from overseas operations?

_____

_____

_____

_____

3. What percentage of the managers in international activities are American (or from the country the corporation considers home)? Are these managers given any special training before their international assignment?

_____

_____

_____

_____

4. What characteristics of the organization have contributed to its success or lack of success in the international marketplace?

_____

_____

_____

_____

SOURCE: R. R. McGrath Jr., *Exercises in Management Fundamentals*, 1st, p. 177. Copyright 1985. Reproduced by permission of Pearson Education, Inc., Upper Saddle River, New Jersey.

6.2   CROSS-CULTURAL COMMUNICATION SIMULATION

In this simulation, you will play the part of a manager employed by one of three firms—a commercial bank, a construction firm, and a hotel development company—that are planning a joint venture to build a new hotel and retail shopping complex in Perth, Australia. They come from three different cultures: Blue, Green, and Red. Each has specific cultural values, traits, customs, and practices.

You are a manager in the company to which you have been assigned. You will attend the kickoff get-together for the three-day meeting during which the three companies will negotiate the details of the partnership. Your management team consists of a vice president and a number of other managers. Consider the types of topics that would be discussed by the various corporations at an initial meeting.

INSTRUCTIONS

Your instructor will provide you with information pertaining to your culture. You will be given about 15 minutes to meet with your fellow corporate members, during which you should

1. Select a leader.

2. Discuss what your objectives and approaches will be at the opening get-together.

3. Using the description of your assigned culture, practice how you will talk and behave until you are reasonably familiar with your cultural orientation. Be sure to practice conversation distance, greeting rituals, and nonverbal behavior.

You will then return to the kick-off meeting where you will meet with the other firms. As the social proceeds, interact with the managers from the other companies. Maintain the role you have been assigned, but do not discuss it explicitly. Notice how other people react to you and how you react to them. You will discuss the experience after it is over.

Upon completing this activity, answer the following questions:

1. In what ways did your perceptions of others and their differences influence how you interacted with them and your ability to achieve your goals?

_____

_____

_____

_____

2. What did you learn about yourself and others through this activity? Discuss your strengths and weaknesses in cross-cultural interaction.

_____

_____

_____

_____

3. What were things you or others did or said that enabled or hindered you from adjusting to other people and their culture (a) in this activity? (b) in similar real-life situations?

_____

_____

_____

_____

4. What lessons did you learn from this activity? What steps can you take to improve your ability to understand and appreciate differences?

_____

_____

_____

_____

SOURCE: D. A. Jameson, "Using a Simulation to Teach Intercultural Communication in Business Communication Courses," *Business Communication Quarterly,* Vol. 55, No. 4, March 1993, pp. 1–10. Copyright 1993. Reprinted by permission of Sage Publications.

CONCLUDING CASE

TRAVEL WISE SPANS THE GLOBE

Travel Wise is a small firm with 25 employees based outside Denver, Colorado. "We take travel to new heights" is the firm's slogan, referring to Denver's mile-high elevation above sea level. For more than a decade, Travel Wise has manufactured and sold travel accessories—wallets, passport holders, travel purses, money belts, and the like. Most of the goods are outsourced to overseas manufacturers, where labor and materials are less expensive than they would be in the United States. However, Travel Wise founder Cindy Kirsch works closely with her suppliers in India and China, visiting them frequently to ensure that workers are paid well and treated fairly, earning an income that affords them a comfortable living.

Kirsch wants Travel Wise to expand, and she has discussed her plans with her design, production, marketing, and financial managers. Although each person has an area of expertise, the size of the company dictates that everyone must know the inner workings of the firm. And Kirsch welcomes ideas from all corners. First, Kirsch wants to increase the number of products offered, adding a line of travel clothing. Second, she wants to investigate the possibility of producing the firm's own guidebooks to exotic destinations. Third, she wants to expand the firm's website to include blogs, travel information services, and the like. Each of these initiatives requires a strategy that must take into consideration the global business environment. Adding a line of clothing would mean evaluating design and manufacturing alternatives, both in the United States and abroad. Creating a series of travel guides would mean hiring travel writers; establishing relationships with travel bureaus, agencies, and governments; and learning the publishing business. Expanding the website would mean determining in which regions of the world most of her customers live and where they want to travel and investigating what types of services consumers might want from the site.

Kirsch and her management staff have several lively discussions before coming up with a plan for the growth of Travel Wise. Then she gathers the entire staff together to discuss the new goals and plans. She solicits ideas from them and later incorporates those that appear to be viable. Ultimately Travel Wise has a strategy for its next level of growth. Kirsch is excited but nervous, knowing that her employees are counting on the firm's success. But she knows that they will work around the clock if necessary to make Travel Wise the brand that travelers turn to for more than just accessories—now it will be clothing, guidebooks, and online support. In the next few years, Travel Wise will be taking travel to even greater heights.

QUESTIONS

1. What type of entry mode would you recommend that Travel Wise use for its new line of clothing in U.S. markets? In foreign markets? Should the clothing be outsourced to suppliers overseas, or should Travel Wise consider building its own manufacturing facility here in the United States?

2. What features and services might Travel Wise offer on its expanded website that would appeal to travelers from Europe, Asia, and other parts of the world?

3. What types of relationships must Travel Wise forge in other countries to produce accurate, up-to-date, insightful travel guides?

7 Entrepreneurship

LEARNING OBJECTIVES

After studying Chapter 7, you will be able to:

LO 1   Describe why people become entrepreneurs and what it takes, personally. p. 249

LO 2   Summarize how to assess opportunities to start new businesses. p. 251

LO 3   Identify common causes of success and failure. p. 258

LO 4   Discuss common management challenges. p. 261

LO 5   Explain how to increase your chances of success, including good business planning. p. 264

LO 6   Describe how managers of large companies can foster entrepreneurship. p. 269

Manager's Brief | Progress Report | Onward

Management Connection

WITH CHIPOTLE, STEVE ELLS TAKES FAST FOOD TO THE NEXT LEVEL

Steve Ells prepared for his business career at the prestigious Culinary Institute of America, where he learned classic cooking techniques and an appreciation for the best, freshest ingredients. He worked in a San Francisco restaurant for a while. Then in 1993, three years after graduating, he opened his first restaurant, Chipotle Mexican Grill, in Denver. His goal was to serve classically prepared food made with fresh raw ingredients in a casual atmosphere. The prices would be reasonable, and the service would be fast. He hoped to generate enough revenues to save up and start a fancier place to eat.

When Ells opened Chipotle, fast food meant manufactured food sold at rock-bottom prices. Ells was driven by his desire to prepare good food, not jump on a trend, but he helped to start the now-popular restaurant segment known as "fast casual." (Panera and Corner Baker are other examples of this type of restaurant.)

With an idea that didn't fit into existing categories, Ells had some trouble convincing his friends that his new business was a good idea. Some said the menu was overly simple; others thought the streamlined decor would look too bare. Another objection was that customers wouldn't know how to pronounce the name, Chipotle.

Diners around Denver quickly came to love Chipotle, lining up to choose freshly made salsa, rice, beans, cheese, and other goodies to have stuffed into burritos. Ells began to expand, adding two more locations in 1995 and another five in 1996. As he gained experience and demonstrated his success as a restaurant owner and manager, Ells attracted investors and expanded into the Midwest with two more restaurants in 1999.[1]

Like many entrepreneurs, Ells is not content to stop at one great idea. As he expanded the number of restaurants and therefore his need for raw ingredients, he learned more about the agriculture and food-processing industries. Some of what he learned disturbed him. For example, seeing that conventionally raised pork comes from pigs that live in confined spaces, he began looking for sources of naturally raised pork. In 2000 his restaurants began serving the naturally raised pork. Ells discovered that it offered a superior taste and that customers were willing to pay a little extra for it.

This eye-opening experience brought Ells to a decision: his commitment to fresh food was no longer enough for Chipotle. From that point, the restaurant's mission would be to know the source of all its ingredients to ensure they come from sources that are respectful of people, animals, and the environment. Chipotle began serving naturally raised chicken in 2002 and naturally raised beef in 2007. By 2008, 40 percent of Chipotle's black beans were certified organic. The dairy products offered come from cows not treated with bovine growth hormone. The company seeks local sources for a growing share of its food. These and other efforts are summarized by the restaurant's promise to serve "food with integrity."

You might think that a professionally trained chef with a commitment to natural foods wouldn't belong in the fast-food business. But Ells doesn't limit his activities to the usual categories. As a matter of fact, opening a fine-dining restaurant no longer seems important to Ells. As he sees it, "Most people eat fast food in [the United States]," so by serving high-quality food in the kind of place where people frequently eat, he is making delicious, fresh, naturally raised food more widely available than it ever has been.

Steve Ells used his love for preparing fresh food and created a popular nationwide chain of restaurants. As you read about the qualities of successful entrepreneurs and the challenges they must overcome, think about which of these you see in Steve Ells and his experience with Chipotle.

entrepreneurship

The pursuit of lucrative opportunities by enterprising individuals.

Bottom Line

Entrepreneurship is inherently about innovation—creating a new venture where one didn't exist before.

How is entrepreneurship different from inventing a new product?

small business

A business having fewer than 100 employees, independently owned and operated, not dominant in its field, and not characterized by many innovative practices.

entrepreneurial venture

A new business having growth and high profitability as primary objectives.

As Steve Ells and countless others have demonstrated, great opportunity is available to talented entrepreneurs who are willing to work hard to achieve their dreams. **Entrepreneurship** occurs when an enterprising individual pursues a lucrative opportunity.[2] To be an entrepreneur is to initiate and build an organization, rather than being only a passive part of one.[3] It involves creating *new* systems, resources, or processes to produce *new* goods or services and/or serve *new* markets.[4]

Entrepreneurship differs from management generally and from small business management in particular. An entrepreneur *is* a manager but engages in additional activities that not all managers do.[5] Whereas managers operate in a more formal management hierarchy, with more clearly defined authority and responsibility, entrepreneurs use networks of contacts more than formal authority. And whereas managers usually prefer to own assets, entrepreneurs often rent or use assets on a temporary basis. Some say that managers often are slower to act and tend to avoid risk, whereas entrepreneurs are quicker to act and actively manage risk.

How does entrepreneurship differ from managing a small business?[6] A **small business** is often defined as having fewer than 100 employees, being independently owned and operated, not dominant in its field, and not characterized by many innovative practices. Small business owners tend not to manage particularly aggressively, and they expect normal, moderate sales, profits, and growth. In contrast, an **entrepreneurial venture** has growth and high profitability as primary objectives. Entrepreneurs manage aggressively and develop innovative strategies, practices, and products. They and their financial backers usually seek rapid growth, immediate and high profits, and sometimes a quick sellout with large capital gains.

Like other business managers, entrepreneurs can strive for sustainability,[7] which you read about in Chapter 5. Their ventures can be domestic or global. For the smaller entrepreneur doing business internationally or globally, the particular challenges include some things you learned about in Chapter 6, such as psychological and cultural barriers and contextual differences (for example, political, regulatory, judicial, tax, and labor environments), plus the need to compete with bigger and/or established incumbents while having fewer resources with which to operate.[8]

The Excitement of Entrepreneurship Consider these words from Jeffry Timmons, a leading entrepreneurship scholar and author: "During the past 30 years, America has unleashed the most revolutionary generation the nation has experienced since its founding in 1776. This new generation of entrepreneurs has altered permanently the economic and social structure of this nation and the world. . . . It will determine more than any other single impetus how the nation and the world will live, work, learn, and lead in this century and beyond."[9] Timmons had written previously, "We are in the midst of a silent revolution—a triumph of the creative and entrepreneurial spirit of humankind throughout the world. I believe its impact on the 21st century will equal or exceed that of the Industrial Revolution on the 19th and 20th."[10]

Overhype? Sounds like it could be,

but it's not.

Overhype? Sounds like it could be, but it's not. Entrepreneurship is transforming economies all over the world, and the global economy in general. In the United States since 1980, more than

95 percent of the wealth has been created by entrepreneurs.[11] It's been estimated that since World War II, small entrepreneurial firms have generated 95 percent of all radical innovation in the United States. The Small Business Administration has found that in states with more small business start-ups, statewide economies tend to grow faster and employment levels tend to be higher than in states with less entrepreneurship.[12] An estimated 20 million Americans are running a young business or actively trying to start one.[13]

The self-employed love the entrepreneurial process, and they report the highest levels of pride, satisfaction, and income. Importantly, entrepreneurship is not about the privileged descendants of the Rockefellers and the Vanderbilts—it provides opportunity and upward mobility for anyone who performs well.[14]

Ryan Clark (bottom), who won the 2009 Student Leadership Award from the Black Engineer of the Year Awards, poses with his twin brother, Ashton, at the Coordinated Science Laboratory in Urbana, Illinois. After graduating from the University of Illinois, the Clark brothers started their own company, Dynamik Duo, where they develop effective websites for various companies in need of showcasing their unique products and/or services.

Myths about Entrepreneurship   Simply put, entrepreneurs generate new ideas and turn them into business ventures.[15] But entrepreneurship is not simple, and it is frequently misunderstood. Read Table 7.1 to start thinking about the myths and realities of this important career option.

Here is another myth, not in the table: being an entrepreneur is great because you can "get rich quick" and enjoy a lot of leisure time while your employees run the company. But the reality is much more difficult. During the start-up period, you are

TABLE 7.1   Some Myths about Entrepreneurs

Myth 1—Entrepreneurs are born, not made.
Reality—While entrepreneurs are born with certain native intelligence, a flair for creating, and energy, these talents by themselves are like unmolded clay or an unpainted canvas. The making of an entrepreneur occurs by accumulating the relevant skills, know-how, experiences, and contacts over a period of years and includes large doses of self-development. The creative capacity to envision and then pursue an opportunity is a direct descendant of at least 10 or more years of experience that lead to pattern recognition.
Myth 2—Anyone can start a business.
Reality—Entrepreneurs who recognize the difference between an idea and an opportunity, and who think big enough, start businesses that have a better chance of succeeding. Luck, to the extent it is involved, requires good preparation. And the easiest part is starting. What is hardest is surviving, sustaining, and building a venture so its founders can realize a harvest. Perhaps only one in 10 to 20 new businesses that survive five years or more results in a capital gain for the founders.
Myth 3—Entrepreneurs are gamblers.
Reality—Successful entrepreneurs take very careful, calculated risks. They try to influence the odds, often by getting others to share risk with them and by avoiding or minimizing risks if they have the choice. Often they slice up the risk into smaller, quite digestible pieces; only then do they commit the time or resources to determine if that piece will work. They do not deliberately seek to take more risk or to take unnecessary risk, nor do they shy away from unavoidable risk.
Myth 4—Entrepreneurs want the whole show to themselves.
Reality—Owning and running the whole show effectively puts a ceiling on growth. Solo entrepreneurs usually make a living. It is extremely difficult to grow a higher-potential venture by working single-handedly. Higher-potential entrepreneurs build a team, an organization, and a company. Besides, 100 percent of nothing is nothing, so rather than taking a large piece of the pie, they work to make the pie bigger.

(continued)

Myth 5—Entrepreneurs are their own bosses and completely independent.

Reality—Entrepreneurs are far from independent and have to serve many masters and constituencies, including partners, investors, customers, suppliers, creditors, employees, families, and those involved in social and community obligations. Entrepreneurs, however, can make free choices of whether, when, and what they care to respond to. Moreover, it is extremely difficult, and rare, to build a business beyond $1 million to $2 million in sales single-handedly.

Myth 6—Entrepreneurs work longer and harder than managers in big companies.

Reality—There is no evidence that all entrepreneurs work more than their corporate counterparts. Some do, some do not. Some actually report that they work less.

Myth 7—Entrepreneurs experience a great deal of stress and pay a high price.

Reality—Being an entrepreneur is stressful and demanding. But there is no evidence that it is any more stressful than numerous other highly demanding professional roles, and entrepreneurs find their jobs very satisfying. They have a high sense of accomplishment, are healthier, and are much less likely to retire than those who work for others. Three times as many entrepreneurs as corporate managers say they plan to never retire.

Myth 8—Start a business and fail and you'll never raise money again.

Reality—Talented and experienced entrepreneurs—because they pursue attractive opportunities and are able to attract the right people and necessary financial and other resources to make the venture work—often head successful ventures. Further, businesses fail, but entrepreneurs do not. Failure is often the fire that tempers the steel of an entrepreneur's learning experience and street savvy.

Myth 9—Money is the most important start-up ingredient.

Reality—If the other pieces and talents are there, the money will follow, but it does not follow that an entrepreneur will succeed if he or she has enough money. Money is one of the least important ingredients in new venture success. Money is to the entrepreneur what the paint and brush are to the artist—an inert tool that in the right hands can create marvels.

Myth 10—Entrepreneurs should be young and energetic.

Reality—While these qualities may help, age is no barrier. The average age of entrepreneurs starting high-potential businesses is in the mid-30s, and there are numerous examples of entrepreneurs starting businesses in their 60s. What is critical is possessing the relevant know-how, experience, and contacts that greatly facilitate recognizing and pursuing an opportunity.

Myth 11—Entrepreneurs are motivated solely by the quest for the almighty dollar.

Reality—Entrepreneurs seeking high-potential ventures are more driven by building enterprises and realizing long-term capital gains than by instant gratification through high salaries and perks. A sense of personal achievement and accomplishment, feeling in control of their own destinies, and realizing their vision and dreams are also powerful motivators. Money is viewed as a tool and a way of keeping score, rather than an end in itself. Entrepreneurs thrive on the thrill of the chase; and, time and again, even after an entrepreneur has made a few million dollars or more, he or she will work on a new vision to build another company.

Myth 12—Entrepreneurs seek power and control over others.

Reality—Successful entrepreneurs are driven by the quest for responsibility, achievement, and results, rather than for power for its own sake. They thrive on a sense of accomplishment and of outperforming the competition, rather than a personal need for power expressed by dominating and controlling others. By virtue of their accomplishments, they may be powerful and influential, but these are more the by-products of the entrepreneurial process than a driving force behind it.

Myth 13—If an entrepreneur is talented, success will happen in a year or two.

Reality—An old maxim among venture capitalists says it all: The lemons ripen in two and a half years, but the pearls take seven or eight. Rarely is a new business established solidly in less than three or four years.

Myth 14—Any entrepreneur with a good idea can raise venture capital.

Reality—Of the ventures of entrepreneurs with good ideas who seek out venture capital, only 1 to 3 out of 100 are funded.

(continued)

Myth 15—If an entrepreneur has enough start-up capital, he or she can't miss.
Reality—The opposite is often true; that is, too much money at the outset often creates euphoria and a spoiled-child syndrome. The accompanying lack of discipline and impulsive spending usually lead to serious problems and failure.
Myth 16—Entrepreneurs are lone wolves and cannot work with others.
Reality—The most successful entrepreneurs are leaders who build great teams and effective relationships working with peers, directors, investors, key customers, key suppliers, and the like.
Myth 17—Unless you attained 600+ on your SATs or GMATs, you'll never be a successful entrepreneur.
Reality—Entrepreneurial IQ is a unique combination of creativity, motivation, integrity, leadership, team building, analytical ability, and ability to deal with ambiguity and adversity.

SOURCE: From J. A. Timmons and S. Spinelli, Jr., *New Venture Creation: Entrepreneurship for the 21st Century* 7th ed, 2007, pp. 19–20. Copyright 2007 The McGraw Hill Companies, Inc. Reprinted with permission.

likely to have a lot of bad days. It's exhausting. Even if you don't have employees, you should expect communications breakdowns and other "people problems" with agents, vendors, distributors, family, subcontractors, lenders, and whomever. Dan Bricklin, the founder of VisiCalc, advises that the most important thing to remember is this: "You are not your business. On those darkest days when things aren't going so well—and trust me, you will have them—try to remember that your company's failures don't make you an awful person. Likewise, your company's successes don't make you a genius or superhuman."[16]

As you read this chapter, you will learn about two primary sources of new venture creation: independent entrepreneurship and intrapreneurship. **Entrepreneurs** are individuals who establish a new organization without the benefit of corporate support. **Intrapreneurs** are new venture creators working inside big companies; they are corporate entrepreneurs, using their company's resources to build a profitable line of business based on a fresh new idea.[17]

entrepreneur
Individuals who establish a new organization without the benefit of corporate sponsorship.

intrapreneurs
New venture creators working inside big companies.

Entrepreneurship

Table 7.2 lists some extraordinary entrepreneurs. The companies they founded are famously successful—and all of the founders started in their 20s. Two young entrepreneurs who started a highly successful business are Tony Hsieh and Nick Swinmurn. In 1999 Swinmurn had the then-new idea to sell shoes online, but he needed money to get started. Hsieh, who at age 24 had already just sold his first start-up (LinkExchange, sold to Microsoft for $265 million), agreed to take a chance on the new venture. Swinmurn has moved on, but Hsieh remains at the helm of the company as the CEO of Zappos.com. In a recent year, Zappos.com enjoyed sales of $1 billion.[18]

The real, more complete story of entrepreneurship is not about the famous people in Table 7.2—it's mostly about people you've probably never heard of.

They have built companies, thrived personally, created jobs, and made positive contributions to their communities through their businesses. Or they're just starting out.

Why Become an Entrepreneur?

Jessica Mah was an entrepreneur before she even finished school. At the age of 13, she went into business using eBay to sell computer parts and templates for websites. While in college at the University of California–Berkeley, she and another student,

Bottom Line
Today's concern for sustainability presents a tremendous variety of opportunities to entrepreneurs who care about the environment.
What are some environmentally friendly start-ups you've heard about? Do you think they have great profit potential?

Tony Hsieh is listed as an extraordinary entrepreneur. At the age of 24, he had already sold off his first venture and took on Zappos.com, where he continues to work today.

Andy Su, founded a business they called InternshipIN, which provided information about internship opportunities. When she graduated, Mah was ready to launch another venture. With support from Y Combinator, which provides funds and advice to selected start-ups, Mah again partnered with Su, this time founding inDinero, a company that helps small business owners manage their money. Customers give inDinero their bank and credit card account numbers, and inDinero keeps track of transactions and analyzes where their money is going. The idea for inDinero came from Mah's own experience that for some people excited about starting a new business, working with customers and products is more exciting and easier to learn than handling money. So far, inDinero has signed up about 6,000 customers and hired seven employees.[19]

Why do Jessica Mah and other entrepreneurs do what they do? Entrepreneurs start their own firms because of the challenge, the profit potential, and the enormous satisfaction they hope lie ahead. People starting their own businesses are seeking a better quality of life than they might have at big companies. They seek independence and a feeling of being part of the action. They feel tremendous satisfaction in building something from nothing, seeing it succeed, and watching the market embrace their ideas and products.

People also start their own companies when they see their progress or ideas blocked at big corporations. When people are laid off, they often try to start businesses of

TABLE 7.2

Mega-Entrepreneurs Who Started in Their 20s

Entrepreneurial Company	Founder(s)
Microsoft	Bill Gates and Paul Allen
Netscape	Marc Andressen
Dell Computers	Michael Dell
Gateway 2000	Ted Waitt
McCaw Cellular	Craig McCaw
Apple Computers	Steve Jobs and Steve Wozniak
Digital Equipment Corporation	Ken and Stan Olsen
Federal Express	Fred Smith
Google	Larry Page
	Sergey Brin
Genentech	Robert Swanson
Polaroid	Edward Land
Nike	Phil Knight
Lotus Development Corporation	Mitch Kapor
Ipix.com	Kevin McCurdy
Yahoo!	David Filo
	Jerry Yang

SOURCES: J. A. Timmons and S. Spinelli, Jr., *New Venture Creation: Entrepreneurship for the 21st Century* 7E, 2007, p. 53. Copyright 2007 The McGraw-Hill Companies, Inc. Reprinted with permission.

their own. And when employed people believe they will not receive a promotion or are frustrated by bureaucracy or other features of corporate life, they may quit and become entrepreneurs. Years ago, Philip Catron became disillusioned with his job as a manager at ChemLawn because he concluded that the lawn care company's reliance on pesticides contributed to illness in its employees, its customers' pets, and even in the lawns themselves. Catron left the company to start NaturaLawn of America, based on the practice of integrated pest management, which uses natural and nontoxic products as much as possible, reducing pesticide use on lawns by 85 percent. Catron built NaturaLawn into 66 franchises in 23 states—and helped integrated pest management become mainstream, as even his former employer, now part of TruGreen ChemLawn, has changed many of its practices.[20]

Immigrants also may find conventional paths to economic success closed to them and turn to entrepreneurship.[21] For example, the Cuban community in Miami has produced many successful entrepreneurs, as has the Vietnamese community throughout the United States. Sometimes the immigrant's experience gives him or her useful knowledge about foreign suppliers or markets that present an attractive business opportunity. Rakesh Kamdar immigrated to the United States from India to study computer science, but he saw a way he could meet the huge U.S. demand for nursing talent. He set up DB Healthcare to recruit nurses from India to work in the United States. Unlike U.S. competitors that had failed, Kamdar set up meetings at DB's Indian offices, and he invited nurses to attend with their husbands, parents, and in-laws. His staff discussed family and individual questions related to the American jobs. With this strategy, DB Healthcare was earning millions of dollars within a few years.[22]

What Does It Take to Succeed?

What can we learn from the people who start their own companies and succeed? What talents enable entrepreneurs to succeed? We express these characteristics in general terms with Figure 7.1. Successful entrepreneurs are innovators and also have good knowledge and skills in management, business, and networking.[23] In contrast, inventors may be highly creative but often lack the skills to turn their ideas into a successful business. Manager–administrators may be great at ensuring efficient operations but aren't necessarily innovators. Promoters have a different set of marketing and selling skills—useful for entrepreneurs, but those skills can be hired, whereas innovativeness and business management skills remain the essential combination for successful entrepreneurs.

What Business Should You Start?

You need a good idea, and you need to find or create the right opportunity. The following discussion offers some general considerations for choosing a type of business.

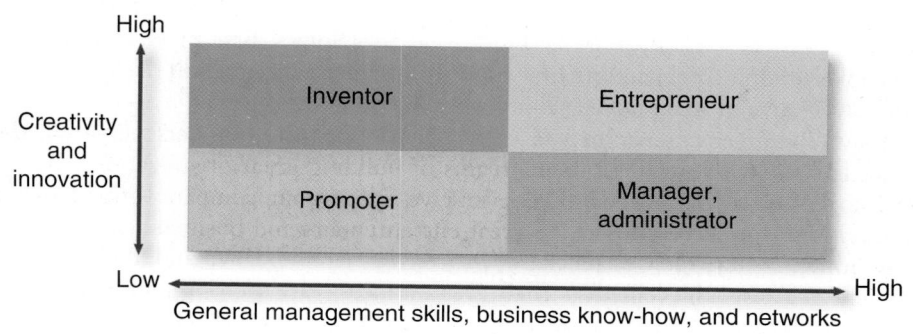

FIGURE 7.1
Who Is the Entrepreneur?

SOURCE: J. A. Timmons and S. Spinelli, Jr., *New Venture Creation: Entrepreneurship for the 21st Century* 7E, 2007, pp. 67–68. Copyright 2007 The McGraw-Hill Companies, Inc. Reprinted with permission.

The Idea   Many entrepreneurs and observers say that in contemplating your business, you must start with a great idea. A great product, a viable market, and good timing are essential ingredients in any recipe for success.

IN PRACTICE

Some of the most exciting ideas today involve products that meet a very basic need at a very low cost. Socially responsible entrepreneurs are combining technological skills with concern for people who live without access to clean water and reliable electricity, creating high-tech projects that can improve lives in poor communities. For example, Nedjip Tozun and Sam Goldman founded D.light Design to develop and sell solar-powered lights, made with low-priced solar panels, efficient LEDs, and sophisticated power management software.

Tozun and Goldman see their market in developing countries, where many people rely on kerosene and diesel lamps, which not only provide a poor quality of lighting but also pollute the air and present a serious danger from fires and serious burns. Although the $25 price tag for a D.light lamp is high for many communities where people earn less than a dollar a day, when family members pool their resources, they find that the lamp allows them to work longer hours, save money spent on fuel, and skip long trips to buy it, so the purchase is a good investment in a cleaner, safer life.

D.light Design is a business, not a charity. Tozun and Goldman see their buyers as "great customers" who see a "clear value proposition" in their product. They also see potential to expand into other solar-powered products, building their business as they meet basic needs.[24]

- How does D.light Design meet the requirements of a great idea (great product, viable market, and good timing)?

Bottom Line
Meeting basic needs profitably can also be good for the planet.
How might solar-powered products deliver environmental as well as social benefits?

Many great organizations have been built on a different kind of idea: the founder's desire to build a great organization, rather than to offer a particular product.[25] Examples abound. Bill Hewlett and David Packard decided to start a company and then figured out what to make. J. Willard Marriott knew he wanted to be in business for himself but didn't have a product in mind until he opened an A&W root beer stand. Masaru Ibuka had no specific product idea when he founded Sony in 1945. Sony's first product attempt, a rice cooker, didn't work, and its first product (a tape recorder) didn't sell. The company stayed alive by making and selling crude heating pads.

You don't have to be first with a product idea if you can figure out a way to execute an existing idea better than the competition. Federal Express succeeded by borrowing DHL's method of using jets to race ahead of UPS in overnight delivery service in the United States. IBM combined existing components and Microsoft's operating system to launch a personal computer that eventually beat Apple's and Atari's earlier models. And Best Buy raised funds in the stock market to expand a line of stores aimed at competing with Circuit City, which is now out of business.[26]

Many now-great companies had early failures. But the founders persisted; they believed in themselves and in their dreams of building great organizations. Be prepared to kill or revise an idea, but never give up on your company—this has been a prescription for success for many great entrepreneurs and business leaders. Think about Sony, Disney, Hewlett-Packard, Procter & Gamble, IBM, and Walmart: their founders' greatest achievements—their greatest ideas—are their organizations.[27]

The Opportunity   Entrepreneurs spot, create, and exploit opportunities in a variety of ways.[28] Entrepreneurial companies can explore domains that big companies avoid and introduce goods or services that capture the market because they are simpler, cheaper, more accessible, or more convenient. While Shayne McQuade was touring Spain, taking a break from his career as a management consultant, he noticed that he had a problem figuring out how to recharge his cell phone. After his trip, McQuade developed a way to make backpacks and messenger bags containing solar panels.[29]

To spot opportunities, think carefully about events and trends as they unfold. Consider, for example, the following possibilities:[30]

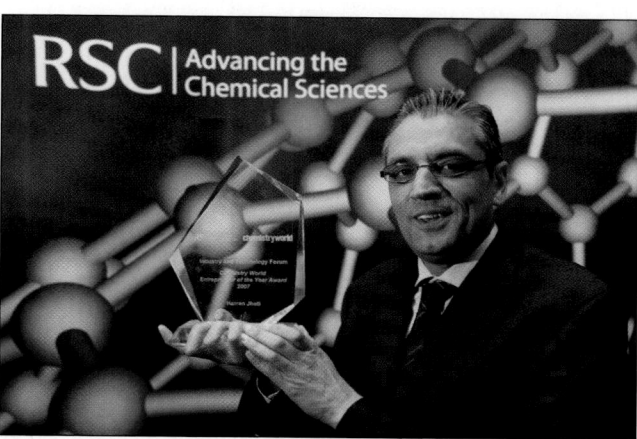

Harren Jhoti, chief executive and founder of a drug discovery and development company called Astex Therapeutics, receives the Chemistry World Entrepreneur of the Year Award at the annual Royal Society of Chemistry Innovations Awards in London. Jhoti built Astex over eight years, raising over £63 million. The annual award is presented to an individual who has established or contributed to the growth of a small or medium-sized chemistry-related company.

Technological discoveries. Start-ups in biotechnology, microcomputers, and nanotechnology followed technological advances. Howard Berke, who has two Nobel prize winners on his payroll, established Konarka Technologies to offer products based on advances in solar cells. In contrast to the older technology of solar panels, solar cells are based on organic chemicals, so they are more flexible and can be installed in a variety of projects.[31]

Demographic changes. All kinds of health care organizations have sprung up to serve an aging population, from Fit After Fifty exercise studios to assisted-living facilities. One business that targets both the aging American population and the growth in single-parent and dual-career households is Errands Done Right. The service assists those who are pressed for time or have difficulty getting around.[32]

Lifestyle and taste changes. Start-ups have capitalized on new clothing and music trends, desire for fast food, and growing interest in sports. In recent years, more consumers want to help take care of the environment, and more businesses are concerned about showing consumers that they care, too.

Economic dislocations, such as booms or failures. Rising oil prices have spurred a variety of developments related to alternative energy or energy efficiency. Howard Berke, the entrepreneur behind Konarka Technologies' solar cells, says, "I don't come at this as an environmentalist. I come at this from good business sense. The cost of renewables . . . is more competitive when compared with fossil fuel."[33]

Calamities such as wars and natural disasters. The terrorist attacks of September 2001 spurred concern about security, and entrepreneurs today are still pursuing ideas to help government agencies prevent future attacks. The hurricanes on the Gulf Coast raised awareness of the importance of preparing for emergencies.

Government initiatives and rule changes. Deregulation spawned new airlines and trucking companies. Whenever the government tightens energy efficiency requirements, opportunities become available for entrepreneurs developing ideas for cutting energy use.

franchising

An entrepreneurial alliance between a franchisor (an innovator who has created at least one successful store and wants to grow) and a franchisee (a partner who manages a new store of the same type in a new location).

Franchises   One important type of opportunity is the franchise. You may know intuitively what franchising is. Or you can at least name some prominent franchises: McDonald's, Jiffy Lube, the Body Shop, Dunkin' Donuts—add your favorites here. **Franchising** is an entrepreneurial alliance between two organizations: the franchisor and the franchisee.[34] The franchisor is the innovator who has created at least one successful store and

In a recent three-year period, almost 900 new franchise concepts were launched in the United States. The categories with the most new concepts were food retailing, service businesses, and sports and recreation. The categories that added the most new franchise units were service businesses, building and construction, and child-related services.[35]

seeks partners to operate the same concept in other local markets. For the franchisee, the opportunity is wealth creation via a proven (but not failureproof) business concept, with the added advantage of the franchisor's expertise. For the franchisor, the opportunity is wealth creation through growth. The partnership is manifest in a trademark or brand, and together the partners' mission is to maintain and build the brand. The Noodles & Company chain of fast casual restaurants first grew by opening 79 company-owned locations. Management concluded that it could grow at a faster pace through franchising. Establishing standard menus and prices took a year, but franchising helped the company almost double its revenues in just two years.[36]

People often assume that buying a franchise is less risky than starting a business from scratch, but the evidence is mixed. One study that followed businesses for six years found the opposite of the popular assumption: 65 percent of the franchises studied were operating at the end of the period, while 72 percent of independent businesses were still operating. One reason may be that the franchises involved mostly a few, possibly riskier, industries. A study that compared only restaurants over a three-year period found that 43 percent of the franchises and 39 percent of independent restaurants remained in business.[37]

If you are contemplating a franchise, consider its market presence (local, regional, or national), market share and profit margins, national programs for marketing and purchasing, the nature of the business, including required training and degree of field support, terms of the license agreement (e.g., 20 years with automatic renewal versus less than 10 years or no renewal), capital required, and franchise fees and royalties.[38]

A flight into space might become as easy as booking a flight to Florida thanks to Burt Rutan. His idea to launch people into space may have opened the door for an entire space tourism industry.

Although some people think success with a franchise is a no-brainer, would-be franchisees have a lot to consider. Luckily, plenty of useful sources exist for learning more, including the International Franchise Association (http://www.franchise.org), the Small Business Administration (http://www.sba.gov), Franchise Chat (http://www.franchise-chat.com), and the Business Franchise Directory (http://www.business-franchisedirectory.com). In addition, the Federal Trade Commission investigates complaints of deceptive claims by franchisors and publishes information about those cases. Take your time in investigating business opportunities, consulting with an accountant or lawyer who has experience.[39]

The Next Frontiers   The next frontiers for entrepreneurship—where do they lie? Throughout history, aspiring entrepreneurs have asked this question. When a business magazine asked prominent investors in new businesses to name the best ideas for a new start-up, their responses included next-generation batteries with enough juice to power cars after a seconds-long charge, longer-lasting tiny batteries to keep cell phones and cameras running for more hours, implantable wireless devices that can monitor heartbeats or blood sugar levels, and online social networking sites that focus on allowing artists and musicians to share and promote their works.[40]

One fascinating opportunity for entrepreneurs is outer space. Historically, the space market was driven by the government and was dominated by big defense contractors such as Boeing and Lockheed Martin. But now, with demand for satellite launches and potential profits skyrocketing, smaller entrepreneurs are entering the field. Some of the most dramatic headlines involve space tourism. Zero Gravity already operates flights in converted Boeing 727 jets that simulate the experience of weightlessness by flying up and down like a roller-coaster 10,000 feet above the earth. Famous passengers who signed up for the $3,500 flights have included business owner Martha Stewart and physicist Stephen Hawking.[41] Other recent ventures in space have included using satellites for automobile navigation, tracking trucking fleets, and monitoring flow rates and leaks in pipelines; testing designer drugs in a near-zero-gravity environment; and using remote sensing to monitor global warming, spot fish concentrations, and detect crop stress for precision farming.

Homeland security is another newly burgeoning industry. A vast number of companies in a wide range of industries are attempting to benefit—for example, baggage screening, smallpox vaccines, capturing arrival and departure information on travelers, explosives detection systems, and sensors for airborne pathogens. Some of the growth is supported by government investment in security-related technology. For example, the state of Illinois gave grants to SSS Research, which develops database software that helps terrorism analysts, and RiverGlass, which develops software that connects databases to find patterns describing high-risk people. In Michigan, the state-funded Venture Michigan I Fund supports investment in Michigan-based start-ups in the security and other growth industries.[42]

The Internet   The Internet is a business frontier that continues to expand. With Internet commerce, as with any start-up, entrepreneurs need sound business models and practices. During the heady days of the Internet rush, many entrepreneurs and investors thought revenues and profits were unimportant and all that mattered was to attract visitors to their websites ("capture eyeballs"). But you need to watch costs carefully, and you want to break even and achieve profitability as soon as possible.[43]

At least five successful business models have proven successful in the e-commerce market: transaction fee, advertising support, intermediary, affiliate, and subscription models.[44] In the **transaction fee model,** companies charge a fee for goods or services. Amazon.com and online travel agents are prime examples. In the **advertising support model,** advertisers pay the site operator to gain access to the demographic group that visits the operator's site.

The **intermediary model** has eBay as the premier example, bringing buyers and sellers together and charging a commission for each sale. With the **affiliate model,** sites pay commissions to other sites to drive business to their own sites. Zazzle.com, Spreadshirt.com, and CafePress.com are variations on this model. They sell custom-decorated gift items such as mugs and T-shirts. Designers are the affiliates; they choose basic, undecorated products (such as a plain shirt) and add their own designs, creating the customized products offered to consumers.[45] Finally, websites using the **subscription model** charge a monthly or annual fee for site visits or access to site content. Newspapers and magazines are good examples.

What about businesses whose primary focus is not e-commerce? Start-ups and established small companies can create attractive websites that add to their professionalism, give them access to more customers, and bring them closer to suppliers, investors, and service providers. Companies can move much more quickly than in the past and save money on activities including customer service/support,

transaction fee model

Charging fees for goods and services.

advertising support model

Charging fees to advertise on a site.

intermediary model

Charging fees to bring buyers and sellers together.

affiliate model

Charging fees to direct site visitors to other companies' sites.

subscription model

Charging fees for site visits.

Customized products are just a click away. Zazzle.com produces customized T-shirts, posters, and postage stamps. It has built a library of over 500,000 digital images, including more than 4,500 items of copyrighted material licensed from Walt Disney's legendary characters such as Mickey Mouse and Goofy. Shown here is a sample of customized postage stamps provided by Zazzle.

technical support, data retrieval, public relations, investor relations, selling, requests for product literature, and purchasing. Setting up shop online costs less than it ever did.

Social entrepreneurship has been around for decades but has surged in recent years in popularity and impact and as a focus for academic research.[46] **Social entrepreneurship** has been defined in many ways, but most fundamentally it refers to leveraging resources to address social problems.[47] D.light Design, described on page 252, is one example.

social entrepreneurship

Leveraging resources to address social problems.

Social entrepreneurship creates social value by stimulating social change or meeting social needs.[48] Like entrepreneurship generally, it can occur in a new or established organizations. Social entrepreneurs engage in for-profit or nonprofit activities, including business enterprises pursuing a mission of creating social value and government or nonprofit organizations operating by using business principles.

One of the best-known examples of social entrepreneurship is the Nobel Prize–winning work of Dr. Muhammad Yunus, formerly of Grameen Bank, which began helping women in South Asia obtain microloans.[49] Another is Fabio Rosa's Agroelectric System of Appropriate Technology (STA), which established low-cost electrification and irrigation in rural Brazil.[50] Additional examples include Nuru Energy, which uses local entrepreneurs to sell high-efficiency LED lighting in Rwanda;[51] the EMR Project, which developed an electronic medical records system to improve patient care in Botswana;[52] the Cookie Project, which trained women to make high-quality cookies with natural ingredients in distressed areas of South Africa;[53] and the Feeds Project, which produces low-cost, high-quality animal feed in Zambia for small-scale chicken farmers, thereby alleviating unemployment and starvation.[54] What other examples can you think of? What has been their impact?

What Does It Take, Personally?

Many people assume that there is an "entrepreneurial personality." No single personality type predicts entrepreneurial success, but you are more likely to succeed as an entrepreneur if you exhibit certain characteristics:[55]

1. *Commitment and determination:* Successful entrepreneurs are decisive, tenacious, disciplined, willing to sacrifice, and able to immerse themselves in their enterprises. Entrepreneurial passion[56] can play an important role in all of these things.
2. *Leadership:* They are self-starters, team builders, superior learners, and teachers. Communicating a vision for the future of the company—an essential component of leadership that you'll learn more about in Chapter 12—has a direct impact on venture growth.[57]
3. *Opportunity obsession:* They have an intimate knowledge of customers' needs, are market driven, and are obsessed with value creation and enhancement.
4. *Tolerance of risk, ambiguity, and uncertainty:* They are calculated risk takers and risk managers, tolerant of stress, and able to resolve problems.
5. *Creativity, self-reliance, and ability to adapt:* They are open-minded, restless with the status quo, able to learn quickly, highly adaptable, creative, skilled at conceptualizing, and attentive to details.
6. *Motivation to excel:* They have a clear results orientation, set high but realistic goals, have a strong drive to achieve, know their own weaknesses and strengths, and focus on what can be done rather than on the reasons things can't be done.

"Even if you think you know it all, there's a lot of life lessons you're going to learn in school. Develop your network while you're there with peers and professors."
Sam Uisprapassorn, Director of Business Development, Solar Pacific Energy[58]

Business professor Saras Sarasvathy conducted an interesting experiment to see if there's something special about the way successful entrepreneurs approach business opportunities. Sarasvathy recruited 45 entrepreneurs, who had created businesses now earning at least $200 million per year, to talk through how they would handle a set of business decisions related to an imaginary enterprise. She also recruited a group of successful corporate managers from large companies to do the same. Sarasvathy found that the entrepreneurs, in contrast to the corporate managers, tended to set very broad goals and shift their approach frequently as they encountered obstacles or spotted new opportunities. Even in terms of the company description she provided, they were apt to think up ways to redefine the company and expand its possibilities. If you've ever watched the TV competition *Iron Chef*, you can imagine how they work—flexibly improvising, taking the unusual ingredients offered, and concocting a surprisingly delicious meal. The corporate managers were effective in a different way, more akin to following a recipe efficiently and beautifully; they tended to work with set goals and define the resources needed to succeed at achieving those goals.[59]

Making Good Choices   Success is a function not only of personal characteristics but also of making good choices about the business you start. Figure 7.2 presents a model for conceptualizing entrepreneurial ventures and making the best possible choices. It depicts ventures along two dimensions: innovation and risk. The new venture may involve high or low levels of *innovation*, or the creation of something new and different. It can also be characterized by low or high *risk*. Risk refers primarily to the probability of major financial loss. But it also is more than that; it is psychological risk as perceived by the entrepreneur, including risk to reputation and ego.[60]

> Success is a function not only of personal characteristics but also of making good choices about the business you start.

The upper-left quadrant, high innovation/low risk, depicts ventures of truly novel ideas with little risk. As examples, the inventors of Lego building blocks and Velcro fasteners could build their products by hand, at little expense. A pioneering product idea from Procter & Gamble might fit here if there are no current competitors and because, for a company of that size, the financial risks of new product investments can seem relatively small.

In the upper-right quadrant, high innovation/high risk, novel product ideas are accompanied by high risk because the financial investments are high and the competition is great. A new drug or a new automobile would likely fall into this category.

FIGURE 7.2
Entrepreneurial Strategy Matrix

SOURCE: Reprinted from *Business Horizons*, May–June 1997, Sonfield and Lussier, "Entrepreneurial Strategy Matrix: A Model of New and Ongoing Ventures," Copyright © 1997, with permission from Elsevier.

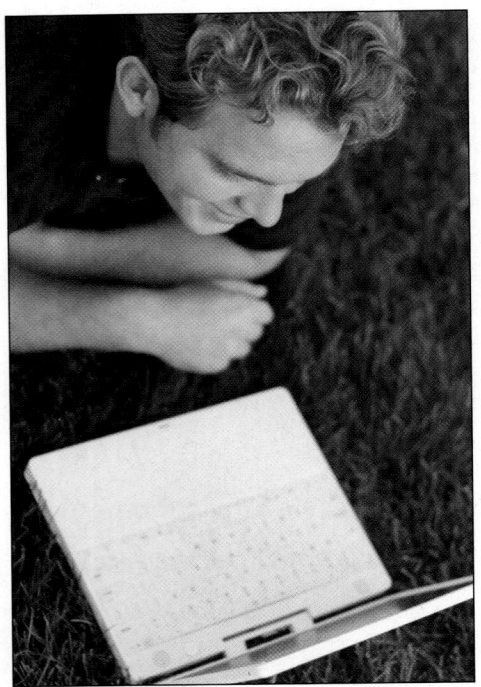

Twitter was launched in July 2006. Thinking about the services it provides and the other social networking websites available, where would you place Twitter in the entrepreneurial strategy matrix (Figure 7.2), and why?

Most small business ventures are in the low innovation/high risk cell (lower right). They are fairly conventional entries in well-established fields. New restaurants, retail shops, and commercial outfits involve high investment for the small business entrepreneur and face direct competition from other similar businesses. Finally, the low innovation/low risk category includes ventures that require minimal investment and/or face minimal competition for strong market demand. Examples are some service businesses having low start-up costs and those involving entry into small towns if there is no competitor and demand is adequate.

How is this matrix useful? It helps entrepreneurs think about their ventures and decide whether they suit their particular objectives. It also helps identify effective and ineffective strategies. You might find one cell more appealing than others. The lower-left cell is likely to have relatively low payoffs but to provide more security. The higher risk/return trade-offs are in other cells, especially the upper right. So you might place your new venture idea in the appropriate cell and determine whether that cell is the one in which you would prefer to operate. If it is, the venture is one that perhaps should be pursued, pending fuller analysis. If it is not, you can reject the idea or take steps to move it toward a different cell.

The matrix also can help entrepreneurs remember a useful point: successful companies do not always require a cutting-edge technology or an exciting new product. Even companies offering the most mundane products—the type that might reside in the lower-left cell—can gain competitive advantage by doing basic things differently from and better than competitors.

IN PRACTICE

For Max Arndt, the choice of a business idea was a requirement for his entrepreneurship class at the University of Minnesota. Pondering what problems of modern society have yet to be solved, it occurred to Arndt that many people hate touching the door handle when they leave a public restroom. How else could they make a sanitary exit? Arndt figured you would need to come up with some kind of metal piece that could be bolted to the bottom of the inside of the door, and that way, you could pull the door open with the toe of your shoe.

That thinking gave birth to the Toepener—basically a metal plate with an L-shaped hook for pulling the door open. Arndt's class loved the idea and voted to make it the one they would back. The school provided a $15,000 loan, and Arndt led his team in setting up the business, with the goal of repaying the loan and earning a profit by the end of the semester. They built a website, set the price at $49.95, and contracted with a manufacturer. Soon they had hundreds of orders and were on track to meet their goals. The editors of *Inc.* magazine also fell in love with the idea, naming the Toepener one of the coolest college start-ups.[61]

• Would you rate this business idea as high or low on innovation? As high or low on risk?

Success and Failure

LO 3

Success or failure lies ahead for entrepreneurs starting their own companies, as well as for those starting new businesses within bigger corporations. Entrepreneurs succeed or fail in private, public, and not-for-profit sectors; in nations at all stages of development; and in all nations, regardless of their politics.[62]

Estimated failure rates for start-ups vary. Most indicate that failure is more the rule than the exception. The failure rate is high for certain businesses like restaurants and lower for successful franchises. Start-ups have at least two major liabilities: newness and smallness.[63] New companies are relatively unknown and need to learn how to be better than established competitors at something that customers value. Regarding smallness, the odds of surviving improve if the venture reaches a critical mass of at least 10 or 20 people, has revenues of $2 million or $3 million, and is pursuing opportunities with growth potential.[64]

> You can find a lot of useful hyperlinks at the MIT Enterprise Forum, http://enterpriseforum.mit.edu/.

Acquiring venture capital is not essential to the success of most start-up businesses; in fact, it is rare. Recent numbers from the Census Bureau say that more than three-fourths of start-up companies with employees were financed by entrepreneurs' own assets or assets of their families. Approximately 1 out of 10 businesses were financed with the owners' credit cards.[65] Still, in a recent quarter, venture capital firms invested more than $6 billion in almost 800 deals;[66] that's a sizable amount of money, even if the fraction of total new companies is small. And venture capital firms often provide expert advice that helps entrepreneurs improve the odds for success.

To understand further the factors that influence success and failure, we'll consider risk, the economic environment, various management-related hazards, and initial public stock offerings (IPOs).

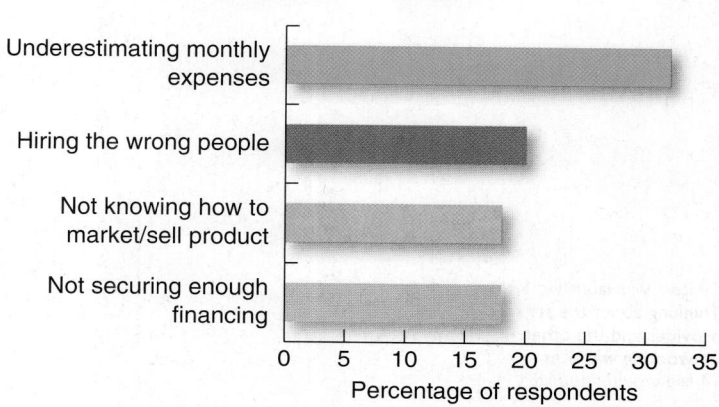

Biggest Start-Up Mistake

Percentage of respondents

> Experts have compiled various lists of missteps that spell doom for a start-up. Often they cite insufficient cash and poor marketing. A recent survey of business owners in companies with fewer than 100 employees found that two of the top mistakes were related to money management.[67]

Risk   You learned about risk in Chapter 3. It's a given: starting a new business is risky. Entrepreneurs with plenty of business experience are especially aware of this. When Chris McGill was evaluating his idea for Mixx.com, a news website that could be personalized based on recommendations by users, he was *USA Today*'s vice president of strategy. To make Mixx succeed, McGill knew he would be leaving a well-paying job for an uncertain future in which he had to line up financing and hire talented people in a turbulent business environment. But McGill also concluded that his experience at *USA Today* and prior management experience with *Yahoo News* gave him the knowledge and connections for a successful Internet business.[68]

Successful entrepreneurs are realistic about risk. They anticipate difficulties and cushion their business to help it weather setbacks. In downtown Seattle, entrepreneurs Ben and Cindi Raykovich saw a risk when a major construction project began disrupting traffic around their store, Sound Sports. The Raykoviches had built their business around serving running enthusiasts who worked downtown and would stop by on their lunch hour or after work. Concerned that the construction would drive away so much business that the store couldn't survive, they opened a second location in the nearby community of Poulsbo. They intend for the second store to supplement revenue, and if they need to close the first store, they can continue to build their business in Poulsbo. Ben Raykovich is hardly cavalier about the situation: "My life is invested in this business. We need to spread out the risk."[69]

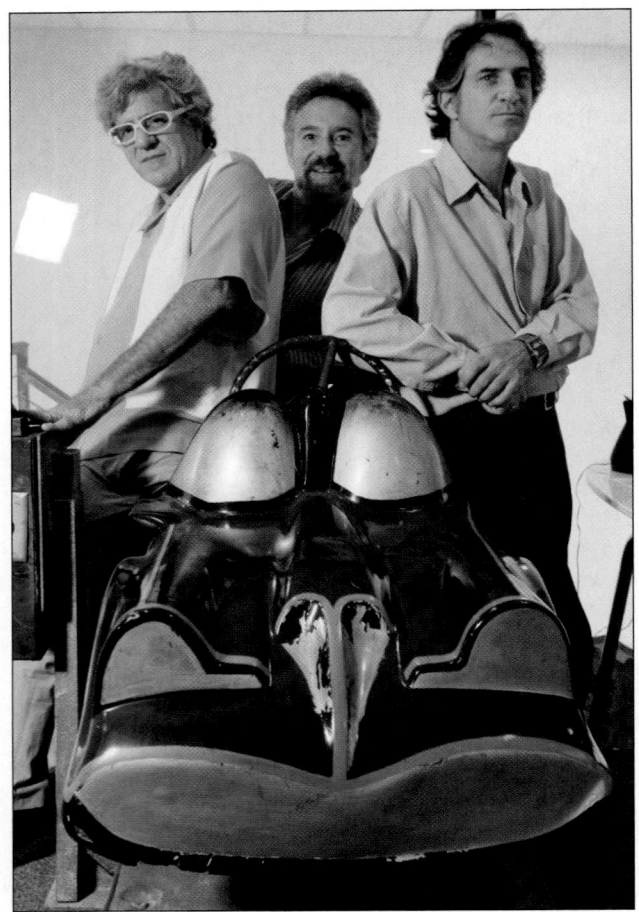

Richard Foos (left), Bob Emmer (center), and Garson Foos are successful entrepreneurs due to their creativity, innovation, and knowledge of their target customers' desires. They are shown here with a circa 1966–1967 Batmobile children's arcade ride in their Shout! Factory headquarters in Los Angeles. As CEO of the Shout! Factory, Richard Foos runs an emporium filled with nostalgia-type collectibles.

business incubators

Protected environments for new, small businesses.

Economic cycles can quickly change favorable conditions into downturns.

The Role of the Economic Environment   Entrepreneurial activity stems from the economic environment as well as the behavior of individuals. For example, money is a critical resource for all new businesses. Increases in the money supply and the supply of bank loans, real economic growth, and improved stock market performance lead to both improved prospects and increased sources of capital. In turn, the prospects and the capital increase the rate of business formation. Under favorable conditions, many aspiring entrepreneurs find early success. But economic cycles can quickly change favorable conditions into downturns. To succeed, entrepreneurs must have the foresight and talent to survive when the environment becomes more hostile.

Although good economic times may make it easier to start a company and to survive, bad times can offer an opportunity to expand. Ken Hendricks of ABC Supply found a business opportunity in a grim economic situation: a serious downturn in the manufacturing economy of the Midwest contributed to the shutdown of his town's largest employer, the Beloit Corporation. Hendricks purchased the company's buildings and lured a diverse group of new employers to town despite the economic challenges. In fact, Hendricks turned around struggling suppliers that ABC acquired.[70] Another silver lining in difficult economic times is that it's easier to recruit talent.

Business Incubators   The need to provide a nurturing environment for fledgling enterprises has led to the creation of business incubators. **Business incubators,** often located in industrial parks or abandoned factories, are protected environments for new, small businesses. Incubators offer benefits such as low rents and shared costs. Shared staff costs, such as for receptionists and secretaries, avoid the expense of a full-time employee but still provide convenient access to services. The staff manager is usually an experienced businessperson or consultant who advises the new business owners. Incubators often are associated with universities, which provide technical and business services for the new companies.

The heyday of business incubators came in the 1990s, when around 700 of them were financing start-ups, mainly emphasizing technology. Eight out of 10 shut down following the collapse of the Internet bubble, but the idea of nurturing new businesses persists. Naval Ravikant, for example, is developing a company tentatively named Hit Forge, which resembles the dot-com incubators. Hit Forge hired four engineers with experience in launching successful Internet concepts. The engineers have wide latitude to try ideas, but they work under strict deadlines. They must go from concept to product within 90 days, and any enterprises that aren't growing after a year will be terminated. Unlike the older-style incubator, Hit Forge lets engineers work from the locations of their choice, and the engineers retain half ownership in the ventures they develop. Also, whereas incubators in the 1990s might have spent $2 million developing an idea, today's launches might cost just $50,000.[71]

As you read "Management Connection: Progress Report," think about which of the preceding ingredients for success and failure were important for Chipotle.

Management Connection

STEVE ELLS'S "FOOD WITH INTEGRITY" STRATEGY FOR CHIPOTLE

When Steve Ells opened his first Chipotle Mexican Grill in Denver, Mexican-themed restaurants were already commonplace, and fast-food restaurants were available just about anywhere. In the words of Ells's co-CEO, Monty Moran, "When creating Chipotle, Steve was making better something that no one wanted to be better, and that was the world of fast food." In effect, Moran says Ells "created something that no one wanted." How did Ells overcome the risks of taking on all of this competition and showing people that they really *did* want better fast food?

Ells seems to have set his business apart based on his single-minded devotion to high-quality, fresh ingredients and his faith that consumers would seek out and pay a bit more for this type of food. (Chipotle raised prices even during the recent recession, but sales barely took a hit.) He eventually built on and extended that commitment with his later theme of food with integrity.

In 2000, after Ells discovered that a family farm called Niman Ranch, where pigs were allowed to range freely, produced the "best pork [he] had tasted," Chipotle restaurants began to phase in the use of naturally raised meats and poultry. By 2008 all of its restaurants were also getting at least some of their produce from local farms, generally located within about 250 miles of the company's distribution centers. (By comparison, Americans today typically eat produce grown an average of 1,500 miles away, according to the company.) Allowing time to find good local sources, the company set goals that 25 percent of at least one produce item would be grown locally, when seasonally available, in 2008, with that percentage rising to 35 percent in 2009 and 50 percent in 2010.

Ells admits that it's harder to find reliable sources of lettuce and tomatoes locally than to tap into established distribution channels. But he insists that the effort is well worthwhile as a way to make his company a leader in good eating: "The more consumers understand the benefits of eating food from more sustainable sources," he says, "the more they're going to want it from everyone." Ells sees his restaurants as an education as well as a dining experience: consumers learn how delicious naturally raised foods can be. He expects they will demand that experience more and more, and restaurants that have identified sources of natural and organic food will be best positioned to satisfy them.

Potentially even more challenging is Ells's commitment to extend integrity to the company's building designs. The newest restaurants are being constructed according to the stringent international standards for LEED certification as energy-efficient and environmentally friendly. A growing number of Chipotle's more than 1,000 restaurants have solar panels, as well as high-efficiency grills and lighting. These efforts have the practical effect of holding down Chipotle's utility bills. However, some observers question a business effort that is unrelated to a restaurant's basic mission of feeding people: consumers have shown they are willing to pay extra for superior food, but will they be as interested in paying extra for the privilege of eating in an environmentally friendly building?

With so many accomplishments aimed at serving food with integrity, has Ells stopped dreaming? Like most entrepreneurs, he continues to see new possibilities, telling a reporter, "We are proud of our accomplishments, but there is still a long way to go."[72]

- Where would you place Chipotle in the strategy matrix shown in Figure 7.2? Why?
- What evidence suggests that Ells made good choices about his strategy?
- What are some risks that Ells faced in starting Chipotle, and how has the economic environment affected his success?

Common Management Challenges   As an entrepreneur, you are likely to face several common challenges that you should understand before you face them, and then manage effectively when the time comes. We next discuss several such challenges.

You Might Not Enjoy It   Some managers and employees can specialize in what they love, whether it's selling or accounting. But entrepreneurs usually have to "do it all," at least in the beginning. If you love product design, you also have to sell what you invent. If you love marketing, get ready to manage the money too. This last challenge was almost a stumbling block for Elizabeth Busch, Anne Frey-Mott, and Beckie Jankiewicz when they launched The Event Studio to run business conferences for their clients. All three women had experience with some aspect of running conferences, but when they started their company, they didn't fully think out all the accounting decisions they would need for measuring their income and cash flow. With some practical advice, they learned some basic accounting lessons that helped them avoid tax troubles later on.[73] If they hadn't been willing to learn new skills, entrepreneurship might not have been the right career path for them.

Survival Is Difficult   Zappos cofounder Tony Hsieh says, "We thought about going under every day—until we got a $6 million credit line from Wells Fargo."[74] Companies without much of a track record tend to have more trouble lining up lenders, investors, and even customers. When economic conditions cool or competition heats up, a small start-up serving a niche market may have limited options for survival. Gary Gottenbusch worried when orders slowed at his Servatii Pastry Shop and Deli, located in Cincinnati. As a recession hit Ohio hard, customers were deciding that fancy breads and cakes were a luxury they could go without. Servatii might have closed, but Gottenbusch was willing to change. He kept afloat and even added to sales by cultivating new distribution channels (sales in hospitals), new products (distinctive pretzel sticks), and cost-cutting measures (a purchasing association with other bakers in the area).[75]

Failure can be devastating. When Mary Garrison wanted to own a business, she chose the women's fitness industry and decided to buy a franchise from Lady of America Franchise Corporation. But when she held her grand opening, not a single person stopped by. Three months later, she closed. Garrison blames the franchisor for not providing the necessary promotional support, a complaint that Lady of America denies.[76]

Growth Creates New Challenges   Just one in three *Inc.* 500 companies keeps growing fast enough to make this list of fastest-growing companies two years running. The reason: they are facing bigger challenges, competing with bigger firms, stretching the founders' capacities, and probably burning cash. Consultant Doug Tatum calls this phase of a company's growth "no man's land."[77] It's a difficult transition.

In the beginning, entrepreneurs keep their business afloat with dogged determination to win customers and keep them happy. They work long hours at low pay, deliver great service, and get good word-of-mouth advertising, and their business grows. When keeping up with all the work becomes physically impossible, entrepreneurs feel they need to bring in help. Julie Ladd, founder of CopyShark.net, says she got ready to contract for help after she spent six months doing everything alone: "I was working 70-plus hours a week and wasn't able to get the turnaround time that my clients needed."[78] The challenge, of course, is that you not only have to come up with the money to keep paying people for the long haul, but also have to figure out who will bring the necessary skills and a level of motivation that can bring them close to the business owner's commitment to the company.

Growth seems to be a consuming goal for most entrepreneurs. But some company founders reach the size where they're happy and don't want to grow any further. Reaching a golden mean is possible.[79] Also, sometimes growth needs to be restrained until the company is ready. Only a year after Gregory Wynn, Komichel Johnson, and Robert A. Jones III set up their homebuilding business, JLW Homes and Communities, they had an opportunity to build a 70-unit condominium project called Heritage Pointe. They determined that getting the job done would require a master builder, two assistants, and at least 100 workers. JLW had two master builders, who were already assigned to projects, and too few workers, so the partners reluctantly decided not to take the job. Jones recalls, "It was way too early for us to do this type of deal, . . . and I'm glad we

Reaching a golden mean is possible.

did [turn it down] because if we didn't, we may have lost our shirts."[80] By carefully planning growth at a sustainable pace, JLW has become a successful Atlanta firm.

It's Hard to Delegate   As the business grows, entrepreneurs often hesitate to delegate to other people work that they are used to doing. Leadership deteriorates into micromanagement, in which managers monitor too strictly, to the minutest detail. For example, during the Internet craze many company founders with great technical knowledge but little experience became "instant experts" in every phase of business, including branding and advertising.[81] Turns out, they didn't know as much as they thought, and their companies crashed. Fortunately, many entrepreneurs observe the consequences of their behavior and figure out how to manage more effectively. Albert Ko, who founded a coupon website called DealPerk, used to handle employees' mistakes by yelling at them; but after he realized he was creating a fear-driven workplace, he began discussing problems privately with an emphasis on improvement. And after losing $500 to mistakes made by an employee who didn't understand directions, Jimmy Tomczak, founder of sandal maker Paper-Feet, has learned to verify that employees understand directions before they get started.[82]

Misuse of Funds   Many unsuccessful entrepreneurs blame their failure on inadequate financial resources. Yet failure due to a lack of financial resources doesn't necessarily indicate a real lack of money; it could mean a failure to properly use the available money. A lot of start-up capital may be wasted—on expensive locations, great furniture, and fancy stationery. Entrepreneurs who fail to use their resources wisely usually make one of two mistakes: they apply financial resources to the wrong uses, or they maintain inadequate control over their resources.

This problem may be more likely when a lucky entrepreneur gets a big infusion of cash from a venture capital firm or an initial offering of stock. For most start-ups, where the money on the line comes from the entrepreneur's own assets, he or she has more incentive to be careful. Tripp Micou, founder of Practical Computer Applications, says, "If all the money you spend is based on what you're bringing in [through sales], you very quickly focus on the right things to spend it on."[83] Micou, an experienced entrepreneur, believes that this financial limitation is actually a management advantage.

Poor Controls   Entrepreneurs, in part because they are very busy, often fail to use formal control systems. One common entrepreneurial malady is an aversion to record keeping. Expenses mount, but records do not keep pace. Pricing decisions are based on intuition without adequate reference to costs. As a result, the company earns inadequate margins to support growth.

Sometimes an economic slowdown provides a necessary alarm, warning business owners to pay attention to controls. When Servatii Pastry Shop and Deli's sales deteriorated even as the prices of ingredients were rising, owner Gary Gottenbusch pushed himself to go "a little out of [his] comfort zone" and consulted with advisers at the Manufacturing Extension Partnership. Besides encouraging him to innovate, the advisers helped him set goals and monitor progress. One problem Gottenbusch tackled was the price of baking commodities, such as shortening and flour. He partnered with other local bakeries to form a purchasing association that buys in bulk and passes along the savings. Keeping costs down helped Servatii stay profitable when customers were trimming their budgets for baked goods.[84]

Blinded by the light of growing sales, many entrepreneurs fail to maintain vigilance over other aspects of the business.

Even in high-growth companies, great numbers can mask brewing problems. In the absence of controls, the business veers out of control. So don't get overconfident; keep asking critical questions. Is our success based on just one big customer?

Is our product just a fad that can fade away? Can other companies easily enter our domain and hurt our business? Are we losing a technology lead? Do we really understand the numbers, know where they come from, and have any hidden causes for concern?

Mortality   One long-term measure of an entrepreneur's success is the fate of the venture after the founder's death. Founding entrepreneurs often fail to plan for succession. When death occurs, estate tax problems or the lack of a skilled replacement for the founder can lead to business failure.

Management guru Peter Drucker offered the following advice to help family-managed businesses survive and prosper.[85] Family members working in the business must be at least as capable and hard-working as other employees; at least one key position should be filled by a nonfamily member; and someone outside the family and the business should help plan succession. Family members who are mediocre performers are resented by others; outsiders can be more objective and contribute expertise the family might not have. Issues of management succession are often the most difficult of all, causing serious conflict and possible breakup of the firm.

initial public offering (IPO)

Sale to the public, for the first time, of federally registered and underwritten shares of stock in the company.

Going Public   Sometimes companies reach a point at which the owners want to "go public." **Initial public stock offerings (IPOs)** offer a way to raise capital through federally registered and underwritten sales of shares in the company.[86] You need lawyers and accountants who know current regulations. The reasons for going public include raising more capital, reducing debt or improving the balance sheet and enhancing net worth, pursuing otherwise unaffordable opportunities, and improving credibility with customers and other stakeholders—"you're in the big leagues now." Disadvantages include the expense, time, and effort involved; the tendency to become more interested in the stock price and capital gains than in running the company properly; and the creation of a long-term relationship with an investment banking firm that won't necessarily always be a good one.[87]

Many entrepreneurs prefer to avoid going public, feeling they'll lose control if they do. That's a viewpoint that has persisted into the second generation of ownership at Half Price Books, a retail chain that was founded four decades ago by Pat Anderson and Ken Gjemre and remains a family business run by Anderson's daughter, Sharon Anderson Wright. Wright sees retaining private ownership as a necessary part of maintaining the company's commitment to employees, pointing out that "not everyone comes out well" when a business is sold. The company, which has more than 100 stores in 16 states, prides itself on hiring bright people and rewarding them with training, a good benefits package, and opportunities for advancement. Concern for employees fits in well with Half Price Books' general commitment to sustainability: 70 percent of the stores' inventory consists of used books, magazines, and music, a business model that promotes reusing rather than throwing out these items. Wright's desire to run an ecofriendly business is another value she can insist on when she is both owner and CEO of the company.[88]

Executing IPOs and other approaches to acquiring capital is complex, legalistic, and beyond the scope of this chapter. Sources for more information include the National Venture Capital Association (www.nvca.org), VentureOne (http://www.ventureone.com), and *VentureWire* (link to this publication from http://www.venturecapital.dowjones.com/).

Increasing Your Chances of Success

LO 5   Aside from financial resources, entrepreneurs need to think through their business idea carefully to help ensure its success. We discuss here the importance of good planning and nonfinancial resources.

Planning   So you think you have identified a business opportunity. And you have the personal potential to make it a success. Now what? Where should you begin?

The Business Plan   Your excitement and intuition may convince you that you are on to something. But they might not convince anyone else. You need more thorough planning and analysis. This effort will help convince other people to get on board and help you avoid costly mistakes.

The first formal planning step is to do an opportunity analysis. An **opportunity analysis** includes a description of the good or service, an assessment of the opportunity, an assessment of the entrepreneur (you), a specification of activities and resources needed to translate your idea into a viable business, and your source(s) of capital.[89] Table 7.3 shows the questions you should answer in an opportunity analysis.

The opportunity analysis, or opportunity assessment plan, focuses on the opportunity, not the entire venture. It provides the basis for making a decision on whether to act. Then the **business plan** describes all the elements involved in starting the new venture.[90] The business plan describes the venture and its market, strategies, and future directions. It often has functional plans for marketing, finance, manufacturing, and human resources.

Table 7.4 shows an outline for a typical business plan. The business plan (1) helps determine the viability of your enterprise, (2) guides you as you plan and organize, and (3) helps you obtain financing. It is read by potential investors, suppliers, customers, and others. Get help in writing up a sound plan!

Key Planning Elements   Most business plans devote so much attention to financial projections that they neglect other important information—information that matters greatly to astute investors. In fact, financial projections tend to be overly optimistic. Investors know this and discount the figures. In addition to the numbers, the best plans convey—and make certain that the entrepreneurs have carefully thought through—five key factors: the people, the opportunity, the competition, the context, and risk and reward.[91]

The *people* should be energetic and have skills and expertise directly relevant to the venture. For many astute investors, the people are the most important variable, more important even than the idea. Venture capital firms often receive 2,000 business plans per year; many believe that ideas are a dime a dozen and what counts is the ability to execute. Arthur Rock, a legendary venture capitalist who helped start Intel, Teledyne, and Apple, stated, "I invest in people, not ideas. If you can find good people, if they're wrong about the product, they'll make a switch."[92]

opportunity analysis

A description of the good or service, an assessment of the opportunity, an assessment of the entrepreneur, specification of activities and resources needed to translate your idea into a viable business, and your source(s) of capital.

business plan

A formal planning step that focuses on the entire venture and describes all the elements involved in starting it.

What market need does my idea fill?
What personal observations have I experienced or recorded with regard to that market need?
What social condition underlies this market need?
What market research data can be marshaled to describe this market need?
What patents might be available to fulfill this need?
What competition exists in this market? How would I describe the behavior of this competition?
What does the international market look like?
What does the international competition look like?
Where is the money to be made in this activity?

TABLE 7.3
Opportunity Analysis

SOURCE: R. Hisrich and M. Peters, *Entrepreneurship: Starting, Developing, and Managing a New Enterprise,* table, p. 41. Copyright © 1998 by The McGraw-Hill Companies, Inc. Reprinted with permission.

TABLE 7.4   Outline of a Business Plan

I. EXECUTIVE SUMMARY
  Description of the Business Concept and the Business
  Opportunity and Strategy
  Target Market and Projections
  Competitive Advantages
  Costs
  Sustainability
  The Team
  The Offering
II. THE INDUSTRY AND THE COMPANY AND ITS PRODUCT(S) OR SERVICE(S)
  The Industry
  The Company and the Concept
  The Product(s) or Service(s)
  Entry and Growth Strategy
III. MARKET RESEARCH AND ANALYSIS
  Customers
  Market Size and Trends
  Competition and Competitive Edges
  Estimated Market Share and Sales
  Ongoing Market Evaluation
IV. THE ECONOMICS OF THE BUSINESS
  Gross and Operating Margins
  Profit Potential and Durability
  Fixed, Variable, and Semivariable Costs
  Months to Breakeven
  Months to Reach Positive Cash Flow
V. MARKETING PLAN
  Overall Marketing Strategy
  Pricing
  Sales Tactics
  Service and Warranty Policies
  Advertising and Promotion
  Distribution
VI. DESIGN AND DEVELOPMENT PLANS
  Development Status and Tasks
  Difficulties and Risks
  Product Improvement and New Products

  Costs
  Proprietary Issues
VII. MANUFACTURING AND OPERATIONS PLAN
  Operating Cycle
  Geographical Location
  Facilities and Improvements
  Strategy and Plans
  Regulatory and Legal Issues
VIII. MANAGEMENT TEAM
  Organization
  Key Management Personnel
  Management Compensation and Ownership
  Other Investors
  Employment and Other Agreements and Stock Option and Bonus Plans
  Board of Directors
  Other Shareholders, Rights, and Restrictions
  Supporting Professional Advisers and Services
IX. OVERALL SCHEDULE
X. CRITICAL RISKS, PROBLEMS, AND ASSUMPTIONS
XI. THE FINANCIAL PLAN
  Actual Income Statements and Balance Sheets
  Pro Forma Income Statements
  Pro Forma Balance Sheets
  Pro Forma Cash Flow Analysis
  Breakeven Chart and Calculation
  Cost Control
  Highlights
XII. PROPOSED COMPANY OFFERING
  Desired Financing
  Offering
  Capitalization
  Use of Funds
  Investor's Return
XIII. APPENDIXES

SOURCE: J. A. Timmons and S. Spinelli, Jr., *New Venture Creation: Entrepreneurship for the 21st Century* 7E, 2007, p. 229. Copyright 2007 The McGraw-Hill Companies, Inc. Reprinted with permission.

The *opportunity* should provide a competitive advantage that can be defended. Customers are the focus here: Who is the customer? How does the customer make decisions? How will the product be priced? How will the venture reach all customer segments? How much does it cost to acquire and support a customer, and to produce and deliver the product? How easy or difficult is it to retain a customer?

> The *opportunity* should provide a competitive advantage that can be defended.

It is also essential to fully consider the *competition*. The plan must identify current competitors and their strengths and weaknesses, predict how they will respond to the new venture, indicate how the new venture will respond to the competitors' responses, identify future potential competitors, and consider how to collaborate with or face off against actual or potential competitors. The original plan for Zappos was for its website to compete with other online shoe retailers by offering a wider selection than they did. However, most people buy shoes in stores, so Zappos cofounders Nick Swinmurn and Tony Hsieh soon realized that they needed a broader view of the competition. They began focusing more on service and planning a distribution method that would make online shopping as successful as visiting a store.[93]

The environmental *context* should be a favorable one from regulatory and economic perspectives. Such factors as tax policies, rules about raising capital, interest rates, inflation, and exchange rates will affect the viability of the new venture. The context can make it easier or harder to get backing and to succeed. Importantly, the plan should make clear that you know that the context inevitably will change, forecast how the changes will affect the business, and describe how you will deal with the changes.

The *risk* must be understood and addressed as fully as possible. The future is always uncertain, and the elements described in the plan will change over time. Although you cannot predict the future, you must contemplate head-on the possibilities of key people leaving, interest rates changing, a key customer leaving, or a powerful competitor responding ferociously. Then describe what you will do to prevent, avoid, or cope with such possibilities. You should also speak to the end of the process: how to get money out of the business eventually. Will you go public? Will you sell or liquidate? What are the various possibilities for investors to realize their ultimate gains?[94]

Entrepreneurs should carefully consider the five key factors when developing a business plan: the people, the opportunity, the competition, the context, and risk and reward. Typically, financial projections dominate the plan while these other important factors are overlooked or undervalued.

Selling the Plan   Your goal is to get investors to support the plan, so the elements of a great plan, as just described, are essential. It's also important whom you decide to try to convince to back your plan.

> According to the State New Economy Index, the most hospitable states for starting an innovative, new-economy business are Massachusetts, Washington, Maryland, New Jersey, and Connecticut.[95]

Many entrepreneurs want passive investors who will give them money and let them do what they want. Doctors and dentists generally fit this image. Professional venture capitalists do not—as they demand more control and more of the returns. But when a business goes wrong—and chances are, it will—nonprofessional investors are less helpful and less likely to advance more (needed) money. Sophisticated investors have seen sinking ships before and know how to help. They are more likely to solve problems, provide more money, and also navigate financial and legal waters such as going public.[96]

View the plan as a way for you to figure out how to reduce risk and maximize reward, and to convince others that you understand the entire new venture process. Don't put together a plan built on naïveté or overconfidence or one that cleverly hides major flaws. You might not fool others, and you certainly would be fooling yourself.

Nonfinancial Resources   Also crucial to the success of a new business are nonfinancial resources, including legitimacy in the minds of the public and the various ways in which other people can help.

Legitimacy   An important resource for the new venture is **legitimacy**—people's judgment of a company's acceptance, appropriateness, and desirability.[97] When the market confers legitimacy, it helps overcome the "liability of newness" that creates a high percentage of new venture failure.[98] Legitimacy helps a firm acquire other resources such as top managers, good employees, financial resources, and government support. In a three-year study tracking business start-ups, the likelihood that a company would succeed at selling products, hiring employees, and attracting investors depended most on how skillfully entrepreneurs demonstrated that their business was legitimate.[99]

A business is legitimate if its goals and methods are consistent with societal values. You can generate legitimacy by visibly conforming to rules and expectations created by governments, credentialing associations, and professional organizations; by visibly endorsing widely held values; and by visibly practicing widely held beliefs.[100]

Networks   The entrepreneur is aided greatly by having a strong *network* of people. **Social capital**—being part of a social network and having a good reputation—helps entrepreneurs gain access to useful information, gain trust and cooperation from others, recruit employees, form successful business alliances, receive funding from venture capitalists, and become more successful.[101] Social capital provides a lasting source of competitive advantage.[102]

Tim Litle has developed several successful innovations and businesses as a result of relationships with business school classmates and customers. Early in his career, a friend in politics wanted to target letters to different groups of citizens, and Litle worked with him to figure out how to do that now-common application with computers. He, the politician, and two other partners eventually built a business to provide the same service to marketers.[103]

IN PRACTICE

An organization set up to build social capital for social entrepreneurs calls itself the Unreasonable Institute. (That name refers to a quote by George Bernard Shaw: "The reasonable man adapts himself to the world; the unreasonable one persists in trying to adapt the world to himself. Therefore all progress depends on the unreasonable man.") The institute's goal is to identify start-ups with innovative and financially sustainable ideas aimed at serving at least a million of the world's poorest people, and then bring 25 of those companies together for a six-week program of meetings with experienced mentors. The expectation is that the planning under expert guidance, as well as the trading of ideas among the entrepreneurs who participate, will get these start-ups off to a running start in solving some of the world's most perplexing problems—at a profit.

The Unreasonable Institute launched the project by reviewing hundreds of applications and selecting 45 finalists. It posted information about the finalists on its website, giving each of them 50 days to raise donations to cover the $6,500 fee to participate. The idea is that these organizations will need to attract capital to succeed, so fund-raising must be an initial hurdle. Finalists have included KITO International, an organization that promotes entrepreneurship among young people living on the streets in various countries; Who Gives a Crap, which intends to make ecofriendly toilet paper and donate the profits to water sanitation projects; and Global Cycle Solutions, which has a plan to use motorcycles and bicycles to run mobile phone chargers and corn shellers in rural areas.[104]

- How does the Unreasonable Institute help start-ups build legitimacy as well as social capital?

Top Management Teams   The top management team is another crucial resource. For example, Sudhin Shahani's start-ups include MyMPO, whose digital media services include Musicane, which lets musicians sell audio and video files and ringtones online at storefronts they create for themselves. The company's head of marketing was singer Will.i.am.[105] Having a musician in that top spot may help Musicane build client relationships with other artists. Also, in companies that have incorporated, a board of directors improves the company's image, develops longer-term plans for expansion, supports day-to-day activities, and develops a network of information sources.

Advisory Boards   Whether or not the company has a formal board of directors, entrepreneurs can assemble a group of people willing to serve as an advisory board. Board members with business experience can help an entrepreneur learn basics such as how to do cash flow analysis; identify needed strategic changes; and build relationships with bankers, accountants, and attorneys.

Partners   Often two people go into business together as partners. Partners can help one another access capital, spread the workload, share the risk, and share expertise. One of the strengths of JLW Homes and Communities, the Atlanta construction business described earlier, is that the three founding partners bring different areas of expertise to the business. Gregory Wynn was a master homebuilder, Komichel Johnson was a financial expert, and Robert A. Jones III was a successful salesperson. Johnson explains the advantage this way: "We don't all agree on the same issues, and we've had some heated arguments. . . . But we realize that through communication and laying out the facts, we can overcome any issues that may arise within our organization."[106]

Despite the potential advantages of finding a compatible partner, partnerships are not always marriages made in heaven. "Mark" talked three of his friends into joining him in starting his own telecommunications company because he didn't want to try it alone. He learned quickly that while he wanted to put money into growing the business, his three partners wanted the company to pay for their cars and meetings in the Bahamas. The company collapsed. "I never thought a business relationship could overpower friendship, but this one did. Where money's involved, people change."

> Partnerships are not always marriages made in heaven.

To be successful, partners need to acknowledge one another's talents, let each other do what they do best, communicate honestly, and listen to one another. That's what the partners in JLW Homes did when they turned down a chance to build a project they were understaffed for completing. Johnson, the financial expert, believed the company would make a good return, and Jones, the salesperson, was eager to move ahead, but homebuilder Wynn said the company was unprepared for a project of that size. Johnson and Jones bowed to Wynn's experience and were later glad they did.[107] Partners also must learn to trust each other by making and keeping agreements. If they must break an agreement, it is crucial that they give early notice and clean up after their mistakes.

Corporate Entrepreneurship

Large corporations are more than passive bystanders in the entrepreneurial explosion. Consider Microsoft. Every spring the company hosts Techfest, essentially a three-day science fair that spotlights innovations the company may pursue. The first day is open to the public, and the second two are for Microsoft employees. About half of Microsoft's researchers come from around the world to be inspired and energized by the glimpse at their colleagues' creative projects.[108]

 LO 6

Even established companies try to find and pursue new and profitable ideas—and they need in-house entrepreneurs (sometimes called intrapreneurs) to do so.

Building Support for Your Idea

A manager who has a new idea to capitalize on a market opportunity will need to get others in the organization to buy in or sign on. In other words, you need to build a network of allies who support and will help implement the idea.

If you need to build support for a project idea, the first step involves *clearing the investment* with your immediate boss or bosses.[109] At this stage, you explain the idea and seek approval to look for wider support.

Higher executives often want evidence that the project is backed by your peers before committing to it. This involves *making cheerleaders*—people who will support the manager before formal approval from higher levels. Some managers refer to this strategy as "loading the gun"—lining up ammunition in support of your idea.

Next, *horse trading* begins. You can offer promises of payoffs from the project in return for support, time, money, and other resources that peers and others contribute.

Finally, you should *get the blessing* of relevant higher-level officials. This usually involves a formal presentation. You will need to guarantee the project's technical and political feasibility. Higher management's endorsement of the project and promises of resources help convert potential supporters into an enthusiastic team. At this point, you can go back to your boss and make specific plans for going ahead with the project.

> Along the way, expect resistance and frustration—and use passion and persistence, as well as business logic, to persuade others to get on board.

Building Intrapreneurship

Building an entrepreneurial culture is the heart of the corporate strategy at Acordia, a successful insurance company that recently changed its name to Wells Fargo TPA.[110] Its success in fostering a culture in which intrapreneurs flourish came from making an intentional decision to foster entrepreneurial thinking and behavior, creating new venture teams, and changing the compensation system so that it encourages, supports, and rewards creative and innovative behaviors. In other words, building intrapreneurship derives from careful and deliberate strategy.

Two common approaches used to stimulate intrapreneurial activity are skunkworks and bootlegging. **Skunkworks** are project teams designated to produce a new product. A team is formed with a specific goal within a specified time frame. A respected person is chosen to be manager of the skunkworks. In this approach to corporate innovation, risk takers are not punished for taking risks and failing—their former jobs are held for them. The risk takers also have the opportunity to earn large rewards.

Bootlegging refers to informal efforts—as opposed to official job assignments—in which employees work to create new products and processes of their own choosing and initiative. Informal can mean secretive, such as when a bootlegger believes the company or the boss will frown on those activities. But companies should tolerate some bootlegging, and some even encourage it. To a limited extent, they allow people freedom to pursue pet projects without asking what they are or monitoring progress, figuring bootlegging will lead to some lost time but also to learning and to some profitable innovations.

Merck, desiring entrepreneurial thinking and behavior in research and development, explicitly rejects budgets for planning and control. New product teams don't *get* a budget. They must persuade people to join the team and commit *their* resources. This creates a survival-of-the-fittest process, mirroring the competition in the real world.[111] At Merck, as at Wells Fargo TPA, intrapreneurship derives from deliberate strategic thinking and execution.

skunkworks

A project team designated to produce a new, innovative product.

bootlegging

Informal work on projects, other than those officially assigned, of employees' own choosing and initiative.

Management Challenges

Organizations that encourage intrapreneurship face an obvious risk: the effort can fail. One author noted, "There is considerable history of internal venture development by large firms, and it does not encourage optimism."[112] However, this risk can be managed. In fact, failing to foster intrapreneurship may represent a subtler but greater risk than encouraging it. The organization that resists entrepreneurial initiative may lose its ability to adapt when conditions dictate change.

The most dangerous risk in corporate entrepreneurship is the risk of overreliance on a single project. Many companies fail while awaiting the completion of one large, innovative project.[113] The successful entrepreneurial organization avoids overcommitment to a single project and relies on its entrepreneurial spirit to produce at least one winner from among several projects.

Organizations also court failure when they spread their entrepreneurial efforts over too many projects.[114] If there are many projects, each effort may be too small in scale. Managers will consider the projects unattractive because of their small size. Or those recruited to manage the projects may have difficulty building power and status within the organization.

The hazards in intrapreneurship, then, are related to scale. One large project is a threat, as are too many underfunded projects. But a carefully managed approach to this strategically important process will upgrade an organization's chances for long-term survival and success.

Entrepreneurial Orientation

Earlier in this chapter, we described the characteristics of individual entrepreneurs. To conclude the chapter, we do the same for companies: we describe how companies that are highly entrepreneurial differ from those that are not. CEOs play a crucial role in promoting entrepreneurship within large corporations.[115]

Entrepreneurial orientation is the tendency of an organization to engage in activities designed to identify and capitalize successfully on opportunities to launch new ventures by entering new or established markets with new or existing goods or services.[116] Entrepreneurial orientation is determined by five tendencies: to allow independent action, innovate, take risks, be proactive, and be competitively aggressive. Entrepreneurial orientation should enhance the likelihood of success and may be particularly important for conducting business internationally.[117]

To *allow independent action* is to grant to individuals and teams the freedom to exercise their creativity, champion promising ideas, and carry them through to completion. *Innovativeness* requires the firm to support new ideas, experimentation, and creative processes that can lead to new products or processes; it requires a willingness to depart from existing practices and venture beyond the status quo. *Risk taking* comes from a willingness to commit significant resources, and perhaps borrow heavily, to venture into the unknown. The tendency to take risks can be assessed by considering whether people are bold or cautious, whether they require high levels of certainty before taking or allowing action, and whether they tend to follow tried-and-true paths.

To be *proactive* is to act in anticipation of future problems and opportunities. A proactive firm changes the competitive landscape; other firms merely react. Proactive firms are forward thinking and fast to act, and are leaders rather than followers. Similarly, some individuals are more likely to be proactive, to shape and create their own environments, than others who more passively cope with the situations in which they find themselves.[118] Proactive firms encourage and allow individuals and teams to *be* proactive.

Finally, *competitive aggressiveness* is the tendency of the firm to challenge competitors directly and intensely to achieve entry or improve its position. In other words, it is a competitive tendency to outperform one's rivals in the marketplace. This might take the form of striking

entrepreneurial orientation

The tendency of an organization to identify and capitalize successfully on opportunities to launch new ventures by entering new or established markets with new or existing goods or services.

Proactive firms are forward thinking and fast to act, and are leaders rather than followers.

fast to beat competitors to the punch, to tackle them head-to-head, and to analyze and target competitors' weaknesses.

What makes a firm "entrepreneurial" is its engagement in an effective combination of independent action, innovativeness, risk taking, proactiveness, and competitive aggressiveness.[119] The relationship between these factors and the performance of the firm is a complicated one that depends on many things. Still, you can imagine how the opposite profile—too many constraints on action, business as usual, extreme caution, passivity, and a lack of competitive fire—will undermine entrepreneurial activities. And without entrepreneurship, how would firms survive and thrive in a constantly changing competitive environment?

Thus management can create environments that foster more entrepreneurship. If your bosses are not doing this, consider trying some entrepreneurial experiments on your own.[120] Seek out others with an entrepreneurial bent. What can you learn from them, and what can you teach others? Sometimes it takes individuals and teams of experimenters to show the possibilities to those at the top. Ask yourself, and ask others: Between the bureaucrats and the entrepreneurs, who is having a more positive impact? And who is having more fun?

| Manager's Brief | Progress Report | **Onward** |

Management Connection

CHIPOTLE GROWS UP

Successful entrepreneurs can sell their company and then start another one, repeating what they know they can do, or they can learn to be managers of a bigger company. Steve Ells has taken the latter option, now running a chain of more than 1,000 restaurants with 25,000 employees and sales approaching $2 billion a year.

Ells's father, an executive in the pharmaceutical industry, helped Ells come up with the cash to start his first restaurant. As customers flocked to Chipotle, Ells spent two years running the first restaurant and saving revenues to start two new locations. In the following year, he added five more. All were located in the Denver area, where Ells himself could keep an eye on them, applying his expertise in the culinary arts.

With an eight-restaurant business and dreams of continued growth, Ells could expand his opportunities by accepting money from people interested in investing in what had become a company with a track record of success. Still keeping the company private, he brought in investors in 1998, which enabled him to expand into the Midwest. Interestingly, one of those investors was McDonald's, a company that is widely respected, although perhaps not so much for its fresh ingredients. By 2001 McDonald's was Chipotle's largest investor.

Eight years after taking its first outside investments, the company went public, selling shares to anyone who wanted to invest. Soon thereafter, McDonald's sold its shares in Chipotle. Being a publicly traded company means Chipotle has to answer not just to Ells, but to the entire investing community. Ells now owns less than 2 percent of his company. As long as the strategy of "food with integrity" is profitable, investors will be happy; if Chipotle loses its appeal to consumers, investors can clamor for new leadership and a new direction for the company. So far, the signs are encouraging: earnings per share of stock have been rising fast.

One kind of freedom may also come with heading up a publicly traded company: Ells might feel freer about positioning his company as an alternative to standard fast food, now that McDonald's is no longer providing the money for expansion. One possible sign of that shift occurred with a costume promotion that Chipotle runs in October. In past years, customers who wore costumes representing a Chipotle menu item got a free burrito. In 2010 the promotion was revised: $2 burritos for anyone dressed as a processed food. For publicity, celebrity chef Jamie Oliver dressed up as a chicken nugget and Steve Ells as a packet of dipping sauce. Proceeds were donated to a nutrition program sponsored by Oliver.

Another challenge of a bigger company is that Ells can't use the same kind of hands-on management that worked with a few restaurants in one city. Instead he has to develop the talent of the people who work for him. Those efforts include a program in which top managers are rewarded for accomplishments such as developing crew members for management positions.

Meanwhile Ells continues to look for new ways to serve great food. Chipotle has opened three test kitchens, including a New York restaurant where the kitchen is headed by a well-respected chef, Nate Appleman. There Appleman dreams up new recipes, such as braised beef shoulder and chicken chorizo, that may shape Chipotle's future menu. And not satisfied just to excel at serving Mexican food, the company is testing a new restaurant concept, serving Asian fast casual fare—with integrity, of course.[121]

- What growth challenges did Steve Ells encounter with Chipotle? How did he handle them?
- How might Ells encourage an entrepreneurial orientation in his company?

KEY TERMS

advertising support model, p. 255	entrepreneurial venture, p. 246	opportunity analysis, p. 265
affiliate model, p. 255	entrepreneurship, p. 246	skunkworks, p. 270
bootlegging, p. 270	franchising, p. 253	small business, p. 246
business incubators, p. 260	initial public offering (IPO), p. 264	social capital, p. 268
business plan, p. 265	intermediary model, p. 255	social entrepreneurship, p. 256
entrepreneur, p. 249	intrapreneur, p. 249	subscription model, p. 255
entrepreneurial orientation, p. 271	legitimacy, p. 268	transaction fee model, p. 255

SUMMARY OF LEARNING OBJECTIVES

Now that you have studied Chapter 7, you should be able to:

LO 1 Describe why people become entrepreneurs and what it takes, personally.

People become entrepreneurs because of the profit potential, the challenge, and the satisfaction they anticipate (and often receive) from participating in the process, and sometimes because they are blocked from more traditional avenues of career advancement. Successful entrepreneurs are innovators, and they have good knowledge and skills in management, business, and networking. While there is no single "entrepreneurial personality," certain characteristics are helpful: commitment and determination; leadership skills; opportunity obsession; tolerance of risk, ambiguity, and uncertainty; creativity, self-reliance, the ability to adapt; and motivation to excel.

LO 2 Summarize how to assess opportunities to start new businesses.

You should always be on the lookout for new ideas, monitoring the current business environment and other indicators of opportunity. Franchising offers an interesting opportunity, and the potential of the Internet is being tapped (after entrepreneurs learned some tough lessons from the dot-bomb era). Trial and error and preparation play important roles. Assessing the business concept on the basis of how innovative and risky it is, combined with your personal interests and tendencies, will also help you make good choices. Ideas should be carefully assessed via opportunity analysis and a thorough business plan.

LO 3 Identify common causes of success and failure.

New ventures are inherently risky. The economic environment plays an important role in the success or failure of the business, and the entrepreneur should anticipate and be prepared to adapt in the face of changing economic conditions. How you handle a variety of common management challenges also can mean the difference between success and failure, as can the effectiveness of your planning and your ability to mobilize nonfinancial resources, including other people who can help.

LO 4 Discuss common management challenges.

When new businesses fail, the causes often can be traced to some common challenges that entrepreneurs face and must manage well. You might not enjoy the entrepreneurial process. Survival—including getting started and fending off competitors—is difficult. Growth creates new challenges, including reluctance to delegate work to others. Funds may be put to improper use, and financial controls may be inadequate. Many entrepreneurs fail to plan well for succession. When needing or wanting new funds, initial public offerings provide an option, but they represent an important and difficult decision that must be considered carefully.

LO 5 Explain how to increase your chances of success, including good business planning.

The business plan helps you think through your idea thoroughly and determine its viability. It also convinces (or fails to convince) others to participate. The plan describes the venture and its future, provides financial projections, and includes plans for marketing, manufacturing, and other business functions. The plan should describe the people involved in the venture, a full assessment of the opportunity (including customers and competitors), the environmental context (including regulatory and economic issues), and the risk (including future risks and how you intend to deal with them). Successful entrepreneurs also understand how to develop social capital, which enhances legitimacy and helps develop a network of others including customers, talented people, partners, and boards.

LO 6 **Describe how managers of large companies can foster entrepreneurship.**

Intrapreneurs work within established companies to develop new goods or services that allow the corporation to reap the benefits of innovation. To facilitate intrapreneurship, organizations use skunkworks—special project teams designated to develop a new product—and allow bootlegging—informal efforts beyond formal job assignments in which employees pursue their own pet projects. Organizations should select projects carefully, have an ongoing portfolio of projects, and fund them appropriately. Ultimately a true entrepreneurial orientation in a company comes from encouraging independent action, innovativeness, risk taking, proactive behavior, and competitive aggressiveness.

DISCUSSION QUESTIONS

1. On a 1 to 10 scale, what is your level of personal interest in becoming an entrepreneur? Why did you rate yourself as you did?

2. How would you assess your capability of being a successful entrepreneur? What are your strengths and weaknesses? How would you increase your capability?

3. Most entrepreneurs learn the most important skills they need after age 21. How does this affect your outlook and plans?

4. Identify and discuss new ventures that fit each of the four cells in the entrepreneurial strategy matrix.

5. Brainstorm a list of ideas for new business ventures. Where did you get the ideas? Which ones are most and least viable, and why?

6. Identify some businesses that recently opened in your area. What are their chances of survival, and why? How would you advise the owners or managers of those businesses to ensure their success?

7. Assume you are writing a story about what it's really like to be an entrepreneur. To whom would you talk, and what questions would you ask?

8. Conduct interviews with two entrepreneurs, asking whatever questions most interest you. Share your findings with the class. How do the interviews differ from one another, and what do they have in common?

9. Read Table 7.1. Which myths did you believe? Do you still? Why or why not? Interview two entrepreneurs by asking each myth as a true-or-false question. Then ask them to elaborate on their answers. What did they say? What do you conclude?

10. With your classmates, form small teams of skunkworks. Your charge is to identify an innovation that you think would benefit your school and to outline an action plan for bringing your idea to reality.

11. Identify a business that recently folded. What were the causes of the failure? What could have been done differently to prevent the failure?

12. Does franchising appeal to you? What franchises would most and least interest you, and why?

13. The chapter specified some of the changes in the external environment that can provide business opportunity (technological discoveries, lifestyle and taste changes, and so on). Identify some important recent changes or current trends in the external environment and the business opportunities they might offer.

14. Choose an Internet company with which you are familiar and brainstorm ideas for how its services or approach to business can be improved. How about starting a new Internet company altogether—what would be some possibilities?

15. Find some inspiring examples of social entrepreneurship and describe them to your class.

16. Brainstorm some new ideas for social enterprise. What challenges do you foresee, and how would you proceed?

EXPERIENTIAL EXERCISES

7.1   TAKE AN ENTREPRENEUR TO DINNER

OBJECTIVES

1. To get to know what an entrepreneur does, how she or he got started, and what it took to succeed.

2. To interview a particular entrepreneur in depth about his or her career and experiences.

3. To acquire a feeling for whether you might find an entrepreneurial career rewarding.

INSTRUCTIONS

1. Identify an entrepreneur in your area you would like to interview.

2. Contact the person you have selected and make an appointment. Be sure to explain why you want the appointment and to give a realistic estimate of how much time you will need.

3. Identify specific questions you would like to have answered and the general areas about which you would like information. (See the following suggested interview questions, although there probably won't be time for all of them.) Using a combination of open-ended questions—such as general questions about how the entrepreneur got started, what happened next, and so forth—and closed-ended questions—such as specific questions about what his or her goals were, if he or she had to find partners, and so

forth—will help keep the interview focused yet allow for unexpected comments and insights.

4. Conduct the interview. If *both* you and the person you are interviewing are comfortable, using a small voice recorder during the interview can be of great help to you later. Remember, too, that you most likely will learn more if you are an "interested listener."

5. Evaluate what you have learned. Write down the information you have gathered in some form that will be helpful to

you later on. Be as specific as you can. Jotting down direct quotes is more effective than statements such as "highly motivated individual." Also be sure to make a note of what you did not find out.

6. Write a thank-you note. This is more than a courtesy; it will also help the entrepreneur remember you favorably should you want to follow up on the interview.

Suggested Interview

QUESTIONS FOR GATHERING INFORMATION

- *Would you tell me about yourself before you started your first venture?*

  Were your parents, relatives, or close friends entrepreneurial? How so?

  Did you have any other role models?

  What was your education/military experience? In hindsight, was it helpful? In what specific ways?

  What was your previous work experience? Was it helpful? What particular "chunks of experience" were especially valuable or relevant?

  In particular, did you have any sales or marketing experience? How important was this in starting your company?

- *How did you start your venture?*

  How did you spot the opportunity? How did it surface?

  What were your goals? What were your lifestyle or other personal requirements? How did you fit these factors together?

  How did you evaluate the opportunity in terms of the critical elements for success? The competition? The market?

  Did you find or have partners? What kind of planning did you do? What kind of financing did you have?

  Did you have a start-up business plan of any kind? Please tell me about it.

  How much time did it take from conception to the first day of business? How many hours a day did you spend working on it?

  How much capital did it take? How long did it take to reach a positive cash flow and break-even sales volume? If you did not have enough money at the time, what were some ways in which you "bootstrapped" the venture (i.e., bartering, borrowing, and the like)? Tell me about the pressures and crises during that early survival period.

  What outside help did you get? Did you have experienced advisers? Lawyers? Accountants? Tax experts? Patent experts? How did you develop these networks and how long did it take?

  What was your family situation at the time?

  What did you perceive to be your own strengths? Weaknesses?

  What did you perceive to be the strengths of your venture? Weaknesses?

  What was your most triumphant moment? Your worst moment?

  Did you want to have partners or do it solo? Why?

- *Once you got going . . .*

  What were the most difficult gaps to fill and problems to solve as you began to grow rapidly?

  When you looked for key people as partners, advisers, or managers, were there any personal attributes or attitudes you were especially seeking because you knew they would fit with you and were important to success? How did you find them?

  Are there any attributes among partners and advisers that you would definitely try to avoid?

  Have things become more predictable? Or less?

  Do you spend more/same/less time with your business now than in the early years?

  Do you feel more managerial and less entrepreneurial now?

  In terms of the future, do you plan to harvest? To maintain? To expand?

  Do you plan ever to retire? Would you explain?

  Have your goals changed? Have you met them?

QUESTIONS FOR CONCLUDING (CHOOSE ONE)

- What do you consider your most valuable asset—the thing that enabled you to "make it"?
- If you had it to do over again would you do it again in the same way?
- Looking back, what do you feel are the most critical concepts, skills, attitudes, and know-how you needed to get your company started and grown to where it is today? What will be needed for the next five years? To what extent can any of these be learned?
- Some people say there is a lot of stress being an entrepreneur. What have you experienced? How would you say it compares with other "hot seat" jobs, such as the head of a big company or a partner in a large law, consulting, or accounting firm?

- What are the things that you find personally rewarding and satisfying as an entrepreneur? What have been the rewards, risks, and trade-offs?
- Who should try to be an entrepreneur? Can you give me any ideas there?

- What advice would you give an aspiring entrepreneur? Could you suggest the three most important "lessons" you have learned? How can I learn them while minimizing the tuition?

SOURCE: J. A. Timmons, *New Venture Creation,* 3rd ed. 1994. Copyright © 1994 The McGraw-Hill Companies, Inc. Reprinted with permission.

7.2   STARTING A NEW BUSINESS

OBJECTIVES

1. To introduce you to the complexities of going into business for yourself.
2. To provide hands-on experience in making new business decisions.

INSTRUCTIONS

1. Your instructor will divide the class into teams and assign each team the task of investigating the start-up of one of the following businesses:
   a. Submarine sandwich shop.
   b. Day care service.
   c. Bookstore.
   d. Gasoline service station.
   e. Other.

2. Each team should research the information necessary to complete the New Business Start-Up Worksheet. The following agencies or organizations might be of assistance:
   a. Small Business Administration.
   b. Local county/city administration agencies.
   c. Local chamber of commerce.
   d. Local small business development corporation.
   e. U.S. Department of Commerce.
   f. Farmer's Home Administration.
   g. Local realtors.
   h. Local businesspeople in the same or a similar business.
   i. Banks and S&Ls.

3. Each team presents its findings to the class.

New Business Start-Up Worksheet

1. *Product*
   What customer need will we satisfy?
   How can our product be unique?

2. *Customer*
   Who are our customers? What are their profiles?
   Where do they live/work/play?
   What are their buying habits?
   What are their needs?

3. *Competition*
   Who/where is the competition?
   What are their strengths and weaknesses?
   How might they respond to us?

4. *Suppliers*
   Who/where are our suppliers?
   What are their business practices?
   What relationships can we expect?

5. *Location*
   Where are our customers/competitors/suppliers?
   What are the location costs?
   What are the legal limitations to location?

6. *Physical Facilities/Equipment*
   Rent/own/build/refurbish facilities? _____
   Rent/lease/purchase equipment? _____
   Maintenance? _____

7. *Human Resources*
   Availability? _____
   Training? _____
   Costs? _____

8. *Legal/Regulatory Environment*
   Licenses/permits/certifications? _____
   Government agencies? _____
   Liability? _____

9. *Cultural/Social Environment*
   Cultural issues? _____
   Social issues? _____

10. *International Environment*
    International issues? _____

11. *Other* _____

CONCLUDING CASE

SHOES WITH SOUL: TWO FRIENDS REALIZE A DREAM

Renee Albertelli and Richard Rodriguez shared a dream ever since they met in college: to start their own business. Both took business and marketing courses and began their careers in established businesses so they could gain experience about what it takes to turn an idea into a business reality. But as they advanced in their careers, the firms they worked for didn't offer the types of challenges they wanted to pursue. They decided they wanted to work for themselves, and they saw an opportunity.

For her job in marketing at a telecommunications firm, Albertelli had traveled to several regions of the world with developing economies, including Africa, Asia, and South America. She became increasingly aware that women in these regions wanted—and needed—to find new ways to earn a living to support and educate their families. Rodriguez, on the other hand, spent his time working in the financial offices of a major U.S. clothing firm that had its own stores nationwide.

During her travels, Albertelli met a group of women who were highly skilled at crafting handmade sandals. They prepared the leather by hand, designed their own shoe patterns, and assembled each pair of sandals with simple tools. Albertelli thought the finished products were beautiful. She was also impressed by the women's desire to operate their own businesses. She thought they would make a great team, if enough sandals could be produced for sale—even in small numbers—in the United States.

Albertelli contacted Rodriguez when she returned from her trip, and the two friends met to create a business plan. Both believed in the product and the cause—they could build a business based on the desire and craftsmanship of small groups of artisans who wanted to band together to form their own businesses and the market for handcrafted goods in the United States. They knew if they could succeed with one group of women and their products, many more would follow. They banked on the assumption that U.S. consumers would fall in love with the idea as well—and buy the products.

Albertelli and Rodriguez took a huge risk—they decided to cash in their retirement savings to fund the creation of the first batch of sandals. They devised a plan for acquiring more financial backing so they could transport and advertise the product. They developed a marketing plan based not only on the beauty of the sandals but also on the lives of the women who created them, so that consumers would feel a connection with the makers. They named their company Shoes with Soul. The two entrepreneurs didn't need to worry initially about locating a manufacturing facility because the shoes would continue to be made in the village where they originated.

Albertelli and Rodriguez worked closely with the woman who had started the shoemaking project in her village. When they had enough prototypes, they began to make the rounds to existing stores. They also considered renting kiosks at certain malls and investigated setting up a booth at specific sporting and cultural events. Although they understood the importance of a website, they decided not to sell the sandals directly online until they had a more complete line of products to offer consumers.

At first, interest in the shoes was limited to small boutiques—entrepreneurs themselves—until a local TV news show heard about the business and decided to do a story on Albertelli, Rodriguez, and the women. Then things began to change, and Shoes with Soul seemed to take off. Rodriguez and Albertelli were excited by their popularity—but how could they fulfill orders, expand their product line, and grow at a sensible pace?

QUESTIONS

1. Describe the personality characteristics that Renee Albertelli and Richard Rodriguez have that should help them navigate the difficulties of starting a business.

2. Rodriguez and Albertelli decided to focus their marketing efforts on the artisans who made the shoes. Do you think this is a wise decision? Why or why not?

3. What management challenges might cause Shoes with Soul to stumble?

4. Describe several steps that Rodriguez and Albertelli could take to avoid these stumbling blocks and guide their new business to success.

PART TWO   SUPPORTING CASE

Can Foxconn Deliver for Apple?

Apple is famous for its attractive and highly prized electronics, including iPhone and iTouch portable devices, iPod and iTunes for music, and iMac and iPad computers. However, Apple doesn't actually make any of its products. Rather, it develops ideas, designs devices, and promotes the products and its brand. To put the devices together, Apple relies on a set of contractors.

One of those contractors is an electronics company called Foxconn, based in Taiwan. With factories located in China, Foxconn has combined manufacturing expertise with low-cost labor to win deals to make computers and key components such as motherboards. As consumers have slowed their spending on laptop computers in favor of smaller devices such as the iPad tablet computer and smartphones, Foxconn has benefited. As of this writing, it was the only company making Apple's iPad and one of just two makers of Apple's iPhone. Workers at Foxconn facilities also produce the Sony PlayStation 3, the Nintendo Wii, Dell and Hewlett-Packard computers, and Nokia cell phones. In China alone, Foxconn employs almost a million workers, making it one of the largest employers in the world. Many of those workers live in on-site dormitories, eat in company-run dining halls, and relax in bookstores and gyms located right at their workplace.

Recently Foxconn has been running into some tragic problems. In 2010 the company drew international media attention when it came to light that several workers at Foxconn's plant in Shenzhen (a city in southern China) had committed suicide. Questions arose about whether working conditions were so horrible as to drive workers to kill themselves. Apple sent executives accompanied by suicide prevention experts to the plant to investigate. Although Apple requires that its contract partners meet specific standards in its code of conduct, and it visits over 100 facilities a year to ensure compliance, it had failed to uncover any problems at Foxconn before the suicides came to light.

In the following year, Foxconn was again in the news about a tragedy when an explosion in its Chengdu, China, plant killed 3 workers and injured 15. Initial investigations suggested that the explosion was the result of a fairly basic manufacturing safety problem: because of improper ventilation, dust collected in the air of a metal-polishing shop, and the dust ignited. If such a problem occurred in the United States, regulators would quickly shut down the facility for violating safety requirements.

Embarrassed by the media and pressured by important customers such as Apple, Foxconn acted to improve working conditions. At the Shenzhen plant, it brought in counselors, improved training of managers and the staff answering calls on the employee hotline, and launched a morale-boosting program called Care–Love, which sponsors employee outings. In the factories in Chengdu and elsewhere, the company took measures to improve ventilation. Along with these changes, Foxconn began giving out raises. In Shenzhen, workers' wages more than doubled.

Since Foxconn launched the effort to improve morale, employee turnover has fallen, and the suicides seem to have ended. Unfortunately the payoff for the company is difficult to measure. Higher costs have erased profits, and Foxconn's stock price has tumbled. So now the company is looking for lower-cost locations. It opened facilities in China's interior cities, where wage rates are about one-third below those of Shenzhen, and is investigating sites in Slovakia, Turkey, and Brazil. Besides saving money, the additional facilities in China may contribute to morale by allowing workers to live closer to their hometowns and families; many of the workers at the Shenzhen facility had traveled far to work there and were homesick.

QUESTIONS

1. What threats, opportunities, strengths, and weaknesses can you identify at Foxconn? How is it addressing these with its strategy?

2. If Foxconn's management hired you to offer advice on improving its ethical decision making and corporate social responsibility, what measures would you suggest? Why?

3. For Foxconn, what management challenges arise from running an exporting business based in China and serving developed nations such as the United States? What management skills does it need under these circumstances?

SOURCES: T. Culpan, Z. Lifei, and B. Einhorn, "Foxconn: How to Beat the High Cost of Happy Workers," *Bloomberg Businessweek*, May 5, 2011, http://www.businessweek.com; D. Nystedt, "Apple: Foxconn 'Saved Lives' with Suicide Prevention Efforts," *PC World*, February 15, 2011, http://www.pcworld.com; J. Bussey, "Measuring the Human Cost of an iPad Made in China," *The Wall Street Journal*, June 3, 2011, http://online.wsj.com; "Apple Report Details Response to Foxconn Suicides," *eWeek*, February 15, 2011, Business & Company Resource Center, http://galenet.galegroup.com; and J. Dalrymple, "Apple Reports on Foxconn, Supplier Workplace Standards," *CNET News*, February 14, 2011, http://news.cnet.com.

Information for Entrepreneurs

If you are interested in starting or managing a small business, you have access to many sources of useful information.

PUBLISHED SOURCES

The first step is a complete search of materials in libraries and on the Internet. You can find a huge amount of published information, databases, and other sources about industries, markets, competitors, and personnel. Some of this information will have been uncovered when you search for ideas. Listed here are additional sources that should help get you started.

Guides and Company Information Valuable information is available in special issues and the websites of *BusinessWeek, Forbes, Inc., The Economist, Fast Company,* and *Fortune,* as well as online in the following:

- Hoovers.com.
- ProQuest.com.
- Investext.com.
- RDS Bizsuite.com.

Valuable Sites on the Internet

- Entreworld (http://www.entreworld.org), the website of the Kauffman Center for Entrepreneurial Leadership, Ewing Marion Kauffman Foundation.
- *Fast Company* (http://www.fastcompany.com).
- Ernst & Young (http://www.ey.com).
- Global Access—SEC documents through a subscription-based website (http://www.primark.com).
- Inc. magazine (http://www.inc.com).
- Entrepreneur.com and magazine (http://www.entrepreneur.com).
- EDGAR database (http://www.sec.gov)—subscription sources, such as ThomsonResearch (http://www.thomsonfinancial.com), provide images of other filings as well.
- Venture Economics (http://www.ventureeconomics.com).

Journal Articles via Computerized Indexes

- Factiva with Dow Jones, *Reuters, The Wall Street Journal.*
- EBSCOhost.
- FirstSearch.
- Ethnic News Watch.
- LEXIS/NEXIS.
- *The New York Times.*
- InfoTrac from Gale Group.
- ABI/Inform and other ProQuest databases.
- RDS Business Reference Suite.
- *The Wall Street Journal.*

Statistics

- Stat-USA (http://www.stat-usa.gov)—U.S. government subscription site for economic, trade, and business data and market research.

- U.S. Census Bureau (http://www.census.gov)—the source of many statistical data including
  - Statistical Abstract of the United States.
  - American FactFinder—population data.
  - Economic programs (http://www.census.gov/econ/www/index.html)—data by sector.
  - County business patterns.
  - Zip code business patterns.
- Knight Ridder . . . CRB Commodity Year Book.
- Manufacturing USA, Service Industries USA, and other sector compilations from Gale Group.
- Economic Statistics Briefing Room (http://www.whitehouse.gov/fsbr/esbr.html).
- Federal Reserve Bulletin.
- Survey of Current Business.
- FedStats (http://www.fedstats.gov/).
- Labstat (http://stats.bls.gov/labstat.htm).
- Global Insight, formerly DRI-WEFA.
- International Financial Statistics—International Monetary Fund.
- World Development Indicators—World Bank.
- Bloomberg Database.

Consumer Expenditures
- New Strategist Publications.

Projections and Forecasts

- ProQuest.
- InfoTech Trends.
- Guide to Special Issues and Indexes to Periodicals *(Grey House Directory of Special Issues).*
- RDS Business Reference Suite.
- Value Line Investment Survey.

Market Studies

- LifeStyle Market Analyst.
- MarketResearch.com.
- Scarborough Research.
- Simmons Market Research Bureau.

Consumer Expenditures

- New Strategist Publications.
- Consumer Expenditure Survey.
- Euromonitor.

Other Sources

- Wall Street Transcript.
- Brokerage House reports from Investext, Multex, etc.
- Company annual reports and websites.

OTHER INTELLIGENCE

Everything entrepreneurs need to know will not be found in libraries because this information needs to be highly specific and current. This information is most likely available from people—industry experts, suppliers, and the like. Summarized here are some useful sources of intelligence.

Trade Associations Trade associations, especially the editors of their publications and information officers, are good sources of information. Trade shows and conferences are prime places to discover the latest activities of competitors.

Employees Employees who have left a competitor's company often can provide information about the competitor, especially if the employee departed on bad terms. Also, a firm can hire people away from a competitor. While consideration of ethics in this situation is important, the number of experienced people in any industry is limited, and competitors must prove that a company hired a person intentionally to get specific trade secrets in order to challenge any hiring legally. Students who have worked for competitors are another source of information.

Consulting Firms Consulting firms frequently conduct industry studies and then make this information available. Frequently, in such fields as computers or software, competitors use the same design consultants, and these consultants can be sources of information.

Market Research Firms Firms doing market studies, such as those listed under the previously mentioned published sources, can be sources of intelligence.

Key Customers, Manufacturers, Suppliers, Distributors, and Buyers These groups are often a prime source of information.

Public Filings Federal, state, and local filings, such as filings with the Securities and Exchange Commission (SEC), Patent and Trademark Office, or Freedom of Information Act filings, can reveal a surprising amount of information. There are companies that process inquiries of this type.

Reverse Engineering Reverse engineering can be used to determine costs of production and sometimes even manufacturing methods. An example of this practice is the experience of Advanced Energy Technology, Inc., of Boulder, Colorado, which learned firsthand about such tactics. No sooner had it announced a new product, which was patented, when it received 50 orders, half of which were from competitors asking for only one or two of the items.

Networks The networks mentioned in this chapter can be sources of new venture ideas and strategies.

Other Classified ads, buyers' guides, labor unions, real estate agents, courts, local reporters, and so on can all provide clues.

The U.S. government is engaging in new and more extensive outreach efforts so that small business owners will use government resources more and understand them more easily. In 2009 the U.S. Small Business Administration launched a community forum, the first government-sponsored online community built specifically for small business owners, on the Business Gateway site of Business.gov. The forum combines discussion threads, blogs, and resource articles. The goals for the SBA and 21 other federal agencies that cosponsor the site are to engage in dialogue with the public, leverage the expertise that exists in both the public and private sectors, and help government better serve entrepreneurs.

SOURCES: J. A. Timmons and S. Spinelli, *New Venture Creation,* 7th ed. (Burr Ridge, IL: McGraw-Hill/Irwin, 2007), pp. 103–4; K. Klein, "Government Resources for Entrepreneurs," *Business Week,* March 3, 2009.

Organization Structure

LEARNING OBJECTIVES

After studying Chapter 8, you will be able to:

LO 1   Explain how differentiation and integration influence an organization's structure. p. 284

LO 2   Summarize how authority operates. p. 287

LO 3   Define the roles of the board of directors and the chief executive officer. p. 287

LO 4   Discuss how span of control affects structure and managerial effectiveness. p. 289

LO 5   Explain how to delegate effectively. p. 291

LO 6   Distinguish between centralized and decentralized organizations. p. 292

LO 7   Summarize ways organizations can be structured. p. 294

LO 8   Identify the unique challenges of the matrix organization. p. 299

LO 9   Describe important integrative mechanisms. p. 305

> " **Take my assets—but leave me my organization and in five years I'll have it all back.** "
>
> — ALFRED P. SLOAN JR.

Manager's Brief	Progress Report	Onward

Management Connection

HOW CISCO SYSTEMS IS CLEANING UP ITS ORGANIZATION CHART

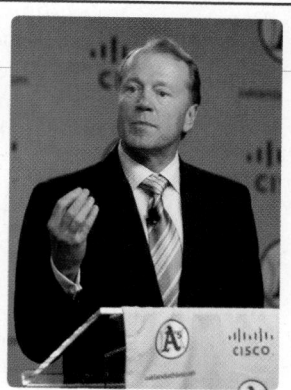

Cisco Systems finds itself in an ironic situation. The Silicon Valley company established itself as the leading provider of hardware for the routing and switching systems that link computers together on the Internet and in wired networks. Thanks to Cisco's hardware, individuals and companies today can collaborate as never before. But after years of rapid expansion, Cisco has become such a cumbersome organization that its own people have struggled to move fast enough in identifying and seizing new business opportunities.

areas, the company will run a separate business unit with its own engineering staff. That way, employees will focus on their particular area of technology. For sales and service, the company is dividing responsibilities into three geographic regions: (1) the Americas, (2) Asia, and (3) Europe, Africa, and the Middle East. The geographic arrangement helps the com-

CEO John Chambers thinks that the way employees are organized into departments, divisions, and councils plays a role in how fast and effectively they can seize new opportunities. As you read this chapter, notice the options available for an organization's structure, and consider whether Cisco's management has made the right choices to enable continued growth.

Although Cisco continues to be the market leader in its major product areas, its share has slipped. Many of its 73,000 employees grew frustrated, and some key executives left Cisco for positions elsewhere. Evidently, developing the latest in networking technology does not guarantee that a company's own people can coordinate their work well enough to stay ahead of the competition.

Cisco's chief executive, John Chambers, recently announced what he hopes will be the solution: a new way of organizing authority and responsibility in Cisco's company structure. The company defined five areas of information technology it intends to focus on: routing and switching, collaboration, video, data center virtualization and cloud (that is, putting these tools online), and "architectures for business transformation" (technology aimed at improving business efficiency). For each of these IT

pany place its people close to customers, and customers will be clear about who at Cisco they should be talking to.

These decisions in some ways reverse some structuring decisions Cisco's leadership made a few years ago, when the company's focus was on building the company rapidly by expanding into new areas. At that time, Cisco set up internal councils of employees drawn from all the company's functional groups—for example, engineering and sales. These councils could draw on resources from throughout the company to expand into new areas. Instead of one manager making decisions to allocate resources in his or her area, the council structure provided an additional path by which people could seek authority and resources to move ahead with an idea. The hope was that this would help the company be more flexible; but in practice, it often meant that managers were distracted and confused about their priorities. The current changes do not end the councils altogether but reduce their number considerably, to just three, each focused on one customer group: service provider, enterprise, and emerging countries. Managers therefore have largely returned to a traditional command-and-control structure where each manager is primarily concerned with his or her own group.

For CEO Chambers, the restructuring of Cisco makes sense because the company's basic strategy is sound and managers need a system in which they can devote themselves more effectively to that strategy. Chambers is betting that with a clearer focus on the targeted business areas, managers will begin making faster decisions, see greater accountability for their results, and seize the valuable opportunities that lie ahead for Cisco.[1]

Although Cisco Systems was the biggest maker of computer networking equipment, investors were nervous to see its market share slipping, and that was taking a toll on employee morale as well as the company's stock price. How could the company respond to this situation? The way in which a company organizes itself to address an issue such as declining market share may well be the most important factor in determining whether its strategy will succeed. Cisco, like many other companies, is working hard to make certain that its strategy and structure are aligned.

Two fundamental concepts around which organizations are structured are differentiation and integration.

This chapter focuses on the vertical and horizontal dimensions of organization structure. We begin by covering basic principles of *differentiation* and *integration*. Next we discuss the vertical structure, which includes issues of *authority*, hierarchy, delegation, and decentralization. We continue on to describe the horizontal structure, which includes functional, divisional, and matrix forms. Finally, we illustrate the ways in which organizations can integrate their structures: coordination by standardization, coordination by plan, and coordination by mutual adjustment.

In the next chapter, we continue with the topic of organization structure but take a different perspective. In that chapter we focus on the flexibility and responsiveness of an organization—that is, how capable it is of changing its form and adapting to strategy, technology, the environment, and other challenges it confronts.

Fundamentals of Organizing

organization chart

The reporting structure and division of labor in an organization.

To get going, let's start simple. We often begin to describe a firm's structure by looking at its organization chart. The **organization chart** depicts the positions in the firm and the way they are arranged. The chart provides a picture of the reporting structure (who reports to whom) and the various activities that are carried out by different individuals. Most companies have official organization charts drawn up to give people this information.

Figure 8.1 shows a traditional organization chart. Note the various types of information that are conveyed in a very simple way:

1. The boxes represent different work.
2. The titles in the boxes show the work performed by each unit.
3. Reporting and authority relationships are indicated by solid lines showing superior–subordinate connections.
4. Levels of management are indicated by the number of horizontal layers in the chart. All persons or units that are at the same rank and report to the same person are on one level.

differentiation

An aspect of the organization's internal environment created by job specialization and the division of labor.

integration

The degree to which differentiated work units work together and coordinate their efforts.

Although the organization chart presents some important structural features, other design issues related to structure—while not so obvious—are no less significant. Two fundamental concepts around which organizations are structured are differentiation and integration. **Differentiation** means that the organization is composed of many different units that work on different kinds of tasks, using different skills and work methods. **Integration** means that these differentiated units are put back together so that work is coordinated into an overall product.[2]

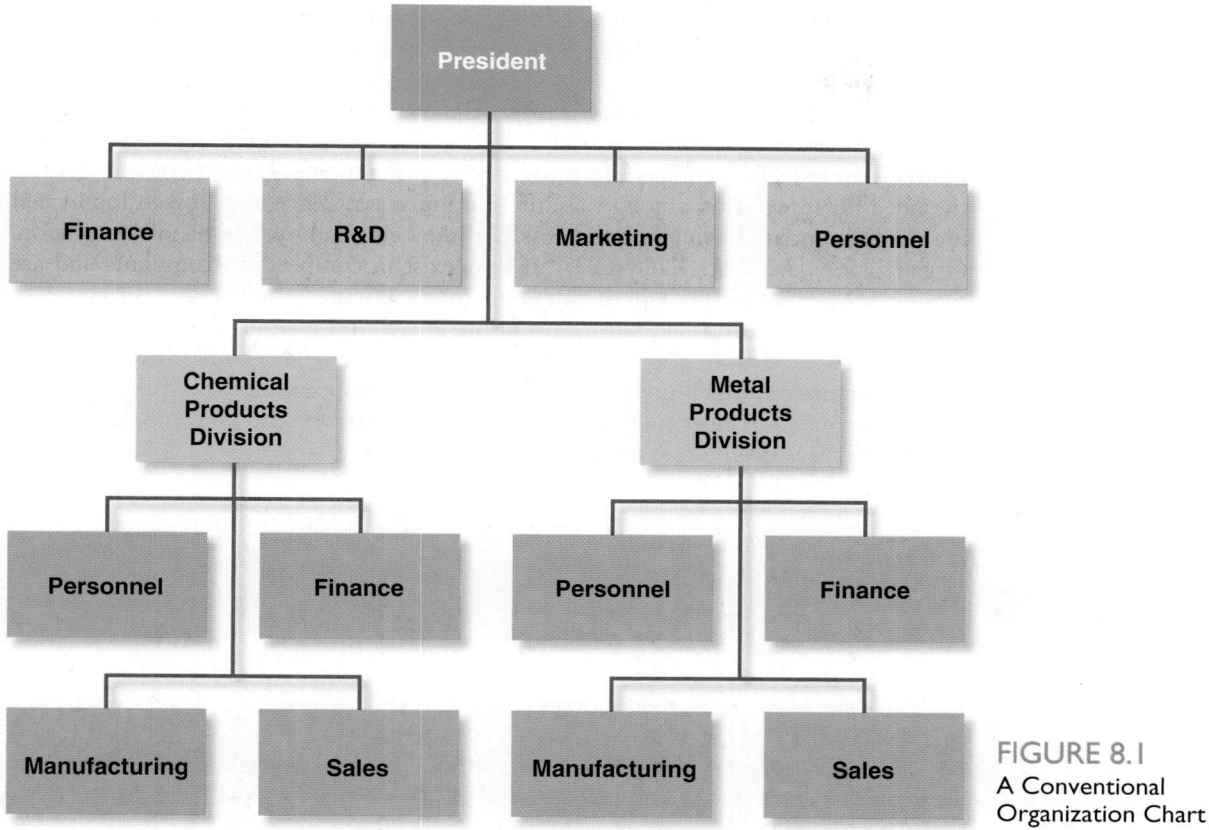

FIGURE 8.1
A Conventional
Organization Chart

Differentiation

Several related concepts underlie the idea of structural differentiation. For example, differentiation is created through division of labor and job specialization. **Division of labor** means the work of the organization is subdivided into smaller tasks. Various individuals and units throughout the organization perform different tasks. **Specialization** refers to the fact that different people or groups often perform specific parts of the larger task. The two concepts are, of course, closely related. Administrative assistants and accountants specialize in, and perform, different jobs; similarly, marketing, finance, and human resources tasks are divided among the respective departments. The many tasks that must be carried out in an organization make specialization and division of labor necessities. Otherwise, the complexity of the overall work of the organization would be too much for any individual.[3]

Differentiation is high when an organization has many subunits and many kinds of specialists who think differently. Harvard professors Lawrence and Lorsch found that organizations in complex, dynamic environments (plastics firms in their study) developed a high degree of differentiation to cope with the complex challenges. Companies in simple, stable environments (container companies) had low levels of differentiation. Companies in intermediate environments (food companies) had intermediate differentiation.[4]

Integration

As organizations differentiate their structures, managers must simultaneously consider issues of integration. All the specialized tasks in an organization cannot be performed completely independently. Because the different units are part of the larger organization, some degree of communication and cooperation must exist among

division of labor

The assignment of different tasks to different people or groups.

specialization

A process in which different individuals and units perform different tasks.

As organizations differentiate their structures, managers must simultaneously consider issues of integration.

coordination

The procedures that link the various parts of an organization for the purpose of achieving the organization's overall mission.

them. Integration and its related concept, **coordination,** refer to the procedures that link the various parts of the organization to achieve the organization's overall mission.

Integration is achieved through structural mechanisms that enhance collaboration and coordination. Any job activity that links different work units performs an integrative function. Remember, the more highly differentiated your firm, the greater the need for integration among the different units. Lawrence and Lorsch found that highly differentiated firms were successful if they also had high levels of integration. Organizations are more likely to fail if they exist in complex environments and are highly differentiated but fail to integrate their activities adequately.[5] In contrast, focusing on integration may slow innovation, at least for a while. In a study tracking the outcomes at information technology companies that acquired other firms, companies with more structural integration were less likely to introduce new products soon after the acquisition, but integration had less of an impact on product launches involving more experienced target companies.[6]

IN PRACTICE

Even though companies are in the same industry, they might take very different approaches to differentiation and integration. Consider two successful developers of video games, Harmonix Music Systems and Valve Software.

Harmonix, known for "Guitar Hero" and "Rock Band," has grown rapidly. As Harmonix added hundreds of employees, management saw a need for greater specialization. Since the company develops several projects at the same time, it has a department devoted to each project, and these departments share the services of an engineering department and an audio department. Each project department has a pair of leaders, one responsible for the game's creative vision, and the other for managing the schedule and budget. Also, Harmonix found that with more people came more diverse experiences and practices, making communication difficult. The company improved coordination by setting formal standards for production methods.

Integration is far less formal at Valve Software, whose games include "Half-Life," "Portal," and "Team Fortress." Valve's structure is based on its organizational culture, which values cooperation and adaptability. The "creative" and "production" roles that Harmonix assigns to its developers are unknown distinctions at Valve, where each employee is a team member who focuses on whatever aspect of the game requires attention. Valve's role is to hire employees it can trust to make the right decisions. The team members working on a project frequently test it and meet to discuss it, and the test results and group input are required to drive any decisions about the product.[7]

- Which company has the higher level of differentiation?

These concepts permeate the rest of the chapter. First we discuss *vertical differentiation* within organization structure. This concept includes issues pertaining to authority within an organization, the board of directors, the chief executive officer, and hierarchical levels, as well as issues pertaining to delegation and decentralization. Next we turn to *horizontal differentiation* in an organization's structure, exploring issues of departmentalization that create functional, divisional, and matrix organizations. Finally, we cover issues pertaining to *structural integration*, including coordination, organizational roles, interdependence, and boundary spanning.

The Vertical Structure

To understand issues such as reporting relationships, authority, responsibility, and the like, we need to begin with the vertical dimension of a firm's structure.

LO 2

Authority in Organizations

At the most fundamental level, the functioning of every organization depends on the use of **authority,** the legitimate right to make decisions and to tell other people what to do. For example, a boss has the authority to give an order to a subordinate.

Traditionally, authority resides in *positions* rather than in people. Thus the job of vice president of a particular division has authority over that division, regardless of how many people come and go in that position and who currently holds it.

In private business enterprises, the owners have ultimate authority. In most small, simply structured companies, the owner also acts as manager. Sometimes the owner hires another person to manage the business and its employees. The owner gives this manager some authority to oversee the operations, but the manager is accountable to—that is, reports and defers to—the owner. Thus the owner still has the ultimate authority.

Formal position authority is generally the primary means of running an organization. An order that a boss gives to a lower-level employee is usually

LO 3

authority
The legitimate right to make decisions and to tell other people what to do.

> "Authority without wisdom is like a heavy axe without an edge, fitter to bruise than polish."
>
> —Anne Bradstreet

carried out. As this occurs throughout the organization day after day, the organization can move forward and achieve its goals.[8] However, authority in an organization is not always position-dependent. People with particular expertise, experience, or personal qualities may have considerable *informal* authority—for example, people who carry themselves with confidence, can deliver valuable information, or work face-to-face with those who have high positions.[9] Effective managers are aware of informal authority as a factor that can help or hinder their achievement of the organization's goals; we will say more about informal authority in the next chapter and Chapter 12. For now, we discuss the formal authority structure of the organization from the top down, beginning with the board of directors.

Board of Directors   In corporations, the owners are the stockholders. But because there are numerous stockholders and these individuals generally lack timely information, few are directly involved in managing the organization. Stockholders elect a board of directors to oversee the organization. The board, led by the chair, makes major decisions affecting the organization, subject to corporate charter and bylaw provisions. Boards perform at least three major sets of duties: (1) selecting, assessing, rewarding, and perhaps replacing the CEO; (2) determining the firm's strategic direction and reviewing financial performance; and (3) ensuring ethical, socially responsible, and legal conduct.[10]

Large corporations have a shareholder-elected board of directors. Small business leaders can benefit from the expertise of outside executives in the same way by forming peer groups or attending monthly meetings with business owners from noncompeting companies to trade advice.

The board's membership usually includes some top executives—called *inside directors.* Outside members of the board tend to be executives at other companies. The trend in recent years has been toward reducing the number of insiders and increasing

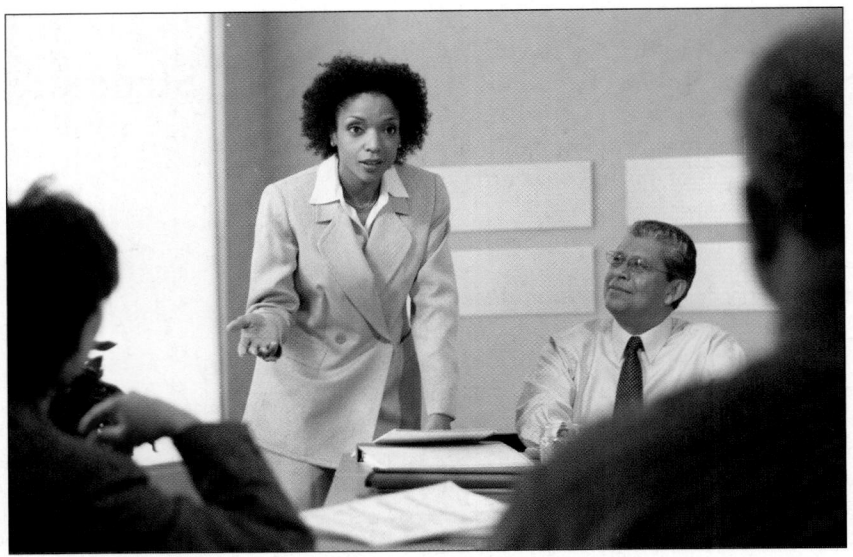

The job of CEO typically consists of leading the board of directors, encouraging employees, and promoting positive change while being accountable for the overall success of the company.

the number of outsiders. Today most companies have a majority of outside directors. Boards made up of strong, independent outsiders are more likely to provide different information and perspectives and to prevent big mistakes. Successful boards tend to be those who are active, critical participants in determining company strategies. Even so, in the wake of scandals and lawsuits, many boards have shifted their focus to compliance issues, such as audits, financial reporting, and laws against discrimination. These issues are critically important, but a board staffed mainly with legal and regulatory experts cannot always give management the necessary direction on strategy.[11]

The owner and managers of a small business may need the expertise of a board of directors at least as much as a large company does. To obtain some of these benefits without the expense or loss of day-to-day control, small business leaders may seek advisers who will hold them accountable for their goals and performance. Some owners set up a board of advisers, such as owners of noncompeting companies, retired executives, and perhaps their banker or accountant. Others hire a business consultant or coach, and they have regular meetings at which they discuss progress toward goals. Owners might even take on a partner who has more skills or experience in an area where the owner is relatively weak. Business development coach Jack Tester advocates such efforts based on his own experience, which has taught him that he works harder when he knows someone is watching and will hold him accountable.[12]

Chief Executive Officer   The authority officially vested in the board of directors is assigned to a chief executive officer (CEO), who occupies the top of the organizational pyramid. The CEO is personally accountable to the board and to the owners for the organization's performance.

In some corporations, one person holds all three positions of CEO, chair of the board of directors, and president.[13] More commonly, however, one person holds two of those positions, with the CEO serving also as either the chair of the board or the president of the organization. When the CEO is president, the chair may be honorary and may do little more than conduct meetings. In other cases, the chair may be the CEO and the president is second in command.

In recent years the trend has been to separate the position of CEO and chairman of the board. Sometimes this change is related to improved corporate governance; board oversight is easier when the CEO is not quite as dominant a figure. In other cases, the board has acted to reduce an unpopular CEO's power or to help prepare for a successor to the CEO.

Top Management Team   Increasingly, CEOs share their authority with other key members of the top management team. Top management teams typically are composed of the CEO, president, chief operating officer, chief financial officer, and other key executives. Rather than make critical decisions on their own, CEOs at companies such as Shell, Honeywell, and Merck regularly meet with their top management teams to make decisions as a unit.[14]

Hierarchical Levels

In Chapter 1 we discussed the three broad levels of the organizational pyramid, commonly called the **hierarchy.** The CEO occupies the top position and is the senior member of top management. The top managerial level also includes presidents and vice presidents. They are the strategic managers in charge of the entire organization.

The key responsibilities at this top level include **corporate governance**—a term describing the oversight of the firm by its executive staff and board of directors. In recent years, as a result of corporate scandals and extremely generous executive pay packages, the public's trust in corporate governance has eroded significantly. As we mentioned in Chapter 5, Congress responded by passing the Sarbanes-Oxley Act, which, along with requirements by the Securities and Exchange Commission, imposed much tighter corporate governance rules. For example, company CEOs and CFOs (chief financial officers) now have to personally certify the accuracy of their firm's financial statements.

The second broad level of the organization is middle management. At this level, managers are in charge of plants or departments. The lowest level is made up of lower management and workers. It includes office managers, sales managers, supervisors, and other first-line managers, as well as the employees who report directly to them. This level is also called the *operational level* of the organization.

An authority structure is the glue that holds these levels together. Generally, but not always, people at higher levels have the authority to make decisions and tell lower-level people what to do. For example, middle managers can give orders to first-line supervisors; first-line supervisors, in turn, direct operative-level workers.

A powerful trend for U.S. businesses over the past few decades has been to reduce the number of hierarchical layers. General Electric used to have 29 levels; today it has only a handful of layers, and its hierarchical structure is basically flat. Most executives today believe that fewer layers create a more efficient, fast-acting, and cost-effective organization. This also holds true for the **subunits** of major corporations. A study of 234 branches of a financial services company found that branches with fewer layers tended to have higher operating efficiency than did branches with more layers.[15]

This trend and research might seem to suggest that hierarchy is a bad thing, but entrepreneur Joel Spolsky learned that a completely flat structure is not necessarily ideal. When Spolsky and Michael Pryor started Fog Creek Software, they decided they would empower employees by having everyone report to the two owners. The system worked fine for a few years until Fog Creek grew to 17 full-time employees. At that size, the company was no longer one small happy family; employees had concerns and were finding it difficult to approach the partners and set up three-way meetings with them. So Spolsky and Pryor tapped two of the employees to serve as leaders of programming teams. Employees found it easier to talk to their team leader, and Spolsky concludes that this layer of "middle management" is helping his company run more smoothly.[16]

Span of Control

The number of people under a manager is an important feature of an organization's structure. The number of subordinates who report directly to an executive or supervisor is called the **span of control.** The implications of differences in the span of control for the shape of an organization are straightforward. Holding size constant, narrow spans build a *tall* organization that has many reporting levels. Wide spans create a *flat* organization with fewer reporting levels. The span of control can be too narrow or too wide. The optimal span of control maximizes effectiveness because it is (1) narrow enough to permit managers to maintain control over subordinates but (2) not so narrow that it leads to overcontrol and an excessive number of managers who oversee a small number of subordinates.

---

hierarchy

The authority levels of the organizational pyramid.

corporate governance

The role of a corporation's executive staff and board of directors in ensuring that the firm's activities meet the goals of the firm's stakeholders.

Bottom Line
A structure with fewer horizontal layers saves time and money.
Why not eliminate all middle layers to save the most time and money?

subunits

Subdivisions of an organization.

LO **4**

span of control

The number of subordinates who report directly to an executive or supervisor.

What is the optimal number of subordinates? Five, according to Napoleon Bonaparte.[17] Some managers today still consider five a good number. At one Japanese bank, in contrast, several hundred branch managers report to the same boss.

Actually, the optimal span of control depends on a number of factors. The span should be wider when (1) the work is clearly defined and unambiguous, (2) subordinates are highly trained and have access to information, (3) the manager is highly capable and supportive, (4) jobs are similar and performance measures are comparable, and (5) subordinates prefer autonomy to close supervisory control. If the opposite conditions exist, a narrow span of control may be more appropriate.[18]

Delegation

As we look at organizations and recognize that authority is spread out over various levels and spans of control, the issue of delegation becomes paramount. **Delegation** is the assignment of authority and responsibility to a subordinate at a lower level. It often requires that the subordinate report back to his or her boss about how effectively the assignment was carried out. Delegation is perhaps the most fundamental feature of management because it entails getting work done through others. Thus delegation is important at all hierarchical levels. The process can occur between any two individuals in any type of structure with regard to any task.

Some managers are comfortable fully delegating an assignment to subordinates; others are not. Consider the differences between these two office managers and the ways they gave out the same assignment in the following example. Are both of these examples of delegation?

Some consider five subordinates under one manager a preferable span of control, though it really depends on the size and nature of the business.

delegation

The assignment of new or additional responsibilities to a subordinate.

Delegation is perhaps the most fundamental feature of management because it entails getting work done through others.

Manager A: "Call Tom Burton at Nittany Office Equipment. Ask him to give you the price list on an upgrade for our personal computers. I want to move up to a quad-core processor with 8 gigs of RAM and at least a 1.5-terabyte hard drive. Ask them to give you a demonstration of the Windows 7 operating system and Microsoft Office 365. I want to be able to establish collaboration capability for the entire group. Invite Cochran and Snow to the demonstration, and let them try it out. Have them write up a summary of their needs and the potential applications they see for the new systems. Then prepare me a report with the costs and specifications of the upgrade for the entire department. Oh, yes, be sure to ask for information on service costs."

Manager B: "I'd like to do something about our personal computer system. I've been getting some complaints that the current systems are too slow, can't run current software, and don't allow for networking. Could you evaluate our options and give me a recommendation on what we should do? Our budget is around $2,000 per person, but I'd like to stay under that if we can. Feel free to talk to some of the managers to get their input, but we need to have this done as soon as possible."

Responsibility, Authority, and Accountability   When delegating work, it is helpful to keep in mind the important distinctions among the concepts of authority, responsibility, and accountability. **Responsibility** means that a person is assigned a task that he or she is supposed to carry out. When delegating work responsibilities, the manager also should delegate to the subordinate enough authority to get the job done. *Authority*, recall, means that the person has the power and the right to make

responsibility

The assignment of a task that an employee is supposed to carry out.

decisions, give orders, draw on resources, and do whatever else is necessary to fulfill the responsibility. Ironically, it is quite common for people to have more responsibility than authority; they must perform as well as they can through informal influence tactics instead of relying purely on authority. More will be said about informal power and how to use it in Chapter 12.

As the manager delegates responsibilities, subordinates are held accountable for achieving results. **Accountability** means that the subordinate's manager has the right to expect the subordinate to perform the job, and the right to take corrective action if the subordinate fails to do so. The subordinate must report upward on the status and quality of his or her performance of the task.

However, the ultimate responsibility—accountability to higher-ups—lies with the manager doing the delegating. Managers remain responsible and accountable not only for their own actions but also for the actions of their subordinates. Managers should not resort to delegation to others as a means of escaping their own responsibilities. In many cases, however, managers refuse to accept responsibility for subordinates' actions. Managers often "pass the buck" or take other evasive action to ensure they are not held accountable for mistakes.[19] Ideally, however, empowering employees to make decisions or take action results in an increase in employee responsibility.

accountability

The expectation that employees will perform a job, take corrective action when necessary, and report upward on the status and quality of their performance.

Advantages of Delegation Delegating work offers important advantages, particularly when it is done effectively. Effective delegation leverages the manager's energy and talent and those of his or her subordinates. It allows managers to accomplish much more than they would be able to do on their own. Conversely, lack of delegation, or ineffective delegation, sharply reduces what a manager can achieve. The manager also saves one of his or her most valuable assets—time—by giving some of his or her responsibility to somebody else. He or she is then free to devote energy to important, higher-level activities such as planning, setting objectives, and monitoring performance.

Another very important advantage of delegation is that it helps develop effective subordinates. Look again at the different ways the two office managers gave out the same assignment. The approach that is more likely to empower subordinates

LO 5

Delegating leadership responsibilities to a new frontline supervisor develops management talent for the organization. But many new supervisors find the experience challenging, stressful, and even overwhelming—probably because few are well prepared ahead of time. Instead they have to learn on the job.[20]

Most influential sources of current leadership skills

(bar chart)

- Trial and error on the job — ~58
- Support from manager/supervisor — ~52
- Formal on-the-job training — ~40
- Support from mentor other than manager — ~27
- Formal educational experience — ~22

Percent (axis: 0 10 20 30 40 50 60)

and help them develop will be obvious to you. (You may also quickly conclude which of the two managers you would prefer to work for.) Delegation essentially gives the subordinate a more important job. The subordinate acquires an opportunity to develop new skills and to demonstrate potential for additional responsibilities and perhaps promotion. In essence, the subordinate receives a vital form of on-the-job training that could pay off in the future. In addition, there is evidence that, at least for some employees, delegation promotes a sense of being an important, contributing member of the organization, so these employees tend to feel a stronger commitment, perform their tasks better, and engage in more innovation.[21]

Bottom Line

Effective delegation raises the quality of subordinates and the service they provide to customers or coworkers. *Under what conditions might an effort at delegation backfire?*

FIGURE 8.2
The Steps in Effective Delegation

Through delegation, the organization also receives payoffs. Allowing managers to devote more time to important managerial functions while lower-level employees carry out assignments means that jobs are done more efficiently and cost-effectively. In addition, as subordinates develop and grow in their own jobs, their ability to contribute to the organization increases as well.

How Should Managers Delegate?   To achieve the advantages we have just discussed, delegation must be done properly. As Figure 8.2 shows, effective delegation proceeds through several steps.[22]

The first step in the delegation process, defining the goal, requires the manager to have a clear understanding of the outcome he or she wants. Then the manager should select a person who is capable of performing the task. Delegation is especially beneficial if you can identify an employee who would benefit from developing skills through the experience of taking on the additional responsibility.

The person who gets the assignment should be given the authority, time, and resources to carry out the task successfully. The required resources usually involve people, money, and equipment, but often they may also involve critical information that will put the assignment in context. ("Review every cost item carefully, because if we're the low bidder, we'll get the account.") Throughout the delegation process, the manager and the subordinate must work together and communicate about the project. The manager should know the subordinate's ideas at the beginning and inquire about progress or problems at periodic meetings and review sessions. Thus, even though the subordinate performs the assignment, the manager is available and aware of its current status. These checkups also provide an important opportunity to offer encouragement and praise.

Some tasks, such as disciplining subordinates and conducting performance reviews, should not be delegated. But when managers err, it usually is because they delegated too little rather than too much. The manager who wants to learn how to delegate more effectively should remember this distinction: If you are not delegating, you are merely *doing* things; but the more you delegate, the more you are truly *building* and *managing* an organization.[23]

Decentralization

LO 6

centralized organization

An organization in which high-level executives make most decisions and pass them down to lower levels for implementation.

decentralized organization

An organization in which lower-level managers make important decisions.

The delegation of responsibility and authority *decentralizes* decision making. In a **centralized organization,** important decisions usually are made at the top. In **decentralized organizations,** more decisions are made at lower levels. Ideally, decision making occurs at the level of the people who are most directly affected and have the most intimate knowledge about the problem. This is particularly important when the business environment is fast-changing and decisions must be made quickly and well. Balanced against these criteria, centralization may be valuable when departments have different priorities or conflicting goals, which need to be mediated by top management. For example, when researchers modeled the search for new ideas in organizations, they found that the worst performance occurred in decentralized organizations where the search for new ideas was carried out at lower levels, because ideas were presented for approval only if they benefited the particular department doing the search.[24]

Sometimes organizations change their degree of centralization, depending on the particular challenges they face. Tougher times often cause senior managements to take charge, whereas in times of rapid growth, decisions are pushed farther down the chain of command. The change to greater or less centralization can also be a response to an opportunity. When Disney's chairman Robert Iger picked Rich Ross to lead Walt Disney Studios, the

The delegation of responsibility and authority decentralizes decision making.

opportunity was Iger's belief that Disney's movies could earn more if they worked with television, theme park, apparel, and other products to build brands. Ross's strategy was to set and enforce a broad goal: releasing movies whose characters would lend themselves to licensing deals or brand extension (for example, a theme park ride). As long as they work toward that objective, Ross gives wide latitude to the heads of his studios, Marvel, Pixar, DreamWorks, and Walt Disney Pictures. He also ensures that employees at the studios and in Disney's other divisions are aware of the projects moving forward, so the divisions can build on each other's work. Within the first two years of Ross's leadership, profits for Walt Disney Studios rose significantly.[25] In this example, Walt Disney Studios moved to greater decentralization. Recent research suggests that a change in this direction tends to go more smoothly than a change toward greater centralization; in that study, teams that became more centralized failed to make the efficiency gains typically associated with a centralized organization.[26]

At times, decentralizing decision making or allowing decisions to be made by middle and lower-level managers can be an advantage to higher-level executives. These are the managers that deal directly with the problem and know the best solution for the company and the employees.

Most American executives today understand the advantages of pushing decision-making authority down to the point of the action. The level that deals directly with problems and opportunities has the most relevant information and can best foresee the consequences of decisions. Executives also see how the decentralized approach allows people to take timelier action.[27]

When times get tough, people tend to want to seize greater control over their situation, and if you're a senior executive, a centralized structure often seems to be the safest course. Nevertheless, executives at Johnson & Johnson have been sticking to decentralization, even during the recent severe recession.

Johnson & Johnson, best known for brands like Band-Aid bandages and Splenda artificial sweetener, operates 250 business units in 57 countries. Besides the famous consumer brands, it also makes medical devices and pharmaceuticals—all products linked to health care. With so many product lines in so many geographic areas, executives at the company's New Jersey headquarters couldn't possibly make all the right decisions. So within the three broad divisions of consumer products, medical devices and diagnostics, and pharmaceuticals, line managers are charged with running business units specializing in particular products and regions.

Not only does this arrangement push decisions closer to the customers, but it also helps J&J develop a huge pool of management talent. Managers can improve their skills while serving a small market segment and take on additional responsibilities as they learn. The company's chief executive officer and chief financial officer both built careers at J&J by working in various businesses to develop broad skills. Similarly, Sheri McCoy, who leads the pharmaceuticals division, held various positions in devices and diagnostics. That kind of experience is hard to get in a company that is smaller or more centralized, so J&J is using its organizational structure as a source of competitive advantage.[28]

• Why is decentralization a competitive advantage for Johnson & Johnson?

According to Raj Gupta, president of Environmental Systems Design (ESD), the engineering design firm decentralized as a necessary response to growth. A traditional "command-and-control" approach to management worked fine when the company was starting out, but now with 240 engineering and design professionals designing for diverse clients working on commercial, transportation, residential, manufacturing, energy, and other projects, it would be impossible for a few people at the top to dictate solutions. In fact, it wouldn't even be desirable, given the diverse expertise of its employees. So instead of grouping staff into functional departments such as sustainable design or electrical work, ESD has a structure in which studios of professionals serve particular clients, making decisions to meet their specialized needs.[29]

The Horizontal Structure

Up to this point, we've talked primarily about vertical aspects of organization structure. Issues of authority, span of control, delegation, and decentralization are important because they give us an idea of how managers and employees relate to one another at different levels. Yet separating discussion of vertical differentiation from horizontal differentiation is a bit artificial because the elements work simultaneously.

As the tasks of organizations become increasingly complex, the organization inevitably must be subdivided—that is, *departmentalized*—into smaller units or departments. One of the first places this can be seen is in the distinction between line and staff departments. **Line departments** are those that have responsibility for the principal activities of the firm. Line units deal directly with the organization's primary goods or services; they make things, sell things, or provide customer service. At General Motors, for example, line departments include product design, fabrication, assembly, distribution, and the like. Line managers typically have much authority and power in the organization. They have the ultimate responsibility for making major operating decisions. They also are accountable for the bottom-line results of their decisions.

Staff departments are those that provide specialized or professional skills that support line departments. They include research, legal, accounting, public relations, and human resources departments. Each of these specialized units often has its own vice president, and some are vested with a great deal of authority, as when accounting or finance groups approve and monitor budgetary activities.

In traditionally structured organizations, conflicts could arise between line and staff departments. One reason was that career paths and success in many staff functions have depended on being an expert in that particular functional area, while success in line functions is based more on knowing the organization's industry. Thus, while line managers might be eager to pursue new products and customers, staff managers might seem to stifle these ideas with a focus on requirements and procedures. Line managers might seem more willing to take risks for the sake of growth, while staff managers seem more focused on protecting the company from risks. But in today's organizations, staff units tend to be less focused on monitoring and controlling performance and more interested in moving toward a new role focused on strategic support and expert advice.[30] For example, human resource managers have broadened their focus from merely creating procedures that meet legal requirements to helping organizations plan for, recruit, develop, and keep the kinds of employees who will give the organization a long-term competitive advantage. This type of strategic thinking not only makes staff managers more valuable to their organizations but also can reduce the conflict between line and staff departments.

As organizations divide work into different units, we can detect patterns in the way departments are clustered and arranged. The three basic approaches to **departmentalization** are functional, divisional, and matrix. We will talk about each and highlight some of their similarities and differences.

line departments

Units that deal directly with the organization's primary goods and services.

staff departments

Units that support line departments.

departmentalization

Subdividing an organization into smaller subunits.

The Functional Organization

In a **functional organization,** jobs (and departments) are specialized and grouped according to *business functions* and the skills they require: production, marketing, human resources, research and development, finance, accounting, and so forth. Figure 8.3 illustrates a basic functional organization chart.

Functional departmentalization is common in both large and small organizations. Large companies may organize along several different functional groupings, including groupings unique to their businesses. For example, Carmike Cinema, which operates more than 2,200 screens in 240 theaters in 36 states, has vice presidents of finance, concessions, film, and entertainment and digital cinema, as well as a general manager of theater operations.

The traditional functional approach to departmentalization has a number of potential advantages for an organization:[31]

1. *Economies of scale can be realized.* When people with similar skills are grouped, more efficient equipment can be purchased, and discounts for large purchases can be used.
2. *Monitoring of the environment* is more effective. Each functional group is more closely attuned to developments in its own field and therefore can adapt more readily.
3. *Performance standards* are better maintained. People with similar training and interests may develop a shared concern for performance in their jobs.
4. People have greater opportunity for *specialized training* and *in-depth skill development.*
5. Technical specialists are relatively *free of administrative work.*
6. *Decision making* and *lines of communication* are simple and clearly understood.

The functional form does have disadvantages, however. People may care more about their own function than about the company as a whole, and their attention to functional tasks may make them lose focus on overall product quality and customer satisfaction. Managers develop functional expertise but do not acquire knowledge of the other areas of the business; they become specialists but not generalists. Between functions, conflicts arise, and communication and coordination fall off. In short, while functional differentiation may exist, *functional integration* may not.

As a consequence, the functional structure may be most appropriate in rather simple, stable environments. If the organization becomes fragmented (or *dis*integrated), it may have difficulty developing and bringing new products to market and responding quickly to customer demands and other changes. Particularly when companies are growing and business environments are changing, organizations need to integrate work areas more effectively so they can be more flexible and responsive. Other forms of departmentalization can be more flexible and responsive than the functional structure.

functional organization

Departmentalization around specialized activities such as production, marketing, and human resources.

Bottom Line

When like functions are grouped, savings often result. *Why might a company centralize its information technology (IT) department?*

The functional structure may be most appropriate in rather simple, stable environments.

One organization that has capitalized on the benefits of integrating functions is pharmaceutical firm AstraZeneca. Developing and bringing a new drug to market is a complex procedure, particularly for a company with global reach, so AstraZeneca brought employees from different functions and regions together on product teams. For example, when the company was working on approvals for its anticholesterol drug, Crestor, it set up a global product team with both technical research and commercial heads to oversee the drug's development and marketing. Communication among the team members not only helped the drug through its clinical trials in various countries but also allowed the marketers who would be responsible for disseminating information to physicians and patients learn about the drug early in its development.[32]

Demands for total quality, customer service, innovation, and speed have made clear the shortcomings of the functional form for some firms. Functional organizations are highly differentiated and create barriers to coordination across functions. Cross-functional coordination is essential for total quality, customer service, innovations, and speed. The functional organization will not disappear, in part because functional specialists will always be needed, but functional managers will make fewer decisions. The more important units will be cross-functional teams that have integrative responsibilities for products, processes, or customers.[33]

The Divisional Organization

divisional organization

Departmentalization that groups units around products, customers, or geographic regions.

The discussion of a functional structure's weaknesses leads us to the **divisional organization**. As organizations grow and become increasingly diversified, they find that functional departments have difficulty managing a wide variety of products, customers, and geographic regions. In this case, organizations may restructure to group all functions into a single division and duplicate each of the functions across all the divisions. In the divisional organization chart in Figure 8.4, Division A has its own operations, marketing, and finance departments, Division B has its own operations, marketing, and finance departments, and so on. In this structure, separate divisions may act almost as separate businesses or profit centers and work autonomously to accomplish the goals of the entire enterprise. Table 8.1 presents examples of how the same tasks would be organized under functional and divisional structures.

TABLE 8.1

Examples of Functional and Divisional Organization

Functional Organization	Divisional Organization
Magazine publisher with editorial, sales, production, web design, and fulfillment departments handling their functions for all magazines.	Magazine publisher with separate teams for each magazine, with editorial, sales, production, web design, and fulfillment employees on each team.
Chain of movie theaters with departments for concessions, films, theater operations, and finance, responsible for all theaters.	Chain of movie theaters with one division for each region of the country handling all functions in that region.
Manufacturer with departments of engineering, production, purchasing, distribution, and sales handling all products.	Manufacturer with product groups each staffed with people to handle that product's engineering, production, purchasing, distribution, and sales.
One human resources department serving the needs of an entire multinational firm, reporting to the corporate leadership.	A human resources group at the offices of each country in which a multinational firm operates, reporting to the vice president in charge of that country's operations.

SOURCE: George Strauss and Leonard R. Sayles, *Strauss and Sayles's Behavioral Strategies for Managers,* © 1980, p. 221. Reprinted by permission of Prentice Hall, Inc., Englewood Cliffs, New Jersey.

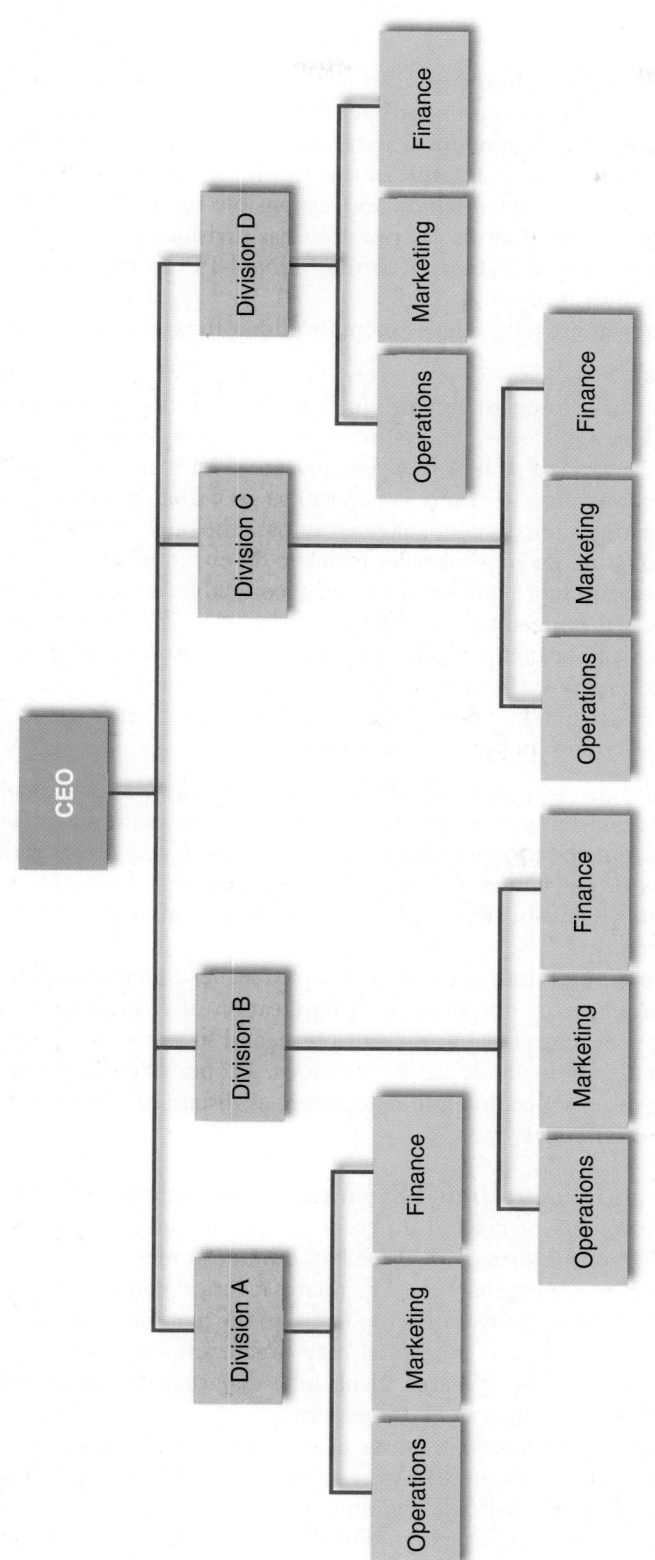

FIGURE 8.4
The Divisional Organization

Organizations create a divisional structure in several ways. It can be created around products, customers, or geographic regions. Each of these is described in the following sections.

Product Divisions   In the product organization, all functions that contribute to a given product are organized under one manager. In the product organization, managers in charge of functions for a particular product report to a product manager. Johnson & Johnson is one example of this form. J&J has more than 250 independent company divisions, many of which are responsible for particular product lines. For example, its subsidiary Cordis Corporation has divisions that develop and sell products for treating vascular diseases, while McNeil-PPC's products include Listerine and Plax mouthwashes.

The product approach to departmentalization offers a number of advantages:[34]

1. *Information needs are managed more easily.* Less information is required because people work closely on one product and need not worry about other products.
2. *People have a full-time commitment to a particular product line.* They develop a greater awareness of how their jobs fit into the broader scheme.
3. *Task responsibilities are clear.* When things go wrong in a functional organization, functional managers can pass the buck ("That other department is messing up, making it harder for us to do our jobs"). In a product structure, managers are more independent and accountable because they usually have the resources they need to perform their tasks. Also, the performances of different divisions can be compared by contrasting their profits and other measures.
4. *People receive broader training.* General managers develop a wide variety of skills, and they learn to be judged by results. Many top executives received crucial early experience in product structures.

Because the product structure is more flexible than the functional structure, it is best suited for unstable environments in which an ability to adapt rapidly to change is important. But the product structure also has disadvantages. It is difficult to coordinate across product lines and divisions. And although managers learn to become generalists, they may not acquire the depth of functional expertise that develops in the functional structure.

Furthermore, functions are not centralized at headquarters, where they are done for all product lines or divisions. Such duplication of effort is expensive. Also, decision making is decentralized in this structure, and so top management can lose some control over decisions made in the divisions. Proper management of all the issues surrounding decentralization and delegation, as discussed earlier, is essential for this structure to be effective.[35]

Customer and Geographic Divisions   Some companies build divisions around groups of customers or around different geographic areas. Pfizer recently replaced divisions based on location with three based on customer groups: primary care, specialty care, and emerging markets. The pharmaceutical company hopes that this structure will make the company more responsive to the needs of doctors and their patients in each group.[36] Similarly, a hospital may organize its services around child, adult, psychiatric, and emergency cases. Bank loan departments commonly have separate groups handling consumer and business needs.

In contrast to customers, divisions can be structured around geographic regions. Sears, for example, was a pioneer in creating *geographic divisions.* Geographic distinctions include district, territory, region, and country. Macy's Group, formerly Federated Department Stores, has geographic divisions for its operations serving particular states or regions of the United States: Macy's East, Macy's Florida, Macy's Midwest, Macy's North, Macy's Northwest, Macy's South, and Macy's West, as well as Macys.com for online shoppers. Avon Products recently restructured into two major business units divided in terms of geography (and economics). Its developed market group will serve customers in North America and Western Europe, while its developing market group will serve customers in Latin America, Central and Eastern Europe, and the Asia-Pacific region.[37]

The primary advantage of both the product and customer/regional approaches to departmentalization is the ability to focus on customer needs and provide faster, better service. But again, duplication of activities across many customer groups and geographic areas is expensive.

IN PRACTICE

Establishing customer divisions improved strategic decisions at Det Norske Veritas (DNV), a Norwegian firm that provides services related to risk management. Initially the company's management assumed that any collaboration across divisions would build sales and profits, but the first effort flopped. Management tried combining the efforts of two business units: its consulting group and a unit that inspects food companies' production chains. The idea was that the combined groups could help food companies reduce risks in their supply chains. However, the group members were slow to share information about customers, thought that time spent on the joint project undermined the work of their own division (which was how their performance was measured), and engaged in conflicts that caused project delays and cost overruns.

Disappointed with these early results, DNV's executives evaluated their decision making and realized they were assembling a collaboration project without first prioritizing the market opportunities, identifying the impact on each division's profits, and rewarding employees for collaborating. To improve future decisions, they restructured the company into business units serving particular markets. With their market knowledge, each unit then investigated where collaboration would make sense to serve its market's needs. Because the whole unit would benefit, it was now easier to tie rewards to collaboration. One success came from the business unit serving the maritime industry. Managers determined that the information technology specialists in this unit could collaborate with the risk management group to help shipping companies manage the risk of their computer systems' malfunctioning. This time, customers *and* employees were enthusiastic.[38]

- What lessons did DNV learn about setting up customer divisions?

The Matrix Organization

A **matrix organization** is a hybrid form of organization in which functional and divisional forms overlap. Managers and staff personnel report to two bosses—a functional manager and a divisional manager. Thus matrix organizations have a dual rather than a single line of command. In Figure 8.5, for example, each project manager draws employees from each functional area to form a group for the project. The employees working on those projects report to the individual project manager as well as to the manager of their functional area.

A good example of the matrix structure can be found at Time Inc., the top magazine publisher in the United States and United Kingdom. At major Time Inc. titles such as *Time, Sports Illustrated,* and *People,* production managers who are responsible for getting the magazines printed report both to the individual publishers and editors of each title *and* to a senior corporate executive in charge of production. At the corporate level, Time Inc. achieves enormous economies of scale by buying paper and printing in bulk and making sure production activities in the company as a whole are coordinated. At the same time, production managers working at each title make sure the different needs and schedules of their individual magazines are being met. Similar matrix arrangements are in place for other key managers, such as circulation and finance. In this

matrix organization

An organization composed of dual reporting relationships in which some employees report to two superiors—a functional manager and a divisional manager.

Matrix organizations have a dual rather than a single line of command.

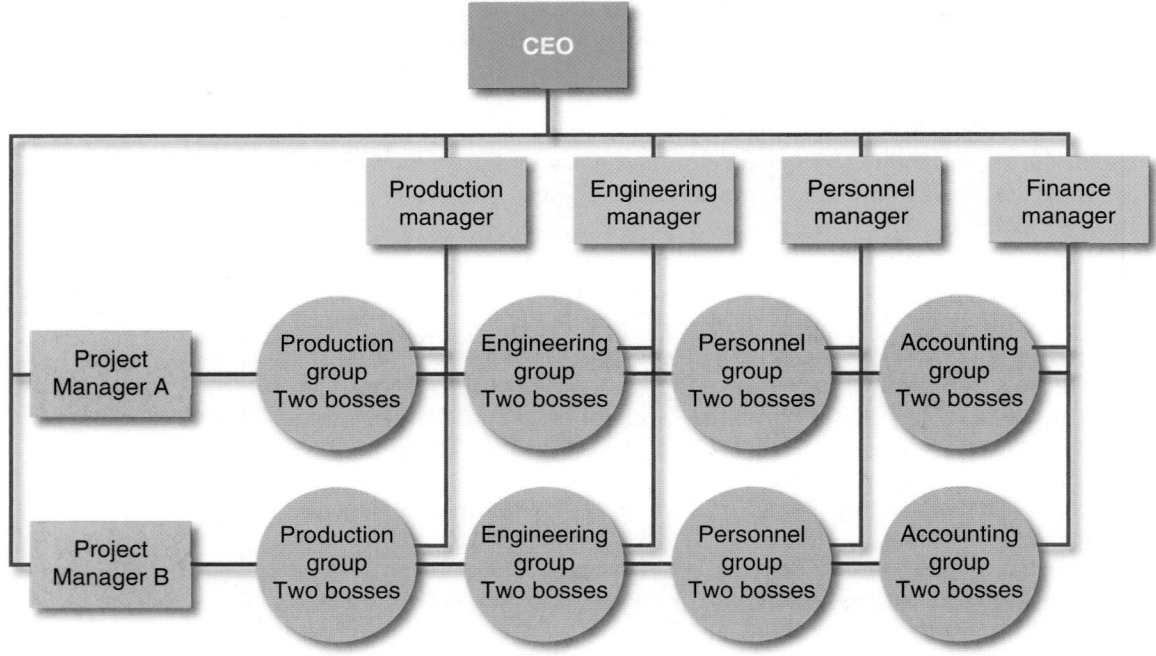

FIGURE 8.5
Matrix Organizational Structure

unity-of-command principle

A structure in which each worker reports to one boss, who in turn reports to one boss.

Organizations with highly specialized staff, such as NASA astronaut Susan J. Helms (left), shown here with Russian cosmonaut Yury V. Usachev in the International Space Station, typically use a matrix structure.

way, the company attempts to gain the benefits of both the divisional and functional organization structure.

The matrix form originated in the aerospace industry, first with TRW in 1959 and then with NASA. Applications now occur in hospitals and health care agencies, entrepreneurial organizations, government laboratories, financial institutions, and multinational corporations.[39] Other companies that have used or currently use the matrix form include IBM, Boeing, Xerox, Wellpoint, Texas Instruments, Bechtel, and Dow Corning.

Pros and Cons of the Matrix Form   Like other organization structures, the matrix has both strengths and weaknesses. Table 8.2 summarizes the advantages of using a matrix structure. The major potential advantage is a higher degree of flexibility and adaptability.

Table 8.2 also summarizes the potential shortcomings of the matrix form. Many of the disadvantages stem from the matrix's inherent violation of the **unity-of-command principle,** which states that a person should have only one boss. Reporting to two superiors can create confusion and a difficult interpersonal situation unless steps are taken to prevent these problems from arising.

Matrix Survival Skills   The value of collaboration is particularly pronounced in a matrix organization. For example, in the kind of structure illustrated in Figure 8.5, project group members may not be permanently assigned to the project manager. They will return to their functional area once the project has been completed. For this group to work effectively, the traditional command-and-control management style may not be the most appropriate; it might gain *compliance* from group members but not their full *commitment*, making it harder to achieve the project's goals. Also, as the matrix organization draws on members of functional groups to tap their expertise, it is very important to get their full contribution. A collaborative process, in which the manager and participants develop a shared sense of ownership for the work they are

Advantages
• Linkage of employees at all levels and in all functions to the company's goals and strategy.
• More information shared across functions.
• Communication fostered—especially valuable for complex assignments where different groups depend on each other.
• Greater responsiveness to customers from bringing together information about customer needs and organizational capabilities.
• Creative ideas from cross-functional work.
• Loyalty to the organization as a whole rather than to a function or division.

Disadvantages
• Unclear responsibilities and competing priorities.
• Violation of the unity-of-command principle.
• Accountability difficult to define.
• Accountability for results under other matrix members' control.
• Possible conflict and stress for employees who must manage a dual reporting role.
• Additional time required for meetings and other communications to coordinate work.
• Extensive collaboration needed but not always easy to reward.

TABLE 8.2

Advantages and Disadvantages of the Matrix Design

Sources: Based on E. Krell, "Managing the Matrix," *HR Magazine*, April 2011, pp. 69–71; R. Lash, "Cracking the Matrix Code," *Canadian HR Reporter*, March 28, 2011, pp. 16, 18; and M. North and C. Coors, "Avoiding Death by Dotted Line," *Healthcare Financial Management*, January 2010, pp. 120–21.

doing, will generate better ideas, participation, and commitment to the project and its outcomes.

To a large degree, problems can be avoided if the key managers in the matrix learn the behavioral skills demanded in the matrix structure.[40] These skills vary depending on the job in the four-person diamond structure shown in Figure 8.6.

The *top executive*, who heads the matrix, must learn to balance power and emphasis between the product and functional orientations. *Product or division managers* and *functional managers* must learn to collaborate and manage their conflicts constructively. Finally, the *two-boss managers* or employees at the bottom of the diamond must learn how to be responsible to two superiors. This means prioritizing multiple demands and sometimes even reconciling conflicting orders. Some people function poorly under this ambiguous, conflictual circumstance; sometimes this signals the end of their careers with the company. Others learn to be proactive, communicate effectively with both superiors, rise above the difficulties, and manage these work relationships constructively.

The Matrix Form Today The popularity of the matrix form waned during the late 1980s, when many companies had difficulty implementing it. But recently it has come back strong. Reasons for this resurgence include pressures to consolidate costs and be faster to market, creating a need for better coordination across functions in the business units, and a need for coordination across countries for firms with global business strategies. Many of the challenges created by the matrix are particularly acute in an international context, mainly because of the distances involved and the differences in local markets.[41]

The key to managing today's matrix is not the formal structure itself but the realization that the matrix is a *process*. Managers who have appropriately adopted the matrix structure because of the complexity of the challenges they confront, but have had

> The key to managing today's matrix is the realization that the matrix is a *process*.

Bottom Line

The matrix structure can speed decisions and cut costs.
How might a matrix structure increase speed?

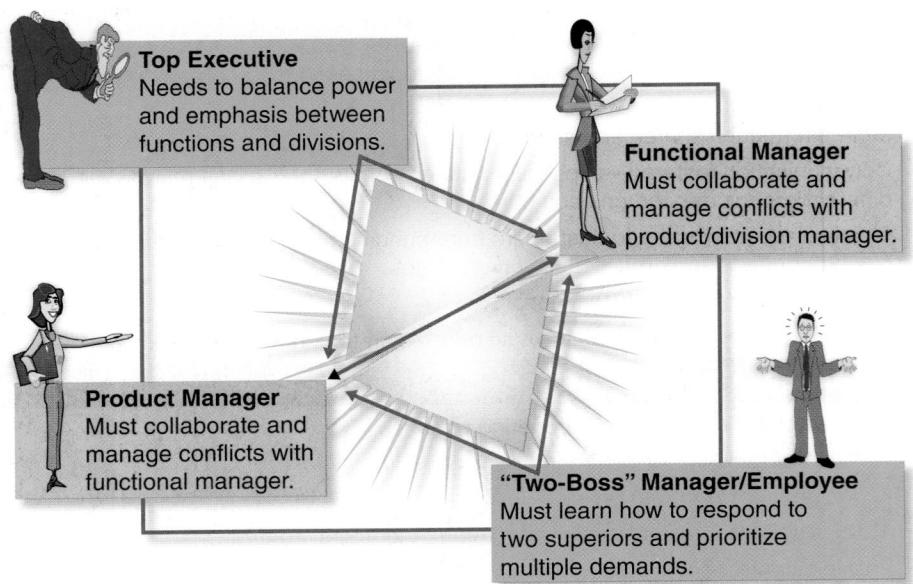

FIGURE 8.6
The Matrix Diamond

trouble implementing it, often find that they haven't changed the employee and managerial relationships within their organizations in ways that make the matrix effective. It is not enough to create a flexible organization merely by changing its structure. To create an environment that allows information to flow freely throughout the organization, managers must also attend to the norms, values, and attitudes that shape how people within their organizations behave.[42] We will address these issues in the next chapter and in Part 4 of the book, which focuses on how to lead and manage people.

As we saw at the beginning of the chapter, Cisco attempted using networks of employees to add flexibility to that organization's structure. Read "Management Connection: Progress Report" for more details on that effort and a chance to evaluate whether it put into practice the principles you have been learning about horizontal structure.

The Network Organization

network organization

A collection of independent, mostly single-function firms that collaborate on a good or service.

dynamic network

Temporary arrangements among partners that can be assembled and reassembled to adapt to the environment.

So far, the structures we have been discussing are variations of the traditional, hierarchical organization, within which all the business functions of the firm are performed. In contrast, the **network organization** is a collection of independent, mostly single-function firms that collaborate to produce a good or service. As depicted in Figure 8.7, the network organization describes not one organization but the web of relationships among many firms. Network organizations are flexible arrangements among designers, suppliers, producers, distributors, and customers where each firm is able to pursue its own distinctive competence, yet work effectively with other members of the network. Often members of the network communicate electronically and share information to be able to respond quickly to customer demands. In effect, the normal boundary of the organization becomes blurred or porous, as managers within the organization interact closely with network members outside it. The network as a whole, then, can display the technical specialization of the functional structure, the market responsiveness of the product structure, and the balance and flexibility of the matrix.[43]

A very flexible version of the network organization is the **dynamic network**—also called the *modular* or *virtual* corporation. It is composed of temporary arrangements among members that can be assembled and reassembled to meet a changing competitive environment. The members of the network are held together by contracts that stipulate results expected (market mechanisms) rather than by hierarchy and authority. Poorly performing firms can be removed and replaced.

Such arrangements are common in the electronics, toy, and apparel industries, each of which creates and sells trendy products at a fast pace. Dynamic networks also

Bottom Line

Networks can improve cost, quality, service, speed, sustainability, and innovation. *Which functions would you include in a network to improve sustainability?*

Management Connections

CISCO SYSTEMS, BEFORE AND AFTER

For a better understanding of how CEO John Chambers is hoping to streamline Cisco's management structure, let's take a closer look at the company's earlier use of internal councils.

In 2009, desiring to promote creative expansion into new product areas, Cisco established a system of working groups, boards, and councils. New ideas start with temporary teams of 2 to 10 employees who work on a particular project and take their ideas to one of Cisco's internal boards—originally there were 47 of these. Each board has about 14 members, including two vice presidents or senior vice presidents. The board reports to a council comprising managers drawn from across the company. There were originally 12 of these councils, each with an average membership of 14 people, including two senior vice presidents or executive vice presidents. The boards and councils include representatives from each of the company's functional areas, including sales, engineering, legal, information technology, manufacturing, and so on. The cross-functional approach is aimed at getting the group to see the impact of each new product idea on each function from the very start so the team can quickly evaluate all the issues and move forward.

Even from the start, industry analysts had doubts about the board structure; one management consultant described the setup as "chaos." However, Chambers insisted that the idea would foster innovation and that by using Cisco's own collaboration hardware, its people could actually move faster than departments in a traditionally structured organization. Cisco entered 30 new markets, and Chambers attributes some of the company's successful acquisitions to the council structure. For example, he says the councils and boards provided a network of people with the expertise to offer electric utilities the secure hardware they needed to set up smart power grids as soon as European utility customers began asking for it. And a council devoted to sports and entertainment was able to win and fulfill a contract to wire the stadium being built for the Yankees in New York—a project that drew on offerings from several of Cisco's businesses.

But participating in the boards and councils was time-consuming; at one point, some managers served in over a dozen groups. One manager who spoke of feeling the pinch was Keith Goodwin, who gave up half the time he spent visiting customers in order to free up time for serving on committees. Early on, Chambers responded to this challenge by expanding the number of executives who serve on councils and boards and by limiting the number of assignments to four or five. However, Chambers said

they should devote at least 30 percent of their time to working on these groups.

Furthermore, the decisions and activities of these groups conflicted with department managers' authority over their budgets and their people's time. Reflecting on the loss of key executives following the implementation of the board structure, venture capitalist Robert Ackerman observed that Cisco had "a lot of talented people feeling like they're beating their head against the wall" in frustration with the complex bureaucracy.

In one case, Hewlett-Packard announced that its switches would offer a warranty including free upgrades and support, and Cisco took over a year to offer its own warranty because the change required approval from several committees. Even Chambers admits that Cisco missed some key industry developments, and critics of his board structure say the blame should partly go to the red tape entangling Cisco's managers. In a memo to his staff, Chambers described talking to Cisco's people and learning that they were longing for a simpler way to do their work and serve their customers' needs.

The decision to shift away from the use of boards and their councils is aimed at giving managers below the executive level greater ability to make the decisions governing their particular divisions and departments. The new structure is a divisional one, with product divisions for engineering activities and geographic divisions for sales and service. Cisco Engineering will be divided into the five areas of information technology Cisco is targeting: routing and switching, collaboration, video, data center virtualization and cloud, and architectures for business transformation. In addition, a senior vice president will lead a group that will investigate emerging new ideas and apply them across the engineering units. The sales unit, called Worldwide Field Operations, will serve the regions of the Americas (the United States, Canada, and Latin America), Asia (including Japan and China), and a third region encompassing Europe, the Middle East, and Africa. Within each region, separate teams will be dedicated to serving large enterprises, public sector organizations, commercial organizations, small businesses, service providers, and Cisco partners. Cisco Services will be organized into groups serving similar segments.[44]

- How did the use of councils and boards affect the responsibility, authority, and accountability of department managers at Cisco?
- In its latest changes, what type of horizontal structure is Cisco adopting? Is this the best choice for Cisco's goals? Why or why not?

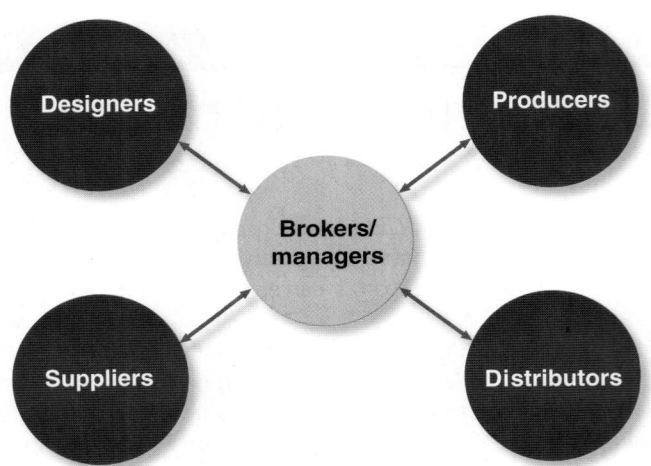

SOURCE: From Raymond E. Miles and Charles C. Snow, "Organizations: New Concepts for New Forms," in California Management Review vol. 28, no. 3 (Spring 1986), pp. 62–73. Copyright 1986 by the Regents of the University of California. Reprinted by permission of University of California Press.

FIGURE 8.7
A Network Organization

are suited to organizations in which much of the work can be done independently by experts. For example, Philip Rosedale set up a virtual company called LoveMachine to commercialize a software tool of the same name: an online communication system that allows users to send one another brief messages. The primary difference from a micro-blogging service like Twitter is that the system is completely transparent; everyone in the system sees the messages. Thus in a company using LoveMachine for employee recognition, everyone sees a message of appreciation, with the intent that public acknowledgment builds morale. For such a transparent application, Rosedale and his partners decided to build a completely transparent company. They launched an online bulletin board where they posted a list of all the tasks to be done for LoveMachine. Freelancers bid on a job by describing how they would carry out the task and what they would charge. For any collaboration required, the freelancers communicate online at the company's chat room or via e-mail and Skype. Rosedale started this virtual arrangement for programming tasks, and it was so successful in delivering great prices and fast turnaround that the company expanded to support tasks such as recruiting contracts and processing payments. One regular contractor is an American who lives in Belgium; other contractors are in India, Russia, and Australia. However, Rosedale acknowledges that he sometimes misses that camaraderie of a face-to-face work team, so he is setting up a San Francisco work space where local workers can gather if they wish.[45]

Successful networks potentially offer flexibility, innovation, quick responses to threats and opportunities, and reduced costs and risk. But for these arrangements to be successful, several things must occur:

The firm must choose the right specialty. It must be something (good or service) that the market needs and that the firm is better at providing than other firms.

The firm must choose collaborators that also are excellent at what they do and that provide complementary strengths.

The firm must make certain that all parties fully understand the strategic goals of the partnership.

Each party must be able to trust all the others with strategic information and also trust that each collaborator will deliver quality products even if the business grows quickly and makes heavy demands.

broker

A person who assembles and coordinates participants in a network.

The role of managers shifts in a network from that of command and control to more like that of a **broker.** Broker/managers serve several important boundary roles that aid network integration and coordination:

Designer role. The broker serves as a network architect who envisions a set of groups or firms whose collective expertise could be focused on a particular good or service.

Process engineering role. The broker serves as a *network co-operator* who takes the initiative to lay out the flow of resources and relationships and makes certain that everyone shares the same goals, standards, payments, and the like.

Nurturing role. The broker serves as a network developer who nurtures and enhances the network (like team building) to make certain the relationships are healthy and mutually beneficial.[46]

Organizational Integration

At the beginning of this chapter, we said organizations are structured around differentiation and integration. So far our discussion has focused on *differentiation*—the way the organization is composed of different jobs and tasks, and the way they fit on an organization chart. But as organizations differentiate their structures, they also need to be concerned about *integration* and *coordination*—the way all parts of the organization will work together. Often the more differentiated the organization, the more difficult integration may be. Because of specialization and the division of labor, different groups of managers and employees develop different orientations. Depending on whether employees are in a functional department or a divisional group, are line or staff, and so on, they will think and act in ways that are geared toward their particular work units. In short, people working in separate functions, divisions, and business units literally tend to forget about one another. When this happens, it is difficult for managers to combine all their activities into an integrated whole.

A variety of approaches are available to managers to help them make certain that interdependent units and individuals will work together to achieve a common purpose. In some situations, managers might see that employees need to work closely together to achieve joint objectives, so they build mutual trust, train employees in a common set of skills, and reward teamwork. In other situations, the organization might rely more on individuals with unique talents and ideas, so they set up flexible work arrangements and reward individual achievements to inspire the best from each individual, while encouraging individual employees to share knowledge and develop respect for one another's contributions.[47] In general, however, coordination methods include standardization, plans, and mutual adjustment.[48]

> "In the end, an organization is nothing more than the collective capacity of its people to create value."
>
> —Louis V. Gerstner Jr., *Who Says Elephants Can't Dance?*

Often the more differentiated the organization, the more difficult integration may be.

Coordination by Standardization

When organizations coordinate activities by establishing routines and standard operating procedures that remain in place over time, we say that work has been standardized. **Standardization** constrains actions and integrates various units by regulating what people do. People often know how to act—and how to interact—because standard operating procedures spell out what they should do. For example, managers may establish standards for which types of computer equipment the organization will use. This simplifies the purchasing and computer-training process—everyone will be on a common platform—and makes it easier for the different parts of the organization to communicate with each other.

To improve coordination, organizations may also rely on **formalization**—the presence of rules and regulations governing how people in the organization interact. Simple, often written, policies regarding attendance, dress, and decorum, for

standardization

Establishing common routines and procedures that apply uniformly to everyone.

formalization

The presence of rules and regulations governing how people in the organization interact.

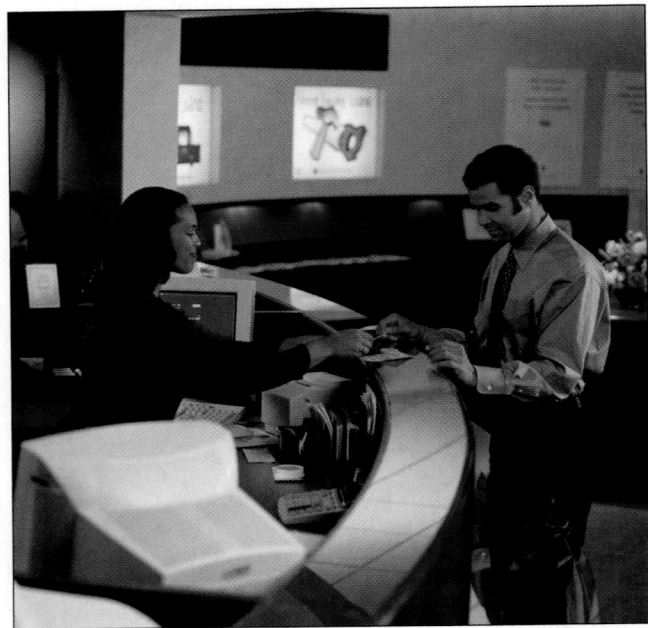

Banks are among the most standardized of organizations, from operating procedures through dress codes, reinforcing to their customers and employees that the organization and their dealings with it are stable and reliable.

coordination by plan

Interdependent units are required to meet deadlines and objectives that contribute to a common goal.

coordination by mutual adjustment

Units interact with one another to make accommodations to achieve flexible coordination.

example, may help eliminate a good deal of uncertainty at work. But an important assumption underlying both standardization and formalization is that the rules and procedures should apply to most (if not all) situations. These approaches, therefore, are most appropriate in situations that are relatively stable and unchanging. In some cases, when the work environment requires flexibility, coordination by standardization may not be very effective. Who hasn't experienced a time when rules and procedures—frequently associated with a slow bureaucracy—prevented timely action to address a problem? In these instances, we often refer to rules and regulations as "red tape."[49]

Coordination by Plan

If laying out the exact rules and procedures by which work should be integrated is difficult, organizations may provide more latitude by establishing goals and schedules for interdependent units. **Coordination by plan** does not require the same high degree of stability and routinization required for coordination by standardization. Interdependent units are free to modify and adapt their actions as long as they meet the deadlines and targets required for working with others.

In writing this textbook, for example, we (the authors) sat down with a publication team that included the editors, the marketing staff, the production group, and support staff. Together we ironed out a schedule for developing this book that covered approximately a two-year period. That development plan included dates and "deliverables" that specified what was to be accomplished and forwarded to the others in the organization. The plan allowed for a good deal of flexibility on each subunit's part, and the overall approach allowed us to work together effectively.

Coordination by Mutual Adjustment

Ironically, the simplest and most flexible approach to coordination may just be to have interdependent parties talk to one another. **Coordination by mutual adjustment** involves feedback and discussions to jointly figure out how to approach problems and devise solutions that are agreeable to everyone. The popularity of teams today is in part due to the fact that they allow flexible coordination; teams can operate under the principle of mutual adjustment.

But the flexibility of mutual adjustment as a coordination device does not come without some cost. Hashing out every issue takes time and may not be the most expedient approach for organizing work. Imagine how long it would take to accomplish even the most basic tasks if subunits had to talk through every situation. At the same time, mutual adjustment can be very effective when problems are novel and cannot be programmed in advance with rules, procedures, or plans. Particularly during crises, in which rules and procedures don't apply, mutual adjustment is likely to be the most effective approach to coordination.

Particularly during crises, mutual adjustment is likely to be the most effective approach to coordination.

Coordination and Communication

Today's environments tend to be complex, dynamic, and therefore uncertain. Huge amounts of information flow from the external environment to the organization and back to the environment. To cope, organizations must acquire, process, and respond to that information. Doing so has direct implications for how firms organize. To function effectively, organizations need to develop structures for processing information.

To foster coordination by mutual adjustment, the libraries that serve some organizations are closing down the traditional book-filled rooms and moving librarians onto the teams that need their research skills.

For example, at Johns Hopkins University, the Welch Medical Library has switched from print journals and reference books to a fully digital system. This frees librarians to be wherever they are needed. The Welch librarians, now called "informationists," are assigned to the departments that formerly came to them for information. They work in their assigned department's facility, where they can readily get to know the doctors and other staff members. Library scientist David Shumaker notes that this type of arrangement is becoming more common in medical settings, where librarians sometimes participate in rounds, equipped with a computer to look up research literature whenever questions arise about a diagnosis.

CH2M HILL, an engineering, construction, and project management firm, also has begun embedding librarians into project teams. Librarian Amy Maule is embedded in a team of engineers investigating new technologies such as renewable energy applications. As they learn about potential new applications, Maule manages the information and suggests additional sources. The longer she works with the team, the more she learns about the technologies, and the more she can contribute her own ideas. Being an embedded librarian has made Maule a subject matter expert as well as a functional expert, increasing her value to the organization.[50]

- How else could an organization increase the integration of its library services?

To cope with high uncertainty and heavy information demands, managers can use the two general strategies shown in Figure 8.8. First, management can act to reduce the need for information. Second, it can increase its capacity to handle more information.[51]

Option 1: Reducing the Need for Information   Managers can reduce the need for information in two ways: (a) creating slack resources and (b) creating self-contained tasks. *Slack resources* are simply extra resources on

> To cope with high uncertainty and heavy information demands, managers can use two general strategies.

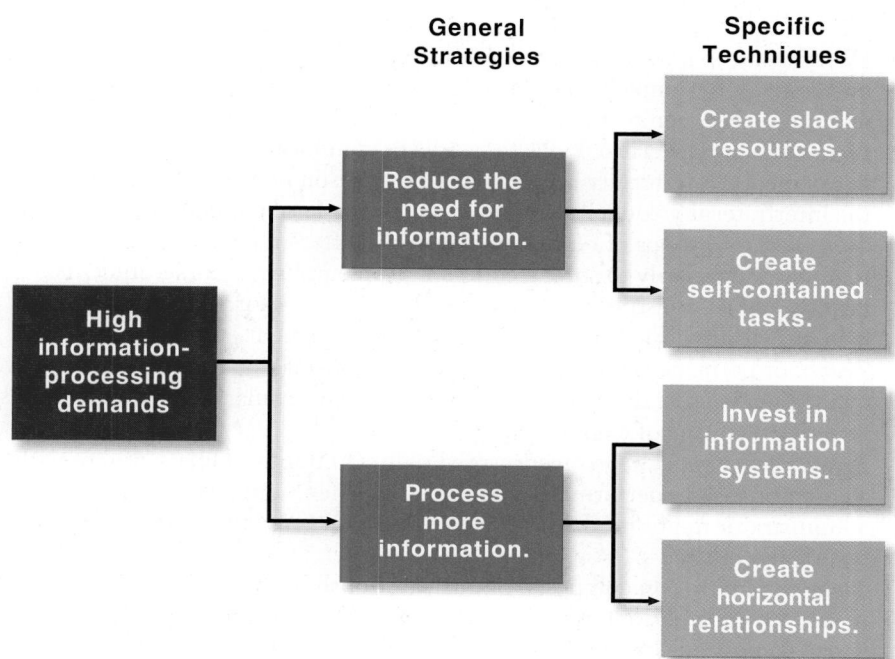

FIGURE 8.8

Managing High Information-Processing Demands

Information sharing is vital at the National Counterterrorism Center, shown here. Technology is used to enable the efficient and safe sharing of this information.

which organizations can rely in a pinch so that if they get caught off guard, they can still adjust. Inventory, for example, is a type of slack resource that provides extra stock on hand in case it is needed. With extra inventory, an organization does not need as much information about sales demand, lead time, and the like. Employees also can be a type of slack resource. For example, many companies augment their full-time staffs with part-time and temporary employees. This way, they do not have to perfectly forecast sales peaks but can rely on supplementary workers to handle irregularities.

Like slack resources, *creating self-contained tasks* allows organizations to reduce the need for some information. Creating self-contained tasks refers to changing from a functional organization to a product or project organization and giving each unit the resources it needs to perform its task. Information-processing problems are reduced because each unit has its own full complement of specialties instead of functional specialties that have to share their expertise among a number of different product teams. Communications then flow within each team rather than among a complex array of interdependent groups.

Option 2: Increasing Information-Processing Capability Instead of reducing the need for information, an organization may take the approach of increasing its information-processing capability. It can *invest in information systems*, which usually means employing or expanding computer systems. But increasing an organization's information-processing capability also means what we referred to in Chapter 1 as *knowledge management*—capitalizing on the intellect and experience of the organization's human assets to increase collaboration and effectiveness. One way to do that is by creating horizontal relationships between units to foster coordination. Such horizontal relationships are effective because they increase integration, which Lawrence and Lorsch suggest is necessary for managing complex environments. As uncertainty increases, the following horizontal processes may be used, ranging from the simplest to the most complex:[52]

1. *Direct contact (mutual adjustment)* among managers who share a problem. In a university, for example, a residence hall adviser might call a meeting to resolve differences between two feuding students who live in adjacent rooms.

2. *Liaison roles,* or specialized jobs to handle communications between two departments. A fraternity representative is a liaison between the fraternity and the interfraternity council, the university, or the local community.

3. *Task forces,* or groups of representatives from different departments, brought together temporarily to solve a common problem. For example, students, faculty, and administrators may be members of a task force charged with bringing distinguished speakers to campus for a current events seminar.

4. *Teams,* or permanent interdepartmental decision-making groups. An executive council made up of department heads might meet regularly to make decisions affecting a college of engineering or liberal arts.

5. *Product, program, or project managers* who direct interdisciplinary groups with a common task to perform. In a college of business administration, a faculty administrator might head an executive education program of professors from several disciplines.

6. *Matrix organizations,* composed of dual relationships in which some managers report to two superiors. Your instructors, for example, may report to department heads in their respective disciplines and also to a director of undergraduate or graduate programs.

Bottom Line

Cross-unit coordination can lead to effective problem solutions.

Why does more information tend to improve solutions?

Several of these processes are discussed further in Chapter 14, where we examine managing teams and intergroup relations.

Looking Ahead

The organization chart, differentiation, integration, authority, delegation, coordination, and the like convey fundamental information about an organization's structure. However, the information so far has provided only a snapshot. The real organization is more like a motion picture—it moves! More flexible and innovative—even virtual— forms of organizations are evolving. Today's organizations are far removed, in many of their fundamental characteristics, from the traditional forms they once had. They may be more networked, flexible, and global, using electronic sharing of information to move faster than 20th century managers could have envisaged.

No organization is merely a set of static work relationships. Because organizations are composed of people, they are hotbeds of social relationships. Networks of individuals cutting across departmental boundaries interact with one another. Various friendship groups or cliques band together to form *coalitions*—members of the organization who jointly support a particular issue and try to ensure that their viewpoints determine the outcome of policy decisions.

Thus the formal organization structure does not describe everything about how the company really works. Even if you know departments and authority relationships, you still have much to understand. How do things really get done? Who influences whom, and how? Which managers are the most powerful? How effective is the top leadership? Which groups are most and which are least effective? What is the nature of communication patterns throughout the organization? These issues are discussed throughout the rest of the book.

Now you are familiar with the basic organizing concepts discussed in this chapter. In the next chapter we will discuss the current challenges of designing the modern organization with which the modern executive constantly grapples. As you read "Management Connection: Onward," consider how the organizing concepts from the chapter help you evaluate the challenges facing Cisco Systems, but also notice where personal relationships and other human factors come into play.

| Manager's Brief | Progress Report | **Onward** |

Management Connection

EVALUATING CISCO'S APPROACH TO INTEGRATION

When Cisco Systems created its structure of boards and councils several years ago, this restructuring was not a replacement for a traditional departmental or divisional structure. Rather, it was added onto the company's existing structure as a way to achieve greater integration while preserving the company's original differentiation and its benefits. There was one hierarchy for the business units and a separate hierarchy of boards reporting to councils, which reported to Cisco's operating committee of 16 top executives. And that second hierarchy had to compete with regular operations for the resources of the company's various functional groups.

This type of structure was seen as flattening the organization to encourage information sharing and collaboration, so that Cisco could avoid the foot dragging that tends to become commonplace in large corporations. It was seen as replacing the rigidity of hierarchy with the flexibility of "leaderless groups" dedicated to pursuing ideas that otherwise might fall through the cracks. However, it also added to the requirements of senior management jobs. Besides accountability for the activities of a function or division, senior managers were required to coach teams moving new ideas toward approval and implementation. They were spending over 30 percent of their time on these extra responsibilities. Some senior managers, including heads of key business units, left the company. People who knew the departed executives said they had grown frustrated with what felt like distractions from running their own units. An industry analyst recently noted, "People at Cisco are constantly going to meetings." Others, inside and outside the company, have questioned whether Cisco under this structure made it clear who was to be held accountable for the results of each board and council.

As we saw, Cisco discontinued most of its councils and restructured its divisions to simplify management, clarify accountability, and speed up decisions. Those changes had to seek the right balance of differentiation and integration for Cisco. When Chambers announced this restructuring, he noted that he was acting because it was "time to simplify the way we execute our strategy." Simplifying in this case meant removing the overlay of boards and councils, setting up divisions focused on customer groups or product types, and dedicating managers' time to command-and-control activities within the traditional hierarchy. Cisco also set up a new position of chief operating office and hired Gary Moore to be responsible for engineering, marketing,

operations, and services, including the implementation of the new structure.

Just as Cisco did not completely abandon hierarchy and divisions when it set up the councils and boards, it did not completely abandon the boards when it refocused on differentiation. It retained three councils: (1) a service provider council, headed by a senior vice president of sales and a senior vice president of engineering; (2) an enterprise council, headed by a senior vice president of sales and a senior vice president who is also chief technology officer; and (3) an emerging countries council, headed by the chief globalization officer and the president of Cisco Asia Pacific and Japan.

In announcing the changes to his employees, Chambers told them that the restructuring would "empower our teams, integrate our major functions, and allow our people to focus on inspiring and important work." If he was right, then when you read about Cisco today, you are reading about a company that is again one of Silicon Valley's great success stories.[53]

- When Cisco shifted from the use of councils and boards to the restructured divisions, how did this change affect the types of coordination it could rely on?
- How did setting up councils and boards affect Cisco's information-processing capability? How might Cisco promote communication after eliminating most of the councils and boards?

KEY TERMS

accountability, p. 291

authority, p. 287

broker, p. 304

centralized organization, p. 292

coordination, p. 286

coordination by mutual adjustment, p. 306

coordination by plan, p. 306

corporate governance, p. 289

decentralized organization, p. 292

delegation, p. 290

departmentalization, p. 294

differentiation, p. 284

division of labor, p. 285

divisional organization, p. 296

dynamic network, p. 302

formalization, p. 305

functional organization, p. 295

hierarchy, p. 289

integration, p. 284

line departments, p. 294

matrix organization, p. 299

network organization, p. 302

organization chart, p. 284

responsibility, p. 290

span of control, p. 289

specialization, p. 285

staff departments, p. 294

standardization, p. 305

subunits, p. 289

unity-of-command principle, p. 300

SUMMARY OF LEARNING OBJECTIVES

Now that you have studied Chapter 8, you should be able to:

 Explain how differentiation and integration influence an organization's structure.

Differentiation means that organizations have many parts. Specialization means that various individuals and units throughout the organization perform different tasks. The assignment of tasks to different people or groups often is referred to as the division of labor. But the specialized tasks in an organization cannot all be performed independently of one another. Coordination links the various tasks in order to achieve the organization's overall mission. An organization with many different specialized tasks and work units is highly differentiated; the more differentiated the organization is, the more integration or coordination is required.

LO 2 Summarize how authority operates.

Authority is the legitimate right to make decisions and tell other people what to do. Authority is exercised throughout the hierarchy, as bosses have the authority to give orders to subordinates. Through the day-to-day operation of authority, the organization proceeds toward achieving its goals. Owners or stockholders have ultimate authority.

LO 3 Define the roles of the board of directors and the chief executive officer.

Boards of directors report to stockholders. The board of directors controls or advises management, considers the firm's legal and other interests, and protects stockholders' rights. The chief executive officer reports to the board and is accountable for the organization's performance.

LO 4 Discuss how span of control affects structure and managerial effectiveness.

Span of control is the number of people who report directly to a manager. Narrow spans create tall organizations, and wide spans create flat ones. No single span of control is always appropriate; the optimal span is determined by characteristics of the work, the subordinates, the manager, and the organization.

LO 5 Explain how to delegate effectively.

Delegation—the assignment of tasks and responsibilities—has many potential advantages for the manager, the subordinate, and the organization. But to be effective, the process must be managed carefully. The manager should define the goal, select the person, solicit opinions, provide resources, schedule checkpoints, and discuss progress periodically.

LO 6 Distinguish between centralized and decentralized organizations.

In centralized organizations, most important decisions are made by top managers. In decentralized organizations, many decisions are delegated to lower levels.

LO 7 Summarize ways organizations can be structured.

Organizations can be structured on the basis of function, division (product, customers, or geographic), matrix, and network. Each form has advantages and disadvantages.

LO 8 Identify the unique challenges of the matrix organization.

The matrix is a complex structure with a dual authority structure. A well-managed matrix enables organizations to adapt to change. But it can also create confusion and interpersonal difficulties. People in all positions in the matrix—top executives, product and function managers, and two-boss employees—must acquire unique survival skills.

LO 9 Describe important integrative mechanisms.

Managers can coordinate interdependent units through standardization, plans, and mutual adjustment. Standardization occurs when routines and standard operating procedures are put in place. They typically are accompanied by formalized rules. Coordination by plan is more flexible and allows more freedom in how tasks are carried out but keeps interdependent units focused on schedules and joint goals. Mutual adjustment involves feedback and discussions among related parties to accommodate each other's needs. It is at once the most flexible and simple to administer, but it is time-consuming.

DISCUSSION QUESTIONS

1. Based on the description of Cisco in this chapter, give some examples of differentiation in that organization. In other words, what specialized tasks have to be performed, and how is labor divided at Cisco? Also, how does Cisco integrate the work of these different units? Based on what you have learned in this chapter, would you say Cisco has an effective structure? Why or why not?

2. What are some advantages and disadvantages of being in the CEO position?

3. Would you like to sit on a board of directors? Why or why not? If you did serve on a board, what kind of organization would you prefer? As a board member, in what kinds of activities do you think you would most actively engage?

4. Interview a member of a board of directors, and discuss that member's perspectives on his or her role.

5. Pick a job you have held, and describe it in terms of span of control, delegation, responsibility, authority, and accountability.

6. Why do you think managers have difficulty delegating? What can be done to overcome these difficulties?

7. Consider an organization in which you have worked, draw its organization chart, and describe it by using terms in this chapter. How did you like working there, and why?

8. Would you rather work in a functional or divisional organization? Why?

9. If you learned that a company had a matrix structure, would you be more or less interested in working there? Explain your answer. How would you prepare yourself to work effectively in a matrix?

10. Brainstorm a list of methods for integrating interdependent work units. Discuss the activities that need to be undertaken and the pros and cons of each approach.

EXPERIENTIAL EXERCISES

8.1   THE BUSINESS SCHOOL ORGANIZATION CHART

OBJECTIVES

1. To clarify the factors that determine organization structure.

2. To provide insight into the workings of an organization.

3. To examine the working relationships within an organization.

INSTRUCTIONS

1. Draw an organization chart for your school of business. Be sure to identify all the staff and line positions in the school. Specify the chain of command and the levels of administration. Note the different spans of control. Are there any advisory groups, task forces, or committees to consider?

2. Review the chapter material on organization structure to help identify both strong and weak points in your school's organization. Now draw another organization chart for the school, incorporating any changes you believe would improve the quality of the school. Support the second chart with a list of recommended changes and reasons for their inclusion.

DISCUSSION QUESTIONS

1. Is your business school well organized? Why or why not?

2. In what ways is the school's structure designed to suit the needs of students, faculty, staff, the administration, and the business community?

8.2   DESIGNING A STUDENT-RUN ORGANIZATION THAT PROVIDES CONSULTING SERVICES

OBJECTIVES

1. To appreciate the importance of the total organization on group and individual behavior.

2. To provide a beginning organization design experience that will be familiar to students.

BACKGROUND

The Industry Advisory Council for your school has decided to sponsor a student-run organization that will provide business consulting services to nonprofit groups in your community. The council has donated $20,000 toward start-up costs and has agreed to provide office space, computer equipment, and other materials as needed. The council hopes that the organization will establish its own source of funding after the first year of operation.

Task 1 The dean of the school wants you to develop alternative designs for the new organization. Your task is to identify the main design dimensions or factors to be dealt with in establishing such an organization and to describe the issues that must be resolved for each factor. For example, you might provide an organization chart to help describe the structural issues

involved. Before jumping ahead with your design, you may also have to think about (1) groups in the community that could use your help and (2) problems they face. Remember, though, your task is to create the organization that will provide services, not to provide an in-depth look at the types of services provided.

You and your team are to brainstorm design dimensions to be dealt with and to develop a one- or two-page outline that can be shared with the entire class. You have one hour to develop the outline. Select two people to present your design. Assume that you will all be involved in the new organization, filling specific positions.

Task 2 After the brainstorming period, the spokespersons will present the group designs or preferred design and answer questions from the audience.

Task 3 The instructor will comment on the designs and discuss additional factors that might be important for the success of this organization.

SOURCE: A. B. (Rami) Shani and James B. Lau, *Behavior in Organizations: An Experimental Approach* 1E, 2005, p. 369. Copyright 2005 The McGraw-Hill Companies, Inc. Reprinted with permission.

8.3   DECENTRALIZATION: PROS AND CONS

OBJECTIVE

To explore the reasons for, as well as the pros and cons of, decentralizing.

INSTRUCTIONS

The following Decentralization Worksheet contains some observations on decentralization. As you review each of the statements, provide an example that illustrates why this statement is important and related problems and benefits of the situation or condition indicated in the statement.

Decentralization Worksheet

A large number of factors determine the extent to which a manager should decentralize. Clearly, anything that increases a manager's workload creates pressure for decentralization because only a finite level of work can be accomplished by a single person. As with many facets of management, there are advantages and disadvantages to decentralization.

1. The greater the diversity of products, the greater the decentralization.

_____

_____

_____

_____

2. The larger the size of the organization, the more the decentralization.

_____

_____

_____

3. The more rapidly changing the organization's environment, the more decentralization.

_____

_____

_____

_____

4. Developing adequate, timely controls is the essence of decentralizing.

_____

_____

_____

_____

5. Managers should delegate decisions that involve large amounts of time but minimal erosions of their power and control.

_____

_____

_____

_____

6. Decentralizing involves delegating authority, and therefore, the principles of delegation apply to decentralization. (List the principles of delegation before you start your discussion.)

_____

_____

_____

_____

SOURCE: R. R. McGrath Jr., *Exercises in Management Fundamentals* (Englewood Cliffs, NJ: Prentice Hall, 1985), pp. 59–60. Reprinted by permission of Prentice Hall, Inc.

CONCLUDING CASE

STANLEY LYNCH INVESTMENT GROUP

The Stanley Lynch Investment Group is a large investment firm headquartered in New York. The firm has 12 major investment funds, each with analysts operating in a separate department. Along with knowledge of the financial markets and the businesses it analyzes, Stanley Lynch's competitive advantage comes from its advanced and reliable computer systems. Thus an effective information technology (IT) division is a strategic necessity, and the company's chief information officer (CIO) holds a key role at the firm.

When the company hired J. T. Kundra as a manager of technology, he learned that the IT division at Stanley Lynch consists of 68 employees, most of whom specialize in serving the needs of a particular fund. The IT employees serving a fund operate as a distinct group, each of them led by a manager who supervises several employees (five employees report to J. T.).

He also learned that each group sets up its own computer system to store information about its projects. The problems with that arrangement quickly became evident. As J. T. tried to direct his group's work, he would ask for documentation of one program or another. Sometimes no one was sure where to find the documentation; it might turn out to be stored in an obscure place such as only on someone's flash drive. Other times he would quickly get three different responses from three different people with three different versions of the documentation. And if he was interested in another group's project or a software program used in another department, getting information was next to impossible. He lacked the authority to ask employees in another group to drop what they were doing in order to hunt down information he needed.

J. T. concluded that the entire IT division could serve the firm much better if all authorized people had easy access to the work that had already been done and the software that was available. The logical place to store that information was online. From experience at a previous company, he believed that the easiest way to compile the information would be to set up a shared web project called a wiki—an online document created through the collaboration of its users, who can look up or contribute information according to their knowledge and needs. The challenge would be how to get everyone to contribute, given that he had authority over so few of the IT workers.

J. T. started by working with his five employees to build a wiki offering basic information presented in a consistent format. Then he met with two higher-level managers who report to the CIO. He showed them the wiki and explained that fast access to information would improve the IT group's quality and efficiency. He suggested that the managers require all the IT employees to put their documentation on the wiki, and he even persuaded them that this behavior should be measured for performance appraisals. This last tactic was especially significant because at an investment company, bonuses for meeting performance targets are a big part of employees' compensation.

The IT employees quickly came to appreciate that the wiki would help them perform better. When they visited it, they could see from the original information that it would be useful. Adoption of the wiki was swift, and before long, the IT employees came to think of it as one of their most important software systems.

QUESTIONS

1. Give an example of differentiation in Stanley Lynch's organization structure and an example of integration in this structure.
2. What role did authority play in the adoption of the wiki by the IT division at Stanley Lynch?
3. Describe how the IT division used coordination to achieve greater integration.

9 Organizational Agility

LEARNING OBJECTIVES

After studying Chapter 9, you will be able to:

LO 1 Discuss why it is critical for organizations to be responsive. p. 318

LO 2 Describe the qualities of an organic organization structure. p. 320

LO 3 Identify strategies and dynamic organizational concepts that can improve an organization's responsiveness. p. 321

LO 4 Explain how a firm can be both big and small. p. 324

LO 5 Summarize how firms organize to meet customer requirements. p. 329

LO 6 Identify ways that firms organize around different types of technology. p. 336

| Manager's Brief | Progress Report | Onward |

Management Connection

HOW PIXAR THRIVES IN A CHANGING INDUSTRY

When was the last time you made a trip to the movie theater to see a movie because it came from your favorite production company? Or for that matter, do you even go to movie theaters? And if you did, would you know a Universal movie from an MGM movie?

It's hard to recall a time when many people regularly paid for movies and cared about who produced them. Today sales of movie tickets and video recordings are down as consumers prefer to find free entertainment online. In that environment, it's hard to be a distinctive and profitable movie producer. One company that has bucked this trend is Pixar. The company's first 11 feature films have earned more than 40 Academy Awards and generated revenues soaring past $6 billion. Titles such as *Toy Story, Cars, Monsters Inc.,* and *Up* are indelibly associated in viewers' minds with the Pixar name, and each new Pixar release is greeted with anticipation.

This tremendous success in an environment being revolutionized by technology was hardly on the radar when Apple's former CEO Steve Jobs acquired Pixar. Under the leadership of Ed Catmull, Pixar was a computer hardware company whose notable achievement was the development of the Pixar Image Computer. The business was operating as a division of Lucasfilms that provided computer graphics. It offered top-of-the-line visual imaging for a variety of applications, including magnetic resonance imaging (MRIs) for medical diagnostics.

As it turned out, business customers weren't very interested in premium visual imaging, but Jobs was open to trying out the technology in creating videos. Pixar had a small animation division headed by John Lasseter, whose role in the company was to make presentations of the hardware's capabilities.

That group was given the green light to try making some animated shorts and then to use those samples to win some TV advertising projects for brands including Listerine and Lifesavers. The revenue stream from the ads helped provide funds for the animation group to develop its capabilities. And they indeed developed their capabilities. The company's animated short film *Tin Toy* won an Academy Award for best animated short in 1988, giving Pixar credibility as a filmmaker.

Building on that foundation, Pixar released its first feature film, *Toy Story,* in 1995. It was the first full-length digitally animated film, and it amazed and delighted its audience while impressing investors by grossing $350 million globally. To keep delighting movie fans, Pixar didn't just repeat that first success. Yes, it has released *Toy Story 2* (in 1999) and *Toy Story 3* (2010), but it has continually tackled projects in spite of—or maybe because of—technical and marketing hurdles that would intimidate a run-of-the-mill studio. Pixar's people figured out how to make fur look real in *Monsters Inc.,* how to make water believable in *Finding Nemo,* how to make rats charming in *Ratatouille,* and how to entice families to a movie about a cranky old widower (*Up*).

Movie lovers and management experts alike have tried to learn what makes Pixar stand out. One conclusion they have come to is that Pixar empowers creative people by giving them freedom to make decisions, coupled with the expectation that they will learn from each project and set the bar higher for the next one. The challenge will be to keep this formula working or be ready with a new one as Pixar grows from a new kid in the industry to an established leader in its current home at Walt Disney Studios (which acquired Pixar from Jobs in 2006).[1]

Pixar grew financially and in creative stature with an organization that both enables and demands innovation. As you read this chapter, consider whether the kind of organization that gets results in a start-up will also enable success for a mature company.

Like Pixar, today's successful companies can't afford to stand still. They cannot rest on their previous accomplishments. If they do, they can all too easily become vulnerable—to a competitor's new product, shifts in customer preferences, or other changes in their environment. Instead they use their current successes to continue to build a competitive advantage for the future, constantly seeking new ways to remain flexible, innovative, efficient, and responsive to their customers. One of the most important ways they have of doing that is to make sure that their organization structures and systems remain *adaptable*—prepared to meet the complex and ever-changing challenges that managers and their organizations constantly confront.

In Chapter 8 we described the formal structure of the organization. Businesses and other organizations are complex; they use the elements of the formal structure, including hierarchical levels, division of labor, and coordination, to manage that complexity. However, concentration on formal structure might leave the false impression that organizations are static structures, in which case they would be ill suited for today's fast-changing environment. But in fact, organizations are complex systems in which many people do many different things at the same time.

> The behavior of organizations does not just pop out of a chart; it emerges from the processes, systems, and relationships.

Therefore, the task of organizing extends to the issues described in this chapter: the design of processes, information flows, and technology. When these are well designed, the organization is flexible and agile enough to succeed in a changing world. Such an organization is often called "ambidextrous." As some people have the gift of writing with either hand, an ambidextrous organization is simultaneously good at *exploitation* (efficiently and quickly meeting needs in areas where it currently excels) and *exploration* (seeking and recognizing new ways to meet future needs).[2] In this chapter, we will see ways to organize people, information, and work that have helped organizations excel at both exploitation and exploration.

The Responsive Organization

mechanistic organization

A form of organization that seeks to maximize internal efficiency.

organic structure

An organizational form that emphasizes flexibility.

The formal structure is put in place to *control* people, decisions, and actions. But in today's fast-changing business environment, *responsiveness*—quickness, agility, the ability to adapt to changing demands—is more vital than ever to a firm's survival.[3]

Many years after Max Weber wrote about the concept of bureaucracy, two British management scholars (Burns and Stalker) described what they called the **mechanistic organization**.[4] The common mechanistic structure they described was similar to Weber's bureaucracy, but they went on to suggest that in the modern corporation, the mechanistic structure is not the only option. The **organic structure** stands in stark contrast to the mechanistic organization. It is much less rigid and, in fact, emphasizes flexibility. The organic structure can be described as follows:

1. Jobholders have broader responsibilities that change as the need arises.
2. Communication occurs through advice and information rather than through orders and instructions.
3. Decision making and influence are more decentralized and informal.
4. Expertise is highly valued.
5. Jobholders rely more heavily on judgment than on rules.

FIGURE 9.1(a)
Organization Chart Shows Who's on Top

FIGURE 9.1(b)
Advice Network Reveals Knowledge Flow

6. Obedience to authority is less important than commitment to the organization's goals.
7. Employees depend more on one another and relate more informally and personally.

Figure 9.1 contrasts the formal structure of an organization—epitomized by the organization chart—to the informal structure, which is much more organic. Astute managers are keenly aware of the network of interactions among the organization's members, and they structure around this network to increase agility. People in organic organizations work more as teammates than as subordinates who take orders from the boss, thus breaking away from the traditional bureaucratic form.[5]

The ideas underlying the organic structure and networks are the foundation for the newer forms of organization described in this chapter. The more organic a firm is, the more responsive it will be to changing competitive demands and market realities.

Managers in progressive companies place a premium on being able to act fast. They want to act in accordance with customer needs and other outside pressures. They want to take actions to correct past mistakes and also to prepare for an uncertain future. They want to be able to respond to threats and opportunities. The particular form—and degree—of organic structure the organization adopts to accomplish these goals will depend on its *strategy*, its *size*, its *customers*, and its *technology*. We will consider each of these in turn.

Strategy and Organizational Agility

Certain strategies, and the structures, processes, and relationships that accompany them, seem particularly well suited to improving an organization's ability to respond quickly and effectively to the challenges it faces. They reflect its managers' determination to fully leverage its people and assets to make the firm more agile and competitive. These strategies and structures are based on the firm's core capabilities, its strategic alliances, its ability to learn, and its ability to engage all the people in the organization in achieving its objectives.

Organizing around Core Capabilities

A recent, different, and important perspective on strategy and organization hinges on the concept of *core competence*.[6] As you learned in Chapter 4, a core competence is the capability—knowledge, expertise, skill—that underlies a company's ability to be a leader in providing a range of specific goods or services. It allows the company to compete on the basis of its core strengths and expertise, not just on what it produces. For example, Barnes & Noble's core competence is book merchandising. A core competence gives value to customers, makes the company's products different from—and better than—those of competitors, and can be used in creating new products. Think of core competencies or core capabilities as the roots of competitiveness and products as the fruits.

Successfully developing a world-class core capability opens the door to a variety of future opportunities; failure means being foreclosed from many markets. Thus a well-understood, well-developed core capability can enhance a company's responsiveness and competitiveness. Strategically, this means that companies should commit to excellence and leadership in capabilities, and strengthen them, before they commit to winning market share for specific products. Organizationally, this means that the corporation should be viewed as a portfolio of capabilities, not just a portfolio of specific businesses. Companies should strive for core competence leadership, not just product leadership.

Managers who want to strengthen their firms' competitiveness via core capabilities need to focus on several related issues:

Identify existing core capabilities.
Acquire or build core capabilities that will be important for the future.
Keep investing in capabilities so that the firm remains world class and better than competitors.
Extend capabilities to find new applications and opportunities for the markets of tomorrow.[7]

Keep in mind that it's not enough for an organization to *have* valuable resources that provide capabilities; those resources have to be *managed* in a way that gives the organization an advantage over competitors.[8] That means managers have to do three things. First, they must accumulate the right resources (such as talented people) by determining what resources they need, acquiring and developing those resources, and eliminating resources that don't provide value. Next, they combine the resources in ways that give the organization capabilities, such as researching new products or resolving problems for customers. These combinations may involve knowledge sharing and alliances between departments or with other organizations. Finally, managers need to leverage

Bottom Line

Core competence can be a source of quality and innovation.

Does your school have a core competence? If so, what is it?

Think of core capabilities as the roots of competitiveness and products as the fruits.

or exploit their resources. They do this by identifying the opportunities where their competencies deliver value to customers—say, by creating new products or by delivering existing products better than competitors—and then by coordinating and deploying the employees and other resources needed to respond to those opportunities.

IN PRACTICE

At Pfizer, Jordan Cohen has helped the pharmaceutical company build on core capabilities by freeing employees from getting bogged down in activities that are not related to those capabilities. While some companies have a strategy of outsourcing activities outside of their core capabilities, Cohen applied this kind of strategic decision to the level of individual employees by creating a system called pfizerWorks.

Cohen arrived at his idea for pfizerWorks at a time when Pfizer was encouraging its employees to look for ways to boost efficiency. Cohen noticed that highly trained colleagues were devoting hours to clerical tasks like creating graphs, transcribing notes from meetings, and conducting data searches. They could be more productive if they focused on the analytical and strategic roles for which they had been hired.

So Cohen recruited several of his coworkers to try a new system for six months: whenever they had a task that was outside their core responsibilities, they could click a pfizerWorks icon on their computer screens, which would take them to a request form to buy outside services. Within an hour, a Pfizer-trained contractor would phone the employee to clarify the details of the assignment and submit a cost estimate. If the employee accepted the arrangement, the contractor would perform the job, and the employee would rate the work.

The trial was a success, and the system was rolled out to the company with Cohen in charge. In its first year, it saved Pfizer almost 70,000 hours of time spent on lower-value work that could be handled more economically by outsiders.[9]

- What would you expect Pfizer's core capabilities to be? How does pfizerWorks help Pfizer invest in these?

Strategic Alliances

As we discussed in Chapter 8, the modern organization has a variety of links with other organizations. These links are more complex than the standard relationships with traditional stakeholders such as suppliers and clients. Today even fierce *competitors* are working together at unprecedented levels to achieve their strategic goals. For example, Federal Express has drop-off boxes at U.S. Postal Service facilities. The New York Times Company and Monster Worldwide formed an alliance in which job advertisements for 19 newspapers will carry the Monster.com brand. The arrangement gives the newspaper company, whose papers include the *New York Times* and *Boston Globe*, a stronger online presence and gives Monster better visibility in local job markets, which have traditionally been dominated by local papers.[10] In these and other examples, strategic alliances allow participants to respond to customer demands or environmental threats far faster and less expensively than each would be able to do on its own.

A **strategic alliance** is a formal relationship created with the purpose of joint pursuit of mutual goals. In a strategic alliance, individual organizations share administrative authority, form social links, and accept joint ownership. Such alliances are blurring firms' boundaries. They occur between companies and their competitors, governments, and universities. Such partnering often crosses national and cultural boundaries. Companies form strategic alliances to develop new technologies, enter new markets, and reduce manufacturing costs. Not only can alliances enable companies to move ahead faster and more efficiently, but they also are sometimes the only practical way to bring together the variety of specialists needed for operating in today's complex and fast-changing environment. Rather than hiring experts who understand the technology and market segments for each new product, companies can form alliances with partners that already have those experts on board.[11]

LO 3

strategic alliance

A formal relationship created among independent organizations with the purpose of joint pursuit of mutual goals.

IN PRACTICE

Airlines, which are fierce competitors as they each try to secure their space in the skies, actually form alliances designed to improve customer service. Member airlines of Star Alliance share ground facilities such as baggage claim, customer lounges, ticketing, and check-in counters. They also share check-in lanes during peak travel times. All of these shared activities help smooth the way for travelers, particularly those with tight connections and who are traveling on multiple airlines. Star Alliance staff (employees of member airlines) notify each other when flights are late, asking them to wait for connecting passengers if possible. And although the alliance makes every effort to make sure passengers' luggage is not lost, those who do come up empty-handed receive a Star Alliance overnight kit. Star Alliance airlines also purchase joint advertising and even make large fuel purchases together, reducing costs. In the future the alliance may begin making joint purchases of such items as coffee and airsick bags.

Although Star Alliance seeks to offer uniformity of ground services, the group encourages individual airlines to maintain their own unique character in the air, such as specialty meals or specific in-flight services.[12]

- What mutual goals does Star Alliance help the airlines achieve?

Bottom Line

Alliances can increase speed and innovation and lower costs.

How might an alliance increase innovation?

Music and coffee—a harmonious strategic alliance! Apple and Starbucks created a partnership that allows Apple customers to sync to the Starbucks wireless Internet network instantly from their iPod Touch, iPads, Macs, and iPhones to download music. Shown here is a Starbucks customer, Steve Carpenter (right), using his iPhone to capture a song at a Starbucks in Miami Beach, Florida.

Managers typically devote plenty of time to screening potential partners in financial terms. But for the alliance to work, the partners also must consider one another's areas of expertise and the incentives involved in the structure of the alliance. A comparison of research and development alliances found that the most innovation occurred when the partners were experts in moderately different types of research. If the partners were very different, they shared ideas and innovated more when the alliance was set up through equity (stock) ownership; for similar partners, a contract to do the research was associated with more innovation.[13]

Managers also must foster and develop the human relationships in the partnership. Asian companies seem to be the most comfortable with the non-financial, "people" side of alliances; European companies the next so; and U.S. companies the least. Thus U.S. companies may need to pay extra attention to the human side of alliances. Table 9.1 shows some recommendations for how to do this. In fact, most of the ideas apply not only to strategic alliances but to any type of relationship.[14]

The Learning Organization

Being responsive requires continually changing and learning new ways to act. Some experts have stated that the only sustainable advantage is learning faster than the competition. This has led to a new term that is now part of the vocabulary of most

The best alliances are true partnerships that meet these criteria:
1. *Individual excellence:* Both partners add value, and their motives are positive (pursue opportunity) rather than negative (mask weaknesses).
2. *Importance:* Both partners want the relationship to work because it helps them meet long-term strategic objectives.
3. *Interdependence:* The partners need each other; each helps the other reach its goal.
4. *Investment:* The partners devote financial and other resources to the relationship.
5. *Information:* The partners communicate openly about goals, technical data, problems, and changing situations.
6. *Integration:* The partners develop shared ways of operating; they teach each other and learn from each other.
7. *Institutionalization:* The relationship has formal status with clear responsibilities.
8. *Integrity:* Both partners are trustworthy and honorable.

TABLE 9.1
How I's Can Become We's

managers: the learning organization.[15] A **learning organization** is an organization skilled at creating, acquiring, and transferring knowledge, and at modifying its behavior to reflect new knowledge and insights.[16] Google, Toyota, and IDEO are good examples of learning organizations. Such organizations are skilled at solving problems, experimenting with new approaches, learning from their own experiences, learning from other organizations, and spreading knowledge quickly and efficiently.

How do firms become true learning organizations? There are a few important ingredients.[17]

learning organization

An organization skilled at creating, acquiring, and transferring knowledge, and at modifying its behavior to reflect new knowledge and insights.

1. Their people engage in disciplined thinking and attention to details, making decisions based on data and evidence rather than guesswork and assumptions.
2. They search constantly for new knowledge and ways to apply it, looking for expanding horizons and opportunities rather than quick fixes to current problems. The organization values and rewards individuals who expand their knowledge and skill in areas that benefit the organization.
3. They carefully review both successes and failures, looking for lessons and deeper understanding.
4. Learning organizations benchmark—they identify and implement the best business practices of other organizations, stealing ideas shamelessly.
5. They share ideas throughout the organization via reports, information systems, informal discussions, site visits, education, and training. Employees work with and are mentored by more experienced employees.

The only sustainable advantage is learning faster than the competition.

These efforts are ideally aimed at two areas of learning.[18] The first is exploitation, or continuously learning ways to operate more efficiently and effectively in the company's first domain. We will see ideas for this kind of learning throughout the remainder of this chapter. The second is exploration, or uncovering new areas in which the company can excel. Chapter 17 will say more about this kind of learning with regard to technology and innovation.

The High-Involvement Organization

Participative management is becoming increasingly popular as a way to create a competitive advantage. Particularly in high-technology companies facing stiff international competition, the aim is to generate high levels of commitment and involvement as employees and managers work together to achieve organizational goals.

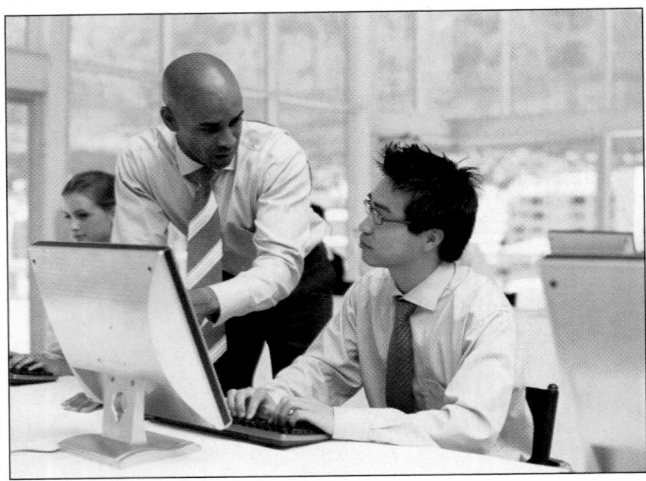

When companies need to be highly responsive, a high-involvement organization is key. Especially in high-technology companies where competition is tough, it's important for all employees to be on the front line and be able to react quickly to change.

In a **high-involvement organization,** top management ensures that there is a consensus about the direction in which the business is heading. The leader seeks input from his or her top management team and from lower levels of the company. Task forces, study groups, and other techniques are used to foster participation in decisions that affect the entire organization. Also fundamental to the high-involvement organization is continual feedback to participants regarding how they are doing compared with the competition and how effectively they are meeting the strategic agenda.

Structurally, this usually means that even lower-level employees have a direct relationship with a customer or supplier and thus receive feedback and are held accountable for a good or service delivery. The organizational form is a flat, decentralized structure built around a customer, good, or service. Employee involvement is particularly powerful when the environment changes rapidly, work is creative, complex activities require coordination, and firms need major breakthroughs in innovation and speed—in other words, when companies need to be more responsive.[19]

Organizational Size and Agility

Bottom Line

Large size often leads to scale economics.
How has General Motors's large size affected its ability to compete?

high-involvement organization

A type of organization in which top management ensures that there is consensus about the direction in which the business is heading.

One of the most important characteristics of an organization—and one of the most important factors influencing its ability to respond effectively to its environment—is its size. Large organizations are typically less organic and more bureaucratic. For example, Unilever, whose many consumer brands include Hellman's, Ben & Jerry's, Lipton, Vaseline, Dove, and Slim-Fast, has more than 200,000 employees worldwide. In many countries, the company has operated as three independent business lines—food, personal care, and ice cream and frozen food—each with its own supply chain and marketing budget.[20]

In large organizations, jobs become more specialized. More distinct groups of specialists get created because large organizations can add a new specialty at lower proportional expense. The complexity created by these numerous specialties makes the organization harder to control. As a result, in the past management added more levels to keep spans of control from becoming too large. To cope with complexity, large companies tend to become more bureaucratic. Rules, procedures, and paperwork are introduced.

Thus with size comes greater complexity, and complexity brings a need for increased control. In response, organizations adopt bureaucratic strategies of control. The conventional wisdom is that bureaucratization increases efficiency but decreases a company's ability to innovate. So are larger companies more responsive to competitive demands or not? Let's see.

The Case for Big

Bigger was better after World War II, when foreign competition was limited and growth seemed limitless. To meet high demand for its products, U.S. industry embraced high-volume, low-cost manufacturing methods. IBM, General Motors (GM), and Sears all grew into behemoths during those decades.

Alfred Chandler, a pioneer in strategic management, noted that big companies were the engine of economic growth throughout the 20th century.[21] Size creates *scale economies,*— that is, lower costs per unit of production. And size can offer specific advantages such as lower operating costs, greater purchasing power, and easier access to capital. Walmart, among the largest companies in America, has the purchasing power to buy merchandise in larger volumes and sell it at lower prices than its competitors can. Size also creates **economies of scope;** materials and processes employed in one product can be used to make other

related products. With such advantages, huge companies with lots of money may be the best at taking on large foreign rivals in huge global markets.

Walmart's huge size has enabled it to set up a highly efficient distribution system in which suppliers work to keep costs low, an important competitive advantage for its low-price strategy.

economies of scope

Economies in which materials and processes employed in one product can be used to make other related products.

The Case for Small

But a huge, complex organization can find it hard to manage relationships with customers and among its own units. Bureaucracy can run rampant. Too much success can breed complacency, and the resulting inertia hinders change. Experts suggest that this is a surefire formula for being left in the dust by hungry competitors. As consumers demand a more diverse array of high-quality, customized products supported by excellent service, giant companies have begun to stumble. Some evidence exists, for example, that as firms get larger and their market share grows, customers begin to view their products as having lower quality. Also, once a company has captured a big share of the market,

Chances are good you'll spend part of your career at a small organization. Just about half of employees in the U.S. private sector work for a small business (defined by the Small Business Administration's Office of Advocacy as an independent business with fewer than 500 employees).[22]

future growth is complicated because winning over more customers requires costlier efforts or a fresh approach. When growth was slowing at Walmart, the company tried

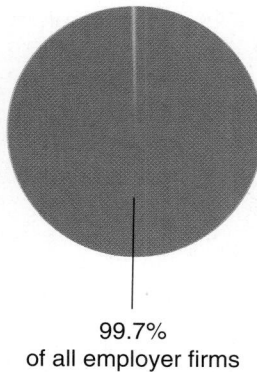
99.7%
of all employer firms

49.7%
of private-sector employees

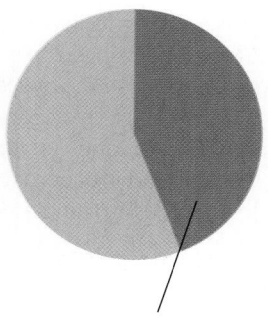
44%
of U.S. private-sector payroll

Role of small businesses in U.S. economy

branching into affordable but fashionable clothing. But cutting-edge fashion has not been an area of expertise for the company, and the initial efforts flopped.[23]

Larger companies also are more difficult to coordinate and control. While size may enhance efficiency by spreading fixed costs over more units, it also may create administrative difficulties that inhibit efficient performance. Unilever not only has three organizations selling different product lines in each country it serves, but until recently it was run by two chairmen–CEOs, an artifact of a merger that took place decades ago. This cumbersome structure has held back Unilever's efficiency and agility, making competition more difficult.[24] To describe this type of problem, a new term has entered the business vocabulary: *diseconomies of scale*, or the costs of being too big. "Small is beautiful" has become a favorite phrase of entrepreneurial business managers.[25]

Smaller companies can move fast, provide quality goods and services to targeted market niches, and inspire greater involvement from their people. Nimble small firms frequently outmaneuver big bureaucracies. They introduce new and better products, and they steal market share. The premium now is on flexibility and responsiveness—the unique potential strengths of the small firm. An extreme example is Kobold Watch, staffed by founder Michael Kobold and three employees. The small company makes and sells premium mechanical wristwatches priced at thousands of dollars each. Kobold advertises online and through word of mouth generated by sales to celebrities, including former president Bill Clinton and actors Kiefer Sutherland and James Gandolfini. When sales surge, Kobold calls on two other watchmakers to help out as needed. He intentionally limits production to 2,500 watches a year—not just to keep his company lean but also to maintain the prestige of his brand.[26]

Bottom Line

Small size may improve speed.
A salesperson learns about a customer's new challenge. Why might a small company be able to react to this information faster?

IN PRACTICE

To keep its flexibility as it grew, Dur-A-Flex became a learning organization. The company started out primarily installing commercial and industrial flooring, but it gradually expanded into manufacturing the flooring systems and related products. After a decade of rapid growth, the company's structure had become rigid, divided into separate manufacturing systems operating on three shifts. Maintaining quality and speed across departments and shifts was sometimes awkward.

Under CEO Bob Smith, Dur-A-Flex embarked on a change program known as "lean," an approach (described later in this chapter) that involves studying and improving every process. Going lean introduced a climate that fostered learning. Every employee is trained in the methods and philosophy behind the lean approach. The company set up its own program, called Dur-A-Flex University, which holds classes mainly during lunch breaks.

According to Bill Greider, who led the lean initiative, "Once our focus turned to learning, everything changed." As employees began interacting in the classes, divisions among groups slipped away. Employees now are encouraged to learn about all aspects of Dur- A-Flex's business, from financial matters to flooring installation methods. Employees also can teach or sign up for a variety of fun Dur-A-Flex University "electives" such as beer making. CEO Smith says the learning approach not only helps employees cut costs and boost sales but also builds their enthusiasm and empowers them.[27]

- How does the focus on learning make Dur-A-Flex more like a small company?

The challenge is to be both big and small to capitalize on the advantages of each.

Being Big and Small

Small *is* beautiful for unleashing energy and speed. But in buying and selling, size offers market power. The challenge, then, is to be both big and small to capitalize on the advantages of each.

When Intuit grew from a software start-up to an established company selling popular accounting software, the company brought in a CEO recruited from General Electric, Steve Bennett, to mesh big-company skills with Intuit's entrepreneurial energy. Managers had plenty of new ideas but needed to build their skill in choosing and implementing the best ideas. Bennett helped the company reevaluate its strategy to find areas of new growth. Popular Intuit products like QuickBooks have already captured most of the market for accounting software, so the company needs to focus less on competitors for its existing products and more on areas of untapped opportunity, which is why Intuit has begun to develop new areas such as online banking and software for managing health care expenses.[28]

From a different angle, companies such as Starbucks and Amazon are very large companies that work hard to act small and maintain a sense of intimacy with employees and customers. Both are considered among the best-managed companies in the world. To avoid problems of growth and size, they decentralize decision making and organize around small, adaptive, team-based work units.

> "When I got [to Intuit], . . . I changed only one word in the operating values: I changed 'Think fast, move fast' to 'Think smart, move smart'. Because doing dumb things faster doesn't get you anywhere."
>
> —Steve Bennett, Intuit CEO[29]

Downsizing   As large companies attempt to regain the responsiveness of small companies, they often face the dilemma of downsizing. **Downsizing** is the planned elimination of positions or jobs. Common approaches to downsizing include eliminating functions, hierarchical levels, or even whole units.[30] Another growing trend has been to replace full-time employees with less expensive part-time or temporary workers.

downsizing

The planned elimination of positions or jobs.

Recognizing that people will be unemployed, frightened, and perhaps unable to pay their bills, managers usually opt for downsizing only in response to some kind of pressure. Traditionally, companies have downsized when demand falls and seems unlikely to rebound in the short run. Laying off workers is a way to avoid paying people who aren't needed to produce and ship goods, as well as to lower costs so that the company remains profitable—or at least viable—until the next upturn in business. More recently, however, global competition forced companies to cut costs even when sales were strong, and technological advances made it possible to produce the same amount of work with fewer employees. As a result, in recent decades, many companies have used downsizing as a way to become more efficient. This trend changed the types of positions that were eliminated. Downsizing in response to a slowdown in demand has tended to have the most impact on operating-level jobs in manufacturing firms. Downsizing to improve efficiency has focused on eliminating layers of management and bureaucratic structures, so those layoffs target "white-collar" middle managers.

The recent recession has forced widespread downsizing across a variety of industries, not just manufacturing. For example, in 2009 Microsoft faced a severe downturn in demand, driven in part by a rare decline in the number of personal computers sold. The company announced that, for the first time in its history, it would have to downsize, laying off about 5,000 employees (about 5 percent of its workforce). The company started with 1,400 job cuts, and several months later announced that another 3,000 workers would lose their jobs, bringing the company near the end of its downsizing plan. In a memo to employees, CEO Steve Ballmer acknowledged the risks of such an approach: "Our success at Microsoft has always been the direct result of the talent, hard work, and commitment of our people."[31] In effect, downsizing runs the risk of eliminating the very source of a company's success.

Done appropriately, with inefficient layers eliminated and resources focused more on adding customer value than on wasteful internal processes, downsizing can indeed lead to a more agile, flexible, and responsive firm. In that case, downsizing can be

rightsizing

A successful effort to achieve an appropriate size at which the company performs most effectively.

called **rightsizing**—arrival at the size at which the company performs most effectively. But even under the best circumstances, downsizing can be traumatic for an organization and its employees. What can be done to manage downsizing effectively, to help make it more effective?

First, firms should avoid excessive (cyclical) hiring to help reduce the need to engage in major or multiple downsizings. But beyond that, firms must avoid common mistakes such as making slow, small, frequent layoffs; implementing voluntary early retirement programs that entice the best people to leave; and laying off so many people that the company's work can no longer be performed. Instead firms can engage in a number of positive practices to ease the pain and increase the effectiveness of downsizing:[32]

Use downsizing only as a last resort, when other methods of improving performance by innovating or changing procedures have been exhausted.

Choose positions to be eliminated by engaging in careful analysis and strategic thinking.

Train people to cope with the new situation.

Identify and protect talented people.

Give special attention and help to those who have lost their jobs.

Communicate constantly with people about the process, and invite ideas for alternative ways to operate more efficiently.

Identify how the organization will operate more effectively in the future, and emphasize this positive future and the remaining employees' new roles in attaining it.

The management practices of high-involvement organizations, described earlier in this chapter, also play a role. In general, the negative consequences of downsizing are greater at high-involvement organizations—but not as bad if the organization continues the high employee involvement after the layoffs.[33]

survivor's syndrome

Loss of productivity and morale in employees who remain after a downsizing.

Interestingly, the people who lose their jobs because of downsizing are not the only ones deeply affected. Those who survive the process—who keep their jobs—tend to exhibit what has become known as **survivor's syndrome**.[34] They struggle with heavier workloads; wonder who will be next to go; try to figure out how to survive; lose commitment to the company and faith in their bosses; and become narrow-minded, self-absorbed, and risk-averse. As a consequence, morale and productivity usually drop.

You will learn more about some of these ideas in later chapters on human resources management, leadership, motivation, communication, and managing change. You might also refer back to our discussion in Chapter 1 about some of the things you can do to successfully manage your own career in an era where downsizing is a normal occurrence. And for an example of a company that has—so far—enjoyed the advantages of being both big and small without downsizing, see "Management Connection: Progress Report."

Manager's Brief	**Progress Report**	Onward

Management Connection

HOW PIXAR KEEPS LEARNING

The critical and financial success of *Toy Story* showed the world that Pixar had great technology and talent. But to deploy those resources in a way that would continue wowing audiences, the company would have to operate in a way that made it a fertile place for innovation.

One way the company does this is by emphasizing collaboration and talent over hierarchy. People at all levels of the organization are expected to submit their work on a film for review by everyone involved. For example, the directors of Pixar movies challenge one another to be great through a required process of reviewing one another's work. Every two or three months, directors present their films to Pixar's other filmmakers and its senior creative staff for a review. Hearing criticisms of one's work can be painful, but most directors apply the feedback and find that their films are better as a result of it. They learn that even mistakes are valued if they are a part of learning. In the worlds of Lee Unkrich, director of *Toy Story 3,* "We know screw-ups are an essential part of making something good. That's why our goal is to screw up as fast as possible." Humor such as this and the laughter that often enlivens conversations at Pixar provide evidence that participants in dialogues are enjoying the give-and-take of equality, rather than merely deferring to the presumed wisdom of the higher-ups.

Similarly, at the end of each day, a movie's animators save their work on the company's computer, regardless of how complete it is, so their colleagues and the movie's director can review it. Each morning, the animation team meets to view and discuss the work in progress. As the team members look at images projected on a screen, all are expected to participate by freely sharing ideas. In addition, after each movie has been released, the team responsible for it is required to go through a process called a "postmortem," in which they compile a list of five things they would do the same way and five things they wouldn't repeat.

The company's team structure reinforces this learning. A traditional organization for making a movie would involve a studio hiring a group of freelancers to spend a few months or a year creating a movie and then move on to their next assignment, perhaps at another company. But at Pixar, the artists and engineers who work on movies are permanent employees. When they finish one project, they review it, learn from it, and take their expanded knowledge to the next Pixar movie team. Being full-time employees also helps employees meet the challenge of having their work peer-reviewed every day. That kind of feedback could be overwhelming to members of a short-term group, but because team members know they will be collaborating again and again on projects, they learn to trust one another and value one another's input. In addition, feedback from the whole team is something the directors respect. Oscar winner Brad Bird, for example, recalls that when working for other studios,

he saw directors ignore input, so "people didn't feel invested in their work, and productivity went down."

The commitment to learning through collaboration is signaled by Pixar's physical architecture. Most of the workforce occupies one main building of Pixar's campus in Emeryville, California, east of San Francisco. Workers on different activities operate out of separate areas of the building, but in the middle is one huge central hall housing the meeting rooms, bathrooms, and cafeteria, where the company clearly hopes people from, say, the art department will run into coworkers from animation and storyboarding, among others. Producer Darla Anderson says "walking to the bathroom or getting a cup of coffee" can be "the most productive part" of her day.

But how does Pixar keep this culture going, even following its acquisition by Hollywood giant Walt Disney Studios? The answer is that the leaders at the top are committed to learning and changing, even if it means making mistakes along the way. When Disney acquired Pixar, John Lasseter was made chief creative officer of both Pixar and Disney Animation Studios, and computer whiz Ed Catmull became president of both groups. So the same drive and fearlessness that enabled Pixar to evolve from a hardware maker to an ad creator to a brilliant movie studio remained the values after Disney's acquisition of Pixar. Pixar remained in Emeryville, where it could enjoy the freewheeling "Let's try it" attitude of Silicon Valley, away from the corporate cautiousness of today's Hollywood. The location decision was based on experience. When Disney, which had bankrolled the early Pixar projects before the acquisition, saw early ideas for the first *Toy Story,* its decision makers were doubtful and pressed for "edgier" characters. The Pixar team persevered with its vision, however, and consumers soon showed that the rosy mood of this and future Pixar movies was quite to their liking after all. Perhaps this is why Disney Studios, as it eyes a need to scale back its workforce, has no layoffs planned for Pixar's responsive, agile organization.[35]

- What are Pixar's core capabilities? How does it build and invest in them?
- In what ways is Pixar both "big" and "small"? How could Disney's downsizing affect Pixar's agility?

Customers and the Responsive Organization

So far we have discussed how an organization's agility, adaptability, and structure are influenced by its *strategy* and *size.* But in the end, the point of structuring a responsive, agile organization lies in enabling it to meet and exceed the expectations of its *customers*—the people it must attract to purchase a good or service and whose

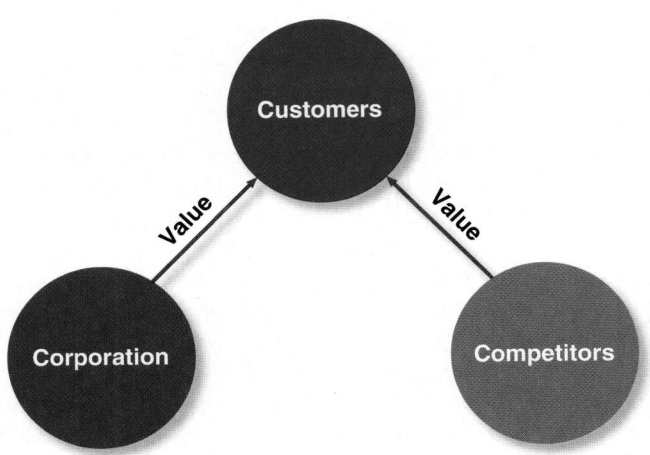

SOURCE: From K. Ohmae et al., *The Mind of the Strategist: The Art of Japanese Business*, 1982, p. 92. Copyright 1982 The McGraw-Hill Companies, Inc. Reprinted with permission.

FIGURE 9.2
The Strategic Triangle

Bottom Line

Today's customers demand excellent service and new high-quality, low-cost products—fast. *How does a rigid bureaucracy make it difficult to meet all these challenges at once?*

customer relationship management (CRM)

A multifaceted process focusing on creating two-way exchanges with customers to foster intimate knowledge of their needs, wants, and buying patterns.

continued patronage and involvement with the organization constitute the fundamental driver of sustained, long-term competitiveness and success.

Recall from Chapter 2 that an organization's environment is composed of many different parts—government, suppliers, competitors, and the like. Perhaps no other aspect of the environment has had a more profound impact on organizing in recent years than a focus on customers. Dr. Kenichi Ohmae points out that any business unit must take into account three key players: the *company* itself, the *competition*, and the *customer*. These components form what Ohmae refers to as the *strategic triangle*, as shown in Figure 9.2. Managers need to balance the strategic triangle, and successful organizations use their strengths to create value by meeting customer requirements better than competitors do. In this section, we will discuss in some depth how organizations maintain and extend a competitive advantage with their customers.

Customer Relationship Management

Customer relationship management (CRM) is a multifaceted process, typically mediated by a set of information technologies, that focuses on creating two-way exchanges with customers so that firms have an intimate knowledge of their needs, wants, and buying patterns. The use of a particular technology to conduct CRM—for example, using cell phone applications to track consumers' locations or social networking to measure what topics they chat about—is less important than figuring out how the organization can use the information to deliver exactly what customers want. Thus at companies that use CRM effectively, it helps them understand, as well as anticipate, the needs of current and potential customers. And in that way, it is part of a business strategy for managing customers to maximize their long-term value to an enterprise.[36]

IN PRACTICE

One of the industry leaders in providing CRM software is San Francisco–based Salesforce. com. The company recently arranged with Toyota to provide a private social network for buyers of new electric and plug-in hybrid vehicles. The network, called Toyota Friend, links drivers in the network to each other, Toyota, dealerships, and their cars. Customers can use Toyota Friend to send short messages to other drivers on the network and communicate with local dealers. Using a technology called telematics, drivers on the network can receive remote diagnostic information, such as battery usage or tire pressure, or direct the car to, for example, start the engine and warm the seats as they head for the parking lot.

The plan was to launch Toyota Friend first in Japan, with a global rollout of the service about a year later. Where the network is available, Toyota customers can access it through any wireless mobile device such as a smartphone or computer. Toyota anticipates that customers will be interested in looking up information such as where the nearest charging station is located and whether the battery needs to be charged. They also can look up maintenance tips provided by Toyota.[37]

- How might Toyota apply the information generated by Toyota Friend to improve how it anticipates and meets customer needs?

As discussed throughout this book, customers want quality goods and services, low cost, innovative products, and speed. Traditional thinking considered these basic customer wants as a set of potential trade-offs. For instance, customers wanted high quality or low costs passed along in the form of low prices. But world-class companies today know that the "trade-off" mentality no longer applies. Customers want it *all*, and they are learning that an organization exists somewhere that will provide it all.

But if all companies seek to satisfy customers, how can a company realize a competitive advantage? World-class companies have learned that almost any advantage is temporary because competitors will strive to catch up. Simply stated—although obviously not simply done—a company attains and retains competitive advantage by continuing to improve. This concept—*kaizen*, or continuous improvement—is an integral part of Japanese operations strategy.

> "Our business is about technology, yes. But it's also about operations and customer relationships."
>
> —Michael Dell

In the realm of customer relations, continuous improvement includes continually changing in order to connect with customers, even without waiting for customers to make the first move. Comcast Cable, Dell, and other companies have adopted Salesforce.com's Service Cloud application, which lets companies find customers who take their questions and problems to Facebook, Twitter, or other social networking communities. Customer service agents can locate messages about their products and then offer to help, potentially saving a customer relationship. Chase Paymentech Solutions is using collaboration software called Greenhouse to invite customers into conversations about new product ideas. Customers can critique and vote on ideas; their feedback not only helps Chase figure out which ideas have potential but also strengthens customer commitment.[38]

World-class companies know that the 'trade-off' mentality no longer applies.

As organizations focus on responding to customer needs, they soon find that the traditional meaning of a customer expands to include "internal customers." The word *customer* now refers to the *next process*, or *wherever the work goes next*.[39] This highlights the idea of interdependence among related functions and means that all functions of the organization—not just marketing people—have to be concerned with customer satisfaction. Any recipient of a person's work, whether coworker, boss, subordinate, or external party, should be viewed as the customer.

A deeper way to understand how organizations can add customer value to their products has been provided by Michael Porter, who popularized the concept of the value chain. A **value chain** is the sequence of activities that flow from raw materials to the delivery of a good or service, with additional value created at each step. You can see a generic value chain illustrated in Figure 9.3. Each step in the chain adds value to the product or service:

value chain

The sequence of activities that flow from raw materials to the delivery of a good or service, with additional value created at each step.

Research and development focus on innovation and new products.
Inbound logistics receive and store raw materials and distribute them to operations.
Operations transform the raw materials into final product.
Outbound logistics warehouse the product and handle its distribution.

SOURCE: M. Porter, *Competitive Advantage: Creating and Sustaining Superior Performance* (New York: Free Press, 1985).

FIGURE 9.3
Generic Value Chain

Marketing and sales identify customer requirements and get customers to purchase the product.

Service offers customer support, such as repair, after the item has been bought.

When the total value created—that is, *what customers are willing to pay*—exceeds the cost of providing the good or service, the result is the organization's profit *margin*.[40]

Managers can add customer value and build competitive advantage by paying close attention to their organization's value chain—not only each step in it, but the way each step interacts with the others. For example, they can achieve economies of scale, as Walmart has, so that their materials and operations costs are lowered, or they can develop innovative distribution channels, as Amazon has done, and add customer value that way. They can also create structures and systems that link the elements of the value chain in innovative ways.

One of the most effective ways to leverage an organization's value chain is to bring together elements of the chain to collaborate to add customer value and build competitive advantage. For example, long-term relationships can be established with suppliers to encourage investment in new technologies and practices that speed product development and turnaround. Nike chooses its suppliers—what it calls its "strategic partners"—to that end and shares its business plans and strategies with them to reinforce close collaboration. Sales staff can communicate with operations staff, before the manufacturing process even starts, to develop products jointly that customers will value highly. Service managers can constantly report back to operations about defects and work with operations and suppliers to reduce and eliminate them. When managers create that type of collaboration, their organization's agility and responsiveness increase significantly.

total quality management (TQM)

An integrative approach to management that supports the attainment of customer satisfaction through a wide variety of tools and techniques that result in high-quality goods and services.

Total Quality and Six Sigma

Often the effort to be more responsive has brought managers face to face with the need to ensure consistently high quality. Systematic ways of meeting that need include total quality management and six sigma.

Total quality management (TQM) is a way of managing in which everyone is committed to continuous improvement of his or her part of the operation. In business, success depends on having high-quality products. As described in Chapter 1 and throughout the book, TQM is a comprehensive approach to improving product quality and thereby customer satisfaction. It is characterized by a strong orientation toward customers (external and internal) and has become an umbrella theme for organizing work. TQM reorients managers toward involving people across departments in improving all aspects of the business. Continuous improvement requires integrative mechanisms that facilitate group problem solving, information sharing, and cooperation across business functions. As a consequence, the walls that separate stages and functions of work tend to come down, and the organization operates more in a team-oriented manner.[41]

One of the founders of the quality management movement was W. Edwards Deming. When he started, his work was largely ignored by American companies, but it was adopted eagerly by Japanese firms that wanted to shed their products of their post–World War II reputation for shoddiness. The quality emphasis of Japanese car manufacturing was one direct result of Deming's work, which has since been adopted by many American and other companies worldwide. Deming's "14 points" of quality emphasized a holistic approach to management that demands intimate understanding of the process—the delicate interaction of materials, machines, and people that determines productivity, quality, and competitive advantage:

1. Create constancy of purpose—strive for long-term improvement rather than short-term profit.
2. Adopt the new philosophy—don't tolerate delays and mistakes.
3. Cease dependence on mass inspection—build quality into the process on the front end.
4. End the practice of awarding business on price tag alone—build long-term relationships.
5. Improve constantly and forever the system of production and service—at each stage.
6. Institute training and retraining—continually update methods and thinking.
7. Institute leadership—provide the resources needed for effectiveness.
8. Drive out fear—people must believe it is safe to report problems or ask for help.
9. Break down barriers among departments—promote teamwork.
10. Eliminate slogans, exhortations, and arbitrary targets—supply methods, not buzzwords.
11. Eliminate numerical quotas—they are contrary to the idea of continuous improvement.
12. Remove barriers to pride in workmanship—allow autonomy and spontaneity.
13. Institute a vigorous program of education and retraining—people are assets, not commodities.
14. Take action to accomplish the transformation—provide a structure that enables quality.

One of the most important contributors to total quality management has been the introduction of statistical tools to analyze the causes of product defects, in an approach called **six sigma quality.** Sigma is the Greek letter used to designate the estimated standard deviation or variation in a process. (The higher the "sigma level," the lower the amount of variation.) The product defects analyzed may include anything that results in customer dissatisfaction—for example, late delivery, wrong shipment, or poor customer service, as well as problems with the product itself. When the defect has been identified, managers then engage the organization in a determined, comprehensive effort to eliminate its causes and reduce it to the lowest practicable level. At six sigma, a product or process is defect-free 99.99966 percent of the time—fewer than 3.4 defects or mistakes per million. Reaching that goal almost always requires managers to restructure their internal processes and relationships with suppliers and customers in fundamental ways. For example, managers may have to create teams from all

> At six sigma, a product or process is defect-free 99.99966 percent of the time.

six sigma quality

A method of systematically analyzing work processes to identify and eliminate virtually all causes of defects, standardizing the processes to reach the lowest practicable level of any cause of customer dissatisfaction.

Nestlé Purina PetCare Company has recently won the Malcolm Baldrige National Quality Award.

parts of the organization to implement the process improvements that will prevent defects from arising. Motorola, where six sigma was developed, and General Electric, whose success with six sigma helped to make the technique popular, credit the method with helping them improve efficiency and quality. Today many companies are combining six sigma's drive to improve quality with a method of improving efficiency known as lean manufacturing, described later in this chapter. This hybrid effort, often called *lean six sigma*, is powerful because it helps an organization to be simultaneously responsive and agile. We will discuss six sigma in more detail in Chapter 16.

Commitment to total quality requires a thorough, extensive, integrated approach to organizing. To encourage American companies to make that commitment and achieve excellence, the Malcolm Baldrige National Quality Award was established in 1987. Named after a former U.S. Secretary of Commerce, the award is given every year to companies and nonprofit organizations that have met specified criteria in seven areas: (1) leadership; (2) strategic planning; (3) customer and market focus; (4) measurement, analysis, and knowledge management; (5) workforce focus; (6) process management; and (7) business results. Recent winners include Nestlé Purina PetCare Company, which outperforms its pet food competitors in customer satisfaction and boasts exceptional performance in worker safety and employee turnover, and K&N Management, a Texas restaurant operator where managers carry handheld computers that deliver daily performance information and any guest comments or complaints so they can make quick course corrections.[42]

ISO 9001

A company can both improve its responsiveness to customers and demonstrate to them that it has done so by being certified for meeting widely recognized standards set by outside organizations. For example, the International Organization for Standardization (known globally as ISO) sets a wide variety of exacting standards for parts, materials, products, and organizational processes, each identified by number. In the area of management systems, ISO standards include the ISO 14000 family of standards for environmental management and the ISO 27001 standard for information security.

In the quality arena, a particularly important family of standards is ISO 9000, which defines good quality management practices. The requirements for a quality management system that will ensure such practices are spelled out in **ISO 9001.** Meeting this standard enables any type or size of organization to improve its total quality for the benefit of producers and consumers by addressing eight principles:[43]

ISO 9001

A series of quality standards developed by a committee working under the International Organization for Standardization to improve total quality in all businesses for the benefit of producers and consumers.

1. *Customer focus*—learning and addressing customer needs and expectations.
2. *Leadership*—establishing a vision and goals, establishing trust, and providing employees with the resources and inspiration to meet goals.
3. *Involvement of people*—establishing an environment in which employees understand their contribution, engage in problem solving, and acquire and share knowledge.
4. *Process approach*—defining the tasks needed to successfully carry out each process and assigning responsibility for them.
5. *System approach to management*—putting processes together into efficient systems that work together effectively.
6. *Continual improvement*—teaching people how to identify areas for improvement and rewarding them for making improvements.
7. *Factual approach to decision making*—gathering accurate performance data, sharing the data with employees, and using the data to make decisions.
8. *Mutually beneficial supplier relationships*—working in a cooperative way with suppliers.

U.S. companies first became interested in ISO 9001 because overseas customers, particularly those in the European Union, embraced it. Companies that comply with the quality guidelines of ISO 9001 can apply for official certification; some countries and companies demand certification as an acknowledgment of compliance before they will do business. Now some U.S. customers as well are making the same demand. Consequently, the number of companies receiving ISO 9001 certification continues to grow; hundreds of thousands of companies in manufacturing and services industries around the world are ISO-certified. For example, Miles Chemical, headquartered in Arleta, California, used ISO 9001 certification as a way to plan how it serves customers. The 27-employee business blends and delivers chemicals to manufacturing customers, and before it entered the certification process, it had operated informally, without standardized processes for getting just the right products to customers on time. By meeting the requirements for ISO 9001, Miles improved service quality, lowered inventory costs, and boosted customer satisfaction scores.[44]

Certification is not the end of the quality effort but a beginning step. Rather than defining how to operate perfectly, ISO 9001 standards establish practices that enable the organization to keep improving—assuming that it continues to follow those practices.

Reengineering

Extending from TQM and a focus on organizing around customer needs, organizations also have embraced the notion of reengineering (introduced in Chapter 1). The principal idea of reengineering is to revolutionize key organizational systems and processes to answer this question: "If you were the customer, how would you like us to operate?" The answer to this question forms a vision for how the organization should run, and then decisions are made and actions are taken to make the organization operate like the vision. Processes such as product development, order fulfillment, customer service, inventory management, billing, and production are redesigned from scratch as if the organization were brand new and just starting out.

For example, Procter & Gamble used reengineering to make its products more competitive. The company learned that the average family buying its products rather than private-label or lower-price brands paid an extra $725 per year. That figure, P&G realized, was far too high and warned that the company's high prices could drive the company to extinction. Other data also signaled the need for P&G to change. Market shares of famous brands such as Comet, Mr. Clean, and Ivory had been dropping for 25 years. P&G was making 55 price changes *daily* on about 80 brands, and inaccurate billings were common. Its plants were inefficient, and the company had the highest overhead in the business. It clearly had to cut prices, and to do that, it had to cut costs.

In response, P&G reengineered. The company tore down and rebuilt nearly every activity that contributed to its high costs. It redesigned the way it develops, manufactures, distributes, prices, markets, and sells products. The reengineering was difficult, time-consuming, and expensive. But after the changes, price changes became rare, factories became far more efficient, inventory levels fell, and sales and profits rose. P&G was able to price its brands nearer to the prices of store brands. P&G might have reinvented itself as a leader in the industry once again and created for itself a long-term competitive advantage that others have scrambled to match.[45]

The kind of reengineering that P&G undertook requires much more than a management directive from the top, a change in the formal organization structure, the introduction of new technology, or even a well-communicated change in strategy. Rather, to be fully effective and successful, reengineering often requires a fundamental change in the way the parts of the organization work together. They need to see each other as partners in a common effort rather than as members of a particular department or unit. Teams made up of all levels of the organization may be involved in the reengineering effort, and information on problems and possible solutions needs

Bottom Line

Effective reengineering can cut costs significantly.
What other drivers of success can reengineering improve?

Reengineering often requires a fundamental change in the way the parts of the organization work together.

to be fully shared between them. Customers and other stakeholders may be interviewed to get their contribution. Often several teams will be working simultaneously. In this way, all the information that is available within and outside the organization can be brought to bear on a problem—and the solution developed will have wider acceptance and can be implemented faster.

As you can see, reengineering is not about making minor organizational changes here and there. It is about completely overhauling the operation, in revolutionary ways, to achieve the greatest possible benefits to the customer and to the organization.

Technology and Organizational Agility

technology

The systematic application of scientific knowledge to a new product, process, or service.

We have discussed the strategic, size, and customer influences on organizational design and agility. We now turn to one more critical factor affecting an organization's structure and responsiveness: its *technology*.

Broadly speaking, **technology** can be viewed as the methods, processes, systems, and skills used to transform resources (inputs) into products (outputs). Although we will discuss technology—and innovation—more fully in Chapter 17, in this chapter we want to highlight some of the important influences technology has on organizational design.

> "Information technology and business are becoming inextricably interwoven. I don't think anyone can talk meaningfully about one without talking about the other."
> —Bill Gates

Types of Technology Configurations

Research by Joan Woodward laid the foundation for understanding technology and structure. According to Woodward, three basic technologies characterize how work is done: small batch, large batch, and continuous process technologies. These three classifications are equally useful for describing either service or manufacturing technologies. Each differs in terms of volume produced and variety of goods/services offered. Each also has a different influence on how managers organize and structure the work of their organizations.[46]

small batch

Technologies that produce goods and services in low volume.

large batch

Technologies that produce goods and services in high volume.

Small Batch Technologies   When goods or services are provided in very low volume or **small batches,** a company that does such work is called a *job shop*. A fairly typical example of a job shop is PMF Industries, a small custom metalworking company in Williamsport, Pennsylvania, that produces stainless steel assemblies for medical and other uses. Less formally, in the service industry, restaurants or doctors' offices are examples of job shops because they provide a high variety of low-volume, customized services.

In a small batch organization, structure tends to be very organic. There tend not to be a lot of rules and formal procedures, and decision making tends to be decentralized. The emphasis is on mutual adjustment among people.

While only a fantasy a few years ago, mass customization is quickly becoming more prevalent.

Large Batch Technologies   As volume increases, product variety usually decreases. Companies with higher volumes and lower varieties than a job shop tend to be characterized as **large batch,** or mass production technologies. Examples of large batch technologies include the auto assembly operations of General Motors, Ford, and Chrysler. In the service sector, McDonald's and Burger King are good examples. Their production runs tend to be more standardized, and all customers receive similar (if not identical) products. Machines tend to replace people in the physical execution of work. People run the machines.

With a large batch technology, structure tends to be more mechanistic. There tend to be more rules and formal procedures, and decision making tends to be centralized with higher spans of control. Communication tends to be more formal in companies where hierarchical authority is more prominent.

Continuous Process Technologies At the very-high-volume end of the scale are companies that use **continuous process** technologies—technologies that do not stop and start. Domino Sugar and Shell Chemical, for example, use continuous process technologies where a very limited number of products are produced. People are completely removed from the work itself. It is done entirely by machines and/or computers. In some cases, people run the computers that run the machines.

Ironically, with continuous process technology, structure can return to a more organic form because less monitoring and supervision are needed. Communication tends to be more informal in companies where fewer rules and regulations are established.

Organizing for Flexible Manufacturing

Although issues of volume and variety often have been seen as trade-offs in a technological sense, today organizations are trying to produce both high-volume and high-variety products at the same time. This is referred to as **mass customization.**[47] Automobiles, clothes, computers, and other products are increasingly being manufactured to match each customer's taste, specifications, and budget. While this seemed only a fantasy a few years ago, mass customization is quickly becoming more prevalent among leading firms. You can now buy clothes cut to your proportions, supplements with the exact blend of the vitamins and minerals you like, CDs with the music tracks you choose, and textbooks whose chapters are picked out by your professor.

How do companies organize to pull off this type of customization at such low cost? As shown in Table 9.2, they organize around a dynamic network of relatively independent operating units.[48] Each unit performs a specific process or task—called a *module*—such as making a component, performing a credit check, or performing a particular welding method. Some modules may be performed by outside suppliers or vendors.

Different modules join forces to make the good or provide a service. How and when the various modules interact with one another are dictated by the unique requests of each customer. The manager's responsibility is to make it easier and less costly for modules to come together, complete their tasks, and then recombine to meet the next customer demand. The ultimate goal of mass customization is a never-ending campaign to expand the number of ways a company can satisfy customers. The Internet has also made it easy for customers to choose their product preferences online and for companies to take an order straight to the manufacturing floor.

Computer-Integrated Manufacturing One technological advance that has helped make mass customization possible is **computer-integrated manufacturing (CIM),** which encompasses a host of computerized production efforts linked together. Two examples are computer-aided design and computer-aided manufacturing, which offer the ultimate in computerized process technologies. The magazine-printing industry has adopted CIM, with editorial and advertising content on publishers' computers linked directly with printing and binding networks at printing plants, producing customized versions of the same magazine for different subscribers.

These systems can produce high-variety and high-volume products at the same time.[49] They may also offer greater control and predictability of production processes,

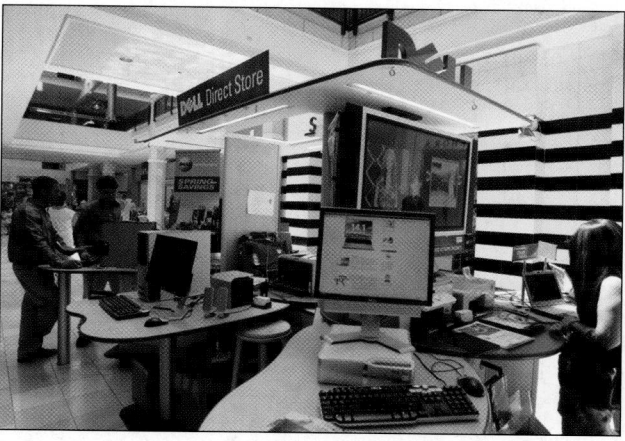

Dell has revolutionized the concept of mass customization. The production process from order to delivery is managed electronically, which allows Dell to build servers very efficiently and their customers to know where their server is during each step of the process.

continuous process

A process that is highly automated and has a continuous production flow.

mass customization

The production of varied, individually customized products at the low cost of standardized, mass-produced products.

Bottom Line

Today's technologies offer customization at low cost.
Give an example of a product you'd like to have customized for your personal preferences. Have you found a customized version yet? If not, you may someday.

computer-integrated manufacturing (CIM)

The use of computer-aided design and computer-aided manufacturing to sequence and optimize a number of production processes.

TABLE 9.2
Key Features in Mass
Customization

Products	High variety and customization
Product design	Collaborative design; significant input from customers Short product development cycles Constant innovation
Operations and processes	Flexible processes Business process reengineering (BPR) Use of modules Continuous improvement (CI) Reduced setup and changeover times Reduced lead times JIT delivery and processing of materials and components Production to order Shorter cycle times Use of information technology (IT)
Quality management	Quality measured in customer delight Defects treated as capability failures
Organizational structure	Dynamic network of relatively autonomous operating units Learning relationships Integration of the value chain Team-based structure
Workforce management	Empowerment of employees High value on knowledge, information, and diversity of employee capabilities New product teams Broad job descriptions
Emphasis	Low-cost production of high-quality, customized products

SOURCE: Reprinted with permission of APICS—The Educational Society for Resource Management, *Production and Inventory Management* 41, no. 1, 2000, pp. 56–65.

reduced waste, faster throughput times, and higher quality. But managers cannot "buy" their way out of competitive trouble simply by investing in superior technology alone. They must also ensure that their organization has the necessary strategic and people strengths and a well-designed plan for integrating the new technology within the organization.

flexible factories

Manufacturing plants that have short production runs, are organized around products, and use decentralized scheduling.

Flexible Factories   As the name implies, **flexible factories** provide more production options and a greater variety of products. They differ from traditional factories in three primary ways: lot size, flow patterns, and scheduling.[50]

First, the traditional factory has long production runs, generating high volumes of a standardized product. Flexible factories have much shorter production runs, with many different products. Second, traditional factories move parts down the line from one location in the production sequence to the next. Flexible factories are organized around products, in work cells or teams, so that people work closely together and parts move shorter distances with shorter or no delays. Third, traditional factories use centralized scheduling, which is time-consuming, inaccurate, and slow to adapt to changes. Flexible factories use local or decentralized scheduling, in which decisions are made on the shop floor by the people doing the work.

Lean Manufacturing   Another organizing approach is **lean manufacturing,** based on a commitment to making an operation both efficient and effective; it strives to achieve the highest possible productivity and total quality, cost-effectively, by eliminating unnecessary steps in the production process and continually striving for improvement. Rejects are unacceptable, and staff, overhead, and inventory are considered wasteful. In a lean operation, the emphasis is on quality, speed, and flexibility more than on cost, efficiency, and hierarchy. If an employee spots a problem, the employee is authorized to halt the operation and signal for help to correct the problem at its source so that processes can be improved and future problems avoided. With a well-managed lean production process, a company can develop, produce, and distribute products with half or less of the human effort, space, tools, time, and overall cost.[51]

Toyota receives much of the credit for modeling and teaching a commitment to "think lean." Many manufacturing companies have tried to adopt a similar lean approach, but Toyota and others have also applied lean methods to nonmanufacturing processes. Toyota's product development, for example, also uses lean principles. The process begins with identifying what customers define as valuable so that employees don't waste time and money on things that customers don't care about. Early in the design process, teams bring together experts from various functions to identify potential problems and identify as many solutions as they can to avoid the need to make design changes later in the process. Managers use their experience with past product development efforts to predict staffing requirements, and employees and technicians working for suppliers are assigned to projects only as they are needed. Further adding to efficiency and quality, the company uses standard parts, procedures, and skill sets wherever possible; detailed checklists help engineers ensure they are using best practices. With methods such as these, Toyota has been able to develop top-quality products faster and more consistently than its competitors. Similar approaches have also been used to improve services, such as operations at hospitals. For instance, St. Agnes Hospital in Baltimore has used lean principles to reduce costs and patient waiting times while improving safety, and the ThedaCare health system in Wisconsin saved more than $3 million in one year of using lean methods.[52]

For the lean approach to result in more effective operations, the following conditions must be met:[53]

People are broadly trained rather than specialized.

Communication is informal and horizontal among line workers.

Equipment is general-purpose.

Work is organized in teams, or cells, that produce a group of similar products.

Supplier relationships are long-term and cooperative.

Product development is concurrent, not sequential, and is done by cross-functional teams.

In recent years, many companies have tried to become leaner by cutting overhead costs, laying off operative-level workers, eliminating layers of management, and utilizing capital equipment more efficiently. But if the move to lean manufacturing is simply a harsh, haphazard cost-cutting approach, the result will be chaos, overworked people, and low morale.

lean manufacturing

An operation that strives to achieve the highest possible productivity and total quality, cost-effectively, by eliminating unnecessary steps in the production process and continually striving for improvement.

Bottom Line

Lean manufacturing strives for high quality, speed, sustainability, and low cost.
Which of the quality improvement approaches is often combined with lean manufacturing?

In a lean operation, emphasis is on quality, speed, and flexibility more than on cost, efficiency, and hierarchy.

Some hospitals have been using lean principles to reduce costs and patient waiting times while improving safety.

IN PRACTICE

Getting lean makes each employee more valuable to the organization because in lean processes, each employee's activities are essential. With waste already eliminated, companies have little to cut if demand falls. In the first recession following widespread use of lean manufacturing, manufacturers did lay off workers, but not as many as an equally severe downturn would have caused in the past, when companies weren't so streamlined.

An example is Parker Hannifin Corporation's factory in Spartanburg, South Carolina, where workers produce a variety of plastic parts. Lean operations and high-tech manufacturing systems enable the company to operate with a few skilled workers. For example, to make seals for aerosol cans, just five workers operate high-speed machinery, each handling a different step of the process. If demand slows, work can be divided so that two workers start the production on one day and the other three finish on a second day, or everyone can work only part of the week. Laying off any of the five workers would be difficult because someone would have to be trained to run that person's machine. Similarly, only two workers are needed to run each shift that produces plastic tubes for blasting caps, down from eight a decade ago. If the company doesn't have enough demand to run two shifts, fewer jobs are at risk.

Parker Hannifin's production levels also are more closely tied to order volume, so fewer goods sit around in inventory. That means staffing is more closely matched to demand as well.[54]

- What would be the consequences of layoffs in a lean organization?

Organizing for Speed: Time-Based Competition

Companies worldwide have devoted so much energy to improving product quality that high quality is now the standard attained by all top competitors. Competition has driven quality to such heights that quality products no longer are enough to distinguish one company from another. *Time* has emerged as the key competitive advantage that can separate market leaders from also-rans.[55]

Time has emerged as the key competitive advantage that can separate market leaders from also-rans.

Companies today must learn what the customer needs and meet those needs as quickly as possible. **Time-based competition (TBC)** refers to strategies aimed at reducing the total time needed to deliver the good or service. TBC has several key organizational elements: logistics, just-in-time (JIT), and concurrent engineering. JIT production systems reduce the time to manufacture products. Logistics speed the delivery of products to customers. Both are essential steps toward bringing products to customers in the shortest time possible. In today's world, speed is essential.

time-based competition (TBC)

Strategies aimed at reducing the total time needed to deliver a good or service.

logistics

The movement of the right goods in the right amount to the right place at the right time.

Logistics The movement of resources into the organization (inbound) and products from the organization to its customers (outbound) is called **logistics.** Like the supply chain, which we discussed in Chapter 2, an organization's logistics are often a critical element in its responsiveness and competitive advantage.

The world of logistics includes the great mass of parts, materials, and products moving via trucks, trains, planes, and ships from and to every region of the globe. Depending on the product, duplication and inefficiency in distribution can cost far more than making the product itself, and slowdowns can cause products to go out of stock so that consumers choose alternatives. One technological advance that is helping some companies improve logistics efficiency and speed is the use of radio frequency identification (RFID) tags. When manufacturers label their products with RFID tags, automated readers can easily track where each product is in the distribution system, including which particular items are selling in each store. Best Buy has had great success with RFID tagging; stores using the system are seeing sales increases as employees more efficiently keep track of which products need to be restocked and where they are located. Walmart, in contrast, is trying to keep its well-known leadership role in distribution by asking suppliers to use RFID, but many of them are finding they cannot afford to institute the new system at this stage of its development while also meeting Walmart's demands to keep prices at a minimum.[56]

In some industries, speedy logistics are essential because products are perishable. For example, Flora-Holland, a flower auctioneer based in the Netherlands, acquires flowers from 8,000 suppliers and stores them in a massive warehouse for auction and distribution to buyers. Using RFID tagging on each cart of flowers, the company can process more than 60,000 transactions within hours. Whenever a pallet of flowers is sorted or moved, the RFID chip transmits the information about its place in the distribution system, along with data about its freshness.[57]

Just-in-Time Operations   An additional element of TBC involves **just-in-time (JIT)** operations. JIT calls for subassemblies and components to be manufactured in very small lots and delivered to the next stage in the process precisely at the time needed, or "just in time." A customer order triggers a factory order and the production process. The supplying work centers do not produce the next lot of product until the consuming work center requires it. Even external suppliers deliver to the company just in time.

Just-in-time is a companywide philosophy oriented toward eliminating waste throughout all operations and improving materials throughout. In this way, excess inventory is eliminated and costs are reduced. The ultimate goal of JIT is to serve the customer better by providing higher levels of quality and service. An example of an effective just-in-time operation is provided by Dell, which does not begin production of a computer customized to a consumer's specifications until after the customer's order has been received. Contrast this approach with traditional production methods, which require extremely costly warehousing of inventory and parts, uncertain production runs, considerable waste, no customizing capability, and lengthy delivery times.

> **just-in-time (JIT)**
> A system that calls for subassemblies and components to be manufactured in very small lots and delivered to the next stage of the production process just as they are needed.

> "Big will not beat small any more. It will be the fast beating the slow."
> —Rupert Murdoch

JIT represents a number of key production and organizational concepts, including the following:

Elimination of waste. Eliminate all waste from the production process, including waste of time, people, machinery, space, and materials.

Perfect quality. Produce perfect parts even when lot sizes are reduced, and produce the product exactly when it is needed in the exact quantities that are needed.

Reduced cycle times. Accomplish the entire manufacturing process more rapidly. Reduce setup times for equipment, move parts only short distances (machinery is placed in closer proximity), and eliminate all delays. The goal is to reduce action to the time spent working on the parts. For most manufacturers today, the percentage of time parts are worked on is about 5 percent of the total production time. JIT seeks to eliminate the other 95 percent—that is, to reduce to zero the time spent not working on the parts.

Employee involvement. In JIT, employee involvement is central to success. The workers are responsible for production decisions. Managers and supervisors are coaches. Top management pledges that there will never be layoffs due to improved productivity.

Value-added manufacturing. Do only those things (actions, work, etc.) that add value to the finished product. If it doesn't add value, don't do it. For example, inspection does not add value to the finished product, so make the product correctly the first time and inspection will not be necessary.

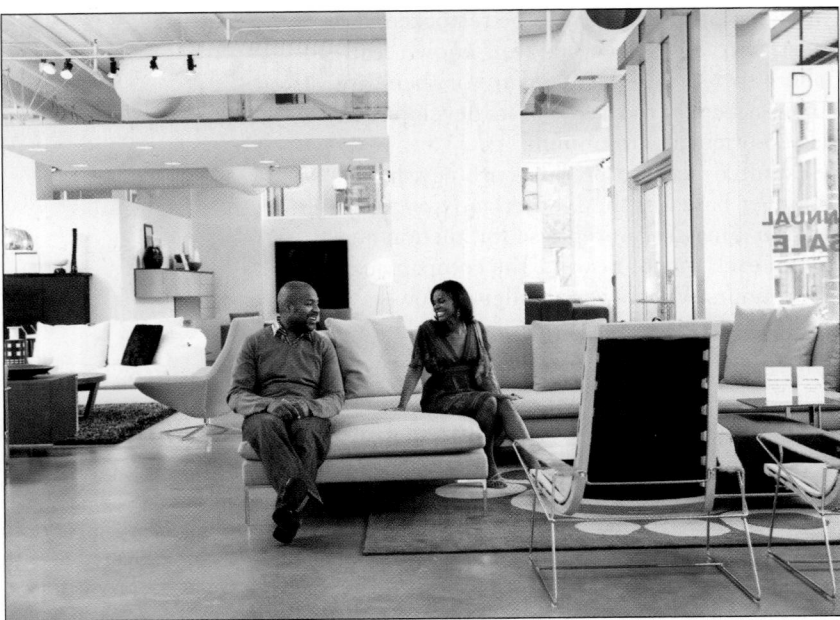

Furniture stores use their showrooms as additional storage space. When something sells, they can easily replace it that same day.

Discovery of problems and prevention of recurrence. Foolproofing, or fail-safing, is a key component of JIT. To prevent problems from arising, their cause(s) must be known and acted on. Thus, in JIT operations, people try to find the "weak link in the chain" by forcing problem areas to the surface so that preventive measures may be determined and implemented.

As organizations have seen the advantages of JIT, they have found applications beyond the factory floor. For example, in the area of information technology, BMC Software used JIT principles to reduce lead times to fulfill orders.[58] And stores are using variations of JIT to minimize the expense of storing products in back rooms. A specialty clothing retailer aims to have shipments move from receiving to the selling floor on the same day. A chain of 30 stores selling furniture and home accessories arranged to have daily deliveries of furniture, so that it could convert storage space to selling space; when a furniture item sells, the store arranges to have the piece replaced the same day.[59]

However, JIT has limits. It's not the most efficient choice when the costs of delivery exceed the costs of storage. And if suppliers have any problems fulfilling orders, the whole system breaks down. JIT requires close ties with suppliers, so finding replacements can be difficult, as the U.S. dealers and manufacturers for Japanese automakers discovered when a massive earthquake and tsunami disrupted production of parts in Japan. Consequently, suppliers in the automotive industry are beginning to see less reliance on the close buyer–seller relationships of JIT. The Automotive Experience group at Johnson Controls used to have arrangements in which one plant served one customer in order to deliver products just in time to the customer's assembly plant. But now the company's Lerma, Mexico, facility designs standard seats that a variety of customers can use; robots switch between the assembly of seats for the Dodge Journey, Ford Fiesta, and Chrysler PT Cruiser.[60]

Concurrent Engineering   JIT is a vital component of TBC, but JIT traditionally concentrates on reducing time in only one function: manufacturing. TBC attempts to deliver speed in *all* functions—product development, manufacturing, logistics, and customer service. Customers will not be impressed if you manufacture quickly but it takes weeks for them to receive their products or get a problem solved.

Many companies are turning to concurrent (sometimes called simultaneous) engineering as the cornerstone of their TBC strategy. **Concurrent engineering**—also an important component of total quality management—is a major departure from the old development process in which tasks were assigned to various functions in sequence. When R&D completed its part of the project, the work was "passed over the wall" to engineering, which completed its task and passed it over the wall to manufacturing, and so on. This process was highly inefficient, and errors took a long time to correct.

In contrast, concurrent engineering incorporates the issues and perspectives of all the functions—and customers and suppliers—from the beginning of the process.

Bottom Line

Time-based competition brings speed to all organization processes.

Give an example of a situation in which speed would be important for a book publisher.

concurrent engineering

A design approach in which all relevant functions cooperate jointly and continually in a maximum effort aimed at producing high-quality products that meet customers' needs.

This team-based approach results in a higher-quality product that is designed for efficient manufacturing *and* customer needs.[61] In the automobile industry, tools such as computer-aided design and computer-aided manufacturing support concurrent engineering by letting various engineers submit elements and showing how these submissions affect the overall design and the manufacturing process. With a modern CAD system, automobile engineers can enter performance requirements into a spreadsheet, and the system will identify a design that meets cost and manufacturing requirements. This technology has helped automakers reduce product development time dramatically.[62] In the realm of computing, some organizations have taken this idea much further, making the programming code for their products available to the public so that anyone at any time can develop new ideas to use with their product, and the organization can decide to license any ideas that seem to have market potential.

Some managers resist the idea of concurrent engineering. Why should marketing, product planning and design, and R&D "allow" manufacturing to get involved in "their" work? The answer is because the decisions made during the early, product concept stage determine most of the manufacturing cost and quality. Furthermore, manufacturing can offer ideas about the product because of its experience with the prior generation of the product and with direct customer feedback. Also, the other functions must know early on what manufacturing can and cannot do. Finally, when manufacturing is in from the start, it is a full and true partner and will be more committed to decisions it helped make.

Final Thoughts on Organizational Agility

As we pointed out in the previous chapter, *any* approach to organizing has its strengths and limitations. The advantages of even the innovative, leading-edge structures and systems we have discussed in this chapter are likely to be short-lived if they become fixed rather than remain flexible. Smart managers and smart competitors soon catch up. Today's advantages are tomorrow's "table stakes"—the minimum requirements that need to be met if an organization expects to be a major player.

To retain, or gain, a competitive edge, managers may want to keep in mind the principle with which we opened this chapter: successful organizations—and that includes the successful managers within them—do not sit still. They do not follow rigid models but maintain structures, systems, organizational designs, and relationships that are adaptive—always sensitive to changes in their environment and able to respond quickly, efficiently, and effectively to them. Their managers focus constantly on exceeding customer expectations and on continuous quality improvement, designing their systems and structures to help them do just that.

The emphasis on agility, quality, flexibility, learning, and leanness to which you have been exposed in this chapter is likely to be a constant in your managerial career—ideally in your own organization, but perhaps as well in the competition you confront. When Jack Welch was chairman of GE, he saw his goal as the creation of the *boundaryless organization*, one in which there were no meaningful barriers between the organization and its environment. In such an organization, structures, technologies, and systems are perfectly aligned with the external challenges and opportunities it confronts. Many forward-thinking managers have embraced this goal.[63]

Management Connection

HOW PIXAR CREATES QUALITY AGAIN AND AGAIN

Pixar is, of course, known for creating animated features that are beloved by viewers across generations. Every Pixar movie made since the 2001 introduction of the Academy Award for Best Animated Feature has been nominated for that award. Whether quality is measured in terms of critical claim, popularity, earnings, or technological leadership in computer animation, the company routinely excels.

Part of the credit for Pixar's repeated success in delivering award-winning, popular movies goes to a production process that drives for excellence. Story ideas come from Pixar's own creative people, who sometimes leave for a company-owned cabin north of headquarters to hold retreats devoted to polishing those ideas. The director and story artists draw these ideas on tens of thousands of digital storyboards, which are converted into story reels, sets of images that can be projected for viewing, with dialogue provided by employees. (The traditional approach would be to go from an idea to a script, but the use of storyboards and story reels enables teams to begin working on a variety of issues immediately to get all the elements of a film just right.) Employees in the art department research details to fill out each scene, set dressers prepare the backgrounds, modelers build the images of each character, and layout draws the overall form and motion. Actors visit the studio to record their lines. Then animators go to work, using complex computer programs to bring the story to life, and the lighting department adds the effects to show how each scene is lit. The visual information is rendered into frames (24 frames per second of the movie). Then the mixers add the music, voices, and sound effects.

The whole process takes about four years and is incredibly painstaking. Problems are sought, identified, and corrected right up until the release of a film, and they may involve matters that seem trivial. In a rainstorm, every rain drop has to be accounted for with a computer program; on an animal, code must be written to draw every strand of fur. Ocean scenes require knowledge of the physics of waves, and lighting design must consider the different ways that light reflects off of skin and plastic. Why bother? Because the attention to detail may not be noticed but is one reason that viewing a Pixar film is such a pleasure. For example, in *Cars 2*, a scene shows two ships being dropped into the sea; one Pixar employee spent three months getting the foam from the spray to look just right. Chief creative officer John Lasseter explains that the splash is crucial because the ships have to feel big—their size relative to the hero of the film is important to the story.

Even as Pixar's teams go from one film to the next, as we saw in the previous part of the case, they are continually looking for where they can improve. In the words of Pixar's president, Ed Catmull, "Success hides problems." He doesn't want to coast on the knowledge that reviewers and families loved the last film; he wants Pixar to figure out how it can make the next film even better. One consequence is that after each movie, Pixar upgrades its software to work more powerfully and effectively for the next project. Another is that the company will take a chance on fresh talent with new ideas. A case in point is Pixar's decision to hire director Brad Bird in 2000 after he produced a film called *The Iron Giant*, which won critical acclaim but lost money. Bird expected tight controls from managers nervous about his previous track record, but instead they gave him wide latitude, and he used his freedom to direct two big winners, *The Incredibles* and *Ratatouille*.

This unrelenting focus on quality has made Pixar a valuable and beloved studio, but it brings its own challenges. Along with Pixar's success have come growth and demand for more and more movies. Early on, Pixar had produced about one movie every two years. That gave employees time to work and learn as a team. Now, as pixar moves toward producing two or three movies a year, that is becoming impossible. On any given day, four or more movies are at some stage of production. As employees involved in the early stages complete their work, they must move to the next project while others are going full steam ahead on the earlier projects. That means only a portion of each team has time to learn the lessons that are occurring on any project at any time. In addition, different teams are using different software, and sometimes the software upgrades require new hardware as well. The pressure to move fast is beginning to divide the company into separate groups with separate production processes.

Being responsive and agile was natural for Pixar in its early years. The challenge facing the company for the future is how to keep its magic alive as success makes it a big enterprise.[64]

- Based on this description of Pixar, do you think it could benefit from a quality process such as adoption of six sigma or ISO 9001? Why or why not?
- Pixar is known more for quality than for speed and efficiency. Which principles of technology and organizational agility could help the company stay agile without sacrificing quality as it grows?

KEY TERMS

computer-integrated manufacturing (CIM), p. 337

concurrent engineering, p. 342

continuous process, p. 337

customer relationship management, (CRM), p. 330

downsizing, p. 327

economies of scope, p. 325

flexible factories, p. 338

high-involvement organization, p. 324

ISO 9001, p. 334

just-in-time (JIT), p. 341

large batch, p. 336

lean manufacturing, p. 339

learning organization, p. 323

logistics, p. 340

mass customization, p. 337

mechanistic organization, p. 318

organic structure, p. 318

rightsizing, p. 328

six sigma quality, p. 333

small batch, p. 336

strategic alliance, p. 321

survivor's syndrome, p. 328

technology, p. 336

time-based competition (TBC), p. 340

total quality management, (TQM), p. 332

value chain, p. 331

SUMMARY OF LEARNING OBJECTIVES

Now that you have studied Chapter 9, you should be able to:

LO 1   Discuss why it is critical for organizations to be responsive.

Organizations have a formal structure to help control what goes on within them. But to survive today, firms need more than control—they need responsiveness. They must act quickly and adapt to fast-changing demands.

LO 2   Describe the qualities of an organic organization structure.

The organic form emphasizes flexibility. Organic organizations are decentralized, informal, and dependent on the judgment and expertise of people with broad responsibilities. The organic form is not a single formal structure but a concept that underlies all the new forms discussed in this chapter.

LO 3   Identify strategies and dynamic organizational concepts that can improve an organization's responsiveness.

New and emerging organizational concepts and forms include core capabilities, strategic alliances, learning organizations, and high-involvement organizations.

LO 4   Explain how a firm can be both big and small.

Historically, large organizations have had important advantages over small organizations. Today small size has advantages, including the ability to act quickly, respond to customer demands, and serve small niches. The ideal firm today combines the advantages of both. It creates many small, flexible units, while the corporate levels add value by taking advantage of its size and power.

LO 5   Summarize how firms organize to meet customer requirements.

Firms have embraced principles of continuous improvement, total quality management, and six sigma quality (often combined with lean manufacturing) to respond to customer needs. Baldrige criteria and ISO 9001 standards help firms organize to meet better quality specifications. Extending these, reengineering efforts are directed at completely overhauling processes to provide world-class customer service.

LO 6   Identify ways that firms organize around different types of technology.

Organizations tend to move from organic structures to mechanistic structures and back to organic structures as they transition from small batch to large batch and continuous process technologies. To organize for flexible manufacturing, organizations pursue mass customization via computer-integrated manufacturing and lean manufacturing. To organize for time-based competition, firms emphasize their logistics operations, just-in-time operations, and concurrent engineering.

DISCUSSION QUESTIONS

1. Discuss evidence you have seen of the imperatives for change, flexibility, and responsiveness faced by today's firms.

2. Describe large, bureaucratic organizations with which you have had contact that have not responded flexibly to customer demands. Also describe examples of satisfactory responsiveness. What do you think accounts for the differences between the responsive and nonresponsive organizations?

3. Considering the potential advantages of large and small size, would you describe the "feel" of your college or university as big, small, or small within big? Why? What might make it feel different?

4. What is a core competence? What would you say are the core capabilities of Toyota, Walmart, and Apple? Brainstorm some creative new products and markets to which these capabilities could be applied.

5. If you were going into business for yourself, what would be your core capabilities? What capabilities do you have now, and what capabilities are you going to develop? Describe what your role would be in a network organization, and the capabilities and roles of other firms you would want in your network.

6. Using an Internet search engine, search for "strategic alliance," and identify three recently formed alliances. For each alliance, identify whether the companies' other products are generally competitors or complementary products. What are the goals of each alliance? What brought them together? Discuss whether you think a strategic alliance is an effective way for these organizations to meet their goals.

7. What skills will you need to work effectively in (a) a learning organization and (b) a high-involvement organization? Be specific, generating long lists. Would you enjoy working in these environments? Why or why not? What can you do to prepare yourself for these eventualities?

EXPERIENTIAL EXERCISES

9.1   MECHANISTIC AND ORGANIC STRUCTURES

OBJECTIVES

1. To think about your own preferences when it comes to working in a particular organizational structure.

2. To examine aspects of organizations by using as an example this class you are a member of.

INSTRUCTIONS

1. Complete the Mechanistic and Organic Worksheet here.

2. Meet in groups of four to six persons. Share your data from the worksheet. Discuss the reasons for your responses, and analyze the factors that probably encouraged your instructor to choose the type of structure that now exists.

Mechanistic and Organic Worksheet

1. Indicate your general preference for working in one of these two organizational structures by circling the appropriate response:

| **Mechanistic** | 1 | 2 | 3 | 4 | 5 | 6 | 7 | 8 | 9 | 10 | **Organic** |

2. Indicate your perception of the form of organization that is used in this class by circling the appropriate response for each item:

A. **Task role definition**

| **Rigid** | 1 | 2 | 3 | 4 | 5 | 6 | 7 | 8 | 9 | 10 | **Flexible** |

B. **Communication**

| **Vertical** | 1 | 2 | 3 | 4 | 5 | 6 | 7 | 8 | 9 | 10 | **Multidirectional** |

C. **Decision making**

| **Centralized** | 1 | 2 | 3 | 4 | 5 | 6 | 7 | 8 | 9 | 10 | **Decentralized** |

D. **Sensitivity to the environment**

| **Closed** | 1 | 2 | 3 | 4 | 5 | 6 | 7 | 8 | 9 | 10 | **Open** |

SOURCE: From John Newstrom and Keith Davis, *Organizational Behavior: Human Behavior at Work*, 1993, p. 358. Copyright 1993 The McGraw-Hill Companies, Inc. Reprinted with permission.

9.2   THE WOODY MANUFACTURING COMPANY

OBJECTIVE

To apply the concepts learned about structure and agility at the individual, group, and organizational levels in designing the Woody Manufacturing Company.

TASK 1 (INDIVIDUAL ASSIGNMENT)

a. Read the following case study of the Woody Manufacturing Company.

b. Review the chapter carefully, and choose the organizational design orientation that you feel can best guide you in developing the design for Mr. Woody.

c. Write down your thoughts on alternative management structures, pay systems, and allocation of work to individuals and groups.

TASK 2 (TEAM ASSIGNMENT)

a. Get together with your team and develop a proposal for Mr. Woody that, if followed, would help him fulfill his vision.

b. Prepare a five-minute presentation. Your typewritten team proposal is due prior to your team presentation in Mr. Woody's conference room.

Designing a New Furniture Company

Mr. Woody, the owner/operator of a small furniture company specializing in the manufacture of high-quality bar stools, has experienced a tremendous growth in demand for his products. He has standing orders for $750,000. Consequently, Mr. Woody has decided to expand his organization and attack the market aggressively. His stated mission is "to manufacture world-class products that are competitive in the world market in quality, reliability, performance, and profitability." He would like to create a culture where "pride, ownership, employment security, and trust" are a way of life. He just finished a set of interviews, and he has hired 32 new workers with the following skills:

Four skilled craftspeople.

Ten people with some woodworking experience.

Twelve people with no previous woodworking experience or other skills.

One nurse.

One schoolteacher.

One bookkeeper.

Three people with some managerial experience in nonmanufacturing settings.

Mr. Woody (with your help) must now decide how to design his new organization. This design will include the management structure, pay system, and the allocation of work to individuals and groups. The bar stool–making process has 15 steps:

1. Wood is selected.
2. Wood is cut to size.
3. Defects are removed.
4. Wood is planed to exact specifications.
5. Joints are cut.
6. Tops are glued and assembled.
7. Legs/bases are prepared.
8. Legs/bases are attached to tops.
9. Bar stools are sanded.
10. Stain is applied.
11. Varnish is applied.
12. Bar stools are sanded.
13. Varnish is reapplied.
14. Bar stools are packaged.
15. Bar stools are delivered to the customer.

Mr. Woody currently manufactures three kinds of bar stools (pedestal, four-legged corner, and four-legged recessed). There is no difference in the difficulty of making the three types of bar stools. Major cost variations have been associated with defective wood, imprecise cuts, and late deliveries to customers. Mr. Woody must decide how to organize his company to maintain high quality and profits.

He has thought about several options. He could have some individuals perform the first step for all types of bar stools; he could have an individual perform several steps for one type of bar stool; or he could have a team perform some combination of steps for one or more bar stools. He wonders whether how he organized would affect quality or costs. He's also aware that while the demand for all types of bar stools has been roughly equal over the long run, there were short periods where one type of bar stool was in greater demand than the others. Because Mr. Woody wants to use his people effectively, he has committed an expert in work design to help him set up an optimal organization.

SOURCE: A. B. (Rami) Shani and James B. Lau, *Behavior in Organizations: An Experimental Approach* 1E, 2005, p. 370. Copyright 2005 The McGraw-Hill Companies, Inc. Reprinted with permission.

CONCLUDING CASE
DIY STORES

DIY Stores is a nationwide chain that offers every tool and supply for repairing and maintaining a home. Shoppers at DIY can find paints and paintbrushes, screwdrivers and lumber, pliers and electrical conduit, spades and shrubs, and much more. Besides the wide variety under one roof, what sets DIY apart is its sales associates. The company hires avid do-it-yourselfers and retired trade workers, assigns them to work in departments where their know-how is relevant, provides training in new products and creative methods, and pays them a little more than they could earn by working for another retailer. The company also makes available fact sheets and lists of tips and building ideas. Together these efforts make DIY Stores a place where shoppers can go to get ideas and advice, so they get more than supplies for a project—they get all the ingredients they need for their project to succeed.

Over the past couple of decades, however, consumers have found an alternative to getting advice in a store: many prefer to do their research online, comfortably seated at a computer. If consumers can use a search engine or chat in an online community to figure out the best way to fix a leaky toilet or make a small bedroom look airy and bright, why would they trek into a store to ask? The answer, DIY's management feared, was that they wouldn't bother. If true, that trend placed DIY's competitive advantage at risk. The retailer needed to change with the times.

DIY's solution was to go where the consumers were: online. Management decided the company needed to supplement its in-store experts with online experts, employees who shared the same kinds of information on the Internet as they did in the stores. The company's corporate communications department was charged with developing a plan for this effort.

The department's people were used to thinking of corporate communications as something that originates at headquarters, so they initially thought the most efficient approach would be to hire a team of writers to work in offices at headquarters, blogging about new products and maintenance tips. But when they presented this plan to top management, one of the vice presidents raised a question: The company's salespeople were its base of knowledge. Why bring in new people? Why not figure out a way to use the human assets the company already had?

The corporate communications people went back to work on the plan. Probably some of the sales associates already were using the Internet themselves and knew how to write a blog and participate in social networking. Probably some of them had the necessary combination of helpfulness and writing skills. So they considered identifying those employees and inviting them to take jobs at headquarters. But as the group discussed this idea, they realized it had a flaw. If employees left the stores, they would no longer be seeing, selling, and watching customers' reactions to products. They would lose the hands-on and face-to-face experiences that kept them up-to-date and in touch with consumers. Also, consumers would quickly figure out that the online exchanges were not with a real DIY sales associate, but with someone who had become a call center employee or professional communicator.

So the team arrived at an unusual plan. The company would identify Internet-savvy sales associates, but it wouldn't remove them from the stores. Rather, the associates who accepted the new position would work three days a week in a store and two days a week in an office, with their schedules staggered so that the online community would be active seven days a week. The company's executives were enthusiastic about this plan.

DIY contacted store managers in cities where it has regional offices. The store managers recommended employees they thought would deliver effective help online, and a team of recruiters interviewed these candidates and selected two dozen to provide an online presence. The typical employee selected had eight years of experience with DIY and submitted an excellent writing sample. Meanwhile, the company built an online "Do It with Us" web page, where customers can submit questions, read tips, share ideas, and find links to information about new products available at DIY's stores.

After a three-day training program, the sales associates started the online conversation with DIY. Within months, they and the site's visitors had started thousands of conversation threads. And in an unexpected development, the sales associates have also become a valued source of knowledge for DIY's other employees. In stores, at headquarters, and in the regional offices, if someone wants product or project information, they often start their search at the "Do It with Us" web page.

QUESTIONS

1. As DIY Stores built its online presence, how well did it organize around its core capabilities?

2. DIY Stores is a large national chain. What impact did its size have on its agility?

3. How could DIY increase its agility in responding to the importance of the Internet?

10 Human Resources Management

LEARNING OBJECTIVES

After studying Chapter 10, you should be able to:

LO 1 Discuss how companies use human resources management to gain competitive advantage. p. 352

LO 2 Give reasons why companies recruit both internally and externally for new hires. p. 358

LO 3 Identify various methods for selecting new employees. p. 359

LO 4 Evaluate the importance of spending on training and development. p. 369

LO 5 Explain alternatives for who appraises an employee's performance. p. 372

LO 6 Describe the fundamental aspects of a reward system. p. 376

LO 7 Summarize how unions and labor laws influence human resources management. p. 382

Management Connection

HOW GOOGLE LANDS THE BEST EMPLOYEES IN A TOUGH JOB MARKET

Year after year, we hear that U.S. schools are not preparing enough new engineers and software developers to meet employers' demand for skilled workers in these fields. Yet Google, the software company known for the popular search engine that bears its name, gets 75,000 job applications a week and is known for hiring the cream of the crop.

How does Google win the competition for talent? One obvious place to look for answers is in how the 24,000-employee company treats its workers. It pays them well, and recently, in a year when many companies were still cutting back, Google gave everyone a 10 percent raise. Knowing that its people hold demanding jobs, Google also tries to make the workplace comfortable with uncommon benefits such as exercise facilities, a free laundry service, and free food in all company cafeterias. It offers flexibility with onsite child care and arrangements for job sharing and telecommuting. Together, these qualities help Google to win a spot, year after year, near the top of *Fortune*'s widely read list of the 100 Best Companies to Work For.

The more important factor, however, is probably the excitement of being part of something that matters. At least since its name, Google, became synonymous with searching the web, the company has been widely seen as a cool place to work, both because the thinking behind the software was advanced and because it makes the Internet such a useful and powerful tool. Newer ventures, such as the development of Gmail and Google Docs and the acquisition of YouTube and the Android mobile operating system, have extended the job opportunities, scope, and significance of working for Google. In a recent survey of young professionals, Google was far and away the top choice as an employer they considered ideal. Universum, the company that conducted the survey, noted that young professionals tend to be attracted to working for companies they already like as consumers.

Because Google is an attractive place to work, it can be picky about whom it hires. The company selects people who are excited about what computers can do and who value intellectual excellence. It retains them by creating a work environment in which employees can contribute creatively and continue to develop. Such people appreciate the 20 hours of training the company provides its salaried employees each year (10 hours per year for hourly workers).

In 2008, when the financial crisis hit just about every business in one way or another, Google slowed its recruiting efforts. Before long, however, the company was again building up its workforce. By 2011, competition was heating up in social networking (where Google wants to catch up with a stronger presence), and the popularity of mobile computing was driving the need for workers in the Android business. Google responded by announcing that it was looking for more than 6,300 new employees— its biggest hiring surge ever. It would need to continue distinguishing itself as a great place for talented people to work.[1]

In receiving tens of thousands of job applications every week, Google has a huge challenge as well as an opportunity. It has to figure out which of these people to hire, how to bring out the best in them, and how to keep them around as long as they are needed. As you read this chapter, think about how the strategic use of people is essential to Google's success.

human resources management (HRM)

Formal systems for the management of people within an organization.

People are a source of competitive advantage when their skills, knowledge, and abilities are not equally available to all competitors.

The opening quote by Thomas Watson, founder of IBM, summarizes our view of the importance of people to any organization. Google's practice of wooing bright people with exciting challenges and generous perks has differentiated the company in important ways. **Human resources management (HRM),** historically known as personnel management, deals with formal systems for managing people at work. For that reason, it is one of the fundamental aspects of organizational and managerial life. Your first formal interaction with an organization you wish to join will likely involve some aspect of its human resources function, and throughout your career as a manager you will be a part of, as well as be affected by, your organization's human resources management.

We begin this chapter by describing HRM as it relates to strategic management. We will also discuss more of the "nuts and bolts" of HRM: staffing, training, performance appraisal, rewards, and labor relations. Throughout the chapter, we discuss legal issues that influence each aspect of HRM. In the next chapter, we expand this focus to address related issues of managing a diverse workforce.

Strategic Human Resources Management

LO 1

HRM has assumed a vital strategic role in recent years as organizations attempt to compete through people. Recall from Chapter 4 that firms can create a competitive advantage when they possess or develop resources that are valuable, rare, inimitable, and organized. We can use the same criteria to talk about the strategic impact of human resources:

1. *Creates value.* People can increase value through their efforts to decrease costs or provide something unique to customers or some combination of the two. Empowerment programs, total quality initiatives, and continuous improvement efforts at companies such as Corning and Xerox are intentionally designed to increase the value that employees bring to the bottom line.
2. *Is rare.* People are a source of competitive advantage when their skills, knowledge, and abilities are not equally available to all competitors. Top companies invest a great deal to hire and train the best and the brightest employees to gain advantage over their competitors. Dow Chemical went to court to stop General Electric from hiring away its engineers. This case shows that some companies recognize both the value and the rareness of certain employees.
3. *Is difficult to imitate.* People are a source of competitive advantage when their capabilities and contributions cannot be copied by others. Disney, Southwest

Airlines, and Whole Foods are known for creating unique cultures that get the most from employees (through teamwork) and are difficult to imitate.

4. *Is organized.* People are a source of competitive advantage when their talents can be combined and deployed rapidly to work on new assignments at a moment's notice. Teamwork and cooperation are two pervasive methods for ensuring an organized workforce. But companies such as Spyglass (a software company) and AT&T have invested in information technology to help allocate and track employee assignments to temporary projects.

Southwest Airlines is known for creating a unique culture that gets the most from employees. Southwest rewards its employees for excellent performance and maintains loyalty by offering free airfare, profit sharing, and other incentives. What benefits would you need to stay motivated?

These four criteria highlight the importance of people and show the closeness of HRM to strategic management. At a growing number of companies, HR experts are participating in strategy meetings to identify key issues where they can analyze data and propose how new methods of acquiring, training, and keeping talent will help the company meet its goals.[2] The evidence is growing that this focus brings positive business results. For example, a study by Deloitte & Touche associated the use of effective human resources practices with higher valuation of a company in the stock market.[3] Global trends make this focus even more important. Competition is intensifying. Rising educational standards and access to technology are increasingly available worldwide. *Innovation*—useful new ideas that emerge from the focused creativity of organization members—has become ever more critical to gaining and maintaining competitive advantage. Because employee skills, knowledge, and abilities are among the most distinctive and renewable resources on which a company can draw, their strategic management is more important than ever. Increasingly, organizations are recognizing that their success depends on what people know— that is, their knowledge and skills. The term **human capital** (or, more broadly, *intellectual capital*) often is used today to describe the strategic value of employee knowledge and abilities.

As more executives have come to appreciate that their employees can be their organization's most valuable resources, human resources managers have played a greater role in contributing to the organization's strategic planning. That means human resources (HR) specialists are challenged to know their organization's business, and line managers are challenged to excel at selecting and motivating the best people. As contributors to the organization's strategy, HR managers also face greater ethical challenges. When they were merely a specialized staff function, they could focus on, say, legal requirements for hiring decisions. But strategy decisions require them to be able to link decisions about staffing, training, and other HR matters to the organization's business success. For example, as members of the top management team, HR managers may be faced with the need for drastic downsizing of the workforce while still retaining top executives through generous salaries or bonuses, or they may fail to aggressively investigate and challenge corrupt practices of colleagues. Such dilemmas are complex and challenging. In the long run, however, organizations are best served when HR leaders are a strong advocate for at least four sets of values: strategic, ethical, legal, and financial.[4]

human capital

The knowledge, skills, and abilities of employees that have economic value.

IN PRACTICE

Tough economic times deliver exciting HR opportunities as well as tough HR challenges. Well-managed firms seize the opportunities and meet the challenges.

One company that prepares well for a slowdown is PriceSpective, a consulting firm. The company's four co-owners meet monthly with senior managers to determine whether their current staffing levels are appropriate for their coming needs. Whenever sales are slow, PriceSpective institutes a temporary hiring freeze. Because these actions are part of a regular planning process, employees don't worry; they know managers are simply making course adjustments to keep the company efficient. Also, even when clients are not signing up for services, PriceSpective keeps talking to prospective employees. For the firm's specialized practice serving pharmaceutical firms, it needs many employees with doctoral degrees, who would be difficult to find and hire quickly when business picks up. Of course, when interviewing during a hiring freeze, managers are careful to explain the company's situation and plans for the future.

Other firms are able to hire during a recession, gaining access to a huge pool of talented people. The recent recession drove more shoppers from higher-priced retailers to Family Dollar Stores, so the company opened more stores, receiving applications from workers with better-than-usual credentials. The company also needed specialists for its information technology department; it found experienced IT workers who left Circuit City when that chain went out of business. Companies that, like Family Dollar, build up their staff when talented people are hungry for work can boost sales, improve efficiency, and gain an advantage over competitors—if they can keep and motivate these employees.[5]

- How would you expect these companies to adjust their HR strategy when the economy is booming?

Managing human capital to sustain a competitive advantage is perhaps the most important part of an organization's HR function. But on a day-to-day basis, HR managers also have many other concerns regarding their workers and the entire personnel puzzle. These concerns include attracting talent; maintaining a well-trained, highly motivated, and loyal workforce; managing diversity; devising effective compensation systems; managing layoffs; and containing health care and pension costs. Balancing these issues is difficult, and the best approach varies depending on the circumstances of the organization. A steel producer facing a cutback in business may need human resources activities to assist with layoffs, whereas a semiconductor company may need more staff to produce enough microchips to meet the demands of the consumer electronics market. The emphasis on different HR activities depends on whether the organization is growing, declining, or standing still. This leads to the practical issues involved in HR planning.

> "Hire the best. Pay them fairly. Communicate freely. Provide challenges and rewards. Get out of their way. They'll knock your socks off."
>
> —Mary Ann Allison

The HR Planning Process

"Get me the right kind and the right number of people at the right time." It sounds simple enough, but meeting an organization's staffing needs requires strategic human resources planning: an activity with a strategic purpose derived from the organization's plans.

The HR planning process occurs in three stages: planning, programming, and evaluating. First, HR managers need to know the organization's business plans to ensure that the right number and types of people are available—where the company is headed, in what businesses it plans to be, what future growth is expected, and so forth. Few actions are more damaging to morale than having to lay off recently hired college graduates because of inadequate planning for future needs. Second, the organization conducts programming of specific human resources activities, such as recruitment, training, and layoffs. In this stage, the company's plans are implemented. Third, human resources activities are evaluated to determine whether they are producing the results needed to contribute to the organization's business plans. Figure 10.1 illustrates the components of the human resources planning process. In this chapter, we focus on human resources planning and programming. Many of the other factors listed in Figure 10.1 are discussed in later chapters.

Demand Forecasts   Perhaps the most difficult part of human resources planning is conducting *demand* forecasts—that is, determining how many and what type of people are needed. Demand forecasts for people needs are derived from organizational plans. To develop the Chevy Volt, General Motors had to determine how many engineers and designers it needed to ensure that such a complex product was ready for a December 2010 U.S. launch. In addition, production managers had to select a manufacturing facility and determine how many workers would be required to produce 10,000 cars in 2011 and ramp up to 45,000 units by the following year. The company also needed to forecast the number of employees needed to provide support services such as crafting marketing plans, administering pay and benefits, and answering questions from customers and the press. Similarly, companies selling an existing product consider current sales and projected future sales growth as they estimate the plant capacity needed to meet future demand, the sales force required, the support staff needed, and so forth. They calculate the number of labor-hours required to operate a plant, sell the product, distribute it, serve customers, and so forth. These estimates are used to determine the demand for different types of workers.

Labor Supply Forecasts   Along with forecasting demand, managers must forecast the *supply of labor*—that is, how many and what types of employees the organization actually will have. In performing a supply analysis, the organization estimates the number and quality of its current employees as well as the available external supply of workers. To estimate internal supply, the company typically relies on its experiences with turnover, terminations, retirements, promotions, and transfers. A computerized human resources information system assists greatly in supply forecasting.

FIGURE 10.1

An Overview of the HR Planning Process

Externally, organizations have to look at workforce trends to make projections. Worldwide, as we discussed in Chapter 6, the highly skilled, higher-paid jobs have been generated mostly in the cities of the industrialized world, where companies have scrambled to find enough qualified workers. At the same time, companies in industrialized nations have used offshoring to move much of their routine and less skilled work to nations with a large population willing to work for lower pay.

In the United States, demographic trends have contributed to a shortage of workers with the appropriate skills and education level. Traditional labor-intensive jobs, in agriculture, mining, and assembly-line manufacturing, are making way for jobs in technical, financial, and customized goods and service industries. These jobs often require much more training and schooling than the jobs they are replacing—or that the education system may currently be producing. Demand for highly qualified employees continues to outpace supply—one reason some jobs are being transferred overseas. Some demographic trends we discussed in Chapter 2 may worsen this situation. For example, the upcoming retirement of the baby boomer generation will remove a large number of educated and trained employees from the workforce. And in math, science, and engineering graduate schools, fewer than half of the students receiving graduate degrees are American born. (To fill U.S. jobs, companies must hire U.S. citizens or immigrants with permission to work in the United States.)

One response managers have made to deal with this skills shortage has been to increase significantly the remedial and training budgets within their own organizations.[6] For example, Caspers Company, which operates 50 McDonald's stores in Tampa, Florida, pays for its non-English-speaking employees to take an intensive English language class. Employees who choose to participate not only provide better customer service but also are able to move into positions of greater responsibility. And Bayer's Baytown, Texas, plant set up an internship program because it can't find enough employees to run its complex chemical-processing equipment and has decided to train them itself. A related approach to training current employees is to retrain and hire workers who were downsized.

Another response has been to increase the labor supply by recruiting workers from other countries. The supply of legal immigrant labor is restricted by various laws and regulations. For example, each year the U.S. government awards H-1B visas to 65,000 college-educated workers in high-skilled, highly demanded jobs such as engineers and scientists. Those people are permitted to work temporarily in the United States. Managers at high-tech companies including Microsoft, Oracle, and Intel complain that the number of H-1B visas is too small to enable companies to meet the demand for technical workers, and some companies address that challenge by aggressively hiring early each year, before the quota has been met. Immigrant workers are also attractive to companies with a low-cost strategy because strong labor demand in the United States enables U.S. workers to insist on higher pay.[7]

IN PRACTICE

Health care is an industry that is growing—in some areas, faster than organizations can hire and train staff. Manufacturing, on the other hand, is shrinking. As sales decline and companies downsize or close altogether, workers are laid off without other job prospects. Recently, some companies and not-for-profit organizations have begun collaborating to meet the needs of both industries by retraining laid-off manufacturing workers to enter the health care field.

The Manufacturers Association of Central New York teamed up with the Northern Area Health Education Center and Syracuse University to evaluate and retrain displaced workers in health care fields. Applicants take aptitude tests to determine what skills they already possess—for example, interpersonal skills, including teamwork, or the ability to interpret graphics. Those who already show a level of proficiency in certain areas can obtain a certificate of competence for those skills. A website hosted by the Northern Area Health

Education Center posts the credential information so that interested employers such as hospitals or nursing homes can find potential job candidates; the site also shows candidates what types of jobs they would qualify for. "We are focusing on jobs that do not have degrees or licenses," says Tom Hadlick, director of the assessment program, which is called WorkKeys. Nursing assistants, pharmacy technicians, and paramedics fall into this category. This collaboration is a way to benefit both the people who need work and the industry that needs them.[8]

- Why do you think an association of manufacturers would participate in a program such as this one?

On the plus side, earlier forecasts of a diverse workforce have become fact, adding greatly to the pool of available talent. The business world is no longer the exclusive domain of white males. In fact, two-career families have become the norm. Minorities, women, immigrants, older and disabled workers, and other groups have made the management of diversity a fundamental activity of the modern manager. Because of the importance of managing the "new workforce," the next chapter is devoted entirely to this topic.

> Earlier forecasts of a diverse workforce have become fact, adding greatly to the pool of available talent.

Reconciling Supply and Demand Once managers have a good idea of the supply of and the demand for various types of employees, they can start developing approaches for reconciling the two. In some cases, organizations find they need more people than they currently have (i.e., a labor deficit). In such cases, organizations can hire new employees, promote current employees to new positions, or outsource work to contractors. In other cases, organizations may find that they have more people than they need (i.e., a labor surplus). If this is detected far enough in advance, organizations can use attrition—the normal turnover of employees—to reduce the surplus. In other instances, the organization may lay off employees or transfer them to other areas.

When managers do need to hire, one tool they can use is their organization's compensation policy. Large companies in particular spend a lot of time gathering information about pay scales for the various jobs they have available and making sure their compensation system is fair and competitive. We discuss pay issues later in this chapter.

Job Analysis Although issues of supply and demand are fairly "macro" activities—conducted at an organizational level—HR planning also has a "micro" side called *job analysis*. **Job analysis** does two things.[9] First, it tells the HR manager about the job itself: the essential tasks, duties, and responsibilities involved in performing the job. This information is called a *job description*. The job description for an accounting manager might specify that the position will be responsible for monthly, quarterly, and annual financial reports, getting bills issued and paid, preparing budgets, ensuring the company's compliance with laws and regulations, working closely with line managers on financial issues, and supervising an accounting department of 12 people.

Second, job analysis describes the skills, knowledge, abilities, and other characteristics needed to perform the job. This is called the *job specification*. For our accounting manager example, the job requirements might include a degree in accounting or business, knowledge of computerized accounting systems, prior managerial experience, and excellent communication skills.

Job analysis provides the information required by virtually every human resources activity. It assists with the essential HR programs: recruitment, training, selection, appraisal, and reward systems. It may also help organizations defend themselves in lawsuits involving employment practices—for example, by clearly specifying what a job requires if someone claims unfair dismissal.[10] Ultimately, job analysis helps increase the value added by employees to the organization because it clarifies what is really required to perform effectively.

job analysis
A tool for determining what is done on a given job and what should be done on that job.

> Job analysis provides the information required by virtually every human resources activity.

Staffing the Organization

 Once HR planning is completed, managers can focus on staffing the organization. The staffing function consists of three related activities: recruitment, selection, and outplacement.

Recruitment

recruitment

The development of a pool of applicants for jobs in an organization.

Recruitment activities help increase the pool of candidates that might be selected for a job. Recruitment may be internal to the organization (considering current employees for promotions and transfers) or external. Each approach has advantages and disadvantages.[11]

Internal Recruiting   The advantages of internal recruiting are that employers know their employees, and employees know their organization. External candidates who are unfamiliar with the organization may find they don't like working there. Also, the opportunity to move up within the organization may encourage employees to remain with the company, work hard, and succeed. Recruiting from outside the company can be demoralizing to employees. Many companies, such as Sears and Eli Lilly, prefer internal to external recruiting for these reasons.

Internal staffing has some drawbacks. If existing employees lack skills or talent, internal recruitment yields a limited applicant pool, leading to poor selection decisions. Also, an internal recruitment policy can inhibit a company that wants to change the nature or goals of the business by bringing in outside candidates. In changing from a rapidly growing, entrepreneurial organization to a mature business with more stable growth, Dell went outside the organization to hire managers who better fit those needs.

Many companies that rely heavily on internal recruiting use a job-posting system. A *job-posting system* is a mechanism for advertising open positions, typically on a bulletin board or the company's intranet. Texas Instruments uses job posting. Employees complete a request form indicating interest in a posted job. The posted job description includes a list of duties and the minimum skills and experience required.

Bottom Line

Outside hires often bring new ideas to the organization. *How might an organization identify candidates with innovative ideas?*

External Recruiting   External recruiting brings in "new blood" to a company and can inspire innovation. Among the most frequently used sources of outside applicants are Internet job boards, company websites, employee referrals, newspaper advertisements, and college campus recruiting.

Recent surveys suggest that employers place the greatest emphasis on referrals by current employees and online job boards.[12] Some companies actively encourage employees to refer their friends by offering cash rewards. In fact, surveys show word-of-mouth recommendations are the way most job positions get filled. Not only is this recruitment method relatively inexpensive, but employees also tend to know who will be a good fit with the company. Web job boards such as CareerBuilder and Monster are widely used because they easily reach a large pool of job seekers. For specialized positions, however,

Just over this employee's shoulder is an internal job listing board, typical for companies who prefer internal recruiting. Companies are increasingly utilizing their intranet sites to post jobs as well.

a growing number of companies are opting to look on professional networking sites such as LinkedIn or to hire a recruiter because the job boards generate many unqualified leads that are overwhelming to process. Many companies accept applications and may post job openings at their corporate websites. When it is worthwhile to pay an outside organization to narrow down the pool of applicants, employers may turn to employment agencies or, for important management positions, an executive search firm. Campus recruiting can be helpful for companies looking for applicants who have up-to-date training and innovative ideas. However, companies that rely heavily on campus recruiting and employee referrals have to take extra care to ensure that these methods do not discriminate by generating pools of applicants who are, say, mostly women or primarily white.[13]

Most companies use some combination of the methods we have been discussing, depending on the particular job or situation. For example, they might use internal recruiting for existing jobs that need replacements, and external recruiting when the firm is expanding or needs to acquire some new skill.

IN PRACTICE

When Walmart Stores was looking for a way to add employees with the leadership potential for management positions in its stores, it decided to aim its recruiting at people with military experience. It charged Gary Profit with military recruiting, a responsibility Profit says makes perfect sense because military personnel not only have received extensive training from the government but also "have a record of performance under pressure." An additional benefit is that military recruiting helps Walmart meet its goal of building a workforce that reflects the diversity of the markets it serves because the U.S. military is a racially and ethnically diverse group. Walmart's military recruiting program looks for junior military officers at job fairs, through military associations, and with the aid of military-focused employment agencies. It promises them a 90-day training program in retail operations and a mentorship with a successful store manager.

One successful candidate Walmart found through its military recruiting effort is Michelle Terry, a graduate of the U.S. Military Academy at West Point. Her service in the U.S. Army as a maintenance platoon leader included responsibility for 80 soldiers, equipment worth more than $10 million, and a warehouse supplying 3,500 troops. Terry wanted a job with a company that would value her experience and give her a chance to advance in her career. She found that at Walmart, which promoted her to managing a Missouri supercenter just six months after she was hired.[14]

- What advantages does Walmart's military recruiting effort have over internal recruiting for management jobs? Should it replace internal recruiting? Why or why not?

Selection

Selection builds on recruiting and involves decisions about whom to hire. As important as these decisions are, they are—unfortunately—at times made in careless or cavalier ways. In this section we describe a number of selection instruments to which you may soon be exposed in your own career.

selection

Choosing from among qualified applicants to hire into an organization.

Applications and Résumés   Application blanks and résumés provide basic information to prospective employers. To make a first cut through candidates, employers review the profiles and backgrounds of various job applicants. Applications and résumés typically include information about the applicant's name, educational background, citizenship, work experiences, certifications, and the like. Their appearance and accuracy also say something about the applicant—spelling mistakes, for example, are almost always immediately disqualifying (something to keep in mind when preparing your own). While providing important information, applications and résumés tend not to be extremely useful for making final selection decisions.

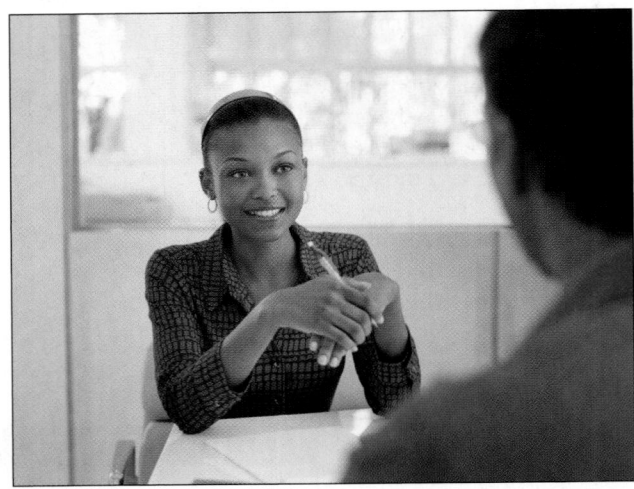

During an interview, employers may opt to hold unstructured interviews, where they ask each potential employee different questions, or they may choose to hold structured interviews where the employer asks all potential employees the same questions.

structured interview

Selection technique that involves asking all applicants the same questions and comparing their responses to a standardized set of answers.

Many interviewers use more than one technique during the same interview.

Interviews   The most popular selection tool is interviewing, and every company uses some type of interview. However, employment interviewers must be careful about what they ask and how they ask it. As we will explain later in the chapter, federal law requires that employers avoid discriminating against people based on criteria such as sex and race; questions that distinguish candidates according to protected categories may be seen as evidence of discrimination.

In an unstructured (or nondirective) interview, the interviewer asks different interviewees different questions. The interviewer may also use probes—that is, ask follow-up questions to learn more about the candidate.[15]

In a **structured interview,** the interviewer conducts the same interview with each applicant. There are two basic types of structured interview. The first approach—called the *situational interview*—focuses on hypothetical situations. Zale Corporation, a major jewelry chain, uses this type of structured interview to select sales clerks. Here is a sample question: "A customer comes into the store to pick up a watch he had left for repair. The watch is not back yet from the repair shop, and the customer becomes angry. How would you handle the situation?" An answer that says "I would refer the customer to my supervisor" might suggest that the applicant felt incapable of handling the situation on his or her own. The second approach—called the *behavioral description interview*—explores what candidates have actually done in the past. In selecting accountants, Bill Bufe of Plante & Moran asks candidates how they handled a difficult person they have worked with, and Art King asks how candidates have handled a stressful situation because he believes this shows how candidates "think on their feet."[16] Because behavioral questions are based on real events, they often provide useful information about how the candidate will actually perform on the job.

Each of these interview techniques offers a manager different advantages and disadvantages, and many interviewers use more than one technique during the same interview. Unstructured interviews can help establish rapport and provide a sense of the applicant's personality, but they may not provide the manager with specific information about the candidate's ability. Structured interviews tend to be more reliable predictors of job performance because they are based on the job analysis that has been done for the position. They are also more likely to be free of bias and stereotypes. And because the same questions are being asked of all candidates for the job, an interview that is at least partially structured allows the manager to compare responses across different candidates.[17]

Reference Checks   Résumés, applications, and interviews rely on the honesty of the applicant. To make an accurate selection decision, employers have to be able to trust the words of each candidate. Unfortunately, some candidates may hide criminal backgrounds that could pose a risk to the employer or exaggerate their qualifications. In a highly publicized incident, the dean of admissions at the Massachusetts Institute of Technology resigned after nearly three decades on the job because the school learned that she had provided false information about her educational background.[18] Although she had certainly demonstrated an ability to perform the job functions, she could no longer claim the level of integrity required by that position. Once lost, a reputation is hard to regain.

Because these and more ambiguous ethical gray areas arise, employers supplement candidate-provided information with other screening devices, including *reference checks.* Virtually all organizations contact references or former employers and educational institutions listed by candidates. Although checking references makes sense, reference information is becoming increasingly difficult to obtain because individuals have won costly lawsuits against former employers who spoke negatively about them. Nevertheless, HR experts encourage prospective employers to make a practice of checking references.[19] One reason is that it does occasionally raise a red flag: past employers will usually just verify dates of employment, job title, and sometimes pay, but sometimes they will advise caution when asked if the candidate is hirable. Checking references also provides a defense for an employer in the event that one of its employees causes harm. It demonstrates that the company was diligent about making the decision to hire that person.

Background Checks   For a higher level of scrutiny, background investigations also have become standard procedure for many companies. Some state courts have ruled that companies can be held liable for negligent hiring if they fail to do adequate background checks. The different types of checks include Social Security verification, past employment and education verification, and a criminal records check. A number of other checks can be conducted if they pertain to the job being hired for, including a motor vehicle record check (for jobs involving driving) and a credit check (for money-handling jobs).

Internet tools have made basic background checks fast and easy to perform. Recent surveys of hiring managers found that roughly half are using social networking sites, especially Facebook and LinkedIn, to learn about job candidates; some prospective employers even ask candidates for user names and passwords.[20] Many companies have chosen not to extend job offers to candidates based on content they have found online. Internet users are advised to remember that anything that carries their name online may become information for potential employers, even years down the road.

Figure 10.2 shows the various screening tools used by many *Fortune* 1000 companies.

FIGURE 10.2

Use of Preemployment Selection Tools (tools that 212 security representatives at *Fortune* 1000 companies said their companies use consistently)

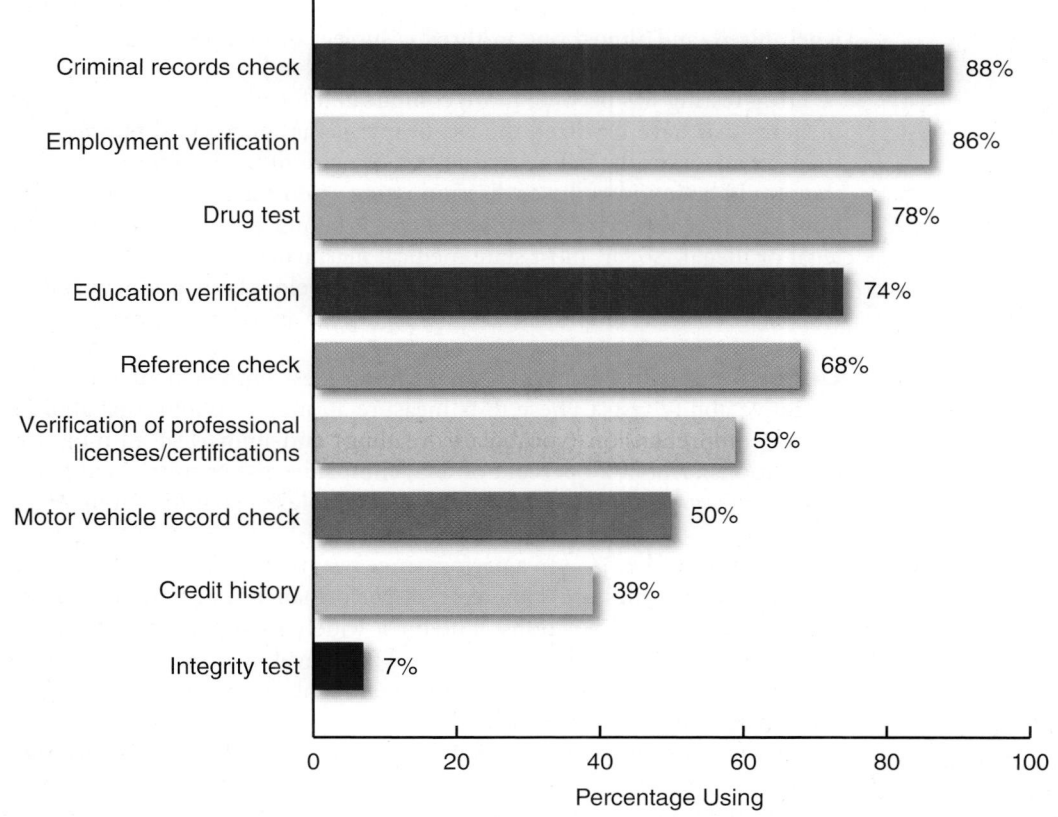

SOURCE: *Top Security Threats and Management Issues Facing Corporate America,* Pinkerton Consulting and Investigations Inc., 2003.

Personality Tests   The popularity of using tests to measure candidates' personalities has risen and fallen, but it currently seems to be on the upswing.[21] Concerns that have discouraged the use of personality tests include the possibility they might be seen as discriminatory or might not accurately predict job performance—perhaps because candidates will "cheat" by trying to guess the right answers or even retaking the test with different answers later if they fail the first screening. However, tests can be constructed using past performance data to find associations between traits and job performance. Some personality types have been associated with greater job satisfaction and performance, especially in situations in which the organization can build groups of people with similar positive traits.[22]

A number of well-known inventories measure personality traits such as sociability, adjustment, and energy. Typical questions are "Do you like to socialize with people?" and "Do you enjoy working hard?" Some personality tests try to determine the type of working conditions that the candidate prefers, to see if he or she would be motivated and productive in the particular job. For example, if the candidate prefers making decisions on his or her own but the job requires gaining the cooperation of others, another candidate might be a better fit. Today many personality tests are taken online rather than with paper and pencil. These online tests can be constructed to deliver certain questions based on answers to preceding questions, so that the test is tailored to the individual test taker.

Drug Testing   *Drug testing* is now a frequently used screening instrument. Since the passage of the Drug-Free Workplace Act of 1988, applicants and employees of federal contractors and Department of Defense contractors and those under Department of Transportation regulations have been subject to testing for illegal drugs. To avoid discrimination against individuals with disabilities, companies typically wait to conduct drug testing until after they have made a conditional job offer. According to statistics from the federal government, about one in four full-time employees is tested when hired, and almost one in three is subject to random drug tests once they have started working.[23]

Drug testing has become more complicated for employers in the growing number of states that have legalized the use of marijuana for medical purposes.[24] Companies that fire a worker for failing a drug test because of medical marijuana use worry that they could be found guilty of discriminating against a disabled person. For many jobs, however, it is also critical that workers not be under the influence of any substance, legal or illegal. So far, most state medical marijuana laws do not include employment protections for workers, but because these developments are new and the laws vary from state to state, employers are in a legal gray area for the time being.

Cognitive Ability Tests   Among the oldest employment selection devices are cognitive ability tests. These tests measure a range of intellectual abilities, including verbal comprehension (vocabulary, reading) and numerical aptitude (mathematical calculations). About 20 percent of U.S. companies use cognitive ability tests for selection purposes.[25] Figure 10.3 shows some examples of cognitive ability test questions.

Performance Tests   In a performance test, the test taker performs a sample of the job. Most companies use some type of performance test, typically for administrative assistant and clerical positions. The most widely used performance test is the typing test. However, performance tests have been developed for almost every occupation, including managerial positions. Assessment centers are the most notable offshoot of the managerial performance test.[26]

Assessment centers originated during World War II. A typical **assessment center** consists of 10 to 12 candidates who participate in a variety of exercises or situations; some of the exercises involve group interactions, and others are performed individually. Each exercise taps a number of critical managerial dimensions, such as leadership,

assessment center

A managerial performance test in which candidates participate in a variety of exercises and situations.

Verbal	1. What is the meaning of the word surreptitious?

Verbal

1. What is the meaning of the word surreptitious?
   - a. covert
   - b. winding
   - c. lively
   - d. sweet

2. How is the noun clause used in the following sentence: "I hope that I can learn this game."
   - a. subject
   - b. predicate nominative
   - c. direct object
   - d. object of the preposition

Quantitative

3. Divide 50 by .5 and add 5. What is the result?
   - a. 25
   - b. 30
   - c. 95
   - d. 105

4. What is the value of 144^2?
   - a. 12
   - b. 72
   - c. 288
   - d. 20736

Reasoning

5. _____ is to boat as snow is to _____
   - a. sail, ski
   - b. water, winter
   - c. water, ski
   - d. engine, water

6. Two women played 5 games of chess. Each woman won the same number of games, yet there were no ties. How can this be so?
   - a. There was a forfeit.
   - b. One player cheated.
   - c. They played different people.
   - d. One game was still in progress.

Mechanical

7. If gear A and gear C are both turning counterclockwise, what is happening to gear B?
   - a. It is turning counterclockwise.
   - b. It is turning clockwise.
   - c. It remains stationary.
   - d. The whole system will jam.

A   B   C

Answers: 1a, 2c, 3d, 4d, 5c, 6c, 7b.

SOURCE: From G. Bohlander, S. Snell, and A. Sherman, *Managing Human Resources*, 12th ed. Copyright © 2001. South-Western, a part of Cengage Learning, Inc. Reproduced by permission. www.cengage.com/permissions

FIGURE 10.3

Sample Measures of Cognitive Ability

decision-making skills, and communication ability. Assessors, generally line managers from the organization, observe and record information about the candidates' performance in each exercise. The first organization to use assessment centers was AT&T. Since then, a number of large organizations have used or currently are using the assessment center technique, including the FBI and Sears.

Integrity Tests   To assess job candidates' honesty, employers may administer integrity tests. Two forms of integrity tests are polygraphs and paper-and-pencil honesty tests. Polygraphs, or lie detector tests, have been banned for most employment purposes.[27] Paper-and-pencil honesty tests are more recent instruments for measuring integrity. These tests include questions such as whether a person has ever thought about stealing and whether he or she believes other people steal ("What percentage of people take more than $1 from their employer?"). Although companies including Payless ShoeSource reported that losses due to theft declined following the introduction of integrity tests, the accuracy of these tests is still debatable.[28]

reliability

The consistency of test scores over time and across alternative measurements.

validity

The degree to which a selection test predicts or correlates with job performance.

Reliability and Validity   Regardless of the method used to select employees, two crucial issues that need to be addressed are a test's reliability and its validity. **Reliability** refers to the consistency of test scores over time and across alternative measurements. For example, if three different interviewers talked to the same job candidate but drew very different conclusions about the candidate's abilities, we might suspect that there were problems with the reliability of one or more of the selection tests or interview procedures.

Validity moves beyond reliability to assess the accuracy of the selection test. The most common form of validity, *criterion-related validity*, refers to the degree to which a test actually predicts or correlates with job performance. Questions about validity are one reason (along with ethical and public policy concerns) why employers were recently criticized for making current employment a requirement for being hired. At a time when unemployment rates were high and employers were flooded with applications, some companies were screening out people based on their unemployed status. Critics of this practice doubted that being jobless during a recession was highly correlated with poor performance.[29] In general, validity is usually established through studies comparing test performance and job performance for a large enough sample of employees to enable a fair conclusion to be reached. For example, if a high score on a cognitive ability test is strongly predictive of good job performance, then candidates who score well will usually be preferred over those who do not. Still, no test by itself perfectly predicts performance. Managers usually rely on other criteria as well before making a final selection.

Another form of validity, *content validity*, concerns the degree to which selection tests measure a representative sample of the knowledge, skills, and abilities required for the job. The best-known example of a content-valid test is a keyboarding test for administrative assistants, because keyboarding is a task a person in that position almost always performs. However, to be completely content-valid, the selection process also should measure other skills the assistant would be likely to perform, such as answering the telephone, duplicating and faxing documents, and dealing with the public. Content validity is more subjective (less statistical) than evaluations of criterion-related validity but is no less important, particularly when one is defending employment decisions in court. As you read "Management Connection: Progress Report," consider whether Google meets these standards with its selection methods.

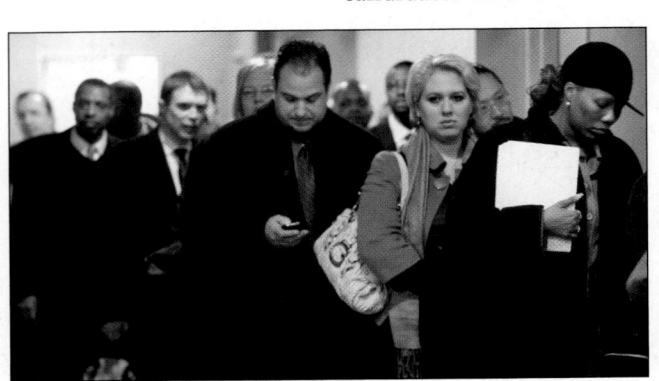

Due to tough economic times, workforce reductions in companies throughout the United States have become commonplace. Job seekers are shown here standing in line to attend a job fair in Chicago.

Manager's Brief   **Progress Report**   Onward

Management Connection

HOW GOOGLE HIRES

The Google search engine provides a model for how the company grew from a few hundred employees to tens of thousands. The idea behind using software like Google is that you'll find the best information if you have an efficient way to sort through the vast amounts of data available online. Google acquired repeat users by delivering relevant links most of the time near the top of the search results. And when it comes to acquiring human resources,

the Google strategy involves positioning the company as a highly attractive place to work, receiving a flood of applications, and making collaborative decisions about which of the applicants will be the best fit with Google's demanding and creative culture.

Promoting Google's reputation as a great place to work might seem unnecessary when so many people already love the company's products and see the Google name on lists of great employers. But in a labor market where experts in computer programming and online marketing are in such demand, the company needs to recruit if it wants to keep attracting the best candidates. Google has expanded its recruiting on college campuses, and it offers generously paid summer internships. It hosts regular open houses and sends people out to give talks on technical topics related to projects for which it is recruiting. Yolanda Mangolini, Google's director of outreach programs, says these activities help participants "imagine themselves at Google." Other efforts include YouTube videos, blogs, and Twitter feeds that provide information about what it's like to work for Google. One enticing post from Alan Eustace, vice president for engineering and research, promised, "We'll hire as many smart, creative people as we can to tackle some of the toughest challenges in computer science." That's no idle boast at a company whose ideas in the pipeline include robot cars, voice search, and an online-only operating system for personal computers. And as Google ramps up hiring, the company is applying its expertise in search technology to go through its database of résumés to identify potentially interesting candidates, find out what they're doing now, and see if any are a good fit with the company's current needs.

Along with its reputation as a great employer, Google developed early on a reputation as a place with a demanding and sometimes quirky process for making hiring decisions. To make sure hiring decisions reflected the company's collaborative approach, job candidates interviewed with people who could provide a variety of perspectives. Sometimes a candidate could wind up participating in a dozen or more interviews before receiving a job offer. Through that process, the interviewers would compile an extensive file of information, and they would make a group decision to avoid the problem of a manager preferring whichever candidate was most like him- or herself. To select creative and intellectually talented people, interviewers came up with questions aimed at stimulating creative thinking. For example, one selection question that became notorious was to ask why manhole covers are round. Other questions could be more complex and quantitative.

But as Google has grown, its management has found that its signature hiring process is a little too quirky and far too slow. In some cases, the company spent so long negotiating job offers (taking as much as 10 days for a counteroffer) that candidates went elsewhere to work. Some people saw the drive to select for intellectual talent as mere elitism; Google acquired a reputation as a place where you could forget about working if your college GPA was less than 3.7 (something the company insists is untrue). So Google is eliminating the problem-solving puzzles from its interviews. The new approach favors selection based on applicants' accomplishments. An attractive candidate at Google is one who can show interviewers something she or he has already created, such as a software app available for sale online. Google also is limiting the number of job interviews to no more than five per candidate and speeding up its decision-making process so candidates don't slip away.

Despite these changes, Google is steadfast in its drive to select people who excel in the areas of Google's core values. The selection methods may be different today, but the selection criteria are still essentially the same: a passion for technology, a passion for the company, creativity, and initiative to go above and beyond the basic requirements of a job.[30]

- How could Google supplement the recruitment practices described here with internal recruiting? What advantages would this offer?
- Discuss your impression of the reliability and validity of the selection methods used by Google.

Workforce Reductions

Unfortunately, staffing decisions do not simply focus on hiring employees. As organizations evolve and markets change, the demand for certain employees rises and falls. Also, some employees simply do not perform at a level required to justify continued employment. For these reasons, managers sometimes must make difficult decisions to terminate their employment.

Layoffs As a result of the massive restructuring of American industry brought about by mergers and acquisitions, divestiture, and increased competition, many organizations have been downsizing—laying off large numbers of managerial and other employees. As mentioned in Chapter 9, dismissing any employee is tough, but when a company lays off a substantial portion of its workforce, the results can rock the foundations of the organization.[31] The victims of restructuring face all the difficulties of being let go—loss of self-esteem, demoralizing job searches, and the stigma of being out of work. To some extent, employers can help employees with these problems by

Validity is usually established through studies comparing test performance and job performance.

outplacement

The process of helping people who have been dismissed from the company regain employment elsewhere.

offering **outplacement,** the process of helping people who have been dismissed from the company regain employment elsewhere. Even then, the impact of layoffs goes further than the employees who leave. For many of the employees who remain with the company, disenchantment, distrust, and lethargy overshadow the comfort of still having a job. In many respects, how management deals with dismissals will affect the productivity and satisfaction of those who remain. A well-thought-out dismissal process eases tensions and helps remaining employees adjust to the new work situation.

Organizations with strong performance evaluation systems benefit because the survivors are less likely to believe the decision was arbitrary. In addition, if care is taken during the actual layoff process—that is, if workers are offered severance pay and help in finding a new job—remaining workers will be comforted. Companies also should avoid stringing out layoffs by dismissing a few workers at a time.

Termination   People sometimes "get fired" for poor performance or other reasons. Should an employer have the right to fire a worker? In 1884 a Tennessee court ruled, "All may dismiss their employee(s) at will for good cause, for no cause, or even for cause morally wrong." The concept that an employee may be fired for any reason is known as **employment-at-will** or *termination-at-will* and was upheld in a 1908 Supreme Court ruling.[32] The logic is that if the employee may quit at any time, the employer is free to dismiss at any time.

employment-at-will

The legal concept that an employee may be terminated for any reason.

Since the mid-1970s, courts in most states have made exceptions to this doctrine. Under the public policy exception (i.e., a ruling designed to protect the public from harm), employees cannot be fired for such actions as refusing to break the law, taking time off for jury duty, or "whistleblowing" to report illegal company behavior.

For example, if a worker reports an environmental violation to a regulatory agency and the company fires him or her, the courts may argue that the firing was unfair because the employee acted for the good of the community. Union contracts that limit an employer's ability to fire without cause are another major exception to the employment-at-will doctrine.

How management deals with dismissals will affect the productivity and satisfaction of those who remain.

Employers can avoid the pitfalls associated with dismissal by developing progressive and positive disciplinary procedures.[33] By *progressive,* we mean that a manager takes graduated steps in attempting to correct a workplace behavior. For example, an employee who has been absent receives a verbal reprimand for the first offense. A second offense invokes a written reprimand. A third offense results in employee counseling and probation, and a fourth results in a paid leave day to think over the consequences of future rule infractions. The employer is signaling to the employee that this is the "last straw." Arbitrators are more likely to side with an employer that fires someone when they believe the company has made sincere efforts to help the person correct his or her behavior.

termination interview

A discussion between a manager and an employee about the employee's dismissal.

The **termination interview,** in which the manager discusses the company's position with the employee, is a stressful situation for both parties. Most experts believe that the immediate superior should be the one to deliver the bad news to employees. However, it is a wise precaution to have a third party, such as an HR manager, present to provide guidance and take notes on the meeting. Because announcing a termination is likely to upset the employee and occasionally leads to a lawsuit, the manager should prepare carefully. Preparation should include knowing all the facts of the situation and reviewing any documents to make sure they are consistent with the reason for the termination. During the termination interview, ethics and common sense dictate that the manager should be truthful but respectful, stating the facts and avoiding arguments.[34] Table 10.1 provides some other guidelines for conducting a termination interview.

Legal Issues and Equal Employment Opportunity   Many laws have been passed governing employment decisions and practices. They will directly affect a good part of your day-to-day work as a manager, as well as the human resource function of your organization. Most of these laws are designed to protect job candidates and

Do's	Don'ts
• Give as much warning as possible for mass layoffs. • Sit down one-on-one with the individual in a private office. • Complete a termination session within 15 minutes. • Provide written explanations of severance benefits. • Provide outplacement services away from company headquarters. • Be sure the employee hears about his or her termination from a manager, not a colleague. • Express appreciation for what the employee has contributed, if appropriate.	• Don't leave room for confusion when firing. Tell the individual in the first sentence that he or she is terminated. • Don't allow time for debate during a termination session. • Don't make personal comments when firing someone; keep the conversation professional. • Don't rush a fired employee offsite unless security is an issue. • Don't fire people on significant dates, like the 25th anniversary of their employment or the day their mother died. • Don't fire employees when they are on vacation or have just returned.

TABLE 10.1
Advice on Termination

SOURCE: S. Alexander, "Firms Get Plenty of Practice at Layoffs, but They Often Bungle the Firing Process," *Wall Street Journal*, 1991. Reproduced with permission of Dow Jones & Company, Inc. via Copyright Clearance Center.

employees against discrimination or sexual harassment and to establish standards of pay and hours worked for certain classes of employee. For example, the 1938 *Fair Labor Standards Act* (FLSA), among other provisions, creates two employee categories: exempt and nonexempt. Employees are normally exempt from overtime pay if they have considerable discretion in how they carry out their jobs and if their jobs require them to exercise independent judgment. Managers usually fall in this category. Nonexempt employees are usually paid by the hour and must be paid overtime if they work more than 40 hours in a week. As a manager you will almost certainly need to specify the exempt or nonexempt status of anyone you hire.

The 1964 *Civil Rights Act* prohibits discrimination in employment based on race, sex, color, national origin, and religion. Title VII of the act specifically forbids discrimination in such employment practices as recruitment, hiring, discharge, promotion, compensation, and access to training.[35] The *Americans with Disabilities Act*, passed in 1990, prohibits employment discrimination against people with disabilities. Recovering alcoholics and drug abusers, cancer patients in remission, and AIDS patients are covered by this legislation. The 1991 *Civil Rights Act* strengthened all these protections and permitted punitive damages to be imposed on companies that violate them.

Failure to comply with any of these laws may expose the organization to charges of unfair practices, expensive lawsuits, and civil and even criminal penalties in some cases. For example, Walmart recently paid $17.5 million to settle a lawsuit in which employees said the company had discriminated against African American workers seeking positions as truck drivers. According to these workers, the company had placed stiffer requirements on African American job candidates. In another case, Union Pacific Railroad paid $75,000 to settle a sex discrimination lawsuit in which a woman was not hired as system material foreman, even though she had more experience than men who applied for the position. And Nordstrom paid $292,500 to settle a lawsuit in which Florida workers said their manager had harassed them because of their race.[36]

One common reason employers are sued is **adverse impact**—when a seemingly neutral employment practice has a disproportionately negative effect on a group protected by the Civil Rights Act.[37] For example, if equal numbers of qualified men and women apply for jobs but a particular employment test results in far fewer women being hired, the test may be considered to cause an adverse impact and, therefore, be subject to challenge on that basis.

adverse impact

When a seemingly neutral employment practice has a disproportionately negative effect on a protected group.

Because of the importance of these issues, many companies have established procedures to ensure compliance with labor and equal opportunity laws. For example, companies frequently monitor and compare salaries by race, gender, length of service, and other categories to make sure employees across all groups are being fairly paid. Written policies can also help ensure fair and legal practices in the workplace, although the company may also have to demonstrate a record of actually following those procedures and making sure they are implemented. In this sense, smart and effective management practices not only help managers motivate employees to do their best work but often help provide legal protection as well.

For example, managers who provide their employees with regular, specific evaluations can often prevent misunderstandings that can lead to lawsuits. And a written record of those evaluations is often useful in demonstrating fair and objective treatment.

Many other important staffing laws affect employment practices. For example, the *Age Discrimination in Employment Act* of 1967 and its amendments in 1978 and 1986 prohibit discrimination against people age 40 and over. One reason for this legislation was the common practice of dismissing older workers to replace them with younger workers who were not as highly paid. The *Worker Adjustment and Retraining Notification Act* of 1989, commonly known as the *WARN Act* or *Plant Closing Bill*, requires covered employers to give affected employees 60 days' written notice of plant closings or mass layoffs. Table 10.2 summarizes many of these major employment laws.

> U.S. businesses spend more than $125 billion annually to provide their employees with formal training.

TABLE 10.2   U.S. Equal Employment Laws

Act	Major Provisions	Enforcement and Remedies
Fair Labor Standards Act (1938)	Creates exempt (salaried) and nonexempt (hourly) employee categories, governing overtime and other rules; sets minimum wage, child labor laws.	Enforced by Department of Labor, private action to recover lost wages; civil and criminal penalties also possible.
Equal Pay Act (1963)	Prohibits gender-based pay discrimination between two jobs substantially similar in skill, effort, responsibility, and working conditions.	Fines up to $10,000, imprisonment up to 6 months, or both; enforced by Equal Employment Opportunity Commission (EEOC); private actions for double damages up to 3 years' wages, liquidated damages, reinstatement, or promotion.
Title VII of Civil Rights Act (1964)	Prohibits discrimination based on race, sex, color, religion, or national origin in employment decisions: hiring, pay, working conditions, promotion, discipline, or discharge.	Enforced by EEOC; private actions, back pay, front pay, reinstatement, restoration of seniority and pension benefits, attorneys' fees and costs.
Executive Orders 11246 and 11375 (1965)	Requires equal opportunity clauses in federal contracts; prohibits employment discrimination by federal contractors based on race, color, religion, sex, or national origin.	Established Office of Federal Contract Compliance Programs (OFCCP) to investigate violations; empowered to terminate violator's federal contracts.
Age Discrimination in Employment Act (1967)	Prohibits employment discrimination based on age for persons over 40 years; restricts mandatory retirement.	EEOC enforcement; private actions for reinstatement, back pay, front pay, restoration of seniority and pension benefits; double unpaid wages for willful violations; attorneys' fees and costs.
Vocational Rehabilitation Act (1973)	Requires affirmative action by all federal contractors for persons with disabilities; defines disabilities as physical or mental impairments that substantially limit life activities.	Federal contractors must consider hiring disabled persons capable of performance after reasonable accommodations.

(continued)

Act	Major Provisions	Enforcement and Remedies
Americans with Disabilities Act (1990)	Extends affirmative action provisions of Vocational Rehabilitation Act to private employers; requires workplace modifications to facilitate disabled employees; prohibits discrimination against disabled.	EEOC enforcement; private actions for Title VII remedies.
Civil Rights Act (1991)	Clarifies Title VII requirements: disparate treatment impact suits, business necessity, job relatedness; shifts burden of proof to employer; permits punitive damages and jury trials.	Punitive damages limited to sliding scale only in intentional discrimination based on sex, religion, and disabilities.
Family and Medical Leave Act (1991)	Requires 12 weeks' unpaid leave for medical or family needs: paternity, family member illness.	Private actions for lost wages and other expenses, reinstatement.

Developing the Workforce

Today's competitive environment requires managers to continually upgrade the skills and performance of employees—and their own. Such constant improvement increases both personal and organizational effectiveness. It makes organization members more useful in their current jobs and prepares them to take on new responsibilities. And it helps the organization as a whole handle new challenges and take advantage of new methods and technologies that emerge. Developing the workforce in this way involves training and development activities. It also involves appraising employees' performance and giving them effective feedback so they will be motivated to perform at their best. We will discuss each of these activities in turn.

Bottom Line

Training improves employee quality.

How might you measure quality improvements from training salespeople?

Training and Development

U.S. businesses spend more than $125 billion annually to provide their employees with formal training. The greatest share of that spending goes to training that the organization itself delivers to its employees. The remainder is spent on training by outsiders, including payments for training companies and tuition reimbursement.[38]

Fortune 500 companies such as General Electric and Procter & Gamble have invested heavily in training. IBM's annual training costs have at times exceeded Harvard University's annual operating expenses. But competitive pressures require that companies consider the most efficient training methods. That means traditional classroom settings are often giving way to computerized methods.

Cold Stone Creamery spends a portion of its training budget in developing computerized simulations to show how employee actions affect store performance. The company uses computer games because they are familiar and attractive to its young employees.

The American Society for Training and Development has argued that as a percentage of total payroll, the average organizational investment in training is too small.[39] This lack of commitment is a great concern in light of the fact that today's jobs require more education but the education level of U.S. workers has not kept pace. What's more, companies need to ensure that employees who have survived layoffs can lead their organizations through tough times.

Overview of the Training Process   Although we use the general term *training* here, training sometimes is distinguished from development. **Training** usually refers to teaching lower-level employees how to perform their present jobs, while **development** involves teaching managers and professional employees broader skills needed for their present and future jobs.

Phase one of training usually starts with a **needs assessment.** Managers conduct an analysis to identify the jobs, people, and departments for which training is necessary. Job analysis and performance measurements are useful for this purpose.

Phase two involves the design of training programs. Based on needs assessment, training objectives and content can be established. For example, Recreational Equipment Inc. (REI) wants its sales associates to learn how to tell whether they are being approached by a transactional customer, who simply wants to find and pay for a specific product, or a consultative customer, who wants to spend some time discussing alternative features and benefits.[40]

Phase three involves decisions about the training methods to be used and whether the training will be provided on or off the job. Common training methods include lectures, role-playing, business simulation, behavior modeling (watching a video and imitating what is observed), conferences, vestibule training (practicing in a simulated job environment), and apprenticeships. The method should be well suited to the objectives defined in phase two. At REI, where the company wants sales associates to identify and respond to various interpersonal situations, much of the training involves role-playing, supplemented with video presentations. The Home Depot emphasizes mentoring for sales associates who work the aisles but has a more efficient computer-based training program for the cashiers, whose jobs are more routine.[41] As shown in Figure 10.4, companies today are increasing the share of training that is conducted electronically (for example, with online videos, games, and quizzes). Computer-based training is easy and inexpensive to deliver, can be provided anywhere an employee has access to a computer, and can be tailored to a trainee's responses. Well-designed computer training also can get trainees highly involved in learning. A recent study found that trainees learned better from an interactive video game than they did from other forms of instruction.[42] Another popular training method is job rotation, where employees are assigned to different jobs in the organization to broaden their experience and improve their skills. It is frequently applied to managers as well as lower-level employees. In fact, smart managers often request assignment to jobs where they can be challenged and their skills broadened.

Finally, *phase four* of training should evaluate the program's effectiveness. Measures of effectiveness include employee reactions (surveys), learning (tests), improved

FIGURE 10.4
Allocation of Training
Time: Instructor-Led vs.
Computer-Based Training

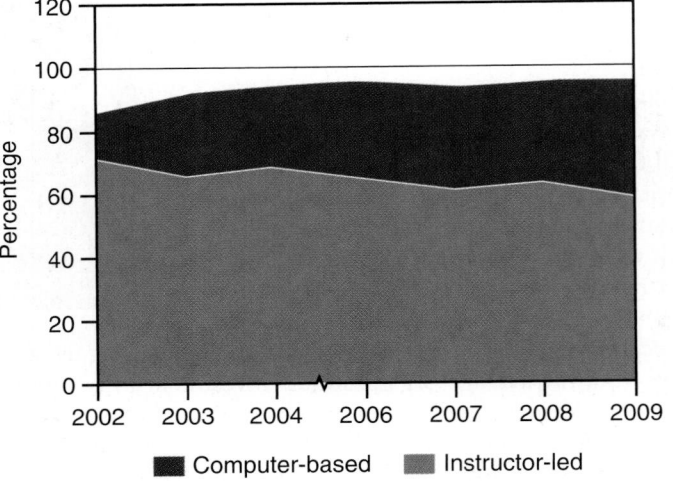

SOURCE: Based on data in L. Patel, "2010 State of the Industry: Continued Dedication to Workplace Learning," *T + D*, November 2010, pp. 48–53.

behavior on the job, and bottom-line results (e.g., an increase in sales or reduction in defect rates following the training program).

Types of Training   Companies invest in training to enhance individual performance and organizational productivity. Programs to improve an employee's computer, technical, or communication skills are quite common, and some types of training have become fairly standard across many organizations. **Orientation training** is typically used to familiarize new employees with their new jobs, work units, and the organization in general. Done well, orientation training has a number of benefits, including lower employee turnover, increased morale, better productivity, and lower recruiting and training costs.

Team training has taken on more importance as organizations reorganize to facilitate individuals working together. Team training teaches employees the skills they need to work together and facilitates their interaction. After General Mills acquired Pillsbury, it used a team training program called Brand Champions to combine the marketing expertise of the two companies and share knowledge among employees handling various functions such as sales and research and development. Most of the time, trainees engaged in team exercises to analyze brands, target customers, and develop marketing messages.[43]

Diversity training focuses on building awareness of diversity issues and providing the skills employees need to work with others who are different from them. This topic is so important that the next chapter is devoted solely to managing diversity.

Today's decentralized and leaner organizations put more demands and responsibility on managers, as has an increasingly competitive environment. And as managers rise in the organization, their technical skills generally become less important than their ability to motivate others. For these reasons, *management training programs* have become another widely used development tool. Such programs often seek to improve managers' *people skills*—their ability to delegate effectively, increase the motivation of their subordinates, and communicate and inspire the achievement of organization goals. *Coaching*—being trained by a superior—is usually the most effective and direct management development tool. Managers may also participate in training programs that are used for all employees, such as job rotation, or attend seminars and courses specifically designed to help them improve their supervisory skills or prepare them for future promotion.

orientation training

Training designed to introduce new employees to the company and familiarize them with policies, procedures, culture, and the like.

team training

Training that provides employees with the skills and perspectives they need to collaborate with others.

diversity training

Programs that focus on identifying and reducing hidden biases against people with differences and developing the skills needed to manage a diversified workforce.

IN PRACTICE

NetApp, a data management company based in Sunnyvale, California, has an engaging approach to management training. The company hired BTS Group to develop a simulation game modeled on NetApp's real-life business. NetApp first used the BTS simulation at a strategy meeting of its top managers. The executives were so enthusiastic and creative about the ways they solved the simulation problem that the company invited middle managers to play the game as a form of training for top posts, where strategic thinking is essential.

In the simulation, the managers were divided into five teams, bringing together managers from various functions. Each team was told to run an imaginary high-growth company named Pet-a-Toaster for three years, competing against the other teams. In the simulation, a year's worth of events were packed into one day of the training program. Each team received a booklet with details about Pet-a-Toaster, based on the market conditions that were actually facing NetApp. Teams allocated the resources they were given, selected from among possible strategies, and reacted to events posed by the game (for example, a request from a big customer). BTS's simulation software analyzed the actions and provided feedback.

At the end of the simulation, BTS reported each team's total sales and operating profits and described the impact of each team's decisions about where to invest resources. Now NetApp's middle managers have a greater appreciation for what it takes to run a company—and a heightened respect for their leaders.[44]

- In this situation, what advantages does simulation have over other training methods, such as lectures, case studies, and computer-based training for individuals?

Performance Appraisal

 LO 5

performance appraisal (PA)

Assessment of an employee's job performance.

One of the most important responsibilities you will have as a manager is **performance appraisal (PA),** the assessment of an employee's job performance. Done well, it can help employees improve their performance, pay, and chances for promotion; foster communication between managers and employees; and increase the employees' and the organization's effectiveness. Done poorly, it actually can have a negative effect—it can cause resentment, reduce motivation, diminish performance, and even expose the organization to legal action.

Performance appraisal has two basic purposes. First, appraisal serves an *administrative* purpose. It provides managers with the information they need to make salary, promotion, and dismissal decisions; helps employees understand and accept the basis of those decisions; and, if necessary, provides documentation that can justify those decisions in court. Second, and at least as important, appraisal serves a *developmental* purpose. The information gathered in the appraisal can be used to identify and plan the additional training, learning, experience, or other improvement employees require. In addition, the manager's feedback and coaching based on the appraisal help employees improve their day-to-day performance and can help prepare them for greater responsibilities in the future.

> "A leader is best when people barely know he exists. Not so good when people obey and acclaim him. Worse when they despise him. But of a good leader who talks little when his work is done, his aim fulfilled, they will say, 'We did it ourselves.'"
>
> — Lao-tse

What Do You Appraise?

Performance appraisals can assess three basic categories of employee performance: traits, behaviors, and results. *Trait appraisals* involve subjective judgments about employee characteristics related to performance. They contain dimensions such as initiative, leadership, and attitude, and they ask raters to indicate how much of each trait an employee possesses. Usually the manager will use a numerical *ratings scale* to specify the extent to which an employee possesses the particular traits being measured. For example, if the measured trait is "attitude," the employee might be rated anywhere from 1 (very negative attitude) to 5 (very positive attitude). Trait scales are quite common because they are simple to use and provide a standard measure for all employees. But they are often not valid as performance measures. Because they tend to be ambiguous as well as highly subjective—does the employee really have a bad attitude, or is he or she just shy?—they often lead to personal bias and may not be suitable for providing useful feedback.

Behavioral appraisals, while still subjective, focus more on observable aspects of performance. They were developed in response to the problems of trait appraisals. These scales focus on specific, prescribed behaviors that can help ensure that all parties understand what the ratings are really measuring. Because they are less ambiguous, they also can help provide useful feedback. Figure 10.5 contains an example of a behaviorally anchored rating scale (BARS) for evaluating quality.

Another common behaviorally focused approach is the *critical incident* technique. In this technique, the manager keeps a regular log and records each significant behavior by the subordinate that reflects the quality of his or her performance. ("Juanita impressed the client with her effective presentation today." "Joe was late with his report.") This approach can be subjective as well as time-consuming, and it may give some employees the feeling that everything they do is being recorded. But it does have the advantage of reminding managers in advance of a performance review what the employee actually did.

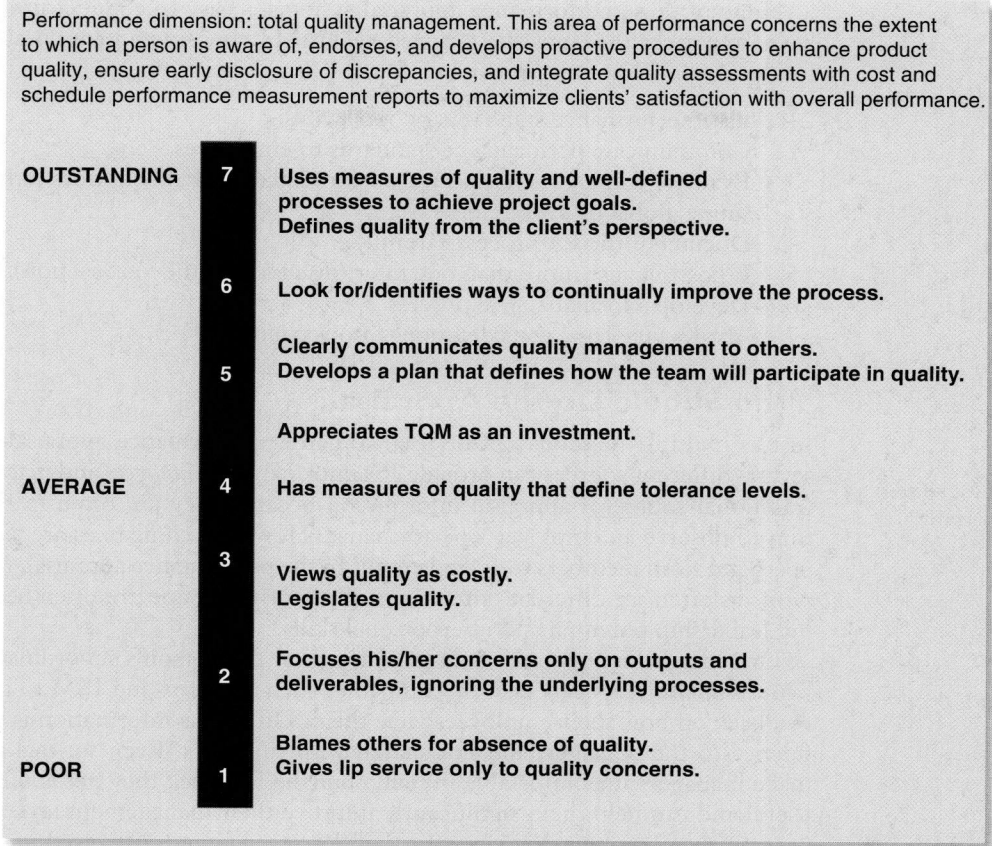

Performance dimension: total quality management. This area of performance concerns the extent to which a person is aware of, endorses, and develops proactive procedures to enhance product quality, ensure early disclosure of discrepancies, and integrate quality assessments with cost and schedule performance measurement reports to maximize clients' satisfaction with overall performance.

OUTSTANDING	7	Uses measures of quality and well-defined processes to achieve project goals. Defines quality from the client's perspective.
	6	Look for/identifies ways to continually improve the process.
	5	Clearly communicates quality management to others. Develops a plan that defines how the team will participate in quality.
		Appreciates TQM as an investment.
AVERAGE	4	Has measures of quality that define tolerance levels.
	3	Views quality as costly. Legislates quality.
	2	Focuses his/her concerns only on outputs and deliverables, ignoring the underlying processes.
POOR	1	Blames others for absence of quality. Gives lip service only to quality concerns.

SOURCE: Landy, Jacobs, and Associates. Used with permission.

FIGURE 10.5
Example of BARS Used for Evaluating Quality

Results appraisals tend to be more objective and can focus on production data such as sales volume (for a salesperson), units produced (for a line worker), or profits (for a manager). One approach to results appraisals—called **management by objectives (MBO)**—involves a subordinate and a supervisor agreeing *in advance* on specific performance goals (objectives). They then develop a plan that describes the time frame and criteria for determining whether the objectives have been reached. The aim is to agree on a set of objectives that are clear, specific, and reachable. For example, an objective for a salesperson might be "Increase sales by 25 percent during the following year." An objective for a computer programmer might be "Complete two projects within the next six months."

MBO has several important advantages. First, it avoids the biases and measurement difficulties of trait and behavioral appraisals. At the end of the review period, the employee either has or has not achieved the specified objective. The employee is judged on actual job performance. Second, because the employee and manager have agreed on the objective at the outset, the employee is likely to be more committed to the outcome, and there is less chance for misunderstanding. Third, because the employee is directly responsible for achieving the objective, MBO can be useful when managers want to empower employees to adapt their behavior to achieve the desired results. But the approach has disadvantages as well. It can result in unrealistic objectives being set, frustrating the employee and the manager. The objectives can also be too rigid, leaving the employee with insufficient flexibility should circumstances change. Finally, MBO often focuses too much on short-term achievement at the expense of long-term goals.

management by objectives (MBO)

A process in which objectives set by a subordinate and a supervisor must be reached within a given time period.

MBO can be useful when managers want to empower employees to adapt their behavior to achieve the desired results.

None of these performance appraisal systems is easy to conduct properly, and all have drawbacks that must be guarded against. In choosing an appraisal method, the following guidelines may prove helpful:

1. Base performance standards on job analysis.
2. Communicate performance standards to employees.
3. Evaluate employees on specific performance-related behaviors rather than on a single global or overall measure.
4. Document the PA process carefully.
5. If possible, use more than one rater (discussed in the next section).
6. Develop a formal appeal process.
7. Always take legal considerations into account.[45]

Who Should Do the Appraisal?

Just as multiple methods can be used to gather performance appraisal information, several different sources can provide PA information. *Managers* and *supervisors* are the traditional source of appraisal information because they are often in the best position to observe an employee's performance. However, companies are also turning to peers and team members to provide input to the performance appraisal. *Peers* and *team members* often see different dimensions of performance and are often best at identifying leadership potential and interpersonal skills.

One increasingly popular source of appraisal is a person's subordinates. Appraisal by *subordinates* has been used by companies such as Xerox and IBM to give superiors feedback on how their employees view them. Often this information is given in confidence to the manager, and not shared with superiors. Even so, this approach can make managers uncomfortable initially, but the feedback they get is often extremely useful and can help them significantly improve their management style. Because this process gives employees power over their bosses, it is generally used for development purposes only, and not for salary or promotion decisions.

Internal and external customers also are used as sources of performance appraisal information, particularly for companies, such as Ford and Honda, that are focused on total quality management. External customers have been used for some time to appraise restaurant employees, but internal customers can include anyone inside the organization who depends on an employee's work output. Finally, it is usually a good idea for employees to evaluate their own performance. Although *self-appraisals* may be biased upward, the process of self-evaluation helps increase the employee's involvement in the review process and is a starting point for establishing future goals.

Because each source of PA information has some limitations, and because different people may see different aspects of performance, Shell, Eastman Kodak, and many other companies have used approaches that involve more than one source for appraisal information. In a process known as **360-degree appraisal**, feedback is obtained from subordinates, peers, and superiors—every level involved with the employee. Often the person being rated can select the appraisers, subject to a manager's approval, with the understanding that the individual appraisals are kept confidential; returned forms might not include the name of the appraiser, for example, and the results may be consolidated for each level.

The 360-degree appraisal offers many advantages. It provides a much fuller picture of the employee's strengths and weaknesses, and it often captures qualities other appraisal methods miss. For example, an employee may have a difficult relationship with his or her supervisor yet be highly regarded by peers and subordinates. The approach can lead to significant improvement, with employees often very motivated to improve their ratings. Improvements in management performance following 360-degree appraisals have been observed in various countries, but cultural differences can affect the impact of this method. Using the cultural measures defined by Geert Hofstede (described in Chapter 6), researchers found that 360-degree appraisals

360-degree appraisal

Process of using multiple sources of appraisal to gain a comprehensive perspective on one's performance.

were most effective with managers in cultures that were individualistic and had relatively low power distance.[46] On the downside, employees are often unwilling to rate their colleagues harshly, so a certain uniformity of ratings may result. In addition, the 360-degree appraisal is less useful than more objective criteria, like financial targets, in measuring performance. Its objective is usually the employee's development, not to provide a basis for administrative decisions like raises. For those, appraisal methods like MBO are more appropriate.[47]

How Do You Give Employees Feedback?

Appraisals are most effective when they are based on an ongoing relationship with employees, and not just a top-down formal judgment issued once a year. Managers of sports teams do not wait until the season is over to perform an appraisal. Instead they work with team members throughout the season, and with the team as a whole, to improve the team's performance. Similarly, in high-functioning organizations informal appraisal and feedback are constantly taking place. Managers discuss the goals of the organization regularly and often to create a shared understanding of the job performance those goals require.

They try to create an atmosphere in which they and their employees are working together on a common agenda. And they communicate with their employ-

> Asked to grade their company's performance appraisal system, a majority of human resources executives chose a C or below. The problem, they said, is that their company's managers need to learn how to give their employees clearer goals and more constructive feedback—especially ideas for improvement.[48]

ees on a day-to-day basis, praising or coaching as appropriate and together assessing progress toward goals. When managers and employees have open communication and employees feel fairly and effectively managed, the kind of appraisal they receive should rarely come as a surprise to them.

Giving PA feedback can be a stressful task for both managers and subordinates. The purposes of PA conflict to some degree. Providing growth and development requires understanding and support; however, the manager must be impersonal and be able to make tough decisions. Employees want to know how they are doing, but typically they are uncomfortable about getting feedback. Finally, the organization's need to make HR decisions conflicts with the individual employee's need to maintain a positive image.[49] These conflicts often make a PA interview difficult; therefore, managers should conduct such interviews thoughtfully.

There is no one "best" way to do a PA interview. In general, appraisal feedback works best when it is *specific* and *constructive*—related to clear goals or behaviors and clearly intended to help the employee rather than simply criticize. Managers have an interest not just in rating performance but in raising it, and effective appraisals take that into account. In addition, the appraisal is likely to be more meaningful and satisfying when the manager gives the employee an opportunity to discuss his or her performance and respond to the appraisal.

One of the most difficult interviews takes place with an employee who is performing poorly. Here is a useful PA interview format to use when an employee is performing below acceptable standards:

1. Summarize the employee's specific performance. Describe the performance in behavioral or outcome terms, such as sales or absenteeism. Don't say the employee has a poor attitude; rather, explain which employee behaviors indicate a poor attitude.
2. Describe the expectations and standards, and be specific.
3. Determine the causes for the low performance; get the employee's input.
4. Discuss solutions to the problem, and have the employee play a major role in the process.

Percentage of HR professionals assigning grade

A   B   C   D   E

Bottom Line

Effective feedback raises employee performance.

What kind of feedback is most likely to be effective?

5. Agree to a solution. As a supervisor, you have input into the solution. Raise issues and questions, but also provide support.
6. Agree to a timetable for improvement.
7. Document the meeting.

"Outstanding leaders go out of their way to boost the self-esteem of their personnel. If people believe in themselves, it's amazing what they can accomplish."
—Sam Walton

Follow-up meetings may be needed. Here are some guidelines for giving feedback to an average employee:

1. Summarize the employee's performance, and be specific.
2. Explain why the employee's work is important to the organization.
3. Thank the employee for doing the job.
4. Raise any relevant issues, such as areas for improvement.
5. Express confidence in the employee's future good performance.

Designing Reward Systems

LO 6

Another major set of HRM activities involves reward systems. Most of this section will be devoted to monetary rewards such as pay and fringe benefits. (We discuss other motivational tools in Chapter 13.) Although traditionally pay has been the primary monetary reward considered, in recent years benefits have received increased attention. Benefits currently make up a far greater percentage of the total payroll than they did in past decades.[50] The typical employer today pays about 30 percent of payroll costs in benefits. Throughout most of the past two decades, benefits costs have risen faster than wages and salaries, fueled by the rapidly rising cost of medical care. Accordingly, employers are attempting to reduce benefits costs, even as their value to employees is rising. Benefits are also receiving more management attention because of their increased complexity. Many new types of benefits are now available, and tax laws affect myriad fringe benefits, such as health insurance and pension plans.

Bottom Line

Organizations today seek new ways to reduce benefits costs. *What benefits have you received from an employer? Did you ever consider the cost of those benefits?*

The typical employer today pays about 30 percent of payroll costs in benefits.

Pay Decisions

Reward systems can serve the strategic purposes of attracting, motivating, and retaining people. The wages paid to employees are based on a complex set of forces. Beyond the body of laws governing compensation, a number of basic decisions must be made in choosing the appropriate pay plan. Figure 10.6 illustrates some of the factors that influence the wage mix.

FIGURE 10.6
Factors Affecting the Wage Mix

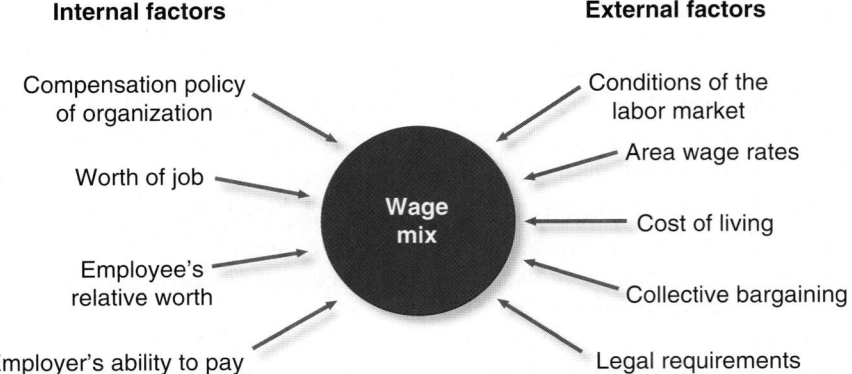

SOURCE: From G. Bohlander, S. Snell, and A. Sherman, *Managing Human Resources,* 12th ed. Copyright © 2001. South-Western, a part of Cengage Learning, Inc. Reproduced by permission. www.cengage.com/permissions

Three types of decisions are crucial for designing an effective pay plan: pay level, pay structure, and individual pay.

Pay level refers to the choice of whether to be a high-, average-, or low-paying company. Compensation is a major cost for any organization, so low wages can be justified on a short-term financial basis. But being the high-wage employer—the highest-paying company in the region—ensures that the company will attract many applicants. Being a wage leader may be important during times of low unemployment or intense competition.

The *pay structure* decision is the choice of how to price different jobs within the organization. Jobs that are similar in worth usually are grouped together into job families. A pay grade, with a floor and a ceiling, is established for each job family. Figure 10.7 illustrates a hypothetical pay structure.

Finally, *individual pay decisions* concern different pay rates for jobs of similar worth within the same family. Differences in pay within job families are decided in two ways. First, some jobs are occupied by individuals with more seniority than others. Second, some people may be better performers who are therefore deserving of a higher level of pay. Setting an individual's pay lower than that of coworkers—like choosing an overall low pay level—may become more difficult for employers to sustain in the future, as more employees use online resources such as Salary.com and PayScale.com to check whether their pay is above or below the average amount for similar job titles.[51]

Unlike many other types of decisions in organizations, decisions about pay, especially at the individual level, often are kept confidential. Is that practice advantageous for organizations? Surprisingly, there is little evidence about this practice even though it affects almost every private sector employee.[52] Some possible ways the organization may benefit from keeping pay decisions secret are by avoiding conflicts, protecting individuals' privacy, and reducing the likelihood that employees will leave to seek better pay if they are earning less than the average for their position. However, if

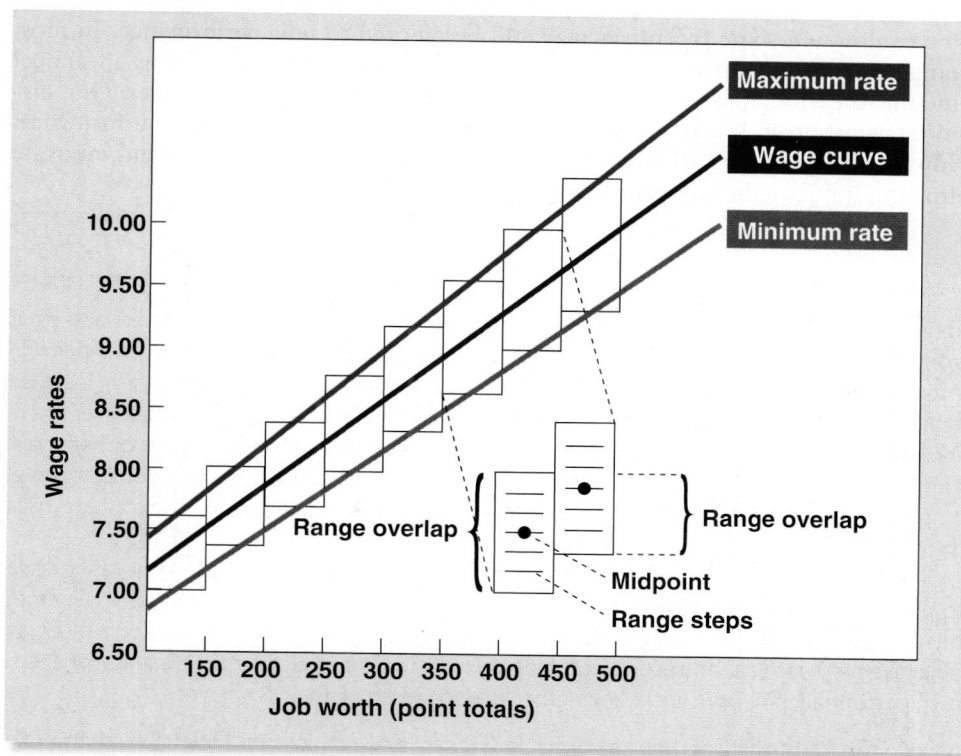

FIGURE 10.7
Pay Structure

decisions about pay are kept secret, employees may worry that decisions are unfair and may be less motivated because the link between performance and pay is unclear. Also, in an economic sense, labor markets are less efficient when information is unavailable, which can reduce organizations' ability to get the best workers at the optimum rate of pay. Given these possible pros and cons of pay secrecy, do you think this practice is wise? Is it ethical? And what about you—do you want to know how much your coworkers earn?

Incentive Systems and Variable Pay

Bottom Line

Incentives can help raise all aspects of organization performance.

Think about the activities of a store employee. What could a Walmart employee do to earn a bonus for meeting quarterly profit goals?

Various incentive systems have been devised to encourage and motivate employees to be more productive.[53] (See Chapter 13 for more discussion of rewarding performance.) *Individual incentive plans* are the most common type of incentive plan. An individual incentive system consists of an objective standard against which a worker's performance is compared. Pay is determined by the employee's performance. Individual incentive plans are used frequently in sales jobs—for example, a salesperson will receive extra compensation for exceeding a sales target. Another widely used individual incentive tool is management bonuses. If effectively designed, individual incentive plans can be highly motivating. Some companies, including Walmart, are even beginning to apply them for nonmanagers. Walmart hopes that using bonuses to reward hourly employees for meeting sales, profit, and inventory targets at their stores each quarter will build employees' job satisfaction and reduce turnover.[54]

Several types of group incentive plans, in which pay is based on group performance, are increasingly used today. The idea behind these plans is to give employees a sense of shared participation and even ownership in the performance of the firm. *Gainsharing plans* concentrate on rewarding employees for increasing productivity or saving money in areas under their direct control.[55] For example, if the usual waste allowance in a production line has been 5 percent and the company wants production employees to try to reduce that number, the company may offer to split any savings gained with the employees.

Profit-sharing plans are usually implemented in the division or organization as a whole, although some incentives may still be tailored to unit performance. In most companies, the profit-sharing plan is based on a formula for allocating an annual amount to each employee if the company exceeds a specified profit target. One disadvantage of profit-sharing plans is that they do not reward individual performance. However, they do give all employees a stake in the company's success and motivate efforts to improve the company's profitability.

IN PRACTICE

Sprint's CEO, Dan Hesse, wants all his employees to be clear about what matters and what they should focus on. He defined a three-pronged strategy for the wireless provider: (1) improve the customer experience; (2) strengthen the brand; and (3) generate cash, increase profits. The HR department works with managers to ensure that everyone's objectives are in line with this strategy because part of each employee's pay is tied to meeting his or her goals. The size of this annual bonus rises with experience and level in the company. For entry-level employees, the bonus is 5 percent of their total pay; for senior executives, that share rises to 50 percent or more.

To make the incentive pay fair, managers no longer have a subjective 5-point rating scale to measure whether employees are eligible. Rather, each employee is scored as having met or not met each of three objectives linked to the strategy. Employees who don't meet an objective are supposed to receive coaching on how to do better next time—and managers' own performance reviews include whether they coached all their employees.[56]

- Why do you think bonuses are larger for higher-level employees? How does that relate to the incentive this kind of pay is intended to provide?

When objective performance measures are not available but the company still wants to base pay on performance, it uses a *merit pay system*. Individuals' pay raises and bonuses are based on the merit rating they receive from their boss. In Rochester, Minnesota, the school superintendent's bonus is an example of merit pay. The school board rates the superintendent's performance in several predetermined areas, such as promoting teamwork between the board and school district staff and supporting the board in developing a strategic plan. In a recent year, the superintendent received an average score of 3 on a four-point scale, so the board awarded him three-quarters of the maximum bonus.[57]

Executive Pay and Stock Options

In recent years the issues of executive pay and stock options, particularly for CEOs, have become major sources of controversy. One reason is that the gap between the pay of top executives and the average pay of employees has widened considerably. In the 1980s CEOs made less than 40 times the average worker's pay. By the next decade, CEOs were earning 140 times more, and the multiple has now reached 500 times the average worker's pay. This gap is considerably wider in the United States than it is abroad. For example, the average CEO of a large British company earns roughly 130 times that of a U.K. worker, and the average top executive in Australia earns about 50 times more than the average Australian worker. In Japan, where the details of executive pay are less public, executive pay has risen relatively slowly, and companies avoid huge income gaps between the top and bottom of the organization, out of concern for employee morale and teamwork.[58]

Besides the difference between executive and average-worker pay, the sheer size and growth of CEO compensation have also contributed to criticism by shareholders and the general public. Top-earning CEOs today can make tens of millions of dollars a year—sometimes even at companies that have performed poorly and even, recently, at companies that received government help during the financial crisis. Still, it's important to keep in mind that the huge awards that make headlines are not necessarily typical. In a recent year, CEOs of companies in the Standard & Poor's stock index earned on average $4.5 million, but the median was $2.5 million because a few executives with far higher earnings pushed the average higher. Also, if we consider only the biggest companies, those in the Standard & Poor's 500, CEO pay averaged $9 million because CEOs of the biggest companies tend to earn more than most CEOs.[59]

Even with these considerations, $9 million or even $2.5 million is a lot of money to earn in one year, and the amount of compensation paid to top executives is growing. While salaries and bonuses have risen at a moderate pace, the fastest-growing part of executive compensation comes from stock grants and *stock options*. Such options give the holder the right to purchase shares of stock at a specified price. For example, if the company's stock price is $8 a share, the company may award a manager the right to purchase a specific number of shares of company stock at that price. If the price of the stock rises to, say, $10 a share after a specified holding period—usually three years or more—the manager can *exercise* the option. He or she can purchase the shares from the company at $8 per share, sell the shares on the stock market at $10, and keep the difference. (Of course, if the stock price never rises above $8, the options will be worthless.) For many top managers, large option grants became a major source of additional compensation. Adding to the scrutiny over this practice is the striking number of situations in which options were dated just before the company's stock price rose, increasing their value—and the suspicion that at least some of these options were backdated to unethically make them more valuable, rather than give executives the incentive to improve the company's performance in the stock market.[60]

Companies issue options to managers to align their interests with those of the company's owners, the shareholders. The assumption is that managers will become even more focused on making the company successful, leading to a rise in its stock price. Assuming that the executives continue to own their stock year after year, the amount of their wealth that is tied to the company's performance—and their incentive to work hard for the company—should continually increase.[61] However, many critics have suggested that excessive use of options encouraged executives to focus on short-term results to drive up the price of their stock, at the expense of their firm's long-run competitiveness. Others suggested that lucrative options motivated questionable or even unethical behavior, as we mentioned in Chapter 2. More recently, a plunging stock market highlighted another problem with stock options: many options became essentially worthless, so they failed to reward employees.[62] While it makes business sense to give employees an incentive to contribute to their company's value, few if any employees could have prevented a widespread global economic downturn. In the future, employees may be wary about accepting stock options in lieu of less risky forms of pay.

Traditionally, companies incurred no expense when they issued stock options. This was another reason options were considered an attractive incentive tool and were sometimes even issued to nonmanagers. However, because of corporate scandals and to curb excessive use of options, the rules were changed in 2004 so that options have to be treated as an expense by companies that issue them. This means that compensation committees have to focus more on whether options motivate executives to focus on what is important for the company's future.

Employee Benefits

Like pay systems, employee benefit plans are subject to regulation. Employee benefits are divided into those required by law and those optional for an employer.

The three basic required benefits are workers' compensation, Social Security, and unemployment insurance. *Workers' compensation* provides financial support to employees suffering a work-related injury or illness. *Social Security*, as established in the Social Security Act of 1935, provides financial support to retirees; in subsequent amendments, the act was expanded to cover disabled employees. The funds come from payments made by employers, employees, and self-employed workers. *Unemployment insurance* provides financial support to employees who are laid off for reasons they cannot control. Companies that have terminated fewer employees pay less into the unemployment insurance fund; thus organizations have an incentive to keep terminations at a minimum.

A large number of benefits are not required to be employer-provided. The most common are pension plans and medical and hospital insurance. Both of these are undergoing significant change. For decades, most Americans under the retirement age were covered by health insurance plans provided by their employers. But as the cost of providing this benefit has soared far faster than other compensation costs, employers started dropping it or providing very limited policies. In 2010 the federal government responded to concern about the rising number of uninsured people and the high cost of care by passing the Affordable Care Act. Among its many provisions, the law requires that, starting in 2014, employers (except small businesses) must either provide their employees with health insurance or else pay a fee to offset the cost of government subsidies for individuals buying their own insurance. As the deadline approaches, organizations have begun considering whether to continue offering health insurance benefits.

Employee benefits include those required by law, such as workers' compensation, Social Security, and unemployment insurance, and those decided by the employer. Retirement plans and paid vacation time are examples of employer-provided, nonrequired benefits.

In one survey, where respondents were invited to compare the costs of insurance versus fees, about 30 percent of managers said they expected to discontinue health insurance benefits. However, most surveys by economists and public policy analysts have predicted a much smaller shift, based on the assumption that employers will consider other factors beyond a cost comparison of fees and insurance. A key reason for expecting continuation of this benefit is that employees place a high value on health insurance, so employers view it as a necessary means of attracting and retaining employees—and also of enabling them to stay healthy and productive.[64]

At the same time, retirement benefits have been shifting away from guaranteed pension payments. While a promised monthly payout used to be the norm, almost no company offers this approach to new employees today.[65] Instead, in many companies, the employer, and perhaps the employee, may contribute to an individual retirement account or 401(k) plan, which is invested.

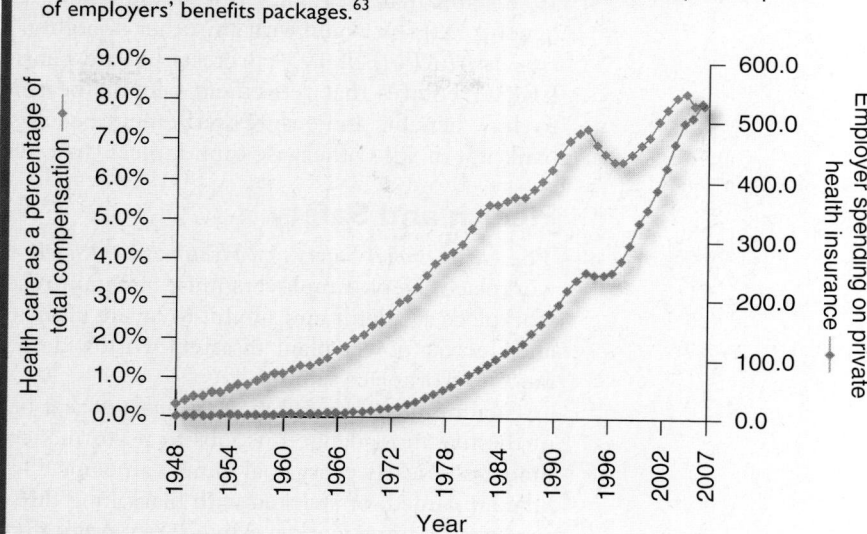

Rapidly rising medical costs have made health care coverage an expensive part of employers' benefits packages.[63]

When the employee retires, he or she gets the total amount that has accumulated in the account.

Because of the wide variety of possible benefits and the considerable differences in employee preferences and needs, companies often use **cafeteria** or **flexible benefit programs**. In this type of program, employees are given credits that they "spend" on benefits they desire. Then employees use their credits toward individualized packages of benefits—medical and dental insurance, dependent care, life insurance, and so on.

Legal Issues in Compensation and Benefits

Several laws affect employee compensation and benefits. We have already mentioned the FLSA, which in addition to distinguishing between exempt and nonexempt employees also sets minimum wage, maximum hour, and child labor provisions.[66] The *Equal Pay Act (EPA)* of 1963, now enforced by the EEOC, prohibits unequal pay for men and women who perform equal work. Equal work means jobs that require equal skill, effort, and responsibility and are performed under similar working conditions. The law does permit exceptions in which the difference in pay is due to a seniority system, a merit system, an incentive system based on quantity or quality of production, or any other factor other than sex, such as market demand. Although equal pay for equal work may sound like common sense, many employers have fallen victim to this law by rationalizing that men, traditionally the "breadwinners," deserve more pay than women or by giving equal jobs different titles (senior assistant versus office manager) as the sole basis for pay differences.

One controversy concerns male and female pay differences within the same company. **Comparable worth** doctrine implies that women who perform *different* jobs of *equal* worth as those performed by men should be paid the same wage.[67] In contrast to the equal-pay-for-equal-work notion, comparable worth suggests that the jobs need *not* be the same to require the same pay. For example, nurses (predominantly female) were found to be paid considerably less than skilled craftworkers (predominantly male), even though the two jobs were found to be of equal value or worth.[68] Under the Equal Pay Act, this would not constitute pay discrimination because the jobs are very different. But under the comparable worth concept, these findings would indicate discrimination because the jobs are of equal worth. To date, no federal law requires comparable worth, and the Supreme Court has made no decisive rulings about it. However, some states, including Iowa, Minnesota, and Washington have comparable worth laws for public sector employees.

cafeteria benefit program

An employee benefit program in which employees choose from a menu of options to create a benefit package tailored to their needs.

flexible benefit programs

Benefit programs in which employees are given credits to spend on benefits that fit their unique needs.

comparable worth

Principle of equal pay for different jobs of equal worth.

Some laws influence mostly benefit practices. The *Pregnancy Discrimination Act* of 1978 states that pregnancy is a disability and qualifies a woman to receive the same benefits that she would with any other disability. The *Employee Retirement Income Security Act (ERISA)* of 1974 protects private pension programs from mismanagement. ERISA requires that retirement benefits be paid to those who vest or earn a right to draw benefits and ensures retirement benefits for employees whose companies go bankrupt or who otherwise cannot meet their pension obligations.

Health and Safety

The *Occupational Safety and Health Act (OSHA)* of 1970 requires employers to pursue workplace safety. Employers must maintain records of injuries and deaths caused by workplace accidents and submit to onsite inspections. Large-scale industrial accidents and nuclear power plant disasters worldwide have focused attention on the importance of workplace safety.

Coal mining is one of many industries that benefit from safety laws. Mining is one of the five most dangerous jobs to perform, according to the U.S. Bureau of Labor Statistics. Nearly every coal miner can name a friend or family member who has been killed, maimed, or stricken with black lung disease. "You die quick or you die slow," reports one mine worker. Mine safety tragically returned to American consciousness in April 2010, when a coal mine explosion at the Massey Energy Company's Upper Big Branch Mine killed 29 workers. An independent investigation found that the accident could have been prevented by standard mine safety practices that evidently had been disregarded by management and missed by regulators.[69] However, according to the Mine Safety and Health Administration, mines have become safer. In the 1960s, hundreds of coal miners died in mine accidents every year; beginning in the mid-1980s, that number fell below 100 per year. During the past decade, even in the year of the Massey disaster, the number of annual fatalities was less than 50.[70]

Another area of concern is the safety of young workers, who may lack the confidence to speak up if they see health or safety problems. A recent study of teenage workers found that many were exposed to hazards and used equipment that should have been off-limits to teens under federal regulations. For example, almost half of teenaged grocery store employees said they had performed prohibited tasks such as using box crushers and dough mixers.[71]

Labor Relations

LO 7

labor relations

The system of relations between workers and management.

Labor relations is the system of relations between workers and management. Labor unions recruit members, collect dues, and ensure that employees are treated fairly with respect to wages, working conditions, and other issues. When workers organize for the purpose of negotiating with management to improve their wages, hours, or working conditions, two processes are involved: unionization and collective bargaining. These processes have evolved since the 1930s in the United States to provide important employee rights.[72]

Labor Laws

Try to imagine what life would be like with unemployment at 25 percent. Pretty grim, you would say. Legislators in 1935 felt that way too. Therefore, organized labor received its Magna Carta with the passage of the National Labor Relations Act.

The *National Labor Relations Act* (also called the *Wagner Act* after its legislative sponsor) ushered in an era of rapid unionization by (1) declaring labor organizations legal, (2) establishing five unfair employer labor practices, and (3) creating the National Labor

Relations Board (NLRB). Prior to the act, employers could fire workers who favored unions, and federal troops were often provided to put down strikes. Today the NLRB conducts unionization elections, hears complaints of unfair labor practices, and issues injunctions against offending employers. The Wagner Act greatly assisted the growth of unions by enabling workers to use the law and the courts to organize and collectively bargain for better wages, hours, and working conditions. Many of the improvements all of us take for granted in the workplace, including minimum wages, health benefits, maternity leave, the 35-hour workweek, and worker protections in general were largely the result of collective bargaining over many years by unions.

Since 2000, unions have aggressively tried to organize workers at Walmart, the world's largest employer with over 2 million employees. So far, the company remains union-free except in China. For a manager, what would be the pros and cons of a union?

Public policy began on the side of organized labor in 1935, but over the next 25 years, the pendulum swung toward the side of management. The *Labor-Management Relations Act*, or *Taft-Hartley Act* (1947), protected employers' free speech rights, defined unfair labor practices by unions, and permitted workers to decertify (reject) a union as their representative.

Finally, the *Labor-Management Reporting and Disclosure Act*, or *Landrum-Griffin Act* (1959), swung the public policy pendulum midway between organized labor and management. By declaring a bill of rights for union members, establishing control over union dues increases, and imposing reporting requirements for unions, Landrum-Griffin was designed to curb abuses by union leadership and rid unions of corruption.

Unionization

How do workers join unions? Through a union organizer or local union representative, workers learn what benefits they may receive by joining.[73] The union representative distributes authorization cards that permit workers to indicate whether they want an election to be held to certify the union to represent them. The National Labor Relations Board will conduct a certification election if at least 30 percent of the employees sign authorization cards. Management has several choices at this stage: to recognize the union without an election, to consent to an election, or to contest the number of cards signed and resist an election.

If an election is warranted, an NLRB representative will conduct the election by secret ballot. A simple majority of those voting determines the winner. Thus apathetic workers who do not show up to vote in effect support the union. If the union wins the election, it is certified as the bargaining unit representative.

During the campaign preceding the election, management and the union each try to persuade the workers how to vote. Most workers, though, are somewhat resistant to campaign efforts, having made up their minds well before the NLRB appears on the scene. If the union wins the election, management and the union are legally required to bargain in good faith to obtain a collective bargaining agreement or contract.

Why do workers vote for a union? The four factors that play a significant role are presented in Figure 10.8.[74] First, economic factors are important, especially for workers in low-paying jobs; unions attempt to raise the average wage rate for their members. Second, job dissatisfaction encourages workers to seek out a union. Poor supervisory practices, favoritism, lack of communication, and perceived unfair or arbitrary discipline and discharge are specific triggers of job dissatisfaction. Third,

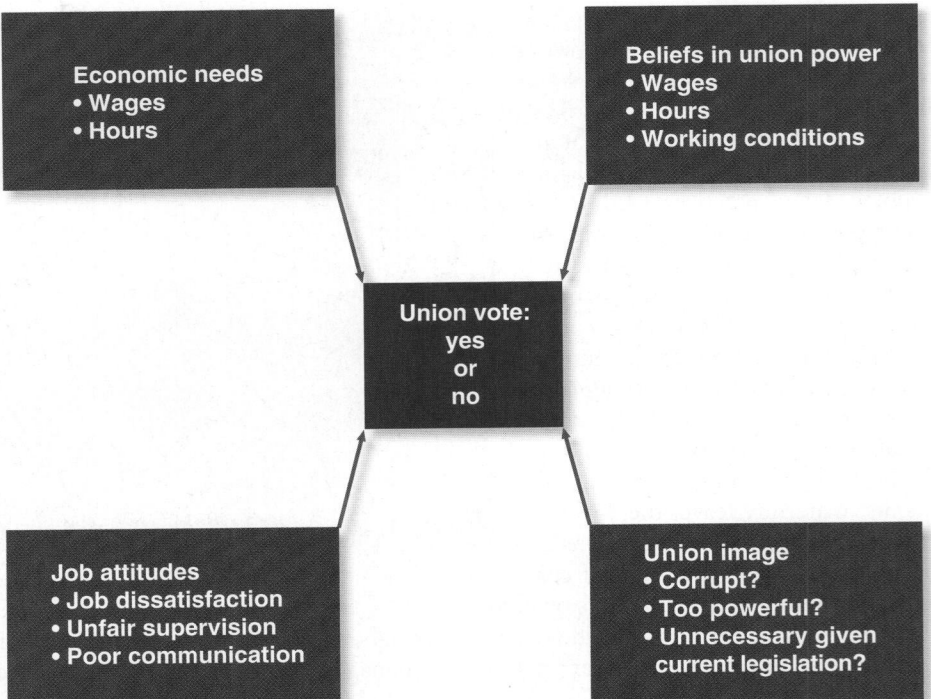

FIGURE 10.8
Determinants of Union Voting Behavior

the belief that the union can obtain desired benefits can generate a pro-union vote. Finally, the image of the union can determine whether a dissatisfied worker will seek out the union. Headline stories of union corruption and dishonesty can discourage workers from unionization.

Collective Bargaining

In the United States, management and unions engage in a periodic ritual (typically every three years) of negotiating an agreement over wages, benefits, hours, and working conditions. Two types of disputes can arise during this process. First, before an agreement is reached, the workers may go on strike to compel agreement on their terms. Such an action is known as an *economic strike* and is permitted by law. However, today strikes are less likely to be used as a bargaining tool, although they sometimes occur as a last resort. Strikers are not paid if they are on strike, and few workers want to undertake this hardship unnecessarily. In addition, managers may legally hire replacement workers during a strike, offsetting some of the strike's effect. Finally, workers are as aware as managers of the tougher competition companies face today, and if treated fairly, they will usually share management's interest in coming to an agreement.

Once an agreement is signed, management and the union sometimes disagree over *interpretation* of the agreement. Usually they settle their disputes through arbitration. **Arbitration** is the use of a neutral third party, typically jointly selected, to resolve the dispute. U.S. companies use arbitration while an agreement is in effect to avoid *wildcat strikes* (in which workers walk off the job in violation of the contract) or unplanned work stoppages.

What does a collective bargaining agreement contain? In a **union shop,** a union security clause specifies that workers must join the union after a set period of time. **Right-to-work** states, through restrictive legislation, do not permit union shops; that is, workers have the right to work without being forced to join a union. The southern United States has many right-to-work states. The wage component of the contract spells out rates of pay, including premium pay for overtime and paid holidays.

arbitration

The use of a neutral third party to resolve a labor dispute.

union shop

An organization with a union and a union security clause specifying that workers must join the union after a set period of time.

right-to-work

Legislation that allows employees to work without having to join a union.

Individual rights usually are specified in terms of the use of seniority to determine pay increases, job bidding, and the order of layoffs.

A feature of any contract is the grievance procedure. Through the grievance procedure, unions perform a vital service for their membership by giving workers a voice in what goes on during contract negotiations and administration.[75] In about 50 percent of discharge cases that go to arbitration, the arbitrator overturns management's decision and reinstates the worker.[76] Unions have a legal duty of fair representation, which means they must represent all workers in the bargaining unit and ensure that workers' rights are protected.

What Does the Future Hold?

In recent years union membership has declined to about 12 percent of the U.S. labor force—down from a peak of more than 33 percent at the end of World War II. Increased automation eliminated many of the types of manufacturing jobs that used to be union strongholds. Employees in today's white-collar office jobs are less interested in joining unions and are also more difficult to organize. Tough global competition has made managers much less willing to give in to union demands, and as a result, the benefits of unionization are less clear to many workers—particularly young, skilled workers who no longer expect to stay with one company all their lives. Some people applaud unions' apparent decline. Others hope for an eventual reemergence. Unions may play a different role in the future, one that is less adversarial and more cooperative with management. Unions are adapting to changing workforce demographics; they are paying more attention to women, older workers, government employees, and people who work at home. Elimination of inefficient work rules, the introduction of profit sharing, and a guarantee of no layoffs were seen as big steps toward a fundamentally different, cooperative long-term relationship.

> In recent years union membership has declined to about 12 percent of the U.S. labor force.

What seems clear is that when companies recognize that their success depends on the talents and energies of employees, the interests of unions and managers may begin to converge. Rather than one side exploiting the other, unions and managers can find common ground in developing, valuing, and involving employees. Particularly in knowledge-based companies, the balance of power is shifting toward employees. Whether or not employees belong to a union, they, not companies, own their own human capital. And these employees are free, within limits, to leave the organization, taking their human capital with them. This leaves organizations in a particularly vulnerable position if they manage poorly. To establish a strong competitive capability, organizations are searching for ways to obtain, retain, and engage their most valuable resources: human resources. "Management Connection: Onward" explores why and how this is a critical issue for Google today. The processes and practices outlined in this chapter form the foundation for effective people management. In the next chapter, we discuss one particularly important people-related issue: managing a diverse workforce.

Manager's Brief   Progress Report   **Onward**

Management Connection

GOOGLE GEARS UP FOR MORE LABOR MARKET COMPETITION

Google's recruiting and selection practices have contributed to its mystique as an exciting place to work, helping it meet its goals for hiring the best talent in the computer industry. But that human resource strategy has been shaken by the appeal of up-and-coming firms in the high-tech sector. Google now risks becoming the established brand. Remember from the beginning of the chapter that young professionals picked Google as the ideal employer? Well, they were picking names from a list of 150 companies. They also could add names to the list, and the top write-in was another high-tech company, Facebook.

Professionals with high-tech expertise still love Google, but many are drawn to opportunities at newly hot enterprises such as Facebook, Twitter, LinkedIn, and Groupon. So even as Google is trying to add thousands of new employees to its ranks, it has to keep its current employees from leaving. That isn't easy: in a recent count, about 200 Facebook employees—10 percent of Facebook's workforce—were former Google workers.

One way to keep employees from leaving is to make sure they feel well compensated. Google has increased its budget for compensation, even though this means profits are growing more slowly than sales. Google considers this a necessary investment; it can't expand into new areas of the fast-moving high-tech industry unless it has the necessary talent to develop ideas. Also, start-ups are in a position to hand out stock before they go public; this compensation is very lucrative when a start-up succeeds and the stock price soars. A Google job feels like the safe bet, not the hot new opportunity.

But it's not just about the money. One reason tech workers leave for a newly hot company is that they want to be part of the excitement of building something new in a small business environment. Former Google employees have told reporters that they doubt a 20,000-plus-employee company can ever be as nimble as the start-ups many of them love. Some complain about too much bureaucracy. Growth changes a company. Google's founders originally held weekly meetings where engineers presented their projects to the leaders. As the company grew, the list of presenters grew so long that the founders lost interest and set up technical reviews for a limited group.

If Google can't (or won't) be small again, it is trying to use its strengths to be worker-friendly in its own way. One notable effort is Project Oxygen, which uses Google's expertise in data search and analysis to improve how employees are managed. Project Oxygen gathered data from managers' performance reviews, employee surveys, and nominations for best manager awards. By analyzing the words used and ratings given, it identified the kinds of management associated with superior team performance and employee satisfaction. After analyzing more than 100 variables, Project Oxygen created a list of management behaviors related to success in leading teams and retaining employees. Training programs incorporated lessons in how to improve on each behavior, and feedback on the behaviors was included in coaching sessions and performance appraisals.

To students of management, the eight behaviors, listed here in order of importance, would come as little surprise: (1) coach effectively; (2) empower team members; (3) express interest in team members; (4) be results-oriented; (5) communicate effectively—including as a listener; (6) support employees' career development; (7) establish a clear vision and strategy; and (8) use key technical skills to advise the team. As obvious as these might sound, the data helped managers at Google think about their role in a new way. In a culture that valued technical know-how, Google's leadership tended to assume that a manager's technical knowledge had to be at least as deep as that of the team members, so they could look to the manager as an expert. The data showed Google's managers that technical skill was indeed important, but it had the least impact on team performance and employee satisfaction. The data also showed what kinds of skills would make the most difference for a manager looking to improve: coaching, delegating, and communicating.

Once Google had data, standards, and training programs for teaching skills, it could begin helping managers improve and measuring the impact of these efforts. Before long, the company saw a statistically significant improvement in the effectiveness of three-quarters of its worst-performing managers. For example, the employees who worked for a manager they considered to be pushy, arrogant, and overly political were restless and wanted to work for someone else. The manager had been denied a promotion on the grounds that he was difficult to work with. With the new data on leadership, Google was able to give him individual coaching aimed at improving in the key areas. Six months later, employee surveys showed an improvement, and after a year, he was doing much better (and earned a promotion). Google was able to quickly track the improvement of managers such as this one because the company conducts performance reviews four times a years rather than waiting for annual reviews.[77]

- Evaluate the effectiveness of Google's approach to performance appraisal. Do you think it will help the company retain good employees? Why or why not?
- How could Google evaluate its reward systems to help it attract and keep employees?

KEY TERMS

SUMMARY OF LEARNING OBJECTIVES

Now that you have studied Chapter 10, you should be able to:

LO 1 Discuss how companies use human resources management to gain competitive advantage.

To succeed, companies must align their human resources to their strategies. Effective planning is necessary to make certain that the right number and type of employees are available to implement a company's strategic plan. It is clear that hiring the most competent people is a very involved process. Companies that compete on cost, quality, service, and so on also should use their staffing, training, appraisal, and reward systems to elicit and reinforce the kinds of behaviors that underlie their strategies.

LO 2 Give reasons why companies recruit both internally and externally for new hires.

Some companies prefer to recruit internally to make certain that employees are familiar with organizational policies and values. In other instances, companies prefer to recruit externally, such as through employee referrals, job boards, newspaper advertising, and campus visits, to find individuals with new ideas and fresh perspectives. External recruiting is also necessary to fill positions when the organization is growing or needs skills that do not exist among its current employees.

LO 3 Identify various methods for selecting new employees.

There are myriad selection techniques from which to choose. Interviews and reference checks are the most common. Personality tests and cognitive ability tests measure an individual's aptitude and potential to do well on the job. Other selection techniques include assessment centers and integrity tests. Background and reference checks verify that the information supplied by employees is accurate. Regardless of the approach used, any test should be able to demonstrate reliability (consistency across time and different interview situations) and validity (accuracy in predicting job performance). In addition, selection methods must comply with equal opportunity laws, which are intended to ensure that companies do not discriminate in any employment practices.

LO 4 Evaluate the importance of spending on training and development.

People cannot depend on a set of skills for all of their working lives. In today's changing, competitive world, old skills quickly become obsolete, and new ones become essential for success. Refreshing or updating an individual's skills requires a great deal of continuous training, designed with measurable goals and methods that will achieve those goals. Companies understand that gaining a competitive edge in quality of service depends on having the most talented, flexible workers in the industry.

LO 5 Explain alternatives for who appraises an employee's performance.

Many companies are using multiple sources of appraisal because different people see different sides of an employee's performance. Typically, a superior is expected to evaluate an employee, but peers and team members are often well positioned to see aspects of performance that a superior misses. Even an employee's subordinates are being asked more often today to give their input to get yet another perspective on the evaluation. Particularly in companies concerned about quality, internal and external customers also are surveyed. Finally, employees should evaluate their own performance, if only to get them thinking about their own performance, as well as to engage them in the appraisal process.

LO 6 Describe the fundamental aspects of a reward system.

Reward systems include pay and benefits. Pay systems have three basic components: pay level, pay structure, and individual pay determination. To achieve an advantage over competitors, executives may want to pay a generally higher wage to their company's employees, but this decision must be weighed against the need to control costs (pay level decisions often are tied to strategic concerns such as these). To achieve internal equity (paying people what they are worth relative to their peers within the company), managers must look at the pay structure, making certain that pay differentials are based on knowledge, effort, responsibility, working conditions, seniority, and so on. Individual pay determination is often based on merit or the different contributions of individuals. In these cases, it is important to make certain that men and women receive equal pay for equal work, and managers may wish to base pay decisions on the idea of comparable worth (equal pay for an equal contribution). Also, the Occupational Safety and Health Act requires that employees have a safe and healthful work environment.

| LO | 7 | **Summarize how unions and labor laws influence human resources management.** |

Labor relations involve the interactions between workers and management. One mechanism by which this relationship is conducted is unions. Unions seek to present a collective voice for workers, to make their needs and wishes known to management. Unions negotiate agreements with management regarding a range of issues such as wages, hours, working conditions, job security, and health care. One important tool that unions can use is the grievance procedure established through collective bargaining. This mechanism gives employees a way to seek redress for wrongful action on the part of management. In this way, unions make certain that the rights of all employees are protected. Labor laws seek to protect the rights of both employees and managers so that their relationship can be productive and agreeable.

DISCUSSION QUESTIONS

1. How will changes in the labor force affect HRM practices for the next decade?

2. Describe the major regulations governing HRM practices.

3. Define job analysis. Why is job analysis relevant to each of the six key HRM activities discussed in the chapter (i.e., planning, staffing, training, performance appraisal, reward systems, labor relations)?

4. What are the various methods for recruiting employees? Why are some better than others? In what sense are they better?

5. What is a "test"? Give some examples of tests used by employers.

6. What purpose does performance appraisal serve? Why are there so many different methods of appraisal?

7. What are some key ideas to remember when conducting a performance appraisal?

8. How would you define an effective reward system? What role do benefits serve in a reward system?

9. Why do workers join unions? What implications would this have for an organization that wishes to remain nonunion?

10. Discuss the advantages and disadvantages of collective bargaining for the employer and the employee.

EXPERIENTIAL EXERCISES

10.1   THE "LEGAL" INTERVIEW

OBJECTIVES

1. To introduce you to the complexities of employment law.

2. To identify interview practices that might lead to discrimination in employment.

INSTRUCTIONS

1. Working alone, review the text material on interviewing and discrimination in employment.

2. In small groups, complete the "Legal" Interview Worksheet.

3. After the class reconvenes, group spokespersons present group findings.

"Legal" Interview Worksheet

The employment interview is one of the most critical steps in the employment selection process. It also may be an occasion for discriminating against individual employment candidates.

The following represents questions that interviewers often ask job applicants. Identify the legality of each question by circling L (legal) or I (illegal) and briefly explain your decision.

Interview Question	Legality	Explanation
1. Could you provide us with a photo for our files?	L I	_____
2. Have you ever used another name (previous married name or alias)?	L I	_____
3. What was your maiden name?	L I	_____
4. What was your wife's maiden name?	L I	_____
5. What was your mother's maiden name?	L I	_____
6. What is your current address?	L I	_____
7. What was your previous address?	L I	_____
8. What is your social security number?	L I	_____
9. Where was your place of birth?	L I	_____
10. Where were your parents born?	L I	_____
11. What is your national origin?	L I	_____
12. Are you a naturalized citizen?	L I	_____
13. What languages do you speak?	L I	_____
14. What is your religious/church affiliation?	L I	_____
15. What is your racial classification?	L I	_____
16. How many dependents do you have?	L I	_____
17. What are the ages of your dependent children?	L I	_____
18. What is your marital status?	L I	_____
19. How old are you?	L I	_____
20. Do you have proof of your age (birth certificate or baptismal record)?	L I	_____
21. Whom do we notify in case of an emergency?	L I	_____
22. What are your height and weight?	L I	_____
23. Have you ever been arrested?	L I	_____
24. Do you own your own car?	L I	_____
25. Do you own your own house?	L I	_____
26. Do you have any charge accounts?	L I	_____
27. Have you ever had your salary garnished?	L I	_____
28. To what organizations do you belong?	L I	_____
29. Are you available to work on Saturdays and Sundays?	L I	_____
30. Do you have any form of disability?	L I	_____

10.2   THE PAY RAISE

OBJECTIVES

1. To further your understanding of salary administration.
2. To examine the many facets of performance criteria, performance criteria weighting, performance evaluation, and rewards.

INSTRUCTIONS

1. Working in small groups, complete the Pay Raise Worksheet.
2. After the class reconvenes, group spokespersons present group findings.

Pay Raise Worksheet

April Knepper is the new supervisor of an assembly team. It is time for her to make pay raise allocations for her subordinates. She has been budgeted $30,000 to allocate among her seven subordinates as pay raises. There have been some ugly grievances in other work teams over past allocations, so Knepper has been advised to base the allocations on objective criteria that can be quantified, weighted, and computed in numerical terms. After she makes her allocations, Knepper must be prepared to justify her decisions. All of the evaluative criteria available to Knepper are summarized as follows:

Employee	Seniority	Output Rating *	Absent Rate	Supervisory Ratings			
				Skills	Initiative	Attitude	Personal
David Bruce	15 yrs.	0.58	0.5%	Good	Poor	Poor	Nearing retirement. Wife just passed away. Having adjustment problems.
Eric Cattalini	12 yrs.	0.86	2.0	Excellent	Good	Excellent	Going to night school to finish his BA degree.
Chua Li	7 yrs.	0.80	3.5	Good	Excellent	Excellent	Legally deaf.
Marilee Miller	1 yr.	0.50	10.0	Poor	Poor	Poor	Single parent with three children.
Victor Munoz	3 yrs.	0.62	2.5	Poor	Average	Good	Has six dependents. Speaks little English.
Derek Thompson	11 yrs.	0.64	8.0	Excellent	Average	Average	Married to rich wife. Personal problems.
Sarah Vickers	8 yrs.	0.76	7.0	Good	Poor	Poor	Women's activist. Wants to create a union.

*Output rating determined by production rate less errors and quality problems.

CONCLUDING CASE

INVINCIBILITY SYSTEMS

The 17,000 employees of Invincibility Systems design and make aerospace and defense equipment such as rockets, spacecraft propulsion systems, and missile propulsion systems. Along with cutting-edge engineering, the company stands out for its cutting-edge human resource management. Invincibility has hired quantitative experts to analyze HR data with the same care it uses to analyze rocket trajectories.

A few years ago, the company hired a statistician and an HR planner to join a team that would collect and analyze data, looking for factors that would predict human resource needs. The team started by looking for ways to improve recruiting. They collected data on the various sources of candidates that the company was using and the candidates actually selected. Then they used a statistical method called regression analysis to identify which sources of candidates generated the most hires—as well as the sources that generated hires who went on to perform well. Using the results of the analysis, Invincibility made its recruiting effort more efficient. By focusing on the most productive sources of top employees, it saves time and money that formerly had gone toward recruiting through channels that were less fruitful.

Next the HR team turned its efforts toward workforce planning. For each department of Invincibility, the team collects data describing the workforce—for example, job categories, years with the company, and labor force projections. It runs regression analysis to predict the likelihood that employees will leave the company in the coming year. The results, coupled with sales forecasts, enable the company to predict how many new employees will need to be hired in each department.

Other companies do this kind of planning, but the extent of the analysis at Invincibility is unusual. For one thing, the analysis is conducted on the level of individual employees. Thus it shows not only that turnover may rise or fall, but also which employees are most likely to leave. That level of analysis is important to Invincibility because unlike organizations where many people perform the same type of work and can step in when someone leaves, employees at Invincibility typically fill highly specialized, highly skilled roles. If an engineer with years of experience in developing high-caliber ammunition suddenly departs, there may be no one else on the team with that person's knowledge and skill set.

Another unusual quality of Invincibility's HR planning is the variety of factors that the planners consider when they run their regression analyses. For example, the company has run regressions to determine whether turnover is related to changes in employee benefits and even the month of the year. If the analysis shows that a factor has been significant in the past, the planners take it into account in their forecasts. In one situation, the planners found that retirements in a department rose after the company announced that it would be phasing out health insurance benefits for retirees. More experienced workers left before the phase-out took effect. When the company prepared to phase out similar benefits in another division, the planners knew they would need to step up recruiting efforts there in preparation for an uptick in retirements.

Some of the data Invincibility uses for planning are unsuitable for other kinds of HR decisions. For example, the company has found that employees' ages and marital status are relevant for predicting whether they are likely to leave the company. Turnover rates are higher among unmarried employees and recently hired employees (who tend to be younger). Thus the company plans greater recruiting efforts in departments where it has higher levels of young and unmarried employees. It also may consider stepping up its efforts to mentor and train employees in these departments. However, it does not make employment decisions such as hiring and promotion based on these factors.

QUESTIONS

1. Besides the factors identified, what other factors should Invincibility Systems take into account in its HR planning?

2. What legal concerns does the data analysis at Invincibility raise? How should the company address those issues?

3. Besides its use for HR planning and recruiting, how might Invincibility's data analysis be applied to improving the company's training programs?

11 Managing the Diverse Workforce

LEARNING OBJECTIVES

After studying Chapter 11, you will be able to:

LO 1 Describe how changes in the U.S. workforce make diversity a critical organizational and managerial issue. p. 396

LO 2 Distinguish between affirmative action and managing diversity. p. 408

LO 3 Explain how diversity, if well managed, can give organizations a competitive edge. p. 408

LO 4 Identify challenges associated with managing a diverse workforce. p. 410

LO 5 Define monolithic, pluralistic, and multicultural organizations. p. 413

LO 6 List steps managers and their organizations can take to cultivate diversity. p. 416

Manager's Brief   Progress Report   Onward

Management Connection

PEPSICO'S DIVERSE WORKFORCE

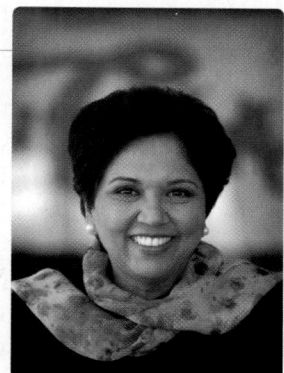

Most of us know PepsiCo as consumers; its popular brands include Pepsi, Mountain Dew, Gatorade, Tropicana, Aquafina, Quaker, Aunt Jemima, Cheetos, Doritos, and many more. By selling these and other brands around the world, PepsiCo, based in Purchase, New York, generates revenues of more than $60 billion a year.

Operating on such a grand scale requires hundreds of thousands of employees. It almost goes without saying that this many people will include quite a variety of backgrounds, personalities, and cultures. Let's look at a few outstanding examples of the members of PepsiCo's diverse workforce.

An obvious place to start is at the top of the organization. PepsiCo's chairman and chief executive officer is Indra Nooyi, a member of the baby boom generation born in India. She studied chemistry, physics, and math for her undergraduate degree in India and later earned a master's degree in management from Yale. After working as a business consultant, she joined PepsiCo, where she worked on global strategy. After leading several significant acquisitions, she moved up to the CEO's job—the first woman to hold that position.

Nooyi is one of only a small percentage of women leading a major U.S. corporation, but she is hardly the only female executive at PepsiCo, where 30 percent of the executives are women. Among these is Maura Abeln Smith, PepsiCo's general counsel (the company's chief lawyer). Smith majored in economics as an undergraduate at Vassar College and earned her law degree from the University of Miami. She worked first at a Miami law firm and then for General Electric. According to Smith, she had a huge advantage: in college she won a prestigious Rhodes scholarship, which opened doors for her, including a full scholarship to law school and a good first job

afterward. She sees difficulty facing many women who want to pursue careers in law but sees far more opportunity for them than existed when she started her own career in the 1970s.

An innovator in the marketing arena is Frank Cooper III. Today's companies are trying to build brand loyalty by finding ways to get consumers actively engaged with their brands online—for example, by entering contests, voting for new flavors, and using brand-related applications in online games. Cooper is spearheading this aspect of marketing as PepsiCo's senior vice president and chief consumer engagement officer. Because online tools make it relatively easy and affordable to target specific segments, Cooper's department first identifies important consumer groups and then builds software applications that appeal to what motivates that group. For example, Cooper led PepsiCo's creation of the We Inspire online community to appeal to African American women, who typically are energized by real stories of people meeting everyday challenges. Besides keeping up with technology applications, this black American business leader has educational credentials that include a law degree from Harvard.

In Chicago, miles away from the corporate headquarters, is PepsiCo's Global Nutrition Group, which aims to improve the healthfulness of PepsiCo's food and beverages, primarily by reducing the salt and sugar they contain. That group's chief executive and chief scientist is Mehmood Khan, a physician who has consulted on diabetes. Khan was born in Pakistan, grew up in England, and studied nutrition and agriculture in the United States. Before accepting his position with PepsiCo, Khan worked as a doctor and medical professor in Minneapolis and was in charge of research and development at Takeda Pharmaceuticals North America, which makes Actos, a drug for treating diabetes. Khan acknowledges that healthful food from a snack company might sound like an oxymoron, but he aims to give people better choices than they have now. And like the company he works for, he thinks globally: what a middle-aged American man will crave and choose is different from a delicious and nutritious treat for a teenage girl in India. PepsiCo wants to serve both of them, and its diverse workforce offers a tremendous array of talent for doing just that.[1]

These descriptions of PepsiCo employees touch on a variety of the characteristics that define people—their age and sex, their places of birth and work, their interests and educational backgrounds, their life experiences and accomplishments. As you read this chapter, think about how bringing together a diverse group and leading it toward a common purpose can be challenging but also a source of opportunity.

In Chapter 10, we described the laws that require equal opportunity and fair treatment in the workplace. In this chapter, we discuss why a proactive approach to developing and managing a diverse workforce has become not only a legal or moral obligation, but a fundamental business requirement as well. Executives at PepsiCo point to their company's exemplary record on diversity as a key element in its success. Managers who lack the ability to work with and effectively manage men and women of different colors, cultures, ages, abilities, and backgrounds will be at a significant disadvantage in their careers. And organizations that do not take the issue of managing diversity seriously will leave their organizations not only open to legal challenge but also far less able to compete effectively, at home and abroad.

In the United States, as we shall see, the number of racial and ethnic minorities is increasing at a far faster rate than the growth in the white, nonminority population, and women make up a sizable share of the workforce. American workers, customers, and markets are already highly diverse and becoming even more so every day. In addition, as we discussed in Chapter 6, businesses are increasingly global. Managers need to be much more aware of, and sensitive to, cultural differences to succeed in a world economy. We have also discussed throughout this book how vital creativity and innovation have become for organization success.

These qualities are fostered in an atmosphere where different perspectives and bright people from all walks of life are celebrated. Few societies have access to the range of talents available in the United States, with its immigrant tradition and racially and ethnically diverse population. Yet getting people from widely divergent backgrounds to work together effectively is not easy. For this reason, managing diversity is one of America's biggest challenges—and opportunities.

Managing diversity involves, first, such basic activities as recruiting, training, promoting, and utilizing to full advantage individuals with different backgrounds, beliefs, capabilities, and cultures. But it means more than just hiring women and minorities and making sure they are treated equally and encouraged to succeed. It also means understanding and deeply valuing employee differences to build a more effective and profitable organization.

This chapter examines the meaning of diversity and the management skills and organizational processes involved in managing the diverse workforce effectively. We also explore the social and demographic changes and economic and employment shifts that are creating this changing U.S. workforce.

> Few societies have access to the range of talents available in the United States, with its immigrant tradition and racially and ethnically diverse population.

managing diversity

Managing a culturally diverse workforce by recognizing the characteristics common to specific groups of employees while dealing with such employees as individuals and supporting, nurturing, and utilizing their differences to the organization's advantage.

Diversity: A Brief History

Managing diversity is not a new management issue. From the late 1800s to the early 1900s, most of the groups that immigrated to the United States were from Italy, Poland, Ireland, and Russia. Members of those groups were considered outsiders because most did not speak English and had different customs and work styles. They struggled, often violently, to gain acceptance in industries such as steel, coal, automobile manufacturing, insurance, and finance. In the 1800s, it was considered poor business practice for white Protestant–dominated insurance companies to hire Irish, Italians, Catholics, or Jews. As late as the 1940s, and in some cases even later than that, colleges routinely discriminated against immigrants, Catholics, and Jews, establishing strict quotas that limited their number, if any were admitted at all. The employment prospects of these groups were severely diminished by this kind of discrimination, and it wasn't until the 1960s that the struggle for acceptance by the various white ethnic and religious groups had on the whole succeeded.

Women's struggle for acceptance in the workplace was in some ways even more difficult. When the women's rights movement was launched in Seneca Falls in 1848, most occupations were off-limits to women, and colleges and professional schools were totally closed to them. Women could not vote and lost all property rights once they were married. In the first part of the 20th century, when women began to be accepted into professional schools, they were subject to severe quotas. There was also a widespread, persistent assumption that certain jobs were done only by men, and other jobs only by women. Even into the 1970s, less than 40 years ago, classified ad sections in newspapers listed different jobs by sex, with sections headed "Help Wanted—Males" and "Help Wanted—Females." Women who wanted a bank loan needed a male cosigner, and married women were not issued credit cards in their own name.[2] Only when the Civil Rights Act of 1964 (see Chapter 10) and other legislation began to be enforced was this kind of sex discrimination gradually eliminated. As we shall see, women are still underrepresented at the most senior levels of corporate life, and major disparities in other areas, like pay, still exist. But most jobs today once considered the exclusive province of men—including frontline military units as well as the executive suite—are now open to and occupied by increasing numbers of women.

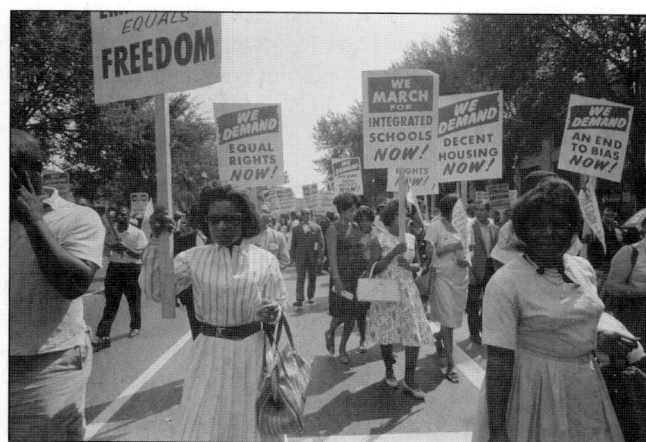

Many of the rights all of us take for granted today—equal opportunity, fair treatment in housing, the illegality of religious, racial, and sex discrimination—received their greatest impetus from the civil rights movement.

The most difficult and wrenching struggle for equality involved America's non-white minorities. Rigid racial segregation remained a fact of American life for 100 years after the end of the Civil War. Black voting rights, particularly in the South, were often viciously suppressed, and racial discrimination in education, employment, and housing throughout the United States was a harsh daily reality. Years of difficult, courageous protest and struggle gradually began to eat away at both legal and social barriers to equality. Organizations like the NAACP, formed by a group of blacks and whites, began to use America's court system and the Constitution to bring equality to African Americans and other people of color. The unanimous *Brown v. Board of Education* Supreme Court decision in 1954 declared segregation unconstitutional, setting the stage for other legislation we discussed in the last chapter, including the Civil Rights Act of 1964. The consequences of America's bitter racial legacy are still with us; the struggle for equality is far from complete. But many of the rights all of us take for granted today—equal opportunity, fair treatment in housing, the illegality of religious, racial, and sex discrimination—received their greatest impetus from the civil rights movement.

Today nearly half of the U.S. workforce consists of women, 14 percent of U.S. workers identify themselves as Hispanic or Latino, and 11 percent are black. Two-thirds of all global migration is into the United States. One-third of all businesses in the United States are owned by women, employing about 20 percent of America's workers.[3]

> The traditional American image of diversity has been one of assimilation.

The traditional American image of diversity has been one of assimilation. The United States was considered the "melting pot" of the world, a country in which ethnic and racial differences were blended into an American purée. In real life, many ethnic and most racial groups retained their identities, but they did not express them at work. Employees often abandoned most of their ethnic and cultural distinctions while at work to keep their jobs and get ahead. Many Europeans came to the United States, Americanized their names, perfected their English, and tried to enter the mainstream as quickly as possible.

Today's immigrants are willing to be part of an integrated team, but they no longer are willing to sacrifice their cultural identities to get ahead. Nor will they have to do so. Companies are recognizing that they should be more accommodating of differences, and that doing so pays off in business. Managers are also realizing that their customers have become increasingly diverse and that retaining a diversified workforce can provide a significant competitive advantage in the marketplace.

Diversity Today

LO 1   Today *diversity* refers to far more than skin color and gender. It is a broad term used to refer to all kinds of differences, as summarized in Figure 11.1. These differences include religious affiliation, age, disability status, military experience, sexual orientation, economic class, educational level, and lifestyle in addition to gender, race, ethnicity, and nationality.

Although members of different groups (white males, people born during the Depression, homosexuals, Iraq war veterans, Hispanics, Asians, women, blacks, etc.) share within their groups many common values, attitudes, and perceptions, much diversity also exists within each of these categories. Every group is made up of individuals who

FIGURE 11.1
Components of a
Diversified Workforce

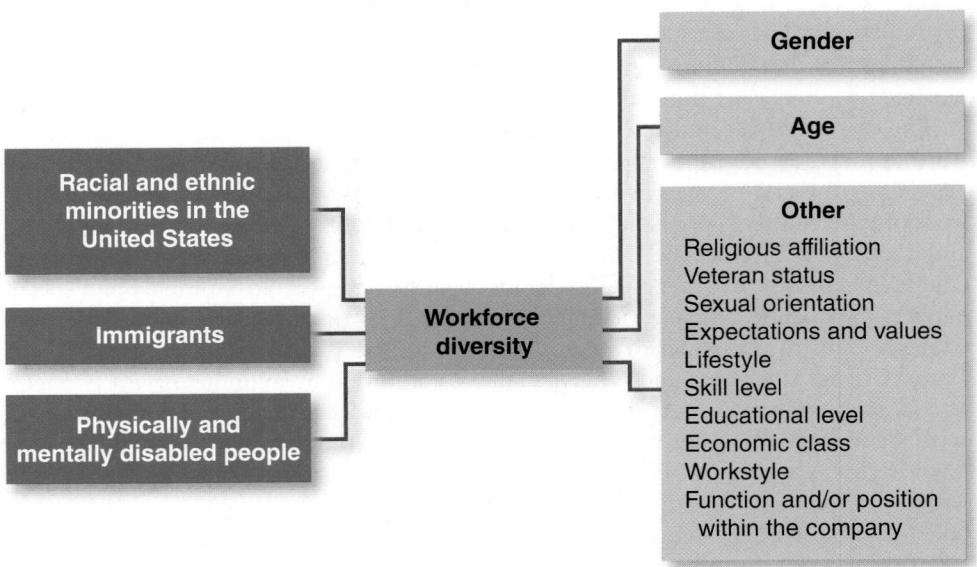

are unique in personality, education, and life experiences. There may be more differences among, say, three Asians from Thailand, Hong Kong, and Korea than among a white, an African American, and an Asian all born in Chicago. And not all white males share the same personal or professional goals and values or behave alike.

Thus managing diversity may seem a contradiction within itself. It means being acutely aware of characteristics *common* to a group of employees, while also managing these employees as *individuals*. Managing diversity means not just tolerating or accommodating all sorts of differences, but supporting, nurturing, and utilizing these differences to the organization's advantage. Borders Books, for example, tries to match up the demographics of its workforce with the demographics of the communities in which its stores operate. Top managers at the company say that sales are better as a result. U.S. businesses will not have a choice of whether to have a diverse workforce; if they want to survive, they must learn to manage a diverse workforce sooner or better than their competitors do.

> Managing diversity means not just tolerating differences, but utilizing differences to the organization's advantage.

As Figure 11.2 shows, a sizable number of HR executives say their companies need to or plan to expand their diversity training programs. Although many companies initially instituted diversity programs to prevent discrimination, more are beginning to see such programs as a crucial way to expand their customer bases both domestically and worldwide. In fact, two out of three companies said they had broadened their diversity programs because of increasing globalization, according to a survey of 1,780 HR and training executives by the Boston-based consulting firm Novations/J. Howard and Associates. A separate survey by Korn/Ferry International showed that approximately 85 percent of European recruiters, 88 percent of recruiters in Asia, and 95 percent of recruiters in Latin America either "strongly agreed" or "somewhat agreed" that being at least bilingual is critical to succeed in today's business environment.

The Size of the Workforce

During most of its history, the United States experienced a surplus of workers. But that is now expected to change. Lower birthrates in the United States and other developed countries are resulting in a smaller labor force. An even more substantial slowdown in the pace of growth of the labor force is projected for the decade ending in 2016 as the baby boom generation retires.[4]

Employers are likely to outsource some work to factories and firms in developing nations where birthrates are high and the labor supply is more plentiful.

> "Human diversity makes tolerance more than a virtue; it makes it a requirement for survival."
>
> —Rene Dubos

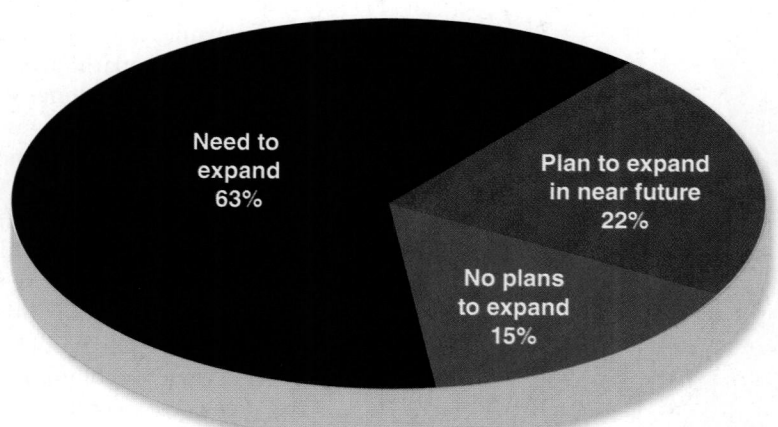

FIGURE 11.2

The Expansion of Diversity Programs in U.S. Companies

SOURCE: From Gail Johnson, "Time to Broaden Diversity," *Training*, September 2004. Copyright 2004. The Lakewood Media Group.

But they will have to compete for the best candidates from a relatively smaller and more diverse U.S. labor pool. Employers will need to know who these new workers are—and must be prepared to meet their needs.

The Workers of the Future

Until recently, white American-born males dominated the U.S. workforce. Businesses catered to their needs. However, while this group still constitutes the largest percentage of workers—about 80 percent of U.S. workers are white, and more than half of them are male—its share of the labor force is declining. Although the number of white male workers is expected to continue growing, the number of women and the numbers of Asian American, black, and Hispanic workers are expected to grow faster.[5] This significant change in the workforce parallels trends in the overall U.S. population. Recently the Census Bureau announced that, for the first time, about one in three residents of the United States is a racial or ethnic minority—a unique milestone in the nation's history. The largest and fastest-growing minority group is Hispanics, closely followed by African Americans. In several states—California, Hawaii, New Mexico, and Texas—and the District of Columbia, these minority groups plus Asians, Native Americans, and Pacific Islanders combine to make a population that is "majority minority."[6] These population trends affect not only the nature of the workforce but also the varied customers and markets managers must attract.

Gender Issues   One of the most important developments in the U.S. labor market has been the growing number of women working outside the home. Social changes during the 1960s and 1970s coupled with financial necessity caused women to enter the workforce and redefine their roles. Consider this:

> Women make up about 47 percent of the workforce.
> The overall labor force participation rate of women rose throughout the 1970s through the 1990s and is now holding steady even as the participation rate of men gradually declines.
> Almost 60 percent of marriages are dual-earner marriages.
> One of every four married women in two-income households earns more than her husband does.[7]

Irene Rosenfeld has broken through the glass ceiling as CEO of Kraft Foods, overseeing the company with revenues of over $30 billion.

For many women, as well as their spouses, balancing work life with family responsibilities and parenting presents an enormous challenge. Although men's roles in our society have been changing, women still adopt the bulk of family responsibilities, including homemaking, child care, and care of elderly parents. Yet some companies may still expect their employees, particularly at the managerial level, to put in long hours and sacrifice their personal lives for the sake of their jobs, organizations, and careers. Not only may these expectations put many women at a disadvantage in the workplace, but they also may cause companies to lose valuable talent. Companies that offer their employees the opportunity to balance work and family commitments are better able to recruit and retain women. These companies are offering family-friendly benefits such as onsite child care, in-home care for elderly family members, and flexible work schedules, and they are taking advantage of newer technologies to permit more work from home. Still, weighing employees' needs for flexibility against the organization's need for productivity entails complex decisions that take into account different job requirements, as well as each employee's contributions and motivation to meet goals under the flexible arrangement. Michele Coleman Mayes, senior vice president and general counsel of Pitney Bowes, agreed to let one attorney leave promptly at five o'clock each evening; the attorney works on her laptop at night as needed to meet her deadlines. But Mayes refused another employee's request to work part-time because the person in that position needed to be available each day to handle requests for other departments. Mayes tells her employees that scheduling decisions "may not always be equal, but I will try to be fair."[8]

The desire for flexible scheduling is often cited as a reason significant pay disparities still exist between men and women. The average full-time working woman earns about 80 percent as much as men in the same job (recall the discussion in Chapter 10 about equal pay and comparable worth). However, the gap has shrunk most years since the 1970s; women's earnings were just 63 percent of men's in 1979. Still, a recent study found that the gap between the earnings of college-educated men and women actually increased after they spent 10 years in the workforce. Some of the difference is explained by women tending to choose lower-paid occupations, work fewer hours, and devote time to bearing and raising children. But even when the researchers controlled for these and other known variables, one-quarter of the pay gap remained unexplained. One of the researchers, Catherine Hill, speculated, "Part of the wage difference . . . is employers' assumptions of what people's choices will be. . . . Employers assume that young women are going to leave the workforce when they have children, and, therefore, don't promote them."[9]

> The average full-time working woman earns about 80 percent as much as men in the same job.

Another concern involving female workers is the low representation of women in top jobs. As women—along with minorities—move up the corporate ladder, they encounter a "glass ceiling." The *glass ceiling* is an invisible barrier that makes it difficult for women and minorities to move beyond a certain level in the corporate hierarchy. For example, just 12 women are chief executives of *Fortune* 500 companies—that's 12 out of 500. Looking at all board members of those companies, 13 percent are white women, and 3 percent are minority women.[10] Still, one positive trend is that women's leadership is beginning to be seen at a broader range of companies. Besides Andrea Jung at the helm of Avon and Irene Rosenfeld at Kraft Foods, the executive ranks now include the likes of Pat Woertz at Archer Daniels Midland and Ursula Burns at Xerox. Table 11.1 lists top women executives and the companies for which they work.

TABLE 11.1   **The A-List: Top Women Executives**

Rank	Name	Company	Title
1	Indra Nooyi	PepsiCo	Chairman and CEO
2	Irene Rosenfield	Kraft Foods	Chairman and CEO
3	Patricia Woertz	Archer Daniels Midland	Chairman, president, and CEO
4	Angela Braly	WellPoint	Chairman, president, and CEO
5	Andrea Jung	Avon Products	Chairman and CEO
6	Oprah Winfrey	Harpo and OWN	Chairman
7	Ellen Kullman	DuPont	Chairman and CEO
8	Ginni Rometty	IBM	Senior vice president, group executive, Sales, Marketing & Strategy
9	Ursula Burns	Xerox	Chairman and CEO

continued

Rank	Name	Company	Title
10	Carol Bartz	Yahoo	President and CEO
11	Safra Catz	Oracle	Copresident
12	Sherilyn McCoy	Johnson & Johnson	Worldwide chairman, Pharmaceuticals Group
13	Melanie Healey	Procter & Gamble	Group president, North America
14	Ann Livermore	Hewlett-Packard	Executive vice president, HP Enterprise Business
15	Anne Sweeney	Walt Disney	Cochair, Disney Media Networks; President, Disney–ABC Television Group
16	Sheryl Sandberg	Facebook	Chief operating officer
17	Carl Meyrowitz	TJX Cos.	President and CEO
18	Judy McGrath	Viacom	Chairman and CEO, MTV Networks
19	Barbara Desoer	Bank of America	President, Home Loans
20	Charlene Begley	General Electric	President and CEO, GE Home and Business Solutions; Senior vice president, GE
21	Abigail Johnson	Fidelity	Vice chairman and director, FMR LLC; President, Fidelity Personal, Workplace, and Institutional Services
22	Susan Ivey	Reynolds American	Chairman, president, and CEO
23	Susan Chambers	Walmart Stores	Executive vice president, Global People Division
24	Sallie Krawcheck	Bank of America	President, Global Wealth and Investment Management
25	Jan Fields	McDonald's	President, McDonald's USA

SOURCE: From "50 Most Powerful Women in Business," from *Fortune* Magazine, October 18, 2010. Copyright 2010 Time Inc. Used under license.

Some companies are helping women break through the glass ceiling. Accenture sponsors monthly networking events for its female employees and offers flexible schedules and part-time arrangements. Such efforts may be behind the results of a survey of managers in which 79 percent of female respondents said they could envision themselves holding a senior management post, compared with only 66 percent feeling that way at the start of their careers.[11] Table 11.2 shows the best companies for women executives according to the National Association of Female Executives.

As women have gained more presence and power in the workforce, some have drawn attention to the problem of **sexual harassment,** which is unwelcome sexual conduct that is a term or condition of employment. Sexual harassment falls into two different categories. The first, *quid pro quo harassment,* occurs when "submission to or

sexual harassment

Conduct of a sexual nature that has negative consequences for employment.

TABLE 11.2
Top 10 Companies for Executive Women

Abbott	KPMG
American Express	Kraft Foods
Bank of America	Marriott International
General Mills	Procter & Gamble
IBM	Prudential Financial

SOURCE: B. Spence, "Top Companies: 2011 NAFE Top Ten," National Association for Female Executives, http://www.nafe.com. Copyright 2011 by National Association for Female Executives. Reproduced with permission of NAFE via Copyright Clearance Center.

CH2M Hill, based in Denver, manages major engineering and construction projects as far afield as London, Abu Dhabi, and the Panama Canal. But one project looked impossible: how to get women into top jobs in a male-dominated industry. CH2M was hiring plenty of talented female engineers, but they never seemed to rise very far.

Determined to find answers, the company investigated and found that although formal policies were equitable, male and female engineers tended to behave in ways that gave the edge to men. Male engineers more actively sought positions involving greater responsibility. Women tended to focus on gaining experience and accomplishing goals, figuring they would eventually be rewarded if they were productive. But they tended to get less helpful coaching because their male managers focused on being polite to them.

To expose and address these style differences, CH2M Hill set up a women's network and began hosting two-day annual meetings at which female managers are encouraged to be assertive in controlling their careers. The meetings include training sessions on negotiation and opportunities to meet with mentors. Eventually the annual meetings were expanded to include men, so the learning can flow both ways.

Along with strengthening the female managers' career strategies, CH2M established a policy that for senior management jobs, any pool of candidates considered for an opening must include at least one woman. Since instituting these changes, the share of women in top jobs at CH2M has grown to 30 percent.[12]

- In breaking its glass ceiling, did CH2M look for a need for change in its female employees' behavior, in its own practices, or both?

rejection of sexual conduct is used as a basis for employment decisions." The second type of harassment, *hostile environment*, occurs when unwelcome sexual conduct "has the purpose or effect of unreasonably interfering with job performance or creating an intimidating, hostile, or offensive working environment." Behaviors that can cause a hostile work environment include persistent or pervasive displays of pornography, lewd or suggestive remarks, or demeaning taunts or jokes. Both categories of harassment violate Title VII of the Civil Rights Act of 1964, regardless of the sex of the harasser and the victim; in a recent year, more than 15 percent of complaints filed with the federal government came from males. If an employee files a complaint of sexual harassment with the Equal Employment Opportunity Commission (EEOC), the commission may investigate and, if it finds evidence for the complaint, may request mediation, seek a settlement, or file a lawsuit with the potential for stiff fines—and negative publicity that may damage the company's ability to recruit the best employees in the future.

Harassment by creation of a hostile work environment is now more typical than quid pro quo harassment. But because it may involve more subjective standards of behavior, it puts an extra burden on managers to maintain an appropriate work environment by ensuring that all employees know what conduct is and is not appropriate and that there are serious consequences for this behavior. In fact, even when managers do not themselves engage in harassment, if they fail to prevent it or to take appropriate action after receiving legitimate complaints about it, they may still be held liable, along with their companies, if a lawsuit is filed. It is also important for managers to know that the "hostile work environment" standard applies to same-sex harassment, as well as to non-gender-related cases, such as a pattern of racial or ethnic slurs. Teenaged workers are a particularly vulnerable population because they are inexperienced, tend to hold lower-status jobs, and often feel hesitant or embarrassed to speak up. The federal EEOC has made this concern a priority and launched a teen-focused page called "Youth at Work" on its website (at http://www.youth.eeoc.gov). The National

TABLE 11.3

Basic Components of an
Effective Sexual Harassment
Policy

1. Develop a comprehensive organizationwide policy on sexual harassment and present it to all current and new employees. Stress that sexual harassment will not be tolerated under any circumstances. Emphasis is best achieved when the policy is publicized and supported by top management.
2. Hold training sessions with supervisors to explain Title VII requirements, their role in providing an environment free of sexual harassment, and proper investigative procedures when charges occur.
3. Establish a formal complaint procedure in which employees can discuss problems without fear of retaliation. The complaint procedure should spell out how charges will be investigated and resolved.
4. Act immediately when employees complain of sexual harassment. Communicate widely that investigations will be conducted objectively and with appreciation for the sensitivity of the issue.
5. When an investigation supports employee charges, discipline the offender at once. For extremely serious offenses, discipline should include penalties up to and including discharge. Discipline should be applied consistently across similar cases and among managers and hourly employees alike.
6. Follow up on all cases to ensure a satisfactory resolution of the problem.

SOURCE: From G. Bohlander and S. Snell, *Managing Human Resources*, 15th ed. Copyright © 2010. South-Western, a part of Cengage Learning, Inc. Reproduced by permission. www.cengage.com/permissions.

Restaurant Association and National Retail Federation also have stepped up efforts to protect teens from harassment.[13]

> A strong commitment to diversity leads to fewer problems with sexual harassment.

One way managers can help their companies prevent harassment from arising, or avoid punitive damages if a lawsuit is filed, is to make sure their organizations have an effective and comprehensive policy on harassment in place. Table 11.3 shows the basic components of such a policy. Companies such as Avon, Corning, and Metro-Goldwyn-Mayer have found that a strong commitment to diversity leads to fewer problems with sexual harassment.[14]

Before moving on, it is important to note that gender issues and the changing nature of work do not apply just to women. In some ways, the changing status of women has given men the opportunity to redefine their roles, expectations, and lifestyles. Some men are deciding that there is more to life than corporate success and are choosing to scale back work hours and commitments to spend time with their families. Worker values are shifting toward personal time, quality of life, self-fulfillment, and family. Workers today, both men and women, are looking to achieve a balance between career and family.

In addition, a growing number of employers are thinking about gender in terms of the issues facing their employees who are gay, lesbian, bisexual, or transgendered (LGBT). These employees may be concerned about work-related issues such as avoiding harassment, obtaining benefits for a same-sex spouse or domestic partner, or simply feeling able to not be secretive about this aspect of who they are. Treatment of LGBT employees is an area of ongoing change, both in societal attitudes and in the law. For example, a few years ago, a person in a same-sex relationship would automatically be assumed to be single, but today some states have laws allowing these people to marry or register as domestic partners and to adopt children together. And the U.S. military has changed policies from banning homosexual service members, to a policy of "don't ask, don't tell" in 1993, to a phased-in repeal of that policy beginning in 2011 that aims at an end of the ban on gay persons serving openly. In situations such as this, where laws, policies, and social norms are in a state of flux, employers must be especially attentive to understand what is required and how employees, customers, and other stakeholders are affected by company policies and practices.

Minorities and Immigrants   In addition to gender issues, the importance and scope of diversity are evident in the growth of racial minorities and immigrants in the workforce. Consider these facts:

> Black, Asian, and Hispanic workers hold more than one of every four jobs in the United States.
> Asian and Hispanic workforces are growing the fastest in the United States, followed by the African American workforce.
> Three in 10 college enrollees are people of color.
> By 2020, most of California's entry-level workers will be Hispanic.
> English has become the second language for much of the population in California, Texas, and Florida.
> Foreign-born workers make up more than 15 percent of the U.S. civilian labor force. About half of these workers are Hispanic, and 22 percent are Asian.
> The younger Americans are, the more likely they are to be persons of color.
> One in 40 people in the United States identifies himself or herself as multiracial, and the number could soar to 1 in 5 by 2050.[15]

These numbers indicate that the term *minority*, as it is used typically, may soon become outdated. Particularly in urban areas where white males do not predominate, managing diversity means more than eliminating discrimination; it means capitalizing on the wide variety of skills available in the labor market. Organizations that do not take full advantage of the skills and capabilities of minorities and immigrants are severely limiting their potential talent pool and their ability to understand and capture minority markets. Those markets are growing rapidly. As the minority share of the population expands, so does their share of purchasing power. And if you sell to businesses, you are likely to deal with some minority-owned companies because the number of businesses started by Asian American, African American, and Hispanic entrepreneurs is growing much faster than the overall growth in new companies in the United States. For example, more than half of the companies that started in California's high-tech Silicon Valley were founded by immigrants, and in a recent year, one-fourth of patent applications in the United States identified an immigrant as the inventor or a co-inventor.[16]

In many urban areas with large Asian, Hispanic, or African American populations, banks have deliberately increased the diversity of their managers and tellers to reflect the population mix in the community and attract additional business. If they did not, customers would readily notice and switch to other banks in the area where they would feel more welcome and comfortable. Such diversity—and collaboration among employees—permits increased customer service, helping banks maintain their competitiveness. For example, tellers approached by new immigrants who do not yet speak English immediately call on their bilingual colleagues for help. The bilingual colleagues are also in a better position to assist the bank customers with special problems, such as income transfers from abroad.

Even so, the evidence shows some troubling disparities in employment and earnings. Unemployment rates are higher for black and Hispanic workers than for whites—twice as high in the case of black men. Earnings of black and Hispanic workers have consistently trailed those of white workers; recent figures put the median earnings for African American employees at 77 percent of median earnings for white workers and the median earnings of Hispanics at just 70 percent. African Americans and Hispanic Americans are also underrepresented in management and professional occupations.[17] This underrepresentation may itself help perpetuate the problem, as it can leave many aspiring young minorities with fewer role models or mentors that are so helpful in an executive career.

The term *minority*, as it is used typically, may soon become outdated.

More than half of the companies that started in California's high-tech Silicon Valley were founded by immigrants.

This disparity may exist even for similar jobs. There is also considerable evidence that discrimination may account for at least some of the disparities in employment and earnings. For example, in one recent study fictitious résumés were used to respond to help-wanted ads in Boston and Chicago newspapers. Each résumé used either African American names like Lakisha and Jamal or white-sounding names like Emily and Greg. The résumés with white-sounding names were 50 percent more likely to get a callback for an interview than the same résumés with African American names. Despite equivalence in credentials, the often unconscious assumptions about different racial groups are very difficult to overcome.[18]

Nevertheless, significant progress has been made. As you can see from the examples in Table 11.4, talented members of minority groups are among the executives running companies and their divisions in a wide variety of industries. And some individuals and groups are highly successful. Average pay and unemployment rates for Asian Americans actually exceed those for white workers.

In addition, virtually every large organization today has policies and programs dedicated to increasing minority representation—including compensation systems that reward managers for increasing the diversity of their operations. Major companies such as FedEx, Xerox, Morgan Stanley Shell, and Sun Microsystems have

TABLE 11.4   Executives of Color: Selected Examples

Name	Company	Title
Jose Maria Alapont	Federal Mogul	CEO
Bruno Almeida	U.S. Media Consulting	CEO and Cofounder
J. Ricky Arriola	Inktel Direct	President and CEO
Ursula M. Burns	Xerox Corporation	Chairman and CEO
Kenneth I. Chenault	American Express	Chairman and CEO
John Echeveste	VPE Public Relations	CEO and Cofounder
Raul J. Fernandez	ObjectVideo	Chairman and CEO
Kenneth C. Frazier	Merck & Co.	CEO
Carlos Ghosn	Renault of France and Nissan of Japan	President and CEO
Tony Hsieh	Zappos	CEO
Tony Jimenez	MicroTech	CEO
Andrea Jung	Avon Products	Chairman and CEO
Shantanu Narayen	Adobe Systems	President and CEO
Rodney O'Neal	Delphi Corporation	President and CEO
Clarence Otis Jr.	Darden Restaurants	President and CEO
Antonio M. Perez	Eastman Kodak Co.	CEO
William Perez	William Wrigley Jr. Co.	CEO
Julian Porras	Omnicam Media Grou	CEO
Ronald A. Williams	Aetna Inc.	Chairman and CEO

SOURCES: DLB Group Worldwide, "DLB Group Worldwide Announces the Top Hispanic CEOs Worldwide," *Hispanic PR Blog*, December 22, 2010, http://www.hispanicprblog.com; "African American CEO's of *Fortune* 500 Companies," *BlackEntrepreneurProfile.com*, http://blackentrepreneurprofile.com, June 21, 2011; and "List of Asian Americans," *Wikipedia*, http://en.wikipedia.org, June 21, 2011.

corporate diversity officers who assist organization managers in their efforts to attract, retain, and promote minority and women executives. Many organizations are also working to ensure a continuing supply of minority candidates by supporting minority internships and MBA programs. Dun and Bradstreet, for example, sponsors summer internship programs for minority MBA students. Lockheed Martin has partnered with the American Management Association's Operation Enterprise to establish two-week paid summer internship programs for high school and college students. These internship programs help students and organizations learn about one another and, ideally, turn into full-time employment opportunities. Table 11.5 shows the top 10 companies for diversity according to DiversityInc.com. For all these companies, developing, hiring, and retaining minority executives is critical for their ability to manage an ever-more-diverse workforce and to serve an increasing number of clients and customers with varied backgrounds.

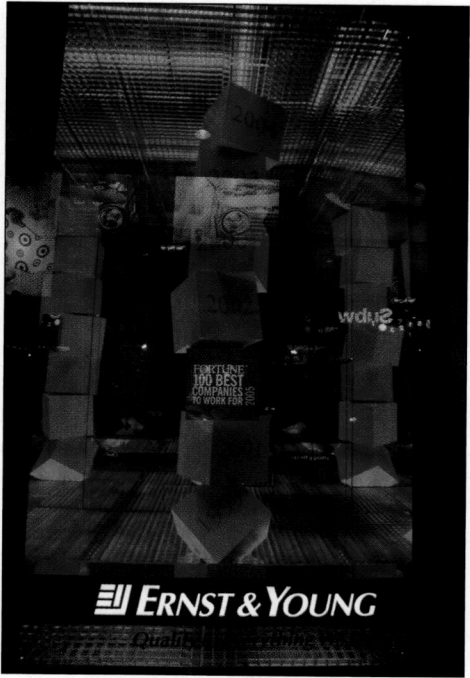

Mentally and Physically Disabled People   The largest unemployed minority population in the United States is people with disabilities. It is composed of people of all ethnic backgrounds, cultures, and ages. The share of the population with a disability is growing as the average worker gets older and heavier.[19] According to U.S. government statistics, people with disabilities represent 10 percent of the working-age civilian population. Many of these people are not in the labor force (meaning they are neither working nor looking for a job), but of the more than 6 million disabled persons who are in the labor force, 14.5 percent were unemployed in 2009. That rate was far above the 9.3 percent unemployment rate for the general population. Persons with a disability are more likely to have jobs if they have higher levels of education, and they are more likely than nondisabled workers to have a part-time job because they can't find full-time work.[20]

According to a recent survey, Ernst & Young has been named as one of the top, most diverse companies based on how it ranked in four key areas—CEO commitment, human capital, corporate and organizational communications, and supplier diversity.

The Americans with Disabilities Act (ADA), mentioned in Chapter 10, defines a disability as a physical or mental impairment that substantially limits one or more major life activities. Examples of such physical or mental impairments include those resulting from conditions such as orthopedic, visual, speech, and hearing impairments; cerebral palsy; epilepsy; multiple sclerosis; HIV infections; cancer; heart disease; diabetes; mental retardation; psychological illness; specific learning disabilities; drug addiction; and alcoholism.[21]

New assistive technologies are making it easier for companies to comply with the ADA and for those with disabilities to be productive on the job. In many cases, state governments will pay for special equipment or other accommodations that workers need. Companies are discovering that making these accommodations can result in unanticipated fringe benefits, too. The National Industries for the Blind (NIB), a Wisconsin company that markets products under the Skilcraft brand name, is a case in point. Seventy-five percent of NIB employees are visually impaired. Because the company's warehouse pickers have trouble reading instructions on paper, NIB installed a voice technology system that conveys instructions to workers through headsets.

1. PricewaterhouseCoopers	6. Johnson & Johnson
2. Ernst & Young	7. Bank of America
3. AT&T	8. Novartis Pharmaceuticals Corp.
4. Kaiser Permanente	9. Procter & Gamble
5. Sodexo	10. Marriott International

TABLE 11.5

Top 10 Companies for Diversity Recruitment and Retention

SOURCE: B. Frankel, "The DiversityInc Top 10 Companies for Recruitment and Retention," *DiversityInc*, March 4, 2011, http://www.diversityinc.com.

An added benefit is that the technology has raised the productivity of the entire operation. Accuracy has improved, and workers—both blind and sighted—are able to pick and ship orders faster using the headsets.

For most businesses, mentally and physically disabled people represent an unexplored but fruitful labor market. Frequently employers have found that disabled employees are more dependable than other employees, miss fewer days of work, and exhibit lower turnover. Tax credits are also available to companies who hire disabled workers. In addition, managers who hire and support employees with disabilities are signaling to other employees and outside stakeholders their strong interest in creating an inclusive organization culture.

Education Levels   When the United States was primarily an industrial economy, many jobs required physical strength, stamina, and skill in a trade, rather than college and professional degrees. In today's service and technology economy, more positions require a college education, and even a graduate or professional degree. Today's prospective employees have responded by applying to college in record numbers. The proportion of the workforce with at least some college education has been growing steadily since the 1970s. The share of workers with a bachelor's degree has more than doubled since 1970. At the same time, the share of workers with less than a high school diploma has tumbled from nearly 4 out of 10 in 1970 to below 1 out of 10 today. People with degrees in science and technology are in especially high demand. Employers often expand their search for scientists and computer professionals overseas, but visa requirements limit that supply. At the other end of the spectrum, in the current labor pool, 28 percent of foreign-born workers have not completed high school.[22]

> The share of workers with a bachelor's degree has more than doubled since 1970.

The Age of the Workforce

The baby boom generation (those born between 1946 and 1964) is aging. Today almost 4 out of 10 workers are age 45 or older, and the median age of America's workforce is rising as the number of older workers swells, while the number of young workers grows only slightly. Industries such as nursing and manufacturing are already facing a tremendous loss of expertise as a result of downsizing and a rapidly aging workforce. Other industries will soon be in similar straits.[23] As a result of these trends, the Bureau of Labor Statistics projects that entry-level workers will be in short supply.

On the plus side, almost 70 percent of workers between the ages of 45 and 74 told researchers with AARP (formerly the American Association of Retired Persons) that they intend to work in retirement. Retirees often return to the workforce at the behest of their employers, who can't afford to lose the knowledge accumulated by longtime employees, their willingness to work nontraditional shifts, and their reliable work habits, which have a positive effect on the entire work group.

> For every young worker entering the workforce, two baby boomers are retiring.[24]

To prevent an exodus of talent, employers need strategies to help retain and attract skilled and knowledgeable older workers. Phased retirement plans that allow older employees to work fewer hours per week is one such strategy. Almost one-third of retiring faculty members at 16 University of North Carolina campuses take advantage of phased retirement, and the concept is catching on in many other public and private organizations.[25] Other strategies include making workplace adaptations to help older workers cope with the physical problems they experience as they age, such as poorer vision, hearing, and mobility. This trend is a significant change from the practice in recent decades, when older workers were given incentives to leave to allow companies to reduce overhead and perhaps hire less expensive replacements. Table 11.6 shows how creative companies are rethinking their retirement policies and solving their skilled labor shortage by finding ways to attract and retain people over 55. These companies save on turnover and training costs and capitalize on the experience of their older employees.

Approaches to More Fully Utilizing Older Employees	Approaches Considered Very or Moderately Effective	Businesses That Have Implemented the Approach
Benefit packages targeted toward older employees	68%	18%
Part-time work arrangements with continuation of benefits	64	30
Educating managers about ways to utilize older employees	60	25
Increased availability of part-time work for older employees (regardless of benefits)	55	36
Skill training for older employees	55	44

TABLE 11.6

Top Five Approaches for More Fully Utilizing Older Employees

SOURCE: From "American Business and Older Employees: A Survey of Findings," Copyright © 2002 AARP.

At the same time, companies need to compete hard for the smaller pool of young talent, being prepared for applicants who know the job market and are ready to demand the working conditions they value and the praise they were raised to expect. Bruce Tulgan, founder of Rainmaker Thinking, which specializes in researching generational differences, says Generation Y—today's young workers—tend to be "high-maintenance" but also "high-performing," having learned to process the flood of information that pours in over the Internet.[26] Many of these workers were raised by highly involved parents who filled their lives with "quality" experiences, so employers are scrambling to design work arrangements that are stimulating, involve teamwork, keep work hours reasonable to allow for outside activities, and provide for plenty of positive feedback. Employers are also updating their recruiting tactics to reach young workers where they are—online. Intermedia, which operates computer centers to host large-scale web and e-mail software for small companies, says the social networking site LinkedIn helps the company reach well-qualified information technology workers. In the government sector, the Central Intelligence Agency and National Security Agency have set up pages on Facebook, where members who register for access can read information about job openings.[27]

IN PRACTICE

Today's companies are learning the value of both young and older workers—and finding new ways to encourage them to collaborate. Pooling the knowledge of experienced workers with the energy and fresh ideas of younger workers can create a powerful workforce. Carolyn Martin of Rainmaker Thinking Inc. encourages her clients to develop mentoring programs so that important company and industry knowledge is passed from older to younger employees. "[Older workers] are walking out the door with a gold mine of experience, product knowledge, and historical perspective, and we're letting them go," she said at a recent economic conference. "Knowledge as power is out. Knowledge shared is in. Everyone, no matter what their age, is a teacher and a learner."

Martin even suggests that employers seek to hire older workers who can teach younger ones. Typically, she says, members of the baby boom generation—who are now beginning to retire—go on to start second careers anyway. "Proactively recruit 50-plus people," she advises. "The older worker is cool. There are not enough Gen-X and -Y to replace them all."[28]

• What do you think younger workers can learn from older ones?

Managing Diversity versus Affirmative Action

LO 2

affirmative action

Special efforts to recruit and hire qualified members of groups that have been discriminated against in the past.

For many organizations, the original impetus to diversify their workforces was social responsibility and legal necessity (recall Chapters 5 and 10). To correct the past exclusion of women and minorities, companies introduced **affirmative action**—special efforts to recruit and hire qualified members of groups that have been discriminated against in the past. The intent is not to prefer these group members to the exclusion of others, but to correct for the long history of discriminatory practices and exclusion. Viewed from this perspective, amending these wrongs is seen as the moral, ethical, and legal approach.

Such efforts, along with legal remedies to end discrimination, have had a powerful impact, transforming our society and organizations in positive ways that would have been unimaginable only a few decades ago. Today the immigrant nature of American society is virtually taken for granted—even seen as a source of pride. And women, African Americans, Hispanics, and other minorities routinely occupy positions that in years past would have been totally closed to them.

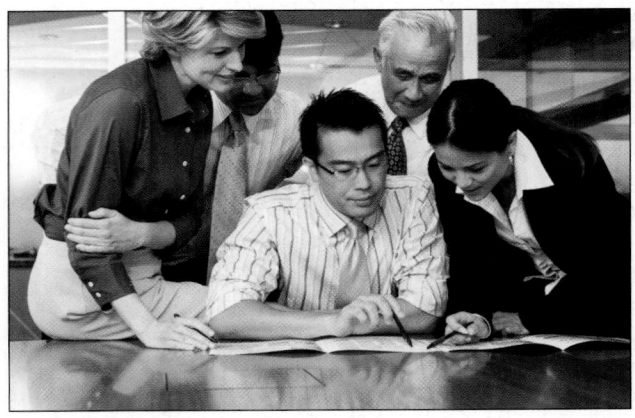

Managing diversity involves organizations making changes to remove obstacles that may keep people from reaching their full potential.

Nevertheless, as we have seen, a legislated approach tends to result in fragmented efforts that have not yet fully achieved the integrative goals of diversity. Employment discrimination still persists, and even after decades of government legislation, equal employment opportunity (EEO) and affirmative action laws have not adequately improved the upward mobility of women and minorities. To move beyond correcting past wrongs to truly inclusive organizations requires a change in organization culture—one in which diversity is seen as contributing directly to the attainment of organization goals.

Seen in this way, affirmative action and diversity are complementary, not the same. In contrast to EEO and affirmative action programs, managing diversity means moving beyond legislated mandates to embrace a proactive business philosophy that sees differences as a positive value. In the end, *all* employees are different. These differences may include the fundamental attributes of race, ethnicity, age, and gender we have been discussing, but they also may include less obvious attributes such as employees' place of origin, their education, or their life experience. All these elements add to the richness of talents and perspectives managers can draw on. Managing diversity in this broader sense involves organizations making changes in their systems, structures, and practices to eliminate barriers that may keep people from reaching their full potential. It means treating people as individuals—

Affirmative action and diversity are complementary, not the same.

equally but not necessarily the *same*—recognizing that each employee has different needs and will need different things to succeed. But it also asks managers to recognize and value the uniqueness of each employee and to see the different ideas and perspectives each brings to the organization as a source of competitive advantage. In short, managing diversity is not just about getting more minorities and women into the organization. It is about creating an environment in which employees from *every* background listen to each other and work better together so that the organization as a whole will become more effective. This emphasis on coming together to benefit the whole has led many companies to now refer to diversity and *inclusion* as their objectives.

Competitive Advantage through Diversity and Inclusion

LO 3

Today many organizations are approaching diversity and inclusion from a more practical, business-oriented perspective. Increasingly, diversity can be a powerful tool for building competitive advantage. Various studies have found links between diversity in an organization's upper ranks and superior financial performance. Some evidence suggests that this correlation may result from investors' preferences for organizations with a policy of inclusion, rather than from superior management of diverse companies. Nevertheless, diversity does not stand in the way of high performance, and it may provide an organizational strength—especially if organizations know how to leverage it.[29]

There are many advantages—and some obvious challenges—to managing a diverse workforce. We discuss some of them in this section.

Ability to Attract and Retain Motivated Employees   For companies facing changing demographics and business needs, diversity makes good sense. Companies with a reputation for providing opportunities for diverse employees will have a competitive advantage in the labor market and will be sought out by the most qualified employees. In addition, when employees believe their differences are not merely tolerated but valued, they may become more loyal, productive, and committed.

Better Perspective on a Differentiated Market   Companies such as Avon, Prudential, Eastman Kodak, and Toys "R" Us are committed to diversity because as the composition of the American workforce changes, so does the customer base of these companies. Just as women and minorities may prefer to work for an employer that values diversity, they may prefer to patronize such organizations.

Many Asian Americans, African Americans, Hispanic Americans, and women have entered the middle class and now control consumer dollars. Similarly, each new generation has its own set of values and experiences, so diversity in ages can help the organization relate to more age groups of customers. A diverse workforce can provide a company with greater knowledge of the preferences and consuming habits of this diversified marketplace. This knowledge can assist companies in designing products and developing marketing campaigns to meet those consumers' needs. In addition, for at least some goods and services, a multicultural sales force may help an organization sell to diverse groups. A diverse workforce also can give a company a competitive edge in a global economy by facilitating understanding of other customs, cultures, and marketplace needs.

Ability to Leverage Creativity and Innovation in Problem Solving   Work team diversity promotes creativity and innovation because people from different backgrounds hold different perspectives on issues. Diverse groups have a broader base of experience from which to approach a problem; when effectively managed, they invent more options and create more solutions than homogeneous groups do. In addition, diverse work groups are freer to deviate from traditional approaches and practices. The presence of diversity also can help minimize "groupthink" (recall Chapter 3).[30]

Many law firms now routinely have diverse legal teams working together on a case. Fresh "out of the box" ideas are often required in complex cases, and a group of lawyers from the same background who all think the same way may not be able to be as innovative as a team that is more diverse. In addition, in jury trials, the impression that a legal team makes on a jury can help or badly hurt the client, and diverse jurors are more likely to be receptive to a visibly diverse team, with different kinds of lawyers participating. The increased importance of legal team diversity has caused some law firms to form alliances with minority firms so they can collaborate on cases.

Enhancement of Organizational Flexibility   A diverse workforce can enhance organizational flexibility because managing diversity successfully requires a corporate culture that tolerates many different styles and approaches. Less restrictive policies and procedures and less standardized operating methods enable organizations to become more flexible and thus better able to respond quickly to environmental

---

Various studies have found links between diversity in an organization's upper ranks and superior financial performance.

Bottom Line
Diversity can help an organization succeed in new markets.
What are some new or diverse markets that Toys "R" Us can serve best with a diverse workforce?

Bottom Line
Diversity can bring new ideas to the organization.
What kinds of innovation are a strength in your generation? In a generation older than yours?

Bottom Line
A diverse workforce can lead to greater responsiveness.
Why might a customer who wants something new get a faster response from a company that tolerates different styles?

changes (recall Chapters 2 and 9). J. P. Morgan, for example, sees valuing diversity as a necessary part of a strategy based on superior talent: "We can only win by creating and encouraging a culture of inclusion, where everyone's opinion counts and all employees have the freedom to deliver their absolute best."[31]

IN PRACTICE

Procter & Gamble considers employee diversity a source of competitive advantage. At a global company, recruiting diversity opens up the largest possible pool of talent and brings in people who understand all customer groups and their needs. Respect for diversity also is a way to ensure the greatest innovation as people feel confident about drawing on their skills and sharing their ideas.

This commitment to diversity is reflected in corporate programs. P&G has established seven "affinity groups" including the African American Leadership Network, Hispanic Leadership Team, and People with Disabilities group. By participating in these voluntary groups, employees can bring up issues of concern, find mentors, and enjoy mutual support. Also, a training program called the Clay Street Project sends employees offsite to practice working effectively on diverse teams.

Commitment to diversity is also reflected in P&G's talented people. The 11-member board of directors is unusually diverse for a big U.S. corporation; it includes five women and a prominent black man, American Express CEO Ken Chenault. P&G's 135,000 employees in 80 countries include Linda Clement-Holmes, the chief diversity officer, who reports directly to the CEO. Clement-Holmes is a 27-year veteran of P&G, a black woman who started in the information technology department. Another successful black woman is Monique Picou, who leads supply operations in the United Kingdom. She started her P&G career in 1989, working in manufacturing and process engineering in Kansas and Louisiana and then holding supply management roles at the Ohio headquarters and in Geneva, Switzerland.[32]

- What strengths does P&G gain from adding these managers into the mix with the white, male, Cincinnati-based managers who dominated the company in the past?

Challenges of Diversity and Inclusion

LO 4

We have discussed the laws guaranteeing equal opportunity and the significant and growing business advantages of diversity and inclusion. Yet every year thousands of lawsuits are filed over issues of discrimination and fair treatment, some involving even the largest and most respected firms.[33] Even when there is no overt discrimination in hiring and pay, managing diversity can be difficult. Often minorities and women who have been hired find themselves in an organization culture or environment that does not give them the opportunity to do their best work. And managers with all the goodwill in the world find it harder than they expected to get people from different backgrounds to work together for a common goal.[34]

To become effective managers of the diverse organization, we first have to identify and overcome a number of challenges. These include unexamined assumptions, lower cohesiveness, communication problems, mistrust and tension, and stereotyping.

Unexamined Assumptions   For most of us, seeing the world from someone else's perspective is difficult because our own assumptions and viewpoints seem so normal and familiar. For example, heterosexuals may not even think about whether to put a picture of their loved ones on their desks; it is a routine, even automatic decision, repeated in a million workplaces across the country. But for gay employees in many companies, displaying such a picture may cause considerable anxiety—if they feel able to consider it at all. Other unexamined assumptions involve the roles of men and women; for example, many people assume that women will shoulder the burden of caring for children, even if it conflicts with the demands of work. In a recent study, researchers sent employers résumés that were identical except that some bore a male name and others a female name, and half implied that the person submitting the résumé was a parent. Employers were less likely to invite the fictional candidate for an interview when the résumé implied the candidate was a parent—but only if the name was female.[35] Because the résumés were otherwise identical, the results suggest that people make assumptions about mothers that do not apply to fathers or to childless women.

In an organization that is oblivious to these different perspectives and does not take an active role in making people from diverse backgrounds feel

> "Among CEOs of *Fortune* 500 companies, 58 percent are six feet or taller. . . . Most of us, in ways we are not entirely aware of, automatically associate leadership with imposing physical stature."
>
> —Malcolm Gladwell

welcome and valued, managers may find it more difficult to develop an enthusiastically shared sense of purpose.

Lower Cohesiveness Diversity can create a lack of cohesiveness. *Cohesiveness* refers to how tightly knit the group is and the degree to which group members perceive, interpret, and act on their environment in similar or mutually agreed-upon ways. Because of their lack of similarity in language, culture, and/or experience, diverse groups typically are less cohesive than homogeneous groups. Often mistrust, miscommunication, stress, and attitudinal differences reduce cohesiveness, which in turn can diminish productivity. This may be one explanation for the results of a study that showed greater turnover among store employees who feel they are greatly outnumbered by coworkers from other racial or ethnic groups.[36] In a diverse group, managers are challenged to take the lead in building cohesiveness by establishing common goals and values. Group cohesiveness will be discussed in greater detail in Chapter 14.

> One way to address problems with low cohesiveness and miscommunication is to provide training in teamwork; another approach is to offer groups where similar kinds of employees can gather and help each other figure out how to navigate the difficulties. The use of these employee resource groups is growing, with the most common targeting women or racial/ethnic groups.[37]

Communication Problems Perhaps the most common negative effect of diversity is communication problems. These difficulties include misunderstandings, inaccuracies, inefficiencies, and slowness. Speed is lost when not all group members are fluent in the same language or when additional time is required to explain things. Sometimes diversity may decrease communication, as when white male managers feel less comfortable giving feedback to women or minorities for fear of how criticism may be received. The result may be employees who do not have a clear idea of what they need to do to improve their performance.

Diversity can also lead to errors and misunderstandings. Group members may assume they interpret things similarly when they in fact do not, or they may disagree because of their

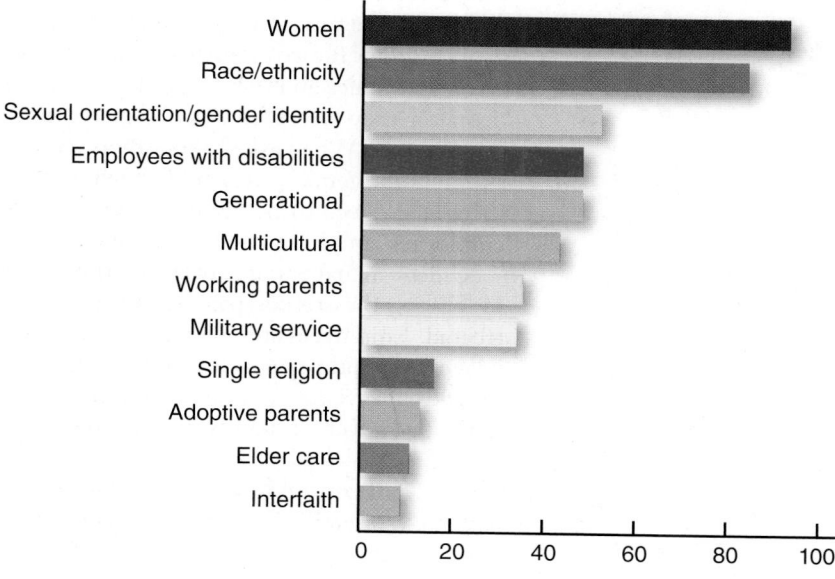
Percentage of organizations with an employee resource group for...

different frames of reference.[38] For example, if managers do not actively encourage and accept the expression of different points of view, some employees may be afraid to speak up at meetings, leaving the manager with a false impression that consensus has been reached. We discuss other problems in communication and how to avoid them in Chapter 15.

Mistrust and Tension   People prefer to associate with others who are like themselves. This is a normal, understandable tendency. But it can often lead to misunderstanding, mistrust, and even fear of those who are different because of a lack of contact and low familiarity. For example, if women and minority group members are routinely excluded, as they sometimes are, from joining white male colleagues at business lunches or after-hour gatherings, they may come to feel isolated from their colleagues. Similarly, tension often develops between people of different ages—for example, what one generation might see as a tasteless tattoo may be a creative example of body art for a member of a different generation. Such misunderstandings can cause stress, tension, and even resentment, making it more difficult to reach agreement on solutions to problems.

Stereotyping   We learn to see the world in a certain way on the basis of our backgrounds and experiences. Our interests, values, and cultures act as filters and distort, block, and select what we see and hear. We see and hear what we expect to see and hear. Group members often inappropriately stereotype their "different" colleagues rather than accurately perceiving and evaluating those individuals' contributions, capabilities, aspirations, and motivations. Such stereotypes are usually negative or condescending. Women may be stereotyped as not dedicated to their careers, older workers as unwilling to learn new skills, minority group members as less educated or capable. But even so-called positive stereotypes can be burdensome. For example, the common stereotype that Asians are good at math may leave unrecognized other attributes that a particular Asian employee might have. Many women and minorities dislike being stereotyped as members of groups that need special help or support, preferring to be treated as individuals.

Stereotypes may cost the organization dearly by stifling employees' ambition so that they don't fully contribute. Research supports the idea that people perform better when they expect that they can. In a study where undergraduate students were purportedly "pretesting" a new graduate admissions test, half the subjects were told that males had greater ability in the test's subject matter. Although all subjects were told they received the same score, the females exposed to the biased message rated their abilities in the subject lower than the males who heard the message, and they set lower goals for their future performance in that area. In another study, playing off the stereotypes that males and Asians excel at math, Asian American women were given a math test after they answered a set of questions either about their Asian identity or about their gender. When asked about their ethnic background, they performed better; when asked about gender, they performed worse.[39] In a corporate setting, managers want their employees to perform to their full ability; stereotypes that dampen individual employees' ambition and performance also detract from the organization's success.

Unless managers are aware of their stereotypes, either their own or those held by others, the stereotypes can directly affect how people in their organizations are treated. Employees stereotyped as unmotivated or emotional will be given less stress-provoking (and perhaps less important) jobs than their coworkers. Those job assignments will create frustrated employees, perhaps resulting in lower commitment, higher turnover, and underused skills.[40]

The Challenge Ahead   For all these reasons, and more, managing diversity is not easy. U.S. organizations are not isolated from the continuing effects of America's racial legacy or the remaining barriers to equal opportunity. Nor are managers immune to the biases, stereotypes, lack of experience, and tensions that make communication,

TABLE 11.7   Beyond Affirmative Action: Key Practices to Leverage Employee Differences

	Key Individual Practices	Key Organizational Practices
Seeing	• Adopt a stance that relevant differences are ubiquitous. • Attend to points of conflict. • Observe silence.	• Attend to intergroup tension. • Reduce the climate of secrecy.
Understanding	Cultivate sources of information about the difference.	

	• Build skill in acquiring data.
	  – Listen.
	  – Ask questions.
	  – Learn and share your own story.
	• Include people who are different in your inner circle or network.
		• Acquire information via survey and other data gathering.
		• Create and institutionalize inclusive structures.

Valuing	• Lower the levels of unnecessary carefulness when dealing with differences. • Be willing to persist in the midst of conflict and its accompanying discomfort. • Incorporate data into your worldview.	• Reward and hold employees accountable for engaging in difference-related activities. • Recruit and develop people who add diversity to the organization.

SOURCE: M. N. Davidson, *The End of Diversity as We Know It: Why Diversity Efforts Fail and How Leveraging Difference Can Succeed* (San Francisco: Berrett-Kohler Press, 2011).

teamwork, and leadership in a diverse workforce much more challenging. Yet managers very much need to confront these issues. They need to develop the skills and strategies diversity requires if they and their organizations are to succeed in our increasingly multicultural business environment.

One constructive way to begin is with what Martin Davidson has called "leveraging difference." This approach sees diversity not as a problem to be tolerated or solved, but as a resource the organization can capitalize on, even though doing so is sometimes difficult. Leveraging difference starts with the recognition that we all bring something different to an organization. Along with surface differences such as sex and race, we contribute different ways of thinking and problem solving, different strengths and values, and so on. To capitalize on these differences, as shown in Table 11.7, people in the organization have to begin by seeing them. Then individuals must make the effort to understand the differences by asking questions and listening carefully. The next step is to value the differences not only through the organization's recruitment and recognition programs but also through willingness to persist despite conflict and to incorporate new perspectives into one's own thinking. This effort provides the information needed to leverage the differences by applying them to the whole spectrum of organization activities, such as innovating, learning, working as a team, and interacting with customers.[41] The remainder of this chapter provides further thinking on how to meet the challenges of diversity and leverage it for organizational success.

> Leveraging difference starts with the recognition that we all bring something different to an organization.

Multicultural Organizations

To capitalize on the benefits and minimize the costs of a diverse workforce, perhaps one of the first things managers need to do is examine their organization's prevailing assumptions about people and cultures. Table 11.8 shows some of the fundamental assumptions that may exist. Based on these assumptions, we can classify organizations as one of three types and describe their implications for managers.

TABLE 11.8   Diversity Assumptions and Their Implications for Management

Common and Misleading Assumptions		Less Common and More Appropriate Assumptions	
Homogeneity	*Melting pot myth:* We are all the same.	**Heterogeneity**	*Image of cultural pluralism:* We are not all the same; groups within society differ across cultures.
Similarity	*Similarity myth:* "They" are all just like me.	**Similarity and difference**	*They are not just like me:* Many people differ from me culturally. Most people exhibit both cultural similarities and differences when compared with me.
Parochialism	*Only-one-way myth:* Our way is the only way. We do not recognize any other way of living or working.	**Equifinality**	*Our way is not the only way:* There are many culturally distinct ways of reaching the same goal, of working, and of living one's life.
Ethnocentrism	*One-best-way myth:* Our way is the best way. All other approaches are inferior versions of our way.	**Culture contingency**	*Our way is one possible way:* There are many different and equally good ways to reach the same goal. The best way depends on the culture of the people involved.

SOURCE: From "Diversity Assumptions and Their Implications for Management" by Nancy J. Adler, *Handbook of Organization,* 1996. Reprinted courtesy of Marcel Dekker Inc., New York.

monolithic organization

An organization that has a low degree of structural integration—employing few women, minorities, or other groups that differ from the majority—and thus has a highly homogeneous employee population.

pluralistic organization

An organization that has a relatively diverse employee population and makes an effort to involve employees from different gender, racial, or cultural backgrounds.

Some organizations are **monolithic.** This type of organization has very little *cultural integration;* in other words, it employs few women, minorities, or any other groups that differ from the majority. For example, in its hiring, an organization might favor alumni of the same college, perhaps even more specifically targeting members of fraternities who are enthusiastic about the school's football team. Such an organization is highly homogeneous in terms of its employee population. In monolithic organizations, if groups other than the norm are employed, they are found primarily in low-status jobs. Minority group members must adopt the norms of the majority to survive. This fact, coupled with small numbers, keeps conflicts among groups low. Discrimination and prejudice typically prevail, informal integration is almost nonexistent, and minority group members do not identify strongly with the company.

Most large U.S. organizations made the transition from monolithic to *pluralistic* organizations in the 1960s and 1970s because of changing demographics as well as societal forces such as the civil rights and women's movements. **Pluralistic organizations** have a more diverse employee population and take steps to involve persons from different gender, racial, or cultural backgrounds. These organizations use an affirmative action approach to managing diversity: they actively try to hire and train a diverse workforce and to ensure against any discrimination against minority group members. They typically have much more integration than do monolithic organizations, but like monolithic organizations, they often have minority group members clustered at certain levels or in particular functions within the organization.

Because of greater cultural integration, affirmative action programs, and training programs, the pluralistic organization has some acceptance of minority group members into the informal network, much less discrimination, and less prejudice. Improved employment opportunities create greater identification with the organization among minority group members. Often the resentment of majority group members, coupled with the increased number of women and minorities, creates more conflict than exists in the monolithic organization.

The pluralistic organization fails to address the cultural aspects of integration. In contrast, in **multicultural organizations** diversity not only exists but is valued. These organizations fully integrate gender, racial, and minority group members both formally and informally. But managers in such organizations do not focus primarily on the visible differences between employees, like race or sex. Rather, managers value and draw on the different *experience* and *knowledge* employees bring to the organization and help it achieve agreed-upon strategies and goals.[42] The multicultural organization is marked by an absence of prejudice and discrimination and by low levels of intergroup conflict. Such an organization creates a *synergistic* environment in which all members contribute to their maximum potential and the advantages of diversity can be fully realized.[43] As you read the "Management Connection: Progress Report" feature, consider whether PepsiCo offers the qualities of a multicultural or a pluralistic organization.

multicultural organization

An organization that values cultural diversity and seeks to utilize and encourage it.

Manager's Brief	**Progress Report**	Onward

Management Connection

DIVERSITY'S STRATEGIC PLACE AT PEPSICO

At the beginning of this chapter, you met the CEO of PepsiCo. This U.S. company's top leader, Indra Nooyi, is an Indian-born, well-educated, business-savvy Hindu woman with high ideals. Those ideals include valuing and nurturing the diversity of PepsiCo's workforce. Nooyi has said that "having women in the organization enhances your ability to make the numbers" and that she wants PepsiCo's employees to be representative of its diverse consumer market.

The implication behind these statements is that diversity is linked to corporate strategy—a corporate strength rather than a regulatory or social hurdle. Indeed, at PepsiCo, diversity management is intended to support the corporate goals, which under Nooyi have been summed up by the slogan "Performance with Purpose." That kind of performance includes meeting financial targets to increase the company's value, but also doing so in a way that is socially and environmentally sustainable so that the company can continue to thrive for the long term. Achieving this "purpose" aspect of Performance with Purpose encompasses what Nooyi thinks of as three kinds of sustainability: human sustainability (offering more wholesome food choices), environmental sustainability (using resources more efficiently), and talent sustainability (creating employment opportunities in the communities served by PepsiCo and enabling all employees to develop in their careers).

Because PepsiCo serves diverse communities, talent sustainability results in a diverse workforce. The effort to recruit from all the communities it serves helps the company to recognize the cultural tastes and nutritional needs of each community, and to communicate how its products help satisfy those tastes and needs. In Nooyi's words, local recruiting is a part of its purpose: "We take seriously our responsibility to find innovative ways to use less energy, water, and packaging, our responsibility to hire local people in the communities where we operate, create products designed for local tastes, and partner with local producers and suppliers." This is true whether the company is selecting an African American–owned agency to create its "We Inspire" social media page aimed at building brand loyalty among African American women, or developing Lehar Iron Chusti spicy snack crackers fortified with iron and B vitamins for teenagers in India, where iron deficiencies (and vegetarian diets) are common.

Talent sustainability also calls for the fostering of career development, ensuring that all members of PepsiCo's diverse workforce see that they have opportunities to advance. This is sustainability in the sense that PepsiCo reflects its customer communities at all levels of the organization, and its people are committed to staying with the company rather than leaving because their careers get stuck. Especially in fast-growing economically developing nations, talent sustainability also is a means to ensure that the company can find enough sales, manufacturing, financial, and other talent as it grows in those markets.

Indra Nooyi has said, "I am everything that this company has stood for in diversity and inclusion; it has all come together with me." Nooyi, a widely respected and successful CEO, did not cause diversity to be valued; rather, her appointment was possible because of the company's longstanding commitment to inclusion. PepsiCo was the first major company to appoint a woman to its board of directors and the first to make an African American a vice president. Back in the 1940s, the company was the first major company to grant a franchise to people of color (soft drink companies sell bottling franchises for distributing their beverages). Building on those early steps, today PepsiCo has reached a point where over 20 percent of its U.S. executives are people of color, and one-third are women. Globally more than 30 percent of PepsiCo's executives are people of color.[44]

- How does PepsiCo's commitment to valuing diversity give it a competitive advantage?
- Would you describe PepsiCo as a multicultural organization? Why or why not?

How Organizations Can Cultivate a Diverse Workforce

LO 6

An organization's plans for becoming multicultural and making the most of its diverse workforce should include (1) securing top management's leadership and commitment, (2) assessing the organization's progress toward goals, (3) attracting employees, (4) training employees in diversity, and (5) retaining employees. A recent study examining the performance of hundreds of companies over a 30-year period found that organizations that assigned responsibility for achieving diversity targets to certain individuals or groups made the most progress in increasing the share of female and black workers on their payrolls. Moderate change occurred in companies that set up programs for mentoring and networking, but formal diversity training programs had little effect unless the organizations also use the other methods.[45] Thus cultivating diversity needs to be a well-planned, organizationwide effort in which each element is supported by the personal commitment of individual managers, who address this issue as seriously as they do other management challenges. These managers actively seek to develop the skills, understanding, and practices that enable people of every background to do their best work in the common pursuit of the organization's goals.

Top Management's Leadership and Commitment

Obtaining top management's leadership and commitment is critical for diversity programs to succeed. Otherwise the rest of the organization will not take the effort seriously. One way to communicate this commitment to all employees—as well as to the external environment—is to incorporate the organization's attitudes toward diversity into the corporate mission statement and into strategic plans and objectives. Managerial compensation can be linked directly to accomplishing diversity goals. Adequate funding must be allocated to the diversity effort to ensure its success. Also, top management can set an example for other organization members by participating in diversity programs and making participation mandatory for all managers.

As we mentioned earlier, some organizations have established corporate offices or committees to coordinate the companywide diversity effort and provide feedback to top management. Honeywell hired a director of workforce diversity, and Avon, a director of multicultural planning and design. Other companies prefer to incorporate diversity management into the function of director of affirmative action or EEO.

Joe Dumars is one of the high percentage of minority NBA presidents.

The work of managing diversity cannot be done by top management or diversity directors alone. Many companies rely on minority advisory groups or task forces to monitor organizational policies, practices, and attitudes; assess their impact on the diverse groups within the organization; and provide feedback and suggestions to top management.

For example, at Equitable Life Assurance Society, employee groups meet regularly with the CEO to discuss issues pertaining to women, African Americans, and Hispanics and make recommendations for improvement. At Honeywell, disabled employees formed a council to discuss their needs.

> "Diversity: The art of thinking independently together."
> —Malcolm Forbes

They proposed and accepted an accessibility program that went beyond federal regulations for accommodations of disabilities.

As you can see, progressive companies are moving from asking managers what they think minority employees need and toward asking the employees themselves what they need.

Organizational Assessment

The next step in managing diversity is to establish an ongoing assessment of the organization's workforce, culture, policies, and practices in areas such as recruitment, promotions, benefits, and compensation. As part of this assessment, managers may evaluate whether they are attracting their share of diverse candidates from the labor pool and whether the needs of their customers are being addressed by the current composition of their workforce. The objective is to identify areas where there are problems or opportunities and to make recommendations where changes are needed. At Aetna, one measure is the percentage of employees who are multilingual; one way the company builds this number is by offering noontime language lessons for interested employees.[46]

Many women and Asians can be at a disadvantage when aggressiveness is a valued part of an organization's culture. Analysis might reveal that this value exists and that it excludes employees who do not share it from full participation. Managers can then decide that the organizational values need to be changed so that other styles of interacting are equally acceptable. Managers can also change their own behaviors to reflect this change—for example, by calling on all individuals in a meeting for their ideas instead of letting more assertive participants dominate. Corporate values and norms should be identified and critically evaluated regarding their necessity and their impact on the diverse workforce.

Attracting Employees

Companies can attract a diverse, qualified workforce by using effective recruiting practices, accommodating employees' work and family needs, and offering alternative work arrangements.

Recruitment   A company's image can be a strong recruiting tool. Companies with reputations for hiring and promoting all types of people have a competitive advantage. Xerox gives prospective minority employees reprints of an article that rates the company as one of the best places for African Americans to work. Hewlett-Packard ensures that its female candidates are familiar with its high rating by *Working Woman* magazine. Many employers are implementing policies to attract more women, ensure that women's talents are used to full advantage, and avoid losing their most capable female employees.

Many minorities, disabled persons, and economically disadvantaged people are physically isolated from job opportunities. Companies can bring information about job opportunities to the source of labor, or they can transport the labor to the jobs.

Diversity is built into the origins of the Philadelphia law firm of Caesar Rivise. The firm's founder was Abraham Caesar, an attorney specializing in intellectual property (for example, patents and trademarks). Back in 1926, Caesar could not land a job at one of the local law firms because he was Jewish. Instead he founded his own firm, joined the next year by partner Charles Rivise. Together the two attorneys built their practice and wrote important reference books on patents, establishing their reputation as experts in the field.

Given Caesar's early experiences, it's not surprising that his law firm committed itself to diversity in hiring. Stanley Cohen, now a partner, noticed that when he joined the firm in the 1960s. Back then, he recalls, his secretary was an African American man. Another Caesar Rivise employee since the 1960s is Bernice Mims. Although Mims graduated at the top of her South Philadelphia High School class, jobs were offered to other students and not Mims because she was black and the employer stipulated "no Jews or Negroes." However, Caesar hired her as a law clerk, and she remained loyal to the firm, eventually working her way up to manager of human resources.

Today Caesar Rivise builds on its historical commitment to diversity in recruiting by sponsoring diversity fellowships at Drexel University's Earle Mack School of Law. The firm assists qualified minority law students with tuition and offers them work experience. Partnering with Drexel is a good strategic fit for the firm because the university emphasizes technology and science—backgrounds that are important for working with corporate clients on technical matters. Cohen, for example, has a chemical engineering degree from Drexel.[47]

• In what ways is Caesar Rivise's image a strong recruiting tool for the firm?

Polycast Technology in Stamford, Connecticut, contracts with a private van company to transport workers from the Bronx in New York City to jobs in Stamford. Days Inn recruits homeless workers in Atlanta and houses them in a motel within walking distance of their jobs. Burger King has done a lot to recruit and hire immigrants in its fast-food restaurants.

Accommodating Work and Family Needs   More job seekers are putting family needs first. Corporate work and family policies are now one of the most important recruiting tools.

Employers that offer onsite child care report decreased turnover and absenteeism and improved morale. In addition to providing child care, many companies now assist with care for elderly dependents, offer time off to care for sick family members, provide parental leaves of absence, and offer a variety of benefits that can be tailored to individual family needs. Some companies are accommodating the needs and concerns of dual-career couples by limiting relocation requirements or providing job search assistance to relocated spouses.

Alternative Work Arrangements   Another way managers accommodate diversity is to offer flexible work schedules and arrangements. Stiff demand for engineering talent is motivating manufacturing companies to accommodate the needs of employees with family responsibilities. Autodesk, which sells design software, sees flexible scheduling as a way to attract and keep female employees. At Freescale Semiconductor, the focus is on meeting performance targets, not on working a set schedule. Section manager Amy Oesch says this approach has enabled her to juggle family responsibilities while moving up to positions of greater authority and earning a graduate degree.[48]

Other creative work arrangements include compressed workweeks (e.g., four 10-hour days) and job sharing, in which two part-time workers share one full-time job. Another option to accommodate working mothers and disabled employees is teleworking (working from home) or telecommuting (working from home via computer hookup to the main work site). This option has been slow to catch on, but the organizations that have tried it report favorable results.

Training Employees

As you learned in Chapter 10, employees can be developed in a variety of ways. Traditionally, most management training was based on the unstated assumption that "managing" means managing a homogeneous, often white-male, full-time workforce. But gender, race, culture, age, educational, and other differences create an additional layer of complexity.[49] Diversity training programs attempt to identify and reduce hidden biases and develop the skills needed to manage a diversified workforce effectively.

The majority of U.S. organizations sponsor some sort of diversity training. Typically, diversity training has two components: awareness building and skill building.

Awareness Building   *Awareness building* is designed to increase awareness of the meaning and importance of valuing diversity.[50] Its aim is not to teach specific skills but to sensitize employees to the assumptions they make about others and the way those assumptions affect their behaviors, decisions, and judgment. For example, male employees who have never reported to a female manager may feel awkward the first time they are required to do so. Awareness building can reveal this concern in advance and help the managers address it.

To build awareness, trainers teach people to become familiar with myths, stereotypes, and cultural differences as well as the organizational barriers that inhibit the full contributions of all employees. They develop a better understanding of corporate culture, requirements for success, and career choices that affect opportunities for advancement.

In most companies, the "rules" for success are ambiguous, unwritten, and perhaps inconsistent with written policy. A common problem for women, minorities, immigrants, and young employees is that they are unaware of many of the unofficial rules that are obvious to people in the mainstream. For example, organizations often have informal networks and power structures that may not be apparent or readily available to women and minority group members. As a result, these employees are less likely to know where to go when they need to get something approved or when they want to build support and alliances. For managers, valuing diversity means teaching the unwritten "rules" or cultural values to those who need to know them and changing the rules when necessary to benefit employees and hence the organization. It also requires inviting "outsiders" in and giving them access to information and meaningful relationships with people in power.

Skill Building   Diversity training that merely identifies problems without giving participants the tools they need to be able to act on what they have learned may leave participants feeling that the training was not useful or worthwhile. For this reason, many organizations include skill building as part of a diversity program. *Skill building* is designed to allow all employees and managers to develop the skills they need to deal effectively with one another and with customers in a diverse environment. Most of the skills taught are interpersonal, such as active listening, coaching, and giving feedback. Ideally, the skills taught are based on the organizational assessment, so the training can be tailored to the specific business issues managers have identified. For example, if too many women and minorities believe they are not getting enough helpful feedback, the skills-building program can be designed to address that issue. Likewise, training in flexible scheduling can help managers meet the company's needs while accommodating and valuing workers who want to be able to set aside time to advance their education, participate in community projects, or look after elderly parents. Tying the training to specific, measurable business goals increases its usefulness and also allows managers to assess whether it is working.

TABLE 11.9

Guidelines for Diversity Training

1. **Position training in your broad diversity strategy.** Training is one important element of managing diversity, but on its own it will probably fail. Culture change means altering underlying assumptions and systems that guide organizational behavior. Training programs must be internally consistent with, and complement, other initiatives focused on culture change.

2. **Do a thorough needs analysis.** Do not start training prematurely. As with any training program, eagerness to "do something" may backfire unless you have assessed what specific aspects of diversity need attention first. Focus groups help identify what employees view as priority issues.

3. **Distinguish between education and training.** Education helps build awareness and understanding but does not teach usable skills. Training involves activities that enhance skills in areas such as coaching, conducting performance appraisals, and adapting communication styles. Education and training are both important, but they're not the same.

4. **Use a participative design process.** Tap a multitude of parties to ensure that the content and tone of the program are suitable to everyone involved. Outside consultants often provide fresh perspectives and have credibility. Insiders have specific company knowledge, sensitivity to local issues, and long-standing relationships with company members. Balance these various sources.

5. **Test the training thoroughly before rollout.** Given the sensitivity, even volatility, of diversity issues, use diversity councils and advocacy groups to pilot the programs. Build in ample feedback time to allow these groups to address sensitive concerns and refine the training.

6. **Incorporate diversity programs into the core training curriculum.** One-time programs do not have a lasting impact. Blend the program's content into other training programs such as performance appraisal, coaching, and so on.

SOURCE: From *Training: The Human Side of Business.* 1993. Copyright 1993. The Lakewood Media Group.

Experiential exercises and videotapes, DVDs, and software often are used in the training programs to help expose stereotypes and encourage employees to discuss fears, biases, and problems. Again, the best exercises are related to the actual problems employees are likely to encounter in the workplace. For example, employees in a hospital diversity training program may practice how to handle a white patient who asks to be treated only by a white doctor or a male patient who wants to be treated only by a male doctor. Training ABC, Advanced Training Source, and American Training Resources are among the companies that offer such products. Table 11.9 provides a set of guidelines for designing effective diversity training.

Retaining Employees

As replacing qualified and experienced workers becomes more difficult and costly, retaining good workers will become much more important. Nationwide, turnover rates have been rising, with companies needing to replace more than 1 percent of their workers every month—and far more in the retailing and services industries. A number of policies and strategies, like the following, can be used to increase retention of all employees, especially those who are "different" from the norm.[51]

Support Groups   Companies can help form minority networks and other support groups to promote information exchange and social support. Support groups, sometimes called affinity groups, provide emotional and career support for members who traditionally have not been included in the majority's informal groups. They also can help diverse employees understand work norms and the corporate culture.

Bottom Line

Retaining qualified employees increases workforce quality.

What makes you feel that your employer values who you are and what you contribute?

At Apple headquarters in Cupertino, California, support groups include a Jewish cultural group, a gay/lesbian group, an African American group, and a technical women's group. Avon encourages employees to organize into African American, Hispanic, and Asian networks by granting them official recognition and assigning a senior manager to provide advice. These groups help new employees adjust and provide direct feedback to management on problems that concern the groups.

Darden Restaurants started support groups, known as employee networks, at its Orlando, Florida, headquarters. Today there are five such groups: the Family Network, aimed at providing support to employees with families; Women's Network; Asian American Network; African American Network; and Hispanic Network. Each network sponsors social activities for the whole company, provides educational activities, and works with executives to develop mentoring relationships and share insights about groups served by Darden's various restaurant chains, including Red Lobster and Olive Garden.

Darden Restaurants's president and chief operating officer Drew Madsen (left) and chief executive officer Clarence Otis are shown in Darden's offices in Orlando, Florida. Improvement at Darden's Red Lobster, combined with continuing strong momentum from its Italian chain, Olive Garden, and the steady growth of its LongHorn Steakhouse chain, could lead Darden to its strongest stock performance in years. The company has 1,800 restaurants, making it the world's biggest casual dining operator.

Darden's employee networks are not meant only to help employees; they also must contribute to business goals. Each network prepared a three-year business plan that details how the network expects to support Darden's growth. For instance, the Family Network sponsored a Take Your Child to Work Day at which children participated in focus groups that generated insights into children's menus. The Hispanic Network hosts events and an intranet where all employees, Hispanic and otherwise, can learn about Hispanic culture and develop ideas for better targeting that part of their clientele.

About 40 percent of Darden's headquarters employees belong to at least one of the networks, which are open to any interested employee. Based on the success of the groups in Orlando, the company is rolling out network membership to its restaurant employees. Darden also trains its managers in diversity issues, such as how to motivate a work group with a wide age range. Given that its restaurants employ both high schoolers and semiretired elders, managers need this opportunity to examine their assumptions about age groups and figure out how to cross the generational divide.[52]

• What characteristics of the support groups at Darden make them effective for retaining employees?

Mentoring   Many people have been puzzled at the apparent inability of women and minorities to move up beyond a certain point on the corporate ladder (the glass ceiling). To help these groups enter the informal network that provides exposure to top management and access to information about organizational politics, many companies have implemented formal mentoring programs. **Mentors** are higher-level managers who help ensure that high-potential people are introduced to top management and socialized into the norms and values of the organization.

In Canada, Ernst & Young makes mentorship an important part of employee development. In fact, the tax and consulting firm has established several mentoring programs aimed at the needs of particular employee groups, including women, minorities, and immigrants. Mentors work with employees to help them develop relevant experience, add skills, and make contact with senior leaders. Ernst & Young sees these mentorships not only as a way to increase what employees can offer but also as a way to fill its talent pipeline with future leaders. In a related but distinct effort, Ernst & Young identifies high-potential employees and has company leaders sponsor them. Sponsorship is similar to mentorship except that the sponsor is more actively involved in the employee's development. Finally, in an unusual twist on mentorship, Ernst & Young has a reverse mentoring program in which women and minority employees counsel leaders on issues related to diversity at the company.[53]

Career Development and Promotions   Because they are hitting a glass ceiling, many of the most talented women and minority group members are leaving their organizations in search of better opportunities elsewhere. In response, companies such as Deloitte & Touche and Honeywell have established teams to evaluate the career progress of women, minorities, and employees with disabilities and to devise ways to move them up through the ranks. One extremely important step is to make sure deserving employees get a chance at line positions. Women in particular are often relegated to staff positions, like human resources, with less opportunity to demonstrate how they can earn money for their employers. Career development programs that give a wide range of employees exposure and experience in line jobs can make senior management positions more available to them.

Systems Accommodation   Managers can support diversity by recognizing cultural and religious holidays, differing modes of dress, and dietary restrictions, as well as accommodating the needs of individuals with disabilities. One important disabling condition is AIDS. Under the ADA, organizations must accommodate employees with AIDS as they would persons with any other disability, permitting and even encouraging them to continue working for as long as they are able and, if warranted, allowing flexible scheduling. Also, accommodations for disability may become increasingly important in the future as the median age of the workforce continues to rise. In addition, the rise in the *weight* of the average U.S. worker may raise disability concerns. Not only are the familiar health consequences such as heart disease, joint problems, and diabetes associated with increased weight, but one study found that obese workers (with a body mass index of 40 or more) had many more workplace injury claims and absences related to injuries.[54] This pattern suggests that managers of the future will be even more concerned than in the past with keeping their workers of all sizes on the job by maintaining safe workplaces and offering benefits that encourage healthy lifestyles (possibly through company-sponsored fitness programs).

Accountability   As we noted at the beginning of this section, one of the most effective ways to ensure that diversity efforts succeed is to hold managers accountable for hiring and developing a diverse workforce. Organizations must ensure that their performance appraisal and reward systems reinforce the importance of effective diversity management. At PepsiCo, each executive reporting to the CEO is assigned responsibility for employee development of a different group—for example, the company's women or Latinos or gay and lesbian employees. The executive responsible for that group must identify leadership talent, learn group members' concerns, identify areas where support is needed, and identify plans for addressing these issues.[55]

For decades, U.S. corporations were striving to integrate their workforces because of regulatory and social responsibility pressures. Today globalization, changing demographics, and the expansion of ethnic markets at home have made managing a diverse workforce a bottom-line issue. Managers at companies like PepsiCo realize that to remain competitive in the coming years, they will have to make managing diversity a strategic priority to attract, develop, keep, and apply the knowledge of their top talent.

Manager's Brief   Progress Report   **Onward**

Management Connection

PEPSICO'S DIVERSITY PROGRAM

PepsiCo's effort to manage diversity is built on the idea of talent sustainability. A sustainable talent pool draws human resources from all the communities where the company operates, and then it provides opportunities for development in order to retain employees and give them a chance to contribute fully. The company sets goals for meeting targets in both areas. The effort is led by PepsiCo's chief personnel officer, supported by three human resource teams: staffing, compensation and benefits, and diversity and inclusion. The efforts have led to international recognition, such as being named a top workplace for women and minorities in the United States (by *Working Mother* and by DiversityInc.) and a top workplace for women's advancement in Turkey (by *Forbes*) and in the United Kingdom (by *The Times*).

Recruiting efforts include developing and promoting a reputation as a company that values diversity. PepsiCo applies its skill at brand marketing to market itself as a great employer. Its most recent campaign included short videos profiling employees to show what it is like to work at the company. In addition, the PepsiCo website provides a full description of its commitment to talent sustainability. PepsiCo also participates in efforts to target underrepresented groups. For example, it was one of the corporate partners recruiting at a Toronto job fair for experienced professionals with disabilities.

For career development that promotes diversity at the top levels of the organization, the company doesn't set quotas. Rather, it identified 300 positions that feed into top management jobs and then requires that when one of those positions is open, candidates should include female and minority candidates. The idea is that getting a diverse group into these high-opportunity positions will create a diverse pool of talent for the top jobs. Without this conscious effort, experience has shown, employees may self-select into certain functions (for example, more women in human resource, finance, and other support functions) so that the candidates for top jobs are not representative of all the company's customers. Along with this, the company set up a performance management system aimed at

ensuring that rewards are based on measurable results, so any talented person should have an equal opportunity to succeed.

In the United States, the company also has established affinity groups it calls diversity and inclusion networks. These include groups for African Americans, Latinos/Hispanics, Asians, Native Americans, women, gay/lesbian/bisexual/transgender employees, and individuals with disabilities. And white males are not ignored; there is also a group called the White Male Inclusion Advisory Group. The affinity groups provide access to mentors, introduce employees to influential coworkers, and sponsor leadership conferences that give members a chance to meet PepsiCo executives.

Along with these efforts, the company realizes that not every manager will know how to manage diversity effectively, and not everyone will know how to participate in a culture that values diversity. PepsiCo provides all employees with training on inclusion, and it measures the impact. After this training began, turnover among minority and female employees fell, and the percentage of employees who say they see "diversity and inclusion reflected in PepsiCo's management" has risen by 16 percent since 2002.

Behind this program is top-level commitment to diversity goals. From the chief executive on down, PepsiCo's management is committed to diversity, both philosophically and in order to meet performance targets. CEO Indra Nooyi says that half her annual bonus is based on meeting goals for talent sustainability. To earn that bonus, she cochairs (with the company's chief diversity officer) a Global Diversity and Inclusion Governance Council. The council meets regularly to ensure the company is, as stated on its website, "enhancing diversity and inclusion capabilities and creating a sustainable and differentiated competitive advantage for PepsiCo." Each of the four geographic divisions has a Diversity and Inclusion Council that focuses on issues relevant to the continent it serves. For example, one issue at PepsiCo India is the widely held assumption that women are not viable candidates for jobs that involve extensive travel to visit customers, so there the company specifically asks that female candidates be included in names from recruiters, and it advertises positions on job portals that target female job hunters. Executives also receive advice from educators, politicians, customers, and other experts serving on its External Diversity Advisory Boards.[56]

- How do you think PepsiCo's program for valuing diversity would be affected if it were simply a human resource management program rather than a part of strategy adopted and advocated by top management?
- Besides the efforts described here, how else could PepsiCo cultivate a diverse workforce?

KEY TERMS

affirmative action, p. 408

managing diversity, p. 394

mentors, p. 422

monolithic organization, p. 414

multicultural organization, p. 415

pluralistic organization, p. 414

sexual harassment, p. 400

SUMMARY OF LEARNING OBJECTIVES

Now that you have studied Chapter 11, you should be able to:

LO 1 Describe how changes in the U.S. workforce make diversity a critical organizational and managerial issue.

The labor force is getting older and more racially and ethnically diverse, with a higher proportion of women. And while the absolute number of workers is increasing, the growth in jobs is outpacing the numerical growth of workers. In addition, the jobs that are being created frequently require higher skills than the typical worker can provide; thus we are seeing a growing skills gap. To be competitive, organizations can no longer take the traditional approach of depending on white males to form the core of the workforce. Today managers must look broadly to make use of talent wherever it can be found. As the labor market changes, organizations that can recruit, develop, motivate, and retain a diverse workforce will have a competitive advantage.

LO 2 Distinguish between affirmative action and managing diversity.

Affirmative action is designed to correct past exclusion of women and minorities from U.S. organizations. But despite the accomplishments of affirmative action, it has not eliminated barriers that prevent individuals from reaching their full potential. Managing diversity goes beyond hiring people who are different from the norm and seeks to support, nurture, and use employee differences to the organization's advantage.

LO 3 Explain how diversity, if well managed, can give organizations a competitive edge.

Managing diversity is a bottom-line issue. If managers are effective at managing diversity, they will have an easier time attracting, retaining, and motivating the best employees. They will be more effective at marketing to diverse consumer groups in the United States and globally. They will have a workforce that is more creative, more innovative, and better able to solve problems. In addition, they are likely to increase the flexibility and responsiveness of the organization to environmental change.

LO 4 Identify challenges associated with managing a diverse workforce.

The challenges for managers created by a diverse workforce include decreased group cohesiveness, communication problems, mistrust and tension, and stereotyping. These challenges can be turned into advantages by means of training and effective management.

LO 5 Define monolithic, pluralistic, and multicultural organizations.

These categories are based on the organization's prevailing assumptions about people and cultures. Monolithic organizations have a low degree of structural integration, so their population is homogeneous. Pluralistic organizations have a relatively diverse employee population and try to involve various types of employees (e.g., engaging in affirmative action and avoiding discrimination). Multicultural organizations not only have diversity but value it, and they fully integrate men and women of various racial and ethnic groups, as well as people with different types of expertise. Conflict is greatest in a pluralistic organization.

LO 6 List steps managers and their organizations can take to cultivate diversity.

To be successful, organizational efforts to manage diversity must have top management support and commitment. Organizations should first undertake a thorough assessment of their cultures, policies, and practices, as well as the demographics of their labor pools and customer bases. Only after this diagnosis has been completed is a company in position to initiate programs designed to attract, develop, motivate, and retain a diverse workforce.

DISCUSSION QUESTIONS

1. What opportunities do you see as a result of changes in our nation's workforce?

2. Is prejudice declining in our society? In our organizations? Why or why not?

3. What distinctions can you make between affirmative action and managing diversity?

4. How can managers overcome obstacles to diversity such as mistrust and tension, stereotyping, and communication problems?

5. How can organizations meet the special needs of different groups (e.g., work and family issues) without appearing to show favoritism to those particular sets of employees?

6. How can diversity give a company a competitive edge? Can diversity really make a difference in the bottom line? How?

EXPERIENTIAL EXERCISES

11.1   BEING DIFFERENT

OBJECTIVES

1. To increase your awareness of the feeling of "being different."

2. To better understand the context of "being different."

INSTRUCTIONS

1. Working alone, complete the Being Different Worksheet.

2. In small groups, compare worksheets, and prepare answers to the discussion questions.

3. When the class reconvenes, group spokespersons present group findings.

DISCUSSION QUESTIONS

1. Were there students who experienced being different in situations that surprised you?

2. How would you define "being different"?

3. How can this exercise be used to good advantage?

Being Different Worksheet

Think back to a recent situation in which you experienced "being different," and answer the following questions:

1. Describe the situation in which you experienced "being different."

_____

_____

2. Explain how you felt.

_____

_____

3. What did you do as a result of "being different"? (That is, in what way was your behavior changed by the feeling of "being different"?)

_____

_____

4. What did others in the situation do? How do you think they felt about the situation?

_____

_____

5. How did the situation turn out in the end?

_____

_____

6. As a result of that event, how will you probably behave differently in the future? In what way has the situation changed you?

_____

_____

11.2 GENDER STEREOTYPES

PART I

Your instructor will divide the group into smaller groups based on gender, resulting in male-only and female-only groups. Groups are to brainstorm a list in response to the following statements. It is not necessary for all members to agree with everything the group generates. Add all inputs to the list.

Female groups complete the following:

- All men are _____
- Men think all women are _____

Male groups complete the following:

- All women are _____
- Women think all men are _____

PART II

After generating your lists, your groups will present a role-play to the class based on the following scenarios by switching gender roles (females portray males, and males portray females):

Two friends (of the same gender) meeting each other back at school for the first time this year.

A person flirting with a member of the opposite sex at a party. (Females play a male flirting with a female; males play a female flirting with a male.)

QUESTIONS

1. What aspects of the role-plays were accurate, distorted, or inaccurate?
2. How did you feel portraying the opposite gender, and how did it feel to see your gender portrayed?
3. On what stereotypes or experiences were these role-plays based?

PART III

Your group will now write its brainstorm lists on the board for discussion. Remember that these lists are a product of a group effort and are generally based on stereotypes and not necessarily the view of any one individual.

Analyze the lists for positive and negative results in both personal and professional settings. Generate a list of ways to dispel, reduce, or counter negative stereotypes.

QUESTIONS

1. What similarities, patterns, or trends developed from the groups?
2. How do you feel about the thoughts presented about your gender?
3. What implications do these thoughts have on actions and situations in the work environment?
4. What can you do to reduce the negative effects of these stereotypes? What can you do to help dispel these stereotypes? (Brainstorm with your group or class.)

SOURCE: Portions of this exercise were adapted from concepts in S. F. Fritz, W. Brown, J. Lunde, and E. Banset, *Interpersonal Skills for Leadership* (Englewood Cliffs, NJ: Prentice Hall, 1999); and A. B. Shani and J. B. Lau, *Behavior in Organizations: An Experiential Approach,* 6th ed. (New York: Irwin, 1996).

11.3   HE WORKS, SHE WORKS

INSTRUCTIONS

1. Complete the He Works, She Works Worksheet. In the appropriate spaces, write what you think the stereotyped responses would be. Do not spend too much time considering any one item. Rather, respond quickly and let your first impression or thought guide your answer.
2. Compare your individual responses with those of other class members or participants. It is interesting to identify and discuss the most frequently used stereotypes.

He Works, She Works Worksheet

The family picture is on *his* desk: *He's a solid, responsible family man.*

His desk is cluttered: _____
_____

He's talking with coworkers: _____
_____

He's not at his desk: _____
_____

He's not in the office: _____
_____

The family picture is on *her* desk: *Her family will come before her career.*

   Her desk is cluttered: _____

_____

   She's talking with coworkers: _____

_____

   She's not at her desk: _____

_____

   She's not in the office: _____

_____

The family picture is on *his* desk: *He's a solid, responsible family man.*

   He's having lunch with the boss: _____

_____

   The boss criticized *him:* _____

_____

   He got an unfair deal: _____

_____

   He's getting married: _____

_____

   He's going on a business trip: _____

_____

   He's leaving for a better job: _____

_____

The family picture is on *her* desk: *Her family will come before her career.*

   She's having lunch with the boss: _____

_____

   The boss criticized *her:* _____

_____

   She got an unfair deal: _____

_____

   She's getting married: _____

_____

   She's going on a business trip: _____

_____

   She's leaving for a better job: _____

_____

SOURCE: F. Luthans, *Organizational Behavior.* 1989. Copyright © 1989 The McGraw-Hill Companies. Reproduced with permission.

CONCLUDING CASE

THE NEW FRONTIER FOR FRESH FOODS SUPERMARKETS

Fresh Foods Supermarkets is a grocery store chain that was established in the Southeast 20 years ago. The company is now beginning to expand to other regions of the United States. First the firm opened new stores along the eastern seaboard, gradually working its way up through Maryland and Washington, DC, then through New York and New Jersey, and on into Connecticut and Massachusetts. It has yet to reach the northern New England states, but executives have decided to turn their attention to the Southwest, particularly because of the growth of population there.

Vivian Noble, the manager of one of the chain's most successful stores in the Atlanta area, has been asked to relocate to Phoenix, Arizona, to open and run a new Fresh Foods Supermarket. She has decided to accept the job, but she knows it will be a challenge. As an African American woman, she has faced some prejudice during her career, but she refuses to be stopped by a glass ceiling or any other barrier. She understands that she will be living and working in an area where several cultures combine and collide, and she will be hiring and managing a diverse workforce. Noble has the support of top management at Fresh Foods, which wants the store to reflect the surrounding community—in both staff makeup and product selection. So she will be looking to hire employees with Hispanic and Native American roots, as well as older workers who can relate to the many retired residents in the area. And she will be seeking their input on the selection of certain food products, including popular ethnic brands, so that customers know they can buy what they need and want at Fresh Foods.

In addition, Noble wants to make sure that Fresh Foods provides services above and beyond those of a standard supermarket to attract local consumers. For instance, she wants the store to offer free delivery of groceries to homebound customers who are either senior citizens or physically disabled. She wants to be sure that the store has enough bilingual employees to translate for and otherwise assist customers who speak little or no English. Noble believes that she is a pioneer of sorts, guiding Fresh Food Supermarkets into a new frontier. "The sky is almost always blue here," she says of her new home state. "And there's no glass ceiling between me and the sky."

QUESTIONS

1. What steps can Vivian Noble take to recruit and develop her new workforce?

2. What other ways can Noble help her company reach out to the community?

3. How will Fresh Foods Supermarkets as a whole benefit from successfully moving into this new region of the country?

PART THREE   SUPPORTING CASE

Zappos

At the turn of the millennium, Zappos, a Las Vegas–based Internet retailer, was a start-up struggling to survive. The company wanted to be *the* online destination for buying shoes, but customers hesitated to pick out shoes online. The company hired a 27-year-old business consultant named Tony Hsieh to figure out what would save Zappos.

Hsieh, a first-generation Taiwanese American with a degree in computer science, already had a couple of successful business start-ups under his belt. Undeterred by Zappos's weak performance, he set an ambitious goal: Zappos would become the largest shoe retailer on the Internet. How? Not by focusing on mainly price or even selection, but by enhancing a company culture designed to make employees happy. Happy employees, Hsieh believed, would deliver superior service. And when customers take a chance on picking out shoes from a website, they want to trust that the seller will ensure they are satisfied with everything about the purchase, from shoe style and fit to fast delivery and an easy returns policy.

The approach quickly began to stimulate sales, and just a year after he started advising Zappos, Hsieh was named chief executive. He works for the startlingly small salary of $36,000. That arrangement doesn't bother Hsieh because he is more motivated by creating a great organization than by earning money. After all, his previous business, LinkExchange, brought him $265 million when he sold it to Microsoft.

The Zappos culture is built on 10 core values:

1. Deliver WOW (an emotional impact and powerful story to tell) through service.

2. Embrace and drive change.

3. Create fun and a little weirdness.

4. Be adventurous, creative, and open-minded.

5. Pursue growth and learning.

6. Build open and honest relationships with communication.

7. Build a positive team and family spirit. (The "family" refers to Zappos coworkers.)

8. Do more with less.

9. Be passionate and determined.

10. Be humble.

These somewhat unconventional values are essential hiring criteria, and the company's career website directs potential applicants to read the values—which are described in whimsical terms—and apply for a job only if they want to be part of this "best thing about the Zappos family." In fact, at the end of the orientation process, employees are offered $3,000 to quit if they feel they aren't a good fit with the company values, and displaying a lack of the values is grounds for being discharged. According to Hsieh, hiring people who share the core values makes it easy to form real friendships, and those relationships, in turn, create an environment in which people think creatively.

The Zappos human resources department, under the leadership of Hollie Delaney, a Salt Lake City native, ensures that job candidates start to experience and participate in this unconventional, fun culture during the application and selection process. An online application invites them to submit video "cover letters" with their applications, and interviews are conducted in a room that looks like the set of a TV talk show, where candidates might answer a question like "What's your theme song?" Employees evaluating candidates consider not only work history, but also the way candidates interact during lunch. They even take into account the observations of the shuttle drivers who take visiting job candidates back to their hotel. Once on board, employees might discover that "fun and a little weirdness" at the company includes an opportunity to dye Hsieh's or another manager's hair blue or shave his or her head at the annual Bald & Blue Day. And the commitment to "wowing" customers spills over into work relationships: given a chance to reward colleagues' good behavior with a $50 monthly bonus, many employees held off, waiting to see exceptional behavior.

Recently performance appraisals also were brought into line with the focus on values. Employees are rated not just on task accomplishment but also on how well they represent the core values. Managers are expected to describe specific instances of employees demonstrating the values at work, and employees who score low on a measure have the chance to receive training in that value. Outside the formal appraisal process, employees also continue to receive regular feedback on task-related measures such as percentage of hours spent talking to customers.

Delaney acknowledges that the company's values result in a work environment that is loud, hardworking, and full of change—conditions that aren't for everyone. Pay also isn't necessarily high, especially for call center workers. But for those who share the values, this kind of workplace is exhilarating. There also are plenty of rewards and perks, including profit sharing, a nap room, and access to a life coach who counsels employees as they sit on a velvet throne.

With this approach to human resources management, Hsieh helped Zappos grow into a billion-dollar company, which was eventually acquired by Amazon. Hsieh negotiated a deal in which Amazon promised to let Zappos continue operating independently, in accordance with its distinctive culture.

Unfortunately, although the 2008 financial crisis didn't keep sales at Zappos from rising, the ongoing economic slowdown eventually hurt, and Zappos laid off some of its workers, letting them down as gently as it could with generous severance packages. Even so, Zappos, unlike many businesses, hasn't outsourced its call center, located in Kentucky, because those employees need to be a part of the company culture. After all, they are the ones who talk directly with customers, and they're trained to wow customers—for example, encouraging them to try multiple sizes because shipping is free in both directions. Now the company's challenge is to reassure the remaining members of the "family" that Zappos is a great place to work even when times are tough.

QUESTIONS

1. Evaluate whether you think Zappos is a responsive organization. How do you expect its recent downsizing to affect its responsiveness?

2. How does human resource management reinforce Zappos's core values?

3. How well do you think Zappos's human resource strategy supports the valuing of employee diversity? What diversity issues does Zappos need to address?

SOURCES: H. Blodget, "Zappos CEO Tony Hsieh Making $36,000 a Year Working for Amazon," *Yahoo Finance,* September 10, 2010, http://finance.yahoo.com; Zappos, Jobs webpage, http://about.zappos.com/jobs/, accessed July 29, 2011; K. Gurchiek, "Delivering HR at Zappos," *HR Magazine,* June 2011, http://www.shrm.org; J. M. O'Brien, "Zappos Knows How to Kick It," *Fortune,* January 22, 2009, http://money.cnn.com; and R. Pyrillis, "The Reviews Are In," *Workforce Management,* May 1, 2011, Business & Company Resource Center, http://galenet.galegroup.com.

12 Leadership

LEARNING OBJECTIVES

After studying Chapter 12, you will be able to:

LO 1   Discuss what it means to be a leader. p. 432

LO 2   Summarize what people want and organizations need from their leaders. p. 432

LO 3   Explain how a good vision helps you be a better leader. p. 434

LO 4   Identify sources of power in organizations. p. 437

LO 5   List personal traits and skills of effective leaders. p. 439

LO 6   Describe behaviors that will make you a better leader, and identify when the situation calls for them. p. 441

LO 7   Distinguish between charismatic and transformational leaders. p. 451

LO 8   Describe types of opportunities to be a leader in an organization. p. 455

LO 9   Discuss how to further your own leadership development. p. 457

Manager's Brief	Progress Report	Onward

Management Connection

HOW HOWARD SCHULTZ LED STARBUCKS TO ITS INITIAL SUCCESS

Although Howard Schultz is now famous for his leadership of Starbucks Coffee Company, there was, in fact, a Starbucks before Schultz was even aware of its existence. The first Starbucks, a coffee store located in Seattle, was started in the 1970s by a trio of owners: Jerry Baldwin, Gordon Bowker, and Zev Siegl.

The story of Schultz's journey to lead a coffee chain began in Brooklyn, New York, where Schultz grew up in a working-class home, not only seeing how hard his father worked but also toiling in a series of tough jobs himself. Beginning with a paper route at age 10, Schultz moved on to jobs such as stretching skins for a furrier and steaming curtains at a garment company. From this, Schultz developed a drive to work as hard as it takes to come out on top.

Schultz won a football scholarship to Northern Michigan University (he played quarterback). Returning to New York after graduation, he took marketing jobs, first with Xerox and then with Hammarplast, a maker of coffee machines. On a business trip to Seattle for Hammarplast, Schultz called on one of

discovered the sense of joy and community that customers could savor in an Italian coffee bar. On his return to the United States, he tried to persuade the owners of Starbucks to create a similar kind of establishment. They weren't interested in shifting away from selling coffee beans, so Schultz went into business for himself, opening a coffeehouse called Il Giornale in 1985. As his business prospered, he opened more locations and then arranged to buy the Starbucks stores and roasting facility, operating them all under the Starbucks brand.

From the beginning, Schultz was driven by his vision not merely to sell coffee, but to sell an exceptional product and create an experience of community. The company buys and roasts all its own coffee beans. It trains baristas and sets up restaurants with the aim of providing the theatrical experience of

Howard Schultz provided his company with a compelling vision and a set of values that drove how the company treated its customers and employees. Some would also say his tremendous drive and passion are signs of a leader. As you read this chapter, compare Schultz's ways of leading with the kinds of practices recommended for successful leadership.

the company's clients, Starbucks. He talked the owners into hiring him as their marketing director, an effort that took a year of building trust because his ambition and intensity were overwhelming in the more laid-back culture of Seattle. Later, as a Starbucks employee, Schultz traveled to Italy, where he

seeing espresso prepared with precision and flair. And with attention to details, from the aroma of roasted coffee to the sounds of its music mixes, it aims to create a comfortable community gathering spot.

That vision extended to his sense of how a company should be run. Even as Schultz launched his first coffee bar, he felt conscious of his employees relying on him and the potential to create something worthwhile with them. Recalling how hard his father worked and how little respect he had received, Schultz felt he should run a company that treated every employee with respect. Beginning in the company's early years, Starbucks began providing health insurance to any employee who worked at least 20 hours a week, a practice that is unusually generous in the food service industry. Schultz has never wavered from that commitment to employees, even when the economy has made the choice difficult.

Schultz also acted out his commitment to employees in his management practices. He set up his office in the Starbucks roasting plant, and at the end of each day, he would walk out onto the plant floor and visit with employees, thanking them for their contributions. Behind that effort was a hope that employees would see a "leadership style" in which he "never put myself above anyone else" or "asked more of anyone than I was willing to do myself."

Schultz's vision and strategy fueled tremendous growth. Schultz's company had 11 stores in 1987, and by 2000 the company was operating 2,600 stores in 13 countries. At that point, Schultz stepped back from running the company full-time to becoming its chairman. Observers agreed that he had been a superb leader. He didn't yet know how much his leadership skills would be tested over the years ahead.[1]

People get excited about the topic of leadership. They want to know what makes a great leader like Howard Schultz. Managers in all industries are interested in this question. They believe the answer will bring improved organizational performance and personal career success. They hope to acquire the skills that will transform an average manager into a true leader.

Based on the idea that leadership can be learned, many large organizations such as Home Depot and Union Pacific actively recruit retired military personnel in the belief that military training and experience prepare those individuals to lead. Of course you don't have to join the armed services to acquire leadership skills. According to one source, "Leadership seems to be the marshaling of skills possessed by a majority but used by a minority. But it's something that can be learned by anyone, taught to everyone, denied to no one."[2]

LO 1

What is leadership? To start, a leader is one who influences others to attain goals. The greater the number of followers, the greater the influence. And the more successful the attainment of worthy goals, the more evident the leadership. But we must explore beyond this bare definition to capture the excitement and intrigue that devoted followers and students of leadership feel when they see a great leader in action, to understand what organizational leaders really do, and to learn what it really takes to become a truly outstanding leader.

Outstanding leaders combine good strategic substance and effective interpersonal processes to formulate and implement strategies that produce results and sustainable competitive advantage.[3] They may launch enterprises, build organization cultures, win wars, or otherwise change the course of events.[4] They are strategists who seize opportunities others overlook, but "they are also passionately concerned with detail—all the small, fundamental realities that can make or mar the grandest of plans."[5]

What Do We Want from Our Leaders?

LO 2

What do people want from their leaders? Broadly speaking, they want help in achieving their goals.[6] These goals include not just more pay and promotions, but support for their personal development; clearing obstacles so they can perform at high levels; and treatment that is respectful, fair, and ethical. Leaders serve people best when they help them develop their own initiative and good judgment, enable them to grow, and help them become better contributors. People want competence and proper management—the kinds of things you will read about in this chapter and that are found in other chapters in this book.

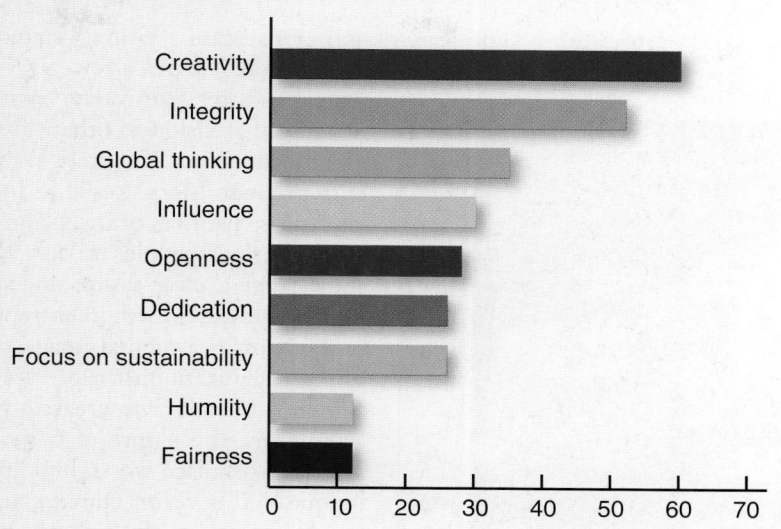

In interviews, the CEOs of business and government agencies around the world said the most important leadership qualities over the next five years would be creativity and integrity. CEOs in North America ranked integrity first.[7]

What do organizations need? Organizations need people at all levels to be leaders. Leaders throughout the organization are needed to do the things that their people want, but also to help create and implement strategic direction. Thus organizations place people in formal leadership roles so these leaders will achieve not their personal goals, but the organization's goals. The world saw a dramatic example of this kind of leadership in Chile recently when miners at a San Jose copper mine became trapped half a mile underground. Their foreman, Luis Urzua, drew on his inner strength and more than three decades of experience to help everyone stay calm and disciplined during the 17 days from when the mine collapsed until they were found, and then for weeks longer as they awaited their rescue. He set up rules and routines to provide a sense of order, make the food last as long as possible, and overcome despair among the frightened men of his crew. To foster a sense of teamwork, he divided the miners into three groups, and to develop a sense of unity and empowerment, he established that everyone would have a vote in making decisions. When the rescuers were ready to bring the miners up one at a time, Urzua chose to be the last one out.[8]

Organizations need people at all levels to be leaders.

These two perspectives—what people want and what organizations need—are neatly combined in a set of five key behaviors identified by James Kouzes and Barry Posner, two well-known authors and consultants.[9] The best leaders

1. *Challenge the process.* They challenge conventional beliefs and practices, and they create constructive change.
2. *Inspire a shared vision.* They appeal to people's values and motivate them to care about an important mission.
3. *Enable others to act.* They give people access to information and give them the power to perform to their full potential.
4. *Model the way.* They don't just tell people what to do—they are living examples of the ideals they believe in.
5. *Encourage the heart.* They show appreciation, provide rewards, and use various approaches to motivate people in positive ways.

You will read about these and other aspects of leadership in this and the following chapters. The topics we discuss will not only help you become a better leader but give you benchmarks that will help you assess the competence and fairness with which your boss manages you.

Vision

LO 3

"The leader's job is to create a vision," stated Robert L. Swiggett, former chair of Kollmorgen Corporation.[10] Until a few years ago, *vision* was not a word one heard managers utter. But today, having a vision for the future and communicating that vision to others are known to be essential components of great leadership. "If there is no vision, there is no business," maintains entrepreneur Mark Leslie.[11] Joe Nevin, an MIS director, described leaders as "painters of the vision and architects of the journey."[12] Practicing businesspeople are not alone in this belief; academic research shows that a clear vision and communication of that vision lead to higher venture growth in entrepreneurial firms.[13]

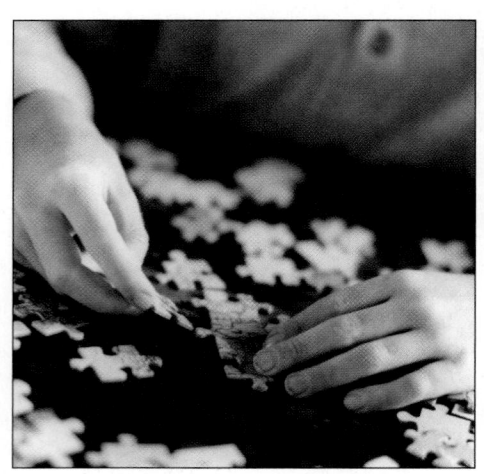

Imagine trying to complete a challenging jigsaw puzzle without the "vision" of what you're working toward.

vision

A mental image of a possible and desirable future state of the organization.

A **vision** is a mental image of a possible and desirable future state of the organization. It expresses the leader's ambitions for the organization.[14] A leader can create a vision that describes high performance aspirations, the nature of corporate or business strategy, or even the kind of workplace worth building. The best visions are both ideal and unique.[15] If a vision conveys an *ideal*, it communicates a standard of excellence and a clear choice of positive values. If the vision is also *unique*, it communicates and inspires pride in being different from other organizations. The choice of language is important; the words should imply a combination of realism and optimism, an action orientation, and resolution and confidence that the vision will be attained.[16]

Visions can be small or large and can exist at any organizational level as well as at the very top. The important points are that (1) a vision is necessary for effective leadership; (2) a person or team can develop a vision for any job, work unit, or organization; and (3) many people, including managers who do not develop into strong leaders, do not develop a clear vision—instead they focus on performing or surviving on a day-by-day basis.

Put another way, leaders must know what they want.[17] And other people must understand what that is. The leader must be able to articulate the vision, clearly and often. Other people throughout the organization should understand the vision and be able to state it clearly themselves. That's a start. But the vision means nothing until the leader and followers take action to turn the vision into reality.[18]

> Visions can be small or large and can exist at any organizational level as well as at the very top.

One leader who articulates and models a clear vision is George Buckley, chief executive of 3M Company, the innovative manufacturer best known for its Scotch tape, Post-It notes, and sandpaper. When the economy recently turned sour, other manufacturers slashed spending on research and development (R&D), but Buckley wanted to retain 3M's commitment to innovation. So even as he tied R&D spending to revenues (R&D spending fell, but not faster than revenues), he challenged his R&D staff to target their efforts toward making products cheaper to produce—and even convinced them that the effort could be satisfying. He accomplished this by recognizing that what drives researchers is a belief that what they do is intellectually stimulating and significant. For example, when Buckley asked the leader of 3M's abrasives business what innovations were in the pipeline, the unit's head commented that abrasives were "not considered sexy." Buckley's replied, "Why not? I think abrasives are sexy. Why can't abrasives be sexy?" Eventually, as researchers saw how their innovations were helping the company serve its markets, they grew enthusiastic about Buckley's vision.[19]

Bottom Line

You can't perform in the long run if you don't have a vision of what you want to accomplish. *Do you have to be a top-level executive to have a vision?*

A metaphor reinforces the important concept of vision.[20] Putting a jigsaw puzzle together is much easier if you have the picture on the box cover in front of you. Without the picture, or vision, the lack of direction is likely to result in frustration and failure. That is what communicating a vision is all about: making clear where you are heading.

Not just any vision will do. Visions can be inappropriate, or fail, for a variety of reasons.[21] First, an inappropriate vision may reflect merely the leader's personal needs. Such a vision can be unethical, or it may fail because of lack of acceptance by the market or by those who must implement it. Second (and related to the first), an inappropriate vision may ignore stakeholder needs. Third, the leader must stay abreast of environmental changes. Although effective leaders maintain confidence and persevere despite obstacles, the time may come when the facts dictate that the vision must change. You will learn more about change and how to manage it later in the book.

Where do visions come from?[22] Leaders should be sensitive to emerging opportunities, develop the right capabilities or worldviews, and not be overly invested in the status quo. You also can capitalize on networks of insightful individuals who have ideas about the future. Some visions are accidental; a company may stumble into an opportunity, and the leader may get credit for foresight. Some leaders and companies launch many new initiatives and, through trial and error, occasionally hit home runs. If the company learns from these successes, the "vision" emerges.

Bottom Line

Imagine a world with clean air, clean water, and enough food for all. In many businesses around the world, managers with vision are helping to make parts of that fantasy become a practical reality.
What is your vision for a better future?

IN PRACTICE

City administrator Steve Hewitt desperately needed a vision when a powerful tornado smashed his town of Greensburg, Kansas. Hewitt emerged after the storm to discover that the tornado had destroyed his own house plus the homes of most of the town's 1,400 residents. It also wiped out Greensburg's hospital, fire station, elementary and high schools, water tower, and business district. Hewitt immediately contacted employees and assessed the extent of the damage. He found a safe place for his family to stay and then turned his full attention to rescue and recovery.

First Hewitt had to deal with the emergency at hand. Supervising crews of city workers and volunteers operating out of tents, Hewitt directed the search and rescue, and later the cleanup. Even as these activities continued, Hewitt had to begin making decisions about the future. Though a small town might understandably give up, Hewitt was determined to rebuild. And out of that tragedy, he seized an opportunity.

Hewitt envisioned a town that would model an energy-efficient and sustainable way of living. He persuaded the city council to pass a resolution that all new municipal buildings meet the stiff LEED (Leadership in Energy and Environmental Design) Platinum certification for "green" buildings, for major energy savings. Hewitt communicated his vision and encouragement in radio broadcasts and flyers handed out at emergency checkpoints. He educated the community about the practical advantages of rebuilding homes to meet LEED standards, persuading many homeowners and store owners to adopt the standards themselves. He developed plans for wind farms to supply electricity to the town. Besides inspiring the locals, these efforts have drawn publicity and donations, including an ecofriendly playground.[23]

• What do you think made Hewitt's vision appealing to the people of Greensburg?

Leading and Managing

Effective managers are not necessarily true leaders. Many administrators, supervisors, and even top executives perform their responsibilities successfully without being great leaders. But these positions afford an opportunity for leadership. The ability to lead effectively, then, will set the excellent managers apart from others.

Good leadership, unfortunately, is all too rare.

Whereas management must deal with the ongoing, day-to-day complexities of organizations, true leadership includes effectively orchestrating important change.[24] While managing requires planning and budgeting routines, leading includes setting the direction (creating a vision) for the firm. Management requires structuring the organization, staffing it with capable people, and monitoring activities; leadership goes beyond these functions by inspiring people to attain the vision. Great leaders keep people focused on moving the organization toward its ideal future, motivating them to overcome whatever obstacles lie in the way.

Good leadership, unfortunately, is all too rare. Managers may focus on the activities that earn them praise and rewards, such as actions that cause a rise in the company's stock price, rather than making tough ethical choices or investing in long-term results. Some new managers, learning that "quick wins" will help them establish their credibility as leaders, push a pet project while neglecting the impact on the very people they were assigned to lead. This approach tends to backfire because employees distrust this type of manager and lose any commitment they might have had to the team's long-term success. Successful leaders, in contrast, enlist the team in scoring *collective* wins that result from working together toward a shared vision.[25]

It is important to be clear here about several things. First, management and leadership are both vitally important. To highlight the need for more leadership is not to minimize the importance of management or managers. But leadership involves unique processes that are distinguishable from basic management processes.[26] Moreover, just because they involve different processes does not mean that they require different, separate people. The same individual can exemplify effective managerial processes, leadership processes, both, or neither.

Some people dislike the idea of distinguishing between management and leadership, maintaining that it is artificial or derogatory toward the managers and the management processes that make organizations run. An alternative distinction is between supervisory and strategic leadership.[27] **Supervisory leadership** is behavior that provides guidance, support, and corrective feedback for day-to-day activities. **Strategic leadership** gives purpose and meaning to organizations. Strategic leadership involves anticipating and envisioning a viable future for the organization, and working with others to initiate changes that create such a future.[28] For example, Indian business leaders prioritize their top responsibilities[29] as providing input for business strategy (which you studied thoroughly in Part I of this book); "keeper" of the organizational culture (introduced in Chapter 2); and guiding, teaching, and serving as a role model for employees (employees being the focus of this part of the book).

supervisory leadership

Behavior that provides guidance, support, and corrective feedback for day-to-day activities.

strategic leadership

Behavior that gives purpose and meaning to organizations, envisioning and creating a positive future.

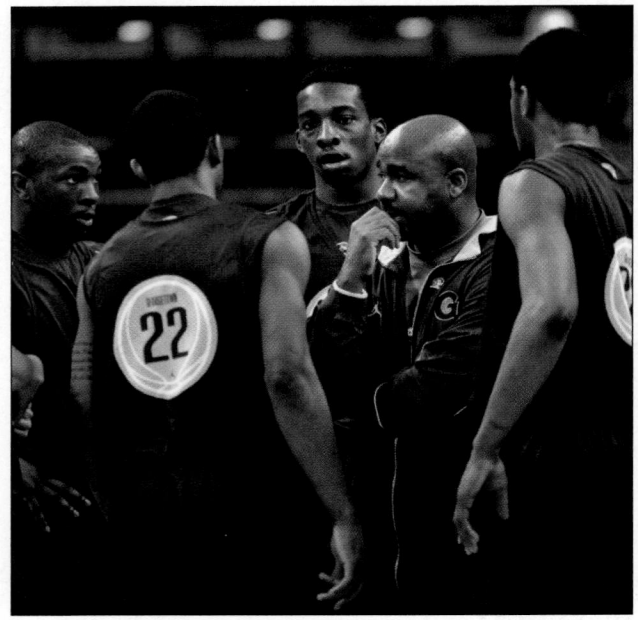

Georgetown head coach John Thompson III talks to his players during practice for the NCAA East Regional basketball tournament.

Leading and Following

Organizations succeed or fail not only because of how well they are led but because of how well followers follow. Just as managers are not necessarily good leaders, people are not always good followers. One leadership scholar stated, "Executives are given subordinates; they have to earn followers."[30] But it's also true that good followers help produce good leaders.

As a manager, you will be asked to play the roles of both leader and follower. As you lead the people who report to you, you will report to your boss. You will be a member of some teams and committees, and you may head others. While the leadership roles get the glamour and therefore are the roles that many people covet, followers must perform their responsibilities conscientiously and well. Good followership doesn't mean merely obeying orders, although some bosses may view it that way. The most effective followers are capable of independent thinking and at the same time are actively committed to organizational goals.[31] Robert Townsend, who led a legendary turnaround at Avis, said that the most important characteristic of a follower may be the willingness to tell the truth.[32]

They master skills that are useful to their organizations, and they hold performance standards

> What are the failures of followership? Here's one answer: apathy, passivity, cynicism, and noninvolvement that invite leaders' abuse of power.[33]

that are higher than required. Effective followers may not get the glory, but they know their contributions to the organization are valuable. And as they make those contributions, they study leaders in preparation for their own leadership roles.[34]

> Effective followers also distinguish themselves from ineffective ones by their enthusiasm and commitment to the organization and to a person or purpose—an idea, a product—other than themselves or their own interests.

Power and Leadership

Central to effective leadership is **power**—the ability to influence other people. In organizations, this influence often means the ability to get things done or accomplish one's goals despite resistance from others.

LO 4

power

The ability to influence others.

IN PRACTICE

Managers are sometimes surprised to discover that their power to influence goes far beyond the scope of their job duties, as less powerful employees are eager to seek their favor. In that context, a behavior as simple as making eye contact with an employee can serve as a kind of reward that inspires the employee.

Linda Parker Hudson discovered this kind of power when she became division president for defense contractor General Dynamics. In her first week on the job, she showed up wearing a distinctively tied scarf. The next day, she spotted more than a dozen female employees wearing scarves tied into identical bows. Hudson admits that the experience was more alarming than flattering; not everyone enjoys that level of scrutiny. But she also recognized that this kind of influence also would enable her to shape the organization's culture.

When Hudson later took charge of the U.S. division of another defense contractor, BAE Systems, she told the managers reporting to her that it was her habit to send e-mail at odd hours and she expected a "rapid response." When she had a thought at 3:00 a.m., she'd send out a message. But it took Hudson by surprise when she received immediate responses from managers who had begun sleeping with their BlackBerry phones within reach. By "rapid," she had not really meant *immediate,* but her staff members were eager to do whatever they thought she wanted. It took Hudson months to persuade them she really expected them to sleep at night.[35]

• Why do you think a manager such as Linda Parker Hudson has so much ability to influence the people in her organization?

Sources of Power

One of the earliest and still most useful approaches to understanding power, offered by French and Raven, suggests that leaders have five important potential sources of power in organizations.[36] Figure 12.1 shows those power sources.

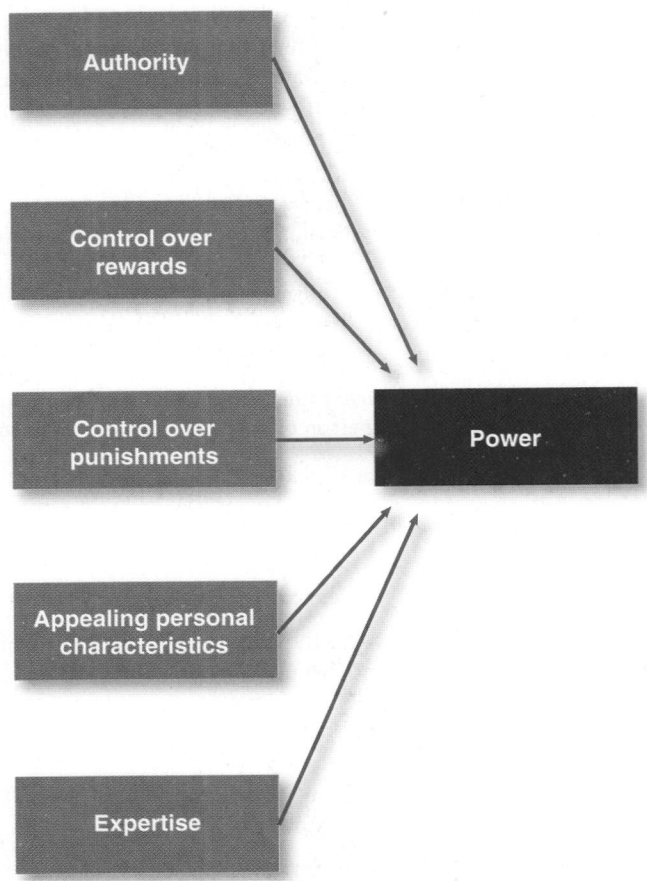

SOURCE: Adapted from J. R. P. French and B. Raven, "The Bases of Social Power," in *Studies in Social Power,* ed. D. Cartwright (Ann Arbor, MI: Institute for Social Research, 1959).

FIGURE 12.1
Sources of Power

Legitimate Power   The leader with *legitimate power* has the right, or the authority, to tell others what to do; employees are obligated to comply with legitimate orders. For example, a supervisor tells an employee to remove a safety hazard, and the employee removes the hazard because he has to obey the authority of his boss. In contrast, when a staff person lacks the authority to give an order to a line manager, the staff person has no legitimate power over the manager. As you might guess, managers have more legitimate power over their direct reports than they do over their peers, bosses, and others inside or outside their organizations.[37]

Reward Power   The leader who has *reward power* influences others because she controls valued rewards; people comply with the leader's wishes to receive those rewards. For example, a manager works hard to achieve her performance goals to get a positive performance review and a big pay raise from her boss. On the other hand, if company policy dictates that everyone receive the same salary increase, a leader's reward power decreases because he or she is unable to give higher raises.

Coercive Power   The leader with *coercive power* has control over punishments; people comply to avoid those punishments. For instance, a manager implements an absenteeism policy that administers disciplinary actions to offending employees. A manager has less coercive power if, say, a union contract limits her ability to punish. In general, lower-level managers have less legitimate, coercive, and reward power than do middle and higher-level managers.[38]

Referent Power   The leader with *referent power* has personal characteristics that appeal to others; people comply because of admiration, personal liking, a desire for approval, or a desire to be like the leader. For example, young, ambitious managers emulate the work habits and personal style of a successful, charismatic executive. An executive who is incompetent, disliked, and commands little respect has little referent power.

Expert Power   The leader who has *expert power* has certain expertise or knowledge; people comply because they believe in, can learn from, or can otherwise gain from that expertise. For example, a sales manager gives her salespeople some tips on how to close a deal. The salespeople then alter their sales techniques because they respect the manager's expertise. However, this manager may lack expert power in other areas, such as finance; thus her salespeople may ignore her advice concerning financial matters.

People who are in a position that gives them the right to tell others what to do, who can reward and punish, who are well liked and admired, and who have expertise on which other people can draw will be powerful members of the organization. All of these sources of power are potentially important. Although it is easy to assume that the most powerful bosses are those who have high legitimate power and control major rewards and punishments, it is important not to underestimate the more "personal" sources such as expert and referent power.

> It is important not to underestimate the more "personal" sources such as expert and referent power.

Traditional Approaches to Understanding Leadership

Three traditional approaches to studying leadership are the trait approach, the behavioral approach, and the situational approach.

Leader Traits

The **trait approach** is the oldest leadership perspective; it focuses on individual leaders and attempts to determine the personal characteristics (traits) that great leaders share. What set Winston Churchill, Alexander the Great, Gandhi, and Martin Luther King Jr. apart from the crowd? The trait approach assumes the existence of a leadership personality and assumes that leaders are born, not made.

From 1904 to 1948, researchers conducted more than 100 leadership trait studies.[39] At the end of that period, management scholars concluded that no particular set of traits is necessary for a person to become a successful leader. Enthusiasm for the trait approach diminished, but some research on traits continued. By the mid-1970s, a more balanced view emerged: although no traits ensure leadership success, certain characteristics are potentially useful. The current perspective is that some personality characteristics—many of which a person need not be born with but can strive to acquire—distinguish effective leaders from other people:[40]

1. *Drive.* Drive refers to a set of characteristics that reflect a high level of effort. Drive includes high need for achievement, constant striving for improvement, ambition, energy, tenacity (persistence in the face of obstacles), and initiative. In several countries, the achievement needs of top executives have been shown to be related to the growth rates of their organizations.[41] But the need to achieve can be a drawback if leaders focus on personal achievement and get so personally involved with the work that they do not delegate enough authority and responsibility. And whereas need for achievement has been shown to predict organizational effectiveness in entrepreneurial

trait approach

A leadership perspective that attempts to determine the personal characteristics that great leaders share.

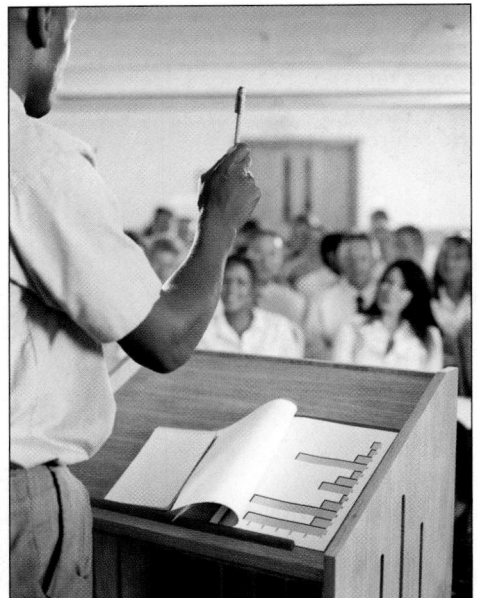

Effective leaders have the drive to succeed, are motivated by power, exude integrity, are self-confident, and thoroughly know the business they are in.

firms, it does not predict success for division heads in larger and more bureaucratic firms.[42]

2. *Leadership motivation.* Great leaders not only have drive; they *want to lead.* In this regard, it helps to be *extraverted*—extraversion is consistently related to both leadership emergence and leadership effectiveness.[43] Also important is a high need for power, a preference to be in leadership rather than follower positions.[44] A high power need induces people to attempt to influence others and sustains interest and satisfaction in the process of leadership. When the power need is exercised in moral and socially constructive ways, rather than to the detriment of others, leaders inspire more trust, respect, and commitment to their vision.

3. *Integrity.* Integrity is the correspondence between actions and words. Honesty and credibility, in addition to being desirable characteristics in their own right, are especially important for leaders because these traits inspire trust in others.

4. *Self-confidence.* Self-confidence is important for a number of reasons. The leadership role is challenging, and setbacks are inevitable. Self-confidence allows a leader to overcome obstacles, make decisions despite uncertainty, and instill confidence in others. Of course you don't want to overdo this; arrogance and cockiness have triggered more than one leader's downfall.

5. *Knowledge of the business.* Effective leaders have a high level of knowledge about their industries, companies, and technical matters. Leaders must have the intelligence to interpret vast quantities of information. Advanced degrees are useful in a career, but ultimately less important than acquired expertise in matters relevant to the organization.[46]

> A senior partner in a law firm told his attorneys about the importance of trust. When a young, ambitious lawyer asked how one can gain trust, the senior partner replied, "Try being trustworthy."[45]

Finally, one personal skill may be the most important: the ability to perceive the needs and goals of others and to adjust one's personal leadership approach accordingly.[47] Effective leaders do not rely on one leadership style; rather, they are capable of using different styles as the situation warrants.[48] This quality is the cornerstone of the situational approaches to leadership, which we will discuss shortly. As you read "Management Connection: Progress Report," think about which leader traits and skills you see Howard Schultz using to lead people at Starbucks.

Arrogance and cockiness have triggered more than one leader's downfall.

Manager's Brief   **Progress Report**   Onward

Management Connection

HOW SCHULTZ LED STARBUCKS BACK FROM THE BRINK OF FAILURE

In the early 2000s, most observers would agree that Starbucks was a tremendous success story, with customers lining up for espressos and lattes in stores located practically around the corner from each other. Howard Schultz was credited as the visionary leader who had taught Americans to enjoy coffee in an entirely new way.

But toward the end of that decade, Schultz began to see signs of trouble. Retailers' crucial measure of success, same-store sales, had grown at 5 percent per year but in the first half of 2008 slowed to 1 percent and even began falling. At times, sales volume in stores dropped so low that the company lost money by paying people to stand behind the counters. The problems grew worse in the second half of the year, when the collapsing economy frightened consumers, and it became a cliché to talk of Starbucks lattes as an unnecessary indulgence.

Even more troubling to Schultz was his belief that the company had lost sight of the vision he originally laid out. As he visited his stores, he no longer saw the verve of the theatrical experience he had sought to create. Instead baristas were hidden behind new automatic espresso machines, which efficiently delivered drinks without the soul of human interaction. New practices for shipping and storing coffee had improved efficiency but eliminated the enticing aroma of freshly ground coffee. Breakfast sandwiches boosted profits but replaced the coffee aroma with the smell of burnt cheese.

Schultz was distressed, as if something "that was an extension of myself" was dying or "turning into something I didn't admire," and that the fault was his for not paying attention. As Schultz interpreted the situation, the company had become so focused on profits and stock price that it had lost sight of the mission that had driven those numbers up in the first place. Growth had been so consistently successful that management had begun to treat success as automatic. He concluded that only he had the in-depth, inside knowledge of the company that could turn the situation around. He persuaded the board of directors to remove CEO Jim Donald, and Schultz returned to that job, committed to leading a turnaround. His goal, he wrote later, was for people to "fall back in love with Starbucks" and for Starbucks to "recapture the essence of what we set out to do: inspire the human spirit."

Drawing on his credibility as the leader who had made Starbucks great, Schultz made difficult, even drastic decisions. To refocus on its core mission, Starbucks would close hundreds of stores, but the employees who remained would continue receiving popular benefits such as health insurance. In a move that demonstrated its vision simultaneously to the public and to its employees, the company closed all its U.S. stores for an afternoon to retrain employees on the art of pouring espresso. Shareholders howled about lost revenue, but Schultz stood firm on the need to remind employees of the company's core

mission. In addition, the espresso machines were replaced with shorter models, and employees returned to grinding coffee in the stores, restoring that wonderful aroma.

Schultz pursued innovation even if it meant making mistakes. He removed smelly sandwiches from the menu but reinstated them after they had been revised so heating them wouldn't compete with the stores' coffee-scented ambience. He launched a sweet drink called Sorbetto in California but pulled it when it flopped.

Schultz also decided that to reinstill the company's vision, he would gather 10,000 store managers and employees at a leadership conference in October 2008. Even though it would cost millions of dollars when investors were growing disenchanted with the company's future prospects, Schultz insisted that the company needed to restore the trust and commitment of its people. Furthermore, for the site of his battered company's gathering, he chose a battered city, New Orleans, still recovering from Hurricane Katrina. Starbucks employees divided their time between discussing how to improve the company and working on projects to restore the city. When Schultz spoke before them, he did so humbly, asking for their help to make the company great again.

Something about all those decisions, delivered by a man who took responsibility for mistakes and admitted he would need help to fix them, renewed Starbucks. Since the turnaround effort began, Starbucks has enjoyed renewed traffic in its stores, rising customer satisfaction scores (up to record levels), and growth in revenues and stock prices. Schultz credits his success as leader of that turnaround to his having "100 percent belief in [the company's] core reason for being." Starbucks chief financial officer Troy Alstead says Schultz's drive and commitment literally saved the company: "A lot of people were questioning, in that span before he came back [as CEO], 'Were we done?' And Howard came back, and it wasn't even a question anymore."[49]

- What sources of power did Howard Schultz have for leading Starbucks's turnaround?
- Which leader behaviors and traits do you see at work in this description?

Leader Behaviors

The **behavioral approach** to leadership attempts to identify what good leaders do. Should leaders focus on getting the job done or on keeping their followers happy? Should they make decisions autocratically or democratically? In the behavioral approach, personal characteristics are considered less important than the actual behaviors that leaders exhibit.

Three general categories of leadership behavior have received particular attention: behaviors related to task performance, group maintenance, and employee participation in decision making.

Task Performance Leadership requires getting the job done. **Task performance behaviors** are the leader's efforts to ensure that the work unit or organization

LO 6

behavioral approach

A leadership perspective that attempts to identify what good leaders do—that is, what behaviors they exhibit.

task performance behaviors

Actions taken to ensure that the work group or organization reaches its goals.

reaches its goals. This dimension is variously referred to as *concern for production, directive leadership, initiating structure,* or *closeness of supervision.* It includes a focus on work speed, quality and accuracy, quantity of output, and following the rules.[50] This type of leader behavior improves leader job performance and group and organizational performance.[51]

Group Maintenance   In exhibiting **group maintenance behaviors,** leaders take action to ensure the satisfaction of group members, develop and maintain harmonious work relationships, and preserve the social stability of the group. This dimension is sometimes referred to as *concern for people, supportive leadership,* or *consideration.* It includes a focus on people's feelings and comfort, appreciation of them, and stress reduction.[52] This type of leader behavior has a strong positive impact on follower satisfaction, motivation, and leader effectiveness.[53]

What *specific* behaviors do performance- and maintenance-oriented leadership imply? To help answer this question, assume you are asked to rate your boss on these two dimensions. If a leadership study were conducted in your organization, you would be asked to fill out a questionnaire similar to the one in Table 12.1. The behaviors indicated in the first set of questions represent performance-oriented leadership; those indicated in the second set represent maintenance-oriented leadership.

Bottom Line

Task performance behaviors focus on achieving work goals.
What shows you that a manager cares about task performance?

group maintenance behaviors

Actions taken to ensure the satisfaction of group members, develop and maintain harmonious work relationships, and preserve the social stability of the group.

TABLE 12.1

Questions Assessing Task Performance and Group Maintenance Leadership

Task Performance Leadership
1. Is your superior strict about observing regulations?
2. To what extent does your superior give you instructions and orders?
3. Is your superior strict about the amount of work you do?
4. Does your superior urge you to complete your work by a specified time?
5. Does your superior try to make you work to your maximum capacity?
6. When you do an inadequate job, does your superior focus on the inadequate way the job is done?
7. Does your superior ask you for reports about the progress of your work?
8. How precisely does your superior work out plans for goal achievement each month?

Group Maintenance Leadership
1. Can you talk freely with your superior about your work?
2. Does your superior generally support you?
3. Is your superior concerned about your personal problems?
4. Do you think your superior trusts you?
5. Does your superior give you recognition when you do your job well?
6. When a problem arises in your workplace, does your superior ask your opinion about how to solve it?
7. Is your superior concerned about your future benefits, such as promotions and pay raises?
8. Does your superior treat you fairly?

SOURCE: Reprinted from J. Misumi and M. Peterson, "The Performance-Maintenance (PM) Theory of Leadership: Review of a Japanese Research Program," *Administrative Science Quarterly* 30, no. 2 (June 1985). Reprinted with permission of Sage Publications, Inc.

Leader–member exchange (LMX) theory highlights the importance of leader behaviors not just toward the group as a whole but toward individuals on a personal basis.[54] The focus in the original formulation, which has since been expanded, is primarily on the leader behaviors historically considered group maintenance.[55] According to LMX theory, and as supported by research evidence, maintenance behaviors such as trust, open communication, mutual respect, mutual obligation, and mutual loyalty form the cornerstone of relationships that are satisfying and perhaps more productive.[56]

Remember, though, the potential for cross-cultural differences. Maintenance behaviors are important everywhere, but the specific behaviors can differ from one culture to another. For example, in the United States, maintenance behaviors include dealing with people face-to-face; in Japan, written memos are preferred over giving directions face-to-face, thus avoiding confrontation and permitting face-saving in the event of disagreement.[57]

Participation in Decision Making

How should a leader make decisions? More specifically, to what extent should leaders involve their people in making decisions?[58] As a dimension of leadership behavior, **participation in decision making** can range from autocratic to democratic. **Autocratic leadership** makes decisions and then announces them to the group. **Democratic leadership** solicits input from others. Democratic leadership seeks information, opinions, and preferences, sometimes to the point of meeting with the group, leading discussions, and using consensus or majority vote to make the final choice.

The Effects of Leader Behavior

How the leader behaves influences people's attitudes and performance. Studies of these effects focus on autocratic versus democratic decision styles or on performance- versus maintenance-oriented behaviors.

Decision Styles   The classic study comparing autocratic and democratic styles found that a democratic approach resulted in the most positive attitudes, whereas an autocratic approach resulted in somewhat higher performance.[59] A **laissez-faire** style, in which the leader essentially made no decisions, led to more negative attitudes and lower performance. These results seem logical and probably represent the prevalent beliefs among managers about the general effects of these approaches.

Democratic styles, appealing though they may seem, are not always the most appropriate. When speed is of the essence, democratic decision making may be too slow, or people may want decisiveness from the leader.[60] Whether a decision should be made autocratically or democratically depends on the characteristics of the leader, the followers, and the situation.[61] Thus a situational approach to leader decision styles, discussed later in the chapter, is appropriate.

Performance and Maintenance Behaviors   The performance and maintenance dimensions of leadership are independent of each other. In other words, a leader can behave in ways that emphasize one, both, or neither of these dimensions. Some research indicates that the ideal combination is to engage in both types of leader behaviors.

A team of Ohio State University researchers investigated the effects of leader behaviors in a truck manufacturing plant of International Harvester.[62] Generally, supervisors who were high on *maintenance behaviors* (which the researchers termed *consideration*) had fewer grievances and less turnover in their work units than supervisors who were low on this dimension. The opposite held for *task performance behaviors* (which the research team called *initiating structure*). Supervisors high on this dimension had more grievances and higher turnover rates.

leader–member exchange (LMX) theory

Highlights the importance of leader behaviors not just toward the group as a whole but toward individuals on a personal basis.

participation in decision making

Leader behaviors that managers perform in involving their employees in making decisions.

autocratic leadership

A form of leadership in which the leader makes decisions on his or her own and then announces those decisions to the group.

democratic leadership

A form of leadership in which the leader solicits input from subordinates.

laissez-faire

A leadership philosophy characterized by an absence of managerial decision making.

> A leader can behave in ways that emphasize one, both, or neither of these dimensions.

When maintenance and performance leadership behaviors were considered together, the results were more complex. But one conclusion was clear: when a leader is high on performance-oriented behaviors, he or she should *also* be maintenance oriented. Otherwise the leader will face high rates of employee turnover and grievances.

At about the same time the Ohio State studies were being conducted, a research program at the University of Michigan was studying the impact of the same leader behaviors on groups' job performance.[63] Among other things, the researchers concluded that the most effective managers engaged in what they called *task-oriented behavior:* planning, scheduling, coordinating, providing resources, and setting performance goals. Effective managers also exhibited more *relationship-oriented behavior:* demonstrating trust and confidence, being friendly and considerate, showing appreciation, keeping people informed, and so on. As you can see, these dimensions of leader behavior are essentially the task performance and group maintenance dimensions.

After the Ohio State and Michigan findings were published, it became popular to talk about the ideal leader as one who is always both performance and maintenance oriented. The best-known leadership training model to follow this style is Blake and Mouton's Leadership Grid®.[64] In grid training, managers are rated on their performance-oriented behavior (called *concern for production*) and maintenance-oriented behavior (*concern for people*). Then their scores are plotted on the grid shown in Figure 12.2. The highest score is a 9 on both dimensions.

As the figure shows, joint scores can fall at any point on the grid. Managers who did not score a 9,9—for example, those who were high on concern for people but low on concern for production—would then receive training on how to become a 9,9 leader.

For a long time, grid training was warmly received by U.S. business and industry. Later, however, it was criticized for embracing a simplistic, one-best-way style of leadership and ignoring the possibility that 9,9 is not best under all circumstances. For example, even 1,1 can be appropriate if employees know their jobs (and therefore don't need to receive directions). Also, they may enjoy their jobs and their coworkers enough that whether the boss shows personal concern for them is not very important. Nonetheless, if the manager is uncertain how to behave, it probably is best to exhibit behaviors that are related to both task performance and group maintenance.[65]

In fact, a wide range of effective leadership styles exists. Organizations that understand the need for diverse leadership styles will have a competitive advantage in the modern business environment over those that believe there is only "one best way."

Situational Approaches to Leadership

situational approach

Leadership perspective proposing that universally important traits and behaviors do not exist, and that effective leadership behavior varies from situation to situation.

According to proponents of the **situational approach** to leadership, universally important traits and behaviors don't exist. They believe effective leader behaviors vary from situation to situation. *The leader should first analyze the situation and then decide what to do.* In other words, look before you lead.

A head nurse in a hospital described her situational approach to leadership:

Look before you lead.

My leadership style is a mix of all styles. In this environment I normally let people participate. But in a code blue situation where a patient is dying I automatically become very autocratic: "You do this; you do that; you, out of the room; you all better be quiet; you, get Dr. Mansfield." The staff tell me that's the only time they see me like that. In an emergency like that, you don't have time to vote, talk a lot, or yell at each other. It's time for someone to set up the order.

I remember one time, one person saying, "Wait a minute, I want to do this." He wanted to do the mouth-to-mouth resuscitation. I knew the person behind him did it better, so I said, "No, he does it." This fellow told me later that I hurt him so badly to yell that in front of all the staff and doctors. It was like he wasn't good enough. So I explained it to him: "That's the way it is. A life was on the line. I couldn't give you warm fuzzies. I couldn't make you look good because you didn't have the skills to give the very best to that patient who wasn't breathing anymore."[66]

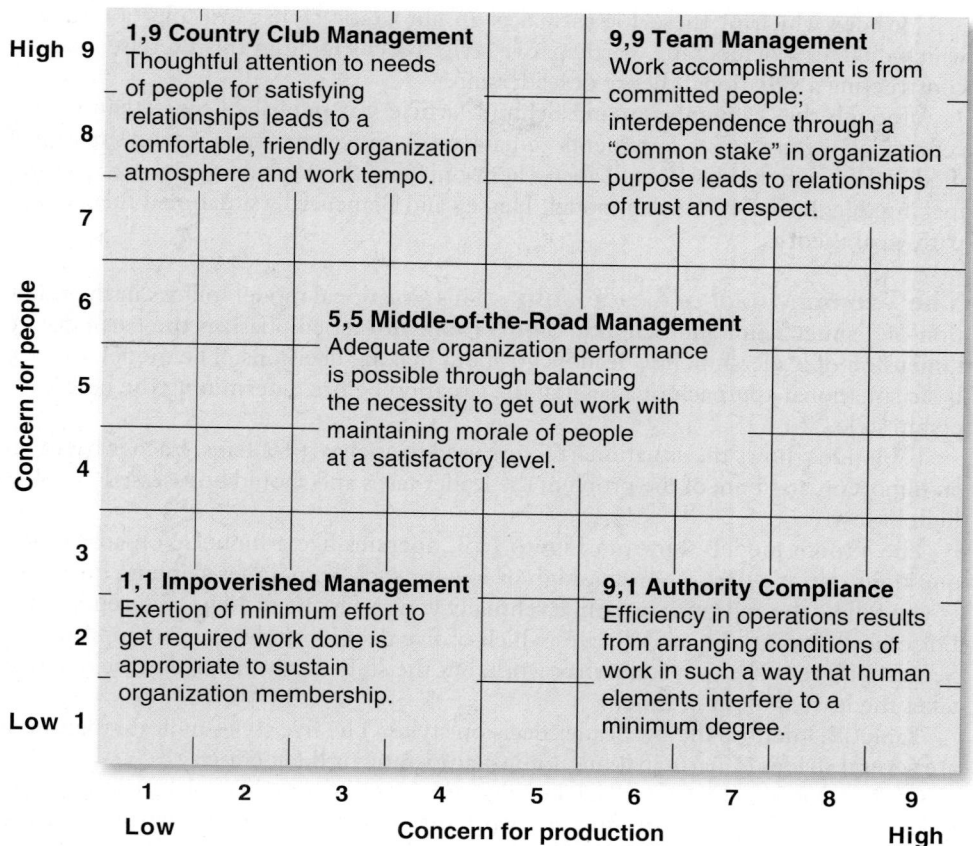

FIGURE 12.2
The Leadership Grid®

This nurse has her own intuitive situational approach to leadership. She knows the potential advantages of the participatory approach to decision making, but she also knows that in some circumstances she must make decisions herself.

The first situational model of leadership was proposed in 1958 by Tannenbaum and Schmidt. In their classic *Harvard Business Review* article, these authors described how

> Managers should consider three factors before deciding how to lead: forces in the manager, forces in the subordinate, and forces in the situation.[67]

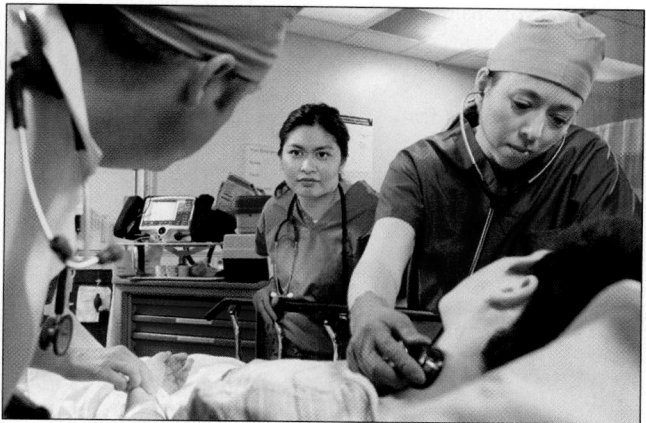

Nurses experience situational leadership on a daily basis. How would you handle a leadership role under pressure?

Forces in the manager include the manager's personal values, inclinations, feelings of security, and confidence in subordinates. Forces in the subordinate include his or her knowledge and experience, readiness to assume responsibility for decision making, interest in the task or problem, and understanding and acceptance of the organization's goals. Forces in the situation include the type of leadership style the organization values, the degree to which the group works effectively as a unit, the problem itself and the type of information needed to solve it, and the amount of time the leader has to make the decision.

Consider which of these forces makes an autocratic style most appropriate and which dictates a democratic, participative style. By engaging in this exercise, you are constructing a situational theory of leadership.

Although the Tannenbaum and Schmidt article was published more than a half-century ago, most of its arguments remain valid. Since that time, other situational models have emerged. We will focus here on four: the Vroom model for decision making, Fiedler's contingency model, Hersey and Blanchard's situational theory, and path–goal theory.

The Vroom Model of Leadership   This situational model follows in the tradition of Tannenbaum and Schmidt. The **Vroom model** emphasizes the participative dimension of leadership: how leaders go about making decisions. The model uses the basic situational approach of assessing the situation before determining the best leadership style.[68]

Table 12.2 shows the situational factors used to analyze problems. Each is based on an important attribute of the problem the leader faces and should be assessed as either high or low.

The Vroom model, shown in Figure 12.3, operates like a funnel. You answer the questions one at a time, choosing high or low for each, sometimes skipping questions as you follow the appropriate path. Eventually you reach one of 14 possible endpoints. For each endpoint, the model states which of five decision styles is most appropriate. Several different decision styles may work, but the style recommended is the one that takes the least amount of time.

Table 12.3 defines the five leader decision styles. The five styles indicate that there are several shades of participation, not just autocratic or democratic.

Of course not every managerial decision warrants this complicated analysis. But the model becomes less complex after you work through it a couple of times. Also, using the model for major decisions ensures that you consider the important situational factors and alerts you to the most appropriate style to use.

Fiedler's Contingency Model   According to **Fiedler's contingency model of leadership effectiveness,** effectiveness depends on two factors: the personal style of the leader and the degree to which the situation gives the leader power, control,

---

Vroom model

A situational model that focuses on the participative dimension of leadership.

Fiedler's contingency model of leadership effectiveness

A situational approach to leadership postulating that effectiveness depends on the personal style of the leader and the degree to which the situation gives the leader power, control, and influence over the situation.

TABLE 12.2
Situational Factors for Problem Analysis

Decision significance:	The significance of the decision to the success of the project or organization.
Importance of commitment:	The importance of team members' commitment to the decision.
Leader's expertise:	Your knowledge or expertise in relation to this problem.
Likelihood of commitment:	The likelihood that the team would commit itself to a decision that you might make on your own.
Group support for objectives:	The degree to which the team supports the organization's objectives at stake in this problem.
Group expertise:	Team members' knowledge or expertise in relation to this problem.
Team competence:	The ability of team members to work together in solving problems.

SOURCE: Reprinted from *Organizational Dynamics*, Vol. 28, No. 4, Victor H. Vroom, "Leadership and the Decision-Making Process," pp. 82–94. Copyright © 2000 with permission from Elsevier.

Time-Driven Model

Instructions: The matrix operates like a funnel. You start at the left with a specific decision problem in mind. The column headings denote situational factors which may or may not be present in that problem. You progress by selecting high or low (H or L) for each relevant situational factor. Proceed down from the funnel, judging only those situational factors for which a judgement is called for, until you reach the recommended process.

Decision Significance	Importance of Commitment	Leader Expertise	Likelihood of Commitment	Group Support	Group Expertise	Team Competence	Process
H	H	H	H	-	-	-	Decide
			L	H	H	H	Delegate
						L	Consult (group)
					L	-	Consult (group)
				L	-	-	Consult (group)
		L	H	H	H	H	Facilitate
						L	Consult (individually)
					L	-	Consult (individually)
				L	-	-	Consult (individually)
			L	H	H	H	Facilitate
						L	Consult (group)
					L	-	Consult (group)
				L	-	-	Consult (group)
	L	H	-	-	-	-	Decide
	L	L	-	H	H	H	Facilitate
						L	Consult (individually)
					L	-	Consult (individually)
				L	-	-	Consult (individually)
L	H	-	H	-	-	-	Decide
			L	-	-	H	Delegate
						L	Facilitate
	L	-	-	-	-	-	Decide

SOURCE: Reprinted from *Organizational Dynamics*, Vol. 28, No. 4, Victor H. Vroom, "Leadership and the Decision-Making Process," pp. 82–94. Copyright © 2000 with permission from Elsevier.

FIGURE 12.3
Vroom's Model of Leadership Style

and influence over the situation.[69] Figure 12.4 illustrates the contingency model. The upper half of the figure shows the situational analysis, and the lower half indicates the appropriate style. In the upper portion, three questions are used to analyze the situation:

1. Are leader–member relations good or poor? (To what extent is the leader accepted and supported by group members?)
2. Is the task structured or unstructured? (To what extent do group members know what their goals are and how to accomplish them?)
3. Is the leader's position power strong or weak (high or low)? (To what extent does the leader have the authority to reward and punish?)

These three sequential questions create a decision tree (from top to bottom in the figure) in which a situation is classified into one of eight categories. The lower the category number, the more favorable the situation is for the leader; the higher the number, the less favorable the situation. Fiedler originally called this variable "situational favorableness," but now it is "situational control." Situation 1 is the best: relations are good, task structure is high, and power is high. In the least favorable situation (8),

TABLE 12.3
Vroom's Leader Decision Styles

Decide: You make the decision alone and either announce or "sell" it to the group. You may use your expertise in collecting information that you deem relevant to the problem from the group or others.
Consult individually: You present the problem to the group members individually, get their suggestions, and then make the decision.
Consult the group: You present the problem to the group members in a meeting, get their suggestions, and then make the decision.
Facilitate: You present the problem to the group in a meeting. You act as a facilitator, defining the problem to be solved and the boundaries within which the decision must be made. Your objective is to get concurrence on a decision. Above all, you take care to ensure that your ideas are not given any greater weight than those of others simply because of your position.
Delegate: You permit the group to make the decision within prescribed limits. The group undertakes the identification and diagnosis of the problem, developing alternative procedures for solving it, and deciding on one or more alternative solutions. While you play no direct role in the group's deliberations unless explicitly asked, your role is an important one behind the scenes, providing needed resources and encouragement.

SOURCE: Reprinted from *Organizational Dynamics*, Vol. 28, No. 4, Victor H. Vroom, "Leadership and the Decision-Making Process," pp. 82–94. Copyright © 2000 with permission from Elsevier.

in which the leader has very little situational control, relations are poor, tasks lack structure, and the leader's power is weak.

Different situations dictate different leadership styles. Fiedler measured leadership styles with an instrument assessing the leader's *least preferred coworker* (LPC); that is, the attitude toward the follower the leader liked the least. This was considered an indication more generally of leaders' attitudes toward people. If a leader can single

FIGURE 12.4
Fiedler's Analysis of Situations in Which the Task- or Relationship-Motivated Leader Is More Effective

SOURCE: From Dennis Organ and Thomas Bateman, *Organizational Behavior*, 4th ed., McGraw-Hill, 1990. © 1990 by The McGraw-Hill Companies, Inc. Reprinted with permission.

out the person she likes the least, but her attitude is not all that negative, she would receive a high score on the LPC scale. Leaders with more negative attitudes toward others would receive low LPC scores.

Based on the LPC score, Fiedler considered two leadership styles. **Task-motivated leadership** places primary emphasis on completing the task and is more likely exhibited by leaders with low LPC scores. **Relationship-motivated leadership** emphasizes maintaining good interpersonal relationships and is more likely from high-LPC leaders. These leadership styles correspond to task performance and group maintenance leader behaviors, respectively.

The lower part of Figure 12.4 indicates which style is situationally appropriate. For situations 1, 2, 3, and 8, a task-motivated leadership style is more effective. For situations 4 through 7, relationship-motivated leadership is more appropriate.

Fiedler's theory was not always supported by research. It is better supported if three broad rather than eight specific levels of situational control are assumed: low, medium, and high. The theory was quite controversial in academic circles; among other arguable things, it assumed that leaders cannot change their styles but must be assigned to situations that suit their styles. However, the model has withstood the test of time and still receives attention. Most important, it initiated and continues to emphasize the importance of finding a fit between the situation and the leader's style.

Hersey and Blanchard's Situational Theory   Hersey and Blanchard developed a situational model that added another factor the leader should take into account before deciding whether task performance or maintenance behaviors are more important. Originally called the *life-cycle theory of leadership*, **Hersey and Blanchard's situational theory** highlights the maturity of the followers as the key situational factor.[70] **Job maturity** is the level of the follower's skills and technical knowledge relative to the task being performed; **psychological maturity** is the follower's self-confidence and self-respect. High-maturity followers have both the ability and the confidence to do a good job.

The theory proposes that the more mature the followers, the less the leader needs to engage in task performance behaviors. The required amount of maintenance behaviors is a bit more complex: maintenance behaviors are not important with followers of low or high levels of maturity but are important for followers of moderate maturity. For low-maturity followers, the emphasis should be on performance-related leadership; for moderate-maturity followers, performance leadership is somewhat less important and maintenance behaviors become more important; and for high-maturity followers, neither dimension of leadership behavior is important.

Little academic research has been done on this situational theory, but the model is popular in management training seminars. Regardless of its scientific validity, Hersey and Blanchard's model provides a reminder that it is important to treat different people differently. Moreover, it suggests the importance of treating the same individual differently from time to time as he or she changes jobs or acquires more maturity in her or his particular job.[71]

Path–Goal Theory   Perhaps the most comprehensive and generally useful situational model of leadership effectiveness is path–goal theory. Developed by Robert House, **path–goal theory** gets its name from its concern with how leaders influence followers' perceptions of their work goals and the paths they follow toward goal attainment.[72]

The key situational factors in path–goal theory are (1) personal characteristics of followers and (2) environmental pressures and demands with which followers must cope to attain their work goals. These factors determine which leadership behaviors are most appropriate.

task-motivated leadership

Leadership that places primary emphasis on completing a task.

relationship-motivated leadership

Leadership that places primary emphasis on maintaining good interpersonal relationships.

Hersey and Blanchard's situational theory

A life-cycle theory of leadership postulating that a manager should consider an employee's psychological and job maturity before deciding whether task performance or maintenance behaviors are more important.

job maturity

The level of the employee's skills and technical knowledge relative to the task being performed.

psychological maturity

An employee's self-confidence and self-respect.

path–goal theory

A theory that concerns how leaders influence subordinates' perceptions of their work goals and the paths they follow toward attainment of those goals.

The four pertinent leadership behaviors are as follows:

1. *Directive leadership*, a form of task performance–oriented behavior.
2. *Supportive leadership*, a form of group maintenance–oriented behavior.
3. *Participative leadership*, or decision style.
4. *Achievement-oriented leadership*, or behaviors geared toward motivating people, such as setting challenging goals and rewarding good performance.

These situational factors and leader behaviors are merged in Figure 12.5. As you can see, appropriate leader behaviors—as determined by characteristics of followers and the work environment—lead to effective performance.

The theory also specifies *which* follower and environmental characteristics are important. There are three key follower characteristics. *Authoritarianism* is the degree to which individuals respect, admire, and defer to authority. *Locus of control* is the extent to which individuals see the environment as responsive to their own behavior. People with an *internal* locus of control believe that what happens to them is their own doing; people with an *external* locus of control believe that it is just luck or fate. Finally, *ability* is people's beliefs about their own abilities to do their assigned jobs.

Path–goal theory states that these personal characteristics determine the appropriateness of various leadership styles. For example, the theory makes the following propositions:

- A directive leadership style is more appropriate for highly authoritarian people because such people respect authority.
- A participative leadership style is more appropriate for people who have an internal locus of control because these individuals prefer to have more influence over their own lives.
- A directive style is more appropriate when subordinates' ability is low. The directive style helps people understand what has to be done.

Appropriate leadership style is also determined by three important environmental factors: people's tasks, the formal authority system of the organization, and the primary work group:

- Directive leadership is inappropriate if tasks already are well structured.
- If the task and the authority or rule system are dissatisfying, directive leadership will create greater dissatisfaction.
- If the task or authority system is dissatisfying, supportive leadership is especially appropriate because it offers one positive source of gratification in an otherwise negative situation.
- If the primary work group provides social support to its members, supportive leadership is less important.

FIGURE 12.5
The Path–Goal Framework

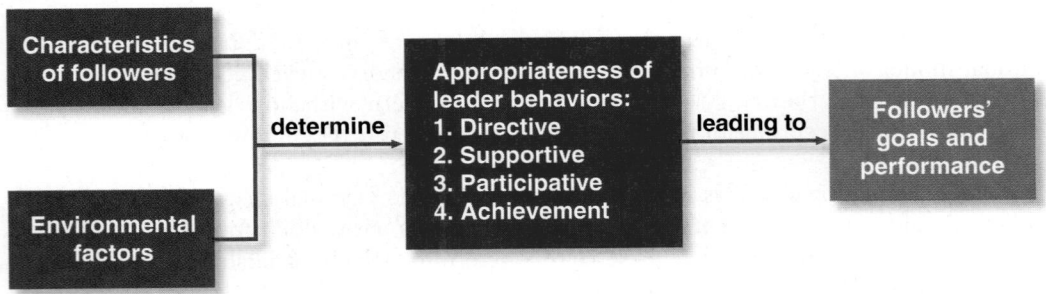

Path–goal theory offers many more propositions. In general, the theory suggests that the functions of the leader are to (1) make the path to work goals easier to travel by providing coaching and direction, (2) reduce frustrating barriers to goal attainment, and (3) increase opportunities for personal satisfaction by increasing payoffs to people for achieving performance goals. The best way to do these things depends on your people and on the work situation. Again, analyze, and then adapt your style accordingly.

Substitutes for Leadership   Sometimes leaders don't have to lead, or situations constrain their ability to lead effectively. The situation may be one in which leadership is unnecessary or has little impact. **Substitutes for leadership** can provide the same influence on people that leaders otherwise would have.

Certain follower, task, and organizational factors are substitutes for task performance and group maintenance leader behaviors.[73] For example, group maintenance behaviors are less important and have less impact if people already have a closely knit group, they have a professional orientation, the job is inherently satisfying, or there is great physical distance between leader and followers. Thus physicians who are strongly concerned with professional conduct, enjoy their work, and work independently do not need social support from hospital administrators.

Task performance leadership is less important and will have less of a positive effect if people have a lot of experience and ability, feedback is supplied to them directly from the task or by computer, or the rules and procedures are rigid. If these factors are operating, the leader does not have to tell people what to do or how well they are performing.

The concept of substitutes for leadership does more than indicate when a leader's attempts at influence will and will not work. It provides useful and practical prescriptions for how to manage more efficiently.[74] If the manager can develop the work situation to the point where a number of these substitutes for leadership are operating, less time will need to be spent in direct attempts to influence people. The leader will be free to spend more time on other important activities.

Research indicates that substitutes for leadership may be better predictors of commitment and satisfaction than of performance.[75] These substitutes are helpful, but you can't put substitutes in place and think you've completed your job as leader. And as a follower, consider this: if you're not getting good leadership, and if these substitutes are not in place, create your own "substitute" for leadership—self-leadership. Take the initiative to motivate yourself, lead yourself, create positive change, and lead others.

substitutes for leadership

Factors in the workplace that can exert the same influence on employees as leaders would provide.

The concept of substitutes for leadership does more than indicate when a leader's attempts at influence will and will not work.

Contemporary Perspectives on Leadership

So far you have learned the major classic approaches to understanding leadership, all of which remain useful today. Now we will discuss a number of new developments that are revolutionizing our understanding of this vital aspect of management.

LO 7

Charismatic Leadership

Like many great leaders, Ronald Reagan had charisma. So does Barack Obama. Thomas Watson, Alfred Sloan, Steve Jobs, and Richard Branson are good examples of charismatic leaders in industry.

Charisma is a rather elusive concept; it is easy to spot but hard to define. What *is* charisma, and how does one acquire it? According to one definition, "Charisma packs

Martin Luther King was a brilliant, charismatic leader who had a compelling vision, a dream for a better world.

charismatic leader

A person who is dominant, self-confident, convinced of the moral righteousness of his or her beliefs, and able to arouse a sense of excitement and adventure in followers.

an emotional wallop for followers above and beyond ordinary esteem, affection, admiration, and trust. . . . The charismatic is an idolized hero, a messiah, and a savior."[76] As you can see from this quotation, many people, particularly North Americans, value charisma in their leaders. But some people don't like the term *charisma;* it can be associated with the negative charisma of evil leaders whom people follow blindly.[77] Nevertheless, charismatic leaders who display appropriate values and use their charisma for appropriate purposes serve as ethical role models for others.[78]

Charismatic leaders are dominant, exceptionally self-confident, and have a strong conviction in the moral righteousness of their beliefs.[79] They strive to create an aura of competence and success and communicate high expectations for and confidence in followers. Ultimately, charismatic leaders satisfy other peoples' needs.[80]

The charismatic leader articulates ideological goals and makes sacrifices in pursuit of those goals.[81] Martin Luther King Jr. had a dream for a better world, and John F. Kennedy spoke of landing a human on the moon. In other words, such leaders have a compelling vision. The charismatic leader also arouses a sense of excitement and adventure. He or she is an eloquent speaker who exhibits superior verbal skills, which help communicate the vision and motivate followers. Walt Disney mesmerized people with his storytelling; had enormous creative talent; and instilled in his organization strong values of good taste, risk taking, and innovation.[82]

Leaders who possess these characteristics or do these things inspire in their followers trust, confidence, acceptance, obedience, emotional involvement, affection, admiration, and higher performance.[83] For example, a recent study of firefighters found them to be happier when working for charismatic officers who expressed positive attitudes.[84] Having charisma not only helps CEOs inspire other employees in the organization but also may enable them to influence external stakeholders, including customers and investors.[85] Evidence for the positive effects of charismatic leadership has been found in a wide variety of groups, organizations, and management levels, and in countries including India, Singapore, the Netherlands, China, Japan, and Canada.[86]

Charisma has been shown to improve corporate financial performance, particularly under conditions of uncertainty—that is, in risky circumstances or when environments are changing and people have difficulty understanding what they should do.[87] Uncertainty is stressful, and it makes people more receptive to the ideas and actions of charismatic leaders. By the way, too, as an organization's performance improves under a person's leadership, that person becomes seen as more charismatic as a result of the higher performance.[88]

transformational leaders

Leaders who motivate people to transcend their personal interests for the good of the group.

Transformational Leadership

Charisma contributes to transformational leadership. **Transformational leaders** get people to transcend their personal interests for the sake of the larger community.[89] They generate excitement and revitalize organizations. At Hewlett-Packard, the ability to generate excitement is an explicit criterion for selecting managers. In the United Kingdom, Richard Branson of Virgin Group is a transformational leader who built a global business empire.[90]

transactional leaders

Leaders who manage through transactions, using their legitimate, reward, and coercive powers to give commands and exchange rewards for services rendered.

The transformational process moves beyond the more traditional *transactional* approach to leadership. **Transactional leaders** view management as a series of transactions in which they use their legitimate, reward, and coercive powers to give commands and exchange rewards for services rendered. Unlike transformational leadership, transactional leadership is dispassionate; it does not excite, transform, empower, or inspire people to focus on the interests of the group or organization. However, transactional approaches may be more effective for individualists than for collectivists (recall Chapter 6).[91]

Generating Excitement   Transformational leaders generate excitement in several ways.[92] First, they are *charismatic*, as described earlier. Second, they give their followers *individualized attention*. Transformational leaders delegate challenging work to deserving people, keep lines of communication open, and provide one-on-one mentoring to develop their people. They do not treat everyone alike because not everyone *is* alike.

Third, transformational leaders are *intellectually stimulating*. They arouse in their followers an awareness of problems and potential solutions. They articulate the organization's opportunities, threats, strengths, and weaknesses. They stir the imagination and generate insights. Therefore, problems are recognized, and high-quality solutions are identified and implemented with the full commitment of followers.

Skills and Strategies   At least four skills or strategies contribute to transformational leadership.[93] First, transformational leaders *have a vision*—a goal, an agenda, or a results orientation that grabs people's attention. Second, they *communicate their vision;* through words, manner, or symbolism, they relate a compelling image of the ultimate goal. Third, transformational leaders *build trust* by being consistent, dependable, and persistent. They position themselves clearly by choosing a direction and staying with it, thus projecting integrity. Finally, they have a *positive self-regard*. They do not feel self-important or complacent; rather, they recognize their personal strengths, compensate for their weaknesses, nurture and continually develop their talents, and know how to learn from failure. They strive for success rather than merely try to avoid failure.

> [Transformational leaders] strive for success rather than merely try to avoid failure.

Transformational leadership has been identified in industry, the military, and politics.[94] Examples of transformational leaders in business include Henry Ford (founder of Ford Motor Company), Herb Kelleher (former CEO of Southwest Airlines), Jeff Bezos (founder of Amazon.com), David Neeleman (entrepreneur and founder of Jet-Blue), and Lee Iacocca (who led Chrysler's turnaround during the 1980s).[95] Transformational leadership exhibited by CEOs predicts firm performance, at least for small and midsized firms.[96]

As with studies of charisma, transformational leadership and its positive impact on follower satisfaction and performance have been demonstrated in countries the world over, including Egypt, Germany, China, England, and Japan.[97] A study in Korean companies found that transformational leadership predicted employee motivation, which in turn predicted creativity.[98] Under transformational leadership, people view their jobs as more intrinsically motivating (see Chapter 13 for more on this) and are more strongly committed to work goals.[99] And top management teams agree more clearly about important organizational goals, which translates into higher organizational performance.[100]

IN PRACTICE

An example of a manager who uses the skills and strategies of transformational leadership is Kathy Savitt, founder and chief executive officer of Lockerz. The company operates an e-commerce website that uses social networking tools to engage teens in shopping online. Teens who visit the site can help themselves and their friends earn points toward discounts on merchandise by clicking on images of the items and viewing various kinds of promotional content. The company grew out of Savitt's passion for serving this young demographic group.

Savitt has a vision not only for the company's place as an Internet marketer, but also for the kind of company it should be for its employees. Her vision is of a business where the employees respect one another and are fearless about innovation. In hiring, Savitt seeks people who not only are highly intelligent but also listen attentively, demonstrate respect for others, and can laugh at themselves. She models her vision of the workplace by addressing problems and setbacks frankly and with a focus on solutions, saying it takes courage to work through failure.

Savitt expresses confidence that by bringing in people who have talent plus a drive to contribute, she can create a company culture that avoids cynical practices she has experienced at other companies in the past. For example, she has seen business meetings that play a kind of stump-the-chump game, where if one employee tries to answer a question or offer an idea, others pile on with criticism. Savitt believes she can avoid that by communicating the values of courage, innovation, and results.[101]

- What kinds of behavior can help Savitt build employees' trust in her and her vision?

Transforming Leaders Importantly, transformational leadership is not the exclusive domain of presidents and chief executives. In the military, leaders who received transformational leadership training had a positive impact on followers' personal development. They also were successful as *indirect* leaders: military recruits under the transformational leaders' direct reports were stronger performers.[102] Don't forget, though: the best leaders are those who can display both transformational and transactional behaviors.[103]

Ford Motor Company, in collaboration with the University of Michigan School of Business, put thousands of middle managers through a program designed to stimulate transformational leadership.[104] The training included analysis of the changing business environment, company strategy, and personal reflection and discussion about the need to change. Participants assessed their own leadership styles and developed a specific change initiative to implement after the training—a change that would make a needed and lasting difference for the company.

Over the next six months, the managers implemented change on the job. Almost half of the initiatives resulted in transformational changes in the organization or work unit; the rest of the changes were smaller, more incremental, or more personal. Whether managers made small or transformational changes depended on their attitude going into the training, their level of self-esteem, and the amount of support they received from others on the job for their efforts. Thus some managers did not respond as hoped. But almost half embraced the training, became more transformational in orientation, and tackled significant transformational changes for the company.

Level 5 leadership, a term well-known among executives, is considered by some to be the ultimate leadership style. Level 5 leadership is a combination of strong professional will (determination) and personal humility that builds enduring greatness.[105] Thus a Level 5 leader is relentlessly focused on the organization's long-term success while behaving with modesty, directing attention toward the organization rather than him- or herself. Examples include John Chambers, CEO of Cisco Systems, and IBM's former chief executive Louis Gerstner. Gerstner is widely credited for turning around a stodgy IBM by shifting its focus from computer hardware to business solutions. Following his retirement, Gerstner wrote a memoir that details what happened at the company but says little about himself. Although Level 5 leadership is seen as a way to transform organizations to make them great, it requires also that the leader exhibit a combination of transactional and transformational styles.[106]

Authenticity

In general, consider **authentic leadership** to be rooted in the ancient Greek philosophy "To thine own self be true."[107] In your own leadership, strive for authenticity in the form of honesty, genuineness, reliability, integrity, and trustworthiness. Authentic transformational leaders care about public interests (community, organizational, or group), not just their own.[108] They are willing to sacrifice their own interests for others, and they can be trusted. They are ethically mature; people view leaders who exhibit moral reasoning as more transformational than leaders who do not.[109] Importantly, ethical leadership flows down from one organizational level to the next[110]—your actions as a leader have an impact beyond your immediate, direct reports.

Pseudotransformational leaders are the opposite: they talk a good game, but they ignore followers' real needs as their own self-interests (power, prestige, control, wealth, fame) take precedence.[111]

Opportunities for Leaders

A common view of leaders is that they are superheroes acting alone, swooping in to save the day. But especially in these complex times, leaders cannot and need not act alone. Effective leadership must permeate the organization, not reside in one or two superstars at the top. The leader's job becomes one of spreading leadership abilities throughout the firm.[112] Make people responsible for their own performance. Create an environment in which each person can figure out what needs to be done and then do it well. Point the way and clear the path so that people can succeed. Give them the credit they deserve. Make heroes out of *them*.

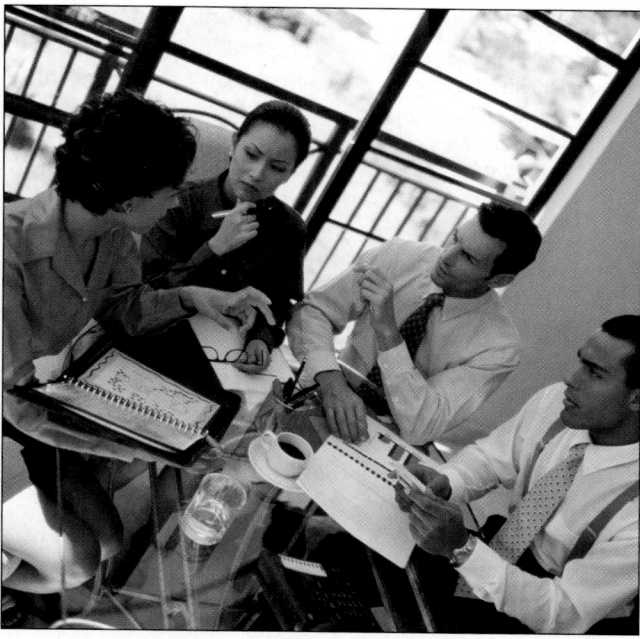

Encouraging and empowering all employees to reach their full potential and grow is an important way managers can strengthen their organization.

Thus what is now required of leaders is less the efficient management of resources, and more the effective unleashing of people and their intellectual capital.

This perspective uncovers a variety of nontraditional leadership roles that are emerging as vitally important.[113] The term **servant–leader** was coined by Robert Greenleaf, a retired AT&T executive. The term is paradoxical in the sense that "leader" and "servant" are usually opposites; the servant–leader's relationship with employees is more like that of serving customers. For the individual who wants to both lead and serve others, servant–leadership is a way of relating to others to serve their needs and enhance their personal growth while strengthening the organization. For example, when David Wolfskehl, founder of Action Fast Print, stopped telling his employees what to do and instead asked how he could help them solve their problems, productivity jumped 30 percent.[114]

A number of other nontraditional roles provide leadership opportunities. **Bridge leaders** are those who leave their cultures for a significant period of time.[115] They live, go to school, travel, or work in other cultures. Then they return home, become leaders, and through their expanded repertoire serve as bridges between conflicting value systems within their own cultures or between their culture and other cultures.

With work often being team-based (see Chapter 14), **shared leadership** occurs when leadership rotates to the person with the key knowledge, skills, and abilities for the issue facing the team at a particular time.[116] Shared leadership is most important when tasks are interdependent, are complex, and require creativity. High-performing teams engaged in such work exhibit more shared leadership than poorly performing teams. In consulting teams, the higher the shared leadership, the higher their clients rated the teams' performance.[117] The role of vertical leader remains important—the formal leader still designs the team, manages its external boundaries, provides task direction, emphasizes the importance of the shared leadership approach, and engages in the transactional and transformational activities described in this chapter. But at the same time, the metaphor of geese in V-formation adds strength to the group: the lead goose periodically drops to the back, and another goose "steps up" and takes its place at the forefront.

LO 8

pseudotransformational leaders

Leaders who talk about positive change but allow their self-interest to take precedence over followers' needs.

servant–leader

A leader who serves others' needs while strengthening the organization.

bridge leaders

A leader who bridges conflicting value systems or different cultures.

shared leadership

Rotating leadership, in which people rotate through the leadership role based on which person has the most relevant skills at a particular time.

lateral leadership

Style in which colleagues at the same hierarchical level are invited to collaborate and facilitate joint problem solving.

Lateral leadership does not involve a hierarchical, superior–subordinate relationship but instead invites colleagues at the same level to solve problems together.[118] You alone can't provide a solution to every problem, but you can create processes through which people work collaboratively. If you can get people working to improve methods collaboratively, you can help create an endless stream of innovations. In other words, it's not about you providing solutions to problems; it's about creating better interpersonal processes for finding solutions. Strategies and tactics can be found throughout this book, including the chapters on decision making, organization structure, teams, communication, and change.

IN PRACTICE

Before his 30th birthday, Robert Chapman stepped into the job of chief executive of his family's business, Barry-Wehmiller Companies (B-W), following the sudden death of his father. Revenues at B-W, which makes packaging equipment and sells related services, grew rapidly during the early years of Chapman's leadership but then plunged as market demand dried up.

Chapman reacted by assembling his management team to evaluate what had gone wrong. The group determined that the earlier growth had been "undisciplined," not directed toward areas where long-term success would be most likely. The team developed a company vision aimed at balanced and sustainable growth. Since then, says Chapman, the company has "never varied" from "executing our vision with discipline and passion."

The passion comes from a commitment to "people-centric leadership." At B-W under Chapman, managers must care about their employees, give them authority to make important decisions, and clarify how their contributions enhance the company's vision. In terms of corporate structure, this is expressed in an Organizational Empowerment Team, staffed with people who develop leaders and apply methods such as lean manufacturing (see Chapter 9) through which employees contribute to improved operations.

Chapman believes companies can literally change the world through their impact on individual employees. Challenging employees to contribute to the corporate vision gives them a chance to feel that their efforts matter; recognition programs show them that they are appreciated. The result is what Chapman calls an "inspirational environment." Oh, and the company is growing again, too.[119]

- In what ways does Chapman's leadership illustrate lateral leadership?

A Note on Courage

To be a good leader, you need the courage to create a vision of greatness for your unit; identify and manage allies, adversaries, and fence sitters; and execute your vision, often against opposition. This does not mean you should commit career suicide by alienating too many powerful people; it does mean taking reasonable risks, with the good of the firm at heart, in order to produce constructive change.

For example, Alan Mulally needed courage when he left Boeing to take charge of Ford Motor Company in 2006, a point at which a series of poor decisions had made Ford a money-losing company. Many of Ford's managers were skeptical of Mulally as their new CEO because he came from outside the automobile industry. Nevertheless, Mullally plunged ahead with two decisions that were controversial at the time: he borrowed heavily and determined that the company would go forward with greater focus by offering fewer brands and models, with each being the best in its class. He also insisted that Ford's executives take a clear look at reality, however perilous it might be. He began calling weekly meetings at which each manager had to grade his or her group's progress. At the first such meeting, the managers all said their situation was fine, and Mulally

> "When you connect with a purpose greater than yourself, you are fearless; you think big."
> —Nancy Barry, founder and president of Enterprise Solutions to Poverty[120]

vehemently registered his disbelief that no one had problems when the company was forecasting a loss of $17 billion. After that, the reports became more honest, and Mulally praised the honesty. Instead of competing to put the best face on what they saw, executives began collaborating for the company's sake, sharing ideas for solutions. A few years later, Mulally's courageous efforts looked brilliant: Ford's borrowing gave the company resources to draw on when other automakers were accepting government loans to survive a financial crisis, and within a few years Ford was recording record profits.[121]

Specifically, fulfilling your vision will require some of the following acts of courage:[122] (1) seeing things as they are and facing them head-on, making no excuses and harboring no wishful illusions; (2) saying what needs to be said to those who need to hear it; and (3) persisting despite resistance, criticism, abuse, and setbacks. Courage includes stating the realities, even when they are harsh, and publicly stating what you will do to help and what you want from others. This means laying the cards on the table honestly: Here is what I want from you . . . what do you want from me?[123]

Developing Your Leadership Skills

As with other things, you must work at *developing* your leadership abilities. Great musicians and great athletes don't become great on natural gifts alone. They also pay their dues by practicing, learning, and sacrificing. Leaders in a variety of fields, when asked how they became the best leader possible, offered the following comments:[124]

- "I've observed methods and skills of my bosses that I respected."
- "By taking risks, trying, and learning from my mistakes."
- "Reading autobiographies of leaders I admire to try to understand how they think."
- "Lots of practice."
- "By making mistakes myself and trying a different approach."
- "By purposely engaging with others to get things done."
- "By being put in positions of responsibility that other people counted on."

How Do I Start?

How do you go about developing your leadership abilities? You don't have to wait until you land a management job or even finish your education. You can begin establishing credibility by behaving with integrity, learning from your mistakes, and becoming competent in your chosen field. You should look for—and then seize—opportunities to take actions that will help the groups you already belong to. Even before you are a supervisor, you can practice empowering others by listening carefully when you are in a group and by sharing what you know so that the whole group will be better informed. Finally, begin building a network of personal contacts by reaching out to others to offer help, not just to request it.[125]

When you are searching for your next job, look for a position with an employer that is committed to developing leadership talent. Ideally, leadership development

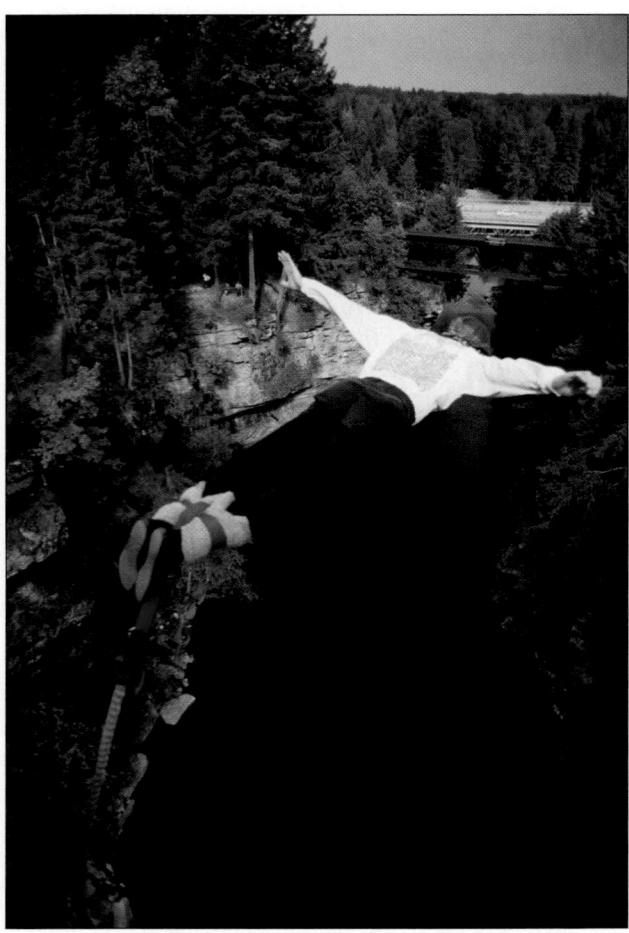

Challenges expand knowledge and experiences. Being open to new ideas allows managers to learn, grow, and succeed even though the challenge may be out of their comfort zone.

is connected to opportunities to practice the skills you are learning about, so ask about chances to lead a project or a team, even for short periods of time.[126] Companies that excel at leadership development include Johnson & Johnson, Hewlett-Packard, and General Electric.[127]

More specifically, here are some developmental experiences you should seek:[128]

- *Assignments:* Building something from nothing; fixing or turning around a failing operation; taking on project or task force responsibilities; accepting international assignments.
- *Other people:* Having exposure to positive role models; increasing visibility to others; working with people of diverse backgrounds.
- *Hardships:* Overcoming ideas that fail and deals that collapse; confronting others' performance problems; breaking out of a career rut.
- *Other events:* Formal courses; challenging job experiences; supervision of others; experiences outside work.

What Are the Keys?

The most effective developmental experiences have three components: assessment, challenge, and support.[129] *Assessment* includes information that gives you an understanding of where you are now, what your strengths are, your current levels of performance and leadership effectiveness, and your primary development needs. You can think about what your past feedback has been, what previous successes and failures you have had, how people have reacted to your ideas and actions, what your personal goals are, and what strategies you should implement to make progress. You can seek answers from your peers at work, bosses, family, friends, customers, and anyone else who knows you and how you work. The information you collect will help clarify what you need to learn, improve, or change.[130]

The most potent developmental experiences provide *challenge*—they stretch you. We all think and behave in habitual, comfortable ways. This is natural, and perhaps sufficient to survive. But you've probably heard people say how important it can be to get out of your comfort zone—to tackle situations that require new skills and abilities, that are confusing or ambiguous, or that you simply would rather not deal with. Sometimes the challenge comes from lack of experience; other times, it requires changing old habits. It may be uncomfortable, but this is how great managers learn. Remember, some people don't bother to learn or refuse to learn. Make sure you think about your experiences along the way and reflect on them afterward, introspectively and in discussion with others.

You receive *support* when others send the message that your efforts to learn and grow are valued. Without support, challenging developmental experiences can be overwhelming. With support, it is easier to handle the struggle, stay on course, open up to learning, and actually learn from experiences. Support can come informally from other people; more formally through the procedures of the organization; and through learning resources in the forms of training, constructive feedback, talking with others, and so on.

What develops in leadership development? Through such experiences, you can acquire more self-awareness and self-confidence, a broader perspective on the organizational system, creative thinking, the ability to work more effectively in complex social systems, and the ability to learn from experience.

Management Connection

HOW SCHULTZ HOPES TO LEAD STARBUCKS INTO THE FUTURE

CEO Howard Schultz has identified some lessons he learned from his return to the helm of Starbucks. One of these is that transformational leadership is not a one-time event. While Schultz insists that the company must always build on its core values and mission, he sees a need for continual innovation.

A case in point was Starbucks's launch of VIA instant coffee in February 2009. Instant coffee had seemed like an improbable product for Starbucks for two main reasons. The first is that Starbucks had built a reputation as a premium brand, and most instant coffee, by comparison, is awful. The technology for making this idea a success simply did not exist. The second problem is that Starbucks had a mission of selling an experience at its stores, whereas instant coffee is generally a routine purchase at a supermarket. The solution to the technological hurdle came from a cell biologist named Don Valencia, who led the development of a high-quality, water-soluble coffee powder that could create a distinctively rich cup of coffee. The solution to introducing the experience to consumers came as the company discovered, through trial and error, that Starbucks could overcome skepticism by offering taste tests in its stores. As Starbucks continued its rollout of VIA, the product's sales exceeded expectations for each market.

Furthermore, the company's growth in international markets is fueling not just greater sales but also opportunities to look around at those new markets and see what opportunities they present. In Schultz's vision, a Starbucks store is more than a place to buy coffee; it is a place to enjoy a sense of community, and in some form, that is something people desire around the world. Starbucks now has hundreds of stores in China and sees India as its next big location for growth. Kuwait also is an important point of entry into a region of the world where coffee drinking is important to the culture. And Europe offers potential for the VIA brand because the custom in many countries is to have a kettle on the stove with hot water for tea—or, perhaps in the future, instant coffee.

Another lesson Schultz recognizes is that the most effective leaders are not just smart but also humble, realizing that the other managers and employees in the company also have good ideas. For instance, when the formula for VIA instant coffee was ready, Schultz was eager for a nationwide introduction of what he was sure would be a hit; but other executives pressed for introducing the product in just two cities to avoid the risk of a huge flop. In the past, Schultz's style would have been to insist on his own ideas, but he listened to the concerns and agreed to a two-city introduction. As it turned out, the company had a lot to learn: free samples handed out in Chicago and Seattle disappeared into consumers' pockets and purses, where they were promptly forgotten. Starbucks revised its marketing plans so that store employees prepared VIA and served it in blind taste tests with Starbucks brewed coffee, and the improved rollout was a success, generating $135 million in sales its first year and nabbing over 10 percent of the instant coffee market in spite of a higher price.

In the words of chief financial officer Troy Alstead, Schultz's reformed leadership style has enabled "more arguing, challenging, and debate in the last two or three years than there's ever been." Schultz agrees that he has become a better leader: "What leadership means is the courage it takes to talk about things that, in the past, perhaps we wouldn't have, because I'm not right all the time."

As of this writing, Starbucks is again prospering, and Schultz is as enthusiastic as ever about the future. However, the Schultz of today has the caution borne of having led his company through a crisis. He recently told a *Financial Times* reporter, "We are back growing again, but I would say not in the same somewhat reckless way."[131]

- How well does Howard Schultz fit the description of a transformational leader?
- How did Schultz continue to develop his leadership skills even after he became a chief executive?

KEY TERMS

SUMMARY OF LEARNING OBJECTIVES

Now that you have studied Chapter 12, you should be able to

LO 1 Discuss what it means to be a leader.

A leader is one who influences others to attain goals. Leaders orchestrate change, set direction, and motivate people to overcome obstacles and move the organization toward its ideal future.

LO 2 Summarize what people want and organizations need from their leaders.

People want help in achieving their goals, and organizations need leaders at all levels. The best leaders challenge the process, inspire a shared vision, enable others to act, model the way, and encourage the heart.

LO 3 Explain how a good vision helps you be a better leader.

Outstanding leaders have vision. A vision is a mental image that goes beyond the ordinary and perhaps beyond what others thought possible. The vision provides the direction in which the leader wants the organization to move and inspiration for people to pursue it.

LO 4 Identify sources of power in organizations.

Having power and using it appropriately are essential to effective leadership. Managers at all levels of the organization have five potential sources of power. Legitimate power is the company-granted authority to direct others. Reward power is control over rewards valued by others in the organization. Coercive power is control over punishments that others in the organization want to avoid. Referent power consists of personal characteristics that appeal to others, so they model their behavior on the leader's and seek the leader's approval. Expert power is expertise or knowledge that can benefit others in the organization.

LO 5 List personal traits and skills of effective leaders.

Important leader characteristics include drive, leadership, motivation, integrity, self-confidence, and knowledge of the business. Perhaps the most important skill is the ability to accurately perceive the situation and then change behavior accordingly.

LO 6 Describe behaviors that will make you a better leader, and identify when the situation calls for them.

Important leader behaviors include task performance behaviors, group maintenance, and decision making. According to the Vroom model, the leadership style should involve individual decisions, consultation with followers, facilitation, or delegation depending on qualities such as the significance of the decision and the importance of followers' commitment. Fiedler's contingency model says a task-motivated leader is more successful when leader–member relations are good and the task is highly structured, or with an unstructured task but low position power for the leader, or with poor leader–member relations when the task structure and leader's position power are both low. In other situations, a relationship-oriented leader will perform better. Hersey and Blanchard's situational theory says that task performance behaviors become less important as the follower's job maturity and psychological maturity increase. Path–goal theory assesses characteristics of the followers, the leader, and the situation; it then indicates the appropriateness of directive, supportive, participative, or achievement-oriented leadership behaviors.

LO 7 Distinguish between charismatic and transformational leaders.

To have charisma is to be dominant and self-confident, to have a strong conviction of the righteousness of your beliefs, to create an aura of competence and success, and to communicate high expectations for and confidence in your followers. Charisma is one component of transformational leadership. Transformational leaders translate a vision into reality by getting people to transcend their individual interests for the good of the larger community. They do this through charisma, individualized attention to followers, intellectual stimulation, formation and communication of their vision, building of trust, and positive self-regard.

<table>
<tr><td>LO 8</td><td>Describe types of opportunities to be a leader in an organization.</td></tr>
</table>

There's plenty of opportunity to be a leader; being a manager of others who report to you is just the traditional one. You can also take or create opportunities to be a servant–leader or bridge leader and engage in shared leadership and lateral leadership. A servant–leader serves others' needs while strengthening the organization. A bridge leader uses experiences of other cultures to create a bridge between systems. Shared leadership involves taking on a leadership role when your skills are most relevant to a particular situation. Lateral leadership is inspiring people to work collaboratively and solve problems together.

<table>
<tr><td>LO 9</td><td>Discuss how to further your own leadership development.</td></tr>
</table>

You can develop your own leadership skills not only by understanding what effective leadership is all about but also by seeking challenging developmental experiences. Such important life experiences come from taking challenging assignments, through exposure in working with other people, by overcoming hardships and failures, by taking formal courses, and by other actions. The most important elements of a good developmental experience are assessment, challenge, and support.

DISCUSSION QUESTIONS

1. What do you want from your leader?

2. Is there a difference between effective management and effective leadership? Explain your views and learn from others' views.

3. Identify someone you think is an effective leader. What traits and skills does this person possess that make him or her effective?

4. Do you think most managers can be transformational leaders? Why or why not?

5. In your own words, define courage. What is the role of courage in leadership? Give examples of acts of leadership you consider courageous.

6. Do you think men and women differ in their leadership styles? If so, how? Do men and/or women prefer different styles in their bosses? What evidence do you have for your answers?

7. Who are your heroes? What makes them heroes, and what can you learn from them?

8. Assess yourself as a leader based on what you have read in this chapter. What are your strengths and weaknesses?

9. Identify the developmental experiences you have had that may have strengthened your ability to lead. What did those experiences teach you? Also identify some developmental experiences you need to acquire, and how you will seek them. Be specific.

10. Consider a couple of decisions you are facing that could involve other people. Use the Vroom model to decide what approach to use to make the decisions.

11. Consider a job you hold or held in the past. Consider how your boss managed you. How would you describe him or her as a leader? What substitutes for leadership would you have enjoyed seeing put into place?

12. Consider an organization of which you are a leader or a member. What could great transformational leadership accomplish in the organization?

13. Name some prominent leaders whom you would describe as authentic and inauthentic, and discuss.

14. Name some leaders you consider servant–leaders, and discuss.

15. Identify some opportunities for you to exhibit shared leadership and lateral leadership.

EXPERIENTIAL EXERCISES

12.1 POWER AND INFLUENCE

OBJECTIVE
To explore the nature of power and influence, and your attitudes toward different kinds of power and influence.

INSTRUCTIONS
Read the introductions and complete sections A, B, and C.

Power and Influence Worksheet

A. Power

Many well-known people have made statements about power and winning (e.g., P. T. Barnum, Mao Tse-tung, Leo Durocher, Lord Acton, Vince Lombardi). Some of these statements are listed in the table that follows. Indicate how you feel about each of the statements by circling number 1 if you strongly disagree, and so on.

	Strongly Disagree	Disagree	Neutral	Agree	Strongly Agree
Winning is everything.	1	2	3	4	5
Nice guys finish last.	1	2	3	4	5
There can be only one winner.	1	2	3	4	5
There's a sucker born every minute.	1	2	3	4	5
You can't completely trust anyone.	1	2	3	4	5
All power rests at the end of the gun.	1	2	3	4	5
Power seekers are greedy and can't be trusted.	1	2	3	4	5
Power corrupts; absolute power corrupts absolutely.	1	2	3	4	5
You get as much power as you pay for.	1	2	3	4	5

B. Influence

During the past week or so you have come in contact with many people. Some have influenced you positively, some negatively. Try to recall recent experiences with employers, peers, teachers, parents, clergy, and the like who may have influenced you in some way. Then try to think about how and why they influenced you as they did.

1. On the following table, list the names of all those who influenced you during the past week or so according to the kind of power that person used. The same person's name may appear under more than one type of power if that person used multiple power bases. Also indicate whether the influence was positive (+) or negative (−).

Power Base	Names and Whether (+) or (−)
Legitimate authority	_____
Reward	_____
Coercive	_____
Referent	_____
Expert	_____

2. After examining your list, check (√) the following questions.

	Yes	No
a. Was there one person who had + marks appearing under several power bases?	_____	_____
b. Was there one person who had − marks appearing under several power bases?	_____	_____
c. Did you find that most of the people with + marks tended to fall under the same power bases?	_____	_____
d. Did you find that most of the people with − marks tended to fall under the same power bases?	_____	_____

3. From your answers to the last two questions, list which power bases you found to be positive (+) and which you found to be negative (−).

+	−
_____	_____
_____	_____
_____	_____
_____	_____
_____	_____

Do you think you personally prefer to use those power bases you listed under + when you try to influence people? Do you actually use them?

C. Power and Influence

From the table in Part B, find the one person who you think had the strongest positive influence on you (Person 1), and the one who had the strongest negative influence (Person 2). These are most likely the persons whose names appear most frequently.

In the following table, place a 1 on the line for each statement that best indicates how you think Person 1 would respond to that statement. Put a 2 on the line for each statement that reflects how you think Person 2 would respond to that item.

	Strongly Disagree	Disagree	Neutral	Agree	Strongly Agree
Winning is everything.	_____	_____	_____	_____	_____
Nice guys finish last.	_____	_____	_____	_____	_____
There can be only one winner.	_____	_____	_____	_____	_____
There's a sucker born every minute	_____	_____	_____	_____	_____
You can't completely trust anyone.	_____	_____	_____	_____	_____
All power rests at the end of the gun.	_____	_____	_____	_____	_____
Power seekers are greedy and can't be trusted.	_____	_____	_____	_____	_____
Power corrupts; absolute power corrupts absolutely.	_____	_____	_____	_____	_____
You get as much power as you pay for.	_____	_____	_____	_____	_____

Now compare your responses in Part A to those in Part C. Do you more closely resemble Person 1 or Person 2? Do you prefer to use the kinds of power that person uses? Which kinds of power do you use most frequently? Which do you use least frequently? When do you feel you have the greatest power? When do you have the least power? How do these answers compare to what you found in Part B3?

SOURCE: Excerpted from Laurence R. Jauch, Arthur G. Bedeian, Sally A. Coltin, and William F. Glueck, *The Managerial Experience: Cases, Exercises, and Readings,* 5th ed. Copyright © 1989. South-Western, a part of Cengage Learning, Inc. Reproduced by permission. www.cengage.com/permissions.

12.2   EVALUATING YOUR LEADERSHIP STYLE

OBJECTIVES

1. To examine your personal style of leadership.
2. To study the nature of the leadership process.
3. To identify ways to improve or modify your leadership style.

INSTRUCTIONS

1. Working alone, complete and score the Leadership Style Survey.
2. In small groups, exchange scores, compute average scores, and develop responses to the discussion questions.

3. After the class reconvenes, group spokespersons present group findings.

DISCUSSION QUESTIONS

1. In what ways did your experience or lack of experience influence your responses to the survey?
2. In what ways did student scores and student responses to survey test items converge? In what ways did they diverge?
3. What do you think accounts for differences in student leadership attitudes?
4. How can students make constructive use of the survey results?

Leadership Style Survey

This survey describes various aspects of leadership behavior. To measure your leadership style, respond to each statement according to the way you would act (or think you would act) if you were a work group leader.

	Always	Frequently	Occasionally	Seldom	Never
1. I would allow team members the freedom to do their jobs in their own way.	5	4	3	2	1
2. I would make important decisions on my own initiative without consulting the workers.	5	4	3	2	1
3. I would allow the team members to make their own decisions.	5	4	3	2	1
4. I would not try to socialize with the workers.	5	4	3	2	1
5. I would allow team members to do their jobs as they see fit.	5	4	3	2	1
6. I would consider myself to be the group's spokesperson.	5	4	3	2	1
7. I would be warm, friendly, and approachable.	5	4	3	2	1
8. I would be sure that the workers understand and follow all the rules and regulations.	5	4	3	2	1
9. I would demonstrate a real concern for the workers' welfare.	5	4	3	2	1
10. I would be the one to decide what is to be done and how it is to be done.	5	4	3	2	1
11. I would delegate authority to the workers.	5	4	3	2	1
12. I would urge the workers to meet production quotas.	5	4	3	2	1
13. I would trust the workers to use good judgment in decision making.	5	4	3	2	1
14. I would assign specific tasks to specific people.	5	4	3	2	1
15. I would let the workers establish their own work pace.	5	4	3	2	1
16. I would not feel that I have to explain my decisions to workers.	5	4	3	2	1
17. I would try to make each worker feel that his or her contribution is important.	5	4	3	2	1
18. I would establish the work schedules.	5	4	3	2	1
19. I would encourage workers to get involved in setting work goals.	5	4	3	2	1
20. I would be action oriented and results oriented.	5	4	3	2	1
21. I would get the workers involved in making decisions.	5	4	3	2	1
22. I would outline needed changes and monitor action closely.	5	4	3	2	1
23. I would help the group achieve consensus on important changes.	5	4	3	2	1
24. I would supervise closely to ensure that standards are met.	5	4	3	2	1
25. I would consistently reinforce good work.	5	4	3	2	1
26. I would nip problems in the bud.	5	4	3	2	1
27. I would consult the group before making decisions.	5	4	3	2	1

CONCLUDING CASE

THE LAW OFFICES OF JETER, JACKSON, GUIDRY, AND BOYER

THE EVOLUTION OF THE FIRM

David Jeter and Nate Jackson started a small general law practice near Sacramento, California. Prior to that, the two had spent five years in the district attorney's office after completing their formal schooling. What began as a small partnership—just the two attorneys and a paralegal/assistant—had now grown into a practice that employed more than 27 people in three separated towns. The current staff included 18 attorneys (three of whom had become partners), three paralegals, and six secretaries.

For the first time in the firm's existence, the partners felt that they were losing control of their overall operation. The firm's current caseload, number of employees, number of clients, travel requirements, and facilities management needs had grown far beyond anything that the original partners had ever imagined.

Attorney Jeter called a meeting of the partners to discuss the matter. Before the meeting, opinions about the pressing problems of the day and proposed solutions were sought from the entire staff. The meeting resulted in a formal decision to create a new position, general manager of operations. The partners proceeded to compose a job description and job announcement for recruiting purposes.

Highlights and major responsibilities of the job description include

- Supervising day-to-day office personnel and operations (phones, meetings, word processing, mail, billings, payroll, general overhead, and maintenance).
- Improving customer relations (more expeditious processing of cases and clients).
- Expanding the customer base.
- Enhancing relations with the local communities.
- Managing the annual budget and related incentive programs.
- Maintaining an annual growth in sales of 10 percent while maintaining or exceeding the current profit margin.

The general manager will provide an annual executive summary to the partners, along with specific action plans for improvement and change.

A search committee was formed, and two months later the new position was offered to Brad Howser, a longtime administrator from the insurance industry seeking a final career change and a return to his California roots. Howser made it clear that he was willing to make a five-year commitment to the position and would then likely retire.

Things got off to a quiet and uneventful start as Howser spent the first few months just getting to know the staff; observing day-to-day operations; and reviewing and analyzing assorted client and attorney data and history, financial spreadsheets, and so on.

About six months into the position, Howser became more outspoken and assertive with the staff and established several new operational rules and procedures. He began by changing the regular working hours. The firm previously had a flex schedule in place that allowed employees to begin and end the workday at their choosing within given parameters. Howser did not care for such a "loose schedule" and now required that all office personnel work from 9:00 to 5:00 each day. A few staff members were

unhappy about this and complained to Howser, who matter-of-factly informed them that "this is the new rule that everyone is expected to follow, and anyone who could or would not comply should probably look for another job." Sylvia Bronson, an administrative assistant who had been with the firm for several years, was particularly unhappy about this change. She arranged for a private meeting with Howser to discuss her child care circumstances and the difficulty that the new schedule presented. Howser seemed to listen half-heartedly and at one point told Bronson that "assistants are essentially a dime a dozen and are readily available." Bronson was seen leaving the office in tears that day.

Howser was not happy with the average length of time that it took to receive payments for services rendered to the firm's clients (accounts receivable). A closer look showed that 30 percent of the clients paid their bills in 30 days or less, 60 percent paid in 30 to 60 days, and the remaining 10 percent stretched it out to as many as 120 days. Howser composed a letter that was sent to all clients whose outstanding invoices exceeded 30 days. The strongly worded letter demanded immediate payment in full and went on to indicate that legal action might be taken against anyone who did not respond in a timely fashion. While a small number of "late" payments were received soon after the mailing, the firm received an even larger number of letters and phone calls from angry clients, some of whom had been with the firm since its inception.

Howser was given an advertising and promotion budget for purposes of expanding the client base. One of the paralegals suggested that those expenditures should be carefully planned and that the firm had several attorneys who knew the local markets quite well and could probably offer some insight and ideas on the subject. Howser thought about this briefly and then decided to go it alone, reasoning that most attorneys know little or nothing about marketing.

In an attempt to "bring all of the people together to form a team," Howser established weekly staff meetings. These mandatory, hour-long sessions were run by Howser, who presented a series of overhead slides, handouts, and lectures about "some of the proven management techniques that were successful in the insurance industry." The meetings typically ran past the allotted time frame and rarely if ever covered all of the agenda items.

Howser spent some of his time "enhancing community relations." He was very generous with many local groups such as the historical society, the garden clubs, the recreational sports programs, the middle and high school band programs, and others. In less than six months he had written checks and authorized donations totaling more than $25,000. He was delighted about all of this and was certain that such gestures of goodwill would pay off handsomely in the future.

As for the budget, Howser carefully reviewed each line item in search of ways to increase revenues and cut expenses. He then proceeded to increase the expected base or quota for attorneys' monthly billable hours, thus directly affecting their profit sharing and bonus program. On the cost side, he significantly reduced the attorneys' annual budget for travel, meals, and entertainment. He considered these to be frivolous and unnecessary. Howser decided that one of the two full-time administrative assistant positions in each office should be reduced to part-time with no benefits. He saw no reason why the current workload could not be completed within this model. Howser wrapped up his initial financial review and action plan by posting notices throughout each office with new rules regarding the use of copy machines, phones, and supplies.

Howser completed the first year of his tenure with the required executive summary report to the partners that included his analysis of the current status of each department and his action plan. The partners were initially impressed both with Howser's approach to the new job and with the changes that he made. They all seemed to make sense and were directly in line with the key components of his job description. At the same time, "the office rumor mill and grapevine" had "heated up" considerably. Company morale, which had always been quite high, was now clearly waning. The water coolers and hallways became the frequent meeting place of disgruntled employees.

As for the marketplace, while the partners did not expect to see an immediate influx of new clients, they certainly did not expect to see shrinkage in their existing client base. A number of individual and corporate clients took their business elsewhere, still fuming over the letter they had received.

The partners met with Howser to discuss the situation. Howser urged them to "sit tight and ride out the storm." He had seen this happen before and had no doubt that in the long run the firm would achieve all of its goals. Howser pointed out that people in general are resistant to change. The partners met for drinks later that day and looked at each other with a great sense of uncertainty. Should they ride out the storm as Howser suggested? Had they done the right thing in creating the position and in hiring Howser? What had started as a seemingly wise, logical, and smooth sequence of events had now become a crisis.

QUESTIONS

1. Do you agree with Howser's suggestion to "sit tight and ride out the storm," or should the partners take some action immediately? If so, what actions specifically?

2. Assume that the creation of the general manager of operations position was a good decision. What leadership style and type of individual would you try to place in this position?

3. Consider your own leadership style. What types of positions and situations should you seek? What types of positions and situations should you seek to avoid? Why?

13 Motivating for Performance

LEARNING OBJECTIVES

After studying Chapter 13, you will be able to:

LO 1   Identify the kinds of behaviors managers need to motivate in people. p. 470

LO 2   List principles for setting goals that motivate employees. p. 471

LO 3   Summarize how to reward good performance effectively. p. 473

LO 4   Describe the key beliefs that affect people's motivation. p. 477

LO 5   Discuss ways in which people's individual needs affect their behavior. p. 480

LO 6   Define ways to create jobs that motivate. p. 484

LO 7   Summarize how people assess fairness and how to achieve fairness. p. 489

LO 8   Identify causes and consequences of a satisfied workforce. p. 492

Manager's Brief	Progress Report	Onward

Management Connection

WHAT MAKES INTUIT A GREAT PLACE TO WORK?

Millions of households and small business owners think of Intuit as the maker of the popular money management software QuickBooks, Quicken, and TurboTax. But Intuit is more than that; it's also a great place to work. Intuit is among the top software companies on *Fortune* magazine's prestigious list of the world's most admired companies and has for a decade landed on *Fortune*'s list of the 100 best companies to work for. And for information technology (IT) professionals, the company also is on *Computerworld*'s list of the 100 best places to work in IT.

One reason Intuit shows up on lists like these is that it offers generous health insurance and retirement plans, plus reimbursements for fitness programs, two weeks' paid leave for a newborn or newly adopted child, discounts on home loans, and access to backup child and elder care for employees' dependents.

But not everyone agrees that generous benefits are what employees care about most. As you will read in this chapter, employees care also about working conditions and their treatment by management and coworkers. In these areas, too, Intuit strives to excel. For example, Intuit programs make it easy for managers and coworkers to recognize employees' accomplishments with praise and prizes. The company also considers flexible schedules that allow employees to do some of their work from home, if possible. To signal that all kinds of talented people are valued, the company makes available nine employee networks in which diverse employees can find support, guidance, and friendship. And as a reflection of its commitment to social responsibility, the company gives employees 32 hours of paid time to perform volunteer services each year.

Concern for people also shows up in Intuit's recent selection to receive the Department of Defense's Employer Support Freedom Award, which recognizes companies that enable members of the armed forces reserves to keep their jobs while serving their country. Tim Graczewski, Intuit's director of corporate strategy and development, nominated Intuit because of its policy of fully compensating reservists while they are mobilized to active duty. Graczewski himself has benefited from that policy: a lieutenant in the U.S. Navy Reserve, he has served in Afghanistan, where he worked on economic issues. Chris Galy, the head of Intuit's recruitment department, says employees are excited and proud that Graczewski can use his business expertise to serve his country. With over 150 Intuit employees having been called to active duty in the past decade and a half, the company also saw a need for a networking group of employees connected with the military; the group quickly signed up 160 members.[1]

Intuit stands out as a company that offers generous benefits to its workers. As you read this chapter, consider whether that is enough to bring out employees' best work, aimed at the company's goals and priorities. If not, what other efforts should managers make?

This chapter tackles an age-old question: How can a manager motivate people to work hard and perform at their best levels? Intuit demonstrates that treating employees as valued contributors to the organization can be a key part of motivating them.

A sales manager in one company had a different approach to this question. Each month, the person with the worst sales performance took home a live goat for the weekend. The manager hoped the goat-of-the-month employee would be so embarrassed that he or she would work harder the next month to increase sales.[2] This sales manager may get high marks for creativity. But if he is graded by results, as he grades his salespeople, he will fail. He may succeed in motivating a few of his people to increase sales, but some good people will be motivated to quit the company.

Motivating for Performance

LO 1

Understanding why people do the things they do on the job is not an easy task for a manager. *Predicting* their response to management's latest productivity program is harder yet. Fortunately, enough is known about motivation to give the thoughtful manager practical, effective techniques for increasing people's effort and performance.

motivation

Forces that energize, direct, and sustain a person's efforts.

Motivation refers to forces that energize, direct, and sustain a person's efforts. All behavior, except involuntary reflexes like eye blinks (which have little to do with management), is motivated. A highly motivated person will work hard toward achieving performance goals. With adequate ability, understanding of the job, and access to the necessary resources, such a person will be highly productive.

To be effective motivators, managers must know what behaviors they want to motivate people to exhibit. Although productive people appear to do a seemingly limitless number of things, most of the important activities can be grouped into five general categories.[3] Managers must motivate people to (1) *join the organization*, (2) *remain in the organization*, and (3) *come to work regularly*. On these points, you should reject the common recent notion that loyalty is dead and accept the challenge of creating an environment that will attract and energize people so that they commit to the organization.[4]

Of course, companies also want people to (4) *perform*—that is, once employees are at work, they should work hard to achieve high *output* and high *quality*. Finally, managers want employees to (5) *exhibit good citizenship*. Good citizens of the organization are committed, satisfied employees who perform above and beyond the call of duty by doing extra things that can help the company. The importance of citizenship behaviors may be less obvious than performance, but these behaviors help the organization function smoothly. They also make managers' lives easier.

Many ideas have been proposed to help managers motivate people to engage in these constructive behaviors. The most useful of these ideas are described in the following pages. We start with the most fundamental *processes* that influence the motivation of all people. These processes—described by goal-setting, reinforcement, and expectancy theories—suggest basic and powerful actions for managers to take. Then we discuss the *content* of what people want and need from work, how individuals differ from one another, and how understanding

A recent survey by a human resource consulting firm found that over half of employees were engaged, defined as knowing what to do (vision) and wanting to do it (commitment). This was a 5 percentage point improvement from three years earlier, when more employees were lacking in commitment.[5]

■ Engaged employees (commitment, vision)
■ Enthusiasts (commitment, no vision)
■ Renegades (vision, no commitment)
■ Disengaged employees (no commitment, no vision)

people's needs leads to powerful prescriptions about designing motivating jobs and empowering people to perform at the highest possible levels. Finally, we discuss the most important beliefs and perceptions about fairness that people hold toward their work, and the implications for job satisfaction.

Setting Goals

Providing work-related goals for people is an extremely effective way to stimulate motivation. In fact, it is perhaps the most important, valid, and useful single approach to motivating performance. Therefore, we discuss it first.

Goal-setting theory states that people have conscious goals that energize them and direct their thoughts and behaviors toward a particular end.[6] Keeping in mind the principle that goals matter, managers set goals for employees or collaborate with employees on goal setting. For example, a satellite TV company might set goals for increasing the number of new subscribers, the number of current subscribers who pay for premium channels, or the timeliness of responses to customer inquiries.[7] Goal setting works for any job in which people have control over their performance.[8] You can set goals for performance quality and quantity, plus behavioral goals like cooperation or teamwork.[9] In fact, you can set goals for whatever is important.[10]

Goals That Motivate

The most powerful goals are *meaningful;* noble purposes that appeal to people's "higher" values add extra motivating power.[11] Johnson & Johnson pursues profit, but it's also about improving health care. Ben & Jerry's makes great ice cream but also is socially responsible. ServiceMaster, the cleaning and maintenance company, and Chick-fil-A have religious commitments that appeal to their employees, and Huntsman Chemical has goals of paying off corporate debt but also relieving human suffering—it sponsors cancer research and a number of charities. Meaningful goals also may be based on data about competitors; exceeding competitors' performance can stoke people's competitive spirit and desire to succeed in the marketplace.[12] This point is not just about the values companies espouse and the lofty goals they pursue; it's also about leadership at a more personal level. Followers of transformational leaders view their work as more important and as highly congruent with their personal goals compared with followers of transactional leaders[13] (recall Chapter 12).

More specifically, much is known about how to manage goals in ways that motivate high job performance. Goals should be *acceptable* to employees. This means, among other things, that they should not conflict with people's personal values and that people have reasons to pursue the goals. Allowing people to participate in setting their work goals—as opposed to having the boss set goals for them—is often a great way to generate goals that people accept and pursue willingly.

Acceptable, maximally motivating goals are *challenging but attainable*. In other words, they should be high enough to inspire better performance but not so high that

Ben & Jerry's is known for making some of the world's finest ice cream. But its social responsibility is also highly important to many employees and customers. When "ONE Cheesecake Brownie" was launched, proceeds were donated to help fight global poverty.

people can never reach them. One team of consultants to an international corporation created more than 40 programs aimed at increasing quality. The company announced it did not expect significant quality improvement until the *fourth year* of the program. Such a goal is not nearly demanding enough.[14]

Ideal goals do not merely exhort employees in general terms to improve performance, start doing their best, increase productivity, or decrease the length of time customers must wait to receive service. Rather, the goals should specify what the employee should do and within what time frame. At the Quick Lane Tire & Auto Center that serves Olathe Ford near Kansas City, Missouri, each service adviser is given a monthly goal for revenues from service orders and receives daily feedback about sales in order to see what categories of products need extra attention. In addition, whenever a customer chooses to postpone needed repairs, these are assigned a red or yellow code. The service center's receptionist has specific goals of calling each red-code customer within seven days and sending a letter within 90 days to each customer who has a yellow code.[15] Such deadlines and measurable performance goals are specific, quantifiable goals that employees are motivated to achieve. Microsoft uses the acronym SMART to create motivating goals: specific, measurable, achievable, results-based, and time-specific.[16]

Goals can generate manipulative game-playing and unethical behavior.

Stretch Goals

stretch goals

Targets that are particularly demanding, sometimes even thought to be impossible.

Some firms today set **stretch goals**—targets that are exceptionally demanding, and that some people would never even think of. There are two types of stretch goals: vertical stretch goals, aligned with current activities including productivity and financial results, and horizontal stretch goals, which involve people's professional development like attempting and learning new, difficult things.[17] Impossible though stretch goals may seem to some, they often are in fact attainable.

Stretch goals can generate a major shift away from mediocrity and toward tremendous achievement. But if someone tries in good faith but doesn't meet their stretch goals, don't punish—remember how difficult they are! Base your assessment on how much performance has improved, how the performance compares with others, and how much progress has been made.[18]

Limitations of Goal Setting

Goal setting is an extraordinarily powerful management technique. But even specific, challenging, attainable goals work better under some conditions than others. For example, if people lack relevant ability and knowledge, a better course to follow might be simply urging them to do their best or setting a goal to learn rather than a goal to achieve a specific performance level.[19] Individual performance goals can be dysfunctional if people work in a group and cooperation among team members is essential to team performance.[20] Individualized goals can create competition and reduce cooperation. If cooperation is important, performance goals should be established *for the team.*

Goals can generate manipulative game-playing and unethical behavior. For example, people can sometimes find ingenious ways to set easy goals and convince their bosses that they are difficult.[21] Or they may find ways to meet goals simply to receive a reward, without necessarily performing in desirable ways. In the earlier example of Quick Lane Tire & Auto Center, goals based on sales dollars are specific and measurable but reward employees for focusing on inventory and margins, not customers and their cars. Similarly, in big law firms it's common for lawyers to keep detailed records of their time and to be rewarded for billing, say, 2,000 hours per year. This system is an invitation to work inefficiently and a dismal, *demotivating* environment for any lawyer who chose the profession out of concern for clients

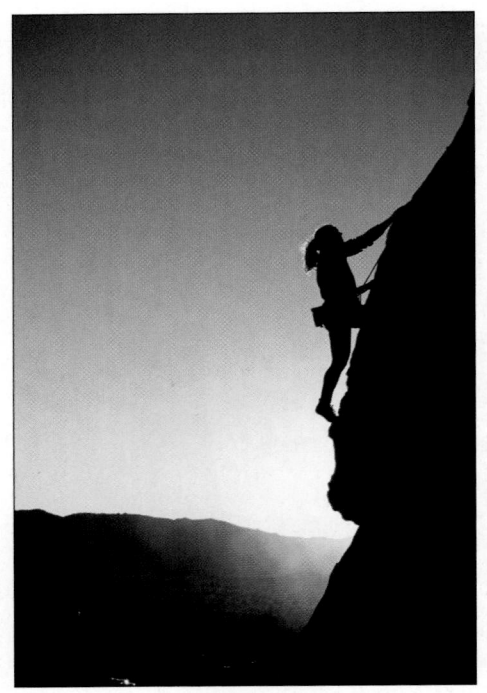
Setting unprecedented goals can push an individual to reach a higher level of achievement.

or love of the law.[22] In addition, people who don't meet their goals are more likely to engage in unethical behavior than are people who are trying to do their best but have no specific performance goals. This is true regardless of whether they have financial incentives, and it is particularly true when people fall just short of reaching their goals.[23]

Another familiar example comes from the pages of financial reports. Some executives have mastered the art of "earnings management"—precisely meeting Wall Street analysts' earnings estimates or beating them by a single penny.[24] The media trumpet, and investors reward, the company that meets or beats the estimates. People sometimes meet this goal by either manipulating the numbers or initiating whispering campaigns to persuade analysts to lower their estimates, making them more attainable. The marketplace wants short-term, quarterly performance, but long-term viability is ultimately more important to a company's success.

It is important *not* to establish a single productivity goal if there are other important dimensions of performance.[25] For instance, if the acquisition of knowledge and skills is important, you can also set a specific and challenging learning goal like "identify 10 ways to develop relationships with end users of our products." Productivity goals will likely enhance productivity, but they may also cause employees to neglect other areas, such as learning, tackling new projects, or developing creative solutions to job-related problems. A manager who wants to motivate creativity can establish creativity goals along with productivity goals for individuals or for brainstorming teams.[26]

Set Your Own Goals

Goal setting works for yourself, as well—it's a powerful tool for self-management. Set goals for yourself; don't just try hard or hope for the best. Create a statement of purpose for yourself comprising three elements: an inspiring distant vision, a mid-distant goal along the way (worthy in its own right), and near-term objectives to start working on immediately.[27] So if you are going into business, you might articulate your goal for the type of businessperson you want to be in five years, the types of jobs that could create the opportunities and teach you what you need to know to become that businessperson, and the specific schoolwork and job search activities that can get you moving in those directions. And on the job, apply SMART and other goal-setting advice for yourself.

law of effect

A law formulated by Edward Thorndike in 1911 stating that behavior that is followed by positive consequences will likely be repeated.

reinforcers

Positive consequences that motivate behavior.

organizational behavior modification (OB mod)

The application of reinforcement theory in organizational settings.

positive reinforcement

Applying consequences that increase the likelihood that a person will repeat the behavior that led to it.

negative reinforcement

Removing or withholding an undesirable consequence.

Set goals for yourself; don't just try hard or hope for the best.

Reinforcing Performance

Goals are universal motivators. So are the processes of reinforcement described in this section. In 1911 psychologist Edward Thorndike formulated the **law of effect:** behavior that is followed by positive consequences probably will be repeated.[28] This powerful law of behavior laid the foundation for countless investigations into the effects of the positive consequences, called **reinforcers,** that motivate behavior. **Organizational behavior modification (or OB mod)** attempts to influence people's behavior, and improve performance,[29] by systematically managing work conditions and the consequences of people's actions.

Four key consequences of behavior either encourage or discourage people's behavior (see Figure 13.1):

1. **Positive reinforcement**—applying a positive consequence that increases the likelihood that the person will repeat the behavior that led to it. Examples of positive reinforcers include compliments, letters of commendation, favorable performance evaluations, and pay raises.[30]
2. **Negative reinforcement**—removing or withholding an undesirable consequence. For example, a manager takes an employee (or a school takes a student) off probation because of improved performance.

punishment

Administering an aversive consequence.

extinction

Withdrawing or failing to provide a reinforcing consequence.

3. **Punishment**—administering an aversive consequence. Examples include criticizing or shouting at an employee, assigning an unappealing task, and sending a worker home without pay. Negative reinforcement can involve the *threat* of punishment by not delivering punishment when employees perform satisfactorily. Punishment is the actual delivery of the aversive consequence. Managers use punishment when they think it is warranted or when they believe others expect them to, and they usually concern themselves with following company policy and procedure.[31]

4. **Extinction**—withdrawing or failing to provide a reinforcing consequence. When this occurs, motivation is reduced and the behavior is *extinguished*, or eliminated. Ways that managers may unintentionally extinguish desired behaviors include not giving a compliment for a job well done, forgetting to say thanks for a favor, and setting impossible performance goals so a person never experiences success. Extinction may be used to end undesirable behaviors, too. The manager might ignore long-winded observations during a meeting or fail to acknowledge unimportant e-mail in the hope that the lack of feedback will discourage the employee from continuing.

The first two consequences, positive and negative reinforcement, are positive for the person receiving them—the person either gains something or avoids something negative. Therefore, the person who experiences these consequences will be motivated to behave in the ways that led to the reinforcement. The last two consequences, punishment and extinction, are negative outcomes for the person receiving them: motivation to repeat the behavior that led to the undesirable results will be reduced.

Managers should be careful to match consequences to what employees will actually find desirable or undesirable. A supervisor once made the mistake of "punishing" an employee for tardiness by suspending him for three days during fishing season. The employee was delighted.[32]

(Mis)Managing Rewards and Punishments

You've learned about the positive effects of a transformational leadership style, but giving rewards to high-performing people is also essential.[33] Unfortunately, sometimes organizations and managers reinforce the wrong behaviors.[34] For example, compensation plans that include stock options are intended to reinforce behaviors that add to the company's value, but stock options also can reinforce decisions that artificially deliver short-term gains in stock prices, even if they hurt the company in the long run. Likewise, programs that punish employees for absenteeism beyond a certain limit may actually encourage them to be absent. People may use up all their allowable absences and fail to come to work regularly until they reach the point where their next absence will result in punishment. Sometimes employees are reinforced with admiration

Sometimes organizations and managers reinforce the wrong behaviors.

and positive performance evaluations for multitasking—say, typing e-mail while on the phone or checking text messages during meetings. This behavior may look efficient and send a signal that the employee is busy and valuable, but multitasking actually slows down the brain's efficiency and can contribute to mistakes.[35] Scans of brain activity show that the brain is not able to concentrate on two tasks at once; it needs time to switch among the multitasker's activities. As a result, managers who praise the hard work of multitaskers may be unintentionally reinforcing inefficiency and failure to think deeply about problems.

To use reinforcement effectively, managers must identify which kinds of behaviors they reinforce and which they discourage (see Table 13.1). The reward system has to support the firm's strategy, defining people's performance in ways that pursue strategic objectives.[36] Reward employees for developing themselves in strategically important ways—for building new skills that are critical to strengthening core competencies and creating value.

Managers should be creative in their use of reinforcers. Sprint, where many workers spend their day sitting in front of a computer, reinforces healthy behavior by providing onsite exercise facilities, where employees can enjoy workouts during their lunch hours.[37] For Steven T. Bigari, owner of 12 McDonald's restaurants, the basic challenge was how to motivate low-wage

> Methodist Hospital System, located in Houston, recently gave each of its employees a $250 gift card to buy gasoline.[38]

workers to stay on the job when faced with struggles to find affordable day care and transportation. Facing stiff competition from Taco Bell, Bigari concluded he couldn't afford higher wages, but he helped a local church set up a day care program, and he visited police auctions during his Saturday lunch breaks to purchase low-priced but reliable cars, which he resold to employees at cost.[39]

Innovative managers use nonmonetary rewards, including intellectual challenge, greater responsibility, autonomy, recognition, flexible benefits, and greater influence over decisions. These and other rewards for high-performing employees, when creatively devised and applied, can continue to motivate when pay and promotions are scarce. Employees at Brown Flynn—a firm that provides services to help companies exercise social responsibility—receive practical benefits such as profit sharing and creative ones like jewelry and shopping sprees, but the intangibles may be what matter most. Employees describe Brown Flynn as offering challenges and rewards, mutual respect, recognition for hard work, and opportunities to exercise leadership.[40] And

Managers should be creative in their use of reinforcers.

"The things that get rewarded get done" is what one author called The Greatest Management Principle in the World. With this in mind, Michael LeBoeuf offered prescriptions for effectively motivating high performance. Companies, and individual managers, should reward the following: 1. *Solid solutions* instead of quick fixes. 2. *Risk taking* instead of risk avoiding. 3. *Applied creativity* instead of mindless conformity. 4. *Decisive action* instead of paralysis by analysis. 5. *Smart work* instead of busywork. 6. *Simplification* instead of needless complication. 7. *Quietly effective behavior* instead of squeaky wheels. 8. *Quality work* instead of fast work. 9. *Loyalty* instead of turnover. 10. *Working together* instead of working against.

TABLE 13.1

The Greatest Management Principle in the World

SOURCE: From *The Greatest Management Principle in the World* by Michael LeBoeuf. Copyright © 1985 by Michael LeBoeuf. Reprinted with permission.

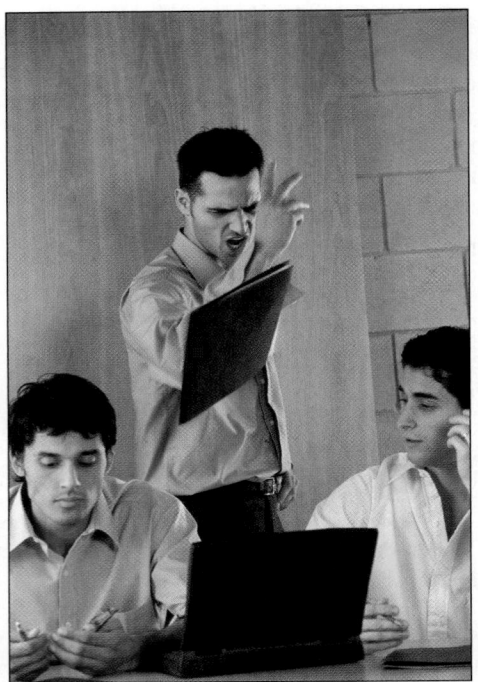

Managers who inappropriately yell at their staff or overuse punishment often create a climate of fear and anxiety in the workplace. How would you deal with a situation like this?

one of Steven Bigari's McDonald's employees said she preferred working for him to earning slightly more at a corporate-owned restaurant because of the way Bigari treats employees: "He's not in it for himself; he's in it for the people."[41]

Managing Mistakes

How a manager reacts to people's mistakes has a big impact on motivation. Punishment is sometimes appropriate, as when people violate the law, ethical standards, important safety rules, or standards of interpersonal treatment, or when they fail to attend or perform like a slacker. But sometimes managers punish people when they shouldn't—when poor performance isn't the person's fault or when managers take out their frustrations on the wrong people.

Managers who overuse punishment or use it inappropriately create a climate of fear in the workplace.[42] Fear causes people to focus on the short term, sometimes creating problems in the longer run. Fear also creates a focus on oneself rather than on the group and the organization. B. Joseph White, president emeritus of the University of Illinois, recalls consulting for a high-tech entrepreneur who heard a manager present a proposal and responded with brutal criticism: "That's the . . . stupidest idea I ever heard in my life. I'm disappointed in you." According to White, this talented manager was so upset she never again felt fully able to contribute.[43] To avoid such damage, managers should think about how they handle mistakes.

Recognize that everyone makes mistakes, and that mistakes can be dealt with constructively by discussing and learning from them. Don't punish, but praise, people who deliver bad news to their bosses. Treat failure to act as a failure but don't punish unsuccessful, good-faith efforts. If you're a leader, talk about your failures with your people, and show how you learned from them. Give people second chances and maybe third chances (Donald Trump claims to give second chances, but never third). Encourage people to try new things, and don't punish them if what they try doesn't work out.

Providing Feedback

Most managers don't provide enough useful feedback, and most people don't receive or ask for feedback enough.[44] As a manager, you should consider all potential causes of poor performance, pay full attention when employees ask for feedback or want to discuss performance issues, and give feedback according to the guidelines you read about in Chapter 10.

Feedback can be offered in many ways.[45] Customers sometimes give feedback directly; you also can request customer feedback and give it to the employee. You can provide statistics on work that the person has directly influenced. A manufacturing firm—high tech or otherwise—can put the phone number or website of the production team on the product so customers can contact the team directly. Performance reviews, described in Chapter 11, should be conducted regularly. And bosses should give more regular, ongoing feedback—it helps correct problems immediately, provides immediate reinforcement for good work, and prevents surprises when the formal review comes.

For yourself, try not to be afraid of receiving feedback; in fact, you should actively seek it. But whether or not you seek the feedback, when you get it, don't ignore it. Try to avoid negative emotions like anger, hurt, defensiveness, or resignation. Think, It's up to me to get the feedback I need; I need to know these things about my performance and my behavior; learning what I need to know about myself will help me identify needs and create new opportunities; it serves my interest best to know rather than not know; taking initiative on this gives me more power and influence over my career.[46]

Bottom Line

Make sure that you reward the right things, not the wrong things. Sound obvious? You'd be surprised how often this principle is violated!

What is rewarding about feedback from your manager?

Try not to be afraid of receiving feedback; in fact, you should actively seek it.

Management Connection

INTUIT IMPROVES AT REINFORCEMENT

Although Intuit is highly respected as an employer, it hasn't always excelled at the details of motivating employees. Management has always sought to reward superior performance, but figuring out just how to do that has involved some trial and error.

About a decade ago, Intuit tried to make it easy for managers to motivate employees by delivering positive reinforcement for superior performance. The company set up an online program in which managers acknowledged individual employees by giving them awards with a designated cash value. The employee who received such an award could go online to a catalog where various kinds of merchandise were available at different price points. So an employee who was granted a $250 reward could exchange it for, say, a piece of electronics priced at $250.

Several problems developed, however. One was that employees weren't very impressed with the rewards. Many items in the catalog seemed to be overpriced (for example, that $250 item in the catalog might be something employees could find in a store for much less). Often the merchandise was out-of-date or arrived late, broken, or without necessary items such as batteries and cables, so the "free" merchandise required the employee to make a purchase. Employees began asking managers to give them gift certificates instead. Participation in the program continued but failed to grow, and only half of employees in the United States were receiving the rewards—implying perhaps that a lot of good performers were receiving no reinforcement through this program. In addition, with all the problems, the program was never rolled out to employees outside the United States.

Intuit wanted to continue with some kind of program that would encourage managers to deliver positive reinforcement, but it wanted to learn from its mistakes. The company decided to turn to an outside expert, Globoforce, which specializes in motivation programs offered internationally. Globoforce implemented a similar kind of online program, but with more options and improved service. In this program the emphasis was placed on delivering

relatively lower-cost (averaging $120) but more frequent rewards (still fully deserved for good performance). Most of these take the form of gift certificates, which give employees control over what they buy and at what price, as well as being easy to deliver rapidly. For example, an employee who chooses a certificate for Amazon.com can receive it via e-mail and spend it at Amazon's website the same day. Furthermore, recognizing that more gadgets are not what every person values most, the recognition program also offers the choice to convert a reward into a charitable donation, which quickly became popular with employees.

Intuit called the new recognition program Spotlight to emphasize its purpose of drawing attention to employees' high performance and great ideas. Two years into implementation of the Spotlight program, over 90 percent of employees had received at least one reward. Employees and their managers both have found the system easy to use. Employees are pleased about the feedback and like knowing that their efforts are appreciated. For example, after Jennifer Lepird, who works in Intuit's human resources department, worked day and night in the weeks before the company completed an acquisition that required her to bring the new employees' pay records into Intuit's system, the manager of the acquisition team sent her a reward worth a few hundred dollars. What thrilled her more than the dollar value of the reward was "the fact that somebody took the time to recognize the effort."

Jim Grenier, Intuit's vice president of human resources, is impressed by the success of the new approach. He finds that by offering smaller awards, the company has a system that makes it easy to surprise many different employees with recognition. The unexpectedness and widespread recognition, he finds, are more powerful than big prizes for a privileged few.[47]

- What motivation principles have Intuit's programs applied?
- How did the Spotlight program improve the use of feedback?

Performance-Related Beliefs

In contrast to reinforcement theory, which describes the processes by which factors in the work environment affect people's behavior, expectancy theory considers some of the cognitive processes that go on in people's heads. According to

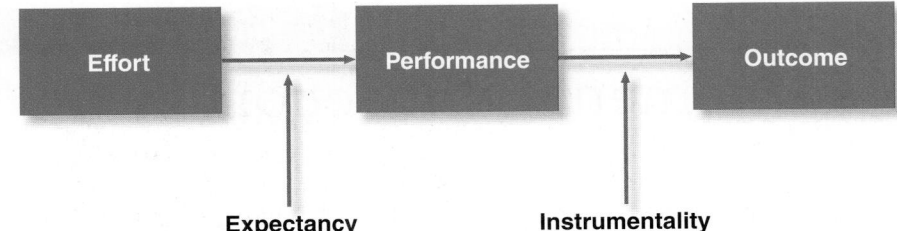

FIGURE 13.2
Basic Concepts of
Expectancy Theory

expectancy theory

A theory proposing that people will behave based on their perceived likelihood that their effort will lead to a certain outcome and on how highly they value that outcome.

expectancy

Employees' perception of the likelihood that their efforts will enable them to attain their performance goals.

outcome

A consequence a person receives for his or her performance.

instrumentality

The perceived likelihood that performance will be followed by a particular outcome.

valence

The value an outcome holds for the person contemplating it.

Will winning the contest really lead to resentment? Will it really lead to increased prestige?

expectancy theory, the person's work *efforts* lead to some level of *performance.*[48] Then performance results in one or more *outcomes* for the person. This process is shown in Figure 13.2. People develop two important beliefs linking these three events: expectancy, which links effort to performance, and instrumentality, which links performance to outcomes.

The Effort-to-Performance Link

The first belief, **expectancy,** is people's perceived likelihood that their efforts will enable them to attain their performance goals. An expectancy can be high (up to 100 percent), such as when a student is confident that if she studies hard, she can get a good grade on the final. An expectancy can also be low (down to a 0 percent likelihood), such as when a suitor is convinced that his dream date will never go out with him.

All else equal, high expectancies create higher motivation than do low expectancies. In the preceding examples, the student is more likely to study for the exam than the suitor is to pursue the dream date, even though both want their respective outcomes.

Expectancies can vary among individuals, even in the same situation. For example, a sales manager might initiate a competition in which the top salesperson wins a free trip to Hawaii. In such cases, the few top people, who have performed well in the past, will be more motivated by the contest than will the historically average and below-average performers. The top people will have higher expectancies—stronger beliefs that their efforts can help them win the competition.

The Performance-to-Outcome Link

The example of the sales contest illustrates how performance results in some kind of **outcome,** or consequence, for the person. Actually, it often results in several outcomes. For example, turning in the best sales performance could lead to (1) a competitive victory, (2) the free trip to Hawaii, (3) feelings of achievement, (4) recognition from the boss, (5) prestige throughout the company, and (6) resentment from other salespeople.

But how certain is it that performance will result in all of those outcomes? Will winning the contest really lead to resentment? Will it really lead to increased prestige?

These questions address the second key belief described by expectancy theory: instrumentality.[49] **Instrumentality** is the perceived likelihood that performance will be followed by a particular outcome. Like expectancies, instrumentalities can be high (up to 100 percent) or low (approaching 0 percent). For example, you can be fully confident that if you do a good job, you'll get a promotion; or you can feel that no matter how well you do, the promotion will go to someone else.

Also, each outcome has an associated valence. **Valence** is the value the person places on the outcome. Valences can be positive, as a Hawaiian vacation would be for most people, or negative, as in the case of the other salespeople's resentment.

Winning a competition for a free trip to Hawaii would be great, but what about all the losers?

Impact on Motivation

For motivation to be high, expectancy, instrumentalities, and total valence of all outcomes must all be high. A person will not be highly motivated if any of the following conditions exist:

1. He believes he can't perform well enough to achieve the positive outcomes that he knows the company provides to good performers (high valence and high instrumentality but low expectancy).
2. He knows he can do the job and is fairly certain what the ultimate outcomes will be (say, a promotion and a transfer). However, he doesn't want those outcomes or believes other, negative outcomes outweigh the positive (high expectancy and high instrumentality but low valence).
3. He knows he can do the job and wants several important outcomes (a favorable performance review, a raise, and a promotion). But he believes that no matter how well he performs, the outcomes will not be forthcoming (high expectancy and positive valences but low instrumentality).

Managerial Implications of Expectancy Theory

Expectancy theory helps the manager zero in on key leverage points for influencing motivation. Three implications are crucial:

1. *Increase expectancies.* Provide a work environment that facilitates good performance, and set realistically attainable performance goals. Provide training, support, required resources, and encouragement so that people are confident they can perform at the levels expected of them. Recall from Chapter 12 that charismatic leaders excel at boosting their followers' confidence.
2. *Identify positively valent outcomes.* Understand what people want to get out of work. Think about what their jobs provide them and what is not, but could be, provided. Consider how people may differ in the valences they assign to outcomes. Know the need theories of motivation, described in the next section, and their implications for identifying important outcomes.
3. *Make performance instrumental toward positive outcomes.* Make sure that good performance is followed by personal recognition and praise, favorable

performance reviews, pay increases, and other positive results. Also, make sure that working hard and doing things well will have as few negative results as possible. It is useful to realize, too, that bosses usually control rewards and punishments, but others do so as well. Peers, direct reports, customers, and others tend to provide rewards in the form of compliments, help, and social punishments.

Organizations may set up formal reward systems as well. Umpqua Bank in Roseburg, Oregon, set up a link called "Brag Box" on its intranet. Employees visit the Brag Box to post comments about good things their coworkers have done. Sandy Hunt, Umpqua's vice president for rewards and recognition, regularly checks the Brag Box and notifies managers when their employees have received a compliment so the managers can further reinforce compliments with praise. In addition, every team at Umpqua has a "recognition fund," which any team member can spend to recognize coworkers for going the extra mile.[50]

IN PRACTICE

Rable Machine, a 72-employee machine shop in Mansfield, Ohio, links employee effort to business value by giving all of its people a stake in the company. When business owner Rick Rupp decided to retire, he created an employee stock ownership plan (ESOP). By participating in the ESOP, all Rable employees are owners, so the more profitable the business, the greater the rewards that flow directly to the employees. Besides owning shares of stock, employees also receive bonuses for saving money and share in Rable Machine's profits.

Linking company performance directly to employees' pocketbooks has created a culture in which employees are open-minded about making changes to keep the business competitive in a highly competitive marketplace. Managers are willing to invest in equipment that will improve efficiency, and employees on the shop floor are willing to learn the latest computerized machinery and automated processes. Managers consult with shop floor employees whenever they consider purchases of a new machine tool, which smoothes the transition to new work methods.

According to Rable's chief executive, Scott Carter, the most important part of managing an employee-owned company is to ensure that employees have full information about how well the company is doing.[51]

• Why would full communication be necessary in order for employee ownership to motivate the employees?

Understanding People's Needs

 So far we have focused on *processes* underlying motivation. The manager who appropriately applies goal-setting, reinforcement, and expectancy theories is creating essential motivating elements in the work environment. But motivation also is affected by characteristics of the person. The second type of motivation theory, *content theories*, indicates the kinds of needs that people want to satisfy. People have different needs energizing and motivating them toward different goals and reinforcers. The extent to which and the ways in which a person's needs are met or not met at work affect his or her behavior on the job.

The most important theories describing the content of people's needs are Maslow's need hierarchy, Alderfer's ERG theory, and McClelland's needs.

Maslow's Need Hierarchy

Abraham Maslow organized five major types of human needs into a hierarchy, as shown in Figure 13.3.[52] **Maslow's need hierarchy** illustrates his conception of people satisfying their needs in a specified order, from bottom to top. The needs, in ascending order, are

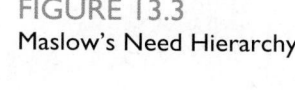

Maslow's need hierarchy

A conception of human needs organizing needs into a hierarchy of five major types.

1. *Physiological* (food, water, sex, and shelter).
2. *Safety or security* (protection against threat and deprivation).
3. *Social* (friendship, affection, belonging, and love).
4. *Ego* (independence, achievement, freedom, status, recognition, and self-esteem).
5. *Self-actualization* (realizing one's full potential, becoming everything one is capable of being).

According to Maslow, people are motivated to satisfy the lower needs before they try to satisfy the higher needs. In today's workplace, physiological and safety needs generally are well satisfied, making social, ego, and self-actualization needs important. But safety issues are still very important in manufacturing, mining, and other work environments. And for months after the terrorist attacks of September 2001, employees still felt fear, denial, and anger—especially among people with children, women, and those close to the events.[53] To deal with such safety issues, managers can show what the firm will do to improve security and manage employee risk, including crisis management plans as discussed in Chapter 3.

Safety issues are still very important in manufacturing, mining, and other work environments.

Once a need is satisfied, it is no longer a powerful motivator. For example, labor unions negotiate for higher wages, benefits, safety standards, and job security. These bargaining issues relate directly to the satisfaction of Maslow's lower-level needs. Only after these needs are reasonably satisfied do the higher-level needs—social, ego, and self-actualization—become dominant concerns.

Maslow's hierarchy, however, is a simplistic and not altogether accurate theory of human motivation.[54] For example, not everyone progresses through the five needs in hierarchical order. But Maslow made three important contributions. First, he identified important need categories, which can help managers create effective positive reinforcers. Second, it is helpful to think of two general levels of needs, in which lower-level

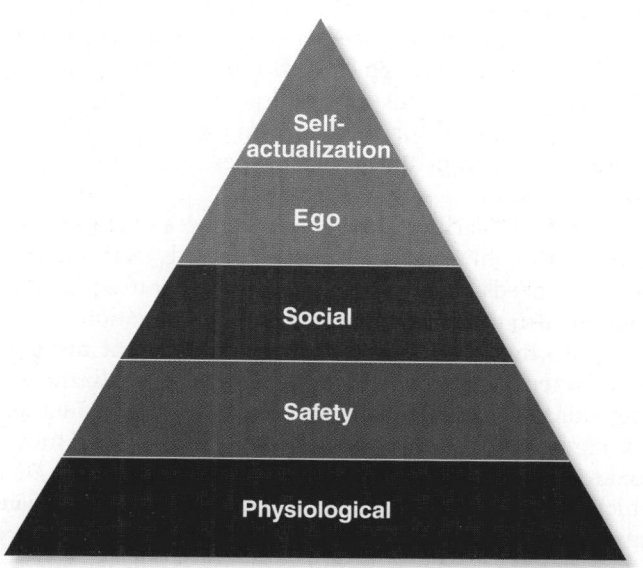

FIGURE 13.3
Maslow's Need Hierarchy

SOURCE: D. Organ and T. Bateman, *Organizational Behavior*, 4th ed., 1991. Copyright 1991 The McGraw-Hill Companies, Inc. Reprinted with permission.

needs must be satisfied before higher-level needs become important. Third, Maslow alerted managers to the importance of personal growth and self-actualization.

Self-actualization is the best-known concept arising from this theory. According to Maslow, the average person is only 10 percent self-actualized. In other words, most of us are living our lives and working at our jobs with a large untapped reservoir of potential. The implication is clear: managers should help create a work environment that provides training, resources, autonomy, responsibilities, and challenging assignments. This type of environment gives people a chance to use their skills and abilities in creative ways and allows them to achieve more of their full potential.

So treat people not merely as a cost to be controlled but an asset to be developed. Many companies have embarked on programs that provide personal growth experiences for their people. An employee at Federal Express said, "The best I can be is what I can be here. Federal Express . . . gave me the confidence and self-esteem to become the person I had the potential to become."[55] Individual managers also can promote employee growth. Pete Wamsteeker's first supervisor, at a feed company, routinely invited him to discuss his career plans, and Wamsteeker did the same for his employees when he became general manager of Cargill Animal Nutrition. When Wamsteeker took that position, he started by learning about his employees so that he could ensure each was in the job where he or she could contribute best.[56]

Organizations gain by making full use of their human resources. Employees also gain by capitalizing on opportunities to meet their higher-order needs on the job. At Campbell Soup Company, managers are rewarded for developing their employees, and Lisa Walker, business director of Campbell USA's wellness team, rises to that challenge. She worked with one employee to help him collaborate better so that he would be seen as a team player with promotion potential. Walker's employee appreciated that her coaching gave him an opportunity for greater achievement, status, and self-esteem.[57]

Alderfer's ERG Theory

A theory of human needs that is more advanced than Maslow's is Alderfer's ERG theory.[58] Maslow's theory has general applicability, but Alderfer aims his theory expressly at understanding people's needs at work.

Alderfer's ERG theory postulates three sets of needs: existence, relatedness, and growth. *Existence* needs are all material and physiological desires. *Relatedness* needs involve relationships with other people and are satisfied through the process of mutually sharing thoughts and feelings. *Growth* needs motivate people to productively or creatively change themselves or their environment. Satisfaction of the growth needs comes from fully utilizing personal capacities and developing new capacities.

What similarities do you see between Alderfer's and Maslow's needs? Roughly speaking, existence needs subsume physiological and security needs, relatedness needs are similar to social and esteem needs, and growth needs correspond to self-actualization.

ERG theory proposes that several different needs can be operating at once. Thus, whereas Maslow would say that self-actualization is important to people only after other sets of needs are satisfied, Alderfer maintains that people—particularly working people in our postindustrial society—can be motivated to satisfy existence, relatedness, and growth needs at the same time.

Consider which theory best explains the motives identified by Diane Schumaker-Krieg to describe her successful career in the financial services industry. Schumaker-Krieg says she was "driven . . . by fear" in October 1987, when she was working for investment firm Dillon Read at the time of the stock market crash. Layoffs were spreading throughout the industry, jobs were scarce, and she was supporting her

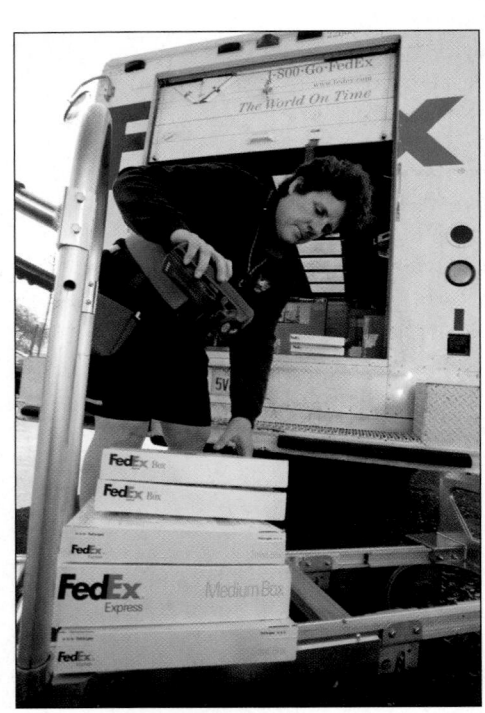

FedEx and some other companies care about and pay attention to the growth and development of their people.

Alderfer's ERG theory

A human needs theory postulating that people have three basic sets of needs that can operate simultaneously.

son following a divorce. Out of determination to take care of her son, Schumaker-Krieg reacted to being laid off by writing a plan for a new business.

> Yarde Metals set up a "nap room" with couches, pillows, soft lighting, and an alarm clock at its headquarters in Southington, Connecticut. Studies suggest that workers who nap may stay healthier—and that means fewer absences and lower costs for health insurance.[59] What do you think—is it worth it to the company?

She persuaded Dillon Read to fund the idea for a year, began building the business, moved it to Credit Suisse, and within years was earning $150 million in profits for her employer. During that time she remarried and earned enough to retire, but she continues working, now with Wells Fargo. She sees her current motivation as enjoyment of her accomplishments, her business relationships, and opportunities to continue innovating.[60] Certainly lower-level needs dominated the early years of Schumaker-Krieg's career, but did the basis for her motivation move one step at a time through all the levels of Maslow's hierarchy?

Maslow's theory is better known to American managers than Alderfer's, but ERG theory has more scientific support.[61] Both have practical value in that they remind managers of the types of reinforcers or rewards that can be used to motivate people. Regardless of whether a manager prefers the Maslow or the Alderfer theory of needs, he or she can motivate people by helping them satisfy their needs, particularly by offering opportunities for self-actualization and growth.

McClelland's Needs

David McClelland also identified a number of basic needs that guide people. The most important needs for managers, according to McClelland, are the needs for achievement, affiliation, and power.[62] Different needs predominate for different people.

> As you read about these needs, think about yourself—which ones are most and least important to you?

The need for *achievement* is characterized by a strong orientation toward accomplishment and an obsession with success and goal attainment. Most managers and entrepreneurs in the United States have high levels of this need and like to see it in their employees.

> "The degree to which you will find the right recognition [of employees' successes] is equal to the degree to which you know the employee, you know their wants and needs."
>
> —Erika Anderson, organizational development consultant[63]

The need for *affiliation* reflects a strong desire to be liked by other people. Individuals who have high levels of this need are oriented toward getting along with others and may be less concerned with performing at high levels.

The need for *power* is a desire to influence or control other people. This need can be a negative force—termed *personalized power*—if it is expressed through the aggressive manipulation and exploitation of others. People high on the personalized power need want power purely for the pursuit of their own goals. But the need for power also can be a positive motive—called *socialized power*—because it can be channeled toward the constructive improvement of organizations and societies.

Low need for affiliation and moderate to high need for power are associated with managerial success for both higher- and lower-level managers.[64] One reason the need for affiliation is not necessary for leadership success is that people high on this need have difficulty making tough but necessary decisions that will make some people unhappy.

Need Theories: International Perspectives

How do the need theories apply abroad?[65] Whereas managers in the United States care most strongly about achievement, esteem, and self-actualization, managers in Greece and Japan are motivated more by security. Social needs are most important in Sweden, Norway, and Denmark. "Doing your own thing"—the phrase from the 1960s that describes

The Japanese are more group-oriented while Americans are more individually oriented when it comes to motivation. How do you think this affects how these two countries do business together?

an American culture oriented toward self-actualization—is not even translatable into Chinese. "Achievement," too, is difficult to translate into most other languages. Researchers in France, Japan, and Sweden would have been unlikely to even conceive of McClelland's achievement motive because people of those countries are more group-oriented than individually oriented.

Clearly, achievement, growth, and self-actualization are profoundly important in the United States, Canada, and Great Britain. But these needs are not universally important. Every manager must remember that need importance varies from country to country and that people may not be motivated by the same needs. One study found that employees in many countries are highly engaged at companies that have strong leadership, work/life balance, a good reputation, and opportunities for employees to contribute; while another found variations from country to country:[66] Employees in Canada were attracted by competitive pay, work/life balance, and opportunities for advancement; workers in Germany by autonomy; in Japan by high-quality coworkers; in the Netherlands by a collaborative work environment; and in the United States by competitive health benefits. Generally, no single way is best, and managers can customize their approaches by considering how individuals differ.[67]

Designing Motivating Jobs

LO 6

extrinsic reward

Reward given to a person by the boss, the company, or some other person.

intrinsic reward

Reward a worker derives directly from performing the job itself.

Here's an example of a company that gave a "reward" that didn't motivate. One of Mary Kay Ash's former employers gave her a sales award: a flounder fishing light. Unfortunately, she didn't fish. Fortunately, she later was able to design her own organization, Mary Kay Cosmetics, around *intrinsic* as well as *extrinsic* motivators that *mattered* to her people.[68] **Extrinsic rewards** are given to people by the boss, the company, or some other person. An **intrinsic reward** is a reward the person derives directly from performing the job itself. An interesting project, an intriguing subject that is fun to study, a completed sale, and the discovery of the perfect solution to a difficult problem all can give people the feeling that they have done something well. This is the essence of the motivation that comes from intrinsic rewards.

Intrinsic rewards are essential to the motivation underlying creativity.[69] A challenging problem, a chance to create something new, and work that is exciting in and of itself can provide intrinsic motivation that inspires people to devote time and energy to the task. So do managers who allow people some freedom to pursue the tasks that interest them most. The opposite situations result in routine, habitual behaviors that interfere with creativity.[70] A study in manufacturing facilities found that employees initiated more applications for patents, made more novel and useful suggestions, and were rated by their managers as more creative when their jobs were challenging and their managers did not control their activities closely.[71]

Conversely, some managers and organizations create environments that quash creativity and motivation.[72] The classic example of a demotivating job is the highly specialized assembly line job; each worker performs one boring operation before passing the work along to the next worker. Such specialization, or the "mechanistic" approach to job design, was the prevailing practice through most of the 20th century.[73] But jobs that are too simple and routine result in employee dissatisfaction, absenteeism, and turnover.

Intrinsic rewards are essential to the motivation underlying creativity.

Especially in industries that depend on highly motivated knowledge workers, keeping talented employees may require letting them design their own jobs so their work is more interesting than it would be elsewhere.[74] Jobs can be designed in the following ways to increase intrinsic rewards and therefore motivation.

Job Rotation, Enlargement, and Enrichment

With **job rotation,** workers who spend all their time in one routine task can instead move from one task to another. Rather than dishing out the pasta in a cafeteria line all day, a person might work the pasta, then the salads, and then the vegetables or desserts. Job rotation is intended to alleviate boredom by giving people different things to do at different times.

As you may guess, however, the person may just be changing from one boring job to another. But job rotation can benefit everyone when done properly, with people's input and career interests in mind. At Thomson, an international publishing company, new information technology (IT) employees can participate in a job rotation program that helps them learn about the company's diverse business units and identify the area that best fits their talents and interests. Harrah's Entertainment also uses job rotation for its IT workers, which gives them a broad knowledge of the business that enhances their value to the company at the same time it opens up opportunities for career development.[75]

Job enlargement is similar to job rotation in that people are given different tasks to do. But whereas job rotation involves doing one task at one time and changing to a different task at a different time, job enlargement means that the worker has multiple tasks at the same time. Thus an assembly worker's job is enlarged if he or she is given two tasks rather than one to perform. In a study of job enlargement in a financial services organization, enlarged jobs led to higher job satisfaction, better error detection by clerks, and improved customer service.[76]

With job enlargement, the person's additional tasks are at the same level of responsibility. More profound changes occur when jobs are enriched. **Job enrichment** means that jobs are restructured or redesigned by adding higher levels of responsibility. This practice includes giving people not only more tasks but higher-level ones, such as when decisions are delegated downward and authority is decentralized. Herzberg's two-factor theory was the first approach to job enrichment, followed by the Hackman and Oldham model.

job rotation

Changing from one task to another to alleviate boredom.

job enlargement

Giving people additional tasks at the same time to alleviate boredom.

job enrichment

Changing a task to make it inherently more rewarding, motivating, and satisfying.

Herzberg's Two-Factor Theory

Frederick Herzberg's **two-factor theory** distinguished between two broad categories of factors that affect people working on their jobs.[77] The first category, **hygiene factors,** are *characteristics of the workplace:* company policies, working conditions, pay, coworkers, supervision, and so forth. These factors can make people unhappy if they are poorly managed. If they are well managed, and viewed as positive by employees, the employees will no longer be dissatisfied. However, no matter how good these factors are, they will not make people truly satisfied or motivated to do a good job.

According to Herzberg, the key to true job satisfaction and motivation to perform lies in the second category: the motivators. The **motivators** describe the *job itself*—that is, what people *do* at work. Motivators are the nature of the work itself, the actual job responsibilities, opportunity for personal growth and recognition, and the feelings of achievement the job provides. When these factors are present, jobs are presumed to be both satisfying and motivating for most people.

Herzberg's theory has been criticized by many scholars, and for that reason we will not go into more detail about his original theory. But Herzberg was a pioneer in the area of job design and still is a respected name among American managers. Furthermore, even if the specifics of his theory do not hold up to scientific scrutiny, he made several very important contributions. First, Herzberg's theory highlights the

two-factor theory

Herzberg's theory describing two factors affecting people's work motivation and satisfaction.

hygiene factors

Characteristics of the workplace, such as company policies, working conditions, pay, and supervision, that can make people dissatisfied.

motivators

Factors that make a job more motivating, such as additional job responsibilities, opportunities for personal growth and recognition, and feelings of achievement.

important distinction between extrinsic rewards (from hygiene factors) and intrinsic rewards (from motivators). Second, it reminds managers not to count solely on extrinsic rewards to motivate workers but to focus on intrinsic rewards as well. Third, it set the stage for later theories, such as the Hackman and Oldham model, that explain more precisely how managers can enrich people's jobs.

The Hackman and Oldham Model of Job Design

Following Herzberg's work, Hackman and Oldham proposed a more complete model of job design.[78] Figure 13.4 illustrates their model. As you can see, well-designed jobs lead to high motivation, high-quality performance, high satisfaction, and low absenteeism and turnover. These outcomes occur when people experience three critical psychological states (noted in the middle column of the figure):

1. They believe they are doing something meaningful because their work is important to other people.
2. They feel personally responsible for how the work turns out.
3. They learn how well they perform their jobs.

These psychological states occur when people are working on enriched jobs—that is, jobs that offer the following five core job dimensions:

1. *Skill variety*—different job activities involving several skills and talents. When cleaning employees in hospitals were given some freedom in how they carried out their work, the employees themselves added skill variety to their work through extra efforts such as engaging patients in small talk and figuring out ways they could make nurses' jobs easier. After adding this skill variety, the employees reported being more satisfied with their jobs.[79]
2. *Task identity*—the completion of a whole, identifiable piece of work. At State Farm Insurance, agents are independent contractors who sell and provide

FIGURE 13.4

The Hackman and Oldham Model of Job Enrichment

SOURCE: From J. Richard Hackman, Greg R. Oldham, Robert Janson, and Kenneth Purdy, "A New Strategy for Job Enrichment," in *California Management Review*. vol. 17, no. 4 (Summer 1975), pp. 57–71. Copyright © 1975 by the Regents of the University of California. Reprinted by permission of University of California Press.

service for State Farm products exclusively. They have built and invested in their own businesses. As a result, agent retention and productivity are far better than industry norms.[80]

3. *Task significance*—an important, positive impact on the lives of others. A study of lifeguards found dramatic improvements in their performance if they were taught about how lifeguards make a difference by preventing deaths. Lifeguards in the study who simply were told that the job can be personally enriching showed no such improvements.[81] Similarly, James Perry, an expert on motivation of government employees, says these workers generally have a strong commitment to serving the public good, including public welfare and stewardship of public resources.[82]

4. *Autonomy*—independence and discretion in making decisions. In a research hospital, a department administrator told her people to do the kinds of research they wanted as long as it was within budget (and legal!). With no other guidelines—that is, complete autonomy—productivity increased sixfold in a year.[83]

5. *Feedback*—information about job performance. Many companies post charts or provide computerized data indicating productivity, number of rejects, and other data. At Whole Foods Market, teams are responsible for hiring and scheduling in their area of the store. Team leaders get information about each month's payroll expense versus the budgeted amount. If the team comes in under budget, everyone knows because everyone gets a share of the savings. This practical feedback inspires teams to hire carefully and work hard.[84]

The most effective job enrichment increases all five core dimensions.

A person's growth need strength will help determine just how effective a job enrichment program might be. **Growth need strength** is the degree to which individuals want personal and psychological development. Job enrichment would be more successful for people with high growth need strength. But very few people respond negatively to job enrichment.[86]

growth need strength

The degree to which individuals want personal and psychological development.

> According to a recent survey of 27,000 people, those most likely to be satisfied with their jobs were clergy members, firefighters, physical therapists, authors, and special education teachers. Job satisfaction was lowest among laborers (except construction), clothing salespeople, hand packers and packagers, food preparers, and roofers.[85] Can you see how the most satisfying jobs have more of Hackman and Oldham's job characteristics?

Empowerment

Today one frequently hears managers talk about "empowering" their people. Individuals may—or may not—feel empowered, and groups can have a "culture" of empowerment that predicts work unit performance.[87] **Empowerment** is the process of sharing power with employees, thereby enhancing their confidence in their ability to perform their jobs and their belief that they are influential contributors to the organization. Unfortunately, empowerment doesn't always live up to its hype. One problem is that managers undermine it by sending mixed messages like "Do your own thing—the way we tell you."[88] But empowerment can be profoundly motivating when done properly.[89]

Empowerment results in changes in employees' beliefs—from feeling powerless to believing strongly in their own personal effectiveness.[90] The result is that people take more initiative and persevere in achieving their goals and their leader's vision even in the face of obstacles.[91] Specifically, empowerment encourages the following beliefs among employees.[92] First, they perceive *meaning* in their work: their job fits their values. Second, they feel *competent*, or capable of performing their jobs with skill. Third, they have a sense of *self-determination*, of having some choice in regard to the tasks, methods, and pace of their work. Fourth, they have an *impact*—that is, they have some influence over important strategic, administrative, or operating decisions or outcomes on the job.

empowerment

The process of sharing power with employees, thereby enhancing their confidence in their ability to perform their jobs and their belief that they are influential contributors to the organization.

Unfortunately, empowerment doesn't always live up to its hype.

When speaking of times when they felt disempowered, people mentioned the following:[93]

- I had no input into a hiring decision of someone who was to report directly to me. I didn't even get to speak to the candidate.
- They treated us like mushrooms. They fed us and kept us in the dark.
- I worked extremely hard—long hours and late nights—on an urgent project, and then my manager took full credit for it.
- My suggestions, whether good or bad, were either not solicited or, worse, ignored.
- The project was reassigned without my knowledge or input.

In contrast, people felt empowered in the following examples:

- I was able to make a large financial decision on my own. I got to write a large check without being questioned.
- After having received a memo that said, "Cut travel," I made my case about why it was necessary to travel for business reasons, and I was told to go ahead.
- I was five years old, and my dad said, "You'll make a great mechanic one day." He planted the seed. Now I'm an engineer.
- My president supported my idea without question.
- All the financial data were shared with me.

Bottom Line

Job enrichment and empowerment don't work magic overnight; people may resist the new approaches and make mistakes along the way. But done right, their potential to achieve real results is undeniable.

Name two ways to ensure that empowerment is done right.

To foster empowerment,[94] management must create an environment in which all the employees feel they have real influence over performance standards and business effectiveness within their areas of responsibility.[95] An empowering work environment provides people with *information* necessary for them to perform at their best, *knowledge* about how to use the information and how to do their work, *power* to make decisions that give them control over their work, and the *rewards* they deserve for the contributions they make.[96] Such an environment reduces costs because fewer people are needed to supervise, monitor, and coordinate. It improves quality and service because high performance is inspired at the source—the people who do the work. It also allows quick action because people on the spot see problems, solutions, and opportunities for innovation on which they are empowered to act.

It is essential to give people clear strategic direction but to leave some room for flexibility and calculated risk taking. For example, Southwest Airlines' strategic principle of "meet customers' short-haul travel needs at fares competitive with the cost of automobile travel" helps employees keep strategic objectives in mind and use their discretion in making complicated decisions about service offerings, route selection, cabin design, ticketing procedures, and pricing.[97] More specific actions include increasing signature authority at all levels; reducing the number of rules and approval steps; assigning nonroutine jobs; allowing independent judgment, flexibility, and creativity; defining jobs more broadly as projects rather than tasks; and providing more access to resources and people throughout the organization.[98]

Empowerment does not mean allowing people to decide trivial things like what color to paint the lunchroom. For empowerment to make a difference, people must have an impact on things about which they care, such as quality and productivity.[99] Companies that have successfully used empowerment programs include Lord Corporation in Dayton, Ohio (which produces engine mounts for aircraft) and Herman Miller (the Michigan-based furniture manufacturer).[100]

You should not be surprised when empowerment causes some problems, at least in the short term. This often occurs with virtually any change, including changes for the better. It's important to remember that with empowerment comes responsibility, and employees don't necessarily like the accountability at first.[101] People may make mistakes at first, especially until they have had adequate training. And because more training is needed, costs are higher. Also, because people acquire new skills and make greater contributions, they may demand higher wages. But if they are well-trained and truly empowered, they will deserve them—and both they and the company will benefit.

Achieving Fairness

Ultimately, one of the most important issues in motivation surrounds how people view their contributions to the organization and what they receive from the organization. Ideally, they will view their relationship with their employer as a well-balanced, mutually beneficial exchange. As people work and realize the outcomes or consequences of their actions, they assess how fairly the organization treats them.

The starting point for understanding how people interpret their contributions and outcomes is equity theory.[102] **Equity theory** proposes that when people assess how fairly they are treated, they consider two key factors: outcomes and inputs. *Outcomes*, as in expectancy theory, refer to the various things the person receives on the job: recognition, pay, benefits, satisfaction, security, job assignments, punishments, and so forth. *Inputs* refer to the contributions the person makes to the organization: effort, time, talent, performance, extra commitment, good citizenship, and so forth. People have a general expectation that the outcomes they receive will reflect, or be proportionate to, the inputs they provide—a fair day's pay (and other outcomes) for a fair day's work (broadly defined by how people view all their contributions).

equity theory

A theory stating that people assess how fairly they have been treated according to two key factors: outcomes and inputs.

But this comparison of outcomes to inputs is not the whole story. People also pay attention to the outcomes and inputs others receive. At salary review time, for example, most people—from executives on down—try to pick up clues that will tell them who got the high raises. As described in the following section, they compare ratios, try to restore equity if necessary, and derive more or less satisfaction based on how fairly they believe they have been treated.

Equity theory suggests that people compare the ratio of their outcomes to inputs against the outcome-to-input ratio of some comparison person. How would you deal with someone you perceive to be a slacker who gets promoted over you?

Assessing Equity

Equity theory suggests that people compare the ratio of their own outcomes to inputs against the outcome-to-input ratio of some comparison person. The comparison person can be a fellow student, a coworker, a boss, or an average industry pay scale. Stated more succinctly, people compare

$$\text{Their own } \frac{\text{Outcomes}}{\text{Inputs}} \text{ versus Others' } \frac{\text{Outcomes}}{\text{Inputs}}$$

If the ratios are equivalent, people believe the relationship is equitable, or fair. Equity causes people to be satisfied with their treatment. But the person who believes his or her ratio is lower than another's will feel inequitably treated. Inequity causes dissatisfaction and leads to an attempt to restore balance to the relationship.

Inequity and the negative feelings it creates may appear anywhere. As a student, perhaps you have been in the following situation.

You stay up all night and get a C on the exam. Meanwhile another student studies a couple of hours, goes out for the rest of the evening, gets a good night's sleep, and gets a B on the exam. You perceive your inputs (time spent studying) as much greater than the other student's, but your outcomes are lower. You are displeased at the seeming unfairness. In business, the same thing sometimes happens with pay raises. One manager puts in 60-hour weeks, has a degree from a prestigious university, and believes she is destined for the top. When her archrival—whom she perceives as less deserving ("she never comes into the office on weekends, and all she does when she is here is butter up the boss")—gets the higher raise or the promotion, she experiences severe feelings of inequity. Motivation problems resulting from perceived pay inequities may be the reason major league baseball teams that have great differences in their player salaries tend to win fewer games.[103]

Many people have felt inequity when they learn about large sums paid to high-profile CEOs. According to one analysis, while the average chief executive officer receives 5.4 times the pay of the average worker in his or her company, that multiple soars in large corporations: 12.5 at corporations with sales of $250 million to $1 billion, 33.2 when sales are $1 billion to $2.5 billion, and 91.8 when sales are more than $2.5 billion. Can it be that the CEO of a large corporation contributes over 90 times more to the company's value than the average employee contributes? One argument in favor of high pay for top executives is that the pay is closely tied to performance and, in fact, can fall drastically at companies that do poorly. Recently, for example, Irene Rosenfeld, CEO of Kraft Foods, saw her compensation tumble by 27 percent to "just" $19.3 million, and Eastman Kodak CEO Antonio Perez saw his pay slashed 66 percent to $5.7 million. Whether that makes the pay fair will be an increasingly public issue at U.S. companies in the near future because the Dodd-Frank Wall Street Reform and Consumer Protection Act requires greater disclosure of performance-based pay details.[104]

Assessments of equity are not made objectively. They are subjective perceptions or beliefs. In the preceding examples, the person who got the higher raise probably felt she deserved it. Even if she admits she doesn't put in long workweeks, she may convince herself she doesn't need to because she's so talented. The student who got the higher grade may believe it was a fair, equitable result because (1) she kept up all semester, while the other student did not, and (2) she's smart (ability and experience, not just time and effort, can be seen as inputs).

Restoring Equity

People who feel inequitably treated and dissatisfied are motivated to do something to restore equity. They have a number of options that they carry out to change the ratios or to reevaluate the situation and decide it is equitable after all.

The equity equation shown earlier indicates a person's options for restoring equity. People who feel inequitably treated can *reduce their inputs* by giving less effort, performing at lower levels, or quitting. ("Well, if that's the way things work around here, there's no way I'm going to work that hard [or stick around].") Or they can attempt to *increase their outcomes.* ("My boss [or teacher] is going to hear about this. I deserve more; there must be some way I can get more.") On the positive side, employees may also put forth extra effort to keep a situation equitable for the group. In the first few months of each year, many accountants face a flood of work related to annual reports and tax preparation. At Gramkow, Carnevale, Seifert & Company, an accounting firm in Oradell, New Jersey, Kenneth Benkow works six days a week and many evenings during tax time. He explains, "What helps motivate me is that I look around the office and I see people who are working as hard or harder than I am. You feel guilty if you're not pulling your own weight."[105]

Other ways of restoring equity focus on changing the other person's ratio. A person can *decrease others' outcomes.* For example, an employee may sabotage work to create problems for his company or his boss.[106] A person can also change her perceptions of inputs or outcomes. ("That promotion isn't as great a deal as he thinks. The pay is not that much better, and the headaches will be unbelievable.") It is also possible to *increase others' inputs,* particularly by changing perceptions. ("The more I think about it, the more I see he deserved it. He's worked hard all year, he's competent, and it's about time he got a break.")

Thus a person can restore equity in a number of ways by behaviorally or perceptually changing inputs and outcomes.

Managers expect employees to show up on schedule, but some managers have heard surprising excuses from absent or tardy employees. Michael Palmer, the owner of K Hotels Sales & Marketing in Los Angeles, told a reporter that an employee once called to ask for the day off because she was so upset about breaking up with her boyfriend. Palmer agreed, but the next day, the employee wanted another day off—so she could allow her new boyfriend to help her get over her grief. At Arcos Inc. in Columbus, Ohio, Mitch McLeod got a call from a software engineer who was running late because the cat had hidden his car keys. That was only one of a series of excuses from that engineer.

Why would employees offer excuses rather than take responsibility? An obvious reason would be hope of avoiding consequences. Also, Patricia Harned of the Ethics Resource Center (ERC) says some employees invent excuses as a way to get a benefit they believe they're entitled to: time off at their convenience. An ERC survey of employees found that about 15 percent say it's OK to call in sick even when they are actually well. Many of them say it's fair because workers deserve more time off.

Managers need an equitable way to handle the excuses. At K Hotels, Palmer tries to encourage good attendance humorously by posting excuses on a dry-erase board to expose their silliness. He and his employee with the new boyfriend eventually agreed she was not a good fit for the company, so she left. At Arcos, the frequently late engineer was a star employee, so McLeod solved the tardiness problem by assigning him later hours.[107]

- What equity issues arise when employees want time off beyond what company policy allows? How fairly did Palmer and McLeod handle the problem?

Procedural Justice

Inevitably, managers make decisions that have outcomes more favorable for some than for others. Those with favorable outcomes will be pleased; those with worse outcomes, all else equal, will be more displeased. But managers desiring to put salve on the wounds—say, of people they like or respect or want to keep and motivate—still can take actions to reduce the dissatisfaction. The key is for people to believe that managers provide **procedural justice**—using fair process in decision making and helping others know that the process was as fair as possible. When people perceive procedural fairness, they are more likely to support decisions and decision makers.[108] For example, one year after layoffs, managers' use of procedural justice (in the form of employee participation in decisions) still predicted survivors' organizational commitment, job satisfaction, and trust toward management.[109]

Even if people believe that their *outcome* was inequitable and unfair, they are more likely to view justice as having been served if the *process* was fair. You can increase people's beliefs that the process was fair by making the process open and visible; stating decision criteria in advance rather than after the fact; making sure that the most appropriate people—those who have valid information and are viewed as trustworthy—make the decisions; giving people a chance to participate in the process; and providing an appeal process that allows people to question decisions safely and receive complete answers.[110]

At an elevator plant in the United States, an army of consultants arrived one day, unexplained and annoying.[111] The rumor mill kicked in; employees thought the plant was to be shut down or that some of them would be laid off. Three months later, management unveiled its new plan, involving a new method of manufacturing based on teams. As the changes were implemented, management did not adequately answer questions about the purpose of the changes, employees resisted,

procedural justice
Using fair process in decision making and making sure others know that the process was as fair as possible.

Utilizing procedural justice allows managers to express the fairness of certain decisions, including layoffs. When employees understand the reasons behind unfavorable decisions, they are more likely to support the choices and the managers that carried them out.

conflicts arose, and the formerly popular plant manager lost the trust of his people. Costs skyrocketed, and quality plummeted.

Concerned, management conducted an employee survey. Employees were skeptical that the survey results would lead to any positive changes and were worried that management would be angry that people had voiced their honest opinions. But management reacted by saying, "We were wrong, we screwed up, we didn't use the right process." They went on to share with employees critical business information, the limited options available, and the dire consequences if the company didn't change. Employees saw the dilemma and came to view the business problem as theirs as well as management's, but they were scared that some of them would lose their jobs. Management retained the right to lay people off if business conditions grew worse but also made several promises: no layoffs as a result of changes made; cross-training programs for employees; no replacements of departing people until conditions improved; a chance for employees to serve in new roles as consultants on quality issues; and sharing of sales and cost data on a regular basis.

The news was bad, but people understood it and began to share responsibility with management. This was the beginning of the restoration of trust and commitment, and of steady improvements in performance.

Job Satisfaction

LO 8

Bottom Line

A single satisfied person doesn't necessarily produce well on every performance dimension. But an organization full of people with high job satisfaction will likely perform well in countless ways.

In an organization with a strategy focused on low cost, is employee satisfaction important? Why or why not?

quality of work life (QWL) programs

Programs designed to create a workplace that enhances employee well-being.

If people feel fairly treated from the outcomes they receive or the processes used, they will be satisfied. A satisfied worker is not necessarily more productive than a dissatisfied one; sometimes people are happy with their jobs because they don't have to work hard! But job dissatisfaction, aggregated across many individuals, creates a workforce that is more likely to exhibit (1) higher turnover; (2) higher absenteeism; (3) less good citizenship among employees;[112] (4) more grievances and lawsuits; (5) strikes; (6) stealing, sabotage, and vandalism; (7) poorer mental and physical health (which can mean higher job stress, higher insurance costs, and more lawsuits);[113] (8) more injuries;[114] (9) poor customer service;[115] and (10) lower productivity and profits.[116] All of these consequences of dissatisfaction, either directly or indirectly, are costly to organizations. Sadly, a survey of U.S. households found that a majority of workers are dissatisfied with their jobs, with the greatest amount of dissatisfaction among workers aged 25 and younger.[117]

Job satisfaction is especially important for relationship-oriented service employees such as realtors, hair stylists, and stockbrokers. Customers develop (or don't develop) a commitment to a specific service provider. Satisfied service providers are less likely to quit the company and more likely to provide an enjoyable customer experience.[118]

Quality of Work Life

Quality of work life (QWL) programs create a workplace that enhances employee well-being and satisfaction. The general goal of QWL programs is to satisfy the full range of employee needs. People's needs apparently are well met at First Horizon National, which offers a flexible benefits package including health and dental insurance, paid vacation, tuition reimbursement, discounts for child care and financial products, and reimbursement for adoption-related expenses. First Horizon extends those benefits to workers who telecommute and work part-time. Web consultant Brenda Fung says, "This company has been so generous to me. There's no way I could even think of leaving."[119]

QWL has eight categories:[120]

1. Adequate and fair compensation.
2. A safe and healthy environment.

3. Jobs that develop human capacities.
4. A chance for personal growth and security.
5. A social environment that fosters personal identity, freedom from prejudice, a sense of community, and upward mobility.
6. Constitutionalism, or the rights of personal privacy, dissent, and due process.
7. A work role that minimizes infringement on personal leisure and family needs.
8. Socially responsible organizational actions.

> "Employee loyalty exists, but it depends upon what the company is willing to do for its employees."
> —Vinnie, an employee at a New York investment bank, on why he turned down a job paying 30 percent more to stay with his current employer[121]

Organizations differ drastically in their attention to QWL. Critics claim that QWL programs don't necessarily inspire employees to work harder if the company does not tie rewards directly to individual performance. Advocates of QWL claim that it improves organizational effectiveness and productivity. The term *productivity*, as applied by QWL programs, means much more than each person's quantity of work output.[122] It also includes turnover, absenteeism, accidents, theft, sabotage, creativity, innovation, and especially the quality of work.

All in all, people's satisfaction and well-being have many important consequences, beneficial to both employees and employers.[123] These range from better attitudes and health to work behaviors and performance, and ultimately include business outcomes.[124] In a well-managed workplace, win–win solutions are indeed possible.

Psychological Contracts

The relationship between individuals and employing organizations typically is formalized by a written contract. But in employees' minds there also exists a **psychological contract**—a set of perceptions of what they owe their employers and what their employers owe them.[125] This contract, whether it is seen as being upheld or violated—and whether the parties trust one another or not—has important implications for employee satisfaction and motivation and the effectiveness of the organization.

psychological contract

A set of perceptions of what employees owe their employers, and what their employers owe them.

Historically, in many companies the employment relationship was stable and predictable. Now mergers, layoffs, and other disruptions have torn asunder the "old deal."[126] As a McGraw-Hill executive put it, "The 'used-to-be's' must give way to the realities of 'What is and what will be.'"[127] The fundamental "used-to-be" of traditionally managed organizations was that employees were expected to be loyal and employers would provide secure employment. Today the implicit contract goes something like this:[128] If people stay, do their own jobs plus someone else's (who has been downsized), and do additional things like participating in task forces, the company will try to provide a job (if it can), provide gestures that it cares, and keep providing more or less the same pay (with periodic small increases). The likely result of this not-very-satisfying arrangement: uninspired people and a business trying to survive.

But a better deal is possible, for both employers and employees.[129] Ideally, your employer will provide continuous skill updating and an invigorating work environment in which you can use your skills and are motivated to stay even though you may have other job options.[130] An example of such a modern psychological contract is Allstate's general employment contract, shown in Table 13.2. Thus you could work for a company that provides the following deal: If you develop the skills we need, apply them in ways that help the company succeed, and behave consistently with our values, we will provide for you a challenging work environment, support for your development, and full, fair rewards for your contributions. The results of such a "contract" are much more likely

A better deal is possible, for both employers and employees.

TABLE 13.2

Allstate Employability Contract

You should expect Allstate to:

1. Offer work that is meaningful and challenging.
2. Promote an environment that encourages open and constructive dialogue.
3. Recognize you for your accomplishments.
4. Provide competitive pay and rewards based on your performance.
5. Advise you on your performance through regular feedback.
6. Create learning opportunities through education and job assignments.
7. Support you in defining career goals.
8. Provide you with information and resources to perform successfully.
9. Promote an environment that is inclusive and free from bias.
10. Foster dignity and respect in all interactions.
11. Establish an environment that promotes a balance of work and personal life.

Allstate expects you to:

1. Perform at levels that significantly increase our ability to outperform the competition.
2. Take on assignments critical to meeting business objectives.
3. Continually develop needed skills.
4. Willingly listen to and act upon feedback.
5. Demonstrate a high level of commitment to achieving company goals.
6. Exhibit no bias in interactions with colleagues and customers.
7. Behave consistently with Allstate's ethical standards.
8. Take personal responsibility for each transaction with our customers and for fostering their trust.
9. Continually improve processes to address customers' needs.

SOURCE: Courtesy of Allstate Insurance Company.

to be a mutually beneficial and satisfying relationship and a high-performing, successful organization.

Consider how business coach Ram Charan assumed this new psychological contract in advising a frustrated human resource (HR) manager.[131] The manager had asked Charan for guidance in coping with bureaucratic red tape that was frustrating to him as a leader and to the employees in his group. Charan encouraged the manager to reframe the situation as a need for learning, creativity, and leadership. The manager, said Charan, should investigate what the managers in other departments need from HR so that his people would truly be serving business needs and helping to solve business problems. Charan also encouraged the manager to learn about his employees' career goals and interests so that he can focus on ways to develop his people's strengths through assignments and greater decision-making authority within the department. If the HR manager accepts Charan's guidance, he and his people will face more interesting challenges than they would by simply defining themselves as a static part of a bureaucracy.

Finally, consider how these ideas for motivation apply at Intuit. Read the "Management Connection: Onward" feature and ask yourself whether old-fashioned stable employment relationships can—or should—be the norm.

Management Connection

HOW INTUIT MOTIVATES FOR INNOVATION

Especially in a high-tech industry such as software development, companies will quickly lose ground if their people aren't constantly innovating. So motivating employees to try new ideas is a key strategy at Intuit.

One way Intuit does this is by communicating to Intuit engineers the value of what they do. Rather than talking just about programming tasks and projects, the company points out that engineers are helping people pay their bills, get maximum tax refunds, understand their financial resources, and boost the profits of their small businesses. Intuit even helps customers be environmentally friendly; the QuickBooks accounting software is the first such program to include a calculator of a company's carbon footprint. Intuit encourages employees to develop a deep understanding of how their customers use its products so they can identify applications or improvements that will be useful. For example, in a practice called follow-me-home, employees may travel to customers' homes and workplaces to observe them directly. And employees can take ideas that have potential to Intuit Labs, which quickly tries out test versions of a new product and solicits feedback from the customers who try it.

Trying to motivate people to innovate is not just empty words. Employees are allowed to use up to four hours of each workweek as "unstructured time" for pursuing whatever ideas they believe will benefit the company. Out of that policy came one of the tools that has been most useful to collaboration: a program called Brainstorm, which gathers and share engineers' ideas online so they can build on what others are thinking. Remarkably, Brainstorm's creators had been with Intuit for just a few months when they saw an opportunity to improve the system the company had been using for idea sharing. Brainstorm proved so popular among Intuit's engineers that the company decided to sell it as a new product.

The company also hosts what it calls idea jams or code jams. At these daylong programs, hundreds of employees gather to share ideas with each other, refine them, and present them to management. The most feasible ideas can win prizes and, better yet, may be implemented if managers—and customers—appreciate their potential. The very experience of participating in an idea jam can be motivating: employees gather in a room full of people who are energized and excited about how they hope to apply their expertise to move the company into the future.

Together, these efforts aim to keep Intuit's work environment like that of what Intuit spokeswoman Julie Miller calls a "bunch of start-ups," alluding to the spirit of collaboration and drive to create something new that often permeate a small, new company. Intuit's founder, Scott Cook, is convinced that for employees, the chance to come up with ideas, develop them, and see them benefiting people is a powerful motivator. When people are working on their own ideas, he told an interviewer, they'll not only work nights and weekends, but really want to: "They love it! They're happy!" And, he adds, "They deliver better results."

This approach to motivation is what has made Intuit a standout in the past; in *Fortune*'s most recent ranking of the world's most admired companies, Intuit was ranked second among software companies for innovation and the quality of its products. Five times as many new products are under development as before. The key, Cook explains, is to direct the enthusiasm to innovate so employees are focused on pleasing customers. That's an approach that is likely to keep the company winning in the future.[132]

- How did Intuit make its engineers' jobs motivating? What additional ideas for job design might encourage even more innovation?
- What elements of Intuit's approach to motivation do you think would contribute most to job satisfaction? Why?

KEY TERMS

SUMMARY OF LEARNING OBJECTIVES

Now that you have studied Chapter 13, you should be able to:

LO 1 Identify the kinds of behaviors managers need to motivate in people.

All important work behaviors are motivated. Managers need to motivate employees to join and remain in the organization and to exhibit high attendance, job performance, and citizenship.

LO 2 List principles for setting goals that motivate employees.

Goal setting is a powerful motivator. Specific, quantifiable, and challenging but attainable goals motivate high effort and performance. Goal setting can be used for teams as well as for individuals. Care should be taken to avoid setting single goals to the exclusion of other important dimensions of performance. Managers also should keep sight of the other potential downsides of goals.

LO 3 Summarize how to reward good performance effectively.

Organizational behavior modification programs influence behavior at work by arranging consequences for people's actions. Most programs use positive reinforcement as a consequence, but other important consequences are negative reinforcement, punishment, and extinction. Care must be taken to reinforce appropriate, not inappropriate, behavior. Innovative managers use a wide variety of rewards for good performance. They also understand how to "manage mistakes" and provide useful feedback.

LO 4 Describe the key beliefs that affect people's motivation.

Expectancy theory describes three important work-related beliefs. Motivation is a function of people's (1) expectancies, or effort-to-performance links; (2) instrumentalities, or performance-to-outcome links; and (3) the valences people attach to the outcomes of performance. In addition, people care about equity and justice.

LO 5 Discuss ways in which people's individual needs affect their behavior.

According to Maslow, important needs arise at five levels of a hierarchy: physiological, safety, social, ego, and self-actualization needs. Focusing more on the context of work, Alderfer's ERG

theory describes three sets of needs: existence, relatedness, and growth. McClelland says people vary in the extent to which they have needs for achievement, affiliation, and power. Because people are inclined to satisfy their various needs, these theories suggest to managers the kinds of rewards that motivate people.

LO 6 Define ways to create jobs that motivate.

One approach to satisfying needs and motivating people is to create intrinsic motivation through the improved design of jobs. Jobs can be enriched by building in more skill variety, task identity, task significance, autonomy, and feedback. Empowerment, the most recent development in the creation of motivating jobs, includes the perceptions of meaning, competence, self-determination, and impact. These qualities come from an environment in which people have necessary information, knowledge, power, and rewards.

LO 7 Summarize how people assess fairness and how to achieve fairness.

Equity theory states that people compare their inputs and outcomes to the inputs and outcomes of others. Perceptions of equity (fairness) are satisfying; feelings of inequity (unfairness) are dissatisfying and motivate people to change their behavior or their perceptions to restore equity. In addition to fairness of outcomes, as described in equity theory, fairness is also appraised and managed through procedural justice.

LO 8 Identify causes and consequences of a satisfied workforce.

A satisfied workforce has many advantages for the firm, including lower absenteeism and turnover; fewer grievances, lawsuits, and strikes; lower health costs; and higher-quality work. One general approach to generating higher satisfaction for people is to implement a quality of work life program. QWL seeks to provide a safe and healthy environment, opportunity for personal growth, a positive social environment, fair treatment, and other improvements in people's work lives. These and other benefits from the organization, exchanged for contributions from employees, create a psychological contract. Over time, how the psychological contract is upheld or violated, and changed unfairly or fairly, will influence people's satisfaction and motivation.

DISCUSSION QUESTIONS

1. Think of a significant mistake made by someone on a job. How did the boss handle it, and what was the effect?

2. Why do you think it is so difficult for managers to empower their people?

3. Think of a job you hold currently or held in the past. How would you describe the psychological contract? How does(did) this affect your attitudes and behaviors on the job?

4. If a famous executive or sports figure were to give a passionate motivational speech, trying to persuade people to work harder, what do you think the impact would be? Why?

5. Give some examples of situations in which you wanted to do a great job but were prevented from doing so. What was the impact on you, and what would this suggest to you in your efforts to motivate other people to perform?

6. Discuss the similarities and differences between setting goals for other people and setting goals for yourself. When does goal setting fail, and when does it succeed?

7. Identify four examples of people inadvertently reinforcing the wrong behaviors, or punishing or extinguishing good behaviors.

8. Assess yourself on McClelland's three needs. On which need are you highest, and on which are you lowest? What are the implications for you as a manager?

9. Identify a job you have held, and appraise it on Hackman and Oldham's five core job dimensions. Also describe the degree to which it made you feel empowered. As a class, choose one job and discuss together how it could be changed to be more motivating and empowering.

10. Using expectancy theory, analyze how you have made and will make personal choices, such as a major area of study, a career to pursue, or job interviews to seek.

11. Describe a time when you felt unfairly treated and explain why. How did you respond to the inequity? What other options might you have had?

12. Provide examples of how outcomes perceived as unfair can decrease motivation. Then discuss how procedural justice, or fair process, can help overcome the negative effects.

13. What are the implications for your career of, and how will you prepare for, the psychological contracts described at the end of the chapter?

14. Set some goals for yourself, considering the discussion of goal setting in the chapter.

EXPERIENTIAL EXERCISES

13.1   ASSESSING YOURSELF

Circle the response that most closely correlates with each of the following items:

	Agree		Neither Agree nor Disagree		Disagree
1. I have developed a written list of short and long-term goals I would like to accomplish.	1	2	3	4	5
2. When setting goals for myself, I give consideration to what my capabilities and limits are.	1	2	3	4	5
3. I set goals that are realistic and attainable.	1	2	3	4	5
4. My goals are based on my hopes and beliefs, not on those of my parents, friends, or significant other.	1	2	3	4	5
5. When I fail to achieve a goal, I get back on track.	1	2	3	4	5
6. My goals are based on my personal values.	1	2	3	4	5
7. I have a current mission statement and have involved those closest to me in formulating it.	1	2	3	4	5
8. I regularly check my progress toward achieving the goals I have set.	1	2	3	4	5
9. When setting goals I strive for performance, not outcomes.	1	2	3	4	5
10. I have a support system in place—friends, family members, and/or colleagues who believe in me and support my goals.	1	2	3	4	5
11. I apply SMART characteristics to my goals.	1	2	3	4	5
12. I prioritize my goals, focusing only on the most important or valuable ones at a particular point in time.	1	2	3	4	5
13. I reward myself when I achieve a goal, or even when I reach a particular milestone.	1	2	3	4	5
14. I revisit my goals periodically, and add and modify goals as appropriate.	1	2	3	4	5

Sum your circled responses. If your total is 42 or higher, you might want to explore ways to improve your skill in the area of goal setting.

SOURCE: Suzanne C. de Janasz, Karen O'Dowd, and Beth Z. Schneider, *Interpersonal Skills in Organizations*, McGraw-Hill, 2002, p. 211. Copyright 2002 The McGraw-Hill Companies, Inc. Reprinted with permission.

13.2   PERSONAL GOAL SETTING

1. In the spaces provided, brainstorm your goals in the following categories. Write down as many as you wish, including goals that are short-, mid-, and long-term.

   Academic, intellectual

   Health, fitness

   Social: family, friends, significant other, community

   Career, job

   Financial

   Other

2. Of the goals you have listed, select from each of the six categories the two most important goals that you would like to pursue in the short term (next 6–12 months). Write these here.

   a. _____

   b. _____

   c. _____

   d. _____

   e. _____

   f. _____

   g. _____

   h. _____

   i. _____

   j. _____

   k. _____

   l. _____

3. From the 12 goals listed, choose the 3 that are the most important to you at this time: the 3 you commit to work on in the next few months. Write a goal statement for each one, using the following guidelines:

   Begin each with the word "To . . ."

   Be specific.

   Quantify the goal if possible.

Each goal statement should be realistic, attainable, and within your control.

Each goal statement should reflect your aspirations—not those of others such as parents, roommates, significant others, and the like.

   a. _____
   _____

   b. _____
   _____

   c. _____
   _____

4. On a separate sheet of paper, develop an action plan for each goal statement. For each action plan,

   List the steps you will take to accomplish the goal.

   Include dates (by when) and initials (who's responsible) for each step.

   Visualize completing the goal and, working backward, specify each step necessary between now and then to reach the goal.

   Identify any potential barriers you might experience in attaining the goal. Problem-solve around these obstacles, and convert them into steps in your action plan.

   Identify the resources you will need to accomplish these goals, and build in steps to acquire the necessary information into your action plan.

5. Transfer the dates of each step for each goal in your action plan to a daily calendar.

6. Keep an ongoing daily or weekly record of the positive steps you take toward meeting each goal.

SOURCE: Suzanne C. de Janasz, Karen O'Dowd, and Beth Z. Schneider, *Interpersonal Skills in Organizations,* McGraw-Hill, 2002, p. 211. Copyright 2002 The McGraw-Hill Companies, Inc. Reprinted with permission.

13.3   WHAT DO STUDENTS WANT FROM THEIR JOBS?

OBJECTIVES

1. To demonstrate individual differences in job expectations.
2. To illustrate individual differences in need and motivational structures.
3. To examine and compare extrinsic and intrinsic rewards.

INSTRUCTIONS

1. Working alone, complete the "What I Want from My Job" survey.
2. In small groups, compare and analyze differences in the survey results and prepare group responses to the discussion questions.
3. After the class reconvenes, group spokespersons present group findings.

DISCUSSION QUESTIONS

1. Which items received the highest and lowest scores from you? Why?
2. On which items were there most and least agreement among students? What are the implications?
3. Which job rewards are extrinsic, and which are intrinsic?
4. Were more response differences found in intrinsic or in extrinsic rewards?
5. In what ways do you think blue-collar workers' responses would differ from those of college students?

What I Want from My Job

Determine what you want from a job by circling the level of importance of each of the following job rewards:

	Very Important	Important	Indifferent	Unimportant	Very Unimportant
1. Advancement opportunities	5	4	3	2	1
2. Appropriate company policies	5	4	3	2	1
3. Authority	5	4	3	2	1
4. Autonomy and freedom on the job	5	4	3	2	1
5. Challenging work	5	4	3	2	1
6. Company reputation	5	4	3	2	1
7. Fringe benefits	5	4	3	2	1
8. Geographic location	5	4	3	2	1
9. Good coworkers	5	4	3	2	1
10. Good supervision	5	4	3	2	1
11. Job security	5	4	3	2	1
12. Money	5	4	3	2	1
13. Opportunity for self-development	5	4	3	2	1
14. Pleasant office and working conditions	5	4	3	2	1
15. Performance feedback	5	4	3	2	1
16. Prestigious job title	5	4	3	2	1
17. Recognition for doing a good job	5	4	3	2	1
18. Responsibility	5	4	3	2	1
19. Sense of achievement	5	4	3	2	1
20. Training programs	5	4	3	2	1
21. Type of work	5	4	3	2	1
22. Working with people	5	4	3	2	1

CONCLUDING CASE

BIG BISON RESORTS: FINDING THE KEY TO WHAT EMPLOYEES VALUE

Frank Schuman, vice president of human resources for Big Bison Resorts, heard laughter as he approached the chief executive's office door. As he stepped into the room, he saw CEO Janette Briggs seated behind her desk, regaling two other executives with a story that the three were obviously enjoying immensely.

"Oh, Frank! Good!" exclaimed Janette when she saw him enter. "I was just telling Pedro and Marlys about my great adventure in TV land." Janette had been away from the office for the past two weeks, taping the popular reality TV show *Executive in Disguise* instead of running her company, a regional chain of indoor water parks.

"How did it go?" asked Frank. "From the laughter I heard outside your door, it must have been hilarious."

"Well, funny, yes," replied Janette. "But mainly it was eye-opening. After spending all that time in our kitchens and cleaning the guest rooms and pools, I see our people and their jobs in a totally new way."

"Is that why you called me here? I was expecting you wanted to review our plans for the Employee of the Month program we're unrolling next month. That is, until I saw—" He waved his hand toward the other two people seated in the room, Pedro Gutierrez, head of operations, and finance chief Marlys Higgenbotham. "Or at least I was guessing they're not here to nominate the first employee of the month."

"No, see, that's the issue. After working directly with our frontline staff, I'm having my doubts about putting resources into Employee of the Month," replied the CEO. Frank swallowed.

Employee of the Month had been a pet idea of Janette's, so he had poured most of his time into developing the program. Each month, a manager at each resort was going to nominate a top-performing employee to be the Employee of the Month and enjoy the glory, not to mention a premium parking space and a framed photo posted in the lobby of the resort where he or she worked. Now it appeared that Janette shared what, he had to admit, were his own doubts about whether the program would really do much to improve performance or lower turnover. Janette continued, "Have a seat, Frank, and let me tell you about what I saw the past two weeks." Frank settled into a chair next to Marlys.

Janette brought Frank up to date: "I've been telling Marlys and Pedro what it was like to work in one of our kitchens. The pace is unbelievable. The workload is unbelievable. And the teamwork is out of this world. Frank, I was amazed, and you would be, too. I know how to make a grilled cheese sandwich, but these folks do a lot more than cook. They're planning and controlling on the fly: How many salads? How many pancakes? How can we make all that without any waste? There's no supervisor on the line; they're *all* thinking like managers—how to please customers, control costs. Honestly, our managers could take lessons from them on teamwork and quality control."

"It sounds like we have a lot of Employees of the Month," Frank said hopefully. Maybe the program wouldn't be canceled after all, and his group's efforts wouldn't have been wasted.

"No, no, no!" broke in Marlys. "The point is, we've tried so many programs to boost productivity. As you know, we were looking at bonuses last year, till the economy got so bad. We simply couldn't justify paying more when occupancy rates were diving. But we have to do something. Now that business is picking up in our market area, other hotels and resorts are going to start recruiting away our best people. The question is, what can we do that will keep employees working as hard as they are now without burning out and leaving us? We thought people would just like a little recognition, but Janette is saying she doubts it now."

"Exactly," said Janette. "And that's why I called you in. We need your expertise about human relations. What do people want? I thought it would be pay, prizes, that sort of thing. And you went along with me. But really, Frank, can that be it? The people I worked with the past two weeks—they have so much skill at what they do, and they're constantly thinking up ways to make our guests happy. They already take pride in what they accomplish. We need to decide what will make their jobs better so they can accomplish more without us getting in their way with, well, Employee of the Month ceremonies."

"OK," replied Frank, "now that you've put it that way, I have to ask if maybe what we *don't* want to do is decide what will make their jobs better."

As Janette and Marlys gazed at Frank quizzically, Pedro spoke up. "That's great, Frank. You're saying we shouldn't make their jobs better? I came up through the ranks at Big Bison, and I can recall that those hourly jobs aren't exactly perfect the way they are."

"What I mean," replied Frank, "is that we need to *listen* before we *decide*."

QUESTIONS

1. What kinds of behavior would an Employee of the Month program, as described here, reinforce at Big Bison Resorts? How might the company apply the principles of reinforcement more effectively?

2. How might Big Bison Resorts get input from employees to make the company's jobs more motivating? What impact would this effort have on the company's performance?

3. How would Big Bison's employees perceive the equity of the Employee of the Month program? Compare their reactions to that program with the response you would expect from an effort to involve employees in improving their jobs.

4. Think about a previous job you have held or are currently at. If you had the power to make such decisions, what would you do to make the job more motivating for employees?

14 Teamwork

LEARNING OBJECTIVES

After studying Chapter 14, you will be able to:

CHAPTER OUTLINE

Manager's Brief	Progress Report	Onward

Management Connection

TEAMWORK, TOYOTA STYLE

Working for Toyota is far more than a mere job for Tim Turner, an assembly safety specialist at Toyota Motor's assembly plant in Georgetown, Kentucky. It's an organization of which he is deeply proud to be a member. A few years ago, when auto sales declined because of an economic downturn, Turner saw Toyota's efforts to keep as many people as possible on the payroll, and he was determined to be a part of the solution. He invited coworkers to write stories about their experiences working for Toyota in Georgetown, and then he compiled their stories into a book he titled *One Team on All Levels: The Story of the Toyota Team Members.* He donates all the proceeds from sales of the book to the Georgetown plant's benevolence fund, which helps out employees in need. (Other workers raise money for the fund by recycling cans and bottles.)

Turner's book includes accounts of workers helping each other out, such as when a group of them arranged to help a coworker with kidney disease. In another story, Shannon Conder tells about Toyota's concern for its Princeton, Indiana, workers when that facility was shut down for nearly a year. The plant was no longer needed to build Tundra pickup trucks, so Toyota decided to retool to build other vehicles there. Some workers were paid to receive training and plan ways to make the new assembly areas safer and more efficient; others, including Conder, were given jobs in Georgetown. "Excellent" is Conder's description of her 11 months in Georgetown. To cover the costs of paying employees when no vehicles were being assembled in Indiana, the company cut managers' pay and workers' bonuses.

What is so special about working for Toyota? Many people point to Toyota's distinctive form of management known as the Toyota Production System (TPS), which focuses on continually improving quality while reducing costs. TPS combines the just-in-time concept of saving money by producing only what is needed, when it is needed, with a concept known as *jidoka,* which introduces a human element into automated processes to ensure quality. Whenever a machine operator spots a problem, that operator is authorized—and expected—to stop the machine immediately so problems can be detected, interpreted, and corrected. Together, these two elements of TPS require that the company use workers with the skill and training to see what they need in order to work efficiently, as well as the willingness and ability to watch for and correct quality problems. Thus TPS works when employees are fully engaged in their working, thinking as well as doing.

TPS is intended to get everyone thinking hard about how to keep making Toyota better at working efficiently and satisfying customers. In this way, everyone is pulling together toward a common goal. With that idea of fully engaged employees, it is not surprising that Toyota refers to its workers as its "team members." And clearly, some of them are pulling hard to ensure that they are on a winning team.[1]

Toyota expresses a strong commitment to its employees, empowers them to make decisions, and expects a high level of commitment to continuous improvement. As you read this chapter, consider whether these ingredients are enough to ensure truly effective teamwork by Toyota's "team members."

Sometimes teams "work," and sometimes they don't. The goal of this chapter is to help make sure that your management and work teams succeed. The employee empowerment at Toyota illustrates one way a company can apply teamwork, with extraordinary results.

Teams are transforming the ways organizations do business.[2] Almost all companies now use teams to produce goods and services, to manage projects, and to make decisions and run the company.[3] For you, this has two vital implications. First, you *will* be working in and perhaps managing teams. Second, the *ability* to work in and lead teams is valuable to your employer and important to your career. Fortunately, coursework focusing on team training can enhance students' teamwork knowledge and skills.[4]

The Contributions of Teams

Team-based approaches to work have generated excitement. Used appropriately, teams can be powerfully effective as a *building block for organization structure*. Organizations such as Semco, Whole Foods, and Kollmorgen, manufacturer of printed circuits and electro-optic devices, are structured entirely around teams. 3M's breakthrough products emerge through the use of teams that are small entrepreneurial businesses within the larger corporation.

Teams also can increase *productivity*, improve *quality*, and reduce *costs*. By adopting a team structure and culture, Battle Creek, Michigan–based Summit Pointe, a mental health organization, has saved millions of dollars while improving patient care.[5] Honeywell's teams saved more than $11 million after reducing production times and shipping more than 99 percent of orders on time.[6] Using engineering teams for its 777 jumbo passenger jet, Boeing received the fastest flight certification ever for a new commercial aircraft. According to Boeing managers, the company could not have developed the 777 without cross-functional teams; it would have been prohibitively expensive.[7] At Nucor's steel plant in Decatur, Alabama, the general manager credits teamwork for high productivity and improved safety.[8]

Teams also can enhance *speed* and be powerful forces for *innovation* and *change*. 3M and many other companies use teams to create new products faster. Lenders cut home mortgage approval times from weeks to hours, and life insurance companies cut time to issue new policies from six weeks to one day.[9] At KPMG Netherlands, a strategic integration team of 12 partners, with 100 other professionals divided into 14 task forces, led strategic and cultural changes by studying future trends and scenarios, defining core competencies, and dealing with organizational challenges.[10] General Mills uses a team approach to make decisions about the packaging for its products. For product divisions such as Big G cereals, Yoplait yogurt, or Green Giant vegetables, teams bring together employees from brand design, engineering, production, research and development, and other relevant functions to figure out how packaging

Bottom Line

Well-managed teams are powerful forces that can deliver all desired results

What do you think makes a team more powerful than a set of individuals?

can reduce waste, cut costs, send a clearer marketing message, and find ways to work more efficiently with suppliers.[11]

Teams also provide many *benefits for their members*.[12] The team is a very useful learning mechanism. Members learn about the company and themselves, and they acquire new skills and performance strategies. The team can satisfy important personal needs, such as affiliation and esteem. Other needs are met as team members receive tangible organizational rewards that they could not have achieved working alone.

Team members can provide one another with feedback; identify opportunities for growth and development; and train, coach, and mentor.[13] A marketing representative can learn about financial modeling from a colleague on a new product development team, and the financial expert can learn about consumer marketing. Experience working together in a team, and developing strong problem-solving capabilities, is a vital supplement to specific job skills or functional expertise. And the skills are transferable to new positions.

IN PRACTICE

The Wells's Dairy production facility in St. George, Utah, has over 90 employees who make and package Blue Bunny ice cream, sherbet, and frozen yogurt. Many of those employees handle either manufacturing or maintenance for the plant's three production lines. On each line, a line owner is responsible for the progress of manufacturing on that line, and another is responsible for maintenance. Each supervisor's group of employees amounts to a kind of team that is committed to a set of goals and feels a sense of team spirit.

The employees working each line are expected to ensure that their work area meets established goals for safety, quality, on-schedule delivery, and cost. They also are authorized—and expected—to stop the line if they see problems with food quality or safety. A results board for each line shows how well each team is performing. Meeting goals becomes a source of great pride for the teams.

Intensifying the team spirit, the facility conducts an expense-cutting contest every quarter. The team that cuts costs the most wins a prize and, of course, a sense of accomplishment and glory.[14]

• What contributions of teams do you see at work in this example?

The New Team Environment

The words *group* and *team* often are used interchangeably.[15]

Modern managers sometimes use the word *teams* to the point that it has become a cliché; they talk about teams while skeptics perceive no real teamwork.

Thus making a distinction between groups and teams can be useful. A *working group* is a collection of people who work in the same area or have been drawn together to undertake a task but do not necessarily come together as a unit and achieve significant performance improvements. A real **team** is formed of people (usually a small number) with complementary skills who trust one another and are committed to a common purpose, common performance goals, and a common approach for which they hold themselves mutually accountable.[16]

Organizations have been using groups for a long time, but today's workplaces are different.[17] Teams are used in many different ways, and to far greater effect,

LO 2

team

A small number of people with complementary skills who are committed to a common purpose, set of performance goals, and approach for which they hold themselves mutually accountable.

Athletic teams are built with people of varying skill levels who work toward a common goal—to win. Teams in a business are often formed with the same mind-set.

work teams

Teams that make or do things like manufacture, assemble, sell, or provide service.

than in the past. Table 14.1 highlights just a few of the differences between the traditional work environment and the way true teams work today. Ideally, people are far more involved, they are better trained, cooperation is higher, and the culture is one of learning as well as producing.

Types of Teams

Your organization may have hundreds of groups and teams, but they can be classified into just a few primary types.[18] **Work teams** make or do things such as manufacture, assemble, sell, or provide service. They typically are well defined; a clear part of the formal organizational structure; and composed of a full-time, stable membership. Work teams are what most people think of when they think of teams in organizations.[19]

Project and development teams work on long-term projects, often over a period of years. They have specific assignments, such as research or new product development, and members usually must contribute expert knowledge and judgment. These teams work toward a one-time product, disbanding once their work is completed. Then new teams are formed for new projects.

Parallel teams operate separately from the regular work structure of the firm on a temporary basis. Members often come from different units or jobs and are asked to do work that is not normally done by the standard structure. Their charge is to recommend solutions to specific problems. They usually do not have authority to act, however. Examples include task forces and quality or safety teams formed to study a particular problem. Whenever Baltimore's Bradford Bank acquires or starts up another operation, it assembles a team of employees drawn from various divisions to smooth the transition for customers. For example, when Bradford signed a deal to acquire deposits from American Bank, a team of employees from branch management, deposit services, and information technology studied American's products to make sure Bradford was ready to offer similar services to its new customers.[20]

Management teams coordinate and provide direction to the subunits under their jurisdiction and integrate work among subunits.[21] The management team is based on authority stemming from hierarchical rank and is responsible for the overall performance of the business unit. Managers responsible for different subunits form a team together, and at the top of the organization resides the executive management team that establishes strategic direction and manages the firm's overall performance.

Transnational teams are work teams composed of multinational members whose activities span multiple countries.[22] Such teams differ from other work teams not only by being multicultural but also by often being geographically dispersed, being psychologically distant, and working on highly complex projects having considerable impact on company objectives.

One example of a project and development team is the Omnica product development team. The 28-person team is responsible for producing medical and high-tech products for their clients faster and more efficiently than they could by any other means.

Transnational teams tend to be **virtual teams,** communicating electronically more than face-to-face, although other types of teams may operate virtually as well. Virtual teams face difficult challenges: building trust, cohesion, and team identity, and overcoming the isolation of virtual team members.[23] Table 14.2 suggests ways that managers can improve the effectiveness of virtual teams.

Traditional Environment	Team Environment
Managers determine and plan the work.	Managers and team members jointly determine and plan the work.
Jobs are narrowly defined.	Jobs require broad skills and knowledge.
Cross-training is viewed as inefficient.	Cross-training is the norm.
Most information is "management property."	Most information is freely shared at all levels.
Training for nonmanagers focuses on technical skills.	Continuous learning requires interpersonal, administrative, and technical training for all.
Risk taking is discouraged and punished.	Measured risk taking is encouraged and supported.
People work alone.	People work together.
Rewards are based on individual performance.	Rewards are based on individual performance and contributions to team performance.
Managers determine "best methods."	Everyone works to continuously improve methods and processes.

SOURCE: From *Leading Teams* by J. Zenger and Associates. Reprinted by permission.

Self-Managed Teams

Today many different types of work teams exist, with different labels.[24] **Traditional work groups** have no managerial responsibilities. The frontline manager plans, organizes, staffs, directs, and controls them, and other groups provide support activities, including quality control and maintenance.

But the trend today is toward giving teams more autonomy so that workers are trained to do all or most of the jobs in the unit, they have no immediate supervisor, and they make decisions previously made by frontline supervisors.[25] Self-managed teams are most frequently found in manufacturing. People often resist self-managed work teams, in part because they don't want so much responsibility and the change is difficult.[26] In addition, people often don't like to do performance evaluation of teammates or to fire people, and poorly managed conflict may be a particular problem in self-managed teams.[27] But compared with traditionally managed teams, self-managed

Leadership Practices of Virtual Team Leader	How Do Virtual Team Leaders Do It?
Establish and maintain trust through the use of communication technology.	Focusing the norms on how information is communicated.
	Revisiting and adjusting the communication norms as the team evolves ("virtual get-togethers").
	Making progress explicit through use of team virtual workspace.
	Equal "suffering" in the geographically distributed world.
Ensure diversity in the team is understood, appreciated, and leveraged.	Prominent team expertise directory and skills matrix in the virtual workspace.
	Virtual subteaming to pair diverse members and rotate subteam members.
Manage virtual work cycle and meetings.	Use the start of virtual meeting (each time) for social relationship building.

TABLE 14.1

The New Team Environment

project and development teams

Teams that work on long-term projects but disband once the work is completed.

parallel teams

Teams that operate separately from the regular work structure, and exist temporarily.

management teams

Teams that coordinate and provide direction to the subunits under their jurisdiction and integrate work among subunits.

transnational teams

Work groups composed of multinational members whose activities span multiple countries.

virtual teams

Teams that are physically dispersed and communicate electronically more than face-to-face.

traditional work groups

Groups that have no managerial responsibilities.

TABLE 14.2

Practices of Effective Virtual Team Leaders

(continued)

Leadership Practices of Virtual Team Leader	How Do Virtual Team Leaders Do It?
	During meeting—ensure through "check-ins" that everyone is engaged and heard from.
	End of meeting—ensure that the minutes and future work plan are posted to team repository.
Monitor team progress through the use of technology.	Make progress explicit through balanced scorecard measurements posted in the team's virtual workspace.
Enhance external visibility of the team and its members.	Frequent report-outs to a virtual steering committee (comprising local bosses of team members).
Ensure individuals benefit from participating in virtual teams.	Virtual reward ceremonies. Individual recognition at the start of each virtual meeting. Making each team member's "real location" boss aware of the member's contribution.

SOURCE: From *Academy of Management Perspectives*, A. Malhotra, A. Majchrzak, and B. Rosen, "Leading Virtual Teams," February 2007, pp. 60–70. Copyright 2007. Reproduced with permission of Academy of Management via Copyright Clearance Center.

quality circles

Voluntary groups of people drawn from various production teams who make suggestions about quality.

autonomous work groups

Groups that control decisions about and execution of a complete range of tasks.

self-managed teams

Autonomous work groups in which workers are trained to do all or most of the jobs in a unit, have no immediate supervisor, and make decisions previously made by frontline supervisors.

self-designing teams

Teams with the responsibilities of autonomous work groups, plus control over hiring, firing, and deciding what tasks members perform.

teams appear to be more productive, have lower costs, provide better customer service, provide higher quality, have better safety records, and are more satisfying for members.

Autonomous work groups, or **self-managed teams,** control decisions about and execution of a complete range of tasks—acquiring raw materials and performing operations, quality control, maintenance, and shipping. They are fully responsible for an entire product or an entire part of a production process. **Self-designing teams** do all of that and go one step further—they also have control over the design of the team. They decide themselves whom to hire, whom to fire, and what tasks the team will perform.

When teams reach the point of being truly self-managed, results have included lower costs and greater levels of team productivity, quality, and customer satisfaction.[28] Overall, autonomous teams are known to improve the organization's financial and overall performance, at least in North America.[29]

Such results have inspired U.S.-based multinational firms to use self-managed teams in their foreign facilities. For example, Goodyear Tire & Rubber initiated self-managed work teams in Europe, Latin America, and Asia; Sara Lee in Puerto Rico and Mexico; and Texas Instruments in Malaysia. Companies that do this learn—and other companies should be forewarned—of the different ways different cultures might respond to self-managed teams, and to customize implementation according to cultural values.[30]

How Groups Become Real Teams

As a manager, you will want your group to become an effective team. To accomplish this, you need to understand how groups can become true teams and why groups sometimes fail to become teams. Groups become true teams via basic group processes, the passage of time, and team development activities.

Group Processes

Assume you are the leader of a newly formed group—actually a bunch of people. What will you face as you attempt to develop your group into a high-performing team? If groups are to develop successfully, they will engage in various processes, including these broad categories:[31]

- *Forming*—group members attempt to lay the ground rules for what types of behavior are acceptable.
- *Storming*—hostilities and conflict arise, and people jockey for positions of power and status.
- *Norming*—group members agree on their shared goals, and norms and closer relationships develop.
- *Performing*—the group channels its energies into performing its tasks.

Groups that deteriorate move to a *declining* stage, and temporary groups add an *adjourning* or terminating stage. Groups terminate when they complete their task or when they disband due to failure or loss of interest and new groups form, as the cycle continues.

Virtual teams also go through these stages of group development.[32] The forming stage is characterized by unbridled optimism: "I believe we have a great team and will work well together. We all understand the importance of the project and intend to take it seriously." Optimism turns into reality shock in the storming stage: "No one has taken a leadership role. We have not made the project the priority that it deserves." The norming stage comes at about the halfway point in the project life cycle, in which people refocus and recommit: "You must make firm commitments to a specific time schedule." The performing stage is the dash to the finish as teammates show the discipline needed to meet the deadline.

Many teams do training exercises to learn team-building techniques. This is the classic "trust fall." The blindfolded person falls backwards, trusting that his teammates will catch him and not let him fall. Trust must be earned, not demanded.

> Optimism turns into reality shock in the storming stage.

Passage of Time

A key aspect of group development is the passage of time. Groups pass through critical periods, or times when they are particularly open to formative experiences.[33] The first such critical period is in the forming stage, at the first meeting, when rules and roles are established that set longer-lasting precedents. A second critical period is the midway point between the initial meeting and a deadline (e.g., completing a project or making a presentation). At this point, the group has enough experience to understand its work; it comes to realize that time is becoming a scarce resource and it must "get on with it"; and there is enough time left to change its approach if necessary.

In the initial meeting, the group should establish desired norms, roles, and other determinants of effectiveness, which are discussed throughout this chapter. At the second critical period (the midpoint), groups should renew or open lines of communication with outside constituencies.

> The group can use fresh information from its external environment to revise its approach to performing its task and ensure that it meets the needs of customers and clients.

Without these activities, groups may get off on the wrong foot from the beginning, and members may never revise their behavior in the appropriate direction.[34]

Developmental Sequence: From Group to Team

As a manager or group member, you should expect the group to engage in all the processes just discussed. But groups are not always successful. They do not always engage in the developmental processes that turn them into effective, high-performing teams.

A useful developmental sequence is depicted in Figure 14.1. The figure shows the various activities as the leadership of the group moves from traditional supervision, through a more participative approach, to true team leadership.[35]

It is important to understand a couple of points about this model. Groups do not necessarily keep progressing from one "stage" to the next; they may remain permanently in the supervisory level or become more participative but never make it to true team leadership. As a result, progress on these dimensions must be a conscious goal of the leader and the members, and all should strive to meet these goals. Your group can meet these goals—and become a true team—by engaging in the activities in the figure.

Why Groups Sometimes Fail

Team building does not necessarily progress smoothly through such a sequence, culminating in a well-oiled team and superb performance.[36] Some groups never do

FIGURE 14.1
Stepping Up to Team Leadership

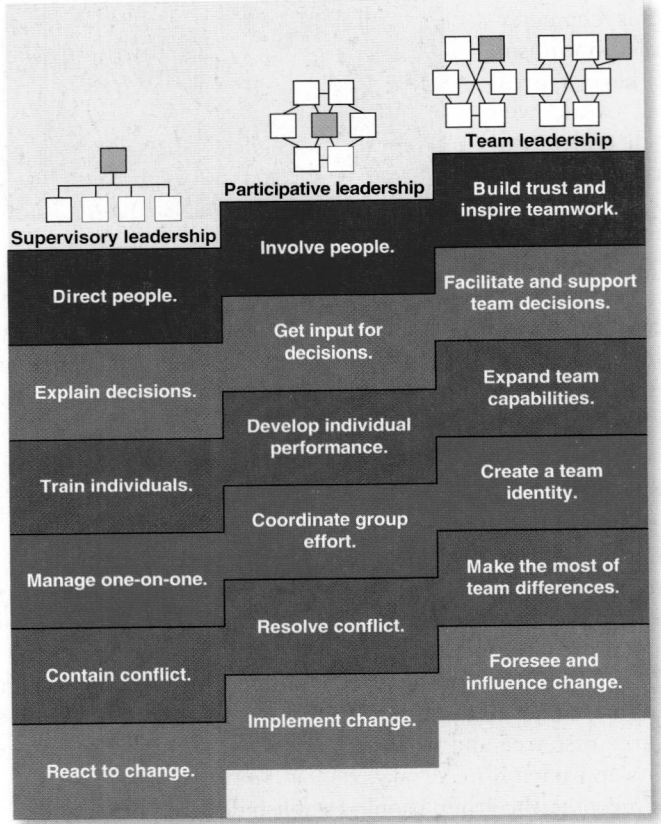

SOURCE: From *Leading Teams* by J. Zenger and Associates. Reprinted by permission.

work out. Such groups can be frustrating for managers and members, who may feel teams are a waste of time and that the difficulties outweigh the benefits.

It is not easy to build high-performance teams. *Teams* is often just a word used by management to describe merely putting people into groups. "Teams" sometimes are launched with little or no training or support systems. For example, both managers and group members need new skills to make a group work. These skills include learning the art of diplomacy, tackling "people issues" head on, and walking the fine line between encouraging autonomy and rewarding team innovations without letting the team get too independent and out of control.[37]

> Giving up some control is very difficult for managers from traditional systems, but they have to realize they will gain control in the long run by creating stronger, better-performing units.

Teams should be empowered, as discussed in Chapter 13. The benefits of teams are reduced when they are not allowed to make important decisions—in other words, when management doesn't trust them with important responsibilities. If teams must acquire permission for every innovative idea, they will revert to making safe, traditional decisions.[38]

Empowerment enhances team performance even among virtual teams. Empowerment for virtual teams includes thorough training in using the technologies and strong technical support from management. Some virtual teams have periodic face-to-face interactions, which help performance; empowerment is particularly helpful for virtual teams that don't often meet face-to-face.[39]

As you read "Management Connection: Progress Report," consider whether Toyota's applications of teamwork are likely to succeed or fail. Failure lies in not knowing and doing what makes teams successful. To be successful, you must apply clear thinking and appropriate practices.[40] That is what the rest of the chapter is about.

| Manager's Brief | **Progress Report** | Onward |

Management Connection

WHEN TROUBLE CALLS, TOYOTA TURNS TO TEAMS

While Toyota generally refers to its employees as "team members," the company has specifically set up distinctive teams to solve particular problems. Two examples include Toyota's use of teamwork to ensure a supply of raw materials and also to address safety concerns in the United States. Both of these show how assembling the right people into an effective team can help a company respond rapidly to unexpected trouble.

In the first example, the problem arose when reports began circulating that China would announce a ban on exporting a group of 17 metals known as rare earth minerals. Some of these minerals, including neodymium and dysprosium, are used to make gasoline–electric hybrid vehicles, including the Toyota Prius. Because China supplies most of the world's demand for these metals, an export ban would essentially stop the manufacturing of the hybrid vehicles. Even before the rumors of a ban, prices had been soaring because of the limited supply and escalating demand. Toyota's response to the situation was to set up a task force charged with developing additional

sources of rare earth minerals. It has pursued ideas such as establishing partnerships to obtain the minerals from sources in Vietnam, Malaysia, and the United States. In addition, the company has been pursuing development of alternative designs that do not require rare earth minerals, not only because they are expensive, but also because mining them takes a heavy toll on the environment.

The second and more widely known use of teamwork came in response to customer complaints that they were experiencing unintended acceleration of their Toyota cars, sometimes leading to crashes. Even as Toyota recalled millions of vehicles for inspections and repairs, Toyota's U.S. sales division set up rapid response teams to evaluate each customer complaint. The teams, named Swift Market Analysis Response Teams (SMART), brought together engineers with research and development backgrounds and technicians who worked in the field. They were charged with contacting customers within 24 hours of a complaint and setting up an appointment to conduct a comprehensive vehicle inspection. The teams worked with North American Toyota dealers, at whose facilities the inspections took place.

At the dealerships, the teams not only inspected the vehicles but also talked to the customers, trying to learn more about how they used the vehicles and what issues concerned them. While inspecting a car can tell Toyota what caused an incident that alarmed a customer, listening to the customer can provide information about the driving conditions and other issues that should be affecting how Toyota designs and tests its vehicles. For example, the company learned that some accelerators became stuck on slipping floor mats that were installed at dealerships or by customers themselves. Toyota made installation of floor mats part of its manufacturing process, making it easier to test for proper function of the gas pedal.[41]

- Based on these descriptions, as what type of team would you categorize the task force on rare earth minerals? The SMART teams?
- What challenges would the SMART teams likely face in their development as effective teams

Building Effective Teams

 All the considerations just described form the building blocks of an effective work team. But what does it really mean for a team to be effective? Team effectiveness is defined by three criteria.[42]

1. The *productive output* of the team meets or exceeds the standards of quantity and quality; the team's output is acceptable to the customers, inside or outside the organization, who receive the team's goods or services. At Lockheed Martin, Clarence L. "Kelly" Johnson's group designed, built, and flew the first U.S. tactical jet fighter, XP80, in 143 days.[43] And a team of doctors, nurses, and administrators at the University of Texas's M. D. Anderson Cancer Center defined goals for improving patient care, identified changes that would meet the goals, and persuaded the center's physicians to adopt the changes. As a result, performance at the center exceeded the team's goals for increasing visits and decreasing the time that elapses between a patient's first visit and his or her surgery.[44]

2. Team members realize *satisfaction* of their personal needs. Johnson gave his Lockheed teams the freedom to innovate and stretch their skills. Team members were enthusiastic and realized great pride and satisfaction in their work.

3. Team members remain *committed* to working together again; that is, the group doesn't burn out and disintegrate after a grueling project. Looking back, the members are glad they were involved. In other words, effective teams remain viable and have good prospects for repeated success in the future.[45]

For help in developing these qualities, teams may use team-building activities or work with an outside coach. Team building usually involves activities focused on relationships among team members. Whether these activities are as simple as a group discussion or as elaborate as a weekend retreat with physical challenges, the team-building event should be followed by an opportunity for participants to evaluate what they learned and how they will apply those lessons at work.[46] Coaching a team focuses on how the group as a whole operates. For example, when the trainers at Dallas-based Cooking Up Collaboration run a team-building event, they assign teams to a cooking challenge such as preparing a four-course dinner or creating dishes out of ingredients such as chutney and papaya. They observe how the team members interact and then offer feedback such as pointing out who listens, who gets ignored, and how tasks are assigned.[47] Team coaching addresses issues such as what the team is focused on, how it sets goals, and how it can improve communication and decision making. Ideally, the coaching helps a team develop enough that it can begin to coach itself.

Based on years of studying team performance, Richard Hackman has identified common barriers to team effectiveness. One is so simple that it would seem obvious: teams need to properly define their membership. However, many don't establish or communicate clear boundaries, perhaps because of discomfort over excluding people. When a team problem came to light, the chief executive of a financial services company determined that the chief financial officer was unable to collaborate effectively with others on the executive team. So the CEO asked the financial executive to skip the "boring" team meetings, keeping their communications one-on-one. Without the CFO, the executive team began to function at a much higher level.

Another barrier is that people tend to focus too much on harmony, assuming that when team members feel good about their participation, the team is effective. In fact, Hackman says, effectiveness comes first: team members feel satisfied when their team works effectively. In a study of symphony orchestras, the relevant measure of satisfaction was how the musicians felt *after* a performance.

A third mistake that Hackman often encounters is the assumption that team members can be together too long. According to this assumption, when the team's membership never changes, the team runs out of ideas. But besides a need for research and development teams to add a new member every few years, Hackman has found that the more common problem is too little continuity: team members haven't been together long enough to learn to work well together. Airplane cockpit crews, for example, perform much better when they have flown together previously.[48]

- How would overcoming the barriers described by Hackman help a team satisfy the criteria for team effectiveness?

Performance Focus

The key element of effective teamwork is commitment to a common purpose.[49] The best teams are those that have been given an important performance challenge by management and then have reached a common understanding and appreciation of their purpose. Without such understanding and commitment, a group will be just a bunch of individuals.

The best teams also work hard at developing a common understanding of how they will work together to achieve their purpose.[50] They discuss and agree on such details as how tasks and roles will be allocated and how they will make decisions. The team should develop norms for examining its performance strategies and be amenable to changing them when appropriate. For example, work teams usually standardize at least some processes, but they should be willing to try creative new ideas if the situation calls for them.[51] With a clear, strong, motivating purpose and effective performance strategies, people will pull together into a powerful force that has a chance to achieve extraordinary things.

The team's general purpose should be translated into specific, measurable performance goals.[52] You learned in Chapter 13 about how goals motivate individual performance. Performance can be defined by collective end products, instead of an accumulation of individual products.[53] Team-based performance goals help define and distinguish the team's product, encourage communication within the team, energize and motivate team members, provide feedback on progress, signal team victories

To ensure the safety of themselves and each other, Boots & Coots firefighters need to maintain trust and communicate under some of the toughest circumstances.

Bottom Line
Teams, with guidance from internal and external customers, should identify the nature of the results they want to achieve.
What qualities should a team's goal have?

social loafing

Working less hard and being less productive when in a group.

social facilitation effect

Working harder when in a group than when working alone.

Accountability to one another, rather than just to "the boss," is an essential aspect of good teamwork.

(and defeats), and ensure that the team focuses clearly on results. Teams with both difficult goals and incentives to attain them achieve the highest performance levels.[54]

The best team-based measurement systems inform top management of the team's level of performance and help the team understand its own processes and gauge its own progress. Ideally, the team plays the lead role in designing its own measurement system. This responsibility is a great indicator of whether the team is truly empowered.[55]

Teams, like individuals, need feedback on their performance.

Feedback from customers is especially crucial. Some customers for the team's products are inside the organization.

Teams should be responsible for satisfying them and should be given or should seek performance feedback. Better yet, wherever possible, teams should interact directly with external customers who make the ultimate buying decisions about their goods and services. External customers typically provide the most honest, and most crucial and useful, performance feedback of all.[56]

Motivating Teamwork

Sometimes individuals work less hard and are less productive when they are members of a group. Such **social loafing** occurs when individuals believe that their contributions are not important, others will do the work for them, their lack of effort will go undetected, or they will be the lone sucker if they work hard but others don't. Perhaps you have seen social loafing in some of your student teams.[57] Conversely, sometimes individuals work harder when they are members of a group than when they are working alone. This **social facilitation effect** occurs because individuals usually are more motivated when others are present, they are concerned with what others think of them, and they want to maintain a positive self-image.

A social facilitation effect is maintained—and a social loafing effect can be avoided—when group members know each other, they can observe and communicate with one another, clear performance goals exist, the task is meaningful to the people working on it, they believe that their efforts matter and others will not take advantage of them, and the culture supports teamwork.[58] Thus, under ideal circumstances, everyone works hard, contributes in concrete ways to the team's work, and is accountable to other team members. Accountability to one another, rather than just to "the boss," is an essential aspect of good teamwork. Accountability inspires mutual commitment and trust.[59] Trust in your teammates—and their trust in you—may be the ultimate key to effectiveness.

Team effort is also generated by designing the team's task to be motivating. Techniques for creating motivating tasks appear in the guidelines for job enrichment discussed in Chapter 13. Tasks are motivating when they use a variety of member skills and provide high task variety, identity, significance, autonomy, and performance feedback.

Ultimately, teamwork is motivated by tying rewards to team performance.[60] Furthermore, combining individual and shared rewards can reduce social loafing and increase team performance.[61] If team performance can be measured validly, team-based rewards can be given accordingly.

It is not easy to move from a system of rewards based on individual performance to one based on team performance and cooperation. It also may not be appropriate unless people are truly interdependent and must collaborate to attain true team goals.[62] Team-based rewards are often combined with regular salaries and rewards based on individual performance. At Nucor, team members earn bonuses based on the tons of steel shipped each week. To ensure high quality, the amount of any bad product is subtracted from total shipments—and if defective products reach the customer, the amount subtracted is multiplied by 3. On average, the amount of the team bonuses equals 170 to 180 percent of the team members' base salary. This type of motivation works because Nucor teams are empowered to make decisions aimed at improving their productivity, and the company actively shares performance data with its employees.[63]

If team performance is difficult to measure validly, then desired behaviors, activities, and processes that indicate good teamwork can be rewarded. Individuals within teams can be given differential rewards based on teamwork indicated by active participation, cooperation, leadership, and other contributions to the team.

If team members are to be rewarded differentially, such decisions are better *not* left only to the boss.[64] They should be made by the team itself through peer ratings or multirater evaluation systems. Why? Team members are in a better position to observe, know, and make valid reward allocations. Finally, the more teams the organization has, and the more a full team orientation exists, the more valid and effective it will be to distribute rewards via gainsharing and other organizationwide incentives.

Member Contributions

Team members should be selected and trained so that they become effective contributors to the team. The teams themselves often hire their new members.[65] MillerCoors Brewing Company and Eastman Chemical teams select members based on the results of tests designed to predict how well they will contribute to team success in an empowered environment. At Texas Instruments, Human Resources screens applicants, and then team members interview them and make selection decisions.

Generally, the skills required by teams include technical or functional expertise, problem-solving and decision-making skills, and interpersonal skills. Some managers and teams mistakenly overemphasize some skills, particularly technical or functional ones, and underemphasize the others. A recent study found that groups in which members shared sad feelings performed better at analytical tasks and difficult decisions, and groups did better at creative tasks if they shared positive emotions.[67] Learning to share emotions appropriately can therefore be an important skill for team success. For the best team performance, it is vitally important that all three types of skills be represented, and developed, among team members.

Along with knowledge about their subject area, teams need members to contribute interpersonal skills, especially listening and building trust.[66]

Norms

Norms are shared beliefs about how people should think and behave. For example, some people like to keep information and knowledge to themselves, but teams should try to establish a norm of knowledge sharing because it can improve team performance.[68] Teams perform better when they think and talk about their tasks (duties, equipment, and resources) and about how they interact with and depend upon one another.[69] From the organization's standpoint, norms can be positive or negative. In some teams, everyone works hard; in other groups, employees are antimanagement and do as little work as possible. Some groups develop norms of taking risks, others of being conservative.[70] A norm could dictate that employees speak either favorably or critically of the company. Team members may show concern about poor safety practices, drug and alcohol abuse, and employee theft, or they may not care about these issues (or may even condone such practices). Health consciousness is the norm among executives at some companies, but smoking is the norm at tobacco companies. Some

norms
Shared beliefs about how people should think and behave.

groups have norms of distrust and of being closed toward one another; but as you might guess, norms of trust and open discussion about conflict are better for group performance.[71]

A professor described his consulting experiences at two companies that exhibited different norms in their management teams.[72] At Federal Express Corporation, a young manager interrupted the professor's talk by proclaiming that a recent decision by top management ran counter to the professor's point about corporate planning. He was challenging top management to defend its decision. A hot debate ensued, and after an hour everyone went to lunch without a trace of hard feelings. But at another corporation, the professor opened a meeting by asking a group of top managers to describe the company's culture. There was silence. He asked again. More silence. Then someone passed him an unsigned note that read, "Dummy, can't you see that we can't speak our minds? Ask for the input anonymously, in writing." As you can see, norms are important and can vary greatly from one group to another.

Roles

roles

Different sets of expectations for how different individuals should behave.

Roles are different sets of expectations for how different individuals should behave. Whereas norms apply generally to all team members, different roles exist for different members within the norm structure.

The mission of Cassini Imaging Science Team is to guide the cameras that take photos of the outer reaches of space. Though the team is widely dispersed (members' locations include New York, California, and Belgium), they are united by a shared sense of purpose and a high value placed on scientific knowledge and technical excellence.

Two important sets of roles must be performed.[73] **Task specialist** roles are filled by individuals who have particular job-related skills and abilities. These employees keep the team moving toward accomplishment of the objectives. **Team maintenance specialists** develop and maintain harmony within the team. They boost morale, give support, provide humor, soothe hurt feelings, and generally exhibit a concern with members' well-being.

Note the similarity between these roles and the important task performance and group maintenance leadership behaviors you learned about in Chapter 12. As suggested in that chapter, some of these roles will be more important than others at different times and under different circumstances. But these behaviors need not be carried out only by one or two leaders; any member of the team can assume them at any time. Both types of roles can be performed by different individuals to maintain an effectively functioning work team.

Beyond what you read about in Chapter 12, what roles should team leaders perform? Superior leaders are better at relating, scouting, persuading, and empowering than are average team leaders.[74] *Relating* includes exhibiting more social and political awareness, caring for team members, and trust building. *Scouting* means seeking information from managers, peers, and specialists, and investigating problems systematically. *Persuading* means not only influencing the team members but also obtaining external support for teams. *Empowerment* includes delegating authority, being flexible regarding team decisions, and coaching. Leaders also should roll up their sleeves and do real work to accomplish team goals, not just supervise.[75]

Finally, recall from Chapter 12 the importance of team leadership, in which group members rotate or share leadership roles.[76]

Self-managed teams report to a management representative who sometimes is called the *coach*. In true self-managed teams, the coach is not an actual member of the team.[77] The reason this is so is that the group is supposed to make its own decisions and also that the perceived power of the management representative could have a dampening

> These behaviors need not be carried out only by one or two leaders; any member of the team can assume them at any time.

effect on the team's openness and autonomy. The role of the coach, then, is to help the team understand its role in the organization and to serve as a resource for the team. The coach can provide information, resources, and insight that team members do not or cannot acquire on their own. And the coach should be an advocate for the team in the rest of the organization.

Cohesiveness

One of the most important properties of a team is cohesiveness.[78] **Cohesiveness** refers to how attractive the team is to its members, how motivated members are to remain in the team, and the degree to which team members influence one another. In general, it refers to how tightly knit the team is.

The Importance of Cohesiveness　Cohesiveness is important for two primary reasons. First, it contributes to *member satisfaction*. In a cohesive team, members communicate and get along well with one another. They feel good about being a part of the team. Even if their jobs are unfulfilling or the organization is oppressive, people gain some satisfaction from enjoying their coworkers.

Second, cohesiveness has a major impact on *performance*. A recent study of manufacturing teams showed that performance improvements in both quality and productivity occurred in the most cohesive unit, whereas conflict within another team prevented any quality or productivity improvements.[79] Sports fans read about this all the time. When teams are winning, players talk about the team being close, getting along well, and knowing one another's games. In contrast, losing is attributed to infighting and divisiveness. Generally, cohesiveness clearly can have a positive effect on performance.[80]

But this interpretation is simplistic; exceptions to this intuitive relationship occur. Tightly knit work groups can also be disruptive to the organization, such as when they sabotage the assembly line, get their boss fired, or enforce low performance norms. When does high cohesiveness lead to good performance, and when does it result in poor performance? The ultimate outcome depends on the task and on whether the group has high or low performance norms.

The Task　If the task is to make a decision or solve a problem, cohesiveness can lead to poor performance. Groupthink (discussed in Chapter 3) occurs when a tightly knit group is so cooperative that agreeing with one another's opinions and refraining from criticizing others' ideas become norms. For a cohesive group to make good decisions, it should establish a norm of constructive disagreement. This type of debating is important for groups up to the level of boards of directors.[81] In top management teams it has been shown to improve the financial performance of companies.[82]

But the effect of cohesiveness on performance can be positive, particularly if the task is to produce some tangible output. In day-to-day work groups for which decision making is not the primary task, cohesiveness can enhance performance. However, that depends on the group's performance norms.[83]

Performance Norms　Some groups are better than others at ensuring that their members behave the way the group prefers. Cohesive groups are more effective than noncohesive groups at norm enforcement. But the next question is, Do they have norms of high or low performance?

As Figure 14.2 shows, the highest performance occurs when a cohesive team has high-performance norms. But if a highly cohesive group has low-performance norms, that group will have the worst performance. In the group's eyes, however, it will have succeeded in achieving its goal of poor performance. Noncohesive groups with high-performance norms can be effective from the company's standpoint. However, they

task specialist

An individual who has stronger job-related skills and abilities than other group members possess.

team maintenance specialist

Individual who develops and maintains team harmony.

cohesiveness

The degree to which a group is attractive to its members, members are motivated to remain in the group, and members influence one another.

Sports fans read about this all the time.

Bottom Line
Cohesive groups are better than noncohesive groups at attaining the goals they want to attain; as a manager you need to ensure that your team's goals represent good business results.
What happens if a team leader builds a cohesive team but fails to set the right goals?

won't be as productive as they would be if they were more cohesive. Noncohesive groups with low-performance norms perform poorly, but they will not ruin things for management as effectively as can cohesive groups with low-performance norms.

Building Cohesiveness and High-Performance Norms

As Figure 14.2 suggests, managers should build teams that are cohesive and have high performance norms. The following actions can help create such teams:[84]

1. *Recruit members with similar attitudes, values, and backgrounds.* Similar individuals are more likely to get along with one another. Don't do this, though, if the team's task requires heterogeneous skills and inputs. For example, a homogeneous committee or board might make poor decisions because it will lack different information and viewpoints and may succumb to groupthink. Recent research has shown that educational diversity and national diversity provide more benefits than limitations to groups' use and application of information.[85]

   > Don't do this, though, if the team's task requires heterogeneous skills and inputs.

2. *Maintain high entrance and socialization standards.* Teams and organizations that are difficult to get into have more prestige. Individuals who survive a difficult interview, selection, or training process will be proud of their accomplishment and feel more attachment to the team.

3. *Keep the team small* (but large enough to get the job done). The larger the group, the less important members may feel. Small teams make individuals feel like large contributors.

4. *Help the team succeed, and publicize its successes.* You read about empowerment in the last chapter; you can empower teams as well as individuals.[86] Be a path–goal leader who facilitates success; the experience of winning brings teams closer together. Then, if you inform superiors of your team's successes, members will believe they are part of an important, prestigious unit. Teams that get into a good performance track continue to perform well as time goes on; groups that don't often enter a downward spiral in which problems compound over time.[87]

5. *Be a participative leader.* Participation in decisions gets team members more involved with one another and striving toward goal accomplishment. Too much autocratic decision making from above can alienate the group from management.

6. *Present a challenge from outside the team.* Competition with other groups makes team members band together to defeat the enemy (witness what happens to school spirit before a big game against an archrival). Some of the greatest teams in business and in science have been focused on winning a competition.[88]

FIGURE 14.2
Cohesiveness, Performance Norms, and Group Performance

But don't *you* become the outside threat. If team members dislike you as a boss, they will become more cohesive—but their performance norms will be against you, not with you.

7. *Tie rewards to team performance.* To a large degree, teams are motivated just as individuals are—they do the activities that are rewarded. Make sure that high-performing teams get the rewards they deserve and that poorly performing groups get fewer rewards. You read about this earlier. Bear in mind that not just monetary rewards but also recognition for good work are powerful motivators. Recognize and celebrate team accomplishments. The team will become more cohesive and perform better to reap more rewards. Performance goals will be high, the organization will benefit from higher team motivation and productivity, and the individual needs of team members will be better satisfied. Ideally, being a member of a high-performing team, recognized as such throughout the organization, will become a badge of honor.[89]

But keep in mind that strong cohesiveness encouraging "agreeableness" can be dysfunctional. For problem solving and decision making, the team should establish norms promoting an open, constructive atmosphere including honest disagreement over issues without personal conflict and animosity.[90]

> Some of the greatest teams in business and in science have been completely focused on winning a competition.

Managing Lateral Relationships

Teams do not function in a vacuum; they are interdependent with other teams. For example, at MillerCoors Brewing Company, major team responsibilities include coordinating with other teams and policy groups. At Texas Instruments, teams are responsible for interfacing with other teams to eliminate production bottlenecks and implement new processes and also for working with suppliers on quality issues.[91] Thus some activities crucial to the team are those that entail dealing with people *outside* the group.

Managing Outward

Several vital roles link teams to their external environments—that is, to other individuals and groups both inside and outside the organization. A specific type of role that spans team boundaries is the **gatekeeper,** a team member who stays abreast of current information in scientific and other fields and informs the group of important developments. Information useful to the group can also include information about resources, trends, and political support throughout the corporation or the industry.[92]

The team's strategy dictates the team's mix of internally versus externally focused roles and how the mix changes over time. General team strategies include informing, parading, and probing.[93] The **informing** strategy entails making decisions with the team and then telling outsiders of the team's intentions. **Parading** means the team's strategy is to simultaneously emphasize internal team building and achieve external visibility. **Probing** involves a focus on external relations. This strategy requires team members to interact frequently with outsiders; diagnose the needs of customers, clients, and higher-ups; and experiment with solutions before taking action.

The appropriate balance between an internal and external strategic focus and between internal and external roles depends on how much the team needs information, support, and resources from outside. When teams have a high degree of dependence on outsiders, probing is the best strategy. Parading teams perform at an intermediate level, and informing teams are likely to fail. They are too isolated from the outside groups on which they depend.

LO 6

gatekeeper

A team member who keeps abreast of current developments and provides the team with relevant information.

informing

A team strategy that entails making decisions with the team and then informing outsiders of its intentions.

parading

A team strategy that entails simultaneously emphasizing internal team building and achieving external visibility.

probing

A team strategy that requires team members to interact frequently with outsiders, diagnose their needs, and experiment with solutions.

Informing or parading strategies may be more effective for teams that are less dependent on outside groups—for example, established teams working on routine tasks in stable external environments. But for most important work teams of the future—task forces, new product teams, and strategic decision-making teams tackling unstructured problems in a rapidly changing external environment—effective performance in roles that involve interfacing with the outside will be vital.

Lateral Role Relationships

Managing relationships with other groups and teams means engaging in a dynamic give-and-take that ensures proper coordination throughout the management system. To many managers, this process often seems like a chaotic free-for-all. To help understand the process and make it more productive, we can identify and examine the different types of lateral role relationships and take a strategic approach to building constructive relationships.

Different teams, like different individuals, have roles to perform. As teams carry out their roles, several distinct patterns of working relationships develop:[94]

1. *Work flow relationships* emerge as materials are passed from one group to another. A group commonly receives work from one unit, processes it, and sends it to the next unit in the process. Your group, then, will come before some groups and after others in the process.
2. *Service relationships* exist when top management centralizes an activity to which a large number of other units must gain access. Common examples are technology services, libraries, and clerical staff. Such units must assist other people to help them accomplish their goals.
3. *Advisory relationships* are created when teams with problems call on centralized sources of expert knowledge. For example, staff members in the human resources or legal department advise work teams.
4. *Audit relationships* develop when people not directly in the chain of command evaluate the methods and performances of other teams. Financial auditors check the books, and technical auditors assess the methods and technical quality of the work.
5. *Stabilization relationships* involve auditing before the fact. In other words, teams sometimes must obtain clearance from others—for example, for large purchases—before they take action.
6. *Liaison relationships* involve intermediaries between teams. Managers often are called on to mediate conflict between two organizational units. Public relations people, sales managers, purchasing agents, and others who work across organizational boundaries serve in liaison roles as they maintain communications between the organization and the outside world.

By assessing each working relationship with another unit (from whom do we receive work, and to whom do we send work? what permissions do we control, and to whom must we go for authorizations?), teams can better understand whom to contact and when, where, why, and how to do so. Coordination throughout the working system improves, problems are avoided or short-circuited before they get too serious, and performance improves.[95]

Managing Conflict

The complex maze of interdependencies throughout organizations provides many opportunities for conflict to arise among groups and teams. Some conflict is constructive for the organization, as we discussed in Chapter 3. Typically, conflict can foster creativity when it is about ideas rather than personalities. In contrast, at a nonprofit organization, team members were committed to maintaining harmony during meetings, but their unre-solved differences spilled over into nasty remarks outside the office.[96]

Many factors cause great potential for destructive conflict: the sheer number and variety of contacts, ambiguities in jurisdiction and responsibility, differences in goals, intergroup competition for scarce resources, different perspectives held by members of

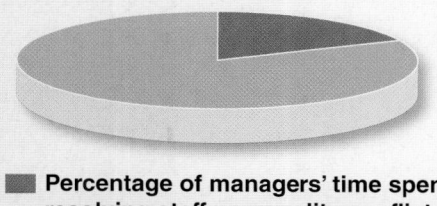

Responding to a survey, senior managers said they spend 18 percent of their time resolving conflicts among their employees. That average response is equivalent to the better part of a day in a five-day workweek.[97]

■ **Percentage of managers' time spent resolving staff personality conflicts**

different units, varying time horizons in which some units attend to long-term considerations and others focus on short-term needs, and others. Tensions and anxieties are likely to arise in teams that are demographically diverse, include members from different parts of the organization, or are composed of contrasting personalities. Both demographic and cross-functional heterogeneity initially lead to problems such as stress, lower cooperation, and lower cohesiveness.[98] Transformational leadership (recall Chapter 13) can reduce the problems and help realize the often-untapped potential benefits of diversity in teams.[99]

> Many factors cause great potential for destructive conflict.

Over time and with communication, diverse groups actually tend to become more cooperative and perform better than do homogeneous groups. In a factory, for example, conflict tends to arise between production workers and the maintenance department, as production workers tend to see maintenance work as either interrupting them when services are preventive or too slow in coming when a machine breaks down. General Cable Corporation smoothed relations and improved efficiency by embedding maintenance employees into production work teams. As daily contact has shaped these relationships, the production workers have come to see the maintenance workers as a ready source of help whenever concerns arise, and the maintenance workers are better able to share the goals of the production team.[100]

Conflict Styles

Teams inevitably face conflicts and must decide how to manage them. The aim should be to make the conflict productive—that is, to make those involved believe they have benefited rather than lost from the conflict.[101] People believe they have benefited from a conflict when (1) a new solution is implemented, the problem is solved, and it is unlikely to emerge again, and (2) work relationships have been strengthened and people believe they can work together productively in the future.

People handle conflict in different ways. You have your own style; others' styles may be similar or may differ. Their styles depend in part on their country's cultural norms. For example, Chinese people are more concerned with collective than with individual interests, and they are more likely than managers in the United States to turn to higher authorities to make decisions rather than resolve conflicts themselves.[102] But culture aside, any team or individual has several options regarding how to deal with conflicts.[103] These personal styles of dealing with conflict, shown in Figure 14.3, are distinguished based on how much people strive to satisfy their own concerns (the assertiveness dimension) and how much they focus on satisfying the other party's concerns (the cooperation dimension).

For example, a common reaction to conflict is **avoidance.** In this situation, people do nothing to satisfy themselves or others. They either ignore the problem by doing nothing at all or address it by merely smoothing over or deemphasizing the disagreement. This, of course, fails to solve the problem or clear the air. In a large retail company, employees in the marketing department decided they were tired of dealing with the limits placed on them by the security team of the company's information

avoidance

A reaction to conflict that involves ignoring the problem by doing nothing at all, or deemphasizing the disagreement.

SOURCE: K. Thomas, "Conflict and Conflict Management." In *Handbook of Industrial and Organizational Psychology,* ed. M. D. Dunnette. Copyright © 1976. Reprinted by permission of the author.

FIGURE 14.3
Conflict Management Strategies

accommodation

A style of dealing with conflict involving cooperation on behalf of the other party but not being assertive about one's own interests.

compromise

A style of dealing with conflict involving moderate attention to both parties' concerns.

competing

A style of dealing with conflict involving strong focus on one's own goals and little or no concern for the other person's goals.

> So imagine you and a friend want to go to a movie together, and you have different movies in mind.

collaboration

A style of dealing with conflict emphasizing both cooperation and assertiveness to maximize both parties' satisfaction.

technology (IT) department. Marketing wanted more communication with consumers, while IT security was obsessed with protecting the company's data from unauthorized access. To avoid the conflict, the marketing group set up a website without telling anyone in IT security.[104]

Accommodation means cooperating on behalf of the other party but not being assertive about one's own interests. **Compromise** involves moderate attention to both parties' concerns, being neither highly cooperative nor highly assertive. This style results in satisficing but not optimizing solutions. **Competing** is a highly competitive response in which people focus strictly on their own wishes and are unwilling to recognize the other person's concerns. Finally, **collaboration** emphasizes both cooperation and assertiveness. The goal is to maximize satisfaction for both parties. At the retail company in the previous example, a consulting firm called Solutionary discovered the website secretly created by the marketing group during a routine test of the company's computer network. Using basic techniques, the consultants were able to hack into the company's network and alter information, such as store prices, very easily. Knowing this would be simple for an outsider to do, the consultants then called together the IT security people and the marketing people to work out a solution that would meet marketing goals without compromising the data in the computer system.[105]

So imagine you and a friend want to go to a movie together, and you have different movies in mind. If he insists that you go to his movie, he is showing the competing style. If you agree, even though you prefer another movie, you are accommodating. If one of you mentions a third movie that neither of you is excited about but both of you are willing to live with, you are compromising. If you realize you don't know all the options, do some research, and find another movie that you're both enthusiastic about, you are collaborating.

Different approaches are necessary at different times.[106] For example, competing can be necessary for cutting costs or dealing with other scarce resources. Compromise may be useful when people are under time pressure, when they need to achieve a temporary solution, or when collaboration fails. People should accommodate when they learn they are wrong or to minimize loss when they are outmatched. Even avoiding may be appropriate if the issue is trivial or resolving the conflict should be someone else's responsibility.

But when the conflict concerns important issues, when both sets of concerns are valid and important, when a creative solution is needed, and when commitment to the solution is vital to implementation, collaboration is the ideal approach. Collaboration can be achieved by airing feelings and opinions, addressing all concerns, and avoiding goal displacement by not letting personal attacks interfere with problem solving. An important technique is to invoke **superordinate goals**—higher-level organizational goals toward which everyone should be striving and that ultimately need to take precedence over personal or unit preferences.[107] Using team-based rewards can give the group a "superordinate identity" that can reduce differences among team members and enhance performance.[108] Collaboration offers the best chance of reaching mutually satisfactory solutions based on the ideas and interests of all parties, and of maintaining and strengthening work relationships.

superordinate goals

Higher-level goals taking priority over specific individual or group goals.

Being a Mediator

Managers spend a lot of time trying to resolve conflict between *other* people. You already may have served as a **mediator,** a "third party" intervening to help settle a conflict between other people. Third-party intervention, done well, can improve working relationships and help the parties improve their own conflict management, communication, and problem-solving skills.[109]

Some insight comes from a study of human resource (HR) managers and the conflicts with which they deal.[110] HR managers encounter every type of conflict imaginable: interpersonal difficulties from minor irritations to jealousy to fights; operations issues, including union issues, work assignments, overtime, and sick leave; discipline over infractions ranging from drug use and theft to sleeping on the job; sexual harassment and racial bias; pay and promotion issues; and feuds or strategic conflicts among divisions or individuals at the highest organizational levels.

In the study, the HR managers successfully settled most of the disputes. These managers typically follow a four-stage strategy. They *investigate* by interviewing the disputants and others and gathering more information. While talking with the disputants, they seek both parties' perspectives, remaining as neutral as possible. The discussion should stay issue oriented, not personal. They *decide* how to resolve the dispute, often in conjunction with the disputants' bosses. In preparing to decide what to do, blame should not be assigned prematurely; at this point they should be exploring solutions. They *take action* by explaining their decisions and the reasoning, and advise or train the disputants to avoid future incidents. And they *follow up* by making sure everyone understands the solution, documenting the conflict and the resolution, and monitoring the results by checking back with the disputants and their bosses. Throughout, the objectives of the HR people are to be fully informed so that they understand the conflict; to be active and assertive in trying to resolve it; to be as objective, neutral, and impartial as humanly possible; and to be flexible by modifying their approaches according to the situation.

mediator

A third party who intervenes to help others manage their conflict.

HR managers encounter every type of conflict imaginable.

IN PRACTICE

In her management career at IBM, Sharon Nunes has participated in a lot of teams. Nunes, now a vice president at the company, has used her experiences to develop ideas about managing conflicts among team members.

First, Nunes has learned to value diverse viewpoints as a source of creative thinking. She saw how creativity was stifled in a work group led by a manager who preferred to hire employees who had graduated from the same business school. Although the manager and employees bonded over conversations about shared experiences, the work group never produced exceptional results because group members' similar ideas were never challenged. Nunes concluded that she would excel by including people who could deliver different outlooks and experiences.

Nunes realized, however, that diverse outlooks are beneficial only if team members share a common goal. That requires shifting attention away from individual wins in a debate and looking for areas of common ground. Nunes found that she and other team members had to gracefully accept challenges to their viewpoints. For example, when Nunes led a team that was setting up a new health care business, she discovered that team members had strong but varied opinions and different styles. Nunes recognized her logical, fact-oriented approach to thinking, which came from her science background, as an approach she sometimes needed to set aside for the sake of listening, persuading, and keeping the focus on team objectives.[111]

- How does Nunes's role as a team leader resemble the role of a mediator?

Here are some other recommendations for more effective conflict management.[112] Don't allow dysfunctional conflict to build, or hope or assume that it will go away. Address it before it escalates. Try to resolve it, and if the first efforts don't work, try others. And remember the earlier discussion (Chapter 13) of procedural justice. Even if disputants are not happy with your decisions, there are benefits to providing fair treatment, making a good-faith effort, giving them a voice in the proceedings, and so on. Caring about others' goals as well as your own will help ensure a collaborative process. Remember, too, that you may be able to ask HR specialists to help with difficult conflicts.

Electronic and Virtual Conflict

When teams are geographically dispersed, as is often the case for virtual teams, team members tend to experience more conflict and less trust.[113] Conflict management affects the success of virtual teams.[114] In a recent study, avoidance hurt performance. Accommodation—conceding to others to maintain harmony rather than assertively attempting to negotiate integrative solutions—had no effect on performance. Collaboration had a positive effect on performance. The researchers also uncovered two surprises: compromise hurt performance, and competition helped performance. Compromises hurt because they often are watered-down, middle-of-the-road, suboptimal solutions. Competitive behavior was useful because the virtual teams were temporary and under time pressure, so having some individuals behave dominantly and impose decisions to achieve efficiency was useful rather than detrimental.

When dealing with external teams, collaboration and competition can benefit your workflow. Merely compromising can generate dull results.

Two surprises: compromise hurt performance, and competition helped performance.

When people have problems in business-to-business e-commerce (e.g., costly delays), they tend to behave competitively and defensively rather than collaboratively.[115] Technical problems and recurring problems test people's patience. The conflict will escalate unless people use more cooperative, collaborative styles. Try to prevent conflicts before they arise; for example, make sure your information system is running smoothly before linking with others. Monitor and reduce or eliminate problems as soon as possible. When problems arise, express your willingness to cooperate, and then *actually be* cooperative. Even technical problems require the social skills of good management.

Consider, for example, the management skills that Toyota required when, as described in "Management Connection: Onward," the company's reputation and bottom line were both at risk.

| Manager's Brief | Progress Report | **Onward** |

Management Connection

TOYOTA REVISITS ITS APPROACH TO TEAMWORK

Over the past few decades, Toyota Motor gained sales in the United States based on its reputation for an unswerving commitment to quality. The Toyota Production System was touted as a means of getting all employees committed to continuous improvement. Then, in 2010, the reputation on which the company had staked its success was suddenly at risk as news media in the United States began reporting claims of unintended acceleration. Over the following months, Toyota—known for getting quality right the first time—recalled millions of vehicles.

What went wrong? Ironically for a study of teamwork, although Toyota's management thinks of the company's employees as "team members," a chief criticism was that Toyota's management failed to allow sufficient collaboration among the company's divisions and disciplines. Maintaining a structure the company established decades ago, Toyota has separate divisions for each function, such as engineering, manufacturing, and purchasing. In North America, managers in each function report to functional managers in Japan, where Toyota is headquartered. If a problem is detected in one area, information is shared with other divisions and regions only after the information about it has made its way back to headquarters.

One consequence of this arrangement is that it reinforces conflict between the functional divisions. Employees in sales, engineering, finance, and so on often have different objectives and focus on different measures of success. If various functions are brought together on one team to solve a problem or serve a customer, they may be forced to work out their differences as they work toward the team's goal. But when employees are isolated in separate functions, power struggles have an opportunity to intensify. Some observers say this is just what happened to Toyota in North America. The result was a delayed and confused response to the complaints of unintended acceleration. Many people were shocked to learn that no manager in the United States had the authority to order the recall of Toyota vehicles when problems began to surface.

Another perspective on Toyota's problems comes from a former Toyota engineer who detailed some of his experiences for *The Wall Street Journal*. According to this former employee, engineering teams were strongly committed to improving designs. Standards were high, and schedules were tight. Under those conditions, teamwork helped. Engineers would assist one another, which enabled the teams to produce remarkable results such as modifying an engine for desert conditions in a few months. However, these successes required such relentless effort that engineers were rushed and exhausted, and mistakes slipped by. In addition, this engineer recalls, much of the effort at improvement targeted design features that customers were likely to notice, even though less noticeable improvements might be more likely to influence a vehicle's safety and performance. Others have contended that Toyota's efforts at continuous improvement in recent years have rewarded primarily improvements that speed production and save money over those that produce a better car.

Fortunately for its future, Toyota has embedded in its culture a commitment to learning and continuous improvement. In this case, executives determined that the company needed changes not in its products as much as in the way that its lines of command can foster collaboration and get everyone aiming toward a shared commitment to quality. Management within Toyota Motor Engineering and Manufacturing North America (TEMA) is taking steps to integrate the work of its teams in various functions.

Back in Japan, the company assigned 1,000 of its engineers to a quality group charged with conducting quality checks to identify potential sources of performance problems. It assigned 20 employees to create and maintain a database of vehicle repairs and customer complaints from around the world; this group is responsible for analyzing the data to look for trends as they emerge. It also began requiring engineering teams to further support one another by cross-checking the designs of other teams' vehicles. The extra series of checks adds to the length of the design process, but the hope is that preventing problems will be less costly than rebuilding the brand's damaged reputation.[116]

- In building effective teams, how did Toyota fall short in the areas of performance focus and motivating teamwork?
- How might Toyota's efforts to improve quality reduce the damage resulting from conflict between employees in different functions?

KEY TERMS

accommodation, p. 522	mediator, p. 523	social facilitation effect, p. 514
autonomous work groups, p. 508	norms, p. 515	social loafing, p. 514
avoidance, p. 521	parading, p. 519	superordinate goals, p. 523
cohesiveness, p. 517	parallel teams, p. 507	task specialist, p. 517
collaboration, p. 522	probing, p. 519	team, p. 505
competing, p. 522	project and development teams, p. 507	team maintenance specialist, p. 517
compromise, p. 522	quality circles, p. 508	traditional work groups, p. 507
gatekeeper, p. 519	roles, p. 516	transnational teams, p. 507
informing, p. 519	self-designing teams, p. 508	virtual teams, p. 507
management teams, p. 507	self-managed teams, p. 508	work teams, p. 506

SUMMARY OF LEARNING OBJECTIVES

Now that you have studied Chapter 14, you should be able to:

LO 1   Discuss how teams can contribute to an organization's effectiveness.

Teams are building blocks for organization structure and forces for productivity, quality, cost savings, speed, change, and innovation. They have the potential to provide many benefits for both the organization and individual members.

LO 2   Distinguish the new team environment from that of traditional work groups.

Compared with traditional work groups that were closely supervised, today's teams have more authority and often are self-managed. Teams now are used in many more ways, for many more purposes, than in the past. Generally, types of teams include work teams, project and development teams, parallel teams, management teams, transnational teams, and virtual teams. Types of work teams range from traditional groups with low autonomy to self-designing teams with high autonomy.

LO 3   Summarize how groups become teams.

Groups carry on a variety of important developmental processes, including forming, storming, norming, and performing. For a group to become a team, it should move beyond traditional supervisory leadership, become more participative, and ultimately enjoy team leadership. A true team has members who complement one another; who are committed to a common purpose, performance goals, and approach; and who hold themselves accountable to one another.

LO 4   Explain why groups sometimes fail.

Teams do not always work well. Some companies underestimate the difficulties of moving to a team-based approach. Teams require training, empowerment, and a well-managed transition to make them work. Groups may fail to become effective teams unless managers and team members commit to the idea, understand what makes teams work, and implement appropriate practices.

LO 5   Describe how to build an effective team.

Create a team with a high-performance focus by establishing a common purpose, translating the purpose into measurable team goals, designing the team's task so it is intrinsically motivating, designing a team-based performance measurement system, and providing team rewards.

Work to develop a common understanding of how the team will perform its task. Make it clear that everyone has to work hard and contribute in concrete ways. Establish mutual accountability and build trust among members. Examine the team's strategies periodically and be willing to adapt.

Make sure members contribute fully by selecting them appropriately, training them, and checking that all important roles are carried out. Take a variety of steps to establish team cohesiveness and high performance norms.

And don't just manage inwardly. Manage the team's relations with outsiders, too.

LO 6   List methods for managing a team's relationships with other teams.

Perform important roles such as gatekeeping, informing, parading, and probing. Identify the types of lateral role relationships you have with outsiders. This can help coordinate efforts throughout the work system.

LO 7   Identify ways to manage conflict.

Managing lateral relationships well can prevent some conflict. But conflict arises because of the sheer number of contacts, ambiguities, goal differences, competition for scarce resources, and different perspectives and time horizons. Depending on the situation, five basic interpersonal approaches to managing conflict can be used: avoidance, accommodation, compromise, competition, and collaboration. Superordinate goals offer a focus on higher-level organizational goals that can help generate a collaborative relationship. Techniques for managing conflict between other parties include acting as a mediator and managing virtual conflict.

DISCUSSION QUESTIONS

1. Why do you think some people resist the idea of working in teams? How would you deal with their resistance?

2. Consider a job you have held, and review Table 14.1 about the traditional and new team environments. Which environment best describes your job? Assess your job on each of the dimensions described in the table.

3. Assess your job as in Question 2, using Figure 14.1. Which leadership "stage" characterized your job environment?

4. Identify some things from a previous job that could have been done differently to move your work group closer toward the "team leadership" depicted in Figure 14.1.

5. Experts say that teams are a means, not an end. What do you think they mean? What do you think happens in a company that creates teams just for the sake of having teams because it's a fad or because it sounds good? How can this pitfall be avoided?

6. Choose a sports team with which you are familiar. Assess its effectiveness and discuss the factors that contribute to its level of effectiveness.

7. Assess the effectiveness, as in Question 6, of a student group with which you have been affiliated. Could anything have been done to make it more effective?

8. Consider the various roles members have to perform for a team to be effective. Which roles would play to your strengths, and which to your weaknesses? How can you become a better team member?

9. Discuss personal examples of virtual conflict and how they were managed, well or poorly.

10. What do you think are your own most commonly used approaches to handling conflict? Least common? What can you do to expand your repertoire and become more effective at conflict management?

11. Generate real examples of how superordinate goals have helped resolve a conflict. Identify some current conflicts and provide some specific ideas for how superordinate goals could be used to help.

12. Have you ever been part of a group that was "self-managed"? What was good about it, and what not so good? Why do many managers resist this idea? Why do some people love the idea of being a member of such a team, while others don't?

13. How might self-managed teams operate differently in different cultures? What are the advantages, disadvantages, and implications of homogeneous versus highly diverse self-managed teams?

EXPERIENTIAL EXERCISES

14.1   PRISONERS' DILEMMA: AN INTERGROUP COMPETITION

INSTRUCTIONS

1. The instructor explains what will take place in this exercise and assigns people to groups. Two types of teams are formed and named Red and Blue (with no more than eight per group) and are not to communicate with the other team in any way, verbally or nonverbally, except when told to do so by the instructor. Groups are given time to study the Prisoners' Dilemma Tally Sheet.

2. (3 min.) Round 1. Each team has three minutes to make a team decision. Write your decisions when the instructor says time is up.

3. (2 min.) The choices of the teams are announced for Round 1. The scores are entered on the Tally Sheet.

4. (4–5 min.) Round 2 is conducted in the same manner as Round 1.

5. (6 min.) Round 3 is announced as a special round for which the payoff points are doubled. Each team is instructed to send one representative to chairs in the center of the room. After representatives have conferred for three minutes,

they return to their teams. Teams then have three minutes, as before, in which to make their decisions. When recording their scores, they should be reminded that points indicated by the payoff schedule are doubled for this round only.

6. (8–10 min.) Rounds 4, 5, and 6 are conducted in the same manner as the first three rounds.

7. (6 min.) Round 7 is announced as a special round, in which the payoff points are "squared" (multiplied by themselves: e.g., a score of 4 would be $4^2 = 16$). A minus sign would be retained (e.g., $-(3)^2 = -9$). Team representatives meet for three minutes; then the teams meet for three minutes. At the instructor's signal, the teams write their choices, and then the two choices are announced.

8. (6 min.) Round 8 is handled exactly as Round 7 was. Payoff points are squared.

9. (10–20 min.) The point total for each team is announced, and the sum of the two team totals is calculated and compared with the maximum positive or negative outcomes ($+108$ or -108 points).

Prisoners' Dilemma Tally Sheet

INSTRUCTIONS:

For 10 successive rounds, the Red team will choose either an A or a B and the Blue team will choose either an X or a Y. The score each team receives in a round is determined by the pattern made by the choices of both teams, according to the following schedule:

PAYOFF SCHEDULE:

AX—Both teams win 3 points.

AY—Red team loses 6 points; Blue team wins 6 points.

BX—Red team wins 6 points; Blue team loses 6 points.

BY—Both teams lose 3 points.

Scorecard:

Round	Minutes	Choice		Cumulative Points	
		Red Team	Blue Team	Red Team	Blue Team
1	3				
2	3				
3*	3 (reps.), 3(teams)				
4	3				
5	3				
6*	3 (reps.), 3(teams)				
7**	3 (reps.), 3(teams)				
8**	3 (reps.), 3(teams)				

*Payoff points are doubled for this round.
**Payoff points are squared for this round. (Retain the minus sign.)
SOURCE: Dorothy Hai, "Prisoner's Dilemma," in *Organizational Behavior: Experiences and Cases*, 1E. Copyright © 1986. South-Western, a part of Cengage Learning, Inc. Reproduced with permission. www.cengage.com/permissions

14.2   THE TRAVELER'S CHECK SCAM GROUP EXERCISE

INSTRUCTIONS

1. (3 min.) Each group selects an observer. The observer remains silent during the group problem-solving process, recording the activities of the group on the Observer's Report Form.

2. (15 min.) Group members read the following problem and proceed to solve it.

3. (2 min.) When the group has a solution to the problem upon which all members agree, it will be written on a note and handed to the instructor.

4. (5 min.) The observer briefs the group on the problem-solving processes observed during the exercise.

5. (25 min.) The small group discusses the following topics:

   a. Did the group decide on a problem solution process before it attempted to solve the problem? If so, what was it?

   b. Was the solution of the problem hindered in any way by the lack of an appropriate agreed-upon group problem-solving process? Explain.

   c. Who were the leaders of the group during the exercise? What did they do? Critique their leadership activities.

   d. What communications patterns were used by the group during the exercise? Who participated the most? Who participated the least? Describe individual behaviors.

   e. Did the group solve the problem? How many members of the group discovered the correct answer on their own?

   f. Was using the group to solve this problem better than assigning the problem to one person? Explain the rationale for your answer.

THE CASE OF MICKEY THE DIP

Mickey the Dip, an expert pickpocket and forger, liked to work the Los Angeles International Airport on busy days. His technique was to pick the pockets of prosperous-looking victims just before they boarded planes to the East Coast. This gave Mickey five hours to use stolen credit cards before the owners could report their losses.

One morning Mickey snatched a fat wallet from a traveler and left the airport to examine his loot. To his surprise he found no credit cards but instead $500 in traveler's checks. After 20 minutes of practice, Mickey could sign a perfect imitation of the victim's signature. He then proceeded to a large department store where all suits were being sold for 75 percent off the regular price. Mickey purchased a suit for $225 and paid for it with $300 in stolen traveler's checks. After the clerk who served him went to lunch, he bought another suit for $150 and paid for it with the remaining $200 of stolen traveler's checks. Later, Mickey switched the labels on the two suits and, using the receipt from the $225 suit, returned the $150 suit at a centralized return desk for a refund. The refund clerk took the suit and gave Mickey eleven $20 bills, which he stuffed into his pocket and disappeared.

When the department store deposited the traveler's checks, they were returned as forgeries. Assuming the store normally sold suits at twice their wholesale price and used 10 percent of sales as an overhead cost figure, what was the cash value of the loss suffered by the store as a result of Mickey's caper? Do not consider taxes in your computations.

THE TRAVELER'S CHECK SCAM EXERCISE OBSERVER'S REPORT

1. What happened during the first few minutes the group met after members finished reading the problem? (List behaviors of specific group members.)

2. Identify the group role played by each group member during the exercise. Give examples of the behavior of each.

3. Were there any conflicts within or among group members during the exercise? Explain the nature of the conflicts and the behavior of the individual(s) involved.

4. How were decisions made in the group? Give specific examples.

5. How could the group improve its problem-solving skills?

SOURCE: Peter P. Dawson, *Fundamentals of Organizational Behavior.* Copyright © 1985 Pearson Education, Inc. Reprinted by permission of Pearson Education, Inc., Upper Saddle River, NJ.

CONCLUDING CASE

ROCKY GAGNON, GENERAL CONTRACTOR

Rocky Gagnon is a 50-year-old journeyman carpenter, laborer, and craftsman. Over the past 30 years, he has worked in almost every job and phase of the house-building process. Gagnon is getting older, and his back is getting sore. He loves the construction business and feels that now is the time for him to start working more with his mind than his back. Gagnon wants to become a general contractor.

Some general contractors have their own facilities, equipment, and employees. Others simply work out of their homes and subcontract all of the work required to complete a particular project.

Gagnon has an idea and a vision for something a little different. He wants to put together a team of tradespeople who will agree to work together toward the successful completion of about 8 to 15 homes per year. At the same time, each individual will be able to continue to operate as an independent contractor during off hours.

One of the results of working for 30 years in the local building trades is a large and varied network of friends and acquaintances. Gagnon has enjoyed many a drink with the local plumbing and heating contractors, roofers, insulation people, land surveyors, and others. He wants to take advantage of those relationships. The general profile of local contractors, according to Gagnon, is that of a highly skilled, very independent group of people with poor communication skills. The workmanship is generally very good—when it finally gets done.

Many jobs and phases of the house-building process take place in a logical sequence. For example, insulation people cannot do their work until the "rough" electrical, plumbing, and heating work is completed. If any of those contractors falls behind schedule or does not complete his or her task, the process is disrupted. Outside factors such as weather, availability of materials, and overlapping schedules and deadlines with other jobs further complicate the challenge of meeting deadlines. Gagnon wants to coordinate all of this and make house building more efficient.

The spirit of cooperation is also severely lacking, according to Gagnon. It seems that many contractors could not care less about the crew that will follow them in the building process.

For example, a framing crew should know about the exact plans for the fireplace, hearth, and chimney on each job and should leave the site properly set up for that contractor. According to Gagnon, the all-too-typical response of the framer (as well as others) is, "That's not my job, so don't tell me about it." Independent contractors are also notorious for leaving their messes behind for someone else to clean up, such as the general contractor or next crew.

Gagnon wants to change all of this by bringing together a group of tradespeople who will agree to work together as a team for the common good. If done right, Gagnon sees this as a win–win situation for all parties.

Rocky Gagnon knows that the opportunity for success clearly exists. He also knows that the key to his success will be the presence of strong organizational and communication skills. Gagnon feels that all of the pieces of the puzzle are there for the taking, and that all he needs is some help in setting up the right team and an organizational structure and work process that will achieve the desired results.

During the past few months, Gagnon put together a list and has met separately with the individuals he considers to be the best craftsmen in the area and, most important, who he knows have the potential and willingness to form the team and working relationship that he envisions. The first of several meetings has been set up for the entire group to meet and work through the particulars. Gagnon has hired a well-known and respected business professor from the local community to serve as an adviser and mediator for the group.

QUESTIONS

1. What type of team would work best in this situation? Support your answer with concepts from the text that apply to this proposed venture.

2. What kinds of problems would you expect this group to encounter? What is the best way to work through those?

3. What are the likely keys to success in motivating these individuals to cooperate and communicate as a team?

15 Communicating

LEARNING OBJECTIVES

After studying Chapter 15, you will be able to:

CHAPTER OUTLINE

Management Connection

ZINGERMAN'S VISION KEEPS EMPLOYEES IN THE KNOW

Zingerman's Community of Businesses started out as Zingerman's Delicatessen in Ann Arbor, Michigan (home of the University of Michigan's main campus). Despite the deli's name, there is, in fact, no one named Zingerman. The company's cofounders, Ari Weinzweig and Paul Saginaw, wanted to open a traditional Jewish deli. They wanted a name that would be easy to pronounce and sounded Jewish, and their own names didn't qualify (Saginaw, in Michigan, is associated with a Native American tribe). They settled on "Greenberg's Deli," but at the last minute learned that another deli in the state already had a claim to that name. So after a quick brainstorming session just a week before opening, they picked Zingerman, partly because a name starting with Z would be easy to spot in a telephone directory.

In the years following its 1982 opening, Zingerman's Deli quickly became popular, owing to its commitment to top quality. As business-savvy people watched the deli thrive, they assumed that Weinzweig and Saginaw would take the next step of most similar businesses and begin to sell franchising opportunities to spread the Zingerman's magic around the region and the nation. However, the two cofounders decided they would be an important fixture in the life of Ann Arbor rather than a national chain, and so they would grow by opening new specialty businesses serving the one community. This principle laid the foundation for the Zingerman's Community of Businesses. Businesses were added as new sources of demand were identified. Today there are nine businesses: the deli, a bakery, a caterer, a creamery that makes cheeses and gelato, a coffee business, a wholesale candy maker, a mail-order service, a restaurant called Zingerman's Roadhouse, and a training organization that teaches the management practices that have made Zingerman's

successful. All are owned by a holding company, Dancing Sandwich Enterprises, and are under the leadership of one or more managing partners hired by Weinzweig and Saginaw. Although they operate independently, they share common values and depend on one another. For example, the deli, restaurant, and caterer feature products from the bakery, creamery, and coffee businesses.

While the Zingerman's businesses are known for dedication to the finest locally grown and made ingredients, Weinzweig sees the businesses' success as being even more closely tied to communication with employees. Excellence in communication is partly a personal commitment to ensure that employees hear from the leadership. When new employees are hired, for example, one of the founders makes a point of leading the first day of orientation so that the founders' ideals come across clearly. And Saginaw realized that as his company grew to hundreds of employees, he had to be intentional about reaching out. He made a habit of thinking about whom he might encounter during the day and planning what they should talk about if they did meet. In addition, Weinzweig and

Saginaw developed two important tools for employee communication: a vision statement and open-book management. Both of these entail sharing information so that all employees are clear about the desired direction and performance of the business.

Whenever leaders at a Zingerman's business launch a new enterprise, they begin by writing a statement of their vision for that enterprise. They use detailed, descriptive language that helps everyone picture what that business will be like, including what will make it distinctive. Putting the vision in writing makes it easy to share with employees, who can refer to it at any time to remind themselves where they, and their organization, should be headed. The writers of the vision succeed when they have expressed ideas that inspire employees so they are excited to come to work and make the vision a reality.

Open-book management, as you will see later in this chapter, is a practice that involves sharing details of the company's performance and training employees to understand how their efforts relate to that performance. It is based on the belief that when employees have a clear sense of how well they are doing, they will be motivated to make improvements if the news is bad or to continue excelling if the news is good. Because Zingerman's is privately owned, the company is not required to make financial data available to the public. Many private companies are very protective of such information—seeing a competitive advantage in secrecy. For Zingerman's, however, greater advantage comes from fully communicating with employees about important issues.[1]

As you read this chapter, consider how important it is for employees to have information about their company's value and performance. Try to identify ways that Zingerman's managers can communicate this information so that employees understand and care about it.

As the founders of Zingerman's are well aware, effective communication is a fundamental component of job performance and managerial effectiveness.[2] It is a primary means by which managers carry out the responsibilities described throughout this book, such as making group decisions, sharing a vision, coordinating individuals and work groups within the organization's structure, hiring and motivating employees, and leading teams. In these and other areas, managers have to be able to share thoughts clearly and convincingly, and they have to listen effectively to others. In this chapter, we present important communication concepts and some practical guidelines for improving your effectiveness. We also discuss communication at the interpersonal and organizational levels.

Interpersonal Communication

communication

The transmission of information and meaning from one party to another through the use of shared symbols.

Communication is the transmission of information and meaning from one party to another through the use of shared symbols. Figure 15.1 shows a general model of how one person communicates with another.

The *sender* initiates the process by conveying information to the *receiver*—the person for whom the message is intended. The sender has a *meaning* he or she wishes to communicate and *encodes* the meaning into symbols (the words chosen for the message). Then the sender *transmits*, or sends, the message through some *channel*, such as a verbal or written medium.

The receiver *decodes* the message (e.g., reads it) and attempts to *interpret* the sender's meaning. The receiver may provide *feedback* to the sender by encoding a message in response to the sender's message.

The communication process often is hampered by *noise*, or interference in the system, that blocks perfect understanding. Noise could be anything that interferes with accurate communication: ringing telephones, thoughts about other things, or simple fatigue or stress.

Person A (Sender)

1. Intended meaning
   ↓
2. Encoding

3. Communication channel

Person B (Receiver)

4. Decoding
   ↓
5. Perceived meaning

FIGURE 15.1
A Model of One-Way Communication

The model in Figure 15.1 is more than a theoretical treatment of the communication process: it points out the key ways in which communications can break down. Mistakes can be made at each stage of the model. A manager who is alert to potential problems can perform each step carefully to ensure more effective communication. The model also helps explain the topics discussed next: the differences between one-way and two-way communication, communication pitfalls, misperception, and the various communication channels.

one-way communication

A process in which information flows in only one direction—from the sender to the receiver, with no feedback loop.

One-Way versus Two-Way Communication

In **one-way communication,** information flows in only one direction—from the sender to the receiver, with no feedback loop. A manager sends an e-mail to a subordinate without asking for a response. An employee phones the information technology (IT) department and leaves a message requesting repairs for her computer. A supervisor scolds a production worker about defects and then storms away.

LO 1

When receivers respond to senders—Person B becomes the sender and Person A the receiver—**two-way communication** has occurred. One-way communication in situations like those just described can become two-way if the manager's e-mail invites the receiver to reply with any questions, the IT department returns the employee's call and asks for details about the computer problem, and the supervisor calms down and listens to the production worker's explanation of why defects are occurring.

True two-way communication means not only that the receiver provides feedback but also that the sender is receptive to the feedback. In these constructive exchanges, information is shared between both parties rather than merely delivered from one person to the other.

two-way communication

A process in which information flows in two directions—the receiver provides feedback, and the sender is receptive to the feedback.

Two-way communication is more difficult and time-consuming than one-way communication. However, it is more accurate with fewer mistakes occurring and fewer problems arising.

Because it is faster and easier for the sender, one-way communication is much more common than it should be. A busy executive finds it easier to dash off an e-mail message than to discuss a nagging problem with a subordinate. Also, he doesn't have to deal with questions or be challenged by someone who disagrees.

Two-way communication is more difficult and time-consuming than one-way communication. However, it is more accurate; fewer mistakes occur, and fewer problems arise. When receivers have a chance to ask questions, share concerns, and make suggestions or modifications, they understand more precisely what is being communicated and what they should do with the information.[3] Effectively sharing information among teammates is a prime contributor to performance.[4]

Consider what happened to Dick Nicholson when he was a sales manager attending a company reception for the sales department. Out of Nicholson's earshot, his company's chairman asked the vice president why a particular employee—a chronic underperformer—was "still a salesman." The vice president then told

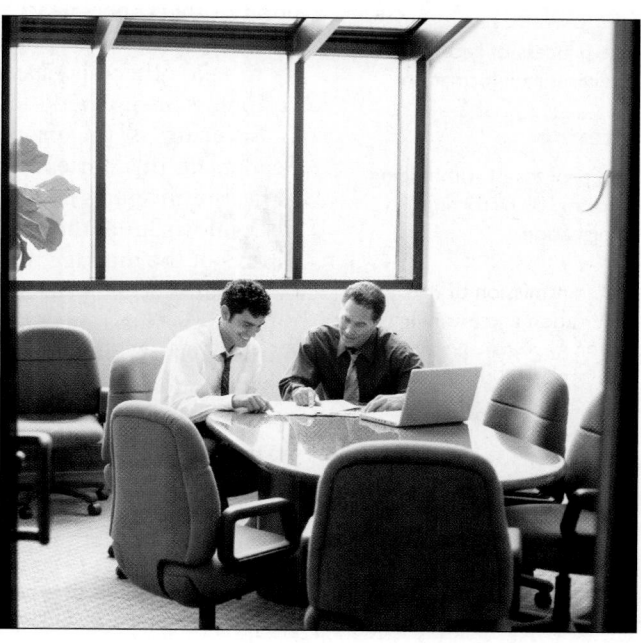

Nicholson what he thought the chairman meant: the chairman wanted to promote the salesperson. If communication were limited to one way, Nicholson could have simply carried out the chairman's apparent order, but instead he visited the chairman later and asked for an explanation. He was relieved when the chairman explained that he was wondering why the ineffective salesperson was still working for the company at all.[5]

Communication Pitfalls

As we know from personal experience, the sender's intended message does not always get across to the receiver. You are operating under an illusion if you think there is a perfect correlation between what you say and what people hear.[6] Errors can occur in all stages of the communication process. In the encoding stage, words can be misused, decimal points entered in the wrong places, facts left out, or ambiguous phrases inserted. In the transmission stage, a memo may get lost on a cluttered desk, the words on the screen could be too small to read from the back of the room, or words might be spoken with ambiguous inflections.

Decoding problems arise when the receiver doesn't listen carefully or reads too quickly and overlooks a key point. And of course receivers can misinterpret the message: as a reader draws the wrong conclusion from an unclear text message, a listener takes a general statement by the boss too personally, or a sideways glance is taken the wrong way.

More generally, people's perceptual and filtering processes create misinterpretations. **Perception** is the process of receiving and interpreting information. As you know, such processes are not perfectly objective. They are subjective, as people's self-interested motives and attitudes toward the sender and toward the message create biased interpretations. People often assume that others share their views, and naturally pay more attention to their own views than to those of

> When George Franks started a new job, his boss always seemed too busy to talk. A mentor suggested that Franks make a habit of asking his boss how he could help. But his boss interpreted the repeated questions as meaning the boss couldn't keep up with his job; offended, he retaliated by "dumping all the projects no one else wanted" on Franks.[7]

others.[8] But perceptual differences get in the way of shared consensus. To remedy this situation, it helps to remember that others' viewpoints are legitimate and to incorporate others' perspectives into your interpretation of issues.[9] Generally, adopting another person's viewpoint is fundamental to working collaboratively. And your ability to take others' perspectives—for instance, to really understand the viewpoints of customers or suppliers—can result in higher assessments of your performance.[10]

perception

The process of receiving and interpreting information.

filtering

The process of withholding, ignoring, or distorting information.

Filtering is the process of withholding, ignoring, or distorting information. Senders do this, for example, when they tell the boss what they think the boss wants to hear or give unwarranted compliments rather than honest criticism. Receivers also filter information; they may fail to recognize an important message or attend to some aspects of the message but not others.

A manager at a magazine who tended to phrase the assignments she gave her reporters as questions—"How would you like to do the X project with Y?" and "I was thinking of putting you on the X project; is that okay?"—was criticized by her male boss, who told her she did not assume the proper demeanor with her staff.[11] Another, the owner of a retail operation, told one of her store managers to do something by saying, "The bookkeeper needs help with the billing. How would you feel about helping her out?" He said fine but didn't do it. Whereas the boss thought he meant he would do it, he said he meant to indicate how he would feel about helping. He decided he had better things to do.[12]

Filtering and subjective perception pervade one interesting aspect of the communications dynamic: how men and women differ in their communicating styles.

Because of such filtering and perceptual differences, you cannot assume the other person means what you think he means or understands the meanings you intend. Managers need to excel at reading interactions and adjusting their communication styles and perceptions to the people with whom they interact.[13] The very human tendencies to filter and perceive subjectively underlie much of the ineffective communication and the need for more effective communication practices that you will read about in the rest of this chapter.

Mixed Signals and Misperception

A common thread underlying the discussion so far is that people's perceptions can undermine attempts to communicate. People do not pay attention to everything going on around them. They inadvertently send mixed signals that can undermine the intended messages. Different people attend to different things, and people interpret the same thing in different ways. All of this creates problems in communication.

If the communication is between people from different cultures, these problems are magnified.[14] Communication breakdowns often occur when business transactions take place between people from different countries. Chapter 6 introduced you to the importance of these cultural issues.

The following example highlights the operation of mixed signals and misperceptions. A bank CEO knew that to be competitive he had to downsize his organization, and the employees who remained would have to commit to customer service, become more empowered, and really *earn* customer loyalty.[15] Knowing that his employees would have doubts and concerns about the coming reorganization, he decided to make a promise to them that he would do his best to guarantee employment to the survivors.

What signals did the CEO communicate to his people by his promises? One positive signal was that he cared about his people. But he also signaled that *he* would take care of *them*, thus undermining his goal of giving them more responsibility and empowering them. The employees wanted management to take responsibility for the market challenge that *they* needed to face—to handle things for them when in fact *they* needed to learn the new ways of doing business. Inadvertently, the CEO spoke to their backward-looking need for security when he had meant to make them see that the bank's future depended on *their* efforts. However, the CEO did avoid one common pitfall at companies that announce plans for downsizing or outsourcing: ignoring the emotional significance of the message.[16] Sometimes managers are so intent on delivering the business rationale for the changes that they fail to acknowledge the human cost of layoffs. When employees hear a message that neglects to address their feelings, they generally interpret the message to mean that managers don't care.

Consider how many problems can be avoided—and how much more effective communication can be—if people take the time to (1) ensure that the receivers attend to the message they are sending, (2) consider the other party's frame of reference and attempt to convey the message with that viewpoint in mind, (3) take concrete steps to minimize perceptual errors and improper signals in both sending and receiving, and (4) send *consistent* messages. You should make an effort to predict people's interpretations of your messages and think in terms of how they could *misinterpret* your messages. It helps to say not only what you mean but also what you *don't* mean. Every time you say "I am not saying X, I am saying Y," you eliminate a possible misinterpretation.[17]

Any interpersonal situation holds potential for perceptual errors, filtering, and other communication breakdowns.

It helps to say not only what you mean but also what you *don't* mean.

Oral and Written Channels

Communication can be sent through a variety of channels (step 3 in the Figure 15.1 model), including oral, written, and electronic. Each channel has advantages and disadvantages.

Oral communication includes face-to-face discussion, telephone conversations, and formal presentations and speeches. Advantages are that questions can be asked and answered, feedback is immediate and direct, the receiver(s) can sense the sender's sincerity (or lack thereof), and oral communication is more persuasive and sometimes less expensive than written. However, oral communication also has disadvantages: it can lead to spontaneous, ill-considered statements (and regret), and there is no permanent record of it (unless an effort is made to record it).

Written communication includes e-mail, memos, letters, reports, computer files, and other written documents. Advantages to using written messages are that the message can be revised several times, it is a permanent record that can be saved, the message stays the same even if relayed through many people, and the receiver has more time to analyze the message. Disadvantages are that the sender has no control over where, when, or if the message is read; the sender does not receive immediate feedback; the receiver may not understand parts of the message; and the message must be longer to contain enough information to answer anticipated questions.[18]

Weigh these considerations when deciding whether to communicate orally or in writing.

You should weigh these considerations when deciding whether to communicate orally or in writing. Also, sometimes use both channels, such as following up a meeting with a confirming memo or writing a letter to prepare someone for your phone call.

Electronic Media

Among other things, electronic media provide opportunities for individuals to multicommunicate: engage in more than one conversation at the same time.[19] In electronic decision rooms, software supports simultaneous access to shared files and allows people to share views and do work collectively.[20] Other means of electronic communication include *teleconferencing*, in which groups of people in different locations interact over telephone lines and perhaps also see one another on television monitors as they participate in group discussions (*videoconferencing*). And you probably are intimately familiar with e-mail, instant messaging, text messaging, and blogging.

E-mail is a fundamental tool of workplace communication; instant messaging (IMing) is less widespread in business settings, but its use is growing. Some companies use blogs to communicate with the external environment—for example, by sharing information about product uses or corporate social responsibility. Blogs also may foster communication within the organization.[21]

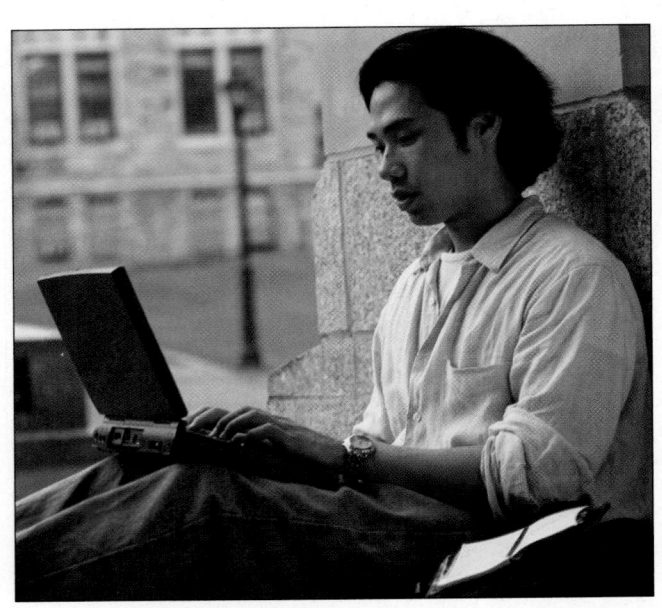

E-mail is one of the most convenient forms of communication, but what are some of the pitfalls? How often have you sent an e-mail, whether personal or professional, and found that someone misinterpreted the message?

A project team might have a blog where the team leader posts frequent updates along with relevant presentations and spreadsheets. When team members need information about the project, searching the blog site can be an easy way to find it. They also can post ideas and comments in response to the blogger's entries. Similarly, blogs can be used to encourage collaboration among employees with a shared interest in particular products, functions, or customers.

Web 2.0

A set of Internet-based applications that encourage user-provided content and collaboration.

Web 2.0 is a set of Internet-based applications that encourage user-provided content and collaboration. Some of the most widely used Web 2.0 applications are social networking, podcasts, RSS (really simple syndication, where users subscribe to receive news, blogs, or other information they select), and wikis (online publications created with contributions from many authors/users). Users of Facebook, YouTube, and Wikipedia have brought the experience to work and applied online collaboration to business needs. Unlike the first generation of Internet applications, Web 2.0 tends not to be formally introduced to organizations when IT departments evaluate it and make a purchase. Instead employees simply begin using the tools to meet a need.

Advantages *Advantages* of electronic communication are numerous and dramatic. Within firms, the advantages include the sharing of more information and the speed and efficiency in delivering routine messages to large numbers of people across vast geographic areas. Business-related wikis such as Socialtext let project teams post their ideas

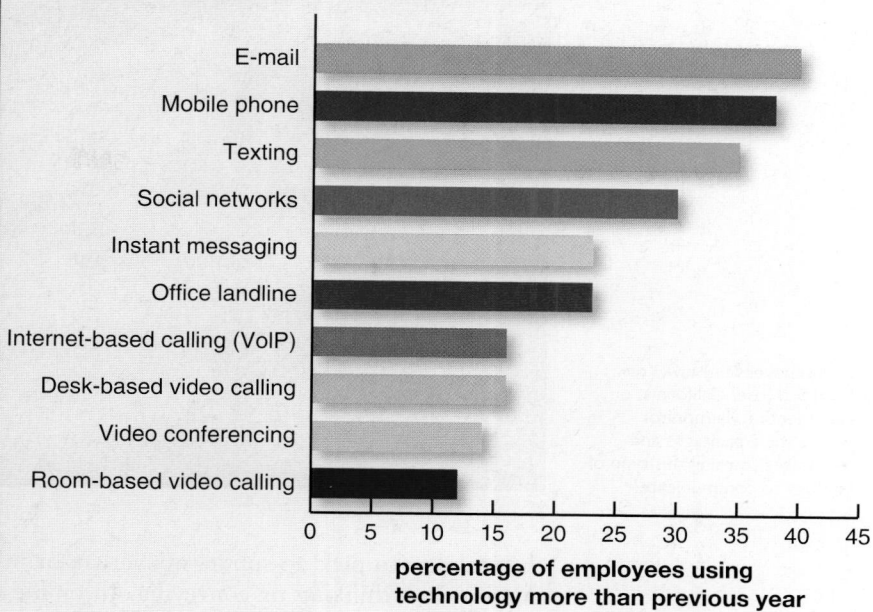

Today's users are spending more time than ever with a variety of communication methods, especially e-mail, mobile phones, and social networking. Notably, although e-mail is often blamed for overloading workers, only 28 percent of technology users call it the top contributor to information overload.[22]

percentage of employees using technology more than previous year

in one forum for others to add contributions. Socialtext allows project leaders to grant users access based on their need to know and participate. Web Crossing uses wikis for product development. The wikis save the company "untold amounts of paper, postage, meetings, travel budgets, conference calls, and the time required to coordinate it all."[23]

Some applications of electronic communication broaden the network of people reached. For example, LinkedIn provides connections to a network of associates, and Facebook lets a business interact with thousands of customers.

Communicating electronically can reduce time and expenses devoted to traveling, photocopying, and mailing. When a fire caused by a truck accident closed a major freeway route in the San Francisco Bay area, Valerie Williamson skipped the traffic mess by visiting with her colleague Brian Friedlander at her company's virtual office in Second Life, the online virtual world. Williamson and Friedlander used avatars (animated images of themselves) to navigate their meeting in the online conference room of their real-world business, Electric Sheep Company.[24] Participants in Second Life can use their avatars to perform such business communication activities as giving PowerPoint presentations, streaming audio and video, and asking questions.

Some companies, including Boeing, use brainstorming software that allows anonymous contributions, presuming it will add more honesty to internal discussions. Some research indicates more data sharing and critical argumentation, and higher-quality decisions, with a group decision support system than is found in face-to-face meetings.[25] Others are concerned that anonymity tempts participants to make careless, rude, or ill-advised statements, so they require that identities be revealed, or they limit access to social networking technologies. However, a growing number of companies see services like LinkedIn, Twitter, and Facebook as necessary for staying in touch with the hundreds of millions of people who use these services—especially the younger generations of coworkers and customers, who are likelier to check tweets and texts than voice mail and e-mail.[26]

Disadvantages *Disadvantages* of electronic communication include the difficulty of solving complex problems that require more extended, face-to-face interaction and

Bottom Line

Imagine how much time you would lose if you couldn't communicate electronically; imagine the savings of money and natural resources you could create if your company and its people sought and used the most cost-effective ways to communicate.

What forms of electronic communication do you use (on the job or for personal use)?

Cisco employees in New York, left, and San Jose, California, on screen, meeting via monitor. What are the advantages and disadvantages to using this type of technology to communicate?

the inability to pick up subtle, nonverbal, or inflectional clues about what the communicator is thinking or conveying. In online bargaining—even before it begins—negotiators distrust one another more than in face-to-face negotiations. After the negotiation (compared with face-to-face negotiators), people usually are less satisfied with their outcomes, even when the outcomes are economically equivalent.[27]

Although organizations rely heavily on computer-aided communication for group decision making, face-to-face groups generally take less time, make higher-quality decisions, and are more satisfying for members.[28] E-mail is most appropriate for routine messages that do not require the exchange of large quantities of complex information. It is less suitable for confidential information, resolving conflicts, or negotiating.[29] Employees have reported being laid off via e-mail and even text messages.[30] Not only do these more impersonal forms of communication cause hurt feelings, but an upset employee can also easily forward messages, and forwarding often has a snowball effect that can embarrass everyone involved. Like e-mail, IMs can help people work together productively, but they can also leak sensitive information.

Companies are worried about leaks and negative portrayals, and they may require employees to agree to specific guidelines before they post information on blogs or networking sites or use a microblogging service such as Twitter. IBM handled this challenge by inviting employees to draft guidelines for using social media. The employees' ideas were reviewed by members of the company's human resources, marketing, finance, communications, and legal departments and then became company policy. When IBM employees use social media, they are expected to follow company rules for business conduct, identify themselves, be respectful, speak for themselves (not say they represent the company), and avoid disclosing company secrets or defaming competitors. The company has concluded that using this policy to train employees is less risky than either trying to keep people away from networking altogether or failing to train them in appropriate conduct.[31]

Two results of electronic communication are a proliferation of negative and nasty messages, and misinterpretations. People hurl insults, vent frustration, snitch on coworkers to the boss, and otherwise breach protocol. The lack of nonverbal cues can result in "kidding" remarks being taken seriously, causing resentment and regret.[32] People see negative meanings in neutral messages[33] and are more likely to lie electronically and to feel justified in doing so.[34] Also, it is not unheard of for confidential messages—including details about people's personal lives and insulting, embarrassing remarks—to become public knowledge through electronic leaks.

Other downsides to electronic communication are important to know.[35] Different people and sometimes different working units latch onto different channels as their medium of choice. For example, many Generation Y workers and customers (born in 1980 or later) tend to ignore voice mail and infrequently check e-mail because they expect these messages to be mostly spam.[36] Another disadvantage is that electronic messages sometimes are seen by those for whom they are not intended. Be careful with your IMs: make sure you don't accidentally send them to the wrong person and that they don't pop up on the screen during a PowerPoint presentation.[37] Deleting electronic messages—whether e-mail, IMs, or cell phone text messages—does not destroy them; they are saved elsewhere. Recipients can forward them to others, unbeknownst to the original sender. Many companies use software to monitor e-mail and IMs. And the messages can be used in court cases to indict individuals or companies. Electronic messages sent from work and on company-provided devices are private property—but they are private property of the system's owner, not of the sender.

> They are private property of the system's owner, not of the sender.

Here's an e-mail golden rule (like the sunshine rule in the ethics chapter): Don't hit "send" unless you'd be comfortable having the contents on the front page of a newspaper, being read by your mother or a competitor. And it's not a bad idea to have a colleague read nonroutine e-mails before sending.

Managing the Electronic Load   Electronic communication media seem essential these days, and people wonder how they ever worked without them. But the sheer volume of communication can be overwhelming.[38]

Fortunately, a few rules of thumb can help you in your electronic communications.[39] For the problem of information overload, the challenge is to separate the truly important from the routine. Effective managers find time to think about bigger business issues and don't get too bogged down in responding to every message that seems urgent but may be trivial. Essential here is to think strategically about your goals, identify the items that are most important, and prioritize your time around those goals. This is easier said than done, of course, but it is essential, and it helps. Most communication software has tools that can help.

Of course, management also has a role to play. Often employees check messages constantly because they believe (perhaps correctly) that this is what their bosses expect of them. Managers can help employees by limiting and communicating the times during which they expect a prompt response.[40]

A few more specific suggestions: with e-mail, don't hit "reply to all" when you should hit just "reply." Get organized by creating folders sorted by subject, priority, or sender, and flag messages that require follow-up. If you receive a copy, you don't need to respond; it's just for your information.

Some companies are recognizing the downsides of electronic media overuse. At U.S. Cellular, an executive vice president took the step of banning e-mail altogether on Fridays. After some resistance, employees found that they were building deeper working relationships through phone calls and face-to-face visits.[41] And at PBD Worldwide Fulfillment Services, Fridays without e-mail have taught new (or old) communication habits that spilled over into the rest of the week. E-mail volume at PBD dropped 75 percent and translated into greater efficiency.[42]

The Virtual Office   Based on the philosophy that management's focus should be on what people do, not where they are, the **virtual office** is a mobile office in which people can work anywhere—their home, car, airport, customers' offices—as long as they have the tools to communicate with customers and colleagues.

In the short run, at least, the benefits of virtual offices appear substantial. Saving money on rent and utilities is an obvious advantage. In Merced, California, Prudential

virtual office

A mobile office in which people can work anywhere as long as they have the tools to communicate with customers and colleagues.

California Realty's agents stay connected with each other and their clients via the Internet, sharing information on individual websites and through e-mail.[43] A virtual office also gives employees access to whatever information they need from the company, whether they are in a meeting, visiting a client, or working from home.[44] Hiring and retaining talented people is easier because virtual offices support scheduling flexibility and may make it possible to keep an employee who wants to relocate—for example, with a spouse taking a new job in another city.

But what will be the longer-term impact on productivity and morale? We may be in danger of losing too many "human moments," those authentic encounters that happen only when two people are physically together.[45] Some people hate being forced to work at home. Some send faxes, e-mail, and voice mail in the middle of the night—and others receive them. Some work around the clock and still feel they are not doing enough. The long hours of being constantly close to the technical tools of work can cause burnout. And some companies are learning that direct supervision at the office is necessary to maintain the quality of work, especially when employees are inexperienced and need guidance. The virtual office requires changes in human beings and presents technical challenges; so although it is much hyped and useful, it will not completely replace real offices and face-to-face work.

> But what will be the longer-term impact on productivity and morale?

Media Richness

Some communication channels convey more information than others. The amount of information a medium conveys is called **media richness**.[46] The more information or cues a medium sends to the receiver, the "richer" the medium is.[47] The richest media are more personal than technological, provide quick feedback, allow lots of descriptive language, and send different types of cues. Thus face-to-face communication is the richest medium because it offers a variety of cues in addition to words: tone of voice, facial expression, body language, and other nonverbal signals. It also allows more descriptive language than, say, a memo does. In addition, it affords more opportunity for the receiver to give feedback to and ask questions of the sender, turning one-way into two-way communication.

media richness

The degree to which a communication channel conveys information.

The telephone is less rich than face-to-face communication, electronic mail is less rich yet, and memos are the least rich medium. In general, you should send difficult and unusual messages through richer media, transmit simple and routine messages through less rich media like memos, and use multiple media for important messages that you want to ensure people attend to and understand.[48] You should also consider factors such as which medium your receiver prefers, the preferred communication style in your organization, and cost.[49] Table 15.1 gives some sample situations for choosing channels based on the message and the audience. Select a channel for each situation, and then compare your answers with those in Table 15.2.

TABLE 15.1
What Communication Channel Would You Use?

Situation 1: A midsize construction firm wants to announce a new employee benefit program.
Situation 2: A manager wishes to confirm a meeting time with 10 employees.
Situation 3: Increase enthusiasm in a midsize insurance company for a program that asks employees from different departments to work on the same project team.
Situation 4: A group of engineers who are geographically dispersed want to exchange design ideas with one another.
Situation 5: Describe a straightforward but somewhat detailed and updated version of a voice mail system to 1,000 employees who are geographically dispersed.

SOURCE: From *Communicating for Managerial Effectiveness* by Phillip G. Clampitt. Copyright © 1991. Reproduced with permission of Sage Publications, Inc. via Copyright Clearance Center.

Situation	Poor Choice	Better Choice
1	Memo	Small group meetings
Rationale: The memo does not offer the feedback potential necessary to explain what may be seen as obscure information. Moreover, with these employees there is a possibility of literacy problems. A group meeting will allow for an oral explanation after which participants can more easily ask questions about any of the complex materials.		
2	Phone	Voice mail or e-mail
Rationale: For a simple message like this, there is no need to use a rich medium when a lean one will do the job.		
3	E-mail, voice mail	Face-to-face, telephone
Rationale: In situations requiring persuasion the sender must be able to quickly adapt the message to the receiver in order to counter objections. This is not a feature of either e-mail or voice mail. Face-to-face communication offers the sender the greatest flexibility. The phone is the next best alternative.		
4	Teleconference	Fax, computer conference
Rationale: A teleconference is apt to overly accentuate the status and personality differences among the engineers. Fax or computer conferencing would allow the quality of the ideas to be the central focus of interaction. Moreover, quick feedback is still possible with these media.		
5	Newsletter	Video
Rationale: If employees are already persuaded of the updated system's merit, you can probably use the newsletter. But a video graphically conveys information that requires demonstration, and will educate people about procedures.		

TABLE 15.2

Suggested Media Choices for Scenarios in Table 15.1

IN PRACTICE

Rashmi Sinha illustrates how busy managers combine face-to-face and electronic communication to stay in touch and on top of work across time zones. Sinha, with her husband, Jon Boutelle, and her older brother, Amit Ranjan, founded a company called SlideShare, which operates a website where customers can share PowerPoint presentations. The company is based in San Francisco (where Sinha and Boutelle live); it has 30 employees there and in Delhi, India (where Ranjan lives). With a 12-hour time difference between the locations, the company's workday is essentially around the clock.

When Sinha arrives in the office at 9:30 a.m., she checks her e-mail to identify any concerns that have arisen. When possible, she addresses each concern immediately to avoid having to reread and reconsider the messages later. Sinha delegates voice mail to her office manager, who lets her know if any messages are important. Although she doesn't check messages on her office phone, she does give out her cell phone number to key contacts and answers her cell phone.

Several times a week, the San Francisco staff members assemble with Sinha and Boutelle for a "scrum meeting" at which participants take a few minutes to say what they've accomplished, what they have planned for the day, and what resources they need from others. Sinha's afternoons are spent in face-to-face meetings with customers, advertisers, and others. Between meetings, Sinha keeps track of employees' progress by monitoring status updates on a program called Pivotal Tracker. Each team posts a list of its assignments, and as employees complete them and receive approval, they update their progress for all to see.

In the evenings around 9:00, Sinha checks in with the Delhi staff, mostly engineers. The Delhi employees assemble in a conference room, and Sinha calls them via the Skype online phone service. She also makes a point of talking to Ranjan each day over the phone or via Skype.

With Skype, Sinha likes to use webcams so the meeting participants can see each other and make a better emotional connection. Of course, even with a webcam, online conferencing has less media richness than being in the same room, so Sinha also arranges a trip to Delhi about once a year. Boutelle, who has an engineering background, travels there more frequently.[50]

- How does Sinha apply the advantages and minimize the disadvantages of electronic communication?

Improving Communication Skills

LO 4 Employers are dismayed by college graduates' poor communication skills. A demonstrated ability to communicate effectively makes a job candidate more attractive and distinguishes him or her from others. You can do many things to improve your communication skills, both as a sender and as a receiver.

Improving Sender Skills

To start, be aware that honest, direct, straight talk is important but all too rare. CEOs are often coached on how to slant their messages for different audiences—the investment community, employees, or the board. That's not likely to be straight talk. The focus of the messages can differ, but they can't be inconsistent. People should be able to identify your perspective, your reasoning, and your intentions.[51]

Beyond this basic point, senders can improve their skills in making persuasive presentations, writing, language use, and sending nonverbal messages. Table 15.3 offers some useful tips on formal presentations; the following discussion focuses more on other keys to persuasion.

Presentation and Persuasion Skills Throughout your career, you will be called on to state your case on a variety of issues. You will have information and perhaps an opinion or proposal to present to others. Typically, your goal will be to "sell" your idea. In other words, your challenge will be to persuade others to go along with your personal recommendation. As a leader, you will find that some of your toughest challenges arise when people do not want to do what has to be done. Leaders have to be persuasive to get people on board.[52]

Persuasion is not what many people think.

Your attitude in presenting ideas and persuading others is very important. Persuasion is not what many people think: merely selling an idea or convincing others to see things your way. Don't assume that it takes a "my way or the highway" approach, with a one-shot effort to make a hard sell and resisting compromise.[53] It usually is more constructive to consider persuasion a process of learning from each other and negotiating a shared solution. Persuasive speakers are seen as authentic, which happens when speakers are open with the audience, make a connection, demonstrate passion, and show they are listening as well as speaking. As a speaker, you can practice this kind of authenticity by noticing and adopting the type of body language you use when you're around people you're comfortable with, planning how to engage directly with your listeners, identifying the reasons why you care about your topic, and watching for nonverbal cues as well as fully engaging yourself when you listen to audience comments and questions.[54]

The most powerful and persuasive messages are simple and informative, are told with stories and anecdotes, and convey excitement.[55] People are more likely to

TABLE 15.3
Ten Ways to Add Power to
Your Presentations

"All the great speakers were bad speakers at first." Ralph Waldo Emerson

1. *Spend adequate time on the **content** of your presentation.* It's easy to get so distracted with PowerPoint slides or concern about delivery skills that the actual content of a presentation is neglected. Know your content inside and out; you'll be able to discuss it conversationally and won't be tempted to memorize. If you believe in what you're saying and *own* the material, you will convey enthusiasm and will be more relaxed.

2. *Clearly understand the **objective** of your presentation.* Answer this question with one sentence: "What do I want the audience to believe following this presentation?" Writing down your objective will help you focus on your *bottom line.* Everything else in a presentation—the structure, the words, the visuals—should support your objective.

3. ***Tell** the audience the **purpose** of the presentation.* As the saying goes, "Tell them what you're going to tell them, then tell them, then tell them what you've told them." Use a clear preview statement early on to help the audience know where you're taking them.

4. *Provide **meaning,** not just data.* Today information is widely available; you won't impress people by overloading them with data. People have limited attention spans and want presenters to help *clarify the meaning* of data.

5. ***Practice, practice, practice.*** Appearing polished and relaxed during a presentation requires rehearsal time. Practice making your points in a variety of ways. Above all, don't memorize a presentation's content.

6. *Remember that a presentation is more like a **conversation** than a speech.* Keep your tone conversational, yet professional. Audience members will be much more engaged if they feel you are talking *with* them rather than *at* them. Rely on PowerPoint slides or a broad outline to jog your memory.

7. *Remember the incredible power of **eye contact.*** Look at individual people in the audience. Try to have a series of one-on-one conversations with people in the room. This will calm you and help you connect with your audience.

8. ***Allow imperfection.*** If you forget what you were going to say, simply pause, look at your notes, and go on. Don't "break character" and effusively apologize or giggle or look mortified. Remember that an audience doesn't know your material nearly as well as you do and won't notice many mistakes.

9. *Be prepared to **answer tough questions.*** Try to anticipate the toughest questions you might receive. Plan your answers in advance. If you don't have an answer, acknowledge the fact and offer to get the information later.

10. *Provide a **crisp wrap-up** to a question-and-answer session.* Whenever possible, follow the Q&A period with a brief summary statement. Set up the Q&A session by saying, "We'll take questions for 10 minutes and then have a few closing remarks." This prevents your presentation from just winding down to a weak ending. Also, if you receive hostile or hard-to-answer questions, you'll have a chance to have the final word.

SOURCE: Lynn Hamilton, class handout (with permission).

remember and buy into your message if you can express it as a story that is simple, unexpected, concrete, and credible and that includes emotional content. For example, Nordstrom motivates employees by passing along stories of times when its people have provided extraordinary service, such as warming up customers' cars while they shopped or ironing a shirt so that a customer could wear it to a meeting. And Rubal Jain sold a customer on his India-based express delivery service Safexpress by recounting how the company had delivered 69,000 copies of the latest Harry Potter release to

Financial guru Suze Orman has been ranked as one of the best presenters by *Business Week* magazine for her ability to relay information in an easy-to-understand format. She delivers financial information using clear, concise, and direct language. Great business communicators use simple language to discuss complex issues.

bookstores around the country all at the precise release time—a far more dramatic case than data about on-time deliveries.[56] To be credible, a communicator backs up the message with actions consistent with the words.

Writing Skills   Effective writing is more than correct spelling, punctuation, and grammar (although these help). Good writing above all requires clear, logical thinking.[57] The act of writing can be a powerful aid to thinking because you have to think about what you really want to say and what the logic is behind your message.[58]

You want people to find your e-mail and reports readable and interesting. Strive for clarity, organization, readability, and brevity.[59] Brevity is much appreciated by readers who are overloaded with documents, including e-mail. Help e-mail recipients manage the flood of information by providing specific subject lines, putting your main point at the beginning of the message, limiting paragraphs to five lines or less, and avoiding sarcasm or caustic humor (which can be misinterpreted, especially when readers are scanning messages in a hurry).[60] Use a dictionary and a thesaurus, and avoid fancy words.

Your first draft rarely is as good as it could be. If you have time, revise it. Take the reader into consideration. Go through your entire letter, memo, or report and delete all unnecessary words, sentences, and paragraphs. Use specific, concrete words rather than abstract phrases. Instead of saying, "A period of unfavorable weather set in," say, "It rained every day for a week."

Language   Word choice can enhance or interfere with communication effectiveness. For example, jargon is actually a form of shorthand and can make communication more effective when both the sender and the receiver know the buzzwords. But when the receiver is unfamiliar with the jargon, misunderstandings result. When people from different functional areas or disciplines communicate with one another, misunderstandings often occur because of language barriers. As in writing, simplicity usually helps.

Therefore, whether speaking or writing, you should consider the receiver's background—cultural as well as technical—and adjust your language accordingly. When you are receiving, don't assume that your understanding is the same as the speaker's intentions. Cisco CEO John Chambers, whose background is in business, simply asks the engineering managers in his high-tech company to explain any jargon. He says, "They do it remarkably well."[61] At the same time, Chambers shows respect and enhances his credibility by being truly interested in their work. Whenever Chambers travels with or reviews engineers, he asks them to teach him a topic—and he listens.

The meaning of word choices also can vary by culture. Japanese people use the simple word *hai* (yes) to convey that they understand what is being said; it does not necessarily mean that they agree. Asian businesspeople rarely use the direct "no," using

> "When [cultivated people] look, they see clearly. When they listen, they think of how to hear keenly. . . . In their demeanor, they think of how to be respectful. In their speech, they think of how to be truthful. . . . When in doubt, they think of how to pose questions."
>
> —Confucius

more subtle or tangential ways of disagreeing.[62] Global teams fail when members have difficulties communicating because of language, cultural, and geographic barriers. Heterogeneity harms team functioning at first. But when they develop ways to interact and communicate, teams develop a common identity and perform well.[63]

When conducting business overseas, try to learn something about the other country's language and customs. Americans are less likely to do this than people from some other cultures; most Americans do not consider a foreign language necessary for doing business abroad, and a significant majority of U.S. firms do not require employees sent abroad to know the local language.[64] But those who do will have a big edge over their competitors who do not.[65] Making the effort to learn the local language builds rapport, sets a proper tone for doing business, aids in adjustment to culture shock, and especially can help you "get inside" the other culture.[66] You will learn more about how people think, feel, and behave, both in their lives and in their business dealings.

Of course, even organizations that operate on a local scale benefit from managers and employees taking their audience into account when choosing their words. To see the importance of writing skills for leaders at Zingerman's, read "Management Connection: Progress Report."

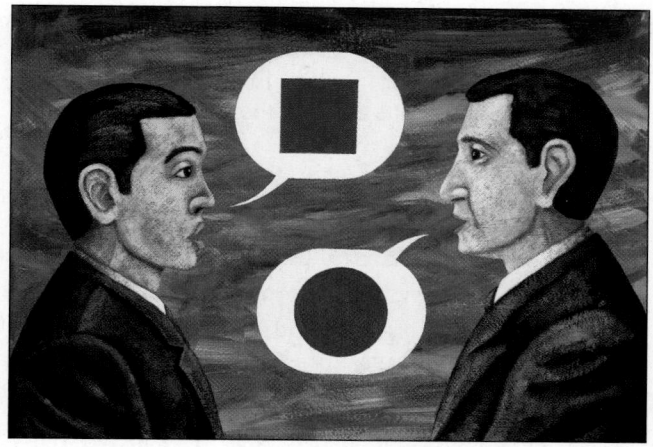

Global teams fail when members have difficulty communicating because of language, cultural, and geographic barriers. What could you do to overcome these barriers?

Those who do will have a big edge over their competitors who do not.

| Manager's Brief | **Progress Report** | Onward |

Management Connection

HOW LEADERS AT ZINGERMAN'S CRAFT AND CONVEY A VISION

Reflecting on the growth of his company from one Ann Arbor delicatessen in 1982 to a collection of nine widely admired, popular, and community-conscious businesses employing hundreds of employees today, Ari Weinzweig says, "It's safe to say we wouldn't be where we are without visioning." For Weinzweig, visioning means developing "a picture of what success will be at a particular time in the future," putting that picture into words employees can understand, and communicating that vision so managers and employees can figure out how to make it a reality.

Early on, cofounders Weinzweig and Paul Saginaw realized they had to make decisions about the company's growth (such as whether to offer franchises of the deli in other locations), and they realized they had certain values to build on. Based on these, they arrived at a vision for their company. They appreciated the clarity that came from a vision, so they began requiring that whenever the company was considering adding a new business, leaders must create a vision for that business.

Weinzweig found that a great vision can emerge when leaders follow several steps of preparation, writing, revising, and sharing the vision. The preparation includes picking the topic (say, vision for the entire organization or a particular unit), picking the time frame (a point within the next 5–10 years), and establishing a positive outlook by listing positive accomplishments or resources. Writing a vision, Weinzweig advises, should start with a quick draft, written from the heart in 30 minutes or less. A list of bullet points or a story is fine, as long as the word *Draft* appears at the top of the document to remind the writer that this is just the start of visioning. Weinzweig encourages personal touches, such as the visioner's personal values and passions related to the businesses. When this step is done, Weinzweig recommends putting the draft aside for a few days.

Next comes the revision process. Good writers recognize that most work can be improved with a fresh reading and input from people with insight. At this stage, Weinzweig recommends adding plenty of specific details, including numbers that provide a measure of success. In addition, the writer should consider whether the vision will inspire the people who read or hear it. Finally, after up to four rounds of revision, Weinzweig says, it's time to share the vision with trusted and respected reviewers—people who have experiences and expertise that will help them offer ideas that are constructive, not destructive. At this point, it's important to keep the focus on description of the vision itself—not on defining action steps, which is a different process. Finally, when reviewers' ideas are taken into account, the vision is ready to be shared.

All the revisions should have helped the writer craft a vision that readers or listeners can picture and will want to help put into action. For example, when Zingerman's Roadhouse decided to expand its commitment to locally sourced food and to serving the community by opening a weekly farmers' market in its parking lot, the leaders wrote a vision that included the following statements:

> It's the longest day of the year; the sun is at its pinnacle of warmth and light. Throngs of people are milling around the Roadhouse parking lot, amazed and excited by the abundance of locally produced goods, ranging from several gorgeous varieties of tomatoes to handmade soap and artisan crafts, to herbs and plants, plus a very strong synergy of Zingerman's items—cheese from the Creamery, breads from the Bakehouse, and the ever-energetic Roadshow crew caffeinating all the vendors and customers. . . .

The West Side Farmers' Market continues to provide our customers with the best products available and serves as a catalyst for community development by offering an educational component and a local music scene.

Applying these methods, Weinzweig, Saginaw, and the managing partners of each business recently completed a company-level visioning process to lay out their vision for what the company will be doing in 2020. Vision 2020 describes Zingerman's growing to 12 to 18 businesses, possibly including new kinds of restaurants, a brewery, a local farm, and a restaurant that charges a sliding scale based on customers' ability to pay. As in the founders' original vision, Vision 2020 makes no provision for franchising, but rather for serving the local community in more varied ways. This is not merely altruism; it is a conviction that each business's uniqueness is an important part of its value. As soon as an idea is franchised, it loses that uniqueness. In addition, Vision 2020 describes the company being run sustainably by fully committed, highly engaged, and happy employees. That vision is almost as irresistible as Zingerman's chewy rye bread or creamy gelato.[67]

- How can Weinzweig's process for writing a vision help managers convey both information and enthusiasm?
- What writing and presentation practices make the farmer's market example effective?

Nonverbal Skills

As you know, people send and interpret signals other than those that are spoken or written. Nonverbal messages can support or undermine the stated message. Often nonverbal cues make a greater impact than other signals. In employees' eyes, managers' actions often speak louder than the words managers choose. Project manager Steve Bailey had already given many presentations when he attended a presentation skills workshop. There a facilitator pointed out Bailey's habit of clasping and unclasping his hands as he spoke. The behavior was distracting and made him appear less in authority. When Bailey stopped making that gesture, he discovered that his audiences tended to be more convinced by his presentations.[68]

In conversation, except when you intend to convey a negative message, you should give nonverbal signals that express warmth, respect, concern, a feeling of equality, and a willingness to listen. Negative nonverbal signals show coolness, disrespect, lack of interest, and a feeling of superiority.[69] The following suggestions can help you send positive nonverbal signals.

First, use *time* appropriately. Avoid keeping your employees waiting to see you. Devote sufficient time to your meetings with them, and communicate frequently with them to signal your interest in their concerns. Second, make your *office arrangement* conducive to open communication. A seating arrangement that avoids separation of people helps establish a warm, cooperative atmosphere (in contrast, an arrangement in which you sit behind your desk and your subordinate sits before you creates a more intimidating, authoritative environment).[70] Third, remember your *body language*.

Research indicates that facial expression and tone of voice can account for 90 percent of the communication between two people.[71] Several nonverbal body signals convey a positive attitude toward the other person: assuming a position close to the person; gesturing frequently; maintaining eye contact; smiling; having an open body orientation, such as facing the other person directly; uncrossing the arms; and leaning forward to convey interest in what the other person is saying.

Silence is an interesting nonverbal signal. The average American is said to spend about twice as many hours per day in conversation as the average Japanese.[72] North Americans tend to talk to fill silences. Japanese allow long silences to develop, believing they can get to know people better. Japanese believe that two people with good rapport will know each other's thoughts. The need to use words implies a lack of understanding.

> Silence is an interesting nonverbal signal.

Nonverbal Signals in Different Countries   Here are just a few nonverbal mistakes that Americans might make in other countries.[73] Nodding the head up and down in Bulgaria means no. The American thumb-and-first-finger circular A-OK gesture is vulgar in Brazil, Singapore, Russia, and Paraguay. The head is sacred in Buddhist cultures, so you must never touch someone's head. In Muslim cultures, never touch or eat with the left hand, which is considered unclean. Crossing your ankle over your knee is rude in Indonesia, Thailand, and Syria. Don't point your finger toward yourself in Germany or Switzerland—it insults the other person.

You also need to correctly interpret the nonverbal signals of others. Chinese scratch their ears and cheeks to show happiness. Greeks puff air after they receive a compliment. Hondurans touch their fingers below their eyes to show disbelief or caution. Japanese indicate embarrassment or "no" by sucking in air and hissing through their teeth. Vietnamese look to the ground with their heads down to show respect. Compared with Americans, Russians use fewer facial expressions, and Scandinavians fewer hand gestures, whereas people in Mediterranean and Latin cultures may gesture and touch more. Brazilians are more likely than Americans to interrupt, Arabs to speak loudly, and Asians to respect silence.

Use these examples not to stereotype but to remember that people in other cultures have different styles and to aid in communication accuracy.

Improving Receiver Skills

Once you become effective at sending oral, written, and nonverbal messages, you are halfway toward becoming a complete communicator. However, you must also develop adequate receiving capabilities. Receivers need good listening, reading, and observational skills.

Listening   In today's demanding work environment, managers need excellent listening skills. Although people frequently assume that good listening is easy and natural, in fact it is difficult and not nearly as common as needed. Catherine Coughlin practiced her listening skills as a customer service representative for Union Electric Company during the summers of the years she was earning her college degree. Whether an individual was calling about an unpaid bill or a power outage, or just looking for an excuse to talk to somebody, Coughlin found that "you've got to respect everyone and their story" and then decide how to respond. Over the following decades, Coughlin used that experience to build a successful career with Southwestern Bell Telephone and its successor companies. She is now a top executive at AT&T and is still committed to careful listening.[74]

reflection
Process by which a person states what he or she believes the other person is saying.

A basic technique called *reflection* will help a manager listen effectively.[75] **Reflection** is a process by which a person states what he or she believes the other person is saying. This technique places a greater emphasis

> "You never learn anything while you're talking."
> —Catherine Coughlin, AT&T[76]

on listening than on talking. When both parties actively engage in reflection, they get into each other's frame of reference rather than listening and responding from their own. The result is more accurate two-way communication.

Besides using reflection, you can improve how well you listen by practicing the techniques described in Table 15.4. For managers, the stakes are high; failure to listen not only causes managers to miss good ideas but can even drive employees away.[77]

Listening begins with personal contact. Staying in the office, keeping the door closed, and eating lunch at your desk are sometimes necessary to get pressing work done, but that is no way to stay on top of what's going on. Better to walk the halls, initiate conversations and go to lunch even with people outside your area, have coffee in a popular gathering place, and maybe even move your desk onto the factory floor.[78]

When a manager takes time to really listen to and get to know people, those same people think, "She's showing an interest in me" or "He's letting me know that I matter" or "She values my ideas and contributions." Trust develops. Listening and learning from others are even more important for innovation than for routine work. Successful change and innovation come through lots of human contact.

Reading   Illiteracy is a significant problem in the United States. Even if illiteracy is not a problem in your organization, reading mistakes are common and costly. As a receiver, for your own benefit, read memos and e-mail as soon as possible, before it's

TABLE 15.4
Ten Keys to Effective Listening

1. *Find an area of interest.* Even if you decide the topic is dull, ask yourself, "What is the speaker saying that I can use?"
2. *Judge content, not delivery.* Don't get caught up in the speaker's personality, mannerisms, speaking voice, or clothing. Instead, try to learn what the speaker knows.
3. *Hold your fire.* Rather than getting immediately excited by what the speaker seems to be saying, withhold evaluation until you understand the speaker's message.
4. *Listen for ideas.* Don't get bogged down in all the facts and details; focus on central ideas.
5. *Be flexible.* Have several systems for note taking, and use the system best suited to the speaker's style. Don't take too many notes or try to force everything said by a disorganized speaker into a formal outline.
6. *Resist distraction.* Close the door, shut off the radio, move closer to the person talking, or ask him or her to speak louder. Don't look out the window or at papers on your desk.
7. *Exercise your mind.* Some people tune out when the material gets difficult. Develop an appetite for a good mental challenge.
8. *Keep your mind open.* Many people get overly emotional when they hear words referring to their most deeply held convictions—for example, *union, subsidy, import, Republican* or *Democrat,* and *big business.* Try not to let your emotions interfere with comprehension.
9. *Capitalize on thought speed.* Take advantage of the fact that most people talk at a rate of about 125 words per minute, but most of us think at about four times that rate. Use those extra 400 words per minute to think about what the speaker is saying rather than turning your thoughts to something else.
10. *Work at listening.* Spend some energy. Don't just pretend you're paying attention. Show interest. Good listening is hard work, but the benefits outweigh the costs.

SOURCE: Ralph G. Nichols, "Listening Is a 10-Part Skill," *Nation's Business* 45 (July 1957), pp. 56–60. Cited in R. C. Huseman, C. M. Logue, and D. L. Freshley, eds., *Readings in Interpersonal and Organizational Communication* (Boston: Allyn & Bacon, 1977).

too late to respond. You may skim most of your reading materials, but read important messages, documents, and passages slowly and carefully. Note important points for later referral. Consider taking courses to increase your reading speed and comprehension skills. Finally, don't limit your reading to items about your particular job skill or technical expertise; read materials that fall outside your immediate concerns.

> You never know when a creative idea that will help you in your work will be inspired by a novel, a biography, a sports story, or an article about a problem in another business or industry.

Observing   Effective communicators are also capable of observing and interpreting nonverbal communications. (As Yogi Berra said, "You can observe a lot by watching.") For example, by reading nonverbal cues, a presenter can determine how her talk is going and adjust her approach if necessary. Some companies train their sales forces to interpret the nonverbal signals of potential customers. People can also decode nonverbal signals to determine whether a sender is being truthful or deceitful. Deceitful communicators tend to maintain less eye contact, make either more or fewer body movements than usual, and smile either too much or too little. Verbally, they offer fewer specifics than do truthful senders.[79]

A vital source of useful observations comes from personally visiting people, plants, and other locations to get a firsthand view.[80] Many corporate executives rely heavily on reports from the field and don't travel to remote locations to observe firsthand what is going on. Reports are no substitute for actually seeing things happen in practice. Frequent visits to the field and careful observation can help a manager develop deep understanding of current operations, future prospects, and ideas for how to fully exploit capabilities.[81]

Of course, you must *accurately interpret* what you observe. A Canadian conducting business with a high-ranking official in Kuwait was surprised that the meeting was held in an open office and was interrupted constantly.[82] He interpreted the lack of a big, private office and secretary to mean that the Kuwaiti was of low rank and uninterested in doing business, and he lost interest in the deal. The Canadian observed the facts accurately, but his perceptual biases and lack of awareness regarding how norms differ across cultures caused him to misinterpret what he saw.

The Japanese are particularly skilled at interpreting every nuance of voice and gesture, putting most Westerners at a disadvantage.[83] When one is conducting business in Asia or other countries, local guides can be invaluable not only to interpret language but to "decode" behavior at meetings, what subtle hints and nonverbal cues mean, who the key people are, and how the decision-making process operates.

Organizational Communication

Being a skilled communicator is essential to being a good manager and team leader. But communication must also be managed throughout the organization. Every minute of every day, countless bits of information are transmitted through an organization. The flow of information affects how well people and units perform. When a group's success depends on discovering new information, individuals who independently tap information from a variety of sources help achieve that success. For evaluating information and arriving at decisions, people in the most effective groups communicate extensively with their team members (a richly connected network). The most productive teams switch back and forth between using centralized networks and using richly connected networks.[84] These patterns of communication may include communications traveling downward, upward, horizontally, and informally within the organization.

Downward Communication

Downward communication refers to the flow of information from higher to lower levels in the organization's hierarchy. Examples include a manager giving an assignment to an assistant, a supervisor making an announcement to his subordinates, and a company president delivering a talk to her management team. Downward communication that provides relevant information enhances employee identification with the company, supportive attitudes, and decisions consistent with the organization's objectives.[85]

People must receive the information they need to perform their jobs and become—and remain—loyal members of the organization. But they often lack adequate information.[86] One problem is *information overload*: they are bombarded with so much information that they fail to absorb everything. Much of the information is not very important, but its volume causes a lot of relevant information to be lost.

A second problem is a *lack of openness* between managers and employees. Managers may believe "No news is good news," "I don't have time to keep them informed of everything they want to know," or "It's none of their business, anyway." Some managers withhold information even if sharing it would be useful.

A third problem is *filtering*, introduced earlier in the chapter. When messages are passed from one person to another, some information is left out. When a message passes through many people, each transmission may cause further information losses. The message can also be distorted as people add their own words or interpretations.

Filtering poses serious problems in organizations. As messages are communicated downward through many organizational levels, much information is lost. The data in Figure 15.2 suggest that by the time messages reach the people for whom they are intended, the receivers may get very little useful information. The smaller the number of authority levels through which communications must pass, the less information will be lost or distorted. Flatter organization offers the advantage of fewer problems caused by filtering of information as it cascades through many layers.

> As messages are communicated downward through many organizational levels, much information is lost.

Coaching   Some of the most important downward communications occur when managers give performance feedback to their direct reports. We discussed earlier the importance of giving feedback and positive reinforcement when it is deserved. It is also important to explicitly discuss poor performance and areas that can be improved.

FIGURE 15.2

Information Loss in Downward Communication

- 100% Board — 0% loss
- 63% Vice presidents — 37% loss
- 56% General managers — 44% loss
- 40% Plant managers — 60% loss
- 30% Supervisors — 70% loss
- 20% Workers — 80% loss

Coaching is dialogue with a goal of helping another be more effective and achieve his or her full potential on the job.[87] When done properly, coaching develops executives and enhances performance.[88] When people have performance problems, or exhibit behaviors that need to be changed, coaching is often the best way to help a person change and succeed. And coaching is not just for poor performers; as even the greatest athletes know, it is for anyone who is good and aspires to excellence. Although coaches for executives sometimes are hired from the outside, coaches from outside your organization may not understand fully the context in which you are working.[89] So don't take advice automatically. The best use of coaches is as sounding boards, helping you think through the potential impact of your ideas, generate new options, and learn from experience.

Companies such as Coca-Cola use coaching as an essential part of their executive development process. When done well, coaching is true dialogue between two committed people engaged in joint problem solving. Thus it is far more than an occasion for highlighting poor performance, delivering reprimands, or giving advice. Good coaching requires achieving real understanding of the problem, the person, and the situation; jointly generating ideas for what to do; and encouraging the person to improve. Good coaches ask a lot of questions, listen well, provide input, and also encourage others to think for themselves. Effective coaching requires honesty, calmness, and supportiveness—all aided by a sincere desire to help. The ultimate and longest-lasting form of help is to help people think through and solve their own problems.

coaching

Dialogue with a goal of helping another be more effective and achieve his or her full potential on the job.

Downward Communication in Difficult Times

Proper downward communication can be particularly valuable during difficult times. During corporate mergers and acquisitions, employees are anxious as they wonder how the changes will affect them. Ideally—and ethically—top management should communicate with employees about the change as early as possible.

But some argue against that approach, maintaining that informing employees about the reorganization might cause them to quit too early. Then too, top management often cloisters itself, prompting rumors and anxiety.

> CEOs and other senior execs are surrounded by lawyers, investment bankers, and so on—people who are paid merely to make the deal happen, not to make it work.

Yet with the people who are affected by the deal, you must increase, not decrease, communication.[90]

In a merger of two *Fortune* 500 companies, two plants received very different information.[91] All employees at both plants received the initial letter from the CEO announcing the merger. But after that, one plant was kept in the dark while the other was continually filled in on what was happening. Top management gave employees information about layoffs; transfers; promotions and demotions; and changes in pay, jobs, and benefits.

Which plant do you think fared better as the difficult transitional months unfolded? In both plants, the merger decreased employees' job satisfaction and commitment to the organization and increased their belief that the company was untrustworthy, dishonest, and uncaring. In the plant whose employees got little information, these problems persisted for a long time. But in the plant where employees received complete information, the situation stabilized and attitudes improved toward their normal levels. Full communication not only helped employees survive an anxious period but also served a symbolic value by signaling care and concern for employees. Without such communications, employee reactions to a merger or acquisition may be so negative as to undermine the corporate strategy and performance.

Open-Book Management

Executives often are proud of their newsletters, staff meetings, videos, and other vehicles of downward communication. More often than

open-book management

Practice of sharing with employees at all levels of the organization vital information previously meant for management's eyes only.

Bottom Line

The more management communicates cost, quality, sustainability, and other data, the more people will care about and pay attention to performance and find new ways to improve.

For employees to be motivated by open-book management, what kinds of information would they need besides sales and profit numbers?

upward communication

Information that flows from lower to higher levels in the organization's hierarchy.

not, the information provided concerns company sports teams, birthdays, and new copy machines. But here is a more unconventional philosophy. **Open-book management** is the practice of sharing with employees at all levels of the organization vital information previously meant for management's eyes only. This information includes financial goals, income statements, budgets, sales, forecasts, and other relevant data about company performance and prospects. This practice is dramatically different from the traditional closed-book approach in which people may or may not have a clue about how the company is doing, may or may not believe the things that management tells them, and may or may not believe that their personal performance makes a difference.

Open-book management is controversial because many managers prefer to keep such information to themselves. Sharing strategic plans and financial information with employees could lead to leaks to competitors or to employee dissatisfaction with compensation. But the companies that share this information claim a favorable impact on motivation and productivity. Laura Ortmann, co-owner of Ginger Bay Salon & Spa in Kirkwood, Missouri, says others in her industry think her commitment to open-book management is strange. But the salon's hair stylists, massage therapists, and nail technicians take a real interest in the sales results they see posted in the break room. When financial results drop below a set level, employees know that the salon will have to start making cuts, so they get involved in looking for creative ways to boost revenue and trim expenses.[92]

Father of scientific management Frederick Taylor, early in the 20th century, would have considered opening the books to all employees "idiotic."[93] But then Jack Stack tried it at Springfield ReManufacturing Corporation, which was on the brink of collapse.[94] The results? Workers were highly motivated and understood the ins and outs of the business. Similarly, at Hilcorp Energy Company, senior managers assemble the 280-plus employees once a month to share data about the company's performance and listen to ideas from the workers. Greg Lalicker, a Hilcorp executive vice president, explains that when employees understand how their work affects profits, they "pull together, not competing against each other."[95]

Upward Communication

Upward communication travels from lower to higher ranks in the hierarchy. Adequate upward communication is important for several reasons.[96] First, managers learn what's going on. Management gains a more accurate picture of subordinates' work, accomplishments, problems, plans, attitudes, and ideas. Second, employees gain from the opportunity to communicate upward. People can relieve some of their frustrations, achieve a stronger sense of participation in the enterprise, and improve morale. Third, effective upward communication facilitates downward communication as good listening becomes a two-way street.

The problems common in upward communication are similar to those for downward communication. Managers, like their subordinates, are bombarded with information and may neglect or miss information from below. Furthermore, some employees are not always open with their bosses; in other words, filtering occurs upward as well as downward. People tend to share only good news with their bosses and suppress bad news because they (1) want to appear competent; (2) mistrust their boss and fear that if he or she finds out about something they have done they will be punished; (3) fear the boss will punish the messenger, even if the reported problem is not that person's fault; or (4) believe they are helping their boss if they shield him or her from problems.

> "Many people believe that if you are doing a good job and accomplishing something, your bosses necessarily know this, but they don't."
> —Jeffrey Pfeffer, professor of organizational behavior, Stanford[97]

For these and other reasons, managers may not learn about important problems. As one leadership expert put it, "If the messages from below say you are doing a flawless job, send back for a more candid assessment."[98]

Managing Upward Communication Generating useful information from below requires managers to both *facilitate* and *motivate* upward communication. For example, they could have an open-door policy and encourage people to use it, have lunch or coffee with employees, use surveys, institute a productivity program for suggestions, or have town hall meetings. They can ask for employee advice, make informal visits to plants, really think about and respond to employee suggestions, and distribute summaries of new ideas and practices inspired by employee suggestions and actions.[99]

Some executives practice MBWA (management by wandering around). That term, coined by Ed Carlson of United Airlines, refers simply to getting out of the office, walking around, and talking frequently and informally with employees.[100] At the headquarters of Secura Insurance in Appleton, Wisconsin, CEO John Bykowski makes a habit of walking through the building to talk with and listen to employees.[101] And in the offices of the *South Florida Sun-Sentinel*, recently retired editor Earl Maucker was known for dropping in to employees' offices and cubicles and for being accessible and frank, so his editorial staff trusted what he said.[102]

Useful upward communication must be reinforced and not punished. The person who tries to talk to the manager about a problem must not be brushed off consistently. An announced open-door policy must truly be open-door. Also, people must trust their supervisor and know that the manager will not hold a grudge if they deliver negative information. To get honesty, managers must truly listen, not punish the messenger for being honest, and act on valid comments.

Horizontal Communication

Much information needs to be shared among people on the same hierarchical level. Such **horizontal communication** can take place among people in the same work team or in different departments. For example, a purchasing agent discusses a problem with a production engineer, and a task force of department heads meets to discuss a particular concern. Communicating with others outside the firm, including potential investors, is another vital type of horizontal communication.[103]

horizontal communication

Information moving between people on the same hierarchical level.

Horizontal communication has several important functions.[104] First, it allows sharing of information, coordination, and problem solving among units. Second, it helps solve conflicts. Third, by allowing interaction among peers, it provides social and emotional support to people. All these factors contribute to morale and effectiveness. For example, the finance–credit and account settlement vice president for Rich Products emphasizes that the staff needs to collaborate with employees in other functions, especially sales and customer service. This horizontal collaboration helps the frozen dessert company ensure that its sales are profitable and that bad debt is kept to a minimum. To foster communication between employees the credit department explains its role in meetings with employees of other departments and learns more about what they do.[106]

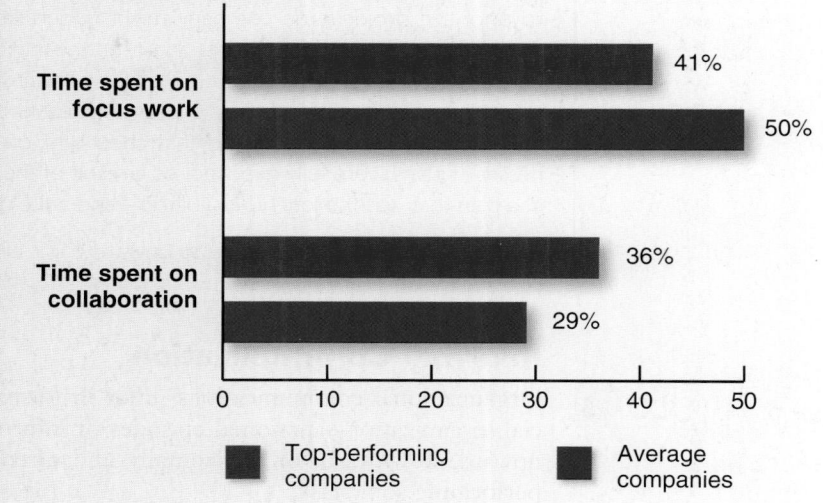

Today's office workers engage in four modes of work: *focus work* (concentrating on a task that may involve thinking, writing, and reflecting), *collaborating* (working with others to generate and evaluate ideas), *learning* (acquiring new knowledge), and *socializing* (developing relationships). Employees of top-performing companies devote more time to the work modes requiring more horizontal communication—including 16 percent more time socializing.[105]

Managing Horizontal Communication   The need for horizontal communication is similar to the need for integration, discussed in Chapter 8. Particularly in complex environments, in which decisions in one unit affect another, information must be shared horizontally. As examples of good horizontal communication, Motorola holds an annual conference for sharing best learnings across functional and business groups throughout the company. NASA colocates scientists from different disciplines. Hewlett-Packard uses common databases for different product groups to share information and ideas.[107]

Applied Materials, a semiconductor equipment manufacturer in Santa Clara, California, took a sophisticated approach to managing horizontal communication. To improve the caliber and efficiency of its information technology (IT) group, the company outsourced routine tasks, cut the in-house IT workforce, and focused the remaining IT employees on supporting strategy. As a result, the IT workers were expected to collaborate with each other (and with customers) to develop and implement creative projects. To improve this kind of collaboration, Applied Materials conducted a survey of the IT staff to determine the existing patterns of communication. Analysis of the survey results showed that about half of the IT employees were, in effect, communication hubs—many of their colleagues consulted with them for ideas and questions. Those highly networked employees weren't necessarily managers; they were people at all levels whom others trusted and respected. The company assembled a team of 12 highly networked IT employees and had them share insights about what conditions affected collaboration in the company. This team identified barriers, and Applied Materials used that information to provide coaching in better communication. A follow-up survey showed that more employees had become highly networked.[108]

IN PRACTICE

In a group gathered to generate or analyze ideas, it is sometimes too easy for everyone to agree with the leader, even if diverse viewpoints would result in a better decision. Thus Richard D. Fain, chairman and chief executive officer of Royal Caribbean Cruises, has found that managing horizontal communications sometimes requires provoking a friendly argument.

Fain learned the value of argument from a mentor, Jay Pritzker, founder of Hyatt Hotels, who served on the board of directors of Fain's company. As a director, Fain recalls, Pritzker would play devil's advocate: "He would argue vociferously against whatever I was proposing and question me in a highly skeptical tone." He would persist until another board member took his side—and then he would concede that Fain had been right all along. But the questions helped the directors fully think through the idea.

Fain applied the idea of provoking positive conflict when he assembled company leaders to prioritize projects the company might undertake. He assembled two teams of leaders, drawn from various departments and representing the company's different cruise lines, and he assigned the teams to debate either for or against each idea. The teams had two months to prepare. As a result of their efforts, the teams delivered well-prepared arguments with conviction. Viewpoints surfaced that shed light on previously unknown situations. Weaknesses in plans were fully exposed. As a result of the debate, the meeting participants arrived at a plan that was thoroughly evaluated—and quite different from what Fain had expected.[109]

• How might Fain's ideas apply to upward communication?

Informal Communication

LO 6   Organizational communications differ in formality. *Formal communications* are official, organization-sanctioned episodes of information transmission. They can move upward, downward, or horizontally and often are prearranged and necessary for performing some task.

Informal communication is more unofficial. People gossip; employees complain about their bosses; people talk about their favorite sports teams; work teams tell newcomers how to get by.[110]

The **grapevine** is the social network of informal communications. Informal networks provide people with information, help them solve problems, and teach them how to do their work successfully. You should develop a good network of people willing and able to help.[111] However, the grapevine can be destructive when irrelevant or erroneous gossip and rumors proliferate and harm operations.[112]

grapevine

Informal communication network.

What does this mean for you personally? Don't engage in e-gossip. Embarrassing episodes become public, and lawsuits based on defamation of character and invasion of privacy have used e-mail evidence. But don't avoid the grapevine, either.[113] Listen, but evaluate before believing what you hear. Who is the source? How credible is he or she? Does the rumor make sense? Is it consistent or inconsistent with other things you know or have heard? Seek more information. Don't stir the pot.

What does this mean for you personally?

Managing Informal Communication Rumors start over any number of topics, including who's leaving, who's getting a promotion, salaries, job security, and costly mistakes. Rumors can destroy people's faith and trust in the company—and in each other. But the grapevine cannot be eliminated. Therefore, managers need to *work with* the grapevine.

The grapevine can be managed in several ways.[114] First, if a manager hears a story that could get out of hand, he or she should *talk to the key people* involved to get the facts and their perspectives. Don't allow malicious gossip.

Second, suggestions for *preventing* rumors from starting include explaining events that are important but have not been explained, dispelling uncertainties by providing facts, and working to establish open communications and trust over time. These efforts are especially important during times of uncertainty, such as after a merger or lay-

No one knows how rumors get started, but we do know they happen. The grapevine can be managed if you talk to the key people involved, suggest ways to prevent the rumors, and neutralize rumors once they've started.

off or when sales slow down, because rumors increase along with anxiety. For example, when advertising revenues fell at R. H. Donnelley, which publishes yellow-pages directories, management stepped up efforts to make sure employees heard any company news straight from management, rather than on the news. Donnelley also encouraged its managers to make regular visits to salespeople to answer their questions.[115]

Third, *neutralize* rumors once they have started. Disregard a rumor if it is ridiculous; openly confirm any parts that are true; make public comments (no comment is seen as a confirmation of the rumor); deny the rumor, if the denial is based in truth (don't make false denials); make sure communications about the issue are consistent; select a spokesperson of appropriate rank and knowledge; and hold town meetings if needed.[116]

Boundarylessness

Many executives and management scholars today consider free access to information in all directions to be an organizational imperative. Jack Welch, when he was CEO of General Electric, coined the term *boundarylessness*. A **boundaryless organization** is one in which no barriers to information flow exist. Instead of separating people, jobs, processes, and places with boundaries, ideas, information, decisions, and actions move to where they are most needed.[117] This free flow does not imply a random free-for-all of unlimited communication and information overload. It implies information

 7

boundaryless organization

Organization in which there are no barriers to information flow.

available *as needed* moving quickly and easily enough so that the organization functions far better as a whole than as separate parts.

GE's chief learning officer used the metaphor of the organization as a house having three kinds of boundaries: the floors and ceilings, the walls that separate the rooms, and the outside walls. These barriers correspond in organizations to the boundaries between different organizational levels, different units and departments, and the organization and its external stakeholders—for example, suppliers and customers. GE adds a fourth wall: global boundaries separating domestic from global operations.[118]

GE's famous Workout program is a series of meetings for business members across multiple hierarchical levels, characterized by extremely frank, tough discussions that break down vertical boundaries. Workout has involved over hundreds of thousands of GE people; in any given week thousands may be participating in a Workout program.[119] Workout is also done with customers and suppliers, breaking down outside boundaries. GE has also reached out to the community by providing this expertise to nonprofits, such as CommonBond Communities, a provider of affordable housing. A GE employee led a Workout session in which CommonBond employees identified how to improve processes and horizontal communication.[120]

GE uses plenty of other techniques to break down boundaries, as well. It relentlessly benchmarks competitors and companies in other industries to learn best practices all over the world. GE places different functions together physically, such as engineering and manufacturing. It shares services across units. And it sometimes shares physical locations with its customers.

Boundaryless organizations intentionally create dialogue across boundaries, turning barriers into permeable membranes. As the GE people put it, people from different parts of the organization need to learn "how to talk."[121] They must also learn "how to walk." That is, dialogue is essential, but it must be followed by commensurate action. To see how the leaders of Zingerman's foster this kind of communication and action among the various businesses, read "Management Connection: Onward."

Manager's Brief   Progress Report   **Onward**

Management Connection

ZINGERMAN'S BUSINESSES OPEN THE BOOKS FOR EMPLOYEES

Inspirational vision statements show the employees of Zingerman's Community of Businesses where their leaders hope they will go. To help employees see whether they are on the road to realizing the vision, managers at Zingerman's use another communication practice: open-book management.

Open-book management is an extension of sharing information about the company's plans and ideals. It includes giving the employees information about expenses, operating margins, revenues, and profits. But for that information to make a difference, open-book management also includes training employees to understand the information and engaging in a dialogue with them, inviting questions and ideas for improvement. As Weinzweig recently told a reporter, "Our employees really get a chance to participate in the business" as they

learn to manage the money and other aspects of running a company.

At Zingerman's, whiteboards posted in each business display that business's sales, expenses, debts, and other financial measures. Once a week, each department meets to discuss the previous week's performance and forecasts for the coming week. Each employee is given responsibility for a line item on his or her group's operating report. For one year, the employee tracks that particular piece of financial information. For example, Izaak Vander Broek, a manager at Zingerman's Delicatessen, recently was responsible for reporting the cost of mistakes made in the deli. As Vander Broek and other employees see how their line item affects the group's overall performance, they tend to care about it more and look for ways to improve results. Financial performance stops looking like mere rows of numbers and becomes seen as the outcome of factors that often can be controlled.

As employees become more engaged, the company has to be prepared for more upward communication, and Zingerman's is ready. As Weinzweig puts it, managers "might not like it, but low-level employees are going to challenge high-level employees." He sees those challenges as a plus now, but years ago, when Zingerman's introduced open-book management, Weinzweig and Saginaw were doubtful that employees would attend the weekly staff meetings, called huddles, to review results. However, employee participation is what makes open-book management deliver results because employees have input into decisions, and they get to see whether their ideas are working. Therefore, the open-book management process makes participating in huddles voluntary but encourages participation. For example, making attendance at the huddles one of the measures tracked on the whiteboards gives participants an incentive to improve that performance measure.

Michael Rogers, vice president of communications for the Small Business Association of Michigan, thinks open-book management makes perfect sense for the Web 2.0 generation. Today's employees are increasingly sharing information on social networking websites, so they are used to being "open and up-front." Rogers says, "If there are no secrets in a company and they are up-front about how they operate, employees are more likely to buy into the mission instead of simply collecting a paycheck."

In a "community" of nine different businesses, upward and downward communication paths aren't enough. The company also has to foster communication among the businesses to ensure that they are all following the same principles and contributing to the overall vision. To ensure formal lateral communication, Zingerman's brings together all the business partners (heads of the business units) every other week to share performance information, troubleshoot any problems that have arisen, and plan for what's ahead. Business-level decisions are made only after the relevant business partners have shared their ideas and sought a consensus.

This level of downward, upward, and lateral communication takes tremendous effort. However, it seems to have paid off in a company that has enjoyed steady growth and tremendous commitment of its employees in an industry dominated by low-wage, high-turnover jobs.[122]

- Most food service jobs do not require a high level of education. What challenges would you expect in using open-book management with employees in this line of work?
- How would you expect Zingerman's approach to communication to help it weather business challenges such as the recent economic downturn?

KEY TERMS

SUMMARY OF LEARNING OBJECTIVES

Now that you have studied Chapter 15, you should be able to:

LO 1 Discuss important advantages of two-way communication.

One-way communication flows from the sender to the receiver, with no feedback loop. In two-way communication, each person is both a sender and a receiver as both parties provide and react to information. One-way communication is faster and easier but less accurate than two-way; two-way communication is slower and more difficult but is more accurate and results in better performance.

LO 2 Identify communication problems to avoid.

The communication process involves a sender who conveys information to a receiver. Problems in communication can occur in all stages: encoding, transmission, decoding, and interpreting. Noise in the system further complicates communication, creating more distortion. Moreover, feedback may be unavailable or misleading. Subjective perceptions and filtering add to the possibility of error.

LO 3 Describe when and how to use the various communication channels.

Communications are sent through oral, written, and electronic channels. All have important advantages and disadvantages that should be considered before choosing a channel. Electronic media have a huge impact on interpersonal and organizational communications and make possible the virtual office. Key advantages of electronic media are speed, cost, and efficiency, but the downsides are also significant, including information overload.

Media richness, or how much and what sort of information a channel conveys, is one factor to consider as you decide which channels to use and how to use them both efficiently and effectively.

 Summarize ways to become a better "sender" and "receiver" of information.

Practice writing, be critical of your work, and revise. Train yourself as a speaker. Use language carefully and well, and work to overcome cross-cultural language differences. Be alert to the nonverbal signals that you send, including your use of time as perceived by other people. Know the common bad listening habits, and work to overcome them. Read widely, and engage in careful, firsthand observation and interpretation.

 Explain how to improve downward, upward, and horizontal communication.

Actively manage communications in all directions. Engage in two-way communication more than one-way. Make information available to others. Useful approaches to downward communication include coaching, special communications during difficult periods, and open-book management. You should also both facilitate and motivate people to communicate upward. Many mechanisms exist for enhancing horizontal communications.

LO 6 Summarize how to work with the company grapevine.

The informal flow of information can contribute as much as formal communication can to organizational effectiveness and morale. Managers must understand that the grapevine cannot be eliminated and should be managed actively. Many of the suggestions for managing formal communications apply also to managing the grapevine. Moreover, managers can take steps to prevent rumors or neutralize the ones that arise.

LO 7 Describe the boundaryless organization and its advantages.

Boundaries—psychological if not physical—exist between different organizational levels, units, and organizations and external stakeholders. The ideal boundaryless organization is one in which no barriers to information flow exist. Ideas, information, decisions, and actions move to where they are most needed. Information is available as needed and freely accessible so that the organization as a whole functions far better than as separate parts.

DISCUSSION QUESTIONS

1. Think of an occasion when you faced a miscommunication problem. What do you think caused the problem? How do you think it should have been handled better?

2. Have you ever *not* given someone information or opinions that perhaps you should have? Why? Was it the right thing to do? Why or why not? What would cause you to be glad that you provided (or withheld) negative or difficult information? What would cause you to regret providing/withholding it?

3. Think back to discussions you have heard or participated in. Consider the differences between one-way and two-way communication. How can two "one-ways" be turned into a true "two-way"?

4. Share with the class some of your experiences—both good and bad—with electronic media.

5. Report examples of mixed signals you have received (or sent). How can you reduce the potential for misunderstanding and misperception as you communicate with others?

6. What makes you want to say to someone, "You're not listening"?

7. What do you think about the practice of open-book management? What would you think about it if you were running your own company?

8. Discuss organizational rumors you have heard: what they were about, how they got started, how accurate they were,

and how people reacted to them. What lessons can you learn from these episodes?

9. Refer to the section on "The Virtual Office." What do you think will be the long-term impact of the mobile office on job satisfaction and performance? If you were a manager, how would you maximize the benefits and minimize the drawbacks? If you worked in this environment, how would you manage yourself to maximize your performance and avoid burnout?

10. Have you ever made or seen mistakes due to people not speaking a common language well? How do you or will you deal with others who do not speak the same language as you?

11. Have you ever tried to coach someone? What did you do well, and what mistakes did you make? How can you become a better coach?

12. Have you ever been coached by someone? What did he or she do well, and what mistakes were made? How was it for you to be on the receiving end of the coaching, and how did you respond? What is required to be successful as the "receiver" of someone else's coaching attempts?

13. Think about how companies communicate with Wall Street and the media, and how analysts on TV communicate with viewers. What concepts from the chapter apply, and how can you become a more astute "consumer" of such information?

EXPERIENTIAL EXERCISES

15.1   NONVERBAL COMMUNICATION

OBJECTIVE
To become more conscious of nonverbal messages.

INSTRUCTIONS
Following is a list of nonverbal communication methods. Pick a day on which you will attempt to keep track of these methods.

Think back at the end of the day to three people with whom you communicated in some way. Record how you responded to these people in terms of their nonverbal communication methods. Identify those that had the greatest and least effect on your behavior.

Nonverbal Communication Worksheet

Medium	What Was the Message?	How Did You Respond?	Which Affected Your Behavior Most and Least?
How they shook hands			
Their posture			
Their facial expressions			
Their appearance			
Their voice tones			
Their smiles			
The expressions in their eyes			
Their confidence			
The way they moved			
The way they stood			
How close they stood to you			
How they smelled			
Symbols or gestures they used			
How loudly they spoke			

SOURCE: Excerpted from Laurence R. Jauch, Arthur G. Bedian, Sally A. Coltin, and William F. Glueck, *The Managerial Experience: Cases, Exercises, and Readings*, 5th ed. Copyright © 1989. South-Western, a part of Cengage Learning, Inc. Reproduced by permission. www.cengage.com/permissions

15.2   LISTENING SKILLS SURVEY

OBJECTIVES
1. To measure your skills as a listener.
2. To gain insight into the factors that determine good listening habits.
3. To demonstrate how you can become a better listener.

INSTRUCTIONS
1. Working alone, complete the Listening Skills Survey.
2. In small groups, compare scores, discuss survey test items, and prepare responses to the discussion questions.
3. After the class reconvenes, group spokespersons present group findings.

DISCUSSION QUESTIONS
1. In what ways did students' responses on the survey agree or disagree?
2. What do you think accounts for the differences?
3. How can the results of this survey be put to practical use?

Listening Skills Survey

To measure your listening skills, complete the following survey by circling the degree to which you agree with each statement.

	Strongly Agree	Agree	Neither Agree nor Disagree	Disagree	Strongly Disagree
1. I tend to be patient with the speaker, making sure she or he is finished speaking before I respond in any fashion.	5	4	3	2	1
2. When listening I don't doodle or fiddle with papers and things that might distract me from the speaker.	5	4	3	2	1
3. I attempt to understand the speaker's point of view.	5	4	3	2	1
4. I try not to put the speaker on the defensive by arguing or criticizing.	5	4	3	2	1
5. When I listen, I focus on the speaker's feelings.	5	4	3	2	1
6. I let a speaker's annoying mannerisms distract me.	5	4	3	2	1
7. While the speaker is talking, I watch carefully for facial expressions and other types of body language.	5	4	3	2	1
8. I never talk when the other person is trying to say something.	5	4	3	2	1
9. During a conversation, a period of silence seems awkward to me.	5	4	3	2	1
10. I want people to just give me the facts and allow me to make up my own mind.	5	4	3	2	1
11. When the speaker is finished, I respond to his or her feelings.	5	4	3	2	1
12. I don't evaluate the speaker's words until she or he is finished talking.	5	4	3	2	1
13. I formulate my response while the speaker is still talking.	5	4	3	2	1
14. I never pretend that I'm listening when I'm not.	5	4	3	2	1
15. I can focus on message content even if the delivery is poor.	5	4	3	2	1
16. I encourage the speaker with frequent nods, smiles, and other forms of body language.	5	4	3	2	1
17. Sometimes I can predict what someone is going to say before she or he says it.	5	4	3	2	1
18. Even if a speaker makes me angry, I hold my temper.	5	4	3	2	1
19. I maintain good eye contact with the speaker.	5	4	3	2	1
20. I try to focus on the speaker's message, not his or her delivery.	5	4	3	2	1
21. If I am confused by a statement someone makes, I never respond until I have asked for and received adequate clarification.	5	4	3	2	1

15.3   ACTIVE LISTENING

This exercise involves triads. Each triad counts off into threes: 1, 2, 3, 1, 2, 3, and so on. In the first round, all the 1s in their respective triads take the pro position (see the topics given later in exercise), all the 2s take the con position, and all the 3s act as observers. After a topic is given, two individuals representing opposing viewpoints have one minute to collect their thoughts, and then five to seven minutes to arrive at a *mutually agreeable position* on that topic.

The observer should use the form here to capture *actual examples* of what the individuals said or did that indicated active and less-than-active listening. When time is called, the pro individuals share their opinion of which listening behaviors they performed well and which ones they'd like to improve.

Then the con individuals do the same. Finally, the observers share their observations and insights, using examples to reinforce their feedback.

If additional rounds are used, rotate the roles so that each person plays a speaking role, and if possible an observing role.

Round 1:
Topic selected: _____
Notes:

Round 2:
Topic selected: _____
Notes:

Listening Feedback Form

Indicators of Active Listening	Pro	Con
1. Asked questions for clarification		
2. Paraphrased the opposing view		
3. Responded to nonverbal cues (e.g., body posture, tone of voice)		
4. Appeared to move toward a mutually satisfying solution		
Indicators of Less-Than-Active Listening		
5. Interrupted before allowing the other person to finish		
6. Was defensive about her or his position		
7. Appeared to dominate the conversation		
8. Ignored nonverbal cues		

Potential topics to be used:
1. Gun control
2. Capital punishment
3. Race as a criterion for college admission
4. Prison reform
5. U.S. intervention in wars outside of the United States
6. Legalization of marijuana
7. Mandatory armed forces draft
8. Interracial adoption
9. Premarital and extramarital sex
10. Prayer in schools
11. Diversity in the workplace
12. Pornography on the Internet

QUESTIONS

1. Did you arrive at a mutually agreeable solution? What helped you get there?
2. What were some factors that hindered this process?
3. How comfortable did you feel "arguing" the position you were given? How did this influence your ability to actively listen?
4. If the position you were given was exactly opposite your values or beliefs, do you see this topic differently now than before the exercise?
5. What steps can you take to improve your ability to listen actively to friends or associates, especially when you don't agree with their viewpoint?

CONCLUDING CASE

BEST TRUST BANK

Best Trust Bank attracts accounts from households and businesses based on its broad name recognition and reputation for integrity. In this way, Best Trust has grown to one of the world's top 25 banks. Its 73,000 employees work at headquarters and in facilities located in 47 different countries.

One of those employees is Paul Wysinsky, who in the 1970s took an entry-level job as a bank teller. As he developed a track record of satisfying customers, working efficiently, and cooperating well with others on his team, Paul moved up to teller supervisor, branch manager, and operations manager. He took business courses during the evening, earned a master's degree, and worked his way up through middle management positions. Twenty years later, he was offered a vice president's job in the human resources division, responsible for recruiting and retaining Best Trust's employees in Houston. Eager to learn about a new part of the company, Paul tackled the new responsibilities so well that when there was an opening for a new executive vice president in charge of corporate human resources, Paul was tapped to run all of HR.

The nature of Paul's work communications changed considerably as he rose through the ranks. When Paul was a teller, he looked forward to chatting with his coworkers during breaks; their enjoyment of each other's company made the days pass pleasantly. His supervisor checked in with him regularly to make sure Paul understood his job. His favorite responsibility, though, was greeting customers and listening to them carefully, trying to guess the unspoken needs that Best Trust might be able to meet. When customers were upset about a problem, he used to get nervous; but with experience, he became an expert at listening attentively, helping the customer find the best possible solution, and speaking in a respectful tone that almost always soothed any frayed nerves.

Now that Paul is an executive vice president, he rarely talks with Best Trust's customers, and more of his communications are structured and formal. Although he cares about attracting, motivating, and retaining employees in all positions, he knows he cannot possibly have a dialogue with 73,000 people in dozens of countries. In fact, he can't even have personal conversations with all of the HR employees—Best Trust has more than 800 of them, including several at each facility.

Consequently, Paul looks for a variety of ways to communicate. He meets weekly with all the department and functional heads involved in formulating strategy. The meeting's agenda includes reviewing HR issues such as leadership development, succession planning, diversity management, and employee satisfaction. Paul is well prepared because he meets at least weekly with each of the managers who report directly to him. In these one-on-one meetings, Paul and the manager review progress on the issues handled by that manager. Paul also uses those meetings to learn what challenges the manager is facing so he can offer coaching and encouragement. And Paul looks for ways to meet with as many employees outside HR as he can. For example, he attends an annual employee recognition gathering held to honor the company's 800 top-performing employees. There he talks to as many people as he can. He asks open-ended questions such as "What are you happy about at Best Trust? What could we do better?"

Talking one-on-one to employees can feel like an escape from one of the chief annoyances of his job: poorly written messages from many of the bank's middle managers. It seems that Best Trust has excelled at finding people with strong analytic and customer service skills, but many of these people stumble at presenting an idea or summarizing their progress in e-mails and reports. Paul feels intense time pressure, and if he gets a suggestion but can't figure out the main idea in the first couple of sentences, he simply passes it to one of his managers for a possible follow-up. Paul suspects that good ideas and real problems are being missed. Rambling reports and presentations loaded with jargon seem to have become a norm at Best Trust, and Paul is thinking about adding a new training program to improve writing skills.

To get out the word about the bank's policies, benefits, and other initiatives, Paul uses a variety of media. He gives presentations at events such as the employee recognition gathering and at branches around the world. Four times a year, he records a video that is posted on the bank's intranet. Topics range from a summary of HR resources to interviews with key leaders at Best Trust. Also on the intranet, Paul leads regular town hall meetings, a live video feed that allows employees to post questions and ideas, which Paul and other executives answer immediately on the video.

Promotions to the executive level are not the only reason communication has changed for Paul at Best Trust. Another source of change is technology. When Paul was a teller, the Internet was just a concept, and transmitting data online was a major undertaking that required computer experts. Now the Internet is a basic tool. On the plus side, it helps Paul deliver information efficiently and keep up with far-flung colleagues. But Paul also has a whole set of policy concerns related to the Internet, such as whether to allow employees to access social networking sites and how closely to monitor blogs and other public information for company-related posts. When Paul thinks about it, he realizes that his communication skills have barely grown as fast as the communication demands of his work.

QUESTIONS

1. How has the media richness of Paul's communications changed since the days when he was a teller?

2. What sender and receiver skills are described in this case? Which ones need improvement? Offer one suggestion for improving the weak skills.

3. How might Paul improve upward communication and the communication culture more generally at Best Trust?

PART FOUR   SUPPORTING CASE

Leading and Motivating When Disaster Strikes: Magna Exteriors and Interiors

The name of Magna Exteriors and Interiors Corporation captures its product mix of vehicle components that give each car or truck model its distinctive look. Some of Magna's exterior products are trim, roof systems, body panels, and front and rear end fascia; interior products include trim, cockpit systems, and cargo management systems. Nowadays auto companies don't make all these components, but instead create the designs and handle the final assembly of components from suppliers such as Magna, delivered to the auto company as needed to meet production plans.

Magna Exteriors and Interiors is a unit of Magna International, which describes itself as "the most diversified automotive supplier in the world." Magna has 263 manufacturing operations plus sales and engineering centers in 26 countries of North America, South America, Africa, Europe, and Asia. These meet the needs of more than two dozen customers, including General Motors, Ford, Chrysler, Toyota, Mack, Harley Davidson, Freightliner, and Volkswagen. The customers sell very different kinds of vehicles, and it is expensive to build and transport large components, so Magna's factories need to be close to customers both geographically and in their working relationships.

Meeting these requirements suddenly became a problem for Magna's factory in Howell, Michigan, on a recent Wednesday evening in March. A fire started on an assembly line at the facility, which makes interior trim such as rear window trays, door panels, and skins for instrument panels. Fortunately the hundred workers who were finishing up the afternoon shift all escaped safely.

The Howell facility employs about 450 workers. Its customers include 16 GM, Ford, Chrysler, Nissan, and Mazda assembly plants. Forecasting a shortage of parts, some of its customers slowed production and canceled shifts in the days immediately after the fire. Magna's managers knew they needed to scramble, or employees would be out of work and important customers would be lost. Robert Brownlee, president of Magna Exteriors and Interiors North America, decided the Howell facility should be running again within just two days. Meeting that goal would require an all-out effort.

While the firefighters were still battling the blaze, Brownlee conferred by phone with his top managers, figuring out what they should do first. Since they couldn't yet assess the extent of the damages, they had to work with a worst-case scenario: destruction of the entire building. They identified four Magna facilities making similar products, where they could ship the Howell plant's tooling on flatbed trucks, if need be. That night, Brownlee directed all four of the plants to increase production and build up their inventories in case they would be needed for the Howell plant's customers.

Next the managers set up a reconstruction team, including electricians, pipe fitters, millwrights, mechanics, toolmakers, and information technology specialists. The team assembled in Howell with a structural engineer, awaiting permission to enter the damaged building. On Thursday night, about 24 hours after the fire, the fire department let the team enter the plant. The structural engineer determined that the fire had been contained in one part of the plant. About 30 percent of the plant, representing one out of four production sectors, was destroyed beyond repair. One of the four remaining production sectors had largely escaped damage.

Now the clock was ticking on Brownlee's two-day recovery goal. On Friday morning, workers pulled damaged tooling out of the rubble and had it moved to Brighton, a city 12 miles away, where they cleaned it and set up a temporary assembly line in a Magna warehouse. Back in Howell, the reconstruction team was building a temporary wall to seal off the undamaged part of the facility and repairing the roof. The heating and electrical systems were destroyed, so they brought in a dozen diesel generators to power heaters and lighting. Until the roof was repaired, they coped with Michigan's wintry March weather by wearing snowmobile suits while clearing out debris and damaged products, working around the clock.

The next morning, spirits rose when power was restored to the least-damaged sector, and the lights came back on. Workers continued to repair, clean, and rewire the tooling. By Saturday night, workers were able to restart some of the machinery and do test runs. Unfortunately they ran into problems with each attempt. Managers were scrambling to keep on top of the plant reconstruction and the attempts to restart machinery. Brownlee saw that this was too much responsibility. He called together the managers, put each one in charge of relaunching one product line, and directed them to put a subordinate in charge of every other duty, including reconstruction.

The efforts to restart continued as representatives from every customer monitored the progress. Magna gave customers daily updates, and as each assembly line resumed, the relevant customer's representative signed off as part of the quality-control practices. By Sunday, limited production had begun at the Howell plant. Six days after the fire department determined that the fire was extinguished, the Howell plant was running at 80 percent of capacity, and its temporary line in Brighton handled the remaining production.

In a statement to the media, the company publicly thanked "the Magna Howell employees who continue to do whatever it takes to meet customer requirements; the Magna group office employees and Magna employees from numerous other divisions who have come to support the effort," the company's contractors and customers, the community's firefighters, and others who helped after the fire.

QUESTIONS

1. As a leader, what vision did Robert Brownlee offer? What combination of task performance and group maintenance behaviors did he use? Was this the appropriate combination after the fire? Why or why not?

2. What do you think the Magna managers and employees were motivated by most after the fire? Why?

3. Management set up a cross-functional reconstruction team, but there is no evidence that this was a self-managed team. Would a self-managed team have been more effective? Why or why not?

SOURCES: D. Sedgwick, "Five-Alarm Planning," *Crain's Detroit Business*, April 18, 2011, Business & Company Resource Center, http://galenet.galegroup.com; Magna International, "About Magna Exteriors and Interiors," http://www.magna.com; T. Van Alphen, "Magna Plant Resumes Full Deliveries after Fire," *Toronto Star*, March 10, 2011, http://www.thestar.com; and Magna International, "Magna Atreum Howell Plant Back in Business Six Days after Fire," news release, March 9, 2011, http://www.magna.com.

16 Managerial Control

LEARNING OBJECTIVES

After studying Chapter 16, you will be able to:

LO 1   Explain why companies develop control systems for employees. p. 566

LO 2   Summarize how to design a basic bureaucratic control system. p. 567

LO 3   Describe the purposes for using budgets as a control device. p. 576

LO 4   Define basic types of financial statements and financial ratios used as controls. p. 579

LO 5   List procedures for implementing effective control systems. p. 584

LO 6   Identify ways in which organizations use market control mechanisms. p. 590

LO 7   Discuss the use of clan control in an empowered organization. p. 592

Management Connection

CONTROLS KEEP SOUTHWEST AIRLINES ON COURSE TO PROFITABILITY

Southwest Airlines has traveled far in the four decades since its founding as a Dallas-based air carrier that flew three Boeing 737s between Houston, Dallas, and San Antonio, Texas. Today it operates over 3,400 flights a day, serving over 70 cities. Based on the number of domestic passengers, it is the largest U.S. carrier (it ranks fifth based on miles flown). Furthermore, as other U.S. airlines have suffered losses and even bankruptcies, Southwest has managed to turn a profit for 38 years in a row. Even during the recent recession, when it posted losses in several quarters, Southwest managed to earn annual profits, and it outperformed American, Delta, and United Continental.

At the heart of Southwest Airlines's success is its mission: "dedication to the highest quality of customer service delivered with a sense of warmth, friendliness, individual pride, and company spirit." Although the company is described as a "discount" carrier and has promoted low fares, others can say the same. What sets Southwest apart is that it tries to make flying fun. A sense of whimsy pervades the company, whether

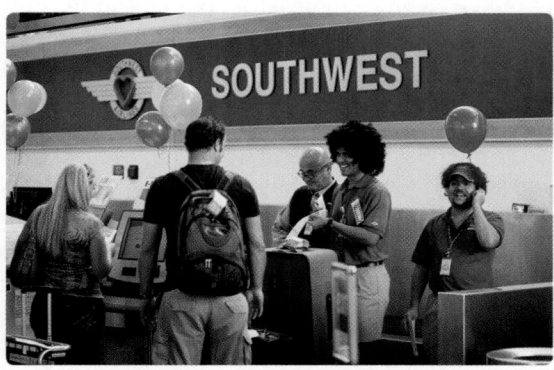

Southwest recently ranked first for its luggage policy, best value, best check-in experience (for domestic airlines), best customer on-time estimate, and top website. Readers of *Smarter Travel* voted Southwest their favorite domestic airline and named it as having the friendliest flight attendants and crew. The American Customer Satisfaction Index consistently gives Southwest Airlines the highest marks in its industry.

Southwest Airlines has become a leader in the airline industry by excelling in superior service, low costs, and cautious funding of growth. As you read this chapter, think about the kinds of control measures and processes that can help a company manage these sometimes-conflicting drivers of success.

in flight attendants who burst into song or the nickname of Southwest's flight between two bastions of high tech, Austin, Texas, and San Jose, California: the "nerd bird." More practically, Southwest aims to make traveling pleasurable by taking care of things that matter to passengers most, such as not charging a fee for checking baggage or changing a reservation.

Success in delivering superior service shows up in travelers' reviews. In the Zagat Airline Survey,

Of course, fun and friendliness do not pay the bills. Even as Southwest instills its distinctive culture in its employees, its managers have to think about how to keep revenues high enough and costs low enough to make a fair profit at the volume of traffic the business can generate. On the revenue side, they have to monitor travelers' buying behavior, especially changes in sales volume in response to price hikes or cuts. In some cases, travelers will actually pay more to fly on

Southwest, perhaps to get frequent-flier miles, enjoy the friendly service, or avoid the dreaded baggage-handling fees. On the cost side, Southwest's managers are cautious about adding routes and flights because adding capacity is expensive when it involves purchasing aircraft and hiring employees. They also have to monitor fuel costs and look for ways to lock in the lowest possible prices for future purchases. When costs go up despite these efforts, the company's excellent reputation with fliers enables it to raise prices more than some less popular competitors can get away with.

Careful control and steady profitability are not merely evidence of past success. They also position the company for future growth. When Southwest's managers determined that a drop in travel volume made it impossible to generate more growth by serving its existing routes, they could turn to a sizable pool of cash on hand to acquire AirTran Airways. Buying AirTran (for $1.4 billion, including $670 million in cash plus company stock) gave Southwest important new routes, including access to the travel hub of Atlanta's airport as well as its first few international routes, serving Mexico and the Caribbean.[2]

Bottom Line

Control is essential for the attainment of any management objective.

What happens in the absence of control?

Even well-intentioned people may not know whether they are directing their efforts toward the activities that are most important.

control

Any process that directs the activities of individuals toward the achievement of organizational goals.

The controls in place at Southwest Airlines have helped the airline write a business success story. Another control-based success was Dell in its early years, when it gained market share as it perfected an individualized but rapid system for getting desktop and laptop PCs into the hands of consumers and business users. But more recently, Dell has stumbled.[3] Consumers have been more interested in low prices from discounters than in Dell's customization. Efforts to save money by outsourcing customer service led to widespread complaints about poor quality. Then the federal government announced that it was investigating financial irregularities in its reporting systems. When Dell said it would restate its earnings, the NASDAQ stock market nearly removed the company from its listing. How can a company that once was so successful run into so many problems, and how can an airline success story like Southwest Airlines occur in an industry loaded with competitors and subject to numerous variables? These examples are two sides of one coin: control—a means or mechanism for regulating the behavior of organization members. Left on their own, people may act in ways that they perceive to be beneficial to them individually, but that may work to the detriment of the organization as a whole. Even well-intentioned people may not know whether they are directing their efforts toward the activities that are most important. Thus control is one of the fundamental forces that keep the organization together and heading in the right direction.

Control is defined as any process that directs the activities of individuals toward the achievement of organizational goals. It is how effective managers make sure that activities are going as planned. Some managers don't want to admit it (see Table 16.1),

TABLE 16.1

Symptoms of an Out-of-Control Company

• **Lax top management**—senior managers do not emphasize or value the need for controls, or they set a bad example.
• **Absence of policies**—the firm's expectations are not established in writing.
• **Lack of agreed-upon standards**—organization members are unclear about what needs to be achieved.
• **"Shoot the messenger" management**—employees feel their careers would be at risk if they reported bad news.
• **Lack of periodic reviews**—managers do not assess performance on a regular, timely basis.
• **Bad information systems**—key data are not measured and reported in a timely and easily accessible way.
• **Lack of ethics in the culture**—organization members have not internalized a commitment to integrity.

but control problems—the lack of controls or the wrong kinds of controls—frequently cause irreparable damage to organizations. Ineffective control systems result in problems ranging from employee theft to peeling tire tread problems. Research in Motion was publicly embarrassed when failure to fully test a "noncritical system routine" for updating its computer servers caused the e-mail service on its BlackBerry devices to crash for hours throughout North America.[4] Employees simply wasting time cost U.S. employers billions of dollars each year![5]

Control has been called one of the Siamese twins of management. The other twin is *planning*. Some means of control are necessary because once managers form plans and strategies, they must ensure that the plans are carried out. They must make sure that other people are doing what needs to be done and not doing inappropriate things. If plans are not carried out properly, management must take steps to correct the problem. This process is the primary control function of management. By ensuring creativity, enhancing quality, and reducing cost, managers must figure out ways to control the activities in their organizations.

Not surprisingly, effective planning facilitates control, and control facilitates planning. Planning lays out a framework for the future and, in this sense, provides a blueprint for control. Control systems, in turn, regulate the allocation and use of resources and, in so doing, facilitate the process of the next phases of planning. In today's complex organizational environment, both functions have become more difficult to implement while they have become more important in every department of the organization. Managers today must control their people, inventories, quality, and costs, to mention just a few of their responsibilities.

According to William Ouchi of the University of California at Los Angeles, managers can apply three broad strategies for achieving organizational control: bureaucratic control, market control, and clan control.[6] **Bureaucratic control** is the use of rules, regulations, and formal authority to guide performance. It includes such items as budgets, statistical reports, and performance appraisals to regulate behavior and results. **Market control** involves the use of pricing mechanisms to regulate activities in organizations as though they were economic transactions. Business units may be treated as profit centers and trade resources (services or goods) with one another via such mechanisms. Managers who run these units may be evaluated on the basis of profit and loss. **Clan control**, unlike the first two types, does not assume that the interests of the organization and individuals naturally diverge. Instead clan control is based on the idea that employees may share the values, expectations, and goals of the organization and act in accordance with them. When members of an organization have common values and goals—and trust one another—formal controls may be less necessary. Clan control is based on many of the interpersonal processes described in the organization culture section of Chapter 2, in Chapter 12 on leadership, and in Chapter 14 on groups and teams (e.g., group norms and cohesiveness).

Table 16.2 summarizes the main features of bureaucratic, market, and clan controls. We use this framework as a foundation for our discussions throughout the chapter.

Government Motors? General Motors former Chairman and CEO Rick Wagoner is shown here talking about the company's restructuring plans during a news conference in February 2009. He later resigned under pressure from the White House, and Fritz Henderson took over as the new CEO. Two months later a historic restructuring plan was implemented that would give the majority ownership of the ailing automaker to the federal government to help it fight off bankruptcy. What type of control is exemplified by this action?

Control has been called one of the Siamese twins of management.

bureaucratic control

The use of rules, regulations, and authority to guide performance.

market control

Control based on the use of pricing mechanisms and economic information to regulate activities within organizations.

clan control

Control based on the norms, values, shared goals, and trust among group members.

Bureaucratic Control Systems

Bureaucratic (or formal) control systems are designed to measure progress toward set performance goals and, if necessary, to apply corrective measures to ensure that performance achieves managers' objectives. Control systems detect and correct significant variations, or discrepancies, in the results of planned activities.

 LO 2

TABLE 16.2
Characteristics of Controls

System Control	Features and Requirements
Bureaucratic control	Uses formal rules, standards, hierarchy, and legitimate authority. Works best where tasks are certain and workers are independent.
Market control	Uses prices, competition, profit centers, and exchange relationships. Works best where tangible output can be identified and a market can be established between parties.
Clan control	Involves culture, shared values, beliefs, expectations, and trust. Works best where there is "no one best way" to do a job and employees are empowered to make decisions.

SOURCES: W. G. Ouchi, "A Conceptual Framework for the Design of Organizational Control Mechanisms," *Management Science* 25 (1979), pp. 833–48; W. G. Ouchi, "Markets, Bureaucracies, and Clans," *Administrative Science Quarterly* 25 (1980), pp. 129–41; and R. D. Robey and C. A. Sales, *Designing Organizations* (Burr Ridge, IL: Richard D. Irwin, 1994).

The Control Cycle

As Figure 16.1 shows, a typical control system has four major steps:

1. Setting performance standards.
2. Measuring performance.
3. Comparing performance against the standards and determining deviations.
4. Taking action to correct problems and reinforce successes.

standard

Expected performance for a given goal: a target that establishes a desired performance level, motivates performance, and serves as a benchmark against which actual performance is assessed.

Step 1: Setting Performance Standards   Every organization has goals: profitability, innovation, satisfaction of customers and employees, and so on. A **standard** is the level of expected performance for a given goal. Standards are targets that establish desired performance levels, motivate performance, and serve as benchmarks against

FIGURE 16.1
The Control Process

which to assess actual performance. Standards can be set for any activity—financial activities, operating activities, legal compliance, charitable contributions, and so on.[7]

We have discussed setting performance standards in other parts of the text. For example, employee goal setting for motivation is built around the concept of specific, measurable performance standards. Such standards should be challenging and should aim for improvement over past performance. Typically, performance standards are derived from job requirements, such as increasing market share by 10 percent, reducing costs 20 percent, and answering customer complaints within 24 hours. But performance standards don't apply just to people in isolation—they frequently reflect the integration of both human and system performance. HealthPartners, a Bloomington, Minnesota, nonprofit organization that operates clinics and a hospital and offers health insurance plans, sets ambitious standards for patient care. To achieve a goal of reducing diabetes complications by 30 percent, HealthPartners measured existing practices and results, and then set up a standard protocol for exams and treatments, including the requirement that any abnormal results receive an immediate response. To encourage its physicians to follow the protocol, HealthPartners offers financial incentives for compliance. In little more than a decade, HealthPartners exceeded its goal for improved diabetes care. A local eye doctor commented that it was easy to tell which diabetic patients have coverage through HealthPartners because so few of them suffer diabetes-related damage to their retinas. HealthPartners has similar programs for treatment of cardiovascular disease and depression and for improving the health status of patients who are obese or smoke.[8]

Performance standards can be set with respect to (1) quantity, (2) quality, (3) time used, and (4) cost. For example, production activities include volume of output (quantity), defects (quality), on-time availability of finished goods (time use), and dollar expenditures for raw materials and direct labor (cost). Many important aspects of performance, such as customer service, can be measured by the same standards—adequate supply and availability of products, quality of service, speed of delivery, and so forth.

Sometimes quality standards involve meeting or exceeding standards set by government agencies. Recently, the U.S. Food and Drug Administration proposed loosening its standards for the ingredients in products labeled "chocolate" to allow the use of vegetable fats other than cocoa butter. If the rule change takes effect, candies like Whoppers malted milk balls and PayDay Chocolatey Avalanche could put "chocolate" in their names. Some true chocolate lovers are horrified, but Nick Malgieri, director of the baking program at the Institute of Culinary Education in New York, says, "No one is going to force a high-class chocolate maker to add vegetable fat to chocolate."[9] At companies that seek a reputation for premium quality, the recipe standards can remain as strict as ever, and chocolate aficionados will be on the alert.

One word of caution: The downside of establishing performance targets and standards is that they may not be supported by other elements of the control system. Each piece of the system is important and depends on the others. Otherwise the system can get terribly out of balance.

Step 2: Measuring Performance   The second step in the control process is to measure performance levels. For example, managers can count units produced, days absent, papers filed, samples distributed, and dollars earned. Performance data commonly are obtained from three sources: written reports, oral reports, and personal observations.

Written reports include computer printouts and on-screen reports. Thanks to computers' data-gathering and analysis capabilities and decreasing costs, both large and small companies can gather huge amounts of performance data.

One common example of *oral reports* occurs when a salesperson contacts his or her immediate manager at the close of each business day to report the accomplishments, problems, or customers' reactions during the day. The manager can ask questions to gain additional information or clear up any misunderstandings. When necessary, tentative corrective actions can be worked out during the discussion.

Personal observation involves going to the area where activities take place and watching what is occurring. The manager can directly observe work methods, employees'

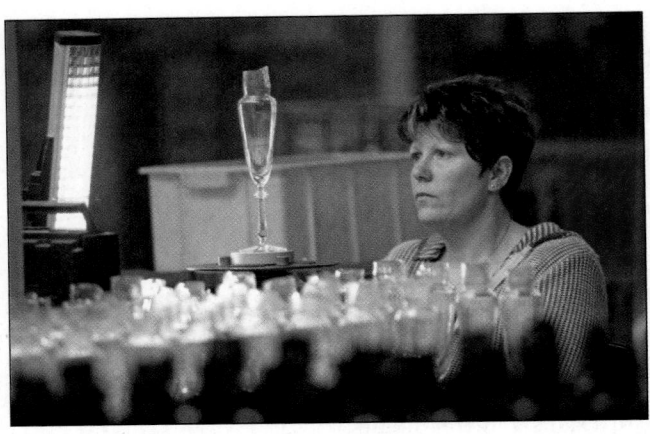

At the Baccarat factory in France, the workers in the quality control area are responsible for the quality and selection of these fine cut crystal glasses.

nonverbal signals, and the general operation. Personal observation gives a detailed picture of what is going on, but it also has some disadvantages. It does not provide accurate quantitative data; the information usually is general and subjective. Also, employees can misunderstand the purpose of personal observation as mistrust or lack of confidence. Still, many managers believe in the value of firsthand observation. As you learned in earlier chapters, personal contact can increase leadership visibility and upward communication. It also provides valuable information about performance to supplement written and oral reports.

Regardless of the performance measure used, the information must be provided to managers on a timely basis. For example, consumer goods companies such as General Foods carefully track new product sales in selected local markets first so they can make any necessary adjustments well before a national rollout. Information that is not available is of little or no use to managers.

Step 3: Comparing Performance with the Standard   The third step in the control process is comparing performance with the standard. In this process, the manager evaluates the performance. For some activities, relatively small deviations from the standard are acceptable, while in others a slight deviation may be serious. In many manufacturing processes, a significant deviation in either direction (e.g., drilling a hole that is too small or too large) is unacceptable. In other cases, a deviation in one direction, such as sales or customer satisfaction that fall below the target level, is a problem, but a deviation in the other, exceeding the sales target or customer expectations, is a sign employees are getting better-than-expected results. As a result, managers who perform the oversight must analyze and evaluate the results carefully.

> Managers can save much time and effort if they apply the principle of exception.

principle of exception

A managerial principle stating that control is enhanced by concentrating on the exceptions to or significant deviations from the expected result or standard.

The managerial **principle of exception** states that control is enhanced by concentrating on the exceptions to, or significant deviations from, the expected result or standard. In other words, in comparing performance with the standard, managers need to direct their attention to the exception—for example, a handful of defective components produced on an assembly line or the feedback from customers who are upset or delighted with a service. Atlanta-based US Security Associates uses information technology to gather performance data on its uniformed security guards and dispatches supervisors to investigate any variances from performance norms, such as a failure of a guard to sign in at a client's location on time.[10]

With the principle of exception, only exceptional cases require corrective action. This principle is important in controlling. The manager is not concerned with performance that equals or closely approximates the expected results. Managers can save much time and effort if they apply the principle of exception.

IN PRACTICE

The accounting and consulting firm of Moody, Famiglietti & Andronico (MFA) uses a formal control process to ensure that it provides exceptional service that is tailored to each client's needs and preferences. The Tewskbury, Massachusetts, firm adopted the U.S. Army's practice of conducting before-action reviews and after-action reviews to learn from its experiences and apply those lessons to future challenges.

At MFA, when employees are preparing to handle an assignment, they begin by calling a short meeting with everyone who has worked with that client during the previous year, as well as employees who have handled similar assignments for other clients. During this before-action review, the participants trade experiences and tidbits of knowledge about the client—say, questions that are likely to arise, efforts that have pleased this client in the past, or existing tools for handling common problems. The input from this meeting helps the team establish goals for the assignment.

During the assignment, team members meet periodically to assess progress and identify any adjustments needed based on what they learn about the client. Within a couple of days of the project's completion, the team reassembles to evaluate its results, comparing outcomes with goals. Participants identify successful actions to recommend in the future, as well as mistakes to avoid next time. Besides noting whether they helped the client meet goals, they also record what they learned about serving the client—data that will be valuable input at the next before-action review for that client. Because the lessons they learn will be the topic of discussion at future before-action reviews, MFA employees are highly motivated to fix mistakes and improve methods.[11]

- How might MFA use the principle of exception in its control process?

Step 4: Taking Action to Correct Problems and Reinforce Successes The last step in the control process is to take appropriate action when there are significant deviations. This step ensures that operations are adjusted to achieve the planned results—or to continue exceeding the plan if the manager determines that is possible. In cases in which significant variances are discovered, the manager usually takes immediate and vigorous action.

> "Mistakes and problems are inevitable in complex enterprises. . . . We shouldn't expect heads of established organizations to be perfect, but we should expect them to catch and correct their mistakes quickly."
> — Rosabeth Moss Kanter, professor, Harvard Business School[12]

An alternative approach is for the corrective action to be taken not by higher-ups, but by the operator at the point of the problem. In computer-controlled production technology, two basic types of control are feasible: specialist control and operator control. With *specialist control*, operators of computer-numerical-control (CNC) machines must notify engineering specialists of malfunctions. With this traditional division of labor, the specialist takes corrective action. With *operator control*, multiskilled operators can rectify their own problems as they occur. Not only is this second strategy more efficient because deviations are controlled closer to their source, but it is also more satisfying because operators benefit by having a more enriched job. At Microscan System, which makes bar-code scanners, every employee is responsible for ensuring the quality of his or her work, resulting in efficient operations. Engineers are responsible for preventing and correcting problems in product and process design, and production workers are responsible for preventing and correcting defects in the processes they carry out.[13]

The selection of the corrective action depends on the nature of the problem.

When corrective action is needed to solve a systemic problem, such as major delays in work flow, often a team approach is most effective. A corrective action is more likely to have greater acceptance in the organization if it is based on a common effort and takes into account multiple points of view. As we discussed in Chapter 14, teams often bring a greater diversity of resources, ideas, and perspectives to problem solving. Knowledgeable team members can often prevent managers from implementing simplistic solutions that don't address the underlying causes of a problem. They are more likely to take into account the effects of any solution on other parts of the organization, preventing new problems from arising later. And they may well develop solutions that managers might not have considered on their own. As a result, any corrective action that is finally adopted will probably be more effective. An important added benefit of bringing employees together to develop corrective actions is that it helps managers build and reinforce an organizationwide culture of high standards.

The selection of the corrective action depends on the nature of the problem. The corrective action may involve a shift in marketing strategy (if, say, the problem is lower-than-expected sales), a disciplinary action, a new way to check the accuracy of manufactured parts, or a major modification to a process or system. Sometimes managers learn they can get better results if they adjust their own practices. Yum Brands, whose franchise restaurants include KFC, Taco Bell, Pizza Hut, and Long John Silver's, conducts regular surveys to learn whether employees feel strong commitment to their jobs. These data are shared with managers to help them measure their performance as leaders and motivators. Jonathan McDaniel, a Houston KFC manager, once learned that his employees were unhappy with their work hours. He began asking them ahead of time whether they wanted particular days off each month—information that helped him create better schedules and end a cause of employee dissatisfaction.[14]

Approaches to Bureaucratic Control

feedforward control

The control process used before operations begin, including policies, procedures, and rules designed to ensure that planned activities are carried out properly.

concurrent control

The control process used while plans are being carried out, including directing, monitoring, and fine-tuning activities as they are performed.

feedback control

Control that focuses on the use of information about previous results to correct deviations from the acceptable standard.

The three approaches to bureaucratic control are feedforward, concurrent, and feedback. **Feedforward control** takes place before operations begin and includes policies, procedures, and rules designed to ensure that planned activities are carried out properly. Examples include inspection of raw materials and proper selection and training of employees. **Concurrent control** takes place while plans are being carried out. It includes directing, monitoring, and fine-tuning activities as they occur. **Feedback control** focuses on the use of information about results to correct deviations from the acceptable standard after they arise.

Feedforward Control   Feedforward control (sometimes called *preliminary control*) is future oriented; its aim is to prevent problems before they arise. Instead of waiting for results and comparing them with goals, a manager can exert control by limiting activities in advance. For example, companies have policies defining the scope within which decisions are made. A company may dictate that managers must adhere to clear ethical and legal guidelines when making decisions. Formal rules and procedures also prescribe people's actions before they occur. For example, legal experts advise companies to establish policies forbidding disclosure of proprietary information or making clear that employees are not speaking for the company when they post messages on blogs, microblogging sites such as Twitter, or social networking sites such as Facebook. Human resource policies defining what forms of body art are acceptable to display at work can avoid awkward case-by-case conversations about a tattoo that offends coworkers or piercings that are incompatible with the company's image.[15]

Recently more managers have grown concerned about the organizational pitfalls of workplace romances, and some have sought a solution in feedforward controls. As wonderful as it is to find love, problems can arise if romantic activities between a supervisor and subordinate create a conflict of interest or charges of sexual harassment. Other employees might interpret the relationship wrongly—that the company sanctions personal relationships as a path to advancement. In addition, romantic ups and downs can spill over into the workplace and affect everyone's mood and motivation. Controls aimed at preventing such problems in an organization include training in appropriate behavior (including how to avoid sexual harassment) and even requiring executives and their romantic interests to sign "love contracts" in which they indicate that the relationship is voluntary and welcome. A copy of the contract goes into the company's personnel files in case the attachment disintegrates and an unhappy employee wants to blame the company for having allowed it in the first place.[16]

Concurrent Control   Concurrent control, which takes place while plans are carried out, is the heart of any control system. On a manufacturing floor, all efforts are directed toward producing the correct quantity and quality of the right products in the specified amount of time. In an airline terminal, the baggage must get to the right airplanes before flights depart. In factories, materials must be available when and where needed, and breakdowns in the production process must be repaired immediately. Concurrent control also is in effect when supervisors watch employees to ensure they work efficiently and avoid mistakes.

Advances in information technology have created powerful concurrent controls. Computerized systems give managers immediate access to data from the most remote corners of their companies. For example, managers can update budgets instantly based on a continuous flow of performance data. In production facilities, monitoring systems that track errors per hour, machine speeds, and other measures allow managers to correct small production problems before they become disasters. Point-of-sale terminals in store checkout lines send sales data back to a retailer's headquarters to show which products are selling in which locations.

For James Skinner, CEO of McDonald's, paying attention to what is happening in the restaurants is critical. Launches of new menu items such as McCafé premium coffee drinks, breakfast burritos, and McGriddle sandwiches have been hits with McDonald's customers looking for value in their food purchases. Skinner and his staff check sales monthly in all stores to assess what is selling well throughout the global chain and to make adjustments. Monitoring these details as they occur has allowed McDonald's to grow even during the recent recession.[17]

Feedback Control   Feedback control is involved when performance data have been gathered and analyzed and the results have been returned to someone (or something) in the process to make corrections. When supervisors monitor behavior, they are exercising concurrent control. When they point out and correct improper performance, they are using feedback as a means of control.

> Timing is an important aspect of feedback control.

Timing is an important aspect of feedback control. Long time lags often occur between performance and feedback, such as when actual spending is compared with the quarterly budget, instead of weekly or monthly, or when some aspect of performance is compared with the projection made a year earlier. Yet if feedback on performance is not timely, managers cannot quickly identify and eliminate the problem and prevent more serious harm.[18]

Some feedback processes are under real-time (concurrent) control, such as a computer-controlled robot on an assembly line. Such units have sensors that continually determine whether they are in the correct position to perform their functions. If they are not, a built-in control device makes immediate corrections.

In other situations, feedback processes require more time. The feedback used by Hertz includes customer ratings of the company's service and the quality of the cars it rents. Patterns of praise and complaints can help the company reinforce or correct practices at particular facilities or throughout the organization, and if a customer is upset about something, Hertz wants to know as soon as possible, so it can correct the problem. In the past, gathering and interpreting customer feedback from surveys and online comments could take about three weeks. Now, however, analytic software collects and tallies data as it flows into the company, and it delivers daily reports to local managers. Armed with the information, the managers are expected to respond to any problems within 24 hours. With these changes, customer satisfaction with Hertz has been rising consistently.[19]

IN PRACTICE

Family Practice Associates (FPA) discovered that the feedback from establishing and using performance standards is a prerequisite for improvement. Without this feedback, the five-doctor medical practice in Wilmington, Delaware, didn't even know how badly it needed to improve, much less what to change.

Several years ago, the physicians at FPA decided to apply for the National Committee for Quality Assurance (NCQA) award for quality of care for diabetes patients. To do that, they would have to submit data summarizing the care they provided. When the doctors began compiling the data, they were shocked to see that test results were sadly out of date. Out of the more than 900 patients with diabetes, hundreds were missing appointments, not receiving follow-up calls, and not scheduling appointments with specialists. Before FPA could even apply for the quality award, it would have to start following up with patients so that FPA could deliver the care they needed.

Once the office staff began contacting patients, the doctors could begin collecting data. Every month, doctors meet to review reports of their progress against the NCQA's quality standards and other quality measures. By becoming more methodical, the practice earned the NCQA award and then was surprised with a bonus from Medicaid—a $10,000 incentive for providing superior care. Buoyed by the recognition, FPA continued to improve by converting from paper to electronic health records. The electronic system lets FPA quickly generate reports that identify additional areas for improvement.[20]

- How might feedforward control supplement these efforts at quality improvement?

The Role of Six Sigma One of the most important quality control tools to emerge is six sigma, which we first discussed in Chapter 9. It is a particularly robust and powerful application of feedback control. Six Sigma is designed to reduce defects in all organization processes—not just product defects but anything that may result in customer dissatisfaction, such as inadequate service, delayed delivery, and excessively high prices due to high costs or inefficiency. The system was developed at Motorola in the late 1980s, when the company found it was being beaten consistently in the competitive marketplace by foreign firms that were able to produce higher-quality products at a lower cost. Since then, the technique has been widely adopted and even improved on by many companies, such as GE, Allied Signal, Ford, and Xerox.

Sigma is the Greek letter used in statistics to designate the estimated standard deviation, or variation, in a process. It indicates how often defects in a process are likely to occur. The lower the sigma number, the higher the level of variation or defects; the higher the sigma number, the lower the level of variation or defects. For example, as you can see in Table 16.3, a two-sigma-level process has more than 300,000 defects per million opportunities (DPMO)—not a very well-controlled process. A three-sigma-level process has 66,807 DPMO, which is roughly a 93 percent level of accuracy. Many organizations operate at this level, which on its face does not sound too bad, until we consider its implications—for example, 7 items of airline baggage lost for every 100 processed. The additional costs to organizations of such inaccuracy are enormous. As you can see in the table, even at just above a 99 percent defect-free rate, or 6,210 DPMO, the accuracy level is often unacceptable—the statistical equivalent of about 50 dropped newborn babies a day.[21]

TABLE 16.3
Relationship between Sigma Level and Defects per Million Opportunities

Sigma Level	DPMO	Is Four Sigma Good Enough?
2σ	308,537	Consider these everyday examples of four sigma quality . . .
3σ	66,807	• 20,000 lost articles of mail per hour.
4σ	**6,210**	• Unsafe drinking water 15 minutes per day.
5σ	233	• 5,000 incorrect surgical operations per week.
6σ	3.4	• 200,000 wrong prescriptions each year.
		• No electricity for 7 hours each month.

SOURCE: Tom Rancour and Mike McCracken, "Applying 6 Sigma Methods for Breakthrough Safety Performance," *Professional Safety* 45, no. 10 (October 2000), pp. 29–32. Reprinted with permission.

At a six-sigma level, a process is producing fewer than 3.4 defects per million, which means it is operating at a 99.99966 percent level of accuracy. Six sigma companies have not only close to zero product or service defects but also substantially lower production costs and cycle times and much higher levels of customer satisfaction. The methodology isn't just for the factory floor, either. Accountants have used six sigma to improve the quality of their audits investigating risks faced by their clients.[22]

The six sigma approach is based on an intense statistical analysis of business processes that contribute to customer satisfaction. For example, a business process could be assembling a product or delivering products to customers. For the given process, the effort begins by defining the outputs and information that flow through each stage of the process and then measuring performance at each stage. A variety of tools are available for analyzing the results. These might include looking for all the root causes of any problem. Suppose some customers are dissatisfied with a company's customer service. Asking "why?" over and over could reveal that customers are dissatisfied because phone calls go unanswered, which happens because support staff cannot keep up with the call volume, which happens because the department is understaffed, which is the result of frozen hiring levels, the result of budget cuts. Any solution will have to address the budget restrictions, either by increasing the budget or by finding a way that a small department can satisfy customers. After the problems are analyzed, process improvements are identified and implemented, and the new process is evaluated again. This cycle continues until the desired quality level is achieved. In this way, the six sigma process leads to continuous improvement in an organization's operations.

Six sigma has come under some criticism for not always delivering business results.[23] One likely reason six sigma doesn't always improve the bottom line is that it focuses only on how to eliminate defects in a process, not whether the process is the best one for the organization. So, for example, at 3M, a drive to improve efficiency through six sigma has been blamed for slowing the flow of innovative ideas. At Home Depot, six sigma has been credited with improving such processes as customer checkout and deciding where to place products in stores, but some say the effort took store workers away from customers. One way managers can apply the strengths of six sigma and minimize the drawbacks is by setting different goals and control processes for the company's mature products than for its areas of innovation.

Management Audits

Over the years, **management audits** have developed as a means of evaluating the effectiveness and efficiency of various systems within an organization, from social responsibility programs to accounting control. Management audits may be external or internal. Managers conduct external audits of other companies and internal audits of their own companies. Some of the same tools and approaches are used for both types of audit.[24]

External Audits   An **external audit** occurs when one organization evaluates another organization. Typically an external body such as a CPA firm conducts financial audits of an organization (accounting audits are discussed later). But any company can conduct external audits of competitors or other companies for its own strategic decision-making purposes. This type of analysis (1) investigates other organizations for possible merger or acquisition, (2) determines the soundness of a company that will be used as a major supplier, or (3) discovers the strengths and weaknesses of a competitor to maintain or better exploit the competitive advantage of the investigating organization. Publicly available data usually are used for these evaluations.[25]

External audits provide essential feedback control when they identify legal and ethical lapses that could harm the organization and its reputation. They also are useful for preliminary control because they can prevent problems from occurring. If a company seeking to acquire other businesses gathers adequate, accurate information

management audit

An evaluation of the effectiveness and efficiency of various systems within an organization.

external audit

An evaluation conducted by one organization, such as a CPA firm, on another.

about possible candidates, it is more likely to acquire the most appropriate companies and avoid unsound acquisitions.

internal audit

A periodic assessment of a company's own planning, organizing, leading, and controlling processes.

Internal Audits   An organization may assign a group to conduct an **internal audit** to assess (1) what the company has done for itself and (2) what it has done for its customers or other recipients of its goods or services. The company can be evaluated on a number of factors, including financial stability, production efficiency, sales effectiveness, human resources development, earnings growth, energy use, public relations, civic responsibility, and other criteria of organizational effectiveness. The audit reviews the company's past, present, and future, including any risks the organization should be prepared to face.[26] A recent study found that the stock prices of companies with highly rated audit committees tended to rise faster than shares of companies with lower-rated internal auditors. It is likely that the higher-rated audit committees do a better job of finding and eliminating undesirable practices.[27]

To perform a management audit, auditors compile a list of desired qualifications and weight each qualification. Among the most common undesirable practices uncovered by a management audit are the performance of unnecessary work, duplication of work, poor inventory control, uneconomical use of equipment and machines, procedures that are more costly than necessary, and wasted resources. At Capital One Financial Corporation, the human resources (HR) department performed an audit of facilities usage. Over several months, staff members walked through headquarters, noting which desks were occupied. The audit determined that more than 4 out of 10 desks were unused each day, and another 3 out of 10 were unused at least part of the day. Employees were away at meetings, visiting clients, or working flexible schedules. The HR staff developed a plan for Capital One to operate more efficiently in one-third of its space. Now most employees keep their work items in a cart, which they take to a desk when they need one. The change saves the company $3 million a year.[28]

Budgetary Controls

LO 3

Budgetary control is one of the most widely recognized and commonly used methods of managerial control. It ties together feedforward control, concurrent control, and feedback control, depending on the point at which it is applied. *Budgetary control* is the process of finding out what's being done and comparing the results with the corresponding budget data to verify accomplishments or remedy differences. Budgetary control is commonly called **budgeting.**

budgeting

The process of investigating what is being done and comparing the results with the corresponding budget data to verify accomplishments or remedy differences; also called *budgetary controlling.*

Fundamental Budgetary Considerations   In private industry, budgetary control begins with an estimate of sales and expected income. Table 16.4 shows a budget with a forecast of expected sales (the *sales budget*) on the top row, followed by several categories of estimated expenses for the first three months of the year. In the bottom row, the profit estimate is determined by subtracting each month's budgeted expenses from the sales in that month's sales budget. Columns next to each month's budget provide space to enter the actual accomplishments so that managers can readily compare expected amounts and actual results.

Although this discussion of budgeting focuses on the flow of money into and out of the organization, budgeting information is not confined to finances. The entire enterprise and any of its units can create budgets for their activities, using units other than dollars, if appropriate. For example, many organizations use production budgets forecasting physical units produced and shipped, and labor can be budgeted in skill levels or hours of work required.

A primary consideration of budgeting is the length of the budget period. All budgets are prepared for a specific time period. Many budgets cover one, three, or six months or one year. The length of time selected depends on the primary purpose of

TABLE 16.4 A Sales Expense Budget

	January		February		March	
	Estimate	Actual	Estimate	Actual	Estimate	Actual
Sales	$1,200,000		$1,350,000		$1,400,000	
Expenses						
General overhead	310,000		310,000		310,000	
Selling	242,000		275,000		288,000	
Producing	327,000		430,500		456,800	
Research	118,400		118,400		115,000	
Office	90,000		91,200		91,500	
Advertising	32,500		27,000		25,800	
Estimated gross profit	80,100		97,900		112,900	

the budgeting. The period chosen should include the enterprise's complete normal cycle of activity. For example, seasonal variations should be included for production and for sales. The budget period commonly coincides with other control devices, such as managerial reports, balance sheets, and statements of profit and loss. In addition, the extent to which reasonable forecasts can be made should be considered in selecting the length of the budget period.

Budgetary control proceeds through several stages. *Establishing expectancies* starts with the broad plan for the company and the estimate of sales, and it ends with budget approval and publication. Next the *budgetary operations* stage deals with finding out what is being accomplished and comparing the results with expectancies. The last stage, as in any control process, involves responding appropriately with some combination of reinforcing successes and correcting problems.

Although practices differ widely, a member of top management often serves as the chief coordinator for formulating and using the budget. Usually the chief financial officer (CFO) has these duties. He or she needs to be less concerned with the details than with resolving conflicting interests, recommending adjustments when needed, and giving official sanction to the budgetary procedures. In a small company, budgeting responsibility generally rests with the owner.

As indicated in the text, there are many types of budgets, but the master budget is the one that brings together and coordinates the activities of the other budgets. It can be referred to as the "budget of budgets."

Types of Budgets   There are many types of budgets. Some of the more common types are as follows:

- *Sales budget.* Usually data for the sales budget include forecasts of sales by month, sales area, and product.
- *Production budget.* The production budget commonly is expressed in physical units. Required information for preparing this budget includes types and capacities of machines, economic quantities to produce, and availability of materials.
- *Cost budget.* The cost budget is used for areas of the organization that incur expenses but no revenue, such as human resources and other support departments. Cost budgets may also be included in the

production budget. Costs may be fixed, or independent of the immediate level of activity (such as rent), or variable, rising or falling with the level of activity (such as raw materials).

- *Cash budget.* The cash budget is essential to every business. It should be prepared after all other budget estimates are completed. The cash budget shows the anticipated receipts and expenditures, the amount of working capital available, the extent to which outside financing may be required, and the periods and amounts of cash available.
- *Capital budget.* The capital budget is used for the cost of fixed assets like plants and equipment. Such costs are usually treated not as regular expenses but as investments because of their long-term nature and importance to the organization's productivity.
- *Master budget.* The master budget includes all the major activities of the business. It brings together and coordinates all the activities of the other budgets and can be thought of as a "budget of budgets."

Traditionally, budgets were often imposed *top-down*, with senior management setting specific targets for the entire organization at the beginning of the budget process. In today's more complex organizations, the budget process is much more likely to be *bottom-up*, with top management setting the general direction, but with lower-level and middle-level managers actually developing the budgets and submitting them for approval. When the budgets are consolidated, senior managers can then determine whether the budget objectives of the organization are being met. The budget will then be either approved or sent back down the organization for additional refinement.

accounting audits

Procedures used to verify accounting reports and statements.

Accounting records must be inspected periodically to ensure they were properly prepared and are correct. **Accounting audits,** which are designed to verify accounting reports and statements, are essential to the control process. This audit is performed by members of an outside firm of public accountants. Knowing that accounting records are accurate, true, and in keeping with generally accepted accounting practices (GAAP) creates confidence that a reliable base exists for sound overall controlling purposes.

FIGURE 16.2

How Dana Discovers What Its True Costs Are

Old way

Old-style accounting identifies costs according to the category of expense. The new math tells you that your real costs are what you pay for the different tasks your employees perform. Find that out and you will manage better.

Salaries
$371,917

Fringes
$118,069

Supplies
$76,745

Fixed costs
$23,614

Total $590,345

New way

Activity-based costing

	Salaries	Fringes	Supplies	Fixed costs
Process sales order.				$144,846
Source parts.				$136,320
Expedite supplier orders.				$ 72,143
Expedite internal processing.				$ 49,945
Receive supplier quality.				$ 47,599
Reissue purchase orders.				$ 45,235
Expedite customer orders.				$ 27,747
Schedule intracompany sales.				$ 17,768
Request engineering change.				$ 16,704
Resolve problems.				$ 16,648
Schedule parts.				$ 15,390
Total				$590,345

SOURCE: Courtesy Dana Corporation.

Activity-Based Costing   Traditional methods of cost accounting may be inappropriate in today's business environment because they are based on outdated methods of rigid hierarchical organization. Instead of assuming that organizations are bureaucratic "machines" that can be separated into component functions such as human resources, purchasing, and maintenance, companies such as Hewlett-Packard and GE have used **activity-based costing (ABC)** to allocate costs across business processes.

ABC starts with the assumption that organizations are collections of people performing many different but related activities to satisfy customer needs. The ABC system is designed to identify those streams of activity and then to allocate costs across particular business processes. The basic procedure is outlined in Figure 16.2 and works as follows: First, employees are asked to break down what they do each day in order to define their *basic activities*. For example, employees in Dana Corporation's material control department engage in a number of activities that range from processing sales orders and sourcing parts to requesting engineering changes and solving problems. These activities form the basis for ABC. Second, managers look at total expenses computed by traditional accounting—fixed costs, supplies, salaries, fringe benefits, and so on—and spread total amounts over the activities according to the amount of time spent on each activity. At Dana, customer service employees spend nearly 25 percent of their time processing sales orders and only about 3 percent scheduling parts. Thus 25 percent of the total cost ($144,846) goes to order processing, and 3 percent ($15,390) goes to scheduling parts. As can be seen in Figure 16.2, both the traditional and ABC systems reach the same bottom line. However, because the ABC method allocates costs across business processes, it provides a more accurate picture of how costs should be charged to products and services.[29]

This heightened accuracy can give managers a more realistic picture of how the organization is actually allocating its resources. It can highlight where wasted activities are occurring or whether activities cost too much relative to the benefits provided. Managers can then take action to correct the problem. For example, Dana's most expensive activity is sales order processing. Its managers might try to find ways to lower that cost, freeing up resources for other tasks. By providing this type of information, ABC has become a valuable method for streamlining business processes.

Financial Controls

In addition to budgets, businesses commonly use other statements for financial control. Two financial statements that help control overall organizational performance are the balance sheet and the profit and loss statement.

The Balance Sheet   The **balance sheet** shows the financial picture of a company at a given time. This statement itemizes three elements: (1) assets, (2) liabilities, and (3) stockholders' equity. **Assets** are the values of the various items the corporation owns. **Liabilities** are the amounts the corporation owes to various creditors. **Stockholders' equity** is the amount accruing to the corporation's owners. The relationship among these three elements is as follows:

$$\text{Assets} = \text{Liabilities} + \text{Stockholders' equity}$$

Table 16.5 shows an example of a balance sheet. During the year, the company grew because it enlarged its building and acquired more machinery and equipment by means of long-term debt in the form of a first mortgage. Additional stock was sold to help finance the expansion. At the same time, accounts receivable were increased, and work in process was reduced. Observe that Total assets ($3,053,367) = Total liabilities ($677,204 + $618,600) + Stockholders' equity ($700,000 + $981,943 + $75,620).

Summarizing balance sheet items over a long period of time uncovers important trends and gives a manager further insight into overall performance and areas in which adjustments need to be made. For example, at some point, the company might decide that it would be prudent to slow down its expansion plans.

---

activity-based costing (ABC)

A method of cost accounting designed to identify streams of activity and then to allocate costs across particular business processes according to the amount of time employees devote to particular activities.

Bottom Line

Activity-based costing can highlight overspending.

If one activity costs the most, how would you decide if this is a case of overspending?

LO 4

balance sheet

A report that shows the financial picture of a company at a given time and itemizes assets, liabilities, and stockholders' equity.

assets

The values of the various items the corporation owns.

liabilities

The amounts a corporation owes to various creditors.

stockholders' equity

The amount accruing to the corporation's owners.

TABLE 16.5
A Comparative Balance Sheet

Comparative Balance Sheet for the Years Ending December 31		
	This Year	**Last Year**
Assets		
Current assets:		
Cash	$161,870	$119,200
U.S. Treasury bills	250,400	30,760
Accounts receivable	825,595	458,762
Inventories:		
Work in process and finished products	429,250	770,800
Raw materials and supplies	251,340	231,010
Total current assets	1,918,455	1,610,532
Other assets:		
Land	157,570	155,250
Building	740,135	91,784
Machinery and equipment	172,688	63,673
Furniture and fixtures	132,494	57,110
Total other assets before depreciation	1,202,887	367,817
Less: Accumulated depreciation and amortization	67,975	63,786
Total other assets	1,134,912	304,031
Total assets	$3,053,367	$1,914,563
Liabilities and stockholders' equity		
Current liabilities:		
Accounts payable	$287,564	$441,685
Payrolls and withholdings from employees	44,055	49,580
Commissions and sundry accruals	83,260	41,362
Federal taxes on income	176,340	50,770
Current installment on long-term debt	85,985	38,624
Total current liabilities	667,204	622,021
Long-term liabilities:		
15-year, 9 percent loan, payable in each of the years 2002–2015	210,000	225,000
5 percent first mortgage	408,600	
Registered 9 percent notes payable	_____	275,000
Total long-term liabilities	618,600	500,000
Stockholders' equity:		
Common stock: authorized 1,000,000 shares, outstanding last year 492,000 shares, outstanding this year 700,000 shares at $1 par value	700,000	492,000
Capital surplus	981,943	248,836
Earned surplus	75,620	51,706
Total stockholders' equity	1,757,563	792,542
Total liabilities and stockholders' equity	$3,053,367	$1,914,563

Comparative Statement of Profit and Loss for the Years Ending June 30			
	This Year	Last Year	Increase or Decrease
Income:			
Net sales	$253,218	$257,636	$4,418*
Dividends from investments	480	430	50
Other	1,741	1,773	32
Total	255,439	259,839	4,400*
Deductions:			
Cost of goods sold	180,481	178,866	1,615
Selling and administrative expenses	39,218	34,019	5,199
Interest expense	2,483	2,604	121*
Other	1,941	1,139	802
Total	224,123	216,628	7,495
Income before taxes	31,316	43,211	11,895*
Provision for taxes	3,300	9,500	6,200*
Net income	$ 28,016	$ 33,711	$5,695*

*Decrease

TABLE 16.6
A Comparative Statement of Profit and Loss

The Profit and Loss Statement   The **profit and loss statement** is an itemized financial statement of the income and expenses of a company's operations. Table 16.6 shows a comparative statement of profit and loss for two consecutive years. In this illustration, the operating revenue of the enterprise has increased. Expense also has increased, but at a lower rate, resulting in a higher net income. Some managers draw up tentative profit and loss statements and use them as goals. Then performance is measured against these goals or standards. From comparative statements of this type, a manager can identify trouble areas and correct them.

Controlling by profit and loss is most commonly used for the entire enterprise and, in the case of a diversified corporation, its divisions. However, if controlling is by departments, as in a decentralized organization in which department managers have control over both revenue and expense, a profit and loss statement is used for each department. Each department's output is measured, and a cost, including overhead, is charged to each department's operation. Expected net income is the standard for measuring a department's performance.

Financial Ratios   An effective approach for checking on the overall performance of an enterprise is to use key financial ratios. Ratios help indicate possible strengths and weaknesses in a company's operations. Key ratios are calculated from selected items on the profit and loss statement and the balance sheet. We will briefly discuss three categories of financial ratios—liquidity, leverage, and profitability:

- *Liquidity ratios.* Liquidity ratios indicate a company's ability to pay short-term debts. The most common liquidity ratio is *current assets to current liabilities,* called the **current ratio** or *net working capital ratio.* This ratio indicates the extent to which current assets can decline and still be adequate to pay current liabilities. Some analysts set a ratio of 2 to 1, or 2.00, as the desirable minimum.

profit and loss statement

An itemized financial statement of the income and expenses of a company's operations.

current ratio

A liquidity ratio that indicates the extent to which short-term assets can decline and still be adequate to pay short-term liabilities.

For example, referring back to Table 16.5, the liquidity ratio there is about 2.86 ($1,918,455/$667,204). The company's current assets are more than capable of supporting its current liabilities.

- *Leverage ratios.* Leverage ratios show the relative amount of funds in the business supplied by creditors and shareholders. An important example is the **debt–equity ratio,** which indicates the company's ability to meet its long-term financial obligations. If this ratio is less than 1.5, the amount of debt is not considered excessive. In Table 16.5, the debt–equity ratio is only 0.35 ($618,600/$1,757,563). The company has financed its expansion almost entirely by issuing stock rather than by incurring significant long-term debt.

- *Profitability ratios.* Profitability ratios indicate management's ability to generate a financial return on sales or investment. For example, **return on investment (ROI)** is a ratio of profit to capital used, or a rate of return from capital (equity plus long-term debt). This ratio allows managers and shareholders to assess how well the firm is doing compared with other investments. For example, if the net income of the company in Table 16.5 were $300,000 this year, its return on capital would be 12.6 percent [$300,000/($1,757,563/$618,600)]— normally a very reasonable rate of return.

debt–equity ratio

A leverage ratio that indicates the company's ability to meet its long-term financial obligations.

return on investment (ROI)

A ratio of profit to capital used, or a rate of return from capital.

Using Financial Ratios   Although ratios provide both performance standards and indicators of what has occurred, exclusive reliance on financial ratios can have negative consequences. Because ratios usually are expressed in compressed time horizons (monthly, quarterly, or yearly), they often cause **management myopia**—managers focus on short-term earnings and profits at the expense of their longer-term strategic obligations.[30] Control systems using long-term (e.g., three- to six-year) performance targets can reduce management myopia and focus attention further into the future.

A second negative outcome of ratios is that they relegate other important considerations to a secondary position. Research and development, management development, progressive human resource practices, and other considerations may receive insufficient attention. Therefore, the use of ratios should be supplemented with other control measures. Organizations can hold managers accountable for market share, number of patents granted, sales of new products, human resource development, and other performance indicators.

management myopia

Focusing on short-term earnings and profits at the expense of longer-term strategic obligations.

The Downside of Bureaucratic Control

So far you have learned about control from a mechanical viewpoint. But organizations are not strictly mechanical; they are composed of people. While control systems are used to constrain people's behavior and make their future behavior predictable, people

> A control system cannot be effective without consideration of how people will react to it.

are not machines that automatically fall into line as the designers of control systems intend. In fact, control systems can lead to dysfunctional behavior. A control system cannot be effective without consideration of how people will react to it. For effective control of employee behavior, managers should consider three types of potential responses to control: rigid bureaucratic behavior, tactical behavior, and resistance.[31]

Rigid Bureaucratic Behavior   Often people act in ways that will help them look good on the control system's measures. This tendency can be useful because it focuses people on the behaviors management requires. But it can result in rigid, inflexible behavior geared toward doing *only* what the system requires. For example, in the earlier discussion of six sigma, we noted that this control process emphasizes efficiency over innovation. After 3M began using six sigma extensively, it slipped from its goal of having at least one-third of sales come from newly released products. When George Buckley took the CEO post, only one-fourth of sales were coming from new products, and Buckley began relying less extensively on efficiency controls. Buckley explained to a reporter, "Invention is by its very nature a disorderly process."[32] The control challenge, of course, is for 3M to be both efficient and creative.

Rigid bureaucratic behavior occurs when control systems prompt employees to stay out of trouble by following the rules. Unfortunately, such systems often lead to poor customer service and make the entire organization slow to act (recall the discussion of bureaucracy in Chapter 10). General Motors is notorious for having a lumbering bureaucracy, which has often been blamed for making the company unresponsive to changes in consumer tastes. For example, several years ago, GM kept engineers at work on the design for a new Hummer SUV even though many of them doubted the vehicles would ever be built. Their pessimism was correct; GM shut down the Hummer group. The company is trying to change. For its new head of vehicle development, GM selected Mary Barra, who has a background in both manufacturing and human resources, as well as a reputation for speaking out and pressing for action. She quickly eliminated layers of management between herself and the top engineer and aggressively supports designers who want to make changes consumers are asking for.[33]

We have all been victimized at some time by rigid bureaucratic behavior. Reflect for a moment on this now classic story of a "nightmare" at a hospital:

> At midnight, a patient with eye pains enters an emergency room at a hospital. At the reception area, he is classified as a nonemergency case and referred to the hospital's eye clinic. Trouble is, the eye clinic doesn't open until the next morning. When he arrives at the clinic, the nurse asks for his referral slip, but the emergency room doctor had forgotten to give it to him. The patient has to return to the emergency room and wait for another physician to screen him. The physician refers him back to the eye clinic and to a social worker to arrange payment. Finally, a third doctor looks into his eye, sees a small piece of metal, and removes it—a 30-second procedure.[34]

Stories such as these have, of course, given bureaucracy a bad name. Some managers will not even use the term *bureaucratic control* because of its potentially negative connotation. That is unfortunate because the control system itself is not the problem. The problems occur when the systems are no longer viewed as tools for running the business but instead as rules for dictating rigid behavior.

Tactical Behavior   Control systems will be ineffective if employees engage in tactics aimed at "beating the system." The most common type of tactical behavior is to manipulate information or report false performance data. People may produce two kinds of invalid data: about what *has* been done and about what *can* be done. False reporting about the past is less common because it is easier to identify someone who misreports what happened than someone who gives an erroneous prediction or estimate of what might happen. Still, managers sometimes change their accounting systems to "smooth out" the numbers. Also, people may intentionally feed false information into a management information system to cover up errors or poor performance. Recently, several customs inspectors at Orlando Sanford International Airport said their supervisors had pressured them to speed up the processing of passengers by entering "generic" data instead of actually questioning the passengers. According to the

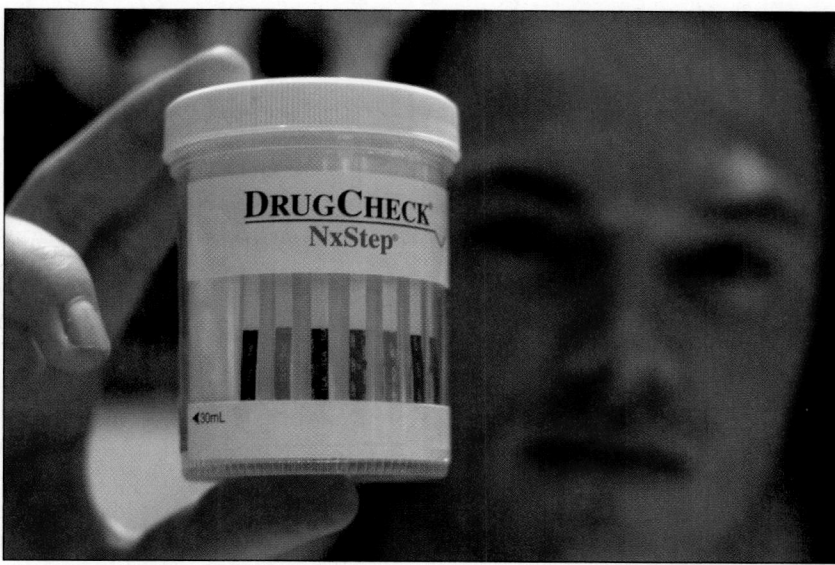

Drug testing is one of the ways organizations monitor employees. Some people favor the control measure but change their minds when personally asked to submit a urine specimen.

inspectors, when the system flagged passengers for additional screening during busy periods, they were told to guess at the information, such as race and length of stay, rather than asking the passengers to provide the information. The justification for this behavior was that time pressure gave them no more than a minute to screen each passenger and keep the line moving, so that the public would be satisfied with their agency's work.[35]

More commonly, people falsify their predictions or requests for the future. When asked to give budgetary estimates, employees usually ask for larger amounts than they need. On the other hand, they sometimes submit unrealistically *low* estimates when they believe a low estimate will help them get a budget or a project approved. Budget-setting sessions can become tugs-of-war between subordinates trying to get slack in the budget and superiors attempting to minimize slack. Similar tactics are exhibited when managers negotiate unrealistically low performance standards so that subordinates will have little trouble meeting them; when salespeople project low forecasts so that they will look good by exceeding them; and when workers slow down the work pace while time-study analysts are setting work pace standards. In these and other cases, people are concerned only with their own performance figures rather than with the overall performance of their departments or companies.

Resistance to Control   Often people strongly resist control systems. They do so for several reasons. First, comprehensive control systems increase the accuracy of performance data and make employees more accountable for their actions. Control systems uncover mistakes, threaten people's job security and status, and decrease people's autonomy.

Second, control systems can change expertise and power structures. For example, management information systems can make the costing, purchasing, and production decisions previously made by managers much quicker. Those individuals may fear a loss of expertise, power, and decision-making authority as a result.

Third, control systems can change the social structure of an organization. They can create competition and disrupt social groups and friendships. People may end up competing against those with whom they formerly had comfortable, cooperative relationships. Because people's social needs are so important, they will resist control systems that reduce social need satisfaction.

Fourth, control systems may be seen as an invasion of privacy, lead to lawsuits, and cause low morale.

Designing Effective Control Systems

LO 5

Effective control systems maximize potential benefits and minimize dysfunctional behaviors. To achieve this, management needs to design control systems that

1. Establish valid performance standards.
2. Provide adequate information to employees.
3. Ensure acceptablity to employees.
4. Maintain open communication.
5. Use multiple approaches.

Establish Valid Performance Standards   An effective control system must be based on valid and accurate performance standards. The most effective standards, as discussed earlier, tend to be expressed in quantitative terms; they are objective rather than subjective. Also, the measures should not be capable of being easily sabotaged or faked. Moreover, the system must incorporate all important aspects of performance. For example, a company that just focused on sales volume without also looking at profitability might soon go out of business. As you learned earlier, unmeasured behaviors are neglected. Often performance standards for delivering training and other HR programs emphasize trainee satisfaction as reported on surveys. But the Philadelphia Department of Licenses and Inspections instead verified that its training actually improved employee performance. The department was notorious for its long lines and rude workers, so it turned for help to the Philadelphia Ritz-Carlton Hotel—part of a chain known for its superb customer service. The hotel's area general manager provided training initially to 40 department workers in how to improve their service skills. As part of its posttraining measurement process, the department checked the wait times for license applicants, which dropped from 82 minutes to 14 minutes. The department is continuing its partnership program with Ritz-Carlton through additional employee training and attendance at each other's management meetings.[36]

> Management also must defend against another problem: too many measures that create overcontrol and employee resistance.

But management also must defend against another problem: too many measures that create overcontrol and employee resistance. To make many controls tolerable, managers can devote attention to a few key areas while setting "satisfactory" performance standards in others. Or they can establish simple priorities. The purchasing agent may have to meet targets in the following sequence: quality, availability, cost, inventory level. Finally, managers can set tolerance ranges. For example, in financial budgeting optimistic, expected, and minimum levels sometimes are specified.

Many companies' budgets set cost targets only. This causes managers to control spending but also to neglect earnings. At Emerson Electric, profit and growth are key measures. If an unanticipated opportunity to increase market share arises, managers can spend what they need to go after it. The phrase "it's not in the budget" is less likely to stifle people at Emerson than it is at most other companies.

Manufacturers spend billions of dollars on test, measurement, and inspection equipment plus millions on software and services to help them monitor whether their products are meeting quality standards. Their top goals for investing in quality control are to improve productivity and reduce waste.[37]

Motives for investing in quality control

This principle applies to nonfinancial aspects of performance as well. At many customer service call centers, control aims to maximize efficiency by focusing on the average amount of time each agent spends handling each phone call. But the business objectives of call centers should also include other measures such as cross-selling products or improving customer satisfaction and repeat business. Carlson Leisure Travel Services is one of a growing number of companies using new technology to analyze the content—not just the duration—of each call and capture information about the amount sold by call center agents.[38]

Business consultant Michael Hammer summarizes these points in terms of what he calls seven "deadly sins" of performance measurement to avoid:[39]

1. *Vanity*—using measures that are sure to make managers and the organization look good. For example, a company might measure order fulfillment in terms of whether products are delivered by the latest date promised by the organization, rather than by the tougher and more meaningful measure of when the customers request to receive the products.
2. *Provincialism*—limiting measures to functional or departmental responsibilities, rather than the organization's overall objectives. If a company's transportation department measures only shipping costs, it won't have an incentive to consider

that shipping reliability (delivery on a given date) will affect performance at the company's stores or distribution centers.

3. *Narcissism*—measuring from the employee's, manager's, or company's point of view, rather than the customer's. For example, a maker of computer systems measured on-time shipping of each component; if 90 percent of the system's components arrived at the customer on time, it was 90 percent on time. But from the customer's point of view, the system wasn't on time at all because the customer needed *all* the components to use the system.

4. *Laziness*—not expending the effort to analyze what is important to measure. An electric power company simply assumed customers cared about installation speed, but in fact, customers really cared more about receiving an accurate installation schedule.

5. *Pettiness*—measuring just one component of what affects business performance. An example would be clothing manufacturers that assume they should consider just manufacturing cost rather than the overall costs of making exactly the right products available in stores when customers demand them.

6. *Inanity*—failing to consider the way standards will affect real-world human behavior and company performance. A fast-food restaurant targeted waste reduction and was surprised when restaurant managers began slowing down operations by directing their employees to hold off on cooking anything until orders were placed.

7. *Frivolity*—making excuses for poor performance rather than taking performance standards seriously. In some organizations, more effort goes to blaming others than to correcting problems.

According to Hammer, the basic correction to these "sins" is to carefully select standards that look at entire business processes, such as product development or order fulfillment, and identify which actions make those processes succeed. Then managers should measure performance against these standards precisely, accurately, and practically, making individuals responsible for their achievement and rewarding success.

Provide Adequate Information   Management must communicate to employees the importance and nature of the control system. Then people must receive feedback about their performance. Feedback motivates people and provides information that enables them to correct their own deviations from performance standards. Allowing people to initiate their own corrective action encourages self-control and reduces the need for outside supervision. *Open-book management*, described in Chapter 15, is a powerful use of this control principle.

Information should be as accessible as possible, particularly when people must make decisions quickly and frequently. For example, a national food company with its own truck fleet had a difficult problem. The company wanted drivers to go through customer sales records every night, insert new prices from headquarters every morning, and still make their rounds—an impossible set of demands. To solve this control problem, the company installed personal computers in more than 1,000 delivery trucks. Now drivers use their PCs for constant communication with headquarters. Each night drivers send information about the stores, and each morning headquarters sends prices and recommended stock mixes.

In general, a manager designing a control system should evaluate the information system in terms of the following questions:

1. Does it provide people with data relevant to the decisions they need to make?
2. Does it provide the right amount of information to decision makers throughout the organization?
3. Does it provide enough information to each part of the organization about how other, related parts of the organization are functioning?[40]

Ritz-Carlton sets performance measures for maintaining its impressive reputation and ensures that employees see how they contribute. The measures are based on the key factors behind the company's success: its mystique, employee engagement, customer engagement, product service excellence, community involvement, and financial performance. Financial performance is viewed as the result of achieving the other goals. For each success factor, cross-functional teams identify targets as detailed as the number of scuff marks on elevator doors or the percentage of satisfied employees at a location. The teams include frontline employees, so that early in the control process, employees already feel their input matters.

At each location, at the beginning of every shift, all employees gather for a meeting to discuss activities, issues, and Ritz-Carlton's business philosophy. They compare recent performance against the company's targets in each area. These conversations reinforce the key performance factors and help employees appreciate the importance of what they do.

Each business unit has up to three priorities to focus on, with each employee working to improve customer, employee, or financial results. Employees appreciate their role in giving each guest a special experience. When Joanne Hanna checked into a Ritz-Carlton after a grueling series of airport delays that caused her to miss several meetings, a hotel employee carried her bags and listened to her frustration. He suggested a spa visit or a masseuse, and when he learned she didn't have time, he brought her a scented candle—and had the information entered into Ritz-Carlton's database. Now, on every visit, Hanna finds a candle in her room, reminding her of one employee's empathy.[41]

- How does Ritz-Carlton ensure that hotel employees have adequate information for meeting quality standards?

Ensure Acceptability to Employees   Employees are less likely to resist a control system and exhibit dysfunctional behaviors if they accept the system. They are more likely to accept systems that have useful performance standards but are not overly controlling. Employees also will find systems more acceptable if they believe the standards are possible to achieve.

The control system should emphasize positive behavior rather than focusing on controlling negative behavior alone. At some companies, managers have concluded that focusing on the number of hours people are at work deteriorates into a negative preoccupation with tardiness, absenteeism, and putting in long hours. Employees lingering at their desks or workstations may not necessarily be efficient and attentive, and employees may become cynical if they see rewards associated with just showing up, rather than delivering results. Best Buy tried the idea of a "results-only work environment" (ROWE), in which employees have great flexibility about their time and activities as long as they meet performance objectives. The successes of this effort included lower employee turnover, suggesting that employees found this type of control system more acceptable. The White House's Office of Personnel Management recently announced that it would try to replicate Best Buy's success by testing ROWE with 400 government workers (Deloitte was engaged to assess the impact).[42]

One of the best ways to establish reasonable standards and thus gain employee acceptance of the control system is to set standards participatively. As we discussed in Chapter 4, participation in decision making secures people's understanding and cooperation and results in better decisions. Allowing employees to collaborate in control system decisions that affect their jobs directly will help overcome resistance and foster acceptance of the system. In addition, employees on the "front line" are more likely to know which standards are most important and practical, and they can inform a manager's judgment on these issues. Finally, if standards are established in collaboration

> The control system should emphasize positive behavior rather than focusing on controlling negative behavior alone.

with employees, managers will more easily obtain cooperation on solving the problem when deviations from standards occur.

Maintain Open Communication   When deviations from standards occur, it is important that employees feel able to report the deviations so that the problem can be addressed. If employees come to feel that their managers want to hear only good news or, worse, if they fear reprisal for reporting bad news, even if it is not their fault, then any controls that are in place will be much less likely to be effective. Problems may go unreported or, even worse, may reach the point where they become much more expensive or difficult to solve. But if managers create an environment of openness and honesty, one in which employees feel comfortable sharing even negative information and are appreciated for doing so in a timely fashion, then the control system is much more likely to work effectively.

Nevertheless, managers may sometimes need to discipline employees who are failing to meet important standards. In such cases, an approach called *progressive discipline* is usually most effective. In this approach, clear standards are established, but failure to meet them is dealt with in a progressive or step-by-step process. For example, the first time an employee's sales performance has been worse than it should have been, the supervising manager may offer verbal counseling or coaching. If problems persist, the next step might be a written reprimand. This type of reasonable and considered approach signals to all employees that the manager is interested in improving their performance, not in punishing them.

> "I've learned that mistakes can often be as good a teacher as success."
> — Jack Welch, former CEO, General Electric

Use Multiple Approaches   Multiple controls are necessary. For example, banks need controls on risk so that they don't lose a lot of money from defaulting borrowers, as well as profit controls including sales budgets that aim for growth in accounts and customers. Southwest Airlines, too, uses multiple controls; "Management Connection: Progress Report" gives examples of these controls.

| Manager's Brief | **Progress Report** | Onward |

Management Connections

PERFORMANCE MEASURES AT SOUTHWEST AIRLINES

Financially, a key part of Southwest Airlines's success has come from a strategy of keeping operations as simple as possible. Unlike most domestic air carriers, Southwest did not build a hub-and-spokes system of routes connecting through a few main airports. Rather, it began serving a few airports point to point, and as it added cities, it continued building point-to-point routes. It operated only one kind of aircraft, the Boeing 737. It tended to avoid the congested Northeast, which has helped it achieve above-average on-time performance.

In carrying out its low-cost strategy, Southwest needs performance measures that look at some of the key costs. First, before an airline can generate revenue, it needs planes flying routes that passengers want to travel. So one key measure is the airline's seating capacity. For most of Southwest's history, the company has enabled steady growth by steadily increasing its seating capacity through purchases of jets. Only during the severe recession of 2009 did Southwest stop buying jets to add to its capacity; that year, the company bought only enough planes to replace the ones it retired from service. That still left Southwest room to maneuver in the short term if demand picked up: it could add flights with existing aircraft during its slower periods at night and on weekends.

In terms of operating costs, one key measure is the cost of fuel, which is Southwest's second-largest expense. Rising fuel prices can spell the difference between a comfortable profit and a loss. Airlines try to manage fuel costs through the practice of hedging, or buying various financial instruments that lock in future prices. Southwest was profitable for years because it skillfully locked in favorable fuel prices during a period when the market price was high. For several years running, Southwest was paying less for fuel than its competitors because of those deals. Southwest also has begun managing fuel prices by looking for ways to fly more efficiently. It has reduced the gallons of fuel per passenger mile by installing "winglets" on the tips of its airplane wings to make the planes more aerodynamic, and it is testing planes built with lighter materials.

On the revenue side, Southwest tracks "yields," which measure the total revenues divided by the number of miles flown. For example, during the 2009 recession, the yield in June was 15.27 cents per mile, down from 16.02 cents per mile the previous year. The company had responded to the economic slowdown by cutting fares, and that was reflected in a lower yield. More recently, a spike in oil prices led airlines across the board to increase their fares, and Southwest raised prices faster than most, a change that improves yields only if passengers don't stay away.

Like other businesses, Southwest also tracks and reports its quarterly and annual profits and its earnings per share. Recently, for example, a slowly strengthening economy led to increased travel, and Southwest reported a 13 percent increase in its quarterly profit. Profits of $131 million represented 18 cents a share, up from 16 cents a share the previous year. Profits during some quarters have dipped, but so far, efforts to offset fuel price increases with fare increases have driven up revenues rather than driving away business. For May 2011 Southwest reported that passenger revenue per available seat mile was up by at least 11 percent.

Behind these financial measures are the customer attitudes that make it possible for Southwest to maintain customer loyalty while charging a profitable price. Southwest is a favorite airline among U.S. travelers. To maintain that attitude, Southwest needs to measure its performance in satisfying customers. By one measure, on-time arrivals, Southwest may have a problem. Until 2010 Southwest was an industry leader, but that year the airline fell to eighth place in data reported by the U.S. Transportation Department. Although its performance slipped a bit from 82.1 percent to 81 percent, the main reason for the slide is that competitors have been improving. Another reason is that it is flying planes that are fuller. The measure for this is passenger load factor, the percentage of the plane that is full. Southwest's load factor recently increased to 82.3 percent, up from 77.2 percent a year earlier. A consequence of fuller planes shows up in another performance measure: Southwest once was notable for turning around planes at the gate in just 20 minutes, but that "turn time" has stretched out to 30 minutes.

Southwest's acquisition of AirTran will make all of these control efforts more complex. The AirTran acquisition adds smaller-capacity Boeing 717s to Southwest's 737-only fleet, so the company needs to hire and train mechanics with a wider range of skills. Scheduling pilots for two different aircraft types also will be more complex. Some of the airports it added by acquiring AirTran's route include congested airports such as New York's LaGuardia and Delta's hub in Atlanta. This could pose a problem for customer service at an airline that is already struggling to turn around performance declines in on-time arrivals and turn times.[43]

- What control measures are described? Identify whether each is a type of feedforward control, concurrent control, or feedback control.
- How might Southwest improve the effectiveness of the control effort described here?

As you learned earlier in this chapter, control systems generally should include both financial and nonfinancial performance targets and incorporate aspects of preliminary, concurrent, and feedback control. In recent years, a growing number of companies have combined targets for managers into a **balanced scorecard,** a combination of four sets of performance measures: (1) financial, (2) customer satisfaction, (3) business processes (quality and efficiency), and (4) learning and growth.[44] The goal is generally to broaden management's horizon beyond short-term financial results so that the company's long-term success is more likely. For example, Hyde Park Electronics had been using a variety of financial controls when it adopted a business scorecard that added metrics such as on-time delivery, employee satisfaction, and sales impact of marketing activities. Profits under the balanced scorecard reached record levels.[45] The balanced scorecard also is adaptable to nonprofit settings. Ocean-Monmouth Legal Services, which provides legal services to poor people in New Jersey, uses a balanced scorecard to track progress in meeting strategic, operational, financial, and client satisfaction goals. The organization's executive director, Harold E. Creacy, credits the approach with helping to cope with the rising costs and tight resources that so often plague nonprofits.[46]

balanced scorecard

Control system combining four sets of performance measures: financial, customer, business process, and learning and growth.

Effective control will also require managers and organizations to use many of the other techniques and practices of good management. For example, compensation systems will grant rewards for meeting standards and impose consequences if they are not met. And to gain employee acceptance, managers may also rely on many of the other communication and motivational tools that we discussed in earlier chapters, such as persuasion and positive reinforcement.

The Other Controls: Markets and Clans

Although the concept of control has always been a central feature of organizations, the principles and philosophies underlying its use are changing. In the past, control was focused almost exclusively on bureaucratic (and market) mechanisms. Generations of managers were taught that they could maximize productivity by regulating what employees did on the job—through standard operating procedures, rules, regulations, and close supervision. To increase output on an assembly line, for example, managers in the past tried to identify the "one best way" to approach the work and then to monitor employees' activities to make certain that they followed standard operating procedures. In short, they controlled work by dividing and simplifying tasks, a process we referred to in Chapter 1 as *scientific management*.

Although formal bureaucratic control systems are perhaps the most pervasive in organizations (and the most talked about in management textbooks), they are not always the most effective. *Market controls* and *clan controls* may both represent more flexible, though no less potent, approaches to regulating performance.

Market Control

LO 6

In contrast to bureaucratic controls, market controls involve the use of economic forces—and the pricing mechanisms that accompany them—to regulate performance. The system works like this: in cases where output from an individual, department, or business unit has value to other people, a price can be negotiated for its exchange. As a market for these transactions becomes established, two effects occur:

- Price becomes an indicator of the value of the good or service.
- Price competition has the effect of controlling productivity and performance.

The basic principles that underlie market controls can operate at the corporate level, the business unit (or department) level, and the individual level. Figure 16.3 shows a few different ways in which market controls are used in an organization.

Market Controls at the Corporate Level
In large, diversified companies, market controls often are used to regulate independent business units. Particularly in large conglomerate firms that act as holding companies, business units typically are treated as profit centers that compete with one another. Top executives may place very few bureaucratic controls on business unit managers but use profit and loss data for evaluating performance. While decision making and power are decentralized to the business units, market controls ensure that business unit performance is in line with corporate objectives.

Use of market control mechanisms in this way has been criticized by those who insist that economic measures do not reflect the complete value of an organization adequately. Employees often suffer as diversified companies are repeatedly bought and sold based on market controls.

Bottom Line

Market controls help maintain low prices.

You manage the tech support department for your company. How might market controls affect your costs?

FIGURE 16.3
Examples of
Market Control

Market Controls at the Business Unit Level   Market control also can be used within business units to regulate exchanges among departments and functions. Transfer pricing is one method that organizations use to try to reflect market forces for internal transactions. A **transfer price** is the charge by one unit in the organization for a good or service that it supplies to another unit of the same organization. For example, in automobile manufacturing, a transfer price may be affixed to components and subassemblies before they are shipped to subsequent business units for final assembly. Ideally, the transfer price reflects the price that the receiving business unit would have to pay for that product or service in the marketplace.

As organizations have more options to outsource goods and services to external partners, market controls such as transfer prices provide natural incentives to keep costs down and quality up. Managers stay in close touch with prices in the marketplace to make sure their own costs are in line, and they try to improve the service they provide to increase their department's value to the organization. Consider the situation in which training and development activities can be done internally by the human resources department or outsourced to a consulting firm. If the human resources department cannot supply quality training at a reasonable price, there may be no reason for that department to exist inside the firm. Similarly, Penske Truck Leasing Company began outsourcing many of its finance processes to a company called Genpact, not only for lower prices but also for the expertise developed by that specialized firm to compete in the marketplace. Penske's senior vice president of finance, Frank Cocuzza, says the department spends $20 million less per year than it did to perform the same functions in-house while it has improved its rate of collections and learned thousands of ways to make his own operation more efficient, modeled after Genpact's lean practices.[47]

Market Controls at the Individual Level   Market controls also are used at the individual level. For example, in situations where organizations are trying to hire employees, the supply and demand for particular skills influence the wages

transfer price

Price charged by one unit for a good or service provided to another unit within the organization.

As much as it would seem that market controls play a significant role in the salary of a professional baseball player or any other professional athlete, are the sometimes ridiculously high salaries that are paid for players today truly indicative of a player's skill—or something else? If the player doesn't live up to the expectation of the previously perceived skill level or, put another way, has a "bad year," should the organization be allowed to cut his pay?

employees can expect to receive and the rate organizations are likely to pay. Employees or job candidates who have more valuable skills tend to be paid a higher wage. Of course, wages don't always reflect market rates—sometimes they are based (perhaps arbitrarily) on internal resource considerations—but the market rate is often the best indicator of an employee's potential worth to a firm.

Market-based controls such as these are important in that they provide a natural incentive for employees to enhance their skills and offer them to potential firms. Even after individuals gain employment, market-based wages are important as controls in that persons with higher economic value may be promoted faster to higher positions in the organization.

Market controls often are used by boards of directors to manage CEOs of major corporations. Ironically, CEOs usually are seen as the ones controlling everyone else in the company; but the CEO is accountable to the board of directors, and the board must devise ways to ensure that the CEO acts in its interest. Absent board control, CEOs may act in ways that make them look good personally (such as making the company bigger or more diversified) but that do not lead to higher profits for the firm. And as recent corporate scandals have shown, without board control CEOs may also artificially inflate the firm's earnings, or not fully declare expenses, making the firm look much more successful than it really is.

Traditionally, boards have tried to control CEO performance mainly through the use of incentive plans, in addition to base salary. These typically include some type of bonus tied to short-term profit targets. In large U.S. companies, most CEO compensation is now at risk, meaning it depends mainly on the performance of the company. In addition to short-term incentives, boards use some type of long-term incentives linked to the firm's share price, usually through stock options, which we discussed in Chapter 10. Also, balanced scorecards are intended to keep CEOs focused on the company's longer-term health. And under the Sarbanes-Oxley Act, described in Chapter 5, board members are expected to exercise careful control over the company's financial performance, including oversight of the CEO's compensation package.

Clan Control: The Role of Empowerment and Culture

Increasingly, managers are discovering that control systems based solely on bureaucratic and market mechanisms are insufficient for directing today's workforce. There are several reasons for this:

- *Employees' jobs have changed.* The nature of work is evolving. Employees working with computers, for example, have more variability in their jobs, and much of their work is intellectual and therefore invisible. Because of this, there is no one best way to perform a task, and programming or standardizing jobs becomes extremely difficult. Close supervision is also unrealistic because it is nearly impossible to supervise activities such as reasoning and problem solving.
- *The nature of management has changed.* The role of managers is evolving, too. Managers used to know more about the job than employees did. Today it is typical for employees to know more about their jobs than anyone else does. We refer to this as the shift from touch labor to knowledge work. When real

expertise in organizations exists at the very lowest levels, hierarchical control becomes impractical.[48]

- *The employment relationship has changed.* The social contract at work is being renegotiated. It used to be that employees were most concerned about issues such as pay, job security, and the hours of work. Today, however, more and more employees want to be more fully engaged in their work, taking part in decision making, devising solutions to unique problems, and receiving assignments that are challenging and involving. They want to use their brains.

For these three reasons, the concept of *empowerment* not only has become more popular in organizations but has become a necessary aspect of a manager's repertoire of control. With no "one best way" to approach a job and no way to scrutinize what employees do every day, managers must empower employees to make decisions and trust that they will act in the best interests of the firm. But this does not mean giving up control. It means creating a strong culture of high standards and integrity so that employees will exercise effective control on their own.

> "As a manager the important thing is not what happens when you are there, but what happens when you are not there."
>
> —Ken Blanchard

Recall our extensive discussion of organization culture in Chapter 2. If the organization's culture encourages the wrong behaviors, then an effort to impose effective controls will be severely hindered. But if managers create and reinforce a strong culture that encourages correct behavior, one in which everyone understands management's values and expectations and is motivated to act in accordance with them, then clan control can be a very effective control tool.[49] As we noted at the beginning of this chapter, *clan control* involves creating relationships built on mutual respect and encouraging each individual to take responsibility for his or her actions. Employees work within a guiding framework of values, and they are expected to use good judgment. For example, at NetApp, an IT company specializing in data storage and protection, a commitment to employee empowerment prompted the switch from a 12-page travel policy to some simple

IN PRACTICE

Netflix establishes clan control with hiring decisions that focus on choosing software engineers (most of the professional staff) who welcome the company's culture of self-determination and professional accomplishment. Interviewers tell job candidates that the company expects them to be problem solvers, not turn to the bureaucracy for rules and policies. Candidates who prefer more structure can readily find positions elsewhere because software engineering talents are in high demand.

Employees at Netflix's headquarters, located in Los Gatos, California, operate free of many constraints that other companies put in place. They don't have to follow a dress code or wear an employee badge. The company keeps everyone informed about strategy, performance targets, and performance. Employees can take days off whenever they want, as long as they meet their goals. Employees on business trips don't have a budget to follow, just a policy that says, "Act in Netflix's best interests."

This freedom doesn't mean Netflix is lax. Rather, the people at headquarters are highly trained and come to Netflix with at least seven years of experience. They need to think creatively, so they need freedom in which to operate. And if an employee's performance is just average, he or she is asked to leave. The result is an atmosphere in which talented people feel that their accomplishments are valued and they don't have to put up with pointless rules or colleagues who don't contribute.[50]

- Are the norms used to control behavior at Netflix as effective as specific rules? Why or why not?

TABLE 16.7

Management Control in an Empowered Setting

1. **Put control where the operation is.** Layers of hierarchy, close supervision, and checks and balances are quickly disappearing and being replaced with self-guided teams. For centuries even the British Empire—as large as it was—never had more than six levels of management, including the queen.
2. **Use "real-time" rather than after-the-fact controls.** Issues and problems must be solved at the source by the people doing the actual work. Managers become a resource to help out the team.
3. **Rebuild the assumptions underlying management control to build on trust rather than distrust.** Today's "high-flex" organizations are based on empowerment, not obedience. Information must facilitate decision making, not police it.
4. **Move to control based on peer norms.** Clan control is a powerful thing. Workers in Japan, for example, have been known to commit suicide rather than disappoint or lose face within their team. Although this is extreme, it underlines the power of peer influence. The Japanese have a far more homogeneous culture and set of values than we do. In North America, we must build peer norms systematically and put much less emphasis on managing by the numbers.
5. **Rebuild the incentive systems to reinforce responsiveness and teamwork.** The twin goals of adding value to the customer and team performance must become the dominant raison d'être of the measurement systems.

SOURCE: Gerald. H. B. Ross, "Revolution in Management Control," *Management Accounting*, November 1990, pp. 23–27. Reprinted by permission.

Clan control takes a long time to develop and an even longer time to change.

Bottom Line

Clan control empowers employees to meet performance standards.

Would you expect more clan control with standardized jobs or creative positions?

guidelines for employees who need to go on a business trip: "We are a frugal company. But don't show up dog-tired to save a few bucks. Use your common sense."[51] The emphasis in an empowered organization is on satisfying customers, not on pleasing the boss. Mistakes are tolerated as the unavoidable by-product of dealing with change and uncertainty and are viewed as opportunities to learn. And team members learn together. Table 16.7 provides a set of guidelines for managing in an empowered world.

The resilience and time investment of clan control are a double-edged sword. Clan control takes a long time to develop and an even longer time to change. This gives an organization stability and direction during periods of upheaval in the environment or the organization (e.g., during changes in the top management). "Management Connection: Onward" provides an example of how this worked during a crisis that faced Southwest Airlines. Yet if managers want to establish a new culture—a new form of clan control—they must help employees unlearn the old values and embrace the new. We will talk about this transition process more in the final chapter of this book.

Manager's Brief	Progress Report	**Onward**

Management Connection

CLAN CONTROL IN A CRISIS AT SOUTHWEST AIRLINES

The strong culture of Southwest Airlines is expressed in its mission dedicated to "the highest quality of customer service delivered with a sense of warmth, friendliness, individual pride, and company spirit." You can see that at the company's website, with its prominent links for getting help. You can learn it from Southwest's definition of company spirit, which includes working hard, being the best, having fun, and not taking oneself too seriously. Along

with hiring for and reinforcing these values, the company entrusts employees to live them out.

This all came into practice dramatically in April 2011, when a Boeing 737 flown by a Southwest crew experienced trouble. On the way from Phoenix, Arizona, to Sacramento, California, the passengers and crew heard a sound like a gunshot. A section of the fuselage had peeled open at 34,000 feet. The plane made an emergency landing at a military base in Yuma, Arizona. Fortunately no passengers were seriously injured. One flight attendant had minor injuries.

Brian Hirshman, the head of maintenance and engineering for Southwest, joined an emergency conference call that night. He listened to Southwest's director of operations explain that airline personnel in Yuma were reporting a fuselage rupture. Hirshman, a former airline mechanic, then briefed the Federal Aviation Administration and drove to headquarters for a 9:30 p.m. meeting with a group of Southwest employees. During the conference at the Dallas headquarters, Hirshman got his first look at photos of the five-foot-long rupture, located just a few feet above the passenger windows. The break crossed three tear straps (vertical pieces secured to the fuselage to keep the skin intact).

The group in Southwest's emergency center reviewed its maintenance records to verify that no safety checks had been missed or improperly done. The damaged jet had passed all the required inspections. Next they contacted Boeing by phone and learned that Boeing also had found no obvious source of the problem. A Boeing engineer recommended that two tests be conducted on all the 737s in Southwest's fleet that were about the same age—a total of 79 planes. Each inspection would take about 16 hours.

More than 1,200 hours' worth of inspections obviously would put a major hurdle in the way of serving the customers who were about to head for Southwest's gates around the nation in the morning. Typically, before grounding so many aircraft, an airline would wait for regulators and manufacturers to make a recommendation. However, the accident had been serious, and no one was yet sure what the problem was.

Hirshman called Southwest's CEO, Gary Kelly, and said he believed they did not have enough information to let the 737s fly. Kelly agreed that the 79 planes should be grounded.

Testing all the aircraft took several days. Five planes needed further maintenance; the rest were found safe to fly. Boeing has continued to investigate the problem, narrowing it down to one generation of planes, most of them made for Southwest. The pattern of problems may suggest that something went wrong during the manufacturing of the planes rather than with Southwest's maintenance practices. It also may have shown up at Southwest because the airline flies its jets on frequent short trips, subjecting them more frequently to the intense stresses that occur during takeoff and landing.

Southwest initially had a public relations nightmare: reports of dramatic damage to one of its planes during a flight. Then it had to help its passengers while canceling and delaying flights over the course of three days. However, by respecting the wisdom of its maintenance chief in putting safety ahead of revenues, Southwest eased passengers' fears and took charge of the inspection process, keeping it to an aggressive schedule and getting the planes back in the air.[52]

- What kinds of behavior did Southwest's culture encourage in this situation?
- Do you think clan control was a more powerful force in this situation than bureaucratic controls? Why or why not?

KEY TERMS

SUMMARY OF LEARNING OBJECTIVES

Now that you have studied Chapter 16, you should be able to:

 Explain why companies develop control systems for employees.

Left to their own devices, employees may act in ways that do not benefit the organization. Control systems are designed to eliminate idiosyncratic behavior and keep employees directed toward achieving the goals of the firm. Control systems are a steering mechanism for guiding resources and for helping each individual act on behalf of the organization.

LO 2 Summarize how to design a basic bureaucratic control system.

The design of a basic control system involves four steps: (1) setting performance standards, (2) measuring performance, (3) comparing performance with the standards, and (4) eliminating unfavorable deviations by taking corrective action. Performance standards should be valid and should cover issues such as quantity, quality, time, and cost. Once performance is compared with the standards, the principle of exception suggests that the manager needs to direct attention to the exceptional cases that have significant deviations. Then the manager takes the action most likely to solve the problem.

LO 3 Describe the purposes for using budgets as a control device.

Budgets combine the benefits of feedforward, concurrent, and feedback controls. They are used as an initial guide for allocating resources, a reference point for using funds, and a feedback mechanism for comparing actual levels of sales and expenses with their expected levels. Recently companies have modified their budgeting processes to allocate costs over basic processes (such as customer service) rather than to functions or departments. By changing the way they prepare budgets, many companies have discovered ways to eliminate waste and improve business processes.

LO 4 Define basic types of financial statements and financial ratios used as controls.

The basic financial statements are the balance sheet and the profit and loss statement. The balance sheet compares the value of company assets to the obligations the company owes to owners and creditors. The profit and loss statement shows company income relative to costs incurred. In addition to these statements, companies look at liquidity ratios (whether the company can pay its short-term debts), leverage ratios (the extent to which the company is funding operations by going into debt), and profitability ratios (profit relative to investment). These ratios provide a goal for managers as well as a standard against which to evaluate performance.

LO 5 List procedures for implementing effective control systems.

To maximize the effectiveness of controls, managers should (1) establish valid performance standards, (2) provide adequate information to employees, (3) ensure acceptability, (4) maintain open communication, and (5) see that multiple approaches are used (such as bureaucratic, market, and clan control).

LO 6 Identify ways in which organizations use market control mechanisms.

Market controls can be used at the level of the corporation, the business unit or department, or the individual. At the corporate level, business units are evaluated against one another based on profitability. At times, less profitable businesses are sold while more profitable businesses receive more resources. Within business units, transfer pricing may be used to approximate market mechanisms to control transactions among departments. At the individual level, market mechanisms control the wage rate of employees and can be used to evaluate the performance of individual managers.

LO 7 Discuss the use of clan control in an empowered organization.

Approaching control from a centralized, mechanistic viewpoint is increasingly impractical. In today's organizations, it is difficult to program "one best way" to approach work, and it is often difficult to monitor performance. To be responsive to customers, companies must harness the expertise of employees and give them the freedom to act on their own initiative. To maintain control while empowering employees, companies should (1) use self-guided teams, (2) allow decision making at the source of the problems, (3) build trust and mutual respect, (4) base control on a guiding framework of norms, and (5) use incentive systems that encourage teamwork.

DISCUSSION QUESTIONS

1. What controls can you identify in the management of your school or at a company where you now work (or recently worked)? If you can, interview a manager or employee of the organization to learn more about the controls in use there. How might the organization's performance change if those controls were not in place?

2. How are leadership and control different? How are planning and control different? How are structure and control different?

3. Imagine you are the sales manager of a company that sells medical supplies to hospitals nationwide. You have 10 salespeople reporting to you. You are responsible for your department achieving a certain level of sales each year. In general terms, how might you go about taking each step in the control cycle?

4. In the situation described in Question 3, what actions would you need to take if sales fell far below the budgeted level? What, if any, actions would you need to take if sales far exceeded the sales budget? If sales are right on target, does effective controlling require any response from you?

(Would your answer differ if the department were on target overall, but some salespeople fell short and others exceeded their targets?)

5. Besides sales and expenses, identify five other important control measures for a business. Include at least one nonfinancial measure.

6. What are the pros and cons of bureaucratic controls such as rules, procedures, and supervision?

7. Suppose a company at which executives were rewarded for meeting targets based only on profits and stock price switches to a balanced scorecard that adds measures for customer satisfaction, employee engagement, employee diversity, and ethical conduct. How, if at all, would you expect executives' performance to change in response to the new control system? How, if at all, would you expect the company's performance to change?

8. Google offers Google Apps, such as Gmail, Google Calendar, and Docs & Spreadsheets, as collaboration tools for employees. Describe how the company could use market controls to determine whether Google employees will

use these software programs or competing software (e.g., Word and Excel).

9. How effective is clan control as a control mechanism? What are its strengths? Its limitations? When would a manager rely on clan control the most?

10. Does empowerment imply the loss of control? Why or why not?

11. Some people use the concept of "personal control" to describe the application of business control principles to individual careers. Thinking about your school performance and career plans, which steps of the control process (Figure 16.1) have you been applying effectively? How do you keep track of your performance in meeting your career and life goals? How do you measure your success? Does clan control help you meet your personal objectives?

EXPERIENTIAL EXERCISES

16.1 SAFETY PROGRAM

OBJECTIVE

To understand some of the specific activities that fall under the management functions *planning, organizing, controlling and staffing,* and *directing.*

INSTRUCTIONS

After reading the following case, briefly describe the kinds of steps you would take as production manager in trying to solve your safety problem. Be sure to relate your answer specifically to the activities of *planning, organizing, controlling and staffing,* and *directing.*

MANAGING THE VAMP CO. SAFETY PROGRAM

If there are specific things that a manager does, how are they done? What does it "look like" when one manages? The following describes a typical situation in which a manager performs managerial functions:

As production manager of the Vamp Stamping Company, you've become quite concerned over the metal stamping shop's safety record. Accidents that resulted in operators' missing time on the job have increased quite rapidly in the past year. These more serious accidents have jumped from 3 percent of all accidents reported to a current level of 10 percent.

Because you're concerned about your workers' safety as well as the company's ability to meet its customers' orders, you want to reduce this downtime accident rate to its previous level or lower within the next six months.

You call the accident trend to the attention of your production supervisors, pointing out the seriousness of the situation and their continuing responsibility to enforce the gloves and safety goggles rules. Effective immediately, every supervisor will review his or her accident reports for the past year, file a report summarizing these accidents with you, and state their intended actions to correct recurring causes of the accidents. They will make out weekly safety reports as well as meet with you every Friday to discuss what is being done and any problems they are running into.

You request the union steward's cooperation in helping the safety supervisor set up a short program on shop safety practices.

Because the machine operators are having the accidents, you encourage your supervisors to talk to their workers and find out what they think can be done to reduce the downtime accident rate to its previous level.

While the program is going on, you review the weekly reports, looking for patterns that will tell you how effective the program is and where the trouble spots are. If a supervisor's operators are not decreasing their accident rate, you discuss the matter in considerable detail with the supervisor and his or her key workers.

SOURCE: From Theodore T. Herbert, *The New Management: Study Guide,* 4th ed., p. 41.

16.2 PRELIMINARY, CONCURRENT, AND FEEDBACK CONTROL

OBJECTIVES

1. To demonstrate the need for control procedures.

2. To gain experience in determining when to use preliminary, concurrent, and feedback controls.

INSTRUCTIONS

1. Read the text materials on preliminary, concurrent, and feedback control.

2. Read the Control Problem Situation and be prepared to resolve those control problems in a group setting.

3. Your instructor will divide the class into small groups. Each group completes the Preliminary, Concurrent, and Feedback Control Worksheet by achieving consensus on the types of control that should be applied in each situation. The group also develops responses to the discussion questions.

4. After the class reconvenes, group spokespersons present group findings.

DISCUSSION QUESTIONS

1. For which control(s) was it easier to determine application? For which was it harder?
2. Would this exercise be better assigned to groups or to individuals?

CONTROL PROBLEM SITUATION

Your management consulting team has just been hired by Technocron International, a rapidly growing producer of electronic surveillance devices that are sold to commercial and government end users. Some sales are made through direct selling, and some through industrial resellers. Direct-sale profits are being hurt by what seem to be exorbitant expenses paid to a few of the salespeople, especially those who fly all over the world in patterns that suggest little planning and control. There is trouble among the resellers because standard contracts have not been established and each reseller has an entirely different contractual relationship. Repayment schedules vary widely from customer to customer. Also, profits are reduced by the need to customize most orders, making mass production almost impossible. However, no effort has been made to create interchangeable components. There are also tremendous inventory problems.

Some raw materials and parts are bought in such small quantities that new orders are being placed almost daily. Other orders are so large that there is hardly room to store everything. Many of these purchased components are later found to be defective and unusable, causing production delays. Engineering changes are made that make large numbers of old components still in storage obsolete. Some delays result from designs that are very difficult to assemble, and assemblers complain that their corrective suggestions are ignored by engineering. To save money, untrained workers are hired and assigned to experienced "worker-buddies" who are expected to train them on the job. However, many of the new people are too poorly educated to understand their assignments, and their worker-buddies wind up doing a great deal of their work. This, along with the low pay and lack of consideration from engineering, is causing a great deal of worker unrest and talk of forming a union. Last week alone nine new worker grievances were filed, and the U.S. Equal Employment Opportunity Commission has just announced intentions to investigate two charges of discrimination on the part of the company. There is also a serious cash flow problem, as a number of long-term debts are coming due at the same time. The cash flow problem could be relieved somewhat if some of the accounts payable could be collected.

The CEO manages corporate matters through five functional divisions: operations, engineering, marketing, finance, and human resources management and general administration.

Preliminary, Concurrent, and Feedback Control Worksheet

Technocron International is in need of a variety of controls. Complete the following matrix by noting the preliminary, concurrent, and feedback controls that are needed in each of the five functional divisions.

Divisions	Preliminary Controls	Concurrent Controls	Feedback Controls
HRM and general administration	_____	_____	_____
Operations	_____	_____	_____
Engineering	_____	_____	_____
Marketing	_____	_____	_____
Finance	_____	_____	_____

CONCLUDING CASE

THE GRIZZLY BEAR LODGE

Diane and Rudy Conrad own a small lodge outside Yellowstone National Park. Their lodge has 15 rooms that can accommodate up to 40 guests, with some rooms set up for families. Diane and Rudy serve a continental breakfast on weekdays and a full breakfast on weekends, included in the room rates they charge. Their busy season runs from May through September, but they remain open until Thanksgiving and reopen in April for a short spring season. They currently employ one cook and two waitpersons for the breakfasts on weekends, handling the other breakfasts

themselves. They also have several housekeeping staff members, a groundskeeper, and a front-desk employee. The Conrads take pride in the efficiency of their operation, including the loyalty of their employees, which they attribute to their own form of clan control. If a guest needs something—whether it's a breakfast catered to a special diet or an extra set of towels—Grizzly Bear workers are empowered to supply it.

The Conrads are considering expanding their business. They have been offered the opportunity to buy the property next door, which would give them the space to build an annex containing an additional 20 rooms. Currently their annual sales total $300,000. With expenses running at $230,000—including mortgage, payroll, maintenance, and so forth—the Conrads' annual income is $70,000. They want to expand and make improvements without cutting back on the personal service they offer to their guests. In fact, in addition to hiring more staff to handle the larger facility, they are considering collaborating with more local businesses to offer guided rafting, fishing, hiking, and horseback riding trips. They also want to expand their food service to include dinner during the high season, which means renovating the restaurant area of the lodge and hiring more kitchen and wait staff. Ultimately, the Conrads would like the lodge to be open year-round, offering guests opportunities to cross-country ski, ride snowmobiles, or hike in the winter. They hope to offer holiday packages for Thanksgiving,

Christmas, and New Year's celebrations in the great outdoors. The Conrads report that their employees are enthusiastic about their plans and want to stay with them through the expansion process. "This is our dream business," says Rudy. "We're only at the beginning."

QUESTIONS

1. Discuss how Rudy and Diane can use feedforward, concurrent, and feedback controls both now and in the future at the Grizzly Bear Lodge to ensure their guests' satisfaction.

2. What might be some of the fundamental budgetary considerations the Conrads would have as they plan the expansion of their lodge?

3. Describe how the Conrads could use market controls to plan and implement their expansion.

17 Managing Technology and Innovation

LEARNING OBJECTIVES

After studying Chapter 17, you will be able to:

Manager's Brief	Progress Report	Onward

Management Connection

IS ALTERNATIVE ENERGY'S FUTURE SPELLED BP?

The initials of the company name BP only hint at its origins. The company started out as Anglo-Iranian Oil, formed to extract and sell oil discovered in Persia near the beginning of the 20th century. In 1954 Iran nationalized the oil industry, and one of the original subsidiaries became British Petroleum. Its largest stockholder was the British government. In the decades that followed, BP made strategic acquisitions, including Standard Oil Amoco and Atlantic Richfield, eventually becoming one of the world's largest energy companies, with about 80,000 employees working in more than 100 countries. The majority of its revenues come from refining and marketing, with another one-fifth of revenues coming from exploration and production of oil and natural gas.

In the late 1990s, CEO Sir John Browne embraced corporate social responsibility for the environment. Browne acknowledged that global climate change was a serious issue affected by his company's practices. In a 1997 speech, he announced that BP would by 2010 reduce its emissions of greenhouse gases (GHGs) by 10 percent from its 1990 levels. A few years later, the company announced that it had met that goal eight years ahead of schedule and intended to continue reducing GHG emissions, even as the company continued to grow.

Under Browne's leadership, environmental concern was not just a social responsibility, but also a business strategy. BP pushed past the bounds of its name to consider providing energy from sources other than petroleum. Initial investments included a manufacturing plant for solar energy and research into biofuels, such as ethanol. In recent years, as BP consistently spent more than $550 million per year on research and development, it rapidly accelerated spending on investments in alternative energy: $50 million in 2007, $99 million in 2008,

and $141 million in 2009. In 2011 the company announced that it intended to invest $2 billion in renewable energy. These efforts were expressed in a shortened company name (BP), a new green sunflower logo, and the company's tagline "Beyond Petroleum."

Among those interested in promoting and investing in green technology, opinions differ as to whether BP is truly a "green" company. Compared with other oil producers, it has invested far more in researching and developing alternative energy sources. Nevertheless, the company's activities are still dominated by oil, natural gas, and coal. Even with the growth of the alternative energy sector, BP expects these fossil fuels to represent 64 percent of its mix in 2030 (lower, however, than Exxon's estimate of 80 percent fossil fuels in 2030). Also, the April 2010 drilling rig explosion and massive oil leak into the Gulf of Mexico tarnished BP's reputation as a company that cares about the environment and strained its resources that might have been devoted to developing new technologies. Furthermore, Sir John Browne retired from BP in 2007 and was replaced with Tony Hayward, who initially was less vigorous in emphasizing alternative energy. The company's investments in alternative energy have, however, continued to grow under Hayward's direction.

Ultimately, BP's decisions to pursue various green technologies will depend heavily on whether the company can do so profitably.[1]

Although solar, wind, biofuels, and other alternative energy sources are advancing quickly, most of the energy that runs power plants and vehicles today still comes from fossil fuels. As you read this chapter, think about the issues that BP's managers must consider as they make decisions about how to include new energy technology in the company's strategy.

Technological innovation is daunting in its complexity and pace of change. And as BP's leadership has figured out, it is vital for a firm's competitive advantage. Not long ago, new products took years to plan and develop, were standardized and mass produced, and were pushed onto the market through extensive selling and promotional campaigns. With sales lives for these products measured in decades, production processes used equipment dedicated to making only those standardized products and achieved savings through economies of scale. But today's customers often demand products that have yet to be designed. Product development is now a race to become the first to introduce innovative products—products whose lives often are measured in months as they are quickly replaced by other, even more technologically sophisticated products.

Today's managers and organizations depend on effective management of technology not only to carry out their basic tasks but, even more important, to ensure the continuing competitiveness of their goods or services. In a marketplace where technology and rapid innovation are critical for success, managers must understand how technologies emerge, develop, and change the ways organizations compete and the ways people work. This chapter discusses how technology can affect an organization's competitiveness and how to integrate technology into the organization's competitive strategy. Then we assess the technological needs of the organization and the means by which these needs can be met.

Bottom Line

Innovation is a key to competitiveness

Why does innovation matter for a service business?

Technology and Innovation

LO 1

technology

The systematic application of scientific knowledge to a new product, process, or service.

innovation

A change in method or technology; a positive, useful departure from previous ways of doing things.

In Chapter 9 we defined **technology** as the methods, processes, systems, and skills used to transform resources into products. More broadly speaking, we can think of technology as the commercialization of science: the systematic application of scientific knowledge to a new product, process, or service. In this sense, technology is embedded in every product, service, and procedure used or produced.[2]

When technology is used to create a new product or service to sell or a new way of working, what has taken place is a form of innovation. *Innovation* differs from *invention*, or making a new idea manifest, which may or may not add value to any organization. In the context of management, **innovation** is any new way of working that creates value. Innovation can result from combining things that are new or from combining existing things in new ways. The resulting innovation can be any one of these three fundamental types:[3]

1. *Product innovation* is a change in the outputs (goods or services) the organization produces. If BP's research into biofuels resulted in a new kind of fuel to sell, this would be an example of product innovation.
2. *Process innovation* is a change in the way outputs (goods or services) are produced. If BP's research into biofuels resulted in a more efficient way to produce fuel from sugarcane, this would be an example of process innovation.

Other examples of process innovation are flexible manufacturing processes discussed in Chapter 9, including mass customization, just-in-time, and concurrent engineering.

3. *Business model innovation* refers to a change in the way the organization creates and delivers value. The change may affect any element of a company's business model: its customer value proposition (the basic problem it solves, such as ecofriendly fuel for about the same cost as fossil fuels), its profit formula (the financial road map for its success), its key resources (people, technology, facilities, brand, etc.), and its key processes. Examples of business model innovation include Amazon (bookselling), Netflix (video rental), and NetJets (business travel).

These categories cover a multitude of creative new ideas, which in businesses can involve changes in product offerings, the basic "platforms" or common features and processes that underlie product creation, the customer problems the organization can solve, the types of customers the organization serves, the nature of the experience provided by the organization, the way the organization earns money from what it does, the efficiency and effectiveness of its processes, the structure of the organization, the supply chain through which it delivers goods and services, the physical or virtual points at which it interacts with customers, the ways the organization communicates, and the brand associated with the organization and its products.[4]

There are definable and predictable patterns in the way technologies emerge, develop, and are replaced. Critical forces converge to create new technologies, which then follow well-defined life cycle patterns. Understanding the forces driving technological development and the patterns they follow can help a manager anticipate, monitor, and manage technologies more effectively.

> "I think there is a world market for maybe five computers."
> —Thomas Watson, IBM chairman, in 1943

1. There must be a *need*, or *demand*, for the technology. Without this need driving the process, there is no reason for technological innovation to occur.
2. Meeting the need must be theoretically possible, and the *knowledge* to do so must be available from basic science.
3. We must be able to *convert* the scientific knowledge into practice in both engineering and economic terms. If we can theoretically do something but doing it is economically impractical, the technology cannot be expected to emerge.
4. The *funding, skilled labor, time, space,* and *other resources* needed to develop the technology must be available.
5. *Entrepreneurial initiative* is needed to identify and pull all the necessary elements together.

IN PRACTICE

These forces have driven technological development and product innovation at Pratt & Whitney, a leading aerospace company. In the market for jet engines, Pratt & Whitney has a strong presence in the military sector but has lagged the competition in selling engines for commercial aircraft. Management decided that its competitive edge would come from offering aircraft companies a far more efficient engine.

It was a daring move. Designing a completely new engine and finding a customer to incorporate it into the design of a plane would take two decades. Management pulled together R&D funds from every source they could tap, eventually spending $1.5 billion before they had signed a single sales contract. Talented engineers and scientists created Pratt's PurePower engine, which uses a technology called a geared turbo fan (GTF). The GTF technology incorporates three product innovations: a lightweight but powerful gearbox, a bigger fan, and a lighter-weight engine housing. Together, these improve fuel efficiency by 16 percent, or roughly three times the improvement engine makers have offered in the past. It also cuts the engine's noise level in half.

Meanwhile, Pratt's sales team found their first customer, Bombardier, a Canadian company that was designing a new line of aircraft called the CSeries, which it hoped would compete with the Boeing 737 and Airbus A319/A320. Bombardier was hoping that offering airlines greater efficiency would enable it to capture 50 percent of the market for jets seating 100 to 150 passengers. Pratt's GTF engine was just what it needed to meet that goal.[5]

- Which forces were driving this innovation at Pratt & Whitney?

Technology Life Cycle

technology life cycle

A predictable pattern followed by a technological innovation, from its inception and development to market saturation and replacement.

Technological innovations typically follow a relatively predictable pattern called the **technology life cycle.** Figure 17.1 depicts the pattern. The cycle begins with the recognition of a need and a perception of a means by which the need can be satisfied through applied science or knowledge. The knowledge and ideas are brought together and developed, culminating in a new technological innovation. Early progress can be slow in these formative years as competitors continually experiment with product design and operational characteristics to meet consumer needs. This stage is where the rate of product innovation tends to be highest. For example, during the early years of the auto industry, companies tried a wide range of machines, including electric and steam-driven cars, to determine which product would be most effective. Eventually the internal combustion engine emerged as the dominant design, and the number of product innovations leveled off.

Once early problems are resolved and a dominant design emerges, improvements come more from process innovations.

Once early problems are resolved and a dominant design emerges, improvements come more from process innovations to refine the technology. At this point managers can gain an advantage by pursuing process efficiencies and cost competitiveness. In the auto example, as companies settled on a product standard, they began leveraging the benefits of mass production and vertical integration to improve productivity. These process innovations were instrumental in lowering production costs and bringing the price of automobiles in line with consumer budgets.[6]

Eventually the new technology begins to reach the upper limits of both its performance capabilities and the spread of its usage. Development slows and becomes increasingly costly, and the market becomes saturated (i.e., there are few new customers). The

FIGURE 17.1
The Technology Life Cycle

604

technology can remain in this mature stage for some time—as in the case of autos—or can be replaced quickly by another technology offering superior performance or economic advantage. The life cycles can take decades or even centuries, as in the case of iron- and steel-making technologies. A dramatic example of technology evolution can be found in the recorded music industry, which moved from the relatively primitive device Thomas Edison invented through the vinyl record to the cassette tape to the digitally recorded CD and then to highly miniaturized but memory-intensive MP3 players like the iPod, which are now being challenged by services, such as Pandora or Rhapsody, that allow users to stream songs from the Internet on their cell phones or computers.

As this example shows, a technology life cycle can be made up of many individual *product* life cycles. Each of these products performs a similar task—delivering recorded music to a listener—yet each product is an improvement over its predecessors. In this way, technological development involves significant innovations, often representing entirely new technologies, followed by a large number of small, incremental innovations. Ongoing development of a technology increases the benefits gained through its use, makes the technology easier to use, and allows more applications. In the process, the use of the technology expands to new adopters.

Diffusion of Technological Innovations

Like the technology life cycle, the adoption of new technology over time follows an S-shaped pattern (see the top line in Figure 17.2). The percentage of people using the technology is small in the beginning but increases dramatically as the technology succeeds and spreads through the population. Eventually the number of users peaks and levels off when the market for the technology is saturated. This pattern, first observed in 1903, has been verified with many new technologies and ideas in a wide variety of industries and settings.[7]

The adopters of a new technology fall into five groups (see the bottom line in Figure 17.2). Each group presents different challenges and opportunities to managers who want to market a new technology or product innovation.

The first group, representing approximately 2.5 percent of adopters, consists of the *innovators*. Typically, innovators are adventurous and willing to take risks. They are willing to pay a premium for the latest and newest technology or product to come along and to champion it if it meets with their approval. The enthusiasm of innovator–adopters is no guarantee of success—for example, the product may still be too expensive for the general market. But a lack of enthusiasm among this group is often a sign that the new technology has serious problems and more development is needed.

> Like the technology life cycle, the adoption of new technology over time follows an S-shaped pattern.

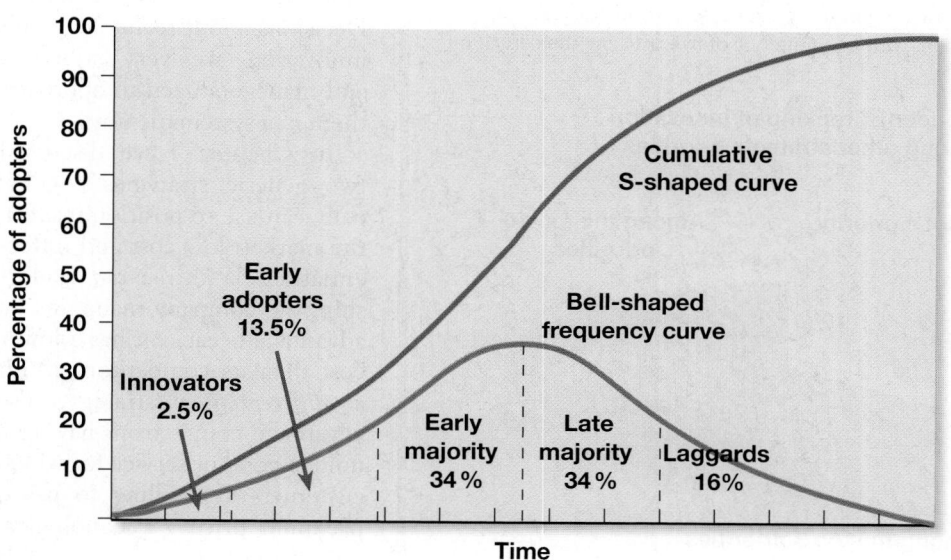

FIGURE 17.2

Technology Dissemination Pattern and Adopter Categories

The next 13.5 percent of adopters are *early adopters*. This group is critical to the success of a new technology because its members include well-respected opinion leaders. Early adopters often are the people or organizations to which others look for leadership, ideas, and up-to-date technological information. Innovators and early adopters are extremely important in new product launches, and marketing managers often spend heavily in promotion among these groups to generate a groundswell of enthusiasm.

The next group, representing 34 percent of adopters, is the *early majority*. These adopters are more deliberate and take longer to decide to use something new. Often they are important members of a community or industry, but typically not the leaders. It may take a while for the technology or new product to spread to this group, but once it does, use will begin to proliferate into the mainstream.

Representing the next 34 percent are the *late majority*. Members of this group are more skeptical of technological change and approach innovation with great caution, often adopting only out of economic necessity or increasing social pressure.

The final 16 percent are *laggards*. Often isolated and highly conservative in their views, laggards are extremely suspicious of innovation and change.

The speed with which an innovation spreads depends largely on five attributes. An innovation will spread quickly if it

- Has a great advantage over its predecessor.
- Is compatible with existing systems, procedures, infrastructures, and ways of thinking.
- Has less rather than greater complexity.
- Can be tried or tested easily without significant cost or commitment.
- Can be observed and copied easily.

Designing products with these technological considerations in mind can make a critical difference in their success.

Technological Innovation in a Competitive Environment

LO 3 Discussions about technology life cycles and diffusion patterns may imply that technological change occurs naturally or automatically. Just the opposite is true: change is neither easy nor natural in organizations (we discuss change more fully in the next chapter). Decisions about technology and innovation are very strategic, and managers need to approach them in a systematic way.

In Chapter 4 we discussed two generic strategies a company can use to position itself in the market: low cost and differentiation. With *low-cost* leadership, the company maintains an advantage because it has a lower cost than its competitors. With a *differentiation* strategy, the advantage comes from having a unique good or service for which customers are willing to pay a premium price.[9] Technological innovations can support either

Executives at a majority of companies consider innovation a top priority, but only about half are satisfied with their company's return on innovation spending. Companies are most likely to measure innovation success in terms of customer satisfaction and growth in revenue, with only one out of five tracking the return on their investment in innovation.[8]

Survey respondents' ranking of innovation spending among other strategic priorities

Not a priority

Among the top 10 priorities

Top priority

25%

10%

26%

39%

Among the top 3 priorities

of these strategies: they can be used to gain cost advantage through pioneering lower-cost product designs and creating low-cost ways to perform needed operations, or they can support differentiation by pioneering unique goods or services that increase buyer value and thus command premium prices.

In some cases, a new technology can completely change the rules of competition within an industry.[10] Technology in those cases is often called *disruptive technology* because companies—even industry leaders—can falter if they fail to respond with effective innovations, and new companies can take over a dominant role. Companies that have struggled with disruptive technology include Kodak, which dominated the photography market until digital cameras replaced the use of film, and radio and television stations as advances in broadband have made the Internet a more exciting option for entertainment.

But industries seldom are transformed overnight. Typically, signals of a new technology's impact are visible well in advance, leaving time for companies and people to respond. For example, almost every competitor in the telecommunications industry fully understood the value of cellular technology. Often the key issue is not *whether* to adopt a new technology but *when* to adopt it and how to integrate the change with the organization's operating practices and strategies.

Bottom Line
Innovation can improve any bottom-line practice.
How can innovation support a low-cost strategy?

Technology Leadership

The adage "timing is everything" is applied to many things, ranging from financial investments to telling jokes. It also applies to the development and exploitation of new technologies. Industry leaders such as 3M, Amazon, Nike, and Merck built and now maintain their competitive positions through early development and application of new technologies. However, technology leadership imposes costs and risks, and it is not the best approach for every organization (see Table 17.1).[11] Apple is well known for its technology leadership, beginning with its Macintosh computer, which pioneered the use of a mouse and graphical desktop icons instead of strings of typed computer commands, and advancing through the wildly popular iPod and iPhone.

> Often the key issue is not *whether* to adopt a new technology but *when* to adopt it.

Advantages of Technology Leadership   What makes innovators and technology leadership attractive is the potential for high profits and first-mover advantages. Being the first to market with new technologies can provide significant competitive advantage. If technology leadership increases an organization's efficiency relative to competitors, it achieves a cost advantage. The organization can use the advantage to reap greater profits than competitors or attract more customers by charging lower prices. Similarly, if a company is first to market with a new technology, it may be able to charge a premium price because it faces no competition. Higher prices and greater profits can defray the costs of developing new technologies.

Advantages	Disadvantages
First-mover advantage	Greater risks
Little or no competition	Cost of technology development
Greater efficiency	Costs of market development and customer education
Higher profit margins	
Sustainable advantage	Infrastructure costs
Reputation for innovation	Costs of learning and eliminating defects
Establishment of entry barriers	
Occupation of best market niches	Possible cannibalization of existing products
Opportunities to learn	

TABLE 17.1

Advantages and Disadvantages of Technology Leadership

Top pharmaceutical companies depend on patents to allow them several years of selling new drugs without competition before cheaper generic versions of their drugs are released. Their competitive strategy is to develop new drugs in the meantime to sustain their success.

This one-time advantage of being the technology leader can be turned into a sustainable advantage. Sustainability of a lead depends on competitors' ability to duplicate the technology and the organization's ability to keep building on the lead quickly enough to outpace competitors. It can do this in several ways. The reputation for being an innovator can create an ongoing advantage and even spill over to the company's other products. For example, 3M's reputation for innovation and quality differentiates some of its standard products, such as adhesive tape, and allows a product to command a premium price. A competitor may be able to copy the product but not the reputation. Patents and other institutional barriers also can be used to block competitors and maintain leadership. The big players in the pharmaceutical industry invest heavily in research and development; they depend on patents to give them several years of selling new drugs without competition before generic versions of their drugs are permitted. For example, the blood thinner Plavix, which has the second-largest level of sales in the world, was protected by patent until 2011. In that year and the next, the patents for one-fifth of current drugs are set to expire, so pharmaceutical companies face a tremendous challenge to develop new drugs in the meantime.[12]

The first mover can also preempt competitors by occupying the best market niches. If it can establish high switching costs (recall Chapter 2) for repeat customers, these positions can be difficult for competitors to capture. Microsoft dominates the software market with its Windows and Vista operating systems because of the large library of software that is packaged with each. Although other companies can offer more advanced software, their products are not as attractive because they are not bundled as the Windows- and Vista-based systems are.

Technology leadership can provide a significant learning advantage. While competitors may be able to copy or adopt a new technology, ongoing learning by the technology leader can keep a company ahead by generating minor improvements that are difficult to imitate. Many Japanese manufacturers use several small, incremental improvements generated with their *kaizen* programs (recall Chapter 9) to upgrade the quality of their products and processes continuously. All these minor improvements cannot be copied easily by competitors, and collectively they can provide a significant advantage.[13]

> The first mover can also preempt competitors by occupying the best market niches.

Disadvantages of Technology Leadership   Being the first to develop or adopt a new technology does not always lead to immediate advantage and high profits, however. While such potential may exist, technology leadership does impose high costs and risks that followers do not have to bear. Being the leader thus can be more costly than being the follower (there's good reason why the forefront of technology is often called the "bleeding edge"). These costs include educating buyers unfamiliar with the new technology, building an infrastructure to support the technology, and developing complementary products to achieve the technology's full potential. For example, when the personal computer was first developed in the 1970s, dozens of computer companies entered the market. Almost all of them failed, usually because they lacked the financial, marketing, and sales ability required to attract and service customers. Also, many new products require regulatory approval. For example, developing a new drug, including testing and obtaining FDA approval, can take 10 years or more and cost upward of $60 million to $1 billion or more. After that, developers enjoy a profitable period of patent protection until competitors move in with low-cost generics. While these followers do not get the benefits of being first to market, they can copy the drug for a fraction of the cost once the original patents expire. This strategy can be highly profitable.[14]

Being a pioneer carries other risks. If raw materials and equipment are new or have unique specifications, a ready supply at a reasonable cost may not be available. Or the technology may not be fully developed and may have problems yet to be resolved. In addition, the unproved market for the technology creates uncertainty in demand. Finally, the new technology may have an adverse impact on existing structures or business. It may cannibalize current products or make existing investments obsolete.

Technology Followership

Not all organizations are equally prepared to be technology leaders, nor would leadership benefit each organization equally. In deciding whether to be a technology leader or follower, managers will consider their company's competitive strategy, the benefits gained through use of the technology, and the characteristics of their organization.

Interestingly, technology followership also can be used to support both low-cost and differentiation strategies. If the follower learns from the leader's experience, it can avoid the costs and risks of technology leadership, thereby establishing a low-cost position. The makers of generic drugs use this type of strategy. Followership also can support differentiation. By learning from the leader, the follower can adapt the products or delivery systems to fit buyers' needs more closely. Microsoft is famous for having built a successful company on this type of followership. The company's products, including music players, video game consoles, spreadsheet and word-processing software, and web browsers, have been launched after technology leaders have paved the way. Likewise, Facebook came to dominate the realm of social networking only after other services such as Friendster and MySpace had burned through money introducing the concept. Newer competitors, such as Google, continue to enter the market with the hope that they can lure away users with a service that improves on Facebook's strengths while avoiding its weaknesses. This follower strategy is more challenging once an industry leader has established widespread customer loyalty.

A manager's decision on when to adopt new technology also depends on the potential benefits of the new technology, as well as the organization's technology skills. As discussed earlier, technologies do not emerge in their final state; rather, they exhibit *ongoing development* (see Figure 17.3). Such development eventually makes the technology easier to use and more adaptable to various strategies. For example, the development of high-bandwidth communication networks has enabled many more companies to work with suppliers located abroad. At the same time, *complementary products and technologies* may be developed and introduced that make the main technology more

> ## Bottom Line
> Following the technology leader can save development expense.
> *How can being a follower help reduce costs?*

FIGURE 17.3
Dynamic Forces of a Technology's Competitive Impact

SOURCE: D. M. Schroeder, "A Dynamic Perspective on the Impact of Process Innovation upon Competitive Strategies," *Strategic Management Journal* 11 (January 1990), pp. 25–42. Reprinted with permission.

useful. For example, the combination of the personal computer with disk drives, printers, e-mail, and other software turned it into an essential business tool.

These complementary products and technologies combine with the *gradual diffusion* of the technology to form a shifting competitive impact from the technology. The appropriate time for an organization to adopt technological innovations is when the costs and risks of switching to the technology are outweighed by the benefits. This point will be different for each organization, with some organizations benefiting from a leadership, early adopter role, and others from a followership role, depending on each organization's characteristics and strategies.[15]

Assessing Technology Needs

The biggest industry sector in the U.S. economy is health care services, where spending is soaring, much to the dismay of the insurers and patients paying the medical bills. One reason U.S. health care costs so much is that the industry has been slower than others to adopt types of technology that can make day-to-day operations more efficient. According to a RAND Corporation study, Americans could save $162 billion a year if health care providers made better investments in information technology. For example, fewer than one out of five hospitals are using a complete bar code system for dispensing medicine, which could save money and reduce medication errors.[16]

In today's increasingly competitive environment, failure to correctly assess the technology needs of the organization can fundamentally impair the organization's effectiveness. Assessing the technology needs of the organization involves measuring current technologies as well as external trends affecting the industry.

Measuring Current Technologies

Before organizations can devise strategies for developing and exploiting technological innovation, they must gain a clear understanding of their current technology base. A **technology audit** helps clarify the key technologies on which an organization depends. The most important dimension of a new technology is its competitive value. One technique for measuring competitive value categorizes technologies as emerging, pacing, key, and base:[17]

technology audit

Process of clarifying the key technologies on which an organization depends.

- *Emerging technologies* are still under development and thus are unproved. They may, however, significantly alter the rules of competition in the future. Managers will want to monitor the development of emerging technologies but may not yet need to invest in them until they have been more fully developed.
- *Pacing technologies* have yet to prove their full value but have the potential to alter the rules of competition by providing significant advantage. For example, when first installed, computer-aided manufacturing (see Chapter 9) was a pacing technology. Its full potential was not yet widely realized, but companies that used it effectively developed significant speed and cost advantages. Managers will want to focus on developing or investing in pacing technologies because of the competitive advantages they can provide.
- *Key technologies* have proved effective, but they also provide a strategic advantage because not everyone uses them. Knowledge and dissemination of these technologies are limited, and they continue to provide some first-mover advantages. For example, a more powerful, proprietary processing chip by Intel is a key technology for that organization. Eventually, alternatives to key technologies can emerge. But until then key technologies can give organization managers a significant competitive edge and make it much more difficult for new entrants to threaten the organization.

The most important dimension of a new technology is its competitive value.

- *Base technologies* are those that are commonplace in the industry; everyone must have them to be able to operate. Thus they provide little competitive advantage. Managers have to invest only to ensure their organization's continued competence in the technology.

Technologies can evolve rapidly through these categories. For example, electronic word processing was considered an emerging technology in the late 1970s. By the early 1980s, it could have been considered pacing. While promising advantages, the technology's cost and capabilities restricted its usefulness to a limited number of applications. With continued improvements and more powerful computer chips, electronic word processing quickly became a key technology. Its costs dropped, its usage spread, and it demonstrated the capacity to enhance productivity. By the late 1980s, it was considered a base technology in most applications. Word-processing technology is now used so widely that it is viewed as a routine activity in almost every office.

Assessing External Technological Trends

Just as with any planning, decisions about technology must balance internal capabilities (strengths and weaknesses) with external opportunities and threats. Managers can use several techniques to better understand how technology is changing within an industry.

Benchmarking   As mentioned in Chapter 4, benchmarking is the process of comparing the organization's practices and technologies with those of other companies. The ability to benchmark technologies against those of competitors varies among industries. While competitors understandably are reluctant to share their secrets, information trading for benchmarking is not uncommon and can prove highly valuable. For example, Harley-Davidson's recovery of its reputation for manufacturing quality motorcycles began only after company executives toured Honda's plant and witnessed firsthand the weaknesses of Harley's manufacturing technologies and the vast potential for improvement.

> ### Bottom Line
> Benchmarking can lower cost and raise speed, quality, sustainability, and customer service.
> *What are some limits on benchmarking as a source of technology ideas?*

Benchmarking against potential competitors in other nations is also important. Companies may find key or pacing technologies in use that can be imported easily and offer significant advantage. Also, overseas firms may be more willing to share their knowledge if they are not direct competitors and if they are eager to exchange information to benefit both companies.

Scanning   Whereas benchmarking focuses on what is being done currently, scanning focuses on what can be done and what is being developed. In other words, benchmarking examines key and perhaps some pacing technologies, while scanning seeks out pacing and emerging technologies—those just being introduced and still in development.

Scanning typically involves a number of tactics, many of them the same as those used in benchmarking. However, scanning places greater emphasis on identifying and monitoring the sources of new technologies for an industry. It also may dictate that executives read more cutting-edge research journals and attend research conferences and seminars. The extent to which scanning is done depends largely on how close to the cutting edge of technology an organization needs to operate.

After Harley-Davidson executives toured a Honda plant, they were able to identify the weaknesses within their own company and use that knowledge to improve and boost their reputation.

Key Factors to Consider in Technology Decisions

LO 5   Once managers have thoroughly analyzed their organization's current technological position, they can plan how to either develop or exploit emerging technological innovations for the future. Managers must balance many interrelated factors in their decisions, such as the technology's potential to support the organization's strategic needs and the organization's skills and capabilities to exploit the technology successfully. The organization's competitive strategy, the technical abilities of its employees to deal with the new technology, the fit of the technology with the company's operations, and the company's ability to deal with the risks and ambiguities of adopting a new technology all must be considered in conjunction with the dynamic forces of a developing technology. This process does not always mean waiting for the technology to develop. Often it requires changing the capabilities and strategies of the organization to match the needs of the technology, including hiring new people, training existing employees, changing internal policies and procedures, and changing strategies. These considerations are discussed next.

Anticipated Market Receptiveness

The first consideration that needs to be addressed in developing a strategy around technological innovation is market potential. In many cases, innovations are stimulated by external demand for new goods and services. For example, the share of Internet users who use a language other than English has been growing rapidly. This trend, along with the globalization of business, has fueled demand for the ability to search the web in different languages. Companies are creating a variety of software innovations to meet this demand. Google will translate a searcher's query into a dozen languages and also translate web pages to present results in the searcher's language. Yahoo Answers will send queries to a native speaker of the user's language. It indexes those responses so they can be searched by future users in that language.[19]

English is still the Internet's top language, but most users speak other languages.[18]

Major languages used on the World Wide Web

- Other 17.8%
- English 27.3%
- Chinese 22.6%
- Spanish 7.8%
- Japanese 5.0%
- Portuguese 4.2%
- German 3.8%
- Arabic 3.3%
- French 3.0%
- Russian 3.0%
- Korean 2.0%

In assessing market receptiveness, executives need to make two determinations:

1. In the short run, the new technology should have an immediate, valuable application.
2. In the long run, the technology must be able to satisfy market needs.

For example, retailers are always looking for ways to get the right goods on their shelves at the right time at a lower cost. They were therefore immediately interested in the introduction of a new technology for tracking inventory, radio frequency identification (RFID). As we saw in Chapter 9's discussion of logistics, RFID tags on pallets of merchandise are an efficient method by which retailers can keep track of inventory moving to warehouses and stores. They provide both cost savings and up-to-the-minute data for measuring demand. With this track record, makers of RFID tags are able to sell additional benefits to existing and new customers. Walmart has begun putting RFID tags on individual products so store employees can measure exactly what is in stock with the wave of a scanner. Hospitals are beginning to place RFID tags on equipment, supplies, and even patients' bracelets so they can ensure adequate supplies and efficiently deliver the right services. And when art collectors transport valuable pieces, they often mark each work with an RFID tag as one of their many security measures.[20]

IN PRACTICE

Drawing on a decade of experience in designing computer games, Damion Schubert has identified several important pitfalls to avoid if a game is to be well received by its market. Schubert, the lead combat designer for BioWare (where his credits include *Star Wars: The Old Republic*), says the first mistake is to innovate too much. He points out that trying to execute every new idea for a game inevitably confuses the message about what is exciting in that game, and it is probably impossible to do well. Instead designers have to think about what they can accomplish well within the constraints of a schedule and then select innovations that users are most likely to enjoy.

Schubert learned of a team that was designing a multiplayer game and thought it would be interesting to allow players to set each other's houses on fire. Really, though, that innovation was something that fed the designers' wish to try something new, not an idea that players would really appreciate. Instead, Schubert says, designers need to ask gamers what *they* think would make the game better.

Similarly, Schubert says, game designers often confuse features with benefits. They might count up the number of races in a game, or the number of creatures or quests. Then they think of ways to add more races, creatures, or quests. But in most genres, the number of such features is limited in the best games because what provides genuine quality in a game is for each choice to be interesting, detailed, and well crafted. Thus it is more important to thoroughly test every innovation so that it works well than to heap on new features. Gamers, Schubert insists, are not just looking for designers "to show them something new" but rather "to show them something better."[21]

- How could an online retailer apply Schubert's ideas for considering market receptiveness?

Technological Feasibility

In addition to market receptiveness, managers must consider the feasibility of technological innovations. Visions can stay unrealized for a long time. Technical obstacles may represent barriers to progress. For example, security experts have for years wanted reliable face recognition systems; if a computer can correctly associate a face with the correct person's identity, this would prevent many of the problems that arise from stolen ID cards, passwords, and other fallible protection systems. But a recent study by the National Research Council found that face recognition technology cannot be improved to the point of making zero errors. Some of the stumbling blocks that are too complex for the computer systems of today and the foreseeable future are picking out facial features from a picture

> "I have not failed. I've just found 10,000 ways that don't work."
>
> —Thomas Edison

with other details, accounting for differences in a person's posture or facial expression, and accounting for differences in lighting levels and time (because people's faces change as they age). Improving performance in one of these areas tends to reduce performance in another. Even testing these systems is difficult: if, say, the lighting is adjusted, the results will diverge from test results under different conditions. At a recent NFL Super Bowl, face recognition technology was tested as a means to spot terrorists in a crowd, but the trial results were disappointing.[22]

Other industries face technological hurdles as well. In the oil industry, for example, technological barriers prevent exploration and drilling in the deepest parts of the ocean. In medicine, scientists and doctors work continuously to identify the causes of and cures for diseases such as cancer and AIDS. Automakers' efforts to develop electric cars have been constrained by the difficulty of designing a battery that can power the long trips Americans love to take. General Motors's widely touted Volt has a range of 40 miles between charges, the same range as an experimental car being tested by Toyota for city driving.[23] Each of these potentially valuable innovations is slowed by the technical limits of currently available technologies.

Economic Viability

Closely related to technological feasibility is economic viability. Apart from whether a firm can "pull off" a technological innovation, executives must consider whether there is a good financial incentive for doing so. The use of hydrogen-powered

Closely related to technological feasibility is economic viability.

fuel cell technology for automobiles is almost feasible technically, but its costs are still too high. In addition, even if those costs were brought down to more acceptable levels, the absence of a supporting infrastructure in the society as a whole—such as the lack of hydrogen refueling stations—would represent another barrier to economic viability. However, if organizations can find niche markets for a high-priced new technology, they often can advance the technology to the point that applications become more affordable. For example, three-dimensional (3D) printers can read plans and translate them into physical objects by applying light or chemicals to plastic to harden it into a desired shape. Originally costing $100,000, today's versions of the machine sell for $15,000 and are used by industrial designers to test part designs before they go into full-scale production. Investing in this technology makes sense because it saves manufacturers the major expense of setting up production processes to make models of parts still in development. The price of a 3D printer is expected to drop as low as $2,000 within a few years, and assuming companies could eventually develop simple versions for under $1,000, 3D printers could start showing up in people's homes. Then if a plastic part of a toy or appliance breaks, you could go online for the plans and "print" out a replacement instantly.[24]

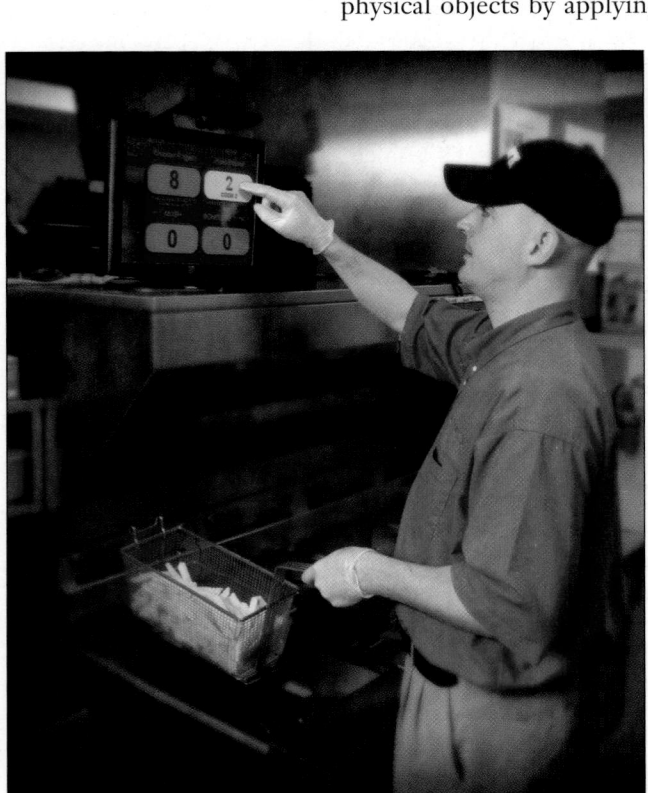

Hyperactive Bob applies robotics technology (computer vision and artificial intelligence) to fast-food operations to make them more efficient. Using this technology is economically feasible because it reduces waste, improves customer satisfaction, and reduces employee turnover.

Less futuristic innovations also require a careful assessment of economic viability and costs. New technologies often represent an expensive and long-term commitment of resources. And integrating them effectively within an organization can require a great deal of management time. Once an organization commits to a technological innovation, a change in direction becomes extremely difficult and costly. For these reasons, a careful, objective analysis of technology costs versus benefits is essential. Of course, benefits can be substantial as well. Fast-food restaurants can adopt a system called Hyperactive Bob. The system scans the parking lot to count vehicles that are arriving; compiles that data with information about time of day, cooking times, ordering patterns, and so on; and then issues orders to employees, telling them which items and how many to begin cooking. Employees touch a screen to indicate when they accept a task and when they are finished. The system, made by Hyperactive Technologies, costs $5,000 to install and $3,000 a year for software licensing, but it saves thousands a year in reduced food waste plus much more in reduced employee turnover—because Bob is an alternative to being shouted at by an anxious supervisor.[25]

The issue of economic viability takes us back to our earlier discussion of adoption timing. Earlier adopters may have first-mover advantages, but costs are associated with this strategic approach. The development costs of a particular technological innovation may be quite high, as in pharmaceuticals, chemicals, and software. Patents and copyrights often help organizations recoup the costs of their investments in technological innovations. Without such protection, the investments in research and development might not be justifiable.

IN PRACTICE

Conversion of paper medical records into electronic systems has been widely touted as an important money-saving technological advance. Savings can come from recommending generic versions of medicines when available, keeping records in one centralized database rather than duplicating them in various locations, and avoiding errors from misreading handwritten orders or prescribing medicines that interact with other drugs the patient is already taking. The hurdle is how to pay for the conversion.

Managers of Midland Memorial Hospital wanted electronic medical records. Nurses were wasting too much time hunting for charts, squinting at messy handwriting, and filling out repetitive forms, but creating a computer system would be expensive. A system with all the features could cost $20 million or more. Midland found the answer at the Veterans Health Administration. When VA facilities went electronic, they put the source code for their software in the public domain, so other programmers could use it, adding unique features for their clients. Using the new system, Midland has lower rates of infection and death and incurred fewer medication errors. The hospital also caught up on its billing backlog.

Doctors face a similar challenge. So far, fewer than 2 out of 10 have computerized medical records. Many are intimidated by the expense and have few if any computer experts on staff. The federal government has addressed the economic hurdle with incentives of about $40,000 for installing and using electronic records systems. Also, in New York City, the Primary Care Information Project developed software and helped more than 1,000 physicians implement it. The project's head concludes that doctors will change but only if they have enough help—financial and technical.[26]

- What might be the advantages and consequences of a hospital delaying the switch to electronic medical records because it isn't economically viable?

Unfortunately, the exploding growth in piracy or even fakery of patented pharmaceuticals, software, and other products has added new barriers to economic viability. Globalization has created a worldwide market for goods produced by low-cost counterfeiters and pirates overseas, who have the added advantage that they do not have to incur research and development expense. In addition, technology has made it easy to copy software without paying for it. Pfizer's anti-impotence drug Viagra, Hewlett-Packard inkjet cartridges, Intel computer chips, GM car designs, Coach handbags, Nike Air Jordan shoes, and countless music and movie recordings—all these and much more have been counterfeited or illegally copied and sold. Worldwide lost sales as a result of this illegal activity—the theft of *intellectual property*—have been estimated at more than $500 billion a year. A major contributor to the problem is China, which accounted for about 80 percent of the fake or pirated goods seized by the U.S. government in a recent year. Some companies have also taken action on their own. Auto parts maker Bendix set up a team charged with enforcing intellectual property rights, has adapted packaging so that it is harder to counterfeit, and educates customers by setting up trade show displays with side-by-side comparisons of its product and knockoffs. Other companies, including Pfizer, are using radio frequency tags on their packages so they can more accurately track products throughout the distribution process.

Bottom Line
Innovation requires financial feasibility.
Say an innovation is exciting but unprofitable. What are the risks of pursuing it anyway?

All these measures are designed to help organizations—and countries—maintain the economic viability of their innovations.[27]

Anticipated Competence Development

We have stated repeatedly in this text that organizations should (and do) build their strategies based on core capabilities. This advice applies to technology and innovation strategies as well. Frequently we can view technological innovations that are the tangible product of intangible—or tacit—knowledge and capabilities that make up a firm's core competence. Merck and Intel are examples of companies in which core capabilities in research and development lead to new technological innovations. Even in these cases, research capabilities are not always a good match with market opportunities. Pharmaceutical companies such as Merck are finding that many of the best new opportunities for fighting disease are in biotechnology, but the companies had developed expertise in chemistry-based drugs. Often these companies add new capabilities by acquiring or setting up ventures with biotechnology start-ups.

A firm may not be technology oriented, but it still must pay attention to changing technology because it sometimes will need new capabilities to survive. For example, when Amazon.com changed the face of e-retailing in the 1990s, traditional brick-and-mortar bookstores had to adapt quickly. To regain competitiveness, they had to bolster their information technology capabilities, which wasn't always an easy thing to do.

> Without the skills needed to implement an innovation, even promising technological advances may prove disastrous.

The upshot of this is that while certain technologies may have tremendous market applicability, managers must have (or develop) the internal capabilities needed to execute their technology strategies. Without the skills needed to implement an innovation, even promising technological advances may prove disastrous.

Organizational Suitability

The final issues that tend to be addressed in deciding on technological innovations have to do with the culture of the organization, the interests of managers, and the expectations of stakeholders. Companies such as 3M and Google, which are seen as proactive "technology-push" innovators, tend to have cultures that are more outward-looking and opportunistic. Executives in these *prospector* firms give considerable priority to developing and exploiting technological expertise, and decision makers tend to have bold intuitive visions of the future. Typically they have technology champions who articulate competitively aggressive, first-mover technological strategies. In many cases, executives are more concerned about the opportunity costs of not taking action than they are about the potential to fail.

By contrast, *defender* firms, such as Kroger and Safeway, tend to adopt a more circumspect posture toward innovation. These firms tend to operate in stable environments. As a result, their strategies are focused more on deepening their capability base through complementary technologies that extend rather than replace their current ones. Strategic decisions are likely to be based on careful analysis and experience in the industry setting. In the United States, supermarkets have competed for decades by emphasizing low-cost distribution over large distances. That strategy has helped the companies survive low-cost pressure from Walmart but has not always translated well when U.S.-based supermarket chains have tried to expand into other parts of the world.[28]

A hybrid *analyzer* firm, such as Microsoft, needs to stay technologically competitive but tends to allow others to demonstrate solid demand in new arenas before it responds. Microsoft's Xbox game console, Office software, and Zune music player all contain innovations, but other companies pioneered the original path-breaking product concepts. As we noted earlier, these types of firms tend to adopt an early follower strategy to grab a dominant position more from their strengths in marketing and manufacturing than through technological innovation.

Every company has different capabilities to deal with new technology. As discussed previously, early adopters have characteristics different from those of late adopters. Early adopters of new technologies tend to be larger, more profitable, and more specialized. Therefore, they are in an economic position to absorb the risks associated with early adoption while profiting more from its advantages. In addition, the people involved in early adoption are more highly educated, have a greater ability to deal with abstraction, can cope with uncertainty more effectively, and have strong problem-solving capabilities. Thus early adopters can more effectively manage the difficulties and uncertainty of a less fully developed technology.[29]

One additional consideration managers need to take into account when introducing new technology is the impact the new technology will have on employees. Often new technology brings with it work flow and other changes that directly affect the organization's work environment. If the organization does not endorse and implement innovation, these changes may create anxiety and even resistance among employees, making integration of the technology more difficult. When managers communicate well in advance about the new technology, explain its purpose, and provide the necessary training, the process of integrating the new technology into the organization's existing processes becomes easier. The cooperation of employees is often a major factor in determining how difficult and costly the introduction of new technology will be. We discuss the issue of managing change in more detail in the next chapter.

Table 17.2 briefly summarizes the five major factors we have been discussing: market receptiveness, technological feasibility, economic viability, anticipated competence development, and organizational suitability. All of these considerations jointly influence the decisions managers will make about technology innovations. A lack in even one of them can derail an otherwise promising project. For example, consider how these factors apply to BP's adoption of alternative energy technologies as you read "Management Connection: Progress Report."

Considerations	Examples
Market receptiveness—assess external demand for the technology (short/long run).	Cell phones, MP3, personal digital assistants (PDAs), HDTV
Technological feasibility—evaluate technical barriers to progress.	Deep-sea oil exploration, physical size of PC microprocessors
Economic viability—examine any cost considerations, and forecast profitability.	Solar fusion, fuel cells for automobiles, missile defense system
Competence development—determine whether current capabilities are sufficient.	Information technology in hospitals, digital technology in cameras
Organizational suitability—assess the fit with culture and managerial systems.	Steel companies focusing on creativity and innovation

TABLE 17.2
Framing Decisions about Technological Innovation

| Manager's Brief | **Progress Report** | Onward |

Management Connection

BP BETS ON TRENDS FAVORING ALTERNATIVE ENERGY

Why is BP ahead of other major oil companies in getting involved with alternative energy? One answer has to be the leadership of former CEO Sir John Browne, who has been concerned about climate change since at least the 1990s. Browne brought in an environmental nonprofit organization, the Environmental Defense Fund, to help BP find ways to reduce greenhouse gas emissions. That commitment to being ecofriendly was a natural impetus to invest in alternatives to fossil fuels (oil, coal, and natural gas).

But alternative energy was not just Browne's pet project; the investments continued—and even grew dramatically—under CEO Tony Hayward. Evidently BP executives were convinced there is a solid business case for committing to these technologies.

With demand for energy rising even as the readiest sources of fossil fuels are used up, energy users are coming to see a need to develop other sources of energy. Currently, burning coal, oil, or natural gas is less expensive than generating wind or solar power. However, as the price of fossil fuels continues to rise and the technology for producing alternative sources of energy advances, that picture could change. Industry analysts have forecast that by 2030, the world's consumption of fossil fuels could actually decrease by 2 percent. Already, the demand for energy from wind turbines and biofuels has risen at a breathtaking rate of 30 percent per year between 2001 and 2008. In the future, demand for solar, wind, and biofuel energy is expected to increase much faster than demand for energy from fossil fuels. One significant challenge, however, is that these alternatives so far have not been very profitable.

Major oil companies have reacted to the profit challenge in various, mostly modest ways. Royal Dutch Shell backed out of early efforts to enter the solar and wind businesses, but it continues to invest in biofuels. Exxon Mobil has largely stayed away from alternative energy altogether, although it did form a partnership with a company developing next-generation biofuels grown from algae. Chevron's portfolio of businesses includes some solar power capacity, and ConocoPhillips has invested in building infrastructure to deliver biofuels for transportation. By contrast, BP's involvement in alternative energy is far more extensive, encompassing biofuels, wind, solar, hydrogen power, and carbon capture and storage (used for making fossil fuels less damaging to the environment). One analyst has estimated that in 2009, 3 percent of BP's total capital expenditures—money spent to acquire or upgrade physical assets such as factories and equipment—were directed toward alternative energy.

Of the biggest oil companies, BP is the only one to report revenues from alternative energy: $794 million, equal to 0.33 percent of its total revenue, in 2009. This is a tiny share, but BP projects the contribution of alternative energy to grow quickly over the coming decades. It has forecast that by 2030, alternative energy sources, led by biofuels, will contribute more to the company's growth than any one of its fossil fuels. By 2030, the company also forecasts, alternative energy sources will represent more than one-third of the company's energy supply mix. With that future in mind, BP invests in researching alternative energy technologies. On average, about one-fourth of BP's R&D budget is devoted to alternative energy projects, with about 70 percent of that spending allocated to bioscience, including biofuels.

To arrive at these conclusions, BP monitors not only the technological environment but also the political one. Like other oil companies, BP's forecasters assume that some governments, especially in Europe, will eventually respond to climate change by imposing a tax on carbon use, which would make oil and coal more expensive. As a result, they expect that demand for cleaner-burning natural gas will rise and that advances in low-carbon technology will make other energy sources more popular. Governments also have provided incentives for alternatives such as building solar farms and growing plants, including corn, to make ethanol. However, such policies are subject to sudden changes, so the company has to proceed cautiously with forecasts when profits depend on government actions. An additional challenge is that some of these technologies are advancing fast in low-wage parts of the world, such as China, where BP may face stiff competition in the sector.[30]

- At what stage of the technology life cycle is alternative energy? What category of adopter of this technology is BP?
- In light of the key factors to consider in technology decisions, how would you rate BP's decision to get involved with alternative energy?

Sourcing and Acquiring New Technologies

Developing new technology may conjure up visions of scientists and product developers working in research and development (R&D) laboratories like that of Bell Labs. However, new technology also can come from many other sources, including suppliers, manufacturers, users, other industries, universities, the government, and overseas companies. While every source of innovation should be explored, each industry usually has specific sources for most of its new technologies. For example, because of the limited resources of most farming operations, innovations in farming most often come from manufacturers, suppliers, and government extension services. Seed manufacturers develop and market new, superior hybrids; chemical producers improve pesticides and herbicides; and equipment manufacturers design improved farm equipment. Land grant universities develop new farming techniques, and extension agents spread their usage.

In many industries, however, the primary sources of new technology are the organizations that use it. For instance, more than three-fourths of scientific innovations are developed by the users of the scientific instruments being improved and subsequently may be licensed or sold to manufacturers or suppliers.[31]

Essentially, the question of how to acquire new technology is a **make-or-buy decision.** In other words, should the organization develop the technology itself or acquire it from an outside source? However, the decision is not that simple. There are many alternatives, and each has advantages and disadvantages. Some of the most common options are discussed in the following sections.

> **make-or-buy decision**
>
> The question an organization asks itself about whether to acquire new technology from an outside source or develop it itself.

Internal Development

Developing a new technology within the company has the potential advantage of keeping the technology proprietary—exclusive to the organization. This provides an important advantage over competitors. The disadvantage of internal development is that it usually requires additional staff and funding for an extended period. Even if the development succeeds, considerable time may elapse before practical benefits are realized. Managers must carefully weigh the potential benefits of proprietary technology against the cost of developing it. Intel balances these risks and benefits by operating research and development laboratories in several locations, including Oregon, Israel, India, and China. Engineers in the various labs have come up with breakthrough ideas in the projects they have tackled, and labs in offshore locations can get around legal restrictions on technology imports, as well as save money relative to the cost of hiring talent in the United States.[32]

Purchase

Most technology already is available in products or processes that can be purchased openly. For example, a bank that needs sophisticated information-processing equipment need not develop the technology itself. It can simply purchase the technology from manufacturers or suppliers. In most situations, this is the simplest, easiest, and most cost-effective way to acquire new technology. However, in this case, the technology itself will not offer a competitive advantage.

> **Bottom Line**
>
> Purchasing may be faster and cheaper than internal development.
>
> *What is the main downside of this way to acquire technology?*

Contracted Development

If the technology is not available and a company lacks the resources or time to develop it internally, it may choose to contract the development from outside sources. Possible contractors include other companies, independent research laboratories, and university and government institutions. Usually outside contracting involves an agreed-upon series of objectives and timetables for the project, with payments made as each part of the project is tested and achieved.

Licensing

Certain technologies that are not easily purchased as part of a product can be licensed for a fee. Television producers license the right to install V-chips (paying a royalty of about $1 per TV set) because the U.S. government requires them so that parents can limit the content to which their children are exposed. Companies that develop video games often license technology, including the software that models the physics behind the activities depicted in the game. The artwork, characters, and music for a particular game may be unique, but the basic laws of real-world physics apply to the action shown in most of today's sophisticated games, so there is no advantage to programming that aspect of each game. Licensing is more economical.[33]

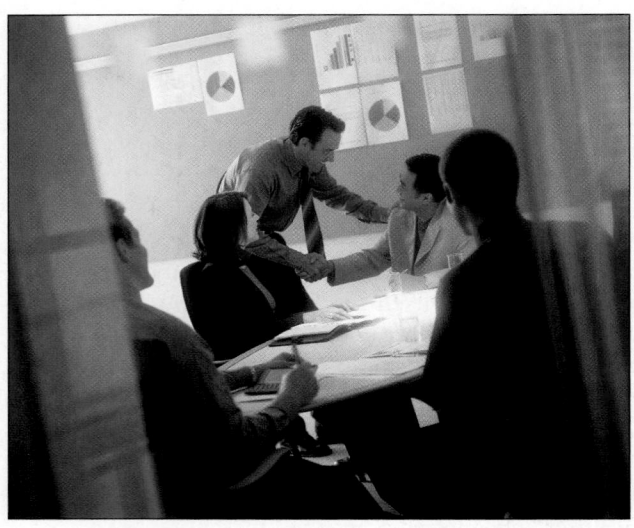

Being open to collaboration can result in ideas to achieve greater success.

Technology Trading

Another way to gain access to new technologies is with technology trading. Representatives from Scotsman Ice Systems have studied other manufacturers' information technology applications. Whether or not those companies were in the same industry, their experiences have provided Scotsman with lessons that would have been expensive to learn from trial and error. Similarly, Mary Jo Cartwright, a director of manufacturing operations for Batesville Casket Company, toured a John Deere farm equipment plant and took note of a technology called visual management screens, which display how-to information for production workers. Although the technology wasn't worthwhile for Batesville at the time, when it later became involved in more customization, the company introduced visual management screens to give workers detailed and understandable assembly instructions.[34]

Sometimes even rival companies use technology trading. Not all industries are amenable to this kind of sharing, but technology trading is becoming increasingly common because of the high cost of developing advanced technologies independently.[35]

Research Partnerships and Joint Ventures

Research partnerships are arrangements designed to jointly pursue specific new technology development. Typically each member enters the partnership with different skills or resources needed for development to succeed. One effective combination is an established company and a start-up. Joint ventures are similar in most respects to research partnerships, but they tend to have greater permanence, and their outcomes result in entirely new companies.[36] But as we described in our discussion on strategic alliances in Chapter 9, sometimes even powerful competitors collaborate on projects. An example is the strategic alliance formed by Tyson Foods, the giant meat producer, and ConocoPhillips, one of the big U.S. oil companies, to develop a renewable diesel fuel that includes beef, pork, and poultry fat discarded during meat processing. This alliance brings together Tyson's knowledge in applying protein chemistry and Conoco's knowledge of refinery technology.[37]

Sometimes even powerful competitors collaborate on projects.

Acquisition of an Owner of the Technology

If a company lacks the needed technology but wishes to acquire proprietary ownership of it, one option is to purchase the company that owns the technology. This transaction can take a number of forms, ranging from an outright purchase of the entire company to a minority interest sufficient to gain access to the technology. For example, Motorola purchased shares of Global Locate, which developed the technology for fast-working global positioning systems. Customers are increasingly interested in GPS applications in cell phones and other mobile devices. More recently, a semiconductor supplier called Broadcom acquired Global Locate outright. That move positioned Broadcom to supply semiconductors featuring GPS navigation without having to license that technology or depend on an outside supplier.[38]

Choosing among these alternatives is simpler if managers ask the following basic questions:

1. Is it important (and possible) in terms of competitive advantage that the technology remain proprietary?
2. Are the time, skills, and resources for internal development available?
3. Is the technology readily available outside the company?

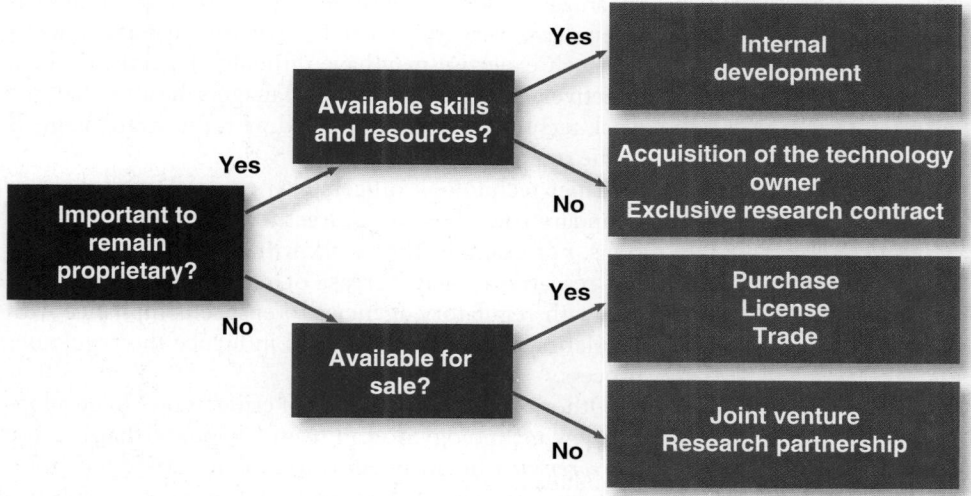

FIGURE 17.4
Technology Acquisition Options

As Figure 17.4 illustrates, the answers to these questions guide the manager to the most appropriate technology acquisition option.

If the preferred decision is to acquire a company, managers take additional steps to ensure the acquisition will make sense for the long term. For example, they try to make sure that key employees will remain with the firm instead of leaving and perhaps taking essential technical expertise with them. Similarly, as with any large investment, managers carefully assess whether the financial benefits of the acquisition will justify the purchase price.

Technology and Managerial Roles

In organizations, technology traditionally has been the responsibility of vice presidents for research and development. These executives are directly responsible for corporate and divisional R&D laboratories. Typically their jobs have a functional orientation. But increasingly companies have the position of **chief information officer (CIO)**, often also called the *chief technology officer (CTO)*. The CIO is a senior position at the corporate level with broad, integrative responsibilities. CIOs coordinate the technological efforts of the various business units; act as a voice for technology in the top management team; identify ways that technology can support the company's strategy; supervise new technology development; and assess the technological implications of major strategic initiatives such as acquisitions, new ventures, and strategic alliances. They also manage their organization's *information technology (IT)* group.[39]

In organizations that value the agility resulting from continuous learning, this position sometimes is a variation on the CTO known as a *chief innovation officer*. The chief innovation officer not only ensures that technology advances in line with the company's strategy, but also ensures that ideas and knowledge freely flow between R&D and other employees, as well as between researchers and the company's management.[40]

Without the CIO's integrative role, different departments in an organization could easily adopt different technology tools and standards, leading to much higher equipment and maintenance expense and difficulties in connecting the different parts of the

LO 6

chief information officer (CIO)

Executive in charge of information technology strategy and development.

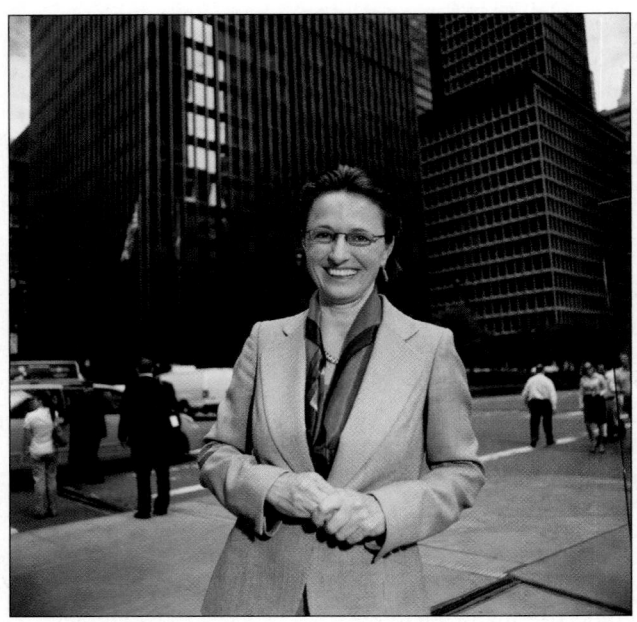

Sophie Vandebroek, chief technology officer of Xerox, took on this role with the goal of making Xerox's systems simpler, speedier, smaller, smarter, more secure, and socially responsible—what she calls the "six S's."

organization. Also, because organization technologists often have very specialized expertise, managers without such expertise may have difficulty supervising them effectively. A CIO can help managers ensure that the work technologists do is aligned with the strategic goals of the organization.

Chief technology officers also perform an important boundary role: they work directly with outside organizations. For example, they work with universities for funding research to stay abreast of technical developments and with regulatory agencies to ensure compliance with regulations, identify trends, and influence the regulatory process.

Other people play a variety of critical roles in developing new technology. Recall from Chapter 7 that it is the *entrepreneur* who, in an effort to exploit untried technologies, invents new products or finds new ways to produce old products. The entrepreneur opens up new possibilities that change the competitive structure of entire industries. For example, Steve Jobs started Apple Computer in his garage, helping to popularize the personal computer and years later the MP3 music player.

Key roles in acquiring and developing new technologies are the technical innovator, product champion, and executive champion.[41] The **technical innovator** develops the new technology or has the key skills needed to install and operate the technology. This person possesses the requisite technical skills, but he or she may not have the managerial skills needed to push the idea forward and secure acceptance within the organization. This is where the product champion gets involved. Introducing new technology into an organization requires that someone promote the idea. The **product champion**—often at the risk of his or her position and prestige—promotes the idea throughout the organization, searching for support and acceptance. The champion can be a high-level manager but often is not. If the champion lacks the power and financial resources to make the required changes independently, she or he must convince people who have such authority to support the innovation. In other words, product champions must get sponsorship.

> "Cost management will never, ever go away. If you can't manage your costs, you can't qualify for the other stuff. Just being strategic isn't sufficient [for a CIO]."
> —Karl Wachs, CIO, Celanese Corporation[42]

technical innovator

A person who develops a new technology or has the key skills to install and operate the technology.

product champion

A person who promotes a new technology throughout the organization in an effort to obtain acceptance of and support for it.

executive champion

An executive who supports a new technology and protects the product champion of the innovation.

Sponsorship comes from the **executive champion,** who has the status, authority, and financial resources to support the project and protect the product champion. Without this support and protection, the product champion, and thus the new technology, could not succeed. Resources needed to develop the innovation would be unavailable, and without protection, the champion would not be allowed to continue promoting the change.

IN PRACTICE

In the hierarchical culture of the military, executive champions are essential to clear the way for innovation. This was the case with the introduction of solar technology to U.S. forces fighting in Iraq and Afghanistan.

Even as technological advances have made U.S. armed forces formidable, they have increased the need for energy to power all the high-tech gear. Supply lines are loaded with batteries and portable generators in addition to food and medical supplies. The supply convoys face danger as they deliver these goods along routes planted with roadside bombs. Particularly perilous is the transportation of fuel, and in Afghanistan, 30 percent of that fuel is used for powering generators.

Since 2001 the U.S. military has been exploring alternative energy options, but these needed an advocate. In Iraq in 2006, Major General Richard Zilmer, commander of the first Marine Expeditionary Force, requested renewable energy gear for forward bases. Nothing came of that request.

Two years later, when marines made a similar request, Navy Secretary Ray Mabus had established a goal that half of the navy's energy come from nonfossil fuels by 2020. (The Marine Corps is part of the U.S. Navy.) Also, the Marine Expeditionary Energy Office was in place to figure out how to apply the navy's energy innovations to marines on active duty. With leaders pushing for innovation, scientists got to work and within months had developed a small solar- and battery-power generator that could be transported on Humvees. They also created small solar panels for marines to carry and open up to recharge their equipment. It was a welcome relief: marines had been carrying up to 20 pounds of batteries in their gear. Best of all, reducing the need for helicopter pilots and truck drivers to deliver batteries and fuel to troops in remote locations can literally save lives.[43]

- What would be the challenges of trying to be a product champion in this situation?

Organizing for Innovation

Successful innovation is a lot more than a great idea. A study by the Boston Consulting Group found that lack of good ideas is hardly ever the obstacle to profitable innovation. More often, ideas fail to generate financial returns because the organization isn't set up to innovate. The culture is risk averse, projects get bogged down, efforts aren't coordinated, and management can't figure out where to direct the company's money.[44] In contrast, as shown in Figure 17.5, innovation has a chance to flourish when positive values are in place, when the organization integrates internal and external knowledge, and when its people are encouraged to own and solve problems and to experiment continuously.

> More often, ideas fail to generate financial returns because the organization isn't set up to innovate.

In Chapter 9 we introduced the concept of "learning organizations"—companies that excel at solving problems, seeking and finding new approaches, and sharing new knowledge with all members of an organization. Such learning organizations are particularly well positioned to develop useful innovations. The innovations may involve a kind of "ambidexterity," or doing two things at once. Some innovations are about *exploiting* existing capabilities—to improve production speed or product quality, for example. Or the innovation may involve *exploring* new knowledge—seeking to develop new products or services.[45] Both innovation processes are necessary. Innovative learning organizations use their existing strengths to improve their operations and thus improve their bottom lines. But they also learn to unleash people's creative energies and capabilities to develop new products and processes that will ensure their long-term competitiveness. In this section we discuss some of the approaches managers use to organize for innovation.

Unleashing Creativity

3M has a strong orientation toward *intrapreneurship* and derives about one-third of its revenues from new products. 3M, Merck, Hewlett-Packard, and Rubbermaid have well-established histories of producing many successful new technologies and

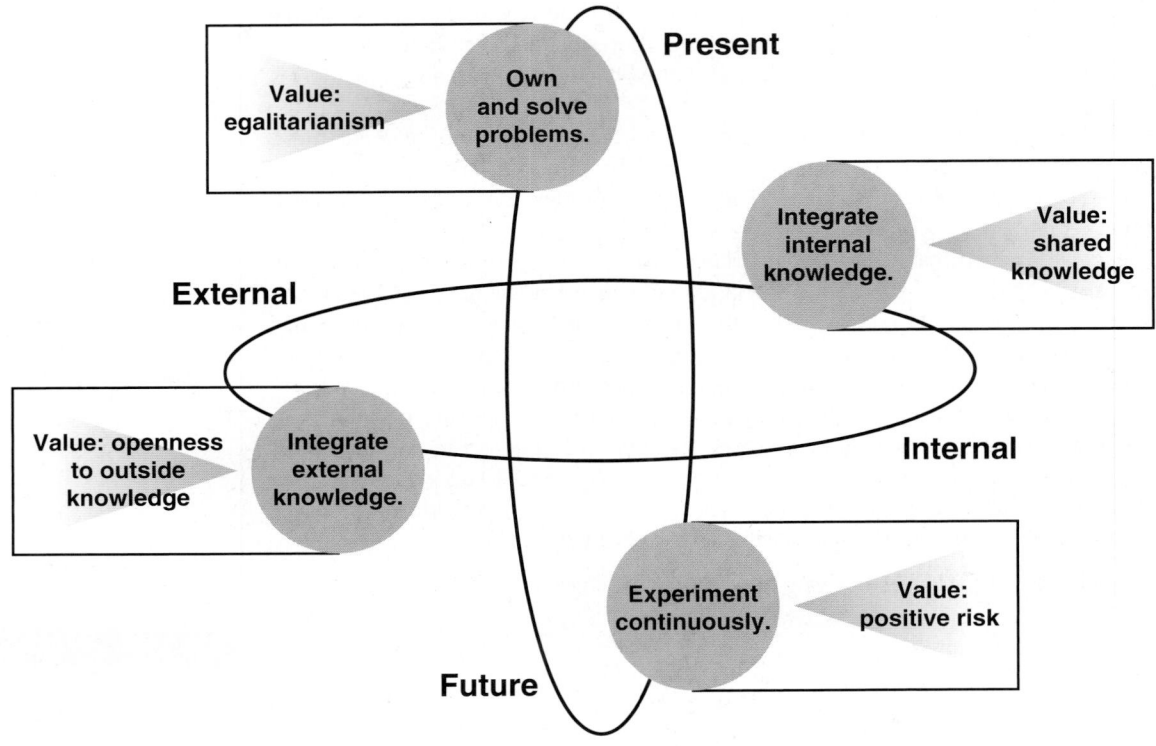

FIGURE 17.5
Requirements for
Innovation

products. What sets these and other continuous innovators apart? The one thing these companies have in common is an organizational culture that encourages innovation.[46]

A culture that permits failure is crucial for fostering the creative thinking and risk taking required for innovation. If 3M hadn't kept Francis G. Okie on board after a few failed inventions, Okie would never have come up with 3M's first success—waterproof sandpaper.

Failure is the essence of learning, growing, and succeeding.

Consider the 3M legend from the early 1920s of inventor Francis G. Okie. Okie dreamed up the idea of using sandpaper instead of razor blades for shaving. The aim was to reduce the risk of nicks and avoid sharp instruments. The idea failed, but rather than being punished for the failure, Okie was encouraged to champion other ideas, which included 3M's first blockbuster success: waterproof sandpaper. A culture that permits failure is crucial for fostering the creative thinking and risk taking required for innovation.

As strange as it may seem, *celebrating* failure can be vital to the innovation process.[47] Failure is the essence of learning, growing, and succeeding. Innovative companies have many balls in the air at all times, with many people trying many new ideas. A majority of the ideas will fail, but it is only through this process that the few big "hits" will emerge that make a company an innovative star. Madison Mount, who leads the design work for food and beverage clients of IDEO, says, "If I'm not taking risks, I feel uncomfortable, because I'm not learning."[48] This type of attitude from a manager can foster creative thinking throughout the ranks.

3M uses the simple set of rules listed in Table 17.3 to help foster innovation. These rules can be—and are—copied by other companies. But 3M has an advantage in that it has followed these rules since its inception and has ingrained them in its culture. This culture is shared and passed on in part through stories. One such legend is about the 3M engineer who was fired because he refused to stop working on a project that his boss thought was wasting

TABLE 17.3
3M's Rules for an
Innovative Culture

- **Set goals for innovation.** By corporate decree, 25 to 30 percent of annual sales must come from new products that are five years old or newer.

- **Commit to research and development.** 3M invests in R&D at almost double the rate of the average U.S. company. One R&D goal is to cut in half the time it takes to introduce new products.

- **Inspire intrapreneurship.** Champions are encouraged to run with new ideas, and they get a chance to manage their products as if they were running their own businesses. 3Mers are allowed to spend 15 percent of their time pursuing personal research interests unrelated to current company projects.

- **Facilitate, don't obstruct.** Divisions are kept small and are allowed to operate with a great deal of independence but have constant access to information and technical resources. Researchers with good ideas are awarded $50,000 Genesis grants to develop their brainstorms into new products.

- **Focus on the customer.** 3M's definition of quality is to demonstrate that the product can do what the customer—not some arbitrary standard—dictates.

- **Tolerate failure.** 3Mers know that if their ideas fail, they still will be encouraged to pursue other innovative ideas. Management knows that mistakes will be made and that destructive criticism kills initiative.

TABLE 17.3
3M's Rules for an
Innovative Culture

SOURCES: Company reports; R. Mitchell, "Masters of Innovation: How 3M Keeps Its New Products Coming," *BusinessWeek,* April 10, 1989, pp. 58–63; T. Katauskas, "Follow-Through: 3M's Formula for Success," *R&D,* November 1990; and T. J. Martin, "Ten Commandments for Managing Creative People," *Fortune,* January 16, 1995, pp. 135–36.

resources. Despite being fired, the engineer came to work as usual, finished the project, and

> "Failure is the best way to clear the fog to see a path to success."
> —Diego Rodriguez and Ryan Jacoby, IDEO, an innovative design firm[49]

demonstrated the value of his innovation. The engineer eventually was promoted to head a new division created to manufacture and market the innovation.

Bureaucracy Busting

Bureaucracy is an enemy of innovation. While bureaucracy is useful to maintain orderliness and gain efficiencies, it also can work directly against innovativeness. Developing radically different technologies requires a more fluid and flexible (organic) structure that does not restrict thought and action. However, such a structure can be chaotic and disruptive to normal operations. Thus, although 3M has been admired for its culture of innovation, during the previous decade it became inefficient, with unpredictable profits and an unimpressive stock price. An efficiency drive beginning in 2001 impressed investors and drove up profits, but breakthrough innovations dried up.[50]

To balance innovation with other business goals, companies often establish special temporary project structures that are isolated from the rest of the organization and allowed to operate under different rules. These units go by many names, including "skunkworks" (recall Chapter 7), "greenhouses," and "reserves."

To foster a culture that values innovation, software maker Intuit set up a program called Innovation Lab. Adapting a policy that Google made famous, the company allows employees to spend 10 percent of their time on unstructured activities aimed at generating and developing new ideas. They can choose an idea they personally feel passionate about or can devote the time to learning about new technologies. Intuit also sponsors "idea jams"—days set aside for employees with an idea to assemble a team to develop the idea. Idea jams are one-day events that take place every three months. Employees also have access to workgroup software called Brainstorm, which helps them share ideas and recruit team members to work on the ideas during the idea jams and their unstructured time. Review groups and mentors ensure that ideas are

Bottom Line

Bureaucracy busting encourages innovation.
Name one way to "bust bureaucracy."

practical and successful. Intuit provides cash awards for winning ideas, but the excitement of Innovation Lab and idea jams is what really motivates Intuit employees to contribute to innovations such as the mobile version of QuickBooks Online.[51]

Bureaucracy-busting managerial systems that encourage collaboration can facilitate innovation. At steel companies such as Chaparral and Nucor, for example, employees work in cross-functional teams to solve problems and create innovative solutions. These flat structures help create an environment that encourages creativity and cooperation. Teams focus on current issues and problems as well as future concerns and opportunities. In addition, teams collaborate with outside partners to bring knowledge into the organization so it can be integrated with existing ideas and information to create innovations. All the while, teams are supported by values of egalitarianism, information sharing, openness to outside ideas, and positive risk. The aim is to destroy the traditional boundaries between functions and departments to create collaborative, less bureaucratic "learning laboratories."[52]

Implementing Development Projects

<table>
<tr><td>LO 8</td></tr>
</table>

development project

A focused organizational effort to create a new product or process via technological advances.

A powerful tool for managing technology and innovations is the **development project**.[53] A development project is a focused organizational effort to create a new product or process via technological advances. For example, when MTV launched channels aimed at various Asian American markets, the company used development projects embedded in a culture that values innovation.

Development projects typically feature a special cross-functional team that works together on an overall concept or idea. Like most cross-functional teams, its success depends on how well individuals work together to pursue a common vision. And in the case of development projects, teams must interact with suppliers and customers frequently, making the complexity of their task that much greater. Because of their urgency and strategic importance, most development projects are conducted under intense time and budget pressures, thus presenting a real-time test of the company's ability to innovate.

Managers should recognize that development projects have multiple benefits. Not only are they useful for creating new products and processes, but they frequently cultivate skills and knowledge that can be used for future endeavors. In other words, the capabilities that companies derive from a development project frequently can be turned into a source of competitive advantage. For example, when Ford created a development project to design an air-conditioning compressor to outperform its Japanese rival, executives also discovered that they had laid the foundation for new processes that Ford could use in future projects. Their new capability in integrated design and manufacturing helped Ford reduce the costs and lead times for other product developments. Thus *organizational learning* had become an equally important criterion for evaluating the success of the project.

For development projects to achieve their fullest benefit, they should build on core capabilities (recall Chapters 4 and 9); have a guiding vision about what must be accomplished and why (Chapter 12); have a committed team (Chapters 12 and 14); instill a philosophy of continuous improvement (Chapter 9); and generate integrated, coordinated efforts across all units (Chapters 8 and 9).

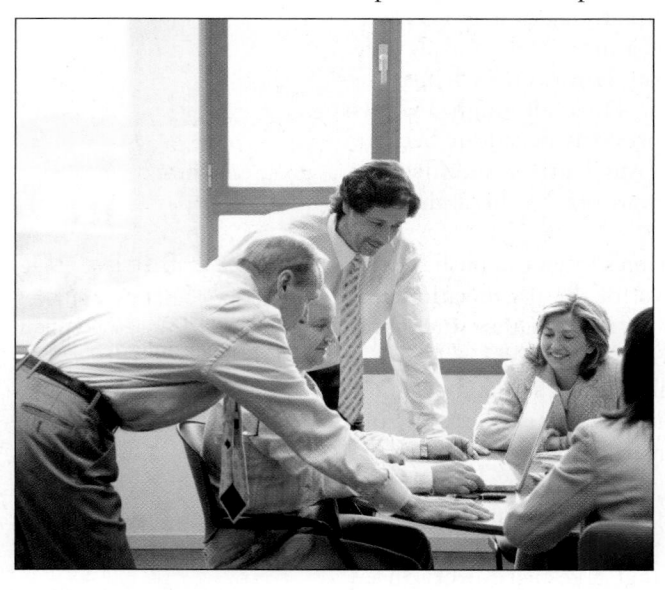

The success of a project is determined by how well a cross-functional team can work together. What traits do good team players have?

Technology, Job Design, and Human Resources

Adopting a new technology typically requires changes in the way jobs are designed. Often the way the task is redefined fits people to the demands of the technology to maximize the technology's operation. But this often fails to maximize total productivity because it ignores the human part of the equation. The social relationships and human aspects of the task may suffer, lowering overall productivity.

The **sociotechnical systems** approach to work redesign specifically addresses this problem. This approach redesigns tasks in a manner that jointly optimizes the social and technical efficiency of work. Beginning with studies on the introduction of new coal-mining technologies in 1949, the sociotechnical systems approach to work design focused on small, self-regulating work groups.[54] Later it was found that such work arrangements could operate effectively only in an environment in which bureaucracy was limited. Today's trends in bureaucracy "bashing," lean and flat organizations, work teams, and an empowered workforce are logical extensions of the sociotechnical philosophy of work design. At the same time, the technologies of the information age—in which people at all organizational levels have access to vast amounts of information—make these leaner and less bureaucratic organizations possible.

Managers face several choices regarding how to apply a new technology. Technology can be used to limit the tasks and responsibilities of workers and "de-skill" the workforce, thus turning workers into servants of the technology. Alternatively, managers can select and train workers to master the technology, using it to achieve great accomplishments and improve the quality of their lives. Technology, when managed effectively, can empower workers as it improves the competitiveness of organizations.

However, as managers make decisions about how to design jobs and manage employees, they also need to consider other human resource systems that complement the introduction of new technology. Table 17.4, for example, shows how compensation systems can be changed to facilitate the implementation of advanced manufacturing technology. In the contemporary setting, the use of group incentives, salary, and skill-based pay systems helps reinforce the collective effort (recall the use of cross-functional teams), professionalism, empowerment, and flexibility required for knowledge work. If a company's pay system is not aligned with the new technologies, it may not reward behavior that is needed to make the changes work. Worse, existing reward systems actually may reinforce old behaviors that run counter to what is needed for the new technology.

sociotechnical systems

An approach to job design that attempts to redesign tasks to optimize operation of a new technology while preserving employees' interpersonal relationships and other human aspects of the work.

TABLE 17.4   Compensation Practices in Traditional and Advanced Manufacturing Firms

Type of Compensation Practice	Traditional Factory	Integrated Manufacturing
Performance-contingent	Focus on *individual incentives* reflects division of labor and separation of stages and functions.	Extensive use of *group incentives* to encourage teamwork, cooperation, and joint problem solving.
Job-contingent	Use of *hourly wage* assumes that differences in employee contribution are captured in job classifications and that performance is determined largely by the production system.	Use of *salary* assumes that the employees' contributions transcend the job per se to substantially affect output. The distinctions between classes of employment are diminished.
Person-contingent	*Seniority pay* rewards experience as a surrogate for knowledge and skill in a stable environment and rewards loyalty to reduce uncertainty within the system.	*Skill-based* pay rewards continuous learning and the value added from increased flexibility in a dynamic environment.

SOURCE: S. A. Snell and J. W. Dean Jr., "Strategic Compensation for Integrated Manufacturing: The Moderating Effects of Jobs and Organizational Inertia," *Academy of Management Journal* 37 (1994), pp. 1109–40.

Taken as a whole, these ideas provide a set of guidelines for managing the strategic and organizational issues associated with technology and innovation. The issues are relevant whether a company is simply automating an activity or, as in the case of BP, entering entirely new high-tech businesses (see "Management Connection: Onward"). In Chapter 18 we expand this discussion to focus on how organizations can reshape themselves to adapt to a dynamic marketplace. Managing change and organizational learning are central elements of what it takes to become a world-class organization.

| Manager's Brief | Progress Report | **Onward** |

Management Connection

BP'S INNOVATION TOOLS AND TACTICS

BP, the company has advertised for years, means "Beyond Petroleum." Although BP has not left petroleum behind, the firm has moved beyond petroleum in several ways and toward several different technologies.

Early in the effort, CEO Sir John Browne announced that BP would invest $100 million in solar energy. While this is a fraction of a percent of the company's total revenues, it was enough for BP to start up what was the world's largest modern solar manufacturing plant. By 2002 BP had an 18 percent share of the solar-power market.

In 2005 BP created a new division, named after the company's Beyond Petroleum slogan. The Beyond Petroleum division had an $8 billion 10-year budget to run businesses in biofuels, wind, solar, hydrogen power, and carbon capture and storage. Many of the businesses are run as partnerships with companies that specialize in each type of energy production or pollution control.

Under CEO Tony Hayward, BP continued its expansion of alternative energy aimed at meeting the company's goals for contributing to a secure, sustainable, affordable energy supply. In the years under Hayward, the Beyond Petroleum division continued expanding its investments in research and development targeting bioscience, carbon capture and storage, and solar and wind energy.

The biggest efforts are in refining, blending, marketing, and distributing biofuels through arrangements such as joint ventures and acquisitions in Brazil and the United Kingdom. Recently, in its largest alternative energy investment so far, the company acquired CNAA, which runs advanced ethanol plants in Brazil that convert sugarcane into fuel for vehicles. BP chose a Brazilian facility because Brazil's climate and geology are ideal for growing vast quantities of sugarcane. The company plans to expand the plant with the expectation that it can produce the equivalent of 8,000 barrels of oil at a competitive cost.

In addition, the company is expanding its involvement with other new technologies. BP's wind farms dominate the U.S. wind energy business, and it has more than 1,700 employees building equipment for producing solar energy. BP also has purchased a hydrogen power business, Hydrogen Energy International, and has partnered with a hydrogen power company in the United Arab Emirates.[55]

- What methods of sourcing and acquiring new technologies has BP used for getting into the alternative energy business? Why do you think BP doesn't develop all of its new technologies internally?
- How should BP's commitment to new technology involving energy efficiency and alternative energy affect the way its jobs are designed?

KEY TERMS

SUMMARY OF LEARNING OBJECTIVES

Now that you have studied Chapter 17, you should be able to:

LO 1 List the types of processes that spur development of new technologies.

Forces that compel the emergence of a new technology include (1) a need for the technology, (2) the requisite scientific knowledge, (3) the technical convertibility of this knowledge, (4) the capital resources to fund development, and (5) the entrepreneurial insight and initiative to pull the components together.

LO 2 Describe how technologies proceed through a life cycle.

New technologies follow a predictable life cycle. First, a workable idea about how to meet a market need is developed into a product innovation. Early progress can be slow as competitors experiment with product designs. Eventually a dominant design emerges as the market accepts the technology, and further refinements to the technology result from process innovations. As the technology begins to approach both the theoretical limits to its performance potential and market saturation, growth slows and the technology matures. At this point the technology can remain stable or be replaced by a new technology.

LO 3 Discuss ways to manage technology for competitive advantage.

Adopters of new technologies are categorized according to the timing of their adoption: innovators, early adopters, the early majority, the late majority, and laggards. Technology leadership has many first-mover advantages but also poses significant disadvantages. The same may be said for followership. After that, technology that helps improve efficiency will support a low-cost strategy, while technologies that help make products more distinctive or unique will support a differentiation strategy. Determining an appropriate technology strategy depends on the degree to which the technology supports the organization's competitive requirements and, if a technology leadership strategy is chosen, the company's ability, in terms of skills, resources, and commitment, to deal with the risks and uncertainties of leadership.

LO 4 Summarize how to assess technology needs.

Assessing the technology needs of a company begins by benchmarking, or comparing, the technologies it employs with those of both competitors and noncompetitors. Benchmarking should be done on a global basis to understand practices used worldwide. Technology scanning helps identify emerging technologies and those still under development in an effort to project their eventual competitive impact.

LO 5 Identify alternative methods of pursuing technological innovation.

New technologies can be acquired or developed. Options include internal development, purchase, contracted development, licensing, trading, research partnerships and joint ventures, and acquisition. The approach used depends on the existing availability of the technology; the skills, resources, and time available; and the importance of keeping the technology proprietary.

LO 6 Define key roles in managing technology.

People play many different roles in managing technology. For example, the chief information officer is the person with broad, integrative responsibility for technological innovation. In addition, the entrepreneur is the person who recognizes the competitive potential of the technology and finds new ways to exploit opportunities. The technical innovator has the key skills needed to develop or install and operate the technology. The product champion is the person who promotes the new idea(s) to gain support throughout the organization. The executive champion is the person with the status and resources to support the project.

LO 7 Describe the elements of an innovative organization.

Organizing for innovation involves unleashing the creative energies of employees while directing their efforts toward meeting market needs in a timely manner. Companies can unleash creativity by establishing a culture that values intrapreneurship; accepts and even celebrates failure as a sign of innovation; and reinforces innovation through goal setting, rewards, and stories of creative employees. The organization's structure should balance bureaucracy for controlling existing processes with a flexibility that allows innovation to take place. Development projects provide an opportunity for cross-functional teamwork aimed at innovation. Job design should take into account both social relationships and the technical efficiency of work so that jobs are within employees' ability but also empower them to work cooperatively and creatively.

LO 8 List characteristics of successful development projects.

For development projects to achieve the fullest benefit, they should (1) build on core capabilities; (2) have a guiding vision about what must be accomplished and why; (3) have a committed team; (4) instill a philosophy of continuous improvement; and (5) generate integrated, coordinated efforts across all teams and units.

DISCUSSION QUESTIONS

1. According to Francis Bacon, "A wise man will make more opportunities than he finds." What does this have to do with technology and innovation? What does it have to do with competitive advantage?

2. What examples of technological innovation can you identify? What forces led to the commercialization of the science behind those technologies? Did the capability exist before the market demand, or was the demand there before the technology was available?

3. Thomas Edison once said that most innovations are 10 percent inspiration and 90 percent perspiration. How does this match what you know about technology life cycles?

4. Why would a company choose to follow rather than lead technological innovations? Is the potential advantage of technological leadership greater when innovations are occurring rapidly, or is it better in this case to follow?

5. If you were in the grocery business, whom would you benchmark for technological innovations? Would the companies be inside or outside your industry? Why?

6. How would you see the executive champion, the chief information officer, and the product champion working together? Could the roles all be played by the same individual? Why or why not?

EXPERIENTIAL EXERCISES

17.1   PLANNING FOR INNOVATION

OBJECTIVES
1. To brainstorm innovative ideas for a company that has become stagnant.
2. To explore the elements of a good innovation plan.

INSTRUCTIONS
1. Read the Mason Inc. scenario.
2. Individually or in small groups, offer a plan for encouraging innovation at Mason Inc. Discuss staffing, rewards, organizational structure, work design, and any other facets of organizational behavior that apply.
3. In small groups, or with the entire class, share the plans you developed.

MASON INC. SCENARIO
Mason Inc. designs, develops, and manufactures personal grooming products. From 1950 to 1980 it was a leader in introducing new, profitable products into the marketplace. Its Research and Development Division grew from 20 to 150 professionals during that time. Since 1980, however, the company has relied on its past successes and has failed to introduce any significant innovative product into the marketplace. Top management wants to reestablish Mason's reputation as the number-one innovator in the industry.

DISCUSSION QUESTIONS
1. What elements do these plans have in common?
2. How well do the plans follow the innovation process?
3. Do the plans incorporate provisions for fulfilling the various roles required for innovation?
4. What are the strengths and weaknesses of each plan?
5. What should be the components of an effective plan?

SOURCE: Judith R. Gordon, *A Diagnostic Approach to Organizational Behavior.* Copyright 1983 Pearson Education, Inc. Reprinted by permission of Pearson Education, Inc., Upper Saddle River, NJ.

17.2   INNOVATION FOR THE FUTURE

OBJECTIVE
To look ahead into the future.

INSTRUCTIONS
Choose a partner. Together, develop an innovative -product or service that will be popular in the year 2025. As you develop your product or service, ask yourselves the following questions:

1. What trends lead you to believe that this product or service will be successful?
2. What current technologies, services, or products will be replaced by your idea?

Present your idea to the class for discussion.

CONCLUDING CASE

WORLDWIDE GAMES

Players of video games often purchase their fun from Worldwide Games, which develops and markets game consoles, portable game devices, and software for playing games either on the company's hardware or on personal computers. Game enthusiasts are always on the lookout for game-playing experiences that are more intense, more lifelike, or more complex, so satisfying them drives constant innovation at Worldwide. The company has developed major and minor advances in screen resolution, processor speed, new kinds of controllers, creative story lines, and more. Its console division focuses on hardware technology, and its online division focuses on powerful new gaming software, often involving elaborate story lines played by subscribers around the world using the Internet to collaborate or compete. Continuous innovation in both divisions essentially keeps Worldwide on a par with its major competitors, who also are constantly on the lookout for the best new idea.

In recent years, two related areas of technology have been essential for the growth of Worldwide and its competitors: social networking and the ability of broadband Internet connections to deliver fast audio and video streams for playing elaborate games online. Worldwide's console division has adopted this technology by inviting purchasers of its latest console to join its Players Network. Those who join the Players Network can use their console to make an Internet connection and play games with other members anywhere in the network. Each player uses his or her controller, console, and television display and sees all the participants' actions on the display. In addition, Worldwide's online division continues to push the limits of online games played with the processing power of the latest personal computers. For the most popular programs, gamers who buy a subscription fee create their own characters, or avatars, to act out the parts in the game. Although the personal data of the players are kept private, players can use the avatars' names to look up other players' track records and invite selected avatars to join their team.

Since a necessary component of both kinds of games—console based and computer based—is for players to register and pay a fee or join the Players Network, Worldwide collects not only money from customers but also information about them. That system came under real risk when hackers recently broke into first the Players Network database and then the registration records of Worldwide Online's subscribers.

As soon as the company detected an intrusion into the Players Network, it shut down the network. When the company's security employees realized they couldn't immediately prevent intrusions within a day or two, Worldwide announced that hackers had obtained the names and possibly the credit card numbers of its tens of millions of network members. Until the problem was fixed, they would be able to play games from disks loaded into their consoles but would not be able to use the network.

While the company was investigating the original security breach, it discovered that the Worldwide Online user database also had been hacked. The company immediately announced that breach, including the fact that some credit card accounts might have been accessed. It shut down that network as well until the security hole could be plugged.

Fixing the problem, which took about a month, included adding firewalls and encryption to the existing security measures. Afterward the company reopened both networks, apologized to consumers, and offered a month of free access to paid services. Returning customers had to download upgraded security software before they could resume play. The entire incident cost the company hundreds of millions of dollars for the investigation, upgrades, and lost sales.

As operations returned to normal, Worldwide tried to minimize the risk of future intrusions by putting an executive in charge of security. The company announced that it had hired a chief information security officer. This manager reports to the company's chief information officer, who reports to the chief transformation officer, who reports to the chief executive officer.

QUESTIONS

1. Is Worldwide Games a technology leader or a technology follower? What are the risks and benefits of staking out this position?

2. What opportunities might Worldwide be missing by not having its chief information officer report directly to the CEO?

3. What makes innovation important for Worldwide? Following the hacking incident, how might bureaucracy be expected to interfere with innovation? How should Worldwide engage in "bureaucracy busting"?

Operations Management in the New Economy

The business of a company—any company—is to take certain inputs and, by means of a process, transform them into outputs. Bringing these outputs (the product) to market cost-effectively will ensure the company's continued existence and well-being. The methods, systems, and mental framework by which a company transforms its inputs into outputs characterize its *operations*. A company maintains the health of its transformation process through *management* of these operations. *Operations management* is the analysis and implementation of this process.

Many varied factors impinge on a company's operations and managers. As company size increases, so do the number of variables. Effective management of the operation and its variables contributes in no small measure to the company's success, whether the company is small or large, diversified or devoted to core businesses, a network organization or a highly structured, centralized body. It holds true whether the company sells a tangible product (goods) or an intangible one (services) because in both cases the customer is buying the object of a desire, or the satisfaction of a need.

EFFECTS OF CHANGE

We often read that operations management is in transition today. In actuality, it has always been in transition because the world is always changing. Changes may take the form of new products (imagine the first traders bringing spices to Europe in the early Middle Ages), new distribution channels (FedEx completely revamped our expectations about package delivery), alterations in the labor pool (women assumed many factory jobs during World War II when men were at war), or new technologies (gunpowder altered all the rules of war in 14th century Europe).

Characteristic of the current age is the quickening *rate* at which change occurs, placing pressure on individuals to adapt quickly and rewarding those able to shift mental gears, personal habits, and priorities easily. Indeed, survival of the fittest applies not only to physical attributes but also to mental agility. Operations managers must be among the most "fit" to function effectively in today's world.

THE CONTEXT OF OPERATIONS MANAGEMENT

What does it mean to be an effective manager of an operation? It means responding to the needs of diverse parties *within* the company, ensuring smooth movement through all stages of the transformation process. We can even take the viewpoint that, within the process, the "customer" is the department receiving the result of the preceding stage. For example, in a printing company, the operator of the press is the customer of the prepress area. An effective manager works with this awareness, ensuring that each area supplies what the next one expects.

Operations management also means satisfying parties in the *larger* arena. For example, investors may want to know how well a new product line is faring in the market or whether a new manufacturing process is delivering as promised. The community may want assurances that wastes from the production process will not cause quality of life to suffer. The government may demand an accounting of any number of activities covered by regulations. Thus the manager of an operation does not exist in isolation but is part of an ongoing interaction among any number of parties.

In ages past, the world was home to many different societies or cultures, which were mostly different one from another, but each was more homogeneous than is the case today. Buyers in a given community needed the same products. Everyone knew what those products were, and common agreement on quality prevailed. Also prevalent was a common understanding of the entitlements of various social levels (what goods of what quality were the prerogative of the wealthy, for example). Because items were individually made, customization was the norm; there was no other way to do business.

As the industrial age dawned in the 19th century, this situation changed. Suddenly the "customer" was no longer a few identifiable individuals, but a growing mass of less well-defined persons, any of whom, with money, could have what was formerly the prerogative of the few. With industrialization came mass production, and one product for all buyers became the norm because there was no other cost-effective way to do business.

The modern-day corporation took shape against this background, and marketing was born. Now in the digital age we are witnessing a phenomenon that once would have sounded like an oxymoron: mass customization. What are the implications for today's managers?

When the product is static or has few variations, operations management quite justifiably focuses on the product (and its cost). This perspective has produced the orientation of traditional operations management. With the ability to manufacture many variations of the same product, with access to increasing amounts of information, the focus today has shifted to the customer's *experience* of the product: how he or she perceives to have been served by the vendor. The customer assesses whether the product contains the desired characteristics and quality at the best price. Management of an operation with this awareness probably will spell the success or failure of the company in today's environment.

But is today's customer truly different? Yes and no: despite the fact that things change, things also stay the same. Human beings still engage in the same activities: they create community; they raise the next generation; they trade; they provide for themselves; and in the process, they learn, fight, and play. And today's managers still shuttle inputs through the transformation process into successful outputs. Most of the traditional notions about human activity still apply.

To explain any activity, however, one may use a variety of lenses (Galileo's lens was different from Ptolemy's, and so he derived a different explanation of the universe). A manager may view the process from the standpoint of product specifications, cost limitations, customer satisfaction, or any number of viewpoints. The lens chosen will reflect a particular view of the world and its priorities, as well as the company's priorities.

Sometimes there are no right or wrong choices, only consequences. The lens that adequately explained a given phenomenon at one time may not serve today. What is reflected through the lens will form the guidelines for decisions, however, and so the choice has far-reaching repercussions.

NEW PERSPECTIVES

From time to time, particular orientations or viewpoints burst onto the stage, altering perceptions and leaving changed priorities in their wake. Such is the case with W. Edwards Deming's *total quality management,* now an article of faith for many of today's managers. The Japanese readily embraced Deming's principles, taking an enviable and now imitated approach to customer satisfaction (see Chapter 9 of the text for Deming's 14 points). Western nations paid scant attention until they saw the results of offering quality in a customer-oriented operation.

For most of us, quality is what we see in the end result (does the product meet manufacturing specifications?). In his lengthy essay *Zen and the Art of Motorcycle Maintenance,* Robert Pirsig associated achievement of quality with a state of mind: "Skilled mechanics and machinists of a certain sort . . . have patience, care and attentiveness to what they're doing, a kind of inner peace of mind that isn't contrived but results from a kind of harmony with the work . . ."[1] More characteristic of the Eastern mind-set, this statement means that quality (good or bad) is not an attribute of the end product, but rather is inherent in the way an individual interacts with the subject of his or her attention.

To achieve good quality requires knowing what is good, and then having the mind-set suitable for achieving it. This attentiveness is related to the Japanese *kaizen,* a willingness and desire to improve constantly. Since the 1980s, Japanese business practices have been the object of study and implementation by Westerners, from specific procedures (such as *kanban,* the basis of just-in-time inventory management) to general philosophies (the *kaizen* that is part of Japanese general operations strategy). A manager anywhere today would be ill served by neglect of these concepts.

Likewise, companies that involve employees in the process are on the way to understanding that the people who interface with the product are crucial to its success. We will see how important this view is in a few pages.

CORPORATE ORGANIZATION

There are many ways to structure a company, and some of today's companies have taken their present form as a result of trends in the economy: mergers or acquisitions, diversification, alliances. With all, certain functions are still identifiable in most corporate organizations. The operation of that function is what commands the attention of its managers. Let us consider how some of these common functions support the operations management system.

Strategic Planning On the highest level, guiding the corporation from the broadest perspective is strategic, or long-range, planning. The firm's upper-level managers provide the corporation's direction, defining and refining its mission in the process. Management of this function entails answering questions such as these: What business are we in? What business should or will we be in? Who are our customers? How can or should we serve them? Do we want to focus on core businesses or diversify? Answers to these questions will help develop corporate goals, which, filtered through the company's management levels, give direction to its operation.

As stated earlier, the world is always changing. Good strategic planning seeks to *anticipate* change and then plan for it. Good

planners also foster a feeling of confidence about what is likely to produce success. During the 1990s, when the rallying cry of much of corporate management was to stick to core businesses, GE chief Jack Welch built a successful conglomerate of widely diverse businesses, finding people with the mind-set to operate well within that structure, and achieving effective coordination of all functions through its many divisions.

Marketing Of all the company's functions, marketing is closest to the customer. Its job is to identify customer needs (latent or manifest) and translate them back to the firm for its reaction. Its role in supporting the operations management system is therefore critical. Operations managers must then restate what marketing has communicated in terms that will bring about the needed response from the production mechanism. To support its efforts, marketing works with advertising to state the company's offerings in terms that are attractive to the buyer. Sales is a part of the marketing function also, salespeople being those who take action to sell within an identified market. This is the front line, the place where information about customer needs and desires penetrates and gains the attention of the company.

A story told in sales circles is about the ABC Company (a shoe manufacturer), whose marketing head visited a remote area of the world to assess the market. He returned to report to his boss, "There's no market; they don't wear shoes." The marketing head of competitor XYZ Company made the same trip for the same purpose, reporting to *his* boss, "It's a terrific market! They've got no shoes!" Marketing's response to a circumstance can take a firm into new areas.

Research and Engineering Suppose the marketing function has identified a new need or potential market. Enter the design and engineering people, whose function is the development and refinement of the product and the processes that manufacture it. They design, develop, and test the product through all stages until it is ready for market launch. They interact with customers who participate in the testing of a new product prior to launching. They also interact with operations—the product attributes and the processes required to make them will become the responsibility of the operations management system. Even as a product is still on the drawing board, its design may change based on customer response, manufacturing procedures (i.e., what is feasible in the current setup), or prices of material or labor.

As researchers and developers, this part of the company is most in touch with what will be available in the future, and one of its functions is identification and implementation of solutions not currently in use. The end result of the designers' work will affect purchasing (of parts, equipment, materials), inventory management (quantities of items to keep on hand), shop floor operation (equipment may need rearrangement), capacity requirements (maximum rate of production), and human resources (human skills needed and cost of acquisition).

Human Resources This brings us to the next function: human resources. A company *is* its people. They form the culture, produce the product, and deliver it. The human resources function must seek, attract, and keep individuals having the skills, human qualities, and experience required by the operations management system. Effective management of human resources thus directly affects the entire production process. Any company wishing to build a plant in a geographically desirable area would be foolish not to take into account the human component: educational level, work ethic, habits, and expectations of the labor pool.

Some believe that there are no bad employees, only employees placed in wrong positions. Effective use of employees will provide operations managers with a valuable source of innovation and productivity gains because the employees are actually in contact with the product (and with the customer, in the case of a service business). They are the interface where quality is born. It cannot be stressed too heavily that one of the most valuable attributes of any employee is the ability to communicate: to articulate what's right about the work experience, what's wrong, and how to improve it. Dissatisfaction unexpressed is potential trouble; ideas not presented represent lost potential.

Purchasing Just as human inputs matter, so do materials. Selecting inputs that will support the company's orientation and vision is the crucial role played by the purchasing function. Optimally, it is a source of expertise for the operations management system, providing information about the variety of materials and systems available for use by the production process. The performance of any operating division is ultimately dependent on goods and services supplied to it by purchasing. Will the materials produce the result intended by the design of the product? Will they allow themselves to be molded as intended by the production process? Will they support the level of quality promised?

Cost-effective supply of the right materials potentially represents enormous savings for the company. A purchasing manager was once heard to say, "The sales division would have to close $500,000 in new business to produce the money I just saved by changing suppliers."

Logistics The logistics of moving inputs through transformation may or may not benefit from an overview of the entire process; the flow may take different names, depending on its location in the process. It may be called *inventory management* as inputs arrive, *scheduling* while in the transformation process, and *distribution* when outputs are en route to the customer. Smooth or poor coordination of the flow from supplier of materials to delivery to the customer has repercussions throughout the channel. If materials are not ready for a specific section of the production apparatus at the right time, equipment and machinery sit idle (a drain on profitability). Delays in delivery to customers mean delays in payment received, and that has an impact on the company's cash flow.

Finance This brings us to the finance area. This function serves as an interface between the firm's managers and the financial community: banks, investment firms, and stockholders. These entities have a stake in the company's success or failure, and at all times are poised to assist, advise, provide support, or withdraw it. Finance must explain the company's performance adequately to elicit the maximum amount of support from financial institutions. In so doing, it makes use of the accounting department. Not merely a mechanism for tracking costs, the accounting department provides information useful to managers in understanding the cost implications of their decisions. Such cost-monitoring information can help managers understand how their own costs compare with standard costs, for example. Accounting also can help derive the cost implications of introducing new equipment or technologies.

In another of its roles, the finance function must be knowledgeable about the firm's creditworthiness. Any decline in the company's ability to pay its bills will weaken its position vis-á-vis competitors. Finance also must monitor the creditworthiness of suppliers. If suppliers are not financially able to deliver what they promise, the operations management system will feel the impact immediately. The financial community watches the impact of all these decisions, basing its ratings (and therefore support) on the wisdom of the decision makers.

A Team Operation The fineness with which one breaks down the preceding functions can vary, but it should be clear at this point that the operations management system is only one of those operating within the corporate context. In the best of all possible worlds, operations management works hand in glove with the other functions, alert to any harmful fragmentation or lack of communication. Communication is, of course, a two-way street, and just as operations people must be aware of the workings of the other functions, the latter must know what the operations management system perceives, needs, and expects.

Satisfying customer expectations is a corporate activity, the work of one body (from *corpus,* Latin for "body"), with the whole dependent on how well its parts work individually and how well they work together. Neglect of any one organ affects the body's ability to perform at optimum level.

PREPARING FOR THE FUTURE IN THE NEW ECONOMY

In addition to awareness of how the company is operating at present, every good manager will give thought to what *could* happen, what is likely to happen, and what is possible, both for the company as a whole and for his or her own sphere of influence. Stated another way, an effective manager has a sense of vision. This means being aware of changes or potential changes in customer demands and changes in the company's resources (technology, labor pool, financial support). A good manager must listen, being attentive to all facts, and then select the useful facts from among the many supplied. A manager must constantly ask, "What if . . . ?"

With good vision and a healthy curiosity, a manager will more adequately handle factors impinging on the operations management system. The objective is to develop a sense of vision adequate to anticipate conceivable consequences. Let us consider some of today's challenges in what is often referred to as the **new economy.**

Globalization A company's sphere of activity has always been what could be reached easily by current means of communication and transportation. What is reachable has constantly expanded. The entire world is today's operating arena, both for buying inputs and for selling outputs. This circumstance presents the operations management system with a new range of possibilities.

The possibility of *outsourcing* has always been present. That is, do we make a particular component of the product, or do we send it out for manufacture pursuant to our specifications? Today a manager may outsource locally or to any facility in the world offering the capability of supplying the need. It takes a lot of information, as well as sound judgment, to know which part of the process would benefit from being handled out of house.

The success of producing elsewhere depends in part on the characteristics of the "elsewhere." In the 20th century, U.S. companies based in northern states sometimes would move certain manufacturing operations to the southern part of the country, taking advantage of lower labor costs. While this required some adjustment in expectations, the adjustment is slight compared to manufacturing in Pacific Rim countries or Latin America, for example. The reason is simple: each culture handles things in a particular way. A wise manager will not assume that a different culture will respond to expectations in the same manner as an American labor force would, and this circumstance may work to one's advantage or to one's detriment. Those who can anticipate potential problem areas are ahead of the game in the decision to manufacture offshore.

Then there is the globe as *marketplace*. To sell globally requires product design that accounts for differing tastes throughout the world's cultures. A small manufacturer of skin care products based on formulas from India began marketing her line in America some years ago. She reports that she had to make alterations to account for the fact that Americans would not use a product with an unusual smell, no matter how beneficial for the skin.[2] Nescafe markets its products all over the globe, but the instant coffee sold in Brazil does not taste like that sold in the United States—in each instance, the product must satisfy the taste of a different culture.[3]

The ease with which the operations management system can make these alterations has increased dramatically in the last few decades. Digital technology has made flexibility in manufacturing a much more attainable situation than was previously the case, offering enormous potential to vary the product.

Environment Another challenge facing today's manager is the environment, meaning both the world and the milieu in which the company operates. In an earlier time, negative effects from a manufacturing process were absorbed unobtrusively by the surroundings. As population density increased and consumption skyrocketed, particularly in the Western nations, this ceased to be true. What occurs in one place on the planet has an impact on the rest of it. The manager's challenge is to care enough about the future without imperiling today's operations, and the decisions are not simple.

It is unfortunate that the issue of environmental responsibility traditionally has been cast in ethical terms. While this stance is valid, and ultimately *the* reason for being good stewards of the planet, it does not help managers handle all the information required to make good decisions or quantify what is needed for decision making. In addition, consumers are often inconsistent, demanding recycled paper, for instance, and then choosing to buy whiter paper that is not recycled.

Certainly the last few decades have witnessed significant progress in the handling of the most blatantly offensive effects of manufacturing processes (waste streaming, emissions control). But making the right decision is not a clear-cut path. Consider the simple example of the supermarket checkout stand. "Would you like paper or plastic for your groceries?" The environmentally responsible buyer must choose between less than desirable alternatives. Paper (even if recycled) uses trees; plastic uses hydrocarbons and is not as easy to recycle. Decisions faced by operations managers are infinitely more complex.

Furthermore, if managers do not see to their societal responsibility, others will demand compliance. A corporation is not its own island in community waters because others are affected by its decisions: property owners, investors, the larger public, and tomorrow's adults. Surely we have learned by now that groups that do not police their own ranks effectively are sure targets for policing by others, be they governmental agencies or community organizations.

The alternatives for an operations manager are therefore to react or to take a leadership role, becoming knowledgeable about potential negative effects of the process managed by him or her and proposing ways to handle them. In the long term, if we are to manage our economy's activities for tomorrow rather than today, responsibility for the environment is not a choice.

Knowledge and Information One of the features of the new economy is that in the transformation process, the major input is intellectual property: knowledge, research, information, and design. These inputs have supplanted (in value) the material inputs required to build physical units. When knowledge is the major raw material, launching the first unit of a product represents millions of dollars; the cost of the second and thereafter is minuscule.

The products themselves are of a different nature, and it often takes greater sophistication to use a new-economy product—thus, for example, people's reluctance to switch from a PC to a Mac, or vice versa. As a result, customers are not as likely to be swayed by advertising, but rather by their increasing knowledge of the product and its technology. Successful companies will be those that increase a customer's knowledge base in general, and skill with their own products in particular.

As the information explosion continues to feed today's consumers and today's workforce, the knowledge acquired gives rise to expectations. As we will discuss later, today's consumers are far from being locked into only a few sources for their information. Rather, they swim in an ocean of facts, figures, perspectives, and opportunities.

Nor are today's employees like those of yesteryear. It is instead the case that, depending on his or her own personal needs or aspirations, an employee is drawn to (and will stay with) a specific job in a given company for two reasons: (1) the possibility of experiencing personal satisfaction or growth and (2) satisfaction in the human interaction prevalent at that company. The balance of these factors varies with the individual, but everyone draws from these two wells. Today's managers therefore must provide more than the means for an employee to put bread on the table. The company must offer ongoing professional development, opportunity for increased responsibility in the firm, and a satisfying place to work. Today's employees do not expect to be *supervised,* but rather *coached* along the path of success. Clearly the manager also must be knowledgeable and continue to grow, increasing in value as a mentor.

Technology The challenge of technology will occupy us for the rest of these pages. Technology has always existed and has always been neutral. That is, just as a knife serves to feed the family or to kill an adversary, new technologies can be used to help or harm. As with any challenge, managers can view technological innovation as something to react to, something to anticipate, something to plan for, or something from which to derive potential improvements and growth.

Technologies exist in various stages of development; that is, some are ready and available for use by the operations management system, some will be cost-effective in 5 or 10 years, and some are in embryo. Any forward-looking manager will be aware of all three. Technology companies (those that market the latest of a given technology, such as cellular phones) must monitor technology on two fronts. They must be aware of similar products on the market, constantly assessing the limits of their own products. They also must be aware of technologies potentially usable by their own operations, just as any nontechnology company would.

In its development, a technology tends to move to the hands of the user. Take the clock as an example. At one time in history, the only clock in the community was the one in the town square. Then wealthier people could purchase large timepieces known as "grandfather clocks." By the middle of the 20th century most adults owned a wristwatch, often a special gift received at graduation. Today children and adults have access to many timepieces, from those on their wrists to the many in the home, office, or car. We could trace a similar progression for other technologies, such as engines and, of course, computers (where the transition from mainframes to portable PCs occurred within a few decades of the last century).

The shift of a technology to the user is not always smooth. One of the potential stumbling blocks when a company embraces a technology is to discount the human factor involved in its use. We see this in small businesses constantly. The local copy shop brings in the latest copying and finishing equipment, offering everything from double-sided, spiral-bound reports graced with photos to personalized, artistic party invitations. The resulting product, however, is in part dependent on the skill and experience of the operator and the availability of sufficient personnel to work with customers.

Larger industrial equipment offers a similar scenario. At an earlier time in history, the operator of, for example, a multistory printing press would have 30 years to become familiar with the operation of that equipment before a new generation came on stream. In today's offices, employees barely become proficient at using the current popular software before a new or different version of it comes out. These "improvements" provide fertile ground for inefficiencies in the final analysis, technology can advance only at the rate at which human beings can use it effectively.

With this knowledge, any effective operations manager will have some type of formal technology management in place—some means of looking ahead, preparing for the effects of new technologies. When envisioning the potential of new technology (or technology in embryo), the best human characteristics to bring to the table are

1. Awareness (information plus perspective).
2. Imagination (the ability to create new scenarios from existing ones).

Awareness is the easiest to acquire. In fact, it can be bought from the many consultants standing ready to assist corporations in preparing for the future. One must cultivate powers of imagination within oneself.

THE INTERNET

That brings us to the current challenge for one's imaginative powers: the Internet. Opportunities and pitfalls abound on the web. What follows are some noteworthy experiences gained from successful and unsuccessful uses of the Internet. By the time this material sees print, much will have changed.

Several methods have emerged as options for exploiting an Internet operation. A regular **bricks and mortar** business can create its own in-house web group, or it can partner with a dot-com company that will operate the web end of its business for it. For example, when the three largest retailers in the country decided to jump on the **e-tailing** bandwagon in the late 1990s, their strategies differed: JC Penney and Sears formed their own in-house website divisions; Kmart, in contrast, contracted with a subsidiary, bluelight.com, to get its site up and running. Last, a business can elect to sell its products only on the Internet. Internet-only companies are referred to as **pure-play** operations. Amazon.com is an example.

Managers also have to figure out how to integrate web activities seamlessly into their operations. Poorly integrated systems can wreak havoc within an organization. For instance, the first Christmas Toys 'R' Us did business on the web, the company had to turn away customers because it couldn't fill the number of orders the site generated. To solve the problem, Toys 'R' Us formed an alliance with Amazon.com. Amazon handled the website and the online ordering process, and Toys 'R' Us managed inventory and shipping. Each company had expertise the other needed to sell toys online.

Alongside web sales, retailers are in various stages of deploying new technologies to offer the benefits of online shopping at the retail site. For example, a kiosk on the shopping floor can make information available electronically, providing shoppers the information they need to make a buying decision. Lamps Plus gives its customers access to high-resolution images they can zoom in on and manipulate to review fabric textures and sample different colors and products in a 360-degree view. Pacific Sunwear lets its customers search for and display clothing for boys or girls by item, color, and price. Other sites, like eBags and Amazon, offer online guides or customer reviews to help buyers make decisions.

These retailers, along with others such as Nordstrom, Eddie Bauer, and Radio Shack, are building on brand-name presence and a familiarity already created at the mall, in the dealership, and through catalog sales—an advantage not enjoyed by companies operating exclusively on the web.

Not long ago, the online auctioneer eBay and a few companies that built e-stores for other firms were the only ones operating in the black. However, pure-play companies can be successful. Approximately one-quarter of the 200 public Internet

Amazon.com was slow to make a profit because of its initial start-up costs—for product and warehouses, for example. However, e-tailers offering travel products, software, and financial services have low overhead and can see a profit much faster.

companies that survived the dot-bomb shakeout are profitable now under standard accounting rules. The biggest moneymakers are online travel, software, and financial services. Why? Because they sell pure information products—there are no products to store or ship. But even Amazon.com, which has long operated in the red, is finally showing a profit despite the fact that every time someone buys a book on Amazon, the company must turn around and purchase a copy from the publisher. Also, once pure-play companies recoup their initial start-up costs, they don't need to spend much more money as sales rise. No additional stores need to be built to reach consumers, for example.[4]

Nonetheless, technology tricks and novel business ideas are not enough. Customers still want speed, convenience, quality, and good service. In this regard, the web is no different from conventional stores and catalogs. Customers ultimately will cast their votes for the companies that provide the best product experience whether they see the product on the web or can touch it in stores.

COMPANYWIDE RESONANCE

Sales and marketing data collection is turned on its head by the Internet as companies record information about a user's habits during a website visit. For instance, if you buy a product on Amazon.com, during future visits, the site will make suggestions about similar products in which you might be interested. Many retailers are of the opinion that this type of **data mining** will make or break the operation in the future. That is, the ability to collect and use information from online customers will be crucial to successful marketing decisions.

Moreover, a company's web page can make it easy or hard for the customer to get the information leading to a purchase. As some have learned the hard way, it is not enough to simply take images that are successful in print and place them on the web; each medium has its own characteristics.

The design of the company's website has a companywide impact. For example, if a customer on the web can verify that an item is available, the chances of closing the sale are increased. If a customer can find out the expected delivery date of the product and the means, the chances of a sale are increased even more. In this scenario, front- and back-end operations touch, and delivering the goods is still key to success.

Mountains of Data The purchasing function benefits from the web through sheer availability of information, as well as ease of response to questions. Today a purchasing manager need not wait for a visit from a sales representative. In fact, under the impact of the web, businesses are seeing a realignment of the traditional relationships among producers, wholesalers, distributors, and retailers. In the business-to-business world, buyers previously faced a number of obstacles to getting the best deal: suppliers were distant, research time was scarce, and intermediaries controlled most of the information. Enter Ariba, a web-based marketplace for industrial goods. Purchasing need only put out a contract on the web, and a flood of bids from suppliers may be the response. In a sense, web-based companies are becoming the new intermediaries, the conduit between producers and buyers.

Purchasing managers can go online to Ariba for industrial goods, National Transportation Exchange for trucking, Chemdex for biochemical supplies, and IMX Exchange for mortgage brokers to find loans, and this is only the start.

The Internet has also become the intermediary between employers and employees. Human resources departments can avail themselves of numerous web-based tools to find candidates. Not only are there gigantic job exchanges such as Monster.com, but intranets exist to keep job searches within companies. Job seekers and potential employers can access one another's information based on geographic preference, salary range, or skill sets.

Logistics, scheduling, and distribution tasks increasingly are plugged into web-based networks, benefiting from the ease of gathering weather data, traffic patterns, and late-breaking news. Tracking information about shipments can be downloaded from FedEx. Zip codes are available online from the U.S. postal service. These factors affect the company's ability to deliver the product on time and the availability of materials from suppliers, effects ultimately felt by the operations management system.

Changing Information Patterns To reduce printing costs and make documents widely available, companies are digitizing information. In some instances, they are posting it on the web. Different people residing in distant places can view the same information this way. Still, digitizing information is not without its obstacles. Not all people have the same hardware and software used for viewing and printing out information. Additionally, miscommunications can occur that otherwise might not if all employees were working under one roof.

Corporations must take these circumstances into account when deciding how to use the web because the decisions affect each of the company's functioning units. Posting certain kinds of information does not usually cause problems. For example, providing company address(es), phone numbers, hours of operation, and the like is more economically done on the web than by a live employee answering the telephone. Many inquiries that in the print age were handled by mailing out an annual report, for example, may be handled more cost-effectively on the web.

Supplying other types of information, however, might not be as free of repercussions as in the preceding examples. Depending on whether the company is a business-to-business or a business-to-consumer operation, buyers will want product information, forms and terms of payment, special sales, return policies, status of an order, shipping rates and turnaround, possibility of changing a current order, tracking information, or status of an order.

Companies can easily track their shipments by downloading the information directly from FedEx.

Providing and maintaining only one piece of this information—for example, change in an order—affects at least three departments: accounting, distribution, and marketing. Each department supplying the information must be aware of the consequences of making the information available and have a mechanism for handling changes. Coordination becomes an issue as well. For example, charges to a credit card account must not occur before the merchandise is shipped. Whether selling to another business or to consumers, online operation requires new networks. Companies forge ahead nonetheless in this burgeoning technology, realizing that the potential advantages are well worth the temporary discomforts.

INTELLECTUAL PROPERTY

We have mentioned that a characteristic of the new economy is the nature of the product: knowledge, design, and engineering, rather than hard manufacturing. Let us look at an environmental engineering firm and how the web affects its operation. The business of such a firm might include devising solutions to improve power plant operation. The activities of firms involved in the planning of any such industrial facility are subject to compliance with government regulations. Handling engineering projects, such as a new power plant, requires submission of an enormous amount of data to demonstrate that the firm has complied with and planned for all impacts on the community. A requirement might be, for example, that notification be given to every property owner within a certain radius of the plant. Downloading that information from title companies and then monitoring the notification process is only one of a multitude of tasks potentially manageable on the web.

The firm must provide the information to the various parties in certain forms, which gives rise to new information needs. For example, one way to verify that it has indeed shipped the requisite print or CD-ROM copies is by downloading tracking information from FedEx. It also can make its compliance documentation available in a read-only format on the web, allowing printing of sections by those who wish to do so.

In preparing to build a plant, all federal, state, and local regulations must be accounted for. The firm must provide information on how its power plant will affect traffic patterns, cultural resources, schools, water supply, flora and fauna, and air quality. It also must state its plans for handling hazardous materials generated during the construction and operation of the plant.

Managing the enormous body of information to respond in the ways illustrated would have been a near impossibility before computer management of data.

PITFALLS

What have been the experiences of those who have succeeded in e-commerce and those who have failed, and what can we learn from them? We already mentioned Toys 'R' Us and its inability to fill its orders on the web. In addition to losing business, it, along with other retailers such as Macys.com and CDNow, was subject to Federal Trade Commission investigation and fines regarding rules for order fulfillment. The FTC regulation states that if retailers cannot meet promised deadlines, they must notify customers, giving them the option of canceling the order. Could the management of these companies have foreseen the inability to fill orders, and if so, how?

Confidentiality of information is an issue. A recent Gallup poll revealed that 66 percent of Americans favor new laws to protect their privacy amid the high-tech revolution.[5] Amazon.com found itself under fire after it began charging different consumers different prices on the basis of information it had collected on them. Toys 'R' Us was hit with a class-action lawsuit claiming that it allowed market researchers to access consumer data from its website. The retailer responded that it had hired the firm to analyze customers' data in order to improve their shopping experience. Although breach of confidentiality predates the web, the enormity of any breach is compounded by the staggering amounts of digital data available for tapping. The Federal Trade Commission and Congress are attempting to pass laws and institute regulations to protect consumers.

Customer familiarity with the web is another issue. Despite what seems to be a flurry of online buying, media reports suggest that many customers are not buying online at all, or only infrequently, or only certain products. As with catalog shopping, the online industry will mature as consumers become more familiar with offerings and as web retailers improve in presentation and fulfillment.

Some customers are concerned about credit card data transmitted online and are therefore hesitant to shop. The misuse of credit card data is present, however, every time a clerk in a store records the data during a purchase. Although this is more a perception than a real problem, perception motivates people's actions, preventing some from making the leap into cybershopping.

Circumstances such as these are forcing the formation of new business models as companies grapple with all the variables, spurred on by the potential benefits.

NEW NEEDS AND DESIRES

Customers themselves are changing as it becomes possible to satisfy latent needs or desires. We have alluded to mass customization. Here are some specific examples of varying product features.

Setting up an assembly line or installing production equipment is part of the cost of manufacturing. Speaking of color choice in automobiles, Henry Ford once said, "They can have any color they want, as long as it's black." Alteration of a manufacturing process to vary a product feature was very costly. With the flexible manufacturing available in the digital age, manufacturers have the option of producing multiple flavors of bottled water, blue jeans tailored for different bodies, and a veritable artist's palette for automobile colors. Levi Strauss and Brooks now offer machine-customized garments, accommodating a vast array of body measurements. Barbie's friends can have hair and skin color, clothing, and even personalities picked by their young owners. Digital technology fuels the manufacturing capability; the web spurs demand.

The result is that customers' desire for customization and personalization has been moved to a new level. Shoppers previously settled for a product that was mostly, or approximately, what they wanted. They are now beginning to see that sometimes they can have a product endowed with *precisely* the features they want. The experience of product acquisition is therefore changing.

THE VALUE OF HUMAN ATTRIBUTES

What are the implications of all this change for traditional operations management? Changes are remembered as negative or positive, depending on how well one has survived them. There is no reason to believe that technological change is any more threatening than other kinds of change. Traditional human qualities still serve: vision, awareness, alertness, imagination, courage, steadfastness, persistence, flexibility, attentiveness, and goodwill.

Today's managers must be aware, noticing shifts in trends, habits and customs, possibilities, and ground rules. They must have or develop the vision to foresee the range of possibilities, and then the imagination to create solutions. They must have the courage to strike out in new directions and be alert to adjustments required by the new direction. An effective manager will be flexible enough to make an adjustment and steadfast in the face of misunderstandings and mistakes. A manager will need to be persistent in following the chosen path, with attentiveness to all facets of the surroundings. Chances of success in any challenge are enhanced by goodwill.

Finally, he or she will need luck. Some say "it comes to you," and some say "you make your own." Most think that both are true.

KEY TERMS

bricks and mortar, p. 636

data mining, p. 637

e-tailing, p. 636

new economy, p. 634

pure-play, p. 636

360-degree view, p. 636

DISCUSSION QUESTIONS

1. What is "mass customization"? How can products be mass-produced yet still be differentiated to appeal to individual market sectors? How has mass customization affected management's focus on the product?

2. Why was Deming's "total quality management" embraced by the Japanese long before Deming's philosophy became key to U.S. operations management? How does it relate to operations management?

3. How has the new economy changed operations management? What is the major input in the operations process as a result?

4. What must businesses consider in deciding to take advantage of new technology? How does new technology affect operations management decisions?

5. Why were many dot-com companies so short-lived at the end of the 20th century? Why would Amazon and Toys 'R' Us form an alliance? Which firm is likely to benefit more? Explain.

6. How can the Internet improve a firm's operations management?

7. What are the implications for operations management of customers being able to satisfy purchasing needs immediately by using the Internet? Have e-business functions fundamentally changed the way firms do business? Explain.

18 Creating and Leading Change

LEARNING OBJECTIVES

After studying Chapter 18, you will be able to:

Manager's Brief | Progress Report | Onward

Management Connection

HOW DR. PRONOVOST IS MAKING HOSPITALS SAFER FOR PATIENTS

The problem, as Dr. Peter Pronovost saw it, was obvious—and appalling. Patients are dying needlessly in U.S. hospitals. The numbers tell a disturbing story: almost 100,000 deaths per year from medical errors and a continuing decline in safety measures over the past decade. One of the leading causes of death in the United States is health care–associated infections—that is, infections acquired while in a hospital, nursing home, or other health care facility. These facts were worse than numbers to Dr. Pronovost, who serves as professor of anesthesiology and critical care medicine at Johns Hopkins University School of Medicine and leads the school's Center for Innovation in Quality Patient Care. The facts represent the suffering of real patients and their families. Years ago Dr. Pronovost witnessed a toddler die as a result of hospital error after the baby had been brought to the hospital for treatment of burns. He became determined to prevent such tragedies from happening to more patients.

Dr. Pronovost decided to find out what must change in order for hospitals to become safer places. What he learned was surprisingly simple. Many infections occur because the people working in health care facilities don't take simple precautions that are known to prevent the spread of infections. To improve, hospitals didn't need new technologies. They needed to change people's behaviors.

Under Dr. Pronovost, Johns Hopkins partnered with the Michigan Health and Hospital Association to try implementing changes that could bring down infection rates in intensive care units (ICUs). The effort, known as the Michigan Keystone ICU Project, targeted a particular kind of infection known as catheter-related bloodstream infections. Central-line catheters are inserted into a patient's neck, chest, or groin to deliver medications and fluids.

Treating a patient who acquires this type of infection adds about $18,000 to the cost of the patient's care, and the treatment sometimes fails: tens of thousands of patients die from these infections every year. However, the infections are rare when care providers keep their hands and the catheters clean. The Centers for Disease Control and Prevention (CDC) has published guidelines for preventing the infections. These guidelines are 120 pages long, which may help to explain why so many ICUs seem not to follow them.

The Keystone Project implemented in Michigan a set of changes Dr. Pronovost had used at Johns Hopkins to reduce the infection rate from 19 per 1,000 catheter days (one of the worst in the nation) to almost zero. The project boiled down the CDC's extensive guidelines for inserting central-line catheters into ICU patients into a five-item checklist:

1. Wash hands with soap and water or an alcohol cleanser.
2. Wear sterile clothing (mask, gloves, hair covering), and cover the patient with a sterile drape.
3. Clean the patient's skin with antiseptic soap when the line is inserted.

4. Avoid placing catheters in the groin, where infection rates are higher.
5. Remove the line when it is no longer needed.

In addition, the ICUs participating in the project measured infection rates so they could see how they were performing before and after the use of the checklist.

In the first year and a half of the Keystone Project, the Michigan hospitals cut the rate of infections by 66 percent to nearly zero infections. That decrease translated into a savings of more than 1,500 lives and $200 million—about $200 for every dollar invested in the project. Changing the way medical teams behave can literally save lives.[1]

Changes such as the ones brought about by the Michigan Keystone Project are not easy, do not happen automatically, and often require that managers overcome a host of obstacles. As you study this chapter, think about why the ability to change is both challenging and essential.

Change happens—constantly and unpredictably. Whatever competitive advantage you may have depends on particular circumstances at a particular time, but circumstances change.[2] The economic environment shifts; competitors pop up everywhere; markets emerge and disappear. The challenge for organizations is not just to produce innovative new products but to balance a culture that is innovative and that builds a sustainable business. And for individuals, the ability to cope with change is related to their job performance, the rewards they receive,[3] and their career success.

But *coping* with change isn't enough. Managers and their organizations need to *create* change and *improve* constantly to achieve world-class excellence and competitive advantage for the future. From his post at Johns Hopkins, Dr. Peter Pronovost sees certain changes in hospitals as literally matters of life and death. In other cases, change is something in the environment that organizations must respond to with their own changes.

Becoming World Class

LO 1

Bottom Line

It's a worthy aspiration: becoming world class at every one of your competitive goals.

What does it mean to be "world class" at a goal such as quality or sustainability?

Managers today want, or *should* want, their organizations to become world class.[4] Being world class requires applying the best and latest knowledge and ideas and having the ability to operate at the highest standards of any place anywhere.[5] Thus becoming world class does not mean merely improving. It means becoming one of the very best in the world at what you do. To some people, striving for world-class excellence seems a lofty, impossible, unnecessary goal. But it is a goal that helps one survive and succeed in today's intensely competitive business world.

World-class companies create high-value products and earn superior profits over the long run. They demolish the obsolete methods, systems, and cultures of the past that impeded their competitive progress and apply more effective and competitive organizational strategies, structures, processes, and management of human resources. The result is an organization capable of competing successfully on a global basis.[6]

Sustainable, Great Futures

Two Stanford professors, James Collins and Jerry Porras, studied 18 corporations that had achieved and maintained greatness for half a century or more.[7] The companies included Sony, American Express, Motorola, Marriott, Johnson & Johnson, Disney, 3M, Hewlett-Packard, Citicorp, and Walmart. Over the years, these companies have been widely admired, been considered the premier institutions in their industries, and made a real impact on the world. Although every company goes through periodic downturns—and these firms are no exceptions over their long histories—these companies have consistently prevailed across the decades. They turn in extraordinary performance *over the long run*, rather than fleeting greatness.

The researchers sought to identify the essential characteristics of enduringly great companies. These great companies have strong core values in which they believe deeply, and they express and live the values consistently. They are driven by goals—not just incremental improvements or business-as-usual goals, but stretch goals (recall Chapter 13). They change continuously, driving for progress via adaptability, experi-

American Express has been considered a highly acclaimed company for over 50 years.

mentation, trial and error, entrepreneurial thinking, and fast action. And they do not focus on beating the competition; they focus primarily on beating themselves. They continually ask, "How can we improve ourselves to do better tomorrow than we did today?"

But underneath the action and the changes, the core values and vision remain steadfast and uncompromised. Table 18.1 displays the core values of several companies that were "built to last." Note that the values are not all the same. In fact, no set of common values consistently predicted success. Instead the critical factor is that great companies *have* core values, *know* what they are and what they mean, and *live* by them—year after year.

> They turn in extraordinary performance *over the long run*, rather than fleeting greatness.

The Tyranny of the *Or*

Many companies, and individuals, are plagued by the **tyranny of the** *or*. This refers to the belief that things must be either A or B and cannot be both. The authors of *Built to Last* provide many common examples: beliefs that you must choose either change or stability; be conservative or bold; have control and consistency or creative freedom; do well in the short term or invest for the future; plan methodically or be opportunistic; create shareholder wealth or do good for the world; be pragmatic or idealistic.[8] Such beliefs, that only one goal but not another can be attained, often are invalid and certainly are constraining—unnecessarily so.

tyranny of the or

The belief that things must be either A or B and cannot be both; that only one goal and not another can be attained.

The Genius of the *And*

In contrast to the tyranny of the *or*, the **genius of the** *and*—more academically, **organizational ambidexterity**—refers to being able to achieve multiple objectives at the same time.[9] It develops via the actions of many individuals throughout the organization. We discussed earlier in the book the importance of delivering multiple competitive values to customers, performing all the management functions, reconciling hard-nosed business logic with ethics, leading and empowering, and others. Authors Collins and Porras have their own list:[10]

genius of the *and*; organizational ambidexterity

Ability to achieve multiple objectives simultaneously.

- Purpose beyond profit *and* pragmatic pursuit of profit.
- Relatively fixed core values *and* vigorous change and movement.
- Conservatism with the core values *and* bold business moves.
- Clear vision and direction *and* experimentation.

TABLE 18.1
Core Ideologies in Built-to-Last Companies

3M	Innovation—"Thou shalt not kill a new product idea."
	Absolute integrity.
	Respect for individual initiative and personal growth.
	Tolerance for honest mistakes.
	Product quality and reliability.
	"Our real business is solving problems."
Sony	To experience the sheer joy that comes from the advancement, application, and innovation of technology that benefits the general public.
	To elevate the Japanese culture and national status.
	Being pioneers—not following others, but doing the impossible.
	Respecting and encouraging each individual's ability and creativity.
Walmart	"We exist to provide value to our customers"—to make their lives better via lower prices and greater selection; all else is secondary.
	Swim upstream, buck conventional wisdom.
	Be in partnership with employees.
	Work with passion, commitment, and enthusiasm.
	Run lean.
	Pursue ever-higher goals.
Walt Disney	No cynicism allowed.
	Fanatical attention to consistency and detail.
	Continuous progress via creativity, dreams, and imagination.
	Fanatical control and preservation of Disney's "magic" image.
	"To bring happiness to millions" and to celebrate, nurture, and promulgate "wholesome American values."

SOURCE: From *Built to Last* by James C. Collins and Jerry I. Porras, Copyright © 1997 by James C. Collins and Jerry I. Porras. Reprinted by permission of the authors, HarperCollins Publishers, Inc. and Random House Group Limited.

- Stretch goals *and* incremental progress.
- Control based on values *and* operational freedom.
- Long-term thinking and investment *and* demand for short-term results.
- Visionary, futuristic thinking *and* daily, nuts-and-bolts execution.

You have learned about all of these concepts throughout this course and should not lose sight of any of them—either in your mind or in your actions. To achieve them requires the continuous and effective management of change.

Organization Development

organization development (OD)

The systemwide application of behavioral science knowledge to develop, improve, and reinforce the strategies, structures, and processes that lead to organizational effectiveness.

How do organizations become more ambidextrous and move in the other positive directions described throughout this book? This chapter discusses several general approaches that will create positive change. We begin here with an umbrella concept called organization development.

Organization development (OD) is a systemwide application of behavioral science knowledge to develop, improve, and reinforce the strategies, structures, and processes that lead to organization effectiveness.[11] Throughout this course, you have acquired knowledge about behavioral science and the strategies, structures, and processes that help organizations become more effective. The "systemwide" component of the definition means that OD is not a narrow improvement in technology or operations but a broader approach to changing organizations, units, or people. The

The strategy of Cirque du Soleil is one of constant innovation: combining circus and theater, and studying other industries like car design, fashion, and restaurants to get ideas for new shows.

"behavioral science" component means that OD is not *directly* concerned with economic, financial, or technical aspects of the organization—although they may benefit through changes in the behavior of the people in the organization. The other key part of the definition—to develop, improve, and reinforce—refers to the actual process of changing for the better and for the long term.

Two features of organization development are important to note.[12] First, it aims to increase organizational effectiveness—improving the organization's ability to deal with customers, stockholders, governments, employees, and other stakeholders, which results in better-quality products, higher financial returns, and high quality of work life. Second, OD has an important underlying value orientation: it supports human potential, development, and participation in addition to performance and competitive advantage.

Many specific OD techniques fit under this philosophical umbrella.[13] The basic types are *strategic interventions*, including helping organizations conduct mergers and acquisitions, change their strategies, and develop alliances; *technostructural interventions* relating to organization structure and design, employee involvement, and work design; *human resources management interventions*, including attracting good people, setting goals, and appraising and rewarding performance; and *human process interventions*, including conflict resolution, team building, communication, and leadership. As you can see, you learned about these topics throughout your management course. You also will learn more about the process of creating change in the rest of this chapter.

Achieving Greatness

A study of 200 management techniques employed by 160 companies over 10 years identified the specific management practices that lead to sustained, superior performance.[14] The authors boiled their findings down to four key factors:

1. *Strategy*—focused on customers, continually fine-tuned based on marketplace changes, and clearly communicated to employees.
2. *Execution*—good people, with decision-making authority on the front lines, doing quality work and cutting costs.
3. *Culture*—one that motivates, empowers people to innovate, rewards people appropriately (psychologically as well as economically), entails strong values, challenges people, and provides a satisfying work environment.
4. *Structure*—making the organization easy to work in and easy to work with, characterized by cooperation and the exchange of information and knowledge throughout the organization.

You have been learning about these concepts throughout this course.

Becoming world class doesn't apply only to the private sector. People worry about globalization's negative effects on local communities as plants shut down and people lose their jobs to overseas workers. But local communities do have options—not easy ones, but doable. A locality can strive to become a world-class center of *thinkers, makers,* or *traders.*[15] Thus Boston creates new ideas and technologies that often dominate world markets; Spartanville–Greenville, South Carolina, is a world-class manufacturing region that is home to more than 80 international firms representing 18 countries; and Miami, Florida, connects Latino and Anglo cultures the way Hong Kong and Singapore have historically bridged Chinese and British cultures. The keys to creating world-class local communities include visionary leadership, a climate friendly to business, a commitment to training workers, and collaboration among businesses and between business and local government.[16]

> Becoming world class doesn't apply only to the private sector.

People are the key to successful change.[17] For an organization to be great, or even just to survive, people have to care about its fate and know how they can contribute. But typically leadership lies with only a few people at the top. Too few take on the burden of change; the number of people who care deeply, and who make innovative contributions, is too small. People throughout the organization need to take a greater interest and a more active role in helping the business as a whole. They have to identify with the entire organization, not just with their unit and close colleagues.

Managing Change

LO 2

Shared leadership is crucial to the success of most change efforts—people must be not just *supporters* of change but also *implementers.*[18]

This shared responsibility for change is not unusual in start-ups and very small organizations. But too often it is lost with growth and over time. In large, traditional corporations, it is all too rare. Organizations need to permanently rekindle individual creativity and responsibility, instituting a true change in the behavior of people throughout the ranks. The essential task is to motivate people fully to keep changing in response to new business challenges.

Motivating People to Change

People must be *motivated* to change. But often they resist changing. Some people resist change more than others, but managers tend to underestimate the amount of resistance they will encounter.[19]

People at all levels of their organizations, from entry-level workers to top executives, resist change. When Foremost Farms USA asked workers to switch goals—instead of making American cheese as fast as they could, they had to aim for getting each block to weigh precisely 640 pounds—the workers complied only as long as managers kept checking. When management's attention turned elsewhere, they reverted to the more familiar emphasis on speed.[20] At IBM executives learned that lower-level managers were getting bogged down because they had to invest so much time and effort in obtaining approval from higher-ups. CEO Sam Palmisano announced that he would give first-level managers authority to spend $5,000 without prior approval—a daring move, considering that the authority applied to 30,000 managers. However, the managers felt uncomfortable with their new authority, and in the first year of the new program, they spent only $100,000 of the $150 million Palmisano had entrusted to them.[21] In other words, they were reluctant to change the way they worked, even though it stood to make their job easier.

Many people settle for mediocrity rather than aspire to excellence. They resist the idea of striving mightily for excellence. When told by their managers, "We have to become world class," their reactions resemble the following statements:

According to human resources leaders surveyed by the Ken Blanchard Companies, some of the toughest challenges in managing change entail getting everyone on board so employees care about and work hard for success.[22]

Challenges faced when managing change (percentage of companies)

- Engaging and energizing employees — 48%
- Sustaining momentum throughout the change process — 48%
- Developing leadership to support the process — 47%
- Getting everyone on the same page — 44%
- Changing rapidly — 23%
- Teaming effectively — 18%

- "Those world-class performance numbers are ridiculous! I don't believe them, they are impossible! Maybe in some industries, some companies . . . but ours is unique . . ."
- "Sure, maybe some companies achieve those numbers, but there's no hurry . . . We're doing all right. Sales were up 5 percent this year, costs were down 2 percent. And we've got to keep cutting corners . . ."
- "We can't afford to be world class like those big global companies; we don't have the money or staff . . ."
- "We don't need to expand internationally. One of our local competitors tried that a few years ago and lost its shirt."
- "It's not a level playing field . . . the others have unfair advantages . . ."

To deal with such reactions and successfully implement positive change, managers must understand why people often resist change. Figure 18.1 shows the common reasons for resistance. Some reasons are general and arise in most change efforts. Other reasons for resistance relate to the specific nature of a particular change.

FIGURE 18.1
Reasons for Resistance to Change

General Reasons for Resistance   Several reasons for resistance arise regardless of the actual content of the change:[23]

- *Inertia.* Usually people don't want to disturb the status quo. The old ways of doing things are comfortable and easy, so people don't want to shake things up and try something new. For example, it is easier to keep living in the same apartment or house than to move to another.
- *Timing.* People often resist change because of poor timing. Maybe you would like to move to a different place to live, but do you want to move this week? Even if a place were available, you probably couldn't take the time. If managers or employees are unusually busy or under stress, or if relations between management and workers are strained, the timing is wrong for introducing new proposals. Where possible, managers should introduce change when people are receptive.
- *Surprise.* One key aspect of timing and receptivity is surprise. If the change is sudden, unexpected, or extreme, resistance may be the initial—almost reflexive—reaction. Suppose your school announced an increase in tuition, effective at the beginning of next term. Wouldn't you at least want more warning so you might be prepared? Managers or others initiating a change often forget that others haven't given the matter much thought; the change leaders need to allow time for others to prepare for the change.
- *Peer pressure.* Sometimes work teams resist new ideas. Even if individual members do not strongly oppose a change suggested by management, the team may band together in opposition. Peer pressure will cause individuals to resist even reasonable changes, especially if a group is highly cohesive and has antimanagement norms (recall Chapter 14). Of course peer pressure can be a positive force, too. Change leaders who invite—and listen to—ideas from team members may find that peer pressure becomes a driving force behind the change's success.

Change-Specific Reasons for Resistance   Other causes of resistance arise from the specific nature of a proposed change. Change-specific reasons for resistance include[24]

- *Self-interest.* Most people care less about the organization's best interest than they do about their own best interests. They will resist a change if they think it will cause them to lose something of value. What could people fear to lose? At worst, their jobs, if management is considering closing down a plant. A merger, reorganization, or technological change could create the same fear. Other possible fears include loss of the feeling of being competent in a familiar job, expectations that the job will become more difficult or time-consuming, and concerns about the organization's future, given that management wasn't satisfied with the status quo.
- *Misunderstanding.* Even when management proposes a change that will benefit everyone, people may resist because they don't fully understand it. People may not see how the change fits with the firm's strategy, or they simply may not see the change's advantage over current practices.[25] One company met resistance to the idea of introducing flexible working hours, a system in which workers have some say regarding the hours they work. This system can benefit employees, but a false rumor circulated among plant employees that people would have to work evenings, weekends, or whenever their supervisors wanted. The employees' union demanded that management drop the flexible hours idea. The president was caught completely off guard by this unexpected resistance and complied with the union's demand.
- *Different assessments.* Employees receive different—and usually less— information than management receives. Even within top management

ranks, some executives know more than others do. Such discrepancies cause people to develop different assessments of proposed changes. Some may be aware that the benefits outweigh the costs, while others may see only the costs and not the advantages. This is a common problem when management announces a change, say, in work procedures, and doesn't explain to employees why the change is needed. Management expects advantages in terms of increased efficiency, but workers may see the change as another arbitrary, ill-informed management rule that causes headaches for those who must carry it out.

- *Management tactics.* Management may attempt to force the change and may fail to address concerns in order to develop employee commitment. Or it may fail to provide the necessary resources, knowledge, or leadership to help the change succeed. Sometimes a change receives so much exposure and glorification that employees resent it and resist. Managers who overpromise what they, or the change, can deliver may discover that the next time they want to introduce a change, they have lost credibility, so employees resist.

It is important to recognize that employees' assessments can be more accurate than management's; employees may know a change won't work even if management doesn't. In this case, resistance to change is beneficial for the organization. Thus, even though management typically considers resistance a challenge to be overcome, it may actually represent an important signal that a proposed change requires further, more open-minded scrutiny.[26]

A General Model for Managing Resistance

Motivating people to change often requires three basic stages, shown in Figure 18.2: unfreezing, moving to institute the change, and refreezing.[27]

Unfreezing   In the **unfreezing** stage, management realizes that its current practices are no longer appropriate and the company must break out of (unfreeze) its present mold by doing things differently. People must come to recognize that some of the past ways of thinking, feeling, and doing things are obsolete.[28] A direct and sometimes effective way to do this is to communicate the negative consequences of the old ways by comparing the organization's performance with that of its competitors. As discussed in Chapter 15, management can share with employees data about costs, quality, and profits.[29] Sometimes employees just need to understand the rationale for changing. In the earlier example of Foremost Farms, big competitors had made it impossible to win with a strategy of working efficiently and selling cheese at a low price. Management had decided to sell more profitable customized products, such as the 640-pound blocks of cheese that one customer planned to repackage in smaller sizes. After Foremost managers took the time to explain the situation to employees, the workers understood the new requirements and began performing as requested.[30]

When managers communicate a problem, they need to take care not to arouse people's defensiveness. Instead of unfreezing resistance, managers are likely to place

unfreezing

Realizing that current practices are inappropriate and that new behavior is necessary.

FIGURE 18.2
Motivating People to Change

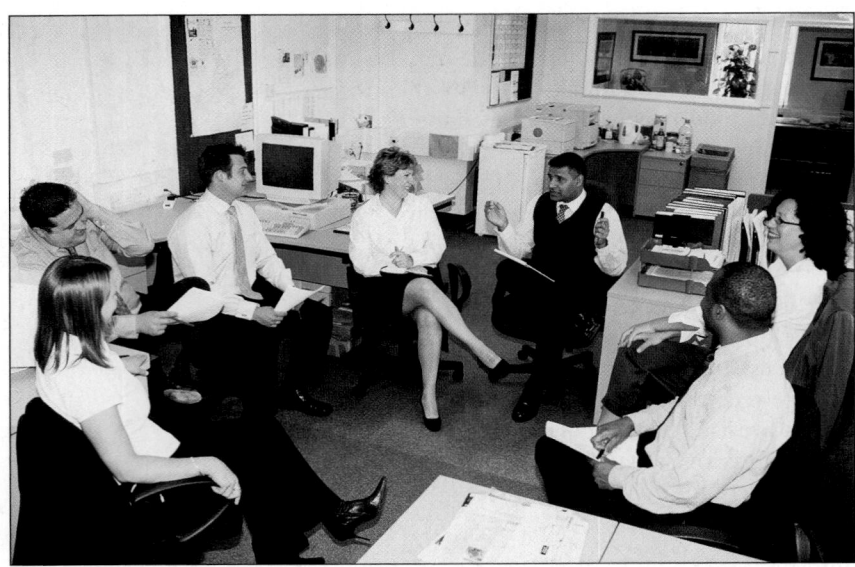

When change is needed, managers should not add to employees' problems any more than necessary. Better yet, they should work together to find ways to reduce the difficulties.

employees on the defensive when they pin the blame for shortcomings directly and entirely on the workers.[31] Similarly, bombarding employees with facts aimed at inducing fear may only add to their resistance. When a problem seems huge, people often decide it is hopeless and don't face it. In *Change or Die*, journalist Alan Deutschman uses that pattern of behavior to explain why heart attack victims often fail to follow diet and exercise plans, even though doctors tell them they will literally die if they don't take care of themselves.[32] Deutschman sees a similar pattern playing out in companies where executives rely on threats of layoffs and corporate bankruptcy to motivate employees to adopt new work practices. In these difficult situations, leaders more effectively unfreeze negative behavior with a message of hope and a commitment to collaborate so that they can accomplish successful change together.

An important contributor to unfreezing is the recognition of a performance gap, which can be a precipitator of major change. A **performance gap** is the difference between actual performance and the performance that should or could exist.[33] As an impetus for change, a performance gap can apply to the organization as a whole; it also can apply to departments, groups, and individuals.

The gap is between what is and what *could be*.

A gap typically implies poor performance; for example, sales, profits, stock price, or other financial indicators are down. This situation attracts management's attention, and management introduces changes to try to correct things. But another, very important form of performance gap can exist. This type of gap can occur when performance is good but someone realizes that it could be better. Thus the gap is between what is and what *could be*. Important changes can and should be made even when performance is good.[34]

Lawrence Ellison, CEO of Oracle, is well-versed in what it takes to convey a vision of change within his organization. Oracle has often acquired other companies, bringing tumultuous change for individual employees and managers within both organizations.

In the realm of change management, employees are mostly motivated by situations that combine the sense of urgency that comes from identifying a problem with the sense of excitement that comes from identifying an opportunity. Furthermore, managers communicating a performance gap should keep in mind that employees care about more than market share and revenues. Employees want to know how making a change can help them have a positive impact on their work group, their customers, their company, their community, and themselves. For example, a financial services company met resistance when it tried to persuade employees that a change would enhance the company's competitive position. Employees got on board only after the change leaders also started talking about how the change would help employees reduce errors, enable teams to avoid duplication of effort, make jobs more interesting, and help the organization fulfill its mission to deliver affordable housing.[35]

Moving   The next step, **moving** to institute the change, begins with establishing a vision of where the company is heading. You learned about vision in the leadership chapter. The vision can be realized through strategic, structural, cultural, and individual change. Strategic ideas are discussed throughout the book. Changes in structure may involve moving to the divisional, matrix, or some other appropriate form (discussed in Chapters 8 and 9). Cultural changes (Chapter 2) are institutionalized through effective leadership (Chapters 12 through 15). Individuals will change as new people join the company (Chapters 10 and 11) and as people throughout the organization adopt the leader's new vision for the future.

One technique that helps to manage the change process, **force-field analysis**, involves identifying the specific forces that prevent people from changing and the specific forces that will drive people toward change.[36] Managers operating under this concept investigate forces acting in opposite directions. Eliminating the restraining forces helps people unfreeze, and increasing the driving forces helps and motivates them to move forward.

The great social psychologist Kurt Lewin developed force-field analysis (and the unfreezing/moving/refreezing model). Lewin theorized that although driving forces may be more easily affected, shifting them may increase opposition (tension and/or conflict) within the organization and add restraining forces. Therefore, to create change, it is crucial to remove restraining forces. An exercise at the end of the chapter provides an example and takes you through this process.

Refreezing   Finally, **refreezing** means strengthening the new behaviors that support the change. Refreezing involves implementing control systems that support the change (Chapter 16), applying corrective action when necessary, and reinforcing behaviors and performance (Chapter 13) that support the agenda. Management should consistently support and reward evidence of movement in the right direction.[37]

In today's organizations, refreezing is not always the best third step if it creates new behaviors that are as rigid as the old ones. The ideal new culture is one of continuous change. Refreezing is appropriate when it permanently installs behaviors that focus on important business results and maintain essential core values. But refreezing should not create new rigidities that might become dysfunctional as the business environment continues to change.[38] The behaviors that should be refrozen are those that promote continued adaptability, flexibility, experimentation, assessment of results, and continuous improvement—in other words, lock in key values, capabilities, and strategic mission, but not necessarily specific practices and procedures.

Specific Approaches to Enlist Cooperation

You can try to command people to change, but the key to long-term success is to use other approaches.[39] Developing true support is better than "driving" a program forward.[40] How, specifically, can managers motivate people to change?

Most managers underestimate the variety of ways they can influence people during a period of change.[41] Several effective approaches to managing resistance and enlisting cooperation are available, as described in Table 18.2 and expanded here.

Education and Communication   Management should educate people about upcoming changes before they occur. It should communicate not only the *nature* of the change but its *logic*. This process can include one-on-one discussions, presentations to groups, and reports and memos. As we discussed in Chapter 15, effective communication includes feedback and listening. That provides an environment in which management can explain the rationale for the change—and perhaps improve it.

performance gap

The difference between actual performance and desired performance.

moving

Instituting the change.

Bottom Line
A useful tactic for innovating toward a positive future is to imagine the difference between what *is* and what *could be*

force-field analysis

An approach to implementing the unfreezing/moving/refreezing model by identifying the forces that prevent people from changing and those that will drive people toward change.

refreezing

Strengthening the new behaviors that support the change.

The ideal new culture is one of continuous change.

TABLE 18.2

Methods for Managing Resistance to Change

Approach	Commonly Used in Situations	Advantage	Drawbacks
Education and communication	Where there is a lack of information or inaccurate information and analysis.	Once persuaded, people will often help with the implementation of the change.	Can be very time-consuming if lots of people are involved.
Participation and involvement	Where the initiators do not have all the information they need to design the change, and where others have considerable power to resist.	People who participate will be committed to implementing change, and any relevant information they have will be integrated into the change plan.	Can be very time-consuming if participators design an inappropriate change.
Facilitation and support	Where people are resisting because of adjustment problems.	No other approach works as well with adjustment problems.	Can be time-consuming and expensive, and still fail.
Negotiation and rewards	Where someone or some group will clearly lose out in a change, and where that group has considerable power to resist.	Sometimes it is a relatively easy way to avoid major resistance.	Can be too expensive in many cases if it alerts others to negotiate for compliance.
Manipulation and cooptation	Where other tactics will not work, or are too expensive.	It can be a relatively quick and inexpensive solution to resistance problems.	Can lead to future problems if people feel manipulated.
Explicit and implicit coercion	Where speed is essential, and the change initiators possess considerable power.	It is speedy and can overcome any kind of resistance.	Can be risky if it leaves people angry at the initiators.

SOURCE: Reprinted by permission of the *Harvard Business Review*. An exhibit from "Choosing Strategies for Change" by John P. Kotter and Leonard A. Schlesinger (March–April 1979). Copyright © 1979 by the Harvard Business School Publishing Corporation; all rights reserved.

Participation and Involvement   The people who are affected by the change should be involved in the change's design and implementation. For major, organizationwide change, participation in the process can extend from the top to the very bottom of the organization.[42] When feasible, management should use the advice of people throughout the organization.

As you learned in Chapter 3, people who are involved in decisions understand them more fully and are more committed to them. People's understanding and commitment are important ingredients in the successful implementation of a change. Participation also provides an excellent opportunity for education and communication.

Facilitation and Support   Management should make the change as easy as possible for employees and support their efforts. Facilitation involves providing the training and other resources people need to carry out the change and perform their jobs under the new circumstances. This step often includes decentralizing authority and empowering people—that is, giving them the power to make the decisions and changes needed to improve their performance.

Offering support involves listening patiently to problems, being understanding if performance drops temporarily or the change is not perfected immediately, and generally being on the employees' side and showing consideration during a difficult period.

Negotiation and Rewards   When necessary and appropriate, management can offer concrete incentives for cooperation with the change. Perhaps job enrichment is acceptable only with a higher wage rate, or a work rule change is resisted until management agrees to a concession on some other rule (say, regarding taking breaks). Even among higher-level managers, one executive might agree to another's idea for a policy change only in return for support on some other issue of more personal importance. Rewards such as bonuses, wages and salaries, recognition, job assignments, and perks can be examined and perhaps restructured to reinforce the direction of the change.[43]

When people trust one another, change is easier. But change is further facilitated by demonstrating its benefits to people.[44] When a pharmaceutical company was trying to make improvements in the way it managed its supply chain, the vice president in charge set a positive tone by calling a meeting at which participants would start by sharing stories of their successes in carrying out their roles within the supply chain. Although suspicious at first, the participants gained enthusiasm and commitment before turning their energy toward making changes. The company was able to measure the improvement: 20 days shaved off the product lead time, saving the company more than $250,000.[45] The participants not only saw themselves as effective problem solvers but also had a dramatic measure of the improvement they could initiate in one meeting.

Manipulation and Cooptation   Sometimes managers use more subtle, covert tactics to implement change. One form of manipulation is cooptation, which involves giving a resisting individual a desirable role in the change process. The leader of a resisting group often is coopted. For example, management might invite a union leader to be a member of an executive committee or ask a key member of an outside organization to join the company's board of directors. As a person becomes involved in the change, he or she may become less resistant to the actions of the coopting group or organization.

Explicit and Implicit Coercion   Some managers apply punishment or the threat of punishment to those who resist change. With this approach, managers use force to make people comply with their wishes. For example, a manager might insist that subordinates cooperate with the change and threaten them with job loss, denial of a promotion, or an unattractive work assignment. Sometimes you just have to lay down the law.

Each approach to managing resistance has advantages and drawbacks and, like many of the other situational management approaches described in this book, each is useful in different situations. Look back at Table 18.2, which summarizes the advantages, drawbacks, and appropriate circumstances for these approaches to managing resistance to change. As the table implies, managers should not use just one or two general approaches, regardless of the circumstances. Effective change managers are familiar with the various approaches and know how to apply them according to the situation.

Throughout the process, change leaders need to build in stability. Recall from the companies that were "built to last" that they all have essential core characteristics of which they don't lose sight. In the midst of change,

> Effective change managers are familiar with the various approaches and know how to apply them according to the situation.

turmoil, and uncertainty, people need anchors onto which they can latch.[46] Making an organization's values and mission constant and visible can often serve this stabilizing function. In addition, strategic principles can be important anchors during change.[47] Maintaining the visibility of key people, continuing key assignments and projects, and making announcements about which organizational components will *not* change can also promote stability. Such anchors will reduce anxiety and help overcome resistance. As you read "Management Connection: Progress Report," consider how Dr. Peter Pronovost applied these methods to the Keystone Project.

Manager's Brief   **Progress Report**   Onward

Management Connection

HOW DR. PRONOVOST'S CHANGES WERE PUT TO THE TEST

Getting the members of a health care team to follow a simple checklist that will prevent dangerous infections and save lives (and save, not cost, money) sounds like the easiest kind of change to introduce to an organization. After all, who could be against saving lives, especially in a hospital? But resistance to change occurs everywhere, and some of the sources of resistance to the Michigan Keystone ICU Project were especially tricky.

Dr. Peter Pronovost learned that preparing a simple five-item checklist for preventing catheter-related bloodstream infections was the easy part of the change process. The hard part was changing the culture of the institutions where he introduced the checklist.

Of course hospitals value preventing illnesses and saving lives. So when Dr. Pronovost introduced his plans, first at Johns Hopkins and then at the Michigan ICUs, everyone agreed to use the checklists. Members of the medical teams were expected to remind one another about any steps that were forgotten or done incorrectly. But in practice, people forgot steps.

Hospital teams tend to have a strong hierarchy, with doctors at the top and registered nurses, then other staff members having less status and power. The hierarchy preserves a culture in which patients and others trust the expertise of their caregivers, especially their doctors. In the case of the change effort to reduce infection rates, that culture was standing in the way of progress because lower-status team members were afraid to enforce the checklist. For the change effort to succeed, it would have to include changing attitudes about upward communication. Everyone would have to feel empowered to speak up for patient safety.

Changing that culture is tricky because hospitals have complicated organizational structures. Typically a hospital's nurses and pharmacists are employees of the hospital, so they are directly subject to its policies, rewards, training, and other means of development and control.

In contrast, the doctors who use a hospital are often self-employed; they have a contractual relationship with the hospital. Hospitals want to keep those relationships positive because it is often the doctor's choice to admit a particular patient to a particular hospital. Furthermore, doctors' training tends to emphasize technical skills rather than management skills such as teamwork and communication, so they may not see successful outcomes as the result of empowering the whole team.

In this context, nurses and other staff members are understandably reluctant to speak up when a doctor doesn't follow a step on a checklist. Not only might they be criticized and ignored by the doctor, but the hospital may be reluctant to back them up in ways that could disturb a valued doctor–hospital relationship.

One way that Dr. Pronovost and the Keystone Project addressed this cultural problem was by ensuring that everyone in the ICU could see the data. Measuring infection rates and publishing the data show doctors and staff members the undeniable need for improvement. Continuing to track the infection rates shows how patient safety improves when the checklist is followed. Surprising as it may seem, hospitals have not routinely collected such data, so this one change makes it harder for hospitals and their people to forget, deny, or ignore the problem.

In addition, Dr. Pronovost has addressed the culture head-on by highlighting the value of speaking up to protect patients' safety. Speaking as a doctor himself, he urges his colleagues to accept the idea that everyone is fallible, no matter how well trained and experienced. Again and again, he urges nurses and other hospital staff to speak up on behalf of their patients.

The efforts paid off. Among the hospitals participating in the Keystone Project, the median rate of central-line infections was about 3 per 1,000 catheter-hours before the change. Eighteen months later, most hospitals were reporting no infections at all.

Three years after the start of the Keystone Project, the ICUs have maintained the change. The combination of culture change, a checklist of procedures, and measurement of results is holding bloodstream infections to near zero in the Michigan ICUs. Pronovost sees the changes as more than a three-year improvement in safety at one state's hospitals. He sees it as a new mind-set: these infections were once seen as inevitable, but "Now we know they are universally preventable. We've reset the benchmark."[48]

- Of the methods for managing resistance to change (Table 18.2), which would be most relevant to the Keystone Project?
- According to the information given, how did Dr. Pronovost carry out the essential activities for leading change (Figure 18.3)?

Harmonizing Multiple Changes

There are no "silver bullets" or single-shot methods of changing organizations successfully. Single shots rarely hit a challenging target. Usually many issues need simultaneous attention, and any single, small change will be absorbed by the prevailing culture and disappear. **Total organization change** involves introducing and sustaining multiple policies, practices, and procedures across multiple units and levels.[49] Such change affects the thinking and behavior of everyone in the organization, can enhance the organization's culture and success, and can be sustained over time.

> **total organization change**
>
> Introducing and sustaining multiple policies, practices, and procedures across multiple units and levels.

A survey at a Harvard Business School conference found that the average attendee's company had five major change efforts going on at once.[50] The most common change programs were practices you have studied in this course: continuous improvement; quality programs; time-based competition; and creation of a learning organization, a team-based organization, a network organization, core capabilities, and strategic alliances. The problem is, these efforts usually are simultaneous but not coordinated. As a result, changes get muddled; people lose focus.[51] The people involved suffer from confusion, frustration, low morale, and low motivation.

Because companies introduce new changes constantly, many people complain about their companies' "flavor of the month" approach to change. That is, employees often see many change efforts as just the company's jumping on the latest bandwagon or fad. The more these change fads come and go, the more cynical people become, and the more difficult it is to get them committed to making the change a success.[52]

> Many people complain about their companies' "flavor of the month" approach to change.

So an important question is, Which change efforts are really worth undertaking? Here are some specific questions to ask before embarking on a change project:[53]

- What is the evidence that the approach really can produce positive results?
- Is the approach relevant to your company's strategies and priorities?
- Can you assess the costs and potential benefits?
- Does it really help people add value through their work?
- Does it help the company focus better on customers and the things they value?
- Can you go through the decision-making process described in Chapter 3, understand what you're facing, and feel that you are taking the right approach?

Management also needs to connect the dots—that is, integrate the various efforts into a coherent picture that people can see, understand, and get behind.[54] You connect the dots by understanding each change program and its goals, by identifying similarities among the programs and also their differences, and by dropping programs that don't meet priority goals or demonstrate clear results. Most important, you do it by communicating to everyone concerned the common themes among the various programs: their common rationales, objectives, and methods. You show them how the various parts fit the strategic big picture and how the changes will make things better for the company and its people. You must communicate these benefits thoroughly, honestly, and frequently.[55]

When looking to implement change, managers should speak candidly to their employees about the poor state of the company. This gives the employees an opportunity to understand how and why important changes need to take place.

Urgency is a reality-based sense of determination, not just fear-based busyness.

Leading Change

Successful change requires managers to actively lead it. The essential activities of leading change are summarized in Figure 18.3.

The companies that lead change most effectively *establish a sense of urgency.*[56] To do so, managers must examine current realities and pressures in the marketplace and the competitive arena, identify both crises and opportunities, and be frank and honest about them. In this sense, urgency is a reality-based sense of determination, not just fear-based busyness. The immediacy of the need for change is an important component, in part because so many large companies grow complacent.

Figure 18.4 shows some common reasons for complacency. To stop complacency and create urgency, a manager can talk candidly about the organization's weaknesses compared with competitors, making a point to back up statements with data. Other tactics include setting stretch goals, putting employees in direct contact with unhappy customers and shareholders, distributing worrisome information to all employees instead of merely engaging in management "happy talk," eliminating excessive perks, and highlighting to everyone the future opportunities that exist but that the organization so far has failed to pursue.

Ultimately, urgency is driven by compelling business reasons for change. Survival, competition, and winning in the marketplace are compelling; they provide a sense of direction and energy around change. Change becomes not a hobby, a luxury, or something nice to do, but a business necessity.[57]

To *create a guiding coalition* means putting together a group with enough power to lead the change. Change efforts fail when a sufficiently powerful coalition is not formed.[58] Major organization change requires leadership from top management, working as a team. But over time, the support must gradually expand outward and downward throughout the organization. Middle managers and supervisors are essential. Groups at all levels are the glue that can hold change efforts together, the medium for communicating about the changes, and the means for enacting new behaviors.[59]

Developing a vision and strategy, as discussed in earlier chapters, directs the change effort. This process involves determining the idealized, expected state of affairs after the change is implemented. Because confusion is common during major organizational change, the clearest possible image of the future state must be developed and conveyed to everyone.[60] This image, or vision, is a target or guideline that can clarify expectations, dispel rumors, and mobilize people's energies. The portrait of the future also should communicate how the transition will occur, why the change is being implemented, and how people will be affected by the change. The power of a compelling vision is one of the most important aspects of change and should not be underestimated or underutilized.

Communicating the change vision requires using every possible channel and opportunity to talk up and reinforce the vision and required new behaviors. It is said that aspiring change leaders undercommunicate the vision by a factor of 10, or even 100 or 1,000, seriously undermining the chances of success.[61] In delivering more messages, however, do not forget that communication is a two-way street. When consultant Steve Schumacher was hired to improve the performance of a division in which quality, productivity, and customer service had been declining, he started by setting

FIGURE 18.3
Leading Change

FIGURE 18.4
Sources of Complacency

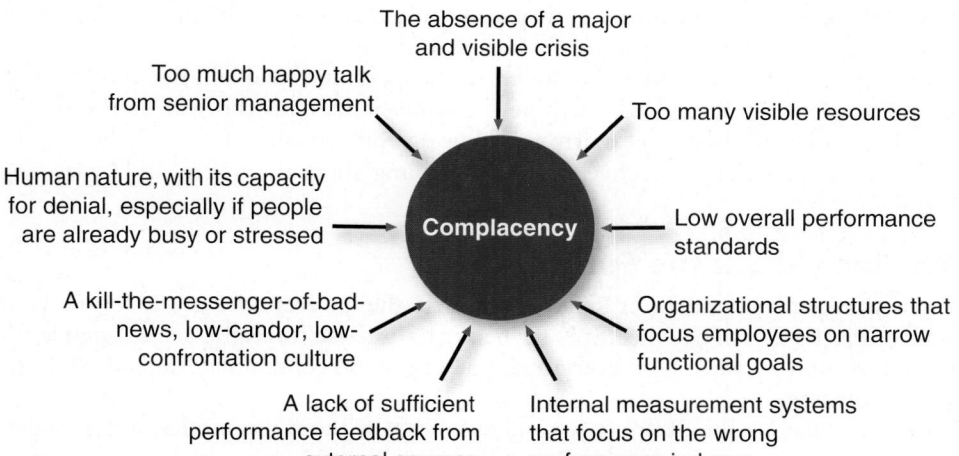

up meetings in which employees described what they saw as the underlying problems. His message to them was simply that the company cared about their views and wouldn't make changes until they had been heard. Schumacher and his team then compiled a list of all the issues and shared it with every employee. Only then did he ask for volunteers to participate in planning solutions. The consulting team was flooded with volunteers. Not only were employees willing to change, but they were excited to be included in planning, and they hungered for a better understanding of where the company wanted to go and how they could contribute to that vision. Before long, as a result of this team effort, performance measures began to rise across the board.[62]

Empowering broad-based action means getting rid of obstacles to success, including systems and structures that constrain rather than facilitate. Encourage risk taking and experimentation, and empower people by providing information, knowledge, authority, and rewards, as described in Chapter 13.

Generate short-term wins. Don't wait for the ultimate grand realization of the vision. You need results. As small victories accumulate, you make the transition from an isolated initiative to an integral part of the business.[63] Plan for and create small victories that indicate to everyone that progress is being made. Recognize and reward the people who made the wins possible, doing it visibly so that people notice and the positive message permeates the organization.

Make sure you *consolidate gains and produce more change.* With the well-earned credibility of previous successes, keep changing things in ways that support the vision. Hire, promote, and develop people who will further the vision. Reinvigorate the organization and your change efforts with new projects and change agents.

> "Change is a verb."
>
> —MimiSilbert, founder, Delancey Street Foundation[64]

Finally, *anchor new approaches in the culture.*[65] Highlight positive results, communicate the connections between the new behaviors and the improved results, and keep developing new change agents and leaders. Continually increase the number of people joining you in taking responsibility for change.[66]

Shaping the Future

reactive change

A change effort that occurs under pressure; problem-driven change.

proactive change

A change effort that is initiated before a performance gap has occurred.

Most change is reactive. A better way to change is to be proactive. **Reactive change** means responding to pressure after a problem has arisen. It also implies being a follower. **Proactive change** means anticipating and preparing for an uncertain future. It implies being a leader and *creating* the future you want.

The road to the future includes drivers, passengers, and road kill. Put another way: on the road to the future, who will be the windshield, and who will be the bug?[67] Needless to say, it's best to be a driver.[68] How do you become a driver? By being proactive more than merely reactive, by really thinking about the future, and by *creating* futures.

Thinking about the Future

If you think only about the present or wallow in the uncertainties of the future, your future is just a roll of the dice. It is far better to exercise foresight, set an agenda for the future, and pursue it with everything you've got. So contemplate and envision the future.

> On the road to the future, who will be the windshield, and who will be the bug?

Before the 20th century, people lived without antibiotics, automobiles, airplanes, tractors, and air conditioning. Imagine how this combination of inventions has revolutionized where and how well people live. And in just the last few decades, we have seen the invention and spread of personal computers, the World Wide Web, cell phones, and the mapping of the human genome. These innovations are still shaping how we learn, communicate, and treat disease.

Will the 21st century bring transformations that are just as dramatic? Some people think the potential for innovation and growth is unprecedented in areas such as information technology, the biological sciences, agriculture, water supply, and clean energy technologies.[69] Futurist Richard Watson sees the cell phone as the device that will most transform how we live in the 21st century. He foresees a cashless society in which consumers use signals from their phones to make payments as well as send messages. Futurist Cynthia Wagner sees career opportunities stemming from researchers' growing knowledge of processes in the human brain. In the future, Wagner surmises, this knowledge will help bioengineers develop microelectrodes to translate paralyzed patients' brain signals into words and movements, and computer scientists will apply the knowledge to make advances in artificial intelligence.[70] Just as technologies change, so do additional trends rise and fall, recently including a (temporary, most likely) damper on globalization, rising distrust of business, a growing role of government, strains on natural resources, and changing patterns of global consumption.[71] Authors Shoshana Zuboff and Jim Maxim claim that vast new markets exist, new kinds of companies are ready to be created, and the new business model hasn't yet emerged.[72] All offer prime opportunity to those who create the future.

Creating the Future

Companies can try different strategic postures to prepare to compete in an uncertain future. **Adapters** take the current industry structure and its future evolution as givens. They choose where to compete. This posture is taken by most companies by conducting standard strategic analysis and choosing how to compete within given environments. In contrast, **shapers** try to change the structure of their industries, creating a future competitive landscape of their own design.[73]

Researchers studying corporate performance over a 10-year period found that 17 companies in the *Fortune* 1000 grew total shareholder return by 35 percent or more per year.[74] How did they do it? They completely reinvented industries. Harley-Davidson turned around by selling not just motorcycles, but nostalgia. Amgen broke the rules of the biotech industry by focusing not on what customers wanted, but on great science. Starbucks took a commodity and began selling it in trendy stores. CarMax and other companies reinvented the auto industry.

You need to create advantages. The challenge is not to maintain your position in the current competitive arena, but to create new competitive arenas, transform your industry, and imagine a future that others don't see. Creating advantage is better than playing catch-up. At best, doing things to catch up buys time; it cannot get you out ahead of the pack or buy world-class excellence.[75] To create new markets or transform industries—these are perhaps the ultimate forms of proactive change.[76]

Figure 18.5 illustrates the vast opportunity to create new markets. Articulated needs are those that customers acknowledge and try to satisfy. Unarticulated needs are those that customers have not yet experienced. Served customers are those to whom your company is now selling, and unserved customers are untapped markets.

Business-as-usual concentrates on the lower-left quadrant. The leaders who re-create the game are constantly trying to create new opportunities in the other three quadrants.[77] For example, as a middle class emerges in populous and fast-developing nations such as India, China, and Brazil, some see problems in the strain this puts on the planet's resources. Others see unexploited opportunities to serve new customers with new kinds of products that are made more sustainably or enable consumers to live a more sustainable lifestyle.[78]

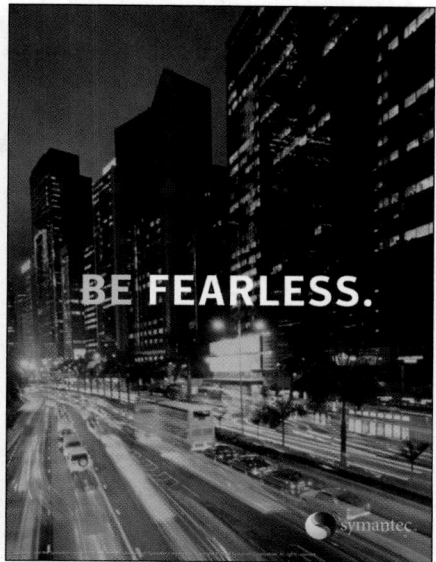

BE FEARLESS.

symantec

Don't think taking risks and being fearless is only for companies; think of your own quest for personal competitive advantage in the same way. Ultimately where you go, what you do, who you become, all are up to you. So be fearless.

adapters

Companies that take the current industry structure and its evolution as givens, and choose where to compete.

shapers

Companies that try to change the structure of their industries, creating a future competitive landscape of their own design.

Create new competitive arenas, transform your industry, and imagine a future that others don't see.

FIGURE 18.5
Vast Opportunity

Other companies hope to meet unarticulated needs by developing and exploiting cutting-edge technology. The nanometer—one-billionth of a meter, 1/100,000 the width of a human hair, or about the size of 10 hydrogen atoms in a row—is the building block of a new industry, nanotechnology. The nanometer is so important because matter at this scale often behaves differently—speeding electrons through circuits faster, conducting heat better, or offering qualities such as greater strength, durability, or reactivity.[79] Large and small companies are beginning to rush nano-based products into the marketplace. Current applications include nanotech silver (which has antimicrobial properties) in grooming products and odor-resistant socks, nanoscale features in semiconductors, and the use of nanoparticles as catalysts in making chemicals for use in coatings, paints, sunscreens, and other products.[80] Applications under development include high-performance rechargeable batteries that can store hydrogen and other high-energy gases, "nano-biochips" that can detect cancer in a patient within minutes, and a nanotechnology material called graphene that can be used to produce a computer touchscreen one atom thick.[81]

Is nanotech—for that matter, are most "industries of the future"—being overhyped? By some estimates, products using nanotech materials could achieve sales of $1 trillion or more by 2015; others say $26 billion would be a more realistic figure. Either way, the expansion of this technology has been impressive, given that it is still under development. Sales of products applying nanotechnology have grown by 7 to 10 times over the past few years.[82] However, there are concerns that the technology is untested and perhaps risky.[83] The particles are so small that they can pass through most filters, and their ability to react at the atomic level could cause unforeseen chemical and biological consequences. At the heart of the problem is a lack of experience with these materials, coupled with the very fact that their properties are different from the same materials at a larger scale. We know that alumina is highly explosive at the nanoscale, but how about carbon's greater conductivity at nanoscale? That doesn't sound so dangerous, but we don't know how this material would affect people if it got into their lungs or skin. Thus industry is challenged to apply this exciting new technology while protecting its workers and customers against the possibility of risks that aren't yet known.[84] Who can best meet such a challenge? As you've read, technological change is a central part of the changing landscape, and competition often arises between newcomers and established companies.

All things considered, which should you and your firm do?

- Preserve old advantages or create new advantages?
- Lock in old markets or create new markets?
- Take the path of greatest familiarity or the path of greatest opportunity?
- Be only a benchmarker or a pathbreaker?
- Place priority on short-term financial returns or on making a real, long-term impact?
- Do only what seems doable or what is difficult and worthwhile?
- Change what is or create what isn't?
- Look to the past or live for the future?[85]

Shaping Your Own Future

If you are an organizational leader and your organization operates in traditional ways, your key goal should be to create a revolution, genetically reengineering your company before it becomes a dinosaur of the modern era.[86] What should be the goals of the revolution? You've been learning about them throughout this course.

But

Maybe you are not going to lead a revolution. Maybe you just want a successful career and a good life.

You still must be able to deal with an economic environment that is increasingly competitive and fast-moving.[87] Creating the future you want for yourself requires setting high personal standards. Don't settle for mediocrity; don't assume that "good" is necessarily good enough—for yourself or for your employer. Think about how not just to meet expectations but to exceed them; to not merely "live with" apparent constraints but break free of the unimportant, arbitrary, or imagined ones; and to seize opportunities instead of letting them pass by.[88]

The most successful individuals take charge of their own development the way an entrepreneur takes charge of a business.[89] More specific advice from the leading authors on career management:[90] consciously and actively manage your own career. Develop marketable skills, and keep developing more. Make career choices based on personal growth, development, and learning opportunities. Look for positions that stretch you, and for bosses who develop their protégés. Seek environments that provide training and the opportunity to experiment and innovate. And know yourself: assess your strengths and weaknesses, your true interests, and ethical standards. If you are not already thinking in these terms and taking commensurate action, you should start now.

Additionally, become indispensable to your organization. Be enthusiastic in your job and committed to doing great work, but don't be blindly loyal to one company. Be prepared to leave, if necessary. View your job as an opportunity to prove what you can do and increase what you can do, not as a comfortable niche for the long term.[92] Go out on your own if it meets your skills and temperament.

> Look for positions that stretch you, and for bosses who develop their protégés.

Although the Bureau of Labor Statistics finds no support for the oft-stated claim that workers will have seven careers in a lifetime, you can expect to change jobs often. In a long-term study of 10,000 U.S. workers, the BLS found that the average worker held 10.8 jobs between the ages of 18 and 42. Separate research shows that few workers stay with the same employer for decades.[91]

Time U.S. Adults Have Spent with the Same Employer

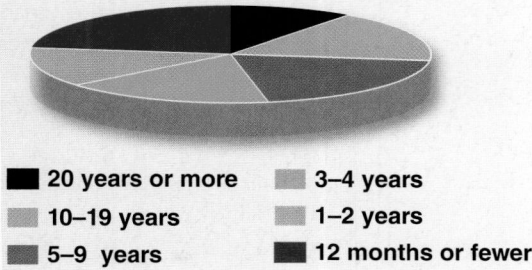

- 20 years or more
- 10–19 years
- 5–9 years
- 3–4 years
- 1–2 years
- 12 months or fewer

This points out the need to maintain your options. More and more, contemporary careers can involve leaving behind a large organization and going entrepreneurial, becoming self-employed in the "postcorporate world."[93] In such a career, independent individuals are free to make their own choices. They can flexibly and quickly respond to demands and opportunities. Developing start-up ventures, consulting, accepting temporary employment, doing project work for one organization and then another, working in professional partnerships, being a constant deal maker—these can be the elements of a successful career. Ideally, this self-employed model can help provide a balanced approach to working and to living life at home and with family, because people have more control over their work activities and schedules.

This go-it-alone approach can sound ideal, but it also has downsides. Independence can be frightening, the future unpredictable. It can isolate "road warriors" who are always on the go, working from their cars and airports, and interfere with social and family life.[94] Effective self-management is needed to keep career and family obligations in perspective and in control.

> Independence can be frightening, the future unpredictable.

Coping with uncertainty and change is easier if you develop resilience. To become more resilient, practice thinking of the world as complex but full of opportunities; expect change, but see it as interesting and potentially rewarding, even if changing is difficult. Also, keep a sense of purpose, set priorities for your time, be flexible when facing uncertainty or a need to change, and take an active role in the face of change rather than waiting for change to happen to you.[95]

IN PRACTICE

An active shaper of her future is Jacqueline F. Woods, whose executive career was a rarity for women in the 1960s, when she studied psychology and communications at Ohio's Muskingum University. Upon graduation, she began working as a customer service training instructor at Ohio Bell, the local phone company. She married Jack Woods and expected she would soon leave the labor force to be a homemaker.

Instead, the first major change occurred. The army drafted Jack to serve in Vietnam, and Jacqueline Woods suddenly was the sole breadwinner. Her dedication to her work helped her land a promotion to director of government affairs, and she enrolled in Ohio Bell's management training program. When her husband returned from military service and was transferred by his employer to Philadelphia, Woods lined up a job with Bell of Pennsylvania, continuing in government affairs, a field she loved.

The next big change came from government. In an antitrust lawsuit, AT&T's Bell System was carved into regional companies. That change opened new horizons. In the regulated monopoly, the best opportunities went to scientists and engineers, but now a business in a newly competitive marketplace required Wood's teamwork skills. She worked her way up to president of Ohio Bell Communications, which sold equipment to businesses.

Later the company offered to make Woods chief financial officer of Ameritch Services. She worried that her financial background was weak, but company executives pointed out that she would need financial skills to be on track for the top jobs. Woods took the CFO post and signed up to study finance on the weekends. A few years later, when AT&T Ohio needed a chief executive, Woods was ready.

Even following retirement, Woods shapes her future. She serves on the boards of foundations involved in a variety of community projects, such as improving local schools and installing wind turbines in Lake Erie.[96]

• What events in Woods's life required her to be flexible? How did she show flexibility?

Learning and Leading

Continuous learning is a vital route to renewable competitive advantage.[97] People in your organization—and you, personally—should constantly explore, discover, and take action, as illustrated in Figure 18.6. With this approach, you can learn what is effective and what is not and adjust and improve accordingly. The philosophy of continuous learning helps your company achieve lower cost, higher quality, better service, superior innovation, greater sustainability, and greater speed—and helps you grow and develop on a personal level.

Commit to lifelong learning. Lifelong learning requires occasionally taking risks, moving outside your "comfort zone," honestly assessing the reasons behind your successes and failures, asking for and listening to other people's information and opinions, and being open to new ideas.[98]

Through a career, a person can "inhabit" and grow through the hierarchy of stages illustrated in Figure 18.7 from Jim Collins's book *Good to Great*. The descriptions in the hierarchy suggest not only that you should do these things, but that you should do them *well*. Your first job may not include managerial responsibilities, but it will require you to be an individual contributor and probably to be part of a team. Level 3 is where managerial capabilities are required, while Level 4 distinguishes true leadership from competent management. Level 5 represents a leadership style that you read about briefly in Chapter 12, which combines strong will and determination with personal humility. The figure shows that Level 5 leadership represents a peak achievement: it is the ultimate contribution of a leader who can turn a good company into a

FIGURE 18.6
Learning Cycle: Explore, Discover, Act

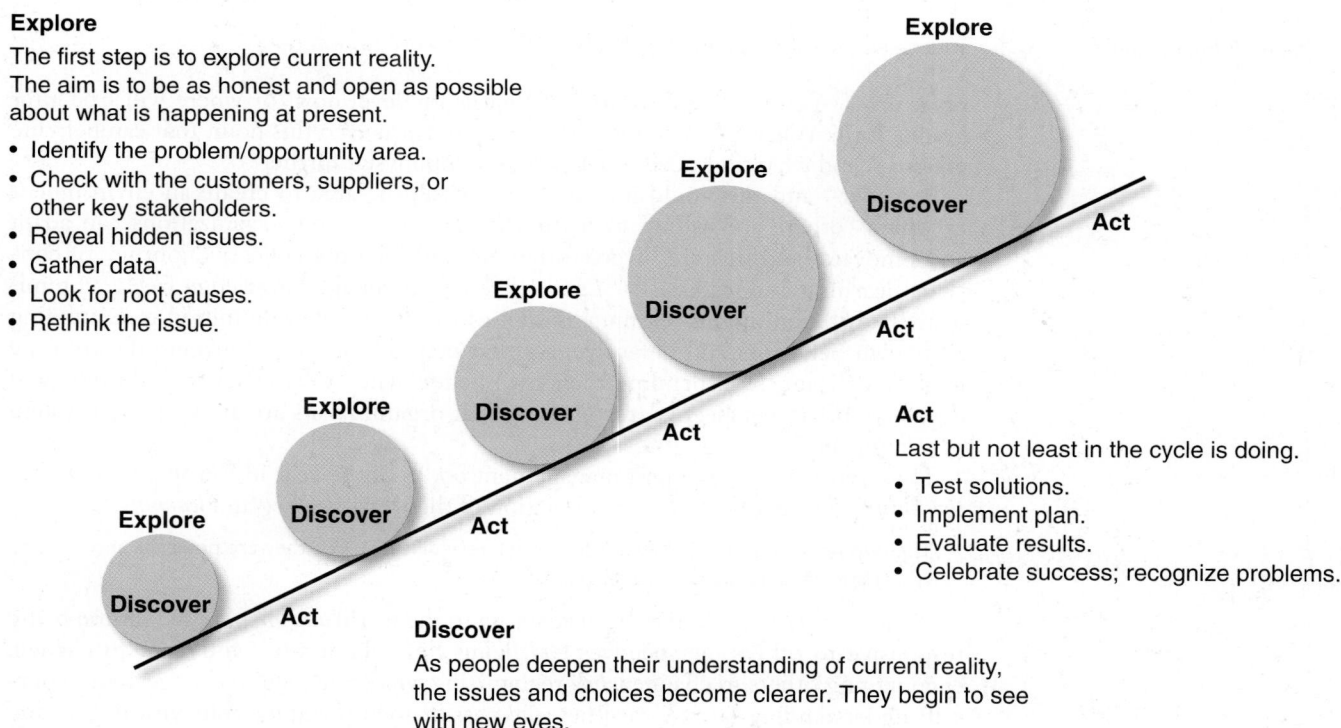

SOURCE: From *Leaning into the Future: Changing the Way People Change Organizations* by George Binney and Collin Williams; published by Nicholas Brealey Publishing Ltd., 1997. Reprinted by permission.

FIGURE 18.7
Level 5 Hierarchy

great one.[99] You might ask yourself, What is my level now (or where will I be after graduation)? What do I aspire to? What have I learned to this point that can help me progress, and what do I need to learn to develop myself further?

A leader—and this could include you—should be able to create an environment in which "others are willing to learn and change so their organizations can adapt and innovate [and] inspire diverse others to embark on a collective journey of continual learning and leading."[100] *Learning leaders* exchange knowledge freely; commit to their own continuous learning as well as to others'; are committed to examining their own behaviors and defensiveness that may inhibit their learning; devote time to their colleagues, suspending their own beliefs while they listen thoughtfully; and develop a broad perspective, recognizing that organizations are an integrated system of relationships.[101]

Honored as one of the best management books of the year in Europe, *Leaning into the Future* gets its title from a combination of the words *leading* and *learning*.[102]

> The two perspectives, on the surface, appear very different. But they are powerful and synergistic when pursued in complementary ways.

A successful future derives from adapting to the world *and* shaping the future; being responsive to others' perspectives *and* being clear about what you want to change; encouraging others to change *while* recognizing what you need to change about yourself; understanding current realities *and* passionately pursuing your vision; learning *and* leading.

This is another example of an important concept from the beginning of the chapter. For yourself, as well as for your organization, be ambidextrous. As you read "Management Connection: Onward," think about how ambidextrous Dr. Peter Pronovost has been in his efforts to improve the safety of hospital patients.

Manager's Brief   Progress Report   **Onward**

Management Connection

CHALLENGES OF SPREADING DR. PRONOVOST'S CHANGES TO MORE HOSPITALS

After the Michigan Keystone ICU Project demonstrated how using a five-point checklist could nearly eliminate catheter-related bloodstream infections, Dr. Peter Pronovost and others were eager to improve patient safety elsewhere. Pronovost's work in patient safety dovetailed with a federal government push to improve health care in the United States. The government backed a voluntary nationwide rollout of the checklist to support a Department of Health and Human Services goal of reducing central-line bloodstream infections by 75 percent over three years. Pronovost and his colleagues at the Johns Hopkins Quality and Safety Research Group joined with state health departments and hospital associations to bring this change effort to hospitals in every state.

As more hospitals enroll in the change effort, Pronovost sees a familiar pattern of resistance to change. At the core is the cultural conflict: staff members are so conscious of the hospital hierarchy that they burst into laughter when Pronovost says nurses should point out doctors' mistakes. He perseveres with his message that everyone is fallible, and everyone makes a mistake occasionally. Pronovost is blunt in expressing the problem—for example, posing this rhetorical question: "Could you imagine any other industry [besides health care] tolerating the violation of an evidence-based standard that kills 31,000 people a year?" Coming from a physician at a prestigious institution, this argument against what Pronovost calls "arrogance" is hard to ignore.

Besides the issues of organizational culture, Pronovost sees shortcomings in hospitals' processes. Many hospitals are not in the habit of collecting and publishing performance data related to patient safety. A hospital might agree that its intensive care unit (ICU) will use the checklist, but the hospital doesn't get around to measuring infection rates. Doctors and staff members don't realize when rates are high or receive feedback showing that following the checklist is preventing illnesses and saving lives.

Some ideas for improving processes can help safety-conscious employees work around cultural barriers to change. In hospitals where nurses can't enforce safety procedures by reminding doctors of the guidelines, Pronovost suggests that nurses carry pagers they can use to call hospital executives if they see a safety threat. Some hospitals have set up websites where employees can report problems anonymously. A notable success story is Tennessee, where the change effort is coordinated by the

Tennessee Center for Patient Safety, a quality improvement organization. The center helped hospitals develop a culture of teamwork by organizing networking meetings at which staff members share experiences and by helping hospitals set up safety teams of nurses, physicians, and hospital executives concerned about promoting patient safety.

As Pronovost pressures doctors, hospital administrators, and staff members to measure and report progress in bringing down infection rates, he sees a role for public policy in promoting and consolidating change. Pronovost would like more states to require their hospitals to collect and report data on bloodstream infections so patients, health care advocates, and other interested people can identify institutions that are poor performers and pressure them to change. By his recent count, 28 states require hospitals to collect data on bloodstream infections, and 14 require public reporting of the data. Pronovost also recommends that hospitals face fines or other sanctions if they fail to meet standards for preventing these readily avoidable infections. State-level sanctions on hospitals could provide pressure otherwise lacking in a system where penalties on doctors have traditionally been handled by a peer review process and hospitals are reluctant to alienate the physicians who send them patients.

Without such requirements, the rollout of the safety effort is slow. About 700 hospitals in 44 states and the District of Columbia have begun participating or agreed to participate. In some states, fewer than one-fifth of the hospitals have signed on. Even among hospitals that agreed to use the checklist, many are slow to adopt the record-keeping part of the change effort, and many others seem comfortable with aiming for an average infection rate rather than the achievable rate of nearly zero infections.

In spite of these challenges, the nationwide rollout has some progress to celebrate. The federal government's Agency for Healthcare Research and Quality (AHRQ) recently assessed the performance of participating hospitals. After 12 to 15 months, these hospitals had reduced their rate of central-line associated bloodstream infections by 35 percent to 1.17 infections per thousand days of central-line use. That was a smaller percentage decrease than in the Michigan pilot study, but it also is a big step toward the ultimate goal of less than 1 infection per thousand days. In Tennessee, where the Tennessee Center for

Patient Safety is pushing the teamwork approach, the change effort has succeeded so well that the Tennessee Hospital Association is now targeting zero infections as its three-year goal.[103]

- Based on the information given, what future does Dr. Pronovost envision for hospitals?
- At what level of the Level 5 hierarchy would you place Dr. Pronovost? Why?

KEY TERMS

adapters, p. 659

force-field analysis, p. 651

genius of the *and*, p. 643

moving, p. 651

organization development (OD), p. 644

organizational ambidexterity, p. 643

performance gap, p. 651

proactive change, p. 658

reactive change, p. 658

refreezing, p. 651

shapers, p. 659

total organization change, p. 655

tyranny of the *or*, p. 643

unfreezing, p. 649

SUMMARY OF LEARNING OBJECTIVES

Now that you have studied Chapter 18, you should be able to:

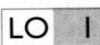 **Discuss what it takes to be world class.**

You should strive for world-class excellence, which means using the very best and latest knowledge and ideas to operate at the highest standards of any place anywhere. Sustainable greatness comes from, among other things, having strong core values, living those values constantly, striving for continuous improvement, experimenting, and always trying to do better tomorrow than today. It is essential to not fall prey to the tyranny of the *or*—that is, the belief that one important goal can be attained only at the expense of another. The genius of the *and* is that multiple important goals can be achieved simultaneously and synergistically.

LO 2 Describe how to manage and lead change effectively.

Effective change management occurs when the organization moves from its current state to a desired future state without excessive cost to the organization or its people. People resist change for a variety of reasons, including inertia, poor timing, surprise, peer pressure, self-interest, misunderstanding, different information about (and assessments of) the change, and management's tactics.

Motivating people to change requires a general process of unfreezing, moving, and refreezing, with the caveat that appropriate and not inappropriate behaviors be "refrozen." More specific techniques to motivate people to change include education and communication, participation and involvement, facilitation and support, negotiation and rewards, manipulation and cooptation, and coercion. Each approach has strengths, weaknesses, and appropriate uses, and multiple approaches can be used. It is important to harmonize the multiple changes that are occurring throughout the organization.

Effective change requires active leadership, including creating a sense of urgency, forming a guiding coalition, developing a vision and strategy, communicating the change vision, empowering broad-based action, generating short-term wins, consolidating gains and producing more change, and anchoring the new approaches in the culture.

LO 3 List tactics for creating a successful future.

Preparing for an uncertain future requires a proactive approach. You can proactively forge the future by being a shaper more than an adapter, creating new competitive advantages, actively managing your career and your personal development, and becoming an active leader and a lifelong learner.

DISCUSSION QUESTIONS

1. Why do some people resist the goal of becoming world class? How can this resistance be overcome?

2. Generate specific examples of world-class business that you have seen as a consumer. Also, generate examples of poor business practice. Why and how do some companies inspire world-class practices, while others do not?

3. How might blogging and other social forms of communication via social media affect the process of managing change? What are the professional and career implications of blogging for you?

4. Generate and discuss examples of problems and opportunities that have inspired change, both in businesses and in you, personally.

5. Review the methods for dealing with resistance to change. Generate specific examples of each that you have seen, and analyze the reasons why they worked or failed to work.

6. Choose some specific types of changes you would like to see happen in groups or organizations with which you are familiar. Imagine that you were to try to bring about these changes. What sources of resistance should you anticipate? How would you manage the resistance?

7. Develop a specific plan for becoming a "continuous learner."

8. In your own words, what does the idea of "creating the future" mean to you? How can you put this concept to good use? Again, generate some specific ideas that you can really use.

9. In what ways do you think the manager's job will be different in 20 years than it is today? How can you prepare for that future?

EXPERIENTIAL EXERCISES

18.1   A FORCE-FIELD ANALYSIS

OBJECTIVE

To introduce you to force-field analysis for managing organizational change.

INSTRUCTIONS

Read the following force-field analysis, and come up with an organizational problem of your own to analyze.

FORCE-FIELD ANALYSIS

As described in the chapter, a force-field analysis is one way to assess change in an organization. The change leader identifies the driving and restraining forces at work at a particular time, assesses organizational strengths, and selects forces to add or remove in order to create change. Using force-field analysis demonstrates the range of forces pressing on an organization at a particular time and can increase optimism that change is possible.

Example—trying to increase student participation in student government.

Driving Forces	Restraining Forces
More money allocated for student government activities. ⟶	⟵ High emphasis on grades—a need to study more.
Better publicity and public relations programs for student government. ⟶	⟵ Other activities—cultural, social, sports—divert interest.
Student government representatives go to classes and explain positive effects of student decisions. ⟶	⟵ Not much public relations work in the past.
Special career programs offered for student government participants. ⟶	⟵ Students do not see student government as effective or helping them get a job.

Present balance point

Force-Field Analysis Worksheet

1. Choose an organizational change in process, complete the Problem Analysis section, and fill in the model. (10–15 min.)

2. In groups of three or four, discuss the driving and restraining forces in each person's problem. (20 min.)

3. Class discussion: (10 min.)

   a. Why is it useful to break up a problem situation into driving and restraining forces?

   b. Would the model be applied any differently to an individual or organizational problem?

PROBLEM ANALYSIS

1. Describe the problem in a few words.

_____

_____

_____

_____

_____

2. A list of forces *driving* toward change would include these:

a. _____

b. _____

c. _____

d. _____

e. _____

f. _____

3. A list of forces *restraining* change would include these:

a. _____

b. _____

c. _____

d. _____

e. _____

f. _____

4. Put the driving and restraining forces of the problem on this force-field analysis, according to their degree of impact on change.

Driving Forces	Restraining Forces
→	←

Present balance point

SOURCE: Dorothy Hai Marcic, *Organizational Behavior: Experiences and Cases,* 1E. Copyright © 1986. South-Western, a part of Cengage Learning, Inc. Reproduced by permission. www.cengage.com/permissions

18.2   NETWORKING SCENARIOS

1. Working on your own, develop a networking strategy for the following three scenarios. (10 min.)

2. Working with your partner or small group, collaborate on identifying the best strategy for dealing with each of the three scenarios. Each group should develop one best strategy for each scenario. (20 min.)

3. Each group reports, sharing its best strategies for each of the three scenarios (or at least one if not enough time is available). (2–3 min. per group per strategy)

4. The large group or class engages in discussion, using the questions at the end. (10 min.)

SCENARIOS

I.   You are running for student government president. What steps would you take to make your candidacy a success?

1. _____

2. _____

3. _____

4. _____

5. _____

6. _____

II. You are in an internship and are interested in becoming a permanent full-time employee at the organization. What people would you approach and what steps could you take to obtain an offer?

1. _____

2. _____

3. _____

4. _____

5. _____

6. _____

III. You just moved to a new community, and your company's business growth relies heavily on referrals. How do you make contacts in a place where you don't know anyone? How can you build a client base?

1. _____

2. _____

3. _____

4. _____

5. _____

6. _____

QUESTIONS

1. What was difficult about this exercise?

2. What creative means were devised to build networks of contacts in these scenarios?

3. Which of these ideas would be easy to implement? Which would be difficult? What makes some strategies easier to do than others?

4. What personal qualities are needed to actually use these strategies?

5. How can someone who is shy about approaching new people use (some or all of) these strategies successfully?

6. What did you learn about yourself and others from this exercise?

SOURCE: Suzanne C. de Janasz, Karen O'Dowd, and Beth Z. Schneider, *Interpersonal Skills in Organizations*, McGraw-Hill/Irwin, 2002, p. 212. © 2002 The McGraw-Hill Companies. Reprinted with permission.

CONCLUDING CASE

BARBARA'S WORLD OF WINDOWS, FABRICS, AND ACCESSORIES—HOME CONSULTANT DIVISION

BUSINESS OVERVIEW AND PERSPECTIVE

Shortly after World War II, Barbara and Jerry Klein opened a small retail store in the northern New Jersey metropolitan area. Their major product lines included cotton, wool, and other fabrics that Jerry was able to buy from a few of his old war buddies who worked in mills located throughout the southeastern United States. The fabrics were purchased by an almost exclusively female clientele from the local area for use in making clothing, curtains, slipcovers, pillows, and other related home furnishings. The store also sold curtain rods, hardware, zippers, sewing supplies, and related accessories.

The store was a great success throughout the 1950s, 1960s, and 1970s. During that time, sales grew from $150,000 to more than $2,500,000 annually. The store employed 30 people, mostly homemakers from the local area who were sewers and clothing makers themselves. The warm, cozy, and friendly atmosphere made the store a favorite of the local and surrounding townspeople. Several competitors came and went over the years—those that survived were very small, posing little threat to Barbara and Jerry, who essentially enjoyed the fruits of a monopoly.

Barbara's (comfortable) world came crashing down during the 1980s, as sales steadily declined to less than $1,800,000 by the decade's end. Their original clientele had gradually retired, moved away, or passed on by that time. The modern-day women from the area were now going to college and establishing professional careers rather than staying at home sewing curtains or making clothes. At the same time, a number of new and more diversified competitors had come onto the scene, capturing more and more market share.

Those new stores carried a much wider range of products, including bridal wear; tablecloths and napkins; miniblinds and assorted shades; quilts; blankets; and limited lines of furniture, lamps, candles, and complementary products.

Barbara and Jerry's daughter Sandy, a recent business school graduate who grew up working part-time in the business, came on board as assistant manager of operations. Sandy was being trained and groomed to eventually take over the business. Given her many years of direct work experience and her newly acquired business management skills, Sandy was given some freedom and encouragement to effect change and turn things around.

A NEW ERA

The store's entire merchandise inventory was counted, assessed, and reorganized. Sandy got rid of slow-moving and stagnant inventory. High-turnover, high-profit merchandise was given more and better shelf space. A number of new products were added to challenge the competition and better reflect the buying trends and needs of the modern-day consumer.

The most significant change was the addition of a new Home Consultant Division. Recognizing the needs and characteristics of today's professional woman shopper, Sandy proceeded to bring the business to the customer in the comfort of her own home. During evening and weekend hours, sales associates visited the homes of working women. Offered a variety of full-color catalogs and fabric samples, customers could simply select the blinds, shades, draperies, wall coverings, slipcovers, and so on of their choosing and write a check for one-half of the total invoice as a deposit. The sales associate took the necessary measurements while on site. The finished products were delivered and installed in approximately two to four weeks. The remaining balance was paid at the time of delivery and installation.

The Home Consultant Division was a huge start-up success. Sales reached $1,000,000 during the first year of operation and $1,500,000 during year 2. As the division grew, so did a number of problems and inefficiencies. A shortage of qualified installers caused the lag time between orders and installations to grow to as much as 6 to 12 weeks. On the home appointment side, where a customer could once expect to have a sales associate visit within a week or two of inquiring, the wait for an appointment had grown to average about one month. On top of all of this, Sandy knew that there was a lot more business out there to capture.

Customers became impatient and unhappy, as Sandy now faced her first serious problem that needed to be fixed fast. The complacency and lack of marketing savvy of her parents had allowed a number of able competitors to come onto the scene, two of which were gearing up to offer their own home shopping divisions.

Sandy asked Barbara Johnson, one of the sales associates, to document the complete and exact process that takes place from the time an inquiry is received to the time that an installation is completed, in the hope of identifying specific inefficiencies and production bottlenecks. Johnson's report can be summarized as follows:

- The process begins with a phone call from people responding to newspaper ads or from in-store shoppers. No

programs are currently in place to actively solicit prospective customers.

- The secretary or whoever happens to answer the phone records the information (name, address, phone number, nature of inquiry) and places a note in the sales associate's mailbox.

- A sales associate (currently two full-time, one part-time) places a phone call to set up an appointment in the order in which the inquiry was received. Most clients are within a 25-mile radius of the store.

- A typical day for a sales associate might include a 4:00 p.m. appointment in one town followed by a 7:30 p.m. appointment in another town. On Saturdays, the sales associate typically has a 9:00 a.m. appointment in one town followed by a 12:00 p.m. appointment in another town.

- The associate then meets with the client, equipped with catalogs and samples, order forms, and measuring equipment. Most appointments result in a sale. The sales associate takes the necessary measurements (window sizes, sofa dimensions, and so on), and leaves with a check for an estimated 50 percent deposit.

- The sales associates spend about one day per week processing orders (calculating the yardage and best source of material, locating the appropriate curtain rods, tabulating the exact invoice total, and so on).

- When all of the materials arrive at the store for a particular order, the sales associate is notified and then proceeds to contact and schedule an installer; this also includes a scheduling call to the client.

- The installer completes the delivery and installation and collects the final payment for the store.

Johnson also provided the following breakdown of each sales associate's average distribution of time spent on the job:

- 40 percent of the time is spent selling at the client's home.
- 30 percent of the time is spent processing orders.
- 30 percent of the time is spent traveling between appointments.

Barbara's report concluded with a summary from the installation side of the division: "Most deliveries and installations are made by two independent subcontractors that have been with the company since the start-up of the division. They have a reputation for doing good work. Several others have come and gone—this due to either poor workmanship or lack of availability or reliability.

"Several customers have complained about the appearance and presentation of the installers and their equipment. Many of the clients are women who live in suburban neighborhoods. These women are often home alone when the deliveries and installations are made. They are apprehensive and fearful when they see unshaven young men with old clothes pull up to their home in a battered old van. A few customers have actually refused to let the installer into their homes without first speaking with someone at the store.

"The two primary installers are working hard and are steadily falling further and further behind the order file."

As for the many untapped markets and additional new business that is out there, Sandy wants her staff to become more proactive—to go after orders rather than just waiting for the phone to ring or for a shopper to inquire while in the store.

Sandy feels that the company is making a big mistake by completely ignoring the local industrial and governmental markets. For example, on the industrial side, hotels, restaurants, banks, offices, and many other establishments regularly purchase and update their furniture, window coverings, and other interior decor. The same is true for prospective governmental customers such as schools, city and town offices, and federal buildings. Sandy also notes that the customers, both in the store and in the home, continue to be almost exclusively women.

QUESTIONS

1. You have inherited a company that must make several internal changes to survive and thrive. How would you plan for and manage each of the changes that must occur? Be sure to address both strategic and tactical aspects of your plan.

2. The text lists and describes a number of operational aspects and components; select each of those that are relevant to this case, and provide a specific example of a technique that you would incorporate into the new operation.

3. In general, what interpersonal skills and management techniques will you use to successfully effect change?

PART FIVE   SUPPORTING CASE

Technology Helps Dollar General Pinch Pennies

More and more consumers determined to save money are winding up at deep-discount retailers popularly known as "dollar stores." These relatively small stores—including Dollar General, Family Dollar, and Dollar Tree—offer food, clothing, and household items at deep discounts. Discounters like Target and Walmart offer a wider selection, but more consumers are trading down to find the best possible prices.

Competing with Walmart on price is hardly an easy strategy. When Kathleen Guion took charge of store operations and store development for Dollar General, she got to work initiating a whole host of changes. Many of these were aimed at controlling costs and helping the stores run more efficiently, and many of the changes involved improving the technology used by store employees, bringing it more in line with industry standards.

Guion found that Dollar General used some truly low-tech approaches to activities involved in running the stores. When trucks pulled up with deliveries, for example, store employees pulled cartons out of the truck one by one and carried them into the store for stocking the shelves. And whenever items languished on shelves too long, the same employees would repack them in boxes and carry them into the back room for storage. Not only were these methods slow, but employees hated lugging the boxes around. Calling her change program EZ Store, Guion simplified those jobs. She bought large wheeled bins called "rolltainers," which employees use to move products from the trucks to back rooms to the sales floor. And when products don't sell as expected, the EZ Store plan calls for marking down the price low enough that the products do get sold. Not only does EZ Store make working for Dollar General more enjoyable by eliminating undesirable chores, but the greater efficiency gives employees more time to serve customers.

Under Guion's direction, Dollar General also upgraded its computer systems to deliver better information faster.

The company introduced handheld scanners connected to an inventory management system so employees can quickly and accurately see which items need to be replenished and when. Computers linked to headquarters have been installed in the back rooms of all the stores (surprising as it may sound, until 2009, headquarters sent messages to stores via postal mail). The company introduced computer-based training programs to improve employees' skills, as well as software for screening job candidates to identify which of them have qualities associated with success. And to reduce thefts in the stores, the company installed closed-circuit television systems.

Managers also have been given better technology. Dollar General bought district managers personal computers with software that monitors performance and flags exceptions to standards. It also gave them BlackBerry handheld devices so they can keep in touch with their people and keep up-to-date on store performance while they travel. The technology has enabled Dollar General to widen the district managers' span of control because fewer managers can keep up with more stores. More efficient management, in turn, has supported the company's program of rapidly opening new stores (it now has more than 9,500 in 35 states).

These efficiency improvements are essential in the difficult retailing industry because Walmart and Target as well as other dollar stores recognize that consumers will move elsewhere if one store doesn't remain competitive. All low-price retailers are constantly looking for ways to improve efficiency. Furthermore, in recent months, costs of transportation and basic goods such as food have been rising, which limits the amount by which retailers can mark up their prices and still offer the best deal. Dollar General CEO Richard Dreiling recently noted that the stores were carrying more than 220 items priced at $1, and that raising the price by even 15 cents would discourage some of the company's regular customers. As Dollar General tries to maintain profitability, it will keep looking for ways to change how it does business, and technology will continue to play a role in the solutions. So far, it's a strategy that has fueled tremendous growth at Dollar General even as other retailers are struggling to maintain sales volume.

QUESTIONS

1. What types of control are important at Dollar General? Why are these important?

2. What technological innovations did Kathleen Guion introduce at Dollar General? How did these innovations support the company's strategy?

3. What challenges would you have expected Guion to face in introducing these changes? What principles of managing change would you have suggested she apply?

SOURCES: Based on "Operational Improvements Benefit Employees, Customers," *MMR*, May 17, 2010, Business & Company Resource Center, http://galenet .galegroup.com; J. Jannarone, "Will Dollar General Lead Retailers into Battle?" *The Wall Street Journal*, June 6, 2011, http://online.wsj.com; A. Zimmerman, "Dollar Stores Find Splurges Drying Up," *The Wall Street Journal*, July 11, 2011, http://online. wsj.com; C. Burritt, "Dollar Stores: More Brands, More Customers," *Bloomberg Businessweek*, July 29, 2010, http://www.businessweek.com; M. Jarzemsky, "Dollar General's Earnings Gain 15%," *The Wall Street Journal*, June 1, 2011, http://online. wsj.com; Dollar General, "About Us," http://dollargeneral.com; and Dollar General, "Dollar General Announces Kathleen Guion, Division President of Store Operations and Store Development, Will Transition to Retirement," news release, July 25, 2011, http://newscenter.dollargeneral.com.

CASE INCIDENTS

Robot Repercussion

Victor Principal, vice president of industrial relations for General Manufacturing, Inc., sat in his office reviewing the list of benefits the company expected to realize from increasing its use of industrial robots. In a few minutes, he would walk down to the labor management conference room for a meeting with Ralph McIntosh, president of the labor union local representing most of the company's industrial employees. The purpose of this meeting would be to informally exchange views and positions preliminary to the opening for formal contract negotiations later in the month, which would focus on the use of computer-integrated robotics systems and the resulting impact on employment, workers, and jobs.

Both Principal and McIntosh had access to similar information flows relevant to industrial robots, including the following. Unlike single-task machines, installed in earlier stages of automation, robots can be programmed to do one job and then reprogrammed to do another one. The pioneering generation of robots was programmed mainly to load machines, weld, forge, spray paint, handle materials, and inspect auto bodies. The latest generation of robots includes vision-controlled robots, which can approximate the human ability to recognize and size up objects by using laser beam patterns recorded by television cameras and transmitted to "smart" computers. The computer software interprets and manipulates the images relayed by the camera in a "smart" or artificially intelligent way.

Experts concluded that the impact of robot installation on employment would be profound, although the extent of the worker replacement was not clear. The inescapable conclusion was that robot usage had the capacity to increase manufacturing performance and to decrease manufacturing employment.

Principal walked down to the conference room. Finding McIntosh already there, Principal stated the company's position regarding installation of industrial robots: "The company needs the cooperation of the union and our workers. We don't wish to be perceived as callously exchanging human workers for robots." Then Principal listed the major advantages associated with robots: (1) improved quality of product as a result of the accuracy of robots; (2) reduced operating costs because the per-hour operational cost of robots was about one-third

of the per-hour cost of wages and benefits paid to an average employee; (3) reliability improvements because robots work tirelessly and don't require behavioral support; and (4) greater manufacturing flexibility because robots are readily reprogrammable for different jobs. Principal concluded that these advantages would make the company more competitive, which would allow it to grow and increase its workforce.

McIntosh's response was direct and strong: "We aren't Luddites racing around ruining machines. We know it's necessary to increase productivity and that robotic technology is here. But we can't give the company a blank check. We need safeguards and protection." McIntosh continued, "We intend to bargain for the following contract provisions:

1. Establishment of labor–management committees to negotiate *in advance* about the labor impact of robotics technology and, of equal importance, to have a voice in deciding how and whether it should be used.

2. Rights to advance notice about installation of new technology.

3. Retraining rights for workers displaced, to include retraining for new positions in the plant, the community, or other company plants.

4. Spreading the work among workers by use of a four-day workweek or other acceptable plan as an alternative to reducing the workforce."

McIntosh's final sentence summed up the union's position: "We in the union believe the company is giving our jobs to robots to reduce the labor force."

Their meeting ended amiably, but Principal and McIntosh each knew that much hard bargaining lay ahead. As Principal returned to his office, the two opposing positions were obvious. On his yellow tablet, Principal listed the requirements as he saw them: (1) a clearly stated overall policy was needed to guide negotiation decisions and actions; (2) it was critical to decide on a company position regarding each of the union's announced demands and concerns; and (3) a plan had to be developed.

As Principal considered these challenges, he idly contemplated a robot possessing artificial intelligence and vision capability that could help him in his work. Immediately a danger alarm sounded in his mind. A robot so constructed might be more than helpful and might take over this and other important aspects of his job. Slightly chagrined, Principal returned to his task. He needed help—but not from any "smart" robot.

SOURCE: J. Champion and J. James, *Critical Incidents in Management: Decision and Policy Issues*, 6th ed. McGraw-Hill/Irwin, 1989. © 1989 The McGraw-Hill Companies.

Implementing Strategic Change

James Fulmer, chief executive officer of Allied Industries, reviewed three notes he had exchanged with Frank Curtis, director of fiscal affairs, now president of a company owned by Allied. The two executives were going to meet in a few minutes to discuss problems that had recently surfaced. During the past decade, Allied had aggressively pursued a growth objective based on a conglomerate strategy of acquiring companies in distress. CEO Fulmer's policy was to appoint a new chief operating officer for each acquisition with instructions to facilitate a turnaround. Fulmer reviewed two of the notes he had written to Curtis.

Date: January 15, 2011

Memorandum

To: Frank Curtis, Director of Fiscal Affairs, Allied Industries

From: James Fulmer, Chairman, Allied Industries

Subject: Your Appointment as President, Lee Medical Supplies

You are aware that Allied Industries recently acquired Lee Medical Supplies. Mr. John Lee, founder and president of the company, has agreed to retire, and I am appointing you to replace him. Our acquisitions group will brief you on the company, but I want to warn you that Lee Medical Supplies has a history of mismanagement. As a distributor of medical items, the company's sales last year totaled approximately $300 million, with net earnings of only $12 million. Your job is to make company sales and profits compatible with Allied standards. You are reminded that it is my policy to call for an independent evaluation of company progress and your performance as president after 18 months.

Date: September 10, 2011

Memorandum

To: Frank Curtis, President, Lee Medical Supplies

From: James Fulmer, Chairman, Allied Industries

Subject: Serious Problems at Lee Medical Supplies

In accord with corporate policy, consultants recently conducted an evaluation of Lee Medical Supplies. In a relatively short period of time, you have increased sales and profits to meet Allied's standards, but I am alarmed at other aspects of your performance. I am told that during the past 18 months, three of your nine vice presidents have resigned and that you have terminated four others. An opinion survey conducted by the consultants indicates that a low state of morale exists and that your managerial appointees are regarded by their subordinates as hard-nosed perfectionists obsessed with quotas and profits. Employees report that ruthless competition now exists between divisions, regions, and districts. They also note that the collegial, family-oriented atmosphere fostered by Mr. Lee has been replaced by a dog-eat-dog

situation characterized by negative management attitudes toward employee feelings and needs. After you have studied the enclosed report from the consultants, we will meet to discuss their findings. I am particularly concerned with their final conclusion that "a form of corporate cancer seems to be spreading throughout Lee Medical Supplies."

As Fulmer prepared to read the third note, written by Frank Curtis, he reflected on his interview with the consultants. While Fulmer considered Curtis a financial expert and a turnaround specialist, his subordinates characterized Curtis as an autocrat and better suited to be a marine boot camp commander.

Date: September 28, 2011

Memorandum

To: James Fulmer

From: Frank Curtis

Subject: The So-Called Serious Problems at Lee Medical Supplies

I have received your memorandum dated September 10, and reviewed the consultants' report. When you appointed me to my present position, I was instructed to take over an unprofitable company and make it profitable. I have done so in 18 months, although I inherited a family-owned business that by your own admission had been mismanaged for years. I found a group of managers and salespeople with an average company tenure of 22 years. Mr. Lee had centralized all personnel decisions so that only he could terminate an employee. He tolerated mediocre performance. All employees were paid on a straight salary basis, with seniority the sole criterion for advancement. Some emphasis was given to increasing sales each year, but none was given to reducing costs and increasing profits. Employees did indeed find the company a fun place to work, and the feeling of being a part of a family did permeate the company. Such attitudes were, however, accompanied by mediocrity, incompetence, and poor performance.

I found it necessary to implement immediate strategic changes in five areas: the organization's structure, employee rewards and incentives, management information systems, allocation of resources, and managerial leadership style. As a result, sales areas were reorganized into divisions, regions, and districts. Managers who I felt were incompetent and/or lacking in commitment to my objectives and methods were replaced. Unproductive and mediocre employees were encouraged to find jobs elsewhere. Authority for staffing and compensation decisions was decentralized to units at the division, region, and district levels. Managers of those units were informed that along with their authority went responsibility for reducing costs and for increasing sales and profits. Each unit was established as a profit center. A new department was established and charged with reviewing performance of those units. Improved accounting and control systems were implemented. A management by objectives program was developed to establish standards and monitor performance. Performance appraisals are now required for all employees. To encourage more aggressive action, bonuses and incentives are offered to managers of units showing increased profits. A commission plan based on measurable sales and profit performances has replaced straight salaries. Resources are allocated to units based on their performance.

My own leadership style has probably represented the most traumatic change for employees. Internal competition is a formally mandated policy throughout the company. It has been responsible for much of the progress achieved to date. Progress, however, is never made without costs, and I recognize that employees are not having as much fun as in the past. I was employed to achieve results and not to ensure that employees remain secure and happy in their work. Don't let a few crybabies unable to adjust to changes lead you to believe that problems take precedence over profits. Does it mean that I am not people oriented if I believe it

is unlikely that a spirit of aggressiveness and competitiveness can coexist with an atmosphere of cooperativeness and family orientation? Do you feel that we are obligated to employees because of past practices? Frankly, I thought I had your support to do whatever was necessary to get this company turned around. In our meeting, tell me if you think my approaches have been wrong and, if so, tell me what I should have done differently.

Just as Fulmer finished reviewing the third memorandum, his secretary informed him that Curtis had arrived for their scheduled meeting. He realized he was undecided about how to communicate to Curtis his ideas and beliefs regarding how changes in an organization can best be implemented. One thing he did know: He didn't appreciate how Curtis had expressed his views in his memorandum, but he recognized that he probably should set aside emotions and respond to the questions Curtis posed.

SOURCE: J. Champion and J. James, *Critical Incidents in Management: Decision and Policy Issues,* 6th ed. McGraw-Hill/Irwin, 1989. © 1989 The McGraw-Hill Companies.

NOTES

Chapter 1

1. Kyle Arnold, "Charging Ahead," *Tulsa World*, November 7, 2010, Business & Company Resource Center, http://galenet.galegroup.com; Hiroko Tabuchi, "An Unlikely Alliance Quickly Results in an All-Electric RAV4," *The New York Times*, November 17, 2010, Business & Company Resource Center, http://galenet.galegroup.com; Hans Greimel, "Panasonic Invests in Tesla," *Automotive News*, November 8, 2010, Business & Company Resource Center, http://galenet.galegroup.com; and Dana Hull, "Empty Auto Factory Gets New Life as Tesla Moves In," *San Jose Mercury News*, September 24, 2010, Business & Company Resource Center, http://galenet.galegroup.com.

2. Michael Abramowitz and Steve Vogel, "Apologies, Anger at Walter Reed Hearing," *Washington Post*, March 6, 2007, http://www.washingtonpost.com. See also Dana Priest and Anne Hull, "Soldiers Face Neglect, Frustration at Army's Top Medical Facility," *Washington Post*, February 18, 2007, http://www.wasingtonpost.com.

3. "Former Hospital Commanders Apologize," *UPI NewsTrack*, March 5, 2007, downloaded from Business & Company Resource Center, http://galenet.galegroup.com.

4. Morten T. Hansen, Herminia Ibarra, and Urs Peyer, "The Best-Performing CEOs in the World," *Harvard Business Review*, January–February 2010, http://hbr.org.

5. S. Green, F. Hassan, J. Immelt, M. Marks, and D. Meiland, "In Search of Global Leaders," *Harvard Business Review*, August 2003, pp. 38–45.

6. "World's Most Admired Companies," *Fortune*, 2011, http://money.cnn.com.

7. John Christoffersen, "Global Ambition: GE Looks Outside U.S. for Growth," *Cincinnati Post*, January 18, 2007, downloaded from Business & Company Resource Center, http://galenet.galegroup.com.

8. Nandini Lakshman, "Cisco's Grand India Ambitions," *BusinessWeek Online*, January 3, 2007, downloaded from Business & Company Resource Center, http://galenet.galegroup.com.

9. Betsy Morris, "The Pepsi Challenge," *Fortune*, February 19, 2008, http://money.cnn.com.

10. Duane Stanford, "Africa: Coke's Last Frontier," *Bloomberg Businessweek*, October 28, 2010, http://www.businessweek.com; and Geoffrey Colvin, "The Great Shakeout," *Fortune*, March 21, 2011, pp. 111–112.

11. T. Bisoux, "Corporate CounterCulture," *BizEd*, November/December 2004, pp. 16–20, quoted on p. 19.

12. G. Huber, *The Necessary Nature of Future Firms* (Thousand Oaks, CA: Sage, 2004).

13. Jay Greene and Cliff Edwards, "Desktops Are So Twentieth Century," *BusinessWeek*, December 8, 2006, http://www.businessweek.com.

14. F. Cairncross, *The Company of the Future* (Cambridge, MA: Harvard Business School Press, 2002).

15. Jessi Hempel, "Web 2.0: The Party's Over," *Fortune*, June 1, 2010, http://tech.fortune.cnn.com.

16. Jean Chatzky, "Confessions of an E-Mail Addict," *Money*, March 2007, downloaded from Business & Company Resource Center, http://galenet.galegroup.com.

17. Robert Austin, "Managing Knowledge Workers," *Science*, July 21, 2006, accessed at ScienceCareers.org, http://sciencecareers.sciencemag.org.

18. David Raths, "Hospital IT Departments Prescribe Portals for Physicians," *KMWorld*, February 2007, downloaded from Business & Company Resource Center, http://galenet.galegroup.com.

19. M. Hansen and B. von Oetinger, "Introducing T-Shaped Managers: Knowledge Management's Next Generation," *Harvard Business Review*, March 2001, pp. 106–16.

20. John Teresko, "Toyota's Real Secret," *Industry Week*, February 2007, downloaded from Business & Company Resource Center, http://galenet.galegroup.com.

21. Ibid.

22. L. Willcocks and R. Plant, "Pathways to E-Business Leadership: Getting from Bricks to Clicks," *Sloan Management Review*, Spring 2001, pp. 50–59.

23. Suzanne Vranica, "P&G Boosts Social-Networking Efforts," *The Wall Street Journal*, January 8, 2007, http://online.wsj.com.

24. James R. Hagerty, "Entrepreneurs Find Gold in Used Phones," *The Wall Street Journal*, February 24, 2011, http://online.wsj.com.

25. B. Kowitt, "Dunkin' Brands' Kitchen Crew," *Fortune*, May 24, 2010, pp. 72–74.

26. "Home and Abroad," *The Economist*, February 10, 2007, Business & Company Resource Center, http://galenet.galegroup.com.

27. A. Wooldridge, "The World Turned Upside Down," *The Economist*, April 17, 2010, pp. 1–3.

28. R. I. Sutton, "The Weird Rules of Creativity," *Harvard Business Review*, September 2001, pp. 94–103.

29. Laura Landro, "Hospitals Take Consumers' Advice," *The Wall Street Journal*, February 7, 2007, http://online.wsj.com.

30. Ibid.

31. O. Port, "The Kings of Quality," *BusinessWeek*, August 30, 2004, p. 20.

32. Karla Ward, "Attracting Opposites," *Lexington Herald-Leader*, December 12, 2006; and Lisa McTigue Pierce, "How to Do It 'My Way,'" *Food & Drug Packaging*, January 2007, both downloaded from Business & Company Resource Center, http://galenet.galegroup.com.

33. Pierce, "How to Do It 'My Way'"; and MyJones website, http://www.myjones.com, accessed March 9, 2007.

34. D. A. Garvin, "Manufacturing Strategic Planning," *California Management Review*, Summer 1993, pp. 85–106.

35. Reported in "Hospital Ratings May Not Be True Quality Measure," *Washington Post*, December 13, 2006, http://www.washingtonpost.com.

36. U.S. Census Bureau, *Statistical Abstract of the United States*, 2007, Table 650, p. 431, http://www.census.gov/prod/www/statistical-abstract.html.

37. Ibid., Tables 607 and 608, pp. 394–95.

38. Sherri Begin, "The Art of Service," *Crain's Detroit Business*, February 12, 2007, downloaded from Business & Company Resource Center, http://galenet.galegroup.com.

39. Adam Lashinsky, "Chaos by Design," *Fortune*, October 2, 2006, http://money.cnn.com.

40. Teresko, "Toyota's Real Secret."

41. Ibid.

42. Gary McWilliams, "Wal-Mart's Radio-Tracked Inventory Hits Static," *The Wall Street Journal*, February 15, 2007, http://online.wsj.com.

43. Kris Maher, "Wal-Mart Seeks New Flexibility in Worker Shifts," *The Wall Street Journal*, January 3, 2007, http://online.wsj.com.

44. S. Cendrowski, "Singapore Airlines," *Fortune*, June 14, 2010, p. 22.

45. F. Gillette, "The Duke of Discomfort," *Bloomberg Businessweek*, September 6, 2010, pp. 58–61.

46. Julie Johnsson, "Jets Reach New Heights," *Chicago Tribune*, February 25, 2007, sec. 5, pp. 1, 4.

47. "Lean and Green: Rucker Applies Lean Practices to Electric Bill," *Internet Wire*, December 14, 2010, Business & Company Resource Center, http://galenet.galegroup.com.

48. P. Bisson, E. Stephenson, and S. P. Vigueire, "Global Forces: An Introduction," *McKinsey Quarterly*, June 2010, pp. 1–4.

49. B. Dumaine, "Searching for Profits in Patagonia," *Fortune*, March 21, 2011, pp. 97–105.

50. B. Doppelt, *Leading Change toward Sustainability* (Sheffield, UK: Greenleaf 2010).

51. Vanessa Fuhrmans, "A Novel Plan Helps Hospital Wean Itself off Pricey Tests," *The Wall Street Journal*, January 12, 2007, http://online.wsj.com.

52. "Avon Regains Some Allure," *BusinessWeek*, February 7, 2007, http://www.businessweek.com.

53. Claudia H. Deutsch, "A Chance to Save Their Skin," *The New York Times*, January 19, 2007, downloaded from Business & Company Resource Center, http://galenet.galegroup.com.

54. J. W. Cortada, *21st Century Business* (London: Financial Times/Prentice Hall, 2001).

55. D. Lepak, K. Smith, and M. S. Taylor, "Value Creation and Value Capture: A Multilevel Perspective," *Academy of Management Review* 23 (2007), pp. 180–94.

56. Joe Light, "Bosses Overestimate Their Managing Skills," *The Wall Street Journal*, November 1, 2010, http://online.wsj.com; and Scott Erker and Bradford Thomas, *Finding the First Rung*, Trend Research report (Pittsburgh: Development Dimensions International, 2010), http://www.ddiworld.com.

57. R. Webber, "General Management Past and Future," *Financial Times Mastering Management*, 1997.

58. Arnold, "Charging Ahead"; Hull, "Empty Auto Factory"; Dave Guilford, "Should EVs Use a Sibling's Architecture?" *Automotive News*, January 31, 2011, Business & Company Resource Center, http://galenet.galegroup.com; Dave Guilford, "Shortage of Engineers? For EVs, Yes," *Automotive News*, December 13, 2010, Business & Company Resource Center, http://galenet.galegroup.com; Associated Press, "Tesla Losses Rise Even as Revenues Grow," *Bloomberg Businessweek*, February 15, 2011, www.businessweek.com; Alan Ohnsman, "Tesla Targets 50% Growth on Roadster, Battery Sales," *Bloomberg Businessweek*, February 22, 2011, www.businessweek.com; and Russell Hensley, Stefan M. Knupfer, and Axel Krieger, "The Fast Lane to the Adoption of Electric Cars," *McKinsey Quarterly*, no. 1 (2011) pp. 10–14.

59. Pui-Wing Tam, "CIO Jobs Morph from Tech Support into Strategy," *The Wall Street Journal*, February 20, 2007, http://online.wsj.com.

60. Ibid.

61. Q. N. Huy, "In Praise of Middle Managers," *Harvard Business Review*, September 2001, pp. 72–79.

62. L. A. Hill, "New Manager Development for the 21st Century," *Academy of Management Executive*, August 2004, pp. 121–26.

63. C. Bartlett and S. Goshal, "The Myth of the Generic Manager: New Personal Competencies for New Management Roles," *California Management Review* 40, no. 1 (1997), pp. 92–116.

64. Ray Fisman, "In Defense of Middle Management," *Slate*, October 13, 2010, http://www.slate.com; and Nicholas Bloom, Benn Eifert, Aprajit Mahajan, et al., "Does Management Matter? Evidence from India," NBER Working Paper 16658 (Cambridge, MA: National Bureau of Economic Research, January 2011), http://www.nber.org/papers/w16658.

65. L. R. Sayles, "Doing Things Right: A New Imperative for Middle Managers," *Organizational Dynamics*, Spring 1993, pp. 5–14.

66. H. Mintzberg, *The Nature of Managerial Work* (New York: Harper & Row, 1973).

67. R. Katz, "Skills of an Effective Administrator," *Harvard Business Review* 52 (September–October), pp. 90–102.

68. Hill, "New Manager Development for the 21st Century."

69. H. Mintzberg, "The Manager's Job: Folklore and Fact," *Harvard Business Review* 53 (July–August 1975), pp. 49–61.

70. Francesca Di Meglio, "Columbia Gets Personal," *BusinessWeek Online*, October 18, 2006 (interview with Michael Morris), downloaded from Business & Company Resource Center, http://galenet.galegroup.com.

71. Colin Stewart, "Program Teaches Corporate Skills to Cure What Ails Them," *Orange County Register*, December 28, 2006, downloaded from Business & Company Resource Center, http://galenet.galegroup.com.

72. "Nontraditional Path: From Pre-Med Dropout to Next Aetna CEO," *DiversityInc.*, October 28, 2010, http://diversityinc.com; and Aetna, "Executive Biographies: Mark T. Bertolini," *About Us: Corporate Profile*, http://www.aetna.com, accessed February 25, 2011.

73. Hill, "New Manager Development for the 21st Century."

74. D. Goleman, R. Boyatzis, and A. McKee, *Primal Leadership: Realizing the Power of Emotional Intelligence* (Boston: Harvard Business School Press, 2002).

75. R. Boyatzis, "Get Motivated," *Harvard Business Review*, January 2004, p. 30.

76. W. George, "Find Your Voice," *Harvard Business Review*, January 2004, p. 35.

77. Stephen Xavier, "Control Yourself: What Role Does Emotional Intelligence Play in Executive Leadership?" *US Business Review*, March 2006, downloaded from Business & Company Resource Center, http://galenet.galegroup.com.

78. Ibid.

79. W. Kiechel III, "A Manager's Career in the New Economy," *Fortune*, April 4, 1994, pp. 68–72.

80. Elizabeth Garone, "Leading the Environmental Charge at Xerox," *The Wall Street Journal*, March 25, 2009, http://online.wsj.com.

81. K. Inkson and M. B. Arther, "How to Be a Successful Career Capitalist," *Organizational Dynamics*, Summer 2001, pp. 48–60.

82. Geoffrey Colvin, "What It Takes to Be Great," *Fortune*, October 19, 2006, http://money.cnn.com.

83. L. M Roberts, J. Dutton, G. Spreitzer, E. Heaphy, and R. Quinn, "Composing the Reflected Best-Self Portrait: Building Pathways for Becoming Extraordinary in Work Organizations," *Academy of Management Review* 30 (2005), pp. 712–36.

84. L. M. Roberts, "Changing Faces: Professional Image Construction in Diverse Organizational Settings," *Academy of Management Review* 30 (2005), pp. 685–711.

85. M. E. P. Seligman, *Authentic Happiness: Using the New Positive Psychology to Realize Your Potential for Lasting Fulfillment* (New York: Free Press, 2002).

86. David Kaplan, "They've Risen through the Ranks," *Houston Chronicle*, April 18, 2010, Business & Company Resource Center, http://galenet.galegroup.com.

87. E. W. Morrison, "Newcomers' Relationships: The Role of Social Network Ties during Socialization," *Academy of Management Journal* 45 (2002), pp. 1149–60.

88. P. Adler and S. Kwon, "Social Capital: Prospects for a New Concept," *Academy of Management Review* 27 (2002), pp. 17–40.

89. Jessi Hempel, "How LinkedIn Will Fire Up Your Career," *Fortune*, April 12, 2010, pp. 74–82.

90. T. Peters, *Liberation Management* (New York: Alfred A. Knopf, 1992).

91. P. Drucker, "What Makes an Effective Executive?" *Harvard Business Review*, June 2004, pp. 58–63.

92. Marshall Goldsmith, "Three Obstacles to a Career Move," *BusinessWeek*, March 7, 2007, downloaded from Business & Company Resource Center, http://galenet.galegroup.com.

93. Guilford, "Should EVs Use a Sibling's Architecture?"; Bill Vlasic, "First Buyers of an All-Electric Car Also Get a Trunkful of Perks," *The New York Times*, October 8, 2010, Business & Company Resource Center, http://galenet.galegroup.com; John Reed and Bernard Simon, "Groups Shift Gear for a Power Revolution," *Financial Times*, September 19, 2010, www.ft.com; Peter Fairley, "Will Electric Vehicles Finally Succeed?" *Technology Review*, January/February 2011, pp. 58–63; Hensley et al., "The Fast Lane to Adoption"; Chester Dawson, "At Auto Show, Hot Wheels Are a Hot Item," *The Wall Street Journal*, January 10, 2011, http://blogs.wsj.com; "Tesla Reports Roadster Deliveries," *Wireless News*, January 13, 2011, Business & Company Resource Center, http://galenet.galegroup.com; Alan Ohnsman, "Tesla Model S Electric Sedan Is in Tests ahead of 2012 Release," *Bloomberg Businessweek*, January 18, 2011, www.businessweek.com; and Dave Guilford, "Green Shoots," *Automotive News*, January 17, 2011, Business & Company Resource Center, http://galenet.galegroup.com.

Appendix A

1. C. George, *The History of Management Thought* (Englewood Cliffs, NJ: Prentice-Hall, 1972).

2. Ibid.

3. A. D. Chandler, *Scale and Scope: The Dynamic of Industrial Capitalism* (Cambridge, MA: Belknap Press of Harvard University Press, 1990).

4. Ibid.

5. J. Schlosser and E. Florian, "*Fortune* 500 Amazing Facts!" *Fortune*, April 5, 2004, pp. 152–59.

6. J. Baughman, *The History of American Management* (Englewood Cliffs, NJ: Prentice-Hall, 1969), chap. 1.

7. George, *The History of Management Thought*, chaps. 5–7; F. Taylor, *The Principles of Scientific Management* (New York: Harper & Row, 1911).

8. J. Case, "A Company of Businesspeople," *Inc.*, April 1993, pp. 70–93.

9. Schlosser and Florian, "*Fortune 500* Amazing Facts!"

10. H. Kroos and C. Gilbert, *The Principles of Scientific Management* (New York: Harper & Row, 1911).

11. H. Fayol, *General and Industrial Management*, trans. C. Storrs (Marshfield, MA: Pitman Publishing, 1949).

12. George, *The History of Management Thought*, chap. 9; J. Massie, "Management Theory," in *Handbook of Organizations*, ed. J. March (Chicago: Rand McNally, 1965), pp. 387–422.

13. C. Barnard, *The Functions of the Executive* (Cambridge, MA: Harvard University Press, 1938).

14. George, *The History of Management Thought*; Massie, "Management Theory."

15. Schlosser and Florian, "*Fortune 500* Amazing Facts!"

16. E. Mayo, *The Human Problems of Industrial Civilization* (New York: Macmillan, 1933): F. Roethlisberger and W. Dickson, *Management and the Worker* (Cambridge, MA: Harvard University Press, 1939).

17. A. Maslow, "A Theory of Human Motivation," *Psychological Review* 50 (July 1943), pp. 370–96.

18. A. Carey, "The Hawthorne Studies: A Radical Criticism," *American Sociological Review* 32, no.3 (1967), pp. 403–16.

19. M. Weber, *The Theory of Social and Economic Organizations*, trans. T. Parsons and A. Henderson (New York: Free Press, 1947).

20. George, *The History of Management Thought*, chap. 11.

21. D. McGregor, *The Human Side of Enterprise* (New York: McGraw-Hill, 1960).

22. C. Argyris, *Personality and Organization* (New York: Harper & Row, 1957).

23. R. Likert, *The Human Organization* (New York: McGraw-Hill, 1967).

24. L. von Bertalanffy, "The History and Status of General Systems Theory," *Academy of Management Journal* 15 (1972), pp. 407–26; D. Katz and R. Kahn, *The Social Psychology of Organizations*, 2nd ed. (New York: John Wiley & Sons, 1978).

25. J. Thompson, *Organizations in Action* (New York: McGraw-Hill, 1967); J. Galbraith, *Organization Design* (Reading, MA: Addison-Wesley, 1977); D. Miller and P. Friesen, *Organizations: A Quantum View* (Englewood Cliffs, NJ: Prentice-Hall, 1984).

26. Schlosser and Florian, "*Fortune 500* Amazing Facts!"

Chapter 2

1. B. Caulfield, "Apple: The Accidental Gaming Giant," *Forbes*, April 25, 2011, http://www.forbes.com; A. Hartung, "Apple Is Better Managed than Microsoft," *Forbes*, April 8, 2011, http://blogs.forbes.com; "How Apple Opened Up—and Made a Fortune," *Bloomberg Businessweek*, April 23, 2010, http://www.businessweek.com; "Report: Apple Is No. 1 Handset Maker," *The Wall Street Journal*, April 21, 2011, http://blogs.wsj.com; J. Valentino-DeVries and Y. I. Kane, "Jobs Defends iPhone Location Practices," *The Wall Street Journal*, April 27, 2011, http://online.wsj.com; and M. Peers, "IPhone's Surprisingly Good Reception," *The Wall Street Journal*, April 22, 2011, http://online.wsj.com.

2. K. Galbraith, "Economy Shifts, and the Ethanol Industry Reels," *The New York Times*, November 4, 2008, http://www.nytimes.com.

3. K. Evans, "Economy Dives as Goods Pile Up," *The Wall Street Journal*, January 31, 2009, http://online.wsj.com.

4. J. Fuller and M. C. Jensen, "Just Say No to Wall Street," *Journal of Applied Corporate Finance* 14, no. 4 (Winter 2002), pp. 41–46.

5. J. Mouawad, "Oil Innovations Pump New Life into Old Wells," *The New York Times*, March 5, 2007, http://www.nytimes.com.

6. U.S. Department of Health and Human Services (DHHS), "Small Employers: Top Five Things to Know," *HealthCare.gov*, http://www.healthcare.gov; Internal Revenue Service (IRS), "Small Business Health Care Tax Credit for Small Employers," http://www.irs.gov; DHHS, "Large Employers: Insurance and Tax Information," *HealthCare.gov*, http://www.healthcare.gov; IRS, "Affordable Care Act Tax Provisions," http://www.irs.gov; and DHHS, "About the Law: Provisions of the Affordable Care Act, by Year," HealthCare.gov, http://www.healthcare.gov.

7. "CEO Dough," *USA Today*, January 20, 2006, http://www.usatoday.com.

8. Bureau of Labor Statistics, "Employment Projections—2008–18," news release, December 10, 2009, http://www.bls.gov/emp.

9. L. Aratani, "Teens Can Multitask, But What Are Costs?" *Washington Post*, February 26, 2007, http://www.washingtonpost.com.

10. M. M. Hamilton, "Age 65 and Not Ready or Able to Go," *Washington Post*, January 14, 2007, http://www.washingtonpost.com.

11. Bureau of Labor Statistics, "Charting the U.S. Labor Market in 2005," June 2006, http://www.bls.gov/cps/labor2005/home.htm. and Bureau of Labor Statistics, "Back to College," *BLS Spotlight on Statistics*, September 2010, http://www.bls.gov/spotlight.

12. See, for example, B. Arnoldy, "Too Prosperous, Massachusetts Is Losing Its Labor Force," *Christian Science Monitor*, January 9, 2007, http://www.csmonitor.com.

13. Bureau of Labor Statistics, "Foreign-Born Workers: Labor Force Characteristics—2009," news release, March 19, 2010, http://www.bls.gov/cps; and BLS, "Employment Projections—2008–18."

14. Bureau of Labor Statistics, "Women in the Labor Force: A Databook," Report 1026, December 2010, http://www.bls.gov/cps/wlf-databook-2010.pdf.

15. "Gaming Goes for the Burn," *PR Week*, February 19, 2007, Business & Company Resource Center, http://galenet.galegroup.com.

16. M. Zitz, "Nintendo Winning Game System Red Hot," *Free Lance–Star (Fredericksburg, VA)*, February 23, 2007, Business & Company Resource Center, http://galenet.galegroup.com.

17. D. Takahashi, "Nintendo Responds to Multiple Gamer Complaints on Game Controller Safety," *Design News*, February 5, 2007, Business & Company Resource Center, http://galenet.galegroup.com.

18. T. Webb, "BP to Cut Production Amid Impact of Deepwater Horizon Spill," *The Observer*, January 30, 2011, http://www.guardian.co.uk; "The Shores of Recovery," *The Economist*, April 23, 2011, Business & Company Resource Center, http://galenet.galegroup.com; and C. Prentice, "Doing Business on the Gulf Coast, Post-Spill," *Bloomberg Businessweek*, April 19, 2011, http://www.businessweek.com.

19. C. J. Murray, "Fast and Cool," *Design News*, February 5, 2007, Business & Company Resource Center, http://galenet.galegroup.com.

20. M. Richtel, "Nintendo's Wii, Radiating Fun, Is Eclipsing Sony," *The New York Times*, January 31, 2007, Business & Company Resource Center, http://galenet.galegroup.com; "EA: Sony's Video Game Dominance Is Over," *ExtremeTech.com*, March 6, 2007, Business & Company Resource Center, http://galenet.galegroup.com; and I. Sherr and N. Becker, "New Nintendo, Sony Gadgets Buck Slump in Videogames," *The Wall Street Journal*, April 16, 2011, http://online.wsj.com.

21. D. J. Collis and C. A. Montgomery, *Corporate Strategy: Resources and Scope of the Firm* (New York: McGraw-Hill/Irwin, 1997).

22. J. DeGaspari, "Pfizer Retrenches," *MMR*, February 12, 2007, Business & Company Resource Center, http://galenet.galegroup.com.

23. M. J. Eyring, "Learning from Tata Motors' Nano Mistakes," *Bloomberg Businessweek*, January 11, 2011, http://www.businessweek.com; and S. Philip, "Tata Motors Profit Rises 100-Fold on Jaguar Land Rover Sales," *Bloomberg Businessweek*, November 10, 2010, http://www.businessweek.com.

24. Sherr and Becker, "New Nintendo, Sony Gadgets"; "Microsoft's Kinect Swings in the Record Books," *The Wall Street Journal*, March 20, 2011, http://blogs.wsj.com; and D. Wakabayashi, "Nintendo Readies Successor for Wii,"

The Wall Street Journal, April 26, 2011, http://online.wsj.com.

25. E. Gwinn, "Shootout at the Top," *Chicago Tribune*, February 27, 2007, Business & Company Resource Center, http://galenet.galegroup.com.

26. A. Ricadela, "Console Wars: Sony Fights Back," *BusinessWeek*, March 8, 2007, Business & Company Resource Center, http://galenet.galegroup.com.

27. "Looking Forward to the Next Level: Electronic Arts," *The Economist*, February 10, 2007, Business & Company Resource Center, http://galenet.galegroup.com.

28. N. Wingfield, "Microsoft Moves to Aid Kinect Hackers," *The Wall Street Journal*, February 21, 2011, http://blogs.wsj.com.

29. B. Bremner, "Nintendo Storms the Gaming World," *BusinessWeek*, January 29, 2007, Business & Company Resource Center, http://galenet.galegroup.com.

30. Adapted from H. L. Lee and C. Billington, "The Evolution of Supply-Chain-Management Models and Practice at Hewlett-Packard," *Interfaces* 25, no. 5 (September–October 1995), pp. 42–63.

31. T. Maylett and K. Vitasek, "For Closer Collaboration, Try Education," *Supply Chain Management Review*, January–February 2007, Business & Company Resource Center, http://galenet.galegroup.com.

32. M. Ramsey and S. Moffett, "Japan Parts Shortage Hits Auto Makers," *The Wall Street Journal*, March 24, 2011, http://online.wsj.com; A. Hesseldahl, "Short Supply of Japanese Electronic Parts Hitting Global Car Industry," *All Things Digital*, March 24, 2011, http://newenterprise.allthingsd.com; and J. Bennett, "Quake Spurs Supplier," *The Wall Street Journal*, March 31, 2011, http://online.wsj.com.

33. D. Tapscott and A. D. Williams, "Hack This Product, Please!" *BusinessWeek*, February 23, 2007, Business & Company Resource Center, http://galenet.galegroup.com.

34. Wingfield, "Microsoft Moves."

35. P. Burrows, "Apple's Effect on Content Partners: More Good than Bad," *Bloomberg Businessweek*, January 27, 2010, http://www.businessweek.com; Peers, "IPhone's Surprisingly Good Reception"; R. Adams, "More Magazines Try iPad," *The Wall Street Journal*, April 11, 2011, http://online.wsj.com; E. Ramstad, "Samsung Sues Apple on Patents," *The Wall Street Journal*, April 22, 2011, http://online.wsj.com; B. Arends, "Move Over, Apple! My Tablet Cost $200," *The Wall Street Journal*, March 9, 2011, http://online.wsj.com; P. Pachal, "Top Four Publisher Objections to Apple Subscriptions," *PC Magazine*, February 22, 2011, http://www.pcmag.com; "Apple's Days in the Sun Are Numbered as Google's Freedom Fight Gains Pace,"

The Independent (London), February 19, 2011, Business & Company Resource Center, http://galenet.galegroup.com; J. Temple, "Vast Apple Influence on Market Challenged," *Houston Chronicle*, February 13, 2011, Business & Company Resource Center, http://galenet.galegroup.com; and R. Adams, "Time Inc. in iPad Deal with Apple," *The Wall Street Journal*, May 2, 2011, http://online.wsj.com.

36. P. Kotler, *Marketing Management: Analysis, Planning, Implementation and Control*, 9th ed. (Englewood Cliffs, NJ: Prentice Hall, 1990).

37. A. A. Buchko, "Conceptualization and Measurement of Environmental Uncertainty: An Assessment of the Miles and Snow Perceived Environmental Uncertainty Scale," *Academy of Management Journal* 37, no. 2 (April 1994), pp. 410–25.

38. A. F. Hagen, "Corporate Executives and Environmental Scanning Activities: An Empirical Investigation," *SAM Advanced Management Journal* 60, no. 2 (Spring 1995), pp. 41–47; R. L. Daft, "Chief Executive Scanning, Environmental Characteristics, and Company Performance: An Empirical Study," *Strategic Management Journal* 9, no. 2 (March/April 1988), pp. 123–39; and M. Yasai-Ardekani, "Designs for Environmental Scanning Systems: Tests of a Contingency Theory," *Management Science* 42, no. 2 (February 1996), pp. 187–204.

39. S. Ghoshal, "Building Effective Intelligence Systems for Competitive Advantage," *Sloan Management Review* 28, no. 1 (Fall 1986), pp. 49–58; and K. D. Cory, "Can Competitive Intelligence Lead to a Sustainable Competitive Advantage?" *Competitive Intelligence Review* 7, no. 3 (Fall 1996), pp. 45–55.

40. P. J. H. Schoemaker, "Multiple Scenario Development: Its Conceptual and Behavioral Foundation," *Strategic Management Journal* 14, no. 3 (March 1993), pp. 193–213.

41. Grant Thornton LLP, "Grant Thornton LLP Business Optimism Index Up 6.7 Points from November as 49% Plan to Hire and 64% Believe U.S. Economy Will Improve," news release, March 14, 2011, http://www.grantthornton.com.

42. R. R. Peterson, "An Analysis of Contemporary Forecasting in Small Business," *Journal of Business Forecasting Methods & Systems* 15, no. 2 (Summer 1996), pp. 10–12; and S. Makridakis, "Business Forecasting for Management: Strategic Business Forecasting," *International Journal of Forecasting* 12, no. 3 (September 1996), pp. 435–37.

43. R. A. D'Aveni, *Hypercompetition—Managing the Dynamics of Strategic Maneuvering* (New York: Free Press, 1994); and M. A. Cusumano, "Strategic Maneuvering and Mass-Market Dynamics: The Triumph of VHS over Beta," *Business History Review* 66, no. 1 (Spring 1992), pp. 51–94.

44. Model adapted from C. Zeithaml and V. Zeithaml, "Environmental Management: Revising the Marketing Perspective," *Journal of Marketing*, Spring 1984. Published by the American Marketing Association.

45. Bremner, "Nintendo Storms the Gaming World."

46. R. King and A. Satariano, "Apple Gets Corporate Sales Backup at Unisys," *Bloomberg Businessweek*, October 25, 2010, http://www.businessweek.com.

47. "Bayer to Axe 6,100 Jobs Worldwide after Schering Takeover," news release, March 2, 2007, *Agence France Presse*, http://www.afp.com.

48. Ricadela, "Console Wars."

49. S. McGrath and J. D. Stoll, "Ford to Sell Aston Martin Unit in Deal Valued at $848 Million," *The Wall Street Journal*, March 12, 2007, http://online.wsj.com.

50. R. Miles and C. Snow, *Organizational Strategy, Structure, and Process* (New York: McGraw-Hill, 1978).

51. C. Zeithaml and V. Zeithaml, "Environmental Management: Revising the Marketing Perspective," *Journal of Marketing* 48 (Spring 1984), pp. 46–53.

52. "Washington Wire," *The Wall Street Journal*, March 16, 2007, http://blogs.wsj.com/washwire/.

53. W. P. Burgers, "Cooperative Strategy in High Technology Industries," *International Journal of Management* 13, no. 2 (June 1996), pp. 127–34; and J. E. McGee, "Cooperative Strategy and New Venture Performance: The Role of Business Strategy and Management Experience," *Strategic Management Journal* 16, no. 7 (October 1995), pp. 565–80.

54. A. Bluestein, L. Buchanan, M. Chafkin, J. Del Rey, A. Joyner, and R. McCarthy, "The Ultimate Business Tune-Up for Times Like These," *Inc.*, January 2009, http://www.inc.com.

55. D. Russakoff, "Building a Career Path Where There Was Just a Dead End," *Washington Post*, February 26, 2007, http://www.washingtonpost.com.

56. Bureau of Labor Statistics, "Contingent and Alternative Employment Arrangements, February 2005," news release, July 27, 2005, http://www.bls.gov/cps/.

57. M. B. Meznar, "Buffer or Bridge? Environmental and Organizational Determinants of Public Affairs Activities in American Firms," *Academy of Management Journal* 38, no. 4 (August 1995), pp. 975–96.

58. D. Lei, "Advanced Manufacturing Technology: Organizational Design and Strategic Flexibility," *Organization Studies* 17, no. 3 (1996), pp. 501–23; and J. W. Dean Jr. and S. A. Snell, "The Strategic Use of Integrated Manufacturing: An Empirical Examination," *Strategic Management Journal* 17, no. 6 (June 1996), pp. 459–80.

59. R. H. Kilmann, M. J. Saxton, and R. Serpa, *Gaining Control of the*

Corporate Culture (San Francisco: Jossey-Bass, 1985); and K. S. Cameron and R. E. Quinn, *Diagnosing and Changing Organizational Culture: Based on the Competing Values Framework* (Englewood Cliffs, NJ: Addison-Wesley, 1998).

60. J. E. Vascellaro and S. Morrison, "Google Gears Down for Tougher Times," *The Wall Street Journal*, December 3, 2008, http://online.wsj.com.

61. C. Hymowitz, "In Deal-Making, Keep People in Mind," *The Wall Street Journal*, May 12, 2008, http://online.wsj.com.

62. Cameron and Quinn, *Diagnosing and Changing Organizational Culture.*

63. S. Desmidt and A. Heene, "Mission Statement Perception: Are We All on the Same Wavelength? A Case Study in a Flemish Hospital," *Health Care Management Review*, January–March 2007, Business & Company Resource Center, http://galenet.galegroup.com.

64. C. Gallo, "How Ritz-Carlton Maintains Its Mystique," *BusinessWeek*, February 13, 2007, http://www.businessweek.com.

65. R. Leifer and P. K. Mills, "An Information Processing Approach for Deciding upon Control Strategies and Reducing Control Loss in Emerging Organizations," *Journal of Management* 22, no. 1 (1996), pp. 113–37; S. A. Dellana and R. D. Hauser, "Toward Defining the Quality Culture," *Engineering Management Journal* 11, no. 2 (June 1999), pp. 11–15; and D. Cohen and L. Prusak, *In Good Company: How Social Capital Makes Organizations Work* (Cambridge, MA: Harvard Business School Press, 2001).

66. J. Koob, "Early Warnings on Culture Clash," *Mergers & Acquisitions*, July 1, 2006, Business & Company Resource Center, http://galenet.galegroup.com.

67. The Kennedy Group Ltd., "Culture vs. Climate," Kennedy Group Executive Strategies, http://thekennedygroup.com; R. L. Manning, "Development of the Psychological Climate Scale for Small Business," *Journal of New Business Ideas and Trends* 8, no. 1 (2010), pp. 50–65, OCLC FirstSearch, http://newfirstsearch.org; and Grapevine Solutions, "Job Climate Surveys," http://www.grapevinesurvyes.com.

68. N. Merchant, "Apple's Startup Culture," *Bloomberg Businessweek*, June 14, 2010, http://www.businessweek.com; A. Frean, "Apple Falls into Serious, Sober, Safe Hands," *The Times* (London), January 22, 2011, Business & Company Resource Center, http://galenet.galegroup.com; C. Newton, "Meet the New Boss: Tim Cook," *San Francisco Chronicle*, January 23, 2011, Business & Company Resource Center, http://galenet.galegroup.com; S. Lohr, "The Missing Tastemaker," *The New York Times*, January 19, 2011, Business & Company Resource Center, http://galenet.galegroup.com; M. Ingram, "Can

Apple's Stock Withstand the Absence of Steve Jobs?" *GigaOM*, January 17, 2011, http://gigaom.com; and "Apple Unlikely to Crash without CEO Jobs," *Bloomberg Businessweek*, January 18, 2011, http://www.businessweek.com.

Chapter 3

1. David Morrill, "Sound of an IPO: Oakland's Pandora," *San Jose Mercury News*, February 14, 2011, updated February 15, 2011, http://www.mercurynews.com; Pandora Media, "Company Overview," press section, http://blog.pandora.com; Tyler Gray, "Pandora Pulls Back the Curtain on Its Magic Music Machine," *Fast Company*, January 21, 2011, http://www.fastcompany.com; Eric Savitz, "CES: Pandora Is Everywhere," *Forbes*, January 8, 2011, http://blogs.forbes.com; Nicole Perlroth, "Pandora Files for IPO, Reveals Founder Owns Less Than 3%," *Forbes*, February 11, 2011, http://blogs.forbes.com; and Antony Bruno, "Thinking Outside the Box," *Billboard*, July 17, 2010, Business & Company Resource Center, http://galenet.galegroup.com.

2. Nancy Doucette, "Stuff Happens," *Rough Notes*, December 2006, downloaded from OCLC FirstSearch, http://firstsearch.oclc.org.

3. M. Blenko, M. Mankins, and P. Rogers, "The Decision-Driven Organization," *Harvard Business Review*, June, 2010, pp. 54–62.

4. M. Magasin and F. L. Gehlen, "Unwise Decisions and Unanticipated Consequences," *Sloan Management Review* 41 (1999), pp. 47–60.

5. M. McCall and R. Kaplan, *Whatever It Takes: Decision Makers at Work* (Englewood Cliffs, NJ: Prentice-Hall, 1985); and Luda Kopeikina, "The Elements of a Clear Decision," *MIT Sloan Management Review* 47 (Winter 2006), pp. 19–20.

6. B. Bass, *Organizational Decision Making* (Homewood, IL: Richard D. Irwin, 1983).

7. J. March, "Bounded Rationality, Ambiguity, and the Engineering of Choice," *Bell Journal of Economics* 9 (1978), pp. 587–608.

8. D. Messick and M. Bazerman, "Ethical Leadership and the Psychology of Decision Making," *Sloan Management Review* (Winter 1996), pp. 9–22.

9. I., Katz and B. Willis, "A CEO's Dilemma: When Is It Safe to Hire Again?" *Bloomberg Businessweek*, 2011. pp. 22–24.

10. Karen Robinson-Jacobs, "Friday's Cutting Portions and Prices," *Dallas Morning News*, March 2, 2007, downloaded from Business & Company Resource Center, http://galenet.galegroup.com; and T.G.I. Friday's, "T.G.I. Friday's Restaurants Take Leadership Role with Portion Control," news release, March 2, 2007, http://fridays.mediaroom.com.

11. Susumu Ogawa and Frank T. Piller, "Reducing the Risks of New Product Development," *MIT Sloan Management Review* 47 (Winter 2006), pp. 65–71.

12. McCall and Kaplan, *Whatever It Takes.*

13. Amy Barrett, "The Case for User Reviews," *Inc.*, September 1, 2010, http://www.inc.com.

14. Barrett, "The Case for User Reviews."

15. Q. Spitzer and R. Evans, *Heads, You Win! How the Best Companies Think* (New York: Simon & Schuster, 1997).

16. C. Gettys and S. Fisher, "Hypothesis Plausibility and Hypotheses Generation," *Organizational Behavior and Human Performance* 24 (1979), pp. 93–110.

17. E. R. Alexander, "The Design of Alternatives in Organizational Contexts: A Pilot Study," *Administrative Science Quarterly* 24 (1979), pp. 382–404.

18. Ogawa and Piller, "Reducing the Risks," p. 68.

19. A. R. Rao, M. E. Bergen, and S. Davis, "How to Fight a Price War," *Harvard Business Review*, March–April 2000, pp. 107–16.

20. Barrett, "The Case for User Reviews."

21. Jason Del Rey, "Case Study: How to Raise Prices," *Inc.*, January 20, 2011, http://www.inc.com.

22. Barrett, "The Case for User Reviews."

23. Dana Mattioli and Sara Murray, "Employers Hit Salaried Staff with Furloughs," *The Wall Street Journal*, February 24, 2009, http://online.wsj.com.

24. Spitzer and Evans, *Heads, You Win!*

25. Morrill, "Sound of an IPO"; Gray, "Pandora Pulls Back the Curtain"; Bruno, "Thinking Outside the Box"; Antony Bruno, "Dashboard Confessional," *Billboard*, January 22, 2011, Business & Company Resource Center, http://galenet.galegroup.com; Clint Cooper, "Music in Motion," *Chattanooga Times/Free Press*, September 30, 2010, Business & Company Resource Center, http://galenet.galegroup.com; John Moe, "Sony's New Music Service: A Good Deal or Not?" *Marketplace*, February 17, 2011, http://www.publicradio.org; Matthew Lasar, "The Perils of Being Pandora," *Ars Technica*, February 15, 2011, http://arstechnica.com; and Andrew Hampp, "Why Pandora Is on Virtually Every Device," *Advertising Age*, January 17, 2011, http://adage.com.

26. L. Bryan and D. Farrell, "Leading through Uncertainty," *McKinsey Quarterly*, 2009, pp. 24–34. "Is Executive Hubris Ruining Companies?" *Industry Week*, January 31, 2007, http://www.industryweek.com (interview of Matthew Hayward).

27. Barrett, "The Case for User Reviews."

28. McCall and Kaplan, *Whatever It Takes.*

29. Barrett, "The Case for User Reviews."

30. J. Pfeffer and R. Sutton, *The Knowing–Doing Gap* (Boston: Harvard Business School Press, 2000).

31. D. Siebold, "Making Meetings More Successful," *Journal of Business*

Communication 16 (Summer 1979), pp. 3–20.

32. Genesis Management Consulting, *Challenges Faced When Taking Strategic Decisions: Results of 2010 Global Survey, Executive Summary* (London: Genesis Management Consulting, December 2010), http://genesismc.files.wordpress.com.

33. Barrett, "The Case for User Reviews."

34. I. Janis and L. Mann, *Decision Making* (New York: Free Press, 1977); and Bass, *Organizational Decision Making.*

35. Kopeikina, "The Elements of a Clear Decision."

36. J. W. Dean Jr. and M. Sharfman, "Does Decision Process Matter? A Study of Strategic Decision-Making Effectiveness," *Academy of Management Journal* 39 (1996), pp. 368–96.

37. R. Nisbett and L. Ross, *Human Inference: Strategies and Shortcomings* (Englewood Cliffs, NJ: Prentice-Hall, 1980).

38. Messick and Bazerman, "Ethical Leadership."

39. Phred Dvorak, "Dangers of Clinging to Solutions of the Past," *The Wall Street Journal*, March 2, 2009, http://online.wsj.com.

40. T. Bateman and C. Zeithaml, "The Psychological Context of Strategic Decisions: A Model and Convergent Experimental Findings," *Strategic Management Journal* 10 (1989), pp. 59–74.

41. Erin White, "Why Good Managers Make Bad Decisions," *The Wall Street Journal*, February 12, 2009, http://online.wsj.com.

42. D. Barton, "Capitalism for the Long Term," *Harvard Business Review*, March, 2011 pp. 84–91.

43. Messick and Bazerman, "Ethical Leadership."

44. N. Adler, *International Dimensions of Organizational Behavior* (Boston: Kent, 1990).

45. Joann S. Lublin, "Recall the Mistakes of Your Past Bosses, So You Can Do Better," *The Wall Street Journal*, January 2, 2007, http://online.wsj.com.

46. L. Perlow, G. Okhuysen, and N. Repenning, "The Speed Trap: Exploring the Relationship between Decision Making and Temporal Context," *Academy of Management Journal* 45 (2002), pp. 931–55.

47. L. Bryan, "Dynamic Management: Better Decisions in Uncertain Times," *McKinsey Quarterly*, 2010, pp. 32–40.

48. K. M. Esenhardt, "Speed and Strategic Choice: How Managers Accelerate Decision Making," *California Management Review* 32 (Spring 1990), pp. 39–54.

49. Stephen Power and Ben Casselman, "BP, Industry Both Blamed in Gulf Spill," *The Wall Street Journal*, January 5, 2011, http://online.wsj.com; Russell Gold and Ben Casselman, "Far Offshore, a Rash of Close Calls," *The Wall Street Journal*, December 8, 2010, http://online.wsj.com; Ben Casselman and Spencer Swartz, "BP: No Single Factor Caused Gulf Spill," *The Wall Street Journal*, September 8, 2010, http://online.wsj.com; and Russell Gold and Ben Casselman, "On Doomed Rig's Last Day, a Divisive Change of Plan," *The Wall Street Journal*, August 26, 2010, http://online.wsj.com.

50. Q. Spitzer and R. Evans, "New Problems in Problem Solving," *Across the Board*, April 1997, pp. 36–40.

51. G. W. Hill, "Group versus Individual Performance: Are *n* +1 Heads Better than 1?" *Psychological Bulletin* 91 (1982), pp. 517–39.

52. N. R. F. Maier, "Assets and Liabilities in Group Problem Solving: The Need for an Integrative Function," *Psychological Review* 74 (1967), pp. 239–49.

53. Ibid.

54. D. A. Garvin and M. A. Roberto, "What You Don't Know about Making Decisions," *Harvard Business Review*, September 2001, pp. 108–16.

55. R. Cosier and C. Schwenk, "Agreement and Thinking Alike: Ingredients for Poor Decisions," *The Executive*, February 1990, pp. 69–74.

56. A. Amason, "Distinguishing the Effects of Functional and Dysfunctional Conflict on Strategic Decision Making: Resolving a Paradox for Top Management Teams," *Academy of Management Journal* 39 (1996), pp. 123–48; and R. Dooley and G. Fyxell, "Attaining Decision Quality and Commitment from Dissent: The Moderating Effects of Loyalty and Competence in Strategic Decision-Making Teams," *Academy of Management Journal* (August 1999), pp. 389–402.

57. C. De Dreu and L. Weingart, "Task versus Relationship Conflict, Team Performance, and Team Member Satisfaction: A Meta-Analysis," *Journal of Applied Psychology* 88 (2003), pp. 741–49.

58. Cosier and Schwenk, "Agreement and Thinking Alike."

59. Ibid.

60. P. LaBerre, "The Creative Revolution," *Industry Week*, May 16, 1994, pp. 12–19.

61. J. V. Anderson, "Weirder Than Fiction: The Reality and Myths of Creativity," *Academy of Management Executive* (November 1992), pp. 40–47; J. Krohe Jr., "Managing Creativity," *Across the Board* (September 1996), pp. 17–21; and R. I. Sutton, "The Weird Rules of Creativity," *Harvard Business Review* (September 2001), pp. 94–103.

62. J. Perry-Smith and C. Shalley, "The Social Side of Creativity: A Static and Dynamic Social Network Perspective," *Academy of Management Review* 28 (2003), pp. 89–106; and J. Perry-Smith, "Social yet Creative: The Role of Social Relationships in Facilitating Individual Creativity," *Academy of Management Journal* 49 (2006), pp. 85–101.

63. "Innovation from the Ground Up," *Industry Week*, March 7, 2007, http://www.industryweek.com (interview of Erika Andersen); A. Farnham, "How to Nurture Creative Sparks," *Fortune*, January 10, 1994, pp. 94–100; and T. M. Amabile, "A Model of Creativity and Innovation in Organizations," in *Research in Organizational Behavior*, ed. B. Straw and L. Cummings, vol. 10 (Greenwich, CT: JAI Press, 1988), pp. 123–68.

64. T. Amabile, C. Hadley, and S. Kramer, "Creativity under the Gun," *Harvard Business Review* (August 2002), pp. 52–61.

65. S. Farmer, P. Tierney, and K. Kung-McIntyre, "Employee Creativity in Taiwan: An Application of Role Identity Theory," *Academy of Management Journal* 46 (2003), pp. 618–30.

66. "Innovation from the Ground Up."

67. Mike Larson, "LEEDing by Example," *Western Builder*, April 6, 2009, downloaded from Business & Company Resource Center, http://galenet.galegroup.com.

68. L. Thompson, "Improving the Creativity of Organizational Work Groups," *Academy of Management Executive* 17 (2003), pp. 96–109.

69. T. Levitt, "Creativity Is Not Enough," *Harvard Business Review* (August 2002), pp. 137–44.

70. Dean and Sharfman, "Does Decision Process Matter?"

71. K. Eisenhardt, J. Kahwajy, and L. J. Bourgeois III, "How Management Teams Can Have a Good Fight," *Harvard Management Review*, July–August 1997, pp. 77–85.

72. C. M. Pearson and I. I. Mitroff, "From Crisis Prone to Crisis Prepared: A Framework for Crisis Management," *Academy of Management Executive* (February 1993), pp. 48–59.

73. Jordan Robertson and Eileen Sullivan, "U.S. Power Grid Hacked, Officials Say," *Chicago Tribune*, April 9, 2009, http://www.chicagotribune.com.

74. S. Moore, "Disaster's Future: The Prospects for Corporate Crisis Management and Communication," *Business Horizons*, January–February 2004, pp. 29–36.

75. G. Meyers with J. Holusha, *When It Hits the Fan: Managing the Nine Crises of Business* (Boston: Houghton Mifflin, 1986); and S. Bacharach and P. Bamberger, "9/11 and New York City Firefighters' Post Hoc Unit Support and Control Climates: A Context Theory of the Consequences of Involvement in Traumatic Work-Related Events," *Academy of Management Journal* 50 (2007), pp. 849–68.

76. McCall and Kaplan, *Whatever It Takes.*

77. Leigh Buchanan, "How I Handled Myself during a Prison Riot," *Inc.*, September 1, 2010, http://www.inc.com (interview with Jerry B. Heftler).

78. J. Dutton, P. Frost, M. Worline, J. Lilius, and J. Kanov, "Leading in Times of Trauma," *Harvard Business Review* (January 2002), pp. 54–61.

79. Morrill, "Sound of an IPO"; Perlroth, "Everything Ventured"; Bruno, "Thinking Outside the Box"; Lasar,

"The Perils of Being Pandora"; Garett Sloane, "Poison Apple for Pandora?" *New York Post*, February 18, 2011, updated February 19, 2011, http://www.nypost.com; Paul Smalera, "Not Pandora's Box," *Fortune*, March 1, 2011, http://tech.fortune.cnn.com; and "The World's 50 Most Innovative Companies: 44 Pandora," *Fast Company*, February 16, 2011, http://www.fastcompany.com.

Chapter 4

1. S. Lohr, "GE Goes with What It Knows: Making Stuff," *The New York Times*, December 5, 2010, Business & Company Resource Center, http://galenet.galegroup.com; D. Brady, "Can GE Still Manage?" *Bloomberg Businessweek*, April 15, 2010, http://www.businessweek.com; E. Crooks and J. Lemer, "Electric Dreams," *Financial Times*, March 31, 2011, Business & Company Resource Center, http://galenet.galegroup.com; L. C. Strauss, "Hope, at Last," *Barron's*, April 4, 2011, http://online.barrons.com; B. Sechler, "GE Earnings Soar on Lending Arm," *The Wall Street Journal*, April 22, 2011, http://online.wsj.com; Bloomberg, "General Electric Co.," *Bloomberg Businessweek*, http://investing.businessweek.com; and GE, "Our Company," http://www.ge.com/company/.

2. J. Bracker and J. Pearson, "Planning and Financial Performance of Small Mature Firms," *Strategic Management Journal* 7 (1986), pp. 503–22; and P. Waalewijn and P. Segaar, "Strategic Management: The Key to Profitability in Small Companies," *Long Range Planning* 26, no. 2 (April 1993), pp. 24–30.

3. P. Glader, "GE Taps Veteran Rice to Lead Global Operations," *The Wall Street Journal*, November 9, 2010, http://online.wsj.com.

4. S. Terlep, "GM Caps Profitable Year," *The Wall Street Journal*, February 24, 2011, http://online.wsj.com; B. Cox, "For Big Three Automakers, an Unlikely Time for a Turnaround," *Fort Worth Star-Telegram*, April 15, 2011, http://www.star-telegram.com; and D. Barkholz, "Dealers: We Want More Cars!" *Automotive News*, August 23, 2010, Business & Company Resource Center, http://galenet.galegroup.com.

5. A. Murray, "JetBlue: Now Just Another Airline in a Lousy Business," *The Wall Street Journal*, February 21, 2007, http://online.wsj.com.

6. B. Bowers, "In Tough Times, Tackle Anxiety First," *The New York Times*, November 13, 2008, Business & Company Resource Center, http://galenet.galegroup.com.

7. G. Farrell, "CEO Profile: Wells Fargo's Kovacevich Banks on Success as a One-Stop Shop," *USA Today*, March 26, 2007, http://www.usatoday.com.

8. D. C. Hambrick and J. W. Fredrickson, "Are You Sure You Have a Strategy?"

Academy of Management Executive 19, no. 4 (2005), pp. 51–62.

9. J. L. Bower and C. G. Gilbert, "How Managers' Everyday Decisions Create or Destroy Your Company's Strategy," *Harvard Business Review*, February 2007, pp. 72–79.

10. Lohr, "GE Goes with What It Knows"; Brady, "Can GE Still Manage?"; Crooks and Lemer, "Electric Dreams"; Strauss, "Hope, at Last,"; P. Glader and M. Ramsey, "GE to Buy 25,000 Electric Vehicles," *The Wall Street Journal*, November 12, 2010, http://online.wsj.com; and J. Muller, "This Is How Change Happens: GE to Buy 12,000 Chevy Volts," *Forbes*, November 11, 2010, http://blogs.forbes.com.

11. R. Kaplan and D. Norton, "Plotting Success with 'Strategy Maps,'" *Optimize*, February 2004, http://www.optimizemag.com; and R. S. Kaplan and D. P. Norton, "Having Trouble with Your Strategy? Then Map It," *Harvard Business Review*, September–October 2000.

12. R. Vosburgh, "Helping Hand," *Supermarket News*, September 1, 2010, Business & Company Resource Center, http://galenet.galegroup.com.

13. Bower and Gilbert, "Managers' Everyday Decisions"; and "Business: Fading Fads," *The Economist*, April 22, 2000, pp. 60–61.

14. S. W. Floyd and P. J. Lane, "Strategizing throughout the Organization: Management Role Conflict in Strategic Renewal," *Academy of Management Review* 25, no. 1 (January 2000), pp. 154–77.

15. Mission statements quoted from the corporate websites: McDonald's, "Student Research," http://www.mcdonalds.com; Microsoft, "Mission and Values," http://www.microsoft.com; and Allstate, Corporate Press Kit, http://www.allstate.com.

16. Vision statements quoted from the organizations' websites: DuPont, "Our Company: DuPont Vision," http://www2.dupont.com; City of Redmond, "City of Redmond Vision Statement," http://www.ci.redmond.wa.us; and Great Lakes Naval Museum Association, "Vision Statement," http://www.greatlakesnavalmuseum.org.

17. A. Martin, "The Happiest Meal: Hot Profits," *The New York Times*, January 11, 2009, http://www.nytimes.com.

18. A. A. Thompson and A. J. Strickland III, *Strategic Management: Concepts and Cases*, 8th ed. (New York: Richard D. Irwin, 1995), p. 23; R. Edward Freeman, J. S. Harrison, and A. C. Wicks, *Managing for Stakeholders* (New Haven, CT: Yale University Press, 2007).

19. R. Gobel, "Inspiring Innovation," *Success*, April 2009, pp. 24–26.

20. M. Kanelios, "Full Steam Ahead for Nevada Solar Project," *CNet News.com*, March 20, 2007, http://news.com.com.

21. D. Porter, "One Man's Garbage Becomes Another's Power Plant," *Yahoo*

News, October 28, 2008, http://news.yahoo.com.

22. D. Michaels, "Pact Ushers in Competitive Skies," *The Wall Street Journal*, March 23, 2007, http://online.wsj.com.

23. A. Loten, "Running a Business in a Disaster Zone," *The Wall Street Journal*, December 30, 2010, http://online.wsj.com.

24. D. J. Collis and C. A. Montgomery, *Corporate Strategy: A Resource-Based Approach*, 2nd ed. (New York, McGraw-Hill/Irwin, 2005).

25. R. L. Priem, "A Consumer Perspective on Value Creation," *Academy of Management Review* 32, no. 1 (2007), pp. 219–35.

26. Farrell, "CEO Profile."

27. A. Wilcox King, "Disentangling Interfirm and Intrafirm Causal Ambiguity: A Conceptual Model of Causal Ambiguity and Sustainable Competitive Advantage," *Academy of Management Review* 32, no. 1 (2007), pp. 156–78.

28. "Beware of Benchmarking Pitfalls Warns AXA Chief," *Europe Intelligence Wire*, May 13, 2010, Business & Company Resource Center, http://galenet.galegroup.com.

29. R. A. Guth, "Microsoft May Shift Strategy to Keep Up," *The Wall Street Journal*, March 29, 2007, http://online.wsj.com.

30. R. A. Guth, D. K. Berman, and K. J. Delaney, "Google Joins Race to Buy DoubleClick," *The Wall Street Journal*, April 2, 2007, http://online.wsj.com.

31. D. G. Sirmon, M. A. Hitt, and R. D. Ireland, "Managing Firm Resources in Dynamic Environments to Create Value: Looking inside the Black Box," *Academy of Management Review* 32, no. 1 (2007), pp. 273–92.

32. A. Bluestein, "The Success Gene," *Inc.*, April 2008, pp. 83–94.

33. D. Barboza, "Google Acquires Stake in Chinese Web Site," *The New York Times*, January 5, 2007, http://www.nytimes.com.

34. P. Haspeslagh, "Portfolio Planning: Uses and Limits," *Harvard Business Review* 60, no.1 (1982), pp. 58–67; R. Hamermesh, *Making Strategy Work* (New York: John Wiley & Sons, 1986); and R. A. Proctor, "Toward a New Model for Product Portfolio Analysis," *Management Decision* 28, no. 3 (1990), pp. 14–17.

35. "PepsiCo Shows Volume, Revenue Growth," *Beverage Industry*, March 2011, p. 8; Business Monitor International, "Company Analysis: PepsiCo," *United States Food and Drink Report*, April 2011, pp. 87–88; and "SN Power 50 for 2010: Indra Nooyi," *Supermarket News*, July 9, 2010, http://supermarketnews.com.

36. "M&A Activity: U.S. and U.S. Cross-Border Transactions," FactSet Mergerstat Free Reports, updated April 14, 2009, http://www.mergerstat.com.

37. S. Higginbotham, "Cisco: What Went Wrong and What Needs to Be Fixed," *Bloomberg Businessweek*, April 7, 2011, http://www.businessweek.com; V. Heiskanen and K. Hoffmann, "Cisco to Close Flip Video-Camera Business as Part of Revamp," *Bloomberg Businessweek*, April 12, 2011, http://www.businessweek.com; I. Sidhu, *Doing Both: Capturing Today's Profit and Driving Tomorrow's Growth*, FT Press, 2010; and Associated Press, "Cisco Share Climb after CEO Promises Changes," *Bloomberg Businessweek*, April 6, 2011, http://www.businessweek.com.

38. M. Porter, *Competitive Advantage* (New York: Free Press, 1985), pp. 11–14.

39. K. Talley, "Wal-Mart Sees Shoppers' Pain," *The Wall Street Journal*, April 28, 2011, http://online.wsj.com.

40. R. Varadarajan, "Think Small," *The Wall Street Journal*, February 14, 2007, http://online.wsj.com.

41. F. F. Suarez and G. Lanzolla, "The Role of Environmental Dynamics in Building a First Mover Advantage Theory," *Academy of Management Review* 32, no. 2 (2007), pp. 377–92.

42. W. M. Bulkeley, "How an IBM Lifer Built Software Unit into a Rising Star," *The Wall Street Journal*, April 2, 2007, http://online.wsj.com; Farrell, "CEO Profile"; and J. L. Lunsford, "Gradual Ascent: Burned by Last Boom, Boeing Curbs Its Pace," *The Wall Street Journal*, March 26, 2007, http://online.wsj.com;

43. J. Scheck and P. Glader, "R&D Spending Holds Steady in Slump," *The Wall Street Journal*, April 6, 2009, http://online.wsj.com.

44. V. Kremer and E. Berggren, "Who Will Win in the Next Economy?" (Accenture; SuccessFactors), available at http://www.the-next-economy.com. This report describes the results of 450 interviews with senior decision makers at organizations in the United States, Europe, Australia, and India, conducted in September and October 2010.

45. R. A. Eisenstat, "Implementing Strategy: Developing a Partnership for Change," *Planning Review*, September–October 1993, pp. 33–36.

46. D. Michaels and J. Lynn Lunsford, "Lack of Seats, Galleys Delays Boeing, Airbus," *The Wall Street Journal*, August 8, 2008, http://online.wsj.com; and J. Flowers, "Boeing Announces Further Delays to 787 Dreamliner Program," *The Wall Street Journal*, April 9, 2008, http://online.wsj.com.

47. Lohr, "GE Goes with What It Knows"; Brady, "Can GE Still Manage?"; Crooks and Lemer, "Electric Dreams"; Strauss, "Hope, at Last,"; Sechler, "GE Earnings Soar on Lending Arm"; R. Layne, "Immelt Sees Economy Improving as GE Growth Accelerates," *Bloomberg Businessweek*, May 6, 2011, http://www.businessweek.com; Bloomberg News, "General Electric Plans to Invest $2 Billion in China," *Bloomberg Businessweek*, November 9, 2010, http://

www.businessweek.com; B. Sechler, "GE to Increase Jobs, Investment in Appliances Unit," *The Wall Street Journal*, October 18, 2010, http://online.wsj.com; and Glader, "GE Taps Veteran Rice."

Chapter 5

1. L. Buchanan, "A Little Enlightened Self-Interest," *Inc.*, June 8, 2010, http://www.inc.com (interview with Yvon Chouinard and Ken Lehman); Patagonia, "Company Info," http://www.patagonia.com; S. Watkins, "Be Honest and Dependable; Take Responsibility," *Investor's Business Daily*, April 16, 2010, Business & Company Resource Center, http://galenet.galegroup.com; Speakeasy blog, "The Latest Online Music Startup: Patagonia," *The Wall Street Journal*, March 3, 2011, http://blogs.wsj.com; and C. Binkley, "How Green Is My Sneaker?" *The Wall Street Journal*, July 21, 2010, http://online.wsj.com.

2. V. Anand, B. Ashforth, and M. Joshi, "Business as Usual: The Acceptance and Perpetuation of Corruption in Organizations," *Academy of Management Executive* (May 2004), pp. 39–53; and B. Ashforth, D. Gioia, S. Robinson, and L. Trevino, "Re-viewing Organizational Corruption," *Academy of Management Review* 33 (July 2008), 670–684.

3. Edelman, "Business More Trusted Than Media and Government in Every Region of the Globe," news release, January 22, 2007, *Trust Barometer 2007* pages of Edelman website, http://www.edelman.com/trust/2007/.

4. M. Banaji, M. Bazerman, and D. Chugh, "How (Un)Ethical Are You?" *Harvard Business Review*, December 2003, pp. 56–64.

5. S. L. Grover, "The Truth, the Whole Truth, and Nothing but the Truth: The Causes and Management of Workplace Lying," *Academy of Management Executive* 19 (May 2005), pp. 148–57.

6. B. L. Toffler, "Five Ways to Jump-Start Your Company's Ethics," *Fast Company*, October 2003, p. 36.

7. D. Gelles, "Blogs That Spin a Web of Deception," *Financial Times*, February 12, 2009, Business & Company Resource Center, http://galenet.galegroup.com.

8. M. E. Guy, *Ethical Decision Making in Everyday Work Situations* (New York: Quorum Books, 1990).

9. B. Sleeper, K. Schneider, and P. Weber, "Scale and Study of Student Attitudes toward Business Education's Role in Addressing Social Issues," *Journal of Business Ethics* 68 (2006), pp. 381–91; Y. J. Chen and T. L. P. Tang, "Attitude toward and Propensity to Engage in Unethical Behavior: Measurement Invariance across Major among University Students," *Journal of Business Ethics* 69 (2006), pp. 77–93; and B. A. Ritter,

"Can Business Ethics Be Trained? A Study of the Ethical Decision-Making Process in Business Students," *Journal of Business Ethics* 68 (2006), pp. 153–64.

10. O. C. Ferrell and J. Fraedrich, *Business Ethics: Ethical Decision Making and Cases*, 3rd ed. (Boston: Houghton Mifflin, 1997).

11. Ibid.

12. Guy, *Ethical Decision Making*.

13. Ferrell and Fraedrich, *Business Ethics*.

14. J. Hechinger and D. Armstrong, "Universities Resolve Kickback Allegations," *The Wall Street Journal*, April 3, 2007, http://online.wsj.com; J. Hechinger, "Probe into College–Lender Ties Widens," *The Wall Street Journal*, April 5, 2007, http://online.wsj.com; and Associated Press, "CIT Executives Placed on Leave Amid Student Loan Investigation," *The Wall Street Journal*, April 9, 2007, http://online.wsj.com.

15. Hechinger and Armstrong, "Universities Resolve Kickback Allegations"; and AP, "CIT Executives."

16. Transparency International, "Persistently High Corruption in Low-Income Countries Amounts to an 'Ongoing Humanitarian Disaster,'" news release, September 23, 2008, http://www.transparency.org.

17. A. Spicer, T. Dunfee, and W. Biley, "Does National Context Matter in Ethical Decision Making? An Empirical Test of Integrative Social Contracts Theory," *Academy of Management Journal* 47 (2004), pp. 610–20; W. Bailey and A. Spicer, "When Does National Identity Matter? Convergence and Divergence in International Business Ethics," *Academy of Management Journal*, 2007, 1462–80; and K. Martin, J. Cullen, J. Johnson, and K. Parboteeah, "Deciding to Bribe: A Cross-Level Analysis of Firm and Home Country Influences on Bribery Activity," *Academy of Management Journal*, 2007, 1401–22.

18. L. Kohlberg and D. Candee, "The Relationship of Moral Judgment to Moral Action" in *Morality, Moral Behavior, and Moral Development*, ed. W. M. Kurtines and J. L. Gerwitz (New York: John Wiley & Sons, 1984).

19. L. K. Trevino, "Ethical Decision Making in Organizations: A Person–Situation Interactionist Model," *Academy of Management Review*, 1992, pp. 601–17.

20. Ferrell and Fraedrich, *Business Ethics*.

21. J. Sharkey, "The Room Is Booked, until the Hotel Says It Isn't," *The New York Times*, December 13, 2010, http://www.nytimes.com; and J. Sharkey, "No Guarantees in Life, Not Even a Booked Room," *The New York Times*, February 7, 2011, http://www.nytimes.com.

22. J. Badarocco Jr. and A. Webb, "Business Ethics: A View from the Trenches," *California Management Review*, Winter 1995, pp. 8–28; and G. Laczniak, M. Berkowitz, R. Brookes, and J. Hale, "The Business of Ethics: Improving or Deteriorating?" *Business Horizons*, January–February 1995, pp. 39–47.

23. M. Gunther, "God and Business," *Fortune*, July 9, 2001, pp. 58–80.

24. Anand, Ashforth, and Joshi, "Business as Usual."

25. S. Glover, "SOX Compliance Proves Beneficial to Organizations, Fuels Risk Consciousness," *National Underwriter Property & Casualty*, November 15, 2010, pp. 34, 36; and P. Sweeney, "Will New Regulations Deter Corporate Fraud?" *Financial Executive*, January–February 2011, pp. 54–57.

26. Corporate Executive Board, "Research Reveals That Integrity Drives Corporate Performance," news release, September 15, 2010, http://news. executiveboard.com; and P. Brotherton, "Corporate Integrity Pays Off in Better Performance," *T + D*, January 2011, p. 24.

27. R. E. Allinson, "A Call for Ethically Centered Management," *Academy of Management Executive*, February 1995, pp. 73–76.

28. R. T. De George, *Business Ethics*, 3rd ed. (New York: Macmillan, 1990).

29. B. W. Heineman Jr., "Avoiding Integrity Land Mines," *Harvard Business Review*, April 2007, pp. 100–108.

30. R. A. Cooke, "Danger Signs of Unethical Behavior: How to Determine If Your Firm Is at Ethical Risk," *Journal of Business Ethics*, April 1991, pp. 249–53.

31. E. Nakashima, "Harsh Words Die Hard on the Web," *Washington Post*, March 7, 2007, http://www.washingtonpost.com.

32. L. K. Trevino and M. Brown, "Managing to Be Ethical: Debunking Five Business Ethics Myths," *Academy of Management Executive*, May 2004, pp. 69–81.

33. Ibid.

34. Heineman, "Avoiding Integrity Land Mines."

35. The results are from a survey of 754 employed U.S. adults and interviews of 300 *Fortune* 1000 executives. Deloitte, "Trust in the Workplace: 2010 Ethics & Workplace Survey," http://www. deloitte.com.

36. D. Messick and M. Bazerman, "Ethical Leadership and the Psychology of Decision Making," *Sloan Management Review*, Winter 1996, pp. 9–22.

37. C. Handy, *Beyond Uncertainty: The Changing Worlds of Organizations* (Boston: Harvard Business School Press, 1996).

38. J. Stevens, H. Steensma, D. Harrison, and P. Cochran, "Symbolic or Substantive Document? The Influence of Ethics Codes on Financial Executives' Decisions," *Strategic Management Journal* 26 (2005), pp. 181–95; and J. Weber, "Does It Take an Economic Village to Raise an Ethical Company?" *Academy of Management Executive* 19 (May 2005), pp. 158–59.

39. J. B. Ciulla, "Why Is Business Talking about Ethics? Reflections on Foreign Conversations," *California Management Review*, Fall 1991, pp. 67–80.

40. R. J. Zablow, "Creating and Sustaining an Ethical Workplace: Ethics Resource Center (ERC), "Code Construction and Content," *The Ethics Resource Center Toolkit*, http://www.ethics.org; and J. Brown, "Ten Writing Tips for Creating an Effective Code of Conduct," Ethics Resource Center, http://www.ethics.org.

41. G. R. Weaver, L. K. Trevino, and P. L. Cochran, "Corporate Ethics Programs as Control Systems: Influences of Executive Commitment and Environmental Factors," *Academy of Management Journal* 42 (1999), pp. 41–57.

42. L. S. Paine, "Managing for Organizational Integrity," *Harvard Business Review*, March–April 1994, pp. 106–17.

43. F. Hall and E. Hall, "The ADA: Going beyond the Law," *Academy of Management Executive*, February 1994, pp. 7–13; and A. Farnham, "Brushing Up Your Vision Thing," *Fortune*, May 1, 1995, p. 129.

44. G. R. Weaver, L. K. Trevino, and P. L. Cochran, "Integrated and Decoupled Corporate Social Performance: Management Commitments, External Pressures, and Corporate Ethics Practices" *Academy of Management Journal* 42 (1999), pp. 539–52.

45. Trevino and Brown, "Managing to Be Ethical," p. 70.

46. Ibid.

47. Banaji, Bazerman, and Chugh, "How (Un)Ethical Are You?"

48. Andrew Taylor, "Execs' Posh Retreat after Bailout Angers Lawmakers," *Yahoo News*, October 7, 2008, http://news. yahoo.com.

49. Anand, Ashforth, and Joshi, "Business as Usual"; and Remi Trudel and June Cotte, "Does Being Ethical Pay?" *The Wall Street Journal*, May 12, 2008, http://online.wsj.com.

50. T. Thomas, J. Schermerhorn Jr. and J. Dienhart, "Strategic Leadership of Ethical Behavior in Business," *Academy of Management Executive*, May 2004, pp. 56–66.

51. Trevino and Brown, "Managing to Be Ethical."

52. B. Rokos and J. Katzanek, "325 Could Lose Jobs When Hemet Call Center Closes," *Press-Enterprise (Riverside, Calif.)*, August 5, 2010, Business & Company Resource Center, http:// galenet.galegroup.com; and B. Rokos, "Hilton Call Center Employees in Hemet Trained Overseas Workers before Losing Jobs," *Press-Enterprise (Riverside, Calif.)*, August 13, 2010, Business & Company Resource Center, http://galenet.galegroup.com.

53. G. Morgenson, "How a Whistle-Blower Conquered Countrywide," *The New York Times*, February 20, 2011, Business & Company Resource Center, http:// galenet.galegroup.com.

54. D. Dahl, "Learning to Love Whistleblowers," *Inc.*, March 2006, OCLC FirstSearch, http://firstsearch. oclc.org.

55. M. E. Schreiber and D. R. Marshall, "Reducing the Risk of Whistleblower Complaints," *Risk Management* 53, no. 11 (November 2006), OCLC FirstSearch, http://firstsearch.oclc.org.

56. R. Bies, J. Bartunek, T. Fort, and M. Zald, "Corporations as Social Change Agents: Individual, Interpersonal, Institutional, and Environmental Dynamics," *Academy of Management Review*, 2007, pp. 788–93.

57. L. Preston and J. Post, eds., *Private Management and Public Policy* (Englewood Cliffs, NJ: Prentice-Hall, 1975).

58. D. Matten and J. Moon, "'Implicit' and 'Explicit' CSR: A Conceptual Framework for a Comparative Understanding of Corporate Social Responsibility," *Academy of Management Review* 33, pp. 404–24.

59. "Graft around the Globe," *Bloomberg Businessweek*, May 17, p. 14.

60. Ferrell and Fraedrich, *Business Ethics*.

61. D. Matten and J. Moon, "'Implicit' and 'Explicit' CSR: A Conceptual Framework for a Comparative Understanding of Corporate Social Responsibility," *Academy of Management Review*, 2008, pp. 404–24.

62. A. Carroll, "Managing Ethically with Global Stakeholders: A Present and Future Challenge," *Academy of Management Executive*, May 2004, pp. 114–20.

63. L. Etter, "Smithfield to Phase Out Crates," *The Wall Street Journal*, January 25, 2007, http://online.wsj.com.

64. P. C. Godfrey, "The Relationship between Corporate Philanthropy and Shareholder Wealth: A Risk Management Perspective," *Academy of Management Review* 30 (2005), pp. 777–98.

65. R. Giacalone, "A Transcendent Business Education for the 21st Century," *Academy of Management Learning & Education*, 2004, pp. 415–20.

66. Patagonia, "Company Info: Corporate Responsibility," http://www.patagonia. com; and Patagonia, "Patagonia Workplace Code of Conduct," http:// www.patagonia.com.

67. M. Witzel, "Not for Wealth Alone: The Rise of Business Ethics," *Financial Times Mastering Management Review*, November 1999, pp. 14–19.

68. D. C. Korten, *When Corporations Ruled the World* (San Francisco: Berrett-Koehler, 1995).

69. Handy, *Beyond Uncertainty*.

70. D. Barton, "Capitalism for the Long Term," *Harvard Business Review*, March 2011, pp. 84–91.

71. D. Quinn and T. Jones, "An Agent Morality View of Business Policy," *Academy of Management Review* 20 (1995), pp. 22–42.

72. B. McKay, "Why Coke Aims to Slake Global Thirst for Safe Water," *The Wall Street Journal*, March 15, 2007, http:// online.wsj.com.

73. N. Varchaver, "Chemical Reaction," *Fortune*, April 2, 2007, Business & Company Resource Center, http:// galenet.galegroup.com.

74. D. Schuler and M. Cording, "A Corporate Social Performance–Corporate Financial Performance Behavioral Model for Consumers," *Academy of Management Review* 31 (2006), pp. 540–58.

75. M. Orlitzky, F. Schmidt, and S. Rynes, "Corporate Social and Financial Performance: A Meta-Analysis," *Organization Studies*, 24 (2003), pp. 403–441.

76. D. Turban and D. Greening, "Corporate Social Performance and Organizational Attractiveness to Prospective Employees," *Academy of Management Journal* 40 (1997), pp. 658–72.

77. A. McWilliams and D. Siegel, "Corporate Social Responsibility: A Theory of the Firm Perspective," *Academy of Management Review 26* (2001), pp. 117–27.

78. M. E. Porter and M. R. Kramer, "Strategy and Society: The Link between Competitive Advantage and Corporate Social Responsibility," *Harvard Business Review*, December 2006, pp. 78–92.

79. Ibid., p. 89.

80. G. Unruh and R. Etternson, "Growing Green," *Harvard Business Review*, June 2010, pp. 94–100.

81. C.K. Prahalad and M.R. Rangaswami, "Why Sustainability Is Now the Key Driver of Innovation," *Harvard Business Review*, September 2009, pp. 56–64.

82. S. L. Hart and M. B. Milstein, "Global Sustainability and the Creative Destructions of Industries," *Sloan Management Review*, Fall 1999, pp. 23–33.

83. P. M. Senge and G. Carstedt, "Innovating Our Way to the Next Industrial Revolution," *Sloan Management Review*, Winter 2001, pp. 24–38.

84. C. Holliday, "Sustainable Growth, the DuPont Way," *Harvard Business Review*, September 2001, pp. 129–34.

85. D. Lubin and D. Esty, "The Sustainability Imperative," *Harvard Business Review*, May 2010, pp. 42–50.

86. P. Shrivastava, "Ecocentric Management for a Risk Society," *Academy of Management Review* 20 (1995), pp. 118–37.

87. Ibid.

88. Ibid.

89. "3M Deploys ChargePoint Electric Vehicle Charging Station at HQ," *Manufacturing Close-Up*, February 16, 2011, Business & Company Resource Center, http://galenet.galegroup.com.

90. M. Herbst, "Gore Rings a Green Alarm," *BusinessWeek*, March 22, 2007; E. Osnos, "In China's Toxic Air, Winds of Change," *Chicago Tribune*, March 13, 2007; and Xinhua News Agency, "Unclean Drinking Water Threatens Health of 320M Chinese: Report," *BBC Monitoring International Reports*, March 13, 2007, all downloaded from Business & Company Resource Center, http://galenet.galegroup.com.

91. Shrivastava, "Ecocentric Management."

92. M. Gunther, "Green Is Good," *Fortune*, March 22, 2007, http://money.cnn.com;

93. S. Waddock, "Leadership Integrity in a Fractured Knowledge World," *Academy of Management Learning & Education*, 2007, pp. 543–57.

94. J. O'Toole, "Do Good, Do Well: The Business Enterprise Trust Awards," *California Management Review*, Spring 1991, pp. 9–24.

95. J. O'Toole, "Do Good, Do Well: The Business Enterprise Trust Awards," *California Management Review*, Spring 1991, pp. 9–24 and Shrivastava, "Ecocentric Management."

96. B. Doppelt, *Leading Change toward Sustainability* (Sheffield, UK: Greenleaf, 2010).

97. Ibid.

98. M. Russo and P. Fouts, "A Resource-Based Perspective on Corporate Environmental Performance and Profitability," *Academy of Management Journal* 40 (1997), pp. 534–59; and R. D. Klassen and D. Clay Whybark, "The Impact of Environmental Technologies on Manufacturing Performance," *Academy of Management Journal* 42 (1999), pp. 599–615.

99. G. Unruh and R. Etternson, "Growing Green," *Harvard Business Review*, June 2010, pp. 94–100.

100. Ibid.

101. Ibid.

102. Ibid.

103. M. LaMonica, "IBM Sees Green in Environmental Tech," *C/Net News.com*, March 6, 2007, http://news.com.com.

104. G. Colvin, "The King of Water," *Fortune*, July 5, 2010, pp. 52–59.

105. "Water as a Scarce Resource: An Interview with Nestle's Chairman," *McKinsey Quarterly*, 2010, Issue 1, pp. 76–80.

106. J. Ball, "Green Goal of 'Carbon Neutrality' Hits Limit," *The Wall Street Journal*, December 30, 2008, http://online.wsj.com; and Google Inc., "Going Green at Google," Corporate Overview: Green Initiatives, Google Corporate home page, http://www.google.com/corporate/green/.

107. G. Pinchot and E. Pinchot, *The Intelligent Organization* (San Francisco: Berrett-Koehler, 1996).

108. S. L. Hart, "Beyond Greening: Strategies for a Sustainable World," *Harvard Business Review*, January–February 1997, pp. 66–76.

109. Buchanan, "A Little Enlightened Self-Interest"; Patagonia, "Company Info: Corporate Responsibility"; Speakeasy, "The Latest Online Music Startup"; Binkley, "How Green Is My Sneaker?"; M. Baker, "Retail Works on an End to Greenwash," *Sydney Morning Herald*, March 8, 2011, http://www.smh.com.au; A. Schwartz, "Patagonia, Adidas, Walmart Team Up on Sustainable Apparel Coalition," *Fast Company*, February 25, 2011, http://www.fastcompany.com; and R. Feitelberg, "Fashion's New Order: Transparency," *WWD*, January 26, 2010, Business & Company Resource Center, http://galenet.galegroup.com.

Appendix B

1. P. Hawken, A. Lovins, and L. Hunter Lovins, *Natural Capitalism* (Boston: Little Brown, 1999).

2. F. Rice, "Who Scores Best on the Environment?" *Fortune*, July 26, 1993, p. 114–22.

3. J. K. Hammitt, "Climate Change Won't Wait for Kyoto," *The Washington Post*, November 29, 2000, p. A39.

4. A. Brown, "Business Leaders Respond to Rio with Self-Regulation," *International Herald Tribune*, June 23, 1997, p. 17.

5. Ibid.

6. K. W. Chilton, "Reengineering U.S. Environmental Protection," *Business Horizons*, March–April 2000, pp. 7–16.

7. K. Dechant and B. Altman, "Environmental Leadership: From Compliance to Competitive Advantage," *Academy of Management Executive*, August 1994, pp. 7–20.

8. R. Stavins, letter in "The Challenge of Going Green," *Harvard Business Review*, July–August 1994, pp. 37–50.

9. N. Walley and B. Whitehead, "It's Not Easy Being Green," *Harvard Business Review*, May–June 1994, pp. 46–51; and C. J. Corbett and L. N. Van Wassenhove, "The Green Fee: Internationalizing and Operationalizing Environmental Issues," *California Management Review*, Fall 1993, pp. 116–33.

10. Walley and Whitehead, "It's Not Easy Being Green."

11. Stavins, "The Challenge of Going Green."

12. Ibid.

13. F. B. Cross, "The Weaning of the Green: Environmentalism Comes of Age in the 1990s," *Business Horizons*, September–October 1990, pp. 40–46.

14. Stavins, "The Challenge of Going Green."

15. J. Singh, "Making Business Sense of Environmental Compliance," *Sloan Management Review*, Spring 2000, pp. 91–100.

16. H. Ellison, "Saving Nature While Earning Money," *International Herald Tribune*, June 23, 1997, p. 18.

17. E. Smith and V. Cahan, "The Greening of Corporate America," *BusinessWeek*, April 23, 1990, pp. 96–103.

18. M. E. Porter, "America's Green Strategy," *Science*, April 1991, p. 168.

19. A. Kleiner, "What Does It Mean to Be Green?" *Harvard Business Review*, July–August 1991, pp. 38–47.

20. D. C. Kinlaw, *Competitive and Green: Sustainable Performance in the Environmental Age* (Amsterdam: Pfeiffer & Co., 1993).

21. Rice, "Who Scores Best on the Environment?"

22. Rice, "Who Scores Best on the Environment?"; J. O'Toole, "Do Good, Do Well: The Business Enterprise Trust Awards," *California Management Review*, Spring 1991, pp. 9–24.

23. O'Toole, "Do Good, Do Well."

24. G. Hardin, "The Tragedy of the Commons," *Science* 162 (1968), pp. 1243–48.

25. D. Kirkpatrick, "Environmentalism: The New Crusade," *Fortune*, February 12, 1990, pp. 44–55.

26. Ibid.

27. R. Carson, *The Silent Spring* (Boston: Houghton Mifflin, 1962); R. Paehlke, *Environmentalism and the Future of Progressive Politics* (New Haven, CT: Yale University Press, 1989), pp. 13–41, 76–143; R. Nash, ed., *The American Environment* (Reading, MA: Addison-Wesley, 1968); R. Revelle and H. Landsberg, eds., *America's Changing Environment* (Boston: Beacon Press, 1970); L. Caldwell, *Environment: A Challenge to Modern Society* (Garden City, NY: Anchor Books, 1971); and J. M. Petulla, *Environmental Protection in the United States* (San Francisco: San Francisco Study Center, 1987).

28. B. Commoner, *Science and Survival* (New York: Viking Press, 1963); and B. Commoner, *The Closing Circle: Nature, Man and Technology* (New York: Bantam Books; 1971).

29. R. Paehlke, *Environmentalism and the Future of Progressive Politics* (New Haven: Yale University Press, 1989).

30. P. Shrivastava, "Ecocentric Management for a Risk Society," *Academy of Management Review* 20 (1995), pp. 118–37.

31. Commoner, *The Closing Circle.*

32. Paehlke, *Environmentalism.*

33. Ibid.

34. Ibid.

35. P. Hawken, J. Ogilvy, and P. Schwartz, *Seven Tomorrows: Toward a Voluntary History* (New York: Bantam Books, 1982); and Paehlke, *Environmentalism.*

36. Porter, "America's Green Strategy."

37. R. Y. K. Chan, "An Emerging Green Market in China: Myth or Reality?" *Business Horizons*, March–April 2000, pp. 55–60.

38. S. Waddock and N. Smith, "Corporate Responsibility Audits: Doing Well by Doing Good," *Sloan Management Review*, Winter 2000, pp. 75–83.

39. C. Morrison, *Managing Environmental Affairs: Corporate Practices in the U.S., Canada, and Europe* (New York: Conference Board, 1991).

40. Ibid.

41. Kleiner, "What Does It Mean to Be Green?"

42. K. Fischer and J. Schot, *Environmental Strategies for Industry* (Washington, DC: Island Press, 1993).

43. J. Howard, J. Nash, and J. Ehrenfeld, "Standard or Smokescreen? Implementation of a Voluntary Environmental Code," *California Management Review*, Winter 2000, pp. 63–82.

44. Rice, "Who Scores Best on the Environment?"

45. M. P. Polonsky and P. J. Rosenberger III, "Reevaluating Green Marketing: A Strategic Approach," *Business Horizons*, September–October 2001, pp. 21–30.

46. Rice, "Who Scores Best on the Environment?"

47. Ibid.

48. W.S. Laufer, "Social Accountability and Corporate Greenwashing," *Journal of Business Ethics* 43 (2003), pp. 253–61.

49. S. Hart and M. Milstein, "Global Sustainability and the Creative Destruction of Industries," *Sloan Management Review*, Fall 1999, pp. 23–32; Ellison, "Saving Nature While Earning Money."

50. Dechant and Altman, "Environment Leadership."

51. Smith and Cahan, "The Greening of Corporate America."

52. J. Elkington and T. Burke, *The Green Capitalists* (London: Victor Gullanez, 1989); and M. Zetlin, "The Greening of Corporate America," *Management Review*, June 1990, pp. 10–17.

53. Smith and Cahan, "The Greening of Corporate America."

54. J. Carey, "Global Warming," *BusinessWeek*, August 16, 2004, pp. 60–69.

55. J. Stevens, "Assessing the Health Risks of Incinerating Garbage," *EURA Reporter*, October 1989, pp. 6–10.

56. Carey, "Global Warming."

57. A. Lovins, L. Hunter Lovins, and P. Hawken, "A Road Map for Natural Capitalism," *Harvard Business Review*, May–June 1999, pp. 145–58.

58. A. Kolk, "Green Reporting," *Harvard Business Review*, January–February 2000, pp. 15–16.

59. L. Blumberg and R. Gottlieb, "The Resurrection of Incineration" and "The Economic Factors," in *War on Waste*, ed. L. Blumberg and R. Gottlieb (Washington, DC: Island Press, 1989).

60. Carey, "Global Warming."

61. L. Blumberg and R. Gottlieb, "Recycling's Unrealized Promise," in Blumberg and Gottlieb; *War on Waste*, pp. 191–226.

62. Carey, "Global Warming."

63. Lovins, Lovins, and Hawken, "A Road Map for Natural Capitalism."

64. J. Elkington, "Towards the Sustainable Corporation: Win-Win-Win Business Strategies for Sustainable Development," *California Management Review*, Winter 1994, pp. 90–100.

65. Lovins, Lovins, and Hawken, "A Road Map for Natural Capitalism."

66. Carey, "Global Warming."

67. Dechant and Altman, "Environmental Leadership."

68. Brown, "Business Leaders Respond to Rio with Self-Regulation."

69. H. Ellison, "Joint Implementation Promotes Cooperation on World Climate," *International Herald Tribune*, June 23, 1997, p. 21.

70. Corbett and Van Wassenhove, "The Green Fee."

71. Polansky and Rosenberger, "Reevaluating Green Marketing."

72. Carey, "Global Warming."

73. D. Lubin and D. Esty, "The Sustainability Imperative," *Harvard Business Review* 42 (May 2010), pp. 42–50.

74. R. D. Klassen and D. Clay Whybark, "The Impact of Environmental Technologies on Manufacturing Performance," *Academy of Management Journal* 42 (1999), pp. 599–615.

75. D. Machalaba, "New Recyclables Market Emerges: Plastic Railroad Ties," *The Wall Street Journal*, October 19, 2004, p. B1.

76. Hart and Milstein, "Global Sustainability."

77. Ibid.

78. Ibid.

79. D. Barton, "Capitalism for the Long Term," *Harvard Business Review*, March 2011, pp. 84–91.

80. D. Lubin and D. Esty, "The Sustainability Imperative," *Harvard Business Review*, May 2010, pp. 42–50.

81. Polansky and Rosenberger, "Reevaluating Green Marketing."

82. Hart and Milstein, "Global Sustainability."

83. Ibid.

84. M. Fong, "Soy Underwear? China Targets Eco-Friendly Clothes Market," *The Wall Street Journal*, December 17, 2004, pp. B1, B4.

85. Polansky and Rosenberger, "Reevaluating Green Marketing."

86. Ibid.

87. Elkington, "Towards the Sustainable Corporation."

88. F. S. Rowland, "Chlorofluorocarbons and the Depletion of Stratospheric Ozone," *American Scientist*, January–February 1989, pp. 36–45.

89. Elkington, "Towards the Sustainable Corporation."

90. M. Lubber, "Sustainability: Ending the 'Tyranny of Short-Termism,'" April 1, 2011, www.ceres.org.

91. Ellison, "Joint Implementation Promotes Cooperation on World Climate."

92. Elkington, "Towards the Sustainable Corporation."

93. H. Ellison, "The Balance Sheet," *International Herald Tribune*, June 23, 1997, p. 21.

94. P. B. Gray and D. Devlin, "Heroes of Small Business," *Fortune Small Business*, November 2000, pp. 50–64.

Chapter 6

1. "The Secret of IKEA's Success," *The Economist*, February 26, 2011, Business & Company Resource Center," http://galenet.galegroup.com; IKEA, "About IKEA," http://www.ikea.com, accessed May 24, 2011; J. Hansegard, "IKEA Profits Rise as Consumers Seek Bargains," *The Wall Street Journal*, January 14, 2011, http://online.wsj.com; J. Hansegard, "IKEA Lifts Lid on Full-Year Earnings," *The Wall Street Journal*, October 1, 2010, http://online.wsj.com; "Retailers in the Top 20: Pathfinders for an Industry," *Businessweek*, February 16, 2010, http://www.businessweek.com; M. Wilson, "Making Energy On-Site," *Chain Store Age*, October 2010, p. 46; M. Glover, "Brief: Eight IKEA Stores in State to Get Solar Panels," *Sacramento Bee*, October 15, 2010, Business & Company Resource Center, http://

galenet.galegroup.com; A. Schwartz, "IKEA Denver Leads the Way for Big Box Geothermal Installations," *Fast Company*, August 24, 2010, http://www.fastcompany.com; R. Mullins, "IKEA Employees Receive Bikes as Thanks," *Tampa (Fla.) Tribune*, December 9, 2010, Business & Company Resource Center, http://galenet.galegroup.com; A. Schwartz, "IKEA Makes First Greentech Investment," *Fast Company*, November 1, 2010, http://www.fastcompany.com; and "The 10 Most Innovative Companies in Retail," *Fast Company*, March 15, 2011, http://www.fastcompany.com.

2. D. Wessel, "Big U.S. Firms Shift Hiring Abroad," *The Wall Street Journal*, April 19, 2011, http://online.wsj.com.

3. E. Smith and J. T. Areddy, "Disney to Begin Shanghai Park," *The Wall Street Journal*, April 4, 2011, http://online.wsj.com.

4. M. S. Malone, "Living in a Bipolar Business World," *ABC News*, November 13, 2009, http://abcnews.go.com.

5. World Trade Organization (WTO), *International Trade Statistics 2008*; and WTO, "WTO Sees 9% Global Trade Decline."

6. See, for example, M. Mandel, "What Spending Slowdown?" *BusinessWeek*, April 23, 2007, http://www.businessweek.com.

7. Census Bureau, *Statistical Abstract of the United States: 2011*, table 1290, p. 797, http://www.census.gov; UN Conference on Trade and Development (UNCTAD), "Inward and Outward Foreign Direct Investment Flows," UnctadStat, http://unctadstat.unctad.org.

8. Reuters, "Deutsche Boerse Set for NYSE Deal as Nasdaq Bows Out," *LiveMint.com*, May 16, 2011, http://www.livemint.com; and F. Yan and A. Leung, "China's Geely Completes Volvo Buy," LiveMint.com, August 2, 2010, http://www.livemint.com.

9. C. Zappone, "China Poised for Global Shopping Spree," *CNNMoney*, March 30, 2007, http://money.cnn.com.

10. R. Rodriguez, "Peach Growers in Valley, China Fight for Market Share," *Fresno (Calif.) Bee*, January 31, 2011, http://www.fresnobee.com; and "AIADA: Imports Increase Market Share," *Auto Remarketing*, December 7, 2010, http://www.autoremarketing.com.

11. Joseph B. White, "What Is an American Car?" *The Wall Street Journal*, January 26, 2009, http://online.wsj.com.

12. T. Heston, "Fitting into the Global Puzzle," *Fabricating and Metalworking*, February 2007, Business & Company Resource Center, http://galenet.galegroup.com.

13. N. Sandler, "Software That Will This Sentence Fix," *BusinessWeek*, February 22, 2007, Business & Company Resource Center, http://galenet.galegroup.com.

14. D. W. Drezner, "The Outsourcing Bogeyman," *Foreign Affairs*, May/June 2004.

15. D. Wessel and B. Davis, "Pain from Free Trade Spurs Second Thoughts," *The Wall Street Journal*, March 28, 2007, http://online.wsj.com.

16. Ibid.

17. Wessel, "Big U.S. Firms Shift Hiring Abroad."

18. Wessel and Davis, "Pain from Free Trade"; P. Levy, "Trade Truths for Turbulent Times: A Reply to Vladimir Masch," *BusinessWeek*, February 14, 2007, Business & Company Resource Center, http://galenet.galegroup.com; P. Restuccia, "Profs Claim the Threat of Outsourcing Is Overblown," *Boston Herald*, February 12, 2007, http://galenet.galegroup.com; and D. Blanchard, "Compete or Retreat," *Industry Week*, January 2007, http://galenet.galegroup.com.

19. D. Whitford, "Where in the World Is Cheap Labor?" *Fortune*, March 22, 2011, http://money.cnn.com.

20. Council on Competitiveness, "Trade Deficit Doesn't Capture U.S. Competitive Edge," news release, November 13, 2006, http://www.compete.org.

21. C. Lombardi, "Survey: Software Companies Increasing Offshoring Work," *C/Net News*, January 12, 2007, http://news.com.com.

22. "When Staying Put Trumps Offshoring," *McKinsey Quarterly*, December 7, 2004, online; and C. Koepfer, "A Look at Total Cost Can Change the View," *Production Machining*, January 2011, p. 6.

23. Koepfer, "A Look at Total Cost"; and Whitford, "Where in the World Is Cheap Labor?"

24. European Union, "About the EU," http://europa.eu; Central Intelligence Agency, "European Union," *The World Factbook*, http://www.cia.gov.

25. "Irish Welcome Portuguese to the 'Debt Club,'" *The Wall Street Journal*, April 7, 2011, http://blogs.wsj.com; S. Rastello and R. Christie, "IMF Will Work on Portugal Bailout Plan with European Union," *Bloomberg Businessweek*, April 8, 2011, http://www.businessweek.com; P. Kowsmann, "Portugal Reaches a Deal on Bailout," *The Wall Street Journal*, May 4, 2011, http://online.wsj.com; and M. Elliott, "Global Crises? Don't Panic," *Fortune*, April 21, 2011, http://money.cnn.com.

26. "Nokia to Build Mobile Phone Factory in Romania," *Agence France Presse*, March 26, 2007, http://news.yahoo.com; and D. Rocks, K. Zachovalova, and N. Saminathaer, "Made in China—er, Veliko Turnovo," *BusinessWeek*, January 8, 2007, Business & Company Resource Center, http://galenet.galegroup.com.

27. R. Casert, "EU Waves New Fines in Face of Microsoft," *Seattle Times*, March 2, 2007; and D. Litterick, "Regulation EU Losing Patience with Reluctant Microsoft," *Daily Telegraph (London)*, March 2, 2007, Business & Company

Resource Center, http://galenet.galegroup.com.

28. "China Surpasses U.S. in Exports," *The Wall Street Journal*, April 12, 2007, http://online.wsj.com.

29. World Trade Organization, *Trade Profiles 2008* (Geneva: WTO, 2009), p. 38, http://www.wto.org; World Trade Organization, *International Trade Statistics 2008* (Geneva: WTO, 2008), p. 5, http://www.wto.org; and World Trade Organization, "WTO Sees 9% Global Trade Decline in 2009 as Recession Strikes," new release, March 24, 2009, http://www.wto.org.

30. J. McDonald, "Intel Plant to Boost Beijing Tech Plans," *Associated Press*, March 26, 2007, http://news.yahoo.com; and M. Kanellos, "Intel to Produce Chips in China," *C/Net News*, March 26, 2007, http://news.com.com.

31. J. T. Areddy and P. Sanders, "Chinese Learn English the Disney Way," *The Wall Street Journal*, April 20, 2009, http://online.wsj.com.

32. Bureau of Labor Statistics, "International Comparisons of Hourly Compensation Costs in Manufacturing, 2007," news release, March 26, 2009, http://www.bls.gov/ilc.

33. G. Anand, "India Graduates Millions, but Too Few Are Fit to Hire," *The Wall Street Journal*, April 5, 2011, http://online.wsj.com.

34. "Citigroup Plans More Branches in India," *Associated Press*, March 26, 2007, http://my.earthlink.net.

35. A. van Agtmael, "Industrial Revolution 2.0," *Foreign Policy*, January–February 2007, Business & Company Resource Center, http://galenet.galegroup.com.

36. Asia-Pacific Economic Cooperation, "Scope of Work" and "Frequently Asked Questions," APEC website, http://www.apec.org.

37. Agtmael, "Industrial Revolution 2.0"; CEMEX website, http://www.cemex.com.

38. C. Simoes and I. Dantas, "Brazil's Economy: Growth May Have a Downside," *Bloomberg Businessweek*, June 10, 2010, http://www.businessweek.com; A. Ragir and D. Kopecki, "Brazil's Credit Boom Could End in Tears," *Bloomberg Businessweek*, January 6, 2011, http://www.businessweek.com; and S. Nielsen, "Wind Power: Brazil's Second Act," *Bloomberg Businessweek*, October 7, 2010, http://www.businessweek.com.

39. Agtmael, "Industrial Revolution 2.0."

40. Office of the United States Trade Representative, "Free Trade Agreements," http://www.ustr.gov.

41. U.S. Energy Information Administration, "Trade," U.S. Department of Energy, http://www.eia.doe.gov.

42. F. Aquila, "Africa's Biggest Score: A Thriving Economy," *Bloomberg Businessweek*, June 28, 2010, http://www.businessweek.com.

43. M. O'Connor, "Teamwork Changes Attitudes in Nation of Entrepreneurs,"

Financial Times, October 14, 2010, Business & Company Resource Center, http://galenet.galegroup.com.

44. E. Markowitz, "A Dating Site Thrives in Delhi," *Inc.,* February 14, 2011, http://www.inc.com; and H. Seligson, "Jilted in the U.S., a Site Finds Love in India," *The New York Times,* February 19, 2011, http://www.nytimes.com.

45. See, for example, "India's Bharti Says to Sign Wal-Mart Deal in April," *Reuters,* April 11, 2007, http://news.yahoo.com.

46. G. A. Fowler, B. Steinberg, and A. O. Patrick, "Mac and PC's Overseas Adventures," *The Wall Street Journal,* March 1, 2007, http://online.wsj.com.

47. P. B. Kavilanz, "U.S. Slaps Tariffs on Chinese Imports," *CNNMoney.com,* March 30, 2007, http://money.cnn.com.

48. Heineken International website, http://www.henekeninternational.com; and Heineken N.V. profile, Vintners.com, http://www.vintners.com.

49. S. Elliott, "Ford Tries a Global Campaign for Its Global Car," *The New York Times,* February 25, 2011, Business & Company Resource Center, http://galenet.galegroup.com.

50. A.-W. Harzing, "An Empirical Analysis and Extension of the Bartlett and Ghoshal Typology of Multinational Companies," *Journal of International Business Studies* 31, no. 1 (2000), pp. 101–20.

51. J. Sandberg, "How Long Can India Keep Office Politics out of Outsourcing?" *The Wall Street Journal,* February 27, 2007, http://online.wsj.com.

52. S. E. Prokesch, "Making Global Connections at Caterpillar," *Harvard Business Review* 74, no. 2 (March–April 1996), pp. 88–89; "Caterpillar Gets a Lift," *BusinessWeek,* February 16, 2007, http://www.businessweek.com; *Off-Highway Engineering: Technical Innovations,* http://www.sae.org/ohmag/techinnovations/02-2001/; L. Freeman, "Caterpillar on a Roll," *B to B* 85, no. 14 (September 11, 2000), pp. 3, 44; I. Buchanan, "The US Experience," *Asian Business* 34, no. 5 (May 1998), pp. 14–16; and Caterpillar website, http://www.cat.com.

53. IKEA, "About IKEA"; "The Secret of IKEA's Success"; Hansegard, "IKEA Profits Rise as Consumers Seek Bargains"; A. D'Innocenzio, "New IKEA CEO Cuts Prices, Targets Frugal U.S. Families," *Houston Chronicle,* October 29, 2010, Business & Company Resource Center, http://galenet.galegroup.com; N. Popper, "IKEA's U.S. Factory Churns Out Unhappy Workers," *Los Angeles Times,* April 10, 2011, http://www.latimes.com; and H. H. Wang, "Why Home Depot Struggles and IKEA Thrives in China," *Forbes,* February 10, 2011, http://blogs.forbes.com.

54. C. H. Moon, "The Choice of Entry Modes and Theories of Foreign Direct Investment," *Journal of Global Marketing* 11, no. 2 (1997), pp. 43–64; and I. Maignan and B. A. Lukas, "Entry Mode Decisions: The Role of Managers' Mental Models," *Journal of Global Marketing* 10, no. 4 (1997), pp. 7–22.

55. A. O. Patrick, "The Race to Get TV Shows Overseas," *The Wall Street Journal,* March 28, 2007, http://online.wsj.com; and B. Barnes, "NBC Faces Trials Bringing 'Law & Order' to France," *The Wall Street Journal,* March 1, 2007, http://online.wsj.com; and E. Smith, "'Pirates' Nabs $346.4 Million at Global Box Office," *The Wall Street Journal,* May 23, 2011, http://online.wsj.com.

56. C. Simons and D. Zehr, "Dell Tries to Win Over Chinese with Scaled-Down PCs," *Atlanta Journal-Constitution,* March 22, 2007, Business & Company Resource Center, http://galenet.galegroup.com.

57. P. Jitpleecheep, "Auntie Anne's Aims to Double Asia Outlets," *Bangkok Post,* April 10, 2007, Business & Company Resource Center, http://galenet.galegroup.com.

58. M. Prewitt, "Breaking Down the Great Wall to Franchising in China," *Nation's Restaurant News,* March 12, 2007, Business & Company Resource Center, http://galenet.galegroup.com.

59. "Hershey's Global Gambit," *BusinessWeek,* April 4, 2007, http://www.businessweek.com.

60. S. Oster, N. Shirouzu, and P. Glader, "China Squeezes Foreigners for Share of Global Riches," *The Wall Street Journal,* December 28, 2010, http://online.wsj.com.

61. R. C. Beasley, "Reducing the Risk of Failure in the Formation of Commercial Partnerships," *Licensing Journal* 24, no. 4 (April 2004), p. 71.

62. J. T. Areddy, "In China, Tire-Espionage Suit Treads Loudly," *The Wall Street Journal,* April 28, 2011, http://online.wsj.com.

63. "IBM's India Hiring Binge Continues," *Associated Press,* February 28, 2007, http://news.yahoo.com.

64. K. Hille, "Western Faces Are Vital to China," *Financial Times,* December 9, 2010, Business & Company Resource Center, http://galenet.galegroup.com; and J. S. Lublin, "Finding Top Talent in China, India, Brazil," *The Wall Street Journal,* April 11, 2011, http://online.wsj.com.

65. A. W. Andreason, "Expatriate Adjustment to Foreign Assignments," *International Journal of Commerce and Management* 13 no. 1 (Spring 2003), pp. 42–61.

66. P. Capell, "Know before You Go: Expats' Advice to Couples," *Career Journal Europe,* May 2, 2006, http://www.careerjournaleurope.com.

67. R. A. Swaak, "Expatriate Failures: Too Many, Too Much Cost, Too Little Planning," *Compensation & Benefits Review,* November/December 1995, pp. 50–52.

68. Capell, "Know before You Go."

69. G. M. Sprietzer, M. W. McCall, and J. D. Mahoney, "Early Identification of International Executive Potential," *Journal of Applied Psychology* 82, no. 1 (1997), pp. 6–29; R. Mortensen, "Beyond the Fence Line," *HRMagazine,* November 1997, pp. 100–9; "Expatriate Games," *Journal of Business Strategy,* July/August 1997, pp. 4–5; and "Building a Global Workforce Starts with Recruitment," *Personnel Journal* (special supplement), March 1996, pp. 9–11.

70. A. Paul, "How the Internet Shrinks the Distance between Us," *The Wall Street Journal,* March 16, 2007, http://online.wsj.com.

71. G. A. Fowler, "In China's Offices, Foreign Colleagues Might Get an Earful," *The Wall Street Journal,* February 13, 2007, http://online.wsj.com.

72. John Slocum, "Coming to America," *Human Resource Executive,* October 2, 2008, http://www.hrexecutive.com.

73. Emily Flitter, "Time Runs Differently in the Emirates," *The Wall Street Journal,* April 16, 2008, http://online.wsj.com.

74. J. Brett, K. Behfar, and M. C. Kern, "Managing Multicultural Teams," *Harvard Business Review,* November 2006, pp. 84–91.

75. D. Stamps, "Welcome to America," *Training,* November 1996, pp. 23–30.

76. L. K. Trevino and K. A. Nelson, *Managing Business Ethics: Straight Talk about How to Do It Right* (New York: John Wiley & Sons, 1995).

77. Transparency International, "Leading Exporters Undermine Development with Dirty Business Overseas," news release, October 4, 2006, http://www.transparency.org.

78. J. G. Longnecker, J. A. McKinney, and C. W. Moore, "The Ethical Issues of International Bribery: A Study of Attitudes among U.S. Business Professionals," *Journal of Business Ethics* 7 (1988), pp. 341–46.

79. D. Searcey, "U.K. Law on Bribes Has Firms in a Sweat," *The Wall Street Journal,* December 28, 2010, http://online.wsj.com.

80. Ibid.; and J. Holzer and S. Raice, "IBM Settles Bribery Charges," *The Wall Street Journal,* March 19, 2011, http://online.wsj.com.

81. UPS, "The UPS Code of Business Conduct: Leading with Integrity," UPS Pressroom, http://www.pressroom.ups.com; and i-Sight, "International Code of Conduct: United Parcel Service," Best Practices, June 17, 2010, http://i-sight.com.

82. A. B. Desai and T. Rittenburg, "Global Ethics: An Integrative Framework for MNEs," *Journal of Business Ethics* 16 (1997), pp. 791–800; and P. Buller, J. Kohls, and K. Anderson, "A Model for Addressing Cross-Cultural Ethical Conflicts," *Business & Society* 36, no. 2 (June 1997), pp. 169–93.

83. "The Secret of IKEA's Success"; Hansegard, "IKEA Lifts Lid on Full-Year

Earnings"; "Retailers in the Top 20"; Popper, "IKEA's U.S. Factory Churns Out Unhappy Workers"; Adams, "IKEA to Sell Second-Hand IKEA Furniture," *Time*, September 2, 2010, http://newsfeed.time.com; M. Cannell, "Is IKEA the Paragon of Discount Wastefulness?" *Fast Company*, July 16, 2009, http://www.fastcompany.com; A. Schwartz, "IKEA Creates a Sustainability Scorecard for Its Products," *Fast Company*, April 1, 2011, http://www.fastcodesign.com; and G. Myles, "IKEA Builds for the Future," *The Mirror (London)*, April 7, 2011, Business & Company Resource Center, http://galenet.galegroup.com.

Chapter 7

1. Chipotle website, http://www.chipotle.com; J. H. Ostdick, "Elevating the Bottom Line," *Success*, December 2010, pp. 59–64; O. Strand, "From Fast-Rising to Fast Food," *The New York Times*, December 15, 2010, Business & Company Resource Center, http://galenet.galegroup.com; J. Hemmerdinger, "Burrito Buzz in South Portland," *Portland (Me.) Press Herald*, December 14, 2010, Business & Company Resource Center, http://galenet.galegroup.com; V. Reklaitis, "Chipotle's Steve Ells Fine-Tunes Fast Food Grow," *Investor's Business Daily*, November 3, 2010, Business & Company Resource Center, http://galenet.galegroup.com; and "Chipotle Increases Its Use of Naturally Raised Beef," *Food & Beverage Close-Up*, June 10, 2010, Business & Company Resource Center, http://galenet.galegroup.com.
2. S. Shane and S. Venkataraman, "The Promise of Entrepreneurship as a Field of Research," *Academy of Management Review* 25 (2000), pp. 217–26.
3. J. A. Timmons, *New Venture Creation* (Burr Ridge, IL: Richard D. Irwin, 1994).
4. G. T. Lumpkin and G. G. Dess, "Clarifying the Entrepreneurial Orientation Construct and Linking It to Performance," *Academy of Management Review* 21 (1996), pp. 135–72.
5. R. W. Smilor, "Entrepreneurship: Reflections on a Subversive Activity," *Journal of Business Venturing* 12 (1997), pp. 341–46.
6. W. Megginson, M. J. Byrd, S. R. Scott Jr., and L. Megginson, *Small Business Management: An Entrepreneur's Guide to Success*, 2nd ed. (Boston: Irwin McGraw-Hill, 1997).
7. D. Shepherd and H. Patzelt, "The New Field of Sustainable Entrepreneurship: Studying Entrepreneurial Action Linking 'What Is to Be Sustained' with 'What Is to Be Developed,'" *Entrepreneurship: Theory & Practice* 35 (2011), pp. 137–63.
8. D.J. Isenberg, "The Global Entrepreneur," *Harvard Business Review*, December 2008, pp. 107–11.

9. J. Timmons and S. Spinelli, *New Venture Creation: Entrepreneurship for the 21st Century*, 6th ed. (New York: McGraw-Hill/Irwin, 2004), p. 3.
10. J. A. Timmons, *The Entrepreneurial Mind* (Andover, MA: Brick House, 1989).
11. Timmons and Spinelli, *New Venture Creation*.
12. A. Loten, "Start-Ups Key to States' Economic Success," *Inc.*, February 7, 2007, http://www.inc.com.
13. Timmons and Spinelli, *New Venture Creation*.
14. Ibid.
15. Ibid.
16. D. Bricklin, "Natural-Born Entrepreneur," *Harvard Business Review* (September 2001), pp. 53–59, p. 58.
17. Alexandra Levit, "'Insider' Entrepreneurs," *The Wall Street Journal*, April 6, 2009, http://online.wsj.com.
18. "For Zappos, the Next Trend Is More Customized Pages for Customers," *InternetRetailer*, February 12, 2009, http://www.internetretailer.com; M. Chafkin, "How I Did It: Tony Hsieh, CEO, Zappos.com," *Inc.*, September 2006, http://www.inc.com.
19. "Coolest College Start-Ups: Where Are They Now?" *Inc.*, March 2011, http://www.inc.com; E. Lee, "The Small-Business Numbers Cruncher," *San Francisco Chronicle*, January 3, 2011, Business & Company Resource Center, http://galenet.galegroup.com; M. Chafkin, "InDinero Fixes Money Management," *Inc.*, December 2010, http://www.inc.com; and A. Gardella, "Can a 20-Year-Old Help You Track Your Finances?" *The New York Times*, September 29, 2010, http://boss.blogs.nytimes.com.
20. L. Kanter, "The Eco-Advantage," *Inc.*, November 2006, pp. 78–103 (NaturaLawn example on page 84).
21. H. Aldrich, *Ethnic Entrepreneurs: Immigrant Business in Industrial Societies* (Newbury Park, CA: Sage, 1990).
22. R. Flandez, "Immigrants Gain Edge Doing Business Back Home," *The Wall Street Journal*, March 20, 2007, http://online.wsj.com.
23. Timmons and Spinelli, *New Venture Creation*.
24. Michael V. Copeland, "Products for the Other 3 Billion," *Fortune*, April 1, 2009, http://money.cnn.com.
25. J. Collins and J. Porras, *Built to Last* (London: Century, 1996).
26. M. V. Copeland, "Start Last, Finish First," *Business 2.0*, January–February 2006, Business & Company Resource Center, http://galenet.galegroup.com.
27. Collins and Porras, *Built to Last*.
28. K. H. Vesper, *New Venture Mechanics* (Englewood Cliffs, NJ: Prentice Hall, 1993).
29. Kanter, "The Eco-Advantage," p. 87.
30. Vesper, *New Venture Mechanics*.
31. Kanter, "The Eco-Advantage," p. 84.
32. J. Berg, "Entrepreneurs Develop Errand Service," *Patriot-News (Harrisburg, PA)*, January 23, 2007, http://galenet.galegroup.com.

33. Kanter, "The Eco-Advantage," p. 84.
34. Timmons and Spinelli, *New Venture Creation*.
35. International Franchise Association, "Study Reveals Significant Growth of Franchising Sector," news release, February 23, 2007, http://www.franchise.org; and International Franchise Association, "The Profile of Franchising: 2006," August 3, 2006, http://www.franchise.org/IndustrySecondary.aspx?id=31604.
36. P. J. Sauer, "Serving Up Success," *Inc.*, January 2007, http://www.inc.com.
37. K. Spors, "Franchised versus Nonfranchised Businesses," *The Wall Street Journal*, February 27, 2007, http://online.wsj.com.
38. Timmons and Spinelli, *New Venture Creation*.
39. R. Gibson, "Learning from Others' Mistakes," *The Wall Street Journal*, March 19, 2007, http://online.wsj.com.
40. M. V. Copeland and S. Hamner, "The 20 Smartest Companies to Start Now," *Business 2.0*, September 2006, General Reference Center Gold, http://find.galegroup.com.
41. A. Pasztor, "Sharper Image Sells New Toy: Zero Gravity's Spacey Flights," *The Wall Street Journal*, March 28, 2007, http://online.wsj.com; and B. Spillman, "Nothing to These Flights," *Las Vegas Review–Journal*, March 5, 2007, Business & Company Resource Center, http://galenet.galegroup.com.
42. A. M. Kukec, "Two Start-Ups Get State Boost to Fight Terrorism," *Daily Herald (Arlington, IL)*, January 10, 2006; and T. Walsh, "State Venture Capital to Be Put to Work," *Detroit Free Press*, August 28, 2006, Business & Company Resource Center, http://galenet.galegroup.com.
43. J. E. Lange, "Entrepreneurs and the Continuing Internet: The Expanding Frontier," in Timmons and Spinelli, *New Venture Creation*, pp. 183–220.
44. Ibid.
45. J. E. Vascellaro, "Selling Your Designs Online," *The Wall Street Journal*, April 5, 2007, http://online.wsj.com.
46. J. Short, T. Moss, and G. Lumpkin, "Research in Social Entrepreneurship: Past, Contributions and Future Opportunities," *Strategic Entrepreneurship Journal* 3 (2009), pp. 161–94.
47. P. Dacin, M.T. Dacin, and M. Matear, "Social Entrepreneurship: Why We Don't Need a New Theory and How We Move Forward from Here," *Academy of Management Perspectives* 24 (2010), pp. 37–57.
48. J. Mair and I. Marti, "Social Entrepreneurship Research: A Source of Explanation, Prediction, and Delight," *Journal of World Business* 41 (2006), pp. 36–44.
49. D. Bornstein and S. Davis, *Social Entrepreneurship: What Everyone Needs to Know* (Oxford, UK: Oxford University Press, 2010).
50. D. Bornstein, *How to Change the World: Social Entrepreneurs and the Power of New*

Ideas (Oxford, UK: Oxford University Press, 2004).

51. B. Dumaine, "Lighting Up Africa," *Fortune*, July 5, 2010, p. 22.

52. J. Thompson and I. MacMillan, "Making Social Ventures Work," *Harvard Business Review*, September, 2010, pp. 66–73.

53. Ibid.

54. Ibid.

55. Timmons, *New Venture Creation.*

56. M. Cardon, J. Wincent, J. Singh, and M. Drnovsek, "The Nature and Experience of Entrepreneurial Passion," *Academy of Management Review* 34 (2009), pp. 511–32.

57. J. R. Baum and E. A. Locke, "The Relationship of Entrepreneurial Traits, Skill, and Motivation to Subsequent Venture Growth," *Journal of Applied Psychology* 89 (2004), pp. 587–98.

58. E. Pak, "Twenty-Something Entrepreneurs Are Helping Transform the Surf and Skate Industry," *Orange County Register (Santa Ana, CA),* February 23, 2007, Business & Company Resource Center, http://galenet.galegroup.com.

59. L. Buchanan, "How Great Entrepreneurs Think," *Inc.*, February 2011, http://www.inc.com.

60. M. Sonfield and R. Lussier, "The Entrepreneurial Strategy Matrix: A Model for New and Ongoing Ventures," *Business Horizons*, May–June 1997, pp. 73–77.

61. C. Lagorio, "Solved! Hands-Free Door Opening," *Inc.*, March 2011, http://www.inc.com; "Coolest College Start-Ups 2011," *Inc.*, March 2011, http://www.inc.com; and Toepener website, http://www.toepener.com.

62. Lange, "Entrepreneurs and the Continuing Internet."

63. S. Venkataraman and M. Low, "On the Nature of Critical Relationships: A Test of the Liabilities and Size Hypothesis," in *Frontiers of Entrepreneurship Research* (Babson Park, MA: Babson College, 1991), p. 97.

64. Timmons and Spinelli, *New Venture Creation.*

65. P. Hoy, "Most Small Businesses Start without Outside Capital," *Inc.*, October 3, 2006, http://www.inc.com.

66. R. Grant, "The Trade-Offs of Venture Capital," *Mortgage Banking*, February 2007, Business & Company Resource Center, http://galenet.galegroup.com.

67. F. Paul, "The #1 Top Start-Up Mistake," *AllBusiness*, March 1, 2011, http://www.allbusiness.com; and "Start-Up Survey: Mistakes Were Made," *The Wall Street Journal*, February 23, 2011, http://blogs.wsj.com.

68. Cari Tuna, "Tough Call: Deciding to Start a Business," *The Wall Street Journal*, January 8, 2009, http://online.wsj.com.

69. H. Dietrich, "Worried about Future Viaduct Construction Woes, Sound Sports Is Planning Ahead," *Minneapolis–St. Paul Business Journal*, http://twincities.bizjournals.com.

70. L. Buchanan, "Create Jobs, Eliminate Waste, Preserve Value," *Inc.*, December 2006, pp. 94–106.

71. M. V. Copeland, "A Studio System for Startups," *Business 2.0*, May 2007, Business & Company Resource Center, http://galenet.galegroup.com.

72. Ostdick, "Elevating the Bottom Line"; Reklaitis, "Chipotle's Steve Ells"; "Chipotle Increases Its Use of Naturally Raised Beef"; M. D. G. Kaplan, "Chipotle Founder: Why Grass-Fed Animals Make a Better Burrito," *SmartPlanet*, April 12, 2010, http://www.smartplanet.com; "Going Green: Will Customers Notice?" *Restaurant Hospitality*, January 2010, p. 20; and K. Harlin, "Chipotle Surges on Hot Profit; Panera Too," *Investor's Business Daily*, February 11, 2011, Business & Company Resource Center, http://galenet.galegroup.com.

73. Norm Brodsky, "Street Smarts: Our Irrational Fear of Numbers," *Inc.*, January 2009, http://www.inc.com.

74. Chafkin, "How I Did It."

75. Anjali Cordeiro, "Sweet Returns," *The Wall Street Journal*, April 23, 2009, http://online.wsj.com.

76. Gibson, "Learning from Others' Mistakes."

77. D. McGinn, "Why Size Matters," *Inc.*, Fall 2004, pp. 32–36.

78. S. E. Needleman, "When It's Time to Take On Help," *The Wall Street Journal*, January 16, 2011, http://online.wsj.com.

79. Kanter, "The Eco-Advantage."

80. W. Harris, "Team Players," *Black Enterprise*, January 2007, Business & Company Resource Center, http://galenet.galegroup.com.

81. S. Finkelstein, "The Myth of Managerial Superiority in Internet Startups: An Autopsy," *Organizational Dynamics*, Fall 2001, pp. 172–85.

82. S. E. Needleman, "Management Flubs Made by Rookie Bosses," *The Wall Street Journal*, January 3, 2011, http://online.wsj.com.

83. R. Weisman, "Bootstrappers Avoid Outside Money Ties," *Boston Globe*, February 5, 2007, Business & Company Resource Center, http://galenet.galegroup.com.

84. Cordeiro, "Sweet Returns."

85. P. F. Drucker, "How to Save the Family Business," *The Wall Street Journal*, August 19, 1994, p. A10.

86. D. Gamer, R. Owen, and R. Conway, *The Ernst & Young Guide to Raising Capital* (New York: John Wiley & Sons, 1991).

87. Ibid.

88. Ostdick, "Elevating the Bottom Line."

89. R. D. Hisrich and M. P. Peters, *Entrepreneurship: Starting, Developing, and Managing a New Enterprise* (Burr Ridge, IL: Irwin, 1994).

90. Ibid.

91. W. A. Sahlman, "How to Write a Great Business Plan," *Harvard Business Review*, July–August 1997, pp. 98–108.

92. Ibid.

93. Copeland, "Start Last, Finish First."

94. Sahlman, "How to Write a Great Business Plan."

95. R. D. Atkinson and D. K. Correa, *The 2007 State New Economy Index* (Ewing Marion Kauffman Foundation and Information Technology and Innovation Foundation, 2007), http://www.kauffman.org; and J. Gangemi, "Ranking the States for the New Economy," *BusinessWeek*, February 27, 2007, http://www.businessweek.com.

96. Ibid.

97. M. Zimmerman and G. Zeitz, "Beyond Survival: Achieving New Venture Growth by Building Legitimacy," *Academy of Management Review*, 27 (2002), pp. 414–21.

98. A. L. Stinchcombe, "Social Structure and Organizations," in J. G. March, ed., *Handbook of Organizations* (Chicago: Rand McNally, 1965), pp. 142–93.

99. L. Taylor, "Want Your Start-Up to Be Successful? Appearance Is Everything," *Inc.*, February 23, 2007, http://www.inc.com.

100. Ibid.

101. R. A. Baron and G. D. Markman, "Beyond Social Capital: How Social Skills Can Enhance Entrepreneurs' Success," *Academy of Management Executive*, February 2000, pp. 106–16.

102. J. Florin, M. Lubatkin, and W. Schulze, "A Social Capital Model of High-Growth Ventures," *Academy of Management Journal* 46 (2003), pp. 374–84.

103. L. Buchanan, "How I Did It: Tim Litle, Chairman, Litle & Co.," *Inc.*, September 2006, http://www.inc.com.

104. D. Fenn, "An Incubator for Unreasonable Ideas," *Inc.*, February 19, 2010, http://www.inc.com; S. Sosa, "The World's Most Unreasonable Entrepreneurs," *Inc.*, November 24, 2010, http://www.inc.com; and "Unreasonable Institute Launches Initiative to Promote High-Impact Social Entrepreneurs," *Wireless News*, January 25, 2011, Business & Company Resource Center, http://galenet.galegroup.com.

105. J. Gangemi, "Young, Fearless, and Smart," *BusinessWeek*, October 30, 2006, http://www.businessweek.com.

106. Harris, "Team Players."

107. Ibid.

108. J. Markoff, "Searching for Michael Jordan? Microsoft Wants a Better Way," *The New York Times*, March 7, 2007, Business & Company Resource Center, http://galenet.galegroup.com; and "Microsoft Researchers Collaborate to Change the World," *Agence France Presse*, March 6, 2007, http://www.afp.com.

109. R. M. Kanter, *The Change Masters* (New York: Simon & Schuster, 1983).

110. D. Kuratko, R. D. Ireland, and J. Hornsby, "Improving Firm Performance through Entrepreneurial Actions: Acordia's Corporate Entrepreneurship Strategy," *Academy of Management Executive* 15 (2001), pp. 60–71.

111. Collins and Porras, *Built to Last.*

112. R. M. Kanter, C. Ingols, E. Morgan, and T. K. Seggerman, "Driving Corporate Entrepreneurship," *Management Review* 76 (April 1987), pp. 14–16.

113. J. Argenti, *Corporate Collapse: The Causes and Symptoms* (New York: John Wiley & Sons, 1979).

114. Kanter et al., "Driving Corporate Entrepreneurship."

115. Y. Ling, Z. Simsek, M. Lubatkin, and J. Veiga, "Transformational Leadership's Role in Promoting Corporate Entrepreneurship: Examining the CEO–TMT Interface," *Academy of Management Journal*, 2008, pp. 557–76.

116. G. T. Lumpkin and G. G. Dess, "Clarifying the Entrepreneurial Orientation Construct and Linking It to Performance," *Academy of Management Review* 21 (1996), pp. 135–72.

117. H. J. Sapienza, E. Autio, G. George, and S. A. Zahra, "A Capabilities Perspective on the Effects of Early Internationalization on Firm Survival and Growth," *Academy of Management Review* 31, no. (2006), pp. 914–33.

118. T. Bateman and J. M. Crant, "The Proactive Dimension of Organizational Behavior," *Journal of Organizational Behavior* (1993), pp. 103–18.

119. Lumpkin and Dess, "Clarifying the Entrepreneurial Orientation Construct."

120. C. Pinchot and E. Pinchot, *The Intelligent Organization* (San Francisco: Barrett-Koehler, 1996).

121. Chipotle website; Strand, "From Fast-Rising to Fast Food"; Hemmerdinger, "Burrito Buzz in South Portland"; Reklaitis, "Chipotle's Steve Ells"; Kaplan, "Chipotle Founder"; Harlin, "Chipotle Surges on Hot Profit"; R. Ruggless, "Ells, Oliver Team Up in 'Boorito' Fundraiser," *Nation's Restaurant News*, October 18, 2010, p. 4; R. Ruggless and P. Frumkin, "Chipotle Plans Asian Fast-Casual Operation," *Nation's Restaurant News*, November 22, 2010, p. 4; and G. M. Stern, "Can a Tex-Mex Grill Dish Up Asian Food?" *Investor's Business Daily*, November 29, 2010, Business & Company Resource Center, http://galenet.galegroup.com.

Chapter 8

1. D. Clark and S. Tibken, "Cisco to Reduce Its Bureaucracy," *The Wall Street Journal*, May 6, 2011, http://online.wsj.com; "Cisco Reorganizes Sales Services Management Units," *eWeek*, May 5, 2011, Business & Company Resource Center, http://galenet.galegroup.com; P. Burrows and J. Galante, "Cisco Reins In Management System That Spurred Exodus at Top," *Bloomberg Businessweek*, May 31, 2011, http://www.businessweek.com; C. Tuna, "Chambers Vows 'Fix' as Cisco Stumbles," *The Wall Street Journal*, April 6, 2011, http://online.wsj.com; "Read John Chambers' Memo to Cisco Staff," *The Wall Street Journal*,

April 5, 2011, http://online.wsj.com; V. G. Kopytoff, "Contrite Cisco Regroups before Skeptical Wall Street," *The New York Times*, May 9, 2011, Business & Company Resource Center, http://galenet.galegroup.com; and J. Gallant, "Chambers: How I'll Make Cisco into IT's Biggest Player," *InfoWorld*, March 20, 2010, Business & Company Resource Center, http://galenet.galegroup.com.

2. R. N. Ashkenas and S. C. Francis, "Integration Managers: Special Leaders for Special Times," *Harvard Business Review* 78, no. 6 (November–December 2000), pp. 108–16.

3. A. West, "The Flute Factory: An Empirical Measurement of the Effect of the Division of Labor on Productivity and Production Cost," *American Economist* 43, no. 1 (Spring 1999), pp. 82–87.

4. P. Lawrence and J. Lorsch, *Organization and Environment* (Homewood, IL: Richard D. Irwin, 1969).

5. Ibid.; and B. L. Thompson, *The New Manager's Handbook* (New York: McGraw-Hill, 1994). See also S. Sharifi and K. S. Pawar, "Product Design as a Means of Integrating Differentiation," *Technovation* 16, no. 5 (May 1996), pp. 255–64; and W. B. Stevenson and J. M. Bartunek, "Power, Interaction, Position, and the Generation of Cultural Agreement in Organizations," *Human Relations* 49, no. 1 (January 1996), pp. 75–104.

6. P. Puranam, H. Singh, and M. Zollo, "Organizing for Innovation: Managing the Coordination-Autonomy Dilemma in Technology Acquisitions," *Academy of Management Journal* 49, no. 2 (2006), pp. 263–80.

7. M. S. Burns, "Taming the Wild West," *Game Developer*, March 1, 2010, Business & Company Resource Center, http://galenet.galegroup.com.

8. A. J. Ali, R. C. Camp, and M. Gibbs, "The Ten Commandments Perspective on Power and Authority in Organizations," *Journal of Business Ethics* 26, no. 4 (August 2000), pp. 351–61; and R. F. Pearse, "Understanding Organizational Power and Influence Systems," *Compensation & Benefits Management* 16, no. 4 (Autumn 2000), pp. 28–38.

9. J. Pfeffer, *Power: Why Some People Have It—and Others Don't* (New York: HarperCollins, 2010).

10. S. F. Shultz, *Board Book: Making Your Corporate Board a Strategic Force in Your Company's Success* (New York: AMACOM, 2000); and R. D. Ward, *Improving Corporate Boards: The Boardroom Insider Guidebook* (New York: John Wiley & Sons, 2000).

11. T. Perkins, "The 'Compliance Board,'" *The Wall Street Journal*, March 2, 2007, http://online.wsj.com.

12. J. Tester, "Who's Your 'Lawnmower'?" *Plumbing and Mechanical*, November 2008, Business & Company Resource Center, http://galenet.galegroup.com.

13. C. M. Daily and D. R. Dalton, "CEO and Board Chair Roles Held Jointly or Separately: Much Ado about Nothing?" *Academy of Management Executive* 11, no. 3 (August 1997), pp. 11–20.

14. T. Simons, L. H. Pelled, and K. A. Smith, "Making Use of Difference: Diversity, Debate, and Decision Comprehensiveness in Top Management Teams," *Academy of Management Journal* 42, no. 6 (December 1999), pp. 662–73; and C. Carl Pegels, Y. I Song, and B. Yang, "Management Heterogeneity, Competitive Interaction Groups, and Firm Performance," *Strategic Management Journal* 21, no. 3 (September 2000), pp. 911–21.

15. S. Vickery, C. Droge, and R. Germain, "The Relationship between Product Customization and Organizational Structure," *Journal of Operations Management* 17, no. 4 (June 1999), pp. 377–91.

16. J. Spolsky, "How Hard Could It Be? How I Learned to Love Middle Managers," *Inc.*, September 2008, http://www.inc.com.

17. D. Van Fleet and A. Bedeian, "A History of the Span of Management," *Academy of Management Review* 2 (1977), pp. 356–72.

18. P. Jehiel, "Information Aggregation and Communication in Organizations," *Management Science* 45, no. 5 (May 1999), pp. 659–69; and A. Altaffer, "First-Line Managers: Measuring Their Span of Control," *Nursing Management* 29, no. 7 (July 1998), pp. 36–40.

19. "Span of Control vs. Span of Support," *Journal for Quality and Participation* 23, no. 4 (Fall 2000), p. 15; J. Gallo and P. R. Thompson, "Goals, Measures, and Beyond: In Search of Accountability in Federal HRM," *Public Personnel Management* 29, no. 2 (Summer 2000), pp. 237–48; C. O. Longenecker and T. C. Stansfield, "Why Plant Managers Fail: Causes and Consequences," *Industrial Management* 42, no. 1 (January/February 2000), pp. 24–32.

20. S. Erker and B. Thomas, "Finding the First Rung," Thought Leadership Research, 2010, http://www.ddiworld.com.

21. Z. X. Chen and S. Aryee, "Delegation and Employee Work Outcomes: An Examination of the Cultural Context of Mediating Processes in China," *Academy of Management Journal* 50, no. 1 (2007), pp. 226–38.

22. "How to Delegate More Effectively," *Community Banker*, February 2009, p. 14; B. Nefer, "Don't Be Delegation-Phobic," *Supervision*, December 2008, Business & Company Resource Center, http://galenet.galegroup.com; J. Mahoney, "Delegating Effectively," *Nursing Management* 28, no. 6 (June 1997), p. 62; and J. Lagges, "The Role of Delegation in Improving Productivity," *Personnel Journal*, November 1979, pp. 776–79.

23. G. Matthews, "Run Your Business or Build an Organization?" *Harvard Management Review*, March–April 1984, pp. 34–44.

24. N. Siggelkow and J. W. Rivkin, "When Exploration Backfires: Unintended Consequences of Multi-level Organizational Search," *Academy of Management Proceedings*, 2006, pp. BB1–BB6.

25. "Rich Ross and His Decentralized Magic Kingdom: Is It Working?" *The Wrap*, April 28, 2011, http://www.thewrap.com; B. Fenton, "Silver Screen Man with a Golden Touch," *Financial Times*, Business & Company Resource Center, http://galenet.galegroup.com; and B. Barnes, "New Team Alters Disney Studios' Path," *The New York Times*, September 27, 2010, Business & Company Resource Center, http://galenet.galegroup.com.

26. J. R. Hollenbeck, A. P. J. Ellis, S. E. Humphrey, A. S. Garza, and D. R. Ilgen, "Asymmetry in Structural Adaptation: The Differential Impact of Centralizing versus Decentralizing Team Decision-Making Structures," *Organizational Behavior and Human Decision Processes* 114 (2011), pp. 64–74.

27. R. Forrester, "Empowerment: Rejuvenating a Potent Idea," *Academy of Management Executive* 14, no. 3 (August 2000), pp. 67–80; and M. L. Perry, C. L. Pearce, and H. P. Sims Jr., "Empowered Selling Teams: How Shared Leadership Can Contribute to Selling Team Outcomes," *Journal of Personal Selling & Sales Management* 19, no. 3 (Summer 1999), pp. 35–51.

28. G. Colvin and J. Shambora, "J&J: Secrets of Success," *Fortune*, April 22, 2009, http://money.cnn.com.

29. L. Gard, "Growth Trifecta," *Construction Today*, January 2009, Business & Company Resource Center, http://galenet.galegroup.com; and Environmental Systems Design, "About ESD," corporate website, http://www.esdesign.com.

30. E. E. Lawler III, "New Roles for the Staff Function: Strategic Support and Services," in *Organizing for the Future*, J. Galbraith, E. E. Lawler III, & Associates (San Francisco: Jossey-Bass, 1993).

31. R. Cross and L. Baird, "Technology Is Not Enough: Improving Performance by Building Organizational Memory," *Sloan Management Review* 41, no. 3 (Spring 2000), pp. 69–78; and R. Duncan, "What Is the Right Organizational Structure?" *Organizational Dynamics* 7 (Winter 1979), pp. 59–80.

32. Company website, http://www.astrazeneca-us.com, accessed June 11, 2007; B. Heffernan, "Avoiding Disconnected DTC," *DTC Perspectives*, http://www.dtcperspectives.com; and "Cross-Functional Teams: Collaboration Best Practices for Pharmaceutical Commercialization Success," *PR Newswire*, May 2, 2007, http://www.prnewswire.com.

33. G. S. Day, "Creating a Market-Driven Organization," *Sloan Management Review* 41, no. 1 (Fall 1999), pp. 11–22.

34. R. Boehm and C. Phipps, "Flatness Forays," *McKinsey Quarterly* 3 (1996), pp. 128–43.

35. B. T. Lamont, V. Sambamurthy, K. M. Ellis, and P. G. Simmonds, "The Influence of Organizational Structure on the Information Received by Corporate Strategists of Multinational Enterprises," *Management International Review* 40, no. 3 (2000), pp. 231–52.

36. L. A. Johnson, "Pfizer Planning to Redraw Its Battle Lines," *America's Intelligence Wire*, October 8, 2008, Business & Company Resource Center, http://galenet.galegroup.com.

37. T. Stynes and P. Ziobro, "Avon Plans Restructuring," *The Wall Street Journal*, February 24, 2011, http://online.wsj.com.

38. M. T. Hansen, "When Internal Collaboration Is Bad for Your Company," *Harvard Business Review*, April 2009, pp. 83–88.

39. W. Bernasco, P. C. de WeerdNederhof, H. Tillema, and H. Boer, "Balanced Matrix Structure and New Product Development Process at Texas Instruments Materials and Controls Division," *R&D Management* 29, no. 2 (April 1999), pp. 121–31; J. K. McCollum, "The Matrix Structure: Bane or Benefit to High Tech Organizations?" *Project Management Journal* 24, no. 2 (June 1993), pp. 23–26; R. C. Ford, "Cross-Functional Structures: A Review and Integration of Matrix," *Journal of Management* 18, no. 2 (June 1992), pp. 267–94; and H. Kolodny, "Managing in a Matrix," *Business Horizons*, March–April 1981, pp. 17–24.

40. D. Cackowski, M. K. Najdawi, and Q. B. Chung, "Object Analysis in Organizational Design: A Solution for Matrix Organizations," *Project Management Journal* 31, no. 3 (September 2000), pp. 44–51; J. Barker, "Conflict Approaches of Effective and Ineffective Project Managers: A Field Study in a Matrix Organization," *Journal of Management Studies* 25, no. 2 (March 1988), pp. 167–78; G. J. Chambers, "The Individual in a Matrix Organization," *Project Management Journal* 20, no. 4 (December 1989), pp. 37–42, 50; and S. Davis and P. Lawrence, "Problems of Matrix Organizations," *Harvard Business Review*, May–June 1978, pp. 131–42.

41. A. Ferner, "Being Local Worldwide: ABB and the Challenge of Global Management Relations," *Industrielles* 55, no. 3 (Summer 2000), pp. 527–29; and C. Bartlett and S. Ghoshal, "Matrix Management: Not a Structure, a Frame of Mind," *Harvard Business Review* 68 (July–August 1990), pp. 138–45.

42. J. Tata, S. Prasad, and R. Thorn, "The Influence of Organizational Structure on the Effectiveness of TQM Programs," *Journal of Managerial Issues* 11, no. 4 (Winter 1999), pp. 440–53; and Davis and Lawrence, "Problems of Matrix Organizations."

43. R. E. Miles and C. C. Snow, *Fit, Failure, and the Hall of Fame* (New York: Free Press, 1994); and G. Symon, "Information and Communication Technologies and Network Organization: A Critical Analysis," *Journal of Occupational and Organizational Psychology* 73, no. 4 (December 2000), pp. 389–95.

44. Clark and Tibken, "Cisco to Reduce Its Bureaucracy"; Burrows and Galante, "Cisco Reins In Management System"; "Read John Chambers' Memo"; Gallant, "Chambers: How I'll Make Cisco into IT's Biggest Player"; R. M. Kanter, "Cisco and a Cautionary Tale about Teams," *Harvard Business Review*, May 9, 2011, http://www.bloomberg.com; B. Worthen, "Seeking Growth, Cisco Reroutes Decisions," *The Wall Street Journal*, August 6, 2009, http://online.wsj.com; and C. Berndtson, "Cisco to Restructure Top Units, Cut Down on Internal Councils," *CRN*, May 5, 2011, http://www.crn.com.

45. D. Dahl, "A Radical Take on the Virtual Company," *Inc.*, March 1, 2011, http://www.inc.com.

46. Miles and Snow, *Fit, Failure, and the Hall of Fame*.

47. S. C. Kang, S. S. Morris, and S. A. Snell, "Relational Archetypes, Organizational Learning, and Value Creation: Extending the Human Resource Architecture," *Academy of Management Review* 32, no. 1 (2007), pp. 236–56.

48. J. G. March and H. A. Simon, *Organizations* (New York: John Wiley & Sons, 1958); and J. D. Thompson, *Organizations in Action* (New York: McGraw-Hill, 1967).

49. P. S. Adler, "Building Better Bureaucracies," *Academy of Management Executive* 13, no. 4 (November 1999), pp. 36–49.

50. N. D. Kho, "Embedded Librarianship: Building Relational Roles," *Information Today*, March 2011, pp. 1, 35–36.

51. J. Galbraith, "Organization Design: An Information Processing View," *Interfaces* 4 (Fall 1974), pp. 28–36. See also S. A. Mohrman, "Integrating Roles and Structure in the Lateral Organization," in *Organizing for the Future*, ed. J. Galbraith, E. E. Lawler III, and Associates (San Francisco: Jossey-Bass, 1993); and B. B. Flynn and F. J. Flynn, "Information-Processing Alternatives for Coping with Manufacturing Environment Complexity," *Decision Sciences* 30, no. 4 (Fall 1999), pp. 1021–52.

52. Galbraith, "Organization Design," and Mohrman, "Integrating Roles and Structure."

53. Clark and Tibken, "Cisco to Reduce Its Bureaucracy"; Burrows and Galante, "Cisco Reins In Management System"; "Read John Chambers' Memo";

Kanter, "Cisco and a Cautionary Tale"; Berndtson, "Cisco to Restructure Top Units"; S. Anthony, "Are Cisco's Committees a Better Way to Innovate?" *Harvard Business Review*, August 12, 2009, http://blogs.hbr.org; T. Poletti, "Cisco Should Ditch Committee Structure," *MarketWatch*, April 14, 2011, http://www.marketwatch.com; and J. Galante, "Cisco Names Moore to Newly Created Operations Chief Position," *Bloomberg Businessweek*, February 22, 2011, http://www.businessweek.com.

Chapter 9

1. P. Sims, "The Case Study: Pixar's Strategy for Improving Constantly," *Financial Times*, April 21, 2011, Business & Company Resource Center, http://galenet.galegroup.com; "Pixar Turns 25," *Fast Company*, February 3, 2011, http://www.fastcompany.com; T. Davenport, "Five Ways Pixar Makes Better Decisions," *Bloomberg Businessweek*, July 20, 2010, http://www.businessweek.com; B. Mirza, "Creative Endeavors," *HR Magazine*, April 2011, pp. 34–35; A. Lane, "The Fun Factory," *New Yorker*, May 16, 2011, pp. 74–87; D. A. Shaywitz, "Where the Action Is," *The Wall Street Journal*, April 22, 2011, http://online.wsj.com; and J. Lehrer, "Animating a Blockbuster: How Pixar Built *Toy Story 3*," *Wired*, May 24, 2010, http://www.wired.com.

2. C. O'Reilly and M. M. Tushman, "Ambidexterity as a Dynamic Capability: Resolving the Innovator's Dilemma," Research Paper no. 1963, Stanford Graduate School of Business, March 2007, http://ssrn.com/abstract=978419.

3. P. M. Wright, L. Dyer, and M. G. Takla, "What's Next? Key Findings from the 1999 State-of-the-Art and Practice Study," *Human Resource Planning* 22, no. 4 (1999), pp. 12–20; and Donald Sull, "How to Thrive in Turbulent Markets," *Harvard Business Review*, February 2009, pp. 78–88.

4. T. Burns and G. Stalker, *The Management of Innovation* (London: Tavistock, 1961).

5. D. Krackhardt and J. R. Hanson, "Information Networks: The Company behind the Chart," *Harvard Business Review*, July–August 1993, pp. 104–11.

6. G. Hamel and C. K. Prahalad, "Competing for the Future," *Harvard Business Review*, July–August 1994, pp. 122–28.

7. G. Hamel and C. K. Prahalad, *Competing for the Future* (Boston: Harvard Business School Press, 1994).

8. D. G. Sirmon, M. A. Hitt, and R. D. Ireland, "Managing Firm Resources in Dynamic Environments to Create Value: Looking inside the Black Box," *Academy of Management Review* 32, no. 1 (2007), pp. 273–92.

9. J. Cohen, "Getting Rid of the Busy Work So You Can Get to Work," *Management Innovation eXchange*, June 25, 2010, http://www.managementexchange.com; and G. Hamel with P. Labarre, "Improving Our Capacity to Manage," *The Wall Street Journal*, April 6, 2011, http://blogs.wsj.com.

10. "Monster, NYT Form Online Jobs Alliance," *Reuters*, February 14, 2007, http://news.yahoo.com.

11. D. Grossman, "Airline Alliances Aim for Integration," *USA Today*, March 25, 2007, http://www.usatoday.com.

12. G. Slowinski, E. Hummel, A. Gupta, and E. R. Gilmont, "Effective Practices for Sourcing Innovation," *Research-Technology Management*, January–February 2009, pp. 27–34.

13. R. C. Sampson, "R&D Alliances and Firm Performance: The Impact of Technological Diversity and Alliance Organization on Innovation," *Academy of Management Journal* 50, no. 2 (2007), pp. 364–86.

14. R. M. Kanter, "Collaborative Advantage: The Art of Alliances," *Harvard Business Review*, July–August 1999, pp. 96–108; J. B. Cullen, J. L. Johnson, and T. Sakano, "Success through Commitment and Trust: The Soft Side of Strategic Alliance Management," *Journal of World Business* 35, no. 3 (Fall 2000), pp. 223–40; and P. Kale, H. Singh, and H. Perlmutter, "Learning and Protection of Proprietary Assets in Strategic Alliances: Building Relational Capital," *Strategic Management Journal* 21, no. 3 (March 2000), pp. 217–37.

15. P. Senge, *The Fifth Discipline* (New York: Doubleday Currency, 1990).

16. D. A. Garvin, "Building a Learning Organization," *Harvard Business Review*, July–August 1993, pp. 78–91; D. A. Garvin, *Learning in Action: A Guide to Putting the Learning Organization to Work* (Boston: Harvard Business School Press, 2000); and V. J. Marsick and K. E. Watkins, *Facilitating Learning Organizations: Making Learning Count* (Aldershot, Hampshire: Gower, 1999).

17. Ibid.; and N. Anand, H. K. Gardner, and T. Morris, "Knowledge-Based Innovation: Emergence and Embedding of New Practice Areas in Management Consulting Firms," *Academy of Management Journal* 50, no. 2 (2007), pp. 406–28.

18. J. G. March, "Exploration and Exploitation in Organizational Learning," *Organization Science* 2, no. 1 (February 1991), pp. 71–87; and S.-C. Kang and S. A. Snell, "Intellectual Capital Architectures and Ambidextrous Learning: A Framework for Human Resource Management," *Journal of Management Studies* 46, no. 1 (2009), pp. 65–92.

19. R. J. Vandenberg, H. A. Richardson, and L. J. Eastman, "The Impact of High Involvement Work Process on Organizational Effectiveness: A Second-Order Latent Variable Approach," *Group & Organization Management* 24, no. 3 (September 1999), pp. 300–39; G. M. Spreitzer and A. K. Mishra, "Giving Up Control without Losing Control: Trust and Its Substitutes' Effects on Managers' Involving Employees in Decision Making," *Group & Organization Management* 24, no. 2 (June 1999), pp. 155–87; and S. Albers Mohrman, G. E. Ledford, and E. E. Lawler III, *Strategies for High Performance Organizations—The CEO Report: Employee Involvement, TQM, and Reengineering Programs in Fortune 1000 Corporations* (San Francisco: Jossey-Bass, 1998).

20. R. Pagnamenta, "Transformation That Could Rescue Unilever from the Slippery Slope," *The Times (London)*, January 3, 2007; and "Unilever on Revival Track after Top Managers Culled," *Evening Standard (London)*, May 3, 2007, Business & Company Resource Center, http://galenet.galegroup.com.

21. "Alfred Chandler," *The Economist*, May 17, 2007, http://www.economist.com; C. Farrell, "Alfred Chandler: Big Business' Big Loss," *Bloomberg Businessweek*, May 14, 2007, http://www.businessweek.com.

22. A. Bianco, "Wal-Mart's Midlife Crisis," *BusinessWeek*, April 30, 2007, http://www.businessweek.com.

23. Small Business Administration, "Advocacy Small Business Statistics and Research," Frequently Asked Questions, http://web.sba.gov.

24. Pagnamenta, "Transformation That Could Rescue Unilever."

25. L. L. Hellofs and R. Jacobson, "Market Share and Customers' Perceptions of Quality: When Can Firms Grow Their Way to Higher versus Lower Quality?" *Journal of Marketing* 63, no. 1 (January 1999), pp. 16–25.

26. J. Dean, "The Greatly Improbable, Highly Enjoyable, Increasingly Profitable Life of Michael Kobold," *Inc.*, May 2007, pp. 126–34.

27. B. Del Conte, "Manufacturing Plant as Classroom: Reinventing Continuous Learning," *Plant Engineering*, March 1, 2009, Business & Company Resource Center, http://galenet.galegroup.com.

28. V. Vara, "After GE," *The Wall Street Journal*, April 12, 2007, http://online.wsj.com.

29. Ibid.

30. W. F. Cascio, "Downsizing: What Do We Know? What Have We Learned?" *Academy of Management Executive* 7 (February 1993), pp. 95–104; and S. J. Freeman, "The Gestalt of Organizational Downsizing: Downsizing Strategies as Package of Change," *Human Relations* 52, no. 12 (December 1999), pp. 1505–41.

31. A. Vance, "Microsoft Slashes Jobs as Sales Fall," *New York Times*, January 23, 2009, http://www.nytimes.com; A. Vance, "Microsoft Profit Falls for First Time in 23 Years," *New York Times*, April 24, 2009, http://www.nytimes.com; and P. Kafka, "Microsoft

Starts the Layoff Machine Again with Thousands of Cuts," *All Things Digital*, http://mediamemo.allthingsd.com.

32. W. F. Cascio, "Strategies for Responsible Restructuring," *Academy of Management Executive* 19, no. 4 (2005), pp. 39–50; Cascio, "Downsizing: What Do We Know?"; Freeman, "The Gestalt of Organizational Downsizing"; and M. Hitt, B. Keats, H. Harback, and R. Nixon, "Rightsizing: Building and Maintaining Strategic Leadership and Long-Term Competitiveness," *Organizational Dynamics*, Fall 1994, pp. 18–31.

33. C. D. Zatzick and R. D. Iverson, "High-Involvement Management and Workforce Reduction: Competitive Advantage or Disadvantage?" *Academy of Management Journal* 49, no. 5 (2006), pp. 999–1015.

34. Cascio, "Strategies for Responsible Restructuring"; Cascio, "Downsizing"; and J. Ciancio, "Survivor's Syndrome," *Nursing Management* 31, no. 5 (May 2000), pp. 43–45.

35. Sims, "The Case Study"; Davenport, "Five Ways Pixar Makes Better Decisions"; Mirza, "Creative Endeavors"; Lane, "The Fun Factory"; Lehrer, "Animating a Blockbuster"; H. Rao, R. Sutton, and A. P. Webb, "Innovation Lessons from Pixar: An Interview with Oscar-Winning Director Brad Bird," *McKinsey Quarterly*, April 2008, https://www.mckinseyquarterly.com; and P. Sims, "In on the Joke: Collaboration through Humor," *Fast Company*, April 22, 2011, http://www.fastcompany.com.

36. T. Wailgum, "CRM Definition and Solutions," *CIO*, March 6, 2007, http://www.cio.com; M. Burns, "CRM Survey 2011," *CA Magazine*, May 2011, http://www.camagazine.com; and M. Burns, "CRM Survey 2010," *CA Magazine*, April 2010, http://www.camagazine.com.

37. C. Dawson, "Toyota, Salesforce.com to Create Social Media Network for Vehicles," *The Wall Street Journal*, May 23, 2011, http://online.wsj.com; A. Eichler, "Prius Drivers Will Get Their Own Social Network," *The Atlantic*, May 23, 2011, http://www.theatlanticwire.com; C. Chiappinelli, "Toyota Taps Salesforce CRM Technology to Link Customers to Their Cars," *Managing Automation*, May 24, 2011, http://www.managingautomation.com; and A. Censky, "Toyota Wants You to Friend Your Car. Really," *CNNMoney*, May 23, 2011, http://money.cnn.com.

38. "Salesforce.com Offers Twitter Customer-Service App," *Information Week*, March 23, 2009, Business & Company Resource Center, http://galenet.galegroup.com; and E. Beck, "Daptiv's Greenhouse: Collaboration Grows," *BusinessWeek Online*, June 12, 2008, Business & Company Resource Center, http://galenet.galegroup.com.

39. K. Ishikawa, *What Is Total Quality Control? The Japanese Way*, trans.

D. J. Lu (Englewood Cliffs, NJ: Prentice-Hall, 1985); and J. Seibert and J. Lingle, "Internal Customer Service: Has It Improved?" *Quality Progress* 40, no. 3 (March 2007), OCLC FirstSearch, http://firstsearch.oclc.org.

40. M. Porter, *Competitive Advantage: Creating and Sustaining Superior Performance* (New York: Free Press, 1985); and Internet Center for Management and Business Administration, "The Value Chain," Strategy pages, *NetMBA*, http://www.netmba.com.

41. B. Creech, *The Five Pillars of TQM: How to Make Total Quality Management Work for You* (New York: Plume Publishing, 1995); and J. R. Evans and W. M. Lindsay, *Management and Control of Quality* (Mason, OH: South-Western College Publishing, 1998).

42. National Institute of Standards and Technology, "Seven U.S. Organizations Honored with the 2010 Baldrige National Quality Award," news release, November 23, 2010, http://www.nist.gov.

43. International Organization for Standardization, "ISO 9000—Quality Management," http://www.iso.org.

44. "Local Chemical Distributor Gets Fourth Quality Certification through CMTC Assistance," *Wireless News*, May 19, 2011, Business & Company Resource Center, http://galenet.galegroup.com; and California Manufacturing Technology Consulting, "Quality Management—Industrial Case Study: Miles Chemical Supply, Inc.," Success Stories, http://www.cmtc.com.

45. J. Champy, *Reengineering Management* (New York: HarperBusiness, 1995). See also M. Hammer and J. Champy, *Reengineering the Corporation* (New York: HarperCollins, 1992).

46. J. Woodward, *Industrial Organization: Theory and Practice* (London: Oxford University Press, 1965).

47. J. H. Gilmore and B. J. Pine, eds., *Markets of One: Creating Customer-Unique Value through Mass Customization* (Cambridge, MA: Harvard Business Review Press, 2000); and B. J. Pine, *Mass Customization: The New Frontier in Business Competition* (Cambridge, MA: Harvard Business School Press, 1992).

48. F. Sahin, "Manufacturing Competitiveness: Different Systems to Achieve the Same Results," *Production and Inventory Management Journal* 41, no. 1 (First Quarter 2000), pp. 56–65.

49. S. Wadhwa and K. S. Rao, "Flexibility: An Emerging Meta-Competence for Managing High Technology," *International Journal of Technology Management* 19, no. 7–8 (2000), pp. 820–45.

50. B. A. Peters and L. F. McGinnis, "Strategic Configuration of Flexible Assembly Systems: A Single Period Approximation," *IIE Transaction* 31, no. 4 (April 1999), pp. 379–90.

51. J. K. Liker and J. M. Morgan, "The Toyota Way in Services: The Case of

Lean Product Development," *Academy of Management Perspectives* 20, no. 2 (May 2006), pp. 5–20; "Strategic Reconfiguration: Manufacturing's Key Role in Innovation," *Production and Inventory Management Journal* (Summer–Fall 2001), pp. 9–17; J. Jusko, "Lean Confusion," *Industry Week*, September 2010, pp. 32–34; and Sahin, "Manufacturing Competitiveness."

52. Liker and Morgan, "The Toyota Way in Services"; and H. Cho, "Squeezing the Fat from Health Care," *Baltimore Sun*, September 17, 2006, Business & Company Resource Center, http://galenet.galegroup.com.

53. Sahin, "Manufacturing Competitiveness"; and G. S. Vasilash, "Flexible Thinking: How Need, Innovation, Teamwork & a Whole Bunch of Machining Centers Have Transformed TRW Tillsonburg into a Model of Lean Manufacturing," *Automotive Manufacturing & Production* 111, no. 10 (October 1999), pp. 64–65.

54. T. Aeppel and J. Lahart, "Lean Factories Find It Hard to Cut Jobs Even in a Slump," *The Wall Street Journal*, March 9, 2009, http://online.wsj.com.

55. C. H. Chung, "Balancing the Two Dimensions of Time for Time-Based Competition," *Journal of Managerial Issues* 11, no. 3 (Fall 1999), pp. 299–314; and D. R. Towill and P. McCullen, "The Impact of Agile Manufacturing on Supply Chain Dynamics," *International Journal of Logistics Management* 10, no. 1 (1999), pp. 83–96. See also G. Stalk and T. M. Hout, *Competing against Time: How Time-Based Competition Is Reshaping Global Markets* (New York: Free Press, 1990).

56. M. Hayes Weier, "Best Buy Sees a Growth Future in RFID," *EE Times*, March 27, 2007, http://www.eetimes.com.

57. A. M. Field, "Where Have All the Flowers Gone?" *Journal of Commerce*, April 16, 2007, Business & Company Resource Center, http://galenet.galegroup.com.

58. M. Settle, "How to Use Virtualization to Save Money and Improve Service Quality," *eWeek*, August 23, 2010, Business & Company Resource Center, http://galenet.galegroup.com.

59. C. Robbins Gentry, "Back-Room Secrets: Just-in-Time Deliveries Optimize Space," *Chain Store Age*, March 2007, Business & Company Resource Center, http://galenet.galegroup.com.

60. R. Miel and D. Sedgwick, "Just-in-Time Seats Die Out," *Automotive News*, August 4, 2010, Business & Company Resource Center, http://galenet.galegroup.com.

61. J. E. Ettlie, "Product Development—Beyond Simultaneous Engineering," *Automotive Manufacturing & Production* 112, no. 7 (July 2000), p. 18; U. Roy, J. M. Usher, and H. R. Parsaei, eds. *Simultaneous Engineering: Methodologies*

and Applications (Newark, NJ: Gordon and Breach, 1999); and M. M. Helms and L. P. Ettkin, "Time-Based Competitiveness: A Strategic Perspective," *Competitiveness Review* 10, no. 2 (2000), pp. 1–14.

62. J. Zygmont, "Detroit Faster on Its Feet," *Ward's Auto World*, July 1, 2006, Business & Company Resource Center, http://galenet.galegroup.com.

63. R. Ashkenas, D. Ulrich, T. Jick, and S. Kerr, *The Boundaryless Organization: Breaking the Chains of Organizational Structure* (San Francisco: Jossey-Bass, 1995); R. W. Keidel, "Rethinking Organizational Design," *Academy of Management Executive*, November 1994, pp. 12–27; and R. Ashkenas, T. Jick, D. Ulrich, and C. Paul-Chowdhury, *The Boundaryless Organization Field Guide: Practical Tools for Building the New Organization* (San Francisco: Jossey-Bass, 1999).

64. Sims, "The Case Study"; "Pixar Turns 25"; Lane, "The Fun Factory"; Lehrer, "Animating a Blockbuster"; Rao et al., "Innovation Lessons from Pixar"; D. Cohen, "As It Ramps Up, Pixar's under Pressure," *Daily Variety*, May 12, 2011, p. 2; and P. Sims, "Pixar's Motto: Going from Suck to Nonsuck," *Fast Company*, March 25, 2011, http://www.fastcompany.com.

Chapter 10

1. J. Light, "Google Is No. 1 on List of Desired Employers," *The Wall Street Journal*, March 21, 2011, http://online.wsj.com; "100 Best Companies to Work For," *Fortune*, February 7, 2011, http://money.cnn.com; R. Waters, "Google Tries New Angle on Hiring," *Financial Times*, February 7, 2011, Business & Company Resource Center, http://galenet.galegroup.com; Digits, "Want to Work for Google? Here's How," *The Wall Street Journal*, June 8, 2011, http://online.wsj.com (video; interview with Joseph Walker); A. Efrati, "High Costs Slow Google's Profit," *The Wall Street Journal*, April 15, 2011, http://online.wsj.com; M. Liedtke and B. Ortutay, "Google Wants to Be Cool Again," *Houston Chronicle*, January 22, 2011, Business & Company Resource Center, http://galenet.galegroup.com; and M. Swift, "Google to Hire at Least 6,000 Workers 'across the Board,'" *San Jose Mercury News*, Business & Company Resource Center, http://galenet.galegroup.com.

2. N. Gardner, D. McGranahan, and W. Wolf, "Question for Your HR Chief: Are We Using Our 'People Data' to Create Value?" *McKinsey Quarterly*, March 2011, https://www.mckinseyquarterly.com.

3. "HR's Impact on Shareholder Value," *Workforce Management*, December 11, 2006, Business & Company Resource Center, http://galenet.galegroup.com.

4. P. M. Wright and S. A. Snell, "Partner or Guardian? HR's Challenge in Balancing Value and Values," *Human Resource Management* 44, no. 2 (2005), pp. 177–82.

5. E. Pofeldt, "Empty Desk Syndrome: How to Handle a Hiring Freeze," *Inc.*, May 2008, pp. 39–40; and C. Tuna, "Some Employers See Hiring Opportunity," *The Wall Street Journal*, April 3, 2009, http://online.wsj.com.

6. R. Mullins, "They're Loving It," *Tampa (Fla.) Tribune*, March 20, 2011, Business & Company Resource Center, http://galenet.galegroup.com; and J. R. Hagerty, "Help Wanted on Factory Floor," *The Wall Street Journal*, May 6, 2011, http://online.wsj.com.

7. S. Lohr, "Parsing the Truths about Visas for Tech Workers," *New York Times*, April 15, 2007, http://www.nytimes.com; "Does Silicon Valley Need More Visas for Foreigners?" *The Wall Street Journal*, March 19, 2007 (interview with Robert Hoffman and Ron Hira), http://online.wsj.com; P. Elstrom, "Work Visas May Work against the U.S.," *BusinessWeek*, February 8, 2007, http://www.businessweek.com; and A. Broache, "Does H-1B Surge Mean Cap Should Be Raised?" *CNet News*, April 5, 2007, http://news.com.com.

8. J. Marquez, "Retrained and Ready," *Workforce Management*, May 7, 2007, http://galenet.galegroup.com.

9. D. E. Hartley, *Job Analysis at the Speed of Reality* (Amherst, MA: HRD Press, 1999); F. P. Morgeson and M. A. Campion, "Accuracy in Job Analysis: Toward an Inference-Based Model," *Journal of Organizational Behavior* 21, no. 7 (November 2000), pp. 819–27; and J. S. Shippmann, R. A. Ash, L. Carr, and B. Hesketh, "The Practice of Competency Modeling," *Personnel Psychology* 53, no. 3 (Autumn 2000), pp. 703–40.

10. J. S. Schippmann, *Strategic Job Modeling: Working at the Core of Integrated Human Resources* (Mahwah, NJ: Lawrence Erlbaum Associates, 1999).

11. D. E. Terpstra, "The Search for Effective Methods," *HR Focus*, May 1996, pp. 16–17; H. G. Heneman III and R. A. Berkley, "Applicant Attraction Practices and Outcomes among Small Businesses," *Journal of Small Business Management* 37, no. 1 (January 1999), pp. 53–74; and J.-M. Hiltrop, "The Quest for the Best: Human Resource Practices to Attract and Retain Talent," *European Management Journal* 17, no. 4 (August 1999), pp. 422–30.

12. G. Crispin and M. Mehler, "10th Annual CareerXroads Source of Hire Report: by the Numbers," CareerXroads, March 2011, http://www.careerxroads.com; and J. Light, "Recruiters Rethink Online Playbook," *The Wall Street Journal*, January 18, 2011, http://online.wsj.com.

13. F. Hansen, "Employee Referral Programs, Selective Campus

14. T. E. Holmes, "Recruiting from the Military," *Black Enterprise*, October 2010, p. 64.

15. R. Myers, "Interviewing Techniques: Tips from the Pros," *Journal of Accountancy* (August 2006), Business & Company Resource Center, http://galenet.galegroup.com; M. McDaniel, D. L. Whetzel, F. L. Schmidt, and S. D. Maurer, "The Validity of Employment Interviews: A Comprehensive Review and Meta-Analysis," *Journal of Applied Psychology* 79, no. 4 (August 1994), pp. 599–616; M. A. Campion, J. E. Campion, and P. J. Hudson Jr., "Structured Interviewing: A Note on Incremental Validity and Alternative Question Types," *Journal of Applied Psychology* 79, no. 6 (December 1994), pp. 998–1002; and R. A. Fear, *The Evaluation Interview* (New York: McGraw-Hill, 1984).

16. Myers, "Interviewing Techniques."

17. U.S. Merit Systems Protection Board, "The Federal Selection Interview: Unrealized Potential," February 2003, mspb.gov/studies/interview.htm.

18. T. Lewin, "Dean at M.I.T. Resigns, Ending a 28-Year Lie," *New York Times*, April 27, 2007, http://www.nytimes.com.

19. D. Meinert, "Seeing behind the Mask," *HR Magazine*, February 2011, pp. 31–37.

20. Ibid., p. 37.

21. T. Ackerman, "Does Psych Testing Result in Better Hires?" *Houston Chronicle*, June 21, 2010, Business & Company Resource Center, http://galenet.galegroup.com; Center for Advanced Human Resource Studies, "Should Personality Testing Be Part of the Hiring Process?" CAHRS ResearchLink, no. 12, November 2010, http://digitalcommons.ilr.cornell.edu; and E. Frauenheim, "Personality Tests Adapt to the Times," *Workforce Management*, February 1, 2010, Business & Company Resource Center, http://galenet.galegroup.com.

22. R. E. Ployhart, J. A. Weekley, and K. Baughman, "The Structure and Function of Human Capital Emergence: A Multilevel Examination of the Attraction-Selection-Attrition Model," *Academy of Management Journal* 49, no. 4 (2006), pp. 661–77.

23. R. Zeidner, "Putting Drug Screening to the Test," *HR Magazine*, November 2010, ProQuest, http://proquest.umi.com.

24. C. Rubin, "Medical Marijuana Laws Leave Employers Dazed and Confused," *Inc.*, February 12, 2010, http://www.inc.com.

25. P. M. Wright, M. K. Kacmar, G. C. McMahan, and K. Deleeuw, "$P = f(M \times A)$: Cognitive Ability as a Moderator of the Relationship between Personality and Job Performance," *Journal of Management* 21, no. 6 (1995),

Recruitment Could Touch Off Bias Charges," *Workforce Management*, June 26, 2006, General Reference Center Gold, http://find.galegroup.com.

pp. 1129–2063; P. R. Sackett and D. J. Ostgaard, "Job-Specific Applicant Pools and National Norms for Cognitive Ability Tests: Implications for Range Restriction Corrections in Validation Research," *Journal of Applied Psychology* 79, no. 5 (October 1994), pp. 680–84; F. L. Schmidt and J. E. Hunter, "Tacit Knowledge, Practical Intelligence, General Mental Ability, and Job Knowledge," *Current Directions in Psychological Science* 2, no. 1 (1993), pp. 3–13; M. Roznowski, D. N. Dickter, L. L. Sawin, V. J. Shute, and S. Hong, "The Validity of Measures of Cognitive Processes and Generability for Learning and Performance on Highly Complex Computerized Tutors: Is the G Factor of Intelligence Even More General?" *Journal of Applied Psychology* 85, no. 6 (December 2000), pp. 940–55; and J. M. Cortina, N. B. Goldstein, S. C. Payne, H. K. Davison, and S. W. Gilliland, "The Incremental Validity of Interview Scores over and above Cognitive Ability and Conscientiousness Scores," *Personnel Psychology* 53, no. 2 (Summer 2000), pp. 325–51.

26. W. Arthur Jr., D. J. Woehr, and R. Maldegen, "Convergent and Discriminant Validity of Assessment Center Dimensions: A Conceptual and Empirical Reexamination of the Assessment Center Construct-Related Validity Paradox," *Journal of Management* 26, no. 4 (2000), pp. 813–35; and R. Randall, E. Ferguson, and F. Patterson, "Self-Assessment Accuracy and Assessment Center Decisions," *Journal of Occupational and Organizational Psychology* 73, no. 4 (December 2000), p. 443.

27. L. A. McFarland and A. M. Ryan, "Variance in Faking across Noncognitive Measures," *Journal of Applied Psychology* 85, no. 5 (October 2000), pp. 812–21. D. E. Terpstra, R. B. Kethley, R. T. Foley, and W. Limpaphayom, "The Nature of Litigation Surrounding Five Screening Devices," *Public Personnel Management* 29, no. 1 (Spring 2000), pp. 43–54.

28. D. S. Ones, C. Viswesvaran, and F. L. Schmidt, "Comprehensive Meta-Analysis of Integrity Test Validities: Findings and Implications for Personnel Selection and Theories of Job Performance," *Journal of Applied Psychology* 78 (August 1993), pp. 679–703.

29. S. Hananel, "Jobless People Need Not Apply?" *Houston Chronicle*, February 17, 2011, Business & Company Resource Center, http://galenet.galegroup.com.

30. Light, "Google Is No. 1"; Waters, "Google Tries New Angle"; Digits, "Want to Work for Google?"; A. Fisher, "So You Want to Work at Google," *Fortune*, April 7, 2011, http://management.fortune.cnn.com; and A. Bryant, "The Quest to Build a Better Boss," *New York Times*, March 13, 2011, Business & Company Resource Center, http://galenet.galegroup.com.

31. R.-L. DeWitt, "The Structural Consequences of Downsizing," *Organization Science* 4, no. 1 (February 1993), pp. 30–40; and P. P. Shah, "Network Destruction: The Structural Implications of Downsizing," *Academy of Management Journal* 43, no. 1 (February 2000), pp. 101–12.

32. See *Adair v. United States*, 2078 U.S. 161 (1908): and D. A. Ballam, "Employment-at-Will; The Impending Death of a Doctrine," *American Business Law Journal* 37, no. 4 (Summer 2000), pp. 653–87.

33. J. A. Segal, "A Warning about Warnings," *HR Magazine*, February 2009, pp. 67–70; International Public Management Association for Human Resources (IPMA-HR), "Progressive Discipline," IPMA-HR Website, http://www.ipma-hr.org; U.S. Chamber of Commerce, "Progressive Discipline," http://business.uschamber.com; and D. Grote, "Positive Approach to Employee Discipline," *ManagerNewz*, March 12, 2007, http://archive.managernewz.com.

34. J. W. Bucking, "Employee Terminations: Ten Must-Do Steps When Letting Someone Go," *Supervision*, May 2008, Business & Company Resource Center, http://galenet.galegroup.com; and M. Price, "Employee Termination Process Is Tough for Those on Both Sides," *Journal Record (Oklahoma City, OK)*, October 23, 2008, Business & Company Resource Center, http://galenet.galegroup.com.

35. *Employer EEO Responsibilities* (Washington, DC: Equal Employment Opportunity Commission, U.S. Government Printing Office, 1996); N. J. Edman and M. D. Levin-Epstein, *Primer of Equal Employment Opportunity*, 6th ed. (Washington, DC: Bureau of National Affairs, 1994).

36. Reuters, "Wal-Mart Settles Lawsuit on Hiring," *New York Times*, February 21, 2009, http://www.nytimes.com; T. L. Gallagher, "UP Settles Discrimination Suit," *Traffic World*, February 4, 2009, Business & Company Resource Center, http://galenet.galegroup.com; and A. Martinez, "Nordstrom Agrees to Pay to Settle Harassment Suit," *Seattle Times*, April 18, 2009, Business & Company Resource Center, http://galenet.galegroup.com.

37. R. Gatewood and H. Field, *Human Resource Selection*, 3rd ed. (Chicago: Dryden Press, 1994), pp. 36–49; and R. A. Baysinger, "Disparate Treatment and Disparate Impact Theories of Discrimination: The Continuing Evolution of Title VII of the 1964 Civil Rights Act," in *Readings in Personnel and Human Resource Management*, ed. R. S. Schuler, S. A. Youngblood, and V. L. Huber (St. Paul, MN: West Publishing, 1987).

38. L. Patel, "2010 State of the Industry: Continued Dedication to Workplace Learning," *T + D*, November 2010, pp. 48–53.

39. A. P. Carnevale, *America and the New Economy: How New Competitive Standards Are Radically Changing American Workplaces* (San Francisco: Jossey-Bass, 1991); M. Hequet, "Doing More with Less," *Training* 31 (October 1995), pp. 77–82; and R. M. Fulmer, P. A. Gibbs, and M. Goldsmith, "Developing Leaders: How Winning Companies Keep on Winning," *Sloan Management Review* 42, no. 1 (Fall 2000), pp. 49–59.

40. G. Anders, "Companies Find Online Training Has Its Limits," *The Wall Street Journal*, March 26, 2007, http://online.wsj.com.

41. Ibid.

42. University of Colorado Denver, "Study Shows Employees Learn Best from Video Games," news release, October 19, 2010, http://www.ucdenver.edu.

43. J. Gordon, "Building Brand Champions: How Training Helps Drive a Core Business Process at General Mills," *Training*, January–February 2007, General Reference Center Gold, http://find.galegroup.com.

44. P. Dvorak, "Simulation Shows What It's Like to Be Boss," *The Wall Street Journal*, March 31, 2008, http://online.wsj.com.

45. For more information, see K. Wexley and G. Latham, *Increasing Productivity through Performance Appraisal* (Reading, MA: Addison-Wesley, 1994).

46. F. Shipper, R. C. Hoffman, and D. M. Rotondo, "Does the 360 Feedback Process Create Actionable Knowledge Equally across Cultures?" *Academy of Management Learning & Education* 6, no. 1 (2007), pp. 33–50.

47. G. Toegel and J. Conger, "360 Degree Assessment: Time for Reinvention," *Academy of Management Learning and Education* 2, no. 3 (September 2003), p. 297; L. K. Johnson, "Retooling 360s for Better Performance," *Harvard Business School Working Knowledge*, February 23, 2004, online.

48. J. Light, "Human-Resources Executives Say Reviews Are off the Mark," *The Wall Street Journal*, November 8, 2010, http://online.wsj.com.

49. M. Edwards and A. J. Ewen, "How to Manage Performance and Pay with 360-Degree Feedback," *Compensation and Benefits Review* 28, no. 3 (May/June 1996), pp. 41–46. See also S. Crabtree, "What Your Employees Need to Know," *Gallup Management Journal*, April 13, 2011, Business & Company Resource Center, http://galenet.galegroup.com; and R. S. Schuler, *Personnel and Human Resource Management* (St. Paul, MN: West Publishing, 1984).

50. Bureau of Labor Statistics, "Employer Costs for Employee Compensation—March 2011," news release, June 8, 2011, http://www.bls.gov.

51. D. Darlin, "Using the Web to Get the Boss to Pay More," *New York Times*, March 3, 2007, http://www.nytimes.com.

52. A. Colella, R. L. Paetzold, A. Zardkoohi, and M. J. Wesson, "Exposing Pay Secrecy," *Academy of Management Review* 32, no. 1 (2007), pp. 55–71.

53. S. Gross and J. Bacher, "The New Variable Pay Programs: How Some Succeed, Why Some Don't," *Compensation and Benefits Review* 25, no. 1 (January–February 1993), p. 51; and G. T. Milkovich and J. M. Newman, *Compensation* (New York: McGraw-Hill/Irwin, 1999).

54. K. Maher and K. Hudson, "Wal-Mart to Sweeten Bonus Plans for Staff," *The Wall Street Journal*, March 22, 2007, http://online.wsj.com.

55. T. Welbourne and L. Gomez-Mejia, "Gainsharing: A Critical Review and a Future Research Agenda," *Journal of Management* 21, no. 3 (1995), pp. 559–609; L. P. Gomez-Mejia, T. M. Welbourne, and R. M. Wiseman, "The Role of Risk Sharing and Risk Taking under Gainsharing," *Academy of Management Review* 25, no. 3 (July 2000), pp. 492–507; D. Collins, *Gainsharing and Power: Lessons from Six Scanlon Plans* (Ithaca, NY: ILR Press, 1998); and P. K. Zingheim and J. R. Schuster, *Pay People Right!* (San Francisco: Jossey-Bass, 2000).

56. E. Krell, "All for Incentives, Incentives for All," *HR Magazine*, January 2011, pp. 35–38.

57. E. Grossfield, "Superintendent Gets a Good Review and Partial Bonus," *Post-Bulletin (Rochester, MN)*, July 13, 2006, Business & Company Resource Center, http://galenet.galegroup.com. See also D. W. Meyers, *Human Management: Principles and Practice* (Chicago: Commerce Clearing House, 1986); and J. P. Guthrie, "Alternative Pay Practices and Employee Turnover: An Organization Economics Perspective," *Group & Organization Management* 25, no. 4 (December 2000), pp. 419–39.

58. R. Kirkland, "The Real CEO Pay Problem," *Fortune*, July 10, 2006, Business & Company Resource Center, http://galenet.galegroup.com; K. Drawbaugh, "Soaring Executive Pay Meets Reforms," *Reuters*, March 9, 2007, http://news.yahoo.com; R. Watts and D. Roberts, "FTSE Pay Spirals out of Control," *Sunday Telegraph (London)*, September 24, 2006, http://galenet.galegroup.com; "Study: Australian Execs Outstrip Workers," *UPI NewsTrack*, January 28, 2006, http://galenet.galegroup.com; and M. Fackler and D. Barboza, "In Asia, Executives Earn Much Less," *New York Times*, June 16, 2006, http://galenet.galegroup.com.

59. M. J. Conyon, "Executive Compensation and Incentives," *Academy of Management Perspectives* 20, no. 1 (February 2006), pp. 25–44.

60. C. Forelle and J. Bandler, "The Perfect Payday," *The Wall Street Journal*, March 18, 2006, http://online.wsj.com.

61. Conyon, "Executive Compensation and Incentives."

62. J. D. Glater, "Stock Options Are Adjusted after Many Share Prices Fall," *New York Times*, March 27, 2009, http://www.nytimes.com; and D. Nicklaus, "Worthless Options Worry Companies," *St. Louis Post-Dispatch*, April 3, 2009, Business & Company Resource Center, http://galenet.galegroup.com.

63. S. Singhal, J. Stueland, and D. Ungerman, "How U.S. Health Care Reform Will Affect Employee Benefits," *McKinsey Quarterly*, June 2011, https://www.mckinseyquarterly.com; Mercer, "Few Employers Planning to Drop Health Plans after Reform Is in Place, Survey Finds," news release, November 9, 2010, http://www.mercer.com; and Avalere Health, "The Affordable Care Act's Impact on Employer Sponsored Insurance: A Look at the Microsimulation Models and Other Analyses," June 17, 2011, http://www.avalerehealth.net.

64. D. Cauchon, "Pension Gap Divides Public and Private Workers," *USA Today*, February 21, 2007, http://www.usatoday.com.

65. Employee Benefit Research Institute, "Employer Spending on Health Insurance," in *EBRI Databook on Employee Benefits*, updated March 2009, http://www.ebri.org.

66. E. C. Kearns and M. Gallagher, eds., *The Fair Labor Standards Act* (Washington, DC: BNA, 1999).

67. C. Fay and H. W. Risher, "Contractors, Comparable Worth and the New OFCCP: Deja Vu and More," *Compensation and Benefits Review* 32, no. 5 (September/October 2000), pp. 23–33; and G. Flynn, "Protect Yourself from an Equal-Pay Audit," *Workforce* 78, no. 6 (June 1999), pp. 144–46.

68. G. W. Bohlander, S. A. Snell, and A. W. Sherman Jr., *Managing Human Resources*, 12th ed. (Mason, OH: South-Western Publishing, 2001).

69. K. Maher, "Mine Probe Faults Massey," *The Wall Street Journal*, May 20, 2011, http://online.wsj.com.

70. Mine Safety and Health Administration, "Coal Fatalities for 1990 through 2010," Mining Fatality Statistics, http://www.msha.gov/stats/centurystats/coalstats.asp.

71. "U.S. Teens Work Late, Long and in Danger, Study," *Reuters*, March 5, 2007, http://news.yahoo.com; and C. K. Johnson, "Teens Tell about On-the-Job Dangers," *Chicago Tribune*, March 5, 2007, http://www.chicagotribune.com.

72. L. Kahn, *Primer of Labor Relations*, 25th ed. (Washington, DC: Bureau of National Affairs Books, 1994); and A. Sloane and F. Witney, *Labor Relations* (Englewood Cliffs, NJ: Prentice-Hall, 1985).

73. S. Premack and J. E. Hunter; "Individual Unionization Decisions," *Psychological Bulletin* 103 (1988), pp. 223–34; L. Troy, *Beyond Unions and Collective Bargaining* (Armonk, NY:

M. E. Sharpe, 1999); and J. A. McClendon, "Members and Nonmembers: Determinants of Dues-Paying Membership in a Bargaining Unit," *Relations Industrielles* 55, no. 2 (Spring 2000), pp. 332–47.

74. R. Sinclair and L. Tetrick, "Social Exchange and Union Commitment: A Comparison of Union Instrumentality and Union Support Perceptions," *Journal of Organizational Behavior* 16, no. 6 (November 1995), pp. 669–79. See also Premack and Hunter, "Individual Unionization Decisions."

75. D. Lewin and Richard B. Peterson, *The Modern Grievance Procedure in the United States* (Westport, CT: Quorum Books, 1998).

76. G. Bohlander and D. Blancero, "A Study of Reversal Determinants in Discipline and Discharge Arbitration Awards: The Impact of Just Cause Standards," *Labor Studies Journal* 21, no. 3 (Fall 1996), pp. 3–18.

77. Light, "Google Is No. 1"; Efrati, "High Costs Slow Google's Profit"; Liedtke and Ortutay, "Google Wants to Be Cool Again"; Swift, "Google to Hire at Least 6,000 Workers"; Bryant, "The Quest to Build a Better Boss"; A. Efrati and P. W. Tam, "Google Battles to Keep Talent," *The Wall Street Journal*, November 11, 2010, http://online.wsj.com; M. Ahmed, "Why Sensible Uncle Is Being Consigned to the Back Seat," *Times (London)*, January 22, 2011, Business & Company Resource Center, http://galenet.galegroup.com; and C. C. Miller, "New Stage, New Skills," *New York Times*, January 22, 2011, Business & Company Resource Center, http://galenet.galegroup.com.

Chapter 11

1. J. S. Lublin, "Nooyi Calls for More Women in Top Management," *The Wall Street Journal*, April 9, 2011, http://online.wsj.com; D. Bullock, "Most Influential CEOs: PepsiCo's Indra Nooyi Pushes for People Power, Diversity," *Minyanville*, May 28, 2010, http://www.minyanville.com; B. Zabcik, "Q&A: PepsiCo GC Maura Abeln Smith," *Corporate Counsel*, June 6, 2011, http://www.law.com; "Top Executives in Marketing and Advertising," *Black Enterprise*, February 2011, pp. 93–101; B. Hutson, "A Lasting Engagement," *Black Enterprise*, July 2010, p. 51; and E. B. York, "Dr. Mehmood Khan Taking on the PepsiCo Nutritional Challenge," *Chicago Tribune*, June 20, 2011, http://articles.chicagotribune.com.

2. B. Eisenberg and M. Ruthsdotter, "Living the Legacy: The Women's Rights Movement 1848–1998," National Women's History Project, http://www.legacy98.org/move-hist.html.

3. Ibid.; and Bureau of Labor Statistics, "Labor Force Statistics from the Current Population Survey," http://www.bls.gov/cps.

4. Bureau of Labor Statistics, "Employment Projections: 2006–16," news release, December 4, 2007, http://www.bls.gov.

5. Ibid.

6. Census Bureau, "Minority Population Tops 100 Million," news release, May 17, 2007, http://www.census.gov.

7. Bureau of Labor Statistics, "Household Data: Annual Averages," *Labor Force Statistics from the Current Population Survey*, http://www.bls.gov/cps/demographis.htm; and Bureau of Labor Statistics, *Women in the Labor Force: A Databook*, Report 1011, December 2008, http://www.bls.gov/cps/wlf-databook-2008.pdf.

8. C. Hymowitz, "Bend without Breaking: Women Executives Discuss the Art of Flex Schedules," *The Wall Street Journal*, March 6, 2007, http://online.wsj.com.

9. Bureau of Labor Statistics, *Charting the U.S. Labor Market in 2005* (Washington, DC: U.S. Department of Labor, June 2006), http://www.bls.gov; and E. Simon, "Women Make Less One Year after College," *Associated Press*, April 23, 2007, http://news.yahoo.com.

10. Catalyst, "Women CEOs of the *Fortune* 1000," May 2011, http://www.catalyst.org; and Alliance for Board Diversity, "Women and Minorities Lose Ground on *Fortune* 500 Corporate Boards, Alliance for Board Diversity Census Shows," news release, May 2, 2011, http://theabd.org.

11. A. Selko, "Gender Still a Large Hurdle to Career Advancement Say Women Execs," *Industry Week*, March 8, 2007, http://www.industryweek.com.

12. D. Carvajal, "The Codes That Need to Be Broken," *New York Times*, January 26, 2011, http://www.nytimes.com.

13. S. Armour, "Companies Try to Educate Teen Workers about Harassment," *USA Today*, October 19, 2006, http://www.usatoday.com.

14. G. Bohlander, S. Snell, and A. Sherman, *Managing Human Resources*, 12th ed. (Mason, OH: South-Western Publishing, 2001); and W. Petrocelli and B. K. Repa, *Sexual Harassment on the Job: What It Is and How to Stop It* (Berkeley, CA: Nolo Press, 1998).

15. Bureau of Labor Statistics, "Labor Force Characteristics of Foreign-Born Workers Summary," news release, April 25, 2007, http://www.bls.gov; and J. Lee and F. D. Bean, "America's Changing Color Lines," *Annual Review of Sociology*, 2004, pp. 221–43.

16. "The United States of Entrepreneurs," *The Economist*, March 14, 2009, http://www.kauffman.org.

17. Bureau of Labor Statistics, "Labor Force Statistics from the Current Population Survey," http://ftp.bls.gov; and BLS, *Charting the U.S. Labor Market*, chart 4–7.

18. M. Bertrand and S. Mullainathan, "Are Emily and Greg More Employable than Lakisha and Jamal?" NBER Working Paper No. 9873, July 2003, http://www.nber.org.

19. M. P. McQueen, "Workplace Disabilities Are on the Rise," *The Wall Street Journal*, May 1, 2007, http://online.wsj.com.

20. U.S. Census Bureau, "Anniversary of Americans with Disabilities Act: July 26," Facts for Features CB11-FF.14, May 31, 2011, http://www.census.gov; and Bureau of Labor Statistics, "Persons with a Disability: Labor Force Characteristics—2009," news release, August 25, 2010, http://www.bls.gov/cps.

21. Equal Employment Opportunity Commission (EEOC), "Disability Discrimination," http://www.eeoc.gov; EEOC, "Notice Concerning the Americans with Disabilities Act (ADA) Amendments Act of 2008," http://www.eeoc.gov; and EEOC, "ADA Charge Data by Impairments/Bases: Resolutions, FY1997–FY2008," http://www.eeoc.gov.

22. Bureau of Labor Statistics, *Charting the U.S. Labor Market in 2006*, http://www.bls.gov/cps/labor2006/; and Bureau of Labor Statistics, "Labor Force Characteristics of Foreign-Born Workers Summary," news release, April 25, 2007, http://www.bls.gov.

23. Census Bureau, *Statistical Abstract of the United States: 2007*, table 574, p. 373; and AARP, "Workforce Trends," Money and Work pages of AARP website, http://www.aarp.org.

24. B. O. Driscoll, "Local Businesses Urged to Build Loyalty, Mentors," *Reno (NV) Gazette-Journal*, February 7, 2007, http://www.rgj.com.

25. S. F. Gale, "Phased Retirement," *Workforce Management*, n.d., http://www.workforce.com.

26. N. A. Hira, "Attracting the Twentysomething Worker," *Fortune*, May 15, 2007, http://money.cnn.com.

27. T. Hoffman, "Eight New Ways to Target Top Talent in '08," *Computerworld*, January 28, 2008, pp. 34, 36; and A. Kingsbury, "The CIA and NSA Want You to Be Their Friend on Facebook," *U.S. News & World Report Online*, February 5, 2009, Business & Company Resource Center, http://galenet.galegroup.com.

28. Driscoll, "Local Businesses Urged to Build Loyalty, Mentors."

29. See, for example, C. Francoeur, R. Labelle, and B. Sinclair-Desgangé, "Gender Diversity in Corporate Governance and Top Management," *Journal of Business Ethics* 81, no. 1 (2008), pp. 83–95; A. McMillan-Capehart, J. R. Aaron, and B. N. Cline, "Investor Reactions to Diversity Reputation Signals," *Corporate Reputation Review* 13 (2010), pp. 184–97; P. Wang and J. L. Schwarz, "Stock Price Reactions to GLBT Nondiscrimination Policies," *Human Resource Management* 49, no. 2 (2010), pp. 195–216; R. C. Anderson, D. M. Reeb, A Upadhyay, and W. Zhao, "The Economics of Director Heterogeneity," *Financial Management* 40, no. 1 (2011), pp. 5–38; and M. Davidson, "Leveraging Difference for Organizational Excellence: Managing Diversity Differently," technical note UVA-OB-0767 (Charlottesville, VA: Darden Business Publishing, 2002).

30. N. Adler, *International Dimensions of Organizational Behavior*, 3rd ed. (Boston: PWS-Kent, 1997); and T. Cox and S. Blake, "Managing Cultural Diversity: Implications for Organizational Competitiveness," *Academy of Management Executives* 5 (August 1991), pp. 45–56.

31. J. P. Morgan, "Diversity," corporate Careers page, http://careers.jpmorgan.com.

32. Procter & Gamble, "Diversity," corporate Careers website, http://www.pg.com/en_US/careers/diversity.shtml; Procter & Gamble, "Fulfilling Our Potential," corporate website, http://www.pg.com/en_US/company/; P. Sellers, "P&G Rates an 'A' for Board Diversity," *Fortune*, May 5, 2011, http://postcards.blogs.fortune.cnn.com; D. Holthaus, "'My Black' Campaign Helps P&G Diversify Workforce," *Cincinnati.com*, July 11, 2010, http://news.cincinnati.com; and A. Beckett, "P&G Appoints Picou as Its Supply Chain Director," *The Grocer*, August 21, 2010, p. 60.

33. See, for example, S. J. Tribble, "Cisco Accused of Bias in Hiring," *San Jose Mercury News*, May 10, 2007, http://www.mercurynews.com; G. Appleson, "Baby Boomers, Often Targeted in Layoffs, Fight Age Discrimination," *St. Louis Post-Dispatch*, April 29, 2007, Business & Company Resource Center, http://galenet.galegroup.com; "Class Action Suits in the Workplace Are on the Rise," *HR Focus*, April 2007, http://galenet.galegroup.com; and M. Schoeff Jr., "Walgreen Suit Reflects EEOC's Latest Strategies," *Workforce Management*, March 26, 2007, http://galenet.galegroup.com.

34. R. R. Thomas Jr., "From Affirmative Action to Affirming Diversity," *Harvard Business Review*, March–April 1990.

35. K. Jesella, "Mom's Mad, and She's Organized," *New York Times*, February 22, 2007, http://www.nytimes.com.

36. G. Avalos, "Study Looks at Diversity, Turnover," *Contra Costa Times (Walnut Creek, CA)*, October 13, 2006, Business & Company Resource Center, http://galenet.galegroup.com.

37. "Study Finds 'Resurgence,' Shifts in Employee Resource Groups," *HR Focus*, March 2011, Business & Company Resource Center, http://galenet.galegroup.com.

38. Adler, *International Dimensions of Organizational Behavior*; and Cox and Blake, "Managing Cultural Diversity."

39. J. D. Nordell, "Positions of Power: How Female Ambition Is Shaped," *Slate*, November 21, 2006, http://www.slate.com.

40. Adler, *International Dimensions of Organizational Behavior.*

41. Davidson, "Leveraging Difference for Organizational Excellence."

42. K. A. Jehn, "Workplace Diversity, Conflict, and Productivity: Managing in the 21st Century," SEI Center for Advanced Studies in Management, Wharton School, University of Pennsylvania, Diversity, http://mktg-sun.wharton.upenn.edu/SEI/diversity.html.

43. A. J. Murrell, F. J. Crosby, and R. J. Ely, *Mentoring Dilemmas: Developmental Relationships within Multicultural Organizations* (Mahwah, NJ: Lawrence Erlbaum Associates, 1999). See a review of this book by M. L. Lengnick-Hall, "Mentoring Dilemmas: Developmental Relationships within Multicultural Organizations," *Personnel Psychology* 53, no. 1 (Spring 2000), pp. 224–27.

44. Bullock, "Most Influential CEOs"; Hutson, "A Lasting Engagement"; York, "Dr. Mehmood Khan"; PepsiCo, "Our Mission and Vision," http://www.pepsico.com; "Top Executives in Diversity," *Black Enterprise*, May 2011, pp. 92–106; and C. Angrisani, "27: Indra Nooyi," *Supermarket News*, July 19, 2010, Business & Company Resource Center, http://galenet.galegroup.com.

45. A. Kalev, F. Dobbin, and E. Kelly, "Best Practices or Best Guesses? Assessing the Efficacy of Corporate Affirmative Action and Diversity Policies," *American Sociological Review* 71 (2006), pp. 589–617.

46. R. Rodriguez, "Diversity Finds Its Place," *HRMagazine*, August 2006, Business & Company Resource Center, http://galenet.galegroup.com.

47. M. Y. Kinney, "Firm Makes a Case for Loyalty," *Philadelphia Inquirer*, April 5, 2009, Business & Company Resource Center, http://galenet.galegroup.com; R. Hightower, "Law Firm to Celebrate Employee's 50-Year Mark," *Philadelphia Tribune*, April 9, 2009, http://www.phillytrib.com; Caesar, Rivise, Bernstein, Cohen & Pokotilow, "About Us," http://www.crbcp.com; Drexel University, "Drexel at a Glance," http://www.drexel.edu; and Drexel University Earle Mack School of Law, "Diversity Initiatives," http://www.drexel.edu/law/diversity.asp.

48. A. Selko, "The Changing Faces of the Workplace," *Industry Week*, April 1, 2007, http://www.industryweek.com; and M. D. Lee, S. M. MacDermid, and M. L. Buck, "Organizational Paradigms of Reduced-Load Work: Accommodation, Elaboration, and Transformation," *Academy of Management Journal* 43, no. 6 (December 2000), pp. 1211–34.

49. L. E. Overmyer Day, "The Pitfalls of Diversity Training," *Training and Development* 49, no. 12 (December 1995), pp. 24–29; S. Rynes and B. Rosen, "A Field Survey of Factors Affecting the Adoption and Perceived Success of Diversity Training," *Personnel Psychology* 48, no. 2 (Summer 1995), pp. 247–70;

L. Ford, "Diversity: From Cartoons to Confrontations," *Training & Development* 54, no. 8 (August 2000), pp. 70–71; and J. M. Ivancevich and J. A. Gilbert, "Diversity Management: Time for a New Approach," *Public Personnel Management* 29, no. 1 (Spring 2000), pp. 75–92.

50. M. Burkart, "The Role of Training in Advancing a Diversity Initiative," *Diversity Factor* 8, no. 1 (Fall 1999), pp. 2–5.

51. "How Bad Is the Turnover Problem?" *HR Focus*, March 2007, Business & Company Resource Center, http://galenet.galegroup.com; B. Thomas, "Black Entrepreneurs Win, Corporations Lose," *BusinessWeek*, September 20, 2006, General Reference Center Gold, http://find.galegroup.com; and P. Shurn-Hannah, "Solving the Minority Retention Mystery," *The Human Resource Professional* 13, no. 3 (May/June 2000), pp. 22–27.

52. L. Bertagnoli, "Group Dynamics: Darden's Employee Networks," *Chain Leader*, September 1, 2008, http://www.chainleader.com; and D. Farkas, "Talkin' 'bout Your Generations," *Chain Leader*, April 2009, pp. 38–41.

53. Ernst & Young, "Mentorship, Sponsorship Keys to Building a Strong and Committed Workforce," news release, April 12, 2011, http://www.ey.com/CA/en/.

54. C. K. Johnson, "Study: Fat Workers Cost Employers More," *Associated Press*, April 23, 2007, http://news.yahoo.com.

55. R. Rodriguez, "Diversity Finds Its Place."

56. Lublin, "Nooyi Calls for More Women in Top Management"; Bullock, "Most Influential CEOs"; PepsiCo, "Our Mission and Vision"; PepsiCo, "PepsiCo Recognized as a Top Employer around the World," news release, December 10, 2010, http://www.pepsico.com; "2011 Best Companies for Multicultural Women," *Working Mother*, http://www.workingmother.com; S. Murray, "Unconscious Bias Still Holding Women Back," *Financial Times*, May 26, 2011, Business & Company Resource Center, http://galenet.galegroup.com; Comtex, "Lime Connect Canada Corporate Recruitment Event for Experienced Professionals with Disabilities," *Internet Wire*, May 23, 2011, Business & Company Resource Center, http://galenet.galegroup.com; S. Bhattacharya and P. Mehra, "In Good Company," *Business Today (India)*, October 17, 2010, Business & Company Resource Center, http://galenet.galegroup.com; and J Light, "In Hiring, Firms Shine Images," *The Wall Street Journal*, May 16, 2011, http://online.wsj.com.

Chapter 12

1. H. Schultz, "How Starbucks Got Its Mojo Back," *Newsweek*, March 21, 2011, pp. 50–55; J. Gapper, "Lunch with the FT: Howard Schultz," *Financial Times*, March 18, 2011, http://www.ft.com; A. Bryant, "Good CEOs Are Insecure (and Know It)," *The New York Times*, October 9, 2010, http://www.nytimes.com (interview with H. Schultz); and J. H. Ostdick, "Elevating the Bottom Line," *Success*, December 2010, pp. 59–64.

2. W. Bennis and B. Nanus, *Leaders* (New York: Harper & Row, 1985), p. 27.

3. J. Petrick, R. Schere, J. Brodzinski, J. Quinn, and M. Fall Ainina, "Global Leadership Skills and Reputational Capital: Intangible Resources for Sustainable Competitive Advantage," *Academy of Management Executive*, February 1999, pp. 58–69.

4. Bennis and Nanus, *Leaders.*

5. Ibid., p. 144.

6. E. E. Lawler III, *Treat People Right! How Organizations and Individuals Can Propel Each Other into a Virtual Spiral of Success* (San Francisco: Jossey-Bass, 2003).

7. A. Carr, "The Most Important Leadership Quality for CEOs? Creativity," *Fast Company*, May 18, 2010, http://www.fastcompany.com.

8. J. P. Rathbone and J. Webber, "Man in the News: An Underground Hero," *Financial Times*, October 16, 2010, Business & Company Resource Center, http://galenet.galegroup.com.

9. J. Kouzes and B. Posner, *The Leadership Challenge*, 2nd ed. (San Francisco: Jossey-Bass, 1995).

10. J. Kouzes and B. Posner, *The Leadership Challenge*, 1st ed. (San Francisco: Jossey-Bass, 1987).

11. Ibid.

12. Ibid.

13. J. Baum, E. A. Locke, and S. Kirkpatrick, "A Longitudinal Study of the Relation of Vision and Vision Communication to Venture Growth in Entrepreneurial Firms," *Journal of Applied Psychology* 83 (1998), pp. 43–54.

14. E. C. Shapiro, *Fad Surfing in the Boardroom* (Reading, MA: Addison-Wesley, 1995).

15. Kouzes and Posner, *The Leadership Challenge* (1995).

16. Ibid.

17. W. Bennis and R. Townsend, *Reinventing Leadership* (New York: William Morrow, 1995).

18. Ibid.

19. D. Mattioli and K. Maher, "At 3M, Innovation Comes in Tweaks and Snips," *The Wall Street Journal*, March 1, 2010, http://online.wsj.com.

20. Kouzes and Posner, *The Leadership Challenge* (1987).

21. J. A. Conger, "The Dark Side of Leadership," *Organizational Dynamics* 19 (Autumn 1990), pp. 44–55.

22. J. Conger, "The Vision Thing: Explorations into Visionary Leadership," in *Cutting Edge Leadership 2000*, ed. B. Kellerman and L. Matusak (College Park, MD: James MacGregor Burns Academy of Leadership, 2000).

23. B. Wolpin, "The Tough Get Going," *American City & County*, November 1, 2008, Business & Company Resource Center, http://galenet.galegroup.com; M. Jackson, "Come-Back Kid," *American City & County*, November 1, 2008, http://galenet.galegroup.com; and B. Zongker, "Museum Features Kansas Town That Went Green," Associated Press, *Yahoo News*, October 26, 2008, http://news.yahoo.com.

24. J. P. Kotter, "What Leaders Really Do," *Harvard Business Review* 68 (May–June 1990) pp. 103–11.

25. M. E. Van Buren and T. Safferstone, "Collective Quick Wins," *Computerworld*, January 26, 2009, pp. 24–25.

26. G. Yukl, *Leadership in Organizations*, 3rd ed. (Englewood Cliffs, NJ: Prentice Hall, 1994).

27. R. House and R. Aditya, "The Social Scientific Study of Leadership: Quo Vadis?" *Journal of Management* 23 (1997), pp. 409–73.

28. R. D. Ireland and M. A. Hitt. "Achieving and Maintaining Strategic Competitiveness in the 21st Century. The Role of Strategic Leadership," *Academy of Management Executive*, February 1999, pp. 43–57.

29. P. Cappelli, H. Singh, J. V. Singh, and M. Useem, "Leadership Lessons from India," *Harvard Business Review*, March 2010, pp. 90–97.

30. J. Gardner, "The Heart of the Matter: Leader–Constituent Interaction," pp. 239–244, quote at p. 240. *Leading & Leadership*, ed. T. Fuller (Notre Dame, IN: University of Notre Dame Press, 2000), pp. 38–45.

31. R. E. Kelly, "In Praise of Followers," *Harvard Business Review* 66 (November–December 1988), pp. 142–48.

32. Bennis and Townsend, *Reinventing Leadership*.

33. Gardner, "The Heart of the Matter."

34. Kelly, "In Praise of Followers."

35. J. S. Lublin, "Bosses' Small Gestures Send Big Signals," *The Wall Street Journal*, December 2, 2010, http://online.wsj.com; and R. I. Sutton, "Why Good Bosses Tune In to Their People," *McKinsey Quarterly*, August 2010, https://www.mckinseyquarterly.com.

36. J. R. P. French and B. Raven, "The Bases of Social Power," in *Studies in Social Power*, ed. D. Cartwright (Ann Arbor, MI: Institute for Social Research, 1959).

37. G. Yukl and C. Falbe, "Importance of Different Power Sources in Downward and Lateral Relations," *Journal of Applied Psychology* 76 (1991), pp. 416–23.

38. Ibid.

39. R. M. Stogdill, "Personal Factors Associated with Leadership: A Survey of the Literature," *Journal of Psychology* 25 (1948), pp. 35–71.

40. S. Kirkpatrick and E. Locke, "Leadership: Do Traits Matter?" *The Executive* 5 (May 1991), pp. 48–60.

41. G. A. Yukl, *Leadership in Organizations*, 2nd ed. (Englewood Cliffs, NJ: Prentice-Hall, 1989).

42. R. Heifetz and D. Laurie, "The Work of Leadership," *Harvard Business Review*, January–February 1997, pp. 124–34.

43. T. Judge, J. Bono, R. Ilies, and M. Gerhardt, "Personality and Leadership: A Qualitative and Quantitative Review," *Journal of Applied Psychology* 87 (2002), pp. 765–80.

44. R. Foti and N. M. A. Hauenstein, "Pattern and Variable Approaches in Leadership Emergence and Effectiveness," *Journal of Applied Psychology* 92 (2007), pp. 347–55.

45. T. Fuller, *Leading & Leadership, 2000* (Notre Dame, IN: University of Notre Dame Press, 2000), p. 243.

46. J. P. Kotter, *The General Managers* (New York: Free Press, 1982).

47. S. Zaccaro, R. Foti, and D. Kenny, "Self-Monitoring and Trait-Based Variance in Leadership: An Investigation of Leader Flexibility across Multiple Group Situations," *Journal of Applied Psychology* 76 (1991), pp. 308–15.

48. D. Goleman, "Leadership That Gets Results," *Harvard Business Review*, March–April 2000, pp. 78–90.

49. Schultz, "How Starbucks Got Its Mojo Back"; Gapper, "Lunch with the FT"; A Ignatius, "We Had to Own the Mistakes," *Harvard Business Review*, July–August 2010, pp. 109–15 (interview with H. Schultz); J. Jargon, "Coffee Talk: Starbucks Chief on Prices, McDonald's Rivalry," *The Wall Street Journal*, March 7, 2011, http://online.wsj.com (interview with Howard Schultz); and C. C. Miller, "A Changed Starbucks, a Changed CEO," *The New York Times*, March 13, 2011, http://www.nytimes.com.

50. J. Misumi and M. Peterson, "The Performance-Maintenance (PM) Theory of Leadership: Review of a Japanese Research Program," *Administrative Science Quarterly* 30 (June 1985), pp. 198–223.

51. T. Judge, R. Piccolo, and R. Ilies, "The Forgotten Ones? The Validity of Consideration and Initiating Structure in Leadership Research," *Journal of Applied Psychology* 89 (2004), pp. 36–51.

52. Misumi and Peterson, "The Performance-Maintenance (PM) Theory."

53. Judge, Piccolo, and Ilies, "The Forgotten Ones?"

54. G. Graen and M. Uhl-Bien, "Relationship-Based Approach to Leadership: Development of Leader-Member Exchange (LMX) Theory of Leadership over 25 Years: Applying a Multi-Level Multidomain Perspective," *Leadership Quarterly* 6, no. 2 (1995), pp. 219–47.

55. House and Aditya, "The Social Scientific Study of Leadership."

56. C. R. Gerstner and D. V. Day, "Meta-Analytic Review of Leader-Member Exchange Theory: Correlates and Construct Issues," *Journal of Applied Psychology* 82 (1997), pp. 827–44.

57. House and Aditya, "The Social Scientific Study of Leadership."

58. J. Wagner III, "Participation's Effect on Performance and Satisfaction: A Reconsideration of Research," *Academy of Management Review*, April 1994, pp. 312–30.

59. R. White and R. Lippitt, *Autocracy and Democracy: An Experimental Inquiry* (New York: Harper & Brothers, 1960).

60. J. Muczyk and R. Steel, "Leadership Style and the Turnaround Executive," *Business Horizons*, March–April 1999, pp. 39–46.

61. A. Tannenbaum and W. Schmidt, "How to Choose a Leadership Pattern," *Harvard Business Review* 36 (March–April 1958), pp. 95–101.

62. E. Fleishman and E. Harris, "Patterns of Leadership Behavior Related to Employee Grievances and Turnover," *Personnel Psychology* 15 (1962), pp. 43–56.

63. R. Likert, *The Human Organization: Its Management and Value* (New York: McGraw-Hill, 1967).

64. R. Blake and J. Mouton, *The Managerial Grid* (Houston: Gulf, 1964).

65. Misumi and Peterson, "The Performance-Maintenance (PM) Theory."

66. J. Wall, *Bosses* (Lexington, MA: Lexington Books, 1986), p. 103.

67. Tannenbaum and Schmidt, "How to Choose a Leadership Pattern."

68. V. H. Vroom, "Leadership and the Decision-Making Process," *Organizational Dynamics*, Spring 2000, pp. 82–93.

69. F. E. Fiedler, *A Theory of Leadership Effectiveness* (New York: McGraw-Hill, 1967).

70. P. Hersey and K. Blanchard, *The Management of Organizational Behavior* (Englewood Cliffs, NJ: Prentice Hall, 1984).

71. Yukl, *Leadership in Organizations*.

72. R. J. House, "A Path Goal Theory of Leader Effectiveness," *Administrative Science Quarterly* 16 (1971), pp. 321–39.

73. J. Howell, D. Bowen, P. Dorfman, S. Kerr, and P. Podsakoff, "Substitutes for Leadership: Effective Alternatives to Ineffective Leadership," *Organizational Dynamics* 19 (Summer 1990), pp. 21–38.

74. R. G. Lord and W. Gradwohl Smith, "Leadership and the Changing Nature of Performance," in *The Changing Nature of Performance*, ed. D. R. Ilgen and E. D. Pulakos (San Francisco: Jossey-Bass, 1999).

75. S. Dionne, F. Yammarino, L. Atwater, and L. James, "Neutralizing Substitutes for Leadership Theory: Leadership Effects and Common-Source Bias," *Journal of Applied Psychology* 87 (2002), pp. 454–64.

76. B. M. Bass, *Leadership and Performance Beyond Expectations* (New York: Free Press, 1985).

77. Y. A. Nur, "Charisma and Managerial Leadership: The Gift That Never Was," *Business Horizons*, July–August 1998, pp. 19–26; and R. J. House, "A 1976 Theory of Charismatic Leadership," in *Leadership: The Cutting Edge*, ed. J. G. Hunt and L. L. Larson (Carbondale,

IL: Southern Illinois University Press, 1977).

78. M. Brown and L. Trevino, "Socialized Charismatic Leadership, Values Congruence, and Deviance in Work Groups," *Journal of Applied Psychology* 91 (2006), pp. 954–62.

79. M. Potts and P. Behr, *The Leading Edge* (New York: McGraw-Hill, 1987).

80. J. Howell and B. Shamir, "The Role of Followers in the Charismatic Leadership Process: Relationships and Their Consequences," *Academy of Management Review* 30 (2005), pp. 96–112.

81. S. Yorges, H. Weiss, and O. Strickland, "The Effect of Leader Outcomes on Influence, Attributions, and Perceptions of Charisma," *Journal of Applied Psychology* 84 (1999), pp. 428–36.

82. Potts and Behr, *Leading Edge*.

83. D. A. Waldman and F. J. Yammarino, "CEO Charismatic Leadership: Levels-of-Management and Levels-of-Analysis Effects," *Academy of Management Review* 24 (1999), pp. 266–85.

84. A. Erez, V. F. Misangyi, D. E. Johnson, M. A. LePine, and K. C. Halverson, "Stirring the Hearts of Followers: Charismatic Leadership as the Transferral of Affect," *Journal of Applied Psychology* 93 (2008), pp. 602–16.

85. A. Fanelli and V. Misangyi, "Bringing Out Charisma: CEO Charisma and External Stakeholders," *Academy of Management Review* 31 (2006), pp. 1049–61.

86. House and Aditya, "The Social Scientific Study of Leadership."

87. D. A. Waldman, G. G. Ramirez, R. J. House, and P. Puranam, "Does Leadership Matter? CEO Leadership Attributes and Profitability under Conditions of Perceived Environmental Uncertainty," *Academy of Management Journal* 44 (2001), pp. 134–43.

88. B. Agle, N. Nagarajan, J. Sonnenfeld, and D. Srinivasan, "Does CEO Charisma Matter? An Empirical Analysis of the Relationships among Organizational Performance, Environmental Uncertainty, and Top Management Team Perceptions of CEO Charisma," *Academy of Management Journal* 49 (2006), pp. 161–74.

89. J. M. Howell and K. E. Hall-Merenda, "The Ties That Bind: The Impact of Leader-Member Exchange, Transformational and Transactional Leadership, and Distance on Predicting Follower Performance," *Journal of Applied Psychology* 84 (1999), pp. 680–94; and B. M. Bass, "Leadership: Good, Better, Best," *Organizational Dynamics*, Winter 1985, pp. 26–40.

90. F. J. Yammarino, F. Dansereau, and C. J. Kennedy, "A Multiple-Level Multidimensional Approach to Leadership: Viewing Leadership through an Elephant's Eye," *Organizational Dynamics*, Winter 2001, pp. 149–63.

91. D. I. Jung and B. J. Avolio, "Effects of Leadership Style and Followers' Cultural Orientation on Performance in Group and Individual Task Conditions," *Academy of Management Journal* 42 (1999), pp. 208–18.

92. Bass, *Leadership*.

93. Bennis and Nanus, *Leaders*.

94. B. Bass, B. Avolio, and L. Goodheim, "Biography and the Assessment of Transformational Leadership at the World-Class Level," *Journal of Management* 13 (1987), pp. 7–20.

95. K. Albrecht and R. Zemke, *Service America* (Homewood, IL: Dow Jones Irwin, 1985).

96. Y. Ling, Z. Simisek, M. Lubatkin, and J. F. Veiga, "The Impact of Transformational CEOs on the Performance of Small to Medium-Sized Firms: Does Organizational Context Matter?" *Journal of Applied Psychology* 93 (2008), pp. 923–34.

97. T. A. Judge and J. E. Bono, "Five-Factor Model of Personality and Transformational Leadership," *Journal of Applied Psychology* 85 (2000), pp. 751–65; and B. Bass, "Does the Transactional-Transformational Paradigm Transcend Organizational and National Boundaries?" *American Psychologist* 22 (1997), pp. 130–42.

98. S. J. Shin and J. Zhou, "Transformational Leadership, Conservation, and Creativity: Evidence from Korea," *Academy of Management Journal* 46 (2003), pp. 703–14.

99. R. Piccolo and J. Colquitt, "Transformational Leadership and Job Behaviors: The Mediating Role of Core Job Characteristics," *Academy of Management Journal* 49 (2006), pp. 327–40.

100. A. Colbert, A. Kristof-Brown, B. Bradley, and M. Barrick, "CEO Transformational Leadership: The Role of Goal Importance Congruence in Top Management Teams," *Academy of Management Journal* 51 (2008), pp. 81–96.

101. A. Bryant, "The Dangers of Cynicism at the Office," *The New York Times*, December 4, 2010, http://www.nytimes.com; and T. Duryee, "How Lockerz Is Making Shopping a Lot More Fun for the 19 and Under Crowd," *Add Things Digital*, February 3, 2011, http://emoney.allthingsd.com.

102. T. Dvir, D. Eden, B. Avolio, and B. Shamir, "Impact of Transformational Leadership on Follower Development and Performance: A Field Experiment," *Academy of Management Journal* 45 (2002), pp. 735–44.

103. B. M. Bass, *Transformational Leadership: Industry, Military, and Educational Impact* (Mahwah, NJ: Lawrence Erlbaum Associates, 1998).

104. G. Spreitzer and R. Quinn, "Empowering Middle Managers to Be Transformational Leaders," *Journal of Applied Behavioral Science* 32 (1996), pp. 237–61.

105. J. Collins, "Level 5 Leadership," *Harvard Business Review* 1 (2001), pp. 66–76; and J. Kline Harrison and M. William Clough, "Characteristics of 'State of the Art' Leaders: Productive Narcissism versus Emotional Intelligence and Level 5 Capabilities," *Social Science Journal* 43 (2006), pp. 287–92.

106. D. Vera and M. Crossan, "Strategic Leadership and Organizational Learning," *Academy of Management Review* 29 (2004), pp. 222–40.

107. F. Luthans, *Organizational Behavior*, 10th ed. (New York: McGraw-Hill/Irwin, 2005).

108. B. M. Bass, "Thoughts and Plans," in *Cutting Edge Leadership 2000*, ed. B. Kellerman and L. R. Matusak (College Park, MD: James MacGregor Burns Academy of Leadership, 2000), pp. 5–9.

109. N. Turner, J. Barling, O. Epitropaki, V. Butcher, and C. Milner, "Transformational Leadership and Moral Reasoning," *Journal of Applied Psychology* 87 (2002), pp. 304–11.

110. D. M. Mayer, M. Kuenzi, R. Greenbaum, M. Bardes, and R. Salvador, "How Low Does Ethical Leadership Flow? Test of a Trickle-Down Model," *Organizational Behavior and Human Decision Processes* 108 (2009), pp. 1–13.

111. Bass, "Thoughts and Plans."

112. W. Bennis, "The End of Leadership: Exemplary Leadership Is Impossible without Full Inclusion, Initiatives, and Cooperation of Followers," *Organizational Dynamics*, Summer 1999, pp. 71–79.

113. L. Spears, "Emerging Characteristics of Servant Leadership," in *Cutting Edge Leadership 2000*, ed. B. Kellerman and L. Matusak (College Park, MD: James MacGregor Burns Academy of Leadership, 2000); and L. Buchanan, "In Praise of Selflessness: Why the Best Leaders Are Servants," *Inc.*, May 2007, pp. 33–35.

114. Buchanan, "In Praise of Selflessness," p. 34.

115. J. Ciulla, "Bridge Leaders," in *Cutting Edge Leadership 2000*, ed. B. Kellerman and L. Matusak (College Park, MD: James MacGregor Burns Academy of Leadership, 2000), pp. 25–28.

116. C. L. Pearce, "The Future of Leadership: Combining Vertical and Shared Leadership to Transform Knowledge Work," *Academy of Management Executive*, February 2004, pp. 47–57.

117. J. Carson, P. Tesluk, and J. Marrone, "Shared Leadership in Teams: An Investigation of Antecedent Conditions and Performance," *Academy of Management Journal* 50 (2007), pp. 1217–34.

118. R. Fisher and A. Sharp, *Getting It Done* (New York: HarperCollins, 1998).

119. Esther Herlzfeld, "Leadership Leads to Growth," *Official Board Markets*, April 11, 2009, Business & Company Resource Center, http://galenet.galegroup.com; and Barry-Wehmiller website, http://www.barry-wehmiller.com.

120. M. Useem, "Thinking Big, Lending Small," *U.S. News and World Report*,

October 22, 2006, http://www.usnews.com.

121. J. Reed and B. Simon, "Adroit in Detroit," *Financial Times*, January 25, 2011, Business & Company Resource Center, http://galenet.galegroup.com; "Epiphany in Dearborn: Ford," *The Economist*, December 11, 2010, Business & Company Resource Center, http://galenet.galegroup.com; and J. LaReau, "Ford Slashes Debt, Spends on Operations," *Automotive News*, January 31, 2011, Business & Company Resource Center, http://galenet.galegroup.com.

122. P. Block, *The Empowered Manager* (San Francisco: Jossey-Bass, 1991).

123. Ibid.

124. Kouzes and Posner, *The Leadership Challenge* (1995).

125. L. W. Boone and M. S. Peborde, "Developing Leadership Skills in College and Early Career Positions," *Review of Business*, Spring 2008, Business & Company Resource Center, http://galenet.galegroup.com.

126. A. Gaines, "Straight to the Top," *American Executive*, August 2008, Business & Company Resource Center, http://galenet.galegroup.com; and S. J. Allen and N. S. Hartman, "Leadership Development: An Exploration of Sources of Learning," *SAM Advanced Management Journal*, Winter 2008, pp. 10–19, 62–63.

127. R. Fulmer, P. Gibbs, and M. Goldsmith, "Developing Leaders: How Winning Companies Keep on Winning," *Sloan Management Review* (Fall 2000), pp. 49–59.

128. M. McCall, *High Flyers* (Boston: Harvard Business School Press, 1998).

129. E. Van Velsor, C. D. McCauley, and R. Moxley, "Our View of Leadership Development," in *Center for Creative Leadership Handbook of Leadership Development*, ed. C. D. McCauley, R. Moxley, and E. Van Velsor (San Francisco: Jossey-Bass, 1998), pp. 1–25.

130. D. S. DeRue and N. Wellman, "Developing Leaders via Experience: The Role of Developmental Challenge, Learning Orientation, and Feedback Availability," *Journal of Applied Psychology* 94 (2009), pp. 859–75.

131. Schultz, "How Starbucks Got Its Mojo Back"; Gapper, "Lunch with the FT"; Ignatius, "We Had to Own the Mistakes"; Jargon, "Coffee Talk"; Miller, "A Changed Starbucks"; "Lex Column: Starbucks," *Financial Times*, November 6, 2010, Business & Company Resource Center, http://galenet.galegroup.com; and E. J. Schultz, "How VIA Steamed Up the Instant-Coffee Category," *Advertising Age*, January 24, 2011, Business & Company Resource Center, http://galenet.galegroup.com.

Chapter 13

1. Intuit, "Intuit Total Rewards Portfolio," Intuit Careers website, http://www.intuitcareers.com, September 2010; B. J. Fikes, "Fortune Magazine Praises Local Companies," *North County Times (Escondido, CA.)*, January 22, 2011, Business & Company Resource Center, http://galenet.galegroup.com; "100 Best Companies to Work For," *Fortune*, February 7, 2011, http://money.cnn.com; "World's Most Admired Companies," *Fortune*, March 21, 2011, http://money.cnn.com; Intuit, "Pay and Recognition," Intuit Careers website, http://intuitcareers.com/professional/pay-recognition; Intuit, "Enduring Innovation with a Profound Impact," Engineering at Intuit website, http://www.innovateforimpact.com; "100 Best Places to Work in IT 2010," *Computerworld*, June 21, 2010, pp. 49–58; and T. Abate, "Feds Give Honors to 15 Employers," *San Francisco Chronicle*, July 24, 2010, Business & Company Resource Center, http://galenet.galegroup.com.

2. R. Kreitner and F. Luthans, "A Social Learning Approach to Behavioral Management: Radical Behaviorists 'Mellowing Out,' " *Organizational Dynamics*, Autumn 1984, pp. 47–65.

3. D. Katz and R. L. Kahn, *The Social Psychology of Organizations* (New York: John Wiley & Sons, 1966).

4. C. A. Bartlett and S. Ghoshal, "Building Competitive Advantage through People," *Sloan Management Review*, Winter 2002, pp. 34–41.

5. R. R. Hastings, "Employee Engagement Gains Are Tenuous," *HR Magazine*, October 2010, p. 16; and Sibson Consulting, "Rewards of Work Study," 2010, http://www.sibson.com.

6. E. Locke, "Toward a Theory of Task Motivation and Incentives," *Organizational Behavior and Human Performance* 3 (1968), pp. 157–89.

7. W. F. Cascio, "Managing a Virtual Workplace," *Academy of Management Executive*, August 2000, pp. 81–90.

8. E. A. Locke, "Guest Editor's Introduction: Goal-Setting Theory and Its Applications to the World of Business," *Academy of Management Executive* 4 (November 2004), pp. 124–25.

9. G. P. Latham, "The Motivational Benefits of Goal-Setting," *Academy of Management Executive* 4 (November 2004), pp. 126–29.

10. E. A. Locke, "Linking Goals to Monetary Incentives," *Academy of Management Executive* 4 (November 2004), pp. 130–33.

11. E. E. Lawler III, *Treat People Right!* (San Francisco: Jossey-Bass, 2003).

12. Ibid.

13. J. Bono and T. Judge, "Self-Concordance at Work: Toward Understanding the Motivational Effects of Transformational Leaders," *Academy of Management Journal* 46 (2003), pp. 554–71.

14. R. H. Schaffer, "Demand Better Results—and Get Them," *Harvard Business Review* 69 (March–April 1991), pp. 142–49.

15. A. Wilson, "Kansas Quick Lane Operation Is Well-Tuned," *Automotive News*, April 5, 2010, Business & Company Resource Center, http://galenet.galegroup.com.

16. K. N. Shaw, "Changing the Goal-Setting Process at Microsoft," *Academy of Management Executive* 4 (November 2004), pp. 139–43.

17. S. Kerr and S. Laundauer, "Using Stretch Goals to Promote Organizational Effectiveness and Personal Growth: General Electric and Goldman Sachs," *Academy of Management Executive* 4 (November 2004), pp. 134–38.

18. Ibid.

19. Latham, "Motivational Benefits of Goal-Setting."

20. T. Mitchell and W. Silver, "Individual and Group Goals When Workers Are Interdependent: Effects on Task Strategies and Performance," *Journal of Applied Psychology* 75 (1990), pp. 185–93.

21. Latham, "Motivational Benefits of Goal-Setting."

22. D. H. Pink, *Drive: The Surprising Truth about What Motivates Us* (New York: Riverhead Books, 2009), pp. 98–99.

23. M. Schweitzer, L. Ordonez, and B. Douma, "Goal Setting as a Motivator of Unethical Behavior," *Academy of Management Journal* 47 (2004), pp. 422–32.

24. M. A. Duran, "Norm-Based Behavior and Corporate Malpractice," *Journal of Economic Issues* 41, no. 1 (March 2007), Business & Company Resource Center, http://galenet.galegroup.com; and D. Durfee, "Management or Manipulation?" *CFO*, December 2006, http://galenet.galegroup.com.

25. G. Seijts and G. Latham, "Learning versus Performance Goals: When Should Each Be Used?" *Academy of Management Executive* 19 (February 2005), pp. 124–31; P. C. Early, T. Connolly, and G. Ekegren, "Goals, Strategy Development, and Task Performance: Some Limits on the Efficacy of Goal Setting," *Journal of Applied Psychology* 74 (1989), pp. 24–33; and C. E. Shalley, "Effects of Productivity Goals, Creativity Goals, and Personal Discretion on Individual Creativity," *Journal of Applied Psychology* 76 (1991), pp. 179–85.

26. R. C. Litchfield, "Brainstorming Reconsidered: A Goal-Based View," *Academy of Management Review* 33 (2008), pp. 649–668.

27. R. Fisher and A. Sharp, *Getting It Done* (New York: HarperCollins, 1998).

28. E. Thorndike, *Animal Intelligence* (New York: Macmillan, 1911).

29. A. D. Stajkovic and F. Luthans, "Differential Effects of Incentive Motivators on Work Performance," *Academy of Management Journal* 44 (2001), pp. 580–90.

30. J. Zaslow, "The Most-Praised Generation Goes to Work," *The Wall Street Journal*, April 20, 2007, http;//online.wsj.com.

31. K. Butterfield, L. K. Trevino, and G. Ball, "Punishment from the Manager's Perspective: A Grounded Investigation and Inductive Model," *Academy of Management Review* 39 (1996), pp. 1479–512.

32. Adam Madison, "Positive Results," *Rock Products*, September 1, 2008, Business & Company Resource Center, http://galenet.galegroup.com.

33. T. Judge and R. Piccolo, "Transformational and Transactional Leadership: A Meta-Analytic Test of Their Relative Ability," *Journal of Applied Psychology* 89 (2004), pp. 755–68.

34. S. Kerr, "On the Folly of Rewarding A While Hoping for B," *Academy of Management Journal* 18 (1975), pp. 769–83.

35. S. Lohr, "Science Finds Advantage in Focusing, Not Multitasking," *Chicago Tribune*, March 25, 2007, sec. 1, p. 10.

36. E. E. Lawler III, *Rewarding Excellence* (San Francisco: Jossey-Bass, 2000).

37. J. Stenson, "Is Your Job Making You Fat?" *MSNBC*, February 6, 2007, http://www.msnbc.msn.com.

38. "100 Best Companies to Work For 2007: Unusual Perks," *Fortune*, January 22, 2007, http://money.cnn.com.

39. M. Fitzgerald, "Thinks Big about the Little Guy," *The New York Times*, February 4, 2007, Business & Company Resource Center, http://galenet.galegroup.com.

40. J. H. Cho, "Lessons in Employee Appreciation," *Star-Ledger* (Newark, NJ), February 8, 2007, Business & Company Resource Center, http://galenet.galegroup.com.

41. Fitzgerald, "Thinks Big."

42. J. Pfeffer and R. Sutton, *The Knowing–Doing Gap* (Boston: Harvard Business School Press, 2000).

43. J. S. Lublin, "Recall the Mistakes of Your Past Bosses, So You Can Do Better," *The Wall Street Journal*, January 2, 2007, http://online.wsj.com.

44. S. Moss and J. Sanchez, "Are Your Employees Avoiding You? Managerial Strategies for Closing the Feedback Gap," *Academy of Management Executive* 18, no. 1 (February 2004), pp. 32–44.

45. Lawler, *Treat People Right!*

46. S. B. Silverman, C. E. Pogson, and A. B. Cober, "When Employees at Work Don't Get It: A Model for Enhancing Individual Employee Change in Response to Performance Feedback," *Academy of Management Executive* 19, no. 2 (May 2005), pp. 135–47; and J. Jackman and M. Strober, "Fear of Feedback," *Harvard Business Review*, April 2003, pp. 101–7.

47. Intuit, "Pay and Recognition"; Globoforce, "Case Study: 'Spotlight' Global Strategic Recognition Program," http://www.globoforce.com; and T. Demos, "Motivate without Spending Millions," *Fortune*, April 5, 2010, http://money.cnn.com.

48. V. H. Vroom, *Work and Motivation* (New York: John Wiley & Sons, 1964).

49. R. E. Wood, P. W. B. Atkins, and J. E. H. Bright, "Bonuses, Goals, and Instrumentality Effects," *Journal of Applied Psychology* 84 (1999), pp. 703–20.

50. Melanie Scarborough, "The Rewards of Recognition: Six Strategies for Successful Employee Programs," *Community Banker*, January 2009, pp. 24–27.

51. D. Korn, "The Employee-Owned Advantage," *Modern Machine Shop*, January 2011, pp. 70–75.

52. A. H. Maslow, "A Theory of Human Motivation," *Psychological Review*, July 1943, pp. 370–96.

53. L. Mainicro and D. Gibson, "Managing Employee Trauma: Dealing with the Emotional Fallout from 9-11," *Academy of Management Executive*, August 2003, pp. 130–43.

54. M. Wahba and L. Birdwell, "Maslow Reconsidered: A Review of Research on the Need Hierarchy Theory," *Organizational Behavior and Human Performance* 15 (1976), pp. 212–40.

55. G. Dessler, "How to Earn Your Employees' Commitment," *Academy of Management Executive*, May 1999, pp. 58–67, quoted on p. 63.

56. C. Hymowitz, "Managers Lose Talent When They Neglect to Coach Their Staffs," *The Wall Street Journal*, March 19, 2007, http://online.wsj.com.

57. Ibid.

58. C. Alderfer, *Existence, Relatedness, and Growth: Human Needs in Organizational Settings* (Glencoe, IL: Free Press, 1972).

59. L. Tanner, "Study: Napping Might Help Heart," *Yahoo News*, February 12, 2007, http://news.yahoo.com.

60. C. Hymowitz, "When the Paycheck Isn't Optional, Ambition Is Less Complicated," *The Wall Street Journal*, April 26, 2007, http://online.wsj.com.

61. C. Pinder, *Work Motivation* (Glenview, IL: Scott, Foresman, 1984).

62. D. McClelland, *The Achieving Society* (New York: Van Nostrand Reinhold, 1961).

63. Quoted in Cho, "Lessons in Employee Appreciation."

64. D. McClelland and R. Boyatzis, "Leadership Motive Pattern and Long-Term Success in Management," *Journal of Applied Psychology* 67 (1982), pp. 737–43.

65. N. Adler, *International Dimensions of Organizational Behavior*, 2nd ed. (Boston: Kent, 1991); and G. Hofstede, *Cultures and Organizations* (London: McGraw-Hill, 1991).

66. N. R. Lockwood, "Leveraging Employee Engagement for Competitive Advantage: HR's Strategic Role," *HRMagazine*, March 2007, Business & Company Resource Center, http://galenet.galegroup.com.

67. E. E. Lawler III and D. Finegold, "Individualizing the Organization: Past, Present, and Future," *Organizational Dynamics*, Summer 2000, pp. 1–15.

68. Ibid.

69. T. M. Amabile, "A Model of Creativity and Innovation in Organizations," in *Research in Organizational Behavior*, ed. B. M. Staw and L. L. Cummings (Greenwich, CT: JAI Press, 1988), pp. 10, 123–67.

70. C. M. Ford, "A Theory of Individual Creative Action in Multiple Social Domains," *Academy of Management Review* 21 (1996), pp. 1112–42.

71. G. Oldham and A. Cummings, "Employee Creativity: Personal and Contextual Factors at Work," *Academy of Management Journal* 39 (1996), pp. 607–34.

72. T. Amabile, R. Conti, H. Coon, J. Lazenby, and M. Herron, "Assessing the Work Environment for Creativity," *Academy of Management Journal* 39 (1996), pp. 1154–84.

73. M. Campion and G. Sanborn, "Job Design," in *Handbook of Industrial Engineering*, ed. G. Salvendy (New York: John Wiley & Sons, 1991).

74. Lawler and Finegold, "Individualizing the Organization."

75. R. Garretson, "Job Rotation Pays Dividends," *Network World*, February 26, 2007, OCLC FirstSearch, http://firstsearch.oclc.org.

76. M. Campion and D. McClelland, "Interdisciplinary Examination of the Costs and Benefits of Enlarged Jobs: A Job Design Quasi-Experiment," *Journal of Applied Psychology* 76 (1991), pp. 186–98.

77. F. Herzberg, *Work and the Nature of Men* (Cleveland: World, 1966).

78. J. R. Hackman, G. Oldham, R. Janson, and K. Purdy, "A New Strategy for Job Enrichment," *California Management Review* 16 (Fall 1975), pp. 57–71.

79. Pink, *Drive*, p. 119.

80. R. Rechheld, "Loyalty-Based Management" *Harvard Business Review*, March–April 1993, pp. 64–73.

81. "Motivation in Today's Workplace: The Link to Performance," *HR Magazine*, July 2010, pp. 1–9.

82. B. Trahant, "Recruiting and Engaging the Federal Workforce," *Public Manager*, Spring 2008, Business & Company Resource Center, http://galenet.galegroup.com.

83. T. Peters and N. Austin, *A Passion for Excellence* (New York: Random House, 1985).

84. P. Kaihla, "Best-Kept Secrets of the World's Best Companies," *Business 2.0*, April 2006, http://galenet.galegroup.com.

85. J. Bryner, "Survey Reveals Most Satisfying Jobs," *Yahoo News*, April 18, 2007, http://news.yahoo.com.

86. Campion and Sanborn, "Job Design."

87. S. Seibert, S. Silver, and W. A. Randolph, "Taking Empowerment to the Next Level: A Multiple-Level Model of Empowerment, Performance, and Satisfaction," *Academy of Management Journal* 47 (2004), pp. 332–49.

88. C. Argyris, "Empowerment: The Emperor's New Clothes," *Harvard*

Business Review, May–June 1998, pp. 98–105.

89. R. Forrester, "Empowerment: Rejuvenating a Potent Idea," *Academy of Management Executive*, August 2000, pp. 67–80.

90. R. C. Liden, S. J. Wayne, and R. T. Sparrowe, "An Examination of the Mediating Role of Psychological Empowerment on the Relations between the Job, Interpersonal Relationships, and Work Outcomes," *Journal of Applied Psychology* 85 (2000), pp. 407–16.

91. Peters and Austin, A *Passion for Excellence*.

92. K. Thomas and B. Velthouse, "Cognitive Elements of Empowerment: An 'Interpretive' Model of Intrinsic Task Motivation," *Academy of Management Review* 15 (1990), pp. 666–81.

93. J. Kouzes and B. Posner, *The Leadership Challenge*, 2nd ed. (San Francisco: Jossey-Bass, 1995).

94. M. M. Butts, R. J. Vandenberg, D. M. DeJoy, B. S. Schaffer, and M. G. Wilson, "Individual Reactions to High Involvement Work Processes: Investigating the Role of Empowerment and Perceived Organizational Support," *Journal of Occupational Health Psychology* 14 (2009), pp. 122–36.

95. Price Waterhouse Change Integration Team, *Better Change* (Burr Ridge, IL: Richard D. Irwin, 1995).

96. E. E. Lawler III, *The Ultimate Advantage: Creating the High Involvement Organization* (San Francisco: Jossey-Bass, 1992).

97. O. Gadiesh and J. L. Gilbert, "Transforming Corner-Office Strategy into Frontline Action," *Harvard Business Review*, May 2001, pp. 72–79.

98. Kouzes and Posner, *The Leadership Challenge*.

99. Price Waterhouse, *Better Change*.

100. J. Jasinowski and R. Hamrin, *Making It in America* (New York: Simon & Schuster, 1995).

101. W. A. Randolph and M. Sashkin, "Can Organizational Empowerment Work in Multinational Settings?" *Academy of Management Executive* 16 (2002), pp. 102–15.

102. J. Adams, "Inequality in Social Exchange," in *Advances in Experimental Social Psychology*, ed. L. Berkowitz (New York: Academic Press, 1965).

103. M. Bloom, "The Performance Effects of Pay Dispersion of Individuals and Organizations," *Academy of Management Journal* 42 (1999), pp. 25–40.

104. T. Jackson, "Dodd-Frank Will Only Deepen Corporate Pay Envy," *Financial Times*, March 21, 2011, Business & Company Resource Center, http://galenet.galegroup.com; and M. E. Podmolik, "Kraft CEO Sees Bonus Cut as Goals Go Unmet," *Chicago Tribune*, April 1, 2011, sec. 1, pp. 21, 23.

105. D. Prial, "Crunch Time for CPAs," *The Record (Bergen County, NJ)*, April 17, 2007, Business & Company Resource Center, http://galenet.galegroup.com.

106. D. Skarlicki, R. Folger, and P. Tesluk, "Personality as a Moderator in the Relationships between Fairness and Retaliation," *Academy of Management Journal* 42 (1999), pp. 100–108.

107. S. E. Needleman, "'The Cat Hid My Car Keys': Excuses Workers Make," *The Wall Street Journal*, May 13, 2010, http://online.wsj.com.

108. J. Brockner, "Making Sense of Procedural Fairness: How High Procedural Fairness Can Reduce or Heighten the Influence of Outcome Favorability," *Academy of Management Review* 27 (2002), pp. 58–76; and D. De Cremer and D. van Knippenberg, "How Do Leaders Promote Cooperation? The Effects of Charisma and Procedural Fairness," *Journal of Applied Psychology* 87 (2002), pp. 858–66.

109. M. Kernan and P. Hanges, "Survivor Reactions to Reorganization: Antecedents and Consequences of Procedural, Interpersonal, and Informational Justice," *Journal of Applied Psychology* 87 (2002), pp. 916–28.

110. Lawler, *Treat People Right!*

111. W. C. Kim and R. Mauborgne, "Fair Process: Managing in the Knowledge Economy," *Harvard Business Review*, July–August 1997, pp. 65–75.

112. T. Bateman and D. Organ, "Job Satisfaction and the Good Sold: The Relationship between Affect and Employee 'Citizenship,' " *Academy of Management Journal* (1983), pp. 587–95.

113. D. Henne and E. Locke, "Job Dissatisfaction: What Are the Consequences?" *International Journal of Psychology* 20 (1985), pp. 221–40.

114. J. Barling, E. K. Kelloway, and R. Iverson, "High-Quality Work, Job Satisfaction, and Occupational Injuries," *Journal of Applied Psychology* 88 (2003), pp. 276–83.

115. D. Bowen, S. Gilliland, and R. Folger, "HRM and Service Fairness: How Being Fair with Employees Spills Over to Customers," *Organizational Dynamics* (Winter 1999), pp. 7–23.

116. J. Harter, F. Schmidt, and T. Hayes, "Business-Unit-Level Relationship between Employee Satisfaction, Employee Engagement, and Business Outcomes: A Meta-Analysis," *Journal of Applied Psychology* 87 (2002), pp. 268–79.

117. T. Schweitzer, "U.S. Workers Hate Their Jobs More Than Ever," *Inc.*, March 6, 2007, http://www.inc.com.

118. T. Bisoux, "Corporate CounterCulture," *BizEd*, November/December 2004, pp. 16–20; and "Motivation in Today's Workplace," pp. 1–2, 4.

119. A. Fisher, "Happy Employees, Loyal Employees," *Fortune*, "100 Best Companies to Work For," January 16, 2007; "100 Best Companies to Work for 2007," *Fortune* Rankings, January 22, 2007, http://money.cnn.com; and First Horizon National Corp., "Careers" and "Our Benefits," http://www.firsthorizon.com.

120. R. E. Walton, "Improving the Quality of Work Life," *Harvard Business Review* (May–June 1974), pp. 12, 16, 155.

121. A. Fisher, "Loyalty Isn't Dead, Employers Have to Earn It," *Fortune*, January 16, 2007, http://money.cnn.com.

122. E. E. Lawler III, "Strategies for Improving the Quality of Work Life," *American Psychologist* 37 (1982), pp. 486–93; and J. L. Suttle, "Improving Life at Work: Problems and Prospects," in *Improving Life at Work*, ed. J. R. Hackman and J. L. Suttle (Santa Monica, CA: Goodyear, 1977).

123. P. B. Warr, "Well-Being and the Workplace," in D. Kahneman, E. Diener, and N. Schwarz (eds.), *Well-Being: The Foundations of Hedonic Psychology* (New York: Russell Sage Foundation, 1999); and T. A. Wright and R. Cropanzano, "The Role of Psychological Well-Being in Job Performance: A Fresh Look at an Age-Old Quest." *Organizational Dynamics* 33 (2004), pp. 338–51.

124. J. K. Harter, F. L. Schmidt, and C. L. M. Keyes, "Well-Being in the Workplace and Its Relationship to Business Outcomes: A Review of the Gallup Studies," in C.L.M. Keyes and J. Haidt (eds.), *Flourishing: The Positive Person and the Good Life* (Washington DC: American Psychological Association, 2003), pp. 205–24.

125. S. L. Robinson, "Trust and Breach of the Psychological Contract," *Administrative Science Quarterly* 41 (1996), pp. 574–99.

126. D. Rousseau, "Changing the Deal While Keeping the People," *Academy of Management Executive* 10 (1996), pp. 50–58.

127. E. Ridolfi, "Executive Commentary," *Academy of Management Executive* 10 (1996), pp. 59–60.

128. E. E. Lawler III, *From the Ground Up* (San Francisco: Jossey-Bass, 1996).

129. Ibid.

130. S. Ghoshal, C. Bartlett, and P. Moran, "Value Creation: The New Management Manifesto," *Financial Times Mastering Management Review*, November 1999, pp. 34–37.

131. Ram Charan, "Stop Whining, Start Thinking," *BusinessWeek*, August 14, 2008, http://www.businessweek.com.

132. Fikes, "Fortune Magazine Praises Local Companies"; "100 Best Companies to Work For"; "World's Most Admired Companies"; Intuit, "Enduring Innovation with a Profound Impact"; "100 Best Places to Work in 2010"; A. Carr, "How to Unleash Your Human Potential," *Fast Company*, September 16, 2010, http://www.fastcompany.com; and J. Borzo, "Intuit Readies Mobile Products for Businesses," *The Wall Street Journal*, October 13, 2010, http://online.wsj.com.

Chapter 14

1. S. Sloan, "It Takes Teamwork to Write Book on Toyota," *Lexington*

(Ky.) Herald-Leader, May 3, 2010, Business & Company Resource Center, http://galenet.galegroup.com; Associated Press, "Toyota Plant Workers Become Lobbyists for a Day," *Cleveland.com*, February 9, 2010, http://blog.cleveland.com; Toyota Motor Corporation Global, "Toyota Production System," Company: Vision and Philosophy, http://toyota-global.com; Toyota Motor Manufacturing, Kentucky Inc., "The Toyota Production System," Manufacturing, http://www.toyotageorgetown.com; and Toyota, "Toyota's Indiana Plant Turns the Corner, Preps for New Sienna," news release, December 21, 2009, http://pressroom.toyota.com.

2. E. C. Wenger and W. M. Snyder, "Communities of Practice: The Organizational Frontier," *Harvard Business Review*, January–February 2000, pp. 139–45.

3. S. Cohen and D. Bailey, "What Makes Teams Work: Group Effectiveness Research from the Shop Floor to the Executive Suite," *Journal of Management* 23 (1997), pp. 239–90.

4. G. Chen, L. Donahue, and R. Klimoski, "Training Undergraduates to Work in Organizational Teams," *Academy of Management Learning and Education* 3 (2004), pp. 27–40.

5. Ken Blanchard Companies, "Client Spotlight: Summit Pointe," *Ignite!*, March 2007, http://www.kenblanchard.com/ignite.

6. K. Wexley and S. Silverman, *Working Scared* (San Francisco: Jossey-Bass, 1993).

7. E. E. Lawler III, *From the Ground Up* (San Francisco: Jossey-Bass, 1996).

8. E. Fleischauer, "Nucor Manager Says Teamwork Key to Success; Q1 Earnings Up," *Decatur (AL) Daily*, April 20, 2007, http://www.decaturdaily.com.

9. Lawler, *From the Ground Up*.

10. R. Heifetz and D. Laurie, "The Work of Leadership," *Harvard Business Review*, January–February 1996, pp. 124–34.

11. P. Demetrakakes, "Packaging a Big Part of General Success," *Food and Beverage Packaging*, October 2008, Business & Company Resource Center, http://galenet.galegroup.com.

12. D. Nadler, J. R. Hackman, and E. E. Lawler III, *Managing Organizational Behavior* (Boston: Little, Brown, 1979).

13. M. Cianni and D. Wnuck, "Individual Growth and Team Enhancement: Moving toward a New Model of Career Development," *Academy of Management Executive* 11 (1997), pp. 105–15.

14. J. Dudlicek, "Stand-Out Performance," *Refrigerated & Frozen Foods*, March 2010, pp. 18–20.

15. Cohen and Bailey, "What Makes Teams Work."

16. J. Katzenbach and D. Smith, "The Discipline of Teams," *Harvard Business Review*, March–April 1993, pp. 111–20.

17. J. Zenger et al., *Leading Teams* (Burr Ridge, IL: Business One Irwin, 1994).

18. S. Cohen, "New Approaches to Teams and Teamwork," in J. Galbraith, E. E. Lawler III, and Associates, *Organizing for the Future* (San Francisco: Jossey-Bass, 1993).

19. Cohen and Bailey, "What Makes Teams Work."

20. L. Mullins, "Integration Crew for Maryland Bank," *American Banker*, February 13, 2007, General Reference Center Gold, http://find.galegroup.com.

21. Ibid.

22. C. Snow, S. Snell, S. Davison, and D. Hambrick, "Use Transnational Teams to Globalize Your Company," *Organizational Dynamics*, Spring 1996, pp. 50–67.

23. B. Kirkman, B. Rosen, C. Gibson, P. Tesluk, and S. McPherson, "Five Challenges to Virtual Team Success: Lessons from Sabre, Inc.," *Academy of Management Executive* 16 (2002), pp. 67–80.

24. R. Banker, J. Field, R. Schroeder, and K. Sinha, "Impact of Work Teams on Manufacturing Performance: A Longitudinal Field Study," *Academy of Management Journal* 39 (1996), pp. 867–90.

25. D. Yeatts, M. Hipskind, and D. Barnes, "Lessons Learned from Self-Managed Work Teams," *Business Horizons*, July–August 1994, pp. 11–18.

26. B. Kirkman and D. Shapiro, "The Impact of Cultural Values on Job Satisfaction and Organizational Commitment in Self-Managing Work Teams: The Mediating Role of Employee Resistance," *Academy of Management Journal* 44 (2001), pp. 557–69.

27. C. Langfred, "The Downside of Self-Management: A Longitudinal Study of the Effects of Conflict on Trust, Autonomy, and Task Interdependence in Self-Managing Teams," *Academy of Management Journal*, 2007, pp. 885–900.

28. B. Kirkman and D. Shapiro, "The Impact of Cultural Values on Employee Resistance to Teams: Toward a Model of Globalized Self-Managing Work Team Effectiveness," *Academy of Management Review* 22 (1997), pp. 730–57.

29. B. Macy and H. Isumi, "Organizational Change, Design, and Work Innovation: A Meta-Analysis of 131 North American Field Studies—1961–1991," *Research in Organizational Change and Development* 7 (1993), pp. 235–313.

30. Ibid.

31. B. W. Tuckman, "Developmental Sequence in Small Groups," *Psychological Bulletin* 63 (1965), pp. 384–99.

32. S. Furst, M. Reeves, B. Rosen, and R. Blackburn, "Managing the Life Cycle of Virtual Teams," *Academy of Management Executive*, May 2004, pp. 6–20. Quotes in this paragraph are from pp. 11 and 12.

33. C. J. G. Gersick, "Time and Transition in Work Teams: Toward a New Model of Group Development," *Academy of Management Journal* 31 (1988), pp. 9–41.

34. J. R. Hackman, *Groups That Work (and Those That Don't)* (San Francisco: Jossey-Bass, 1990).

35. Zenger et al., *Leading Teams*.

36. R. Cross, "Looking before You Leap: Assessing the Jump to Teams in Knowledge-Based Work," *Business Horizons*, September–October 2000, pp. 29–36.

37. J. Case, "What the Experts Forgot to Mention," *Inc.*, September 1993, pp. 66–78.

38. A. Nahavandi and E. Aranda, "Restructuring Teams for the Reengineered Organization," *Academy of Management Executive*, November 1994, pp. 58–68.

39. B. Kirkman, B. Rosen, P. Tesluk, and C. Gibson, "The Impact of Team Empowerment on Virtual Team Performance: The Moderating Role of Face-to-Face Interaction," *Academy of Management Journal* 47 (2004), pp. 175–92.

40. J. R. Katzenbach and D. K. Smith, *The Wisdom of Teams* (Boston: Harvard Business School Press, 1993).

41. M. Kitamura and J. Scott, "Toyota Forms Rare-Metals Team amid China Export Ban," *Bloomberg Businessweek*, September 29, 2010, http://www.businessweek.com; M. Ramsey, "Toyota Tries to Break Reliance on China," *The Wall Street Journal*, January 14, 2011, http://online.wsj.com; S Biggs, "Rare Earth Metals Leave Toxic Trail to Toyota, Vestas," *Bloomberg Businessweek*, January 6, 2011, http://www.businessweek.com; Associated Press, "Toyota Looks to Cut Dependence on Rare Earth Minerals in Electric Cars," *Fox News*, January 17, 2011, http://www.foxnews.com; A. Ohnsman, "Toyota Forms Teams to Review Acceleration Complaints (Update1)," *Bloomberg Businessweek*, April 8, 2010, http://www.businessweek.com; N. O'Leary, "Lexus' David Nordstrom on Hyping a Luxury Hybrid," *Brandweek*, May 17, 2010, Business & Company Resource Center, http://galenet.galegroup.com; L. Chappell, "N.A. Gets a Key Role in Toyota Quality Control," *Automotive News*, Business & Company Resource Center, http://galenet.galegroup.com; and M. Ramsey, "U.S. Ends Toyota Probe," *The Wall Street Journal*, February 25, 2011, http://online.wsj.com.

42. Nadler et al., *Managing Organizational Behavior*.

43. T. Peters and N. Austin, *A Passion for Excellence* (New York: Random House, 1985).

44. D. Wood, "Multidisciplinary Team Eliminates Inefficiencies in a Busy GYN Oncology Clinic," *Oncology Nursing News*, April 2009, Business & Company Resource Center, http://galenet.galegroup.com.

45. Nadler et al., *Managing Organizational Behavior*.

46. S. Adams, "Making All Your Teams into A-Teams," *Training Journal*, August

2008, Business & Company Resource Center, http://galenet.galegroup.com.

47. C. Hall, "Corporate Coaches Cook Up Recipe for Teamwork," *Dallas Morning News*, May 30, 2010, Business & Company Resource Center, http://galenet.galegroup.com.

48. D. Coutu, "Why Teams Don't Work," *Harvard Business Review*, May 2009, pp. 99–105 (interview of J. Richard Hackman).

49. Katzenbach and Smith, "The Discipline of Teams."

50. Ibid.

51. L. Gibson, J. Mathieu, C. Shalley, and T. Ruddy, "Creativity and Standardization: Complementary or Conflicting Drivers of Team Effectiveness?" *Academy of Management Journal* 48 (2005), pp. 521–31.

52. C. Meyer, "How the Right Measures Help Teams Excel," *Harvard Business Review*, May–June 1994, pp. 95–103.

53. J. R. Katzenbach and J. A. Santamaria, "Firing Up the Front Line," *Harvard Business Review*, May–June 1999, pp. 107–17.

54. D. Knight, C. Durham, and E. Locke, "The Relationship of Team Goals, Incentives, and Efficacy to Strategic Risk, Tactical Implementation, and Performance," *Academy of Management Journal* 44 (2001), pp. 326–38.

55. B. L. Kirkman and B. Rosen, "Powering Up Teams," *Organizational Dynamics* (Winter 2000), pp. 48–66.

56. Lawler, *From the Ground Up.*

57. A. Jassawalla, H. Sashittal, and A. Maishe, "Students' Perceptions of Social Loafing: Its Antecedents and Consequences in Undergraduate Business Classroom Teams," *Academy of Management Learning and Education*, 2009, pp. 42–54.

58. M. Erez, "Is Group Productivity Loss the Rule or the Exception? Effects of Culture and Group-Based Motivation," *Academy of Management Journal* 39 (1996), pp. 1513–37.

59. Katzenbach and Smith, "The Discipline of Teams."

60. M. Bolch, "Rewarding the Team," *HRMagazine*, February 2007, General Reference Center Gold, http://find.galegroup.com; P. Pascarelloa, "Compensating Teams," *Across the Board*, February 1997, pp. 16–22; and M. Johnson, J. Hollenbeck, S. Humphrey, D. Ilgen, D. Jundt, and C. Meyer, "Cutthroat Cooperation: Asymmetrical Adaptation to Changes in Team Reward Structures," *Academy of Management Journal*, 2006, 103–19.

61. M. J. Pearsall, M. S. Christian, and A. P. J. Ellis, "Motivating Interdependent Teams: Individual Rewards, Shared Rewards, or Something In Between?" *Journal of Applied Psychology* 95 (2010), pp. 183–91.

62. R. Wageman, "Interdependence and Group Effectiveness," *Administrative Science Quarterly* 40 (1995), pp. 145–80.

63. Bolch, "Rewarding the Team."

64. Lawler, *From the Ground Up.*

65. R. Wellins, R. Byham, and G. Dixon, *Inside Teams* (San Francisco: Jossey-Bass, 1994).

66. Institute for Corporate Productivity, "Virtual Teams Now a Reality," news release, September 4, 2008, http://www.i4cp.com.

67. R. Preidt, "Work Teams Who Share Negative Emotions Better at Problem-Solving," *Bloomberg Businessweek*, November 23, 2010, http://www.businessweek.com.

68. A. Srivastava, K. Bartol, and E. Locke, "Empowering Leadership in Management Teams: Effects on Knowledge Sharing, Efficacy, and Performance," *Academy of Management Journal*, 2006, pp. 1239–51.

69. L. A. DeChurch and J. R. Mesmer-Magnus, "The Cognitive Underpinnings of Effective Teamwork: A Meta-Analysis." *Journal of Applied Psychology* 95 (2010), pp. 32–53.

70. J. M. Levine, E. T. Higgins, and H. Choi, "Development of Strategic Norms in Groups," *Organizational Behavior and Human Decision Processes* 82 (2000), pp. 88–101.

71. K. Jehn and E. Mannix, "The Dynamic Nature of Conflict: A Longitudinal Study of Intragroup Conflict and Group Performance," *Academy of Management Journal* 44 (2001), pp. 238–51.

72. J. O'Toole, *Vanguard Management: Redesigning the Corporate Future* (New York: Doubleday, 1985).

73. R. F. Bales, *Interaction Process Analysis: A Method for the Study of Small Groups* (Reading, MA: Addison-Wesley, 1950).

74. V. U. Druskat and J. Wheeler, "Managing from the Boundary: The Effective Leadership of Self-Managing Work Teams," *Academy of Management Journal* 46 (2003), pp. 435–57.

75. Katzenbach and Smith, *The Wisdom of Teams.*

76. J. Carson, P. Tesluk, and J. Marrone, "Shared Leadership in Teams: An Investigation of Antecedent Conditions and Performance," *Academy of Management Journal*, 2007, pp. 1217–34.

77. C. Stoner and R. Hartman, "Team Building: Answering the Tough Questions," *Business Horizons*, September–October 1993, pp. 70–78.

78. S. E. Seashore, *Group Cohesiveness in the Industrial Work Group* (Ann Arbor, MI: University of Michigan Press, 1954).

79. Banker et al., "Impact of Work Teams on Manufacturing Performance."

80. B. Mullen and C. Cooper, "The Relation between Group Cohesiveness and Performance: An Integration," *Psychological Bulletin* 115 (1994), pp. 210–27.

81. D. P. Forbes and F. J. Milliken, "Cognition and Corporate Governance: Understanding Boards of Directors as Strategic Decision-Making Groups," *Academy of Management Review* 24 (1999), pp. 489–505.

82. T. Simons, L. H. Pelled, and K. A. Smith, "Making Use of Difference: Diversity, Debate, and Decision Comprehensiveness in Top Management Teams," *Academy of Management Journal* 42 (1999), pp. 662–73.

83. Seashore, *Group Cohesiveness in the Industrial Work Group.*

84. B. Lott and A. Lott, "Group Cohesiveness as Interpersonal Attraction: A Review of Relationships with Antecedent and Consequent Variables," *Psychological Bulletin*, October 1965, pp. 259–309.

85. K. Dahlin, L. Weingart, and P. Hinds, "Team Diversity and Information Use," *Academy of Management Journal* 48 (2005), pp. 1107–23.

86. B. L. Kirkman and B. Rosen, "Beyond Self-Management: Antecedents and Consequences of Team Empowerment," *Academy of Management Journal* 42 (1999), pp. 58–74.

87. Hackman, *Groups That Work.*

88. W. Bennis, *Organizing Genius* (Reading, MA: Addison-Wesley, 1997).

89. Cianni and Wnuck, "Individual Growth and Team Enhancement."

90. K. Jehn, "A Multimethod Examination of the Benefits and Detriments of Intragroup Conflict," *Administrative Science Quarterly* 40 (1995), pp. 245–82.

91. Wellins et al., *Inside Teams.*

92. D. G. Ancona, "Outward Bound: Strategies for Team Survival in an Organization," *Academy of Management Journal* 33 (1990), pp. 334–65.

93. Ibid.

94. L. Sayles, *Leadership: What Effective Managers Really Do, and How They Do It* (New York: McGraw-Hill, 1979).

95. Ibid.

96. P. Lencioni, "How to Foster Good Conflict," *The Wall Street Journal*, November 13, 2008, http://online.wsj.com; and D. Schachter, "Learn to Embrace Opposition for Improved Decision Making," *Information Outlook*, October 2008, Business & Company Resource Center, http://galenet.galegroup.com.

97. Accountemps, "Keeping the Peace," news release, March 15, 2011, http://accountemps.rhi.mediaroom.com.

98. J. Chatman and F. Flynn, "The Influence of Demographic Heterogeneity on the Emergence and Consequences of Cooperative Norms in Work Teams," *Academy of Management Journal* 44 (2001), pp. 956–74; and R. T. Keller, "Cross-Functional Project Groups in Research and New Product Development: Diversity, Communications, Job Stress, and Outcomes," *Academy of Management Journal* 44 (2001), pp. 547–55.

99. E. Kearney and D. Gebert, "Managing Diversity and Enhancing Team Outcomes: The Promise of Transformational Leadership." *Journal of Applied Psychology* 94 (2009), pp. 77–89.

100. J. Cable, "Lean for Machines," *Industry Week*, July 2010, pp. 36–40.

101. D. Tjosvold, *Working Together to Get Things Done* (Lexington, MA: Lexington Books, 1986).

102. C. Tinsley and J. Brett, "Managing Workplace Conflict in the United States and Hong Kong," *Organizational Behavior and Human Decision Processes* 85 (2001), pp. 360–81.

103. K. W. Thomas, "Conflict and Conflict Management," in *Handbook of Industrial and Organizational Psychology*, ed. M. D. Dunnette (Chicago: Rand McNally, 1976).

104. D. Tynan, "IT Turf Wars," *InfoWorld.com*, February 14, 2011, Business & Company Resource Center, http://galenet.galegroup.com.

105. Ibid.

106. K. W. Thomas, "Toward Multidimensional Values in Teaching: The Example of Conflict Behaviors," *Academy of Management Review*, 1977, pp. 484–89.

107. C. O. Longenecker and M. Neubert, "Barriers and Gateways to Management Cooperation and Teamwork," *Business Horizons*, September–October 2000, pp. 37–44.

108. M. Johnson, J. Hollenbeck, S. Humphrey, D. Algen, D. Jundt, and C. Meyer, "Cutthroat Cooperation: Asymmetrical Adaptation to Changes in Team Reward Structures," *Academy of Management Journal* 49 (2006), pp. 103–119.

109. P. S. Nugent, "Managing Conflict: Third-Party Interventions for Managers," *Academy of Management Executive* 16 (2002), pp. 139–54.

110. M. Blum and J. A. Wall Jr., "HRM: Managing Conflicts in the Firm," *Business Horizons*, May–June 1997, pp. 84–87.

111. S. Nunes, "How to Work outside Your Comfort Zone," *Bloomberg Businessweek*, July 6, 2010, http://www.businessweek.com.

112. J. A. Wall Jr. and R. R. Callister, "Conflict and Its Management," *Journal of Management* 21 (1995), pp. 515–58.

113. J. Polzer, C. B. Crisp, S. Jarvenpaa, and J. Kim, "Extending the Faultline Model to Geographically Dispersed Teams: How Collocated Subgroups Can Impair Group Functioning," *Academy of Management Journal* 49 (2006), pp. 679–92.

114. M. Montoya-Weiss, A. Massey, and M. Song, "Getting It Together: Temporal Coordination and Conflict Management in Global Virtual Teams," *Academy of Management Journal* 44 (2001), pp. 1251–62.

115. R. Standifer and J. A. Wall Jr., "Managing Conflict in B2B Commerce," *Business Horizons*, March–April 2003, pp. 65–70.

116. Chappell, "N.A. Gets a Key Role"; Ramsey, "U.S. Ends Toyota Probe"; A. Taylor III, "What's Really behind the Toyota Debacle," *Fortune*, April 14, 2010, http://money.cnn.com; D. Mehri, "Kaizen Goes Kaput," *The Wall Street Journal*, February 13, 2010, http://online.wsj.com; H. Greimel, "Toyota Adds a Cross-Check to Development Process," *Automotive News*, August 9, 2010, Business & Company Resource Center, http://galenet.galegroup.com; C. Dawson and Y. Takahashi, "Toyota Makes New Push to Avoid Recalls," *The Wall Street Journal*, February 24, 2011, http://online.wsj.com; and A. Ohnsman, "Toyota Extends Auto Development Time to Boost Quality," *Bloomberg Businessweek*, July 7, 2010, http://www.businessweek.com.

Chapter 15

1. A. Weinzweig, "Creating a Company Vision," *Inc.*, February 1, 2011, http://www.inc.com; Zingerman's Community of Businesses, "About Us," http://www.zingermanscommunity.com; Zingerman's Community of Businesses, "Our Businesses," http://www.zingermanscommunity.com; K. Gabert, "Baking Up the Perfect Batch," *Food Manufacturing*, September 2010, pp. 8–10; J. Baldoni, "Reengineering a Leader's Value," *Fast Company*, May 25, 2010, http://www.fastcompany.com; and M. Shuman, A. Barron, and Wasserman, *Community Food Enterprise: Local Success in a Global Marketplace* (Arlington, VA: Wallace Center at Winrock International, 2009), http://www.communityfoodenterprise.org.

2. L. Penley, E. Alexander, I. E. Jernigan, and C. Henwood, "Communication Abilities of Managers: The Relationship to Performance," *Journal of Management* 17 (1991), pp. 57–76.

3. W. V. Haney, "A Comparative Study of Unilateral and Bilateral Communication," *Academy of Management Journal* 7 (1964), pp. 128–36.

4. J. R. Mesmer-Magnus and L. A. DeChurch, "Information Sharing and Team Performance: A Meta-Analysis." *Journal of Applied Psychology* 94 (2009), pp. 535–46.

5. J. Sandberg, "What Exactly Was It That the Boss Said? You Can Only Imagine," *The Wall Street Journal*, September 19, 2006, http://online.wsj.com.

6. M. McCormack, "The Illusion of Communication," *Financial Times Mastering Management Review*, July 1999, pp. 8–9.

7. J. Sandberg, "Not Communicating with Your Boss? Count Your Blessings," *The Wall Street Journal*, May 22, 2007, http://online.wsj.com.

8. R. Cross and S. Brodt, "How Assumptions of Consensus Undermine Decision Making," *Sloan Management Review* 42 (2001), pp. 86–94.

9. S. Mohammed and E. Ringseis, "Cognitive Diversity and Consensus in Group Decision Making: The Role of Inputs, Processes, and Outcomes," *Organizational Behavior and Human Decision Processes* 85 (2001), pp. 310–35.

10. S. Parker and C. Axtell, "Seeing Another Viewpoint: Antecedents and Outcomes of Employee Perspective Taking," *Academy of Management Journal* 44 (2001), pp. 1085–100.

11. D. Tannen, "The Power of Talk: Who Gets Heard and Why," *Harvard Business Review*, September–October 1995, pp. 138–48.

12. Ibid.

13. Ibid.

14. L. K. Larkey, "Toward a Theory of Communicative Interactions in Culturally Diverse Workgroups," *Academy of Management Review*, April 1996, pp. 463–91.

15. C. Argyris, "Good Communication That Blocks Learning," *Harvard Business Review*, July–August 1994, pp. 77–85.

16. E. Krell, "The Unintended Word," *HRMagazine*, August 2006, General Reference Center Gold, http://find.galegroup.com.

17. C. Deutsch, "The Multimedia Benefits Kit," *The New York Times*, October 14, 1990, sec.3, p. 25.

18. T. W. Comstock, *Communicating in Business and Industry* (Albany, NY: Delmar, 1985).

19. N. L. Reinsch Jr., J. W. Turner, and C. H. Tinsley, "Multicommunicating: A Practice Whose Time Has Come?" *Academy of Management Review* 33 (2008), pp. 391–403.

20. J. Taylor and W. Wacker, *The 500 Year Delta: What Happens after What Comes Next* (New York: HarperCollins, 1997).

21. S. J. Leandri, "Five Ways to Improve Your Corporate Blogs," *Information Outlook*, January 2007, Business & Company Resource Center, http://galenet.galegroup.com.

22. A. Rane and T. Agrawal, *The Future of Workplaces* (GigaOm Pro, March 2011), http://livingworkplace.skype.com.

23. J. Dye, "Collaboration 2.0: Make the Web Your Workspace," *EContent*, January–February 2007, General Reference Center Gold, http://find.galegroup.com.

24. E. Lee, "The Maze Meltdown: Crash May Virtually Change Commuting," *San Francisco Chronicle*, May 6, 2007, http://www.sfgate.com.

25. S. S. K. Lam and J. Schaubroeck, "Improving Group Decisions by Better Pooling Information: A Comparative Advantage of Group Decision Support Systems," *Journal of Applied Psychology* 85 (2000), pp. 565–73.

26. M. Schmulen, "Memo to the Boss: Twitter's Not a Time Suck," *Fortune*, January 19, 2010, http://tech.fortune.cnn.com; D. Lindorff, "Facing Up to Facebook," *Treasury & Risk*, April 2011, Business & Company Resource Center, http://galenet.galegroup.com; and S. Ali, "Why No One under 30 Answers Your Voicemail," *DiversityInc*, August 27, 2010, http://www.diversityinc.com.

27. C. Naquin and G. Paulson, "Online Bargaining and Interpersonal Trust," *Journal of Applied Psychology* 88 (2003), pp. 113–20.

28. B. Baltes, M. Dickson, M. Sherman, C. Bauer, and J. LaGanke, "Computer-Mediated Communication and Group

Decision Making: A Meta-Analysis," *Organizational Behavior and Human Decision Processes* 87 (2002), pp. 156–79.

29. R. Rice and D. Case, "Electronic Message Systems in the University: A Description of Use and Utility," *Journal of Communication* 33 (1983), pp. 131–52; and C. Steinfield, "Dimensions of Electronic Mail Use in an Organizational Setting," *Proceedings of the Academy of Management*, San Diego, 1985.

30. M. Gardner, "You've Got Mail: 'We're Letting You Go,'" *Christian Science Monitor*, September 18, 2006, http://www.csmonitor.com; and Linton Weeks, "Read the Blog: You're Fired," *National Public Radio*, December 8, 2008, http://www.npr.org.

31. Lindorff, "Facing Up to Facebook."

32. Reuters, "Is That Really What Your E-mail Meant to Say?" *Yahoo News*, February 14, 2007, http://news.yahoo.com.

33. K. Byron, "Carrying Too Heavy a Load? The Communication and Miscommunication of Emotion by Email," *Academy of Management Review* 33 (2008), pp. 309–27.

34. C. E. Naquin, T. R. Kurtzberg, and L. Y. Belkin, "The Finer Points of Lying Online: E-mail versus Pen and Paper," *Journal of Applied Psychology* 95 (2010), pp. 387–94.

35. B. Glassberg, W. Kettinger, and J. Logan, "Electronic Communication: An Ounce of Policy Is Worth a Pound of Cure," *Business Horizons*, July–August 1996, pp. 74–80.

36. Ali, "Why No One under 30 Answers Your Voicemail."

37. A. Joyce, "Never Out of IM Reach," *The Washington Post*, December 26, 2004, p. F5; and G. Hughes, "Quick Guide to IM-ing at Work," *Yahoo Tech*, January 24, 2007, http://tech.yahoo.com.

38. M. Totty, "Rethinking the Inbox," *The Wall Street Journal*, March 26, 2007, http://online.wsj.com. Reuters, "BlackBerrys, Laptops Blur Work/Home Balance: Poll," *Yahoo News*, April 5, 2007, http://news.yahoo.com; and M. Locher, "BlackBerry Addiction Starts at the Top," *PC World*, March 6, 2007, http://www.pcworld.com.

39. Taylor and Wacker, *The 500 Year Delta*; Locher, "BlackBerry Addiction"; and Hughes, "Quick Guide to IM-ing."

40. Locher, "BlackBerry Addiction."

41. E. Horng, "No E-mail Fridays Transform Office," *ABC News*, March 10, 2007, http://abcnews.go.com.

42. Ibid.

43. B. Van Der Meer, "Realty Companies Making Internet Home," *Modesto (CA) Bee*, December 15, 2006, General Reference Center Gold, http://find.galegroup.com.

44. T. Mackintosh, "Is This the Year You Move to a Virtual Office?" *Accounting Technology*, May 2007, General Reference Center Gold, http://find.galegroup.com.

45. E. M. Hallowell, "The Human Moment at Work," *Harvard Business Review*, January–February 1999, pp. 58–66.

46. R. Lengel and R. Daft, "The Selection of Communication Media as an Executive Skill," *Academy of Management Executive* 2 (1988), pp. 225–32.

47. J. R. Carlson and R. W. Zmud, "Channel Expansion Theory and the Experiential Nature of Media Richness Perceptions," *Academy of Management Journal* 42 (1999), pp. 153–70.

48. L. Trevino, R. Daft, and R. Lengel, "Understanding Managers' Media Choices: A Symbolic Interactionist Perspective," in *Organizations and Communication Technology*, ed. J. Fulk and C. Steinfield (London: Sage, 1990).

49. J. Fulk and B. Boyd, "Emerging Theories of Communication in Organizations," *Journal of Management* 17 (1991), pp. 407–46.

50. L. Welch, "The Way I Work: Rashmi Sinha of SlideShare," *Inc.*, April 1, 2011, http://www.inc.com.

51. L. Bossidy and R. Charan, *Confronting Reality: Doing What Matters to Get Things Right* (New York: Crown Business, 2004).

52. M. McCall, M. Lombardo, and A. Morrison, *The Lessons of Experience: How Successful Executives Develop on the Job* (Lexington, MA: Lexington, 1988).

53. J. A. Conger, "The Necessary Art of Persuasion," *Harvard Business Review*, May–June 1998, pp. 84–95.

54. N. Morgan, "How to Become an Authentic Speaker," *Harvard Business Review*, November 2008, pp. 115–19.

55. N. Nohria and B. Harrington, *Six Principles of Successful Persuasion* (Boston: Harvard Business School Publishing Division, 1993).

56. J. Ewers, "Making It Stick," *U.S. News & World Report*, January 29–February 5, 2007, pp. EE2–EE8 (review of *Made to Stick* by Chip Heath and Dan Heath).

57. H. K. Mintz, "Business Writing Styles for the 70's," *Business Horizons*, August 1972. Cited in *Readings in Interpersonal and Organizational Communication*, ed. R. C. Huseman, C. M. Logue, and D. L. Freshley (Boston: Allyn & Bacon, 1977).

58. C. D. Decker, "Writing to Teach Thinking," *Across the Board*, March 1996, pp. 19–20.

59. M. Forbes, "Exorcising Demons from Important Business Letters," *Marketing Times*, March–April 1981, pp. 36–38.

60. T. Flood, "Top Ten Mistakes Managers Make with Email," *The Wall Street Journal*, February 3, 2010, http://online.wsj.com.

61. D. Jones, "Cisco CEO Sees Tech as Integral to Success," *USA Today*, March 19, 2007, p. 4B (interview with John Chambers).

62. G. Ferraro, "The Need for Linguistic Proficiency in Global Business," *Business Horizons*, May–June 1996, pp. 39–46.

63. P. C. Early and E. Mosakowski, "Creating Hybrid Team Cultures: An Empirical Test of Transnational Team Functioning," *Academy of Management Journal* 43 (2000), pp. 26–49.

64. Ferraro, "The Need for Linguistic Proficiency."

65. C. Chu, *The Asian Mind Game* (New York: Rawson Associates, 1991).

66. Ferraro, "The Need for Linguistic Proficiency."

67. Weinzweig, "Creating a Company Vision"; Shuman et al., *Community Food Enterprise*; and Zingerman's Community of Businesses, "Zingerman's 2020 Vision," accessed at www.zingermanscommunity.com, April 14, 2011.

68. J. S. Lublin, "Improv Troupe Teaches Managers How to Give Better Presentations," *Career Journal*, February 7, 2007, http://www.careerjournal.com.

69. Comstock, *Communicating in Business and Industry*.

70. M. Korda, *Power: How to Get It, How to Use It* (New York: Random House, 1975).

71. A. Mehrabian, "Communication without Words," *Psychology Today*, September 1968, p. 52. Cited in M. B. McCaskey, "The Hidden Message Managers Send," *Harvard Business Review*, November–December 1979, pp. 135–48.

72. Ferraro, "The Need for Linguistic Proficiency."

73. *Business Horizons*, May–June 1993. Copyright 1993 by the Foundation for the School of Business at Indiana University. Used with permission.

74. A. T. Palmer, "Art of Listening Picked Up Young," *Chicago Tribune*, April 29, 2007, sec. 5, p. 3.

75. A. Athos and J. Gabarro, *Interpersonal Behavior* (Englewood Cliffs, NJ: Prentice-Hall, 1978).

76. Ibid.

77. M. K. Pratt, "Five Ways to Drive Your Best Workers out the Door," *Computerworld*, August 25, 2008, pp. 26–27, 30.

78. J. Kouzes and B. Posner, *The Leadership Challenge* (San Francisco: Jossey-Bass, 1995).

79. G. Graham, J. Unruh, and P. Jennings, "The Impact of Nonverbal Communication in Organizations: A Survey of Perceptions," *Journal of Business Communications* 28 (1991), pp. 45–62.

80. Ibid.

81. D. Upton and S. Macadam, "Why (and How) to Take a Plant Tour," *Harvard Business Review*, May–June 1997, pp. 97–106.

82. N. Adler, *International Dimensions of Organizational Behavior*, 2nd ed. (Boston: Kent, 1991).

83. Chu, *The Asian Mind Game*.

84. Alex Pentland, "How Social Networks Network Best," *Harvard Business Review*, February 2009, p. 37.

85. A. Smidts, A. T. H. Pruyn, and C. B. M. van Riel, "The Impact of Employee Communication and Perceived External Prestige on Organizational Identification," *Academy of Management Journal* 49 (2001), pp. 1051–62.

86. J. W. Koehler, K. W. E. Anatol, and R. L. Applebaum, *Organizational Communication: Behavioral Perspectives* (Orlando, FL: Holt, Rinehart & Winston, 1981).

87. J. Waldroop and T. Butler, "The Executive as Coach," *Harvard Business Review*, November–December 1996, pp. 111–17.

88. D. T. Hall, K. L. Otazo, and G. P. Hollenbeck, "Behind Closed Doors: What Really Happens in Executive Coaching," *Organizational Dynamics*, Winter 1999, pp. 39–53.

89. T. Judge and J. Cowell, "The Brave New World of Coaching," *Business Horizons*, July–August 1997, pp. 71–77; E. E. Lawler III, *Treat People Right!* (San Francisco: Jossey-Bass, 2003); and L. A. Hill, "New Manager Development for the 21st Century," *Academy of Management Executive*, August 2004, pp. 121–26.

90. J. Gutknecht and J. B. Keys, "Mergers, Acquisitions, and Takeovers: Maintaining Morale of Survivors and Protecting Employees," *Academy of Management Executive*, August 1993, pp. 26–36.

91. D. Schweiger and A. DeNisi, "Communication with Employees Following a Merger: A Longitudinal Field Experiment," *Academy of Management Journal* 34 (1991), pp. 110–35.

92. L. Buchanan, "Opening the Books and Motivating Workers," *Inc.*, June 8, 2010, http://online.wsj.com; and "Top Small Company Workplaces: Ginger Bay Salon & Spa," *Inc.*, June 2010, http://www.inc.com.

93. J. Case, "Opening the Books," *Harvard Business Review*, March–April 1997, pp. 118–27.

94. T. R. V. Davis, "Open-Book Management: Its Promise and Pitfalls," *Organization Dynamics*, Winter 1997, pp. 7–20.

95. P. Patel, "Houston's Top Workplaces 2010: No. 1 Midsize Company, Hilcorp Energy Company," *Houston Chronicle*, November 7, 2010, Business & Company Resource Center, http://galenet.galegroup.com; and P. Patel, "Houston's Top Workplaces 2010 Q&A," *Houston Chronicle*, November 7, 2010, Business & Company Resource Center, http://galenet.galegroup.com.

96. W. V. Ruch, *Corporate Communications* (Westport, CT: Quorum, 1984).

97. J. Sandberg, "Working for a Boss Who Only Manages Up Can Be a Real Downer," *The Wall Street Journal*, May 16, 2006, http://online.wsj.com.

98. J. Gardner, "The Heart of the Matter: Leader-Constituent Interaction," in *Leading & Leadership*, ed. T. Fuller (Notre Dame, IN: Notre Dame University Press, 2000), pp. 239–44.

99. R. Ashkenas, D. Ulrich, T. Jick, and S. Kerr, *The Boundaryless Organization* (San Francisco: Jossey-Bass, 1995).

100. Ruch, *Corporate Communications*.

101. P. Bach, "Staying in Touch a Changing Picture," *Post-Crescent* (Appleton, WI), April 18, 2006, General Reference Center Gold, http://find.galegroup.com.

102. M. Fitzgerald, "The Earl of Florida," *Editor & Publisher*, February 1, 2007, General Reference Center Gold, http://find.galegroup.com.

103. A. Hutton, "Four Rules for Taking Your Message to Wall Street," *Harvard Business Review*, May 2001, pp. 125–32.

104. Koehler et al., *Organizational Communication*.

105. Janet Pogue, "Working around the Water Cooler," *Employee Benefit News*, February 1, 2009, Business & Company Resource Center, http://galenet.galegroup.com; Gensler, "Gensler Survey Measures Connection between Workplace Design and Business Performance," news release, October 23, 2008, http://www.gensler.com; and Gensler, *2008 Workplace Survey: United States*, 2008, http://www.gensler.com.

106. W. Atkinson, "Let's Work Together Right Now," *Collections & Credit Risk*, May 2006, Business & Company Resource Center, http://galenet.galegroup.com.

107. Ashkenas et al., *The Boundaryless Organization*.

108. T. Harbert, "Teamwork for Techies," *Computerworld*, December 20, 2010, pp. 24–27.

109. A. Bryant, "Want Clarity? Learn to Play Devil's Advocate," *The New York Times*, February 26, 2011, http://www.nytimes.com (interview with R. D. Fain).

110. N. B. Kurland and L. H. Pelled, "Passing the Word: Toward a Model of Gossip and Power in the Workplace," *Academy of Management Review* 25 (2000), pp. 428–38.

111. L. Abrams, R. Cross, E. Lesser, and D. Levin, "Nurturing Interpersonal Trust in Knowledge-Sharing Networks," *Academy of Management Executive* 17 (November 2003), pp. 64–77.

112. R. L. Rosnow, "Rumor as Communication: A Contextual Approach," *Journal of Communication* 38 (1988), pp. 12–28.

113. L. Burke and J. M. Wise, "The Effective Care, Handling, and Pruning of the Office Grapevine," *Business Horizons*, May–June 2003, pp. 71–76.

114. K. Davis, "The Care and Cultivation of the Corporate Grapevine," *Dun's Review*, July 1973, pp. 44–47.

115. "Office Politics Is on the Rise According to a Survey by Accountemps," *Bradenton (FL) Herald*, October 25, 2008, Business & Company Resource Center, http://galenet.galegroup.com; and Alan M. Wolf, "A Morale Boost," *Raleigh (NC) News & Observer*, March 15, 2009, http://galenet.galegroup.com.

116. N. Difonzo, P. Bordia, and R. Rosnow, "Reining in Rumors," *Organizational Dynamics*, Summer 1994, pp. 47–62.

117. Ashkenas et al., *The Boundaryless Organization*.

118. R. M. Hodgetts, "A Conversation with Steve Kerr," *Organizational Dynamics*, Spring 1996, pp. 68–79.

119. R. M. Fulmer, "The Evolving Paradigm of Leadership Development," *Organizational Dynamics*, Spring 1997, pp. 59–72.

120. General Electric, "GE Shares Skills, Intellectual Capital with CommonBond Communities," news release, December 4, 2006, http://www.genewscenter.com.

121. Ashkenas et al., *The Boundaryless Organization*.

122. Shuman et al., *Community Food Enterprise*; D. Walsh, "No Secrets," *Crain's Detroit Business*, January 18, 2010, Business & Company Resource Center, http://galenet.galegroup.com; D Walsh, "There's More to Open Book Than Simply Opening Books," *Crain's Detroit Business*, January 18, 2010, Business & Company Resource Center, http://galenet.galegroup.com; and University of Michigan Ross School of Business, "Implementing Open-Book Finance," news release, October 19, 2010, http://www.bus.umich.edu.

Chapter 16

1. J. C. Collins and J. I. Porras, *Built to Last: Successful Habits of Visionary Companies* (New York: HarperBusiness, 1994).

2. Southwest Airlines, "About Southwest," http://www.southwest.com; "Smiles and Free Peanuts: Southwest Airlines," *The Economist*, June 4, 2011, Business & Company Resource Center, http://galenet.galegroup.com; S. Carey, "Airlines' Consumer Rating Falls Further," *The Wall Street Journal*, June 21, 2011, http://online.wsj.com; M. J. Credeur, "Southwest Capping Fleet Marks Record No-Growth Period," *Bloomberg Businessweek*, July 29, 2010, http://www.businessweek.com; M. Schlangenstein, "Southwest Profit Rises 13%, Fuel Outlook Spurs Concern," *Bloomberg Businessweek*, January 20, 2011, http://www.businessweek.com; M. Schlangenstein and J. Hughes, "Southwest Risks Keep-It-Simple Focus to Spur Growth," *Bloomberg Businessweek*, September 28, 2010, http://www.businessweek.com; "Southwest Charts a New Flight Plan," *Bloomberg Businessweek*, September 30, 2010, http://www.businessweek.com; and S. McCartney, "Can't Call Southwest a Discount Airline These Days," *The Wall Street Journal*, June 2, 2011, http://online.wsj.com.

3. B. Kenney, "Dell Inc.: Coach Michael Dell's New Game Plan," *Industry Week*, June 7, 2007, http://www.industryweek.com.

4. "BlackBerry Outage Explained," *Chicago Tribune*, April 21, 2007, sec. 3, p. 2; and N. Weil, "BlackBerry Service Restored, Slow Response Irks Users," *InfoWorld*, April 18, 2007, http://www.infoworld.com.

5. W. G. Ouchi, "Markets, Bureaucracies, and Clans," *Administrative Science Quarterly* 25 (1980), pp. 129–41.

6. R. Simons, A. Davila, and R. S. Kaplan, *Performance Measurement & Control*

Systems for Implementing Strategy (Englewood Cliffs, NJ: Prentice Hall, 2000).

7. E. D. Pulakos, S. Arad, M. A. Donovan, and K. E. Plamondon, "Adaptability in the Workplace: Development of a Taxonomy of Adaptive Performance," *Journal of Applied Psychology* 85, no. 4 (August 2000), pp. 12–24; and K. A. Merchant and T. Sandino, "Four Options for Measuring Value Creation: Strategies for Managers to Avoid Potential Flaws in Accounting Measures of Performance," *Journal of Accountancy* 208, no. 2 (2009), pp. 34–38.

8. E. Gardner, "High-Quality Information," *Modern Healthcare*, March 5, 2007, General Reference Center Gold, http://find.galegroup.com.

9. M. S. Rosenwald, "Chocolate Purists Alarmed by Proposal to Fudge Standards," *Washington Post*, April 27, 2007, http://www.washingtonpost.com.

10. J. T. Burr, "Keys to a Successful Internal Audit," *Quality Progress* 30, no. 4 (April 1997), pp. 75–77; and J. Zorabedian, "Uniform Security," *American Executive*, June 2008, Business & Company Resource Center, http://galenet.galegroup.com.

11. L. Buchanan, "Leadership: Armed with Data," *Inc.*, March 2009, http://www.inc.com.

12. R. M. Kanter, "The Matter with the Mainstream," *U.S. News & World Report*, October 30, 2006, General Reference Center Gold, http://find.galegroup.com.

13. "Quality Leadership 100," *Quality*, September 2006, Business & Company Resource Center, http://galenet.galegroup.com.

14. E. White, "How Surveying Workers Can Pay Off," *The Wall Street Journal*, June 18, 2007, http://online.wsj.com.

15. B. Roberts, "Stay Ahead of the Technology Use Curve," *HRMagazine*, October 2008, Business & Company Resource Center, http://galenet.galegroup.com; and K. A. Carr, "Broaching Body Art," *Crain's Cleveland Business*, September 29, 2008, http://galenet.galegroup.com.

16. T. Hals, "Beware the Pitfalls of Office Romance," *Yahoo News*, February 13, 2007, http://news.yahoo.com; and M. Selvin, "'Love Contract'? It's Office Policy," *Los Angeles Times*, February 13, 2007, http://www.latimes.com.

17. "McDonald's Sales Rise 7.1%," *CNNMoney*, February 9, 2009, http://money.cnn.com; and "CEOs Who Don't Get Out Often Enough, and Some Who Do," *24/7 Wall Street*, May 7, 2008, http://247wallst.com.

18. V. U. Druskat, "Effects and Timing of Developmental Peer Appraisals in Self-Managing Work Groups," *Journal of Applied Psychology* 84, no. 1 (February 1999), p. 58.

19. "Business Analytics: Numbers and Nuance," *CIO Insight*, January 12, 2011, Business & Company Resource Center, http://galenet.galegroup.com.

20. M. Lewis Jr., "Eyes on the Prize," *Medical Economics*, February 10, 2011, pp. 34–42.

21. S. Waddock and N. Smith, "Corporate Responsibility Audits: Doing Well by Doing Good," *Sloan Management Review* 41, no. 2 (Winter 2000), pp. 75–83; L. L. Bergeson, "OSHA Gives Incentives for Voluntary Self-Audits," *Pollution Engineering* 32, no. 10 (October 2000), pp. 33–34.

22. S. Aghili, "A Six Sigma Approach to Internal Audits," *Strategic Finance*, February 2009, Business & Company Resource Center, http://galenet.galegroup.com.

23. See, for example, B. Hindo, "At 3M, a Struggle between Efficiency and Creativity," *BusinessWeek*, June 11, 2007, General Reference Center Gold, http://find.galegroup.com; B. Hindo and B. Grow, "Six Sigma; So Yesterday?" *BusinessWeek*, June 11, 2007, http://find.galegroup.com; and J. Rae, "Viewpoint: Have It Both Ways," *BusinessWeek*, June 11, 2007, http://find.galegroup.com.

24. T. Rancour and M. McCracken, "Applying 6 Sigma Methods for Breakthrough Safety Performance," *Professional Safety* 45, no. 10 (October 2000), pp. 29–32; and G. Eckes, "Making Six Sigma Last," *Ivey Business Journal*, January–February 2002, p. 77.

25. J. L. Colbert, "The Impact of the New External Auditing Standards," *Internal Auditor* 5, no. 6 (December 2000), pp. 46–50.

26. Aghili, "A Six Sigma Approach"; Y. Giard and Y. Nadeau, "Improving the Processes," *CA Magazine*, December 2008, Business & Company Resource Center, http://galenet.galegroup.com; and G. Cheney, "Connecting the Dots to the Next Crisis," *Financial Executive*, April 2009, pp. 30–33.

27. J. D. Glater, "The Better the Audit Panel, the Higher the Stock Price," *New York Times*, April 8, 2005, p. C4; and M. Alic and B. Rusjan, "Contribution of the ISO 9001 Internal Audit to Business Performance," *International Journal of Quality and Reliability Management* 27, no. 8 (2010), pp. 916–37.

28. B. Roberts, "Data-Driven Human Capital Decisions," *HRMagazine*, March 2007, General Reference Center Gold, http://find.galegroup.com.

29. T. P. Pare, "A New Tool for Managing Costs," *Fortune*, June 14, 1993, pp. 124–29; P. Pretko, "The ABCs of Activity-Based Costing," *Electrical Wholesaling*, October 1, 2010, Business & Company Resource Center, http://galenet.galegroup.com; and P. C. Zelinski, "What Is Your Cost Model Costing You?" *Modern Machine Shop*, March 2011, p. 20.

30. K. Merchant, *Control in Business Organizations* (Boston: Pitman, 1985); and C. W. Chow, Y. Kato, and K. A. Merchant, "The Use of Organizational Controls and Their Effects on Data Manipulation and Management Myopia," *Accounting, Organizations, and Society* 21, nos. 2/3 (February/April 1996), pp. 175–92.

31. E. E. Lawler III and J. Rhode, *Information and Control in Organizations* (Pacific Palisades, CA: Goodyear, 1976); A. Ferner, "The Underpinnings of 'Bureaucratic' Control Systems: HRM in European Multinationals," *Journal of Management Studies* 37, no. 4 (June 2000), pp. 521–39; and M. S. Fenwick, "Cultural and Bureaucratic Control in MNEs: The Role of Expatriate Performance Management," *Management International Review* 39 (1999), pp. 107–25.

32. Hindo, "At 3M, a Struggle between Efficiency and Creativity."

33. S. Terlep, "GM's Latest Change Agent Tackles Designs, Red Tape," *The Wall Street Journal*, June 15, 2011, http://online.wsj.com.

34. J. Veiga and J. Yanouzas, *The Dynamics of Organization Theory*, 2nd ed. (St. Paul, MN: West, 1984).

35. P. R. Gutierrez, "Airport Workers Report Breach," *Orlando Sentinel*, May 26, 2007, General Reference Center Gold, http://find.galegroup.com.

36. M. Gelbart, "L&I Gets Ritz-Carlton Image Tips," *Philadelphia Inquirer*, March 10, 2009, http://www.philly.com.

37. G. Campbell, "Special Report: Gaining Ground," *Quality*, December 1, 2010, http://www.qualitymag.com.

38. J. Fleischer, "New Methods to Measure Performance," *Call Center*, February 1, 2007, General Reference Center Gold, http://find.galegroup.com.

39. M. Hammer, "The Seven Deadly Sins of Performance Measurement and How to Avoid Them," *MIT Sloan Management Review* 48, no. 3 (Spring 2007), pp. 19–28.

40. Lawler and Rhode, *Information and Control in Organizations;* and J. A. Gowan Jr. and R. G. Mathieu, "Critical Factors in Information System Development for a Flexible Manufacturing System," *Computers in Industry* 28, no. 3 (June 1996), pp. 173–83.

41. J. Robison, "How the Ritz-Carlton Manages the Mystique," *Gallup Management Journal*, December 11, 2008, Business & Company Resource Center, http://galenet.galegroup.com.

42. The Juggle, "Getting Results without Face Time," *The Wall Street Journal*, May 3, 2011, http://blogs.wsj.com; P. Moen, E. L. Kelly, and R. Hill, "Does Enhancing Work-Time Control and Flexibility Reduce Turnover? A Naturally Occurring Experiment," *Social Problems* 58, no. 1 (2011), pp. 69–98; and The Juggle, "Obama Administration's Experiment: Work Wherever, Just Get It Done," *The Wall Street Journal*, April 1, 2010, http://blogs.wsj.com.

43. Credeur, "Southwest Capping Fleet"; Schlangenstein, "Southwest Profit Rises 13%"; Schlangenstein and Hughes, "Southwest Risks Keep-It-Simple Focus";

"Southwest Charts a New Flight Plan"; McCartney, "Can't Call Southwest a Discount Airline"; S. Carey, "Airlines Wrestle with Capacity," *The Wall Street Journal*, April 22, 2011, http://online.wsj.com; J. Hughes and M. Schlangenstein, "Southwest Loses On-Time 'Bragging Rights' as 2010 Ranking Slips," *Bloomberg Businessweek*, June 28, 2011, http://www.businessweek.com; D. Fitzgerald, "Southwest, AirTran Report Traffic Growth in May," *The Wall Street Journal*, June 7, 2011, http://online.wsj.com; "Southwest/AirTran," *Financial Times*, September 28, 2010, Business & Company Resource Center, http://galenet.galegroup.com; and D. Hull, "A Push to Make Air Travel More Environmentally Friendly," *San Jose (Calif.) Mercury News*, December 27, 2010, Business & Company Resource Center, http://galenet.galegroup.com.

44. R. S. Kaplan and D. P. Norton, *The Balanced Scorecard: Translating Strategy into Action* (Boston: Harvard Business School Press, 1996); and A. Gumbus and R. N. Lussier, "Entrepreneurs Use a Balanced Scorecard to Translate Strategy into Performance Measures," *Journal of Small Business Management* 44, no. 3 (July 2006), General Reference Center Gold, http://find.galegroup.com.

45. Gumbus and Lussier, "Entrepreneurs Use a Balanced Scorecard."

46. M. A. Reed-Woodard, "The Business of Nonprofit," *Black Enterprise*, June 2007, General Reference Center Gold, http://find.galegroup.com.

47. R. Myers, "Going Away," *CFO*, May 2007, General Reference Center Gold, http://find.galegroup.com.

48. K. Moores and J. Mula, "The Salience of Market, Bureaucratic, and Clan Controls in the Management of Family Firm Transitions: Some Tentative Australian Evidence," *Family Business Review* 13, no. 2 (June 2000), pp. 91–106; and A. Walker and R. Newcombe, "The Positive Use of Power on a Major Construction Project," *Construction Management and Economics* 18, no. 1 (January/February 2000), pp. 37–44.

49. P. H. Fuchs, K. E. Mifflin, D. Miller, and J. O. Whitney, "Strategic Integration: Competing in the Age of Capabilities," *California Management Review* 42, no. 3 (Spring 2000), pp. 118–47; M. A. Lando, "Making Compliance Part of Your Organization's Culture," *Healthcare Executive* 15, no. 5 (September/October 1999), pp. 18–22; and K. A. Frank and K. Fahrbach, "Organization Culture as a Complex System: Balance and Information in Models of Influence and Selection," *Organization Science* 10, no. 3 (May/June 1999), pp. 253–77.

50. R J. Grossman, "Tough Love at Netflix," *HR Magazine*, April 2010, http://galenet.galegroup.com.

51. "100 Best Companies to Work For, 2009," *Fortune*, February 2, 2009, http://money.cnn.com.

52. Southwest Airlines, "About Southwest"; T. W. Martin, A. Pasztor, and P. Sanders, "Southwest's Solo Flight in Crisis," *The Wall Street Journal*, April 8, 2011, http://online.wsj.com; A. Pasztor and P. Sanders, "Manufacturing Issues Suspected in Southwest Jet Rupture," *The Wall Street Journal*, April 23, 2011, http://online.wsj.com; and D. Robinson, "No Problems Reported Here for Southwest," *Buffalo (N.Y.) News*, April 5, 2011, Business & Company Resource Center, http://galenet.galegroup.com.

Chapter 17

1. G. Yemen, M. J. Lenox, and J. D. Harris, "BP: Beyond Petroleum," case UVA-S-0182 (Charlottesville, VA: University of Virginia Darden School Foundation, December 15, 2010); BP, "About BP," http://www.bp.com; "Long-Term Outlooks Reflect BP, Exxon 'Books,'" *Energy Intelligence Finance*, February 9, 2011, p. 5; "DJ BP Plans to Invest $2B in Alternative Energy in 2011—Executive," *FWN Financial News*, April 5, 2011, Business & Company Resource Center, http://galenet.galegroup.com; and K. Pender, "BP No Longer Seen as Green," *San Francisco Chronicle*, June 6, 2010, Business & Company Resource Center, http://galenet.galegroup.com.

2. R. A. Burgelman, M. A. Maidique, and S. C. Wheelwright, *Strategic Management of Technology and Innovation* (New York: McGraw-Hill, 2000).

3. D. C. L. Prestwood and P. A. Schumann Jr., "Revitalize Your Organization," *Executive Excellence* 15, no. 2 (February 1998), p. 16; C. Y. Baldwin and K. B. Clark, "Managing in an Age of Modularity," *Harvard Business Review* 75, no. 5 (September–October 1997), pp. 84–93; S. Gopalakrishnan, P. Bierly, and E. H. Kessler, "A Reexamination of Product and Process Innovations Using a Knowledge-Based View," *Journal of High Technology Management Research* 10, no. 1 (Spring 1999), pp. 147–66; J. Pullin, "Bombardier Commands Top Marks," *Professional Engineering* 13, no. 3 (July 5, 2000), pp. 40–46; M. Johnson, C. Christensen, and H. Kagermann, "Reinventing Your Business Model," *Harvard Business Review* (December 2008), pp. 50–59; C. M. Christensen, *The Innovator's Dilemma* (Boston: Harvard Business Publishing, 1997); and C. M. Christensen, S. D. Anthony, and E. A. Roth, *Seeing What's Next* (Boston: Harvard Business Publishing, 2004).

4. M. Sawhney, R. C. Wolcott, and I. Arroniz, "The 12 Different Ways for Companies to Innovate," *MIT Sloan Management Review* 47, no. 3 (Spring 2006), pp. 75–81.

5. B. Saporito, "How to Build a Job Engine," *Time*, May 19, 2011, http://www.time.com.

6. G. P. Pisano, *The Development Factory: Unlocking the Potential of Process Innovation* (Boston: Harvard Business School Press, 1996); and R. Leifer, C. M. McDermott, G. C. O'Connor, L. S. Peters, M. Rice, and R. W. Veryzer, *Radical Innovation: How Mature Companies Can Outsmart Upstarts* (Cambridge MA: Harvard Business School Press, 2000).

7. H. M. O'Neill, R. W. Pounder, and A. K. Buchholtz, "Patterns in the Diffusion of Strategies across Organizations: Insights from the Innovation, Diffusion Literature," *Academy of Management Review* 23, no. 1 (January 1998), pp. 98–114; E. M. Rogers, *Diffusion of Innovations* (New York: Free Press, 1995); and B. Guilhon, ed., *Technology and Markets for Knowledge: Knowledge Creation, Diffusion and Exchange within a Growing Economy*, Economics of Science, Technology and Innovation 22 (Dordrecht, Netherlands: Kluwer Academic Publishing, 2000).

8. J. P. Andrew, K. Haanæs, D. C. Michael, H. L. Sirkin, and A. Taylor, *Innovation 2009: Making Hard Decisions in the Downturn*, Boston Consulting Group Senior Management Survey, http://www.bcg.com.

9. M. E. Porter, *Competitive Strategy* (New York: Free Press, 1980).

10. J. A. Schumpeter, *The Theory of Economic Development* (Boston: Harvard University Press, 1934); and K. DesMarteau, "Information Technology Trends Drive Dramatic Industry Change," *Bobbin* 41, no. 12 (August 2000), pp. 48–58.

11. S. A. Zahra, S. Nash, and D. J. Bickford, "Transforming Technological Pioneering in Competitive Advantage," *Academy of Management Executive* 9, no. 1 (1995), pp. 17–31; and M. Sadowski and A. Roth, "Technology Leadership Can Pay Off," *Research Technology Management* 42, no. 6 (November/December 1999), pp. 32–33.

12. A. Weintraub, "Who Might Be Eyeing Bristol?" *BusinessWeek*, June 20, 2007, General Reference Center Gold, http://find.galegroup.com; and D. Cust, "Pharma Sector Faces 'Perfect Storm,'" *Acquisitions Monthly*, June 2007, http://find.galegroup.com.

13. M. Imai and G. Kaizen, *A Commonsense, Low-Cost Approach to Management* (New York: McGraw-Hill, 1997); and M. Imai and G. Kaizen, *The Key to Japan's Competitive Success* (New York: McGraw-Hill, 1986).

14. M. Hiltzik, "How Big Pharma Distorts the Costs of Developing New Drugs," *Los Angeles Times*, April 3, 2011, http://articles.latimes.com; "Brand Drugs Soar as Generics Rise," *Journal of Nursing*, April 1, 2011, http://www.asrn.org; and J. J. Castellani, "The Role of Innovation in Addressing Global Health,"

remarks from the Under Secretary for Economic, Energy and Agricultural Affairs, U.S. Department of State, March 31, 2011, http://www.state.gov.

15. P. A. Geroski, "Models of Technology Diffusion," *Research Policy* 29, no. 4/5 (April 2000), pp. 603–25; and L. A. Thomas, "Adoption Order of New Technologies in Evolving Markets," *Journal of Economic Behavior & Organization* 38, no. 4 (April 1999), pp. 453–82.

16. G. Colvin, "McKesson: Wiring the Medical World," *Fortune*, February 5, 2007, http://money.cnn.com.

17. R. E. Oligney and M. I. Economides, "Technology as an Asset," *Hart's Petroleum Engineer International* 71, no. 9 (September 1998), p. 27.

18. J. E. Vascellaro, "Found in Translation," *The Wall Street Journal*, May 24, 2007, http://online.wsj.com.

19. "Internet World Users by Language: Top 10 Languages," *Internet World Stats*, http://www.internetworldstats.com.

20. M. Bustillo, "Wal-Mart Radio Tags to Track Clothing," *The Wall Street Journal*, July 23, 2010, http://online.wsj.com; "RFID: Challenges and Opportunities," *MoreRFID*, June 30, 2011, http://www.morerfid.com; and D. Steinberg, "The $25 Billion Art Move," *The Wall Street Journal*, June 24, 2011, http://online.wsj.com.

21. D. Schubert, "Focusing Your Innovation," *Game Developer*, February 1, 2009, Business & Company Resource Center, http://galenet.galegroup.com.

22. "Not Dead Yet? Maybe Face Recognition Just Needs Re-purposing," *Security Director's Resport*, June 2011, pp. 2–5.

23. A. Taylor III, "The Great Electric Car Race," *Fortune*, April 14, 2009, http://money.cnn.com.

24. S. Hansell, "Beam It Down from the Web, Scotty," *New York Times*, May 7, 2007, http://www.nytimes.com.

25. M. Kanellos, "For Fast-Food Help, Call in the Robots," *CNet News*, March 26, 2007, http://news.com.com.

26. L. Landro, "An Affordable Fix for Modernizing Medical Records," *The Wall Street Journal*, April 30, 2009, http://online.wsj.com; and St. Lohr, "How to Make Electronic Medical Records a Reality," *New York Times*, March 1, 2009, http://www.nytimes.com.

27. J. Jusko, "Foiling Fakes," *Industry Week*, May 2007, General Reference Center Gold, http://find.galegroup.com.

28. "Fresh, but Far from Easy," *The Economist*, June 23, 2007, General Reference Center Gold, http://find.galegroup.com.

29. R. Dewan, B. Jing, and A. Seidmann, "Adoption of Internet-Based Product Customization and Pricing Strategies," *Journal of Management Information Systems* 17, no. 2 (Fall 2000), pp. 9–28; P. A. Geroski, "Models of Technology Diffusion," *Research Policy* 29, no. 4/5 (April 2000), pp. 603–25; Rogers, *Diffusion of Innovations*.

30. Yemen et al., "BP: Beyond Petroleum"; "Long-Term Outlooks"; "DJ BP Plans to Invest $2B"; Pender, "BP No Longer Seen as Green"; and "BP: Nonfossil Fuels to Be 'Major' Energy Sources by 2030," *Chemical Business Newsbase*, January 31, 2011, Business & Company Resource Center, http://galenet.galegroup.com.

31. E. Von Hippel, *The Sources of Innovation* (Oxford, UK: Oxford University Press, 1994); and D. Leonard, *Wellsprings of Knowledge: Building and Sustaining the Sources of Innovation* (Cambridge, MA: Harvard Business School Press, 1998).

32. T. Krazit, "Intel R&D on Slow Boat to China," *CNet News*, April 16, 2007, http://news.com.com.

33. K. MacQueen, "Cashing in His V-Chips," *Maclean's*, June 11, 2007, General Reference Center Gold, http://find.galegroup.com; and "Online Gaming's Netscape Moment?" *The Economist*, June 9, 2007, http://find.galegroup.com.

34. T. Purdum, "Benchmarking Outside the Box: Best Practices Can Rise from Where You Least Expect Them," *Industry Week*, March 2007, General Reference Center Gold, http://find.galegroup.com.

35. Von Hippel, *The Sources of Innovation;* and Leonard, *Wellsprings of Knowledge.*

36. J. Hagedoorn, A. N. Link, and N. S. Vonortas, "Research Partnerships," *Research Policy* 29, no. 4/5 (April 2000), pp. 567–86; and S.-S. Yi, "Entry, Licensing and Research Joint Ventures," *International Journal of Industrial Organization* 17, no. 1 (January 1999), pp. 1–24.

37. R. Dorn, "Chicken, Pork or Beef?" *Fleet Equipment*, May 2007, General Reference Center Gold, http://find.galegroup.com; and "One of the Nation's Largest Producers of Animal Fat and a Major Oil Company Have Decided to Make Diesel Fuel Together," *Diesel Progress*, North American ed., May 2007, http://find.galegroup.com.

38. "Broadcom Acquires GPS Specialist Global Locate for $146 Million," *Information Week*, June 12, 2007, General Reference Center Gold, http://find.galegroup.com.

39. T. Hoffman, "Change Agents," *ComputerWorld*, April 23, 2007, General Reference Center Gold, http://find.galegroup.com; Center for CIO Leadership, "Center for CIO Leadership Unveils 2008 Survey Results," news release, November 18, 2008, http://www.marketwire.com; and Center for CIO Leadership, "CIO Leadership Survey Executive Summary," abstract, 2008, http://www.cioleadershipcenter.com; and G. H. Anthes, "The CIO/CTO Balancing Act," *ComputerWorld* 34, no. 25 (June 19, 2000), pp. 50–51.

40. "Information Resources: The Evolution of R&D," *Research-Technology Management*, May–June 2011, pp. 65–66; and J. C. Spender and B. Strong, "Who Has Innovative Ideas? Employees," *The Wall Street Journal*, August 23, 2010, http://online.wsj.com.

41. D. L. Day, "Raising Radicals: Different Processes for Championing Innovative Corporate Ventures," *Organization Science* 5, no. 2 (May 1994), pp. 148–72; C. Siporin, "Want Speedy FDA Approval? Hire a 'Product Champion,'" *Medical Marketing & Media*, October 1993, pp. 22–28; C. Siporin, "How You Can Capitalize on Phase 3B," *Medical Marketing & Media*, October 1994, pp. 72–72; and E. H. Kessler, "Tightening the Belt: Methods for Reducing Development Costs Associated with New Product Innovation," *Journal of Engineering and Technology Management* 17, no. 1 (March 2000), pp. 59–92.

42. Hoffman, "Change Agents."

43. K. Johnson, "Solar Updates Marines' Arsenal," *The Wall Street Journal*, May 9, 2011, http://online.wsj.com.

44. Andrew et al., *Innovation 2009*, p. 11.

45. J. G. March, "Exploration and Exploitation in Organizational Learning," *Organization Science* 2, no. 1 (1991), pp. 71–87; and S. C. Kang and S. A. Snell, "Intellectual Capital Architectures and Ambidextrous Learning: A Framework for Human Resource Management," *Journal of Management Studies* 46, no. 1 (2009), pp. 65–92.

46. B. Hindo, "At 3M, a Struggle between Efficiency and Creativity," *BusinessWeek*, June 11, 2007, http://www.businessweek.com; K. Palmer, "Creativity on Demand," *U.S. News & World Report*, April 30, 2007, pp. EE2–EE4; E. Figueroa and P. Conceicao, "Rethinking the Innovation Process in Large Organizations: A Case Study of 3M," *Journal of Engineering and Technology Management* 17, no. 1 (March 2000), pp. 93–109; and D. Howell, "No Such Thing as a Daft Idea," *Professional Engineering* 13, no. 4 (February 23, 2000), pp. 28–29.

47. D. A. Fields, "How to Stop the Dumbing Down of Your Company," *Industry Week*, March 7, 2007, http://www.industryweek.com; L. K. Gundry, J. R. Kickul, and C. W. Prather, "Building the Creative Organization," *Organizational Dynamics* 22, no. 2 (Spring 1994), pp. 22–36; and T. Kuczmarski, "Inspiring and Implementing the Innovation Mind-Set," *Planning Review*, September–October 1994, pp. 37–48.

48. D. Rodriguez and R. Jacoby, "Embracing Risk to Grow and Innovate," *BusinessWeek*, May 16, 2007, http://www.businessweek.com.

49. Ibid.

50. Hindo, "At 3M, a Struggle."

51. D. Tsuruoka, "Intuit Innovation Lab, 'Idea Jams' Aim to Spur Creativity," *Investor's Business Daily*, April 14, 2009, Business & Company Resource Center, http://galenet.galegroup.com.

52. D. Leonard, *Wellsprings of Knowledge: Building and Sustaining the Sources of Innovation* (Cambridge MA: Harvard Business School Press, 1998); D. Leonard-Barton, "The Factory as a

Learning Laboratory," *Sloan Management Review*, Fall 1992, pp. 23–38; and A. K. Gupta and V. Govindarajan, "Knowledge Management's Social Dimension: Lessons from Nucor Steel," *Sloan Management Review* 42, no. 1 (Fall 2000), pp. 71–80.

53. H. K. Bowen, K. B. Clark, C. A. Holloway, and S. C. Wheelwright, "Development Projects: The Engine of Renewal," *Harvard Business Review*, September–October 1994, pp. 110–20; C. Eden, T. Williams, and F. Ackermann, "Dismantling the Learning Curve: The Role of Disruptions on the Planning of Development Projects," *International Journal of Project Management* 16, no. 3 (June 1998), pp. 131–38; and M. V. Tatikonda and S. R. Rosenthal, "Technology Novelty, Project Complexity, and Product Development Project Execution Success: A Deeper Look at Task Uncertainty in Product Innovation," *IEEE Transactions on Engineering Management* 47, no. 1 (February 2000), pp. 74–87.

54. E. Trist, "The Evolution of Sociotechnical Systems as a Conceptual Framework and as an Action Research Program," in *Perspectives on Organizational Design and Behavior*, ed. A. Van de Ven and W. F. Joyce, pp. 19–75 (New York: John Wiley & Sons, 1981); and A. Molina, "Insights into the Nature of Technology Diffusion and Implementation: The Perspective of Sociotechnical Alignment," *Technovation* 17, nos. 11/12 (November/December 1997), pp. 601–26.

55. Yemen et al., "BP: Beyond Petroleum"; R. Lea, "Browne Firm Sells Stake in BP's Green Deal," *The Times* (London), March 12, 2011, Business & Company Resource Center, http://galenet.galegroup.com; and S. Pearson and S. Pfeifer, "BP Strikes $680M Brazilian Fuel Deal," *Financial Times*, March 12, 2011, Business & Company Resource Center, http://galenet.galegroup.com.

Appendix D

1. R. M. Pirsig, *Zen and the Art of Motorcycle Maintenance* (New York: William Morrow and Company, 1974).
2. P. Raichur, *Absolute Beauty* (New York: HarperPerennial, 1986).
3. Nescafe: Nestle (verified by T. Haywood via 1/16/01 e-mail that Nescafe and Nesquik flavors are modified for the market in which they are sold).
4. T. J. Mullaney and R. D. Hof, "Information Technology Annual Report," *BusinessWeek Online*, June 24, 2002.
5. J. Black, "The Fight for Privacy Has Just Begun," *BusinessWeek Online*, January 10, 2002.

Chapter 18

1. K. Herzer and M. Seshamani, "A Success Story in American Health Care: Eliminating Infections and Saving Lives in Michigan," U.S. Department of Health and Human Services, http://www.healthreform.gov; J. Rose, "Making a List," *Inside Healthcare*, January 2011, pp. 16–17; "Changing Hospital Culture," *Industrial Engineer*, April 2010, pp. 14–15; L. Landro, "The Secret to Fighting Infections," *The Wall Street Journal*, March 28, 2011, http://online.wsj.com; L. Landro, "Building Team Spirit," *The Wall Street Journal*, February 26, 2010, http://online.wsj.com; and "Bringing True Accountability to Health Care," *Europe Intelligence Wire*, July 13, 2010, Business & Company Resource Center, http://galenet.galegroup.com.
2. C. M. Christensen, "The Past and Future of Competitive Advantage," *Sloan Management Review*, Winter 2001, pp. 105–9.
3. T. A. Judge, C. J. Thoresen, V. Pucik, and T. M. Welbourne, "Managerial Coping with Organizational Change: A Dispositional Perspective," *Journal of Applied Psychology* 84 (1999), pp. 107–22.
4. C. Giffi, A. Roth, and G. Seal, *Competing in World-Class Manufacturing: America's 21st Century Challenge* (Homewood, IL: Business One Irwin, 1990).
5. R. M. Kanter, *World Class: Thriving Locally in the Global Economy* (New York: Touchstone, 1995).
6. Giffi, Roth, and Seal, *Competing in World-Class Manufacturing*.
7. J. Collins and J. Porras, *Built to Last* (London: Century, 1996).
8. Collins and Porras, *Built to Last*.
9. C. Gibson and J. Birkinshaw, "The Antecedents, Consequences, and Mediating Role of Organizational Ambidexterity," *Academy of Management Journal* 47 (2004), pp. 209–26.
10. Collins and Porras, *Built to Last*.
11. T. Cummings and C. Worley, *Organization Development and Change*, 8th ed. (Mason, OH: Thomson/South-Western, 2005).
12. Ibid.
13. Ibid.
14. N. Nohria, W. Joyce, and B. Roberson, "What Really Works," *Harvard Business Review*, July 2003, pp. 42–52.
15. R. M. Kanter, "Thriving Locally in the Global Economy," *Harvard Business Review*, August 2003, pp. 119–27.
16. Ibid.
17. D. R. Conner, *Managing at the Speed of Change* (New York: Random House, 2006); and R. Teerlink, "Harley's Leadership U-Turn," *Harvard Business Review*, July–August 2000, pp. 43–48.
18. E. E. Lawler III, *Treat People Right!* (San Francisco: Jossey-Bass, 2003).
19. P. Zigarmi and J. Hoekstra, "Leadership Strategies for Making Change Stick," *Perspectives* (Ken Blanchard Companies, 2008), http://www.kenblanchard.com.
20. Conner, *Managing at the Speed of Change*; and S. Oreg, "Resistance to Change: Developing an Individual Differences Measure," *Journal of Applied Psychology*, 2003, pp. 680–93.
21. P. Dvorak, "How Understanding the 'Why' of Decisions Matters," *The Wall Street Journal*, March 19, 2007, http://online.wsj.com.
22. A. Deutschman, *Change or Die* (Los Angeles: Regan, 2007), pp. 164–78.
23. J. Stanislao and B. C. Stanislao, "Dealing with Resistance to Change," *Business Horizons*, July–August 1983, pp. 74–78; and J. D. Ford and L. W. Ford, "Decoding Resistance to Change," *Harvard Business Review*, April 2009, pp. 99–103.
24. J. P. Kotter and L. A. Schlesinger, "Choosing Strategies for Change," *Harvard Business Review*, March–April 1979, pp. 106–114; Ford and Ford, "Decoding Resistance to Change"; and Zigrami and Hoekstra, "Leadership Strategies."
25. D. Zell, "Overcoming Barriers to Work Innovations: Lessons Learned at Hewlett-Packard," *Organizational Dynamics*, Summer 2001, pp. 77–85.
26. E. B. Dent and S. Galloway Goldberg, "Challenging Resistance to Change," *Journal of Applied Behavioral Science*, March 1999, pp. 25–41; Ford and Ford, "Decoding Resistance to Change"; Zigarmi and Hoekstra, "Leadership Strategies"; and J. Ford, L. Ford, and A. D'Amelio, "Resistance to Change: The Rest of the Story," *Academy of Management Review* 33 (2008), pp. 362–77.
27. G. Johnson, *Strategic Change and the Management Process* (New York: Basil Blackwell, 1987); and K. Lewin, "Frontiers in Group Dynamics," *Human Relations* 1 (1947), pp. 5–41.
28. E. H. Schein, "Organizational Culture: What It Is and How to Change It," in *Human Resource Management in International Firms*, ed. P. Evans, Y. Doz, and A. Laurent (New York: St. Martin's Press, 1990).
29. M. Beer, R. Eisenstat, and B. Spector, *The Critical Path to Corporate Renewal* (Cambridge, MA: Harvard Business School Press, 1990).
30. Dvorak, "How Understanding the 'Why' of Decisions Matters."
31. E. E. Lawler III, "Transformation from Control to Involvement," in *Corporate Transformation*, ed. R. Kilmann and T. Covin (San Francisco: Jossey-Bass, 1988).
32. Deutschman, *Change or Die*, pp. 1–15.
33. D. Hellriegel and J. W. Slocum Jr., *Management*, 4th ed. (Reading, MA: Addison-Wesley, 1986).
34. F. Vermeulen, P. Puranam, and R. Gulate, "Change for Change's Sake," *Harvard Business Review* 88 (June 2010), pp. 70–76.
35. C. Aiken and S. Keller, "The Irrational Side of Change Management," *McKinsey Quarterly*, April 2009, http://www.mckinseyquarterly.com.
36. Lewin, "Frontiers in Group Dynamics."
37. Schein, "Organizational Culture."
38. E. E. Lawler III, *From the Ground Up* (San Francisco: Jossey-Bass, 1995).
39. Q. Nguyen Huy, "Time, Temporal Capability, and Planned Change," *Academy of Management Review* 26 (2001), pp. 601–23.
40. B. Sugarman, "A Learning-Based Approach to Organizational Change: Some Results and Guidelines,"

Organizational Dynamics, Summer 2001, pp. 62–75.

41. Kotter and Schlesinger, "Choosing Strategies for Change."

42. R. H. Miles, "Beyond the Age of Dilbert: Accelerating Corporate Transformations by Rapidly Engaging all Employees," *Organizational Dynamics*, Spring 2001, pp. 313–21.

43. D. A. Nadler, "Managing Organizational Change: An Integrative Approach," *Journal of Applied Behavioral Science* 17 (1981), pp. 191–211.

44. D. Rousseau and S. A. Tijoriwala, "What's a Good Reason to Change? Motivated Reasoning and Social Accounts in Promoting Organizational Change," *Journal of Applied Psychology* 84 (1999), pp. 514–28.

45. E. Oakley, "Leading Change without Authority," *Material Handling Management*, May 2007, General Reference Center Gold, http://find.galegroup.com.

46. C. F. Leana and B. Barry, "Stability and Change as Simultaneous Experiences in Organizational Life," *Academy of Management Review* 25 (2000), pp. 753–59.

47. O. Gadiesh and J. Gilbert, "Transforming Corner-Office Strategy into Frontline Action," *Harvard Business Review*, May 2001, pp. 72–79.

48. "Changing Hospital Culture"; Landro, "The Secret to Fighting Infections"; Landro, "Building Team Spirit"; "Bringing True Accountability to Health Care"; and "Three Years Out, Safety Checklist Continues to Keep Hospital Infections in Check," *Blood Weekly*, February 18, 2010, Business & Company Resource Center, http://galenet.galegroup.com.

49. B. Schneider, A. Brief, and R. Guzzo, "Creating a Climate and Culture for Sustainable Organizational Change," *Organizational Dynamics*, Spring 1996, pp. 7–19.

50. The Price Waterhouse Change Integration Team, *Better Change: Best Practices for Transforming Your Organization* (Burr Ridge, IL: Irwin, 1995).

51. M. Beer and N. Nohria, "Cracking the Code of Change," *Harvard Business Review*, May–June 2000, pp. 133–41.

52. N. Nohria and J. Berkley, "Whatever Happened to the Take-Charge Manager?" *Harvard Business Review*, January–February 1994, pp. 128–37.

53. D. Miller, J. Hartwick, and I. Le Breton-Miller, "How to Detect a Management Fad—and Distinguish It from a Classic," *Business Horizons*, July–August 2004, pp. 7–16.

54. Price Waterhouse Change Integration Team, *Better Change*.

55. Ibid.

56. E. M. Heffes, "You Need Urgency Now!" *Financial Executive*, January–February 2009, Business & Company Resource Center, http://galenet.galegroup.com (interview with John P. Kotter).

57. Lawler, *From the Ground Up*.

58. J. Kotter, *Leading Change* (Boston: Harvard Business School Press, 1996).

59. Schneider, Brief, and Guzzo, "Creating a Climate and Culture."

60. R. Beckhard and R. Harris, *Organizational Transitions* (Reading, MA: Addison-Wesley, 1977).

61. Kotter, *Leading Change*.

62. S. Schumacher, "Waking Employees," *Rock Products*, September 1, 2010, Business & Company Resource Center, http://galenet.galegroup.com.

63. G. Hamel, "Waking Up IBM," *Harvard Business Review*, July–August 2000, pp. 137–46; and Deutschman, *Change or Die*.

64. Deutschman, *Change or Die*, p. 202.

65. Kotter, *Leading Change*.

66. D. Smith, *Taking Charge of Change* (Reading, MA: Addison-Wesley, 1996).

67. G. Hamel, "Killer Strategies That Make Shareholders Rich," *Fortune*, June 23, 1997, pp. 22–34.

68. G. Hamel and C. K. Prahalad, *Competing for the Future* (Boston: Harvard Business School Press, 1994).

69. Mckinley Conway, "Coming: The Biggest Boom Ever!" *The Futurist*, May–June 2010, Business & Company Resource Center, http://galenet.galegroup.com.

70. M. Cheung, "Phones to Replace the Wallet, a Smarter Internet, and More Futurist Predictions," *Computer Dealer News*, October 2010, p. 8; and C. G. Wagner, "70 Jobs for 2030," *The Futurist*, January–February 2011, pp. 30–33.

71. E. Beinhocker, I. Davis, and L. Mendenca, "The 10 Trends You Have to Watch," *Harvard Business Review* 87 (July/August 2009), pp. 5–60.

72. S. Zuboff and J. Maxim, *The Support Economy* (New York: Penguin, 2004).

73. H. Courtney, J. Kirkland, and P. Viguerie, "Strategy under Uncertainty," *Harvard Business Review*, November–December 1997, pp. 66–79.

74. J. O'Shea and C. Madigan, *Dangerous Company: The Consulting Powerhouses and the Business They Save and Ruin* (New York: Times Books, 1997).

75. Hamel and Prahalad, *Competing for the Future*.

76. Ibid.

77. Ibid.

78. A. Scott, "Sustainability: Building Better Practices," *Chemical Week*, October 11, 2010, pp. 24–27.

79. M. Courtney, "Small Is Beautiful," *Computing*, August 5, 2010, Business & Company Resource Center, http://galenet.galegroup.com; and G. E. King and L. Gibbs, "The Little Unknown," *Industrial Engineer*, July 2010, pp. 33–37.

80. King and Gibbs, "The Little Unknown"; P. Livingstone, "Billions of Pieces, Billions of Questions," *R&D Magazine*, October 2010, pp. 8–13; and J. Katz, "Nanotechnology: Beyond the Hype," *Industry Week*, November 2010, pp. 22–26.

81. Courtney, "Small Is Beautiful"; Livingstone, "Billions of Pieces"; and Katz, "Nanotechnology."

82. King and Gibbs, "The Little Unknown"; Livingstone, "Billions of Pieces"; and Katz, "Nanotechnology."

83. See, for example, J. Truini, "EPA Needs to Address Tiny Concerns, Report Says," *Waste News*, May 28, 2007, General Reference Center Gold, http://find.galegroup.com.

84. King and Gibbs, "The Little Unknown"; and Katz, "Nanotechnology."

85. Hamel and Prahalad, *Competing for the Future*.

86. J. Kotter, *The New Rules: How to Succeed in Today's Post-Corporate World* (New York: Free Press, 1995).

87. Ibid.

88. T. Bateman and C. Porath, "Transcendent Behavior," in *Positive Organizational Scholarship*, ed. K. Cameron, J. Dutton, and R. Quinn (San Francisco: Barrett-Koehler, 2003).

89. L. A. Hill, "New Manager Development for the 21st Century," *Academy of Management Executive*, August 2004, pp. 121–26; and D. A. Ready, J. A. Conger, L. A. Hill, "Are You a High Potential?" *Harvard Business Review* 88 (June 2010), pp. 78–84.

90. Lawler, *From the Ground Up*; and Kotter, *The New Rules*.

91. Lawler, *Treat People Right!*

92. C. Bialik, "Seven Careers in a Lifetime? Think Twice, Researchers Say," *The Wall Street Journal*, September 4, 2010, http://online.wsj.com.

93. M. Peiperl and Y. Baruck, "Back to Square Zero: The Post-Corporate Career," *Organizational Dynamics*, Spring 1997, pp. 7–22.

94. Ibid.

95. Conner, *Managing at the Speed of Change*, pp. 235–45.

96. L. Thompson, "Service Operator," *Inside Business*, November/December 2010, pp. 76–80.

97. J. W. Slocum Jr., M. McGill, and D. Lei, "The New Learning Strategy Anytime, Anything, Anywhere," *Organizational Dynamics*, Autumn 1994, pp. 33–37.

98. Kotter, *The New Rules*.

99. J. Collins, *From Good to Great* (New York: HarperBusiness, 2001).

100. Hill, "New Manager Development for the 21st Century," p. 125.

101. J. A. Raelin, "Don't Bother Putting Leadership into People," *Academy of Management Executive*, August 2004, pp. 131–35.

102. G. Binney, and C. Williams, *Leaning into the Future* (London: Nicholas Brealey, 1997).

103. "Changing Hospital Culture"; Landro, "The Secret to Fighting Infections"; Landro, "Building Team Spirit"; "Bringing True Accountability to Health Care"; "Three Years Out"; Health Blog, "Progress on Reducing Bloodstream Infections," *The Wall Street Journal*, April 5, 2011, http://blogs.wsj.com; M. McKinney, "Stalling States," *Modern Healthcare*, May 3, 2010, Business & Company Resource Center, http://galenet.galegroup.com; and K. Terry, "Do You Hold Staff Accountable for Safety?" *H&HN Hospitals and Health Networks*, February 2010, Business & Company Resource Center, http://galenet.galegroup.com.

PHOTO CREDITS

Chapter 1

Page 3 Sandy Huffaker/Corbis; **5** Royalty-free/CORBIS; **Page 7** David Handschuh/NY Daily News Via Getty Images; **Page 9** AP Photo/Laurent Rebours; **Page 11** The McGraw-Hill Companies, Inc./Ken Cavanagh, photographer/DAL; **Page 12** The McGraw-Hill Companies, Inc./John Flournoy, photographer; **Page 15** Courtesy of Google.com; **Page 23** Courtesy of the Xerox Corporation; **Page 26** Ingram Publishing; **Page 37** Public domain image from the Library of Congress Prints and Photographs Division/DAL; **Page 38** © Stock Montage, Inc.

Chapter 2

Page 47 Justin Sullivan/Getty Images; **Page 53** Photodisc/Getty Images; **Page 57** Oliver Berg/dpa/Corbis; **Page 61** AP Photo/Toby Talbot; **Page 62** JGI/Jamie Grill/Getty Images; **Page 69** AP Photo/M. Spencer Grant; **Page 72** Courtesy of Nordstrom, Inc.

Chapter 3

Page 85 Laura Morton/Corbis; **Page 89** © Threadless.com/Jérémie Royer; **Page 94** Comstock/PunchStock; **Page 95** Photodisc/Getty Images; **Page 98, 101** Ingram Publishing; **Page 105** Blend Images/SuperStock

Chapter 4

Page 127 Colorblind Images/Photolibrary.com; **Page 131** Richard Cummins/Corbis; **Page 133** AP Photo/Charles Rex Arbogast; **Page 139** AP Photo/The Idaho State Journal, Joshua Duplechian; **Page 142** (c)1998 EyeWire, Inc.; **Page 145** The McGraw-Hill Companies, Inc./Christopher Kerrigan, photographer; **Page 152** Courtesy of Nordstrom, Inc.

Chapter 5

Page 165 Jean-Marc Giboux/Liaison Agency/Getty Images; **Page 167** AP Photo/Louis Lanzano; **Page 170** Michael Newman/PhotoEdit, Inc.; **Page 175** AP Photo/Pat Sullivan; **Page 177** Royalty-Free/Corbis; **Page 184** Chip East/Reuters/Corbis; **Page 185** © The McGraw-Hill Companies, Inc./John Flournoy, photographer; **Page 189** Courtesy of Timberland Company

Chapter 6

Page 203 British Retail Photography/Alamy; **Page 209** AP Photo/Mustafa Quaishi; **Page 215** 2007 Getty Images, Inc.; **Page 217** John Neubauer/PhotoEdit, Inc.; **Page 220** Image courtesy of The Advertising Archives; **Page 221** Courtesy of Toyota Motor North America, Inc.; **Page 227** Courtesy of Cold Stone Creamery; **Page 232** Digital Vision/Getty Images

Chapter 7

Page 245 AP Photo/Mark Lennihan; **Page 247** AP Photo/The News-Gazette, Heather Coit; **Page 250** Courtesy of Zappos.com. © 2009 Zappos.com, Inc.; **Page 253** Dominic Lipinski/PA Wire/AP Images; **Page 254** Courtesy of Scaled Composites; **Page 255** AP Photo/Pat Sullivan; **Page 258** Ingram Publishing; **Page 260** AP Photo/Reed Saxon; **Page 267** Digital Vision/Photodisc/Getty Images

Chapter 8

Page 283 Jed Jacobsohn/Getty Images; **Page 287** Eric Audras/Photoalto/PictureQuest; **Page 288** Jon Feingersh/Blend Images LLC; **Page 290** Getty Images/Digital Vision; **Page 293** Digital Vision/Getty Images; **Page 300** Courtesy of NASA; **Page 306** Digital Vision/Alamy; **Page 308** Paul J. Richards/AFP/Getty Images

Chapter 9

Page 317 Jordan Strauss/WireImage; **Page 322** Joe Raedle/Getty Images; **Page 324** Stockbyte/Getty Images; **Page 325** Davis Barber/PhotoEdit, Inc.; **Page 334** G.K. & Vikki Hart/Getty Images; **Page 337** AP Photo/Paul Sakuma; **Page 339** Blend Images/Getty Images; **Page 342** Thomas Barwick/Photographer's Choice RF/Getty Images

Chapter 10

Page 351 Courtesy of Google; **Page 353** NBAE/Getty Images; **Page 358** Tim Boyle/Getty Images; **Page 360** Chris Ryan/Getty Images; **Page 364** AP Photo/M. Spencer Green; **Page 369** Courtesy of Persuasive Games; **Page 380** Digital Vision; **Page 383** Robyn Beck/AFP/Getty Images

Chapter 11

Page 393 Neville Elder/Corbis; **Page 395** Library of Congress, Prints and Photographs Division, LC-U9-10364-37; **Page 398** AP Photo/Thibault Camus; **Page 405** Lars Niki; **Page 408** Beathan/Corbis; **Page 416** Alan Einstein/NBAE/Getty Images; **Page 421** AP Photo/Williams Perry

Chapter 12

Page 431 Dan Callister/Alamy; **Page 434** Mel Curtis/Getty Images; **Page 436** AP Photo/Chuck Burton; **Page 440** BananaStock/PictureQuest; **Page 445** Jupiterimages/Imagesource; **Page 452** Associated Press; **Page 455** Stockbyte/Getty Images; **Page 458** Karl Weatherly/Getty Images

Chapter 13

Page 469 Compassionate Eye Foundation/Rob Daly/OJO Images Ltd/Getty Images;

Page 471 AP Photo/Tammie Arroyo; **Page 472** Brand X/Jupiterimages; **Page 476** Imagesource/PictureQuest; **Page 479** Robert Glusic/Getty Images; **Page 482** AP Photo/Paul Sakuma; **Page 484** Kaz Chiba/The Image Bank/Getty Images; **Page 489** Tom & Dee Ann McCarthy/Corbis; **Page 491** Ingram Publishing / AGE Fotostock

Chapter 14

Page 503 Sean Gallup/Getty Images; **Page 506** (t)Comstock Images/Getty Images, (b)Courtesy of Omnica Corporation; **Page 509** Marc Pokempner/Getty Images; **Page 513** Courtesy of Boots & Coots; **Page 516** NASA, ESA, R. O'Connell (University of Virginia), and the Hubble Heritage Team (STScI/AURA); **Page 524** Jon Feingersh/Getty Images

Chapter 15

Page 531 Jeff Greenberg/Alamy; **Page 533** Jack Hollingsworth/Corbis; **Page 535** BananaStock Ltd.; **Page 536** Comstock/PunchStock; **Page 538** Hiroko Masuike/The New York Times/Redux; **Page 544** Frazier Harrison/Getty Images; **Page 545** Chuan Khoo/Getty Images; **Page 555** Bill Varie/Corbis

Chapter 16

Page 565 Joe Raedle/Getty Images; **Page 567** AP Photo/Carlos Osorio; **Page 570** Chamussy/Sipa/AP Images; **Page 577** Keith Brofsky/Getty Images; **Page 583** Ron Wurzer/Getty Images; **Page 592** David Madison/Getty Images

Chapter 17

Page 601 Sean Gardner/-Pool/Getty Images; **Page 608** Thinkstock/Jupiterimages; **Page 611** AP Photo/Nati Harnik; **Page 614** Courtesy of HyperActive Technologies; **Page 620** Photodisc/Getty Images; **Page 622** Alyson Aliano; **Page 624** no credit needed; **Page 626** Ned Frisk/Corbis; **Page 636** Macduff Everton/Corbis; **Page 637** AP Photo/Mark Humphrey

Chapter 18

Page 641 2006 Crosskeys Media®; **Page 643** TongRo Image Stock/Alamy; **Page 645** Simon Fergusson/Getty Images; **Page 650** (t)Digital Vision, (b)David Paul Morris/Getty Images; **Page 656** Digital Vision; **Page 659** Copyright © 2008 Symantec Corporation. Reprinted with permission.

GLOSSARY / SUBJECT INDEX

A

Abbott, 400
ABC Supply, 260
Accenture, 400
Accommodating work/family needs, 418

Accommodation *A style of dealing with conflict involving cooperation on behalf of the other party but not being assertive about one's own interests,* 422, **522**

Accountability *The expectation that employees will perform a job, take corrective action when necessary, and report upward on the status and quality of their performance,* 290–**291**, 422–423

Accounting audits *Procedures used to verify accounting reports and statements,* **578**

Achievement, need for, 483
Achievement-oriented leadership, 450
Acordia, 270

Acquisition *One firm buying another,* **67**

    mergers and, 150
    of new technology, 618–621
Action Fast Print, 455
Active employee, 25–26

Activity-based costing (ABC) *A method of cost accounting designed to identify streams of activity and then to allocate costs across particular business processes according to the amount of time employees devote to particular activities,* **579**

ADA, 178, 367, 369, 405, 422

Adapters *Companies that take the current industry structure and its evolution as givens, and choose where to compete,* **659**

Adhocracy, 76
Adjourning stage, 509
Adjustment, mutual, 306, 308
Administrative management, 39
Advanced Training Source, 420

Adverse impact *When a seemingly neutral employment practice has a disproportionately negative effect on a protected group,* **367**

Advertising support model *Charging fees to advertise on a site,* **255**

Advisory boards, 269
Advisory relationships, 520
Aéropostale, 62
Aetna, 13, 22, 176, 417

Affective conflict *Emotional disagreement directed toward other people,* **103**

Affiliate model *Charging fees to direct site visitors to other companies' sites,* **255**

Affiliation, need for, 483

Affirmative action *Special efforts to recruit and hire qualified members of groups that have been discriminated against in the past,* **408–413**

Affordable Care Act, 52, 380
Age Discrimination in Employment Act, 368
Age of the workforce, 406–407
Aggression, competitive, 68
Agroelectric System of Appropriate
        Technology, 256
Air Tran Airways, 566

Alderfer's ERG theory *A human needs theory postulating that people have three basic sets of needs that can operate simultaneously,* **482–483**

Alliances, strategic, 69, 321–322, 323
Allied Signal, 574
Allstate Insurance, 139, 493–494
Alternative work schedules, 418–419
Amazon, 6, 7, 10, 63, 91, 144, 255, 327, 332,
        453, 607, 616, 636–637
American Airlines, 143, 565
American Association of Community Colleges,
        186
American Bank, 506
American Electric Power Co., 199
American Express, 68, 400, 410, 642, 643
American International Group, 179
American Management Association, 405
American Society for Training and
        Development, 369
American Training Resources, 420
Americans with Disabilities Act (ADA), 178,
        367, 369, 405, 422
Amgen, 659
Analysis
    competitor, 141
    cost-benefit, 198
    environmental, 64–66, 80–81, 141–143
    external opportunities and threats,
        141–143
    financial, 144
    force-field, 651
    human resources, 141, 144
    industry, 141
    internal strengths and weaknesses,
        143–146
    job, 357
    life cycle, 188
    macroeconomic, 141
    market, 141
    operations, 144
    opportunity, 146–153, 160–161, 265
    political and regulatory, 141
    quantitative, 41
    self-SWOT, 147
    situational, 129
    social, 141
    SWOT, 146–153, 160–161
    technological, 141
Analyzer firms, 616
Anheuser-Busch, 146
Anticipated competency development, 616
Anticipated market receptiveness, 612–613
Antitrust, 213
AOL, 42, 150
A&P, 147
APEC, 216, 226
Apple, 4, 9, 41, 47–48, 63–64, 67, 73, 77–78,
        109, 188, 199, 216, 220, 252, 265, 322,
        421, 607, 622
Applications for jobs, 359–360
Applied Materials, 554
Appraisal by subordinates, 374

Appraisal of performance; *see* Performance
    appraisal

Arbitration *The use of a neutral third party to resolve a labor dispute,* **384**

Archer Daniels Midland, 399
Arcos, 491
Ariba, 637
Arm & Hammer, 188
Articulated needs, 659–660
ASEAN, 216
Asia-Pacific Economic Cooperation (APEC),
    216

Assessment center *A managerial performance test in which candidates participate in a variety of exercises and situations,* **362**

Assets *The values of the various items the corporation owns,* 144, **579–580**

Assistive technologies, 405
Association for the Advancement of Retired
        People (AARP), 406
Association of Certified Fraud Examiners,
        181
Association of Southeast Asian Nations, 216
Assumptions, unexamined, 410–411
Astex Therapeutics, 253
AstraZeneca, 296
Astroturfing, 168
At-will employment, 366
Atari, 252
ATI Technologies, 60, 62
Atlantic Richfield, 601
AT&T, 23, 63, 132, 150, 227, 229, 353, 363,
        405, 455, 547
Audit relationships, 520
Audits
    accounting, 578
    external, 575–576
    internal, 576
    management, 575–576
    marketing, 144
    technology, 610
Auntie Anne's, 227

Authentic leadership *A style in which the leader is true to himself or herself while leading,* **454–455**

Authoritarianism, 450

Authority *The legitimate right to make decisions and to tell other people what to do,* **287**

    decentralized, 69–70, 292–294
    delegating, 263, 290–292
    informal, 287
    in organizations, 287–289
AutoAdmit, 175

Autocratic leadership *A form of leadership in which the leader makes decisions on his or her own and then announces those decisions to the group,* **443**

Autodesk, 418

Autonomous work groups *Groups that control decisions about and execution of a complete range of tasks,* **508**

Autonomy, 487
Avis, 437

Caux Principles *Ethical principles established by international executives based in Caux, Switzerland, in collaboration with business leaders from Japan, Europe, and the United States,* **169**

Centralized organization *An organization in which high-level executives make most decisions and pass them down to lower levels for implementation,* **292**

Certainty *The state that exists when decision makers have accurate and comprehensive information,* **87**

Charismatic leader *A person who is dominant, self-confident, convinced of the moral righteousness of his or her beliefs, and able to arouse a sense of excitement and adventure in followers,* **451–452**

Chief information officer (CIO) *Executive in charge of information technology strategy and development,* **18, 621**

Clan control *Control based on the norms, values, shared goals, and trust among group members,* **567–568, 592–594**

Coaching *Dialogue with a goal of helping another be more effective and achieve his or her full potential on the job,* 371, 512, 516–517, 550–**551**

Coalitional model *Model of organizational decision making in which groups with differing preferences use power and negotiation to influence decisions,* **106**

Cognitive conflict *Issue-based differences in perspectives or judgments,* **103**

Cohesiveness *The degree to which a group is attractive to its members, members are motivated to remain in the group, and members influence one another,* 411, **517–519**

Collaboration *A style of dealing with conflict emphasizing both cooperation and assertiveness to maximize both parties' satisfaction,* 7–8, **522–523**

Communication *The transmission of information and meaning from one party to another through the use of shared symbols,* 530–563, **532**

Comparable worth *Principle of equal pay for different jobs of equal worth,* **381**

Competing *A style of dealing with conflict involving strong focus on one's own goals and little or no concern for the other person's goals,* **522**

Competitive aggression, 68

Competitive environment *The immediate environment surrounding a firm; includes suppliers, customers, rivals, and the like,* **49**

competitors, 56–57, 267
customers, 62–64
suppliers, 60–61
threat of new entrants, 57–58
threat of substitutes, 58–60

Competitive intelligence *Information that helps managers determine how to compete better,* **65**

Competitive pacification, 68
Competitive position, 149
Competitor analysis, 141
Competitors, 56–57, 267
Complacency, reasons for, 656–657
Complements, product, 58–60
Complexity, environmental, 64

Compliance-based ethics programs *Company mechanisms typically designed by corporate counsel to prevent, detect, and punish legal violations,* **177–178**

Complimentary products and technologies, 609
Compressed workweek, 418

Compromise *A style of dealing with conflict involving moderate attention to both parties' concerns,* **522**

Computer-controlled production, 571

Computer-integrated manufacturing (CIM) *The use of computer-aided design and computer-aided manufacturing to sequence and optimize a number of production processes,* **337–338**

Computer-numerical control (CNC), 571

Concentration *A strategy employed for an organization that operates a single business and competes in a single industry,* **147–148**

Concentric diversification *A strategy used to add new businesses that produce related products or are involved in related markets and activities,* **147–148**

Conceptual and decision skills *Skills pertaining to the ability to identify and resolve problems for the benefit of the organization and its members,* **21**

Concern for people, 442, 444
Concern for production, 442, 444

Concurrent control *The control process used while plans are being carried out, including directing, monitoring, and fine-tuning activities as they are performed,* **572–573**

Concurrent engineering *A design approach in which all relevant functions cooperate jointly and continually in a maximum effort aimed at producing high-quality products that meet customers' needs,* **342–343**

Confidentiality, of information, 638

Conflict *Opposing pressures from different sources, occurring on the level of psychological conflict or conflict between individuals or groups,* **89**

affective, 103
cognitive, 103
constructive, 103
managing, 520–521
styles, 521–523
virtual, 524–525
Conflict of interest, 167, 171

Conglomerate diversification *A strategy used to add new businesses that produce unrelated products or are involved in unrelated markets and activities,* **148**

ConocoPhillips, 620
Conservation, 197
Consideration, 442
Consolidated Natural Gas, 200
Constructive conflict, 103
Constructive feedback, 375
Consumer Protection Act, 490
Consumers, 62–64
Contemporary approaches to management, 41–42
Content theories, 480
Content validity, 364
Continental Airlines, 143
Contingencies, 42
Contingency models of leadership, 446–449
Contingency perspective, 42

Contingency plans *Alternative courses of action that can be implemented based on how the future unfolds,* **92, 130–131**

Contingent workers, 71
Continuous improvement, 10, 331
Continuous learning, 663–664

Continuous process *A process that is highly automated and has a continuous production flow,* **337**

Contracted development, 619
Contraction, 69
Contracts
labor, 37
psychological, 493–494

Control *Any process that directs the activities of individuals toward the achievement of organizational goals,* **566**

as a function of management, 16
illusion of, 97
market, 567–568, 590–592
monitoring and, 133
resistance to, 584
Control systems, 564–599
bureaucratic systems
approaches to, 572–575
budgetary controls, 576–579
control cycle, 568–572
designing effective, 584–590
downside of, 582–584

financial controls, 579–582
management audits, 575–576
causes of problems with, 566–567
clan control, 567–568, 592–594
concurrent, 572–573
defined, 566
feedback, 572–573
feedforward, 572
market control, 567–568, 590–592
resistance to, 584
six sigma, 333–334, 574–575, 582
span of, 289–290
strategic, 154–155

Controlling *The management function of monitoring performance and making needed changes,* **16**

Converse, 68
Cooking Up Collaboration, 512

Cooperative strategies *Strategies used by two or more organizations working together to manage the external environment,* **68–69**

Cooptation, 69, 653

Coordination *The procedures that link the various parts of an organization for the purpose of achieving the organization's overall mission,* **286**

Coordination and communication, 306–309

Coordination by mutual adjustment *Units interact with one another to make accommodations to achieve flexible coordination,* **306, 308**

Coordination by plan *Interdependent units are required to meet deadlines and objectives that contribute to a common goal,* **306**

Coordination by standardization, 305–306
Copyright laws, 52
CopyShark.net, 262
Cor Business, 132
Cordis Corporation, 298

Core competence *A unique skill and/or knowledge an organization possesses that give it an edge over competitors,* **145–146, 320–321, 626**

Core values, 643–644
Corning, 146, 352, 402
Corporate culture, 72–78
Corporate entrepreneurship, 269–272

Corporate governance *The role of a corporation's executive staff and board of directors in ensuring that the firm's activities meet the goals of the firm's stakeholders,* **289**

Corporate social responsibility (CSR) *Obligation toward society assumed by business,* **181–186;** see also Ethics

Corporate strategy *The set of businesses, markets, or industries in which an organization competes and the distribution of resources among those entities,* **147–150**

Corrective action, 571–572
Corruption, in foreign transactions, 236

Lord Corporation, 488
L'Oreal, 188
Louisiana-Pacific, 199
Louisville Gas and Electric, 200
LoveMachine, 304
Low-cost leadership, 606

Low-cost strategy *A strategy an organization uses to build competitive advantage by being efficient and offering a standard, no-frills product,* **151**

Lying, outcome of, 167–168

M

Maastricht Treaty, 212
MacMillan Bloedel, 199
Macroeconomic analysis, 141

Macroenvironment *The general environment; includes governments, economic conditions, and other fundamental factors that generally affect all organizations,* **49**

demographics, 53–54
economy, 49–51
laws and regulations affecting, 52–53
social issues, 54–55
technology, 51–52
Macy's, 298, 638
Maintenance behaviors, 443–444

Make-or-buy decision *The question an organization asks itself about whether to acquire new technology from an outside source or develop it itself,* **619**

Makers, 646
Malcolm Baldrige National Quality Award, 334

Management *The process of working with people and resources to accomplish organizational goals,* **14**

across international borders, 229–232
administrative, 39
bonuses for, 378
bureaucracy approach to, 40–41, 70, 625–626
classical approach to, 37–41
coaching, 371, 512, 516–517, 550–551
contemporary approaches, 41–42
crisis, 107–109
ecocentric, 187–188
versus entrepreneurship, 246
evolution of, 36–42
functions of, 14–17
human relations approach, 39–40
knowledge, 6–7, 308
versus leadership, 435–437
levels, 18–20
open-book, 551–552, 586
participative, 41
principles of, 39
quantitative, 41
scientific, 37–39, 590
systematic, 37
systems theory, 42
training programs for, 371

Management audit *An evaluation of the effectiveness and efficiency of various systems within an organization,* **575–576**

Management by objectives (MBO) *A process in which objectives set*

by a subordinate and a supervisor must be reached within a given time period, **373**

Management by wandering around (MBWA), 553
Management information systems (MIS), 51

Management myopia *Focusing on short-term earnings and profits at the expense of longer-term strategic obligations,* **582**

Management principles, 475

Management teams *Teams that coordinate and provide direction to the subunits under their jurisdiction and integrate work among subunits,* **506–507**

Managerial control, 564–599
bureaucratic systems
approaches to, 572–575
budgetary controls, 576–579
control cycle, 568–572
designing effective, 584–590
downside of, 582–584
financial controls, 579–582
management audits, 575–576
causes of problems with, 566–567
clan control, 567–568, 592–594
concurrent, 572–573
defined, 566
feedback, 572–573
feedforward, 572
market control, 567–568, 590–592
resistance to, 584
six sigma, 333–334, 574–575, 582
span of, 289–290
strategies, 154–155
Managers
best and worst, 14
as brokers, 304–305
delegating responsibilities, 263, 290–292
division, 301
effective, 32–33
frontline, 16, 19
functional, 301
line, 294
middle-level, 18–19, 289
minority, 404
operational, 19
Personal Assessment of Management Skills (PAMS), 29–32
product, 301
role of, 21
skills needed, 20–22, 229–232, 301–302
span of control, 289–290
strategic, 18
t-shaped, 7–8
tactical, 18
top-level, 18–19
two-boss, 301
types of, 18–20
as working leaders, 20

Managing diversity *Managing a culturally diverse workforce by recognizing the characteristics common to specific groups of employees while dealing with employees as individuals and supporting, nurturing, and utilizing their differences to the organization's advantage,* **394**

Manipulation, 653
Manufacturing
computer-integrated, 337–338
concurrent engineering, 342–343
flexible, 71, 337–339

JIT, 341–342
job losses in, 209
large batch, 336–337
lean, 339
mass customization, 71, 337–338
scientific management, 37–39, 590
small batch, 336
value-added, 341
Manufacturing Extension Partnerships, 263
Market analysis, 141

Market control *Control based on the use of pricing mechanisms and economic information to regulate activities within organizations,* **567–568, 590–592**

Market receptiveness, anticipating, 612–613
Marketing audit, 144
Marketing function, 633
Markets
barriers to entry into, 57–58
bull and bear, 51
threat of substitutes, 58–60
Marriott, 147, 400, 405, 642
Marsh & McLennan, 167
Mary Kay Cosmetics, 484

Maslow's need hierarchy *A conception of human needs organizing needs into a hierarchy of five major types,* **40, 481–482**

Mass customization *The production of varied, individually customized products at the low cost of standardized, mass-produced products,* **71, 337–338**

Master budget, 578
Master Lock, 211
MasterCard, 132

Matrix organization *An organization composed of dual reporting relationships in which some employees report to two superiors—a functional manager and a divisional manager,* **299–302**

Matsushita, 206
Mattel, 231

Maximizing *A decision realizing the best possible outcome,* **94**

McClelland's needs, 483
McDonald's, 5, 62, 139–140, 181, 182, 198, 199, 200, 227, 253, 272, 336, 400, 475–476, 573
McGraw-Hill, 493

Mechanistic organization *A form of organization that seeks to maximize internal efficiency,* **318**

Media richness *The degree to which a communication channel conveys information,* **540**

Mediator *A third party who intervenes to help others manage their conflict,* **523–524**

Medtronic, 22
Member satisfaction, 517
Mentally and physically disabled, 405–406

NAME INDEX